# THE STUDY OF BIOLOGY

**Jeffrey J. W. Baker** *Wesleyan University*, **Garland E. Allen** *Washington University*

▲ **ADDISON-WESLEY PUBLISHING COMPANY**

# THE STUDY OF BIOLOGY

### SECOND EDITION

*Reading, Massachusetts · Menlo Park, California · London · Amsterdam · Don Mills, Ontario · Sydney*

This book is in the

**Addison-Wesley Series in the Life Sciences**

Harper Follansbee and Johns W. Hopkins III, *Consulting Editors*

*Publisher's Note:* A number of the illustrations
in this text are adapted from figures
in *Biology* by John Kimball, second edition, Addison-Wesley, 1968.

*Cover Illustration:* Web pattern produced by a spider drugged
with phenobarbitol. (Photo courtesy Peter N. Witt, North
Carolina Department of Mental Health, Raleigh, N.C.)

ISBN 0-201-00377-5
DEFGHIJKLM-HA-798765

*To Barbara and Sue*

# PREFACE TO THE SECOND EDITION

The gratifying acceptance of the first edition of *The Study of Biology* has helped greatly in encouraging the necessary effort involved in this major revision. Since the biology instructor is primarily interested in precisely how much and in what way this second edition differs from the first, some attention will be devoted to this point.

Those familiar with the first edition of *The Study of Biology* are aware that it approaches the subject matter of biology from a different viewpoint than many other current biology textbooks. Nothing has convinced us that this approach should be changed, and it has not been. Indeed, we are more than ever convinced that with the vast body of important biological information available today, it is absurd to attempt to teach it all in an introductory course. Thus this text continues to deal with selected areas of biology in a manner designed to illustrate the underlying logic of scientific investigation. It is our experience and apparently that of others that so doing enables the student to handle other areas of biology (and science) with considerable ease and understanding. In brief, then, in terms of its *approach* to the subject matter of biology, *The Study of Biology* remains nontraditional.

On the other hand, in terms of *content* and emphasis, the second edition differs greatly from the first. How could it not? In terms of genetics alone, for example, since the first edition of *The Study of Biology* appeared in 1967 the genetic code has been virtually solved (see pp. 560–572), a gene has been isolated, photographed (see p. 576), and synthesized (see pp. 576–577), and the "traditional" viewpoint of its replication questioned (see pp. 552–556). The vast strides forward made in the past three years in almost all areas of biology have necessitated at least some changes in every chapter, major changes in most of them, and the incorporation of additional chapters in certain areas.

The most notable example of the incorporation of additional chapters deals with animal behavior. In the first edition, the authors decided to omit this area because it did not seem at the time to be as crucial as others which were given a higher priority. We were wrong. The past few years have seen ethology become a major field of biology and one increasing in stature and importance. Thus we have gone from the extreme of no treatment of animal behavior to a fairly extensive one, extending through two chapters and portions of others. The appearance of this subject late in the book (Chapters 22 and 23) does not indicate a minor position for animal behavior, but rather the reverse; it was felt that a thorough grounding in the principles of genetics, development, ecology, and evolution should precede the consideration of behavior. Special thanks must be extended here to Drs. Peter H. Klopfer of Duke University and Jack P. Hailman of the University of Wisconsin for their extremely valuable reviews of the behavior material while it was being prepared; their suggestions were uniformly helpful and fitted in perfectly with the underlying philosophy of *The Study of Biology*.

Since both authors are zoologically rather than botanically oriented, it is not surprising, perhaps, that the first edition of *The Study of Biology* should reflect this prejudice. In this second edition, however, a conscientious effort has been made to correct this imbalance, and we believe this effort has been successful. In particular, the chapter on plant physiology has been greatly expanded and updated, as has the material on plant evolution. Invaluable in this effort has been the guidance of Dr. Preston W. Adams of DePauw University, whose enthusiastic adoption and conversion of our approach into a separate textbook, *The Study of Botany* (Addison-Wesley, 1970), has proved of immense value in preparing this revision.

The first edition of *The Study of Biology* relied heavily on the use of our supplementary text, *Matter, Energy, and Life* (Addison-Wesley, second edition, 1970), and several users (with justification, we think) objected to this arrangement. Thus the treatment of the fundamental principles of physics and chemistry essential for modern biology has been expanded into two full chapters, to make the text more self-sufficient. In other words, *Matter, Energy, and Life* is now a helpful but no longer essential supplementary text for users of *The Study of Biology*.

Other deletions, additions, and modifications have been made in this second edition, but they are far too numerous to receive attention here. As has already been implied, in preparing this revision we have relied heavily on feedback from users of the first edition, and virtually all suggestions concerning corrections, modifications, and additions that did not run counter to the book's philosophy have been followed. Besides the aforementioned persons, special thanks must go to the following reviewers in their particular areas of interest: Dr. Oscar P. Chilson, Washington University, biochemistry; Drs. Philip C.

Laris, University of California, Santa Barbara and Georgia E. Lesh, Western Reserve University, animal physiology; Dr. Jason Wolfe, Wesleyan University, cell reproduction; Dr. Edward Simon, Purdue University, genetics; and Drs. James Norman Dent, University of Virginia, and George M. Malacinski, Indiana University, developmental biology. The reviews of these individuals were tremendously valuable in our work, but any shortcomings found in this second edition of *The Study of Biology* are the responsibility of the authors alone.

We sincerely hope that the use of *The Study of Biology* will prove to be an enjoyable educational experience for both students and instructors.

*Middletown, Connecticut*                       J.J.W.B.
*St. Louis, Missouri*                          G.E.A.
*January 1971*

# PREFACE TO THE FIRST EDITION

In recent years, at both the secondary school and college levels, there has been a revolution in the teaching of biology—a revolution which reflects, perhaps, the degree of change which has occurred at the forefronts of biological research. To reflect advances in molecular biology, for example, courses and textbooks have changed the subject matter with which they deal. Biology teaching has turned from mostly descriptive material toward the more experimental aspects of the biological sciences.

Few biologists would deny that these changes in their discipline and in their outlook concerning its teaching are for the better. Yet, there is one aspect of this biological revolution which seems to have received less than its due share of attention. Most especially on the introductory level of instruction, the inclusion of new information has often taken precedence over an analysis of the reasoning through which this new information was obtained. It is laudable to include within an introductory textbook the experiment by which a certain bit of biological knowledge was gained, as well as that bit of knowledge itself. Yet, we often find that a student can read a detailed description of an experiment without fully comprehending the hypothesis that the experiment purports to be testing . . . or, at times, even what the hypothesis *is*.

To correct this deficiency is the primary aim of this book. Those instructors who think they might like to try the book in their courses will gain considerable insight into its philosophy by a quick reading of Chapter 3. The entire book is based on our conviction that although there is no one scientific method, *there is still an underlying pattern of deductive logic in every scientific experiment or observation*, and that this pattern should continually be stressed to the student reader. At times, as a quick leafing through the book will reveal, this stress is accomplished by an indented format, allowing a separation of the hypothesis from its prediction(s). At other times, to avoid monotony, a deductive format is stressed within the regular text material itself. In either case, the aim is the same: To aid the student in understanding just what predictions follow from the tentative acceptance of an hypothesis, and which of these predictions a particular experiment or observation attempts to verify or refute.

In concentrating on the deductive and experimental aspect of biological ideas, we have made liberal use of historical material. Where possible, we have tried to present the relevant information which was available to given investigators (to Mendel, for example, or to Bayliss and Starling) as they set out to solve a problem, and then, with knowledge of the experiments they designed—or the questions they asked—we have tried to show the various hypotheses developed and the deductive format implicit in the final result. The purpose of this emphasis is to reveal something of the pattern of logic involved in a wide variety of biological problems. In this way we hope that the student will develop a sense of how to analyze the results of scientific work.

From the standpoint of the writers, there are disadvantages to this approach. Chief among them is the fact that it takes a great deal more space to analyze the logical basis of an experiment than it does to merely describe it. Thus we were faced with two alternatives: either write a textbook comparable in length to the Old and New Testaments, or be willing to eliminate certain sacred topics completely. Not *entirely* due to laziness, we have chosen the second alternative. Thus devotees of animal physiology may be dismayed to discover that this book contains virtually nothing about eye and ear physiology; aficionados of human evolution may be unhappy to find that we have little to say on this topic, *per se*. However, by being exposed to the topics which *are* included, and given the manner in which those topics are presented, students will, we feel, be better prepared to more meaningfully handle supplementary materials on the omitted topics without the aid of a textbook.

The instructor will, we hope, make clear to the student the fact that the breaking down of an experiment into its deductive logic format *in no way recreates the thought processes that originally went into the work*. It is extremely doubtful that such a recreation can ever be brought about. One of the more unfortunate aspects of the "new" curricula in science is that the student has often been led to believe that he is actually being a research scientist as he carries out "inquiry oriented" exercises. In reality, he is only discovering the pattern of logic that underlay the original investigation and which made it a valid scientific one. It is easy, for example, to discover the deductive framework underlying Spemann's experiment with the organizer. Yet, when reading Spemann's description of his thoughts at the time, one has the strong suspicion that not even he knew the precise path of reasoning that led him to the answer.

A word is in order here as to the dichotomy between "content" and "process" that is frequently posed in discussions of biological curricula. We believe that this distinction is an artificial one—that *without scientific content, a study of scientific process becomes meaningless.* In the present book, we hope to make the point that scientific statements are not sacred. To grasp this idea, so contrary to the public image of science, the student must understand *what* statements biologists make about the world (the "content") as well as *how* these statements are supported through research (the "process").

Because our major effort has been directed toward emphasis of important principles and ideas, scientific terminology has been reduced to a minimum; where it is needed, however, it is introduced. The same is true of descriptive material such as the phases of mitosis or the anatomy of the digestive system. There is little reason to attempt to convert such material into experimental exercises; historically they did not develop that way. Further, despite its current disfavor, descriptive biology has been and still is an important part of the field.

Finally, for the benefit not only of science majors, but also of those students who will take no further science courses, we have attempted to make clear the meaning of scientific "truth," the limitations of science, and the importance of pure or basic research. Even the most intelligent layman cannot hope to be thoroughly familiar with even a small part of scientific research. He can, however, gain a general understanding of the nature of all science and thereby make more intelligent decisions concerning its many political and sociological ramifications.

*Washington, D.C.*                                              J.J.W.B.
*Cambridge, Massachusetts*                                      G.E.A.
*November 1966*

# CONTENTS

**1 Characteristics of Living Things**

Introduction *1*    Specific organization *3*    Metabolism and excretion *4*
Movement and responsiveness *6*    Growth *7*    Reproduction *7*
Differentiation *8*    Adaptation *10*    Conclusion *10*

**2 Major Generalizations in Biology**

Introduction *12*    The cell concept *12*    The gene concept *15*
The mutation theory *17*    The continuity of the germ plasm *17*
Evolution and natural selection *19*    Ecological interrelations *21*
The molecular foundation of biology *22*    Mechanism and vitalism *23*
Conclusion *24*

**3 The Nature and Logic of Science**

Introduction *26*    The "scientific method" *27*    Inductive logic *33*
The application of logic: a case study *38*    The limitations of science *43*
Conclusion *46*

**4 Testing Hypotheses and Predictions**

Introduction *49*    Eijkman's experiments *49*
Chance and trial-and-error in scientific discovery *53*
A case history of scientific experimentation *55*    Conclusion *62*

## 5  The Analysis and Interpretation of Data

Introduction 66    Frames of reference for biological data 66
Normal curves and the analysis of distributions 69    From table to graph 71
Correlations 76    Interpolation and extrapolation 77
Generalizing points on a graph 79    The sigmoid curve 80
Scalar transformations 81    Conclusion 85


## 6  Cells

Introduction 90    Tools and techniques 90    The general plan of cells 96
The cytoplasm 97    The nucleus 104    How do we know? 105
The function of the nucleus 106    Cell sizes 111
The cell membrane: a study of function 113    Osmosis 118
Procaryotes vs. eucaryotes 120    Conclusion 121


## 7  Cellular Metabolism:  Matter, Energy, and Chemical Change

Introduction 127    Matter and energy 129    Atomic structure 131
The polarity of molecules 141    Ions and radicals 143
Oxidation and reduction: redox reactions 146
The collision theory and activation energy 147
Energy exchange and chemical reactions 148    Rates of reaction 153
Reversible and irreversible reactions 155    Chemical equilibrium 156
Classes of molecules in living systems 159    Enzymes 168
Theories of enzyme activity 173    Conclusion 180


## 8  The Dynamics of Living Cells:  Metabolic Pathways

Introduction 184    ATP: the energy currency in cells 185
Electron transport and energy release: the generation of ATP 188
The release of electrons: pathways for the breakdown of sugars 197
Life without air: anaerobic oxidation 205
Characteristics of metabolic pathways as illustrated by the oxidation of sugars 208
How biochemical systems are studied 219    Conclusion 221


## 9  Photosynthesis

Introduction 228    Some background notes 228    The problem 230
Water into wood? 231    Another fact is added 232    Chemists enter the scene 234
Ingenhousz sees the light 237    A new problem to solve 239
An old problem is solved 244    The oxygen problem is solved 246
Photosynthesis: the modern view 249    The dark reactions 255
The light reactions 257    The efficiency of photosynthesis 262    Conclusion 263


## 10  Plant Anatomy

Introduction 268    General organization of a vascular plant 269
Plant tissues 271    The root system 285    The shoot system 287
Increase in thickness of the plant body 294    Conclusion 298

## 11  Plant Physiology

Introduction *302*    Translocation: the movement of material through plants *302*
Movement of water and minerals into the plant *306*
Mechanism of stomatal movement *310*    The movement of gases in plants *314*
Movement through the xylem *319*    Movement through the phloem *325*
Movement of liquid out of the plant *330*
Movement of metabolic wastes: excretion *331*
Plant hormones *332*    Photoperiodism *342*    Tropisms *349*
Apical dominance and the control of plant form *354*    Conclusion *359*

## 12  Animal Anatomy and Physiology I:
## The Intake and Processing of Food

Introduction *363*    Animal tissues *363*    Digestion *369*
Digestion: techniques of study *372*    An open-and-shut case *377*
Hunger and thirst *378*    Absorption *380*    Elimination *382*
The transport of materials: circulation *383*    The heartbeat *385*
Respiratory exchange *388*    The control of breathing *390*
Breathing: a chemical basis? *391*    Gas exchange in the lungs *393*
Respiratory gases in the blood *393*    Partial pressure and tension *394*
Excretion *397*    The kidneys *399*    The filtration process *401*
Reabsorption: the final step *402*    Conclusion *404*

## 13  Animal Anatomy and Physiology II:  Movement and Coordination

Introduction *410*    Nerves and muscles: electrochemical potential *410*
The structure of muscle tissue *413*    Muscle contraction: the biochemical approach *414*
Muscle contraction: the biophysical approach *417*
Vertebrate movement: the relation of muscle to bone *421*
The nature of the nerve impulse *423*
Neuron-to-neuron connections: the synapse *435*
The neuromuscular junction *438*    The nervous system *439*
The reflex arc *443*    The autonomic nervous system *447*
The system of chemical control *448*    Conclusion *452*

## 14  Self-Regulation:  The Principle of Homeostasis

Introduction *458*    A mechanical analogy of self-regulation *459*
A simple biological control system: temperature regulation *460*
Physiological control at a higher level: breathing rate *463*
A homeostatic system involving several organs: the regulation of blood sugar *465*
Biochemical control mechanisms *466*    Conclusion *468*

## 15  Cell Reproduction

Introduction  *470*    Cell division: some problems of study *470*   Mitosis *471*
Mitosis: some problems *479*    The reduction division: meiosis *482*
Self-duplication of mitochondria and chloroplasts *490*    Conclusion *491*

## 16  Genetics I:  From Math to Mendel

Introduction *495*    Genetics: a mathematical basis *495*    Binomial expansions *499*
Experimental genetics *504*    Mendelian genetics *506*    Two pairs of genes *514*
Binomial expansions and mendelian genetics *518*    Conclusion *521*

## 17  Genetics II:  From Mendel to Molecule

Introduction *525*    Linkage *525*    Broken links *528*    Mapping *529*
Chromosomal aberrations *532*    Genetics: the fruit fly era *533*    Epistasis *535*
Multiple alleles *537*    In search of the gene *539*    Viral and other evidence *541*
Gene structure *543*    Testing the model *549*    DNA replication—some doubts *552*
Gene function *556*    The genetic code and mutations *560*    The gene *572*
Extrachromosomal inheritance *577*    Conclusion *578*

## 18  Developmental Biology

Introduction *583*    The background *583*    A new approach *585*
Some theories important to embryology *587*    Energy for development *589*
The beginning of development *590*    Early development *593*
Evolution of development *597*    Experimental embryology *599*
Regeneration *605*    Genes, regulation, and development *618*
Evidence for gene regulation in growth and development *622*
The inheritance of sex: a developmental hypothesis *627*
Congenital malformations *628*    Conclusion *629*

## 19  Taxonomy:  The Classification of Living Organisms

Introduction *633*    Development of taxonomic schemes *634*
The system of binomial nomenclature *638*    The problem of species definition *640*
Some modern approaches in taxonomy *644*    Taxonomic charts *647*
Taxonomy and the process of science *648*    Conclusion *649*

## 20  Ecological Relationships:  Competition for Energy

Introduction *652*    Ecological niches, habitats, and the ecosystem *653*
The food chain *657*    The cyclic use of materials *659*
Interactions between organisms in the ecosystem *665*
Changes in ecosystems through time: succession *667*
The growth and regulation of populations *672*
Human population and environmental exploitation *677*
Ecology and evolution *679*    Conclusion *682*

## 21  The Process of Evolution

Introduction *688*    The evidence for evolution *688*    Darwinian natural selection *694*
Direction of natural selection *700*    The population concept of evolution *702*

Natural selection and changes in gene frequency *704*    Sexual selection *706*
The role of isolation in the origin of species *707*    Migration and genetic drift *711*
Adaptive radiation: evolutionary opportunity and exploitation *712*
Adaptation and survival *717*    Conclusion *719*

## 22  Animal Behavior I:  The Higher Levels of Complexity

Introduction *723*    Animal behavior in historical perspective *726*
Anthropomorphism and the razor's edge *727*    The difficulty of simplicity *729*
The rise of "instinct" *733*    Behavior: genetic and evolutionary aspects *742*
Motivation *746*    Model behavior *748*
A contrast of learning: insight and imprinting *752*
Communication *756*    Conclusion *760*

## 23  Animal Behavior II:  Contemporary Concepts and Concerns

Introduction *763*    This land is my land *764*    Agonistic behavior and aggression *766*
Aggression in man *772*    The development of behavior *776*
The density problem *781*    Conclusion *784*

## 24  The Origin of Life

Introduction *787*    The idea of spontaneous generation *787*
The origin of life by chemosynthesis *790*    Viruses and the origin of life *798*
The geological time scale and the origin of life *801*    Conclusion *802*

## 25  The Evolution of Plants

Introduction *808*    Evolution of the procaryotes *808*
Origin of eucaryotic organisms *812*
The origin and diversification of eucaryotes: two alternative hypotheses *819*
Origin and adaptive significance of multicellularity *823*
Origin and diversification of sexual systems *825*    The primary invasion of the land *830*
Migration to the land: an hypothesis *833*    The early land plants *834*
Evolution of reproductive systems in the early land plants *840*
Secondary invasions of the land: the bryophytes *844*
Secondary invasions of the land: the fungi *846*
Secondary invasions of the land: lichens *851*    The gymnosperms *853*
The evolution of the angiosperms *855*    Conclusion *857*

## 26  The Evolution of Animals

Introduction *863*    The role of evolution *863*    Evolution: a working hypothesis *866*
The problem of phylogenetic relationships *872*
Phylogenetic relationships: the invertebrates *875*    "Reasons for being" *879*
Animal evolution: the molecular level of investigation *880*    Conclusion *884*

## Appendixes

1   Conversion of temperature scales *891*
2   Calculation of variance of a sample of data *893*
3   Table of amino acids *895*
4   Sample key to trees, using fruits *899*
5   Some taxonomic charts *902*

## Glossary *919*

## Index *953*

## Color Plates   *Between pages 510 and 511*

# CHARACTERISTICS OF LIVING THINGS

# CHAPTER 1

If a drop of mercury is placed in a watch glass with a small amount of dilute nitric acid and a crystal of potassium dichromate, an interesting phenomenon takes place. As the potassium dichromate dissolves, the mercury drop begins to move about the watch glass in a variety of directions. Long, armlike extensions flow first in one direction, then in another. The entire phenomenon bears a striking resemblance to "amoeboid movement," the pattern of movement demonstrated by a one-celled organism called an *Amoeba*. The *Amoeba* moves by projecting part of its mass into similar long, armlike extensions, or *pseudopods.**

Unlike an *Amoeba*, however, the mercury system is clearly not alive. In addition to moving of its own accord, the *Amoeba* can perform a variety of other activities. It takes food particles into its cell mass, converts this food into usable substances, gives off waste products, and reproduces. The mercury system cannot perform any of these activities. Nevertheless, in the way it moves, the mercury system represents a *model* of a living organism; that is, it performs a function which we normally associate only with life. This fact raises some questions in the mind of the biologist as to what exactly are the defining characteristics of life. Now, it may seem odd that biologists have any difficulty in deciding what is alive and what is not. Let us, therefore, examine the reasons for this difficulty.

---

* The explanation for the mercury's behavior is as follows. The surface tension of the mercury drop is very high. Potassium dichromate in nitric acid chemically interacts with the surface of the mercury, momentarily decreasing the surface tension at a given point. Mercury from inside the drop flows out at such points. Such reactions occur randomly over the surface of the drop, producing temporary pseudopods.

1

One school of modern biology is based upon the assumption that the functions of living systems can be explained ultimately in terms of physical and chemical processes. A living organism is thus viewed as a highly complex and well-organized chemical system. But in reducing the study of life to the study of individual chemical reactions, an inevitable question arises: Where does the "livingness" of an organism end and the "nonlivingness" begin? Or, to phrase the question another way: When does a collection of molecules cease to be merely a chemical mixture and become a living organism?

This problem can be illustrated by considering some of the information known about viruses. A **virus** is a small particle composed of two types of substance: protein and nucleic acid. The nucleic acid carries a program of information for producing more viruses; the protein forms a coat around the acid (Fig. 1–1). Viruses invade living cells, such as those of bacteria or higher organisms. Inside the host cell, the virus reproduces itself by means of the cell's metabolic machinery. Often this destroys the host cell. The virus cannot, however, reproduce outside of living cells, no matter what organic substances are supplied to it. That is, apparently the virus can reproduce only when it has at its disposal the chemical machinery of a living cell. On the other hand, viruses can be crystallized, placed in a bottle, and stored for many years. When the crystals are resuspended in aqueous solution, they are capable of infecting cells just as before. In view of these characteristics, many biologists have found it impossible to classify viruses as either living or nonliving. Instead, they place viruses in an undefined category between "life" and "nonlife."

The viruses may complicate the problem of defining life, but the causative agent of the disease known as "scrapie" appears to make the situation an impossible one. Scrapie is so called because it causes the sheep and goats it infects to rub themselves against objects which scrape off pieces of fleece and skin. It appears to be caused by an infectious agent smaller than the smallest known virus. This agent can remain infective after being heated at 212°F for half an hour. It can survive cycles of rapid freezing and thawing, and some samples have been shown to be infective after being kept in 10% formalin for more than two years. Most significant, the scrapie infectious agent is resistant to ultraviolet light of the specific wavelength absorbed by nucleic acid, yet still retains its reproductive and infectious capacity. The disease is of significance not only to sheep and goat herders but also because of its close resemblance to the human disease called kuru.

The existence of forms such as viruses and the causative agent of scrapie has important implications for any attempt to arrive at a definition of life. It indicates that a meaningful and all-inclusive definition of life is virtually impossible. In fact, research in both biochemistry and biophysics over the past twenty-five years points to the conclusion that there is simply no sharp line of distinction between living and nonliving things, and that living systems are perhaps best considered as a special kind of organization of the same elements as are found in the rest of the universe.

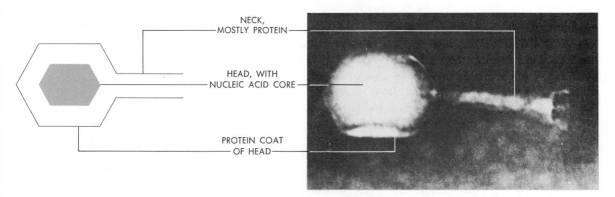

FIG. 1–1  Electron photomicrograph and schematic drawing of a virus of the T2 strain.  This type of virus, which attacks bacteria, is called a *bacteriophage*.  (From *J. Mol. Biol.* **1,** 1959, 281–292.  Courtesy S. Brenner, R. W. Horne, Academic Press, Inc.  Magnification ✕335,000.)

In any case, biologists have found that it is much more fruitful to *characterize* living things (i.e., to describe their essential qualities) than to try to define life.  It is more meaningful in the long run to describe viruses—their beauty as structural objects, and how their chemical composition affects host cells—than to argue that they are either living or nonliving.

In the characterization of living things which follows, we shall include only those features which can be directly or indirectly measured.  On this basis, we may say that the majority of living things are characterized by:

1)  having a specific chemical and structural organization,

2)  the use of raw materials from the environment to provide energy as well as structural elements for various cell activities (metabolism),

3)  elimination of certain by-products of their metabolism (excretion),

4)  the ability to make copies of themselves (reproduction),

5)  responsiveness to stimuli from the environment (sensitivity),

6)  the ability to move in some way,

7)  the ability to adapt to a variety of changes in the external environment (adaptation), and

8)  death and disintegration.

Not all known organisms possess every one of these characteristics in a way that is immediately recognizable.  Yet it *is* safe to say that these characteristics apply to the majority of organisms with which biologists work.

Living organisms usually show definite size and shape as well as physical and chemical composition.  These characteristics are inherited by the organism from its parents.  Nonliving objects, such as a rock, show no specific, set pattern of

**1-2
SPECIFIC
ORGANIZATION**

size or shape. It is true, of course, that crystals exhibit definite patterns of both shape and size. However, the *level* of complexity of even the simplest virus or bacterium is, in general, thought to be considerably greater than that of the most complex crystal. Compared to nonliving things, then, living organisms tend to show a very high degree of organization.

The organization displayed by living things can be viewed on several different levels. One of the lowest is the molecular level. The molecules which compose living things are, themselves, organized groups of atoms. Groups of molecules may, in turn, be organized into **cells**, and cells of similar types may be organized into **tissues**. Muscle cells, for example, are generally united to form muscle tissue. Tissues of one or more different types may unite to form **organs**—the liver, the kidney, or the eye, for example. Several organs are further combined into **systems,** such as the digestive, excretory, or visual system, and systems, working together in an integrated manner, make up an entire living **organism.** Thus we can view the organization of a living animal or plant as extending all the way from the level of atoms and molecules to that of the entire organism. Single-celled organisms, of course, lack the intermediate levels of tissue, organ, and system. Yet, on the molecular level, they are indeed highly organized.

Larger organisms require an organization of parts which is proportionately greater than that required by small organisms. They may, for example, require muscular and nervous coordination, visual and other sensory mechanisms, chemical control mechanisms, and so on. In such complex organisms, the many parts are heavily interdependent. Damage to even a small organ, or its failure to operate properly, may cause complete disorganization of the entire organism. In terms of living systems, the words disorganization and death are often synonymous.

## 1-3
## METABOLISM
## AND EXCRETION

Life without energy is a contradiction in terms. The sum total of chemical processes involved in the release and utilization of energy within living cells is known as **metabolism.** The metabolic processes of living organisms are responsible for growth, maintenance, and repair of the organism. The term "metabolism" can be used to refer either to the chemical activities of a single cell or to the sum total of such activities in an entire organism.

The energy exchanges involved in metabolism are concerned with the breakdown or buildup of chemical bonds. Chemical bonds represent the potential energy which holds atoms together in a molecule. Energy is required to build many types of chemical bonds; when such bonds are broken, as in the metabolism of food substances, that energy is released, and can be used to drive other reactions which require an input of energy. Although there are hundreds of different metabolic reactions which occur within even a single cell, all of these may be grouped into three main categories. Those which involve the breakdown of larger molecules into smaller are called **degradation processes.** Those which involve the buildup of smaller molecules into larger ones are referred to as **synthetic processes.** Those which involve the changing of one molecule to another at the same level of complexity are called **transformation processes.**

Degradation—the breakdown of large molecules into small molecules—may release energy for use in the many activities of the organism. At one time or another, virtually all the molecules in an organism undergo degradation, although each may be broken down at a different rate. The construction of protein molecules from simpler units in the living cell is an example of a synthetic process. The buildup of proteins requires the expenditure of energy from the cell's energy supply. This energy goes into forming chemical bonds which hold the various protein components together. The cell may be looked upon as a metabolic factory, constantly active with the breakdown and buildup of all sorts of molecules. Even in seemingly inactive tissues such as bone, these processes occur as long as the cells are alive.

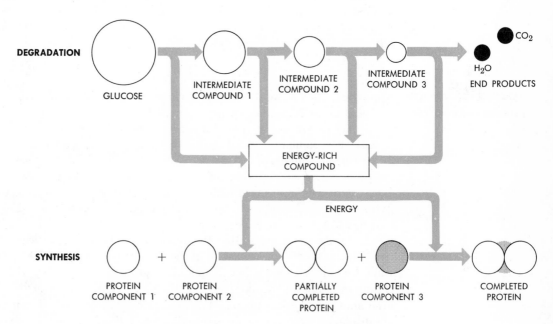

FIG. 1–2   The relation between synthesis and degradation, shown in schematic form. The breakdown of glucose involves a series of degradation processes. The energy released from such reactions is stored in an "energy-rich" compound, and is subsequently utilized to build the chemical bonds required in putting proteins together.

The energy required for synthetic processes to take place in living systems is supplied by certain degradation reactions. For example, the breakdown of sugars in cellular respiration supplies the energy for such synthetic processes as the buildup of proteins. One of the important links in this metabolic chain is the energy-harnessing mechanism. The cell has certain pathways by which the energy released in degradation of fuel molecules can be transferred to storage molecules in the cell. In this way, energy is available for later use in the synthesis of other compounds. The energy relationship between these processes is shown in Fig. 1–2.

**Excretion** is another characteristic life process. Excretion is the removal of waste products which result from the various metabolic processes within cells. Metabolic waste products may include such substances as water, carbon dioxide, ammonia, or urea. In single-celled organisms, excretion involves the passage of materials from inside the cell out to the surrounding medium. In multicelled organisms, the problem is more complex. Wastes from individual cells must be carried to the outside through a liquid medium, the so-called **extracellular fluid.** Many multicelled organisms also possess special organs, such as kidneys in the mammals, which extract wastes from the extracellular fluid (in this case, blood) as it passes through the organs. The elimination of metabolic wastes is essential to the normal functioning of the organism. If metabolic wastes are allowed to accumulate above a certain threshold value, they can become toxic to the organism. It is for this reason that kidney failure in human beings is a serious and eventually fatal affliction.

**1–4**
**MOVEMENT AND**
**RESPONSIVENESS**

**Movement** is one of the most obvious characteristics of living organisms. Although most plants, and some animals, lead a generally stationary life, they all display movement of some form or another. For example, vascular plants usually show some movement during the course of a day as their stems twist to follow the movements of the sun across the sky (see Fig. 1–3). Such movements are particularly characteristic of the sunflower, but may be observed to some extent in nearly all forms of higher plant life. Other plants, such as the Venus's flytrap, are capable of very rapid movements. Certain leaves of this plant are modified to act as a trap in capturing flies attracted to their surfaces. The leaves are designed in such a way that the moment the fly touches at least three sensitive hairs on a leaf, the two halves of the leaf clamp together. The fact that these traps are quite successful in catching flies indicates the rapidity with which the closing movement can take place. Still other types of movement are common even among one-celled plants. For example, rhythmic and swimming motions are displayed by many of the one-celled algae, found in ponds, rivers, and the oceans. It is clear, then, that plant movements, while on the whole less extensive than those shown by animals, nevertheless exist in a variety of forms.

In higher animals, movement is brought about by **muscular contraction.** Muscle is a type of tissue specially modified to contract when stimulated. By contracting, the muscle is shortened, and thus exerts a pulling force. Since the muscles are attached to movable body parts, a variety of different motions are possible.

Another characteristic of living organisms is their response to **stimuli** in the environment. A **stimulus** is any change in the environment—chemical or physical—which brings about a **response** or change in behavior on the part of the organism. Responsiveness is of obvious importance to living organisms, for it allows them to approach food and to avoid something harmful in the environment. The responses of lower organisms to various stimuli are often much simpler

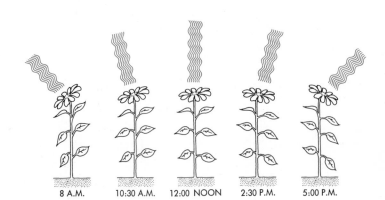

FIG. 1–3  Slow movements of the sun-flower stem and leaves during the course of a day. By responding to the position of the sun, the plant gains maximum exposure of its leaf surface to light.

8 A.M.    10:30 A.M.    12:00 NOON    2:30 P.M.    5:00 P.M.

than those displayed by higher organisms. However, even the simplest one-celled organism is capable of responding to a large number of different stimuli.

The response of an organism to a given stimulus is often very specific. Dogs, for example, have a very keen sense of smell. A dog which smells food will respond by salivating, while one which smells a rabbit may attempt to follow its trail by its scent. It may respond to the odor of an unfamiliar person by assuming a defensive position, curling its upper lip, and showing upright bristles on the back of the neck. In all these cases the stimulus was one of odor. Yet differences in the nature of the specific odor produced observably different responses.

All organisms show increases in size during their lifetime. This phenomenon is known as **growth.** Animals generally have limited or **determinate** periods of growth, which result in an adult of characteristic size. However, many plants and a few animals (such as sponges) continue to grow throughout their entire lifetime (**indeterminate** growth).

Growth is the result of the buildup of structural molecules at a rate more rapid than the rate at which they are broken down. In other words, during periods of growth, synthesis occurs to a greater extent than degradation. One-celled organisms grow by increasing the size of their single cell. Growth of a many-celled organism is generally the result of an increase in the size of individual cells, an increase in the number of cells, or both.

Reproduction—the means by which organisms produce more of their kind—is one of the most universally recognized characteristics of living things. The reproduction of nearly all animals and plants is either **sexual** or **asexual.** The most common example of asexual reproduction is **cell division** or **fission.** During cell division, a single parent cell splits into two daughter cells, each exactly like the original parent. Although asexual reproduction is most common

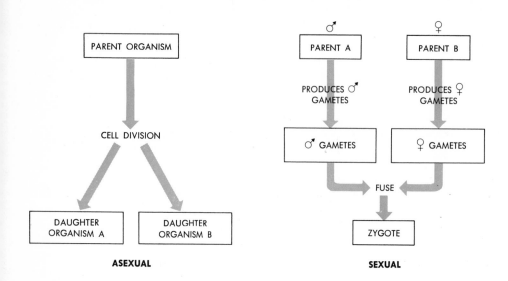

FIG. 1–4 Schematic diagram illustrating the basic difference between sexual and asexual reproduction. The symbols ♂ and ♀ stand for male and female, respectively.

among the one-celled plants and animals, it is by no means limited to simple organisms, for the cells of all organisms undergo the process of cell division sometime in the course of their existence.

Sexual reproduction, on the other hand, results from the **union** of two cells, called **gametes**. In most cases, gametes can be distinguished as belonging to two distinct sexes—male and female. The male gamete (called a **sperm**) fuses with the female gamete (called an **ovum** or **egg**) by a process known as **fertilization**. This results in the formation of a single-celled **zygote**. The zygote, by repeated cell divisions, eventually develops into a complete organism (see Fig. 1–4).

**1-7**

**DIFFERENTIATION**   During the growth of a many-celled organism from a single zygote or asexual cell, cells take on different shapes and functions as a result of changes that are not only structural, but also biochemical. Thus from the same zygote there emerge cells as different in every respect as those of a nerve and muscle. These changes which occur during the growth of an organism after fertilization are known as **differentiation**.

The process of differentiation is a necessary stage in the **specialization** of cells (see Fig. 1–5). A one-celled organism must carry out all its own life activities.

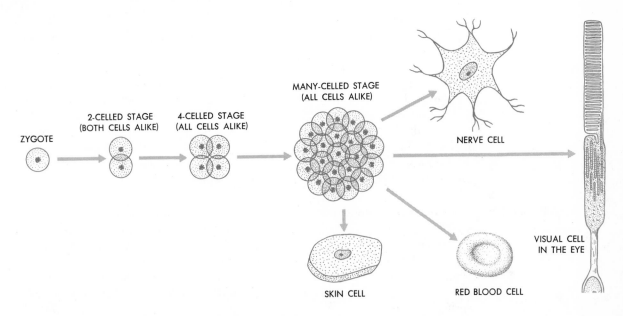

FIG. 1–5   Diagrammatic representation of differentiation.   At a certain point in the growth of an organism from zygote to adult, cells begin to become different, both in structure and in chemical composition.   Starting from similar cells, differentiation results in such different forms as the nerve cell, skin cell, visual cell, or red blood cell.   (The four cells drawn above are not scaled to true relative size.)

In many-celled organisms, however, specialization becomes not only possible, but advantageous.   For example, if certain cells can specialize to carry messages between one part of the organism and another (nerve cells), while others specialize in producing movement by contraction (muscle cells), a greater degree of coordination is possible.   The organism can thus make more complex responses, and its chances for survival are enhanced.

In specializing, cells lose their ability to live independently.   A nerve cell cannot live outside the animal body except in very highly controlled laboratory conditions.   Since the nerve cell specializes in carrying messages, other cells must function to carry an oxygen supply to the nerve cells, while still others remove their waste products.   By virtue of such complex interrelations among cells, however, organisms attain increased efficiency and a high level of coordination that would not be possible unless cell differentiation occurred.

Study of the process of differentiation is one of the most important and exciting fields of modern biology.   Current research is attempting to understand the chemistry of differentiation.   How, for instance, are embryonic cells signaled to develop in one direction rather than another?   Answers to questions about cell differentiation may prove to be extremely important in such areas of medicine as cancer research, for, in some cases, at least, cancer seems to involve a *dediffer-*

*entiation* of cells. This means that the affected cells revert to their embryonic or near-embryonic state, losing both their structural and their chemical specialization. Characteristically, they then begin to divide at an embryonic rate, consuming large amounts of energy, and thus robbing normal cells of needed energy. Moreover, because of dedifferentiation, cancer cells are unable to perform the specialized functions which they previously carried out for the organism. In order to determine how cancerous tissue can be treated, it is first necessary to understand how differentiation of cells occurs in the first place. This knowledge should make it possible to understand how the extraordinary process of dedifferentiation is brought about, and under what conditions.

**1–8**
**ADAPTATION**    The ability of an animal or plant to adapt to its environment is a characteristic which helps it to survive the changes which it must constantly face. **Adaptation** is any change in structure, physiology, or behavioral habits which allows an organism to exploit its environment more efficiently (i.e., to take advantage of resources in its environment in such a way as to increase chances of survival). Successful adaptation enables the organism to live longer and leave more offspring.

Biologically speaking, the term "adaptation" may be used in two different senses. On the one hand, an individual organism may be said to adapt to specific conditions during its own lifetime. A tree may grow very tall and straight if shaded from the sun by other trees around it. Or, it may grow in a crooked and bent direction out of a crevice, in response to the light. An animal transported from a temperate to an Arctic climate might develop an extra-heavy coat of hair. All these examples illustrate specific adaptations shown by individual organisms in the course of their own lifetime. Such adaptations are *temporary*; they are *not* transmitted to the next generation.
Such adaptations are *temporary*; they are *not* transmitted to the next generation.

However, the term "adaptation" is also used to refer to permanent changes which occur in a given species over many generations. Among the mammals, for example, some are adapted to land (man, horse, dog), others to a wholly aquatic existence (porpoise, whale), others to tree habitats (squirrels, monkeys). Each form is specialized to live in a certain environment. Adaptation of this kind comes about in quite a different way than adaptation of the individual; it is a hereditary feature of the organisms within the species. Such adaptations develop through random mutation and natural selection.

**1–9**
**CONCLUSION**    In this chapter we have discussed some of the major characteristics of life. A characterization is *not* a definition. Definitions involve drawing a limiting boundary around some object, process, or idea. A definition thus shows what something is by excluding other possibilities. We have seen how difficult this is in relation to "life." To characterize, on the other hand, means to describe the peculiar qualities of something. In characterizing life we have seen some of its most important qualities. We have not attempted to define life because, in the long run, such a definition is not particularly pertinent to the biologist's work.

He is more interested in describing how an organism accomplishes certain tasks, how it deals with aspects of its surroundings, and how its kind has changed over historical time. The biologist studies these questions because they appear to be answerable. Asking how to define life, on the other hand, poses a problem of semantics which neither the biologist nor anyone else is likely to be able to solve.

**EXERCISES**

1. Why is it so difficult to arrive at a workable definition of life?
2. How has the study of viruses contributed to the problem of defining life?
3. How are the processes of synthesis and degradation related in the metabolism of the organism?
4. What is responsiveness in organisms? How does the response of an organism relate to stimuli?
5. What are the two major patterns of growth in many-celled organisms?
6. Describe the generalized cycle of reproduction for organisms with male and female sex, for example, a higher animal or a flowering plant.
7. What is differentiation? What is the advantage to an organism of having differentiated tissues?
8. It has been said that the problem of differentiation is one of the most important areas of research in modern biology and medicine. For what reasons might this field be so important?
9. Distinguish between tissue, organ, and system in reference to many-celled organisms.
10. What are the two types of adaptation? How do these differ from each other?

**SUGGESTED READINGS**

SCHRÖDINGER, E., *What Is Life? And Other Scientific Essays* (New York: Anchor, 1956). This book, by a Nobel Prize winner, examines some of the mechanistic interpretations of life. Schrödinger, a physicist, is particularly interested in bringing his knowledge of the atom to bear on problems of biological significance. Not an easy book, this series of essays is rewarding to those who follow them from beginning to end.

VON BERTALANFFY, L., *Problems of Life: An Evaluation of Modern Biological and Scientific Thought* (New York: Harper Torchbooks, 1960). This book deals with the thesis that biology is based on physics and chemistry, the tools necessary for understanding life. The author, a well-known biologist, shows how these tools are used in studying living organisms.

# CHAPTER 2

# MAJOR GENERALIZATIONS IN BIOLOGY

Generalizations are statements which relate a number of specific and isolated items of information. The statement "All cats have four legs" is a generalization because it says something about a whole category of objects called cats. It relates a specific item of information such as "That white cat has four legs" to another specific item of information, "This gray cat has four legs." Generalizations are very important to everyday thinking. They are no less so to science. Generalizations provide a means of telescoping and condensing experience. They also allow a person to go beyond the specific individual event (for example, that a given cat has four legs) and predict aspects of experience with which he has not had direct contact. In summary, then, generalizations have two important functions: (1) They relate aspects of experience and so provide a way by which people organize their thinking, and (2) they provide a basis for prediction.

There are a number of biological generalizations of great importance. Although each of these will be discussed in some detail in later parts of the book, it will be helpful to introduce them in broad outline at this point.

The cell is the basic unit of life. The importance of viewing organisms on the cellular level is perhaps best summarized in the words of a German physiologist of the nineteenth century, Max Verworn:

*It is to the cell that the study of every bodily function sooner or later drives us. In the muscle cell lies the problem of the heartbeat and that of muscular contraction; in the gland cell reside the causes of secretion; in the lining cells of the digestive tract lies the problem of the absorption of food; and the secrets of the mind are hidden in the ganglion [i.e., nerve] cell.*

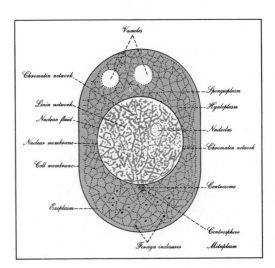

FIG. 2–1 Biology textbooks of the 1920's contained diagrams of "typical" cells like the one shown here. Such drawings were based on cell anatomy as revealed by the light microscope.

What is a cell? As was seen in Chapter 1, cells take many forms. There are nerve cells, muscle cells, digestive cells, skin cells, bone cells, visual cells in the eye, and many others. Although different in a variety of ways, most cells have certain fundamental similarities. A simplified diagram of a cell, showing just a few of the essential parts, can be seen in Fig. 2–1. This diagram shows that cells possess an outer limiting membrane, the **cell** or **plasma membrane.** Inside the plasma membrane are the **nucleus** and the **cytoplasm.** The cytoplasm is a watery medium in which a variety of molecules and larger structures called **organelles** (*-elle* = little, thus "little organ") are suspended. The nucleus, which is surrounded by its own limiting membrane, contains nucleic acid, shown to be responsible for the transmission of genetic information.

The "cell concept" as viewed today can be summarized in the following four propositions.

1) *Virtually all living organisms are composed of cells.* This generalization extends from simple one-celled organisms such as an amoeba or a bacterium to complex many-celled forms such as a man or a tree. Cells are thus the basic structural units of which organisms are composed.

2) *Cells are the site of all metabolic reactions in an organism.* Even in a complex form such as man, all metabolism takes place within individual cells. Thus, for example, the chemical processes which provide the energy for contraction of a muscle cell take place within the muscle cell itself.

3) *Cells arise only from preexisting cells.* No spontaneous generation of cells occurs. A multicelled organism grows by duplication of its individual cells. By special cell divisions, some organisms produce gametes, which are capable of

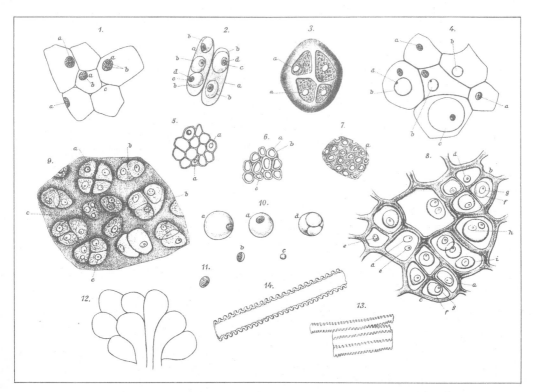

FIG. 2–2  Drawings from Schwann's *Microscopical Investigations* (1839).  This work shows that by the mid-nineteenth century a great deal of detail was known about the structure of cells.

generating a whole new organism.  The idea of **biogenesis**—that all living cells originate only from preexisting living cells, or that life originates from life—is fundamental to the modern cell concept.

4)  *Cells contain hereditary material* **(nucleic acid)** through which specific characteristics are passed on from parent cell to daughter cell.  The hereditary material contains a "code" which ensures that there will be continuity of species from one cell generation to the next.

The modern cell concept (sometimes called "the cell theory") is not the work of any one man.  Cells were first observed and described by some of the early seventeenth-century microscopists.  Robert Hooke's *Micrographia* (1665) contains some of the first clear plant-cell drawings, made from observations of thin sections of cork.*  Hooke coined the term "cell" to refer to these boxlike struc-

* The term "cork" refers to a portion of the bark, or outer covering layer, of any woody plant.  The cork used for thermos bottles is part of the bark of the cork oak tree, found mostly in Spain.

tures. The fact that all living organisms are composed of cells was not recognized, however, until the nineteenth century. The most important generalized statement about the cellular nature of living organisms was made by two German biologists, Matthias Schleiden and Theodor Schwann, in 1838 and 1839. Schleiden, a botanist, and Schwann, a zoologist, studied many types of tissue in their respective fields. Both came to the conclusion that the cell was the basic structural unit of all living things. Some of Schwann's diagrams of various animal cells can be seen in Fig. 2–2. Schleiden and Schwann thus contributed the first of the propositions listed above. The second and third propositions were added by the German pathologist and statesman Rudolf Virchow (1821–1902). In his work *Cellular Pathology* (1858), Virchow spoke of the cell as the basic metabolic as well as structural unit. In this same work he emphasized the continuity in living organisms by the statement: "omnis cellula e cellula"—"all cells come from (preexisting) cells." The last proposition in the modern cell concept is a more recent addition.

There have been many ideas put forth to explain the way in which characteristics are determined in the offspring of any two parent organisms. One view is that the offspring shows a mixture, or blending, of all the characteristics from each parent. This idea was accepted by many people in the nineteenth century. It holds that such characteristics as hair color, bone size, or flower color are a blend between the parental characteristics. In morning glories, for example, a cross between a plant with red flowers and one with white flowers would be expected to produce a first generation of plants with pink flowers. Observation shows that this is, indeed, the case. The idea of **blending inheritance** is analogous to that of mixing two different-colored paints in one bucket. The resulting mixture shows characteristics which are a "blend" between the two "parental" characteristics.

The theory of blending inheritance explains very well the hereditary process in many organisms such as the morning glory. But there are some situations which it does not explain. For example, if several pink (first generation) morning glories are crossed, the second generation shows red, pink, and white morning glories in a ratio of 1:2:1. The theory of blending inheritance is unable to account for the reappearance of both the red and white characteristic. Here is where the paint-mixing analogy falls down. There was thus a need for some explanation of how ancestral characteristics, hidden for one generation or more, could reappear seemingly unchanged.

This need was met by the concept of **particulate inheritance.** There were several particulate theories current in the late nineteenth century, but after 1900 only one of these, that proposed by the Austrian monk Gregor Mendel in 1865, proved useful in understanding the hereditary process in a wide variety of organisms. All particulate theories of heredity maintain that parent organisms pass on definite units or particles, each of which determines or influences one characteristic of the offspring (flower color, hair color, bone size, etc.). The mendelian concept holds that the offspring inherits two particles for each characteristic, one particle from each parent. If the two particles are different in the form of the characteristic (i.e., one determining red flowers, the other white flowers) there can be two possible results. In the case of morning glories, both particles (which we would refer to today as **genes**) show their effects. The offspring is correspondingly midway between the two parents and is a true blend for that characteristic. A different result is seen in the case of eye color in human beings; here, blending does not occur. If a blue-eyed and brown-eyed set of parents have children, all will probably show brown eyes. However, sometimes brown-eyed parents have blue-eyed children, but blue-eyed parents never have brown-eyed children. According to the mendelian theory, the gene for brown eyes is said to be **dominant** over the gene for blue eyes. The latter, in turn, is said to be **recessive** to the gene for brown eyes. Thus a person with blue eyes is known to have only the genes for blue eyes. A person with brown eyes, however, may have two genes for brown, or one for brown and one for blue. Since the gene for brown eyes masks the effects of the gene for blue eyes, the latter is not expressed in the appearance of the organism. Yet, as in the case of the second-generation morning glories, the blue-eye gene can reappear in subsequent generations, apparently unaltered by its association with the dominant brown gene.

The mendelian concept of heredity is especially capable of explaining these inheritance patterns, where the concept of blending inheritance is wholly inadequate. According to the mendelian scheme, each gene for a certain characteristic is unchanged by its association with other genes. Thus, in the case of morning glories, the gene for "red flower" is unaltered by existing next to a gene for "white flower" in the first-generation organisms. When these organisms are crossed, some offspring of the second generation get two "red" genes (thus showing only red flowers), some get a "red" and a "white" gene (thus showing the pink condition) and still others receive two "white" genes (thus showing the white flower). Thus, although the first generation offspring showed neither red nor white flowers, the genes, when properly matched up in the second generation, produced the original parental characteristics again.

Mendel's particulate concept not only offers a more complete explanation of heredity than the idea of blending inheritance, but it also affords the means of predicting with considerable accuracy the results of crosses between a variety of parental types. For these reasons, Mendel's theory gained wide acceptance among biologists in the twentieth century. It is basically this theory, expanded through new work in molecular biology, which forms the substance of the modern-day view of heredity.

Acceptance of a particulate theory of inheritance raises many questions. What is the actual nature of the genes? How are these units passed on to the next generation? How does a gene determine, physiologically, a given characteristic? How do variations in the organism arise? These and many other questions have provided the stimulus for much genetic research in the present century. In the past decade, remarkable progress has been made in understanding the transmission and action of genetic material. Many of these topics will be discussed in later chapters of this book.

One of the important features of the modern theory of inheritance is that it explains how organisms produce nearly perfect copies of themselves. However, heritable variations sometimes do arise in offspring. That is, there appear to be mistakes in the process by which genes reproduce themselves, in passing from one generation to the next. Such mistakes, if they cannot be shown to arise in accordance with mendelian rules, are said to be **mutations.** Mutations are due to changes in the hereditary code comprising the gene itself. Such changes generally show up as differences in the physical or chemical structure of an organism. A condition known as vestigial wing in the fruit fly is the result of a mutation of the gene for normal wing size. Flies bearing the mutant gene have very short, useless wings (see Fig. 2–3). Most mutations produce only very slight changes in the organism—so slight that only an expert can detect their presence. Occasionally, however, as in the vestigial-wing example, mutations may be quite noticeable.

2–4
**THE MUTATION
THEORY**

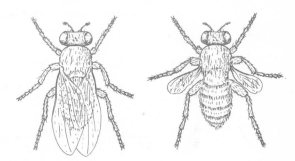

FIG. 2–3   The fruit fly *Drosophila melanogaster.* The drawing to the left shows a normal or wild individual. To the right can be seen a mutant form, vestigial wing. Note the short, shriveled wings of the mutant.

Once mutations occur, they are generally passed on to subsequent generations. That is, a mutant gene "breeds true" until such time as it mutates further. Biologists do not know exactly what causes mutations to occur under normal conditions of life. However, there are various experimental means of speeding up the rate of mutation. X-radiation or chemical compounds such as mustard gas and colchicine will do this very effectively. Such experiments indicate that mutations occur at random. Thus, although it is possible to increase the rate at which mutations occur, it is not possible to cause a specific gene to mutate by applying any of the above experimental methods.

2–5
**THE CONTINUITY
OF THE
GERM PLASM**

In 1889 the German biologist August Weismann formulated the theory of the "continuity of the germ plasm." In this theory, Weismann postulated that, for animals, from the very first divisions of the fertilized egg, certain cells are "set aside" to become the reproductive or gamete-forming tissue of the developing organism. These he referred to as germ cells, or the **germ plasm.** The other

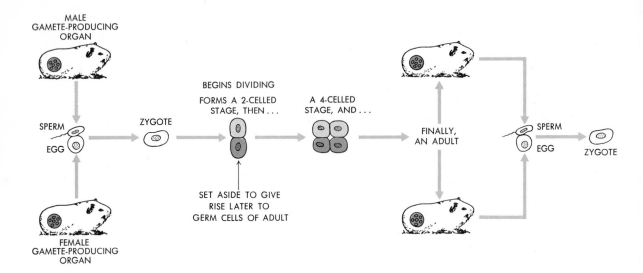

FIG. 2–4  Weismann's concept of the continuity of the germ plasm.  Note that from the first division of the zygote, certain cells are set aside to become the future germ plasm which will later form sperm or eggs.

cells develop into body cells, or **somatoplasm** (muscle cells, nerve cells, skin cells, etc.).  The germ plasm was thus viewed as distinct from the somatoplasm from the very beginning of embryonic development.  The germ plasm of the offspring descends directly from the germ plasm of the parent.

Weismann's theory provides a way of looking at the inheritance of various characteristics.  It shows an unbroken continuity existing between the germ plasm of the parent and the germ plasm of the offspring.  The somatic cells can be viewed as the agent involved in maintaining and transmitting the germ plasm. Weismann's concept extended the continuity which Virchow saw (continuity from one *cell* generation to the next) to include generations of entire organisms (see Fig. 2–4).  It must be pointed out that Weismann's generalization is limited to the animal world only.  No such separation of germ plasm and somatoplasm occurs in the embryonic development of plants.

Weismann's work indicated that in animals, at least, *acquired characteristics are not inherited.*  Only changes which affect the genetic material in the germ plasm of an organism will be transmitted to the offspring.  Thus, for example, any kind of change that may occur to genes in skin tissue will not affect the offspring of that individual.  Mutations in the genetic code of gamete-forming tissue will, however, be passed on to the next generation.

The concept of evolution and of the means by which it occurs is probably the most important generalization in modern biology. Our present theory of the evolution of plants and animals consists of two conceptually and historically different ideas. One is the idea of evolution itself—the view that the many species of plants and animals existing today have descended, through modification, from earlier, different species. The other is the more theoretical consideration of natural selection—the mechanism by which this development is brought about.

The theory of evolution is an attempt to explain the diversity of animal and plant species. Modern evolutionary theory holds that groups of organisms change in the course of geological time. Species living today have descended, in modified form, from species which existed millions of years ago. The modifications which occur from one generation to the next are in general very small. Once these modifications have occurred a first time, however, they are passed on to succeeding generations unless canceled by other variations. After thousands or millions of years, accumulation of these slight modifications results in an animal or plant significantly different from its remote ancestors.

The theory of natural selection describes a *mechanism* by which evolution may occur. The concept of natural selection is closely linked with the name of Charles Darwin (1809–1882). It was primarily through Darwin's work that the idea of natural selection was firmly established as an important biological generalization.

The idea of natural selection as a mechanism for evolution is based upon several ideas:

1) Hereditary differences occur among members of a given species. Some of the variations will increase the individual organism's chances of survival, while others will decrease the chances.

2) More organisms are generally born than can survive in view of limited food supply, available habitats, etc. Thus there is a continual struggle for existence.

3) Limited availability of the necessities of life produces *competition* among organisms. Competition is most severe between individuals of the same kind, because these have identical, or nearly identical, requirements.

4) Organisms which are successful in competition will have a better chance to reproduce. In other words, the fittest will survive.

5) The basic unit of evolution is the *species*. A species is a population of individuals, the members of which interbreed freely.

These are the ingredients of the natural-selection process. How do they produce evolution? Note first that those individuals whose hereditary variations enable them to get more food or better living conditions will survive longer and thus reproduce more. They thus pass on their genes to a larger percentage of the next generation than the less successful organisms. Over a period of many generations, then, the genetic character of the breeding population will change,

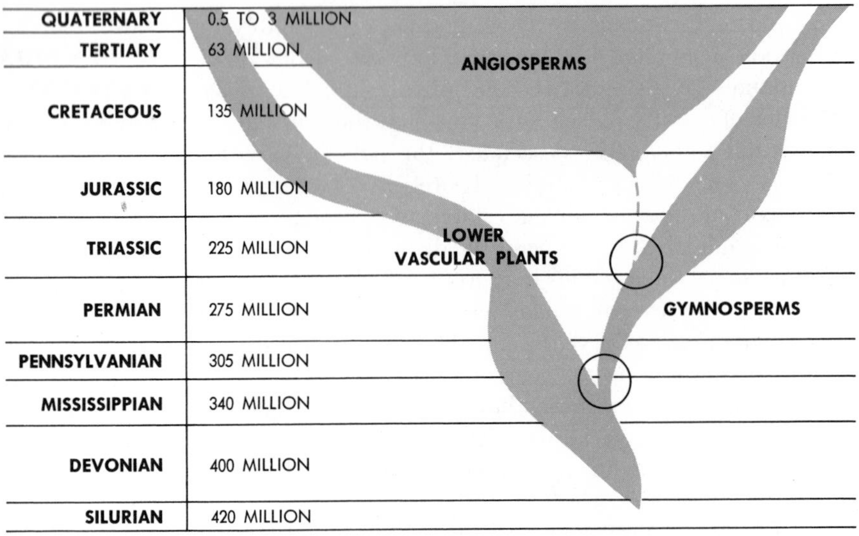

| | | | |
|---|---|---|---|
| QUATERNARY | 0.5 TO 3 MILLION | | |
| TERTIARY | 63 MILLION | ANGIOSPERMS | |
| CRETACEOUS | 135 MILLION | | |
| JURASSIC | 180 MILLION | | |
| TRIASSIC | 225 MILLION | LOWER VASCULAR PLANTS | |
| PERMIAN | 275 MILLION | | GYMNOSPERMS |
| PENNSYLVANIAN | 305 MILLION | | |
| MISSISSIPPIAN | 340 MILLION | | |
| DEVONIAN | 400 MILLION | | |
| SILURIAN | 420 MILLION | | |

FIG. 2–5  Phylogenetic chart of land plants.  Various geological periods are shown on the scale to the left, with the oldest at the bottom.  The figures beside each period indicate approximately how many years ago the period began.  The two points in time where a common ancestor gave rise to two branches are circled.  The width of the shaded area indicates the relative number of genera in each major branch at each point in time. (Adapted from *Scientific American*, February 1963, p. 81.)

favoring the more successful variations.  Individuals in the population will gradually become better and better adapted to their environment.

The concept of natural selection is an extremely important one.  It provides a single generalization by which the evolution of all known living forms can be explained.  It is integrally connected to the ideas of heredity, ecology, taxonomy, cytology (the study of cells), paleontology (the study of fossils), embryology, and even biochemistry.  It thus brings together a number of areas of biological thought.

Evolution by natural selection has resulted in the proliferation of many kinds of organisms on earth.  There are many more species alive today than there were several million years ago.  For example, the many varieties of dog living today probably evolved from a common ancestral type.  Thus not only does evolution include the gradual modification of a given kind of organism into a new kind, but also the divergence of a single kind of organism into many.  Darwin especially emphasized the divergence pattern of evolution.

A family tree, or **phylogenetic chart,** may be used to make clear the historical relationships between groups evolving from a common ancestor.

Figure 2–5 shows the broad outline of a family tree for the evolution of land plants. The points representing common ancestors are circled. At these points divergence occurred, giving rise to two separate groups of plants in each case.

The term "missing link" has often been used to refer to some undiscovered stage in the evolution of a group of organisms. The term "link" is unfortunate. It implies something like the link in a chain—one direct connection in a straight sequence of objects or events. A common ancestor is not at all like a link. Rather, it represents a starting point from which two different groups have diverged to evolve in their own separate ways.

Darwin's concept of natural selection emphasized the important interrelation between an organism and its environment. Survival depends on how well an organism copes with the various aspects of this environment. Detailed studies have shown that all living things in a given area are closely interrelated, both with each other and with the nonliving aspects of the environment. The environment of an organism is the sum of its biological and physical surroundings. The biological environment of any organism includes the other plants and animals in the region; the physical environment includes such features as temperature, amount of light, moisture, minerals, and so on. The aspect of biology which studies the relations between an organism and its environment is known as **ecology.**

Organisms exist together in **communities.** The groups of organisms which inhabit the forest, the field, the pond, or the ocean bottom are all examples of biological communities. All communities in a given region (for example, in a valley between two mountain ranges) are interdependent. The phrase "web of life" has often been used to express this interdependence, because disturbance to any one aspect of the community interrelations will have profound effects on all other aspects, just as breaking a single strand in a delicately woven spider's web may totally alter the entire pattern of the web. Man has learned, often the hard way, that to disturb the balance of nature in any region can produce far-reaching effects.

Around the turn of the century, air pollution from the smoke of a copper smelter destroyed much of the vegetation in Copper Basin, Tennessee. The result was rainwater-caused erosion* which in turn restricted the type of plants which could regain foothold. Even present attempts to reforest the area have been greatly hampered by continual erosion. This example illustrates in a dramatic way how closely the biological and physical environments are interrelated.

2-7
**ECOLOGICAL
INTERRELATIONS**

---

* Rainfall in a region is affected to some extent by the amount of moisture released into the atmosphere locally by plants. The loss of plant life over an extensive area like Copper Basin could thus significantly affect the average rainfall in this region, and it has been speculated that the loss of plant life which did occur may account for a recorded change in annual rainfall.

The generalization of ecological interrelations is of great practical as well as theoretical importance. It provides the basis for all efforts to conserve wildlife, preserve forests, and to make better use of land for agriculture. All sound conservation programs are based upon an intimate knowledge of the principles of ecology. Since conservation is one of the most crucial social and technological issues which mankind faces today, ecology is one of the most important areas of modern biological research.

**2–8
THE MOLECULAR
FOUNDATION
OF BIOLOGY**

One general tenet underlies much current biological research. This is the idea that ultimately, living processes can be explained in terms of the interaction of molecules, atoms, and subatomic particles such as electrons. This does not mean, of course, that research in areas of ecology or evolutionary theory must be concerned with molecular explanations in order to be important. We must always keep a concern for the whole organism. Yet current study in molecular biology indicates that areas such as genetics, evolution, general physiology, and even classification of organisms, can all be carried to the molecular level.

The molecular approach to biology is based on our present-day understanding of physics and chemistry, and their applicability to biological problems. As an area of current research, molecular biology is extremely important for a variety of reasons. One is that by using the tools of physics and chemistry, it is possible to treat many biological problems with precision and with rigor. For instance, through nineteenth- and twentieth-century studies on the physics and chemistry of energy processes in living systems, it is possible to predict with great accuracy the amount of heat which an organism will release in performing a specific task. It is possible too, to calculate exactly how much energy is released in the breakdown of a given number of food molecules, or how much energy is used in building a certain complex molecule like a protein. Studies in molecular biology have also yielded a very precise indication of how hereditary information is coded so that the offspring duplicates the characteristics of the parental type. By using the methods of chemistry and physics, such principles have become well established. Much less has been left to speculation or to guesswork than would otherwise be the case.

Another important reason for the central role of molecular biology in much current research is that such studies have revealed clearly how similar the chemical processes are in all organisms. The processes involved in energy transformation or in the passing on of coded heredity information seem to be quite similar in organisms as different as a maple tree, a bacterium, and man. In other words, molecular biology has brought to light the great biochemical unity which seems to underlie the living world. The fact that in quite different organisms the same molecules can be found performing the same chemical jobs indicates how much seemingly different organisms have in common. It gives strong support to the idea that all organisms have descended ultimately from a common ancestor.

There may be some doubt as to whether the ideas of "mechanism" and "vitalism," as ways of looking at living organisms, are generalizations in the same sense as those of natural selection or the gene concept. Some people might argue that they are only philosophies. Clearly however, they represent opposing views of what is an acceptable biological explanation of the nature of life. Although debated more hotly in the past than at the present, their basic assumptions strike more closely to the problem of "What is life?" than perhaps any other biological issue.

**Mechanism** is that view of living organisms which holds that life is completely explicable in physical and chemical terms. A mechanist believes that organisms are extremely complex organizations of various atoms and molecules. He also believes that the interrelation between these atoms and molecules can be understood by applying the tools of the chemist or physicist. He does not believe that there is anything to a living cell that goes beyond the physical or chemical concepts which we accept today. He is willing to accept the fact that modern techniques are not perfect, and that newer methods will have to be developed before we can completely understand how a living cell functions. The important point is that to him, the possibility of gaining such an understanding is a real one.

**Vitalism,** on the other hand, maintains that life is an expression of something more than the mere interaction of a group of molecules. To the vitalist, the living organism is more than the sum of its parts. There resides in the living matter some vital principle which cannot be explained in physical or chemical terms. An example of vitalist thinking is provided in the memoirs of Assistant Surgeon Edward Curtis of the Washington, D.C. Army Medical Museum. After President Abraham Lincoln died on April 15, 1865, an autopsy took place in the Northeast Corner guest room of the White House. In the words of Dr. Curtis,

...*Silently, in one corner of the room, I prepared the brain for weighing. As I looked at the mass of soft gray and white substance that I was carefully washing, it was impossible to realize that it was that mere clay upon whose workings, but the day before, rested the hopes of the nation. I felt more profoundly impressed than ever with the mystery of that unknown something which may be named "vital spark" as well as anything else, whose absence or presence makes all the immeasurable difference between an inert mass of matter owing obedience to no laws but those governing the physical and chemical forces of the universe and, on the other hand, a living brain by whose silent, subtle machinery a world may be ruled.*

The vitalist does not deny that chemical analyses of living organisms are important. But he feels that "life" involves something more than the principles of physics and chemistry.

It is essentially over this question of whether or not a "something more" actually exists that the mechanists and the vitalists have argued for so long.

**2-9
MECHANISM
AND VITALISM**

Much debate by a number of scientists in the later nineteenth and early twentieth centuries did very little to settle the issue. In any case, the point seems largely academic. In their daily research, most biologists today are mechanists. They look for biological explanations which agree with those of physics and chemistry. Yet, such a biologist could also believe (and some do) that this approach will never provide a complete understanding of the living organism. They would maintain that there is something beyond this which will always defy man's laboratory analysis.

**2-10**
**CONCLUSION**

The generalizations discussed in this chapter have two major functions for the biologist. First, they provide a means by which he can relate many individual pieces of information. Second, they allow him to make predictions. As will become clear in the next several chapters, the predictive value of scientific generalizations is of fundamental importance.

Of the generalizations which we have discussed, some offer a higher level of generality than others; that is, they cover a larger number of cases than those with a low level of generality. Darwin's idea of natural selection is a high-level generalization because it applies to all known organisms. Plants, animals, bacteria, even viruses, evolve over time in accordance with Darwin's idea. Weismann's concept of continuity of the germ plasm, however, is a lower-level generalization because it applies only to animals. Thus not all of the generalizations discussed in this chapter have the same weight, or the same value, to the biologist. More will be said about the nature and validity of scientific generalizations in the following chapter.

**EXERCISES**

1. What is the cell concept as we understand it today? What did the following men contribute to the development of that concept: (a) Matthais Schleiden? (c) Theodor Schwann? (c) Rudolf Virchow?

2. Describe the difference between the concepts of blending inheritance and particulate inheritance.

3. What is a mutation?

4. Briefly outline Darwin's conception of natural selection. How is the idea of mutations related to that of natural selection?

5. What is the distinction between germ plasm and somatoplasm?

6. What is meant by the phrase "continuity of the germ plasm"?

7. In darwinian terms, what is the criterion of "success" in any species?

8. Read the viewpoints of a mechanist and a vitalist as given in the suggested readings. Which arguments seem most valid? What loopholes, if any, do you find in each type of argument?

9. What is meant by saying that all biological processes have a molecular basis? What support is there for this assertion?

Since all the generalizations discussed in this chapter will be studied in depth in later sections of the book, no readings will be given here for individual concepts. The mechanist-vitalist controversy, however, represents some attempts to arrive at a philosophy of biology. Two books, each expressing quite different views on the subject, will provide the basis for stimulating thought about the nature and limitations of biological investigation.

DRIESCH, HANS, *The Science and Philosophy of the Organism* (London: Adam and Charles Black, 1908). Driesch was the most prominent and vocal of the late nineteenth- and early twentieth-century vitalists. The experiments which led him to his vitalism are described in this book.

LOEB, JACQUES, *The Mechanistic Conception of Life* (Cambridge: Harvard University Press, 1964). This is a reprint of a book which originally appeared in 1912. Loeb represents the extreme mechanistic outlook. The book is not too technical to provide a thorough introduction to the mechanist's arguments.

# CHAPTER 3

# THE NATURE AND LOGIC OF SCIENCE

First and foremost, biology is a science, the biologist a scientist. Science can be distinguished from other fields of intellectual endeavor by two main features. Obviously, it differs in its content—the type of organized knowledge with which it is concerned. A more important difference, however, lies in the *procedure* of science—its strictly empirical approach to problems. Science deals only with rational beliefs which can be verified or disproved by observation or experiment. In the words of Roger Bacon (1210–1292), "experimental science has one great prerogative . . . that it investigates its conclusions by experience."

Science is frequently said to consist of collecting and organizing facts. This, however, is only one aspect of science. Far more important is what the scientist does with the facts he has at hand. The way in which the scientist draws conclusions, makes generalizations, and tests predictions forms the method of science. In a general way, then, it is useful to make a distinction between content and procedure in science. Scientific content is the subject matter of science—the generalizations which the scientific community may recognize as valid. The concepts embodied in Mendel's laws, the concepts of natural selection and mutation—these represent scientific content. The methods by which such concepts were obtained—by experiments, observations, or reasoning from known examples—represent scientific procedure.

The number of scientists in the United States in 1900 was approximately 8000. In 1960 the number was more than 100,000. At least four out of five of all the professional scientists who ever lived are alive today. No one can live in the 1970's and not be aware of the tremendous impact that this growth in science and the resulting growth in technology have had on the world, both for good and for bad. The influence of science has spread even to the arts. For example,

26

Sir Isaac Newton's famous equation

$$F \propto \frac{m_1 m_2}{s^2},$$

which simply states that the gravitational force ($F$) between two bodies is proportional ($\propto$) to the product of their masses ($m_1 m_2$) divided by the square of the distance ($s^2$) between their centers of gravity, influenced the poet Francis Thompson (1859–1907) to write:

*When to the new eyes of thee*
*All things by an immortal power*
*Near or far,*
*Hiddenly*
*To each other linked are*
*That thou canst not stir a flower*
*Without troubling of a star.*

Johann Wolfgang von Goethe (1749–1832) wrote:

*In nature we never see anything isolated but everything in connection with something else which is before it, beside it, under it and over it.*

Science is the discipline that tries to sort out these connections and to make some kind of order out of them.  Not even the seemingly most insignificant detail can be overlooked, for, as the physicist Sir George Thomson puts it,

*It is the greatest discovery which science has made that the apparently trivial, the merely curious, may be the clues to an understanding of the deepest principles of Nature.*

But again it is not the nature of the trivial or nontrivial matters with which science deals that accounts for science's astounding impact on society; rather it is the *manner* in which the scientist approaches these matters.  It is to this "manner" that attention must now be directed.

3-2
THE "SCIENTIFIC
METHOD"

The popular, man-on-the-street concept of the scientist and his methods is a poor one.  According to this concept, the scientist is a man with secret means of obtaining knowledge to benefit mankind.  The fact that explanations put forth by research scientists may be wrong as often as they are right, and that not all of their discoveries directly benefit man (indeed, many seem to be completely useless), is not widely known.  This is possibly due to the fact that wrong guesses are not given much publicity, and right guesses which do not directly benefit man attract less public attention.

Even among scientists, however, there is wide disagreement as to what is meant by the "scientific method."  Some science textbooks list a series of six or seven steps involved in the scientific method.  Such a formal and highly structured description is quite unrealistic. No research scientist follows any such formalized ritual in performing his experiments.

Some writers, however, have gone to the other extreme in their description of the scientific method. One states that "science is simply doing one's damnedest with one's mind with no holds barred." This view has one positive attribute. It correctly indicates that the means used by scientists in solving problems are not necessarily unique to science. As a definition of the scientific method, however, the statement is not very successful. Followed to its logical conclusion, it indicates that philosophers, mechanics, mathematicians, plumbers, or any other persons who work diligently to solve problems are also scientists. Most certainly this is not the case.

*Science proceeds by postulating and testing hypotheses.* **Hypotheses** are simply tentative explanations put forth to account for observed phenomena.

Let us take a specific example:

The silver salmon, *Oncorhyncus kisutch*, hatches in the freshwater streams of our Pacific Northwest. The young fish swim downstream to the Pacific Ocean, where they may spend five years attaining full size and sexual maturity. Then, in response to some undetermined stimulus, they return to fresh water to spawn (lay their eggs).

By tagging the fish, a remarkable fact is discovered. Nearly always, *the fish return to the precise stream where they were born.*

Here is an observed phenomenon which arouses the curiosity. *How* are the fish able to locate the precise stream in which they were born? This is no easy task. Some of the fish must swim up high waterfalls and go as far inland as the state of Idaho in order to return to their place of birth.

An hypothesis is needed to explain the phenomenon. In a sense, an hypothesis is simply an "educated guess." In this case, the hypothesis will probably be based on pertinent observations of the salmon and their habits. Perhaps the fish find their way to their homes by recognizing certain objects they saw when they passed downstream as young fish on their way to the sea. Or perhaps they recognize the "taste" or "odor" of their home streams. Several other hypotheses are possible, of course, but let us settle on these two. What next?

Clearly, to stop here, after merely formulating hypotheses, is not very satisfying. It is natural to want to find out which hypothesis (if either) is correct. The scientist, in his attempts to find the answer, proceeds by designing and performing experiments. *The primary purpose of scientific experiments is to test hypotheses.* Thus any hypothesis selected by a scientist to explain a natural phenomenon must meet a very important requirement: *It must be testable.*

Both hypotheses which we selected to explain the homing behavior of salmon meet this requirement; they *can* be tested by experimentation. But *how* do experiments test hypotheses? The answer is quite simple. *Experiments test hypotheses by testing the correctness of the predictions that can be derived from them.*

Consider, for example, the first hypothesis, which explained the salmon's ability to find their home stream solely on the basis of visual recognition. If this hypothesis is correct, then salmon with shields placed over their eyes should be unable to find their way home. This reasoning can be expressed more formally as follows:

**Hypothesis:** *If . . . Oncorhyncus kisutch* salmon use visual stimuli alone to find their way to their home streams to spawn, . . .

**Prediction:** *then* . . . blindfolded salmon of this species should not be able to find their way home.

Suppose that the fish find their way home when blindfolded just as well as they did before. If we assume that no other factors (or variables) have been overlooked which might influence the results, can it be stated that the experimental results *disprove* our hypothesis? Yes. Suppose, on the other hand, that the blindfolded fish did *not* find their way to their home streams. Would these results *prove* the visual-stimulus hypothesis? No. The experimental results can only be said to *support* the hypothesis.

FIG. 3–1 This "truth table" shows the relation between an hypothesis and its predictions. Note that a true prediction may be derived from a false hypothesis as well as from a true one. Thus true predictions do not constitute proof of the truth of an hypothesis.

**A TRUTH TABLE**

| HYPOTHESIS | CONCLUSION OR PREDICTION |
|---|---|
| TRUE | TRUE |
| FALSE | TRUE or FALSE |

This raises an interesting question. Why should it be possible to *disprove* an hypothesis by one set of experimental results, yet not be able to *prove* the same hypothesis by obtaining the predicted set of results? The answer lies in the nature of the relation between hypotheses and the predictions which can be derived from them. This relation, which is shown in the "truth table" of Fig. 3–1, forms the basic framework for the operations of **deductive logic.**

Deductive logic (often called *if . . . , then* reasoning) is the heart and soul of mathematics. It becomes most evident in plane geometry, e.g., "*If* two points of a line lie in a plane, *then* the line lies in the same plane." However, deduction plays no less of a role in other fields of mathematics as well, e.g., "*If* $a < b$ and $x \leq y$, *then* $a + x < b + y$" (the addition law), or "*If* $x < y$ and $a > 0$, *then* $ax < ay$" (the multiplication law).

In science, and therefore in biology, deduction is just as vital as it is in mathematics. (Recall our breakdown of the salmon experiment into an *if . . . , then* framework.) Yet, there are important differences between the way deduction is used in mathematics and the way it is used in experimental science. Mathematicians generally deal with symbols. They are not so concerned with physical entities such as migrating salmon. Furthermore, the mathematician can manipulate his symbols at will. He can create situations in his proofs in which he is certain that only one hypothesis is being tested, only one question being asked. Not so the biologist. The salmon he is studying cannot be so easily manipulated. Therefore, the biologist can never be absolutely certain that his experiment has eliminated all the variables which might influence his results. Shielding the eyes of the salmon, for example, may cause the animals to use another sensory system in order to find their way home. Perhaps, normally, they *do* use their eyes to find their way home. Such a possibility may seem far-fetched, and highly unlikely. In the case of the salmon, it probably is. But the fact that such things are even remotely possible must constantly be in back of the biologist's mind.

A major problem in biological research, then, becomes one of experimental design (to which considerable attention will be devoted in Chapter 4). The biologist recognizes the impossibility of eliminating all the variables which might affect his experimental results, but he tries to design his experiments to decrease the *likelihood* that these variables will occur (see Fig. 3–2).

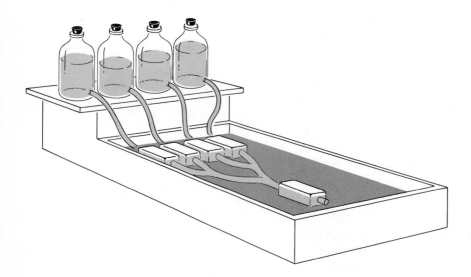

FIG. 3–2   Whenever possible, the biologist attempts to construct an experimental apparatus which allows him to test his hypotheses in the laboratory, rather than in the field. In this way, variables which might influence his results can be more easily controlled. This apparatus tests the ability of young eels to detect minute quantities of dissolved substances in the water. The object of the experiment is to discover whether these substances play a role in the eels' instinctive ability to find their way home from the Sargasso Sea (a region in the Atlantic Ocean) where they were born to the freshwater streams where they spend most of their lives. In this experiment, it was shown that the eels had no preference for tap water over seawater, but definitely preferred natural inland water to seawater. They were able to detect certain organic substances in the water even when these were diluted to $3 \times 10^{-20}$ parts per million. This means that the eels must be reacting to the presence of only two or three molecules of such a substance in their scent-detecting olfactory sacs.

Examine again the truth table in Fig. 3–1. Note that the word "conclusion" as used by a mathematician is interchangeable with the word "prediction" as used by the biologist, for the predictions which can be made from an hypothesis are simply the conclusions that one must draw from accepting it. In the case of the salmon, it must be concluded (or predicted) that the blindfolded salmon could not find their way home if the visual-stimulus hypothesis is accepted as being correct. If blindfolded salmon *do* find their way home, our conclusion has proved false. From the truth table, we see that this automatically means that our hypothesis is false, for note that *a true hypothesis can never give rise to a false conclusion.* In other words, predictions derived from a true hypothesis should never lead to contradictions.

The truth table also shows that we can never *prove* that an hypothesis is true. For, while a true hypothesis always gives rise to true predictions, *so also may a false hypothesis.* The importance of this last fact cannot be over-emphasized, for it shows that science can only deal with its "truths" in terms of probabilities, and never in terms of certainties.

In the past, many false hypotheses have been held by scientists and laymen alike, simply because accurate predictions could be made from these hypotheses despite their falsity. Acceptance of the belief that the sun orbits the earth leads one to predict that the sun will rise on one horizon, cross over the sky, and set on the other horizon . . . and so it does.* The fact that this prediction turns out to be correct does not, of course, mean that the sun *does* orbit the earth. In order to demonstrate that this hypothesis is false, other tests must be devised which show it to yield false predictions.†

Although the truth table shows that a true hypothesis never gives rise to a false conclusion (prediction), only in mathematics does the obtaining of just one false conclusion spell certain death for the hypothesis. Biologists rarely deal with cases in which *every* prediction made by an hypothesis turns out to be correct. The question then becomes one of *how many* or *what proportion* of a given number of predictions must be verified in order to make the hypothesis a useful one. For this reason, experimental data are often subjected to a **statistical analysis,** in which mathematics is employed to determine whether deviations from the pattern that is predicted by the hypothesis are significant. This topic will be dealt with more thoroughly in Chapter 5.

---

* It is likely that the observation of this aspect of the sun's behavior contributed to the idea that the sun orbits the earth. This illustrates the fact that hypotheses frequently arise from observations of the very phenomena which the hypotheses would predict. It is often difficult to establish which came first.

† One such test is to predict the future relative positions of the sun, earth, and other planets, given that the sun does orbit the earth. Such predictions are invariably shown to be false, thus disproving the hypothesis. On the other hand, accepting the hypothesis that the earth, along with the other planets, orbits the sun leads to very accurate predictions regarding the relative positions of the sun, earth, and other planets at any point in time. Every such accurate prediction supports the earth-orbiting-the-sun hypothesis.

Let us return once more to the problem of explaining salmon homing behavior and test the second hypothesis, which proposes that the fish find their way back to their home stream by their sense of smell. This hypothesis is supported by a chemical analysis of the water in several different streams. Such an analysis shows the water of each stream to be somewhat different from that of any other, due primarily to the different kinds and quantities of dissolved minerals which each contains.

We can proceed, then, to test experimentally this second hypothesis by testing the validity of a prediction which can be made from it:

**Hypothesis:** *If . . .   Oncorhyncus kisutch* salmon find their way to their home stream by following its distinctive odor upstream, . . .

**Prediction:** *then . . .* blocking the olfactory sacs (with which the fish detect odors) should prevent the salmon from finding their home stream.

This experiment was performed by Dr. A. D. Hasler and his associates, of the University of Wisconsin. The results strongly supported the odor hypothesis; a large majority of the fish were unable to find their way to their home stream to spawn. Nevertheless, some fish *did* find their way. Each one that did represents a false prediction which, according to the truth table, proves the hypothesis to be false. However, the laws of probability must be taken into consideration here. Statistical analysis shows that a certain number of the fish would be expected to end up in their home streams purely by chance. Since the number of experimental fish which found their way home was not significantly greater than the number which would be predicted to get there by chance, the odor hypothesis can still be considered a valid one.

Let us take a second example of experimentation in biology to illustrate another point concerning the interpretation of experimental results:

It has been shown many times that exposure of certain strains of mice to X-ray beams of 600 roentgens or more (a roentgen is a unit of measure of the amount of energy delivered in X-ray beams) causes death within two weeks or less. The death seems to be due to secondary rather than primary effects of the radiation. But it is uncertain just what is the primary cause of death at any one time, especially in the period of one to five days after exposure. It was thought that death might possibly be due to bacterial infection resulting from a migration of bacteria through the intestinal epithelium (lining), which histological (tissue) examination showed had been severely damaged by the X-rays. In order to test this hypothesis, antibiotics of various types were administered to the irradiated mice in several different ways to see whether this had any effect on the time of death. However, no such effect was shown, as the mice still died in the same length of time as the control animals, which had been irradiated under the same conditions but given no antibiotics. It was tentatively concluded, therefore, that death in the period tested (from one to five days after exposure) was not due to bacterial infection.*

Note the deductive *if . . . , then* reasoning here. The experimental logic can be simply stated as follows:

*Hypothesis: If . . .* the deaths of irradiated mice within one to five days after exposure are due to bacterial infection, . . .

*Prediction: then . . .* administration of antibiotics should lower the death rate of mice which receive them.

The experimental results showed the prediction to be a false one. The mice still died in the same length of time after exposure to the X-rays. Thus we know, barring experimental error, that the hypothesis explaining the deaths as being due to bacterial infection was also false, and therefore must be either discarded or modified.

Suppose that the administration of antibiotics *had* caused a lengthening of life. Would this have shown that our hypothesis must be the correct explanation? Absolutely not, although this result would have lent strong support to the *probability* of its being correct.

Could it be stated that death from radiation *in animals* is not due to bacterial infection? No, for the word "animals" includes many more forms of life than just mice. Could it be stated that death from radiation *in mice* is not due to bacterial infection? No, for not all strains of mice were tested. When the research paper is written for publication in a research journal, the biologist will carefully word his interpretations, limiting them to the precise strains of mice tested and to the time period of death (one to five days after exposure) with which he worked.

Despite the limitational care with which experimental results are generally interpreted, biologists often *do* extend their experimental results from one organism to another. Modern medical drugs, for example, are usually tested first on laboratory animals; if successful, their use may be extended to humans. But there is always an element of uncertainty involved. All organisms do not necessarily react the same way to the same drugs . . . "One man's meat is another man's poison."

## 3-3
## INDUCTIVE LOGIC

All the generalizations discussed in Chapter 2 are based on observations and/or experiments extending, in many cases, over a considerable number of years. The cell concept, Mendel's ideas of heredity, and Darwin's theory of natural selection are generalizations drawn from observations made on many different organisms. They are **inductive generalizations** attained through a process of **inductive logic.**

---

* J. J. W. Baker, Roscoe B. Jackson Memorial Laboratory, 1960, unpublished notes.

Inductive logic involves coming to a probable conclusion on the basis of many particular instances. Suppose, for example, that a person tastes a green apple and finds that it is sour. He tastes a second green apple; it also is sour. A third and fourth green apple yield the same results. From these separate, individual observations, a general conclusion might be drawn: "All green apples are sour." Inductive logic, then, involves proceeding from the specific to the general. In this case, it involves going from specific observations on four green apples, to a general conclusion about *all* green apples. Inductive logic is therefore an opposite of deductive logic, for the latter proceeds from the general to the specific.

Although inductive and deductive logic are two distinct types of thought processes, scientists do not tend to think exclusively in one way or the other at different times. In the solution of scientific problems there is constant interplay between inductive and deductive thinking. Consider again the generalization, "All green apples are sour." After tasting the first apple, a person might conclude that only this one apple was sour. After tasting the second, however, he might immediately conclude that *every* green apple is sour. It might be said that this is "jumping to conclusions." In more precise terms, it is simply making an inductive generalization on the basis of only two items of information. From this generalization, a prediction can be made:

*If* all green apples are sour, . . .*

*then*, the next green apple tasted should be sour.

A quick test confirms the prediction. This, in turn, lends support to the original inductive generalization. Thus we see a constant interplay between deductive and inductive reasoning in problem solving.

From the above example it is evident that the more observations are available, the more reliable are the inductive generalizations which can be drawn from them. An inductive generalization based on two items of information is less likely to be reliable than one based on ten or a hundred. However, inductive generalizations never attain absolute certainty. They only attain high degrees of probability. The degree of certainty attained depends on both the amount and the kind of information used in drawing the generalization. There are some apple varieties, for example, which are both sweet and green. Should the apple-taster encounter such apples, it would be necessary for him to modify the initial generalization accordingly, i.e.: "All green apples are sour, except for variety X."

The following experiment illustrates the interplay of inductive and deductive logic which often occurs in science. The experiment was designed to answer the question of how mutations arise in living organisms. For many years, some biologists maintained that mutations (see Section 2–4) were triggered within the or-

---

* Note that despite the deductive format, the statement, "All green apples are sour," is not the same type of hypothesis as "Salmon find their home streams by sense of smell." The latter hypothesis attempts to *explain* a phenomenon, the former, simply to test the validity of the inductive generalization. Both types of hypothesis occur in science.

ganism by specific changes in its environment. Other biologists disagreed. They felt that mutations occurred entirely at random, and were quite independent of environmental influences. The conflict existing between these views may be expressed in the form of a question: Do mutations arise spontaneously on their own, or are they due to environmental influences? In 1943, using bacteria as their experimental organism, the geneticists Luria and Delbrück performed an experiment which suggested an answer to this question.

BACTERIOPHAGE ——

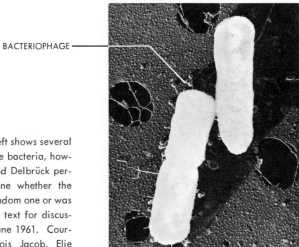

FIG. 3–3 The bacterial cell at the left shows several bacteriophages attached to it. Some bacteria, however, are immune to them. Luria and Delbrück performed an experiment to determine whether the mutation causing immunity was a random one or was due to exposure to the phages (see text for discussion). (From *Scientific American*, June 1961. Courtesy Thomas F. Anderson, Francois Jacob, Elie Wollman.)

Bacteria are parasitized by certain viruses called **bacteriophages.** Figure 3–3 shows an electron micrograph of several such bacteriophages (called "phages" for short). If a culture of bacteria is allowed to grow for several days and then exposed to phages, most of the cells are killed. A few may survive, however. These survivors are "resistant" varieties. Their resistance is passed on to their descendants; it is, therefore, the result of a genetic mutation.

On the basis of this information, two working hypotheses can be formulated:

1) The resistance to phages arises in the bacteria by spontaneous mutation. Such mutant bacteria will appear whether or not the bacterial culture is exposed to phages. In the absence of the selecting agent (the phages), resistant cells are simply not detected among the greater masses of nonmutant bacterial cells. When phages are introduced, however, only the mutant forms survive and reproduce.

2) The resistance is caused to appear in some of the bacteria as a result of their contact with the phages. The bacteria which respond to this change in environment (i.e., the introducing of the phages) by mutating, survive. The bacteria which do not respond are destroyed.

In other words, the second hypothesis holds that the presence of the phages is the causal agent for mutation and that mutants for phage resistance do not appear until the bacteria come in contact with the phages. By contrast, the first hypothesis holds that the mutants are present all along but are simply not detectable until the phages are introduced.

To test the first hypothesis, Luria and Delbrück set up a number of bacterial cultures of the same species. Each culture was grown from a small group of bacterial cells. All the bacterial cultures were simultaneously exposed to phages, and the number of resistant cells, or survivors, were counted.*

The experimenters reasoned in the following way.

*Hypothesis I:* *If . . .*   mutations occur spontaneously, . . .

*Prediction:*     *then . . .* the number of resistant cells in the various culture dishes should be quite different.

If, for example, the mutation occurs early, when the growing culture contains few cells, the mutant cell will multiply and leave a large number of offspring each bearing the mutation. By the time the phages are introduced into the culture, many resistant bacteria may be present. Conversely, if the mutation takes place just before the introduction of phages, only a few resistant cells will be present. The laws of chance predict that there would be considerable variation in the number of surviving cells per culture dish.

*Hypothesis II:* *If . . .*   mutations occur in response to the presence of phages, . . .

*Prediction:*     *then . . .* the number of resistant cells per culture dish should be quite uniform.

Since each culture dish contains roughly the same number of bacteria, and the amount of phages introduced in each case is the same, hypothesis II predicts that the number of mutants should be roughly the same from one culture to the next.

The results of this experiment (Fig. 3–4) show that the variation in number of surviving cells per culture dish is quite large. Some cultures have only two or three surviving colonies, while others have twelve, fifteen, or more. The experimental results bear out the prediction of hypothesis I. Thus hypothesis I can be said to be supported. The results contradict the prediction of hypothesis II. Thus, barring experimental error, hypothesis II can be said to be disproved. Mutations *do* occur at random, and are entirely independent of the environmental changes which may give them selective value. Note that the Luria and Delbrück experiment can be said to test both hypotheses. Since the pre-

---

* The number of survivor cells can be counted quite easily by allowing the culture to incubate for a few days. Each surviving cell will reproduce to form a colony which can be detected by simply examining the culture dish.

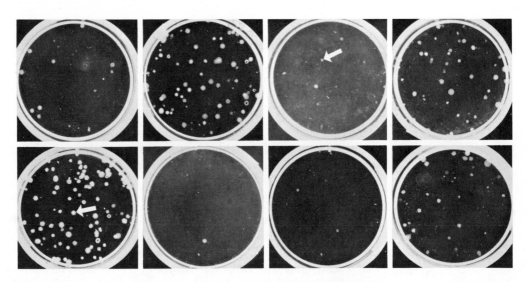

FIG. 3–4   The random variation in bacterial colony numbers obtained in the Luria and Delbrück experiments clearly supports the hypothesis proposing that mutations occur spontaneously and at random (see text for discussion).

dictions made by hypotheses I and II are contradictory, the results can support only one of them. Such an experiment is called a **crucial** experiment. Another example of a crucial experiment will be discussed in Chapter 4.

In the case just discussed, the experimental results overthrew a rather widely held concept. Most of the time, however, the results are not so dramatic. Far more often, experimental results either support already well-established hypotheses, or cause minor modifications of them. For example, simple experiments on the respiratory physiology of a tree, a man, a robin, a frog, and a fish might disclose that the simple sugar glucose is oxidized as energy is released. At the same time, oxygen is used up, and carbon dioxide and water are released as waste products. From these facts, one might propose hypothesis I: "The energy needed by organisms is obtained from the oxidation of glucose by oxygen." In summary form, we may write the balanced equation as follows:

$$C_6H_{12}O_6 + 6O_2 \rightarrow 6CO_2 + 6H_2O.$$

If no further work is done, hypothesis I might attain the status of a full-fledged theory or law. But investigations that have been carried out on the cells of other organisms, such as yeast, disclose that these cells can tap the energy of glucose without oxygen. Another oxidizing agent (pyruvic acid) is used. Thus our original hypothesis I must be modified to read: "The energy needed by organisms is obtained from glucose by some oxidizing agent." The discovery that some organisms use substances other than glucose as the source of their energy leads to further modification of hypothesis I: "The energy needed by organisms is obtained from energy-rich substances by oxidation of these substances."

Thus each new discovery necessitates new modifications of previously acceptable hypotheses. The whole apple is not discarded; its bad parts are merely pared away. As Chapter 7 will show, because of many modifications and additions our current hypotheses regarding respiratory physiology are considerably more refined than those discussed here.

In a very real sense, then, scientific "truths" are only *approximate* truths. In the words of the chemist G. N. Lewis:

*The scientist is a practical man and his are practical aims. He does not seek the* **ultimate** *but the* **proximate.** *He does not speak of the last analysis but rather of the next approximation. His are not those beautiful structures so delicately designed that a single flaw may cause the collapse of the whole. The scientist builds slowly and with a gross but solid kind of masonry. If dissatisfied with any of his work, even if it be near the very foundations, he can replace that part without damage to the remainder. On the whole, he is satisfied with his work, for while science may never be wholly right it is certainly never wholly wrong; and it seems to be improving from decade to decade.*

It is true that a deductive-logic framework is present in every scientific experiment, but this does not mean that every research scientist is constantly examining his experiments to make sure this framework is present. Rather, the deductive-logic framework is there because the designer of the experiment is accustomed to thinking this way when designing experiments. In the laboratory, it is a kind of "second nature" to him.

It should be noted that many biologists never carry out scientific experiments in the full sense of the word. These biologists concern themselves with the gathering of factual material. The detailed anatomical examination of a new plant or animal species is an example of such work. No hypothesis is being tested here; no predictions are being made. Yet, such work is often of great value. It provides the factual tools which others may use to design and carry out significant experiments on the organisms involved.

## 3–4
## THE APPLICATION
## OF LOGIC:
## A CASE STUDY

It is now known that a fluid called **semen,** produced by the males of higher animals, contains **spermatozoa,** or sperm. Sperm are living cells, consisting of a headpiece and a tail. They carry the inheritance factors of the male, and are capable of independent movement. In sexual reproduction, the sperm swim toward the female egg cell and unite with it to achieve fertilization. It is fertilization which causes the egg to begin its development into a new animal.

In the eighteenth century, however, scientists were still uncertain as to just *how* the male semen caused fertilization of the egg. The importance of the spermatozoa was not recognized. Thus only two possibilities were considered:

1) The seminal fluid of the male must make actual contact with the egg before it would begin development; or

2) It was only necessary that a gas or vapor, arising from the semen by evaporation, make contact with the egg.

From their examination of the human female reproductive system, physicians saw that the semen would be deposited a considerable distance from the egg. Since the role played by the spermatozoa was not recognized, the fact that they might be able to swim toward the egg was not taken into account. It was therefore assumed that only a vapor diffusing from the semen could possibly reach the egg to fertilize it.

On the basis of these anatomical observations, the vapor hypothesis gained considerable support. In 1785, it was put to experimental testing by the Italian, Lazaro Spallanzani (1729–1799).

The following examination of excerpts from Spallanzani's report analyzes his experiments and conclusions and demonstrates their logical basis.

Is fertilization affected by the spermatic vapor?
It has been disputed for a long time and it is still being argued whether the visible and coarser parts of the semen serve in the fecundation of (i.e., here, in triggering the development of) man and animals, or whether a very subtle part, a vapor which emanates therefrom and which is called the *aura spermatica,* suffices for this function.

*Here the problem is defined: Does the semen itself cause the egg to develop? Or, is it merely the vapor arising from the semen that does so?*

It cannot be denied that doctors and physiologists defend this last view, and are persuaded in this more by an apparent necessity than by reason or experiments.

*The lack of experimental evidence to support the vapor hypothesis is pointed out here by Spallanzani. In the full text of his report, he cites some of the anatomical observations noted in the introductory part of this section.*

Despite these reasons, many other authors hold the contrary opinion, and believe that fertilization is accomplished by means of the material part of the semen.

*The alternative hypothesis—that the semen must actually make contact with the egg—is stated.*

These reasons advanced for and against do not appear to me to resolve the question; for it has not been demonstrated that the spermatic vapor itself arrives at the ovaries, just as it is not clear whether the material part of the semen that arrives at the ovaries, and not the vaporous part of the semen, is responsible for fertilization.

*The statement, ''. . . it has not been demonstrated that . . . (etc.)'' again shows Spallanzani's recognition of the lack of concrete evidence to support either hypothesis.*

Therefore, in order to decide the question, it is important to employ a convenient means to separate the vapor from the body of the semen and to do this in such a way that the embryos are more or less enveloped by the vapor;

*An experimental design is suggested. Some sort of experimental apparatus must be constructed to properly answer the questions to be posed by the experiments.*

for *if* they are born, [*then*] this would be evidence that the seminal vapor has been able to fertilize them; or [*if*] on the other hand, they might not be born, *then* it will be equally sure that the spermatic vapor alone is insufficient and that the additional action of the material part of the sperm is necessary.

*Note the two occurrences here of the ''if . . . , then'' format as Spallanzani cites the deductive basis of his experimentation.*

(*Note:* Spallanzani had shown earlier that the semen could be diluted several times, yet still remain capable of fertilization. In terms of what is known today regarding the role of the spermatozoa in fertilization, this is not surprising. However, Spallanzani interpreted these results as support for the vapor hypothesis, since he considered the vapor to be merely diluted semen. The following experiment, however, convinced him otherwise.)

In order to bathe tadpoles [eggs]* thoroughly with this spermatic vapor, I put into a watch glass a little less than 11 grains of seminal liquid from several toads. Into a similar glass, but a little smaller, I placed 26 tadpoles [eggs] which, because of the viscosity of the jelly, were tightly attached to the con-

*Spallanzani here describes his experimental apparatus (see Fig. 3–5). Often an important part of an experiment is the design of such apparatus.*

---

* Like many men of his day, Spallanzani believed that the animal egg contained a tiny miniature of the adult form, which needed only fertilization to grow to full size. Hence his reference to the unfertilized eggs as tadpoles. The belief in the existence of a preformed individual in the egg (the *preformation theory*) will be discussed in Chapter 16.

cave part of the glass. I placed the second glass on the first, and they remained united thus during five hours in my room where the temperature was 18°. The drop of seminal liquid was placed precisely under the eggs, which must have been completely bathed by the spermatic vapor that arose; the more so since the distance between the eggs and the liquid was not more than 1 ligne [2.25 mm]. I examined these eggs after five hours and I found them covered by a humid mist, which wet the finger with which one touched them; this was however only a portion of the semen, which had evaporated and diminished by a grain and a half. The eggs had therefore been bathed by a grain and a half of spermatic vapor; for it could not have escaped outside of the watch crystals since they fitted together very closely.

But in spite of this, the eggs, subsequently placed in water, perished.

Although the experiment overthrows the spermatic vapor theory . . .

. . . it was nevertheless unique and I wished to repeat it.

Having previously used spermatic vapor produced in closed vessels, I wished to see what would happen in open vessels in order to eliminate a doubt produced by the idea that the circulation of air was necessary to fertilization . . .

. . . but fertilization did not succeed any better than in the preceding experiments.

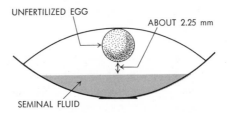

FIG. 3–5 Apparatus setup similar to the one used by Spallanzani to answer the question, "Is fertilization effected by the spermatic fluid?" Vapor rising from the seminal fluid freely bathed the egg, but no contact between egg and fluid occurred. The egg did not become fertilized.

*The lack of development corresponds to a false conclusion; that is, the prediction which follows acceptance of the hypothesis being tested does not come true . . .*

*. . . and thus the vapor hypothesis must be false.*

*Spallanzani recognizes the need for further evidence that the vapor hypothesis is, indeed, incorrect. (His results in this second series of experiments were the same.)*

*A variable is recognized that might influence the results; the experiment is modified to eliminate it. If air plays a role in fertilization, then the eggs should develop if air is allowed to circulate, etc.*

*Again, negative results. The prediction is shown to be incorrect.*

The last experiment of this type was to collect several grains of spermatic vapor and to immerse a dozen eggs in it for several minutes; I touched another dozen eggs with the small remnant of semen which remained after evaporation, and which did not weigh more than half a grain; eleven of these tadpoles hatched successfully although none of the twelve that had been plunged into the spermatic vapor survived.

The conjunction of these facts evidently proves that fertilization in the terrestrial toad is not produced by the spermatic vapor but rather by the material part of the semen.

As might be supposed, I did not do these experiments only on this toad, but I have repeated them in the manner described on the terrestrial toad with red eyes and dorsal tubercles, and also on the aquatic frog, and I have had the same results. I can even add that although I have only performed a few of these experiments on the tree frog, I have noticed that they agree very well with all the others . . .

Shall we, however, say that this is the universal process of nature for all animals and for man?

The small number of facts which we have does not allow us, in good logic, to draw such a general conclusion.

One can at the most think that this is most probably so . . . ,

*Still another variation of the original experiment is performed for further evidence against the vapor hypothesis; even immersion in a concentration of spermatic vapor does not result in fertilization. Certainly the hypothesis being tested would have predicted fertilization in this case. Yet, fertilization does not occur.*

*In their deductive format, Spallanzani's results do, indeed, show the vapor hypothesis to be false. They do not, however, prove the validity of the alternative hypothesis, but only lend it support. Note that Spallanzani is careful not to generalize beyond the animal used for his experiments.*

*Spallanzani now wishes to extend his results to other organisms, and so performs other experiments using different kinds of animals.*

*Spallanzani asks, ''Can the generalization be extended to other organisms not yet tested in these experiments?''*

*Spallanzani is cautious in considering an extension of his generalization regarding the necessity of contact with the semen rather than its vapor.*

*Spallanzani shows his awareness of the nature of scientific ''proof'' with this statement;*

... more especially as there is not a single fact to the contrary ...

*that is, no wrong predictions (false conclusions) have been obtained in the experimental testing of this hypothesis.*

and the question of the influence of the spermatic vapor in fertilization is at least definitely decided in the negative for several species of animals, and with great probability for the others.*

*Note the awareness on the part of Spallanzani that his negative results give him positive disproof of the hypothesis tested, yet give only probable verification rather than absolute proof to the opposite hypothesis.*

Spallanzani later performed other experiments which further supported the results reported here. He discovered, for example, that if he filtered the semen through cotton, it lost much of its fertilizing powers, and that the finer he made the filter, the more the powers were diminished. He found, too, that several pieces of blotting paper completely removed the semen's ability to fertilize, but that the portion left on the paper, when put into water, *did* successfully fertilize eggs. Despite the obviousness (to us) of the role played by the spermatozoa in fertilization—a role to which the results of these experiments point—Spallanzani had previously decided that semen without spermatozoa *was* capable of fertilization, and he was unable to shake this belief ... even in the light of his own experimental results! If nothing else, this nicely demonstrates that scientists are just as prone to overlook the obvious solution as anyone else, and often refuse to give up preconceived notions despite evidence to the contrary. It was not until the nineteenth century that the role of the spermatozoa in fertilization was definitely established.

3-5
**THE LIMITATIONS
OF SCIENCE**

In its own right, science is one of man's most productive ways of exploring, exploiting, and trying to understand his environment. But it is by no means the *only* way. The historian tries to understand the present and, occasionally, to predict the future, by studying the record of man's past. Religion attempts to find certain truths by operating mostly from a platform of faith. Philosophers draw on science, history, religion, and many other fields of endeavor in an attempt to consolidate the findings of each field and draw meaningful conclusions from them.

Further, we should note that despite the many contributions it has made to man's intellectual growth, as well as to his health and general welfare, science does have serious limitations. Oddly, one of these stems from one of its greatest

---

* From M. L. Gabriel and S. Fogel (eds.), *Great Experiments in Biology* (Englewood Cliffs, N.J.: Prentice-Hall, 1955). Used by permission.

attributes.  As the philosopher George Boas points out,

*. . . what science wants is a rational universe, by which I mean a universe in which the reason has supremacy over both our perceptions and our emotions.*

This rational basis of experimental science, rooted by necessity in concrete experiences, is, indeed, a strength.  But it is also a weakness.  By dealing only with that set of phenomena which can directly or indirectly be experienced through man's senses and placed into an experimental situation, science is necessarily excluded from that set of phenomena whose members do not have these qualifications.  Experimental science can only attempt to explain *how* a natural phenomenon may occur, and hypothesize its causes.  It cannot even begin to speculate *why* these phenomena occur, in the teleological sense of the word, and there is no reason, of course, why it should attempt to do so.

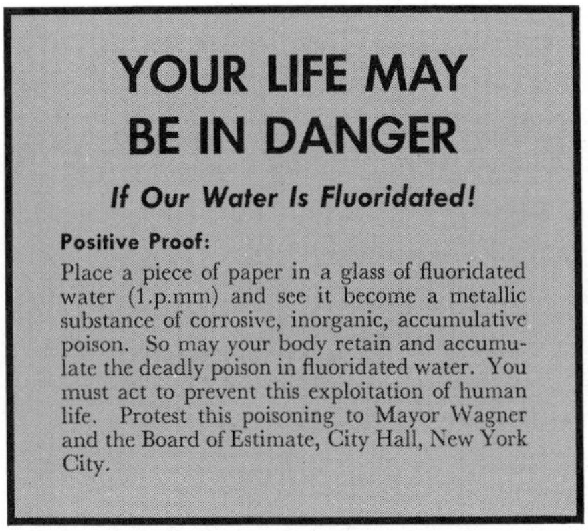

## YOUR LIFE MAY BE IN DANGER

### If Our Water Is Fluoridated!

**Positive Proof:**

Place a piece of paper in a glass of fluoridated water (1.p.mm) and see it become a metallic substance of corrosive, inorganic, accumulative poison.  So may your body retain and accumulate the deadly poison in fluoridated water.  You must act to prevent this exploitation of human life.  Protest this poisoning to Mayor Wagner and the Board of Estimate, City Hall, New York City.

FIG. 3–6  As a field of endeavor, science is fairly immune to the blatant appeals to the emotions which an advertisement like this attempts to make.  As an individual, however, the scientist is probably no more or less averse to emotional judgments than any other man.

The unemotional basis of science is another strength which is at the same time a weakness.  This does not mean, of course, that scientists as individuals are at all unemotional or detached.  They are in no way different from any other persons in this regard, being just as liable to personal prejudices and weaknesses as the next man.  However, as a field of endeavor, science, at least in the long run, is necessarily objective and detached from emotional prejudice.  (See Fig. 3–6.)  Yet, there are times when man may not wish to let reason have supremacy over his emotions.  Certainly we would not wish to deal with today's very real problems of human poverty and injustice in an entirely unemotional and detached manner.  To retain its basic nature, however, and succeed in dealing with contemporary social problems, experimental science must do just that.

Despite the logical basis of science, it would be a mistake to give the impression that scientists are never wrong.  Nothing could be further from the truth.  The astronomer Johannes Kepler once wrote, "How many detours I had to make, along how many walls I had to grope in the darkness of my ignorance until I found the door which lets in the light of truth." It is doubtful, in fact, that there has ever been a scientist who has not made mistakes. James Bryant Conant states,

*One could write a large volume on the erroneous experimental findings in physics, chemistry, and biochemistry which have found their way into print in the last one hundred years; and another whole volume would be required to record the abortive ideas, self-contradictory theories and generalizations recorded in the same period.*

For example, Lord Rutherford stated that man would never tap the energy within the atomic nucleus. The first atomic bomb exploded a few years after his death. The famous nineteenth-century physiologist Johannes Müller asserted that the speed of the nerve impulse would never be measured. Six years later, Hermann von Helmholtz did it in a frog nerve only a few inches long.

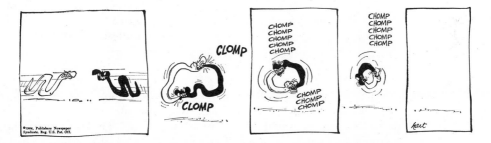

FIG. 3–7   The consequences of logical thinking do not always lead to "correct" conclusions. It is a well-known fact that snakes can and sometimes do swallow other snakes, even ones larger than themselves. If it is assumed that the one which is swallowed disappears from sight, the situation pictured above is the logical conclusion! (Courtesy Johnny Hart and Publishers Newspaper Syndicate.)

Nor is it safe to think that scientists always reason correctly. As a matter of fact, some scientists are notorious for "going off the deep end," particularly when writing in areas other than their own specialty. Furthermore, if scientists can be wrong, *so can science.* Ask a physicist about "ether," a chemist about "phlogiston," or a biologist about "lamarckism." Science has had incorrect theories in the past, it has them now, and it will continue to have them in the future. The strength of science does not lie in any infallibility. Nor does it lie in its logical basis, for the conclusion of a perfectly logical argument can be utter nonsense (see Fig. 3–7). Rather, it lies in the self-criticizing nature of science—the constant search for "truth" by the elimination of experimentally established error.

Science is an organized and continually changing body of knowledge based on observation, generalization, and experimentation. As a disciplined endeavor, it can be said to be a tradition of beliefs that have rational foundations, subject to continual review and discussion. Thus as a field, science is separate from the scientists who have contributed to its growth. As an individual, the scientist is only a human being, with all the emotions and weaknesses that are part and parcel of being so.

The scientist A. J. Lotka stated in 1925 that "Science does not explain anything . . . science is less pretentious. All that falls within its mission is to observe phenomena and to describe them and the relations between them." We might amplify this and state again that any absolute truth is beyond the reach of science. *In science, "truth" is a well-supported hypothesis.* Should the hypothesis fall, a new "truth" takes its place.

Yet, despite its built-in limitations, science must still be recorded as a remarkably successful way of accumulating knowledge. In **applied research,** scientists may use the methods of science for the purpose of developing products to improve human comfort and welfare. In **pure** or **basic research,** the scientist searches for knowledge—knowledge for its own sake—regardless of whether or not his discoveries will benefit mankind. It is important to note, however, that *the results of basic research have contributed as much as or more than those of applied research,* and, indeed, it can be said that the former leads to the latter. It seems that science is productive by its very nature.

## 3-6
## CONCLUSION

Science can be considered as organized scientific knowledge or as the process by which such knowledge is obtained. Experimental science uses the format of deductive logic in the design of its experiments. The purpose of these experiments is to test the validity of the predictions which are made on the basis of accepting the hypotheses as true. If the experiment is properly designed, and the predictions are not borne out by the experimental data, the hypothesis may be considered disproved. If, on the other hand, the results of the experiment are as predicted, the hypothesis can be said to be supported, *but not proved.* The absolute proof attainable by the use of deduction in mathematics lies forever beyond the reach of experimental science. The validity of scientific "truths" can only be measured statistically in terms of probabilities.

The demand of science for rational, unemotional, experimentally demonstrable bases for its beliefs lend to its greatest strengths. At the same time, these demands limit science's working range to the perceivable and manipulatable environment. Science is only one of several highly successful ways available to man in his attempts to understand the universe and his role within it.

## EXERCISES

1. Distinguish between basic (pure) and applied research. Why is it important for both kinds of research to be supported?

2. Explain why the attainment of any absolute truths lies beyond the realm of science.

3. List some of the limitations of science.

4. Why must a scientist be careful not to extend his experimental conclusions to organisms other than those with which he worked?

5. In a recent presidential campaign, some noted scientists and engineers formed a group to support one of the candidates. A spokesman for this group made the following statement:

*By the time we were through, any guy in Pittsburgh in a T-shirt with a can of beer in his hand knew that the smartest people in this country considered ——— to be unfit [for the presidency].**

What are the tacit assumptions made in this statement? Can you see any possible dangers which might develop from the acceptance of such reasoning?

6. Explain why the following hypothesis is an unacceptable one to scientists: Life originated on another planet somewhere else in the universe and came to earth millions of years ago enclosed in a meteorite.

7. Devise an hypothesis to explain each of the following observations. Then outline an experiment to test your hypothesis.

   a) There are more automobile accidents at dusk than at any other time.

   b) In washing glass tumblers in hot soapsuds and then immediately transferring them face downwards onto a cool, flat surface, bubbles at first appear on the outside of the rim, expanding outwards. In a few seconds, they reverse, go under the rim, and expand inside the glass tumbler.

   c) It has been noticed that one species of mud-dauber wasp will build its nests from highly radioactive mud, although the radiation received by the developing young may be enough to kill them. Another species of mud-dauber wasp, under the same environmental conditions, avoids this mud, and selects nonradioactive mud to build its nests.

   d) In mice of strain A, cancer develops in every animal living over 18 months. Mice of strain B do not develop cancer. However, if the young of each strain are switched immediately after birth, cancer does *not* develop in the switched strain-A animals, but *does* develop in the switched strain-B animals living over 18 months.

ARBER, AGNES, *The Mind and The Eye* (Cambridge: Cambridge University Press, 1964). A discussion of some facets of scientific work by a noted botanist. The book is one of the few attempts to discuss the philosophy of science using biological examples.

BAKER, JEFFREY J. W., and GARLAND E. ALLEN, *Hypothesis, Prediction and Implication in Biology* (Reading, Mass.: Addison-Wesley, 1968). Part II contains further analyses of scientific papers of the type applied to the Spallanzani paper in this chapter; one of these analyses involves an controversy between researchers. Part III deals with a Letters-to-the-Editor debate on the need (or lack of it) for a scientific investigation of racial differences and intelligence.

BRONOWSKI, J., "The Creative Process." *Scientific American*, September, 1958, p. 58. In this article the author tries to show that innovation in science is not different

**SUGGESTED READINGS**

---

from innovation in fields of arts or social sciences. In all these cases, innovation comes from a person's seeing deep unity in a number of different situations.

CONANT, J. B., *On Understanding Science* (New Haven: Yale University Press, 1947). A clear, well-written account of the nature of science and its development. Uses many specific examples.

CONANT, J. B., *Science and Common Sense* (New Haven: Yale University Press, 1961). This book is an attempt to make science more intelligible by showing the way in which a number of scientists came across their discoveries. Conant presents a number of "case histories" of scientific discovery.

GARDNER, M., *Fads and Fallacies in the Name of Science* (New York: Dover Publications, 1957). A well-written, very interesting account of a number of pseudoscientific theories, how they gained adherents, and how most of them can be shown to be invalid. Discusses "Bridey Murphy," "Atlantis," "flying saucers," Lysenkoism, and extrasensory perception (ESP).

HARDIN, GARRET, *Biology, Its Principles and Implications* (San Francisco: W. H. Freeman, 1961). An excellent discussion of scientific hypotheses, their modifications, etc., as well as many good examples are provided in this exceptionally well-written book.

STANDEN, ANTHONY, *Science Is a Sacred Cow* (New York: E. P. Dutton Co., 1950). A light-hearted debunking of the traditional view of science and scientists as infallible. Easy reading, written by a scientist.

TATON, RENE, *Reason and Chance in Scientific Discovery* (New York: John Wiley & Sons, 1962). A well-presented account of the role of chance, error, and inspiration in scientific discoveries, as well as an analysis of the relation between science and the culture of the times. A very intriguing and thought-provoking work.

WEILL, ANDREW T., NORMAN E. ZINBERG, and JUDITH M. NELSEN, "Clinical and Psychological Effects of Marihuana in Man," in *The Process of Biology: Primary Sources*, ed. by Jeffrey J. W. Baker and Garland E. Allen (Reading, Mass.: Addison-Wesley, 1970). An excellent example of a paper showing the strengths as well as the limitations of scientific investigation.

The September, 1958 *Scientific American* is devoted to the topic "Innovation in Science." There are a number of articles in this issue on the growth of various sciences, and the conditions under which science is thought to flourish. The articles in this issue devote particular attention to the role of imagination and creativity in science (see also the Bronowski article above).

# TESTING HYPOTHESES AND PREDICTIONS

# CHAPTER 4

Beri-beri is the common name for a degenerative and paralytic condition found in man and other vertebrates. Until about fifty years ago, this disease was relatively common in human populations, especially in places such as Borneo and Java. Toward the end of the nineteenth century many people had voiced ideas as to what might cause the condition. The most popular idea was that beri-beri resulted from bacterial infection, for this was the period of the great influence of Louis Pasteur and his germ theory of disease. Bacteria were looked upon as the causal agent of all known human maladies.

In 1893 the Dutch government sent a commission to the East Indies to investigate beri-beri, which was particularly prevalent there. One member of that commission, Christian Eijkman (1858–1930), made observations which led him to formulate an alternative hypothesis as to the cause of the disease. Eijkman went on to design an experiment to test his hypothesis. This work provides a classic example of the design and execution of an experiment.

Eijkman observed that experimental chickens kept around the laboratory were fed on a diet consisting mainly of polished rice. Many of these chickens seemed to have a condition which resembled beri-beri. Eijkman decided to see whether there might be any relationship between a diet of polished rice and the occurrence of beri-beri. He began by formulating two initial hypotheses:

*Hypothesis I:* Beri-beri is a result of dietary disturbance, and is not due to bacterial infection.

*Hypothesis II:* A factor present in rice husks seems to prevent appearance of the condition.

From these hypotheses Eijkman could make a simple prediction:

**Hypothesis I:**  *If . . .*   beri-beri is a dietary condition, . . .

and

**Hypothesis II:**  *If . . .*   beri-beri is a result of eating polished rice, . . .

**Prediction:**      *then . . .* feeding chickens polished rice should produce the condition.   Conversely, feeding them unpolished rice should keep them healthy.

To test this prediction, Eijkman set up a simple experiment.  He procured two groups of normal, healthy chickens.  To one group he fed polished rice, to the other, unpolished rice.  The chickens were placed in pens and kept under identical conditions for a period of two weeks.  At the end of this period, many of those chickens fed on polished rice showed symptoms of beri-beri.  Among those fed on unpolished rice, however, there were no symptoms.  This experiment seemed to support Eijkman's hypothesis that beri-beri is a dietary condition.

Eijkman's experiment, simple as it is, has some very important features. First, it was designed to test a prediction made from a preliminary hypothesis. A good experiment is one designed to test a specific prediction, which the experiment can then either confirm or reject.  If the prediction from a given hypothesis is verified, the hypothesis may be correct—although, as we saw in Chapter 3, it is not *necessarily* so.  On the other hand, if the prediction proves to be false, then the hypothesis itself *must* be false.  Note that the most conclusive experiments are often ones which disprove a specific prediction, for they make it possible to reject the hypothesis from which the prediction was drawn.

Second, Eijkman's experiment made use of *controls*.  In a controlled experiment, two groups of organisms are treated alike in all but one respect.  The one difference is the factor being studied, such as polished or unpolished rice in the diet.  In Eijkman's experiment, the chickens fed on polished rice form the **control group**, while those fed on unpolished rice form the **experimental group**.  In general, control groups represent the normal situation, whereas experimental groups represent the *variation*.  A control group provides a basis for comparison—a standard against which changes in the experimental group can be measured.

Scientific experiments are generally designed to test one prediction at a time. If Eijkman had set up his experiment as described above, but had used ducks for his experimental group and chickens for control, this would have introduced *two variables* into the experiment: the difference in diet and the difference in type of organism.  If the experimental group had shown a high incidence of beri-beri, Eijkman would have been much less certain of his results than in the experiment as actually performed.  It could be argued, for instance, that ducks are highly susceptible to beri-beri, and contract the condition under circumstances where chickens do not.  This is not a far-fetched objection; many diseases are known to appear frequently in some organisms, and seldom or never in others. Thus, if he had used two different types of organism, Eijkman would not have been able to conclude that beri-beri was a dietary condition.

Although Eijkman's original experiment did support his hypothesis, it did not eliminate all other possibilities. Eating polished rice, for example, might merely lower an animal's resistance to infectious organisms. Thus chickens fed on polished rice would be more susceptible to beri-beri germs, but would contract the condition only if such infectious organisms were present. Although subsequent research showed that this possibility was not correct, the experiment described above did not provide evidence to that effect. Furthermore, Eijkman could not conclude from his experiment that because a diet of polished rice caused beri-beri in chickens, it must necessarily have the same effect on other animals. He needed to test his hypothesis in relation to human beings.

It is normally difficult to carry out large-scale experiments with human beings, especially under conditions which are likely to produce harmful effects. An already existing situation, however, helped Eijkman solve this problem. Beri-beri was especially common among the penal institutions of Java. Eijkman ordered unpolished rice to be introduced into the diets of the inmates in a few of those prisons where beri-beri was quite common. A definite improvement was shown, but still the results were not conclusive. There was always the possibility, however remote, that the prisoners would have recovered anyway, due to changes in the nonrice portion of their diet during the period under observation. A control group was needed.

Luckily, local customs provided just what was needed. Prison diets throughout Java were remarkably similar, except for one factor. Although rice was a staple in every prison, in some areas polished rather than unpolished rice was used. By collecting information gathered by the Supervisor of the Civil Health Department of Java, Eijkman had data for his control and experimental groups right at hand. Data were available for 100 prisons throughout Java and a neighboring island. It was important to have as many experimental situations as possible. As we saw in Chapter 3, the more data there are from which to work, the more valid a generalization will be. Data from 100 prisons are adequate to avoid any significant source of error.

From this sample Eijkman found the following results: Out of 27 prisons where unpolished rice was fed to prisoners, beri-beri occurred in only *one* prison. On the other hand, beri-beri occurred in 36 out of the remaining 73 prisons, where polished rice was a main part of the diet. Then, finding that actually three rice diets were being used, Eijkman made a new classification of diets:

1) polished rice (husks entirely or at least 75% removed),

2) unpolished rice (husks entirely or at least 75% preserved),

3) a mixture of (1) and (2), being served in some prisons.

TABLE 4–1

| DIET CONSISTING OF | PERSONS CONTRACTING BERI-BERI, % |
|---|---|
| POLISHED RICE | 70.6 |
| UNPOLISHED RICE | 2.7 |
| MIXTURE OF POLISHED AND UNPOLISHED RICE | 46.1 |

Data for this new series of categories were tabulated as shown in Table 4–1. It is apparent that Eijkman's hypothesis (that beri-beri is caused by a dietary factor) is well supported by these data.

However, these experiments did not answer all the questions which this investigation into beri-beri had raised. For example, it was suggested by some people that beri-beri was caused by eating old spoiled rice; others said that rice imported from Saigon or Rangoon was the causative agent. Still others claimed that hygienic factors in the various prisons were the cause. Eijkman was able to answer all these objections, and thus gained even more support for his hypothesis. He fed chickens polished and unpolished rice of all sorts—old and new, from Saigon and from the East Indies. In all cases, those chickens which showed beri-beri were fed on polished rice.

In meeting other objections, Eijkman studied the age of prison buildings, their ventilation, and the population density in all prisons. His findings for age of building and ventilation are given in Table 4–2. It can be seen that there is no relation between either of these factors and the percentage of persons contracting beri-beri. These data effectively ruled out hygienic factors as possible causes of beri-beri.

TABLE 4–2

| AGE OF BUILDINGS | PERSONS CONTRACTING BERI-BERI, % | VENTILATION | PERSONS CONTRACTING BERI-BERI, % |
|---|---|---|---|
| 40–100 YEARS | 50 | GOOD | 41.2 |
| 21–40 YEARS | 34.4 | MEDIUM | 72.7 |
| 2–20 YEARS | 45.2 | FAULTY | 33.3 |

In addition to those features discussed earlier, Eijkman's experiments illustrate two additional features of some importance in experimental analysis. Eijkman used a large number of samples in order to avoid *sampling error*, and he collected *numerical data*. The importance of using a large number of samples has already been discussed. The importance of numerical data deserves special mention.

Information collected from observation or experiment may be of two kinds: *quantitative* and *qualitative*. Quantitative data are those which are the result of measurement, or which can be expressed in some definite and precise form, usually in numbers. Qualitative data, on the other hand, are those data which do not lend themselves to precise numerical expression, Differences in height of a group of people, stated in terms such as "taller," "shorter," "tallest," etc., would be an example of qualitative data. The same differences, stated as results of measurement of height (as in inches or centimeters), would be an example of quantitative data.

In general, scientists prefer numerical data because they are more easily subject to verification. Suppose that an experiment is performed in which the amount of growth of plants is studied under different intensities of light, and that the results are presented as follows: Plant #1 grew a little under a dull light, Plant #2 grew somewhat more than this under a medium-bright light, and Plant #3 grew very much under a bright light. These findings are based on subjective judgments. It would be difficult to repeat the experiment and know whether the new results agreed with the old. On a numerical basis, the data might be presented as follows: Plant #1 grew 5 inches under light intensity of 500 candlepower; Plant #2 grew 8 inches under light intensity of 700 candlepower; Plant #3 grew 10 inches under light intensity of 1000 candlepower, etc. This kind of data is easy to check. The experiment can be performed again, and the degree of difference or similarity between the two sets of data can be observed.

Numerical data are also valuable because relationships between two factors are more readily apparent (as between light intensity and amount of growth). In the above case, the fact that plants show greater growth under high light intensity than under low light intensity is more evident when the data are presented in numerical form. Although subjective data do not necessarily obscure such a relationship, they make it much less apparent.

Finally, numerical data are valuable because they make possible more precise and meaningful communication between scientists. To say that a plant grows "a little" or "very much" may mean different things to different people. Hence ambiguity arises. The use of numerical data prevents such ambiguity, and the results of experiments are less easily subject to misunderstanding.

**4-3
CHANCE AND
TRIAL-AND-ERROR
IN SCIENTIFIC
DISCOVERY**

In this chapter and the preceding one, we have stressed the logical, planned approach to scientific discovery. This is indeed a very important part of scientific research. Yet, other factors are involved in science which cannot be called logical or predictable. The roles played by trial-and-error and chance in scientific discovery have often been neglected in discussions of scientific procedure, but both these factors play important roles.

**The role of trial-and-error.** A rat in a maze tries first one passage, then another, until it reaches the end and is rewarded by a piece of cheese. If the rat has no previous experience with the maze, the only method it can use to reach the cheese is that of trial-and-error. This method is one which is frequently thrust on an organism, be it rat or man, that is faced with solving a problem for which no definite and clear-cut clues are available.

Consider the following example of trial-and-error in scientific research. Dr. Paul Muller, who won the Nobel Prize in 1948 for his discovery of dichloro-diphenyl-trichloro-ethane (DDT), said in his acceptance speech: "After fruitless testing of hundreds of different substances, I realized that it is not easy to find a good contact insecticide." The problem was to find a substance which would be lethal to insects but relatively harmless to man and animals. For Muller, there was no other way than to test many substances, one after the other, until he finally hit upon DDT, which seemed to be effective. The discovery was made only by long hours of testing a variety of possible compounds.*

The method of trial-and-error has one disadvantage. It is inefficient. If an experimenter has some clues from which he can formulate an hypothesis at the beginning, he can reduce the number of experiments which he has to perform. In fact, if all knowledge were gained only by trial-and-error, scientific advances would be very slow in coming.

**The role of chance.** To ignore the role of chance discovery would be to present a false picture of scientific research. There is a difference, however, between being lucky and being observant enough to take advantage of this luck. The history of science is filled with examples of "missed discoveries." Although many individuals have hit upon important discoveries during the course of their investigations, they ignored their discovery because they were looking for something else. To some extent, an investigator must be prepared to seize upon chance observation.

An interesting case of the role of chance occurs in the work of the French biologist Louis Pasteur (1822–1895) on the problem of immunity. In 1798, Edward Jenner had shown that animals and people could be immunized against the infectious disease smallpox by injection of small amounts of material extracted from the sores of cattle affected by a similar condition known as cowpox. This was a specific case, however, and Jenner had not attempted to extend his findings to other diseases. However, by the middle of the nineteenth century the question of a more general application of Jenner's technique to immunization against all sorts of diseases was widely discussed in medical circles. Could immunization be established for other diseases, just as Jenner had shown it could be done for cowpox? Pasteur had pondered this problem for several years, while engaged in other fields of research. Then a chance occurrence gave him the clue from which there developed a whole theoretical science of **immunology.**

Pasteur had begun experiments on chicken cholera in the spring of 1879, but had discontinued his work during the summer. When he returned toward the beginning of September, the cultures of chicken cholera bacteria (which had

---

* In view of the current status of DDT, it is difficult to picture an award being made today for its discovery.

been kept in the laboratory untended for several months), failed to produce the disease when injected into chickens. A new, virulent (capable of causing disease) culture was obtained and used to inoculate not only new animals, but also the chickens which had been inoculated previously with the old culture. The new animals quickly contracted the disease as expected. To his surprise, however, Pasteur found that the previously inoculated chickens showed no signs of cholera and remained quite healthy.

As a result of his own reading and thinking on the general problem of immunity, Pasteur immediately recognized the similarity between this situation and Jenner's immunization of animals against smallpox. The evidence was as yet too scanty for any really valid conclusions to be drawn. But Pasteur was sufficiently thoughtful to suspect the general application of a new principle. By transferring pox material taken from an infected cow to man, Jenner had altered the human constitution so as to render it "immune" to infection from other pox microorganisms. Pasteur now recognized that the Jenner effect was a manifestation of a general law. The old bacteria culture which had remained in Pasteur's laboratory over the summer had lost its ability to produce the disease symptoms in an organism. But it had not lost the ability to elicit from the host animal the immunization response which makes that organism unreceptive to virulent microorganisms of the same type in the future. Jenner had used the term "vaccine" to refer to the substance removed from the sores of diseased cows for injection into other animals and people. Pasteur now coined the term "vaccination" to refer to the creation of immunity by similar means in any organism against any of a number of infectious diseases.

Pasteur's chance observation allowed him to make a speculative leap from Jenner's specific case to the general biological principle that nonliving microorganisms of infectious diseases can be utilized to build an immunological response in host animals. Chance was not all that was involved, however; Pasteur's own awareness of the *importance* of his observation made possible his recognition of such a generalization. In other words, chance is often a key ingredient in scientific discoveries, but it is seldom enough by itself to produce an important theory or idea. As Pasteur himself pointed out, "Chance favors the prepared mind."

## 4-4 A CASE HISTORY OF SCIENTIFIC EXPERIMENTATION

Having gained some general ideas as to the character and properties of scientific experimentation, we may now proceed to analyze a complete research project. This will provide a better understanding of the way in which observation, experiment, and logical reasoning interact to lead to a final conclusion. As an example, we shall consider the work of two English physiologists, W. M. Bayliss and E. H. Starling. Their experimentation was simple but ingenious, and thus serves as an excellent model to illustrate some of the important characteristics of scientific work. However, in order to understand exactly what is involved in the work of Bayliss and Starling, it is first necessary to be familiar with (1) the general anatomy of the digestive system in the area of the pancreas,

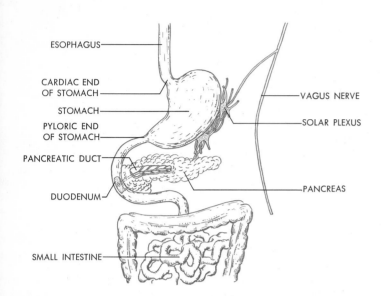

ESOPHAGUS

CARDIAC END
OF STOMACH

STOMACH

PYLORIC END
OF STOMACH

PANCREATIC DUCT

DUODENUM

SMALL INTESTINE

VAGUS NERVE

SOLAR PLEXUS

PANCREAS

FIG. 4–1    Generalized scheme of the alimentary tract from the esophagus to the upper part of the small intestine.  Shown also is the vagus nerve on the left-hand side of the body, and the solar plexus, a reflex center for many organs in this region of the abdomen.

and (2) the nature of the dispute among physiologists which led to the formulation of the basic problem in the minds of Bayliss and Starling.

In the early part of this century, Bayliss and Starling had discovered that the pancreas, one of the digestive organs, is stimulated to release its digestive enzymes at precisely the right moment, as food passes from the stomach into the upper portion of the small intestine.  The question left unanswered was basically, "What is the mechanism by which the pancreas is stimulated to release its digestive juice at precisely this moment?"

In the normal digestive process, food passes from the mouth into the **esophagus**, a long tube which leads to the stomach.  Figure 4–1 shows the basic organization of the alimentary canal in the region of the pancreas.  At the point where the esophagus joins the stomach (the **cardiac** end of the stomach), there is a special type of muscle which, when contracted, acts like a drawstring, closing off the stomach from the esophagus.  Another valve, at the lower or **pyloric** end of the stomach, serves a similar function in closing the stomach off from the intestines.  Inside the sealed-off stomach, the food is churned by the action of muscles of the stomach itself and mixed with gastric juices secreted from the tissue which lines the stomach walls.  When the food is thoroughly mixed and partly broken down, the pyloric valve opens.  The food passes into the **duodenum**, a portion of the upper end of the small intestine approximately 10 to 12 inches long.  At this point, the food is in a semiliquid condition known as **chyme**. Opening into the duodenum is a duct leading from the pancreas.  The pancreas produces a digestive juice which contains enzymes specialized to act upon each of the major types of food: carbohydrates, fats, and proteins.  Within several

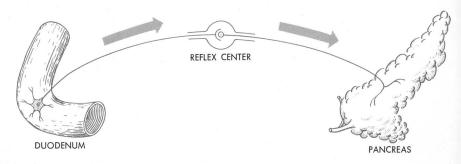

FIG. 4–2   Schematic representation of a reflex system, specifically referring to that idea hypothesized before the work of Bayliss and Starling. A nerve leading from the duodenum passes to a ganglion (reflex center), such as the solar plexus. From here, the message is relayed out to appropriate nerve tracts leading to other organs, in this case to the pancreas. The reflex center thus acts like a telephone switchboard.

minutes after the chyme has entered the duodenum, the pancreas begins to secrete its digestive juice. This juice mixes with the chyme, and the entire mass is moved slowly through the small intestine.

The following information was available at the time Bayliss and Starling began their work. If the pyloric valve was tied off so that food could not pass from the stomach into the duodenum, there was no pancreatic secretion. Thus the passage of food from the stomach into the duodenum somehow provided the signal to begin pancreatic secretion. It was also known that the chyme passing into the duodenum was highly acidic. It was suggested that the acid nature of the chyme was responsible for triggering pancreatic secretion. Previous workers had shown that introduction of dilute hydrochloric acid into the duodenum of an anesthetized animal brought about prominent activity of the pancreas. Introduction of similar but nonacid control substances yielded no secretory activity.

Given this information, two hypotheses were put forward in the late nineteenth century to explain the exact mechanism by which the chyme, as it passed into the duodenum, caused the pancreas to begin secretion.

*Hypothesis I:* The pancreas is controlled by the nervous system. Food entering the duodenum stimulates nerve endings in the walls of this organ. These nerves carry an impulse to various centers in the spinal cord and brain. From these central relay points, appropriate stimuli are sent back to the pancreas, bringing about a release of digestive juice. The basic nerve-reflex pattern is shown in Fig. 4–2.

*Hypothesis II:* The stimulation is carried from the walls of the duodenum to the pancreas by means of a "chemical messenger" in the blood. This messenger is perhaps produced by the cells in the wall of the duodenum.

Evidence for hypothesis I came from the work of several earlier physiologists. They had shown that stimulation of certain nerves, especially those in a prominent tract known as the *vagus*, caused an increase in pancreatic secretion. It was also known that the vagus did not stop pancreatic secretion.

Those adhering to hypothesis II also had good evidence to support their view. One of the most interesting experiments was performed in Germany in the 1870's. Two dogs were anesthetized and joined together in such a way that their blood streams were interconnected. When the duodenum of *one* of these two dogs was exposed and injected with dilute acid, the pancreas of both dogs began to secrete pancreatic juice. Since there were no nervous-system interconnections between the two animals, the experimental result was good indication that a blood-borne messenger was indeed responsible for triggering the pancreas.

With two opposing hypotheses to explain the same phenomenon, there was need for a crucial experiment, i.e., one that would serve to disprove one hypothesis. Recall from Chapter 3 that a crucial experiment is one based on a point of disagreement between two rival hypotheses. If two such hypotheses are compared point for point and a situation found where each hypothesis yields a different prediction, a crucial experiment may be designed around this point of difference. Bayliss and Starling developed such a test. They reasoned:

*Hypothesis: If* . . .  the pancreas is stimulated by a chemical substance in the blood rather than by central or peripheral nervous reflexes, . . .

*Prediction:*  *then* . . . removal of all ganglia and severing of all possible nervous pathways between the duodenum and the pancreas should not interfere with pancreatic secretion when acid is introduced into the duodenum.

This was the point of difference between the two hypotheses, since according to hypothesis I, if all possible nerve pathways were cut from the duodenum, then injection of acid should fail to elicit the normal pancreatic secretion.

In 1902, Bayliss and Starling performed their crucial experiment. Opening the abdomen of an anesthetized animal, they removed all the nerves from the duodenum and cut the vagus nerves on each side of the body. They carefully tied a loop of the duodenum in two places, so that it was no longer connected to other parts of the digestive tract by any direct opening. All other nerve connections to the duodenum were also carefully cut away; thus this particular loop of the duodenum was connected to the body of the animal only by its arteries and veins. A glass tube, its free end leading out of the animal's body, was inserted into the pancreatic duct so that the number of drops of pancreatic juice secreted for any unit of time could be accurately recorded on a revolving drum or **kymograph**. The experimental setup is diagrammed in Fig. 4–3.

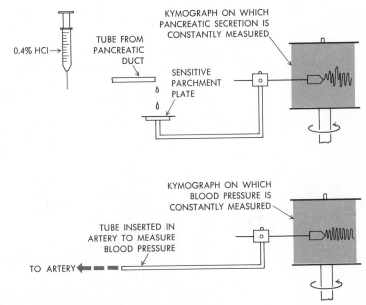

FIG. 4–3  Experimental setup for the Bayliss and Starling experiment. Injection of acid solution into the duodenum produces flow of pancreatic fluid, measured on drum at upper right. All connections to the duodenum from the rest of the body have been severed except arteries and veins.

To guard against possible sources of error, Bayliss and Starling took the precaution of recording, on a separate revolving drum, the blood pressure of the animal under investigation. It is important to see why this step was necessary. For their normal functioning, tissues depend on a certain amount of blood flowing through them at a certain pressure. If the pressure falls, materials in the blood do not move from the capillaries to the tissues as rapidly, and thus the physiological activity of these tissues is altered. If the blood pressure in the experimental animal were to fall during the course of the experiment, the amount of pancreatic juice would also be expected to fall. By keeping a running record of the dog's blood pressure, the experimenters would be able to tell when the reduction of pancreatic juice was a result of a change in blood pressure, and when it was due to some condition of the experiment.

Injecting a small amount of dilute (0.4%) hydrochloric acid into the isolated loop of the duodenum, Bayliss and Starling found that after a delay of two minutes or so, the pancreas began to secrete digestive juice at a relatively rapid rate. It seemed apparent that the two-minute delay ruled out nervous transmission of the stimulus, which would have been much faster. It was considered possible, therefore, that the secretion-causing agent might be transmitted via the more slowly moving bloodstream.

As a control, Bayliss and Starling recorded the rate of pancreatic secretion in an anesthetized animal whose nervous connections to the duodenum and pancreas were left intact. This rate, brought about by the introduction of 0.4% HCl into the duodenum, served as a comparison for the rate observed in the experimental animals. Note that the chief difference between the experimental and control animals was the absence or presence of nervous connection between the duodenum and pancreas. Thus a similarity in the rates of secretion in the two animals would indicate that nerve impulses were not the major factor in bringing about the activation of the pancreas, because *if* nerve pathways were involved in stimulating the pancreas, *then* the rate of flow would be greater in the control (nerves intact) than in the experimental (nerves severed) animal. Since the rate of flow in both turned out to be the same, Bayliss and Starling concluded that it was possible to account for the stimulation of the pancreas by mechanisms other than the nervous reflex. Hypothesis I was thus disproved, and hypothesis II supported.

But this was not enough. Once the nerve-pathway hypothesis was ruled out, it became an important phase of Bayliss and Starling's work to show exactly what the hypothetical blood-borne messenger was, where it was produced, and how it had its effects. These problems formed the foundation for the next phase of experimentation.

It was known that direct injection of hydrochloric acid into the blood did not increase the rate of pancreatic secretion. Hence the acid itself was not the immediate stimulus. Bayliss and Starling now concentrated on the tissue of the wall of the duodenum and intestine. Since the acid chyme entered the duodenum from the stomach and came into contact with the epithelial (lining) cells which composed the wall of the duodenum, it was reasonable to assume that perhaps the chyme stimulated the production of some chemical substance in the cells of the intestinal walls. This chemical messenger, then, carried in the blood to the pancreas, served as the stimulant to trigger the release of digestive juices by the latter organ.

The experimenters tested this hypothesis in the following way. They scraped some of the epithelial cells from the inside wall of the duodenum and intestine, and mixed these scrapings with dilute hydrochloric acid. Then they filtered this liquid and injected it into the bloodstream. A minute or two thereafter, an enormously large secretion of pancreatic fluid was recorded, indicating that the action of acid on the epithelial cells caused the formation of a messenger substance which passed into the blood. Although this substance passed to all tissues of the body, it would stimulate only the cells of the pancreas itself. Bayliss and Starling called the messenger substance **secretin**. Today we know that secretin is one of many substances, called **hormones**, which act in this general way. A hormone is a chemical messenger produced by one area of the body (usually by an **endocrine gland**) to have some influence in another, very specific area. Certain cells of the walls of the duodenum thus constituted an endocrine gland producing the hormone secretin.

Further investigation showed that if the scrapings were taken from successively lower portions of the intestine and mixed with acid, the magnitude of their effect on the pancreas decreased. Thus the lower ends of the small intestine would not produce any secretion when brought in contact with dilute hydrochloric acid. In order to explain exactly how this might occur, Bayliss and Starling hypothesized that the cells of the upper portions of the intestinal tract contained a large amount of a substance they called *prosecretin*, which was converted into secretin by the action of dilute acid on the cells. They expressed this as:

PROSECRETIN + HYDROCHLORIC ACID → SECRETIN.

The further along the intestine the cells were located, however, the less prosecretin they contained, hence the less secretin they produced when stimulated by acid. Finally, the cells of the lower end of the intestine contained no prosecretin whatsoever, and hence could not function as a hormone-producing gland. It was logical that the most active area of the intestine should be the duodenum—that area closest to the lower end of the stomach. There the acid food has its greatest effect, and thus causes the relatively rapid secretion of digestive juice by the pancreas.

The work of Bayliss and Starling served to end a long-standing controversy. For this reason it is important in the history of physiology. In addition, it highlights many of the features which often are part of scientific experimentation. Let us consider some of the main features which this experimental work emphasizes.

1) Bayliss and Starling were led to their work because of an existing controversy. This controversy developed between two rival hypotheses, both of which might explain the phenomenon of pancreatic secretion in an acceptable way. Comparing the two hypotheses point for point, Bayliss and Starling were able to find an area in which one theory predicted one result, while the other predicted something different. They were thus able to organize a crucial experiment which served to settle the controversy. In other words, they formulated their reasoning in such a way that only *one question* was at stake in the experimental design: Would the pancreas secrete digestive juice if the duodenum were isolated from the animal in all ways except through the bloodstream?

2) The experimenters were able to carry the investigation further than answering just a single question. They were able to suggest a physiological mechanism by which the acid chyme from the stomach actually produced the stimulation of the pancreas by way of the bloodstream. This enhanced their original finding in the crucial experiment because it offered a replacement for the nerve-pathway hypothesis—some type of chemical explanation which was consistent with their new findings. This is an important feature of scientific experimentation. It is not enough to destroy an old hypothesis; it is also necessary to carry the work far enough to offer some type of replacement theory which is in agreement with

all available data. In other words, a crucial experiment should not only explain all the old findings, but also any new findings which the old hypothesis could not explain.

3) Bayliss and Starling set up their experiment in such a way as to record their data precisely and quantitatively. By using the parchment plate and the revolving drum, they were able to get an accurate record of the number of drops of digestive juice which the pancreas secreted under different experimental conditions. They also took the precaution of recording the blood pressure, so that any changes which this might make in the activity of the pancreas could be accounted for. They tried to leave no loopholes which could detract from the significance of their findings.

4) The experimenters introduced a control factor, the animal in which the nervous connections between duodenum and pancreas were left intact. In this way the rate of pancreatic flow with the nerves severed could be compared to some standard. The control was important, in this case, since a major purpose of the work of Bayliss and Starling was to show that nerve reflex was not a significant cause of pancreatic secretion.*

**4-5**
**CONCLUSION**    In this chapter, we have gained some insight into the nature of scientific experiments, their characteristics and their design. The characteristics discussed are not the only ones found in good experiments, nor do all valid experiments *necessarily* have these features. Yet, all good experiments do have certain things in common. It will be important to look for these characteristics as experiments are discussed in later sections of this book. The validity of the experimental results rests upon the degree to which the important criteria of experimental design are met.

**EXERCISES**    1. What is the relation between an hypothesis and an experiment?

2. What is a controlled experiment? Why is it essential to have controls whenever possible in experimental work? List some of the most important characteristics of a controlled scientific experiment.

3. A biologist finds that removal of organ A, an endocrine gland, from an adult mammal causes organs B and C to cease functioning. Organ B is also an endocrine gland. The three possible explanations for this occurrence are diagrammed below. (For A → B, read "A is necessary to B," etc.)

$$A \nearrow^{B}_{\searrow C} \qquad A \rightarrow B \rightarrow C \qquad A \rightarrow C \rightarrow B$$

---

* For a thorough analysis of the Bayliss and Starling work, it is suggested that the student read an abridged version of the original paper of 1902, listed in the readings at the end of this chapter. The paper, incidentally, can serve the reader as a model for the general format of scientific articles.

Design an experiment or experiments which would test these possibilities and which would distinguish between them.

4. In order to give his experimental results validity, a scientist wanted to test the effectiveness of a certain vaccine. He went to a village which was made up of equal numbers of natives and persons of another race. The vaccine was supposed to prevent a certain disease to which the entire village population was susceptible. Which of the following should he do in order to test his serum in a valid way?

a) Give vaccine to the natives but not to the non-natives, and watch the results.

b) Give vaccine to the non-natives but not to the natives, and watch the results.

c) Give vaccine to the natives and a harmless salt solution to the non-natives, and watch the results.

d) Give half of the natives and half of the non-natives the serum, and half of the natives and half of the non-natives a harmless salt solution, and watch the results.

e) You cannot run a validly controlled experiment with human beings, since they are so complex.

5. From the following experimentally obtained observations regarding mineral nutrition in plants, draw a conclusion as to the factor or factors necessary for the development of chlorophyll in green plants.

*Observation 1.* Plants grown in soil containing chloride and magnesium, and supplied with light, became green.

*Observation 2.* Plants grown in soil containing chloride but not magnesium, and supplied with light, remained white.

*Observation 3.* Plants grown in soil containing chloride and magnesium, but kept in the dark, remained white.

*Observation 4.* Plants grown in soil containing magnesium but no chloride, and supplied with light, became green.

*Observation 5.* Plants grown in soil containing chloride but not magnesium, and kept in the dark, remained white.

*Observation 6.* Plants grown in soil containing neither magnesium nor chloride, but supplied with light, remained white.

*Observation 7.* Plants grown in soil containing magnesium but not chloride, and kept in the dark, remained white.

*Observation 8.* Plants grown in soil containing neither chloride nor magnesium, and kept in the dark, remained white.

*Conclusion:* The factor (or factors) necessary for the development of chlorophyll, as judged from the above experiment, are: . . .

6. A few years ago a number of psychological experiments were performed with a "consciousness-expanding drug" known as psilocybin. This drug, an extract from certain fungi, heightens the senses, makes a person more aware of his surroundings, and supposedly gives each individual a deeper understanding of himself. To measure the effects of the drug, several people, including the experimenter himself, would take a dose simultaneously. Researchers claimed that only when the experimenter was also

under the influence of the drug could he properly evaluate the subjects' responses. Discuss the way or ways in which such an experiment fails to meet the requirements of a valid scientific experiment.

7. A group of scientists wanted to know what factor or factors cause rats to be susceptible to a certain disease induced by viruses.

*Hypothesis:* Diet is the factor which is responsible for susceptibility to the condition induced by a particular virus.

*Experimental Procedure:* Six pens were prepared, each to house 20 laboratory rats chosen at random from a stockroom. A special food was prepared, containing an adequate amount of carbohydrates, fats, proteins, vitamins, and minerals. The rats in the six pens were subjected to the following feeding formulas:

*Pen A* – These 20 rats were fed the special food (F).

*Pen B* – These 20 rats were fed the special food (F) with carbohydrates omitted.

*Pen C* – These 20 rats were fed the special food (F) with both fats and carbohydrates omitted.

*Pen D* – These 20 rats were given food containing vitamins and minerals only.

*Pen E* – These 20 rats were given food containing minerals only.

*Pen F* – These 20 rats were given no food at all.

Evaluate each of the occurrences or results I–IV on the basis of such considerations as the following:

   a) Is it a logical step in experimental procedure?

   b) Is there adequate control of all variables, or are additional variables introduced?

   c) Is the result observed (if it is a result) expected or unexpected?

   d) Is the occurrence related to the success or failure of the experiment?

I. The rats used to introduce the virus into the rats in pens A, B, C, D, and E were trapped at the city dump and placed in the pens as soon as they showed symptoms of virus V.

II. The rats in pens E and F appeared to lose weight most rapidly but failed to show symptoms of virus V.

III. All the rats in pen F outlived all the rats in all the other pens.

IV. Adequate water and suitable temperature were provided for all the rats in the six pens throughout the experiment.

SUGGESTED READINGS    BAYLISS, W. M., and E. H. STARLING, "The Mechanism of Pancreatic Secretion." *Journal of Physiology* **28** (1902), 325–353. Reprinted in *The Process of Biology: Primary Sources*, Jeffrey J. W. Baker and Garland E. Allen, eds. (Reading, Mass.: Addison-Wesley, 1970). This is an abridged reprint of Bayliss and Starling's original paper. A good insight into how they designed the crucial experiment.

DUBOS, RENE, *Louis Pasteur, Free Lance of Science* (Boston: Little, Brown & Co., 1950). This biography and the shorter paperback version, *Pasteur and Modern Science* (New York: Anchor Books, 1960), provide further insight into Pasteur's many areas of research, and his experimental approach to problems. Both books are very well written, and show the roles of chance and luck, coupled with Pasteur's own genius, in leading him to so many important discoveries.

GOLDSTEIN, PHILIP, *How to Do an Experiment* (New York: Harcourt, Brace, 1957).

YOUDEN, W. J., *Experimentation and Measurement* (Washington: NSTA Books, 1962). A valuable and well-organized booklet containing much information about the design of experiments and the handling of biological data.

CHAPTER 5  **THE ANALYSIS AND
INTERPRETATION OF DATA**

**5-1
INTRODUCTION**

As important to the scientist as the collection of data is how he extracts from it the significant information it may contain. A large collection of data is of limited value if it is not arranged in such a way as to show important relationships. For example, random samples of age and height measurements for a population of human beings would not show what relation exists between these factors. Grouping the measurements by age in one column with corresponding height in another would yield much more information. It would show, for example, the ages during which growth occurred most rapidly, as well as the ages at which growth slowed down and ceased.

As a means of extracting as much information as possible from their measurements, working scientists subject their data to many kinds of analysis. They may arrange their data in tables or graphs, or subject them to specific mathematical procedures known as statistical analysis. Such treatment provides the researcher with a more complete understanding of his experimental results and of the scientific principles involved. This chapter will discuss some of the ways in which data can be handled, and how such procedures are of great importance in scientific work.

**5-2
FRAMES OF
REFERENCE FOR
BIOLOGICAL DATA**

Measurements are the bases of a quantitative approach to biology. Any system of measurement establishes a basic frame of reference within which comparisons can be made. In the United States, for example, the common units of linear measurement are the inch, the foot, the yard, and the mile. Within this frame of reference, comparisons of distance can be made with relative ease because these units of measurement have become familiar to everyone.

66

A single unit for measuring distance will not usually be convenient for all possible situations.  Different units must be employed in making different kinds of measurements.  For example, the astronomer uses the *light-year* as his basic unit for measuring distances outside our solar system.  A light-year is the distance which light can travel in one year's time.  The distance to the nearest star (Alpha Centauri) can be expressed conveniently as 4.4 light-years, whereas if it were expressed in terms of miles, the figure would be very awkward to work with.*  Similarly, scientists in other fields use different units of measure for distance, volume, or mass, the choice depending on the magnitudes which they wish to measure.  One unit can generally be converted into another, if necessary. For example, a light-year *can* be expressed in terms of miles if this is desired. The most convenient frames of reference are those where one unit can be converted into another with relative ease.

Nearly all scientists use the **metric system** of measurement.  In the metric system, the standard unit of linear measure is the **meter**, equivalent to 39.37 inches.  The standard unit of mass is the **gram**, the mass of one milliliter of water at a temperature of 4° centigrade.  The standard unit of volume is the **liter**, equivalent to approximately 1.06 quarts.

The metric system has two important advantages.  First, all units are divided and subdivided on the basis of tens.  Thus 1 liter is composed of 10 deciliters, or 1000 milliliters.  Similarly, 1 meter is composed of 10 decimeters, 100 centimeters, or 1000 millimeters, and 1 gram is composed of 10 decigrams, 100 centigrams, or 1000 milligrams.

A second advantage of this system is that units can be easily converted from one type of measure to the other; thus the capacity measure 1000 milliliters (ml) equals the volume measure 1000.027 cubic centimeters (cc or $cm^3$), and so on.  For ordinary purposes, 1000 ml is considered equivalent to 1000 cc. Such flexibility greatly simplifies routine calculations.

One of the very helpful features of the metric system is that the unit names are to some extent *descriptive* of the unit values.  For example, a centimeter is one-hundredth of a meter (from the Latin word *centum*, meaning "hundred"), and a millimeter is one-thousandth of a meter (from the Latin word *mille*, meaning "thousand").  The prefix *micro-*, which literally means "small," has come to mean one-millionth; thus a microgram is one-millionth of a gram. The Greek prefix *kilo-*, meaning "thousand," is used in the multiple rather than the fractional sense.  Thus a kilometer is 1000 meters, and a kilogram, 1000 grams.  Table 5–1 compares some of the major metric units.  English equivalents for most of these metric units are shown in the right-hand column of the table.

Like the standards for mass, volume, and distance, the temperature scale which scientists use is different from the traditional Fahrenheit system.

---

* Light travels about 5,865,696,000,000 miles per year.  To say that the nearest star is 25,809,062,400,000 miles away is so cumbersome as to be almost meaningless.

**TABLE 5–1**  CHIEF UNITS OF THE METRIC SYSTEM

| LINEAR MEASURE | | SYMBOL | ENGLISH EQUIVALENT |
|---|---|---|---|
| 1 KILOMETER | = 1000 METERS | km | 0.62137 MILE |
| 1 METER | = 10 DECIMETERS | m | 39.37 INCHES |
| 1 DECIMETER | = 10 CENTIMETERS | dm | 3.937 INCHES |
| 1 CENTIMETER | = 10 MILLIMETERS | cm | 0.3937 INCH |
| 1 MILLIMETER | = 1000 MICRONS | mm | |
| 1 MICRON | = 1/1000 MILLIMETER OR | $\mu$ | |
| | 1000 MILLIMICRONS | | NO ENGLISH |
| 1 MILLIMICRON | = 10 ANGSTROM UNITS | m$\mu$ | EQUIVALENTS |
| 1 ANGSTROM UNIT | = 1/100,000,000 CENTIMETER | $\overset{\circ}{\text{A}}$ | |

| MEASURES OF CAPACITY | | | |
|---|---|---|---|
| 1 KILOLITER = 1000 LITERS | | kl | 35.15 CUBIC FEET OR |
| | | | 264.16 GALLONS |
| 1 LITER      = 10 DECILITERS | | l | 1.0567 U.S. LIQUID |
| | | | QUARTS |
| 1 DECILITER = 100 MILLILITERS | | dl | .03 FLUID OUNCES |
| 1 MILLILITER = VOLUME OF 1 g OF WATER AT | | ml | |
| STANDARD TEMPERATURE AND | | | |
| PRESSURE | | | |

| MEASURES OF MASS | | | |
|---|---|---|---|
| 1 KILOGRAM = 1000 GRAMS | | kg | 2.2046 POUNDS |
| 1 GRAM      = 100 CENTIGRAMS | | g | 15.432 GRAINS |
| 1 CENTIGRAM = 10 MILLIGRAMS | | cg | 0.1543 GRAINS |
| 1 MILLIGRAM = 1/1000 GRAM | | mg | ABOUT .01 GRAIN |

| MEASURES OF VOLUME | | | |
|---|---|---|---|
| 1 CUBIC METER | = 1000 CUBIC DECIMETERS | $m^3$ | |
| 1 CUBIC DECIMETER | = 1000 CUBIC CENTIMETERS | $dm^3$ | |
| 1 CUBIC CENTIMETER | = 1000 CUBIC MILLIMETERS | $cm^3$ | |
| 1000 CUBIC MILLIMETERS | = 1 MILLILITER (ml) | $mm^3$ | |

Table 5–2 shows three temperature scales in common use today.  In our daily affairs, most of us use the Fahrenheit scale.  Biologists use the centigrade system most frequently.  It has the advantage of being based on units of ten—there are 100 degrees between the boiling point and freezing point of water.  The absolute or Kelvin (K) scale is also frequently used in scientific work, for temperatures falling below the normal range encountered in most situations.  Simple formulae for conversion from one temperature scale to another are given in Appendix 1.

**TABLE 5–2** COMPARISON OF TEMPERATURE SYSTEMS

|  | °F | °C | °K |
|---|---|---|---|
| BOILING POINT OF WATER | 212 | 100 | 373 |
| FREEZING POINT OF WATER | 32 ↑180°↓ | 0 ↑100°↓ | 273 ↑100°↓ |
| LOWEST TEMPERATURE OF UNIVERSE | −459 | −273 | 0 |

Many types of measurements in biology involve sampling small amounts of data from the vast amounts which are potentially available. For instance, it would be impossible from a practical point of view to measure the height of all the human beings in a large city in order to determine the average height of the city's population. Not only would such a procedure be time-consuming and laborious, it would also be unnecessary, since by choosing sample individuals from among the population at large, acceptably accurate results are obtained with a minimum of effort. This means that if the sampling is **unbiased** (*i.e.*, if all the individuals are not taken from one neighborhood, or from one age group), the average height calculated from a fraction of the total population should be nearly the same as that from the entire population. Thus measurements of height on 1000 adult males between the ages of 25 and 35 out of a population of 500,000 should be equivalent to that found for all adult males between 25 and 35 in the population. One of the chief problems in any sampling technique, however, is the possibility that the chosen few measurements will be **biased**— that they will not be representative of the population as a whole. There are several ways in which the degree of bias, affecting the validity of sampling data, can be determined. Some of the ways in which such data can be treated will be discussed in this section. First, however, let us consider how sampling is done, and how the raw data collected from field or laboratory measurements are converted into a useful form.

Several years ago a group of biologists set out to measure a specific characteristic, tail length, in two closely related species of deer mice (genus *Peromyscus*). They suspected from previous reports that the two populations were different in this characteristic, and wanted to see whether this difference was statistically significant. The first collecting trip in the field yielded only 15 specimens from population A. Although this was a small sample, the organisms were brought back to the laboratory and their tail lengths measured. The values that were recorded are shown in Table 5–3.

**TABLE 5-3**

| ORGANISM NO. | TAIL LENGTH, mm | | |
|---|---|---|---|
| | OBSERVER 1 | OBSERVER 2 | OBSERVER 3 |
| 1 | 60.5 | 60.2 | 60.3 |
| 2 | 61.0 | 59.9 | 61.1 |
| 3 | 62.2 | 62.0 | 63.0 |
| 4 | 68.1 | 68.0 | 67.9 |
| 5 | 60.7 | 60.6 | 60.2 |
| 6 | 58.3 | 58.4 | 58.5 |
| 7 | 66.6 | 66.0 | 66.3 |
| 8 | 56.7 | 56.6 | 56.6 |
| 9 | 62.5 | 62.6 | 62.5 |
| 10 | 60.8 | 50.9 | 60.7 |
| 11 | 58.0 | 58.2 | 58.1 |
| 12 | 54.5 | 54.5 | 54.5 |
| 13 | 56.7 | 56.2 | 56.1 |
| 14 | 58.9 | 58.8 | 58.7 |
| 15 | 60.2 | 60.3 | 60.2 |

Note that for the sake of accuracy, three different observers measured each organism. The slight discrepancies in the values recorded for each organism reflect a type of error that inevitably results when measurements are made. All measurements involve some element of estimation (for example, where does one start measuring a mouse's tail?), and thus some differences will always arise. Despite the fact that measurements are objective and quantitative, they still involve human judgment, and thus the element of subjectivity. Where big discrepancies in data arise, it is important to know whether those discrepancies are a valid measure of some difference found in nature or are the result of an error in measurement. For example, observer 2 gave the value of 50.9 mm for organism 10, whereas observers 1 and 3 gave it as 60.8 and 60.7, respectively. In this case, with three observers checking each item, we would be safe in concluding that the value of 50.9 was in error. However, if we had only the data from observer 2 to work with, it would not be so easy to discard the suspect measurement. The low value of 50.9 (compared to the other 14 organisms) could be due to a mutilation (in which case it could be discarded as atypical) or a mutation (in which case it would be of statistical importance to the biologist). Now, considering for further statistical purposes only the data collected by observer 1, let us see what information these measurements can yield.

There are a number of ways in which data can be analyzed and its validity checked. One important step in the analysis is to calculate the **mean** or average value of tail length for the sample at hand. The mean (symbolized $\overline{X}$) is determined by adding up (summing, symbolized by the Greek letter $\Sigma$) all the individual values (1 through 15) and dividing by the total number of values

(15) in the sample. This can be expressed mathematically as

$$\overline{X} = \frac{\Sigma X}{N},$$

where $\Sigma X$ represents the sum of all the individual measurements, and $N$ the total number in the population. Using the values from observer 1, we find that

$$\overline{X} = 60.3.$$

The mean value is useful in comparing one sample with another.

The data collected in Table 5–3 represent a survey of 15 organisms from a large natural population. The average of these 15 individuals, 60.3, may not be typical of the whole population. The smaller the sample, the greater the chance of **sampling error**—of results not typical of the whole. After all, finding the mean of a sample of data is nothing more than making a generalization, and as was shown in Chapter 3, it is dangerous to generalize from a small sample of data. It is therefore important to have as large a sample of measurements as possible. For instance, if organisms 14 and 15, as recorded in Table 5–3, had values of 40.0 (and, let us say, represented mutations), the mean would be lowered from 60.3 to 57.6. This is a large difference if one is talking about the average for the entire population. The question would then become: Are 2 out of every 15 mice mutants for tail length, or did 2 mutants just happen to turn up in the present sample?

Sampling error is a significant problem in the collection of data. A large sample helps to reduce the misleading effects of such error. The data shown in Table 5–4 show further measurements made from the original field population. How well does the mean value of 60.3 hold when a larger sample of measurements is included? (Check, using the values for observer 1.)

The data in Tables 5–3 and 5–4, in their present form, yield only a small amount of information. Calculation of the mean is one step toward analysis of the results in a meaningful form. A second step is organization of the data into a graphical form that will tell us not only what the average value is, but how each measurement relates to that average.

One of the most common ways to graph data such as those given above is to construct a **histogram.** A histogram is a form of bar graph. The height of each bar measures the number of individuals. The placement of the bar along a horizontal line indicates the specific range of value for each measurement. For example, the extremes of tail length given in Tables 5–3 and 5–4 run from 52.4 to 68.0, excluding organism 85.* On this basis, nine categories, each rep-

**5–4**
**FROM TABLE**
**TO GRAPH**

---

\* For the sake of this example, let us assume that organism 85 represented a mutilation rather than a mutation.

**TABLE 5–4**

| ORGANISM NO. | TAIL LENGTH, mm | | | ORGANISM NO. | TAIL LENGTH, mm | | |
|---|---|---|---|---|---|---|---|
| | OBSERVER 1 | OBSERVER 2 | OBSERVER 3 | | OBSERVER 1 | OBSERVER 2 | OBSERVER 3 |
| 16 | 60.3 | 60.3 | 60.5 | 51 | 57.2 | 57.5 | 57.3 |
| 17 | 64.5 | 64.6 | 64.5 | 52 | 59.1 | 59.2 | 59.0 |
| 18 | 61.1 | 61.5 | 61.7 | 53 | 62.5 | 62.4 | 62.0 |
| 19 | 62.1 | 62.2 | 62.0 | 54 | 63.6 | 63.6 | 63.5 |
| 20 | 62.7 | 62.7 | 62.7 | 55 | 57.0 | 57.1 | 57.2 |
| 21 | 61.0 | 59.8 | 61.2 | 56 | 55.1 | 55.5 | 55.0 |
| 22 | 65.9 | 65.8 | 65.7 | 57 | 56.5 | 56.6 | 56.5 |
| 23 | 64.4 | 62.9 | 63.0 | 58 | 62.5 | 62.6 | 62.4 |
| 24 | 61.0 | 61.2 | 61.0 | 59 | 56.7 | 56.5 | 56.3 |
| 25 | 57.7 | 57.6 | 57.5 | 60 | 58.5 | 58.6 | 58.5 |
| 26 | 60.5 | 60.4 | 60.5 | 61 | 60.1 | 60.0 | 60.2 |
| 27 | 58.5 | 58.8 | 58.6 | 62 | 59.8 | 59.9 | 60.0 |
| 28 | 60.1 | 60.3 | 60.5 | 63 | 65.5 | 65.4 | 65.0 |
| 29 | 61.8 | 61.9 | 62.0 | 64 | 58.1 | 58.2 | 58.3 |
| 30 | 59.5 | 59.7 | 59.6 | 65 | 62.2 | 62.2 | 62.2 |
| 31 | 61.5 | 62.0 | 61.7 | 66 | 56.5 | 56.6 | 56.6 |
| 32 | 64.5 | 65.0 | 64.8 | 67 | 63.6 | 63.1 | 63.5 |
| 33 | 63.0 | 63.1 | 63.2 | 68 | 61.0 | 61.0 | 61.0 |
| 34 | 61.9 | 61.8 | 61.8 | 69 | 58.7 | 58.6 | 58.8 |
| 35 | 60.2 | 60.2 | 60.2 | 70 | 62.0 | 62.2 | 62.4 |
| 36 | 56.5 | 56.6 | 56.4 | 71 | 67.1 | 67.2 | 67.0 |
| 37 | 64.0 | 64.1 | 64.0 | 72 | 59.8 | 59.7 | 59.8 |
| 38 | 60.8 | 60.6 | 60.6 | 73 | 62.5 | 62.6 | 62.6 |
| 39 | 61.0 | 61.1 | 61.1 | 74 | 58.0 | 58.7 | 58.6 |
| 40 | 65.1 | 65.1 | 65.3 | 75 | 62.5 | 62.3 | 62.6 |
| 41 | 62.5 | 62.5 | 52.6* | 76 | 65.1 | 65.0 | 65.2 |
| 42 | 63.0 | 63.0 | 63.0 | 77 | 58.5 | 58.7 | 59.0 |
| 43 | 60.1 | 60.4 | 59.9 | 78 | 62.5 | 62.6 | 62.7 |
| 44 | 52.5 | 52.3 | 52.4 | 79 | 56.5 | 56.5 | 56.5 |
| 45 | 65.5 | 65.1 | 65.7 | 80 | 63.4 | 63.6 | 63.8 |
| 46 | 62.0 | 62.1 | 62.1 | 81 | 54.0 | 54.2 | 54.2 |
| 47 | 60.8 | 60.7 | 60.7 | 82 | 62.2 | 62.4 | 62.3 |
| 48 | 58.8 | 58.7 | 58.6 | 83 | 64.5 | 64.4 | 64.4 |
| 49 | 59.1 | 60.0 | 59.5 | 84 | 57.8 | 58.0 | 57.8 |
| 50 | 63.1 | 63.0 | 63.2 | 85 | 49.1 | 49.2 | 49.0 |

* Possible error in measurement or in recording of data.

resenting a range of 2 mm, can be set up along the horizontal axis of the bar graph. Along the vertical axis the number of organisms can be measured off, from 1 to 25. The histogram is constructed by making the bar for each category correspond in height to the number of organisms in that category. The completed histogram is shown in Fig. 5–1.

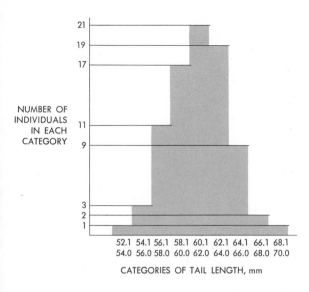

NUMBER OF INDIVIDUALS IN EACH CATEGORY

CATEGORIES OF TAIL LENGTH, mm

FIG. 5–1    Histogram of data compiled in Tables 5–3 and 5–4. Histograms show clearly the number of individuals in each category. The largest single category (in this case, 60.1–62.0 mm) is called the mode.

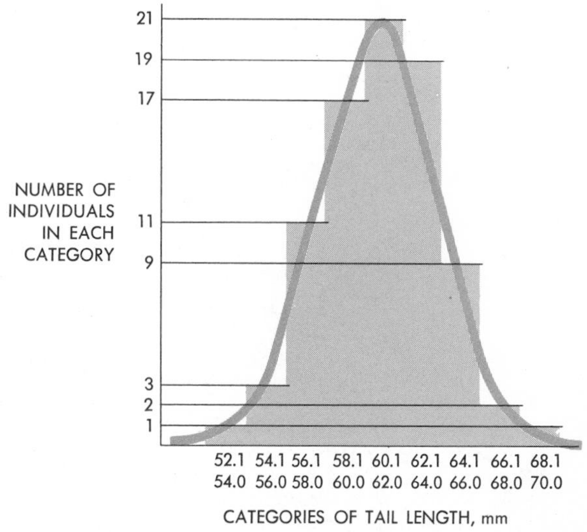

FIG. 5–2    Line graph of data presented in Tables 5–3 and 5–4, superimposed on the histogram of these data.

The histogram has the advantage of showing immediately on inspection the category containing the largest number of organisms. This is called the **mode.** The histogram also has the advantage of showing immediately the way in which other categories are grouped around the mode. In Fig. 5–1, the other categories are grouped roughly evenly to both sides of the mode, and thus represent what is called a **normal distribution.**

In a perfectly normal distribution, the mean and the mode are identical; however, the mode is not necessarily the same as the mean, and the two should not be confused. In principle they represent different quantities. It is true that in many of the sampling procedures which biologists deal with, the two are identical or very close together. To determine the mean accurately, however, it is still necessary to make the calculations that we discussed in the previous section.

If a line is drawn through the bars on the histogram, the data can be shown as a **line graph** (see Fig. 5–2). This graph shows a **normal distribution curve.** It is more or less symmetrical, with the value having the greatest frequency in the center and with values decreasing equally on both sides.

We have already discussed two statistics relating to graphs: the mean and the mode. On a graph, the mean is a measure of the degree to which the values fall in the middle of the range of observed values. The mode, as in the histo-

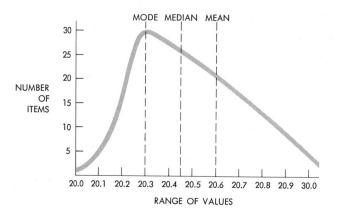

FIG. 5–3   Asymmetrical curve showing mode, median, and mean, each having a separate value.

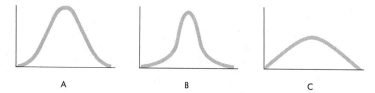

FIG. 5–4   Three curves of frequency distribution with the same mean, but different dispersion of data around the mean. The variance for curve C would be the greatest, whereas that for B would be the least.

gram, represents the category containing the largest number of individual items of data.

One other statistic is of importance—the **median.** This is the value of the observation which has an equal number of observations to either side. The median always defines the recorded value that is the midpoint of a number of observations. If a distribution curve is symmetrical (*i.e.*, if it is a normal curve) the median and the mean are the same. If the curve is asymmetrical, the two are different. Figure 5–3 shows an assymetrical curve with the mean and the median marked. The median occurs between the values of 20.4 and 20.5. The mean, however, is found at 20.59, that is, nearly at the value 20.6. The mean, median, and mode thus represent different ways of describing the degree of symmetry of a curve.

Despite the methods developed thus far to describe the distribution of data, we still have no adequate way to estimate the *dispersion* of the observations. For example, all three curves shown in Fig. 5–4 are symmetrical and have identical means, modes, and medians. Yet it is obvious that in each case the data are dispersed quite differently around the mean.

One statistic that provides an estimate of dispersion is called the **variance,** and is symbolized by $s^2$. The method of calculating $s^2$ is given in Appendix 2. Here we need only note that the greater the value for the variance, the more widely dispersed are the data around the mean. Of the three curves shown in Fig. 5–4, curve C obviously has the greatest variance. To relate this to our earlier example, we should expect that the variance for a distribution of tail length should be much greater in a natural population of mice than in an inbred laboratory strain. Both types of mice will show approximately normal distribution curves but the laboratory mice, because they are genetically more similar to each other, will show less variance in the dispersion of the measurements. The dispersion could also be measured by the **range,** *i.e.,* the difference between the minimum and maximum measurements in the data. But then we would know only the lower and upper limits of measurement, irrespective of how great the frequency of the various measurements might be. Variance has the advantage of taking frequency of distribution into account; for this reason, it is capable of yielding much more information about the actual dispersion of measurements around the mean.

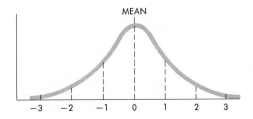

FIG. 5–5   A normal distribution curve showing the units of standard deviation marked off from the mean. If the sampling of data is valid, the standard deviation for most items of data will, in general, be within one unit on either side of the mean.

A second statistic which is of considerable value in describing dispersion of data on distribution graphs is called **standard deviation.** Standard deviation is merely the square root of the variance. It provides a way of showing the limits within which any given items in a distribution may be expected to deviate from the mean. All, or nearly all, of the observations in a sample usually lie within three standard deviations of the mean. As is shown in Fig. 5–5, 68% of the observations fall between the −1 and +1 values on the graph. In other words, 68% of the observations can be expected to lie within one standard deviation unit from the mean. Similarly, 95% of the observations are expected to fall within two standard deviation units of the mean, and over 99% of the observations are expected to fall within three standard deviation units from the mean.

Mean, median, mode, variance, and standard deviation all provide ways of describing characteristics of distribution curves. Since the distribution curve is one of the most common types of graph encountered in biological research, familiarity with these statistical concepts is important to the biologist. Not only do they help him to express differences between one set of data and another, they also help him to determine the validity of sample information. If the standard deviation for an item is more than three units, it is apparent that the data represent a very far spread from the mean. In addition, once the standard deviation and variance have been calculated for any sampling, the relation of each item to the mean for the whole sample can be calculated very easily. A questionable item of data can thus be checked for its uniqueness. Through use of such statistical tools, measurements can be treated to a variety of tests that help the researcher draw more information from them than is found in the raw data themselves.

**5–5
CORRELATIONS**

We have seen that graphs summarize a large amount of data very succinctly. Graphs are also useful in that they can show correlations between factors. For example, suppose that we release a large number of microorganisms, say *Paramecia* (singular, *Paramecium*), in a large culture dish. Assume that the central part of the dish is marked off with a circle, and all the *Paramecia* start out within this circle. If we observe the circle once an hour for 6 hours, we find that the number of individuals within the circle gradually decreases. Data for these observations are collected in Table 5–5, and graphed in Fig. 5–6.

TABLE 5–5*

| NUMBER OF HOURS AFTER RELEASE | 1 | 2 | 3 | 4 | 5 | 6 |
|---|---|---|---|---|---|---|
| NUMBER OF *PARAMECIA* IN CENTRAL CIRCLE | 104 | 31 | 16 | 8 | 5 | 5 |

* Taken from Andrewartha, H. G., *An Introduction to the Study of Animal Populations* (Chicago: University of Chicago Press, 1963), p. 214.

In Fig. 5–6, it can be seen that there is definite relationship between time after release and number of *Paramecia* in the central circle. This is not unexpected. Since the organisms swim about randomly, they gradually disperse themselves throughout the entire dish; the number in the central circle thus gradually decreases.

The graph provides more than just this information, however, for the line does not descend in a straight path, but rather in a curve of decreasing slope. The steepness of the slope between the first hour and the second indicates that more organisms left the central circle in that interval than in any other interval observed. In other words, from the graph we learn something about the *rate* at which the number of individuals in the starting circle decreases. If treated mathematically, the slope of the line gives a quantitative measure of this rate. Such analysis of several parts of the curve gives even further information—namely, the *change* in rate. Thus we see that from a simple graph a large quantity of information can be derived.

To **interpolate** means, literally, to "polish between." In terms of data analysis, the term refers to filling in between two items of data. In Fig. 5–6, we did not measure the number of *Paramecia* in the circle between hours 1 and 2. If we did, however, we would expect the number to be about 52, i.e., on a direct line between 104 and 31. It is on the basis of this assumption that we drew the graph line connecting these two items of data. Drawing such a graph line is an example of interpolation, for it involves the estimate of an unmeasured quantity, based on the trend shown by items of data on either side of it.

Note carefully the basic assumption involved in interpolation—that the trend shown by the two items of data is representative of points between them not directly measured. There is no guarantee that this is true for any individual case; however, experience has shown that when a reasonably large sample of data is available, interpolation is a quite valid process. Since there is theoretically an infinite number of possible measurements which could be made in constructing the graph shown in Fig. 5–6, some form of interpolation is essential.

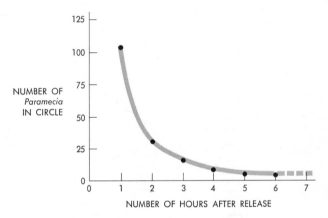

FIG. 5–6  Graph of data presented in Table 5–5. This graph shows that the number of *Paramecia* in the region where released decreases with time.

On other occasions, however, it is desirable to go *beyond* the data which are available. For example, in Fig. 5–6, we might wish to estimate the number of *Paramecia* in the circle after 7 or 8 hours. On the basis of the curve at the last two measured points (5 and 6 hours), it would be logical to extend the curve to the right in a horizontal line. At 7 hours the number of *Paramecia* within the circle would thus be 5. The process of extending the graph line beyond the measured data is an example of **extrapolation.**

In extrapolation, as in interpolation, projection is made by inference from a known into an unknown situation. In general, however, *extrapolation is less certain than interpolation.* A simple example will illustrate this point. Suppose that an oil prospector finds oil in three wells, all in a straight line with each other. By interpolation he would be reasonably certain of finding oil at a fourth well, dug somewhere on this line between the other three. He could infer that all three wells were tapping the same vein as an oil source. By extrapolation, however, the prospector would be much less certain of finding oil in a fourth well dug on an extension of the line. The vein could well end just beyond the third point, thus providing no source of oil for the fourth drilling.

The validity of certain extrapolations is often the subject of heated scientific controversy. One of the most widely discussed topics in modern biology is based on the question of the effects which atomic radiation may have on living organisms. There is little doubt that the mutation rate in organisms is directly proportional to the amount of radiation received—as long as the dosage is above a certain level. Below that level, however, a sufficient quantity of valid data is difficult to obtain. On the basis of data available at the present time, if a graph is plotted comparing the dosage of radiation received against the number of mutations observed, a proportional relation is observable (see Fig. 5–7).

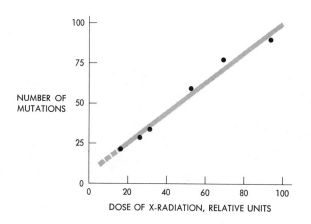

FIG. 5–7    Graph showing relative number of mutations observed in irradiated organisms against the dose of radiation received. (Adapted from B. M. Duggar, *Biological Effects of Radiation*, Chapter VI: "Statistical Treatment of Biological Problems in Irradiation," by Lowell Reed. New York: McGraw-Hill, 1936.)

For small doses, such as those that could conceivably result from nuclear fallout, experimental evidence is still scanty, and no valid conclusions have yet been drawn. In discussing the question of banning nuclear tests, physicists have taken the viewpoint (in general) that downward from about 20 units (on the graph of Fig. 5–7) the curve drops off and runs along the base line—in other words, they contend that below this point virtually no mutations occur. Biologists, on the other hand, claim that the evidence gained so far indicates that the line should continue its downward trend on the same proportional basis—that every dose of radiation, no matter how small, would produce its proportional number of mutations. As the reader can quickly see, the question is one of extrapolation. Until more evidence on small-dosage radiation is available, no satisfactory answer can be given.

Physicists claim that their viewpoint is substantiated by many such graphs of certain physical phenomena, where careful measurement has shown that the graph line does level off as it approaches the zero point. Biologists feel that their viewpoint has validity on the basis of the measurements made at higher dosage rates. The controversy is by no means trivial, since the future development of civilization may hinge, in part, on which case proves to be more nearly correct. We bring the human survival question to bear on the problem of extrapolation to underscore the importance which lies in the *uncertainty* of this method.

Both interpolation and extrapolation show only what *most probably*, or *might* be the case; nevertheless, they are important to scientists because they are ways of thinking which human beings naturally tend to use. Both involve inferring from known information, or data, by an inductive path toward general conclusions. The conclusion in these cases does not inevitably follow—at best it is only highly probable. Yet, interpolation and extrapolation afford the scientist fairly reliable methods of prediction. Without venturing to extend his conclusions beyond the small items of data which he has collected, the scientist would be hard put to draw *any* conclusions. This would render all data meaningful only in context of the specific situation in which they were collected. All generalizations would be meaningless if we could not have some faith in our extrapolations and interpolations.

Interpolation and extrapolation represent one type of generalizing activity in which researchers engage when analyzing data. In constructing graphs, another type of generalizing also occurs. Consider Fig. 5–8 (a). A biologist plotted these data in an attempt to learn whether any correlation existed between the diameter of nerve fibers and the maximum velocity at which the fiber would conduct an impulse. The data present a scatter across the graph. This is characteristic of most plots of raw data. Scattering is due to experimental error, error in measurement, and to slight physiological differences among nerve fibers.

In constructing a graph line from these data, the investigator has two choices: (1) He can draw a line connecting every point, thus producing a zigzag effect, or (2) he can draw a single straight line which passes roughly through the midline of the scatter. The second choice is preferable in this case (see Fig. 5–8b). Drawing a single straight line has the advantage of showing more definitely the trend which the data indicate. It is, then, a means of generalizing the data. From the graph line shown in Fig. 5–8 (b), we conclude that there is a regular, proportional relation between the diameter of a nerve fiber and the rate at which the fiber conducts an impulse.

Not every case of scattering is best treated by generalizing the trend. In graphs of the stock market, for example, the small fluctuations from day to day or week to week may be as important for some purposes as the general trend shown over the entire year. Here is a case of having to decide when small varia-

**5-7
GENERALIZING
POINTS
ON A GRAPH**

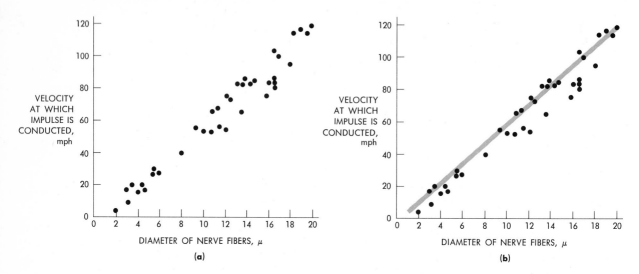

FIG. 5–8   Graphs showing the relation between the diameter of nerve fibers and the rate at which they conduct a nerve impulse. (a) Plot of raw data, showing scattering. (b) Same data generalized with a graph line which shows the trend. Such generalizations are permissible because the data are scattered along a definite plane. (Data from *Ohio J. Science* **41**, p. 145.)

tions in data are important and when they are not.  The nature of the data and the purposes of the investigator determine to what extent graph lines may be validly used to generalize a scattered number of points.  It is important to recognize, however, that in many instances such generalizations are not only permissible, but desirable.

**5–8**
**THE SIGMOID**
**CURVE**

The **sigmoid curve** is found commonly in measurements of total growth in individual organisms or populations.  Figure 5–9 provides an example of this type of graph line.  Sigmoid curves are typical of two general areas of biological investigation: (1) studies of the growth pattern that organisms display in response to certain growth-promoting or -inhibiting substances, and (2) ecological studies where the growth of a whole population is measured.

The graph of Fig. 5–9 shows that an organism or population does not grow at an even rate.  The greatest rate of growth seems to occur between the eighth and thirteenth unit of time (in this case, days).  After this, the rate slows down until, around the twentieth day, the organism or population has ceased to grow at all.  It is then said to remain in equilibrium.

Note that the graph can be roughly divided into four phases, each representing a different rate of growth.  First comes the **positive acceleration phase,** where the organism or population is just beginning to increase; it is "getting on its feet," so to speak.  Soon, however, the growth rate increases rapidly, and the curve shoots sharply upward.  This is the **logarithmic phase,**

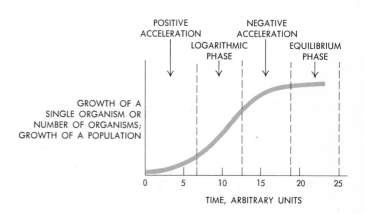

POSITIVE
ACCELERATION

NEGATIVE
ACCELERATION

LOGARITHMIC
PHASE

EQUILIBRIUM
PHASE

GROWTH OF A
SINGLE ORGANISM OR
NUMBER OF ORGANISMS;
GROWTH OF A POPULATION

TIME, ARBITRARY UNITS

FIG. 5–9 Typical growth curve for either a single organism or an entire population, showing the four phases into which such a curve can be divided. Each phase indicates a different rate of growth.

so called because the increase is occurring in an exponential manner. For a single growing organism, the cells are multiplying most rapidly in this phase; for a population, the number of individuals is increasing most rapidly. Then, however, for various reasons which depend upon the situation under consideration, the growth rate slows down and enters the **negative acceleration phase.** The growth rate finally levels off in the **equilibrium phase.** Here, the number of cells produced in a single organism just equals the number which die off or, in a population of organisms, birth rate equals death rate. In this phase, the size of the individual or the population remains about the same.

Since it is a typical representation of the growth of living organisms, the sigmoid curve is one of the most common graph patterns in biology. Its occurrence is not limited to growth studies, for there are other biological situations where a sigmoid curve may be found. One example will be considered in the next section.

**5-9**
**SCALAR**
**TRANSFORMATIONS**

We have talked earlier in this chapter about the problem of choosing the proper scale for making measurements and for plotting data in a table or graph. Let us now consider a more subtle aspect of this problem. Suppose that a biologist is investigating the relation between body mass and metabolic rate* in a series of mammals. Body mass is measured in grams, and metabolic rate by the amount of oxygen consumed per gram of body mass per hour. Data on seven animals are shown in Table 5–6.

---

* Metabolic rate is the rate at which an organism releases energy (i.e., oxidizes its food supply). The most accurate measure for metabolic rate is to observe how great a volume of oxygen the organism consumes in a given period of time. The more oxygen used, the higher the metabolic rate, and vice versa.

**TABLE 5–6**  THE METABOLIC RATES OF MAMMALS OF
VARIOUS BODY SIZES

|  | BODY MASS, g | OXYGEN CONSUMPTION, $mm^3$/g-hour |
|---|---|---|
| MOUSE | 25 | 1,580 |
| RAT | 225 | 872 |
| RABBIT | 2,200 | 466 |
| DOG | 11,700 | 318 |
| MAN | 70,000 | 202 |
| HORSE | 700,000 | 106 |
| ELEPHANT | 3,800,000 | 67 |

This table shows that there is some kind of *inverse relation* between body mass and metabolic rate. An inverse relation is one in which as one quantity is increased (for example, body mass), the other decreases (metabolic rate). Thus the smallest animal has the highest metabolic rate, and *vice versa*. Unfortunately, the table itself does not show the exact nature of the relation between the two factors. If the data in Table 5–6 are plotted on a graph, however, the relation becomes much more apparent (see Fig. 5–10).

As the graph indicates, body mass and metabolic rate do not vary in the same proportion. Maximum oxygen consumption (mouse) is 23 times as great as minimum oxygen consumption (elephant). On the other hand, maximum mass (elephant) is over 15,000 times as great as minimum mass (mouse). The graph shows that as body mass increases from 25 to 11,700 grams (from mouse to dog), metabolic rate drops drastically. Thereafter the curve begins to level off, and eventually approaches the horizontal.

There are two difficulties with the graph as shown in Fig. 5–10. Both result from the fact that the range of values being measured is very great (for example, body mass varies from 25 grams in the mouse to 3,800,000 in the elephant). The first difficulty is that it is impossible to get all the items of data plotted on a single graph. In order to include data for the elephant, the horizontal axis would have to be three times as long as it is in Fig. 5–10. The second difficulty arises from the fact that the data for low body masses are greatly cramped. With each subdivision of the horizontal axis representing 100,000 grams, it is virtually impossible to show the difference between 25 and 225 grams. Both these difficulties are related to the type of scale used for the graph; thus the solution to the difficulties is provided by **scalar transformation**. Scalar transformation is the process by which values for data plotted on one type of scale are converted into values on another scale.

In Fig. 5–10, the data have been plotted on an **arithmetic scale**. That is, the jump between any two adjacent values (markings on the scale) contains the same number of units as the jump between any other two adjacent values. There are as many grams represented between the 100,000 and 200,000 marks

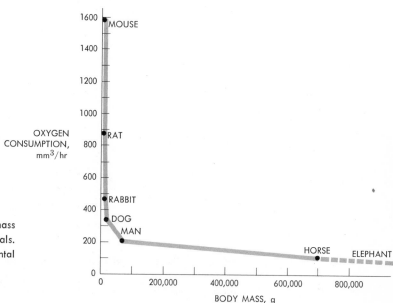

FIG. 5–10   Plot of relation between body mass and oxygen consumption for several mammals. Data are taken from Table 5–6. Both the horizontal and vertical axes show arithmetic scales.

FIG. 5–11   A logarithmic scale, with 10 as the base number. On this scale, we see that a jump from 1 to 2 is much different from a jump from 2 to 3, in terms of the arithmetic numbers involved.

on the horizontal axis as there are between the 200,000 and 300,000 marks. By performing scalar transformation, we can convert arithmetic scales to **logarithmic (or exponential) scales.** Logarithmic scales are very useful in scientific work. In constructing such scales, the logarithm of a number is used rather than the number itself. A **logarithm** is simply an **exponent.** The logarithm of the number $x$ is simply the exponential power to which another number (called the *base*) must be raised in order to equal $x$. For example, 1 can be said to be the log (abbreviation for logarithm) of the number 10 (written as log 10), since $10^1 = 10$. In this example, the base number is 10 and the exponent 1. Similarly, log 100 = 2, since $10^2 = 100$; again, 10 is the base number. Log 1000 = 3, since $10^3 = 1000$. The most commonly encountered log scales are based on powers of the number 10. However, log scales can be developed using any number as the base. Since 10 is used as the base number so much of the time, logarithms with base 10 are sometimes referred to as "common" logarithms. Unless otherwise indicated, log values are assumed to be those of common logarithms.

    A log scale is shown graphically in Fig. 5–11. Note that each successive unit on the log scale increases by a factor of 10, rather than by a constant increment as on an arithmetic scale. Thus the increase in arithmetic units

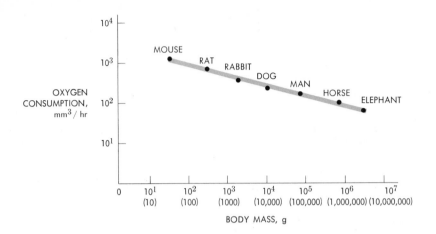

FIG. 5–12   The data plotted on an arithmetic scale in Fig. 5–10 are shown here plotted on a log or exponential scale.  Exponential scales have two advantages: (1) They make it possible to plot greater extremes of data on a single graph, and (2) they show certain types of relations which are not so apparent on arithmetic scales.

between log-scale 1 and 2 is not equal to that between 2 and 3.  From 1 to 2 would be a jump of 10 units, from 2 to 3 would be a jump of 100 units, from 3 to 4 would be a jump of 1000 units, and so on.

If we plot the data from Table 5–6 on a log scale (see Fig. 5–12), we find that we avoid the two difficulties discussed in connection with Fig. 5–10.  We also find that the curved graph line becomes a straight one.  (Compare Figs. 5–10 and 5–12.)  Now, whenever data plotted on a graph produce a straight line, the investigator knows that some consistent relation exists between the two factors he is measuring.  Thus we can see that there is a consistent relation between body mass and metabolic rate—a fact that was not so evident in Fig. 5–10.  The relation has become evident only after scalar transformation.  Often, data plotted on an arithmetic scale seem to show relatively less consistent relation than the same data plotted on a log or exponential scale.

The question which now arises is: Why should the dependent and consistent relation between body mass and metabolic rate show up when the data are plotted on a log scale, but not when the data are plotted on an arithmetic scale?

Living organisms have both a surface area and a volume.  As the size of the organism increases, volume and surface area increase at different rates.  Although this problem will be considered in more detail in studying the shape and size of cells, it is interesting to note here that volume increases more rapidly than surface area as the organism enlarges.  This means that a large organism has a larger volume in relation to surface area than a small organism.

The significant feature of this relationship is that surface area provides the point of exchange of heat between the organism and the environment. For a large animal, the volume is large enough to compensate for the loss of heat at the surface. For a small animal, however, with proportionately much more surface area in relation to its volume, a great deal of heat is lost to the outside. The correspondingly higher metabolic rate that is characteristic of small animals releases more energy in a given period of time and some of this energy serves to keep the body temperature at a relatively constant rate.

**5-10
CONCLUSION**

In the present chapter we have discussed several of the most important principles in the collection and analysis of data. The design of an experiment is of crucial importance in modern science. Collection and analysis of the data resulting from that experiment, however, is the heart of scientific discovery. The conclusions, the relationships, the trends which data can be made to yield depend upon how the data are handled. It is important not only for scientists, but also for those approaching science for the first time, to become familiar with procedures used in analyzing data. We have seen in this chapter how a formidable array of numbers such as that shown in Tables 5–3 and 5–4 can yield important information. With patience and imagination, the researcher can extract much meaningful information from raw data.

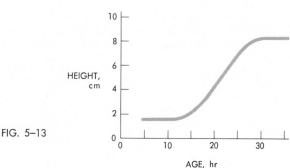

FIG. 5–13

Answer each part of each question specifically.

**EXERCISES**

1. Figure 5–13 shows the growth curve of a mushroom.

a) What is the phase between 0 and about 15 hours called? What is probably happening within the mushroom in this phase?

b) What is the phase between 15 and 25 hours called? Between 25 and 30 hours? Compare what is happening within the mushroom in these two stages.

c) What is the phase from 30 hours onward called?

d) Can you offer any hypothesis as to why the mushroom curve should level off after about 30 hours?

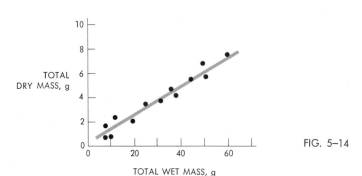

FIG. 5–14

2. Figure 5–14 shows a comparison of wet mass to dry mass in mushrooms.  Wet mass is the mass of the whole mushroom, including the water which makes  up a great percentage of the bulk; dry mass is the mass of the solid material in the  mushroom, with all the water evaporated.

   a) What will be the approximate dry mass of a mushroom whose wet mass is  40 g?  What will be the approximate wet mass of a mushroom whose dry mass is  2.1 g?

   b) Since this graph represents the relative masses *during growth*,  what do we see about the amount of water which a mushroom contains as it grows  larger?

   c) Biologists have long been interested in exactly how a mushroom manages to grow so rapidly.  One hypothesis offered was that the mushroom absorbs a great quantity of water at one stage in its growth and therefore greatly increases its size in a relatively short time.  Evaluate this hypothesis in light of the graph.

3. The curves shown in Fig. 5–15 illustrate the total amount of growth in length of roots subjected to a certain experimental treatment (the units could be milliliters of poison or hormones, roentgens of radiation, etc.).  The amount of this treatment increases

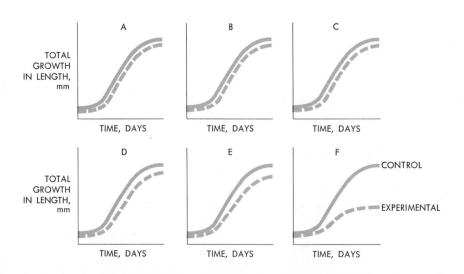

FIG. 5–15

steadily from curves A to F.  From the six graphs, which of the following statements may be validly made?

a) The experimental treatment had no effect on the growth of these roots.

b) After being exposed to the experimental treatment, the roots took much longer to arrive at their maximum length.

c) Low dosages of the experimental treatment probably have little effect upon the growth of these roots.

d) The exposure to the experimental treatment resulted only in a slowing down or inhibition of root growth; there was no effect upon the final length of the mature root.

e) If we graphed a comparison of the concentration of the experimental substance used in treatment with the effect upon total growth of the roots, we would get a line of perfect positive correlation.

4. The data given below are the weight in pounds and the height in inches of a group of men.

| WEIGHT | 147 | 149 | 153 | 151 | 155 | 154 |
|--------|-----|-----|-----|-----|-----|-----|
| HEIGHT | 67  | 68  | 70  | 69  | 72  | 71  |

Which one (or ones) of the graphs in Fig 5–16 represents a reasonably correct plotting of these data?  If you were writing a scientific paper on this subject, which graph would you select to illustrate your data?  Why?

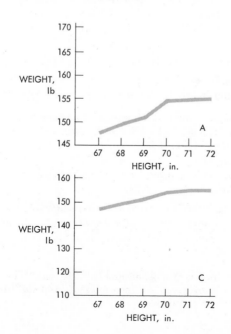

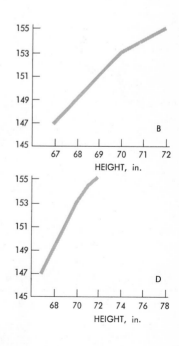

FIG. 5–16

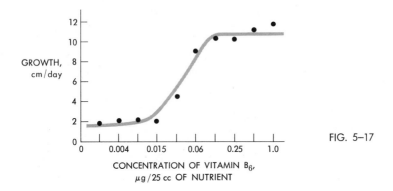

FIG. 5–17

5. Figure 5–17 is a graph* plotting growth (measured in centimeters per day) against the amount of vitamin $B_6$ in a nutrient solution fed to *Neurospora,* the red bread mold. *Note:* The amount of vitamin $B_6$ supplied in the nutrient is the *only* variable factor in this experiment. Read the lettered statements below and write on your paper: A, if the statement is in agreement with the data; B, if the statement is contradicted by the data; C, if the statement cannot be judged either valid or invalid on the basis of the evidence.

a) There is a positive correlation between the amount of growth of *Neurospora* and the concentrations of vitamin $B_6$ fed to the culture.

b) A *Neurospora* culture will grow most rapidly on a vitamin $B_6$ concentration of from 0.03 to 0.08 micrograms per cc of nutrient fluid.

c) A *Neurospora* culture will grow more rapidly at a vitamin $B_6$ concentration of 1.0 than at either of the figures given above in (2).

d) Increasing the concentration of vitamin $B_6$ to 1.5 micrograms per 25 cc of nutrient solution would probably not increase the rate of growth to any appreciable degree.

e) Vitamin $B_6$ is a building block necessary for the construction of some necessary compound in the living *Neurospora.*

6. Figure 5–18 is a graph showing population cycles in a laboratory culture dish of three organisms. The original culture dish contained the protozoan *Paramecium;* a second organism, *Didinium,* slightly smaller than *Paramecium,* was introduced into the culture dish when *Paramecium* was multiplying rapidly. A third organism, which happens to feed exclusively on *Didinium,* was introduced into the culture when *Didinium* first began to decline.

a) Offer a hypothesis to explain the data shown in the graph. Include a discussion of why the *Paramecium* curve rises a second time, and some ideas as to the cause-effect relationships shown here. Be as specific and complete as possible.

---

* Graph taken from G. W. Beadle and E. L. Tatum, "The Genetic Control of Biochemical Reactions in *Neurospora.*" *Proceedings of National Academy of Sciences* **27** (1941), 499–506. Used by permission.

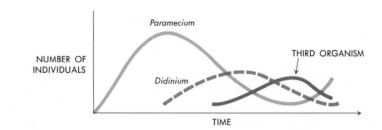

FIG. 5–18

b) What would be the probable effect on the population of *Paramecium* and the third organism if *Didinium* were removed?

c) What would be the probable effect on the population of *Paramecium* and *Didinium* if the third organism were removed?

LINN, CHARLES, *Probability and Statistics* (Columbus, Ohio: American Education Publications, 1964). A highly readable discussion of this subject, with sections of considerable importance for the treatment of biological data.

MORONEY, M. J., *Facts from Figures* (New York: Penguin Books, 1958). This book is very well written. It presents some interesting problems in the handling of data, and is easy to read.

MOSTELLER, F., R. E. K. ROURKE, AND G. B. THOMAS, *Probability and Statistics* (Reading, Mass: Addison-Wesley, 1961). This is a standard textbook on theories of probability and statistical analysis.

TIPPETT, L. H. C., *Statistics* (New York: Oxford University Press, 1944). This is one part of the "Home University Library of Modern Knowledge." It is very elementary, providing a good introduction for those who have no previous knowledge about statistics or the handling of data.

WALLIS, W. A., AND H. V. ROBERTS, *Statistics: A New Approach* (Glencoe, Ill.: The Free Press, 1956). Although written by professional statisticians, this book represents a very readable and interesting account of various methods and problems involved in statistical analysis.

YOUDEN, W. J., *Experimentation and Measurement* (Washington: National Science Teachers' Association, 1962). This is a simple, well-written introduction to the problems of setting up experiments, collecting data, and analyzing them. Some mathematics is introduced, but is carefully explained.

**SUGGESTED READINGS**

## CHAPTER 6  CELLS

### INTRODUCTION

The "cell theory" (see Section 2–2), which states that virtually all living organisms are composed of individual units called cells, is one of biology's broadest generalizations. In Chapter 2, it was pointed out that in all complex organisms, cells are organized into units called *tissues*. In higher animals, for example, certain cells are united to form muscle, bone, cartilage, etc. These tissues, in turn, are generally united to form *organs*, such as the stomach, lungs, brain, etc., and organs, working together, form the body *systems* (digestive, nervous, reproductive, etc.). Taken all together, these systems form the complex organism in its entirety.

Quite obviously, the key to this structural hierarchy is the cell. Cells are often referred to as *units of structure*. They are the bricks, so to speak, of an organism's body. Bricks, of course, can be broken into smaller pieces. So can cells. In each case, however, both form and function are changed.

Cells are also *units of function*. Respiration, growth, excretion, reproduction, etc., are all ultimately the result of cellular activity. It is not surprising, then, that biologists are concerned with **cytology,** the study of cells.

### 6-2
### TOOLS AND
### TECHNIQUES

Advances in our knowledge of cellular anatomy are tied directly to improvements made in the techniques and instruments used in examining cells. The nineteenth and early twentieth centuries saw the introduction and refinement of certain techniques, such as staining and microtoming. In the former, parts of cells and tissues are colored with dyes, causing them to stand out in sharp contrast to other structures left unstained or stained different colors (see Fig. 6–1). In microtoming, cells and tissues are cut into thin sections so that they may be examined under a microscope (see Fig. 6–2). (See also Color Plate I.)

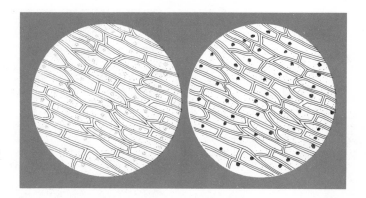

FIG. 6–1 Cytological staining. The nuclei of onion cells become more clearly visible after staining with iodine.

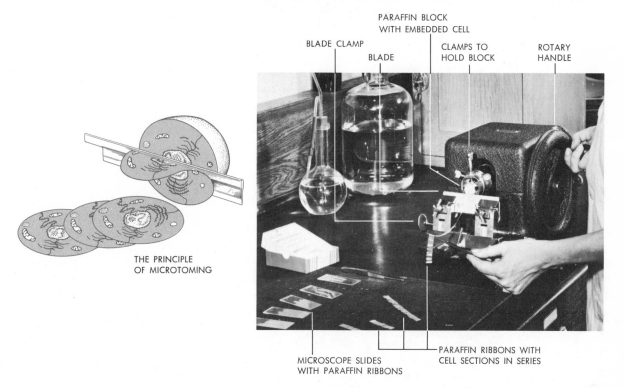

PARAFFIN BLOCK
WITH EMBEDDED CELL

BLADE CLAMP

BLADE

CLAMPS TO
HOLD BLOCK

ROTARY
HANDLE

THE PRINCIPLE
OF MICROTOMING

MICROSCOPE SLIDES
WITH PARAFFIN RIBBONS

PARAFFIN RIBBONS WITH
CELL SECTIONS IN SERIES

FIG. 6–2 A rotary microtome in use. The cells are permeated with paraffin to hold them rigid when cut by the blade. When the wheel is turned, the cells are pushed against the blade and a section is cut. The next turn of the wheel moves the cells forward a predetermined number of microns and another section is cut. The entire section series is then stained and studied under the microscope. From such studies, it is possible to recreate the cell in three-dimensional perspective. (Photo courtesy Douglas C. Anderson, Department of Forestry, Ontario, Canada.)

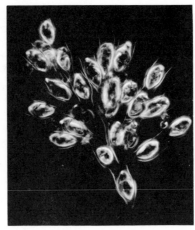

BRIGHT-FIELD                    DARK-FIELD                    PHASE-CONTRAST

FIG. 6–3  Three microscope techniques are shown here in viewing the same organism, *Dynobryon sertularia*. Bright-field microscopy directs light up through the specimen toward the viewer. Dark-field microscopy sends light in at an angle from the side. Thus only light bent upward by the specimen is seen in the field. Phase-contrast microscopy utilizes knowledge of the wave nature of light to produce a three-dimensional image. (Photos courtesy Dr. Earl Hanson, Wesleyan University.)

The primary instrument for cell study is the light microscope. From the seventeenth century to the 1920's, detailed knowledge of cellular anatomy increased as the resolving powers of the light microscope increased. The resolving power of a microscope is its capability of making closely adjacent objects appear separated.* Unfortunately, the resolving power of the light microscope is limited by the wavelength of the visible light it uses. Certain techniques of light microscopy, however, have helped to extend the range of this instrument. One method is known as **dark-field** microscopy. In this method, the light rays are bent by the lenses in such a way that only the light passing through the specimen passes upward to the viewer's eye. Thus the object appears bright against a dark background. Another method is known as **phase-contrast** microscopy. In this technique, light waves are bent and deflected in such a way as to make adjacent objects in the field stand out sharply from each other. Figure 6–3 presents a comparison between images viewed by these techniques and one viewed by normal (**bright-field**) microscopy.

---

* The human eye has a resolving power of approximately 0.1 mm. Thus two lines placed closer together than 0.1 mm will appear as a single line to the naked eye, no matter how close to them the observer may get. Since most cells are smaller than 0.1 mm across, the need for a microscope in cytology becomes obvious.

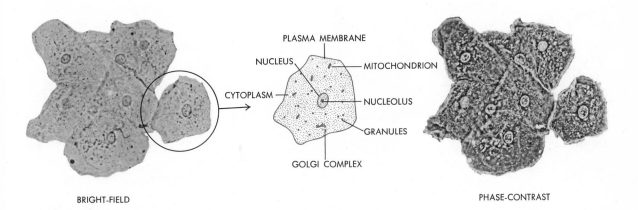

BRIGHT-FIELD                            PHASE-CONTRAST

FIG. 6–4 The center drawing, of a human cheek-lining cell, shows most of the knowledge of cellular anatomy as established by the 1920's. The phase-contrast microscope, not commercially produced until 1946, greatly improved the image (right). However, the electron microscope has played the greatest part in making this drawing obsolete. (Photos courtesy Unitron Instrument Company, Newton Highlands, Mass.)

In 1924, the physicist Louis de Broglie theorized that electrons had a wave nature. The length of that wave was found to be only 0.05 Å (recall from Table 5–1 that one angstrom unit equals 1/100,000,000 cm). Therefore, it was reasoned, if a beam of electrons were substituted for a beam of light, the shorter wavelength of the electrons should cause a corresponding increase in resolving power. This prediction proved to be correct. In 1934, an electron microscope was used to obtain pictures that had greater resolution than those which could be obtained through the light microscope. The electron microscope uses a beam of electrons rather than a beam of light. Magnetic coils serve to focus the beam, much as the objective lenses focus light beams in the light microscope. The electron microscope has uncovered more new knowledge of cell structure in the past thirty years than was discovered with the light microscope in the previous three hundred. The light microscope can magnify an object only to about 2000 times its actual size, whereas the electron microscope magnifies about 300,000 times.

Figure 6–4 represents most of what was known about cellular anatomy before the development of the electron microscope. Seen through the light microscope, the living matter outside the cell nucleus appears as a semiliquid medium, with certain structures embedded in it. From a distance, a forest-covered mountain appears to be a solid green or bluish color. Close to the mountain, however, one

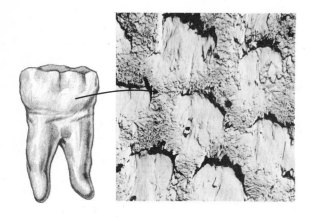
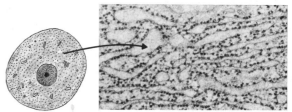

FIG. 6–5   Although a clean tooth may feel smooth to the tongue, the electron microscope reveals the surface to be otherwise.   Analogously, the electron microscope reveals the cell cytoplasm to be a highly structured region, rather than a more or less uniform semiliquid. (Tooth photo courtesy Eric Berger, from *Frontiers of Dental Science*, an NSTA and Scholastic Book Services publication; cytoplasm photo courtesy Dr. George E. Palade, Rockefeller Institute.)

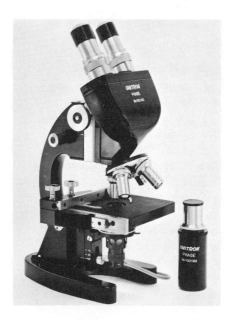

LIGHT MICROSCOPE                                          ELECTRON MICROSCOPE

FIG. 6–6   The light microscope and the electron microscope.   (Photos courtesy Unitron Instrument Company, Newton Highlands, Mass. and the Radio Corporation of America.)

can see that this apparently solid green blanket is highly structured, composed of individual trees differing widely in size and kind. In an analogous manner, this is what the development of the electron microscope did to the study of cellular anatomy; it enabled the biologist to view the cell "up close." And like the blanket of trees, the cytoplasm showed itself to be not a uniform semiliquid substance, but rather a highly structured region, with intricate design and detail (see Figs. 6–5 and 6–6).

Recently, a new instrument called the scanning electron microscope has been used to study the fine structure of organisms. In the scanning electron microscope, a beam of electrons scans the surface of an opaque specimen, rather than passing through an extremely thin section of it, as in the conventional electron microscope. Thus, whole specimens rather than thin slices can now be examined at magnifications much greater than is possible with the light microscope. Also, since specimens are easier to prepare for study with the scanning electron microscope, it is possible to examine many specimens in a short time. The new instrument is greatly facilitating the study of specimens with complex surface architecture, e.g., pollen grains (see Fig. 6–7).

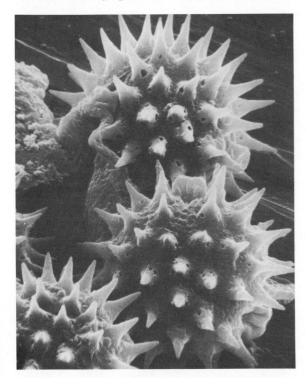 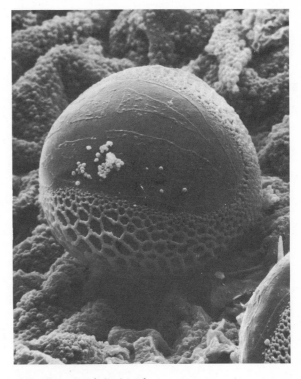

FIG. 6–7    The scanning electron microscope allows high-magnification three-dimensional viewing of objects such as cells or, in this case, pollen grains. Shown above are pollen grains of two different species of plants: *Cosmos bipinnatus* (left), magnification ✕6500 approximately; and the lily *Lilium longiflorum* (right), magnification ✕2000 approximately. (Photos courtesy J. Heslop-Harrison, University of Wisconsin.)

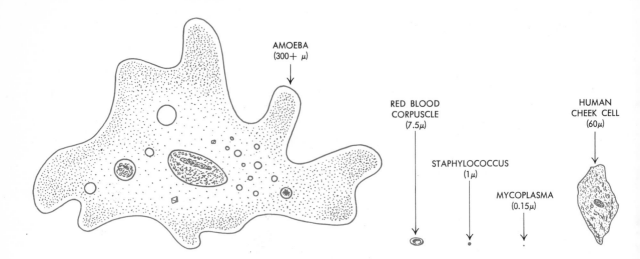

FIG. 6–8   A comparison of cell sizes.  A large amoeba is visible to the naked eye.  Mycoplasmas can be clearly distinguished only with the electron microscope.  (From John W. Kimball, *Biology*, 2nd edition.  Reading, Mass.: Addison-Wesley, 1968.)

## 6-3
### THE GENERAL PLAN OF CELLS

The "typical cell" does not exist; cells come in too many assorted shapes and sizes.  Some cells are so small as to be beyond the resolving power of a light microscope, while others may be inches across (see Fig. 6–8).  A nerve cell may be three or four feet long, yet thin as a thread throughout most of its length.  There are exceptions to almost any statement one can make about cells,* but a start must be made somewhere.  It is obviously not possible to discuss the anatomical idiosyncrasies of each of the many kinds of cells.  Therefore, it is reasonable to discuss those cytological attributes which apply to *most* cells, mentioning exceptions only when they are important enough to be noted.

Cells can be viewed as tiny containers of matter which, collectively, exhibit the qualities of "life."  The sides of each container are composed of the **cell** or **plasma membrane.**  In many plant cells, the plasma membrane is often pressed flat against a rigid **cell wall,** mostly composed of the insoluble polysaccharide, cellulose.  The cell wall gives plant tissue its rigidity; it is the combined strength of many fused cell walls that keeps trees upright and makes celery tough.

Most cells have a rounded body within them which is called the **nucleus.**  Thus the matter within the confines of a plasma membrane can be roughly divided into two regions.  The living matter within the nucleus is called the

---

* For example, every cell has a nucleus (except for certain muscle cells, which have several; and mature red blood cells, which have none; and bacteria and blue-green algae, which lack membrane-bounded nuclei); every cell has centrioles (but none have been found in cells of vascular plants); etc.

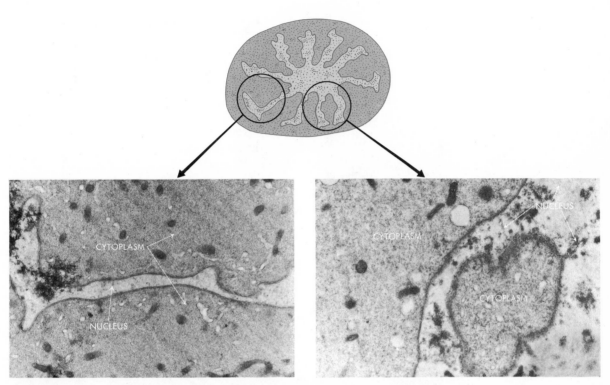

FIG. 6–9    These two cells, shown in high magnification, are highly "untypical" in the shape of the nucleus and its relationship to the surrounding cytoplasm.   Yet in terms of the developing insect "nurse cells" which they represent, these cells are quite "typical."   The "island" of cytoplasm shown in the photo on the right indicates a three-dimensional relationship in which the cytoplasm sends fingerlike projections into a highly infolded nuclear membrane.   (Photo courtesy Dr. Spencer Berry, Wesleyan University.)

**nucleoplasm.**  The material not within the nucleus, but still within the body of the cell, is the **cytoplasm** (see Fig. 6–9).

As just indicated, the cytoplasm is that living matter in the cell which lies inside the plasma membrane but outside the nucleus.   The plasma membrane itself (Fig. 6–10a) is a cytoplasmic structure through which materials pass in and out of the cell.   Chemical studies of red blood cells show their isolated plasma membranes to be composed mainly of phospholipids and proteins. Lipids are fatlike substances which dissolve in fatty solvents (benzene, chloroform, alcohol, etc.) but not in water, and phospholipids are simply lipids that contain phosphorus.   Phospholipids consist, at one end, of a long chain of atoms with nonpolar properties, and at the other end of a shorter group with polar properties.*   Molecules with polar properties tend to dissolve in water.   Thus phospholipid

* See pp. 141–143.

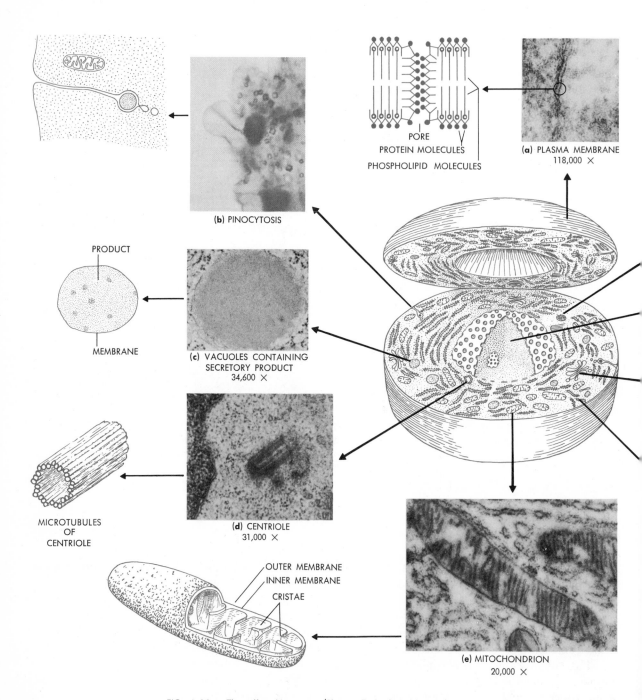

**(a)** PLASMA MEMBRANE
118,000 ×

PORE
PROTEIN MOLECULES
PHOSPHOLIPID MOLECULES

**(b)** PINOCYTOSIS

PRODUCT

MEMBRANE

**(c)** VACUOLES CONTAINING
SECRETORY PRODUCT
34,600 ×

MICROTUBULES
OF
CENTRIOLE

**(d)** CENTRIOLE
31,000 ×

OUTER MEMBRANE
INNER MEMBRANE
CRISTAE

**(e)** MITOCHONDRION
20,000 ×

FIG. 6–10   The cell and its parts. (Photos: Endoplasmic reticulum courtesy Dr. George E. Palade and
Dr. Keith Porter, from *The Cell*, by the Upjohn Company; lysosome courtesy Dr. Fritz Miller, University
of Munich; plasma membrane courtesy Dr. George E. Palade and Dr. Marilyn G. Farquhar, from

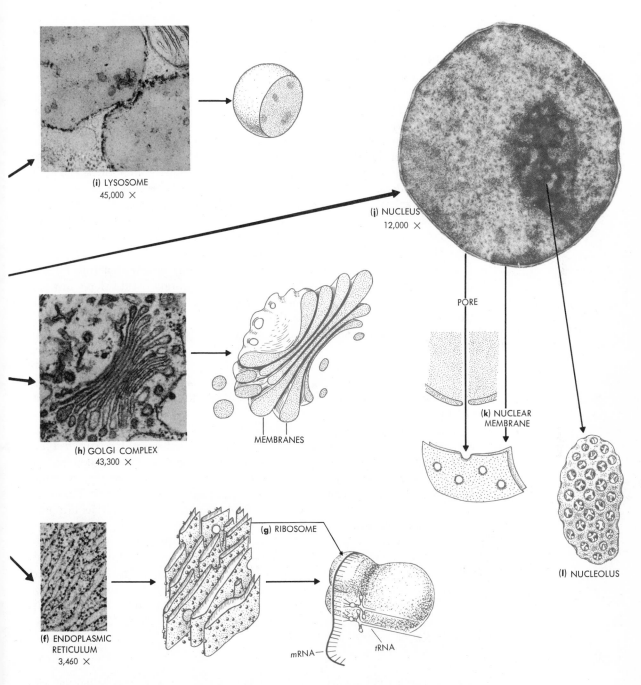

**(i)** LYSOSOME
45,000 ×

**(j)** NUCLEUS
12,000 ×

**(h)** GOLGI COMPLEX
43,300 ×

MEMBRANES

PORE

**(k)** NUCLEAR
MEMBRANE

**(l)** NUCLEOLUS

**(g)** RIBOSOME

**(f)** ENDOPLASMIC
RETICULUM
3,460 ×

mRNA

tRNA

*J. Cellular Biology* **17,** p. 63; nucleus, mitochondrion, Golgi complex, vacuole, all courtesy Dr. George
E. Palade, Rockefeller Institute; pinocytosis courtesy Dr. and Mrs. Ronald C. Rustad; centriole courtesy
Robert Capone and George Chapman, Cornell University Medical School.)

molecules in contact with water tend to line up with their polar ends in the water and their lipid ends away from it.

In 1937, Dr. H. Davson and J. F. Danielli put forth a hypothesis to describe the spatial arrangement of the phospholipid and protein molecules within the membrane on the basis of the known physical and chemical characteristics of phospholipids and proteins and the behavior of intact plasma membranes. Briefly, this hypothesis proposed that the plasma membrane is a *unit membrane*, composed of phospholipid molecules sandwiched between layers of protein. Since the size of the molecules involved is known, this information permits us to predict that the unit membrane should be in the range of 75 Å thick and that when it is under high magnification, the differing natures of the two kinds of molecules involved will cause it to appear as a triple layered structure. Electron-microscope studies bear out these predictions. Further, this hypothesized unit structure for cell membranes nicely explains some of their characteristics, such as a wide permeability to such lipid solvents as alcohol.

It should be emphasized here that the hypothesized unit structure for the plasma membrane is only a tentative one. Cell membranes still behave in ways not explained by the static unit-membrane model, a fact to which considerable attention will be directed later in this chapter.

It has been shown in the cells of many animals, such as the amoeba, that substances can and do enter cells without passing through the plasma membrane. This process is called **pinocytosis.** The outer membrane invaginates, with the entering substance occupying the invagination space. The invagination then pinches off, and the pinocytic vesicle thus formed is free to be moved within the cell (Fig. 6–10b).

Within the cytoplasm are found many kinds of nonliving inclusions. Plant cells, for example, contain bubblelike structures called **vacuoles** (Fig. 6–10c). These vacuoles often serve as reservoirs, holding sap or waste products. A **vacuolar membrane** separates the contents of the vacuoles from the surrounding cytoplasm. The vacuolar membrane has a structure similar to the outer plasma membrane of the cell, and it regulates the passage of materials into and out of the vacuole and the cytoplasm.

Many plant cells have small bodies called **plastids** (Fig. 6–11). **Chloroplasts** are perhaps the most important kind of plastid. Chloroplasts contain the pigment **chlorophyll,** which gives the plant its green color and is essential to its manufacture of food. **Leucoplasts** are believed to serve as centers for storage of certain materials in the cytoplasm. **Chromoplasts,** due to the pigments they contain, are the plastids that give color to the flowers and fruits of many plants. Plastids do not occur in animal cells.*

---

* Certain marine slugs are known which contain functional chloroplasts within the cells of their body tissues. However, the chloroplasts are obtained by feeding on algae; not all the chloroplasts are digested and some end up inside the slug's body cells. The chloroplasts are not found in slug eggs, and thus each animal must become newly infected.

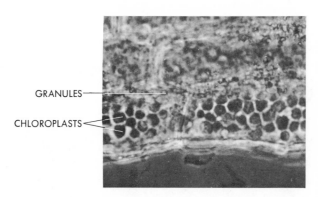
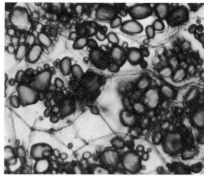

GRANULES

CHLOROPLASTS

FIG. 6–11    Plant cells often show many inclusions. Here food granules are shown in *Elodea* cells in the photo to the left. At right are shown starch grains in the cells of a white potato. (Photos courtesy Dr. Kulbir Gill, Panjab University, left and John Kimball, right.)

**Centrioles** (Fig. 6–10d) are small, deeply staining particles, seen lying near the nuclear membrane in cells which are not dividing. Under the electron microscope the centriole appears as a small hollow cylinder, the walls of which are formed by nine sets of triplet microtubules. In cells that have two centrioles, the centrioles separate from each other and move toward opposite sides of the cell shortly before the cell begins to divide. In cells with only one centriole, a new centriole appears to grow from the side of the other, with the two resulting centrioles separating. It has been hypothesized that the centriole may play a role in the formation of fiberlike structures called **spindle fibers,** along which the chromosomes of the cell migrate during cellular division. The centriole does not seem to be essential for cellular division, however, since many higher plant cells manage to divide without them. Of course, it may simply be that centrioles have not yet been detected within these cells.

During the 1960's, detailed electron-microscope studies of cells verified the existence of **microtubules** in the cytoplasm. Microtubules are long, straight cylinders about 230 to 270 Å in diameter. In cross section, each microtubule is composed of 13 filaments arranged radially around a 45 Å central core. Each filament consists largely of protein molecules. Microtubules are very abundant immediately adjacent to the plasma membrane. There is some evidence to support the hypothesis that these structures may be involved in the flowing of cytoplasm within the cell (cytoplasmic streaming). In wheat, a band of microtubules encircles the nucleus just before the cell begins to undergo division. During cell division, some of the microtubules become attached to each of the chromosomes and apparently help to move the chromosomes during the division process. A full discussion of cell division will be presented in Chapter 15.

**Mitochondria** (Fig. 6–10e) are seen as spherical or sausage-shaped structures scattered throughout the cytoplasm. They are usually found in the region

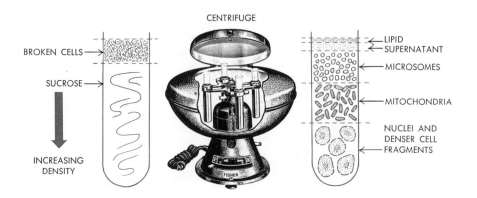

FIG. 6–12    Cell parts, such as mitochondria, can be studied after being isolated by centrifuging at speeds up to 15,000 times the force of gravity. The centrifuge shown here is not capable of the high speeds necessary to produce such a force, but its principle is the same as that used in the more powerful ultracentrifuge. Since the respiratory rate of the mitochondrial fraction is so high, it is reasonable to assume that mitochondria are responsible for energy release in the intact, living cell. (Centrifuge reproduced by permission of the Fisher Scientific Co.)

of the cell that shows the greatest metabolic activity, and are found in their greatest numbers in the cells which are most active metabolically, such as liver or muscle cells. If the mitochondria are separated from the rest of the cellular parts by centrifugation (Fig. 6–12), their metabolic characteristics can be studied. Such isolated mitochondria can break down certain organic compounds to carbon dioxide and water. In so doing, they release energy. Thus the mitochondria seem to be the centers of respiratory activity of the cell, and in them originate the carbon dioxide and water exhaled in breathing.

The electron microscope reveals in considerable detail the structure of the mitochondrion. Seen in section, the innermost of the mitochondrion's two membranes shows infoldings. These infoldings, called **cristae,** form partitions extending into the cavity of the mitochondrion. The presence of cristae increases surface area within a mitochondrion. It is on cristae that collections of enzymes and other types of molecules, collectively called **respiratory assemblies,** are located. Within each respiratory assembly, molecules resulting from the breakdown of sugar and other carbon compounds react during respiration. As might be predicted, there is a direct relationship between the number of cristae and the activity of the cells from which the mitochondrion comes. Mitochondria from active cells show a large number of cristae. This greatly increases the surface area on which the energy-releasing reactions can take place (Fig. 6–13).

The electron microscope also reveals a complex network of channels extending throughout the cytoplasm. These channels often appear to be infoldings which are continuous with the plasma membrane. They also appear to connect

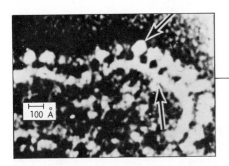 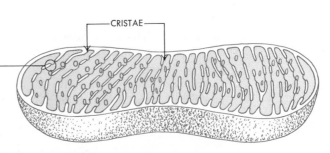

FIG. 6–13   As might be predicted on the basis of their hypothesized function, mitochondria from cells of tissues with high respiratory rates show a correspondingly high number of cristae.  This drawing shows part of a mitochondrion from the wing muscle of the blowfly, *Caliphora*.  Compare this drawing to the cristae shown in the pancreas mitochondria (Fig. 6–10).  The pancreas is metabolically less active than insect-wing muscle.  In highly active tissue, not only do mitochondria have more cristae, but there are larger numbers of mitochondria.  The arrows in the EM photomicrograph show the bodies with which the respiratory assemblies are thought to be associated.  The uppermost arrow points to a spherical $F_1$ particle, hypothesized to be molecules of ATP-coupling enzymes necessary for oxidative phosphorylation, to be discussed in Chapter eight.  The lower arrow points to the suggested site of the respiratory enzymes.  (Photo courtesy Institute of Enzyme Research, University of Wisconsin.)

with the nuclear membrane, but agreement on this point is not universal.  The entire system of channels is called the **endoplasmic reticulum** (Fig. 6–10f).  It is thought that the endoplasmic reticulum may play a role in speeding the transport of materials from the extracellular environment into the cytoplasm, as well as from the nucleus to the cytoplasm.  Support for this hypothesis comes from the observation that tiny bodies called **ribosomes** (Fig. 6–10g) are often found along the outer surface of a channel.  Ribosomes are so named because they contain high concentrations of ribonucleic acid (RNA).  By "tagging" the smaller molecules (amino acids) of which proteins are composed with radioactive atoms, it can be shown that the amino acids go first to the ribosomes and later show up in protein molecules.  Thus it is reasonable to deduce that proteins are synthesized either in or on the ribosomes.  Since virtually all living cells synthesize proteins, ribosomes are one of the few subcellular particles which must be present in all living things.  The hypothesis that the ribosomes are the site of protein synthesis would predict their presence in larger numbers in cells that are very active in protein synthesis than in cells that are less active.  This proves to be the case; a typical bacterium, growing rapidly (and thus synthesizing large quantities of protein), may contain some 15,000 ribosomes.

Electron-microscope examination of bacterial ribosomes shows that they have a diameter of about 200 Å, whereas those from mammalian cells are a few angstroms larger.  Unfortunately, the electron microscope does not provide the detail necessary to study the *precise* structure of ribosomes.  Thus what is now known about ribosome structure has been established by indirect experimental

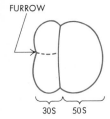

FURROW

30S    50S

evidence. It has been shown that the bacterial ribosome consists of two subunits, which after centrifugation divide into different fractions by a process of sedimentation. These fractions are labeled 50S and 30S respectively.* Neither subunit can synthesize protein by itself, but to date it remains a mystery why this two-subunit structure is essential to ribosomal functioning. The subunits themselves differ in structure, with the 50S bacterial ribosome subunit consisting of 23S ribosomal RNA, about 35 different proteins, and the furrowed 30S subunit consisting of 16S ribosomal RNA and about 20 different proteins. The proteins appear to be present as globular spheres with a diameter of 32 to 40 Å. Ribosomes are often found associated in groups know as **polyribosomes** or **polysomes.**

The **Golgi complex** (Fig. 6–10h) is a cluster of flattened, parallel, smooth-surfaced sacs found within the cytoplasm. The sacs, often referred to collectively as the **dictyosome,** contain numerous smaller infoldings or pockets. At times, the Golgi complex resembles the endoplasmic reticulum without its ribosomes. The precise function of the Golgi complex is uncertain. There is evidence to indicate that it may be concerned with excretion and the transport of particles into and out of the cell.

The electron microscope reveals another structure in the cytoplasm which rather resembles a mitochondrion. This is the **lysosome** (Fig. 6–10i). The lysosome is a saclike structure containing enzymes which catalyze the breakdown of molecules such as fats, proteins, and nucleic acids, into smaller molecules. These smaller molecules can then be used as energy sources. It may be that the lysosomes serve to isolate these digestive enzymes from the cell cytoplasm, thereby keeping the cell from digesting itself. This hypothesis is supported by the fact that when the lysosome membrane is ruptured, the cell undergoes chemical breakdown, or **lysis.** There is experimental evidence linking the lysosomes to the muscle atrophy which occurs after surgical denervation or disease-caused (e.g., by polio) nerve paralysis. It has further been noticed that at death the mitochondria and lysosomes are broken down. It may be that the breakdown of the lysosomes contributes to the early, irreversible changes which occur after death.

The nucleus (Fig. 6–10j) is usually the most obvious anatomical feature of a cell. Most cell nuclei can easily be seen under the light microscope; the nucleus stands out as a rounded body slightly denser than the surrounding cytoplasm. A nucleus has a limiting membrane, the **nuclear membrane** or **envelope** (Fig. 6–10k), which separates the nuclear contents, or **nucleoplasm,** from the surrounding cytoplasm. This membrane bears the same relationship to the nucleus that the plasma membrane bears to the cytoplasm; it serves as a reg-

---

* The S stands for Svedberg units. A Svedberg unit is a sedimentation constant, a measure of the rate of sedimentation of, for example, a ribosomal subunit in a centrifuge.

ulatory device through which materials pass in and out of the nucleus. The electron microscope reveals that the nuclear membrane has distinct pores through which substances may pass in going from the nucleus into the cytoplasm and vice versa. The membrane is a double one, consisting of two unit membranes.

When we stain a living onion cell with iodine, the nucleus takes up the reddish-brown stain far more readily than does the cytoplasm. Thus the nucleus stands out well against the cytoplasm. Closer examination reveals that only certain portions of the nucleoplasm have taken up the stain. Particularly visible are one or more **nucleoli** (Fig. 6–10l), which are small, spherical bodies. The nucleoli are extremely variable structures, often changing in size and shape. When a cell is dividing, the nucleoli disappear, then reappear shortly after division is completed. Their precise function is not entirely understood. Chemical analysis shows that the nucleoli are rich in ribonucleic acid, a fact which supports an hypothesis proposing that they play an indirect role in synthesis of proteins.

The majority of the stain taken up by the nucleoplasm is found in the substance called **chromatin.** Chromatin (from the Greek word for color) is so called because of its affinity for certain stains. It is found in strands within the nucleus. These strands run through the nucleoplasm in an irregular pattern, at times exhibiting a network or a granular appearance. We shall give the nature and function of chromatin further consideration in Section 6–7.

Thus far we have discussed only the *facts* of cellular anatomy, as revealed mostly by the light and electron microscopes, and briefly listed the functions of each cell organelle. Such a discussion cannot begin to impart a feeling for the tremendous amount of work which went into the determination of the structure and function of these organelles. The case of the plasma membrane has already been cited.

**6–6**
**HOW DO WE KNOW?**

There is considerable uncertainty about the function of some cell organelles. The Golgi complex is an example. Some cytologists think that the Golgi complex may serve as an area in which substances produced by the ribosomes can be stored temporarily before these substances are conducted out of the cell. Some support for this hypothesis comes from the fact that the Golgi complex does, indeed, seem to be only a specialized portion of the endoplasmic reticulum. It does not have ribosomes attached to it, and possesses vacuole-like structures (which often contain cell secretory products produced by the ribosomes). Other cytologists hypothesize that the Golgi complex may play a role in the formation of additional membranes as the cell grows and divides, basing this hypothesis partly on the observation that the Golgi complex, via the endoplasmic reticulum, seems continuous with both the nuclear and plasma membranes (though this obviously is not the only possible interpretation).

Note that we have here two different hypotheses to explain the function of one cell organelle. This is not at all an unusual occurrence in science. First of all, the two hypotheses in this case are not mutually exclusive; they may *both* be correct. The predictions which would be made from the acceptance of one

FIG. 6–14    The alga *Acetabularia mediterranea*. Each umbrella and stem comprise just one cell. (Photo courtesy General Biological Supply House, Inc., Chicago.)

do not necessarily exclude predictions which would be made from acceptance of the other. Both hypotheses survive because no observations have been made or experiments performed which *contradict* their predictions. Until the time such observations or experiments *are* made, there is no way to reject either of these two hypotheses—nor any others which are consistent with what we know about the Golgi complex. Dr. D. J. Morre and his co-workers at Purdue University have recently succeeded in isolating a fraction of almost pure dictyosome from rat liver cells. It may thus not be much longer before the precise function of the Golgi apparatus is determined, as well as the way this function is carried out.

**6–7**
**THE FUNCTION OF**
**THE NUCLEUS**

A combination of the proper experimental organism and certain experimental techniques often opens the way for a series of experiments which conclusively establish and affirm scientific hypotheses. Such a combination is found in the experiments of Hämmerling on the marine alga *Acetabularia*. Figure 6–14 shows a photograph of some *Acetabularia* cells. Each stalk and umbrellalike cap compose just one cell, which may be up to five centimeters in length. The nucleus of the cell is always found located in the stalk. This fact, coupled with its large size, makes *Acetabularia* an ideal organism through which to discover the role played by the nucleus in the life of the cell.

Hämmerling's first experiment simply involved cutting an *Acetabularia* cell in half, as shown in Fig. 6–15. The half without a nucleus continued to live

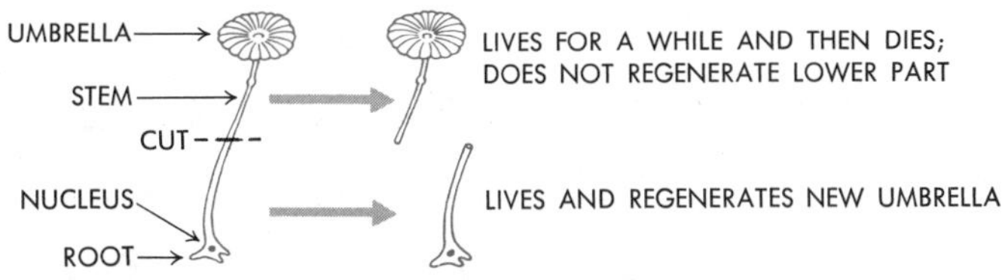

FIG. 6–15

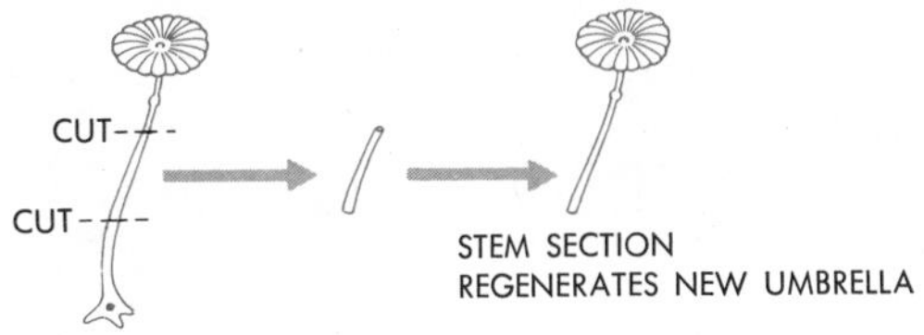

UMBRELLA  
STEM  
CUT  
NUCLEUS  
ROOT

LIVES FOR A WHILE AND THEN DIES;  
DOES NOT REGENERATE LOWER PART

LIVES AND REGENERATES NEW UMBRELLA

FIG. 6–16

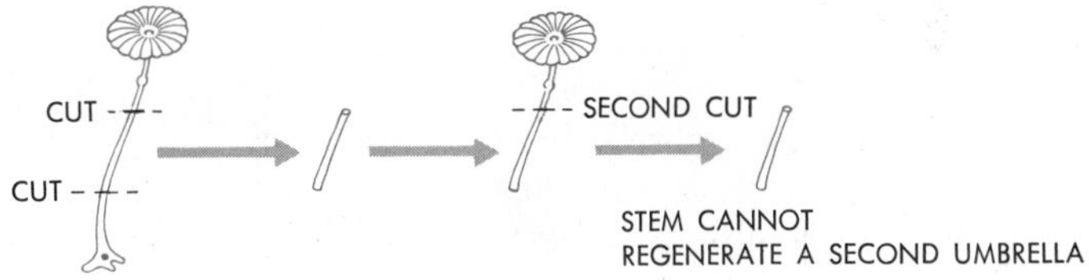

CUT  
CUT

STEM SECTION  
REGENERATES NEW UMBRELLA

FIG. 6–17

CUT  
CUT

SECOND CUT

STEM CANNOT  
REGENERATE A SECOND UMBRELLA

for a while, but eventually died. The half with a nucleus regenerated a new umbrella, and continued to live and reproduce. Hämmerling performed this same experiment on many *Acetabularia* cells, always with the same results. He therefore concluded that while the presence of the nucleus in *Acetabularia* is *not* essential to the cell's short-term existence, it *is* to the continuation of life and regeneration of the lost part.

The fact that the upper part of the *Acetabularia* cell did not regenerate the lower part, while the lower part, with the nucleus, did regenerate the upper part, makes it reasonable to hypothesize that the presence of the nucleus is required if regeneration is to occur.

**Hypothesis:** *If . . .*   the nucleus of an *Acetabularia* cell plays an essential role in regeneration, . . .

**Prediction:** *then . . .* an isolated *Acetabularia* stem without a nucleus should not be able to regenerate an umbrella.

To test this hypothesis, Hämmerling performed the experiment shown in Fig. 6–16. Note here that the stalk, without a nucleus, still managed to regenerate an umbrella. This result contradicted the hypothesis.

However, after a *second* operation on the same stem that regenerated the first umbrella, the stem section could not regenerate a second umbrella (Fig. 6–17). Thus the original hypothesis needed merely to be modified to state

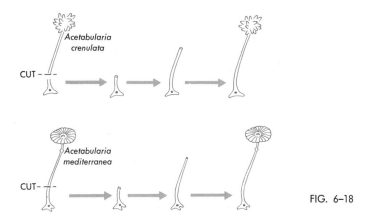

CUT –

*Acetabularia crenulata*

CUT –

*Acetabularia mediterranea*

FIG. 6–18

that the presence of the nucleus is essential to the *continued* regeneration of the lost umbrella by an *Acetabularia* cell.

It is now possible to suggest a slightly different hypothesis to explain the results of these first experiments. Perhaps the nucleus secreted some sort of "regenerative substance" into the cytoplasm surrounding it. It was the presence of this regenerative substance that enabled the *Acetabularia* stem section to regenerate the first umbrella. The stem section was unable to regenerate a second umbrella because it had used up all the regenerative substance given it by the nucleus and was unable to produce the substance itself.

This hypothesis can be tested by cutting the stem of the cell at varying distances from the nucleus. If the hypothesis is correct, we could predict a correlation between the amount of regenerative power possessed by some section and its closeness to the nucleus; the section closest to the nucleus should have the highest powers of regeneration.

Experiments of this sort, performed on many different types of cells, lead to the conclusion that the nucleus is the control center for virtually all the life processes carried on by the cell. It is true that cells that have had their nuclei removed will continue to live for a while. However, such cells are incapable of reproduction and growth, and sooner or later they die. It was noted earlier that certain cytoplasmic elements of the cell are responsible for the synthesis of proteins and the respiratory, energy-supplying processes of the cell. Yet, even this factor does not make the cell independent of the nucleus for its continued life. Even these specialized cytoplasmic structures seem dependent on the nucleus for their continued functioning. Thus the nucleus emerges as the most important single portion of most cells.

There is another feature of the nucleus that can be demonstrated by experiments on two different species of *Acetabularia*. These two species, *Acetabularia mediterranea* and *Acetabularia crenulata*, are chosen for the unique and

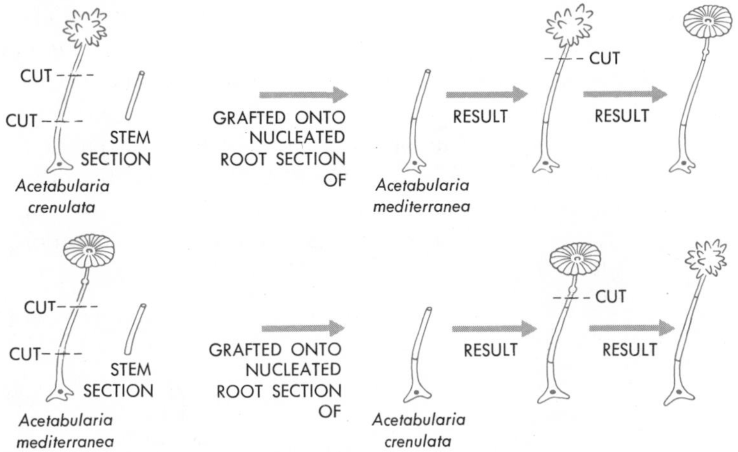

FIG. 6–19

easily recognized shape of their umbrellas. In this experiment, we note that when the umbrellas are cut off, each species regenerates an umbrella typical of its kind (Fig. 6–18).

These results are hardly surprising. We somehow take it for granted that this will happen, just as we always expect lions to have lion cubs and humans to have human children. Suppose, however, that a section of the cut stem of one species is grafted onto the cut end of a nucleated piece of the other species. Two such experiments can be performed: the grafting of a stem section from *A. mediterranea* onto a nucleated root section of *A. crenulata*, and the grafting of a stem section from *A. crenulata* onto a nucleated root section of *A. mediterranea*. The object is to see which portion of the cell (i.e., cytoplasm or nucleus) determines the characteristics of the regenerated umbrella. The results of these experiments are shown in Fig. 6–19. Note that in both experiments the first umbrella regenerated is identical to that of the species from which the stem section came. However, if this first regenerated umbrella is cut off and a second one allowed to regenerate, the second umbrella will be characteristic of the species from which the nucleated root section came.

How can these results be explained? Consider the hypothesis that the cell nucleus secretes a regenerative substance into the cytoplasm. This hypothesis can be nicely modified and expanded to fit the experimental observations. Perhaps the first regenerated umbrella looks like that of the species from which the stem section came because the grafted stem section still contains some of the regenerative substance given to it by the nucleus of its own species. It uses up this regenerative substance in producing the new umbrella. Then, unable to produce more of the regenerative substance of its own species, it has to rely on the nucleus of the other species for the substance used in building the second umbrella. According to this hypothesis, the second umbrella will resemble the *Acetabularia* species from which the nucleated section came—and it does.

From the results of these experiments, it can also be predicted what might happen if two nucleated root sections from *A. mediterranea* and *A. crenulata* are fused so that both nuclei contribute to the regeneration of one new umbrella. Figure 6–20 shows the results of such an experiment. In this case, a mixed or hybrid type of umbrella is formed which has characteristics of the umbrellas of both species. These results fit well with our hypothesis. We can visualize both nuclei sending out their own type of regenerative substance. Since both types of these substances are used in umbrella regeneration, a hybrid umbrella would be predicted.

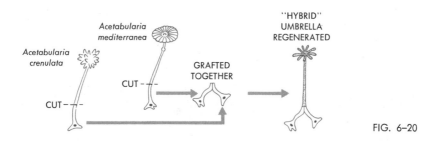

FIG. 6–20

From these experiments with *Acetabularia*, we can draw tentative conclusions about the function of the nucleus in this alga. Similar work has been done on enough other plant and animal cells to indicate that these conclusions can be extended to include almost every other kind of cell.

1) *The nucleus is responsible for the continuing life of the cell and seems to be necessary for its reproduction and the regeneration of lost parts.* In support of this hypothesis, it can be noted that cells that have no nucleus when fully developed (such as most mammalian red blood cells) are unable to reproduce. Nor do such cells live very long. They must, therefore, be produced by other groups of cells. In the case of red blood cells, the producing cells are found in the bone marrow.

2) *The nucleus, by certain interactions with the cytoplasm, determines what type of new cytoplasm will be reproduced.* The nucleus seems to produce substances that cause the cytoplasm to function in a definite way. To draw an analogy with a construction job, the nucleus corresponds to the foreman's office in which are contained blueprints for the entire building operation. The foreman passes on the architect's ideas to the work bosses directly under him. These work bosses leave the office, corresponding to the nucleus, and go out into the area where the laborers are working. This area corresponds to the cytoplasm. It is here that the orders of the foreman will be put into effect.

It is now pertinent to examine the nature of the deep-staining chromatin of the nucleus. Chemical analysis reveals chromatin to be composed of a **nucleo-protein.** Nucleoproteins are complex substances, composed of nucleic acids and

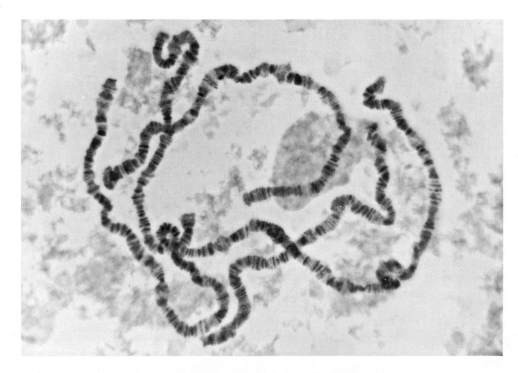

FIG. 6–21    Photo of chromosomes from the salivary gland cells of the fruit fly. The dark bands represent areas of different density of materials. Chromosomes are mostly composed of protein and deoxyribonucleic acid (DNA). (Courtesy General Biological Supply House, Inc., Chicago.)

proteins. In chromatin, this nucleic acid is deoxyribonucleic acid or DNA. When cells begin the reproductive process, the existence of the chromatin in the form of **chromosomes** becomes evident. One of the so-called "giant chromosomes" from salivary gland cells of the fruit fly is shown in Fig. 6–21.

Also found within the nucleus, associated with the nucleoli, is one type of ribonucleic acid (RNA). Some of this RNA is free to pass out of the nucleus into the cytoplasm, where it moves to the ribosomes to play a role in protein synthesis. In the light of these facts, a third function of the cell nucleus can be hypothesized. This function was perhaps suggested by the last series of experiments on the two species of *Acetabularia*.

3) *The nucleus carries the inheritance factors of a cell, enabling it to pass on to its descendants its own special characteristics.* These factors for inheritance are located within that portion of the nucleoplasm known as the chromatin.

**6-8
CELL SIZES**

Cells vary widely in size and shape. The difference in size between the smallest cell and the largest cell is comparable to the difference in size between a bacterium and a whale. Even in common types of cells, a range of from 1 to 100 microns is common, with the latter dimension being just barely visible to the

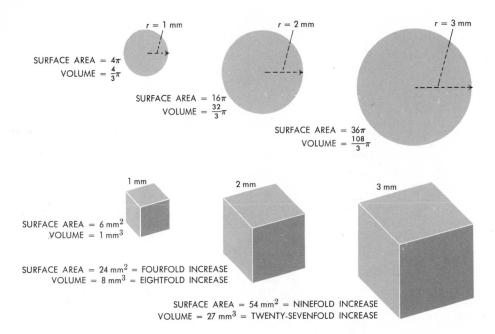

FIG. 6–22   The problem of when a cell must divide is related to a principle of solid geometry.  As soon as the mass volume of a cell increases to a point at which the surface area is no longer sufficient to supply nutrients and remove wastes, the cell must divide.

naked eye.  Such huge cells as those of *Acetabularia* (up to 5 cm) or an ostrich egg cell (almost 8 cm) are definitely the exception rather than the rule.

It might be wondered, then, just what the size limit upon any cell is, or, indeed whether a size limit exists.  The answer becomes obvious when we recall that all cells are dependent upon food materials which pass into the cell from their outside environment.  Cells are also dependent upon the plasma membrane for the intake of an oxidizing agent for respiration and the excretion of waste products.  The diffusion of materials into and out of the cells must take place through the plasma membrane.

Thus the question of just how large a particular cell may grow becomes a simple problem of solid geometry.  As a sphere becomes greater in size, its volume increases as the cube of the radius.  The surface area, on the other hand, increases only as the square of the radius.  This same principle, slightly modified, applies to the other three-dimensional shapes a cell may assume.  A cell may become no larger than the maximum size at which it can successfully carry out its life processes.  If it exceeds this limit, the cell must either divide into two parts or die (Fig. 6–22).

Knowing this, we can make a prediction about the relation between the size of the cell and the rate of its metabolic activity.  Cells in the growth region or stems of plants, for example, are constantly dividing, and so are very active metabolically. Such cells are very small. The smaller the cell, the greater the amount of surface area per unit volume of living material. Thus a rapid exchange of food and waste materials is possible. The large size obtained by certain egg cells is directly related to the fact that they are relatively inactive until fertilized, and so can afford a low ratio of plasma membrane surface to the volume of living material the membrane encloses. After fertilization the egg must become extremely active; therefore, its first activity must be one of rapid division. This division brings its surface area into a proportionate relationship with the inner living material which will enable the cell to supply its greatly increased demands for rapid exchange of materials.

Using radioactive tracers and very delicate microchemical techniques, biologists have devoted considerable attention to the problem of how substances pass through the plasma membrane when entering or leaving the cell. The experiment diagrammed in Fig. 6–23 shows an animal membrane inside of which has been placed a solution of blood plasma (protein), a monosaccharide sugar

**6–9**
**THE CELL MEMBRANE: A STUDY OF FUNCTION**

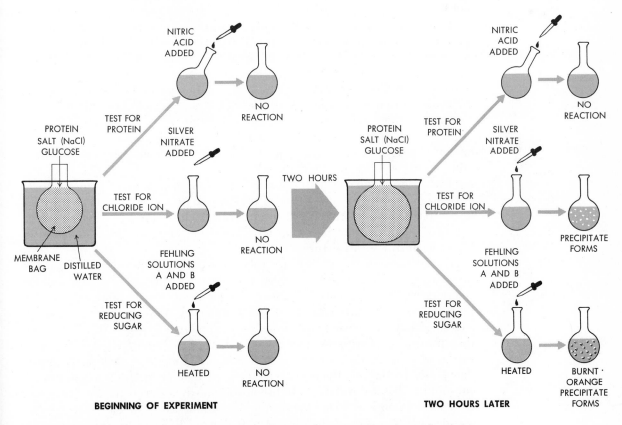

FIG. 6–23   A series of experiments performed to investigate the nature of membranes in relation to the solutions within them. Note the change in size of the membrane bag after two hours.

(glucose), and an inorganic salt (sodium chloride).  The membrane, with its enclosed substances, is lowered into distilled water.

After two hours have passed, the distilled water outside the animal membrane is chemically analyzed for the presence of plasma, glucose, and salt.  The test for plasma is negative; no plasma has passed through the membrane to the distilled water.  The tests for glucose and salt, however, are positive.  Evidently, then, these compounds have passed through the membrane into the water.  These results show this membrane to be **permeable** to glucose and sodium chloride, but **impermeable** to plasma.  A membrane that is partially permeable to solvent, but not permeable to solutes is said to be **semipermeable.**  A membrane allowing one substance (solute or solvent) to pass through more easily than another substance (solute or solvent) is called **differentially permeable.**

Note, however, that something else happened in the experiment.  The membrane bag became swollen, indicating that something had moved in from the outside.  Since nothing but water is present in the beaker it can only be concluded that as molecules of glucose and ions of sodium chloride moved out, molecules of water moved in.  This membrane, then, is permeable to water molecules.

If the amounts of salt and glucose present in the distilled water outside the membrane are quantitatively compared with the amounts of salt and glucose on the inside, they will be found to be equal.  Molecules and ions in the solution are in a constant state of random motion.  For example, if the salt copper sulfate is dissolved in distilled water, the copper and sulfate ions will spread out among the water molecules.  In time, every area of the container will contain the same amount of copper and sulfate ions.  This is because *all molecules, atoms, or ions in a solution tend to move from an area of greater concentration to one of lesser concentration.*  We call such movement **diffusion.**  When all the copper and sulfate ions are equally dispersed throughout the water, an *equilibrium* has been reached.  This does *not* mean that the ions have stopped moving.  It means that, in terms of probability, for every ion that moves from the left side of the container to the right, another ion moves from the right to the left.  The net effect is as if the ions had not moved at all.  The equilibrium in such a situation is thus a **dynamic equilibrium.**

It is now easy to hypothesize an explanation for the results of the experiment involving the animal membrane filled with blood plasma, glucose, and sodium chloride.  Molecules of glucose and ions of sodium and chlorine must have passed through the membrane into the distilled water by diffusion.  At first, more molecules and ions passed out through the membrane into the distilled water than passed in.  This is because the *concentration* of these molecules and ions was greater inside the membrane than outside.  For every molecule and ion that passed in through the membrane, perhaps 1000 molecules and ions passed out into the distilled water.  As diffusion continued, however, the concentration of molecules and ions inside the membrane became closer to the concentration outside, and the rate of diffusion slowed down.  Eventually, the number of molecules passing out through the membrane became equal to the number passing in. At this point, a dynamic equilibrium was attained. No such equilibrium was attained with the protein molecules in the blood plasma, since they were unable to pass through the membrane. The swelling of the containing membrane can be accounted for by assuming that the water molecules entered more rapidly than the glucose, sodium, and chloride ions escaped.

The results obtained in this experiment with the membrane are duplicated in experiments using individual cells. In general, proteins are not passed through the plasma membrane of such cells. It is logical to wonder why this should be so. One hypothesis is suggested by the fact that electron-microscope photographs reveal the plasma membrane to be perforated by pores so small that they must be measured in angstrom units. It might be hypothesized, then, that only those molecules small enough to pass through the pores in the plasma membrane will pass into the cell. This hypothesis is supported by the fact that small molecules, such as those of water, generally pass freely in and out of cells, while larger molecules, such as proteins, generally do not.

Other observations, however, contradict this hypothesis. Ions of sodium are kept out of resting nerve cells, yet such ions are far smaller than the smallest pore in the plasma membrane. Conversely, under certain conditions large molecules of nucleic acid will pass into some cells. Thus the pore hypothesis may account for the movements of some substances in and out of cells, but it cannot account for others. The cells of many different organisms can concentrate molecules or ions to a far higher degree than the surrounding medium. Many of these molecules and ions are of such small dimensions that they could easily pass out of the cell, and since diffusion occurs from a region of greater to a region of lesser concentration, it would be predicted that they would do so. But they do not. We might ask, then, why the experiment with the membrane resulted in equal concentrations of glucose molecules and sodium and chlorine ions on both sides of the membrane, when such an equilibrium is not necessarily attained with other types of cells.

The answer is suggested by additional experiments. It has been shown that the respiratory rate of cells that are concentrating ions or molecules against the normal concentration gradient is far higher than the respiratory rate of similar cells that are not concentrating the same molecules or ions. It seems evident, then, that these cells maintain a high concentration of dissolved substances within them by expending energy. A similar group of cells, intact but nonliving, is unable to maintain a high concentration of salts. Not being alive, these cells are unable to expend the energy necessary to hold the ions and molecules within their membranes. The laws of diffusion have the upper hand, and the concentration of substances inside and outside these nonliving cells soon becomes equal (Fig. 6–24).

As reported by one investigator, the pores in the plasma membranes of red blood cells have a diameter of 7 Å. Yet glucose molecules 8 Å across are able to pass into the cells. Here again, experiments show that energy is being expended

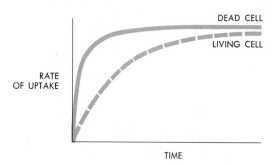

FIG. 6–24   This graph shows the uptake of ions introduced into a liquid medium surrounding dead and living cells. Note that the living cells are able to offer some resistance to diffusion of ions into the cell. A graph of the respiratory rates of such cells shows that they must expend energy to accomplish this.

by the red blood cells; it would seem as if they must perform work in order to get the glucose inside. The process is spoken of as one of **active transport,** as opposed to the passive transport of substances into and out of the cell by diffusion. In the latter process, the cell need expend no energy.

As yet, no single hypothesis has explained all the types of movements of materials known to occur across the plasma membrane. It has been suggested that the polarity of the phospholipid molecules composing part of the plasma membrane, as well as the polarity of the molecules passing through it, may determine whether the substance gets through. In the light of our present knowledge it seems best to view the plasma membrane as an active boundary layer, rather than as a rigid, inflexible structure. It might be pictured as being similar to a line of men standing a few feet apart. Their duty is to guard a certain area, making certain that only properly identified persons or vehicles get through. If a large vehicle must pass through the line, the men can move aside to make room. If a small person without the proper credentials approaches the line, the men can move together to prevent his passage. We cannot use this example in the case of nonliving cells. Instead, we can picture the plasma membrane of the nonliving cell as similar to a line of posts stuck in the ground around a guarded area. In this situation, the openings between the posts cannot be adjusted, and the dynamic equilibrium is attained between the ions or molecules of only those substances able to pass between the posts.

The hypothesis pictured by this analogy views the plasma membrane as more than a passive, inactive structure. Such an hypothesis helps to explain why a balanced equilibrium is not always attained between similar substances inside and outside the cell. The hypothesis also pictures the cell as playing an active role in determining which substances enter it by diffusion and which do not, as well as how much of a substance may do so. Occasionally, therefore, cells must expend energy in obtaining or holding needed ions or molecules.

The Davson-Danielli unit membrane concept discussed earlier (see Section 6–4) provides an excellent example of a hypothetical "model." Such models

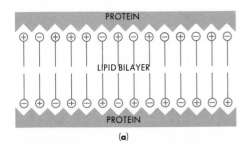 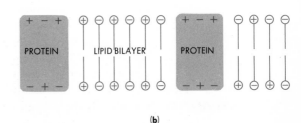

(a)    (b)

FIG. 6–25    The Davson-Danielli unit-membrane model of the plasma membrane (a) has recently been modified to the model shown at right (b) (see text for discussion).

are often put forth to account for observed phenomena (in this case, the functioning of the plasma membrane) and to suggest experiments to test the accuracy of the model. It is important to realize that there is absolutely no requirement that the model in any way resemble the actual structure it is intended to represent; no biologist, including Davson and Danielli, would make such a claim. It is only essential that the proposed model be consistent with observed facts about plasma membranes and that it allow accurate predictions to be made concerning their structure and function.

The Davson-Danielli model of the plasma membrane, consisting of lipid bilayers sandwiched between protein, has proven remarkably successful in accounting for the electrical and passive-permeability characteristics of plasma membranes. Further, artificial membranes have been made on the basis of the model which closely resemble real plasma membranes in both structure and function. Yet it is difficult to see how the protein components of the membrane can perform all the functions they must surely perform during active transport if, as the Davson-Danielli model indicates, they are merely spread out over the lipid surface. Evidence that the Davson-Danielli unit-membrane model needs considerable revision comes from the observation that the enzyme phospholipase can remove up to 70% of the phosphorus from an intact plasma membrane's phospholipids and yet leave its basic structure intact. If there was an even layer of protein spread over the phospholipid bilayer, as the Davson-Danielli model holds, the enzyme would not have been able to get to the phospholipid layers inside.

Electron-microscope examinations of membranes after treatment with phospholipase were carried out by A. Otholenghi and M. Bowman at Ohio State University. These examinations show that the membrane is not digested all over, but only in patches. Presumably these patches are areas where exposed phospholipid molecules are concentrated. Further, M. Glazer and his colleagues at the University of California at La Jolla and Pasadena have shown that when red blood cell membranes are heated, the areas assumed to be those attacked by phospholipase are left intact but areas sensitive to temperatures of the range that affects proteins are altered.  Thus the California workers have proposed a new model of cell membrane structure in which there are whole areas composed largely of protein (see Fig. 6–25).  Note that the new model does not overthrow the Davson-Danielli model, but merely modifies it to make it consistent with new experimental observations.

6–10<br>OSMOSIS

**Osmosis** is the passage of a solvent through a semipermeable membrane from a region of greater to a region of lesser concentration.  In a living organism, the solvent is usually water and the semipermeable membrane is usually that of the cell.  Since water molecules are small, the cell is somewhat limited in the amount of direct control it can impose on their passage across the membrane.

Figure 6–26(a) shows the diffusion of water and sugar molecules (sucrose) across a membrane permeable to both molecules.  At the start, water is present on both sides of the membrane, but sucrose is present only on the right.  Since there are only water molecules on the left side of the membrane, while the right side has both water and sucrose molecules, the greater concentration of water is on the left side of the membrane.  Thus, by simple diffusion, water molecules will tend to move through the membrane from the left side to the right, and sucrose molecules will move from the right to the left.  Each compound is passing from its area of greater to lesser concentration.  As time passes, the concentration of sucrose molecules on the left will increase until it balances the concentration on the right.  At the same time, the concentration of water molecules on the right will increase until it balances the concentration on the left.  Eventually, the ratio of sugar molecules to water molecules will be the same for both sides

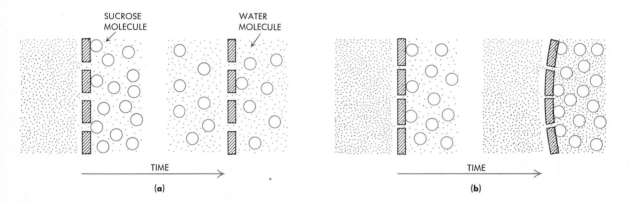

FIG. 6–26    (a) Diffusion of sucrose and water molecules through a membrane which is permeable to both.  Eventually, the rates of each kind of molecule passing through the membrane from either side become equal.  (b) A membrane which is impermeable to sucrose but permeable to water. The water molecules pass from left to right, since their concentration is greater at left. The resulting osmotic pressure exerts a force on the membrane.

of the membrane. After this point has been reached, both sucrose molecules and water molecules will continue to pass through the membrane, but the concentration on both sides will remain constant. The system will have attained dynamic equilibrium for both kinds of molecules.

Now consider the situation diagrammed in Fig. 6–26(b). In this case, the membrane is semipermeable. In other words, this membrane allows free passage of the small water molecules, but restricts the passage of the larger sucrose molecules. At the start, sucrose is in greater concentration on the right and water is in greater concentration on the left. In this system, the sucrose molecules cannot pass from an area of greater to lesser concentration; the membrane is impermeable to them. The water molecules, on the other hand, can pass freely through the membrane. Thus they pass from an area of greater to lesser concentration, i.e., from left to right. Of course, as a result of a random motion, water molecules are also passing from right to left. However, since the concentration of water molecules is greater on the left side of the membrane than on the right, far more molecules pass in from left to right. The passage of these water molecules is an example of osmosis.

Figure 6–26(a) showed a system which attained dynamic equilibrium. The system shown in Fig. 6–26(b) could never attain that condition, and here is why: The concentration of water on the left side is 100%. Now, the sugar molecules must stay on the right side, since they cannot pass through the membrane; therefore, no matter how many water molecules move from the area of greater concentration (the left) to the area of lesser concentration (the right), the concentration of water on the right can never equal that on the left (that is, 100%).

OSMOTIC
RATE

TIME

FIG. 6–27    The relation between osmotic rate and time.

In the diffusion of water across the membrane in Fig. 6–26(b), do the molecules pass from left to right at the same rate from the beginning of the experiment to its end? The graph in Fig. 6–27, which plots the rate of osmosis against time, indicates the answer to this question. Note that the rate of osmosis *decreases* with time; the longer the process goes on, the slower the rate at which it occurs.  Thus, if 25 units of water molecules pass through the cell membrane the first minute, 15 may pass through the second minute, 8 during the third minute, and so on.  The passage of water through the membrane constantly changes the relative concentrations of both water and sugar molecules on the right side.  Since osmotic rate is directly proportional to concentration differences between the substances involved, the osmotic rate is constantly changing.  At the beginning of the experiment represented in Fig. 6–26(b), there are many water molecules passing from left to right, and we can say that the system has a high osmotic rate at the start.

On first thought, one might well be tempted to view osmosis as simply a special case of diffusion by which water (or a solvent) passes through submicroscopic pores in semipermeable membranes.  Certainly it is true that the direction and equilibrium of osmotic processes can be accurately predicted by an hypothesis which interprets osmosis in this manner.  Yet careful measurements, using isotopically labeled $H_2O^{18}$, uncover a contradiction to this hypothesis; water traverses a porous semipermeable membrane faster than would be predicted, even if the theoretical maximum rate of diffusion is assumed to prevail.  Current hypotheses concerning osmotic flow are based on concepts of bulk flow resulting from hydrostatic pressure differences working in conjunction with diffusion.  Thus even the seemingly "simple" processes occurring in living matter often turn out to be far from simple when subjected to more thorough analyses.

An understanding of the principles of diffusion, osmosis, and active transport is essential to the understanding of plant and animal physiology.  It is primarily through these processes that living organisms obtain the nutrients and oxidizing agents used by their cells and dispose of the waste products of their metabolic activities.

## 6–11
## PROCARYOTES VS. EUCARYOTES

Fairly recently, biologists have begun to realize that the differences between plants and animals are not as significant as the differences between two basic cellular types, **procaryotic** and **eucaryotic.**  In the process of genetic evolution, the division of cells into procaryotic and eucaryotic types has been estimated to be more than two and a half times as remote from the present stage as the division of living forms into plant and animal kingdoms.

As the footnote in Section 6–3 indicates, the bacteria and blue-green algae are "exceptional" cell types.  For one thing, they lack a nuclear membrane.  For a long time, such cells were thought not to have a nucleus at all, but it is now known that there is a distinct region in the cytoplasm where the genetic material is found (see Fig. 6–28).  These are procaryotic cells.  Such cells also lack mitochondria, an endoplasmic reticulum, Golgi, and lysosomes.  Procaryotic cells do not exhibit the cytoplasmic streaming and amoeboid movement of many eucaryotic cells, and their cell walls are of a different chemical composition.  The genetic material of a procaryotic cell is not organized into chromosomes, being composed only of nucleic acid with no accompanying protein.  When

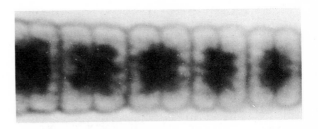

FIG. 6–28    Cells of the blue-green alga *Oscillatoria*, showing the central region of nuclear material characteristic of the procaryotic cells of blue-green algae and bacteria. (Photo from W. W. Robbins and T. E. Weier, *Botany*. New York: John Wiley, 1950, p. 304. Used by permission.)

chlorophyll is present in a procaryotic cell, it is not organized into chloroplasts. In addition, the flagella of procaryotic cells lack the 9 + 2 fibrillar structure characteristic of the flagella of eucaryotic cells.

Obviously, procaryotic cells exhibit a very "primitive" structure. Since the difference between eucaryotes and procaryotes seems to be primarily one between "haves" and "have-nots," it is reasonable to ask how procaryotic cells manage to survive without such vital organelles as mitochondria and an endoplasmic reticulum. There is now some evidence that the plasma membrane of procaryotic cells folds inward at several points, and that this membrane is able to carry out many of the chemical functions performed by the organelles of eucaryotic cells.

**6-12
CONCLUSION**

The cell is the unit of structure and function in virtually all living organisms. Especially since the advent of the electron microscope, the cell has come to be recognized as a highly organized unit, with many specialized organelles. The most important of these organelles have been discussed in this chapter, as well as some of the hypotheses that have been proposed to explain their role in cellular activity. Some of the supporting experimental evidence for these hypotheses has also been discussed, particularly that obtained by Hämmerling with the alga *Acetabularia*. These experiments indicate that the cell nucleus plays a role in determining structural inheritance through its regulation of building processes. The chromatin was shown to be that material within the nucleus which most probably carries the hereditary message.

The size of a cell is at least partly a function of its metabolic activity. A cell must remain small enough for its surface area to adequately handle its respiratory and excretory needs.

The cell takes more than a passive role in the moving of substances into and out of it. By expending energy, cells can engage in the active transport of substances through their plasma membrane in either direction. Thus, for example, cells can concentrate substances within them which would ordinarily pass out by diffusion. The cell can also absorb substances whose molecules are larger than the pores in the plasma membrane. This indicates that the latter structure plays a role in active transport by virtue of an adjustable molecular structure.

**EXERCISES**    1. Discuss briefly the functions of the following parts of a cell: (a) plasma membrane, (b) cell wall, (c) ribosomes, (d) endoplasmic reticulum, (e) mitochondria, (f) centriole, (g) plastids, (h) lysosomes.

2. What is significant about the fact that most cells contain almost all the same structures?

3. Describe the plasma membrane of a living cell. In what way is the structure of the membrane closely correlated with its function?

4. If electron micrographs show that mitochondria are grouped around a particular structure or region of the cell, what might you infer is happening in this region?

5. What is the major conclusion to be drawn from Hämmerling's experiments?

6. Distinguish between osmosis and diffusion.

7. Explain what is meant by calling a membrane permeable, semipermeable, or impermeable.

8. A particular membrane is said to be permeable to water and sodium chloride, yet impermeable to glucose molecules. Explain how this might be possible.

9. Figure 6–29 is a diagram of an osmometer, similar to those used to demonstrate osmosis. At the beginning of an experiment there is a 50% glucose solution within the membrane, which is impermeable to glucose. Draw a graph representing the rate of osmosis in this system, indicated by the rate at which the water climbs up the tube.

10. Indicate on the graph you drew for Exercise 9 what the line would look like if the glucose concentration within the membrane were only 10% at the beginning of the experiment.

11. A snail can be killed by throwing salt on it; you get very thirsty (indicating that your body cells are low on water) after eating a salty meal; in growing living cells in test tubes, physiologists are very careful to use a medium known as Ringer's solution, in which the salt concentration is exactly that found in body and cellular fluids. Explain all three of these facts in terms of osmosis and dialysis (see Glossary).

12. Plasmolysis is a term used to refer to the collapse of a cell from excessive loss of water. Describe the conditions that probably exist if a cell undergoes plasmolysis when it is placed in a solution.

For Exercises 13–17, read the following directions carefully, and refer to Fig. 6–30.

*Necessary data:* At the beginning of the experiment the solutions in the two arms of the tube are as pictured. They are separated at the bottom of the tube by a differentially permeable membrane. The volumes on either side of the tube are the same, and thus the level of the liquid in both arms is also the same. The apparatus is allowed to stand for several days.

13. During the experiment what will happen to the water level?

   a) It will rise in side A, since water (not the substances in it) will tend to pass from its area of greater concentration to its area of lesser concentration.

   b) It will rise in side A, since the water (not the substances in it) will tend to pass from its area of lesser concentration to its area of greater concentration.

   c) It will remain the same, because atmospheric pressure is equal on both sides of the system.

   d) None of the above.

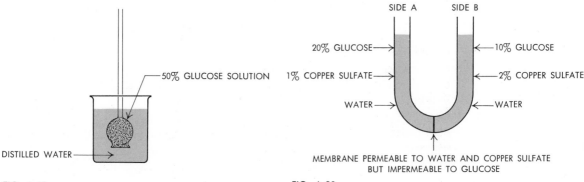

FIG. 6–29                    FIG. 6–30

14. What will happen to the glucose solution of side A?

   a) It will become more concentrated, and that on side B will become less concentrated, since water moves from A to B.

   b) It will become more concentrated, and that on side B will become less concentrated, since water passes from B to A.

   c) It will become less concentrated, and that on side B will become more concentrated, since water passes from A to B.

   d) It will become less concentrated, and that on side B will become more concentrated, since water passes from B into A.

15. Which of the following best describes what will happen to the copper sulphate as the experiment proceeds?

   a) There will be no passage of copper sulphate because solutes do not go through semipermeable membranes.

   b) There will be a slight passage of this substance, but the passage will be restricted by the size of the pores in the membrane.

   c) There will be a slow movement, since the concentrations are nearly equal.

   d) There will be no passage, since copper sulphate is insoluble.

16. Osmotic pressure will be greatest on:

   a) Side A at the beginning of the experiment.

   b) Side A at the end of the experiment.

   c) Side B at the beginning of the experiment.

   d) Side B at the conclusion of the experiment.

17. Which of the following substances show the phenomenon of dialysis in the above?

   (a) Water (b) glucose (c) copper sulphate

18. Table 6–1 lists the concentrations of various substances inside and outside a cell. Study these data and answer the questions that follow.

   a) Indicate whether each substance listed in Table 6–1 will tend to pass into or out of the cell by the process of simple diffusion.

**TABLE 6–1**

|  | EXTRACELLULAR FLUID | INTRACELLULAR FLUID |
|---|---|---|
| SODIUM ION | 137 mEq/liter* | 10 mEq/liter |
| POTASSIUM ION | 5 mEq/liter | 141 mEq/liter |
| CALCIUM ION | 5 mEq/liter | 0 mEq/liter |
| MAGNESIUM ION | 3 mEq/liter | 62 mEq/liter |
| CHLORIDE ION | 103 mEq/liter | 4 mEq/liter |
| BICARBONATE ION | 28 mEq/liter | 10 mEq/liter |
| PHOSPHATES | 4 mEq/liter | 75 mEq/liter |
| GLUCOSE | 90 mg%† | 0 to 20 mg% |
| AMINO ACIDS | 30 mg% | 200 mg% |
| OXYGEN PRESSURE | 35 mm Hg | 20 mm Hg |
| CARBON DIOXIDE PRESSURE | 46 mm Hg | 50 mm Hg |

\* mEq/liter stands for milliequivalent per liter. It is a relative value.

† mg% stands for milligram percent. This, too, is useful here as a relative figure.

b) The various concentrations listed in Table 6–1 will remain constant under normal conditions. This indicates that some processes are at work to counteract the diffusion process. What mechanism, operating on the cellular level, may be responsible for this?

The experiment shown in Fig. 6–31 was performed on the multinucleated protozoan *Pelomyxa*. For the purpose of this experiment, the effect of many nuclei is no different than that of a single nucleus. The amount of radiation in all cases was equal to a lethal dose.

Examine separately each statement in Exercises 19–28. If the statement is possible on the basis of the experimental results given, write A opposite that number on your paper. If the statement cannot be evaluated on the basis of the experimental results, write B. If the statement is contradicted by the evidence given, write C.

19. Under normal conditions radiation (a dosage equal to the lethal dose) kills a cell.

20. Radiation undoubtedly affects the nucleus of a cell more than the cytoplasm.

21. The cells on the left-hand side of Fig. 6–31 died because the nucleus was unable to govern protein synthesis.

22. The mechanical effect of transplanting a portion of cytoplasm could counteract the effects produced by radiation.

23. Unirradiated cytoplasm will enable the cell to survive in the presence of radiated cytoplasm.

24. The transplanted, unirradiated cytoplasm may produce a repair substance which enables the nucleus to recover from the radiation.

25. On the right-hand side of Fig. 6–31, the critical damage from the radiation may have been restricted to the cytoplasm.

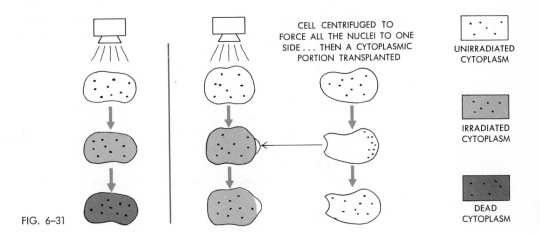

FIG. 6-31

26. The transplanted portion of cytoplasm may have contained all the necessary components for the continuing existence of the cell.

27. Centrifuging a cell causes its death.

28. Radiation does not kill cells.

29. Offer an hypothesis to account for the results shown in Fig. 6-32. Consider closely the comparative effects of the radiation (which in all cases was of equal dosage) on the nucleus and the cytoplasm. Does the radiation affect the cytoplasm and the nucleus equally? Explain your hypothesis completely.

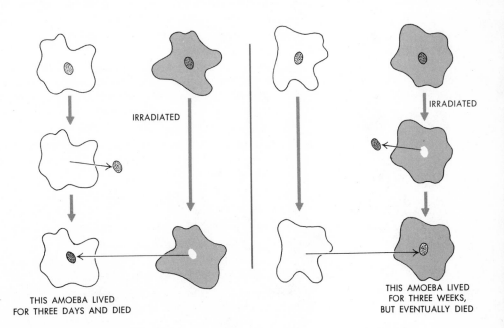

FIG. 6-32    THIS AMOEBA LIVED FOR THREE DAYS AND DIED

THIS AMOEBA LIVED FOR THREE WEEKS, BUT EVENTUALLY DIED

SUGGESTED
READINGS

BAKER, JEFFREY J. W., *Cell* (Columbus, Ohio: American Education Publications, 1966). Paperback book describing modern cellular anatomy as revealed by the electron microscope and artist's reconstructions.

MERCER, E. A., *Cells: Their Structure and Function* (New York: The Natural History Press, 1962).

SCHWANN, THEODOR, "Microscopical Researches into the Accordance in the Structure and Growth of Animals and Plants," in *The Process of Biology: Primary Sources*, ed. by Jeffrey J. W. Baker and Garland E. Allen (Reading, Mass.: Addison-Wesley, 1970). The original 1838 "cell theory" paper of zoologist Schwann in which he compares his own observations on animals with those of Schleiden on plants.

WILSON, G. B., and JOHN H. MORRISON, *Cytology* (New York: Reinhold Publishing Corporation, 1961). Good discussion in Chapter 11 of cytological techniques.

# CELLULAR METABOLISM: MATTER, ENERGY, AND CHEMICAL CHANGE

# CHAPTER 7

Cells are chemical machines. They consume fuels (e.g., sugars) and release waste products (e.g., carbon dioxide and water). The energy they extract from their fuel is used to perform **work,** which is defined as the force required to move matter through a distance. Work is involved whether the matter being moved is as small as an electron, or as large as a rock or an automobile. All cells perform general types of work, such as building up or synthesizing molecules, or actively transporting various substances across cell membranes. In addition, some cells also do specialized work, such as physical movement (e.g., the movement of an amoeba or the contraction of a muscle cell) or electrochemical work (e.g., the conduction of an impulse by a nerve cell).

Like machines, cells release energy from fuels in an orderly way to accomplish specific tasks. In both cases, the release of energy is accomplished by breaking down fuels, in a process known as "oxidation." But here the comparison between the cell and the machine begins to break down. When looked at more closely, the details of energy extraction and use show the cell to be a far more complex and delicate unit than any known machine. In the long run, the differences between a cell and a machine are far more important than the similarities in adding to our understanding of the nature of life.

To understand these differences, consider a comparison between a cell and an internal combustion engine, such as an automobile engine. The comparison will be limited here to just two points: (a) the mechanism of energy release and (b) the rate of energy release. In the automobile engine, energy is released from the fuel (gasoline) by a series of rapid, single-step oxidations, each of which is a single explosion in a cylinder. All the available energy from a given quantity of fuel is released in one step at each ignition. The power from these small explosions pushes the pistons up and down, thereby generating forward motion. Work is thus performed, since a mass (the car) has been moved a distance. Much of the energy, however, is lost as heat and thus wasted. Living cells, on the other hand, release energy from their fuel substances (sugars, fats) in a number of successive but interconnected oxidation reactions, each of which releases a small amount of energy. Thus, in place of the one-step, rapid burning process which occurs in the automobile engine, the cell breaks down its fuels by a multi-step, "slow burning" process.

The rate at which an internal combustion engine operates is usually controlled by an outside agent (the driver) through a mechanical device called the accelerator. But some engines also have an internal, self-controlling mechanism called a "governor," a mechanical device designed to retard the motor's rate of activity. The faster the motor goes, the more the governor is brought into action to slow the motor down. A governor is an example of an internal, self-regulating device, in contrast to the driver, who is an *external*, autonomous regulator. Cells have no counterpart to the "driver" of an automobile. Yet, to respond to changing external conditions and use their energy most efficiently, cells must be able to control the rate at which their internal processes occur. To accomplish this, cells have a variety of internal chemical mechanisms. Some of these mechanisms regulate what substances come into or go out of the cell; some regulate the rate of one particular step in a long series of biochemical reactions. All the controls are internal and are thus analogous to the governor in an automobile engine. The chief difference between control in cells and control in machines lies in the ability of the former to exercise high levels of precision not through the regulation of gross mechanical processes (as in a motor), but by regulating small-scale chemical reactions.

The totality of the processes by which cells obtain and use energy to do work and maintain themselves is known as **metabolism.** All metabolic activity is ultimately chemical in nature; i.e., it involves the interaction of atoms and molecules. The metabolism of all cells is carried out by many series of interconnected chemical reactions known as **metabolic pathways.** Any particular metabolic pathway usually consists of many individual reactions whose total effect is the synthesis or degradation of molecules and the use or release of energy.

The metabolic activity of any cell is closely related to cell structure. Indeed, the remarkable efficiency and precision of control which cells are able to achieve is largely a result of the intimate relation between cell structures and the metabolic pathways associated with them. In this and the next chapter some of the characteristics of metabolic pathways will be discussed. However, before looking directly at the characteristics of specific metabolic pathways, it will be helpful to consider some basic problems relating to chemical reactions in general. These include:

1) The nature of matter and energy, and the changes which occur in them during chemical reactions.

2) The types of molecules found in living systems.

3) The nature of catalysis and catalysts, especially the organic catalysts, or **enzymes.**

4) The common energy currency of living cells.

5) The various types of metabolic pathways found in cells.

These topics will form the subject matter of Chapter 7. In Chapter 8, we will look in somewhat greater detail at some specific metabolic pathways in living cells.

**7-2
MATTER AND
ENERGY**

**Matter** can be directly defined as anything that has mass and occupies space. The fundamental unit of matter is the **atom,** which in turn consists of particles known as **protons, neutrons,** and **electrons. Energy,** on the other hand, must be defined *indirectly* in terms of the movement of matter, i.e., in terms of work.

It is often useful to speak of energy as existing in one of two states, **kinetic** and **potential.** Potential energy is energy which is stored or inactive. This energy is capable of performing work and is frequently referred to as **free energy** (symbolized as $G$).* A stick of dynamite represents a great deal of potential energy; in quantitative terms it can be said to have a high free-energy value. In a biological context, sugar or fat also represents potential energy, though the free-energy value of either of these substances would be considerably less than that of an equivalent quantity of dynamite.

Kinetic energy is energy in action. It is energy in the process of having an effect on matter, and thus in the process of doing work. A boulder perched on the top of a hill has potential energy. If the boulder is given a slight push and begins rolling down the hill, the potential energy is released as kinetic energy. By the time the boulder has reached the bottom of the hill, all of its potential energy (in relation to the hill) has been released. For the boulder to get back to the top of the hill, its potential energy must be restored. This can occur only if an input of energy comes from some outside agent (such as someone pushing the boulder back up the hill).

In addition to the potential and kinetic states of energy, it is also useful to recognize five forms of energy. These forms are chemical energy, electrical energy, mechanical energy, radiant energy, and atomic energy. The last of these has little direct relationship to the normal functioning of the individual organism, but the others are all directly involved in living systems in one way or another.

---

* The letters $F$ and $G$ are both used to represent "free energy." $F$ is an older term taken from Free energy; $G$ is a more recently used symbol from the name of J. Willard Gibbs (1790–1861), one of the founders of the field of thermodynamics.

**Chemical energy** is the energy involved in putting atoms together into compounds, or in breaking down compounds to form individual atoms. Compounds such as gasoline, for example, represent considerable amounts of potential chemical energy. The burning of gasoline inside of an engine releases the potential energy of the fuel molecule.

**Electrical energy** is produced by the flow of electrons along a conductor. A battery which is charged contains potential electrical energy in the sense that it has the power to produce a flow of electrons. When the battery is hooked up, allowing the electrons to flow along a conductor, kinetic electrical energy is released.

**Mechanical energy** is energy directly involved in moving matter. The rolling of a boulder down a hill and the movement of a piston in a motor are examples of kinetic mechanical energy.

**Radiant energy** is energy which travels in waves. Two well-known examples of radiant energy are light and heat. However, the category of radiant energy also includes radio waves, infrared and ultraviolet light, X-rays, gamma rays, and cosmic rays.

**Atomic energy** is the energy within the nucleus of atoms. It is released when nuclei are split apart (nuclear fission), or when protons and neutrons are joined together to form a new nucleus (nuclear fusion). During atomic fission or fusion a certain quantity of mass is lost, i.e., is converted into energy. Thus, in proportion to the number of atoms involved, nuclear reactions release (or consume) far more energy than normal chemical reactions. Like other forms of energy, nuclear energy can also be stored as well as released.

All forms of energy listed above are interrelated and interconvertible. The conversion of one form of energy to another goes on continually. It is the basis upon which all living organisms maintain themselves. For example, kinetic radiant energy from the sun is converted into potential chemical energy in green plant cells by the food-making process (**photosynthesis**). When an animal eats the plant, it transforms the potential chemical energy of the plant substance into further kinds of chemical energy (by building its own kind of molecule) or into mechanical energy (for movement). Energy transformation is the basis of all life.

If the total amount of radiant energy transmitted to a green plant in a given period of time is measured, it will be found that only a small percentage of the total available energy is captured as potential chemical energy. The same is true of any step in the transformation from one form of energy to another. Careful recordings show that a leaf exposed to the sunlight has a higher temperature than one which is in the dark. This example illustrates the fact that *the transformation of energy is never 100% efficient*. Much of the solar energy which strikes the leaf is transformed into heat and lost to the environment. Of course, none of the energy in such transformations is actually lost in the sense of being unaccounted for. Long ago physicists formulated the very important **law of conservation of energy** or, as it came to be called, the **first law of thermo-**

**dynamics.** This law states that, during ordinary chemical or physical processes, energy is neither created nor destroyed; it is only changed in form.*

The first law of thermodynamics provides a useful framework for studying energy transformations in living systems. Some of the energy an organism derives from its food is recaptured in a useful form as potential chemical energy, while the rest is lost as heat. In one sense, the success of an organism in its struggle for existence depends on the effectiveness (or efficiency) with which it can use the energy available to it, converting as much as possible into potential chemical energy. The more energy lost as heat, the more food the organism must consume in order to accomplish the same amount of work.

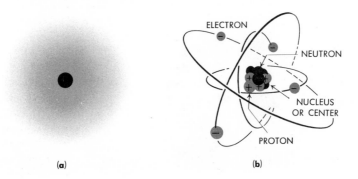

(a)                                                   (b)

FIG. 7–1    (a) The modern conception of the atom, showing the dense centrally located nucleus and the outer haze of electrons. (b) Diagrammatic sketch of the atom showing its parts. Negatively charged electrons circle the nucleus, composed of protons and neutrons. This diagram represents a working model of the atom. It does not, in any real sense, represent a ''picture'' of the atom.

**7-3
ATOMIC
STRUCTURE**

As was stated earlier, atoms are composed of three primary building blocks: protons, neutrons, and electrons. The only exception is hydrogen-1 (protium), the lightest element, which has no neutrons.

Early in this century it was suggested that atoms were composed of a small, dense, central portion—the nucleus—which in turn was surrounded by various numbers of other particles—the electrons. In 1913, Niels Bohr (1885–1962) suggested that the atom resembled a tiny solar system, with the nucleus representing the sun and the electrons the orbiting planets. Later, the nucleus was shown to contain two types of particles: protons, which are positively charged, and neutrons, which carry no charge. The nucleus was seen to carry a positive charge because of the protons. The electrons circling the nucleus were found to have a negative charge, offsetting the positive charge of the protons. Figure 7–1 shows this general conception of the atom.

* This generalization does *not* apply to atomic fission or fusion reactions, where a certain quantity of mass is converted into energy.

Electrons are now conceived of as a negatively charged haze or cloud of particles outside the positively charged nucleus of an atom. Electrons move about the nucleus at varying distances from it, traveling at a high velocity. It is the electrons that are most directly involved in chemical reactions. Electrically neutral atoms have equal numbers of electrons and protons. Under certain conditions, however, an atom can gain or lose electrons. In this way, it acquires a negative or positive charge and becomes an **ion.** When atoms interact with one another by giving up, taking on, or even sharing electrons, a chemical reaction occurs. The exchanges and interactions of electrons among atoms form the basis of chemical reactions and thus of all life processes.

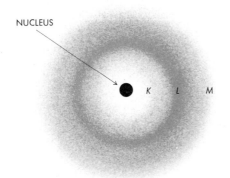

NUCLEUS

FIG. 7–2 Diagrammatic representation of an atom, showing three energy levels: *K* represents the lowest energy level, *L* the next highest, and so on. The electrons are shown as a haze since their positions can be determined only in statistical terms.

The electron cloud around the nucleus of an atom is composed of electrons in different **energy levels.** Energy levels are roughly analogous to the "planetary orbits" suggested by Niels Bohr. The term "energy level" is an expressive one, since it leads to the consideration of electrons as particles possessing certain amounts of potential energy. Electrons can be pictured as moving in specific energy levels outside the atomic nucleus (see Fig. 7–2). The electrons neither absorb nor radiate energy so long as they remain in these energy levels. However, should one or more electrons fall from the energy level which they occupy to a lower one, they will radiate a precise amount of energy. If energy is absorbed by the atom, one or more electrons may jump from a lower energy level to a high one.

The amount of energy an electron possesses depends first and foremost on the energy level it occupies in an atom. The energy levels are analogous to successively higher steps cut into a cliff. The electrons in the energy levels are analogous to rocks of equal size distributed among the various steps, from the ground up. It takes a certain amount of energy to get individual rocks to each higher level. Thus the position which each rock occupies represents a certain amount of potential energy.

An atom can have a large number of energy levels. In all atoms it is possible to recognize seven energy levels in which the electrons can be found. These seven energy levels are known as the *K, L, M, N, O, P,* and *Q* levels. Each energy level has a certain maximum number of electrons which it can hold. The seven energy levels are listed in Table 7–1 along with the maximum number of electrons actually found in the isolated, ground-state (i.e., lowest energy state) atoms. More electrons are theoretically possible than are actually found, especially in the $N, O, P$, and $Q$ levels; the maximum number of electrons theoretically possible in each energy level is given by the expression $2n^2$, where $n$ is number of the energy level ($K = 1, L = 2, M = 3$, etc.).

An attractive force exists between the negatively charged electrons and the positively charged nucleus of the atom. This force is greatest at the first energy level and falls off in successively more distant levels. This means that electrons in the outer energy levels are more easily removed from an atom than are those close to the nucleus. In general, it will take less energy to remove an electron from the $Q$ energy level than from the $P$, less energy to remove an electron from the $P$ than from the $O$ level, and so forth.

**TABLE 7–1**

| MAJOR ENERGY LEVEL | $K$ | $L$ | $M$ | $N$ | $O$ | $P$ | $Q$ |
|---|---|---|---|---|---|---|---|
| MAXIMUM NUMBER OF ELECTRONS | 2 | 8 | 18 | 32 | 32 | 18 | 2 |

Electrons, then, are attracted to the nucleus of the atom. Hence, like the rocks on the higher steps, electrons farther from the nucleus contain more potential energy.* More energy was required to get them to this greater distance from the nucleus. An electron in an outer energy level releases more energy in falling to the lowest inner level than an electron in an intermediate level does in falling to the same position. Similarly, a satellite 1000 miles from the earth's surface releases more energy in falling to the ground than does one which is 500 miles up.

Carrying this last analogy further, we see also that the satellite which is 1000 miles high could be more easily influenced than the one only 500 miles high by a gravitational field outside that of the earth. In an analogous way, electrons close to the nucleus contain less potential energy than electrons farther from the nucleus but are also less easily attracted away from the atom.

If a hypothetical atom is stripped of its electrons and is then brought back into contact with an electron source, it regains the lost electrons. In doing so the innermost energy levels are filled first. The total number of electrons an atom regains under such circumstances depends on the number of protons in the nucleus, since the number of protons must equal the number of electrons.

---

* This should not be interpreted to mean that the nucleus represents ground zero for an electron. Rather, the first orbital represents the lowest potential energy for an electron.

Under ordinary conditions, an atom of a given element has all its energy levels filled in the manner characteristic for that element. It is in an "unexcited" state. In this sense, it is analogous to a pinball machine which is not being played. All the steel balls are in the trough at the lower level of the playing board (see Fig. 7–3). Thus they possess the least possible potential energy. If energy is supplied to the balls by a player, they reach a higher energy state. In other words, they gain kinetic energy and are moved out of the tray and go up across the surface of the board.

Eventually, each ball rolls back down across the board's surface and returns to the trough. As the ball rolls, it loses a certain amount of energy. As a matter of fact, theoretically, it loses exactly the amount of energy needed to raise it that same distance. When all the balls reach the trough again, they are not necessarily in the same order as they were at the start of the game. Some may have taken a longer time to return than others. However, as long as all the positions in the trough are filled, it makes no difference whether or not the order is the same. This situation is comparable to what happens when energy is supplied to an atom. Increasing the energy of an atom does not just increase its vibrational motion. It also serves to move electrons from lower to higher energy levels. It takes a definite amount of energy to move an electron from one level to another. This process is often referred to as "exciting" an atom. "Exciting"

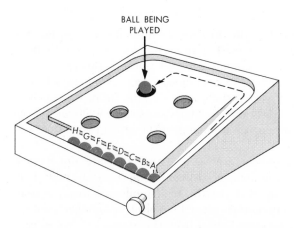

FIG. 7–3    Diagram illustrating the analogous relationship between a pinball machine and an atom in terms of excitation levels. The pinball in position A is in the lowest energy level for this particular system. When it is removed by the addition of energy from the player, an unstable situation is created, and all the other pinballs move down to fill the vacated spot. This is analogous to raising electrons to higher energy levels by supplying energy to an atom. The pinball at the highest energy level on top of the board eventually returns to the more stable level in the trough by giving off the same amount of energy as was needed to move it from the lower level.

an atom involves capturing a certain amount of energy for each upward jump of an electron. The term **electron transition** or **quantum shift** is used to describe the movement of electrons from lower to higher energy levels and vice versa.

In an atom, however, electrons can jump to a large number of energy levels, depending on the amount of energy supplied. A small but definite amount of energy will cause an electron to jump only to the next higher level. The right amount of additional energy, however, may cause the electron to jump farther, perhaps so far from the nucleus that it escapes completely from the atom to which it originally belonged (just as a satellite may escape the earth's gravitational field and go off into space). In the case of the atom, the loss of an electron gives the atom a charge of +1, since it now has one more proton than electrons. The electrically charged atom is now an ion. Loss of two electrons would give the atom a charge of +2, and so on. Ions can also be formed by the *gain* of electrons. Such ions would be negatively charged. The process of supplying energy to an atom to bring about a loss or gain of electrons is called **ionization.**

Raising electrons to a higher energy level produces some gaps below. Some of the lower energy levels are thus incomplete. These are usually filled by other electrons which fall down from higher energy levels. Just as an electron absorbs energy to jump to a higher energy level, so it releases the same amount of energy in falling back to a lower position.

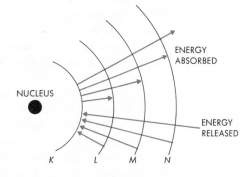

FIG. 7–4   Electron jumps occur when an atom is supplied with energy. Outward jumps may occur from any energy level to any other, depending on how much energy the electron absorbs. In the above diagram, outward jumps are shown only from the *K* level. When electrons fall inward they give off precise amounts of energy, which appears as X-rays, visible light, and other types of radiant energy.

The movement of electrons to lower energy levels may release energy as X-rays, visible light, or other wavelengths of radiation. The wavelength emitted by an electron in making a downward transition depends on the distance which it falls and the type of atom in which the transition occurs (see Fig. 7–4). To pass from the *M* to the *L* level in atoms of one element involves emitting a certain amount of energy. Going from the *L* to the *K* level in the same atom produces a different amount. Going from the *M* to the *K* level produces still a third amount, and so on. Transitions of the same sort in atoms of other elements would produce a somewhat different series of energy emissions. When light from excited atoms is passed through a spectroscope (a device which bends light through a prism), it is possible to identify many specific electron transitions by the characteristic bright lines which they produce on the spectrum. Every time an electron falls from a higher energy level to a lower one, a specific wavelength of energy is emitted. This shows up as a line on the observed spectrum. Such spectrum analysis is based on the principle that for each distance of fall (say from the $M$ to the $L$ energy level), a specific line will appear on the spectroscope. The number of electrons making any given downward transition in a given period of time (and under specified conditions) determines the brightness of the line. Furthermore, the number and kind of transitions which occur depends on the electron configuration of the atoms or molecules involved. Hence, study of such spectra gives a good clue to the electron structure of atoms, molecules, or ions.

When an electron makes a transition, it absorbs or releases distinct amounts of energy. The quantum theory, first proposed by the German physicist Max Planck in 1900, holds that energy can be described as coming in discrete packets, or **quanta.** The light emitted by an incandescent lamp, for example, consists of millions of discrete quantities of energy which, because they have some physical properties, can interact with matter. Although the reality of energy "packets" is debated among physicists, the quantum model is useful in understanding how energy can cause or result from electron transitions. If an atom absorbs one or more quanta of radiant energy, electrons at certain energy levels jump to a higher level. The energy is thus temporarily captured by the atom. It may then be released in ways which will allow electrons in other atoms to make transitions also. Thus energy can be transferred among groups of atoms by the movement of electrons from one energy level in one atom to a different energy level in another.

Under ordinary conditions, atoms are often combined with other atoms. Such a combination of two or more atoms is called a **molecule.** When atoms unite to form molecules, the energy levels of the individual atoms interact to form **molecular energy levels.** Electron transitions are possible in the energy levels of molecules, just as they are among energy levels of individual atoms. When a molecule of chlorophyll, for example, absorbs quanta of light energy from the sun, electrons are raised to higher energy levels. The electrons are temporarily lost to the molecule as a whole. But when the electrons make the downward transitions, they release the same amount of energy they absorbed. This energy is captured by the plant cell and used to power certain chemical reactions during photosynthesis.

The atoms making up a molecule are held together by **chemical bonds.** A chemical bond is not a physical structure. It is simply an energy relationship between atoms which holds them together in a molecule. The chemical bond which unites the atoms can therefore be measured in units of energy. The units of energy are frequently expressed as kilocalories (kcal)* of potential energy per mole of compound.† Thus kilocalories can be used to compare the potential energy that the chemical bonds of various chemical compounds contain.

To understand how chemical bonds are formed, consider the interaction of atoms A and B to form molecule AB. First, A and B must come close enough together for their electron clouds to overlap; rearrangements of electrons between the two atoms is the basis for the formation of chemical bonds. As A and B approach each other, however, they exhibit mutual repulsion as the result of their negatively-charged electron clouds (like charges repel, unlike attract). We have to do work (put in energy) to push the atoms still closer together. It is not until the atoms are forced so close together that an electron from one is attracted to the positively-charged nucleus of the other that the rearrangements which make the two atoms have a net attraction for each other can take place. If energy is now supplied to move the electron back where it was in the first place, the repulsion between the atoms is enough to force them apart with an appreciable velocity. This velocity corresponds to an energy of motion which is equal to the energy initially expended in forcing the atoms together.

All interactions between atoms to make or break chemical bonds involve the exchange of energy. To break any chemical bond, a certain input of energy (called dissociation energy) is required to overcome the stable state and move the atoms far enough apart so that their mutual repulsion again takes over and sends them on their opposite ways. This energy varies from one type of atom to another. For example, it takes a large amount of energy (104.2 kcal/mole) to break hydrogen-to-hydrogen bonds, but a smaller amount (50.9 kcal/mole) to break sulfur-to-sulfur bonds.

The above description does not refer to the overall, or net, energy exchange during chemical reactions, but only to the part leading from the top of the energy hill downward toward stable bond formation. It may require more or less energy than is released in this downhill phase to get the reacting molecules to the top of the rise. Consideration of the overall energy changes during chemical reactions will be reserved for Section 7–8.

The overlapping of electron clouds causes rearrangement of electrons in the outermost energy level of each atom. This rearrangement involves one of two possibilities: (1) one atom will give up one or more of its electrons to the other or (2) each atom will share one or more electrons with the other. In either case, the

---

* A calorie is the amount of heat energy required to raise the temperature of one gram of water (at 15°C) one centigrade degree. A kilocalorie would thus be the amount of heat required to raise the temperature of 1000 grams of water the same amount. In biology, the kilocalorie is often written as Calorie, with the first letter capitalized to distinguish it from the smaller physical calorie used by physical scientists.

† A mole is a measure of the number of particles (molecules, ions, etc.) of any substance in a given sample of that substance. The number of particles per mole is a multiple of the same constant number for all substances. This constant number, called Avogadro's number, is $6.024 \times 10^{23}$ particles. Thus one mole of sodium chloride contains $1 \times 6.024 \times 10^{23}$ sodium ions and $1 \times 6.024 \times 10^{23}$ chloride ions. Two moles of sodium chloride contain $2 \times 6.024 \times 10^{23}$ sodium ions and $2 \times 6.024 \times 10^{23}$ chloride ions.

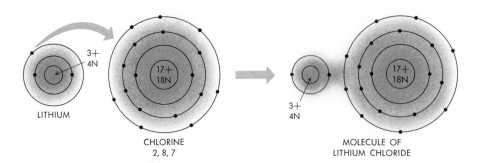

FIG. 7–5    The formation of lithium chloride.

total electric charge of one atom may be either less positive or more positive than that of the other.

The interaction between outer electrons is the result of a process in which each atom approaches a stable outer electron configuration. This process requires closer examination. It is central to an understanding of current thinking about the formation of a chemical bond.

With the exception of the $K$ or innermost energy level, a stable outer electron configuration is achieved with eight electrons. The atoms of any element with eight outer electrons are stable. Neon, argon, krypton, xenon, and radon are all examples of such elements.* Such atoms do not generally react with other atoms. Most atoms have fewer than eight electrons in their outer energy level. These atoms tend to reach the stable configuration by giving up, taking on, or sharing electrons. The driving force behind any chemical reaction originates in the process by which the atoms involved attain a stable outer energy level.

Two major types of chemical bonds are found in chemical compounds. The distinction between the two is based on the way in which the stable condition of the outer energy levels is reached.

The first type of chemical bond, found most frequently in inorganic compounds, is the **ionic** or **electrovalent** bond. In the formation of this type of bond, one atom gives up its outermost electrons to one or more other atoms. When this occurs, the outermost energy level of each atom becomes more stable. The formation of lithium chloride from the elements lithium and chlorine is an example of ionic bonding (see Fig. 7–5).

The electron configuration for chlorine, counted from the nucleus outward, is 2, 8, and 7. Atoms of lithium have a single electron in the $L$ level. Lithium

---

* Until recently, it was thought that none of these elements formed any compounds. For this reason they were known as "inert" gases. Their lack of chemical activity is due to the fact that they have a stable electron configuration in their energy levels. It is now known that certain compounds, such as xenon tetrafluoride, can be formed under special conditions.

can reach stability by giving up its one *L* electron to chlorine. This gives the chlorine atom a total of eight electrons in its *M* level—which represents stability for this element. Both atoms now have a stable electron configuration in their outer energy levels.

When lithium gives up its electron, the atom has one less negative charge. Hence it is positively charged (+1). Chlorine, by accepting an electron, now has one more negative charge than positive charges. Thus it is negatively charged (−1). Since opposite charges attract, the positively charged lithium atom and the negatively charged chlorine atom attract each other. This attraction holds the two atoms together. In this way a molecule of lithium chloride, LiCl, is formed.

*There is no 100% ionic bond.* Though one atom tends to give its electrons to another, this "handing over" is not complete. The donated electron may still occasionally circle the nucleus of the donor atom.

In the formation of ionic bonds, which atoms will give up electrons and which will receive them? In general, those atoms with fewer than four electrons in the outer energy level tend to lose electrons. Those with more than four tend to gain electrons. Atoms such as sodium, potassium, hydrogen, calcium, and iron possess three or fewer outer electrons. Thus all of these atoms tend to give up electrons. Atoms such as oxygen, chlorine, sulfur, and iodine need one or two electrons to complete their outer energy levels. Thus these atoms tend to take on electrons.

What about an atom such as carbon, which has four electrons in its outer energy level? Does such an atom tend to give up or take on electrons when combining with other atoms?

Carbon combines with atoms of many other elements by forming **covalent** chemical bonds, a sort of "compromise" between the giving up and the taking on of one or more pairs of electrons between atoms. In such bonding, atoms combine by undergoing a rearrangement of electrons in their outer energy levels. Neither atom loses its electrons completely. Instead, the electrons are shared and may circle the nucleus of any atom in the molecule.

The formation of a molecule of the gas methane illustrates the principle of covalent bonding. Under suitable conditions carbon reacts with hydrogen to form molecules of methane. Four atoms of hydrogen react with each atom of carbon to produce a symmetrical molecule, $CH_4$:

$$\begin{array}{c} H \\ | \\ H-C-H. \\ | \\ H \end{array}$$

Each line between the carbon atom and each hydrogen atom represents a single pair of shared electrons. The pair consists of one electron from the carbon atom and one from the hydrogen atom. This may be shown more clearly by

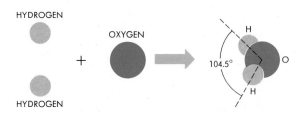

FIG. 7–6    The formation of water from hydrogen and oxygen. Since the outer electron level of oxygen contains only six electrons and each hydrogen has only one electron to donate, two hydrogen atoms are required to satisfy the stability requirements of the oxygen.

writing the molecular formula in the following manner:

$$\begin{array}{c} \text{H} \\ \text{ox} \\ \text{H} \; \text{\char"D7}_\text{\char"B0} \; \text{C} \; {}^\text{\char"B0}_\text{\char"D7} \; \text{H.} \\ \text{ox} \\ \text{H} \end{array}$$

The open dots represent the outer electrons originally in the $L$ energy level of carbon. The crosses represent the electrons originally in the $K$ level of each hydrogen atom.

Consider why this type of bonding takes place. The carbon atom has four electrons in its outer energy level. To attain stability, carbon needs eight electrons. Each hydrogen atom has one electron in its $K$ level. Hydrogen can reach stability by either losing or gaining one electron. In the formation of the covalent bond between carbon and hydrogen, the electrons in the outer energy levels of each atom circle the nuclei of both hydrogen and carbon. As a result, each of the four hydrogen atoms has its own electron plus one electron from the carbon to circle its nucleus. In turn, the carbon atom has not only its own four electrons but also one from each of the hydrogen atoms to circle its nucleus. This completes the requirements for stability in the outer energy levels of both atoms. It is the sharing of these outer electrons that produces the covalent chemical bond.

When three or more atoms combine to form a molecule, a definite and predictable geometric relationship is established between the atoms involved. In other words, the molecule takes on a definite shape. For example, an angle of 104.5° is formed between the two hydrogen atoms and one oxygen atom of a water molecule (Fig. 7–6). Such angles are called **bond angles.** By certain physical techniques, bond angles can be accurately measured. The determination of bond angles allows the scientist to establish the relative positions of atoms in a molecule.

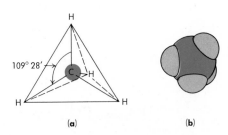

FIG. 7–7    Two representations of the geometry of a molecule of methane ($CH_4$). (a) A diagram of the tetrahedral structure, showing the central carbon surrounded by four hydrogens all at equal distances from the carbon and from each other. (b) A space-filling model of methane showing the actual volumes and geometric relations of the atoms. The green atom in the center is carbon. The fourth hydrogen is partly hidden on the other side of the molecule.

The way in which one molecule reacts with another depends in part on the shape of each molecule. The geometric configuration of water molecules (with a molecular weight of only 18) is crucial to the properties of water which make life possible (polarity, ability to form ice crystals, cohesiveness, etc.). Similarly, the chemical characteristics of some proteins (with molecular weights in the millions) may be completely changed by changing the physical shape of one small part of the molecule.

For the most part, molecules are represented in diagrams as if they were flat, two-dimensional structures. In reality, they are three-dimensional, having depth in addition to length and breadth. For example, the organic compound methane, shown in a face-on view on page 140, actually forms a solid, four-sided pyramid known as a tetrahedron (Fig. 7–7a). The bond angles between the four hydrogen atoms, rather than 90°, are actually 109°28′. It is therefore desirable to show the three-dimensional structure with a "space-filling" model (Fig. 7–7b). Here the space occupied by the atoms, as well as their orientation within the molecule, is taken into consideration.

The concepts of molecular configuration and bond angles play a role in explaining chemical reactions between molecules. These concepts will be important in later considerations of large molecules found in living organisms.

**7-4**
**THE POLARITY OF**
**MOLECULES**

A frequent consequence of the geometric shapes of molecules is a distinct separation of electric charge. This means that one portion of a molecule is positive or negative in relation to another portion of the same molecule. When such an uneven distribution of charge occurs, the molecule is said to exhibit **polarity.** The molecule has a positive and a negative end, separated from each other like the poles of a bar magnet. The charge results because the nuclei of individual atoms in the molecule hold more electrons close to them than do the nuclei of other atoms in the same molecule. Thus the area surrounding these electron-

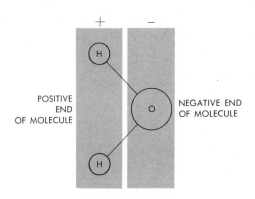

POSITIVE
END
OF MOLECULE

NEGATIVE END
OF MOLECULE

FIG. 7–8   The polarity of a water molecule is indicated in this highly schematic diagram.

attracting nuclei becomes negatively charged, while the area around the "deprived" nuclei becomes positively charged.

The water molecule illustrates this point. Although, as a whole, the water molecule is electrically neutral, it does have a positive and a negative end (Fig. 7–8). The geometric configuration of the molecule places both hydrogen atoms at one end. The nucleus of the oxygen atom attracts electrons more than the nuclei of the hydrogen atoms. This results in two positively charged regions on one end of the molecule and a single negatively charged region on the other. The result is a molecule with a positive and a negative end, or two poles; the molecule is therefore polar.

Molecular polarity is significant to the biological sciences in two main areas. First, polar molecules tend to become oriented in precise spatial patterns with respect to other molecules (either polar or nonpolar). Because of this, polar molecules are important in certain structural elements of organisms. For example, molecules of fatty acids, found in all living matter, are composed of a nonpolar carbon chain with a polar carbon-oxygen (carboxyl) group (COOH) at one end. When placed in water, the polar ends of the fatty acid molecules are attracted to water molecules, also polar. The nonpolar carbon chains are at the same time repelled by the water. As a result, fatty acid molecules are oriented on the water's surface (Fig. 7–9). Of particular importance to living things is the orientation of **phospholipid** molecules each of which is a combination of a fat molecule with a phosphate group. Phospholipids are among the most important parts of cell membranes. They tend to become oriented on surface or boundary regions in a manner similar to fatty acids on water. It is partly in this way that cell membranes assume their distinct structure.

Second, polarity is important in understanding both the geometry and the chemical characteristics of large molecules such as proteins or nucleic acids. Proteins are so large they may possess a number of polar groups on one molecule. Polar groups are groups of atoms which as a unit bear a positive or negative charge. Polarity thus tends to bring small molecules, or specific regions of large molecules, into definite geometric relation with each other. In this way, the

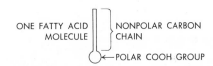

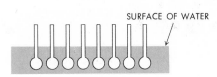

FIG. 7–9   Polar molecules, such as fatty acids, tend to orient themselves in respect to other polar molecules.  Here the molecules of a fatty acid line up in a specific fashion on the surface of water.  The COOH groups are in the water (also polar) and the carbon chains protrude above the surface.

chemical bonding between individual molecules or between specific regions on the same molecule is brought about more easily.

In living organisms, one of the most common types of chemical bond produced by polar attraction is the **hydrogen bond.**  Hydrogen bonds are produced by the electrostatic attraction between positively charged hydrogen atoms (protons) on one part of a molecule and negatively charged atoms of oxygen or nitrogen on the same or another molecule.  The oxygen and nitrogen atoms tend to be negatively charged because their electrons are held closer to the nuclei and are shared less easily.  Because the hydrogen bond occurs between polar regions of a molecule it is, like all polar attractions, relatively weak.

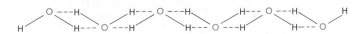

FIG. 7–10   Water serves as a good example of the polar orientation of molecules which results specifically in hydrogen bonding.  Note that molecular shape is an important factor.

A simple example of hydrogen bonding can be seen between water molecules. The hydrogen atoms of one water molecule form a hydrogen bond with the oxygen atom of the adjacent molecule (Fig. 7–10).

At room temperature, the compound hydrogen chloride (HCl) is a gas.  If molecules of this gas are dissolved in water, the hydrogen is separated from the chlorine.  The separation or ionization occurs in such a way that the hydrogen atom does not take back the electron which it loaned to chlorine in forming the bond.  Thus the hydrogen atom, now a hydrogen ion or simply one proton, bears a charge of $+1$.  The chlorine retains the extra electron which it received from the hydrogen atom.  Since it has one more electron than protons, the chlorine bears a negative charge of $-1$ and is thus a chloride ion.  The hydrogen ion is written as $H^+$, and chloride ion as $Cl^-$.

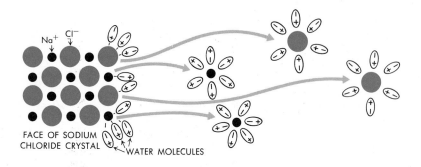

FIG. 7–11    A representation of the dissolving of sodium chloride in water. The negative ends of the polar water molecules are attracted to the positive sodium ions, and pull them off the crystal lattice. The positive ends of the water molecules are attracted to the negative chloride ions, and pull them off. As indicated, each sodium and chloride ion is probably surrounded by at least six water molecules.

Recall that ions are formed whenever an atom loses or gains electrons. The dissolving of sodium chloride in water results in a separation, or **dissociation,** of the sodium and chloride ions (see Fig. 7–11). Since sodium chloride is an ionic compound, its component atoms are already in the ion state. Molecular substances, on the other hand, such as hydrogen chloride, lithium chloride, and acids, undergo ionization when entering into solution. As soon as the water is removed, the oppositely charged particles recombine to form the same molecules or **ion pairs.** The molecule of lithium chloride shown in Fig. 7–5 is an example of an ion pair.

The process of ionization can be represented by an ionization equation. In chemical language, an equation indicates what goes into and what comes out of a certain reaction. For example, the ionization equation for HCl, given below, indicates that one molecule of this compound yields, upon ionization, a positively charged hydrogen ion ($H^+$) and a negatively charged chloride ion ($Cl^-$):

$$HCl \longrightarrow H^+ + Cl^-.$$

Similarly, the dissociation of sodium chloride (table salt) gives

$$NaCl \longrightarrow Na^+ + Cl^-.$$

When calcium chloride ionizes, it produces two chloride ions for every ion of calcium:

$$CaCl_2 \longrightarrow Ca^{++} + 2Cl^-.$$

This equation tells us several things. First, it shows that a molecule of calcium chloride consists of one atom of calcium and two atoms of chlorine. The subscript after the symbol for any atom indicates the number of atoms of that element in the molecule. Second, in writing the ionization equation for this compound, the two atoms of chlorine must be accounted for by showing that there are two chloride ions in the solution. To indicate that these two ions do occur, a 2 is placed in front of the $Cl^-$. The equation is now balanced. Each of the atoms on the left side of the equation is accounted for on the right.

When some compounds ionize, one of the products is a **complex ion.** Complex ions are associations of two or more atoms which bear an overall positive or negative charge. They are thus collections of two or more atoms which act as a single ion. For example, the ionization of sulfuric acid yields hydrogen ions and a sulfate ion:

$$H_2SO_4 \longrightarrow 2H^+ + SO_4^=.$$
(sulfate ion)

The sulfate ion is composed of one atom of sulfur and four atoms of oxygen. These five atoms have an overall electric charge of $-2$.

Molecules of calcium nitrate contain two nitrate ions bonded to one calcium atom. They are written as

$$Ca(NO_3)_2.$$

Aluminum sulfate, which contains three sulfate ions bonded to two aluminum atoms, is written as

$$Al_2(SO_4)_3.$$

The parentheses enclose the complex ion itself. The subscript number after the parentheses indicates the number of radical groups contained in the molecule.

Not all compounds which ionize in water do so with equal readiness. In all the ionization equations listed above, nearly 100% of the molecules dissociate to release the appropriate ions. However, water molecules ionize only very slightly, so that the reaction

$$H_2O \longrightarrow H^+ + OH^-$$
(hydroxide ion)

occurs in approximately one out of every 554 million molecules.

Carbonic acid ionizes more than water, but still only about 1% of the molecules dissociate:

$$H_2CO_3 \longrightarrow H^+ + HCO_{3-}$$
(bicarbonate ion)

Solubility, the degree to which a molecule will enter into solution, depends on several characteristics of the molecule, such as the presence or absence of charged or uncharged regions of the molecule, and the types of chemical bonds holding the atoms in the molecule together. Most molecules bound by ionic bonds are soluble as are some with covalent bonds. Molecules demonstrating polarity also tend to be soluble. Solubility simply means that the molecules separate from each other when placed in a solvent.

Atoms held together by ionic bonds can separate more easily because one atom has given up electrons while another has accepted them. In this way, the outer energy level of each atom has been satisfied. Thus, when such molecules dissociate, no further exchange of electrons is required. Dissociation in this case merely involves overcoming the electrostatic attraction between positive and negative particles. The action of water molecules accomplishes this dissociation (see Fig. 7–11).

In covalent bonds, the outer energy level of each atom is satisfied only as long as the shared electrons revolve about both nuclei. For this to be possible, the atoms must remain close together. It is very difficult to separate one from another if, in so doing, the atoms are forced to assume unstable outer electron configurations. For this reason water molecules generally cannot force covalently bonded atoms apart. Such molecules thus fail to show ionization in water.

**7–6
OXIDATION AND
REDUCTION:
REDOX REACTIONS**

The process of losing electrons is called **oxidation;** the atom which loses electrons is said to be **oxidized.** The process of gaining electrons is called **reduction;** the atom which gains electrons is said to be **reduced.**

The process of oxidation does not necessarily involve the element oxygen. The name "oxidation" was originally derived from the class of reactions involving the combination of various elements (mostly metals) with oxygen. Now, however, the term oxidation is used more broadly to refer to any loss of electrons in a chemical reaction, whether or not oxygen is involved.

Oxidation and reduction are useful terms when employed to describe what happens when two atoms, such as sodium and chlorine, combine to form a compound—in this instance, sodium chloride. Sodium atoms undergo a change from a neutral to an electrically charged condition (from 0 to +1) by losing an electron. Chlorine goes from neutral to a negatively charged condition (0 to −1) by gaining an electron. The sodium is thus oxidized and the chlorine reduced. Thus the formation of ionic chemical bonds often (though not always) involves an oxidation-reduction reaction.

By contributing electrons which reduce chlorine, sodium acts as a **reducing agent.** By accepting electrons from sodium, chlorine acts as an **oxidizing agent.** An oxidizing agent, then, is one which accepts electrons, while a reducing agent is one which gives up electrons.

When most biological molecules are oxidized, electrons are removed in combination with protons, rather than alone. In other words, a whole hydrogen atom, in the form of one proton and one electron, is removed during biological oxidation. Thus biological oxidation is frequently associated with hydrogen removal, or "hydrogen transfer," as it is sometimes called. This fact should not obscure the important point that the process is still one of oxidation, i.e., the loss of electrons.

No one knows exactly what causes atoms or molecules to interact during a chemical reaction. As a model hypothesis, however, the collision theory has been of much value in formalizing our ideas about how reactions occur. This hypothesis offers an explanation of how atoms and molecules actually interact, and leads to accurate predictions. It also helps to explain how factors such as temperature, concentration of reactants, and catalysts affect reaction rates.

The collision theory is derived from the idea that all atoms, molecules, and ions in any system are in constant motion. For any particle to interact chemically with another, both must first come into contact so that electron exchanges or rearrangements are possible. The collision of any two particles is considered to be a completely random event. If two negatively charged particles approach each other, each will mutually repel the other so that direct collision is not likely. The same will be true of two positive particles. If a positive and a negative particle approach each other, however, a collision is more likely. Furthermore, this collision may be successful in the sense that it produces an interaction and hence a chemical change.

Not every collision between oppositely charged particles will produce a chemical interaction. Several other factors are involved. First, the average velocity of the particles determines what percentage of collisions will be successful for any given kind of reactants. The more rapidly the particles travel, the more likely it is that they will yield successful collisions.

Second, particles of each element or compound have their own minimum energy requirements for successful interaction. Imagine a system in which molecules of A and B interact to produce C and D. For any collision between A and B to produce a reaction, each molecule must have a certain minimum kinetic energy. This energy is usually referred to in terms of particle velocity. Greater kinetic energy of a particle means greater velocity. Greater velocity means greater probability that a collision will be successful. If the average kinetic energy of a system is increased, the number of successful collisions will also generally be increased.

Third, molecular geometry plays a role in determining whether or not a collision is successful. If a molecule collides with an atom or another molecule in such a way that the reactive portion of the molecule is not exposed to the other particle, no reaction will occur. This is true in spite of the fact that the particles may have possessed the proper amount of kinetic energy. For this reason, molecular geometry, though a factor in any chemical reaction, is particularly important in reactions between very large molecules. Here, the relative position of two colliding molecules is crucial to successful interaction. Living systems have developed means of holding large molecules in specific positions which aid in exposing the reactive portion of the molecule. This is one of the main functions of organic catalysts, or enzymes.

The minimum kinetic energy required by any system of particles for successful chemical reaction is known as the **activation energy**. Activation energy is a characteristic of any reacting chemical system. If the average energy of the particles is below this minimum, the reaction will proceed slowly or not at all. If the average is above the minimum, the reaction will proceed more rapidly.

Not all particles are traveling at the same speed within a chemical system. For instance, some of the particles may have almost no velocity, perhaps because they have just collided head-on with a particle of similar charge traveling at the same speed. Others may be moving so rapidly that they pass out of the system completely.

The average velocity of the particles in this system would be expected to lie somewhere between these two extremes. If we plot a graph comparing velocity with the number of particles moving at each velocity, we should get a normal distribution curve. This means that the largest number of particles have velocities somewhere around the average. Such a graph is shown in Fig. 7–12. The dotted line down the center represents the average velocity. The solid line to the right indicates the minimum energy or velocity requirement for reaction. All particles to the left of this line do not have this energy of activation. Therefore, these particles cannot be expected to react. All particles to the right of this line have velocities greater than the activation energy. They can be expected to produce successful collisions. This graph emphasizes the fact that *chemical interaction between atoms or molecules can be discussed only in terms of probability.* The rate of a chemical reaction is influenced by factors which increase or decrease the probability that collisions between particles will be successful.

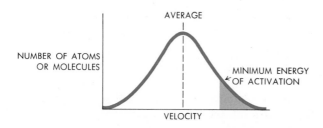

FIG. 7–12  A bell-shaped curve indicates the distribution of velocities among a large group of atoms or molecules. The largest number of particles show average velocity. Some particles have a low velocity (at extreme left of horizontal axis) while some have a very high velocity (at right). The hatched area represents those particles which have enough activation energy to enter into chemical combination.

## 7-8 FREE ENERGY EXCHANGE AND CHEMICAL REACTIONS

All chemical reactions involve an exchange of free energy. On the basis of these exchanges, chemical reactions can be divided into two classes. Those reactions which absorb more energy than they release are called **endergonic** reactions. Those which release more free energy than they absorb are called **exergonic** reactions.

Endergonic and exergonic reactions can be compared in terms of the energy hill analogy. Endergonic reactions occur in an uphill direction. Exergonic reactions occur in a downhill direction. This means that, like rolling a stone uphill, endergonic reactions require an input of free energy. And, like a stone rolling downhill, exergonic reactions release free energy (see Fig. 7–13).

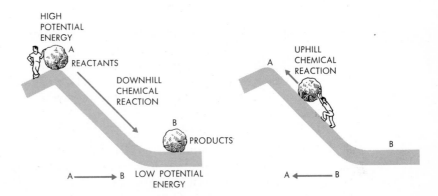

FIG. 7–13 In this analogy, a free energy-releasing chemical reaction is compared to a stone rolling down a hill. When the stone has reached the bottom, it has less potential energy than when at the top. To go in the reverse direction, i.e., back up the hill, the stone will have to absorb the same amount of energy that it released while rolling down. Under natural conditions, absorbing this amount of energy is quite unlikely. Only very rarely, if at all, would a stone ever get back to the top. The same is true of chemical reactions which release large amounts of energy. They are considered to be irreversible. Unless energy is supplied from the outside, the reverse reaction will not occur.

As was pointed out earlier, the energy which is available in any particular chemical system for doing useful work is known as free energy $(G)$. If a net change in free energy occurs during a chemical reaction, the system has either more or less free energy after the reaction than before. An exergonic reaction always involves the loss of free energy. We can say that such a system shows negative free-energy change, $-\Delta G$, where $\Delta$ means "change." An endergonic reaction takes in free energy. Thus it shows an increase in free energy, $+\Delta G$. It is possible, therefore, to show whether a given reaction involves an overall increase or decrease in free energy simply by putting the symbol $-$ or $+$ after the equation.

Like the energy in chemical bonds, free energy exchange in reactions is measured in kilocalories per mole of reactant. For example, in the reaction between hydrogen and oxygen to produce water, we find

$$H_2 + \tfrac{1}{2}O_2 \longrightarrow H_2O,^* \qquad \Delta G = -56.56 \text{ kcal/mole}. \qquad (7\text{–}1)$$

---

* In equations where energy equivalents are given, the numbers before each molecule refer to numbers of moles. The one-half $O_2$ thus means one-half mole of oxygen.

The reaction has a negative $\Delta G$, and hence is one which gives off energy. The more negative the value for $\Delta G$, the more energy the reaction releases. Consider the reaction of the sugar glucose and oxygen which, in several steps, releases the energy for many life processes. These steps can be summarized in the following equation:

$$C_6H_{12}O_6 + 6O_2 + 6H_2O \longrightarrow 6CO_2 \uparrow + 12H_2O, \qquad \Delta G = -680 \text{ kcal/mole.} \qquad (7\text{–}2)$$

This overall reaction releases a great deal more energy than the reaction shown in Eq. (7–1).

In a similar manner, the numerical value for reactions with a positive $\Delta G$ indicates how much energy the reaction requires. In Eq. (7–3), iodine reacts with hydrogen to form the compound hydrogen iodide:

$$\tfrac{1}{2}I_2 + \tfrac{1}{2}H_2 \longrightarrow HI, \qquad \Delta G = +0.315 \text{ kcal/mole.} \qquad (7\text{–}3)$$

This reaction requires a small amount of energy, as shown by the low positive value for $\Delta G$. On the other hand, the process of photosynthesis, in which green plants produce carbohydrates from carbon dioxide and water, requires a large intake of energy. This energy is supplied by light. The overall process can be written as

$$6CO_2 + 12H_2O \longrightarrow C_6H_{12}O_6 + 6H_2O + 6O_2 \uparrow, \qquad \Delta G = +686 \text{ kcal/mole.} \qquad (7\text{–}4)$$

Knowing the value of $\Delta G$ makes it possible to compare the amounts of energy which various reactions absorb or release.

All exergonic reactions show an overall loss of free energy. Many of these same reactions, however, require an energy input to get them started. If left to themselves, many reactants will never show any chemical activity. However, if the right amount of energy is supplied, the reaction begins. It then goes to completion without the addition of more energy from the outside.

How can this be explained? In such chemical systems, the reactants have relatively high activation energies. The addition of energy gets a larger percentage of particles in the system up to the required kinetic energy. In absorbing this energy, the particle becomes activated. When particles are in an activated state, a successful reaction is much more probable.

A specific example will clarify this point. Formic acid, HCOOH, is the pain-causing substance in wasp and bee stings. Under certain conditions, formic acid decomposes into carbon monoxide (CO) and water, with a slightly positive $\Delta G$. However, for this reaction to occur, a formic acid molecule must first absorb enough energy to become activated. In being activated, the molecule undergoes a rearrangement of one hydrogen atom. The molecular structure is changed, and along with it the stability of the whole molecule. It splits into two parts, carbon monoxide and water:

$$HCOOH \longrightarrow CO + H_2O. \qquad (7\text{–}5)$$

Energy exchanges in chemical systems are often given on a graph, which shows the changes in potential energy during the course of reaction. These changes are then compared with the time it takes the reaction to go to completion. Such a graph for the formic acid reaction is shown in Fig. 7–14.

Analysis of this graph shows some important things about this chemical reaction. The graph describes the changes in energy for one molecule as that molecule undergoes the decomposition reaction shown in Eq. (7–5). Before reacting, an individual molecule is in a relatively low energy state. By absorbing energy, this molecule passes to a higher potential-energy level. It is now in an activated state. The appropriate rearrangement occurs, and the product molecules are formed. Note that the product molecules are at a slightly higher energy state than the original molecule of formic acid. This indicates that the overall reaction absorbed a small amount of energy. The reaction is endergonic.

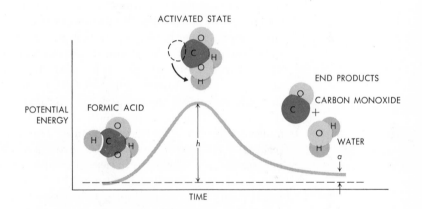

FIG. 7–14   Changes in potential energy during the decomposition of formic acid. The original molecule, to the left, is in a relatively low energy state. By collision with another molecule of high kinetic energy, this molecule becomes activated. The potential energy of such an activated molecule is greater. During activation, a molecular arrangement occurs and the molecule splits. The end products, carbon monoxide and water, are at a higher energy state than the original molecule, $a$ on the graph. Distance $h$ represents the height of the energy barrier.

The distance $h$ on the graph indicates the energy of activation for this chemical system. The height of the graph line can thus be considered an **energy barrier:** a "hill" over which the molecule has to climb before it can roll down the other side to completion. After absorbing the required activation energy the reaction proceeds spontaneously, just as a stone rolls down a hill once it is pushed over a rise at the top. Figure 7–15 shows an energy diagram for a spontaneous exergonic reaction. The products of exergonic reactions are always at lower potential-energy states than the reactants.

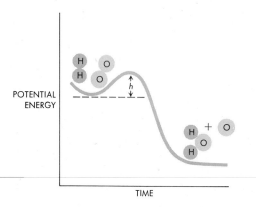

POTENTIAL
ENERGY

TIME

FIG. 7–15   A spontaneous exergonic reaction, the formation of water from $H_2$ and $O_2$. The end products are at a lower energy state than the two starting reactants, indicating that the reaction releases energy. This reaction has a small energy barrier, as indicated by the size of $h$.

Under standard conditions* hydrogen and oxygen exist together in a single container without the least indication of reacting to produce water. The molecules simply do not have the necessary energy of activation. However, if a small electric spark is introduced into the chamber, an explosive reaction takes place. Thus hydrogen and oxygen react quickly to form water if given the necessary push to get them started. The fact that a spark is all that is needed to provide this push shows that the energy barrier for this reaction is not very high. Passing the spark through hydrogen and oxygen provides enough energy to put some molecules of each in the activated state. The activated molecules spontaneously react to form molecules of water. From Eq. (7–1) we see that this reaction releases energy. The energy released from one reaction is enough to get several other molecules of each element over the energy barrier. The spark provides an initial push. The rest of the reaction occurs by a chain-reaction effect, just as a house of cards collapses when one card is disturbed.

How does the energy involved in chemical reactions relate to the formation and breaking of chemical bonds? In exergonic reactions, the end products are at a lower energy state than the reactants; in endergonic reactions, the end products are at a higher energy state. Some exergonic reactions result in the formation of chemical bonds, while others result in the breaking of bonds. There is no necessary correspondence between exergonic reactions and the breaking of bonds, and between endergonic reactions and the building of bonds. However, quite frequently those reactions which result in the building or synthesis of a large molecule from smaller components are, indeed, endergonic, while those which result in the breaking down of larger molecules into smaller parts are exergonic.

As we saw in Section 7–3, the fact that activated atoms always release a certain amount of energy in the formation of chemical bonds does not mean that

---

* *Standard conditions* means standard temperature (25° on the celsius or centigrade scale) and one atmosphere of pressure (760 millimeters of mercury).

all chemical reactions in which bonds are formed show an overall release of energy. The net energy exchange of any reaction (i.e., whether the reaction as a whole is exergonic or endergonic) is a result of the energy required to activate the atoms (move them to the top of the rise), combined with the energy released in attaining stability. If more energy is required to move the reacting atoms to the top of the rise than is released as the atoms combine to form a molecule, then the reaction as a whole will be *endergonic*. If less energy is required, then the reaction as a whole will be *exergonic*. Thus, every particular set of possible reactants will have its own energy characteristics. It is important to remember, however, that net energy exchange must always account for both the energy of activation necessary to drive the two (or more) atoms close enough together to interact, and the energy released as the atoms interact in the formation of chemical bonds.

**7-9
RATES OF
REACTION**

The rate of any chemical reaction is defined as *the amount of reaction in a given period of time*. The amount of reaction is generally measured in terms of the change in concentration of reactants or products. The basic relationship between amount of reaction and time can be expressed as a word equation:

$$\text{RATE OF REACTION} = \frac{\text{CHANGE IN CONCENTRATION}}{\text{CHANGE IN TIME}}. \tag{7-6}$$

The concept of rate in chemical reactions is vital to an understanding of chemical equilibrium. In addition, knowledge about reaction rates allows a clearer understanding of the mechanisms by which a particular chemical process occurs. Under given conditions, the rate of a reaction is a predictable characteristic of chemical systems. Such systems can thus be described in terms of reaction rates as well as direction or energy exchange.

A specific example will help in understanding the concept of rate as it applies to chemical reactions. Consider the reaction below, where molecules of A and B combine to yield the product C + D:

$$A + B \rightarrow C + D. \tag{7-7}$$

If we begin with molecules of A and B only, the rate of reaction at the outset is very high. Rate in this case can be measured in terms of how rapidly the reactant molecules A and B disappear in specific units of time. If we were to stop the reaction every thirty seconds and determine the amount of A and B present, these data would, plotted on a graph, give a line like that shown in Fig. 7–16(a).

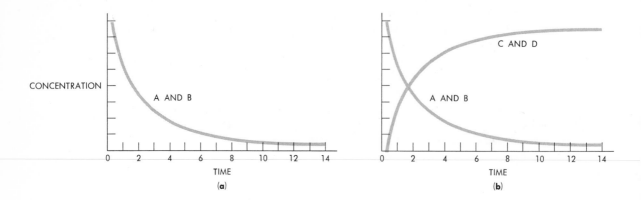

FIG. 7–16    Changes in concentration of reactants A and B and products C and D during the course of a chemical reaction. This relationship between change of concentration and time indicates the rate of reaction. Graph (a) shows only change in concentration of reactants. Graph (b) also shows the change in concentration of products. Change in concentration of either reactants or products is most rapid during the first few minutes of reaction.

We can see that the rate at which A and B disappear from solution changes with time. For instance, the concentration of A and B decreases most rapidly in the first two minutes and begins to level off about the sixth minute. By the ninth minute nearly all of A and B have been used up in the reaction. At this point, the rate at which A and B combine to yield C and D is almost zero.

If we also plot the rate of appearance of products C and D in this reaction, a curve is obtained which is just the opposite of that for the disappearance of A and B, as shown in Fig. 7–16(b). This is not surprising, since the rate at which C and D appear depends directly on the rate at which A and B interact.

The molecular explanation for the change in rate of chemical reactions goes back to the collision theory. The rate at which a chemical reaction progresses toward completion depends on the number of effective collisions between reacting molecules or atoms. This number is determined for any given reaction by the concentration of reactants. The more molecules or atoms of reactants, the greater the number of effective collisions.

During the course of any chemical reaction in a closed system the concentration of reactants decreases as the chance of collision between a molecule of A and a molecule of B decreases. At the same time, the concentration of product molecules C and D is increasing. This means that collisions between C and D molecules will become more frequent. This increase in the frequency of collisions has effects on the course of chemical reactions which will be discussed in Sections 7–10 and 7–11.

There are many factors which influence the rate of chemical reactions: temperature, concentration of reactants, pH (hydrogen ion concentration), and the presence or the absence of catalysts. Each of these factors influences the rate of chemical reactions by increasing or decreasing the number of effective collisions. *Temperature* effects reaction rates by changing the average velocity of particles in a chemical system. It also affects reaction rates by changing the fraction of molecules possessing the minimum energy for reaction. Higher temperatures mean faster velocities and a greater fraction of molecules possessing the minimum energy; lower temperatures mean slower velocities and a smaller fraction of molecules possessing minimum energy. This works as follows: change in velocity means a change in the possibility of collision; the faster the velocities of the reacting particles, the greater the frequency of collision. In general, for every rise of 10°C the rate of a chemical reaction is doubled, or, conversely, for a fall of 10°C, the rate is cut in half.

The concentration of reactants has a similar effect. The greater the concentration of one or both reactants, the greater the chance that a collision will occur. The smaller the concentration of reactants, the less chance of collision, hence the slower the rate of reaction. Catalysts affect the rate of reaction by increasing the effectiveness of any given collision once it has occurred or by increasing the chances of the reaction occurring by providing a surface on which the reactants can meet. Catalysts are molecules (or sometimes atoms) which facilitate a particular reaction without themselves being permanently changed in the reaction. Catalysts do not cause a reaction to occur which would not occur on its own. They do, however, speed up the rate of reactions which would occur anyway.

It follows from the collision theory that chemical reactions are **reversible;** i.e., the reaction can go in either direction. In any chemical system, then, two reactions are usually taking place:

## 7–10
## REVERSIBLE AND IRREVERSIBLE REACTIONS

$$A + B \rightarrow AB \tag{7–8}$$

and the reverse:

$$AB \rightarrow A + B. \tag{7–9}$$

The forward and reverse equations can be combined into one, with the reversibility indicated by double arrows:

$$A + B \rightleftharpoons AB. \tag{7–10}$$

Equation (7–10) indicates that at the same time that reactants A and B on the left are combining to form product AB on the right, product AB is decomposing to yield the two reactants again. Thus, within one test tube, the forward and the reverse reactions are occurring simultaneously.

In Eq. (7–10) the two arrows are of equal length. This shows that the forward reaction occurs just as readily as the reverse. In some reactions, however, this is not the case. Equation (7–11) below shows a longer arrow to the right than to the left:

$$A + B \rightleftharpoons AB. \tag{7–11}$$

This indicates that the reaction occurs more readily in the forward direction than in the reverse direction. Since the forward reaction is favored in this case, the reaction is shifted to the right. The relative size of the two arrows indicates the general direction of reversible reactions.

In principle, all chemical reactions are reversible. There is no reaction known which, under suitable conditions, cannot proceed (however slowly) in the reverse direction. Yet under ordinary conditions some reactions are far less reversible than others. In these cases, the reaction from right to left occurs so slowly that its rate is barely detectable. For all practical purposes, such reactions are said to be irreversible.

What conditions tend to produce irreversibility? Two factors are important. First, there is the consideration of energy. Some reactions release a great deal of energy going in one direction. Such reactions will tend to go in the reverse direction only if the same amount of energy can be absorbed. An irreversible reaction can be compared to rolling a stone down a hill. The downward path releases potential energy. To get back up the hill, the stone requires the input of the same amount of energy. Obviously, it is likely that far more stones will roll down a hill than will be pushed back up.

Second, chemical reactions are irreversible if one of the products leaves the site of reaction. This may occur if the product escapes as a gas:

$$A + B \rightarrow C + D \uparrow, \tag{7–12}$$

or if one product is a **precipitate** (i.e., an insoluble substance which settles out of solution):

$$A + B \rightarrow C + D \downarrow. \tag{7–13}$$

In each case the reverse reaction is inhibited by the removal of one of the product substances (D). Because removal of their products occurs frequently, many biochemical reactions can be considered irreversible.

**7-11
CHEMICAL
EQUILIBRIUM**

Within a certain period of time, reactions reach a state of equilibrium. When this condition is reached, the *proportion* of reactants in relation to products remains the same. Note that this does *not* mean that the *amounts* of reactant and of product are necessarily equal.

An example will illustrate this point. Consider the reaction in which molecules A and B yield products C and D:

$$A + B \rightleftharpoons C + D. \tag{7–14}$$

The different lengths of the arrows indicate that the conversion of A and B to C and D occurs more readily than the conversion of C and D to A and B. In other words, the energy barrier is lower for a successful interaction of A and B than for C and D. This means that, in a given period of time and at the same

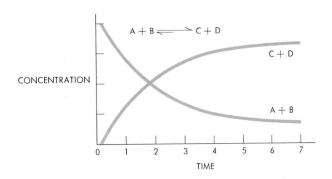

FIG. 7–17    Graph showing the change in concentration of reactants and products in a reversible reaction. The point of chemical equilibrium is reached where the two curves level off (at about the fifth minute). Here, the rate of the forward reaction is equal to the rate of the reverse reaction.

concentrations, more A and B will react with each other than will C and D. Under the same conditions, the initial rates of the two reactions are different.

If the reaction begins with only molecules of A and B present, it will occur at first only to the right. The graph in Fig. 7–17 plots change in concentration of reactants and products. It is apparent that the change in concentration ceases after about the fifth minute. Beyond this point, there is no further change. Furthermore, when these curves level off, the concentration of C and D is greater than the concentration of A and B. The reaction is thus directed to the right, as the relative lengths of the arrows indicate. The energy of activation for the forward reaction is less than that for the reverse reaction.

As long as molecules of reactant and product are still present in a system, chemical reactions never cease. In the above reaction, C and D accumulate because of the relatively high activation energy required to convert them back into A and B. Eventually the number of collisions between molecules of C and D will be higher than the number of collisions between molecules of A and B. As a result, the rate of the reverse reaction will increase, despite the higher energy of activation which tends to oppose it. At the same time, the rate of the forward reaction will decrease because of the decreasing concentrations of A and B.

Eventually, a point will be reached at which the forward rate equals the reverse rate. When this condition is reached, we say that a state of **chemical equilibrium** exists. Note that the concentration of reactants does *not* have to equal the concentration of products in order for equilibrium to be established. In the above case, the concentrations of C and D are much greater than the concentration of either A or B at the equilibrium point. The important feature of equilibrium is that *the rates of forward and reverse reactions are the same.* This means that as many molecules of A and B are being converted into C and D as molecules of C and D are being converted to A and B.

Those reactions which are completely reversible can be symbolized by arrows of equal lengths, pointing in both directions, as in the equation

$A + B \rightleftharpoons C + D.$                                      (7–15)

A graph showing rates of reaction for completely reversible systems can be seen in Fig. 7–18. The converging of the two lines indicates that the concentration of reactants and products is equal after the reaction reaches equilibrium.

When a point of equilibrium is reached in a chemical reaction, *the rate of reaction in one direction is equal to the rate of reaction in the other*. The reaction is still occurring both to the right and to the left. Since the rates of these reactions are equal, however, the concentration of reactants and products remains the same.

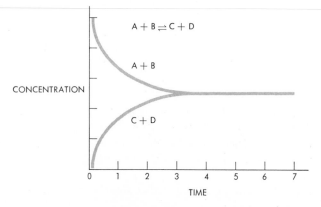

FIG. 7–18    A graph showing changes in concentration over a period of time for a completely reversible reaction. Note that an equilibrium is established about $3\frac{1}{2}$ minutes after the reaction has begun. At this point, concentration of reactants equals concentration of products.

The condition which exists at chemical equilibrium is referred to as **dynamic equilibrium.** While the overall characteristics of a given system at dynamic equilibrium remain relatively constant, its individual parts are in a state of continual change.

Left to itself, the direction which any reaction takes is toward a condition of equilibrium. The point at which chemical equilibrium lies is characteristic for any given chemical reaction.

What happens when a chemical reaction at equilibrium is disturbed by the removal or addition of substances on either side? Suppose that the reaction

$$A + B \rightleftharpoons AB \qquad\qquad (7\text{–}16)$$

exists in perfect equilibrium. If we add a quantity of either substance A or B, or both simultaneously, we will push the reaction to the right so that more molecules of AB will be formed. We can accomplish the same effect by another method. Without adding more of either A or B, the reaction may be shifted to the right by removal of some AB. If we add molecules of AB to the system in equilibrium, the reaction is shifted to the left. The eventual point at which equilibrium will again be reached in such reactions has not been changed by adding or removing substances. Only the direction or rate of the reaction has been changed momentarily. Reversible reactions eventually return to dynamic equilibrium.

In all animal life, from bacteria to man, there are three major types of compounds involved in metabolic reactions. These are **carbohydrates, lipids (fats),*** and **proteins.** All three types of molecules contain the elements carbon, hydrogen, and oxygen, with proteins containing other elements, such as nitrogen and sometimes sulfur, as well. The ratios of these elements differ between one type of molecule and the next, as do the three-dimensional arrangements of the atoms that form the molecules.

Carbohydrate is a general category containing two major types of substance, sugars and starches. Sugars serve as the primary fuel molecules for all living cells. Starches serve as reserve fuels, and are composed of many simple sugar units linked together. Carbohydrates generally contain hydrogen and oxygen in the ratio of 2:1. A generalized carbohydrate formula can thus be written as $(CH_2O)_n$, where the subscript $n$ means that molecules of carbohydrates are multiples of this basic unit. The formula for glucose, one of the most common carbohydrates in living systems, is $C_6H_{12}O_6$ ($n = 6$). Another common carbohydrate is ribose, whose formula is $C_5H_{10}O_5$ ($n = 5$). A structural formula, showing the basic arrangement of atoms in a molecule of glucose, a simple sugar, is given below:

Glucose, ribose, and several other five- or six-carbon sugars are the basic building blocks of all types of larger carbohydrate molecules. Glucose is accordingly called a simple sugar, or **monosaccharide.** Two simple sugars joined together (such as glucose and glucose, or glucose and fructose) are called double sugars, or **disaccharides.** Large carbohydrate molecules, such as starch or cellulose, are composed of the simpler glucose units joined end-to-end, forming very large, complex carbohydrates called **polysaccharides.** Large starch molecules can have molecular weights up to 500,000 or more. The term **macromolecule** is sometimes used to refer to any type of large molecule.

---

*The terms "lipid" and "fat" are often used interchangeably. They are not identical, however. Fats are a specifically defined class of molecules, composed mostly of fatty acids combined with glycerol. Lipid is a more general category of substances having no structural features in common but made up of molecules which are soluble in nonpolar solvents. Thus, all fats are lipids, but not all lipids are fats.

The following example illustrates how glucose units can be joined together to produce a larger molecule, in this case, the disaccharide maltose. Equation (7–17) shows that during this process one molecule of water is eliminated:

$$C_6H_{12}O_6 + C_6H_{12}O_6 \rightarrow C_{12}H_{22}O_{11} + H_2O. \tag{7–17}$$
$$\text{(maltose)}$$

This process of joining, with the elimination of a water molecule, is called **dehydration synthesis** and is shown with the following molecular formulas:

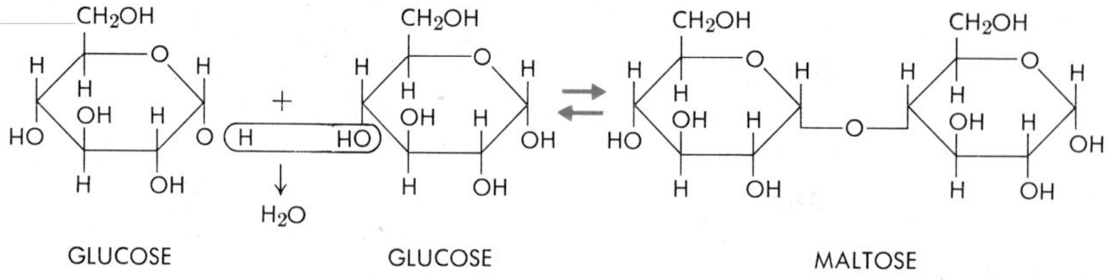

GLUCOSE          GLUCOSE          MALTOSE

The reverse process, whereby maltose is broken down by the chemical *addition* of water between two units, is called **hydrolysis.** Both dehydration synthesis and hydrolysis occur in the formation and degradation of all major macromolecules in the living cell. The chemical bond which joins two glucose units (or glucose and a maltose) is known as an $\alpha$-glycosidic bond. Some disaccharides (such as lactose, shown below) have a $\beta$-glycosidic bond. This bond is formed in the same way as the $\alpha$-bond, but has a different orientation in space. Whereas the $\alpha$-glycosidic bond projects below the plane of the two rings, the $\beta$-bond projects above it:

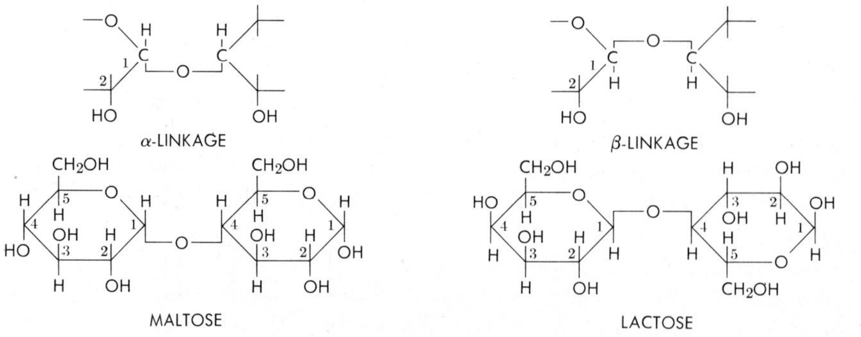

$\alpha$-LINKAGE          $\beta$-LINKAGE

MALTOSE          LACTOSE

Disaccharides bound together by $\alpha$-glycosidic bonds thus have a different overall three-dimensional shape from those bound together by $\beta$-bonds; accordingly, the two types of molecules behave differently in cellular metabolism.

The lipids are a group of organic chemical compounds including the fats, oils, and sterols. They are an important tissue component and a major foodstuff. A lipid molecule, like that of a carbohydrate, contains the elements carbon, hydrogen, and oxygen. However, unlike the carbohydrates, the ratio of hydrogen to oxygen is far greater than $2:1$.

The true fat molecule has two parts. These are (1) *alcohol* (usually glycerol) and (2) a group of compounds known as *fatty acids*. Fats are broken down into these two parts during digestion. The glycerol portion of the molecule has the following structural formula:

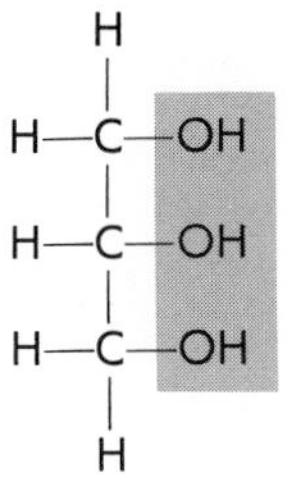

```
      H
      |
 H —  C — OH
      |
 H —  C — OH
      |
 H —  C — OH
      |
      H
```

The shaded portion, the alcohol groups, indicates the region where fatty acids can be attached.

There are many kinds of fatty acids, which differ most in molecular size and in the degree to which the carbon atoms are completely bonded to or **saturated** with hydrogen atoms. The following is the formula for a saturated fatty acid, stearic, $C_{17}H_{35}COOH$:

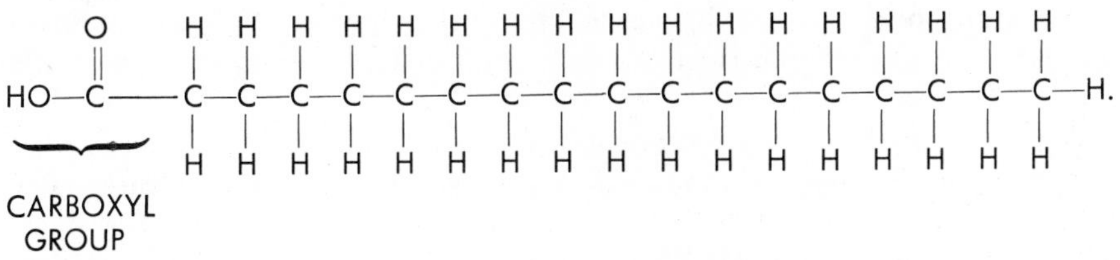

```
        O     H  H  H  H  H  H  H  H  H  H  H  H  H  H  H  H  H
        ||    |  |  |  |  |  |  |  |  |  |  |  |  |  |  |  |  |
 HO — C —— C— C— C— C— C— C— C— C— C— C— C— C— C— C— C— C— C— H.
              |  |  |  |  |  |  |  |  |  |  |  |  |  |  |  |  |
              H  H  H  H  H  H  H  H  H  H  H  H  H  H  H  H  H
```

CARBOXYL
GROUP

The following is the formula for a singly unsaturated fatty acid (i.e., one in which two hydrogens are replaced by a double bond between two adjacent carbons), oleic, $C_{17}H_{33}COOH$:

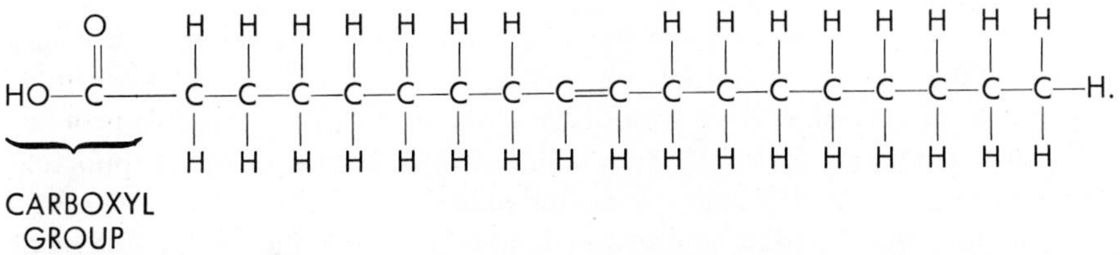

```
        O     H  H  H  H  H  H  H        H  H  H  H  H  H  H  H
        ||    |  |  |  |  |  |  |        |  |  |  |  |  |  |  |
 HO — C —— C— C— C— C— C— C— C=C— C— C— C— C— C— C— C— C— H.
              |  |  |  |  |  |  |  |  |  |  |  |  |  |  |  |
              H  H  H  H  H  H  H  H  H  H  H  H  H  H  H  H
```

CARBOXYL
GROUP

All fatty acids consist of a **carboxyl** group (—COOH) attached to varying numbers of carbon and hydrogen atoms. The carboxyl group is found in all organic acids. The joining of a fatty acid to the glycerol molecule is accomplished by the removal of an $H^+$ from the glycerol molecule and an $OH^-$ group from the fatty acid. The $H^+$ and $OH^-$ unite to form water. Since glycerol has three $OH^-$ groups available, three fatty acid molecules can be attached, as shown below (the R represents the hydrocarbon region of the fatty acid):

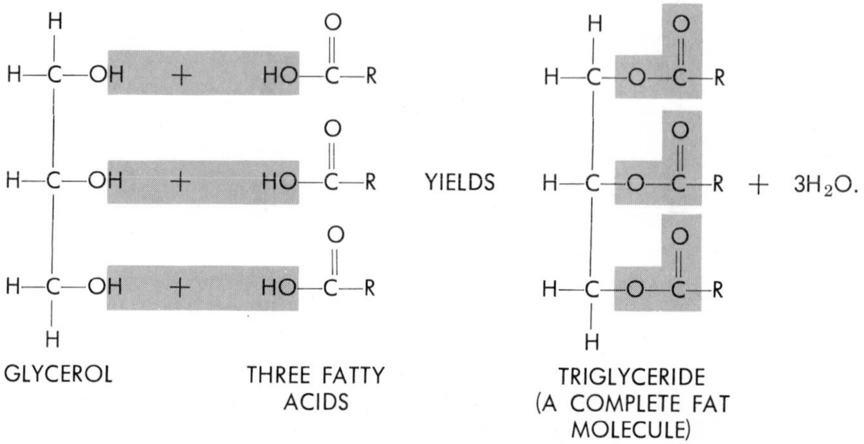

GLYCEROL                THREE FATTY                    TRIGLYCERIDE
                             ACIDS                        (A COMPLETE FAT
                                                             MOLECULE)

The glycerol and fatty acid are joined by dehydration synthesis, yielding in this case an **ester bond.** The splitting of fats during human digestion involves breaking the ester bond, and the reaction is catalyzed by an enzyme (pancreatic lipase).

*Fats are an organism's most concentrated source of biologically usable energy.* Most of them provide twice as many calories per gram as do carbohydrates. The chemical reason for this is evident from a comparison of molecular formulas: $C_{57}H_{110}O_6$ is a fat, while $C_6H_{12}O_6$ is the carbohydrate glucose. Energy is released in these compounds by oxidation, i.e., by the removal of electrons. The greater hydrogen content of fats means that they can be more fully oxidized than carbohydrates and can thus supply more energy. Relative to fats, carbohydrates are already partially oxidized, and thus yield less energy upon completion of the oxidation process.

Proteins play the most varied roles of any molecules in the living organism. As enzymes, proteins serve to keep all the various chemical reactions within a cell operating smoothly and continuously. As structural elements, proteins serve in such places as the contractile fibers of muscle, the spongy supporting tissue between bones, and in hair, nails, and skin.

The fundamental building block of protein is the **amino acid.** Amino acids are nitrogen-containing compounds with an amino group ($NH_2$) and a carboxyl group ($COOH$). Amino groups give basic properties to amino acids, while carboxyl groups give acidic properties.

A diagram of a generalized amino acid is shown below. Attached to a carbon atom in every amino acid is a characteristic group of atoms, symbolized as R.

AMINO (OR BASE) GROUP

$$
\begin{array}{c}
H \qquad\qquad R \qquad\qquad O \\[2pt]
\backslash \qquad\quad | \qquad\quad \parallel \\[2pt]
N - C - C \\[2pt]
/ \qquad\quad | \qquad\quad \backslash \\[2pt]
H \qquad\qquad H \qquad\quad OH
\end{array}
$$

CARBOXYL (OR ACID) GROUP

*It is in the number and arrangement of atoms comprising the R group that one amino acid differs from another.*

From about twenty different amino acids (see Appendix 3 for structural formulas), all the proteins known to exist in plants and animals are constructed. Amino acids are to proteins as letters of the alphabet are to words. A group of amino acids can be joined together in a specific order to produce a given protein, just as a group of letters can be arranged to form a specific word. For this reason, amino acids are often referred to as the "alphabet" of proteins.

Amino acids are linked in end-to-end fashion to form long protein chains. *The variety found among proteins is the result of the types of amino acids composing each and the order or sequence in which these types are arranged.*

The comparison of amino acids to letters of the alphabet is helpful in representing how a small change in a protein molecule can completely change its chemical properties. Changing one letter in a word may cause that word to become meaningless. For example, the word "skunk" conveys one idea, while the word "skank" means nothing at all. Likewise, a change or substitution of one amino acid for another may make an entire protein molecule "meaningless" to the cell. The molecule is no longer able to carry out its function. For example. a certain portion of the human population possesses a condition known as sickle-cell anemia. Hemoglobin molecules (protein) in afflicted persons differs from normal hemoglobin in only one amino acid out of about 300. Such hemoglobin molecules will not combine as readily with oxygen. Persons with this type of hemoglobin generally have a shortened life span. Thus a change in one amino acid in one type of protein can have far-reaching effects on the entire organism.

Sometimes the removal or addition of one or two letters in a word may change the meaning without making the word senseless. For example, the word "live" can become "liver" or "olive." Similarly, one protein may be changed into another by the removal or addition of one or a few amino acids.

In one way, however, the comparison of proteins to words falls short. This is in the matter of length. Words are generally composed of relatively few letters. Even the name of the New Zealand village Taumatawhakatangihanga-koauauotamateapokaiwhenuakitanatahu only approaches the complexity and length of a small to average protein. Proteins are macromolecules, often consisting of several hundred to over a thousand amino acids. Their molecular weights range from 6000 to 2,800,000.

The great size of proteins gives them added versatility in cell chemistry. They can take on a variety of shapes and sizes, each of which may serve very specialized functions. For this reason, biochemists speak of **chemical specificity** as being characteristic of many proteins. It is through the use of such chemically specific proteins as enzymes that living organisms are able to carry out their many different reactions so efficiently.

When amino acids unite to form proteins, the amino end of one amino acid molecule forms a chemical bond with the carboxyl end of the other, with the removal of one molecule of water:

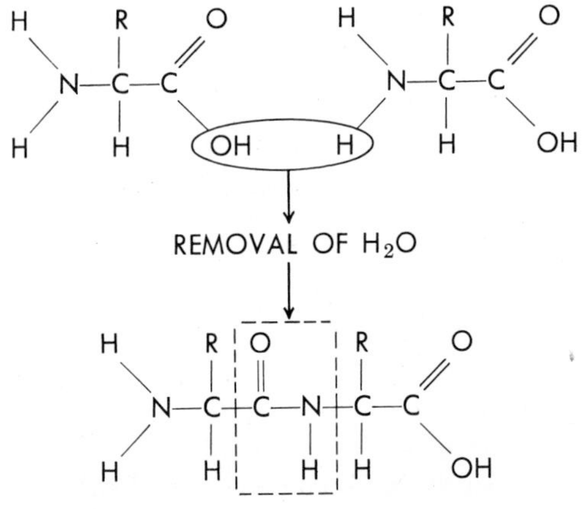

REMOVAL OF $H_2O$

The result is the formation of a connecting link between the two, much like the connection of railroad cars. This linkage process continues until all the amino acids necessary to form the protein are joined together in the order characteristic for that particular molecule. Note in the diagram above that this process involves the loss of one water molecule between each two amino acids and is thus a dehydration synthesis. The resulting linkage is called a **peptide bond.**

The joining of amino acids in this manner forms a larger unit called a **peptide.** Peptides may contain from two to thirty or more amino acids. Several peptides joined together form a **polypeptide.** In turn, various numbers of polypeptides unite to form a complete protein. In some proteins, the polypeptide chains line up end-to-end to form one very long molecule. In others, they line up side-by-side, with connecting chemical bonds.

The molecular structure of a peptide consisting of four amino acids is shown below:

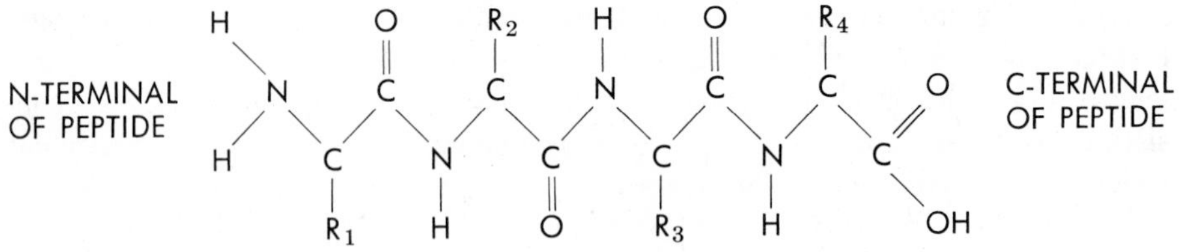

The sequence of amino acids formed from a series of covalent peptide bonds may be considered the most fundamental level of organization of proteins, their "backbone."* This sequence of amino acids is responsible, in part, for the uniqueness of each type of protein.

Few proteins exist as extended polypeptide chains stretched out like a rope. Most polypeptide chains are coiled or twisted in a variety of ways by the formation of hydrogen bonds between adjacent portions of the molecule. The most prominent form produced by hydrogen bonding is the **alpha helix.**

An alpha helix is produced by spiral twisting of the amino acid chain. To visualize the geometry of a helix, think of a ribbon as a straight-chain polypeptide. A helical structure can be formed by twisting the ribbon several times around a pencil. The spiral which remains after the pencil is removed is the general shape of an alpha helix. The alpha helix is held in position by the formation of hydrogen bonds between amino acids on one part of the chain with those on another part of the same chain.

The hydrogen bonds are formed between the $C\!=\!O$ group of one amino acid and an N—H group nearby. Hydrogen bonding is the result of an electrostatic attraction between an unshared electron pair of one atom and the positively charged hydrogen end of a polar molecule. Only a few atoms will form hydrogen bonds, and three of these—oxygen, sulfur, and nitrogen—are found in proteins. Thus, for example, a hydrogen bond can be formed when the two groups shown below approach each other (the dashed line represents the hydrogen bond):

$$\begin{array}{c}\diagdown \qquad\qquad\qquad\qquad\diagup\\[-2pt] C\ \overset{\times\times}{\underset{\times\times}{\times}}\ \overset{\times\times}{O}\ \overset{\times}{\underset{\times}{\phantom{.}}}\ \text{-----}\ H\ \overset{\circ}{\underset{\times}{\phantom{.}}}\ N\\[-2pt] \diagup \qquad\qquad\qquad\qquad\qquad\diagdown\end{array}$$

It is difficult to overestimate the importance of hydrogen bonding to our present concept of protein structure. Although, individually, hydrogen bonds are quite weak, many hydrogen bonds reinforce each other to produce a relatively stable structure (see Fig. 7–19).

---

* Currently, the terms *primary, secondary,* and *tertiary* structure of proteins are often used to refer, respectively, to: (1) the amino acid sequence; (2) the coiling of the polypeptide chain into the *alpha helix,* or the interaction of two polypeptides to produce the *beta configuration;* and (3) the folding of the alpha helix into various shapes to produce a more or less globular protein molecule (see following sections). However, the terms primary, secondary, and tertiary structure actually refer to types of forces stabilizing a protein molecule, and not to any actual geometric shape. Thus "primary structure" refers to the covalent bonding of peptides within a protein. "Secondary structure" refers to hydrogen bonding, as well as to various ionic and so-called salt bonds. "Tertiary structure" refers to ionic bonds, interactions between atoms placed extremely close to each other, and the like, such as disulfide bonds. In order to avoid discussing the numerous types of bonds which contribute to the overall stability of a protein molecule, we have chosen to discuss only the major geometric patterns which proteins may take.

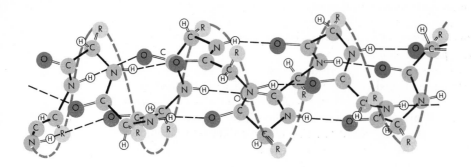

FIG. 7–19    A diagram of a peptide backbone wound into an alpha-helix configuration. The heavy dashed curve traces the helical structure. The broken lines going from the C—O to the N—H groups represent the hydrogen bonds which hold the chain in the alpha-helix form. (After R. B. Corey and Linus Pauling, *Proc. Intern. Wood Textile Research Conf.* **B. 249,** 1955.)

Hydrogen bonds can be broken by many physical and chemical means. For example, a change in pH or temperature is very effective in weakening hydrogen bonds. When the pH or temperature of a protein solution is raised, a sudden change occurs in the number of protein molecules existing in helical form. At certain critical pH or temperature values, the weak forces such as hydrogen bonds break, and the molecule unrolls or unwinds; it is then said to be **denatured.** Up to a limit, such a process is reversible. If the pH or temperature is lowered to its original value the hydrogen bonds re-form, and the helical structure spontaneously re-forms itself. However, at certain extremes of pH (low or high), or at certain critically high temperatures, denaturation becomes an effectively irreversible process, for other forces than hydrogen bonds have been destroyed. A hard-boiled egg is an example of irreversibly denatured protein (the egg white, or albumin). The white does not become liquid again upon cooling. The effects of denaturation are represented in Fig. 7–20.

From what has been said so far, it might appear that soluble proteins are like thin threads or ropes. However, they are actually globular or spherical in shape. The helical polypeptide chain is folded into a compact, rounded molecule. Twisting and folding of the alpha helix gives further chemical specificity to the protein. An extremely important feature of proteins is the fact that the entire molecule has a specific structural form. For each protein, folding of the polypeptide chain is slightly different, giving each molecule its own unique configuration. The shapes of three proteins are shown in Fig. 7–21.

Changes in the folding of an alpha helix can alter the **biological activity** of a protein. When we speak of biological activity of a protein we mean that each protein will react chemically with only one type of molecule, or with a small group of other types of molecules. It is thought that molecules of various substances are able to fit onto the surface of the protein molecules with which

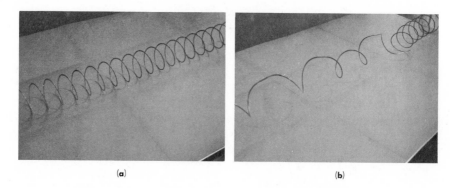

(a)                                    (b)

FIG. 7–20    (a) A coiled spring toy known as a "slinky." This represents the alpha-helix structure of certain proteins. When the slinky is pulled out of shape, as shown in photograph (b), it cannot recoil into the original helical structure. It has been irreversibly altered. This is analogous to denaturing a protein by such physical means as heating or by such chemical means as placing the protein in a concentrated solution of urea.

FIG. 7–21    The various sizes and molecular configurations for several types of protein found in living systems. Hemoglobin is the oxygen-carrying protein of the blood. It consists of four polypeptide chains. $\beta_1$-lipoprotein is found in the liquid portion of blood and in the tissue fluids of higher organisms, such as mammals. It is composed of lipid elements bound to protein and serves in maintaining the stability of certain enzymes. Fibrinogen is also found in the liquid portion of blood and is involved in forming clots. The glucose molecule is included for size comparison.

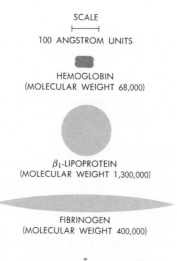

SCALE
⊢——————⊣
100 ANGSTROM UNITS

HEMOGLOBIN
(MOLECULAR WEIGHT 68,000)

$\beta_1$-LIPOPROTEIN
(MOLECULAR WEIGHT 1,300,000)

FIBRINOGEN
(MOLECULAR WEIGHT 400,000)

GLUCOSE MOLECULE ON
SAME SCALE
(MOLECULAR WEIGHT 186)

they normally react. In order for any reaction to occur, therefore, the fit must be a good one so that appropriate atoms of the reacting substance and the protein are brought close enough together. This depends on the surface configuration of the protein. It is thus possible to see that even slight changes in any one of the three levels of organization in a protein could render that protein nonfunctional. Since soluble proteins play such an important part in nearly all biochemical reactions, changes in shape of these molecules can greatly disrupt metabolic processes within a cell.

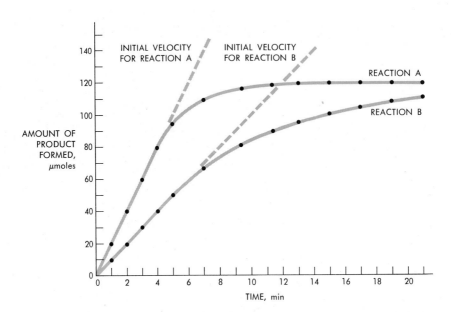

FIG. 7–22   The relationship between total amount of product formed and the time for two enzyme-catalyzed reactions.  The initial rates of reactions A and B are different, measuring a difference in turnover number.  As shown in this figure, A acts more effectively on its substrate (in a given period of time) than B (it is assumed that both reactions will ultimately reach the same equilibrium, i.e., concentration of reactants and products).  If both reactions begin with the same concentration of substrate, eventually equivalent amounts of product will be formed (and the curves will level off at the same height).  Only the time required to yield the same total amount of product will differ.

## 7-13
## ENZYMES

There are many varieties of proteins in the bodies of living plants and animals. However, one group deserves special attention: the enzymes.  Enzymes are involved in virtually all of the chemical reactions within living organisms. Without these specialized proteins, life as we know it could not possibly exist.

*Enzymes are organic catalysts.*  Catalysts, recall, are molecules which speed up a chemical reaction without themselves being chemically changed in the process.  After participation in one reaction, a catalyst can go on to participate in a second, a third, and so on.  As catalysts, enzymes participate in almost all of the chemical reactions which keep organisms alive.  They enable a human being to be a beehive of chemical activity at only 98.6°F.  They enable Antarctic fish to remain alive and active at near 0°C.  Furthermore, since they come out of chemical reactions unchanged, a few enzyme molecules can go a long way.  This means that the organism does not have to expend a great deal of energy in order to constantly resynthesize enzymes at a rate proportional to the rate of the reaction they catalyze.

Much can be learned about the nature of enzyme-catalyzed reactions by studying the kinetics of reactions· i.e., the various changes in rate which a reaction shows during its course. For example, it is possible to measure the amount of product formed in an enzyme-catalyzed reaction from the moment the reactants (called the "substrate") and enzyme are brought together, until the reaction has stopped (i.e., reached an end-point, or equilibrium).

If the amount of product formed is measured at one-minute intervals and this quantity is plotted against time on a graph, curves such as those shown in Fig. 7–22 are obtained. This graph shows data for two different reactions, designated here as A and B. Observe the solid line for reaction A as an example. At time 0 there is no product detectable in the reaction system; this represents the beginning of the reaction. After 1 minute 20 $\mu$moles have been formed, after 2 minutes 40, after 3 minutes 60, and after 4 minutes 80. The rate of the reaction could be given as 20 $\mu$moles of product formed per minute for this initial period. Note, however, that by the fifth minute this rate has begun to slow down. Instead of a total of 100 $\mu$moles of product formed by the five-minute mark, only about 92 have been formed. In the interval between the fourth and the fifth minute only about 12 $\mu$moles, rather than 20, have been formed. During the first four minutes, the rate has been constant, and the change in rate has been zero. But from the fourth minute on through about the twelfth minute, the rate is changing; i.e., it is slowing down. For each successive minute, the amount of product formed in that interval is less than in the preceding minute. From the twelfth minute onward, the reaction rate again becomes constant; no more product is being formed, and the change in rate is again zero.

Using the principles of chemical kinetics discussed earlier, how can we explain these changes? During the first four minutes of reaction A, the number of substrate molecules greatly exceeds the number of enzyme molecules (this is usually true for all catalyzed reactions). This means that every enzyme molecule is working at its maximum capacity. There are so many substrate molecules around that, each time an enzyme finishes with one substrate molecule, it is confronted with others. After a period of time, however (in this case, after four minutes), the number of substrate molecules begins to dwindle and the concentration is lowered. As the concentration of reactants (substrate) is lowered, the chance of successful collisions is reduced (see Section 7–9). In the present case we are concerned not only with successful collisions between the reactants, but also between reactants (substrate) and the enzyme. As time goes on, the substrate concentration becomes less and less since more substrate is being converted into product. The leveling off of the curve after twelve minutes indicates that the total amount of product is remaining constant. The reaction system has reached equilibrium.

A similar curve can be seen for reaction B. The difference in the shape of this curve represents the difference in effectiveness of enzyme A and enzyme B in acting on their respective substrates. Given the same initial concentrations of both enzyme and substrate, it is apparent that enzyme B acts less rapidly on its substrate than enzyme A. Since the initial substrate concentrations in the two reaction systems are the same, the total amount of product formed in B, given enough time, will eventually be equivalent to that formed in A, as long as the two reactions have the same equilibria—i.e., as long as the reactions normally reach equilibrium with the concentration of reactants and products the same for the two reactions.

In comparing the kinetics of reactions A and B, it is necessary to have a common reference point. For example, do we want to compare the two reactions at the two-minute mark, the twelve-minute mark, or later? It is obvious that comparisons made at different times will give different values for the total product formed in reactions A and B. The reason for this is that we are faced with two variables (given equal concentrations of enzyme molecules): (1) the rate at which the two different enzymes can act on their substrates (which is a characteristic of the enzyme molecule); and (2) the constantly changing substrate concentrations during the course of reaction. There is, however, a means of eliminating one of these variables. In the first few minutes of the reaction, the number of substrate molecules is so large compared to the number of enzyme molecules that changing the concentration does not, for a period at least, affect the number of successful collisions. Note that during this early period the rate of change is constant; i.e., the enzyme is acting on substrate molecules at a constant rate. The slope of the graph line during these early minutes defines what biochemists call the **initial velocity** of the reaction. The initial velocity of any enzyme-catalyzed system is determined by the characteristics of the enzyme molecule and is always the same for the enzyme and its substrate as long as temperature and pH are constant and substrate is present in excess. As shown in Fig. 7–22 the initial velocities of reactions A and B are different and represent a difference in effectiveness between the two enzymes. This difference is measured as the **turnover number,** a term which indicates the maximum rate at which an enzyme can act on substrate molecules in a given period of time. It is important to understand why substrate should be present in excess to measure the true initial velocity of an enzyme-substrate reaction.

Suppose that we run a series of reactions with enzyme system A, in which the concentration of enzyme is held constant but the starting concentration of substrate is varied. If we measure the initial velocity (say, for the first two minutes) of each reaction and plot this value on a graph against substrate concentration, we get a curve like that shown in Fig. 7–23. Note that at low substrate concentrations, the initial velocity of the reaction is low. This means that when there are few substrate molecules in solution to begin with, the enzyme can never reach its maximum rate of conversion (since the frequency of successful collisions becomes the limiting factor). In other reactions, where the starting concentration of substrate is greater, the initial velocity is greater. As the graph line shows, the increase in initial velocity with increasing substrate concentration is linear, but only up to a point. By the time the starting concentration of substrate has reached 0.1 mole per liter, the curve has begun to level off. This suggests that the enzyme is approaching its maximum initial velocity. In other words, beyond about 0.5 moles per liter an increase in substrate concentration

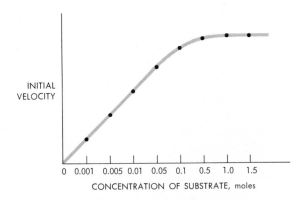

INITIAL
VELOCITY

0   0.001   0.005   0.01   0.05   0.1   0.5   1.0   1.5
CONCENTRATION OF SUBSTRATE, moles

FIG. 7–23   Graph showing the relationship between substrate concentration and initial velocity of an enzyme-catalyzed reaction. The reaction volume and enzyme concentration are held constant. Each point on the graph represents the measured initial velocity of a specific reaction where substrate concentration was the only variable.

does not affect the initial velocity of the reaction. Enzyme molecules are working as fast as they can; the presence of more and more substrate at the start of the reaction will not affect the initial velocity. Thus, at this point we can measure true initial (maximum) velocity because one variable has been eliminated: substrate concentration. Rate of conversion now depends solely on characteristics of the enzyme molecule.

The above phenomena are understandable in terms of our general knowledge of the kinetics of any chemical reactions, whether enzyme-catalyzed or not. However, enzyme-catalyzed reactions have some characteristics which are distinct from non-enzyme-catalyzed reactions. Recognition of the nature of some of these characteristics will help to understand a second important question: By what mechanism do enzymes speed up the rate of biochemical reactions?

1) *The rate of enzyme-catalyzed reactions is greatly affected by temperature.* If the initial velocity of a specific enzyme-catalyzed reaction is measured at a number of different temperatures (with enzyme and substrate concentrations held constant), a curve like that shown in Fig. 7–24 is obtained. Note that at low temperatures the rate of reaction is quite slow, and that with increasing temperature, up to about 36°C, the rate increases. Beyond 36°C, however, the rate begins to slow down again even though the temperature is raised. From our knowledge of all chemical reactions, we can explain the first half of this curve: why the initial velocity increases with an increase in temperature. The higher the temperature, the more rapidly the reacting molecules (in this case, substrate and enzyme molecules) move about, and the greater the fraction of molecules which possess minimum energy of activation. However, this principle should apply to temperatures above 36°C as well. In non-enzyme-catalyzed reactions,

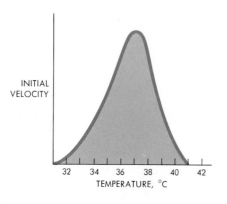

INITIAL
VELOCITY

FIG. 7–24    The effect of temperature on
the activity of one enzyme.

TEMPERATURE, °C

initial velocity does indeed increase as the temperature is raised beyond 36°C. Why, then, are enzyme-catalyzed reactions so sensitive? To answer this question requires that we develop a model to explain how enzymes function, a topic that will be taken up in the next section.

The initial velocity-temperature curve shown in Fig. 7–24 varies from one type of enzyme to another. Every specific enzyme has its so-called **optimum temperature**: that temperature at which the enzyme achieves its maximum rate (i.e., initial velocity). Thus, for the particular reaction shown above, 38°C is the optimum temperature; for another enzyme-catalyzed reaction, 25° or 40° might be the optimum.

The term optimum temperature is somewhat misleading and should be viewed not only in a chemical but also a biological context. Seldom in nature do biochemical reactions operate at their maximum rate. It is not often advisable, for example, for an organism to be carrying out a particular biochemical reaction as rapidly as possible. Thus, while a particular enzyme may work at a maximum rate at 38°C, we cannot assume that this is the temperature at which the enzyme usually functions. The enzyme could normally exist inside a mammal which maintains a fairly constant internal temperature of 37°C, or it could exist in a bacterium which lives in the soil, where the temperature varies considerably. In general, the optimum temperature of an enzyme-catalyzed reaction, as measured in a chemical sense, is often close to the average temperature at which the enzyme functions in nature. But we must not assume that this is always true. And, more important, we must not assume that whatever temperature (or other conditions) may be optimal when the system is measured in a test tube is the "optimum" at which the system operates in terms of the survival of organisms. The fastest rate is not always the best from the standpoint of an organism's operating efficiency.

2) *Enzymes can be "poisoned"* by certain compounds, such as bichloride of mercury or hydrogen cyanide. These chemicals are deadly poisons to all living organisms. They exert their effect by inactivating one or many enzymes.

Hydrogen cyanide blocks one of the enzymes involved in the chemistry of respiration. The way in which this is believed to occur will be considered shortly.

3) *Enzymes are specific in their action.* This is one of the most distinctive characteristics of enzymes. They will often catalyze only one particular reaction. For example, the enzyme sucrase will catalyze only the breakdown of sucrose to glucose and fructose. It will not split lactose or maltose. Lactase and maltase, respectively, must be used as the catalytic agent for these two sugars.* With other enzymes, specificity of action is not quite so obvious. Trypsin, for example, is a **proteolytic** (protein-splitting) enzyme which acts upon many different proteins.

Why should some enzymes work on only one compound while others will work on several? Enzymes act upon a specific chemical linkage group. In the case of trypsin, only those peptide linkages of protein molecules which are formed with the carboxyl group of the amino acids lysine or arginine are acted on by trypsin:

Since peptide linkages involving the carboxyl groups of lysine and arginine are characteristic of many proteins, it is not surprising that trypsin will act on more than one.

We now come to one of the most important questions in the study of enzymes: By what mechanism do enzymes operate?

The most important hypothetical model proposes that enzymes have certain surface configurations produced by the three-dimensional folding of their poly-

7-14
THEORIES OF
ENZYME ACTIVITY

---

* The *-ase* ending indicates that the compound is an enzyme. Other enzymes, such as trypsin, end with *-in*. This signifies that they, like all enzymes, are proteins. Enzymes ending in *-in* were discovered and named before an international ruling was made in favor of the *-ase* ending. A few changes have been made. For example, the mouth enzyme ptyalin is now called salivary amylase. Enzymes are also named after the compounds they attack. Thus peptides are attacked by peptidases; peroxides by peroxidases; lipids by lipases; ester linkages by esterases; hydrogen atoms are removed by dehydrogenases; and so on.

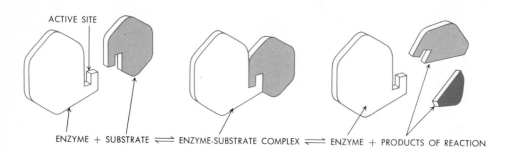

ACTIVE SITE

ENZYME + SUBSTRATE ⇌ ENZYME-SUBSTRATE COMPLEX ⇌ ENZYME + PRODUCTS OF REACTION

FIG. 7–25    A schematic representation of the interaction of an enzyme and its substrate. The specificity of enzymes for certain substrates is thought to be due to the surface geometry of the enzyme and substrate molecules, which allows them to fit together in a precise manner. Arrows indicate that each phase of the reaction is reversible.

peptide chains. On this surface, there is an area to which the substrate molecule is fitted. This area is called the **active site** of the enzyme. It is thought that, when the substrate molecule becomes attached to the enzyme at this site, the internal energy state of the substrate molecule is changed, bringing about the reaction (Fig. 7–25).

A helpful analogy for visualizing how enzymes work is to picture the substrate as a padlock and the enzyme as the key which unlocks it. The notched portion of the key thus becomes the active site, since it is here that the "reaction," or the unlocking of the padlock, takes place. The padlock comes completely apart, just as a molecule is broken apart by enzyme action. The key serves equally well, however, to run the reaction in the reverse direction, i.e., to lock the padlock again. The key comes out unchanged and ready to work again on another padlock of the same type; similarly, the enzyme is ready to catalyze another reaction of the same type. In light of this analogy, trypsin becomes a sort of "skeleton key" enzyme. It can open several types of padlocks (proteins) as long as they have similar engineering designs (certain peptide linkages).

The lock-and-key model has been nicely supported by X-ray diffraction studies. The structure of the complex that results when the enzyme lysozyme reacts with a molecule very similar to its normal substrate shows that the substitute "substrate" molecule fits snugly into a groove or cleft in the lysozyme molecule's surface, where the enzyme's catalytic groups are held in just the right position to break the substrate's bonds. Yet there is some evidence that the lock-and-key model of enzyme action is not completely satisfactory in terms of always yielding accurate predictions with all enzymes. For example, the enzyme specific for the amino acid isoleucine must often "choose" between its proper substrate (isoleucine) and valine. The only difference between these two molecules is one methylene ($-CH_2-$) group:

$$
\begin{array}{c}
CH_3 \\
| \\
CH_2 \quad CH_3 \\
\diagdown \;\; \diagup \\
CH \\
| \\
{}^+NH_3-C-CO_2^- \\
| \\
H \\
\text{ISOLEUCINE}
\end{array}
\qquad
\begin{array}{c}
CH_3 \quad CH_3 \\
\diagdown \;\; \diagup \\
CH \\
| \\
{}^+NH_3-C-CO_2^- \\
| \\
H \\
\text{VALINE}
\end{array}
$$

The chemist and Nobel laureate Linus Pauling estimates that if an enzyme discriminated between these two highly similar molecules purely on their ability to form a complex with it (in the manner described by the lock-and-key model), then from these physicochemical grounds alone the enzyme should make a "mistake"—i.e., it should bind to valine instead of isoleucine—about 1 time in 20. However, it has been shown experimentally that "mistakes" are made at a frequency of less than 1 in 3000.

We may avoid this seeming contradiction if we look upon many enzymes as "flexible" rather than rigid. When proper substrates bind to these enzymes, a change is induced in the structure of the latter which results in a reorientation of the enzyme groups actually involved in the catalysis. In other words, the enzymes' "bond-snapping" portions are brought into the proper position for action. Thus this "induced fit" hypothesis suggests that enzyme specificity is only partly due to complementarity of structure between enzyme and substrate molecules, and that the ability of substrates to induce in the enzyme the structural changes necessary for catalysis must also be taken into account.

Recent X-ray diffraction work on the proteolytic (protein-splitting) enzyme carboxypeptidase A provides very strong evidence in support of the "induced fit" hypothesis. It has been shown that the binding of this enzyme to its substrate causes movement of the side-chain amino acid number 248, tyrosine (known to be involved in the actual catalysis), some eight angstroms toward the substrate, so that tyrosine's hydroxyl ($-OH$) group is near the substrate peptide bond to be split (see Fig. 7–26). Furthermore, the positively charged group of the arginine (145) moves two angstroms toward the substrate carboxyl group, where it binds it. It has further been shown that an inhibitor of carboxypeptidase A binds to the enzyme as does the normal substrate, but does not bring about a change in the tyrosine (248) side-chain.

The lock-and-key analogy, including the "induced fit" hypothesis, helps us to interpret the characteristics of enzyme action described in the previous section; for example, refer to Fig. 7–24. The effect of increase in initial velocity with increasing temperature (up to 38°C) is a result of increasing the kinetic energy of the substrate and enzyme molecules. At temperatures higher than 38°C, however, the decrease in initial velocity is the result of changes in the configuration

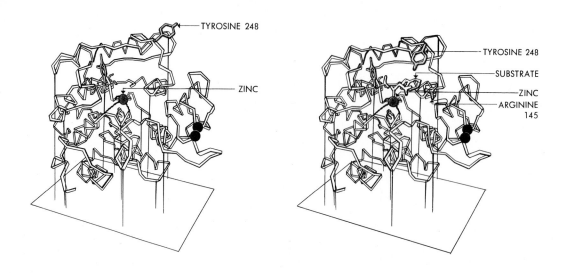

FIG. 7–26    At left is shown a drawing of a three-dimensional model of the enzyme carboxypeptidase A, as reconstructed from X-ray diffraction data. The groove or cleft into which the substrate molecule fits is shown above and to the right of the zinc atom. At right is shown a drawing of the same enzyme, but with the substrate molecule bound to it at the zinc atom and a side-group of arginine. After the substrate molecule is in position, both tyrosine and arginine move toward it. This observation supports the "induced fit" hypothesis of enzyme action.

of the enzyme molecule, a protein. We know that most proteins are heat sensitive. High temperatures denature the proteins by breaking hydrogen bonds or other types of bonds which hold the molecule in its specific three-dimensional shape. When the enzyme's shape is altered, the active site no longer fits the specific configuration of the substrate molecule. The result is that no reaction can occur. Thus, when an enzyme system is exposed to increasing temperatures, more and more of the enzyme molecules become denatured. Though with increasing temperature more molecules are colliding with each other, the number of effective collisions between enzyme and substrate is becoming less. In other words, by "tampering" with the key and changing its shape, we have affected the ability of the key to open a specific lock.

A similar situation exists for the effects of different pH ranges on the action of enzymes. Changing pH affects hydrogen bonds of proteins; at high or low pH values many hydrogen bonds are broken, and thus the enzyme molecules change their three-dimensional structure. The effect of both pH and heat on enzymes emphasizes the importance which preserving a specific molecular shape has on the biochemical activity of enzymes.

Especially interesting in light of the lock-and-key analogy is the effect of inhibitors, or "poisons," on enzyme activity. A very simple case, diagrammed

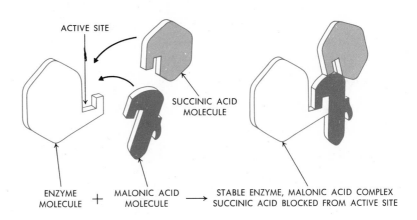

ACTIVE SITE

SUCCINIC ACID
MOLECULE

ENZYME      +    MALONIC ACID    ⟶    STABLE ENZYME, MALONIC ACID COMPLEX
MOLECULE         MOLECULE              SUCCINIC ACID BLOCKED FROM ACTIVE SITE

FIG. 7–27   A diagrammatic representation of competitive inhibition in enzymatic reactions.

in Fig. 7–27, will illustrate this problem. In almost all cells glucose may be stored indefinitely without ever releasing its chemical energy. The reason for this is that there is no activation energy present. In terms of the energy hill, there is nothing to lift the glucose over the hump at the top and start it rolling down the hill. Outside of a living system, it is necessary to supply a relatively large amount of activation energy (heat, for example) to glucose in order to get it started down the energy hill.

One step in the breakdown of sugars involves the conversion of a four-carbon molecule, succinic acid, to another four-carbon molecule, fumaric acid, with the removal of two electrons (and two protons). This reaction is catalyzed by the enzyme succinic dehydrogenase, which is highly specific for its succinic acid substrate. If the reaction is run in a test tube with just enzyme and substrate, a particular initial velocity can be observed; if malonic acid is added to the test tube along with succinic acid, the rate of formation of fumarate is greatly reduced. Malonic acid is a three-carbon molecule whose overall molecular shape is very similar to that of succinic. It is thought that the malonic acid molecule can fit into the active site of succinic dehydrogenase and "fool" the enzyme. However, because malonic acid is slightly different from succinic, the enzyme cannot convert it into fumaric. Hence, whenever a malonic acid molecule gets into the active site of succinic dehydrogenase, no reaction occurs. Malonic acid inhibits the enzyme system, a feat which it accomplishes by virtue of its similar shape to the normal substrate. Malonic acid is like a key which fits into a lock but which is just different enough from the proper key not to be able to turn. For a moment it "jams" the lock. Malonic acid molecules can fall out of the

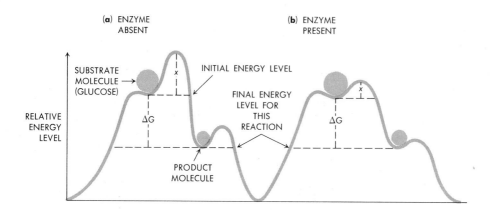

FIG. 7–28    The effect of an enzyme on the activation energy requirements of a molecule undergoing chemical degradation. The amount of activation energy required is represented by the distance $x$. The net gain in free energy is symbolized by $\Delta G$ (it is assumed that the molecule falls to the lowest energy level). Note that the uncatalyzed reaction (a) has a far higher activation energy barrier than the catalyzed reaction (b) on the right. The new molecule must overcome another energy barrier, requiring more activation energy, before it can be broken down and release more energy. In a living organism another enzyme, specific for this reaction, would be needed.

active site, however, and, if they are around, it is possible for succinic acid molecules to enter once the site is free. Malonic acid is thus an example of a **competitive inhibitor:** it competes with the normal substrate for the enzyme's active site. However, it does not permanently deactivate the enzyme.

Certain molecules can also affect enzyme molecules more or less permanently. These are called **noncompetitive inhibitors,** two examples of which are carbon monoxide and cyanide. Carbon monoxide molecules attach to the active site of certain oxygen carriers (e.g., hemoglobin) and certain respiratory enzymes (e.g., the cytochromes). When either of these inhibitors is attached to a respiratory protein, normal function is impossible (i.e., the cytochrome or hemoglobin cannot interact with oxygen). Unlike malonic acid, however, neither carbon monoxide nor cyanide becomes detached from the active site of the protein. As a result, the effect of noncompetitive inhibitors is permanent; this is why both carbon monoxide and cyanide are such deadly poisons.

Since most biochemical reactions are to one degree or another reversible, it is not surprising that enzymes can catalyze reactions in either direction. In a completely reversible reaction, the enzyme can catalyze the reverse reaction as readily as the forward. If the equilibrium is shifted to the right, the enzyme can catalyze the forward direction more easily than the backward, and so forth. This observation suggests the aforementioned point that enzymes do not make reactions occur which would not occur on their own, but only increase the *rate* at which the reactions take place. *Enzymes speed up reactions by changing the energy requirements for getting the reaction started.* Enzymes do not affect the net energy changes (the $\Delta G$) of any reaction; that would be thermodynamically impossible.

How, then, do enzymes increase reaction rate? The energy hill analogy, discussed earlier in this chapter, will help to elucidate this point. The glucose molecule at the top of the energy hill shown in Fig. 7–28 represents a certain amount of potential chemical energy. However, glucose may be stored indefinitely without ever releasing its chemical energy. In terms of the energy hill, there is nothing to lift it over the hump at the top and start it rolling down the hill.

This is where enzymes fit into the picture. Their presence lowers the amount of activation energy ($x$) needed to start the reaction. Thus by expending only a small amount of energy, a living organism can release the chemical energy available in the glucose molecule.

Many enzymes, besides requiring environmental conditions such as proper temperature, pH, etc., also need the presence of certain other substances before they will work. For example, salivary amylase will work on amylose only if chloride ions ($Cl^-$) are present. Magnesium ions ($Mg^{++}$) are needed for many of the enzymes involved in the breakdown of glucose.

Some enzymes require another organic substance in the medium in order to function properly. In a few cases, enzymes actually consist of two molecular parts. One of these is a protein, called an **apoenzyme.** The other molecular part is a smaller, nonprotein molecule. This smaller molecule is called a **coenzyme.** Its name signifies that it works with the main apoenzyme molecule as a coworker in bringing about a reaction.

In an apoenzyme-coenzyme case, the two molecular parts are chemically bonded to each other. In other cases, the coenzyme is combined only briefly with the enzyme. In either case, the presence of the coenzyme is needed before any catalytic activity takes place.

Chemical analysis of the smaller coenzymes has shown that they often contain a vitamin as part of the molecule. This finding has led to the idea that vitamins serve as coenzymes. This would explain why the absence of certain vitamins causes such remarkable physical effects on the organism. The enzyme which works with the vitamin-based coenzyme cannot work by itself. Therefore, an entire series of important physiological reactions may be blocked (see Fig. 7–29). The hypothesis that vitamins serve as coenzymes also explains why only a small supply of vitamins is sufficient to fulfill the requirements for good health. Like enzymes, coenzyme molecules must be replaced only from time to time, at a relatively slow rate.

Small molecules such as coenzymes could affect enzyme activity by interacting with specific active sites (not those for the substrate necessarily) on the enzyme molecule. It is thought that such an interaction could cause the three-dimensional shape of the enzyme to shift slightly, thus opening up the substrate active

FIG. 7–29    (1) A series of five chemical reactions, each catalyzed by its own specific enzyme (a, b, c, d, and e).    (2) Enzyme c is removed, preventing the conversion of C to D.    (3) Since the reactions are reversible, A, B, and C begin to accumulate.   Since no more D, E, or F is being produced, these substances begin to disappear as F is used by the organism in its life processes.   (4) Further accumulation of A, B, and C and depletion of D, E, and F.   (5) Death of the organism due to lack of the vital substance F.   Had the reactions been irreversible, there would have been accumulation of only C, continuing until the death of the organism.   This figure demonstrates the far-reaching effects of the removal of one important enzyme and the dynamic chemical balance which exists in living systems.

sites for easier access by the substrate itself.  Not much is known at present about how accurate this model is, but certain kinds of evidence suggest that something like a configurational shift does occur when enzymes are in the presence of certain small molecules such as coenzymes.  More will be said on this subject in the following chapter.

**7-15
CONCLUSION**    This chapter has provided background information concerning the structure of matter, especially those compounds which characterize living matter (such as carbohydrates, fats, and proteins).  The relationship of electron orbital configurations of atoms, molecules, and ions to these substances was also stressed, as were some important principles of chemical equilibrium.  Special attention was paid to some of the means used by the cell for splitting apart and joining molecules, with particular emphasis on the nature and role of enzymes.  In the next chapter, this knowledge will be applied toward gaining an understanding of how the cell operates as an energy-utilizing functional unit within a living organism.

1. The reaction $A + B \rightarrow AB$ takes place slowly at 20°C unless either compound $x$ or $y$ is present. Compound $x$ is a metallic catalyst and $y$ is an enzyme; both compounds catalyze the reaction. Ten milliliters of a solution of A and B is placed in each of four test tubes to which varying amounts of $x$ or $y$ are added, as shown below:

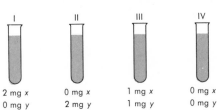

| I | II | III | IV |
|---|---|---|---|
| 2 mg $x$ | 0 mg $x$ | 1 mg $x$ | 0 mg $x$ |
| 0 mg $y$ | 2 mg $y$ | 1 mg $y$ | 0 mg $y$ |

   a) Predict which tubes would show the greatest and which the least rate of reaction at 20°C. Explain your reasons.

   b) If A and B are heat-stable at 100°C, in which tube(s) would the reaction rate be greatest at this temperature? Least? Why?

   c) Increasing the temperature from 20° to 30° will probably double the reaction rate in which tube(s)? How do you know?

   d) If the reaction is allowed to reach equilibrium, in which tube(s) will the amount of AB be greatest? Least? What are your reasons?

   e) The contents of tubes I, II, III, and IV are poured into separate dialyzing sacks made from cellophane. The sacks are placed in separate containers of distilled water. The reaction slows down in sacks I and III but continues at the previous rate in sacks II and IV. If A and B are added to the distilled water from outside of sacks II and IV (each tried separately), the reaction proceeds at a very slow rate. When A and B are added to distilled water from outside sacks I and III, the reaction speeds up. Explain the results (assume that A, B, and AB are all large molecules).

2. Describe the difference between an *endergonic* and an *exergonic* reaction. How does this feature relate to the equilibrium of the reaction (i.e., is there any relation between whether the equilibrium is shifted to the right or left, and whether the reaction is endergonic or exergonic)? How does it relate to how spontaneous the reaction is (spontaneous reactions require very little to get them started)? How does this relate to whether the reaction involves synthesis (the building of chemical bonds) or breakdown (the breaking of chemical bonds)?

3. What is a chemical bond? Why is the term "bond" misleading?

4. Discuss the three graphs in Fig. 7–30 in terms of the chemical events which they represent. What does the change in concentration of reactants and products indicate? Relate these graphs to the concept of chemical equilibrium.

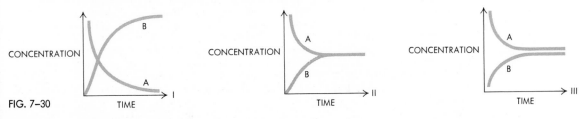

FIG. 7–30

5. What are the major differences between carbohydrates, fats, and proteins in terms of (a) molecular weight, (b) molecular geometry (size and shape), and (c) general biological uses (in cell metabolism)?

6. Explain the lock-and-key model of enzyme function. How is this model useful? In what ways could it be misleading?

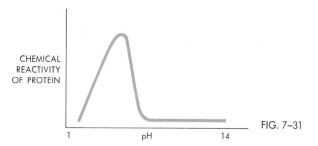

CHEMICAL REACTIVITY OF PROTEIN

1    pH    14

FIG. 7–31

7. Proteins are said to display optimal ranges of activity within any environment, for example, within a range of pH values, temperatures, etc. In terms of the graph in Fig. 7–31, explain how changes in pH could affect the chemical reactivity of protein molecules. Include in your answer a discussion of the following points:

   a) Where on a protein molecule (and at what level of organization of the molecule—primary, secondary, or tertiary structure) changes in hydrogen ion ($H^+$) concentration in the medium have their effect.

   b) How changes in the protein brought about by change in $H^+$ concentration could affect chemical reactivity of the protein.

   c) Why is the curve relatively steep on either side of the optimal peak?

8. How do upward electron transitions represent a form of potential energy? How is such potential energy released as kinetic energy?

9. The following data represent optical density readings for three enzyme-catalyzed reactions.

| TABLE I | | TABLE II | | TABLE III | |
|---|---|---|---|---|---|
| ENZYME + SUBSTRATE | | ENZYME + SUBSTRATE + INHIBITOR | | ENZYME + INHIBITOR + OVERABUNDANCE OF SUBSTRATE | |
| TIME (min) | OPTICAL DENSITY | TIME | OPTICAL DENSITY | TIME | OPTICAL DENSITY |
| 0 | .030 | 0 | .011 | 0 | .033 |
| 15 | .064 | 15 | .030 | 15 | .055 |
| 30 | .095 | 30 | .049 | 30 | .085 |
| 45 | .125 | 45 | .068 | 45 | .110 |
| 60 | .150 | 60 | .088 | 60 | .135 |

Assuming that the more reaction which occurs, the greater the optical density of the solution, interpret the data in light of current knowledge of enzyme structure and function. Include in your answer the following:

a) Why does the curve have the shape it does for Table I? Why does the change in optical density occur as it does? Explain this in terms of interaction between enzyme and substrate molecules.

b) What is happening in Tables II and III? What kind of inhibition is shown here? On what evidence is your answer based?

c) How can these graphs be explained in terms of the concept of active site or the lock-and-key analogy of enzyme function?

It was further found that when the enzyme and inhibitor were first heated together in solution, the inhibitor subsequently removed, the protein solution slowly cooled, and a normal amount of substrate added, the reaction occurred in much the same way as indicated in Table I. Explain this phenomenon in terms of your knowledge of the nature of the forces involved in determining protein structure.

The following books contain more detailed treatment of atomic structure, chemical bonding, and formation of molecules.

**SUGGESTED READINGS**

BAKER, J. J. W., and G. E. ALLEN, *Matter, Energy, and Life*, 2nd edition (Reading, Mass.: Addison-Wesley, 1970).

BOREK, ERNEST, *The Atoms Within Us* (New York: Columbia University Press, 1961). A paperback, this book is a simplified introduction to the chemistry of living material. Somewhat less technical than *Matter, Energy, and Life*.

CHELDELIN, VERON H., and R. W. NEWBURGH, *The Chemistry of Some Life Processes* (New York: Reinhold, 1964). An introduction to organic chemistry with special reference to biochemical processes. Assumes more background in chemistry and atomic structure (bonding, etc.) than *Matter, Energy, and Life*, but covers certain biochemical processes in greater detail.

HENDRICKSON, JAMES B., *The Molecules of Nature* (New York: W. A. Benjamin, 1965).

HOFFMAN, KATHERINE B., *Chemistry of Life* (Washington, D.C.: National Science Teachers' Association, 1964). A very readable introduction to some basic biochemical processes. Amply illustrated.

MOROWITZ, HAROLD J., *Life and the Physical Sciences: An Introduction to Biophysics* (New York: Holt, Rinehart, and Winston, 1963).

RYSCHKEWITSCH, GEORGE E., *Chemical Bonding and the Geometry of Molecules* (New York: Reinhold, 1963). A simple introduction to types and properties of chemical bonding in terms of orbital theory.

SISLER, HARRY H., *Electronic Structure, Properties, and the Periodic Law* (New York: Reinhold, 1963). An up-to-date treatment of orbital theory and its relation to bond formation. Requires some simple mathematical background.

STEINER, ROBERT F., and HAROLD EDELHOCH, *Molecules and Life* (New York: Van Nostrand, 1965).

WHITE, EMIL, *Chemical Background for the Biological Sciences* (Englewood Cliffs, N. J.: Prentice-Hall, 1964). This paperback serves well as the text for a one-semester course in organic chemistry. It is primarily concerned with a variety of organic rather than biochemical reactions.

# CHAPTER 8  THE DYNAMICS OF LIVING CELLS: METABOLIC PATHWAYS

## 8-1
### INTRODUCTION

Far from being a bag of randomly interacting molecules, a cell is a complex and highly organized unit which carries out its many chemical reactions in a rapid and highly efficient manner, following many different metabolic pathways. In their overall detail, metabolic pathways are highly intricate and involved processes. To understand such pathways and to grasp their particular significance, it is helpful to ask a number of general questions which are relevant to all biochemical systems:

1) What specific steps are actually involved in a particular pathway? How many individual reactions comprise the pathway, and what is the nature of the changes they represent?

Answering the latter question involves mapping the particular steps in any pathway from beginning to end.

2) How specific is each step in the pathway and how specific is the entire pathway itself?

In other words, in how many directions can each intermediate in a given pathway go? And how is the specificity of steps in any pathway preserved?

3) Where do particular metabolic pathways occur in the cell and with what cell organelles are they associated?

This question is concerned specifically with the problem of localization—of how certain metabolic pathways are bound up with specific cell structures which bring together and keep various intermediates in proximity.

4) What are the energy requirements of the pathway as a whole and of its individual steps? Is the overall pathway endergonic or exergonic? What happens to the energy from those individual steps which are exergonic? And what drives the individual endergonic steps?

Investigating the energetics of a metabolic pathway is one of the most important means of understanding precisely what keeps the pathway going.

5) How are metabolic pathways controlled?  In other words, how is the direction of an overall pathway maintained and what controls the rate at which the pathway operates?

This question brings us back to the "governor" analogy discussed at the beginning of Chapter 7. One of the most crucial distinctions between a living cell and a machine is the ability of the former to control its own rate of activity.

6) How are various metabolic pathways interrelated? What interconnections exist between the various pathways, and how do these function?

To illustrate the major characteristics of metabolic pathways, it is helpful to look in some detail at the series of reactions involved in the breakdown of sugar and the consequent release of energy in cells. Sugars are fuels and provide the basic energy source of all living processes. Furthermore, the reactions involved in sugar breakdown are quite similar in all cells, from bacteria to man. Since the getting and expending of energy is one of the most important and crucial life processes, understanding the specific reactions involved in the release of energy not only furnishes some information about how cells themselves function, but also provides a means of showing some general characteristics of all metabolic pathways.

Before examining the specific pathways by which energy is released from fuel molecules, it is necessary to understand something of the mechanism by which energy is stored and used in cells. Living cells do not use directly the energy released from the breakdown of a fuel molecule, but rather convert that energy into a molecular "currency" which can be "spent" at a later time for any energy-requiring process. Within each cell, energy released from the breakdown of fuel molecules is captured in the form of **high-energy phosphate bonds.*** These high-energy bonds serve as the major energy source in all living things. High-energy phosphate bonds are found primarily in a molecule called **adenosine triphosphate** or **ATP.** This consists of a molecule known as adenine, a five-carbon sugar (ribose), and three phosphate groups. The ATP molecule is shown in diagrammatic form below:

**8–2
ATP: THE ENERGY
CURRENCY IN
CELLS**

---

* There is some dispute about the exact energy equivalents for each of these bonds. The general range for the estimates is as follows: ATP high-energy phosphate bonds contain 7 kcal/mole; low-energy phosphate bonds contain 3–4 kcal/mole.

The two wavy lines between the end phosphate groups of the ATP molecule indicate high-energy bonds. The bond of the first phosphate linked to the ribose is a low-energy bond. The difference between high- and low-energy phosphate bonds lies in the overall amount of energy that each makes available to biological systems upon hydrolysis. High-energy phosphate bonds release **about seven kilocalories (kcal) per mole. Low-energy phosphate bonds release approximately three to four kcal per mole.**

High-energy phosphate bonds result from internal rearrangements of electrons between phosphorus and oxygen atoms. The same numbers of atoms and electrons are involved in both low-energy and high-energy phosphate bonds. The difference in the amount of energy released when each is broken is the result of a difference between the electron configurations in the respective bonds.

Molecules of ATP, which contain two high-energy phosphate bonds, serve as the major packets of energy in living cells. When energy is required for any cellular activity (e.g., the synthesis of a protein), one or two of the three phosphate groups from an ATP molecule are removed. This removal process leaves a compound which is less rich in energy: either **adenosine diphosphate (ADP)** or **adenosine monophosphate (AMP)**, according to the particular reaction. Molecules of ADP and AMP are rebuilt into ATP by the energy released from the breakdown of glucose molecules. Thus a constant cycle of breakdown and reformation of ATP occurs in living systems (Fig. 8–1).

The amount of energy released by breaking one high-energy phosphate bond in ATP is slightly more than is necessary to drive most endergonic reactions.

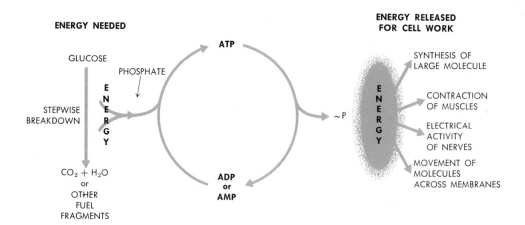

FIG. 8–1    The ATP cycle. Molecules of ATP, the "small-change currency" of the cell, give up one or two phosphate groups, releasing the energy locked in the high-energy bonds to perform cell work. Some of the types of work for which energy is needed are shown to the right. The "energy-poor" compounds ADP and AMP are built back up into ATP by addition of one or two phosphate groups. The energy for this is derived from the breakdown of glucose.

Hydrolysis of 1 mole of ATP to ADP yields about 7 kcal. About 5.5 kcal are required to build a glycosidic bond, about 5 kcal to form an ester bond, and about 3.5 kcal to form a peptide bond. Thus ATP can provide enough energy for all the major synthetic reactions within a cell.

Energy can be transferred from the processes involved in the breakdown of one type of molecule to the processes involved in the synthesis of another by means of **coupled reactions.** For example, the formation of a glycosidic bond between two simple sugars is coupled to the reaction in which ATP breaks down to form ADP. This reaction provides a good example of the principle on which coupled reactions take place.

Consider the overall reaction in which glucose and fructose join together to form the double sugar sucrose:

$\Delta G = +5.5$ kcal/mole

As indicated, the overall net energy change is $+5.5$ kcal per mole (i.e., the reaction is endergonic). Two important details are missing from this overall representation of the reaction, however: (1) ATP is involved, and (2) the reaction takes place in two separate steps. The two steps and the exact role of ADP are shown in Fig. 8–2. In the first reaction a molecule of ATP interacts with a molecule of glucose; during this reaction one phosphate group is transferred from the ATP to form glucose-1-phosphate, leaving ADP. This reaction is exergonic, releasing approximately 7 kcal per mole of ATP and glucose. Glucose-1-phosphate is thus now an energy-rich intermediate, containing some of the energy originally held in the high-energy phosphate bond of ATP. In the second reaction, hydrolysis of the phosphate bonds of glucose-1-phosphate yields about the same amount of energy as required to form the glycosidic bond. Thus the second reaction proceeds spontaneously as long as a supply of glucose-1-phosphate and fructose is present. In the transfer of the terminal phosphate of ATP to glucose, electrons are rearranged around carbon 1 of the glucose; the result is the formation of a relatively high-energy phosphate bond (equivalent to about 5.5 kcal

ATP  +  GLUCOSE  ⟶  ADP  +  | GLUCOSE-1-PHOSPHATE |

| GLUCOSE-1-PHOSPHATE |  ⟶  SUCROSE + $P_i$ (INORGANIC PHOSPHATE, $HPO_4^{=}$)

+

FRUCTOSE

FIG. 8–2    The two-step process by which glucose is activated by picking up a phosphate group from ATP and subsequently reacts with fructose to form the double sugar or disaccharide sucrose. The reaction shows an overall increase in free energy obtained from the breakdown of ATP to ADP. The exergonic breakdown of ATP is coupled to the endergonic formation of the glycosidic bond between glucose and fructose.

per mole).  The rearrangement of electrons forming this new chemical bond represents potential chemical energy.  This potential energy is realized as kinetic chemical energy when the glucose-1-phosphate interacts with fructose to form a new chemical arrangement (the glycosidic bond).  Coupled reactions, then, involve the creation of a high-energy intermediate by rearrangement of atoms within at least one reactant.  This first step in the process is exergonic.  The "activated," high-energy intermediate now contains the energy which directly drives the second, or endergonic, step.  When exergonic and endergonic reactions are coupled in this way, relatively little of the total potential energy is lost.

ATP is not the only molecule that can provide energy for biochemical reactions.  Other molecules, similar in structure to adenine, may also have high-energy phosphate bonds, e.g., uridine triphosphate (UTP), cytidine triphosphate (CTP), and guanosine triphosphate (GTP).  In addition, high-energy sulfur bonds are involved in a few biochemical reactions.  Nevertheless, ATP is rightly considered the main energy source of the living cell.  It serves in far more biochemical reactions than any other single molecule.

**8-3
ELECTRON
TRANSPORT AND
ENERGY RELEASE:
THE GENERATION
OF ATP**

To remain alive, cells constantly fight an uphill battle.  Most of the chemical reactions necessary for the maintenance of life are endergonic.  ATP is constantly being used to drive these uphill reactions.  Where, then, does the ATP come from?  How does the energy-poor compound, ADP, go back to form the energy-rich compound, ATP?  In other words, what exergonic reactions are necessary to drive the uphill processes of ATP formation?

The answer to this question lies in a phenomenon known as **electron transport.**  In Section 7–8 it was seen that energy is captured in the formation of chemical bonds by the transition of electrons from lower to higher energy levels in atoms and molecules.  Similarly, energy is released in the breaking of chemical bonds by the downward transition of electrons. The energy to move electrons upward in the formation of ATP comes from the release of energy in the downward transition of electrons from other molecules. These other molecules are the fuels (primarily carbohydrates and lipids) which come to the cell as its food. A main function of fuel molecules in living systems, therefore, is to provide a source of electrons which, through downward transition, can be coupled to the formation of particular chemical bonds in ATP. In living cells, electrons are removed from fuel molecules and passed through a series of "acceptor" molecules, coming to occupy successively lower energy levels as the process continues. The relation between electron transport and the degradation of fuel molecules is shown diagrammatically in Fig. 8–3. As electrons are passed from one acceptor to another, their potential energy levels are lowered and some of the released energy is bound into high-energy phosphate bonds of ATP. At least five different acceptor molecules are involved in the electron transport system (Fig. 8–3). At three points in the process the drop in energy level during electron transfer is sufficient to generate a high-energy phosphate bond. Since electrons are usually transported in pairs, the complete passage of a pair of electrons along the electron transport system results in the generation of three ATP molecules from three molecules of ADP and inorganic phosphate ($P_i$). Thus the endergonic reactions associated with ATP's formation are coupled to the exergonic reactions in which electrons are removed from fuel molecules.

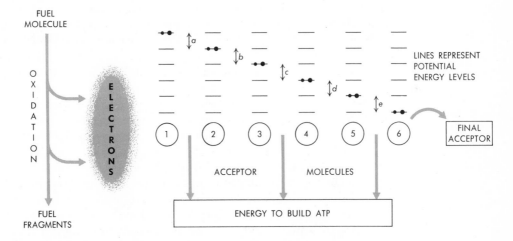

FIG. 8–3   Generalized diagram showing the principle involved in biological oxidation and the capturing of energy as ATP. The circular structures labeled 1 through 6 represent specific electron transport molecules. The electron drops in potential-energy level as it passes from one transport molecule to another. These drops occur within the electron cloud of each transport molecule and are indicated by the distances a, b, c, d, and e. The drop in energy level with each transfer results in the release of small amounts of energy. This is captured in the formation of ATP.

What molecules act as acceptors in the electron transport system and what properties allow them to serve this special function? Of particular importance in the electron transport system are the **cytochromes.** In Fig. 8–3, the cytochromes are represented by the last four molecules in the electron transport system (numbers 3, 4, 5, and 6). The first two acceptors in the transport system are coenzymes known respectively as nicotinamide adenine dinucleotide (NAD) and flavin adenine dinucleotide (FAD). The cytochromes, sometimes referred to as "respiratory enzymes," are iron-containing molecules.

The existence of the cytochromes and the nature of their cellular function were first noted in 1925 by the British biochemist David Keilin. Keilin started out to study the chemical composition of different kinds of living tissues by a process known as microspectroscopy. In this process, a piece of living tissue is placed on a microscope slide and light is passed through it. The ocular lens of the microscope, however, is replaced by a prism so that light emerging from the tube is diffracted and a spectrum produced. Such spectra show a broad, continuous background ranging in color from red on one end to violet on the other. This represents the spectrum of light emitted by the light source. Onto this continuous background are superimposed a number of dark absorption lines, representing various types of molecules in the tissue being observed. Each type of molecule absorbs light at different specific wavelengths. Thus by examining the absorption spectrum it is possible to identify some of the major components of living tissue.

Keilin was interested in studying a particular group of molecules (known at the time as "myohaematin") found in all types of living cells. In particular, Keilin was studying the characteristics of these molecules in the thoracic muscles (which control wing movements) of the bee. He placed the entire organism on a microscope slide and allowed light to pass through the wing muscle at the joint between the wing and thorax (see Fig. 8–4). He noted that, when the insect was quiet, no particular absorption bands could be observed. When the insect moved its wings, however, several distinct absorption bands appeared on the spectrum (see Fig. 8–5). Studies on myohaematin in yeast cells showed another interesting result. Yeast growing normally in a suspension, when examined with the microspectrograph, showed the major absorption bands. When oxygen was bubbled through the yeast culture, the absorption bands disappeared. If nitrogen was bubbled through the culture, however, the absorption bands persisted, and even became more intense. These observations suggested that myohaematin underwent oxidation and reduction and that the absorption bands were characteristic of the reduced state, their absence characteristic of the oxidized state. Chemical studies with isolated myohaematin confirmed these conclusions.

One more interesting piece of information was added to Keilin's observations. He found that the appearance and disappearance of absorption bands was markedly affected by the presence of such agents as carbon monoxide and cyanide. As we saw in Section 7–14, these same agents strongly affect the respira-

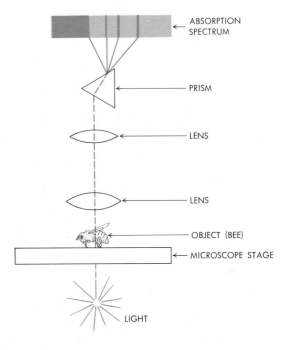

FIG. 8–4   Schematic view of Keilin's experimental setup. An insect (a bee) is placed on the microscope stage, so that light coming up through the stage passes through the wing muscle. The light is then passed through the rest of the lens system of the microscope and out through a prism. The prism diffracts the light to form a spectrum, on which are imposed dark absorption lines produced by particular molecular types in the muscle. This technique provides a means of studying in action the chemical components of living tissue.

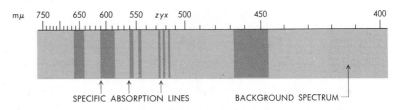

FIG. 8–5   The absorption spectrum which Keilin obtained by the technique of microspectroscopy. The continuous spectrum forming the background is produced by the light source and ranges from red on the left to violet on the right. The dark lines represent specific wavelengths of light which molecules in the tissue have absorbed. Each type of molecule absorbs at one or two specific wavelengths. If the molecule is absent from the tissue, its corresponding line on the spectrum is also absent.

tory pigment hemoglobin in the blood. It was known that hemoglobin was an iron-containing compound which could both pick up and discharge oxygen molecules, thus serving as the oxygen-carrier molecule of the blood. When carbon monoxide is added to a hemoglobin solution, however, the hemoglobin molecules are permanently reduced and are thus unable to pick up oxygen. Similarly, when carbon monoxide or cyanide is added to a solution of myohaematin, the dark absorption bands occur and persist even if oxygen is added later. Thus oxygen is unable to reverse the effects of cyanide or carbon monoxide on myohaematin just as it also fails to reverse the effect of these molecules on hemoglobin.

Keilin drew the following specific conclusions from his observations:

1)  The oxidation-reduction reactions of myohaematin are normally reversible; reduced myohaematin appears conspicuously when oxygen is absent; it disappears when oxygen is present.

2)  Molecules of myohaematin behave in some ways quite similar to those of hemoglobin with specific poisons such as cyanide or carbon monoxide. Thus myohaematin might well be an iron-containing molecule with many structural properties of hemoglobin.*

3)  The existence of a number of different dark bands on the absorption spectrum of reduced myohaematin suggested that several different kinds of this molecule were present in the cell.

Fifteen years later, Keilin and one of his coworkers, Hartree, showed that the dark lines of the absorption spectrum were produced by several different molecules (rather than the single substance myohaematin) which they renamed cytochromes. Each set of bands turned out to represent one of several types of cytochromes called, in order of their sequence in the electron transport process, cytochrome $b$, cytochrome $c$, cytochrome $a$, and cytochrome $a_3$ (or cytochrome oxidase). Chemical analysis showed that all of these cytochromes had certain molecular features in common. Each was composed of a basic ring structure (called a porphyrin ring) in the center of which was an iron atom bonded to four nitrogens. The porphyrin ring structure is also found in the hemoglobin and myoglobin molecules. In cytochromes, the porphyrin ring is bonded at several points to a polypeptide chain in the manner shown in Fig. 8–6. The protein segment of the molecule stabilizes the active site in the region of the iron atom. The work of Keilin, Hartree, and others showed that reversible changes involved in cytochrome activity were the result of successive oxidations and reductions. When muscle tissue is active and using the energy from the breakdown of sugar to produce ATP, electrons are being transported at a rapid rate along the electron assembly. Each transport molecule (e.g., one of the cytochromes) picks up an electron and thus becomes reduced. It passes the electron on to the next cytochrome molecule in the transport system, and thus becomes oxidized. The ability of cytochromes to successively undergo oxidation and reduction in a reversible manner is a function of the electron configuration about the central iron atom. Iron is one of several types of atoms which can exist in one of several valence states: i.e., iron can give up either two or three electrons, and thus exist as either the ferrous ion ($F^{++}$) or the ferric ion ($F^{+++}$). The ferric ion can pick

---

* Hemoglobin, however, does not normally undergo oxidation and reduction when picking up or discharging oxygen. The cytochromes, as Keilin showed, obviously do, as a normal part of their biochemical function.

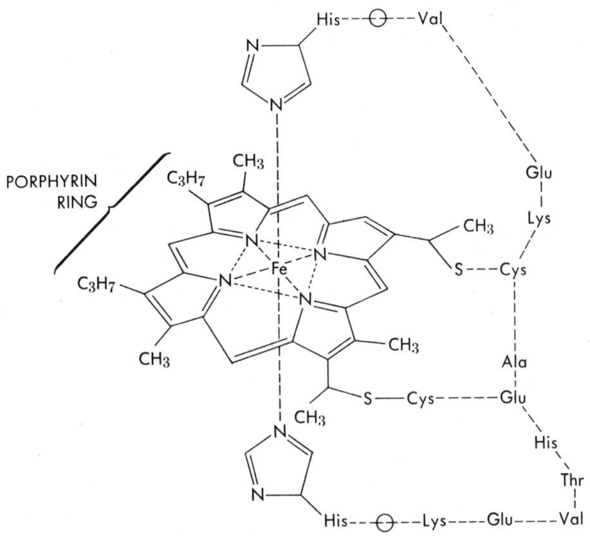

FIG. 8–6  Simplified representation of a molecule of cytochrome c. The porphyrin ring, shown at left, forms a flat plane, with the iron atom at the center. The iron is bonded to the porphyrin by four nitrogens, and to the amino acid histidine both above and below the plane of the ring. The complete amino acid sequence of the polypeptide chain is not shown, only some selected residues. The protein is thought to stabilize the molecule, giving it a specific shape. In a manner not yet completely understood, the protein part of the molecule keeps the iron atom in an easily reversible oxidation state.

up an electron and thus become reduced to the ferrous ion. The ferrous ion, in turn, can give up the electron and thus be oxidized back to the ferric ion. The ability of cytochrome molecules to easily pick up and release electrons allows them to function efficiently in the electron transport process.

The complete electron transport assembly is shown diagrammatically in Fig. 8–7. Electrons are removed two at a time from glucose and picked up first by oxidized NAD or $NAD^+$ (which then becomes reduced NAD, symbolized $NADH + H^+$).* Reduced NAD passes its electrons to oxidized FAD, which in turn becomes reduced FAD (abbreviated $FADH_2$). $FADH_2$ then passes electrons on to the cytochromes, first to $b$, which passes them on to $c$, $a$, and $a_3$.

---

* This way of symbolizing reduced NAD emphasizes that what each NAD molecule picks up as a carrier is not two complete hydrogen atoms, but rather two electrons and one proton; the extra proton (the $H^+$) is given off to the medium where it combines with a water molecule to form the hydronium ion ($H_3O^+$). $H_3O^+$ can give up its extra proton to oxygen at the end of the electron transport system to yield water, as shown in Fig. 8–7. The equation would be: $H_3O^+ + O = \rightarrow 3H_2O$.

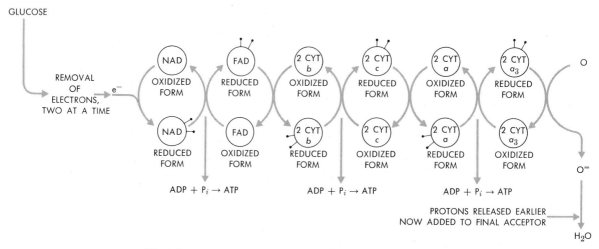

FIG. 8–7   Diagram of the various electron transport molecules involved in the passage of electrons from a fuel molecule to a final acceptor.  During the course of this process, the energy from the electrons is used to add inorganic phosphate ($PO_4$) onto ADP molecules, forming ATP.  The sites of ATP production are shown by the arrows leading downward from three transfer points.  $P_i$ stands for inorganic phosphate.

What is the ultimate fate of the electrons on cytochrome $a_3$?  Obviously, if the electrons cannot be passed somewhere, the electron transport system will soon grind to a halt, since all the transport molecules will be in the reduced form.

Here is where one of Keilin's observations becomes crucial.  Recall, he found that when the tissue was kept in a nitrogen atmosphere (where no oxygen was present) the dark bands persisted even when the tissue was at rest.  Molecular oxygen must thus be involved somehow in returning the reduced cytochromes to the oxidized state.  The exact role was unknown at the time Keilin did his major work on this problem, but it has since been shown that *the function of oxygen in cellular respiration is to act as a final electron acceptor.*  As shown in Fig. 8–7, oxygen picks up electrons from reduced cytochrome $a_3$ and thereby becomes negatively charged ($O^-$).  This negatively charged oxygen ion picks up protons from the medium to produce water.*  Here is one of the chief differences between the use of a fuel (such as gasoline) in a motor and the use of a fuel (such as sugar) in a living organism.  Both processes generally consume oxygen and release carbon dioxide.  When gasoline burns, however, oxygen reacts directly with the molecules of the fuel.  In cellular oxidation, oxygen does *not* unite directly with molecules of sugar.  Rather, electrons are removed in successive stages from the fuel molecules and ultimately transferred to oxygen.  Although both cellular oxidation and the oxidation of fuel in a motor may produce the same end products ($CO_2$ and $H_2O$), the chemical mechanisms by which these processes occur are very different.  This difference is vitally important in understanding the energy-harnessing process involved in the rebuilding of ATP.  Release of energy in small steps, such as occurs in the cell, allows more energy to be captured in a usable form. The one-step oxidation of fuel through burning produces a great deal of heat. The many-step oxidation of sugars in the cell produces a minimum of heat. For organisms, as for the machine, heat represents wasted energy. Thus the stepwise breakdown which occurs in cells, although more intricate, is ultimately more efficient.

The electron transport system has a structural as well as functional basis in cells. Found in virtually all types of cells, it is usually associated with membranes —in bacteria as parts of intracellular membranes, and in cells of higher organisms as part of the mitochondrial membranes (see Chapter 6). Recent evidence has shown that the inside walls or cristae of mitochondria contain many small globular units, believed to represent groupings of respiratory enzymes. Each respiratory assembly is thought to contain one set of cytochrome molecules, arranged in a specific order on a membrane. It is also probable (though not definitely established) that at least FAD is also bound to the membrane with the cytochromes. The specific structural arrangement of the cytochrome molecules makes possible the effective passing of electrons from one acceptor to the other. Like workers lined up on an assembly line, the electron transport molecules are arranged in an order corresponding to their function in transporting electrons. The generation of ATP by electron transport, then, occurs on the inner membraneous walls of the mitochondria.

**TABLE 8–1**   OXIDATION-REDUCTION POTENTIALS FOR VARIOUS ELECTRON ACCEPTORS

| ELECTRON ACCEPTOR | OXIDATION-REDUCTION POTENTIAL |
|---|---|
| NAD | −0.3 |
| FAD | −0.1 |
| CYT $b$ | +0.1 |
| CYT $c$ | +0.28 |
| CYT $a$ | +0.29 |
| CYT $a_3$ | DATA NOT AVAILABLE |
| MOLECULAR OXYGEN | ∼+0.80 |

How are electrons passed in a specific order along the electron transport system? Why, for example, does cytochrome $c$ pass the electron only to cytochrome $a$, and not back to cytochrome $b$? Furthermore, why does cytochrome $a_3$ pass the electron to oxygen rather than back to cytochrome $a$? The answer to these questions is obtained by measuring the so-called oxidation-reduction potentials in each molecule of the respiratory assembly. Essentially, oxidation-reduction potentials measure the affinity of a particular atom or molecule for electrons. The more positive the attraction for electrons in a given atom or molecule, the greater potential that atom or molecule possesses. When oxidation-reduction potentials for NAD, FAD, and the cytochromes are measured, data similar to those shown in Table 8–1 are obtained. These data indicate that each successive molecule in the electron transport system has a greater affinity for electrons than the molecules preceding it (i.e., has a stronger oxidation-reduction potential). Thus, as soon as any one electron transport molecule picks up electrons, they will be pulled away from it by the adjacent molecule, which possesses a more powerful oxidation-reduction potential. In this way the flow of electrons through the respiratory assembly is always maintained in one direction.

Why is ATP generated at only three points during electron transport? The answer to this question lies in the amount of energy released at each successive step in the transfer process. As we have seen, energy is released as electrons pass from one carrier to the next, as a result of the stepwise, downward transition of electrons from higher to lower energy levels. If the amount of energy given off at each step of the transfer process is measured, data such as those shown in Table 8–2 are obtained. To drive the uphill reaction involved in ATP formation, 7 kcal per mole are required. According to Table 8–2, only three specific points in the electron transport process generate more than 7 kcal (per mole of electrons transported). These points occur in the transfer from NAD to FAD, from cytochrome $b$ to cytochrome $c$, and from cytochrome $a$ to $a_3$ to molecular oxygen.

**TABLE 8–2**  POTENTIAL ENERGY RELEASED AS ELECTRONS ARE PASSED THROUGH EACH STEP OF THE ELECTRON TRANSPORT SYSTEM

| ELECTRON PASSAGE | $\Delta G$, kcal/mole |
| --- | --- |
| NAD $\rightarrow$ FAD | $-12.4$ |
| FAD $\rightarrow$ CYT $b$ | $-4.1$ |
| CYT $b$ $\rightarrow$ CYT $c$ | $-10.1$ |
| CYT $c$ $\rightarrow$ CYT $a$ | $-1.3$ |
| CYT $a$ $\rightarrow$ CYT $a_3$ $\rightarrow$ $O_2$ | $-24.4$ |

The stepwise release of potential energy during electron transport allows the capture of a significant percentage of the total potential energy as high-energy phosphate bonds. There is some evidence that some cytochrome systems located outside of mitochondria and possibly bound to other membranes may be able to power the active transport of materials across cell membranes independently of the hydrolysis of ATP. For example, Dr. George W. Kidder III of Wesleyan University in Connecticut has found evidence in frog stomach lining tissue that active acid secretion (a major function of this tissue and one which involves hydrogen ion transport) is driven by a direct interaction between a component or components of the cytochrome system, which is the energy source, and the transport of hydrogen ions. In this view, active transport in the frog tissue is seen as a thermodynamic alternative to ATP production, rather than a result of that production.

Having seen the complex forms of energy release and use in cell processes, we can now look at the ultimate source of energy for the cell: the sugars, starches, and fats. How are sugars oxidized, step by step, to release usable energy? What changes must the sugar molecule undergo during this process so that only two electrons are removed at a time, and how are these changes specifically controlled by enzymes? How can the cell be as efficient as it is in extracting energy from glucose? Where does the process of sugar breakdown occur in cells, and how is it regulated? How is the metabolism of sugars related to the metabolism of other molecules in the cell, such as proteins and nucleic acids? These and other questions will form the basis for a closer look at the metabolic pathways involved in biological oxidation.

In most cells the breakdown of sugars occurs in two main stages:

1) **Glycolysis or fermentation** is the partial breakdown of sugars into simpler components without the presence of molecular oxygen. Some electrons are removed from the sugars during glycolysis, though only a small amount of the total potential energy of the sugar is extracted. In certain specific cells the end product of glycolysis, pyruvic acid, is converted into alcohol in a process called alcoholic fermentation (for example, yeasts).

2) **Aerobic respiration** is the series of changes by which the products of glycolysis undergo further oxidation and ultimate degradation to $CO_2$ and $H_2O$. During respiration, many pairs of electrons are removed from the sugar fragments, with oxygen acting as the final electron acceptor. If oxygen is not available, only glycolysis occurs.

A generalized reaction for respiration can be written as follows:

$$FUEL\ MOLECULE + O_2 \rightarrow FUEL\ FRAGMENTS + H_2O + ENERGY. \tag{8–1}$$

In more specific terms, the equation for respiration can be given as

$$C_6H_{12}O_6 + 6O_2 + 6H_2O \rightarrow 6CO_2 + 12H_2O. \tag{8–2}$$

The general reaction for glycolysis can be written as

$$FUEL\ MOLECULE \rightarrow FUEL\ FRAGMENTS + ENERGY. \tag{8–3}$$

In particular, the equation for glycolysis can be written as

$$
\begin{array}{l}
C_6H_{12}O_6 \rightarrow C_3H_4O_3 \nearrow 2C_2H_5OH\ (alcohol) + 2CO_2 + ENERGY\ (yeast) \\
\text{(glucose)}\quad \text{(pyruvic} \\
\qquad\qquad \text{acid)} \searrow 2C_3H_6O_3\ (lactic\ acid) + ENERGY\ (bacteria,\ muscle\ cells)
\end{array}
\tag{8–4}
$$

The differences between the outcomes of glycolysis and respiration reflect differences in the individual steps, in the enzymes involved, and in the total energy extracted. Most cells of higher organisms are able to carry out both glycolysis and respiration. The cells of some lower organisms, however, are able

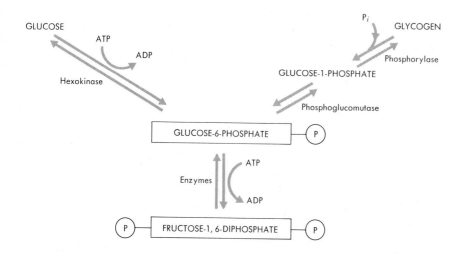

FIG. 8–8    Carbohydrate breakdown, phase I: mobilization. In this phase an activated 6-carbon unit, fructose-1,6-diphosphate, is produced, starting with either free glucose or glucose bound up in glycogen. Two ATP molecules are used per glucose converted into fructose-1,6-diphosphate. The cell thus spends energy to mobilize its carbohydrates for further oxidation. This can be considered an initial "investment."

to carry out only glycolysis. We will discuss their metabolic pathways in a later section. For the moment, let us consider the complete pathway of carbohydrate metabolism, including both glycolysis and respiration, as it occurs in the cells of higher plants and animals.

The process of sugar breakdown involves three phases: (1) mobilization of reserve carbohydrates, (2) glycolysis, and (3) aerobic respiration.

Mobilization entails preparing various carbohydrate stores in the cells for entry into the glycolytic pathway. The starting point of mobilization can be either single, free glucose units or glucose bound together as animal starch or **glycogen** (see Fig. 8–8). Both glucose and glycogen are converted to glucose-6-phosphate and, ultimately, to fructose-1,6-diphosphate. The mobilization of glucose requires the expenditure of ATP, while that of glycogen does not. The expenditure of ATP is necessary to form glucose units into glycogen in the first place. Therefore, the retrieval of glucose from glycogen does not require the direct expenditure of ATP itself, but uses from the surrounding medium inorganic phosphate groups which become attached to the glucose units as they are broken down from the glycogen chain. In the long run, then, whether the starting point is free glucose or glycogen, the creation of glucose-6-phosphate requires the expenditure of one ATP molecule at some point along the way.

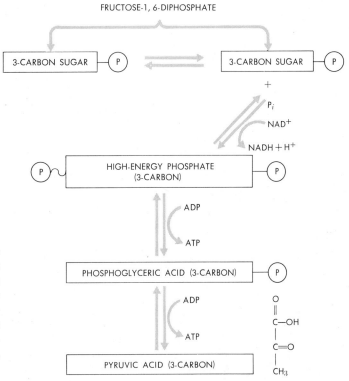

FIG. 8–9   Carbohydrate breakdown, phase II: glycolysis.   Once glucose has been mobilized as fructose-1,6-diphosphate, the 6-carbon sugar is broken down into two 3-carbon sugars.   These 3-carbon sugars are interconvertible between themselves, and exist in equilibrium.   Thus both pass through the glycolytic pathway shown on the right. The ultimate products of glycolysis are pyruvic acid, ATP, and reduced NAD (NADH + H$^+$).

A second ATP molecule, as shown in Fig. 8–8, is involved in the conversion of glucose-6-phosphate into fructose-1,6-diphosphate.   This represents the end of the mobilization phase.   As a result of mobilization, we have a 6-carbon, "energized" molecule which is ready to undergo the first of the oxidative pathways: glycolysis.

Glycolysis begins with the activation of glucose and involves essentially the breakdown of this 6-carbon sugar into two 3-carbon sugars, each of which proceeds along the same pathway and ultimately produces pyruvic acid (see Fig. 8–9).   The 3-carbon sugars each contain a phosphate group bonded by a low-energy phosphate bond.   Although these 3-carbon sugars are more energy-rich than they would be if they did not have the phosphate group attached to them, they are not high-energy phosphate compounds.   Each 3-carbon sugar undergoes a series of enzymatically catalyzed reactions in which two hydrogens (two electrons and two protons) are removed and a second phosphate group from the medium is added.   This series of reactions creates a high-energy phosphate bond out of one of the two phosphate groups and thus puts the 3-carbon sugar into a high potential-energy state.

As seen previously, a source of electrons is crucial for the generation of energy.   By interacting with NAD$^+$, the 3-carbon sugar is oxidized, giving up

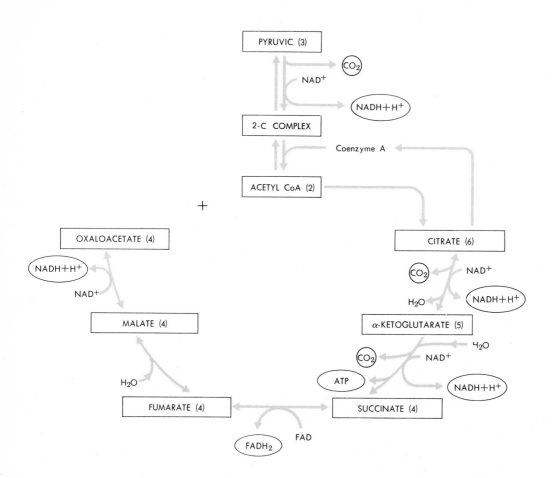

FIG. 8–10    Diagram of the Krebs cycle, showing several of the intermediate stages in the oxidation and decarboxylation of pyruvic acid.

two electrons. Electrons are negatively charged and tend to remain with the positively charged protons of the atom or molecule of which they are a part. However, metabolic pathways have a means of getting around this difficulty. With each electron removed from the fuel molecule, a proton is also removed. Together, an electron and a proton constitute a hydrogen atom. In reality, then, two hydrogen atoms are removed from the fuel molecule (the 3-carbon sugar). NAD, as the first electron acceptor in the transfer process, picks up from the oxidized fuel molecule one proton. The other proton is generally picked up by a water molecule in the medium, producing a positively charged hydronium ion ($H_3O^+$).

The 3-carbon, high-energy phosphate compound now interacts with ADP directly to generate a molecule of ATP. This process is known as **substrate-level**

**phosphorylation** and generates a low-energy phosphate compound known as **phosphoglyceric acid** (see Fig. 8–9). Substrate phosphorylation is distinct from electron transport in that it involves the generation of ATP by transfer of the high-energy phosphate bond from a substrate molecule directly to ADP. Substrate-level phosphorylation is a means of generating ATP without electron transport. Phosphoglyceric acid now undergoes a series of rearrangements in which its low-energy phosphate bond is converted into a high-energy phosphate bond. This high-energy phosphate bond is then transferred to ADP, generating another molecule of ATP. The end product of this series of rearrangements is a 3-carbon, nonphosphate compound, pyruvic acid ($C_3H_4O_3$).

The end product of glycolysis, from one original starting glucose molecule, is as follows: two molecules of pyruvic acid, two molecules of reduced NAD (NADH + $H^+$), and four molecules of ATP (from substrate phosphorylation). Since two ATP's were invested to mobilize the carbohydrate in glycolysis, the cell has achieved a net gain of two ATP's without electron transport.

The final phase of carbohydrate breakdown is called either the **Krebs cycle** (named for the English biochemist Hans Krebs, who first worked out the chemical details of the pathway), the **citric acid cycle** (since citric acid is a major intermediate in the process), or the **tricarboxylic acid cycle** (since a number of 3-carbon sugars are involved). The Krebs cycle involves further oxidation of the 3-carbon pyruvic acid to its lowest potential-energy level: carbon dioxide and water. During this process a number of electron pairs and carbon dioxide molecules are removed from intermediates. Some of the major stages in the Krebs cycle are shown in Fig. 8–10.

Specific enzymes are involved in the conversion of the 3-carbon pyruvic acid into a 2-carbon acetic acid molecule. During this conversion, one carbon dioxide molecule is removed and two electrons are picked up by NAD, forming a complex which combines immediately with **coenzyme A,** which is always present in the cell. This reaction forms acetyl coenzyme A (referred to as acetyl CoA), which is able to enter directly the pathways involved in the Krebs cycle. The 2-carbon acetyl CoA combines with the 4-carbon oxaloacetic acid, also abundant to the cells, to yield the 6-carbon citric acid.* In this reaction the 2-carbon acetate molecule is separated from coenzyme A, which is then returned to the medium and can be used for combination with another acetate. As a result of this process, two NADH + $H^+$ molecules are generated, one from each pyruvic acid. Each NADH + $H^+$ can generate three ATP's.

The 6-carbon citric acid molecule undergoes a series of oxidations and decarboxylations (removal of carbon dioxide molecules) as shown in Fig. 8–10. After the removal of each carbon dioxide or each pair of electrons (i.e., hydrogen atoms), internal rearrangements of the molecule are necessary to preserve its stability. Note that during the progress of the Krebs cycle, the 6-carbon molecule is converted successively into a 5-carbon molecule ($\alpha$-ketoglutarate) and a series of 4-carbon molecules (succinate, fumarate, malate, and oxaloacetate). Thus each turn of the cycle begins with a 4-carbon compound combining with a 2-carbon compound to yield a 6-carbon intermediate which is broken down to the original 4-carbon compound by a stepwise series of reactions. Because one molecule of oxaloacetic acid is regenerated from each molecule of oxaloacetate which originally combined with acetyl CoA, this series of reactions is truly a cycle.

Two sources of potential chemical energy are produced during the Krebs cycle. One is the direct production of ATP by substrate phosphorylation, such as occurs in the conversion of $\alpha$-ketoglutarate to succinate. A second is the production of reduced electron transport molecules, including both $NADH + H^+$ and $FADH_2$. In the complete oxidation of one pyruvic acid molecule, four $NADH + H^+$ molecules are generated; in addition, one $FADH_2$ is generated (in the conversion of succinate to fumarate). Through the process of electron transport, these molecules can generate a considerable amount of ATP. Each $NADH + H^+$ molecule yields three ATP's (except the one produced during glycolysis which generates only two) by passing its two electrons along the complete electron transport chain (as shown in Fig. 8–7). In the reaction where electrons are picked up from succinate by FAD, one step (from NAD to FAD) in the electron transport system is bypassed. Thus each pair of electrons passing from $FADH_2$ down the chain generates two ATP's instead of the customary three. From one pyruvic acid, then, 14 ATP's are generated by electron transport. An additional ATP per pyruvic acid comes from substrate phosphorylation.

Each glucose molecule which enters the breakdown process generates two pyruvic acid molecules. Thus the complete oxidation of a single glucose results in two turns of the Krebs cycle. To obtain an accurate tally of the input and output of glucose oxidation, it is necessary to remember that every reaction after the breakdown of fructose-1,6-diphosphate occurs twice for each original starting glucose. The relationship among glycolysis, the Krebs cycle, and the generation of ATP by electron transport is shown diagrammatically in Fig. 8–11.

ATP is thus generated in the breakdown of glucose both by substrate phosphorylation and by electron transport. Through both of these processes, but particularly through electron transport, an enormous amount of potential energy of glucose is harnessed as the potential energy of high-energy phosphate bonds. Table 8–3 shows the precise amount of ATP generated by each process, and the particular steps where energy is harnessed. As the data show, for each starting glucose molecule, six ATP's are generated by substrate phosphorylation and 32 ATP's are generated by electron transport. Two ATP's were required to get the process going, so that from the complete oxidation of a single glucose molecule, a net total of 36 ATP's is produced.* Or, put another way, from a mole of glucose molecules, 36 moles of ATP become available to the cell for work. Considering that only two ATP's were spent to get the process started, this represents a substantial return on investment in potential energy.

---

* Based upon recent calcuations which lower the number from 38.

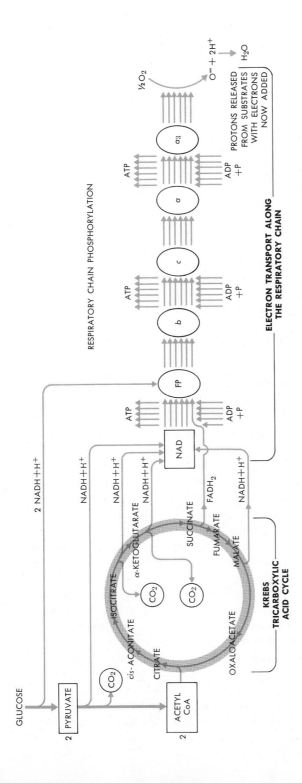

FIG. 8–11    The relation between glycolysis, the Krebs cycle, and the generation of ATP by electron transport. Every NADH + H² molecule passes its electrons along the complete electron transport assembly, generating three ATP's. Each FADH₂ molecule passes its electrons along only part of the assembly, thus generating only two ATP's. For each glucose molecule mobilized at the beginning, two of each of the reactions shown here take place. This is a result of the breakdown of the original 6-carbon sugar into 3-carbon fragments early in the pathway.

**TABLE 8–3**   ENERGY HARNESSED IN ATP'S DURING COMPLETE GLUCOSE OXIDATION

**BY SUBSTRATE PHOSPHORYLATION**

| | | |
|---|---|---|
| **GLYCOLYSIS:** | | |
| HIGH-ENERGY PHOSPHATE (HEXOSE) SUGAR $\rightarrow$ 2 PHOSPHOGLYCERIC ACID | | 2 ATP |
| 2 PHOSPHOGLYCERIC ACID $\rightarrow$ 2 PYRUVIC ACID | | 2 ATP |
| **KREBS CYCLE:** | | |
| 2 $\alpha$-KETOGLUTARIC ACID $\rightarrow$ SUCCINIC ACID | | 2 ATP |
| TOTAL FROM SUBSTRATE PHOSPHORYLATION | | 6 ATP |

**BY ELECTRON TRANSPORT**

| | | |
|---|---|---|
| **GLYCOLYSIS:** | | |
| 2 3-CARBON SUGAR PHOSPHATE $\rightarrow$ HIGH-ENERGY SUGAR DIPHOSPHATE | 2 NADH $\rightarrow$ | 6 ATP |
| **KREBS CYCLE:** | | |
| 2 PYRUVIC ACID $\rightarrow$ ACETIC ACID | 2 NADH | 6 ATP |
| 2 CITRIC ACID $\rightarrow$ $\alpha$-KETOGLUTARIC ACID | 2 NADH | 6 ATP |
| 2 $\alpha$-KETOGLUTARIC ACID $\rightarrow$ SUCCINIC ACID | 2 NADH | 6 ATP |
| 2 SUCCINIC ACID $\rightarrow$ FUMARIC ACID | 2 FADH | 4 ATP |
| 2 MALIC ACID $\rightarrow$ 2 OXALOACETIC ACID | 2 NADH | 6 ATP |
| TOTAL FROM ELECTRON TRANSPORT | | 34 ATP |
| TOTAL FROM SUBSTRATE PHOSPHORYLATION | | 6 ATP |
| TOTAL | | 40 ATP |

Note that, in many of the reactions diagrammed above, various intermediates and other molecules are constantly exchanged between the pathway and the surrounding medium. It is very important to realize that cells contain pools of molecules of various sorts which are constantly available for interactions with one or another intermediate during a particular metabolic reaction. For example, coenzyme A is plentiful in the cell and is available to react with acetic acid to produce acetyl CoA (Fig. 8–10). Coenzyme A is also used in other metabolic reactions, but is always returned to the medium. As another example, water is constantly being used in various reactions of the Krebs cycle. The water comes, of course, from the liquid medium which comprises a good part of the cell mass, and is "repaid" to the medium by the formation of water at the end of the electron transport process.

Cells, like whole organisms, are "open systems." This means that they must continually exchange materials with the external environment. Cells cannot produce ATP without oxidizing some fuel molecule, and that fuel must come from somewhere. For animals, it comes from the food they eat: plants and other animals. Like animals, plants also oxidize carbohydrates via glycolysis and the Krebs cycle. Unlike animals, however, plants can produce their own carbohydrates internally by photosynthesis. The energy which drives that uphill reaction is obtained externally from sunlight. Though more self-sufficient than animals, plants are still "open systems" in the sense that they require an external energy source. The ultimate source of all energy in living systems is external, whether in the form of specific fuel molecules which can be oxidized to regenerate ATP, or in the form of sunlight for the synthesis of carbohydrates. Without this continual input of energy from the environment, life would quickly come to a halt.

The precise molecular mechanism by which phosphorylation is carried out is still something of a mystery. Several hypotheses have been advanced to account for it. For example, Drs. Peter Mitchell and Janet Boyle of the Glynn Research Laboratories in England suggest that mitochondria (and chloroplasts and bacteria also) operate a "proton pump." This proton pump model proposes that the primary output of the energy conversion process is a flow of protons to one side of a membrane. The resulting concentration gradient of protons, and the electrical field produced by their concentration, can be used to drive a variety of metabolic processes, including the synthesis of ATP and the active uptake of ions or molecules. An attractive feature of the Mitchell-Boyle hypothesis is that it offers a very simple explanation for the action of a number of antibiotics that uncouple oxidation from the manufacture of ATP. It has been found that such antibiotics literally short-circuit the membranes by making them passively permeable to various ions. In other words, the antibiotics make the membranes leak. It is possible, of course, that the introduction of anti-biotics may affect the normal working state of the mitochondria. However, work on the anaerobic bacterium *Streptococcus faecalis*, which makes ATP by an entirely different process from mitochondria, shows that a proton-impermeable membrane is essential for active transport. This observation does not by any means provide conclusive support for the Mitchell-Boyle hypothesis, but it does illustrate nicely that a scientific model, in this case the proton pump, need not necessarily be correct to be useful. It will serve its purpose well if it merely suggests the right experiments to carry out.

**8–5
LIFE WITHOUT AIR:
ANAEROBIC
OXIDATION**

While human liver cells can exist for several hours without an oxygen supply, brain cells will cease to function properly if oxygen is cut off for only five or six minutes. In fact, most cells (especially in multicellular organisms) live on such a high-energy budget that constant electron transport is necessary to generate a sufficient supply of ATP to keep the cells alive. These cells are thus dependent on oxygen to keep the electron transport system in operation. Such cells are known as **aerobes,** a term which indicates that they require a supply of oxygen-containing air for continued existence. Some types of cells, however, have a different type of electron transport system and thus do not require oxygen to generate ATP. These cells, called **anaerobes,** produce ATP solely by substrate phosphorylation.

There are two types of anaerobic cells. **Obligate anaerobes** are those which completely lack an electron transport system and cannot use molecular oxygen whether it is present or not. Obligate anaerobes never use oxygen, and consequently exist on a very low ATP budget. **Facultative anaerobes,** on the

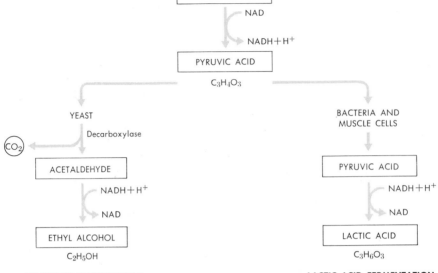

FIG. 8–12  Diagrammatic representation of two possible pathways of anaerobic oxidation. Since the electron transport system is not used in either pathway, some means must be available for disposing of the NADH + H$^+$ generated during the breakdown of glucose to pyruvate. This is accomplished by passing the electrons back to pyruvate to generate lactic acid, as in bacteria and muscle cells; or by passing the electrons to an intermediate produced from decarboxylating pyruvate to generate ethyl alcohol, as in yeast.

other hand, are those cells which can exist anaerobically for relatively long periods of time, even indefinitely, if oxygen is not present. Yet facultative anaerobes can, given a supply of oxygen, carry out electron transport (because they have the electron transport molecules) and thus generate larger quantities of ATP. Certain kinds of bacteria are examples of obligate anaerobes, since not only does their growth not require oxygen but in some instances is actually *hindered* by oxygen. Yeasts and the muscle cells of higher organisms are examples of facultative anaerobes. If oxygen is absent, yeast cells carry out the process of fermentation, producing ATP only by substrate phosphorylation. Similarly, when muscle cells are exercising very rapidly, the oxygen supply brought by the blood to the tissue is not sufficient to completely oxidize glucose to ATP. Thus muscle cells exist anaerobically during these periods of vigorous contraction, producing ATP by substrate phosphorylation. When a sufficient oxygen supply becomes available to either type of cell, much more ATP is generated by electron transport.

The end products of anaerobic breakdown are slightly different in different types of cells. Two common pathways of anaerobic respiration, one for yeasts and one for bacteria and muscle cells, are shown diagrammatically in Fig. 8–12. In its initial stages, anaerobic oxidation follows the pathway of glycolysis, during which glucose is converted to pyruvic acid. In this process, two $NADH + H^+$ molecules and two pyruvic acid molecules are produced for each starting glucose. Anaerobes share the glycolytic pathway with aerobic organisms, even to the extent of having most of the same enzymes involved in mobilization and initial oxidation of the glucose molecule. It is in the fate of the pyruvic acid molecule that anaerobes differ markedly from aerobes.

When no oxygen is available, bacterial and muscle cells dispose of the electrons picked up by $NAD^+$ by passing them (and their accompanying protons) back to the pyruvic acid, producing lactic acid:

$$C_3H_4O_3 + 2\,NADH + H^+ \rightarrow C_3H_6O_3 + 2\,NAD^+. \tag{8–5}$$
(pyruvic                          (lactic acid)
  acid)

Lactic acid is the end product of this form of anaerobic oxidation, and is as far as the facultative anaerobe is able to carry the oxidative process without molecular oxygen or as far as the obligate anaerobe can carry the process under any circumstances. It is the accumulation of lactic acid which produces muscle fatigue after extended use. It is also the accumulation of lactic acid by anaerobic bacteria that produces the characteristic taste of sour milk. Because lactic acid is the end product, this pathway is sometimes called **lactic fermentation.**

In yeast cells, the pyruvic acid molecule is decarboxylated to form an intermediate compound known as acetaldehyde. The 2-carbon acetaldehyde picks up electrons (and accompanying proton) from reduced NAD to produce ethyl alcohol, as shown in the following equation:

$$C_3H_4O_3 \xrightarrow{\text{decarboxylase}} C_2H_4O + CO_2 \xrightarrow[\text{NADH} + H^+ \quad \text{NAD}]{\text{alcohol dehydrogenase}} C_2H_3OH \tag{8–6}$$

(pyruvic                                    (ethyl
  acid)                                    alcohol)

Because ethyl alcohol is the end product of this anaerobic pathway, the process is sometimes referred to as **alcoholic fermentation.**

Anaerobic organisms get their ATP by substrate phosphorylation during the conversion of glucose to pyruvic acid. The reactions from pyruvic acid onward, as outlined above, are simply means of disposing of the end products of the earlier reactions (i.e., pyruvic acid and $NADH + H^+$). Man has been able to take advantage of the anaerobic process of alcoholic fermentation to produce a variety of alcoholic beverages; his wine, beer, and distilling industries all depend on this fermentation process.

In facultative anaerobic cells, such as human muscle tissue, lactic fermentation represents only a temporary pathway that is brought into play when the oxygen supply is low. As lactic acid accumulates, muscles become less and less able to carry out normal contraction. This occurs primarily because the ATP supply is gradually diminishing. During a period of rest, muscle cells can reoxidize the lactic acid through the electron transport system and generate more ATP which can be stored for further use.

It is apparent that anaerobic organisms gain far less ATP from the oxidation of each glucose molecule than do aerobic organisms. For this reason, anaerobic cells are relatively simple, and cannot achieve the high level of metabolic activity characteristic of aerobic cells. Anaerobes exist just above a "poverty line," gaining only a small return in energy currency for their initial investment.

**8–6
CHARACTERISTICS
OF METABOLIC
PATHWAYS AS
ILLUSTRATED BY
THE OXIDATION OF
SUGARS**

At the beginning of the chapter a series of questions was asked concerning the basic characteristics of metabolic pathways. Each of these questions can now be considered in relation to the specific examples of aerobic and anaerobic respiration.

1) **The stepwise nature of pathways.** Both glycolysis and the Krebs cycle involve a number of individual steps by which the original glucose molecule is broken down into smaller fragments and the potential energy extracted. As has been seen, the stepwise nature of the pathway ensures that maximum energy can be extracted in a usable form from the fuel molecule. For example, only a few electrons can be removed at a time from the molecule without creating a condition of instability. In order to extract energy in the most controlled (and therefore efficient) manner, the molecule is dismembered a few atoms at a time. Since life itself depends on the efficient use both of the substances present in a cell and of the available energy, the stepwise breakdown or buildup of molecules is essential for continued functioning.

2) **The specificity of individual steps in metabolic pathways.** Each step in the metabolic pathways of glycolysis and the Krebs cycle is catalyzed by specific enzymes which ensure that only certain chemical changes occur. For example, NAD can pick up electrons only from certain intermediate products in the Krebs cycle: it can interact with malate to form oxaloacetate and $NADH + H^+$, but it cannot interact with fumarate. The conversion of malate to oxaloacetate (with the production of $NADH + H^+$) is catalyzed by a specific enzyme (NAD-malic dehydrogenase). If this enzyme is not present, the reaction will not occur and the entire cycle can be stopped.

Similarly, malate must be formed from fumarate in order for the subsequent reactions of the Krebs cycle to proceed. This is accomplished through the action of an enzyme (fumarase) which catalyzes only this particular reaction. Every step throughout the Krebs cycle and glycolysis depends on such specific reactions. It is obvious that if fumarate, for example, could be converted into a very large number of intermediates other than malate, the specific production of ATP would be greatly retarded. All metabolic pathways depend on a similar high level of specificity of each component step to yield specific products.

Another aspect of specificity is apparent in glucose oxidation. Given the same starting reactant, the differences between two metabolic pathways are the result of the differences in enzymes present. For example, aerobic organisms can oxidize pyruvic acid to $CO_2$ and $H_2O$, with the production of a considerable amount of ATP, because they possess (a) enzymes for the Krebs cycle and (b) electron transport molecules, the cytochromes. Obligate anaerobes lack all of these enzymes and consequently cannot carry out the Krebs cycle pathways. Similarly, yeast and bacteria differ in the pathways by which they act upon pyruvic acid. Yeast has an enzyme (decarboxylase) which converts pyruvate to acetaldehyde. Acetaldehyde is then converted by another specific enzyme into ethyl alcohol. Some bacteria, on the other hand, lack decarboxylase and thus convert pyruvic acid directly into lactic acid. Again, the specific fate of any molecule in the metabolic pathways depends on the specific enzymes which are present.

3) **Localization of pathways.** In the cells of most organisms, pathways are localized to some extent in various parts of the cell. The example of complete glucose oxidation illustrates this principle clearly. The glycolytic pathway occurs in the cytoplasm of cells and is catalyzed by soluble enzymes not bound to any particular cell organelles. The enzymes for the Krebs cycle, however, are not free in the cytoplasm, but rather are dissolved in the liquid matrix inside mitochondria. These enzymes are apparently not bound to the mitochondrial membranes, but are too large to pass through the walls of the mitochondria into the cytoplasm. The electron transport molecules (the cytochromes, FAD to some extent, and possibly NAD) are generally bound to the cristae (Fig. 6–13). Pyruvic acid, generated in the cytoplasm by glycolysis, can pass through the mitochondrial wall and come into contact with the enzymes of the Krebs cycle. As soon as electrons are removed from intermediates in the Krebs cycle, they are carried by NAD (or FAD) to the respiratory assembly where electron transport can take place. The by-products of the Krebs cycle ($CO_2$, water, and ATP) can pass out of the mitochondria into the cytoplasm for elimination or involvement in other metabolic pathways.

We see here, then, three levels of localization. Glycolysis is the least localized of the pathways, occurring throughout the cytoplasm. The Krebs cycle is much more localized, being confined to the liquid medium within the rather small mitochondria. Electron transport is the most highly confined of all the pathways, taking place within a respiratory assembly less than 50 angstroms in diameter. The advantages of this localization are obvious. When all the reactants and intermediates as well as the enzymes of a particular pathway are confined in a small space, the rate of reaction is markedly increased and thus efficiency improved. The electron transport system shows one of the most highly developed localizations in all of biochemistry. Here, not only are the molecules tightly bound together in close physical proximity, but they seem even to be arranged in an order appropriate to their functioning in the electron transport process. A diagram of one respiratory assembly, attached to the mitochondrial wall, is

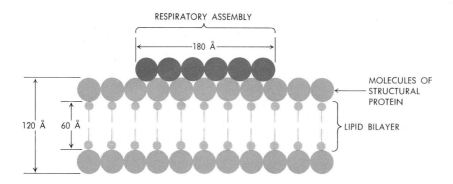

FIG. 8–13   Cross section of a mitochondrial wall, showing ordered molecules of a single respiratory assembly attached to the wall.  Note that the electron transport molecules of the assembly are arranged in the precise order in which they receive and pass on electrons.  (Adapted from A. L. Lehninger, *Bioenergetics.*  New York: Benjamin, 1965, p. 113.)

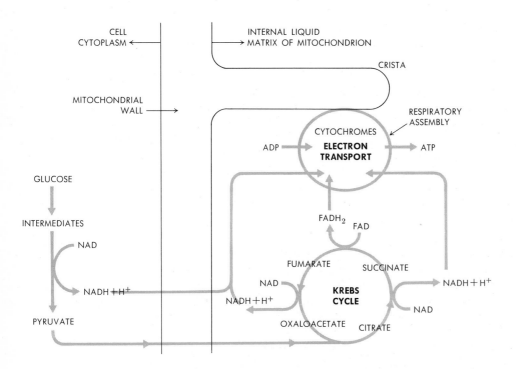

FIG. 8–14   Schematic summary of localization of various pathways in the complete oxidation of glucose in aerobic cells.  The reactions of glycolysis occur in the cell cytoplasm by enzymes located there.  The pathway of the Krebs cycle occurs through soluble enzymes located in the liquid matrix inside the mitochondrion.  Electron transport, during which ATP is generated from ADP, occurs in the respiratory assembly, a group of molecules attached to the inside wall of the mitochondrion.

shown in Fig. 8–13. With this highly ordered spatial arrangement, electrons can be transmitted rapidly from one carrier to the next in line. In the reactions for glycolysis, the Krebs cycle, and electron transport, the relation between structure and function on a subcellular level is clearly evident. A summary of the localizations involved in glucose breakdown is given in Fig. 8–14.

4) **Energetics of metabolic pathways.** In looking at any metabolic pathway, it is important to distinguish between the energetics of the pathway as a whole and the energetics of individual steps. For example, some of the steps in the oxidation of glucose are *endergonic*, as is the conversion of glucose to glucose-6-phosphate or the conversion of glucose-6-phosphate to fructose-1,6-diphosphate (both of which require the input of ATP). Yet the overall reaction is strongly exergonic. In looking at the energetics of glucose oxidation, we are concerned with (a) the total free-energy change and (b) the efficiency of the entire process, i.e., the amount of energy recaptured in a usable form compared to the total free-energy change. In the case of glucose oxidation, the amount of work accomplished is equivalent to the number of high-energy phosphate bonds built for a given amount of glucose oxidized. As seen earlier, the total free-energy change in the complete oxidation of a mole of glucose is 680 kcal. This figure represents the total potential energy released during the process. From calculations made earlier (Section 8–4), it was seen that a total of 38 ATP molecules were generated per mole of glucose oxidized. At a value of 7 kcal per mole of ATP, roughly 252 out of 680 kcal were regained by the cells in a usable form. Recall, however, that two moles of ATP are required to mobilize a mole of glucose for the oxidative pathways. The cell, therefore, shows a net gain of 6 moles of ATP, or 252 kcal per mole of glucose oxidized. Since 252 is approximately 37% of 680, glycolysis and the Krebs cycle combined extract 37% of the energy released during glucose oxidation. This is a remarkable degree of efficiency when compared to the best internal combustion engines, which achieve considerably less efficiency.*

If the efficiency of glucose oxidation in aerobic and anaerobic organisms is compared, an astounding difference is observed. Anaerobic organisms, carrying out only glycolysis, generate a total of four moles of ATP per mole of glucose. Since two ATP's were required to start the process, the actual net gain is two ATP's. This is equivalent to 14 kcal (per mole) out of a possible 680 which would be released if the glucose molecule could be broken down to its lowest energy states ($CO_2$ and $H_2O$). Anaerobic organisms are thus able to extract less than 1% of the energy available to them in the glucose molecule. However, anaerobic organisms do not break glucose down nearly as far as aerobic organisms do. The total energy released in the partial breakdown of glucose to alcohol or lactic acid is 56 kcal per mole. At a net gain of two moles of ATP per mole of glucose oxidized, anaerobic cells can reach an efficiency of 35%. Thus, for the reactions

---

* The average automobile engine is seldom better than 25% efficient; i.e., it extracts as usable work (forward motion) 25% of the energy released during combustion of gasoline.

which they actually do carry out, anaerobic organisms are only slightly less efficient than aerobic.

Every metabolic pathway has a relative degree of efficiency which can be calculated in a similar fashion. It is particularly important to understand that the relatively high efficiency of cellular metabolic pathways is brought about by (a) their stepwise nature, (b) the fact that they are frequently localized in specific regions of the cell, and (c) the role of enzymes in reducing the amount of activation energy necessary to get the reactions going.

5) **The control of metabolic pathways.** Controls affect both the overall directionality and the rate at which metabolic pathways occur. Such controls are usually exerted on specific steps of the pathway, and can occur in a number of ways. One is by the **law of mass action** or **Le Châtelier's principle,** which states that the rate and the direction of a reaction (or series of reactions) are affected by the relative concentrations of reactants and products. In a reversible reaction, the greater the concentration of reactant and the less the concentration of products, the more the reaction is shifted to the right. Conversely, the greater the concentration of products and the less the concentration of reactants, the more the reaction is shifted to the left. Concentration of either reactants or products is determined by several factors. One is the availability of reactants, in turn determined by what can get into and leave the cell. A second is the fate of the end products—whether they are removed from the site of the reaction, packaged up and stored in the cell, broken down, or simply transported out of the cell. In aerobic respiration, for example, $CO_2$ diffuses out of the cell, thus "pulling" the reaction toward more sugar breakdown. An alternative fate is that the end products build up and accumulate in the cell. All these factors affect both the direction and the rate at which a pathway operates by exerting "pushes" and "pulls" on both reactants and products.

A second means by which metabolic pathways are controlled is through the energy requirement—the degree of reversibility—of the individual steps of the reaction series. For example, most of the individual reactions in the Krebs cycle are reversible, having relatively low free-energy changes in either direction. However, from Fig. 8–10 it can be seen that at least two steps—conversion of oxaloacetate and acetyl CoA to citrate, and the conversion of $\alpha$-ketoglutarate to succinate—are shifted heavily to the right (i.e., in the forward direction). This means that the energy requirement for the forward reaction is considerably less than the reverse. Thus, although it is theoretically possible for succinate to go back and reform $\alpha$-ketoglutarate or for citrate to go back and reform acetyl CoA and oxaloacetate, neither of these reactions is very likely to occur. From the standpoint of equilibrium and energy requirements, both reactions are virtually nonreversible. Thus the Krebs cycle is kept moving in a single direction, even though most of the steps are individually reversible. A few essentially irreversible steps in a metabolic pathway act in a manner analogous to a series of one-way turnstiles in a subway station: they prevent the whole reaction series (i.e., the passage of people) from backing up by stopping the reverse flow at specific points. The existence of irreversible steps does not change the *rate* of the overall reaction, which is controlled by other factors, including the concentration of reactants and products. But it does keep the reaction series moving in one direction.

Another example of how directionality is controlled can be seen in the electron transport system. Each successive transport molecule has a greater affinity for electrons than the molecule preceding it in the series. There is thus little chance for the electrons to move in a reverse direction and slow down, or to avoid being passed in the sequence necessary to generate ATP.

The rate at which metabolic reactions take place can be controlled by a third and highly subtle device: controlling the activity of enzymes operating on specific steps in the pathway. This control can be exerted in two ways: (a) by controlling the rate at which enzyme molecules are synthesized, and (b) by controlling the rate at which existing molecules catalyze specific reactions with their substrate. The first method is essentially a genetic mechanism (i.e., controlling the rate at which enzymes are synthesized by the genes) and will be dealt with in more detail in a later chapter. The second process operates by an elaborate feedback mechanism, whereby certain molecules associated with a given pathway directly interact with enzymes controlling early stages in the same pathway. This interaction can serve either to increase (activate) or decrease (inhibit) the rate at which the enzyme acts on the substrate.

A single example will illustrate both activation and inhibition of enzymes by products of the pathway. The conversion of citric acid to $\alpha$-ketoglutaric acid involves several steps, one of which is catalyzed by the enzyme isocitrate dehydrogenase, as shown below:

$$\text{CITRATE} \xleftrightarrow{}\xleftrightarrow{}\xleftrightarrow[\text{dehydrogenase}]{\text{isocitrate}} \alpha\text{-KETOGLUTARATE} + \text{NADH} + \text{H}^+ + \text{CO}_2.$$

As part of the Krebs cycle, this reaction leads ultimately to the production of usable energy (NADH + H$^+$ or, ultimately, ATP). Chemical investigation has shown that both of these molecules are capable of inhibiting the action of the enzyme isocitrate dehydrogenase. In other words, in the presence of these two molecules the enzyme greatly slows down the conversion of citrate to $\alpha$-ketoglutarate. Thus, as the cell builds up a greater concentration of energy-rich compounds, the pathway for energy production is signaled to slow down. Conversely, it has been found that molecules of ADP or AMP stimulate isocitrate dehydrogenase to convert citrate into $\alpha$-ketoglutarate. Thus, as the energy supply of the cell begins to run low, enzymes in the energy-producing pathway are signaled to speed up their action.

The advantage of sensitive control mechanisms from the standpoint of the efficiency of metabolic pathways is obvious. Such controls keep the cell from producing more of a certain compound than is needed and also prevent the concentration of needed substances within the metabolic pool from falling below a critical level in the cells.  In other words, such control mechanisms help to adjust the cell's supply of molecules to ever-changing metabolic needs.

How can such elaborate control mechanisms go accounted for on the molecular level?  How is it possible at this level to provide a precise explanation of how such molecules as ATP or ADP respectively inhibit or activate enzymes such as isocitrate dehydrogenase?  In the last several years an interesting model has been proposed by J. P. Changeux and Arthur Pardee for how this might be brought about.  The model is based on two assumptions:

a)   Enzymes can have more than one combining site.  In addition to a site (or sites) for the substrate, enzymes can also have binding sites for other molecules, such as certain intermediates or end products of the particular metabolic pathway.  Thus an enzyme molecule could have a binding site for an inhibitor molecule and a binding site for an activator molecule in addition to an active site for the substrate.

b)   Enzymes, being proteins, can exist in one of several three-dimensional shapes, all of which are interconvertible and exist in the cell in equilibrium with one another.  The enzyme molecule can, without any input of energy, shift back and forth between one conformation and another.

The model can be thought of as operating in the following manner.  The two conformational forms of the enzyme can be thought of as existing in equilibrium in the cell, as shown below:

$$E \rightleftharpoons E*$$
RELAXED    CONSTRAINED

In the relaxed state, the enzyme has a high affinity for both its substrate, S, and a smaller molecule, the activator, A.  The activator retards the shift of the enzyme from the relaxed to the constrained conformation.  In the relaxed state, the enzyme also has a low affinity for an inhibitor molecule, I.  The inhibitor retards the shift of the enzyme from the constrained back to the relaxed conformation.  In the constrained state, the enzyme has a low affinity for both its substrate and the activator, but a high affinity for the inhibitor molecule.  The inhibitor does not remain permanently bound to the enzyme.  The characteristics of the model can be summarized as follows:

$$E \rightleftharpoons E*$$

| RELAXED | CONSTRAINED |
|---|---|
| HIGH AFFINITY FOR S | LOW AFFINITY FOR S |
| HIGH AFFINITY FOR A | LOW AFFINITY FOR A |
| A RETARDS $E \rightarrow E*$ | I RETARDS $E* \rightarrow E$ |
| LOW AFFINITY FOR I | HIGH AFFINITY FOR I |

If much A is present in the cell, the relaxed state of the enzyme is favored; A binds to E, preventing the normal shift of E molecules to E*.  Because E*

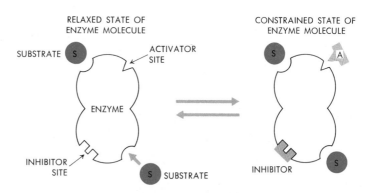

FIG. 8–15   Schematic picture of an enzyme molecule subject to mechanisms which control its rate of activity. The enzyme contains three types of active sites: two substrate sites, one "activator" site, and one "inhibitor" site. The activator and inhibitor sites are specific for two different types of molecules and are both different in shape from the substrate sites. When in the constrained state the enzyme does not easily combine with the substrate or activator.

has a low affinity for A, E* molecules are able to shift back to E. As a result, the equilibrium shifts towards the formation of relaxed enzyme (E). Because E can react readily with the substrate, the enzyme-catalyzed reaction proceeds. However, if there is much inhibitor, I, present in the cell, the situation is completely different: E* has a high affinity for I, which, when bound to E*, prevents the conformational shift back to the relaxed state, E. All molecules of E* are prevented from reverting to E, but E is not prevented from converting to E*. The equilibrium is shifted toward the right, and more E* is formed. It, too, combines with I, so that gradually most of the population of the enzyme in the cell is inactivated. Thus the number of active or inactive enzyme molecules is controlled by the concentrations of activator, inhibitor, and substrate in the cell (or the *in vitro* system) acting on the equilibrium between E and E*. The mechanisms postulated for these changes are shown schematically in Figs. 8–15, 8–16, and 8–17.

To date, there is not a great quantity of data indicating that this model necessarily explains the *exact* mechanism by which enzyme activation and inhibition can take place. However, the model *is* consistent with many facts of protein structure and enzyme specificity, and thus provides at least a starting point for reviewing how subtle control mechanisms can operate on the biochemical level.

The picture of enzyme regulations presented above is another example of a scientific or hypothetical model. Models serve to suggest further lines of investigation and experimentation; they are definitely *not* meant to represent unalterable dogma. One difficulty with model-building in science or any other field is the

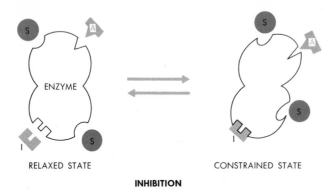

**INHIBITION**

FIG. 8–16    Inhibition operates by the binding of an inhibitor to a specific active site on the enzyme's surface. This binding causes the three-dimensional shape or conformation of the enzyme to shift to the ''constrained'' state, in which the substrate active sites will not accept substrate molecules. The rate of catalytic activity is thus greatly reduced.

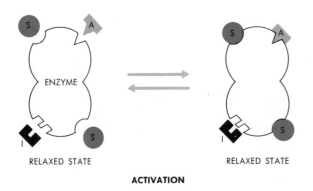

**ACTIVATION**

FIG. 8–17    Model for enzyme activation by the binding of an activator to a specific active site. The activator prevents the enzyme from undergoing normal, random shifts to the constrained state, and thus keeps it working at full capacity. In the relaxed state, the inhibitor molecule may also be kept from fitting easily into its site on the enzyme surface.

ever-present tendency to accept models as proven facts. However, as was seen in Chapter 3, scientific models are simply hypotheses and thus cannot be "proven." The model of enzyme action just discussed is *useful*, because it allows accurate predictions to be made and suggests some specific further experiments. For example, many enzymes are composed of one or more subunits, each of which consists of a polypeptide chain. The subunits are held together in the enzyme molecule by hydrogen bonds or various forms of weak attraction. If the subunits of an enzyme are separated so that the subunit (or subunits) containing the substrate active site are no longer in contact with the inhibitor

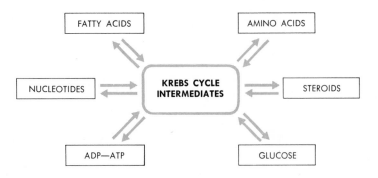

FIG. 8–18　The Krebs cycle as a metabolic hub. Intermediates in the cycle form the takeoff points for other metabolic pathways involved in the synthesis (and breakdown) of various classes of molecules.

site, it would be predicted that the presence of an inhibitor should not affect the catalytic rate of the enzyme. Such experiments have been performed, and it has been shown that as predicted, when the subunits of a particular enzyme are separated, the inhibitor has no effect. While such data do not provide "proof" that the model is accurate, they do lend support to its general conception.

6) **The interrelationship between metabolic pathways.** Thus far, glycolysis and the Krebs cycle have been considered primarily as pathways for the breakdown of glucose and the production of energy. However, nearly all the intermediates in these two pathways are starting reactants, intermediates, or end products in other metabolic pathways within the cell. For example, Krebs cycle intermediates form connecting points with pathways for the synthesis (and breakdown) of all the major types of molecules found in the cell: fatty acids, amino acids, steroids, carbohydrates, and nucleotides (Fig. 8–19). This relationship is shown still more specifically in Fig. 8–19. Consider, for example, the very important intermediate acetyl coenzyme A, the specific form in which the oxidation products of glucose enter the Krebs cycle. Acetyl CoA represents an intermediate in the breakdown of carbohydrates. In addition, the condensation of several acetyl CoA molecules (each containing two carbons) can produce the hydrocarbon chains, which are major structural components of fatty acid molecules. Thus, when fatty acids are broken down to be used as fuel, they can enter the Krebs cycle as acetyl CoA. Acetyl CoA can also be converted, by a series of reactions, into one of several amino acids. Furthermore, it is the starting point for the synthesis of steroids, molecules which form the basis of several important hormones.

Note also from Fig. 8–19 that the conversion of acetyl CoA to each of these other types of molecules occurs by reversible pathways, a very important factor in the regulation of cell metabolism. If a greater amount of carbohydrates

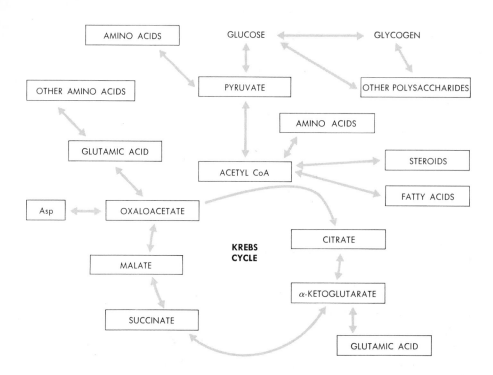

FIG. 8–19   The Krebs cycle as a metabolic hub, showing details of the various intermediates from which synthesis of other types of molecules can occur.

comes into the cell than is needed to build ATP, much of the carbohydrate can be shunted off through acetyl CoA to form fatty acids. Fats are an important storage form of fuel molecules, and thus can be held in reserve until needed. The existence of this pathway is responsible for the buildup of fat in human beings on a carbohydrate-rich diet.

As Fig. 8–19 shows, many intermediates in the Krebs cycle, e.g., α-keto-glutarate and oxaloacetate, can be converted into other types of molecules, principally amino acids. Pyruvate can enter a pathway for the formation of several types of amino acids, and glucose can be converted into a variety of polysaccharides including, most prominently, glycogen. The existence of these many interconvertible steps between the Krebs cycle and other metabolic pathways allows for maximum efficiency in the use of molecules in the cells. If every pathway started with its own reactants, proceeded through its own particular set of intermediates, and produced its own individual set of products, far more types of molecules would be needed in a cell than are actually found there. The fact that the end product of one pathway can serve as an intermediate or a reactant for another pathway can conserve both the number and the different types of molecules necessary as well as the amount of work the cell must do.

Cells are small, and space and energy are usually at a premium. Thus the interconvertibility of pathways not only allows the exercise of more effective control but also increases the efficiency of metabolic activity.

The series of reactions involved in glycolysis and the Krebs cycle are numerous and intricate. How do we know the intermediate steps involved, and the sequence in which they occur? Several examples will illustrate the way in which biochemists have learned about the respiratory reactions.

In 1935 the Hungarian biologist Albert Szent-Gyorgyi studied the respiration of isolated pigeon-breast muscle. He found that the rate of oxygen uptake, quite rapid at first, fell off slowly with time. Pigeon-breast muscle respires very rapidly, thus producing little lactic acid. Its by-products are $CO_2$ and $H_2O$. Szent-Gyorgyi noted something else of importance in his experiments: The fall in rate of respiration paralleled the rate at which succinic acid disappeared from the muscle. He found, however, that the respiratory rate could be restored to its normal level by the addition of small amounts of succinic or fumaric acid. Szent-Gyorgyi concluded that these substances must somehow be involved in the oxidation of carbohydrate. Later studies showed that if succinic, fumaric, or oxaloacetic acid were added to muscle preparation, a large amount of citric acid would be produced. This gave such workers as Hans Krebs the idea that something like the following must be taking place:

SUCCINIC ACID ⎫
FUMARIC ACID ⎬ → CITRIC ACID
OXALOACETIC ACID ⎭

However, the exact sequence of reactions was not at all clear.

The task of determining the exact reaction series was complicated by the fact that several of these substances are chemically interconvertible. For example, succinic acid can be converted into fumaric acid, and vice versa. This **reversible reaction** is catalyzed by the enzyme succinic dehydrogenase. When succinic acid is added to isolated muscle, fumaric acid and citric acid accumulate. When fumaric acid is added, succinic acid and citric acid accumulate. There is, therefore, no conclusive way to distinguish between the two alternative hypotheses for the sequence of reactions:

*Hypothesis I:* Succinic acid → fumaric acid → citric acid.

*Hypothesis II:* Fumaric acid → succinic acid → citric acid.

One experimental technique does make it possible to decide between these alternatives, however. The enzyme succinic dehydrogenase acts only in the chemical reactions by which succinic acid is converted to fumaric acid, and vice versa. Now, we know from an earlier chapter that a substance called malonic acid (Fig. 7–27) selectively inhibits succinic dehydrogenase. This means that when malonic acid is present in the system, only molecules of succinic dehydrogenase will cease to function. On the basis of the two hypotheses given above, it is possible to make a prediction.

**Hypothesis I:** *If* . . .     the correct sequence of reactions is:
Succinic acid → fumaric acid → citric acid, . . .

**Prediction:**     *then* . . . addition of malonic acid along with succinic acid should *not* produce an increase in the amount of citric acid.

**Hypothesis II:** *If* . . .     the correct sequence of reactions is:
Fumaric acid → succinic acid → citric acid, . . .

**Prediction:**     *then* . . . addition of malonic acid along with succinic acid *should* produce an increase in the amount of citric acid.

Performing the experiment shows that citric acid does not accumulate in the muscle tissue. These results thus support the predictions of hypothesis I and contradict those of hypothesis II.

The above examples illustrate two major types of the techniques involved in working out biochemical reaction series. The first technique involves the addition of large amounts of a suspected intermediate to a biochemical system, measurement of its disappearance rate, and identification of the new substance that will then begin to build up. This was the technique applied by Szent-Gyorgyi. The second technique involves the addition to a biochemical system of some substance known to inhibit a certain enzyme. The alteration of the rate at which certain products accumulate will indicate at which point in the reaction series the particular enzyme acts. For example, consider this series:

$$A \xrightarrow{\text{enzyme 1}} B \xrightarrow{\text{enzyme 2}} C \xrightarrow{\text{enzyme 3}} D \xrightarrow{\text{enzyme 4}} E \text{ (END PRODUCT).}$$

BLOCKED WITH
METABOLIC POISON

If enzyme 3 is put out of commision by a known inhibitor, the intermediate products B and C will accumulate while D disappears (it is converted to E). This indicates that C precedes D in the reaction series. It also indicates that enzyme 3 catalyzes the conversion of C to D. Several substances, such as cyanide and carbon monoxide, are known to block the action of certain cytochromes. By employing these poisons, it has been possible to work out the sequence of reactions in electron transport.

There are, of course, many other techniques frequently used in biochemical analysis. One such technique involves radioactively labeled molecules. These are fed to a biochemical system and the reaction series is stopped at various places. The distribution of radioactive atoms in various intermediate products gives an idea of the pathway taken by the series of reactions. In summary, the biochemist must use a variety of methods to study living processes on the molecular level.

In this chapter we have explored some of the characteristics of metabolic pathways by looking at the reactions involved in carbohydrate breakdown and the generation of energy as ATP. We have specifically examined the pathways of glycolysis, the Krebs cycle, and electron transport in terms of the individual steps involved, their specificity, the localization of pathways within the cell, the energetics of pathways, how the rate and directionality of pathways are controlled, and how various metabolic pathways in the cells are interconnected. A cell is not a bag of randomly mixed molecules, but a highly organized structure in which chemical events occur with a frequency and efficiency far greater than could be obtained by pure chance. Cell structures serve to aid this efficiency by forming localized regions where contact between appropriate molecules is not left to pure chance.

8-8
CONCLUSION

It has also been noted that the dynamics of cells can be controlled in highly subtle ways. Because cells cannot afford to synthesize molecules they do not need and must respond to changing external conditions rapidly, built-in signaling devices which redirect various intermediates to appropriate pathways are necessary. A molecule such as glucose which starts down a particular metabolic pathway (such as in glycolysis) is like a train starting out from the roundhouse. It is initially headed in one direction, but can be diverted along any number of interconnecting tracks according to special needs. The interconvertibility of metabolic pathways, combined with the sensitive control mechanisms which regulate their direction and rate, provide the cell with maximum flexibility. Thus, despite constantly changing external conditions, cells are able to maintain their many vital activities in a relatively constant way.

1. Explain why the equation

EXERCISES

$$C_6H_{12}O_6 + 6O_2 + 6H_2O \rightarrow 6CO_2 + 12H_2O$$

is a more accurate representation of the process of respiration than the equation

$$C_6H_{12}O_6 + 6O_2 \rightarrow 6CO_2 + 6H_2O.$$

What is the role of water in the process of aerobic respiration?

2. Give several reasons for the fact that energy-releasing reactions in living cells occur in a number of steps.

3. Figure 8–20 relates the amount of carbon dioxide produced by yeast fermentation to time. Answer the following questions on the basis of the information contained in this graph.

a) Why does the addition of inorganic phosphate at about the 75-minute mark increase the amount of $CO_2$ produced? What does this show about the role of phosphate in the process of respiration?

b) Compare the *rates* of $CO_2$ production for the first 25 minutes with those for the second 25 minutes [rate of respiration is determined by dividing the total amount of reaction (in this case measured as the number of ml of $CO_2$ produced) by duration of the reaction (25 minutes for each period)]. Are the *rates* the same or

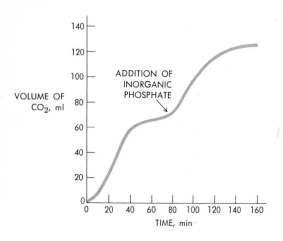

FIG. 8-20

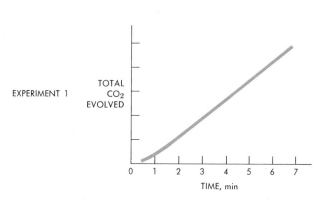

FIG. 8-21

different? Is this expected in terms of the role we think phosphate plays in the process of respiration? Why or why not?

4. A slice of liver tissue (an aerobic type of cell) was prepared with cells intact, and allowed to carry out respiration. The culture medium in which the cells were incubated contained all the necessary precursors for respiration: glucose, oxygen, ADP, and inorganic phosphate ($P_i$). Respiration rate was measured by the total amount of carbon dioxide evolved in given periods of time. As long as the culture was carefully maintained, respiration occurred normally and the graph for $CO_2$ evolution was as shown in Fig. 8-21.

The enzyme hexokinase catalyzes the conversion of glucose into glucose-6-phosphate. If a competitive inhibitor for hexokinase is added to the incubating liver cells, the curve for $CO_2$ evolution is as shown in Fig. 8-22.

The enzyme succinic dehydrogenase catalyzes the conversion of succinic acid to fumaric acid. When an inhibitor for this enzyme is added, the curve for $CO_2$ evolution is much the same as shown in Experiment 2 (see Fig. 8-23).

If cyanide is added to the incubating cells (no other inhibitors added), the curve for $CO_2$ evolution appears as in Fig. 8-24.

Assume that oxygen is readily available to all the cells and that its delivery does not depend on the presence of hemoglobin or myoglobin. Answer the following questions based on these data:

a) Explain the difference between the graph lines for Experiments 2, 3, and 4 and that for Experiment 1. Discuss each experiment separately, showing the metabolic basis for the observed effects. Relate your answers to occurrences on the molecular level in the various pathways involved. Discuss the molecules affected by the various inhibitors, and how these molecules affect equilibrium in the pathway.

b) Dinitrophenol (DNP) is a drug which uncouples ATP production from the electron transport system, thereby interfering with ATP production but allowing electron transport to occur. Supposing that DNP is added to each of the cultures

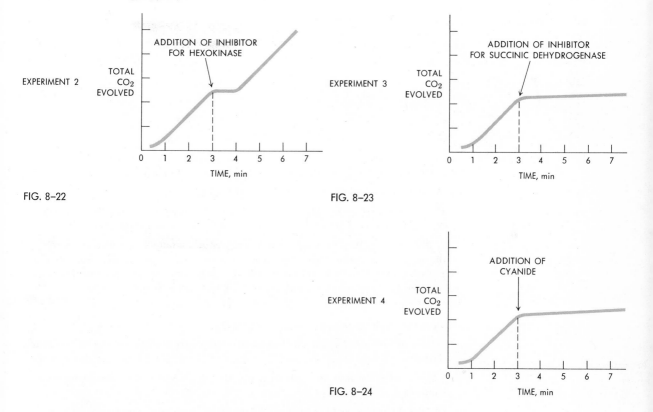

EXPERIMENT 2

FIG. 8–22

EXPERIMENT 3

FIG. 8–23

EXPERIMENT 4

FIG. 8–24

in Experiments 2, 3, and 4 at time period 3 (the same time point at which each of the inhibitors is added), predict what the resulting line for $CO_2$ evolution will be like. Draw the graph for each experiment. Explain your reasons for each graph.

c) Predict the changes, if any, in the graph lines, if pyruvate were added to the culture system for Experiments 2, 3, and 4. Give your reasons.

5. How is it that the anaerobic respiration of glucose yields different end products in yeast and animal tissues? What must be the principal differences in the two types of cells?

6. Tables 8–4 and 8–5 show the amounts of carbon dioxide produced and oxygen consumed during the respiration of germinating seedlings. To compare the respiratory processes of different organisms, these data can be treated in two ways: They may be plotted on a graph (ml of $O_2$ used on the horizontal axis, and $CO_2$ produced on the vertical) and the slope of the lines compared, or the *respiratory quotient* for each type of organism may be determined. Respiratory quotient is determined by dividing the amount of oxygen consumed by the amount of $CO_2$ produced. This can be done by averaging the amounts of each gas, then using these mean values for cal-

**TABLE 8–4**

DATA ON GERMINATING WHEAT SEEDLINGS

| $CO_2$ PRODUCED, ml | $O_2$ CONSUMED, ml |
|---|---|
| 9.2 | 9.6 |
| 14.8 | 17.1 |
| 15.6 | 14.9 |
| 16.6 | 13.8 |
| 17.0 | 17.4 |
| 20.1 | 19.9 |
| 21.6 | 21.2 |

**TABLE 8–5**

DATA ON GERMINATING CASTOR-BEAN SEEDLINGS

| $CO_2$ PRODUCED, ml | $O_2$ CONSUMED, ml |
|---|---|
| 5.1 | 7.4 |
| 13.1 | 17.4 |
| 9.1 | 13.2 |
| 2.5 | 4.4 |
| 5.0 | 6.6 |
| 11.3 | 15.1 |
| 18.8 | 26.7 |

culation. On the basis of this information, answer the following questions:

a) What are the respiratory quotients for the wheat seed and the castor-bean seed?

b) Plot the data for each table on a graph. How do the slopes for the two lines compare to each other? How do the slopes relate to respiratory quotient?

c) A difference in respiratory quotient indicates that one organism uses more $O_2$ during its respiration than the other. Knowing that the oxygen used in this process unites with hydrogens from a foodstuff, can you account for the *differences* between the respiratory quotients of wheat and castor bean?

d) What additional information would you need to verify your answer for (c)?

7. Observe the experiments described by Fig. 8–25.

a) Which of the graphs *best* illustrates the temperature–time curves of the four flasks?

b) Explain why the line for each flask (on the graph you chose) should have the shape that it does.

c) On the molecular level, why should rate of respiration in yeast cells vary with temperature?

8 Why are carbohydrates said to be fattening?

9. In what sense is the citric acid cycle a central metabolic hub in the biochemistry of living cells?

10. Inorganic phosphate ($P_i$) is a competitive inhibitor for the enzyme alkaline phosphatase (APase). APase catalyzes the removal of a terminal phosphate group from several kinds of compounds by a reversible reaction of the type shown below:

$$\text{GLUCOSE-6-PHOSPHATE} \xrightleftharpoons{\text{APase}} \text{GLUCOSE} + P_i.$$

If this reaction is allowed to occur in a system with excess substrate, and a concentrated solution of $P_i$ is added as an inhibitor at some point after the reaction has started, the graph of Fig. 8–26 is obtained. If a concentrated solution of sodium arsonate ($NaHAsO_4$), also a competitive inhibitor for APase, is added to a second reaction in place of the $P_i$, the graph of Fig. 8–27 is obtained.

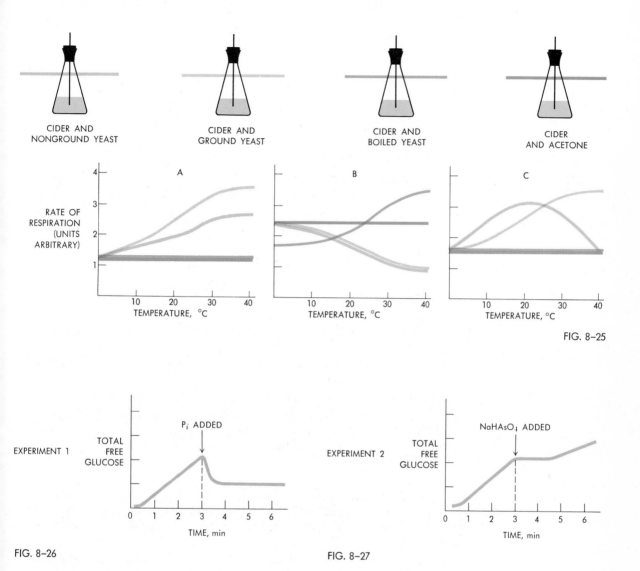

CIDER AND
NONGROUND YEAST

CIDER AND
GROUND YEAST

CIDER AND
BOILED YEAST

CIDER
AND ACETONE

FIG. 8-25

EXPERIMENT 1

TOTAL
FREE
GLUCOSE

$P_i$ ADDED

TIME, min

FIG. 8-26

EXPERIMENT 2

TOTAL
FREE
GLUCOSE

NaHAsO$_4$ ADDED

TIME, min

FIG. 8-27

Explain the differences between these two graphs in terms of molecular interactions between substrate, enzyme, and inhibitor. Discuss the following points:

a) In both experiments, why does the graph line stop climbing after inhibitor is added?

b) In Experiment 1, why does the graph line fall to a lower level after the addition of inhibitor, whereas the line remains horizontal for Experiment 2?

c) The effect of each inhibitor on the equilibrium of the reaction.

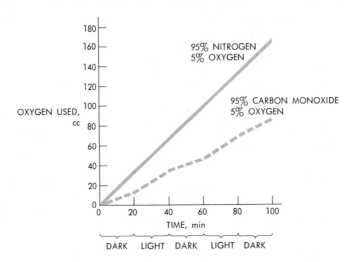

FIG. 8–28

11. The graph in Fig. 8–28 shows the effect of carbon monoxide on the respiration of yeast cells.

a) Offer an hypothesis to explain the difference in respiratory rates of yeast cells treated with carbon monoxide.

b) What seems to be the effect of light on the inhibitory effect of CO?

12. Which substance would you take for quick energy, glucose or sucrose? Why? Find out the carbohydrate ingredients of some particular chocolate candy bar. Why is chocolate candy said to be a source of quick energy?

SUGGESTED
READINGS

A great mass of material has been published recently concerning cellular metabolism, ATP, electron transport, and the like. Below are listed some of those articles and books which might be most useful in providing both additional background and recent information in the field.

BAKER, J. J. W., and G. E. ALLEN, *Matter, Energy, and Life*, 2nd edition (Reading, Mass.: Addison-Wesley, 1970). A more detailed account of the background material discussed in this chapter. Various chapters of the book deal with such topics as the structure of matter, formation of molecules, the course and mechanism of chemical reactions, acids and bases, the chemical composition of living matter, carbohydrates and lipids, proteins, enzymes, and nucleic acids. The book assumes no formal knowledge of chemistry or physics.

BALDWIN, E., *The Nature of Biochemistry* (Cambridge: Cambridge University Press, 1962). A number of chapters in this book are devoted to principles of fat and protein metabolism, respiration, and energy transformation. Each chapter is short and well explained.

BASERGA, R., and W. E. KISIELESKI, "Autobiographies of Cells." *Scientific American*, August 1963, p. 103. This article shows how techniques of labeling molecules with radioactive atoms make it possible to trace the life history of a cell. A good article in what it reveals about cells and the methods used to study them.

CHAMBERS, ROBERT W., and ALMA PAYNE, *From Cell to Test Tube* (New York: Charles Scribners, 1962). A well-written survey of some aspects of cellular metabolism.

GERARD, R. W., *Unresting Cells* (New York: Harpers, 1949). A well-written book dealing with many problems of nutrition, digestion, and the metabolism of carbohydrates, fats, and proteins. This book is enjoyable reading and very informative.

GREEN, D. E., "The Mitochondrion." *Scientific American*, January 1964, p. 63.

GREEN, D. E., "The Synthesis of Fat." *Scientific American*, February 1960, p. 46.

HAFFNER, R., and J. BAKER, *The Vital Wheel: Metabolism* (Columbus, Ohio: American Education Publications, 1963). A concise treatment of a number of topics in intermediary metabolism. The articles in this book are reprints from *Science and Math Weekly*, and show in very lucid form the basic patterns of energy exchange.

KAMEN, MARTIN, "A Universal Molecule of Living Matter." *Scientific American*, August 1958, p. 77. This article discusses the tetrapyrrole ring, which is found as the basic molecular architecture of chlorophyll, hemoglobin, various enzymes, and the cytochromes. A good review article on molecular evolution.

LEHNINGER, A. L., "Energy Transformation in the Cell." *Scientific American*, May 1960, p. 102. A good summary discussion of the way in which energy is extracted from breakdown of carbohydrates.

MIRSKY, A. E., and V. G. ALLFREY, "How Cells Make Molecules." *Scientific American*, September 1961, p. 74. An excellent article which deals with the process of protein synthesis from the template of DNA.

SIEKEVITZ, P., "The Powerhouse of the Cell." *Scientific American*, July 1957, p. 131.

STUMPF, PAUL K., "ATP." *Scientific American*, April 1953, p. 84. A short article dealing with the chemical structure and mode of action of ATP. The article also deals with the ways in which ATP is generated in the Krebs cycle.

# CHAPTER 9

# PHOTOSYNTHESIS

**Photosynthesis**—the manufacture of energy-rich compounds in plants—is one of the most important chemical processes in the world. Experimental investigations of photosynthesis extend back over three hundred years, yet the problem is still not completely solved. In this chapter, we shall study the work done on the problem and follow it from the earliest times through to its present state. It is hoped that the reader will gain a clear understanding of the problems involved, in addition to seeing the historical development of a vitally important scientific idea.

When reading of the ideas held by the early natural scientists, one is often tempted to scoff at their work. One may wonder how they could ever have held certain beliefs. It is all too easy, however, to look back from the twentieth century to an earlier period and point out scientific mistakes or false hypotheses; hindsight is much more accurate than foresight. We have at our disposal a great deal of factual knowledge which was entirely unknown to earlier scientists.

In the early seventeenth century, when the experimental study of plant physiology began, there was little evidence to show how chemical reactions occurred. Men noted that some substances went into a chemical reaction and other substances came out. From such observations, the **transmutation theory** evolved. Transmutation was believed to be a process by which one substance could change into another. For example, early investigators noted that when water was boiled away in a flask, a small residue of crystals remained. This they interpreted to mean that some of the water had been transmuted into "earthy material." Many of these early experimenters were called alchemists. Although alchemists are frequently referred to as men who sought to change base metals into gold, only a small number of them actually put much serious effort into the attempt. The early development of chemistry owes a great deal to alchemists. By their many investigations with a variety of inorganic and organic substances, alchemists collected a great many empirical data. Some of these data formed a foundation for the development of the first chemical theories, of which the theory of transmutation is a prime example.

In the seventeenth century, little or nothing was known about the nature of gases or, as they were then called, "aeroform substances." Many believed them to be spirits released when certain solids were heated, while others considered them to be actually alive. Furthermore, if there was little understanding of the nature of gases, there was certainly no more comprehension of their significance to living organisms. As we shall see, this lack of knowledge played an important part in the early investigations of photosynthesis.

The "phlogiston theory" was as important to the seventeenth-century scientist as the atomic theory is to chemistry today. The phlogiston theory was advanced to explain many phenomena, especially the burning of substances. It was thought that the flames leaping upward and away from a burning object represented something escaping from the object. This unknown something was called "phlogiston." Today, it is known that a burning substance unites with oxygen. If all the products of the burning process are measured (including the gaseous compounds released), the weight is greater after burning than before. The additional weight can be accounted for by the amount of oxygen used in the burning process. The seventeenth-century scientist was also aware that a burning substance gained rather than lost weight, and one might think that this fact would pose a serious problem to holders of the phlogiston theory. To those early scientists, however, this posed no problem. Phlogiston was simply assigned a negative weight! In other words, due to the loss of the negatively weighted phlogiston, a substance would weigh more after burning than before.

The phlogiston theory actually accounted for a considerable number of observable phenomena. It is a prime example of a false hypothesis that gives rise to many true conclusions. For example, the early scientists noted that a candle burned under a sealed bell jar eventually goes out. This, of course, is due to the fact that there is no more oxygen available in the air within the jar. To adherents of the phlogiston theory, however, the air was simply referred to as being "phlogisticated." Such phlogisticated air was said to be "fixed," and no longer capable of supporting burning. The air present under the bell jar before the candle burned was referred to as being "dephlogisticated air." The phlogiston theory thus adequately explained the phenomenon of burning without running into any contradictions which might disprove it. For this particular event, the burning of a candle, the phlogiston theory is just as good as the modern theory involving oxygen.

A belief in transmutation, a lack of any concept of the nature and significance of gases, and an acceptance of the phlogiston theory mark the mental framework within which early plant physiologists approached their investigations of photosynthesis.

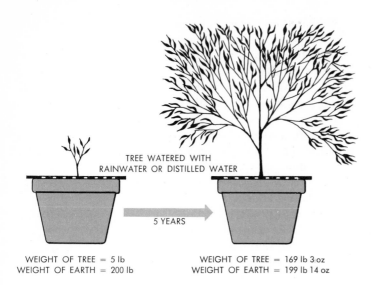

TREE WATERED WITH
RAINWATER OR DISTILLED WATER

5 YEARS

WEIGHT OF TREE = 5 lb
WEIGHT OF EARTH = 200 lb

WEIGHT OF TREE = 169 lb 3 oz
WEIGHT OF EARTH = 199 lb 14 oz

FIG. 9–1　Van Helmont's experiment. He concluded that the gain in weight shown by the plant was due entirely to the water he had given it over the five-year period.

**9-3**
**THE PROBLEM**

The problem of plant nutrition may seem a simple one. How does a plant grow? Where does it get the materials to build more plant matter? It seems easy to understand how animals may grow. They are seen devouring food which, it is assumed, they use to build more animal matter. With rare exceptions, however, plants do not feed in this manner.

One of the first men to study this problem was Jan Baptista van Helmont (1577–1644). While most of his studies were of a chemical nature, van Helmont performed a significant experiment with a willow tree. In this experiment he intended to discover the source of plant nutrients. In his own words:

*I took an earthen vessel, in which I put 200 pounds of earth that had dried in a furnace, which I moistened with rainwater, and I implanted therein the trunk or stem of a willow tree, weighing five pounds. And at length, five years being finished, the tree sprung from thence did weigh 169 pounds and about three ounces. When there was need, I always moistened the earthen vessel with rainwater or distilled water, and the vessel was large and implanted in the earth. Lest the dust that flew about should be co-mingled with the earth, I covered the lip or mouth of the vessel with an iron plate covered with tin and easily passable with many holes. I computed not the weight of the leaves that fell off in four autumns. At length, I again dried the earth up in the vessel, and there was found the same 200 pounds, wanting about two ounces. Therefore, 164 pounds of wood, bark, and roots, arose out of water only.\**

* All excerpts quoted in this chapter by permission, from L. K. Nash, "Plants and the Atmosphere," in *Harvard Case Histories in Experimental Science*, Vol. II (Cambridge: Harvard University Press, 1957), pp. 325–436.

Van Helmont's experiment is shown in Fig. 9–1. It seemed to him that the plant matter accounting for the gain in weight had come from the water alone, since the earth had not lost any appreciable weight. In his last sentence, van Helmont states his conclusion. He assumed that water had transmuted into wood, which he regarded as an "earthy" material.

To van Helmont, this conclusion seemed both logical and inescapable. It agreed well with the predictions of the transmutation hypothesis, widely accepted in his day. Thus, in the light of the time at which this experiment was performed, van Helmont's conclusions are both understandable and reasonable. The experiment itself was a rather good one. (At that time, the use of a control was not considered to be essential). What of the gases that surround the plant in the atmosphere? Van Helmont did not consider them capable of adding to the plant material. Although van Helmont here overlooked an extremely important variable, he must still be given credit for beginning an investigation which others were stimulated to extend much farther.

Does the water itself actually provide all the matter used by the plant in making its stems, leaves, and roots? This conclusion of van Helmont's was questioned during the 1690's by John Woodward, a physician and professor at Cambridge University. From his own observation, Woodward knew that "even the clearest Water is very far from being pure." Even when "fresh and newly taken out of the Spring," he wrote, it exhibits "great numbers of exceeding small terrestrial particles disseminated through all parts of it." In an account of his investigations published in 1699, Woodward remarked:

**9-4
WATER INTO
WOOD?**

*Upon the whole, 'tis palpable and beyond reasonable Contest, that Water contains in it a very considerable Quantity of terrestrial Matter. Now the Question is to which of these, the Water, or the Earthy Matter sustain'd in it, Vegetables owe their Growth and Augment. For deciding of which I conceive the following Experiments may afford some Light: And I can safely say they were made with due Care and Exactness.*

Woodward placed measured amounts of water solutions in glass containers. To prevent the water from evaporating, he covered each container with a piece of parchment. After carefully weighing each plant, he inserted it through a small hole in the covering so that the roots were immersed in the water solution. From time to time he added measured amounts of water (as the water level in the containers dropped during the experiment). All of the containers were kept in a window with equal exposure to the air and sunlight. During the summer and early fall of 1691, one series of experiments was continued for 77 days; the following summer, a second series was terminated after 56 days. The results of Woodward's experiments are shown in Table 9–1.

From his data on the amount of water expended by the plants (last column in Table 9–1), Woodward concluded: "The much greatest part of the Fluid Mass [water solution] is thus drawn off and convey'd through the Pores [stomata] of them, and exhales up into the Atmosphere." Since the containers used as

TABLE 9–1   RESULTS OF JOHN WOODWARD'S WATER CULTURE EXPERIMENTS DURING 1691 AND 1692*

| CONTAINER | KIND OF PLANT | SOURCES OF WATER | WEIGHT OF PLANTS (IN GRAINS) | | GAIN IN WEIGHT (IN GRAINS) | | AMOUNT OF WATER USED, OZ |
|---|---|---|---|---|---|---|---|
| | | | WHEN PUT IN | WHEN TAKEN OUT | AFTER 77 DAYS | AFTER 56 DAYS | |
| A | MINT | SPRING WATER | 27 | 42 | 15 | | 2558 |
| B | MINT | RAIN WATER | 28¼ | 45¾ | 17½ | | 3004 |
| C | MINT | RIVER WATER | 28 | 54 | 26 | | 2493 |
| D | MINT | CANAL WATER | 127 | 255 | | 128 | 14,190 |
| E | MINT | CANAL WATER 1½ OZ OF GARDEN SOIL | 76 | 244 | | 168 | 10,731 |
| F | NIGHTSHADE | SPRING WATER | 49 | 106 | 57 | | 3708 |
| G | SWEET PEA | SPRING WATER | 98 | 101½ | 3½ | | 2501 |

*Taken from John Woodward's paper "Some Thoughts and Experiments Concerning Vegetation." *Philosophical Transactions of the Royal Society of London* **21** (1699), 193–227.

controls (water solution only) seemed to have "a larger quantity of terrestrial Matter" than those with plants, Woodward concluded that "A great part of the terrestrial Matter that is mixt with the Water, ascends up into the Plant as well as the Water." In addition, the mint plants in the canal water enriched with garden soil grew the most.

It seemed clear to Woodward, therefore, that "Vegetables are not form'd of Water: but of a certain peculiar terrestrial Matter . . . we may very reasonably infer, that Earth, and not Water, is the Matter that constitutes Vegetables . . . Water serves only for a Vehicle to the terrestrial Matter which forms Vegetables: and does not itself make any addition unto them."

**9–5**
**ANOTHER FACT**
**IS ADDED**

In the late seventeenth century, development of the microscope and its use in natural science led to the discovery that the leaves of plants have many openings (**stomata**) on their surfaces (see Color Plate II, p. 510). One early microscopist (Nehemiah Grew) reports on these structures as follows:

*But as the skins of animals, especially in some parts, are made with certain open pores or orifices, either for the reception, or the elimination of something for the benefit of the body; so likewise the skins of at least many plants are formed with several orifices or passports, either for the better avoleotion [evaporation] of superfluous sap, or the admission of air.*

Still other microscopists identified the leaves of plants as digestive organs and the functioning pores as outlets for digestive waste products. But the author of the above quotation hit on a very striking possible function for these openings. *Could it be that they allowed exchange of substances between the plant and the atmosphere?*

The English clergyman Stephen Hales (1677–1761) became interested in the whole problem of the flow of materials through plants. He seems to have been one of the first men to note (although indirectly) that perhaps water is not the only substance involved in plant nutrition. He wrote:

*That the leaves and stems of plants do imbibe elastic air, there is some reason to suspect, from the following experiment . . . I set a well rooted plant of peppermint in a glass cistern full of earth, and then poured in as much water as it would contain; over this glass cistern I placed an inverted glass zz, aa [Fig. 9–2], the water being drawn up by means of a siphon to aa. At the same time also, I placed in the same manner another inverted glass zz, aa of equal size with the former, but without any plant under it.*

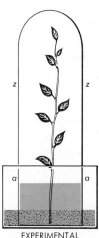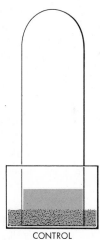

FIG. 9–2  Stephen Hales's experiment. He concluded that plants remove something from the air. He also showed that the plant changed the composition of the air, although he was not sure what this change was.

EXPERIMENTAL            CONTROL

Continuing, Hales wrote:

*The capacity of these vessels above the water aa was equal to 49 cubic inches. In a month's time the mint had made several weak slender shoots, and many small hairy roots shot out at the joints that were above water, occasioned probably by the great moisture of the air, in which the plant stood; half the leaves of the old stem were now dead; but the leaves and stem of the young shoots continued green most part of the following winter: The water in the two inverted glasses rose and fell as it was either affected by the different weight of the atmosphere or by the dilation and contraction of the air above aa.* [That is, the water rose or fell according to the external barometric pressure and according to the prevailing temperature of the air enclosed in the systems. Since these short-term fluctuations occurred in both systems, it is fairly certain that they were not due to the presence of the growing plant.] *But the water in the vessel in which the peppermint stood [finally] rose so much above aa and above the surface of the water in the other vessel that one seventh part of that air must have been reduced to a fixt state, either by being imbibed into the substance of the plant, or by the vapours which arose from the plant.* [Inasmuch as this long-term shrinkage of volume occurred only in the system containing the plant, it could reasonably be regarded as an effect springing from the latter's presence.] *This was chiefly done in the two or three summer months, for after that no more air was absorbed. The beginning of April in the following Spring, I took out the old mint and put a fresh plant in its place to try if it would absorb any more of the air, but it faded in four or five days. Yet a fresh plant put into the other glass, whose air had also been confined for nine months, lived near a month, almost as long as another plant did in fresh confined air.*

Hales's experiment is significant for several reasons, one of which is that he very skillfully employed the use of a control, the empty container. Had he used only the system in which the mint was growing, it would have been very difficult for him to tell which of the fluctuations of water level were due to increases in barometric pressure and which were due to changes brought about by the plant. In Hales's experiment, however, any changes which occurred in *both* systems would obviously not be the result of the plant, but of some outside force (in this case, atmospheric pressure). Thus the use of a control helped Hales to clearly define what effects his plant had upon the atmosphere in its container.

Another important factor is noted from Hales's experiment. Placing a fresh mint plant into the jar from which the original plant had been removed, Hales noticed that the new plant "faded in four or five days." This allowed him to make a very significant conclusion. He could see that the first plant had caused some *change* in the air. From this experiment, then, Hales was able to draw some very important conclusions:

1) Plants interact with the atmosphere. As a result, there was a smaller volume of gas in Hales's glass after the reaction than there was before it.

2) Plants in some way affect the condition of the atmosphere with which they come in contact. The atmosphere in the glass was slightly changed from its original composition.

Hales did not find it easy to interpret the results of his experiments. He saw two possible reasons why the water level in the glasses might have risen. First, it might have been because the leaves imbibed gases. Second, it might have been because the plant exhaled a substance which, on combining with particles already in the air, caused a shrinkage. (For example, when equal volumes of alcohol and water are added together, the total volume is less than the sum of the two.) Hales leaned towards this last explanation, though he did not understand how it could occur. Through Hales's work, the interaction of plants and the atmosphere became established (something that van Helmont had completely overlooked). The exact nature of this interaction, however, remained obscure.

**9–6
CHEMISTS ENTER
THE SCENE**

Antoine Laurent Lavoisier (1743–1794) was a brilliant French chemist. He was responsible for the eventual overthrow of the phlogiston theory. He read widely of the works of van Helmont, Hales, and others who worked on the problem of plant nutrition. In doing so, he compiled much of the work done in the past and unified it into a simple hypothesis:

*Here, then, are two sources from which plants raised in water alone can draw the* [earthy] *materials that are found in them by analysis: first, from the water itself and the small amount of foreign earth material that must have been present* [in solution] *in all cases; second, from the air and the substances of all kinds with which it is charged.*

Lavoisier was not, however, primarily interested in the physiological processes within a plant. As a chemist, he was far more concerned with the substances plants used: water, earth, and gases. He had, however, further pinpointed the problem: Plants get the material from which they grow *either* from the water and a small amount of earth (recall that van Helmont's earth *did* lose two ounces in weight) *or* from the air surrounding the plant.

The British chemist Joseph Priestley (1733–1804) also became interested in the investigation of gases involved with plant life. By experimentation, Priestley had discovered that a candle will burn in an enclosed space (such as an inverted bell jar) for only a certain period of time. He also noticed that mice soon suffocate when placed in a similar situation. He recognized, therefore, that animals and burning candles somehow "damaged" the air, rendering it no longer capable of supporting life. In reflecting on this observation, Priestley wrote:

*. . . and when once any quantity of air has been rendered noxious by animals breathing in it as long as they could, I do not know that any methods have been discovered of rendering it fit for breathing again. It is evident, however, that there must be some provision in nature for this purpose, as well as for that of rendering the air fit for sustaining flame: for without it the whole mass of the atmosphere would, in time, become unfit for the purpose of animal life; and yet there is no reason to think that it is, at present, at all less fit for respiration than it has ever been . . .*

*The quantity of air which even a small flame requires is prodigious. It is generally said that an ordinary candle consumes, as it is called, about a gallon in a minute. Considering this amazing consumption of air, by fires of all kinds, volcanoes, etc. it becomes a great object of philosophical inquiry, to ascertain what change is made in the constitution of the air by flame, and to discover what provision there is in nature for remedying the injury which the atmosphere receives by this means.*

Priestley's statement, ". . . there must be some provision in nature for this purpose" (i.e., for restoring air "rendered noxious" by animals and burning flames) shows his awareness of the need for a balance in nature as far as the atmosphere was concerned. It seemed evident to him that life could not long exist if there was not some such restorative function, for he could see how even a small candle flame contributed heavily to the "damaging" of its surrounding atmosphere. Priestley was, indeed, coming very close to the heart of the matter. At the time he wrote the above passage, however, he was unaware of just how the balance he envisioned as a necessity was accomplished.

One day, quite by accident, Priestley discovered something.   In his own words:

*I flatter myself that I have accidentally hit upon a method of restoring air which has been injured by the burning of candles, and that I have discovered at least one of the restoratives which nature employs for this purpose.   It is vegetation.*

Indeed an important discovery.   Priestley continued:

*In what manner this process in nature operates, to produce so remarkable an effect, I do not pretend to have discovered; but a number of facts declare in favor of this hypothesis.   I shall introduce my account of them by reciting some of the observations which I made on the growing of plants in confined air, which led to this discovery.*

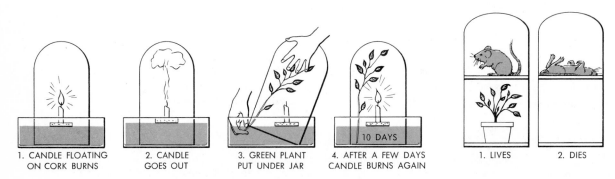

1. CANDLE FLOATING ON CORK BURNS    2. CANDLE GOES OUT    3. GREEN PLANT PUT UNDER JAR    4. AFTER A FEW DAYS CANDLE BURNS AGAIN    1. LIVES    2. DIES

FIG. 9–3   Priestley's experiments.   From his results, he concluded that plants "reverse the effects of breathing."

Priestley went on to state that he had earlier hypothesised that both plants and animals affect the atmosphere in the same manner.   To test this hypothesis, he did an experiment similiar to that performed by Hales; i.e., he put a sprig of mint into a glass jar which stood inverted in a vessel of water.   He was surprised to see it continue to grow there for several months, for this result contradicted his hypothesis.   He also found that the air surrounding this plant allowed a candle to burn and a mouse to live.   These discoveries led Priestley to perform another experiment (Fig. 9–3).   In Priestley's own words:

*Accordingly, on the seventeenth of August, 1771, I put a sprig of mint, into a quantity of air, in which a wax candle had burned out, and found that on the twenty-seventh of the same month, another candle burned perfectly well in it.   This experiment I repeated, without the least variation in the event, not less than eight or ten times in the remainder of the summer.   Several times I divided the quantity of air in which the candle had burned out, into two parts, and putting the plant into some of them, left the other the control in the same exposure, contained, also, in a glass vessel immersed in water, but without any plant; and never failed to find, that a candle would burn in the former, but not in the latter. I generally found that five or six days were sufficient to restore this air, when the plant was in its vigour; whereas I have kept this kind of air in glass vessels for months, without being able to perceive that the least alteration had been made in it . . .*

Up to this point, Priestley's work with plants involved air which had been "vitiated," or made unfit for a living animal, by a burning candle. He next turned to air which had been exposed over long periods of time to decaying plant and animal materials in a water-sealed vessel. Such materials also "vitiated" the air. He found that almost exactly the same thing happened—the introduction of living plants purified the air.

Priestley thus came to the conclusion that plants "reverse the effects of breathing." He concluded that animals affect the atmosphere by adding something to it, while plants subtract something from it when they purify the atmosphere. His findings were not accepted by many other workers. Attempts to repeat his experiments with the mint often failed, and Priestley was unable to explain why. However, his early experiments had laid a strong foundation on which others would build. His experiments, though he himself later questioned them, gave clear evidence to other investigators that plants *do* have a "purifying" effect on the air.

Priestley's works were read carefully by a Dutch physician, Jan Ingenhousz (1730–1799). Ingenhousz carried on investigations of his own at a remarkable pace. By performing variations of the experiments done by Priestley, Ingenhousz made several important discoveries. He wrote:

## 9-7 INGENHOUSZ SEES THE LIGHT

*I found that plants have, moreover, a most surprising faculty of elaborating [i.e., changing] the air which they contain, and undoubtedly absorb continually from the common atmosphere, into real and fine dephlogisticated air; . . .*

Here, Ingenhousz was merely confirming the discovery of Priestley that plants somehow restore the air. Ingenhousz saw plants as constantly absorbing gases from the atmosphere and changing them into dephlogisticated air. (Recall that a burning candle or respiring animal was thought to release phlogiston into the air and thus render it unfit for breathing. In light of the phlogiston theory, then, plants removed phlogiston from the air, thereby making it fit to support the burning candle or a living animal again). Ingenhousz concluded:

*. . . that they [i.e., plants] poured down continually . . . a shower of this depurated [i.e., purified] air, which, diffusing through . . . the atmosphere . . . render[s] it more fit for human life; that this operation [i.e., purification of air] is far from being carried on constantly, but begins only after the sun has . . . made his appearance above the horizon, and has, by his influence, prepared the plants to begin anew their beneficial operation . . . upon the animal creation, which was stopped during the darkness of the night; . . . that this operation of plants diminishes towards the close of the day, and ceases entirely at sunset . . .*

Here, indeed, was a major discovery. For the first time, light was seen as being necessary for the photosynthetic process. But Ingenhousz went on to make another contribution:

*. . . that this office is not performed by the whole plant, but only by the leaves and the green stalks that support them . . .*

A second major discovery: Ingenhousz noted that only green portions of plants will perform this photosynthetic process. Thus the stage was set for later discoveries of the importance of the green pigment chlorophyll to the photosynthetic process. Continuing, he remarked:

*. . . that all plants contaminate the surrounding air by night, and even in the daytime in shaded places; . . . that all flowers render the surrounding air highly noxious, equally by day and by night; . . . that the roots removed from the ground do the same, some few, however, excepted; . . . but that in general fruits have the same general deleterious quality at all times, though principally in the dark, . . .*

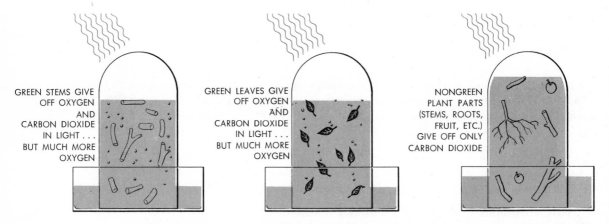

FIG. 9–4   These experiments demonstrate Ingenhousz' discovery that green matter is necessary for plants to manufacture "plant matter." He also noted that both green and nongreen plants respired (i.e., gave off $CO_2$). Finally, and most important, Ingenhousz discovered that even the green plant parts needed light to give off oxygen.

Here, Ingenhousz discovered a variable overlooked by Priestley. He saw that not all of the plant contributes to restoring the atmosphere. Some portions of the plant act just as burning candles or animals; i.e., they give off carbon dioxide and use oxygen. It is now known, of course, that all living organisms carry on respiration, and that plants are no exception. However, plants, by virtue of their photosynthetic activity, contribute more oxygen to the air than they remove by their respiratory processes.

Thus Ingenhousz, through a few simple experiments, moved the study of photosynthesis three giant steps forward. First, he showed that light was necessary for the process to occur. Second, he showed that only the green parts of plants actually perform photosynthesis. Third, he showed that all living parts of the plant respire. Representations of all of Ingenhousz' experiments and their results are shown in Fig. 9–4.

Ingenhousz did not understand *why* light was important. Nor did he recognize the significance of the green coloring. His interpretation of his experimental results is interesting. Ingenhousz saw two possibilities that would account for the production of pure air by plants. First, the pure or dephlogisticated air arose from the plant, which had drawn in phlogiston from the atmosphere. Figure 9–5 illustrates what Ingenhousz must have imagined to happen.

AIR CONTAINING PHLOGISTON  ⟶  PHLOGISTON + DEPHLOGISTICATED AIR

FIG. 9–5    One of two hypotheses proposed by Ingenhousz to explain photosynthesis.

Second, Ingenhousz suggested that plants completely immersed in water produced dephlogisticated air because of a vital force which, under the influence of light, transmuted water or other substances into plant materials. He wrote:

*I should rather incline to believe that that wonderful power of nature, of changing one substance into another, and of promoting perpetually that transmutation of substances, which we may observe everywhere, is carried out in this green vegetable matter in a more ample and conspicious way. . . . water itself, or some substance in the water, [is] . . . changed into this vegetation, and undergoes, by the influence of the sun shining upon it . . . such a metamorphosis as to become what we call now dephlogisticated air.*

This explanation sounds quite similar to van Helmont's hypothesis of transmutation of water into plant material. Nonetheless, it was Ingenhousz' final working hypothesis. Its value was far less than that of the experiments which Ingenhousz performed. It remained for later workers to properly interpret the results of these experiments.

By the late eighteenth century, quite independently of work on plant physiology, the phlogiston theory was slowly abandoned. The element oxygen was isolated and many of its physical and chemical properties were described. In the light of these advances, the steps of the photosynthetic process were suspected to be as shown in Fig. 9–6.

**9–8**
**A NEW PROBLEM**
**TO SOLVE**

FIG. 9–6        SOMETHING FROM AIR  +  WATER  —LIGHT + GREEN COLORING→  PLANT MATTER  +  "RESTORED AIR"

Note that no distinction was made between the actual final product of photosynthesis (carbohydrate) and the other plant growth materials, such as proteins.

Today, we write the process in a simplified form:

CARBON DIOXIDE + WATER → GLUCOSE + OXYGEN

$$CO_2 + H_2O \rightarrow C_6H_{12}O_6 + O_2 \text{ (unbalanced)}$$

Since only oxygen is released as a waste product of this reaction, the problem boils down to one of discovering what parts of the water and carbon dioxide molecules go into making new plant materials. There are three possibilities:

1) The carbon of the carbon dioxide ($CO_2$) unites with the water ($H_2O$) to form glucose ($C_6H_{12}O_6$), the oxygen of the $CO_2$ being released into the atmosphere.

2) The hydrogen of the $H_2O$ unites with the $CO_2$, the oxygen of the $H_2O$ being released into the atmosphere.

3) Both of the reactions described in 1 and 2 occur, the oxygen being released from both the $CO_2$ and the $H_2O$.

These three alternatives actually serve to point up the main question: *Where does the oxygen released by the plant come from*, the water, the carbon dioxide, or both? The answer to this question indirectly tells us where the plant matter comes from, *for whatever is left over after the oxygen is removed must go into the glucose.*

Conflicting hypotheses were put forth and tested by two men. The French scientist M. Berthollet (1748–1822) decided that the released oxygen came from the water molecules. He reasoned that if plants were grown in a medium free of hydrogen and were given only water, then any hydrogen found in their tissues would have to come from the water. The removal of hydrogen from the water would leave its oxygen free to pass into the atmosphere. We can express his reasoning in a deductive format as follows:

**Hypothesis:** *If* . . .   the oxygen released into the air does not come from the water molecules, . . .

**Prediction:** *then* . . . plants grown in a hydrogen-free medium should contain no hydrogen in their tissues.

Note that this reasoning could be stated conversely—i.e., *if* the oxygen that plants release into the air does come from the water molecules, *then* plants grown in a hydrogen-free medium should contain hydrogen in their tissues.

Berthollet performed an experiment to test his hypothesis, growing plants in a medium which did not contain hydrogen. He then chemically analyzed the plant material for the presence of this element. As Fig. 9–7 indicates, hydrogen *was* found in the tissues. Berthollet saw that the hydrogen could have come only from the water, since carbon dioxide contains no hydrogen. By taking the hydrogen, Berthollet reasoned, the plant releases the oxygen in the water molecules into the air. Therefore, he said, *the oxygen released by the plant comes from the water molecule.*

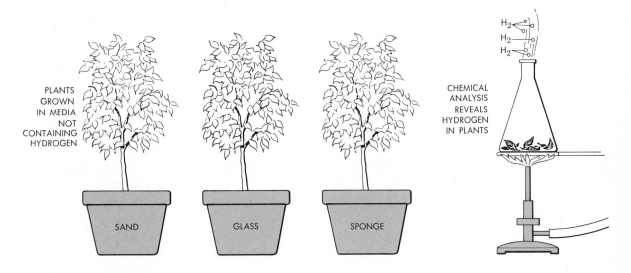

FIG. 9–7  Berthollet's experiment, supporting his hypothesis that the oxygen given off in photo-synthesis comes from the water molecule.

Another Frenchman, Jean Senebier (1742–1809), took issue with Berthollet's conclusion.  Senebier wrote:

... [hypothesis] *if the decomposition of the water were the only cause of the pure air produced by plants exposed under water to the sun,* [prediction: then] *it is clear that the irradiation of plants placed in distilled water and in well-boiled water should furnish pure air as well as when carbonated water is used.  This almost never occurs* [contradiction of prediction] *as I have shown in my experiments* [Fig. 9–8], *since leaves that have given no pure air when exposed to the sun in boiled water, did admit pure air when, on the following day, they were placed in a water-*

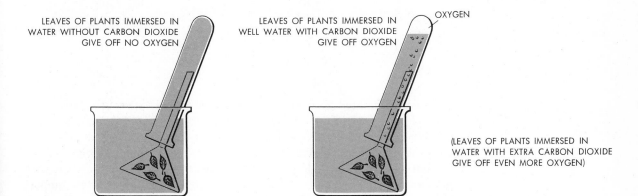

FIG. 9–8  Senebier's first experiment.

*containing fixed air. Besides, the quantity of pure air produced by plants irradiated under water is too nearly proportional to the quantity of fixed air contained in the water for one to believe that the production of the pure air is not worked by leaves primarily through the decomposition of the fixed air* [i.e. the carbon dioxide] *dissolved in the water that they have imbibed.*

Senebier's reasoning is as follows:

**Hypothesis:** *If* . . . the oxygen comes from the water molecule (as Berthollet believed), . . .

**Prediction:** *then* . . . the leaves should give off oxygen when immersed in water.

However, Senebier's data contain a contradiction; leaves immersed in water give off oxygen *only when carbon dioxide is present*. This indicated to Senebier that *the oxygen released comes from the carbon dioxide molecule.*

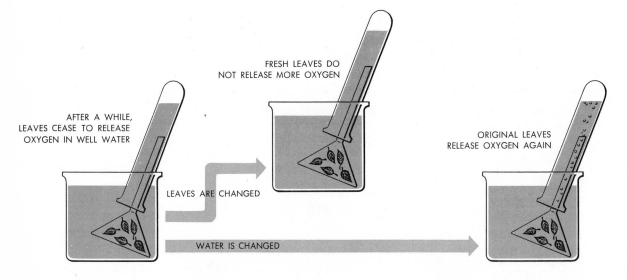

FIG. 9–9   Senebier's second experiment.

Senebier eliminated a possible variable by a second experiment (Fig. 9–9). After the leaves used in the first experiment had stopped releasing oxygen, he replaced them with fresh leaves. The fresh leaves, however, released no oxygen. This showed that it was a lack of carbon dioxide rather than a "tiring" of the leaves that caused oxygen release to stop. When fresh water containing carbon dioxide was put in, oxygen release began again. This appeared to support Senebier's hypothesis that carbon dioxide molecules were the source of the released oxygen.

Senebier's experimental data also seemed to show that the amount of oxygen produced by submerged leaves is directly related to the amount of fixed air (i.e., carbon-dioxide-laden air) available to those leaves. In other words, the more fixed air supplied, the more oxygen released.*

Who was right about the origin of oxygen released during photosynthesis, Berthollet or Senebier? Another investigator, Nicholas Theodore de Saussure (1767–1845) entered the dispute. As an experimenter, de Saussure was extremely concerned with quantitative measurements, and herein may rest his real importance. He was not content just to know what happened; he also wanted to know *how much* of it happened. In one experiment performed with plants grown in sunlight, the data of which are given in Table 9–2, de Saussure showed that Senebier was wrong in assuming a positive correlation between the amount of oxygen given off by a plant and the amount of carbon dioxide with which it is supplied. He saw that Senebier's conclusion applied only within a limited range, and that too much carbon dioxide could actually kill the plant.

**TABLE 9–2**  DE SAUSSURE'S FINDINGS

| COMPOSITION OF GASES IN ATMOSPHERE | GAIN IN WEIGHT | REMARKS |
|---|---|---|
| NORMAL ATMOSPHERE | 425 mg | |
| 100% $CO_2$ | 0 | DIED ALMOST IMMEDIATELY |
| 75% | 0 | DIED ALMOST IMMEDIATELY |
| 66% | 0 | DIED ALMOST IMMEDIATELY |
| 50% | — | GREW 7 DAYS, THEN CEASED |
| 25% | 265 mg | GREW 10 DAYS, ONLY SLIGHTLY |
| 12.5% | 371 mg | |
| 8.5% | 583 mg | THRIVED BETTER THAN IN ATMOSPHERE |

By growing plants in enclosed containers and comparing them with plants grown open to the atmosphere, de Saussure was able to show that plants grown in enclosed atmospheres were unable to increase their carbon content to any great extent. He saw that the carbon within the plants came from the carbon dioxide. De Saussure concluded, therefore, that the process of photosynthesis results from the breakdown of carbon dioxide, the release of the oxygen, and the joining of carbon with water to produce plant compounds (**carbon fixation**). Thus de Saussure supported Senebier's hypothesis that the oxygen released dur-

---

* While performing these experiments, Senebier made an interesting discovery. He noted that shredded bits of leaves, when immersed in water and irradiated with light, released oxygen just as well as whole leaves (Fig. 9–11). These results indicated that the photosynthetic process is not performed by the leaf as an organ. Today it is known that photosynthesis is carried on within the chloroplasts found in living green plant cells.

ing photosynthesis comes from the carbon dioxide molecules.  This conclusion also seems reasonable in terms of our knowledge of the molecular formula for carbohydrates, which shows hydrogen and oxygen to be usually in the same ratio in carbohydrates as in water molecules.  Glucose ($C_6H_{12}O_6$), for example, has six carbon atoms and six molecules of water.

Areas of agreement notwithstanding, none of the three—Berthollet, Senebier, de Saussure—was ever to learn which hypothesis concerning the origin of the oxygen evolved by green plants during photosynthesis was correct.  The problem was not solved for another century.

**9-9**
**AN OLD PROBLEM**
**IS SOLVED**

The reader will recall that in van Helmont's experiment with the willow tree, the soil in the earthen vessel had decreased two ounces in weight during the course of the experiment.  In John Woodward's experiment, the plants grew better when he enriched canal water with garden soil.  Many years later, de Saussure discovered that when plants are kept in distilled water (free of chemicals), they grow very little.  When he added nitrate to the culture solution, however, the growth of the plants was enhanced considerably.  It seemed obvious, therefore, that a green plant requires for its proper nutrition not only sunlight and carbon dioxide, but also various minerals of the soil.  This hypothesis was in direct opposition to one then popular proposing that the green plant, like animals, uses carbon in the organic form and obtains it from partly decomposed plant and animal remains in the soil (humus).  This idea, of course, is actually that propounded by Aristotle some 21 centuries earlier.

To test the hypothesis that green plants absorb and use various minerals from the soil, the water culture technique pioneered by Woodward in 1691 was refined and used by many nineteenth century investigators, especially after about 1860.  In this method, plants were placed in distilled water and various chemicals added.  The investigators reasoned that if plants were kept in a medium free of chemical A, then none of that particular chemical should appear in the tissues of the plant.  Further, if chemical A is lacking from the culture solution, then the plant should show signs of its absence, such as stunted growth, discolored leaves, or some other symptom.

Some of the earliest water culture experiments were performed around 1860 by the German botanist Julius Sachs.  Sachs placed seedlings of beans, corn, and buckwheat into glass jars (Fig. 9–10) containing the following nutrient solution:

| | |
|---|---|
| WATER (DISTILLED) | 1000 cc |
| POTASSIUM NITRATE | 1.0 gm |
| SODIUM CHLORIDE | 0.5 gm |
| CALCIUM SULFATE | 0.5 gm |
| MAGNESIUM SULFATE | 0.5 gm |
| CALCIUM PHOSPHATE | 0.5 gm |

Other seedlings of these same species were placed in jars containing only the distilled water.  A few days later, Sachs noticed that the plants in the mineral solution appeared more vigorous than those whose roots had remained in distilled

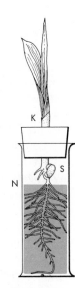

FIG. 9–10   Water culture jar used by the plant physiologist Julius Sachs. A corn seedling is shown suspended by a cork (K). Note the seed (S), the level of the nutrient solution (N), and the roots immersed within the nutrient solution. (From Julius Sachs, *Lectures on the Physiology of Plants*. Oxford: Clarendon Press, 1887.)

water. New lateral roots had begun to grow from the roots of the plants in the mineral solution; new leaves also appeared. Following the unfolding of the third or fourth leaf of the experimental plants, the newly appearing leaves were completely white, i.e., lacked chlorophyll. When Sachs examined the cells of these white leaves with the microscope, he saw no chloroplasts.

It was clear that Sachs' water solution of various chemicals still lacked something. Perhaps, Sachs hypothesized, the missing nutrient element might be iron. To test this new hypothesis, he prepared a dilute solution of iron chloride and painted the surface of one of the white leaves with a small brush. In only a day or two, Sachs observed that the white leaf had begun to turn green.

To obtain additional support for his hypothesis that the absence of iron was causing the leaves to be lacking in chlorophyll, Sachs added a few drops of iron chloride solution to the water in the jars containing the plants with colorless leaves. Within two days, the white leaves of the seedlings had begun to turn green. After several more days, they became the normal green color. These experiments offered strong support for the hypothesis that the absence of iron results in the leaves' not producing chlorophyll. They also suggest that the iron may be involved in the synthesis of chlorophyll. In additional water culture experiments, Sachs found that only extremely small amounts of iron are necessary; in fact, in quantities larger than a few milligrams, the iron becomes a poison.

Using the water culture technique, Sachs and various other investigators of the late nineteenth century were able to establish that green plants require the elements phosphorus, potassium, nitrogen, sulfur, calcium, iron, and magnesium. With this knowledge about plant nutrition, botanists had conclusive evidence that the green plant obtains most of its nutrient elements from the soil. From the atmospheric carbon dioxide, the green plant gets its carbon (as de Saussure had shown earlier). The exact source of the hydrogen present in the plant was still unknown, however.

The old problem was not yet completely solved. The soil in which plants grow contains numerous elements. When the chemical composition of the plant body was analyzed, several elements other than those mentioned in the preceding paragraph were found to be present (although usually in very small amounts). Were these elements actually used by plants in their metabolism?

Before this question could be answered conclusively, the techniques of water culture had to be more highly refined. In early studies using this technique, investigators used chemicals that they thought were pure, i.e., free of chemicals other than the ones desired. During the 1920's, it was discovered that many so-called "pure" chemicals actually contain at least traces of other elements. In addition, it was discovered that minute amounts of certain elements may dissolve out of the glass of the culture containers. Even the distilled water was found to contain trace quantities of certain elements (presumably contaminated by the apparatus used to distill the water). Once these sources of contamination were recognized, the investigators were able to refine the water culture. Within a few years, conclusive evidence was uncovered supporting the hypothesis that green plants require very small amounts of such elements as boron, manganese, copper, zinc, and molybdenum for normal growth. More recently, it has been found that some plants require chlorine, sodium, cobalt, and vanadium.

Thus, by the early 1930's, an ancient problem had been almost completely solved. The green plant does not get all of its matter from the soil; nor does it get its entire substance from the water. Rather, it obtains a dozen or more elements from the soil, or soil water. It secures all of its carbon from the carbon dioxide of the air. However, the exact origins of the oxygen used by the green plant (and that given off during photosynthesis) as well as of the hydrogen of its molecules had yet to be determined.

## 9–10
## THE OXYGEN PROBLEM IS SOLVED

Clues leading to the solution of a problem in one area of biological research are often provided by investigations in a slightly different area. So it was with plant photosynthesis. The Dutch-born microbiologist C. B. Van Niel had been studying photosynthesis in purple sulfur bacteria. Like the cells containing chlorophyll in green plants, these bacteria use light energy to synthesize carbohydrate materials. However, purple sulfur bacteria use hydrogen sulfide ($H_2S$) instead of water. This fact suggests a deduction which might determine the origin of the oxygen given off by green plants during photosynthesis.

*Hypothesis: If ...*   the oxygen released by plants during photosynthesis comes from the carbon dioxide molecule, ...

*Prediction: then ...* the purple sulfur bacteria will release oxygen as a result of their photosynthetic activity.

On the other hand,

**Hypothesis:** *If . . .*    the oxygen released by plants during photosynthesis comes from a water molecule, . . .

**Prediction:** *then . . .* the purple sulfur bacteria will release sulfur as a result of their photosynthetic activity.

From his observations, Van Niel already knew the answer. Photosynthesizing purple sulfur bacteria release sulfur as a waste product, not oxygen. The process can be summarized as follows:

$$CO_2 + 2H_2S \rightarrow (CH_2O)_n + H_2O + 2S.$$

Van Niel reasoned that light decomposes the hydrogen sulfide into hydrogen and sulfur. The hydrogen atoms are then used to reduce the carbon dioxide to carbohydrate. It was an easy step to suggest that the same process occurs in green plants, except that *water*, rather than hydrogen sulfide, is decomposed by light. The hydrogen atoms so released can then be used to reduce carbon dioxide, while the oxygen is given off. Van Niel hypothesized, therefore, that *the oxygen given off by green plants during photosynthesis comes from the water molecules*, and not those of carbon dioxide.

There is one basic premise made here, of course. It is assumed that, other than the raw materials involved, there is no difference between the photosynthetic process carried out by the purple sulfur bacteria and that performed by green plants. Purple sulfur bacteria are quite primitive organisms; most green plants are not. Therefore, in terms of evolutionary status, it might seem unlikely that the food-making process in both forms is similar.

On the other hand, the conversion of light energy to chemical energy is truly a remarkable feat for a living system to perform, and so it is even less likely (though by no means impossible) that more than one way to accomplish such a conversion would have evolved. This consideration lends strength to Van Niel's extrapolation from the photosynthetic processes of the purple sulfur bacteria to the same processes in green plants. The basic premise is still present, however, with all its accompanying doubts, and prevents Van Niel's observations of the purple sulfur bacteria in relation to the origin of the oxygen evolved in green plant photosynthesis from being conclusive.

It often happens that the crucial experiment which would resolve the issue between two conflicting hypotheses cannot be performed until the proper experimental instrument or technique is developed. Such was the case here. The introduction of tracer experiments by George Hevesy (1885–) in 1923 opened many new experimental pathways in biology. Hevesy used radioactive isotopes of lead to trace the pathways through which materials moved from place to place in plants.

In 1941, a team of scientists at the University of California performed the crucial experiment that determined the source of oxygen released in photosynthesis. They exposed the green alga *Chlorella* to water which had been labeled with $O^{18}$. This isotope can be detected by a technique known as **mass spectrometry** (see Glossary). The reasoning in the experiment was as follows:

**Hypothesis:** *If...*   the oxygen released in green plant photosynthesis comes from the water molecules, . . .

**Prediction:**   *then . . .* the oxygen released by the experimental *Chlorella* should be $O^{18}$.

On the other hand,

**Hypothesis:** *If...*   the oxygen released in green plant photosynthesis comes from the carbon dioxide molecule, . . .

**Prediction:**   *then . . .* the oxygen released by the experimental *Chlorella* should be $O^{16}$, the regular isotope of oxygen.

The results were definite and conclusive: The $O^{18}$ turned up in the released oxygen; none appeared in the carbohydrate produced.

A "clincher" experiment seemed obvious, and was performed. The carbon dioxide was labeled with $O^{18}$, rather than the water. In this case, it was predicted that none of the $O^{18}$ introduced would be detected in the oxygen released. The experimental data showed this prediction also to be correct.

Thus both Berthollet and Van Niel were right; the oxygen released in photosynthesis *does* come from the water molecules. The modern picture of photosynthesis, however, shows Berthollet's experiment to be a poor one, and his correct guess mostly good luck.

It is interesting to reexamine Senebier's experiments—which seemed so conclusively to establish carbon dioxide molecules as the source of oxygen released by the plant during photosynthesis—and see where his reasoning went wrong. An experiment performed early in this century by the British plant physiologist F. F. Blackman suggests the answer. Blackman measured the oxygen output of the water plant *Anacharis densa* while exposing it to varying intensities of light. He found that the oxygen output (and therefore photosynthetic activity) varied directly with light intensity *only within a certain limited range*. Beyond this range, further increase in light intensity resulted in no further increase in oxygen output. Blackman concluded that light was responsible for only one phase of the photosynthetic process (the "light reactions") and that there must be a second phase (the "dark reactions") which was independent of light. As we shall see, later research bore out this hypothesis.

However, Blackman also found that when the light intensity was lowered to zero, oxygen release slowed and stopped. Senebier had obtained the same result when the concentration of carbon dioxide in the water was reduced to zero. Senebier therefore concluded that the evolved oxygen had originated from the carbon dioxide molecules. But the same reasoning applied to Blackman's experiment would lead one to conclude that the oxygen evolved by the *Anacharis densa* plants came from the light!

Actually, both these experiments demonstrate that photosynthesis has certain *limiting factors* on which it depends. For example, no matter how much water and light are available, photosynthesis will not proceed without carbon dioxide; therefore, carbon dioxide is a limiting factor of photosynthesis. Likewise, no matter how much water and carbon dioxide are available, photosynthesis will not proceed without light; therefore, light is also a limiting factor of photosynthesis. Water and temperature are two other limiting factors. In a similar manner, the unavailability of spark plugs will prevent the manufacture of functional automobiles, even if all the other parts are readily available.

The experiment that showed the water molecule to be the source of the oxygen evolved during photosynthesis was performed about a quarter-century ago. Besides showing the source of this oxygen, this experiment showed that the atoms used to build the energy-rich molecules produced by photosynthesis are carbon and oxygen from atmospheric carbon dioxide molecules and hydrogen from water molecules.*

## 9–11
## PHOTOSYNTHESIS:
## THE MODERN VIEW

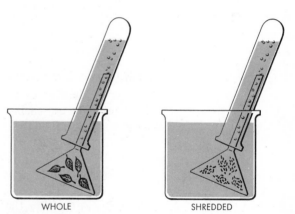

FIG. 9–11 Another of Senebier's experiments, showing that oxygen is released by shredded leaves as well as by whole leaves.

WHOLE           SHREDDED

However, knowing where the matter produced by photosynthesis comes from is one thing; knowing how it is produced is something entirely different. In the past 30 years, the use of many modern instruments and techniques has enabled us to learn more about the process of photosynthesis than was learned in the previous 300 years.

Let us follow an idea first suggested by another one of Senebier's experiments. He found that shredded bits of leaves, when placed in water and irradiated with light, were capable of releasing oxygen into the air just as well as whole or entire leaves (Fig. 9–11). What is the significance of this discovery? It shows that the leaf is not a photosynthesizing organ in the sense that the human stomach is an organ of digestion. If the leaf were a photosynthesizing organ, then chopping it into pieces would prevent photosynthetic activity.

---

* It is interesting to look back on van Helmont's simple experiment with the willow tree and interpret his results in the light of this knowledge.

CH₂
CH   H   CH₃
...

FIG. 9–12  Structural formula of chlorophyll *a*. Note the central magnesium (Mg) atom. Compare with the cytochrome molecule shown in Fig. 8–6. Chlorophyll *b* has the same basic structure as chlorophyll *a*, but differs in having a —CHO group instead of the —CH₃ group at the location indicated by the colored circle.

FIG. 9–13  Structure of a chloroplast as seen in increasingly finer resolution. (a) Cell of *Elodea*, showing numerous chloroplasts as seen with the aid of the light microscope. (Photo courtesy Kulbir Gill, Panjab University, India.) (b) Electron-microscope micrograph of a corn leaf cell, showing one chloroplast in cross section. Note that each granum has the appearance of a closely spaced array of dark and light lines but is connected to other grana by intergrana lamellae, which appear as less closely spaced lines separated by spaces or stromata. (EM photo courtesy L. K. Shumway, Washington State University.) (c) Artist's conception (based on electron-microscope study of ultrastructure) of one chloroplast. (d) Artist's conception of one granum, showing stacks of thylakoids. Where surfaces are removed at right, individual quantasomes can be seen. (e) One thylakoid, with top membrane partially removed revealing quantasomes underneath. Since it is only on the quantasomes that chlorophyll molecules are believed to be found normally, the grana are pigmented, while the intergrana lamellae and stromata are unpigmented. (f) Electron-microscope micrograph of a thylakoid similar to that on which the artist's conception of thylakoid structure in (e) is based. (Photo courtesy R. B. Park, University of California, Berkeley.) ▶

Obviously, it is necessary to look within the leaf, perhaps within its cells, to see the center of photosynthetic activity.

The principle of Senebier's experiment was extended a step further in 1954, when it was found that the complete photosynthetic process could be performed by isolated chloroplasts. This shows that for much of the photosynthetic activity, not even the entire cell is necessary.

The problem can be approached from a different direction. Jan Ingenhousz, you recall, made two important discoveries. First, he noted that a green coloring must be present within the plant if the plant is to carry on photosynthesis. This green pigment is the complex compound **chlorophyll** (Fig. 9–12), which bears a distinct chemical resemblance to the cytochrome enzymes and to hemoglobin. Chlorophyll's chief distinguishing features are its possession of a magnesium atom (rather than iron as in hemoglobin), and a side group of atoms called a phytol group. There are actually several variations of chlorophyll molecules known. Chlorophyll *a* is found in all green plants and all algae. Chlorophyll *b* is found in plants and the green algae, along with chlorophyll *a*. Other chlorophyll types are found in certain algae and in those bacteria that are photosynthetic. The relationship between chlorophyll and chloroplasts is represented in Fig. 9–13. Chloroplasts are highly structured bodies, each of which is made up of columns called **grana** interconnected and held intact by **lamellar membranes**. Each granum is a pile of **thylakoids**, arranged in a manner rather resembling a stack of wafers. Within the thylakoids, bodies called **quantasomes** are found; these are thought to contain enzymes for coupling the light reaction to ATP generation.

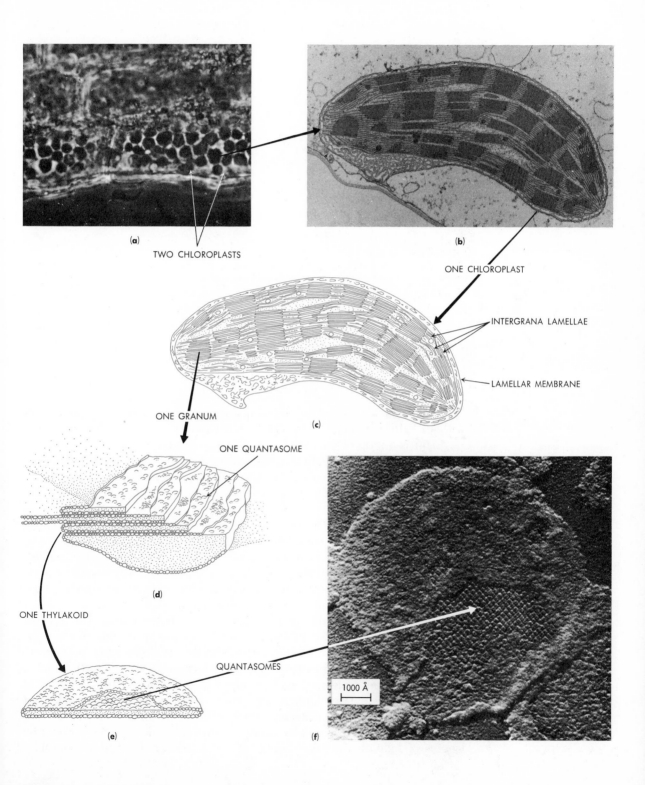

(a)

TWO CHLOROPLASTS

(b)

ONE CHLOROPLAST

INTERGRANA LAMELLAE

LAMELLAR MEMBRANE

ONE GRANUM

(c)

ONE QUANTASOME

(d)

ONE THYLAKOID

QUANTASOMES

1000 Å

(e)

(f)

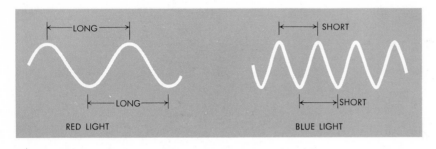

FIG. 9–14   Light energy travels in waves, the longer wavelengths conveying less energy than the shorter ones.

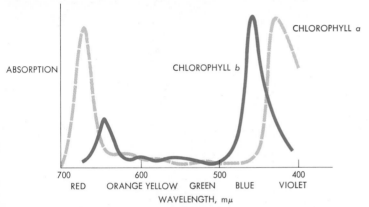

FIG. 9–15   The absorption spectra of chlorophylls *a* and *b*. (From John W. Kimball, *Biology,* 2nd edition. Reading, Mass.: Addison-Wesley, 1968.)

Ingenhousz's second major discovery was that photosynthesis cannot occur without light. It is now known that light supplies the energy for the process.

Light is a form of radiant energy. Physicists have proposed two models to explain the behavior of light in certain situations. The first model is the **wave theory** of light. This model pictures light as traveling in waves, similar to the waves on the surface of a body of water. As with water, the **wavelength** of light may vary from one type of wave to another. Figure 9–14 shows how wavelengths are measured. *The longer the wavelength, the less energy conveyed. The shorter the wavelength, the more energy conveyed.*

Various wavelengths of light are detected by the human eye as different colors. At one end of the visible spectrum is red light, which has a long wavelength. At the other end is violet light, which has a short wavelength. Violet light, of course, conveys more energy than red light.

There are other wavelengths of light to which the human eye does not respond, since they lie beyond the range of the visible spectrum. For example, ultraviolet light has a wavelength shorter than that of violet, and is not detected by the human eye. Infrared light waves, which are longer than those of red light (and so convey less energy) are also invisible to man. Thus the human eye is selective in that it reacts to certain wavelengths of light while other wavelengths pass it by undetected.

Like the eye, the green plant pigment chlorophyll is selective in the wavelengths of light it absorbs. The graph in Fig. 9–15 shows that chlorophyll

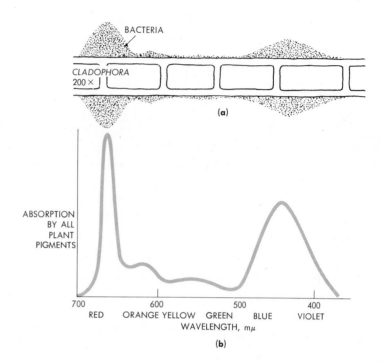

FIG. 9–16  A comparison of the "action spectrum" of photosynthesis (as determined by the congregating of large numbers of bacteria at regions of high oxygen concentration along an alga filament exposed to a spectrum of light) with the absorption spectrum of the plant's pigments.   Note the close correlation between the numbers of bacteria and the peaks of high absorption of light by the pigments.   (From John W. Kimball, *Biology*, 2nd edition.   Reading, Mass.: Addison-Wesley, 1968.)

absorbs most of the blue and violet light and also some red.  Other colors are allowed to pass through or are reflected.  The fact that the plant is green shows that chlorophyll rejects the wavelength of light which causes this color and reflects it back to the eye.  A color such as yellow is allowed to pass through unabsorbed.  It can be assumed, then, that the plant does not use, to any great extent, the wavelengths of light yielding green or yellow as an energy source for photosynthesis.

There are other kinds of pigments besides the chlorophylls in plants.  Blue-green, brown, red, golden, and green algae, for example, receive their names from their own particular pigments, most of which are probably accessory to the photosynthetic process.  However, in green plant cells, pigments called **carotenoids** are found closely associated with the chlorophyll molecules.  Carotenoids generally range in color from yellow to red.  The red of a tomato and the orange of a carrot are caused by their carotenoid pigments.  The brilliant colors of autumn are due to a dwindling of the chlorophyll supply in the leaf, which allows the previously masked carotenoid pigments to become visible.

In 1881, a filamentous green alga (*Cladophora*) and some motile aerobic bacteria were used in an ingenious experiment.  Being aerobic, the bacteria move from regions of low oxygen concentration to regions of high oxygen concentration.  This fact suggested to the German plant physiologist T. W. Engelmann a way to determine which wavelengths of light were used in photosynthesis.  He caused a tiny spectrum to shine on a filament of *Cladophora* which was immersed in a medium containing the bacteria.  Engelmann's results are shown in Fig. 9–16(a).  It is from experiments such as these that an "action spectrum" of photosynthesis can be drawn.  By "action spectrum" is meant the relationship between the degree of photosynthetic activity and the various wavelengths of light under which this activity occurs.  The action spectrum for Engelmann's experiment is shown in Fig. 9–16(b).  A comparison of part (a) of this figure with part (b) shows that the bacteria congregate mostly around those regions of the filament illuminated by the red and blue portions of the spectrum.  One may conclude that these regions release the most oxygen; thus they must carry on the greatest amount of photosynthetic activity.

Superimposition of Fig. 9–16(b) on Fig. 9–15 discloses more interesting information on the subject of photosynthesis.  The resulting three-curve graph (Fig. 9–17) indicates that the action spectrum of photosynthesis closely approximates the absorption spectra—i.e., the wavelengths of light absorbed by these pigments, as well as the degree of this absorption—of chlorophylls *a* and *b*. Therefore, it can be hypothesized that the energy absorbed by these chlorophylls is used to power photosynthetic activity.  The fact that the action and absorption spectra are not identical suggests that the carotenoids may also absorb some light energy and contribute to the photosynthetic process.

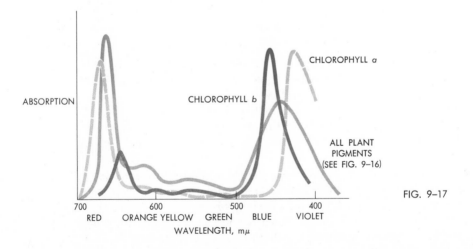

FIG. 9–17

The wave theory does not explain the behavior of light under all conditions. The **quantum theory** holds that light is composed of tiny particles called **quanta** or **photons**.  These particles are given off by any light-emitting object and travel through space until they reach and interact with a material object. Knowledge of both the wave and the quantum theories of light is essential to the biologist interested in photosynthesis, for while light absorption by chlorophyll can be explained in terms of the wave theory, the quantum theory must be employed to explain what happens after light is absorbed.  In other words, light seems to travel as a wave, but interacts with matter as a particle.

Precisely *why* chlorophyll absorbs only certain wavelengths of light is not known. It would seem that these wavelengths supply precisely the correct amount of energy to initiate the photosynthetic process. You have probably ridden in an automobile that developed a rattle at a certain speed. Below this critical speed, or above it, the rattle stopped. Apparently it took just the right amount of energy, neither more nor less, to cause the rattle.

Like respiration, photosynthesis is a multistep process. And, like modern research on respiration, modern research on photosynthesis involves the use of experimental techniques which, though simple in principle, often entail years of intense and difficult work. Much of this work has been done by Melvin Calvin and his associates at the University of California.

Very briefly, the experimental techniques involved placing the green alga *Chlorella* in a culture medium containing carbon dioxide labeled with radioactive $C^{14}$. It was found that the radioactive carbon turns up in glucose molecules within 30 seconds after the start of photosynthesis. To discover how this occurs, it was necessary to find out what compounds are involved in the intermediate steps of the dark reactions, those steps between the raw materials, carbon dioxide and water, and the final product, glucose. For this purpose, the reactions were stopped at various time intervals within the 30 seconds after placing cells in tracer medium. After five seconds, the $C^{14}$ was found in one intermediate phosphoglyceric acid (PGA), and a few seconds later, in phosphoglyceraldehyde (PGAL).

The compounds containing the radioactive isotopes were separated and identified by chromatography and chemical analysis. The radioactive isotopes were identified by being exposed to X-ray film, whereupon they literally "took their own pictures." This technique of photography is known as autoradiography.

Figure 9–18 shows the pathway of carbon in the dark reactions, so far as it has been worked out. While detailed study of this reaction series is hardly necessary here, there are a few things to be noted. First, the dark reactions involve a partial cycle. Ribulose phosphate enters the dark reactions to become activated by ATP and form ribulose diphosphate. The ribulose diphosphate then reacts with the carbon dioxide to form a six-carbon sugar molecule, which in turn breaks down to form two molecules of PGA (a three-carbon compound). The next step is essentially a reversal of what occurs in respiration (see Section 8–4). PGA is reduced by nicotinamide-adenine dinucleotide phosphate (NADPH) to form the three-carbon PGAL. Six molecules of PGAL are formed, of which five are used to reform the three starting molecules of ribulose diphosphate. Thus the cycle beings again.

The net input to the cycle is 3 molecules of $CO_2$ for each complete turn. Two turns thus generate two 3-carbon molecules which can condense to form glucose

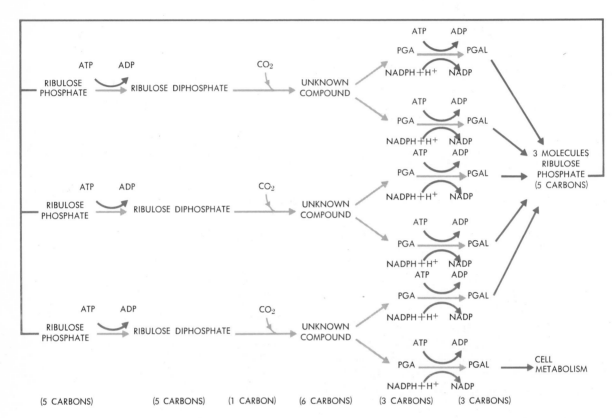

FIG. 9–18   Diagrammatic representation of the dark reactions of photosynthesis. The darker arrows indicate the places where energy-rich compounds resulting from the light reactions (to be discussed shortly) enter the chemical system. (Adapted from John W. Kimball, *Biology*, 2nd edition. Reading, Mass.: Addison-Wesley, 1968.)

or fructose. Fructose and glucose, in turn, may be used to build disaccharides such as sucrose and the complex polysaccharides, starch and cellulose.

Direct synthesis of compounds other than carbohydrates can occur in photosynthetic systems. For example, 30% of the photosynthesized compounds in the green alga *Chlorella* appear as amino acids.

The dark reactions of photosynthesis are not unique to green plants. The same processes have also been shown to occur in certain animal cells. However, since they must oxidize glucose to get the necessary ATP and NADPH + H$^+$, animal cells must expend more energy performing this process than they obtain from it. Green plant cells do not need to oxidize glucose to obtain these energy-rich compounds. Where, then, do they get the energy? From the light reactions.

Van Niel's work with the purple sulfur bacteria did more than simply point to the water molecule as the source of oxygen released during photosynthesis. Noting that these organisms could release sulfur from the hydrogen-sulfide molecule only in the presence of light, Van Niel formulated the idea that in the photosynthetic activity of these bacteria, the splitting of the hydrogen-sulfide molecule was actually accomplished by light. It therefore seemed reasonable to him that in green-plant photosynthesis, the splitting of the water molecule might also be accomplished by light. He reasoned that light energy causes water molecules to split into hydrogen and oxygen, the latter being released. The hydrogen atoms could then be used to reduce carbon dioxide to energy-rich compounds in the dark reactions.

Van Niel was not entirely correct, however. As we have just seen, the reducing agent for carbon dioxide is $NADPH + H^+$, not hydrogen atoms. In 1951 it was discovered that chloroplasts exposed to light could reduce $NADP^+$ to $NADPH + H^+$. This indicated that Van Niel had been essentially correct, though unaware of the intermediate step (from $NADP^+$ to $NADPH + H^+$) between the free hydrogen atoms and the reduction of carbon dioxide. It still is not certain, however, just how the chloroplast can reduce $NADP^+$ to $NADPH + H^+$ using the hydrogen atoms released by the splitting of water molecules.

If fresh green leaves are crushed in acetone, the leaves are killed and the chlorophyll may be extracted from their chloroplasts. If a beam of white light is then directed into the solution, the chlorophyll fluoresces, giving off a red light. However, if the same leaf chloroplasts are exposed to the same beam of white light while intact, *no fluorescence is seen.*

How can these two observations be explained? It is known that substances give off light as the electrons within their atoms or molecules fall from higher to lower energy levels. The electrons jump to these higher energy levels by absorbing the energy to which the atoms or molecules are exposed. The emission of light from the filament of a light bulb, for example, is due to the falling of electrons from the higher energy levels to which they were moved by the absorption of the incoming electrical energy.

We can hypothesize, then, that isolated chlorophyll fluoresces for the same reason. Incoming photons "excite" its electrons, causing them to jump to higher energy levels. In falling back to their original energy levels, the chlorophyll electrons give up their absorbed energy as red light.

Why, then, do the intact chlorophyll-containing chloroplasts not give off red light? If one throws a rubber ball into a darkened room and it immediately returns, it is reasonable to assume that the ball has hit a wall and bounced back. Several more throws with the same results support this hypothesis. If however, the ball does not return after a throw, it is logical to hypothesize that it has been diverted, and the kinetic energy that caused it to bounce back has been absorbed by something else.

Precisely the same assumption is made with the intact chloroplast. Since it does not fluoresce, it can be hypothesized that the energy which would be used in fluorescence, like the ball that did not return, has been absorbed by "something else." This "something else" is not present in an acetone solution of chlorophyll, and thus the energy is free to return as red light—the ball bounces back.

But what is this "something else"? Again bacteria helped provide the answer. There are certain kinds of anaerobic bacteria that live in the soil, growing without oxygen and light. These bacteria use hydrogen gas to synthesize energy-rich molecules. Neither light nor chlorophyll are necessary, then, for these bacteria to synthesize their nutrients. Yet it seems obvious that they must possess a compound capable of accepting free hydrogen and passing it on for the reducing reactions of nutrient synthesis. This compound was finally isolated from these bacteria by Dupont scientists in 1963. It proved to be an iron-rich protein, **ferredoxin.**

The great attraction for electrons demonstrated by ferredoxin made it a likely candidate to be the "something else" that received the light energy absorbed by intact chloroplasts. The situation can be diagrammed as follows:

$$\text{LIGHT} \rightarrow \underset{\text{"EXCITED" ELECTRONS}}{\text{CHLOROPHYLL WITH}} \xrightarrow{2e^-} \underset{\text{(FERREDOXIN?)}}{\text{"SOMETHING ELSE"}} \xrightarrow{2e^-}$$

$$NADP^+ + 2H \rightarrow NADPH + H^{+*} \rightarrow \text{DARK REACTIONS}$$

Drs. Daniel I. Arnon, K. Tagawa, and H. Y. Tsujimoto, of the University of California, performed an experiment to test the hypothesis that ferredoxin was, indeed, the missing "something else." The experimental reasoning was as follows:

*Hypothesis: If* . . .  ferredoxin is the compound that accepts the electrons removed from chlorophyll by light energy, . . .

*Prediction: then* . . . ferredoxin previously reduced by chlorophyll should reduce $NADP^+$ to $NADPH + H^+$ without further aid from light energy.

Working with Dr. Frederick R. Whatley (who, with Drs. D. I. Arnon and Mary B. Allen, had first shown in 1954 that isolated chloroplasts could perform the complete photosynthetic process), Drs. Tagawa and Arnon succeeded in isolating reduced ferredoxin formed through the interaction of light and chlorophyll in spinach chloroplasts. They then exposed this "charged" ferredoxin to NADP. As the hypothesis predicted, the ferredoxin passed on the excess electrons it had absorbed from chlorophyll and reduced the $NADP^+$ to $NADPH + H^+$. Still other experiments provided further support for this hypothesis. Yet, despite the

---

* Before 1963, $NADP^+$ was known as triphosphopyridine nucleotide, or TPN, and often appears in older references under this name. Similarly, $NAD^+$ was known as diphosphopyridine nucleotide, or DPN. As the name indicates, $NAD^+$ differs from NADP in possessing one less phosphate group.

favorable evidence, doubt has recently been cast upon the role of ferredoxin as the *primary* electron acceptor following the absorption of light by chlorophyll. A still more likely candidate, tentatively called **ferredoxin-reducing substance** (**FRS**), has been discovered.

Still another problem exists, however. By absorbing light energy and passing two electrons along to a ferredoxin molecule, the chlorophyll molecule is left "electron deficient." Yet it can be shown that this deficiency does not last; an instant later the same chlorophyll molecule will pass on two more electrons to ferredoxin. It is evident that there must be a fresh supply of electrons to replace those expelled from the chlorophyll molecule by the absorbed photons.

In the formation of $NADPH + H^+$ from $NADP^+$, two hydroxide ions ($OH^-$) are released. Each one of these ions has an extra electron. If an energy source could be found, it would seem likely that the electron-replacement source for chlorophyll could be these $OH^-$ ions. For every four $OH^-$ ions oxidized, two molecules of water and one of oxygen would be formed. The hypothesis proposing that these $OH^-$ ions are the electron-replacement source for chlorophyll is thus an attractive one, since it also accounts for the source of the known waste products of photosynthesis.

Dr. Arnon and his associates have recently performed experiments that support this hypothesis. They have further shown that the energy needed to remove the electrons from the $OH^-$ ions also comes from light. This light energy, however, is absorbed by another pigment; in higher plants and green algae this pigment is chlorophyll *b*. The light absorbed by the chlorophyll *b* causes the pigment to lose electrons, and thereby to become an oxidizing agent. It can thus remove an electron from an $OH^-$ ion.

From chlorophyll *b*, the electrons must be passed through intermediate compounds to chlorophyll *a*. This reaction pathway is not yet entirely clear. It is known that at least part of the electron-transferal process involves cytochrome enzymes in the chloroplasts, and that some ATP is manufactured as it proceeds. Arnon has labeled this entire process one of **noncyclic photophosphorylation**. The last term indicates production of the high-energy phosphate bonds in ATP through the use of light energy. The process is noncyclic because electrons must constantly be fed into the cycle to keep it going. These electrons come via chlorophyll *b* from the $OH^-$ ions produced by the decomposition of water.

Measurements of the energy stored by the noncyclic photophosphorylation process and the amount necessary to drive the dark reactions to completion show a discrepancy. Not enough energy is obtained from the former process to drive the latter. Somewhere, there must be another source of energy to power the dark reactions. What is this energy source?

You may recall that in cellular respiration, $NADH + H^+$ donates its electrons to the cytochrome system, where they are eventually passed on to oxygen, generating some ATP along the way. Since $NADP^+$ is similar in structure and function to NAD, it is reasonable to suppose that $NADP^+$ might serve as an intermediate electron carrier. It appears that $NADP^+$ does indeed pick up electrons from chlorophylls; in returning to the chlorophylls from which they came, the electrons are passed from $NADPH + H^+$ through a cytochome system similar to that found in mitochondria. It is during this process that additional ATP is generated to run the dark reaction.

Examination of the chloroplasts shows that their internal structure bears a certain resemblance to mitochondria: both have a series of membranes, whose surfaces are composed of a mosaic of individual units. In the chloroplast, these units, the quantasomes, are on the surface of the lamellar membranes, (see Fig. 9–13 (d), (e), and (f)). Recall that the analogous structures on the inner surface of the mitochondrial cristae are involved with coupling electron transport to ATP formation. The quantasomes appear to serve a similar function in the chloroplasts. This can be determined in the following way. If chloroplasts are treated in such a way as to cause the quantasomes to be removed from the lamellae, the chloroplasts can still carry on electron transport but are no longer able to generate ATP. It thus appears that the quantasomes must contain phosphorylating enzymes and others which couple electron transport to ATP production.

The pathway by which this process is hypothesized to occur is shown in Fig. 9–19. It is called **cyclic photophosphorylation.** Here the electrons expelled from the chlorophyll molecule by photons pass from ferredoxin to plastoquinone, and thence to the system of cytochromes in the chloroplast itself. As the electrons pass down the line, the energy they release is taken directly into the high-energy bonds of ATP. At the bottom of the cyclic "hill," they regain their lost energy by absorbing more light energy in the chlorophyll $a$ molecule. This is truly a cycle, for *no outside source of electrons is required.*

Cyclic photophosphorylation is an important and necessary part of photosynthesis. Its plentiful yield of ATP more than compensates for the lower yield of ATP obtained from noncyclic photophosphorylation. As long as the proper frequencies of light are provided, cyclic photophosphorylation continues to yield ATP. The ATP excess not used to power the dark reactions can be used for such activities as the synthesis of disaccharide, starch, and protein.

The reader may have noticed that we have referred to the "light reactions" (plural) rather than the "light reaction" (singular). We have done this, of course, partly because a whole series of chemical reactions is involved, instead of just one. However, there is another, more important reason. In 1956 Dr. Robert Emerson and his colleagues at the University of Illinois showed that although photosynthesis is very inefficient at wavelengths greater than 680 m$\mu$ (see Fig. 9–17), it can be enhanced by the addition of light at a shorter wavelength, e.g., 650 m$\mu$. Most significant, the rate of photosynthesis in the presence of both wavelengths is greater than the sum of the rates when the two wavelengths are applied separately. This phenomenon, called the **Emerson enhancement effect,** is consistent with a hypothesis proposing that photosynthesis requires

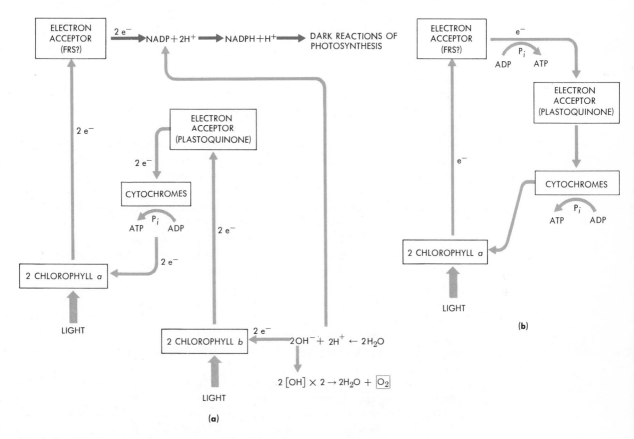

FIG. 9–19 Diagrammatic representation of the light reactions of photosynthesis, showing both (a) noncyclic and (b) cyclic photophosphorylation. (Adapted from John W. Kimball, *Biology*, 2nd edition. Reading, Mass.: Addison-Wesley, 1968.)

*two* light-driven reactions or photochemical systems, both of which can be driven by light of less than 680 m$\mu$ but only one by light of longer wavelengths.

  In any important physiological process, structure usually complements function. The arrangement of cytochromes in the mitochondrion, for example, is one that increases the efficiency with which the electrons pass from acceptor to acceptor. Like the mitochondrion, the chloroplast shows an intricate design which seems to be in accord with its function (Fig. 9–13). It has been shown that the light reactions occur in the pigment-containing lamellae, while the dark reactions are primarily the function of the nonpigmented stroma. Undoubtedly this intricate and highly organized structure is an important factor in the ability of an illuminated chloroplast to synthesize glucose from carbon dioxide and water in 30 seconds.

**9–14**
**THE EFFICIENCY OF**
**PHOTOSYNTHESIS**

The solar energy that strikes the surface of the earth every day is the equivalent of 100,000,000 Hiroshima-size atomic bombs. Some of this energy evaporates water in the seas, water which may later fall back on the land and form potential energy sources as it runs downward through streams and rivers on its way back to the sea.

Of much greater significance, however, is the solar energy captured by green plants. The fall of excited electrons in chlorophyll is far more important than all the waterfalls on earth. The chemical energy resulting from carbon dioxide fixation comprises virtually all of the fuel for living matter. Indeed, the use of light energy in the building of energy-rich molecules is so important that those organisms capable of using light for that purpose are given a special title, the **autotrophs.** The autotrophs are truly great contributors to the world of living organisms. Without their constant conversion of light energy into a chemical form usable by all kinds of organisms, virtually all life on earth would perish. For, directly or indirectly, most nonphotosynthesizing organisms (**heterotrophs**) are dependent upon the autotrophs for the fuels that keep them going. Thus Joseph Priestley's original concept of the need for plant life to "render air fit for breathing again" has been greatly enlarged to include many other needs as well.

Since the photosynthetic process is of utmost importance to all forms of life, including mankind, the efficiency of that process must also be a matter of great importance.

There are several ways of looking at the subject. It can be noted, for example, that of the amount of the sun's energy that reaches the earth (most is wasted by being radiated elsewhere in space), only one part in 2000 is actually captured by photosynthesizing plants. This very low efficiency would be far lower were it not for the fact that about 70% of the earth's surface is covered with water. Though we often tend to think of the familiar green land plants whenever we consider photosynthesis, about 90% of all photosynthetic activity is carried on by microscopic plants in the oceans, rivers, and lakes of the world. Indeed, *as far as man is concerned*, many land plants are actually very inefficient food producers. A great deal of the energy they capture and store is used to build their own complex bodies. A single-celled alga, on the other hand, is almost entirely food, and when it is eaten, most of its body and stored energy enter the food chain. Compare this with the inefficiency of the apple tree, in which only the fruit is eaten. It must be stressed again, however, that the plant is inefficient *only* so far as man is concerned. For the apple tree, apple production must have been an efficient means of seed dispersal or the structure would not have evolved. Though man has often acted as if it were otherwise, no plant or animal has evolved for the purpose of supplying man with food, efficiently or inefficiently.

It is a basic principle of thermodynamics that whenever energy is transformed from one form to another, some of that energy is lost for useful work. The problem is one directly connected to that of photosynthesis, and the use of photosynthetic products by all forms of life. Quite obviously (and fortunately) photosynthesis is an immensely profitable venture for the plant. The energy investment costs nothing; the dividends are so great that they can support those forms of life which do not contribute to them (i.e., do not photosynthesize). The Biblical quotation "All flesh is grass" is quite literally true.

Fortunately, once light is absorbed by chlorophyll molecules of the green plant, the synthetic process becomes remarkably efficient. Better than half of the absorbed light energy ends up locked within glucose molecules as potential chemical energy. Any further chemical transformations of this energy are bound to draw on this stored chemical energy, losing more of it for useful work. The feeding of plant material to animals to fatten them for human consumption is, in terms of energy expenditure, an extremely wasteful process. Only the wealthiest nations can afford it. It is certainly no accident that the overpopulated poor nations of the Far East are primarily vegetarian, relying for their nourishment mostly on crops such as rice. Such nations cannot afford the considerable energy "leakage" that must inevitably accompany the transformation of plant food matter into animal food matter.

It is evident, then, that it behooves man to study photosynthesis in detail. It is often possible to increase the efficiency of photosynthetic food production at the points at which energy may be wasted; educating the farmer to plant high-yield crop strains is one way. Laboratory duplication of the photosynthetic reaction on a commercially practicable scale would be a breakthrough of immense proportions. Such an achievement would go a very long way toward solving the problems of a world in which too many persons do not get nearly enough to eat.

**9-15**
**CONCLUSION**

The study of photosynthesis began over 300 years ago with van Helmont's investigations into the origins of plant matter. The problem is still not entirely solved, but new experimental techniques (such as the use of isotopic tracers), plus the knowledge of ultrastructure provided by the electron microscope, have provided a body of information such that duplication of the process now seems an attainable goal.

The modern view of photosynthesis pictures a system of "electron flow" among various acceptor compounds. As the falling electrons move from one such compound to another, their kinetic energy (provided initially by light) is trapped as potential chemical energy in ATP.

The entire photosynthetic process is divided into two main parts. In the dark reactions, $NADPH + H^+$ and ATP produced by the light reactions are used to power a reaction in which carbon dioxide is progressively reduced to form the three-carbon compound PGAL. The PGAL may then be oxidized directly for the energy needs of the cell or it may continue up the energy hill for synthesis into larger fuel or structural molecules. The dark reactions have been shown to occur in animal cells as well, although, unlike plant cells, animal cells must expend more energy than they gain by the process.

In the light reaction, light energy raises the electrons of chlorophyll $a$ to higher energy levels. In the intact chloroplast, these "excited" electrons are transferred to ferredoxin and eventually reduce NADP to NADPH + $H^+$, which then proceeds into the dark reactions of photosynthesis. The electrons lost by chlorophyll $a$ are replenished by the $OH^-$ ions resulting from the splitting of the water molecule. The exciting of electrons in other plant pigments, such as chlorophyll $b$, provides the energy for the oxidation of the $OH^-$ ions. Since the process involving a transferal of electrons from chlorophyll $a$ results in the production of ATP, and since light is required, the process is known as noncyclic photophosphorylation. Noncyclic photophosphorylation does not provide enough ATP and NADPH + $H^+$ to power the dark reactions, however. Fortunately, a second reaction series, called cyclic photophosphorylation, is more profitable. When electrons are exposed to light, inorganic phosphate, and ADP, they flow from chlorophyll $a$ to ferredoxin to plastoquinone, and thence down the cytochrome system of the chloroplast back to chlorophyll $a$, where the cycle is repeated. During the round trip, the kinetic energy of the electrons is used to convert ADP to ATP. The energy provided by cyclic photophosphorylation is more than sufficient to power the dark reactions.

Organisms that provide energy-rich molecules through processes such as photosynthesis are called autotrophs. Those that do not, and are thereby directly or indirectly dependent on the autotrophic organisms for their food, are called heterotrophs. All animals, and many nongreen plants, are heterotrophic.

By far the greater amount of solar energy striking the earth is wasted, but once this energy is trapped by chlorophyll, the photosynthetic process is remarkably efficient (about 55%). It is evident that studies of ways to increase the overall efficiency of photosynthesis, as well as ways to duplicate the process on a commercially practicable scale, must become increasingly important to mankind.

**EXERCISES**

1. Answer the following questions in relation to van Helmont's experiment.

   a) What did van Helmont conclude from this experiment about the origin of the plant material that led to the gain in weight?

   b) What variable did he fail to recognize in this experiment?

   c) How did Stephen Hales modify van Helmont's experimental conclusions?

2. What contribution did each of the following make to the problem of plant interaction with air and water? (a) Joseph Priestley (b) Nicholas de Saussure (c) Jan Ingenhousz

3. What does the controversy between Berthollet and de Saussure (concerning the origin of the oxygen given off in photosynthesis) illustrate about the characteristics of scientific research?

4. In what way was the origin of the oxygen evolved during photosynthesis eventually determined? Explain the technique involved.

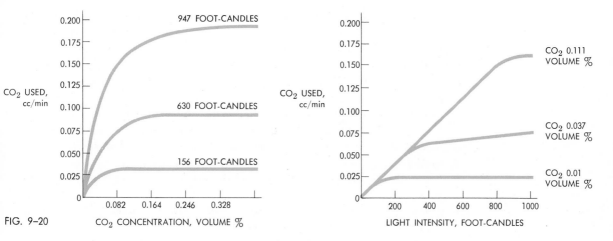

FIG. 9–20

5. See Fig. 9–20. Evaluate each of the statements below only in terms of the data given in the graphs. Explain why you agree or disagree with each statement.

a) Both carbon dioxide concentration and light intensity have upper limits beyond which they will not stimulate photosynthesis.

b) A concentration of 18% $CO_2$ would have an inhibiting action on the rate of photosynthesis at *any* light intensity.

c) When the concentration of $CO_2$ is 0.111% by volume, a doubling of the light intensity in foot-candles approximately doubles the rate of photosynthesis.

d) Up to a certain limiting value, a change in either the concentration of $CO_2$ or the intensity of light produces a change in the rate of photosynthesis.

e) Carbon dioxide and light energy are each involved in two separate phases of the photosynthetic cycle. Therefore, the rate of utilization of one does not affect the rate of utilization of the other.

6. What does the fact that most leaves are green tell you about the wavelengths of the light used in photosynthesis?

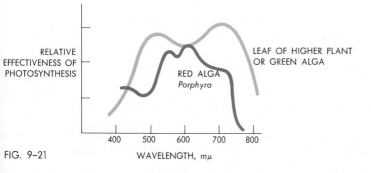

FIG. 9–21

7. Observe the action spectra of two organisms (Fig. 9–21). Evaluate each of the following statements in relation to this graph.

   a) The red alga and green plant, both exposed to roughly the same light source, would absorb the same wavelengths of light with the same degree of effectiveness.

   b) Which single wavelength of light would produce about equal photosynthesis in the red algae and the green plant: (i) 450; (ii) 500; (iii) 510; (iv) 585; (v) 600; (vi) 650; (vii) 700?

   c) If a green alga and a red alga were inhabiting the same region of the ocean, in general they (would, would not) compete for the same wavelengths of light energy.

   d) The red alga is more effective in absorbing the total range of solar energy than the green plant (compare to diagram of solar energy spectrum, Fig. 9–15).

8. Chlorophyll serves to "capture" light energy for use in the process of photosynthesis. It does this by absorbing the light from the sun (radiant energy) and making this usable by:

   a) losing an electron which is transferred by acceptor molecules, thus producing chemical energy for the splitting-up of water,

   b) gaining an electron which, when it joins the chlorophyll molecule, releases some energy which is used to build up ATP and to split water,

   c) losing an electron which is transferred by acceptor molecules, thus producing small amounts of energy used to build up ATP and also to split water,

   d) gaining an electron, which is then immediately transferred for the sole purpose of splitting up the water.

9. What is the function of the carotenoid pigments in plants?

10. Distinguish between the "light reactions" and the "dark reactions" of photosynthesis.

11. Which of the following substances, supplied to a plant kept in the dark, would make it possible for the plant to remain alive?   a) NADP alone; b) NADP and $CO_2$; c) PGAL; d) NADH alone; e) NADH and $CO_2$. Explain your answer.

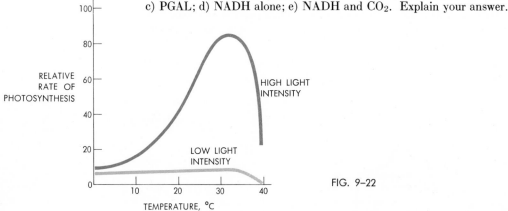

FIG. 9–22

12. Observe the graph in Fig. 9–22. Propose an hypothesis to account for the way in which temperature may affect the rate of photosynthesis differently at different light intensities.

13. The process of respiration is said to be the opposite of that of photosynthesis. In what sense is this statement true? In what ways is it not true?

14. Which aspects of the photosynthetic process are not yet understood by scientists?

ARNON, D. I., "The Role of Light in Photosynthesis." *Scientific American*, November 1960, p. 104. The author discusses how light energy is captured by the photosynthetic pigments and converted into a usable form: ATP. A good article but somewhat technical. It is well worth the effort to understand how the light reactions of photosynthesis are being studied.

BASSHAM, J. A., "The Path of Carbon in Photosynthesis." *Scientific American*, June 1962, p. 88. This article discusses how, by radioactive labeling techniques, the major intermediate compounds in photosynthesis have been isolated.

GALSTON, A. W., *The Life of the Green Plant* (Englewood Cliffs, N.J.: Prentice-Hall, 1961). Chapter 3 contains a discussion of photosynthesis. This is less detailed than the Steward book listed below. A good coverage of the basic process.

NASH, LEONARD K., "Plants and the Atmosphere," in *Harvard Case Histories in Experimental Science* Vol. II (James Bryant Conant, ed.) (Cambridge: Harvard University Press, 1957). Contains a more complete case study of the history of photosynthesis than has been possible to give in the present chapter.

OVERBEEK, JOHANNES VAN, *The Lore of Living Plants* (New York: Scholastic Books, Inc., 1964). Chapter 1 is devoted to an up-to-date treatment of photosynthesis. Well-written and not too detailed. Good as a review and new viewpoint of material covered in the textbook.

RABINOWITCH, EUGENE, "Progress in Photosynthesis." *Scientific American*, November 1953, p. 80. Despite the fact that many details of photosynthesis have been worked out since this article was written, it is still correct in its essentials and is a well-presented survey of the light and dark reactions. The same article is also available, slightly revised, in the *Scientific American* booklet, *The Chemistry and Physics of Life*.

STEWARD, F. C., *Plants at Work* (Reading, Mass.: Addison-Wesley, 1964). Chapter 6 contains a thorough but not too detailed discussion of the physics and chemistry of photosynthesis. This is the best treatment in terms of depth and completeness of any book outside a technical reference. Recommended for those who wish to go beyond the discussion in the text.

WALD, GEORGE, "Life and Light." *Scientific American*, October 1959, p. 92. This article discusses the way that light is used by, and even produced by, living organisms. The main emphasis is on photosynthesis and the vision process.

# CHAPTER 10 PLANT ANATOMY

To primitive man, the appearance of leaves and flowers in the spring must have signified an awakening, a return to life after the hardships of winter. Plants, dormant for so many months, seemed suddenly to become active. Even to modern man, this rapid growth and development of plants in the spring is often highly symbolic, providing inspiration for countless works of music, poetry, and art.

To the **botanist**—a biologist interested specifically in plants—the activity of plant life in the spring has a further significance. It puts him face to face with a number of important problems, and raises many questions. What forces are involved in the movement of materials through a plant? How are new leaves produced? What triggers the unfolding of leaves and flowers in the spring? What controls the growth and development of plants? Why do roots grow downward and stems upward? How do stimuli outside the plant (such as light) affect its growth and development?

These and other such questions demand an understanding of the way in which a plant functions as a complete organism. Up to this point, only the internal organization of individual cells has been discussed. Although study of isolated cell organelles is important for understanding their special characteristics, we must view the organism as a whole—as a continuity of cells, tissues, and organs working together to carry out an integrated series of activities. Only when the individual parts of an organism are viewed in relation to the whole can we begin to understand the intricate mechanisms by which living things maintain themselves.

Much of the dynamics of plant structure and function can be understood simply by viewing them as ways in which the green plant survives as an auto-

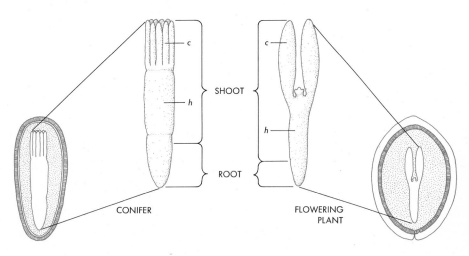

FIG. 10-1    Diagrammatic sketches of young embryos showing basic root-shoot organization. The shoot is further differentiated into young leaves (c, cotyledons) and embryonic stem (h, hypocotyl).

trophic organism. Chapter 9, for example, discussed how the process of photosynthesis enables the autotrophic organism to use solar energy to build energy-rich molecules. There is thus great selective value in the development by a green plant of light-accessible surface area. Some of the ways in which the many problems of autotrophism are solved will be considered in this and the following chapter.

A plant begins its life as a one-celled zygote, a cell produced by the union of an egg cell with a sperm cell (fertilization). The zygote grows and develops into the embryo and finally into a fully mature plant. Even in the very young embryo, there is already a polarized differentiation into an axis composed (in the vascular plants) of a **root** and a **shoot** with leaves attached to a stem (see Fig. 10–1). This basic organization of root and shoot is maintained throughout the life of the plant (Fig. 10–2). Each of these parts performs special functions. Changes in the function of one part necessarily affect the other. For example, the amount of carbohydrate synthesis in the leaves of the shoot is dependent upon the amount of water uptake by the root, as well as the conduction of water upward by the stem of the shoot. Almost all land plants have this basic division of labor. In some species, however, a portion of the shoot may have become modified during evolution for specific functions (e.g., the modifications of stems into many kinds of thorns and tendrils).

In function and general organization, roots and shoots are conspicuously different systems of the plant body. Roots are naked axes, bearing no superficial appendages other than small, one-celled projections, the **root hairs** (Fig. 10–3). Shoots display a segmented appearance due to the presence of conspicuous lateral

**10-2
GENERAL
ORGANIZATION OF
A VASCULAR
PLANT**

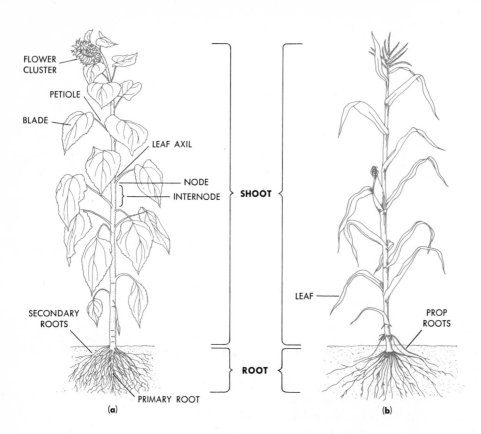

FLOWER
CLUSTER

PETIOLE

BLADE

LEAF AXIL

NODE
INTERNODE

**SHOOT**

SECONDARY
ROOTS

**ROOT**

PRIMARY ROOT

(a)

LEAF

PROP
ROOTS

(b)

FIG. 10–2    The basic root-shoot organization of a vascular plant.    (a) Sunflower, a dicotyledonous flowering plant.    (b) Corn, a monocotyledonous flowering plant.    (After Gilbert M. Smith *et al.*, *A Textbook of General Botany*, 3rd edition.    New York: Macmillan, 1935.)

appendages, the **leaves** (Fig. 10–3).    Roots anchor the plant body firmly in the soil and absorb water and various minerals.    In many species, the root system serves as a storage structure for carbohydrates and other molecules synthesized by the plant.    The main functions of shoots include photosynthesis (especially in the leaves), transport of carbohydrates and other materials between the leaf-bearing portion and the roots, movement of water and dissolved minerals from root to leaves, storage of various molecules used in the normal functioning of cells in the stem itself, and the production of reproductive structures (e.g., flowers). Both externally and internally, the form and structure of roots and shoots are well adapted for the performance of these different tasks.

While roots and shoots differ significantly in structure and function, they are still similar in important ways.    Both have a common origin in the zygote and the embryo.    The tissues of each merge with the other almost imperceptibly; this arrangement obviously makes possible the performance of joint functions such as the transport of materials longitudinally from one part of the plant body to

FIG. 10–3  Conspicuous differences in shoots and roots.  Left, leaves (and fruits) on stem of the basswood (*Tilia*) tree.   Right, root hairs on primary root of germinating radish.  (From John W. Kimball, *Biology*, 2nd edition. Reading, Mass.: Addison-Wesley, 1968.)

another.  Both root and shoot appear to have evolved from a common structure; support for an hypothesis proposing such a common evolutionary origin comes from certain ancient extinct plants which show no differentiation of the body into roots and leafy shoots (see Fig. 25–23).

## 10–3
## PLANT TISSUES

While the individual cells of a living organism may be considered as its units of structure and function, only in a one-celled organism is an individual cell the whole story.  Undoubtedly, one of the largest forward steps in the evolution of multicellular plants was the joining of individual cells into groups.  Such a union allows cell differentiation and specialization.  Some cells can serve for protection, some for transport of food and waste materials, some for perception of the surrounding environment, some for photosynthesis, some for reproduction, and so on.

During its development from the zygote, the cells of the plant divide, enlarge, and differentiate into many different kinds and become organized into complexes or associations (the tissues).  The formation of various kinds of cells and tissues is closely correlated with the following four main functions which the land-dwelling plant has to perform:

1. Restriction of water loss from the plant body, especially via the aerial portion.

2. Absorption of water from the soil and its distribution throughout the plant body.

3. Strengthening of the plant body against the force of gravity.

4. Production of new cells and tissues necessary for the continued life of the plant.

The several tissues of the plant body may be classified into four main groups as follows:

1) **Embryonic or meristematic tissues.** From the time the zygote divides, the plant produces new cells, tissues, and organs throughout its entire life. In the embryo, the production of new cells occurs anywhere. As the embryo grows, however, the production of new cells and tissues is gradually limited to certain regions of the body, the **meristems** (Fig. 10–4). The remainder of the plant body becomes specialized for functions other than the formation of new cells. Thus, unlike an animal, which usually completes the construction of all of its tissues and organs during an early period of embryonic development, a plant body is partially embryonic and partially adult throughout its entire life. Similarly, in a plant, additional organs, e.g., leaves, are formed throughout the life span of the individual, while in the animal body the number of organs is fixed at a certain definite number early in the development of the embryo.

The meristems located at the apices of root and shoot (**apical meristems**) are often cone-shaped (Fig. 10–4). In the root, the apical meristem is covered by a conical sheath, the **root cap,** which protects the embryonic cells as the root forces its way into the soil. In the shoot, the apical meristem is located at the very tip of the stem and receives some protection by the developing leaves. Just below the growing cone of cells, in the apical meristem of the shoot, the young leaves and branches are formed. The plant body produced by the apical meristems is called the **primary body,** composed of fully differentiated and mature primary tissues. In many plants, most of the body is primary: these are the **herbs** or **nonwoody** plants.

In addition to the primary body, many other species of plants have an increase in the thickness of the shoot and root due to the production of additional cells and tissues by a lateral meristem, the **vascular cambium** (Fig. 10–4). Thus, woody plants (trees and shrubs) have secondary tissues comprising a secondary body superimposed throughout most of the plant over the primary body produced by activity of the apical meristem.

Since they are constantly dividing, the metabolic rate of meristem cells is generally far higher than that of cells composing other plant tissues. Consequently, meristem cells must remain small enough to keep a high ratio of surface area per cell unit volume. They also have a smaller amount of endoplasmic reticulum, their plastids and mitochondria are less elaborate, and their cell walls are usually much thinner than those of fully differentiated living cells of the plant body.

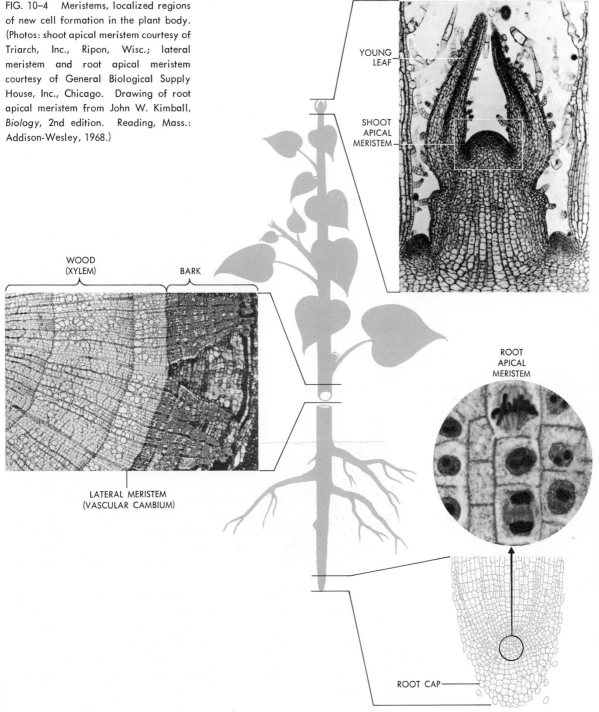

FIG. 10–4 Meristems, localized regions of new cell formation in the plant body. (Photos: shoot apical meristem courtesy of Triarch, Inc., Ripon, Wisc.; lateral meristem and root apical meristem courtesy of General Biological Supply House, Inc., Chicago. Drawing of root apical meristem from John W. Kimball, *Biology*, 2nd edition. Reading, Mass.: Addison-Wesley, 1968.)

YOUNG LEAF

SHOOT APICAL MERISTEM

WOOD (XYLEM)

BARK

LATERAL MERISTEM (VASCULAR CAMBIUM)

ROOT APICAL MERISTEM

ROOT CAP

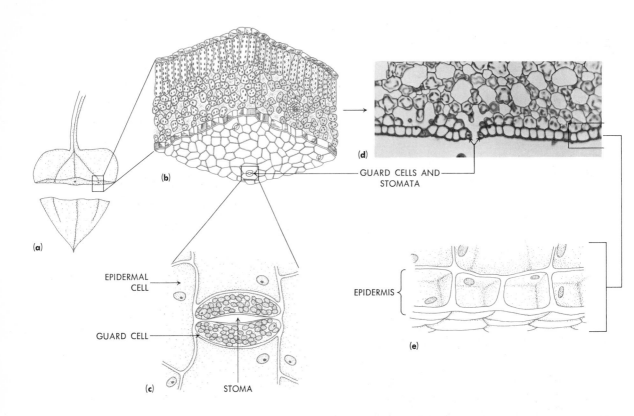

EPIDERMAL
CELL

GUARD CELL

STOMA

GUARD CELLS AND
STOMATA

EPIDERMIS

FIG. 10–5    Protective or surface tissues. (a, b, and c) Epidermis of a leaf. (d, e) Epidermis of stem of
buttercup. [Photo courtesy Triarch, Inc., Ripon, Wisc. Drawings (a) and (e) from John W. Kimball,
*Biology*, 2nd edition. Reading, Mass.: Addison-Wesley, 1968.]

2) **Protective or surface tissues.** As the names imply, protective tissues are
generally located on the outer surfaces of the plant body for its protection. The
entire body of young plants and fully mature herbs is covered with a protective
tissue, the **epidermis** (Fig. 10–5). The epidermis, usually a single layer of living
cells, forms a continuous covering over all portions of the primary body (the
leaves and reproductive structures as well as the stems and roots). The epidermal
cells of the aerial portion of the plant body usually produce a waxy substance,
**cutin,** which impregnates the outer walls and forms a distinct layer, the cuticle,
over the outer surface of the cells. In many species the waxy cuticle forms a
light-grey "bloom" which can be easily wiped off, e.g., the leaves of red cabbage
and fruits such as unwashed plums and grapes. The epidermis helps to prevent
the aerial parts of the plant body from losing excessive quantities of water
through transpiration (see Section 11–5).

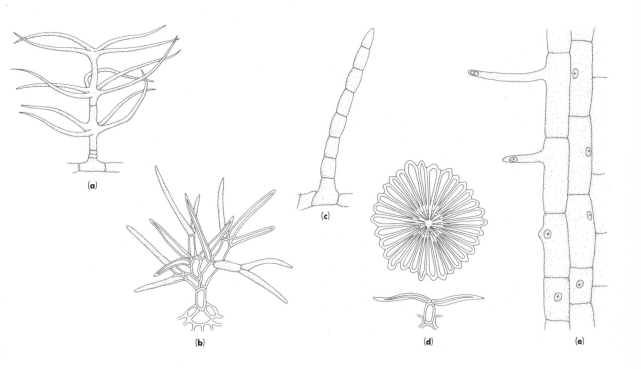

FIG. 10–6    Appendages (trichomes) of the epidermal tissue of vascular plants. (a) Branched hair from sycamore. (b) Dendroid hair from lavender. (c) Unbranched hair from *Coreopsis*. (d) Peltate scale from olive in surface (upper drawing) and side (lower drawing) views. (e) Root hairs. [(a) and (b) after K. Esau, *Plant Anatomy*. New York: John Wiley, 1953. (d) after K. Esau, *Anatomy of Seed Plants*. New York: John Wiley, 1960.]

The epidermis of aerial portions of the plant body possesses very distinctive, usually bean-shaped pairs of cells with a small opening between them. Since the size of the opening can vary through changes in the shape of the pair of cells, they are known as **guard cells** (Fig. 10–5c, d). The opening between the guard cells is called a **stoma** (plural: **stomata**). Stomata are adaptions which facilitate the exchange of gases between the interior of the plant body and the atmosphere.

Many species of vascular plants possess appendages extending from the epidermis of the stems and leaves. These **trichomes** (Fig. 10–6), which may consist of one cell or many cells, appear in the form of hairs or scales. In some species, the hairs may be many-branched and sufficiently dense so as to form a wooly covering over the epidermis. The hairs of many other species are glandular, producing and secreting droplets of oily materials. This phenomenon is especially

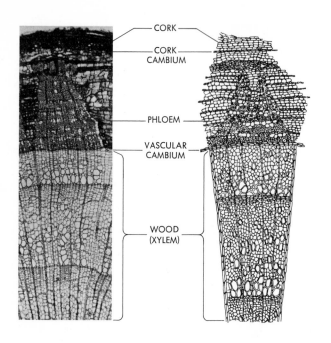

CORK
CORK CAMBIUM
PHLOEM
VASCULAR CAMBIUM
WOOD (XYLEM)

FIG. 10–7    Protective or surface tissues: periderm (cork plus cork cambium) in stem of basswood tree. The epidermis has already been ruptured and shed. (Photo courtesy General Biological Supply House, Inc., Chicago. Drawing from John W. Kimball, *Biology*, 2nd edition. Reading, Mass.: Addison-Wesley, 1968.)

noticeable in petunia and tobacco plants. The hairs of the nettle (*Urtica*) have a spherical tip. If lightly touched with one's hand, this tip breaks off and penetrates the skin. The fluid contents of the hair escape into the wound. The fluid is poisonous and produces a stinging sensation and inflammation around the puncture. The epidermis of seeds of the cotton plant produces hairs (the cotton fibers) which may grow as long as $\frac{1}{2}$ to $2\frac{1}{2}$ inches. This length, plus the high composition of cellulose in their thick walls, renders cotton very useful in making cloth.

The epidermal tissue of young roots has long slender appendages, the root hairs, at some distance from the tip where the root cells have reached their maximum length (Fig. 10–6e). Each root hair, a tubular outgrowth of a single epidermal cell, greatly increases the surface area of the root for absorption of water and minerals in solution. For example, one rye plant was calculated to have some 14 billion living root hairs with a total area of 4300 square feet. The same plant had 13,800,000 roots with a surface area of 2500 square feet. Thus, a single rye plant had a total of 6800 square feet of surface contact between its roots and root hairs and the soil. In fact, it had 130 times more surface in contact with the earth than it had exposed to the atmosphere by its aboveground parts. Root hairs commonly live only a few days. They are rapidly replaced, however, by new ones forming just back of the root apex.

In those species of plants in which the stems and roots increase in thickness by the formation of new cells and tissues by the cambium, the epidermis becomes stretched and finally ruptured. Before the epidermis is destroyed, however, a secondary protective layer tissue, the **periderm,** is developed through the activity of a special lateral meristem, the **cork cambium** (Fig. 10–7). When fully functional, the cells in the outer layer of the periderm (known as cork cells) are dead and usually filled with air (this characteristic gives cork its excellent insulating qualities, and thus makes it an ideal choice for thermos bottle stoppers). Before they die, cork cells produce wax and a fatty substance, **suberin,** which accumulate as distinct alternating layers over the primary cellulose wall. Since the wax and suberin layers are practically impervious to water, the cork cells are well adapted to protect the plant body from excessive loss of water.

3) **Fundamental tissues.** Fundamental tissues generally compose the greatest mass of the plant body. The soft portions of the leaves, flowers and fruits, the cortex regions of the stem and root, and the pith region of the stem are all composed of fundamental tissues. The chief function of fundamental tissues is the production and storage of food. In their form and structure, the cells of the fundamental issues are highly diverse. A brief examination of some of this diversity will be helpful in understanding the morphology and physiology of the plant body.

**Parenchyma** cells occur in continuous masses throughout the plant body. They are especially abundant in the region between the epidermis and the vascular tissues (see Fig. 10–8a, b, c), in the pith of the stem, in the photosynthetic tissue (**mesophyll**) of leaves, in the flesh of juicy fruits, and in the food storage region of the seed (usually the **endosperm**). Parenchyma cells are also present in the conducting tissues of both the primary and secondary body, i.e., in both herbs and woody plants. Parenchyma cells are relatively unspecialized; even when fully mature, these cells are more similar in form and structure to the cells of the meristem than any other cells inside the plant body. In fact, parenchyma cells retain the ability to divide, a characteristic which enables the plant body to heal wounds and regenerate organs. Parenchyma cells usually have relatively thin primary walls; thick walls are present only in certain tissues (e.g., secondary xylem). A large vacuole, which may contain large quantities of water and other materials, is usually present. In fact, the water-filled vacuoles of parenchyma cells give considerable support and shape to the plant body.

Closely similar to parenchyma in both structure and function is **collenchyma** tissue (Fig. 10–8g, h). As with parenchyma cells, collenchyma cells are functional while living (some cells must die before they can function). Collenchyma cells have adaptations enabling them to help support the plant body, not only in its growing portions but also the fully mature primary body. These adaptive features include an elongate shape, irregularly thickened walls, and close packing. All of these characteristics make collenchyma a very strong tissue, capable of considerable stretching, yet still flexible and plastic. Such characteristics are especially valuable in the growing stem or leaf. Collenchyma tissue is

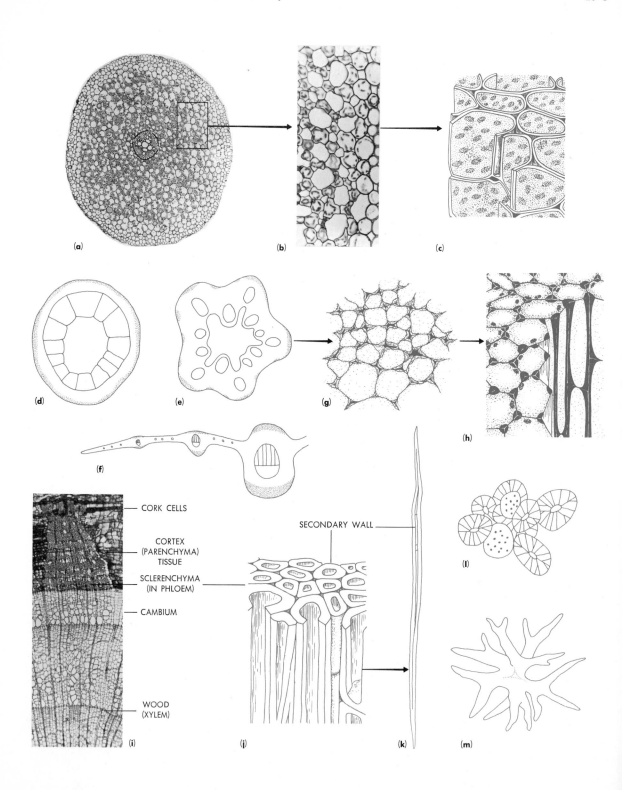

(a)

(b)

(c)

(d)

(e)

(g)

(h)

(f)

CORK CELLS

CORTEX
(PARENCHYMA)
TISSUE

SCLERENCHYMA
(IN PHLOEM)

CAMBIUM

WOOD
(XYLEM)

SECONDARY WALL

(i)

(j)

(k)

(l)

(m)

◀FIG. 10–8    Fundamental tissues. (a) Parenchyma tissue in root of buttercup (indicated by rectangle). (b, c) Enlarged views of parenchyma cells from (a). (d, e, f) Diagrams indicating location of collenchyma tissue in stems (d, e) and leaf (f). (g, h) Enlarged views of cells in collenchyma tissue. (i) Location of sclerenchyma tissue (fibers) in food-conducting tissue of basswood stem. (j, k) Enlarged views of fibers; note secondary wall. (l) Sclereids ("stone cells") from fruit of pear. (m) A leaf sclereid. [Photos: (a) and (b) courtesy Triarch, Inc., Ripon, Wisc.; (i) courtesy General Biological Supply House, Inc., Chicago. Drawings: (c), (h), and (j) from John W. Kimball, *Biology*, 2nd edition. Reading, Mass.: Addison-Wesley, 1968; (d), (e), (f), and (l) after K. Esau, *Anatomy of Seed Plants*. New York: John Wiley, 1960.]

usually located on the periphery of stems and leaves, often just beneath the epidermis (see Fig. 10–8d, e, f).

Collenchyma tissue and water-filled parenchyma cells may enable the young growing plant to maintain its characteristic shape and rigidity. In the mature herb, however, much of the strength and support of the body is provided by **sclerenchyma** tissue. The cells of sclerenchyma possess features enabling the plant body to withstand considerable bending and stretching without much damage to the softer cells of the parenchyma tissue. During their development, each sclerenchyma cell forms a very thick secondary wall as an additional deposit over the primary cell wall (see Fig. 10–8j). The great strength of sclerenchyma cells comes from a framework of cellulose molecules (often reinforced with lignin) which composes the secondary wall.

Some cells of sclerenchyma may be conspicuously elongated. These **fibers** (Fig. 10–8j, k) may be as long as 7 centimeters (in the flax plant, used in making linen cloth) or even 25 centimeters long (the ramie plant, formerly used in making Chinese linen). Fiber cells add considerable strength to plant parts no longer growing in length. They often occur as separate strands, bundles, or cylinders in various parts of the plant.

A second kind of sclerenchyma cell is the **sclereid**, a type of cell that is highly diverse in shape and size (Fig. 10–8l, m). Sclereid cells may occur anywhere in the plant body, either singly or in groups. The gritty texture of pear fruits is due to small clusters of sclereids known as "stone cells" (Fig. 10–8l). The hardness of nut shells and seed coats is also due to sclereids.

**4) Vascular or conducting tissues.** The possession of special tissues for transporting water, food, and other materials throughout the plant body is a characteristic feature of most land-dwelling plants. The cells comprising these conducting tissues are usually tubelike and enlongated in the direction in which the conduction occurs. Two kinds of conducting tissues are present in the body of most land plants: **xylem** and **phloem.** Each tissue consists of several different kinds of cells.

Xylem tissue is the most abundant conducting tissue in the body of the vascular plant. It forms a continuous system running from near the root tips, upward through the stem, and out into the leaves. Xylem contains several kinds of cells, some of which are alive at functional maturity while others must die

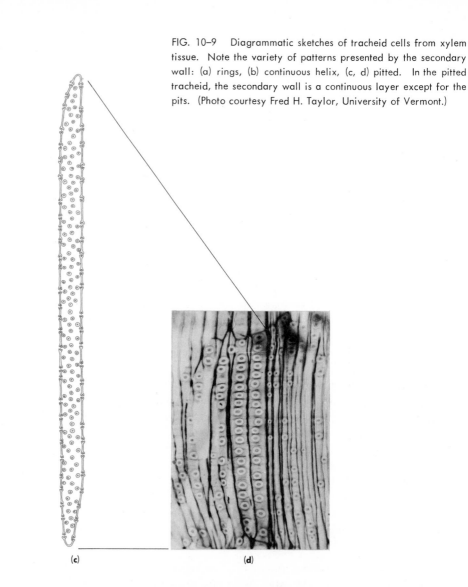

FIG. 10–9   Diagrammatic sketches of tracheid cells from xylem tissue.  Note the variety of patterns presented by the secondary wall: (a) rings, (b) continuous helix, (c, d) pitted.  In the pitted tracheid, the secondary wall is a continuous layer except for the pits.  (Photo courtesy Fred H. Taylor, University of Vermont.)

(a)          (b)          (c)                    (d)

before they can do their main task.  The most characteristic cells in the xylem are **tracheids** and **vessel elements;** both conduct water.*  During their development, both types of cells produce secondary walls: these add extra strength and rigidity to the xylem tissue as well as to the entire plant body.  These wall thickenings also prevent the water-conducting cells from collapsing during periods when much water is being lost from the plant by transpiration (see

---

* Tracheids and vessel elements are found in angiosperms, while in gymnosperms tracheids are the only conducting elements.

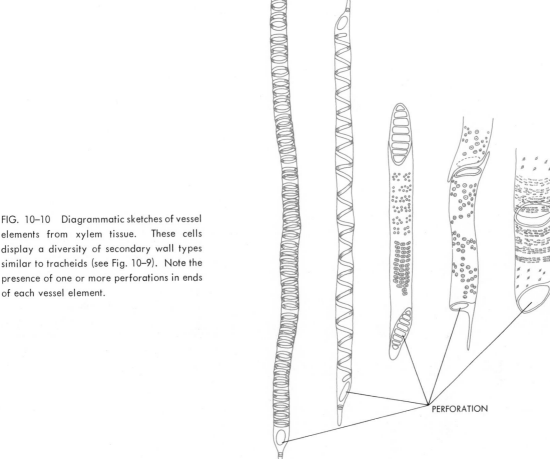

FIG. 10–10 Diagrammatic sketches of vessel elements from xylem tissue. These cells display a diversity of secondary wall types similar to tracheids (see Fig. 10–9). Note the presence of one or more perforations in ends of each vessel element.

PERFORATION

Section 11–5). When first formed by apical meristems or vascular cambium, both tracheids and vessel elements are living. When fully developed, however, the cytoplasm and nucleus disappear, leaving only the thickened cell wall. The result is either a long hollow cell (tracheid), admirably suited for the movement of water (Fig. 10–9), or the **xylem vessel** (a series of vessel elements joined end to end), which is an even more efficient structure for water movement. During the development of a vessel, the transverse walls separating adjacent cells of the series break down and are absorbed. The cytoplasm and nucleus also disappear. The result is a long tubular structure which greatly accelerates the rate of water conduction (Fig. 10–10).

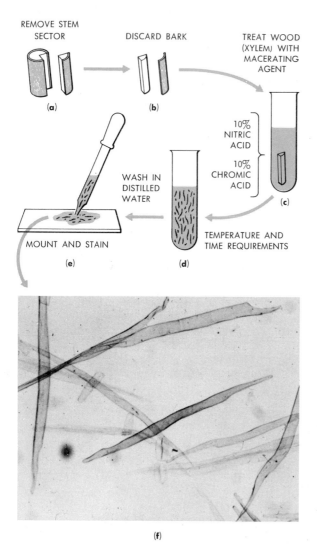

REMOVE STEM
SECTOR                  DISCARD BARK          TREAT WOOD
(XYLEM) WITH
MACERATING
AGENT

(a)                        (b)

10%
NITRIC
ACID

10%
CHROMIC
ACID

WASH IN
DISTILLED
WATER                                                (c)

MOUNT AND STAIN          TEMPERATURE AND
TIME REQUIREMENTS

(e)                      (d)

(f)

FIG. 10–11   The often extreme hardness of
plant tissues calls for special separation processes. Here is shown the technique of xylem
maceration and its results. (a–e) Diagrams illustrating the maceration procedure. Small pieces
about the thickness of a match are placed in a
chemical solution that dissolves the material
which cements the cells together in tissues. (f) A
photograph of the results of macerating xylem of
ash (*Fraxinus pennsylvanica*). (Courtesy U. S.
Forest Products Laboratory, Madison, Wisc.)

During the development of individual tracheids and vessel elements, the
secondary wall thickening may be deposited over almost all of the primary wall
except for scattered, isolated areas. These areas form small cavities or **pits** in
the secondary wall. The pits of adjacent cells usually meet each other (Fig.
10–12). Separating the two adjacent pits is a **pit membrane,** composed of the
primary wall of each cell and the cementing material which binds the cells
together. (It is this cementing material that is dissolved in the process of
xylem maceration; see Fig. 10–11.) Since the pit membrane is quite permeable,
water can move easily from one cell to the next. Around each pit there is usually
a circular border which overhangs the pit cavity (Fig. 10–12). Thus, bordered

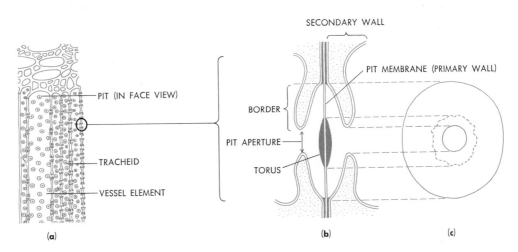

FIG. 10–12   Diagrams of pairs of adjacent pits, each with a circular border composed of the over-
arching secondary wall.  Bordered pits are present in both tracheids and vessel elements.  [(a) from
John W. Kimball, *Biology*, 2nd edition.  Reading, Mass.: Addison-Wesley, 1968; (b) and (c) adapted
from K. Esau, *Plant Anatomy*.  New York: John Wiley, 1953.]

pit-pairs of adjacent tracheids and vessel elements constitute an adaptation for
increasing the area of the thin, water-permeable parts of the primary walls
without enlarging the cavities or pits in the secondary walls.  Such an adaptation
provides for rapid movement of water without greatly reducing the strength and
rigidity of the tracheids and vessel elements.

  While the pit membranes of the majority of vascular plants are rather thin,
those of conifers have a conspicuous central thickening, or **torus** (Fig. 10–12).
The torus may function as a valve between cells.  When the pressure in one cell
becomes considerably greater than in the adjacent cell, the torus is forced
against the border of the pit in the adjacent cell, blocking the pit opening and
impeding the movement of water from one tracheid to another.

  In addition to tracheids and vessel elements, xylem tissue also contains
parenchyma cells.  These living cells may either be scattered among the dead
tracheids and vessel elements or aggregated into **rays** (Fig. 10–13).  Each ray is
a radial system of cells in the xylem.  They function in the lateral movement of
materials across the xylem and in the storage of carbohydrates.

  Finally, xylem tissue may contain elongate, very thick-walled **fiber cells**
(Fig. 10–8j, k).  Fibers add strength to xylem tissue, especially in species where
the xylem contains many wide, relatively thin-walled vessels.  In some species,
fiber cells develop cross-walls after the secondary wall is deposited along their
longitudinal walls.  Fiber cells may also retain their cytoplasm and nucleus and
function in the storage of starch and other reserve foods.

  In addition to xylem, the conducting tissues include phloem.  As does xylem,
the phloem also forms a continuous system, running from near the tips of the

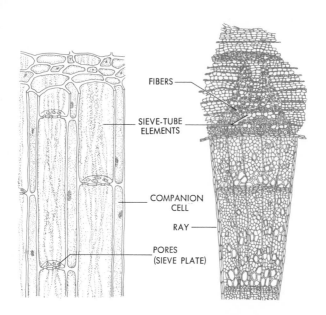

FIBERS

SIEVE-TUBE
ELEMENTS

COMPANION
CELL

RAY

PORES
(SIEVE PLATE)

FIG. 10–13    Cells of the phloem tissue. Left, sieve-tube elements (in longitudinal section). Right, same in cross section of basswood stem. Note that the phloem tissue in basswood also contains thick-walled supporting fibers. (Both drawings from John W. Kimball, *Biology*, 2nd edition. Reading, Mass.: Addison-Wesley, 1968.)

roots upward through the stem to the leaves. Like xylem, phloem contains several kinds of cells; both fibers and parenchyma are present. The main conducting cells of the phloem are the **sieve cells** and **sieve-tube elements;** both transport food materials.* As implied by their name, these cells have characteristic clusters of small pores on their end walls which, in surface view, resemble a sieve (Fig. 10–13). Through these pores, strands of cytoplasm extend from one cell to its neighbor.

Sieve cells and sieve-tube elements have one unique characteristic; during development, the nucleus becomes disorganized and disappears as a distinct organelle. Yet even without a nucleus, the cell cytoplasm continues to live and the cell performs its part in the conduction of food materials.

How can a cell continue to live and function without a nucleus? You may recall the experiments on the green alga *Acetabularia* (Section 6–7) in which the stalk and umbrella portion were cut off, leaving the nucleus in the rhizoid part. The isolated stalk which lacked a nucleus lived for a time and then died. From this and other experiments with this alga, it was concluded that the nucleus apparently produces substances which cause the cytoplasm to function in a definite way. Without the nucleus, the life of the cell does not continue for long. One hypothesis proposes that the cytoplasm of the sieve cells and sieve-tube elements may be controlled by nuclei-produced substances from nearby specialized parenchyma cells (the **companion cells**). No satisfactory experimental test for this hypothesis has yet been performed, however.

---

* Sieve-tube elements are characteristic of angiosperms, while sieve cells are found in gymnosperms and lower forms.

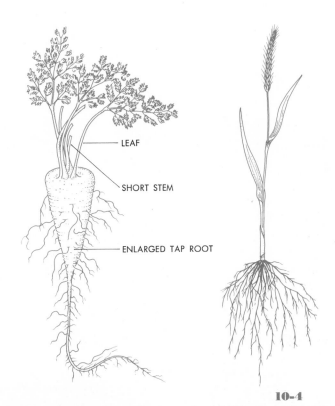

LEAF

SHORT STEM

ENLARGED TAP ROOT

FIG. 10–14   Root systems of flowering plants.  Left, taproot of carrot.  Right, fibrous root system of foxtail grass.

## 10-4
## THE ROOT SYSTEM

In patterns of growth, two types of root system are generally recognized.*  Most trees and shrubs and many herbs have a root system that is basically a **taproot** and its branches.  Taproot systems are characterized by a large, central **primary root** which grows straight downward.  From this taproot, lateral or branch roots develop in sequence, the youngest near the apical meristem and the oldest near the base.  Taproots are especially effective in anchoring the plant in the earth, as anyone who has tried to pull up a dandelion from a lawn will readily attest. Since they can penetrate far into the soil, taproots can also obtain deeper, more permanent sources of water.  The taproots of many species may be specially adapted for the storage of the products of photosynthesis.  The familiar edible portion of a carrot plant, for example, is a taproot packed with stored food (Fig. 10–14).

Grass plants, their relatives, and most ferns possess a **fibrous** root system, composed of numerous **adventitious roots** arising from the stem.  In monocots (e.g., corn), these adventitious roots replace the primary root, which dies.  While fibrous root systems do not anchor plants in the ground as well as do taproot systems, they are well adapted for absorbing water near the surface.

---

* A third type, called **diffuse,** is recognized by some botanists.  It is similar to the fibrous type.

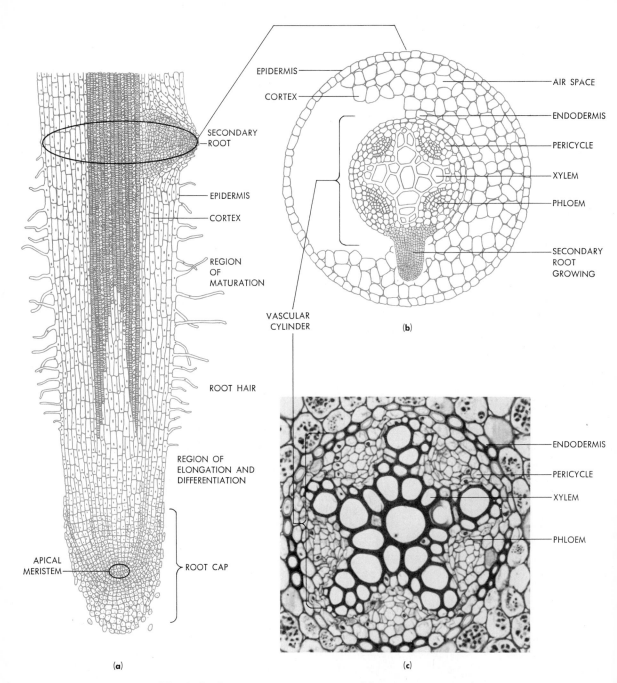

FIG. 10–15   Tissue organization of a root.  (a) Longitudinal section (greatly shortened in order to show the various stages in development).  (b) Cross section showing location of various tissues.  (c) Vascular cylinder of root of buttercup.  Compare with (b) for identity of tissues.  (Photo courtesy of Carolina Biological Supply Company.  Drawings adapted from John W. Kimball, *Biology*, 2nd edition. Reading, Mass.: Addison-Wesley, 1968.)

Internally, fibrous roots differ little from taproots. For convenience, the taproot can be considered as a typical example of root structure. A longitudinal section of the tip of a root is shown in Fig. 10–15(a). The end of the root is covered by a root cap. As the root grows, the cells of the root cap are worn away. They are continually replaced, however, by the apical meristem.

Behind the root cap is the apical meristem, a growing or embryonic region which provides new cells for the tissues of the root as well as for the root cap itself. Behind the apical meristem is a region of elongation, where cells increase in length. During elongation, the cells also begin to differentiate, i.e., to become specialized. Further up the root is the region of maturation, where the cells reach their full size and become completely specialized. In this region, root hairs project from many of the epidermal cells.

Seen in cross section, the cells and tissues of the root in the maturation region present a definite pattern (see Fig. 10–15b, c). Three principal regions are discernible: **epidermis, cortex,** and **vascular cylinder** or **stele.** The cortex tissue consists mainly of parenchyma cells which are characteristically separated from each other by spaces of various sizes. These intercellular spaces, which develop during the early growth of the root, appear to be adaptations for aeration of the root cells. The cortex helps move water and dissolved minerals across the root from the epidermis to the xylem, and it stores various molecules transported downward from the shoot. The innermost layer of cells in the cortex usually differentiates as an **endodermis,** composed of cells whose walls become thickened during their development. There is some evidence that the endodermis functions in the movement of water and dissolved minerals from the cortex to the xylem.

The vascular cylinder begins with one or more layers of parenchyma cells, the **pericycle,** immediately inside the endodermis. Cells of the pericycle tissue retain the ability to undergo cell division, producing the secondary roots. On the inner surface of the pericycle are the vascular tissues, which in many species are arranged in a star-shaped pattern. Comprising the core of this star are the cells of the xylem. Between the points of the star are small groups of phloem cells. They are usually separated from the xylem by a layer of cambium which, in those species whose roots undergo increase in thickness, produces both secondary xylem and phloem.

One of the most characteristic features of the shoot system is its differentiation into a central axis (the stem) to which a series of lateral appendages (the leaves) is attached. The leaves are arranged on the stem in patterns more or less characteristic of each species. The point of attachment of each leaf to the stem is called the **node;** and the portion of the stem between two nodes, the **internode** (Fig. 10–2). Depending upon the species, the internodes may be long and distinct or very short and indistinct. In plants bearing their leaves in a rosette, e.g., the dandelion, internodes can be distinguished only with difficulty. The internodes are also very short in the spur shoots of fruit trees and the needle-bearing shoots of pines. In trees, the division of the stem into nodes and inter-

**10–5
THE SHOOT
SYSTEM**

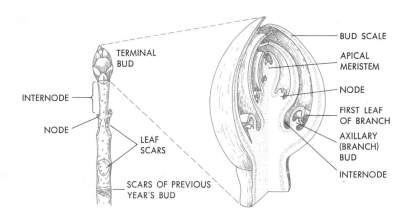

FIG. 10–16   The bud, a stem in miniature.  A series of overlapping leaves, the bud scales protect the apical meristem.   These scales usually fall off the tree as the bud develops into a new shoot, leaving bud scale scars on the twig.   (Drawing on right adapted from Willis H. Johnson et al., Biology, 3rd edition. New York: Holt, Rinehart, and Winston, 1966.)

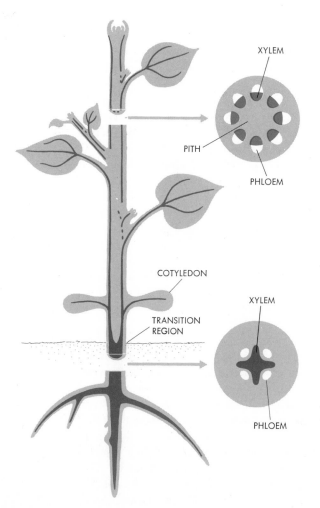

FIG. 10–17   A diagrammatic representation of the vascular system of a flowering plant. The plant body is shown as it would appear if split lengthwise.   Note that the xylem and phloem tissues form a continuous system throughout the entire body.

nodes is eventually obscured by the growth in thickness, due to the activity of the vascular cambium. Thus, except for young twigs, external evidence for the spatial relationship between the stem and the leaves can no longer be seen in a tree.

New leaves and tissues of the shoot arise in the apex of the stem, a region called the shoot apical meristem. This meristem is usually enclosed by older leaves; the whole comprises a **bud** (Fig. 10–16). If the older leaves are carefully removed, the very tip of the shoot appears as a minute dome or mound; this is the apical meristem proper, the ultimate source of the cells of the shoot. Embryonic leaves in various stages of development can be seen arising beneath this tip. The older leaves overarch the younger ones, thus protecting them (and the apical meristem proper) from drying out (desiccation).

Internally, the shoot apex (Fig. 10–4) presents an appearance considerably different from that of the root apex. The most obvious difference is the lack of a cap of tissue comparable to a root cap. Thus, in the shoot apex, the apical meristem itself terminates the shoot. In addition, while the root apical meristem adds new cells both outwardly to the root cap and inwardly to the root proper, the shoot apical meristem contributes new cells only to future leaf and stem tissues. Just as in the young root, after the new cells are formed by the meristem, they gradually elongate and differentiate into the various kinds of cells characteristic of the mature tissues of the plant.

As in the root, the cells and tissues of the stem present a definite pattern when viewed in cross section. In some species (e.g., certain ferns and a few aquatic flowering plants), three main regions can be distinguished: **epidermis, cortex,** and **vascular cylinder.** In such plants the vascular cylinder forms a solid rod in the center of the stem. In most plant species, however, the center of the stem axis (Fig. 10–17) is occupied by the **pith** composed largely of parenchyma tissue.

Beneath the epidermis of the stem is the cortex which, as in the root, consists largely of parenchyma cells. Collenchyma and fibers are also present in some species. In ferns, the innermost layer of the cortex is usually differentiated into an endodermis. In most flowering plants, however, the endodermis does not develop.

The vascular or conducting system occupies the region of the stem inside the cortex. In most seed-producing plants, the stem vascular system has the form of either a continuous cylinder surrounding a central pith, or a split cylinder enclosing a pith. In the case of the split cylinder, the xylem and phloem tissues are in segments or strands called **vascular bundles.** If the cortex and the pith tissues are removed from the stem of such a plant, the vascular system may be seen as a network of individual vascular bundles which occasionally meet and fuse and then branch again (Fig. 10–18). At each node, one or more vascular bundles enter each leaf and each branch bud.

Within the stem, the vascular bundles of many species are situated so that the phloem tissue lies outside the xylem. In some plants (e.g., the potato,

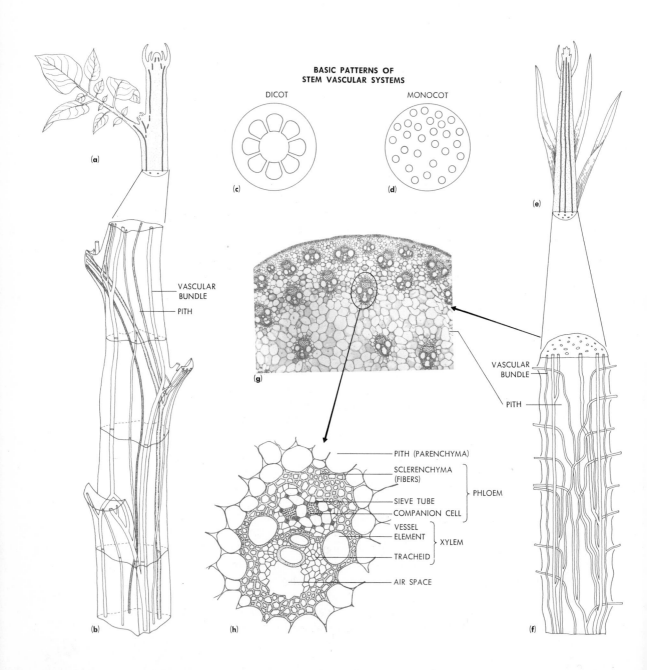

BASIC PATTERNS OF
STEM VASCULAR SYSTEMS

DICOT

MONOCOT

(a)

(b)

(c)

(d)

(e)

(f)

(g)

(h)

VASCULAR
BUNDLE

PITH

VASCULAR
BUNDLE

PITH

PITH (PARENCHYMA)

SCLERENCHYMA
(FIBERS)

SIEVE TUBE

COMPANION CELL

PHLOEM

VESSEL
ELEMENT

TRACHEID

XYLEM

AIR SPACE

watermelon, milkweed, and sunflower), phloem may be present on both sides of the xylem. By looking at the arrangement of vascular bundles in the stem, two distinct patterns can be distinguished among the flowering plants (Fig. 10–18c, h). If the vascular bundles are arranged in a circular pattern around the central pith, like spokes radiating from the hub of a wheel, the plant is put in a taxonomic category known as the **dicotyledonous** plants ("dicots"). The vascular bundles are replaced by cylinders early in the life of woody plants. If the vascular bundles are dispersed throughout the stem, the plant is placed in a group called the **monocotyledonous** plants ("monocots").

It can be seen that there are significant differences in the kind and arrangement of tissues between the stem and the root. In the root, the xylem is usually in the form of a star-shaped or fluted column occupying the central region (see Fig. 10–17). In the stem, however, the xylem is either a hollow or split cylinder with the central portion of the stem consisting of pith tissues (see Fig. 10–17). Despite these obvious differences in arrangement, the vascular systems of the root and stem meet and become adapted to one another in a transition region, generally located between the root and the cotyledons. The structure of this transition region varies from one group of plants to another, and is often highly complex. In the flax plant, for example, the vascular tissue pattern in the lower part of the transition region is similar to that of the root. Some distance higher up, a pith develops in the center of the vascular cylinder. Just above this point, the vascular system becomes arranged into vascular bundles, some of which enter the cotyledons while others continue into the stem.

In its form and anatomy, the leaf portion of the shoot is the most variable organ of the plant. Due to this variability, several kinds of leaves have been distinguished including: **foliage leaves, scale leaves, bracts,** and **cotyledons.** Foliage leaves are the main photosynthetic structures. Scale leaves occur as bud scales and on underground stems, and function in protection and storage of reserve molecules. Bracts are usually associated with the flowers, where they too appear to serve a protective role. Sometimes the bracts are colored (as in poinsettia, *Euphorbia pulcherrima*), and function the same as petals. Cotyledons are the first leaves to be formed by the young plant, and it is the presence of one or two of them that give the monocotyledonous and dicotyledonous plants their respective names.

◀FIG. 10–18    Patterns of vascular tissues in flowering plant. (a–c) Diagrams of the primary vascular system of the stem of potato. (d–h) Vasculature in stem of corn. (h) Cross section of a vascular bundle showing arrangement of tissues. Note that the phloem lies outside the xylem (with reference to the epidermis). [Photo courtesy General Biological Supply House, Inc., Chicago. Drawings: (b) adapted from E. F. Artschwager, *Journal of Agricultural Research* **14** (1918), 221–252; (f) adapted from M. Kumazawa, *Phytomorphology* **11** (1961), 128–139; (h) from John W. Kimball, *Biology*, 2nd edition. Reading, Mass.: Addison-Wesley, 1968.]

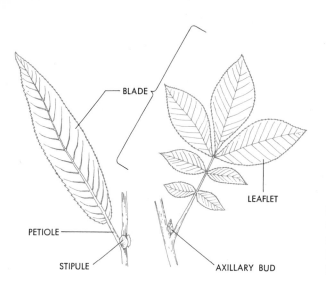

BLADE

LEAFLET

PETIOLE

STIPULE

AXILLARY BUD

FIG. 10–19  Leaf forms.  Left, a simple leaf of willow.  Right, a compound leaf (with seven leaflets) of hickory.  One or more lateral buds occur in the leaf axil, the angle formed by the leaf base and the internode above.

A foliage leaf usually consists of three parts: **blade, petiole,** and **stipule** (Fig. 10–19).  In the course of evolution, the blade has become greatly flattened, an adaptation which has greatly increased the efficiency of the surface areas in the capture of light energy and exchange of gases.  The blade may be divided into **leaflets** (*compound leaf*) or it may be undivided (*simple leaf*) and its margin may be even or variously notched.  In some species, the blade is directly attached to the stem and no petiole is present.  In most plants, however, the blade is attached to the stem by a stalk, or petiole.  The petiole serves to transport water and dissolved minerals from the stem to the blade, where they are used in photosynthesis.  The photosynthetic products are sent back through the petiole into the stem for translocation to other parts of the plant.  In some plants (such as corn), the base of the leaf is expanded into a sheath which surrounds the stem.  This sheath often serves to protect the young terminal region of the shoot as well as the buds in the axil of the leaves.  The leaves of many species of flowering plants (especially the dicots) have outgrowths of the leaf base, the stipules.  These function mostly to protect the young leaf before it unfolds.

Leaves grow from the **leaf primordia,** contained within the terminal bud of a plant and just beneath the dome of apical meristem cells.  In the spring, rapid growth brings about the unfolding of the leaves and their subsequent development into mature organs.  Once they reach their mature size, the leaves of most plants do not grow any longer or wider; they remain at their mature size until they die.  Depending upon the species, leaves may live for only a few weeks (as in some desert annual herbs), a few months (as in most deciduous trees that drop their leaves in the fall), or for three or four years in some evergreen plants (as in pines).

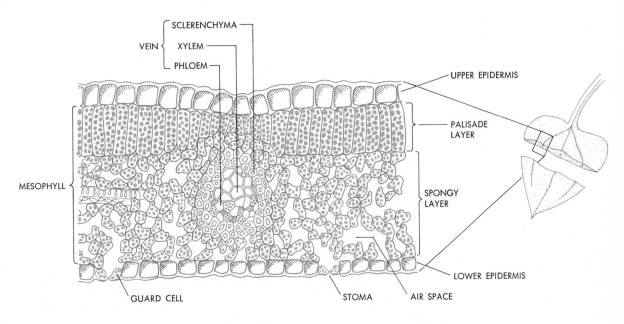

FIG. 10–20    Internal organization of a leaf as seen in cross section. There may be two or three layers of palisade cells in some species. Stomata are generally limited to, or are most numerous on, the lower surface of the leaf. (Drawing on left from John W. Kimball, *Biology*, 2nd edition. Reading, Mass.: Addison-Wesley, 1968.)

Internally, foliage leaves are constructed of three main tissue systems: **epidermis, mesophyll,** and **vascular tissue** (Fig. 10–20). The outer cells, on both surfaces, form the protective layers as epidermis. The cells of both epidermal layers secrete a waxy material, **cutin.** Inside the epidermis is the mesophyll, a tissue composed of parenchyma cells rich in chloroplasts. In many species, especially the dicots, the mesophyll is differentiated into **palisade** parenchyma and **spongy** parenchyma. In cross section, the cells are seen to be elongated at right angles to the epidermis and arranged like a row of stakes (thus the name, "palisade"). If a section is cut through the leaf just beneath the epidermis, the cells of the palisade parenchyma are seen to be more or less separated from each other by spaces; these facilitate aeration of these photosynthetic cells. Occupying the bottom half of the mesophyll is the spongy parenchyma, so-called because of the conspicuous system of intercellular spaces which spreads throughout this tissue. Since these spaces connect with the numerous stomata present in the lower epidermis, the movement of water vapor, carbon dioxide, and oxygen is facilitated. Thus, the leaf possesses an internal aerating system of impressive proportions. For example, one study of leaves from a *Catalpa* tree showed the internal surface to be some 12 times greater in extent than the external surface. The leaf, therefore, is well-adapted for highly efficient photosynthesis.

As we have already seen, one to several branches of the vascular system of the stem enter the leaf at its attachment to the node. Within the leaf blade of dicots, the vascular bundles (veins) branch, fuse, and become smaller, forming a network; such a pattern of venation is said to be **reticulate** or **netted.** In many monocots, e.g., corn, the principal veins continue almost **parallel** throughout most of the entire leaf blade. Very small veins interconnect these parallel main veins. Surrounding the veins is a layer of tightly packed parenchyma cells, the **bundle sheath,** which extends to the ends of the veins, completely enclosing each one. The cells of the bundle sheath increase the contact between the cells of the xylem and phloem and the cells of the mesophyll. There is evidence that the bundle sheath takes part in the movement of materials between the veins and the mesophyll.

Much of the support for a leaf with a flat blade is provided by the system of veins which ramify throughout it. Additional support for the leaf blade is provided by the turgor pressure of the water inside the vacuoles of the mesophyll cells. Due to the compact arrangement of its cells and the strength of the cuticle layer, the epidermis also provides considerable support for the leaf. Collenchyma cells and sclerenchyma fibers may occur beneath the epidermis, close to the larger veins and along the blade margin; this arrangement also provides support for the leaf blade.

## 10–6
## INCREASE IN
## THICKNESS OF THE
## PLANT BODY

"Great oaks from tiny acorns grow." This old saying contains a capsule summary of a great deal of botany. The seedling may in time grow into an enormous tree with a trunk many feet in diameter and hundreds of feet in height. The longer a plant lives and the larger it grows, the greater must be its ability to withstand the increasing weight of its leaves and branches, as well as the strain imposed by high winds. Further, in the young plant there is only a small amount of food- and water-conducting tissue, and the quantity of supporting tissue is also small. As the oak seedling grows into a tree, some provision must be made for increasing the amount of conducting and supporting tissues.

During the course of plant evolution, these problems have been solved in different ways by various groups of plants. The tree ferns, for example, may have trunks 4 to 12 inches or more in diameter. Much of this thickness is due to a thick sheath of intertangled roots which arise close to the shoot apex and grow downward through the trunk. At the base of the trunk a dense mat of these roots forms a buttress which gives the plant support. The palm tree attains a diameter of two feet or more by a rapid thickening which occurs just below the apical meristem in the seedling. Cells in the region below the very young leaves act as a

FIG. 10–21  Diagrams showing the development of the stem (left) and root (right) of a dicotyledonous plant. Note that the tissue patterns of both organs become closely similar after secondary growth has occurred. (Left: from R. M. Holman and W. W. Robbins, *Elements of Botany.* New York: John Wiley, 1940. Right: from K. Esau, *Plant Anatomy,* 2nd edition. New York: John Wiley, 1965.)  ▶

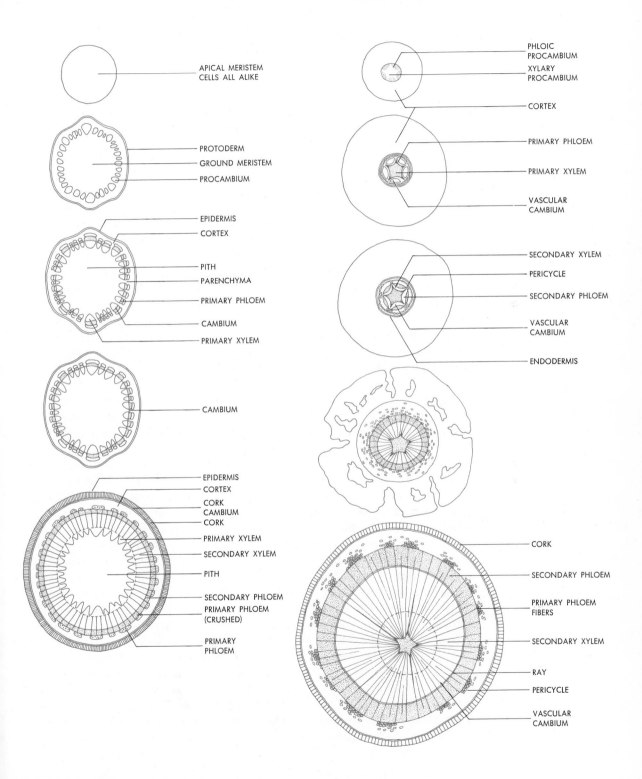

primary thickening meristem which enlarges the stem of the young palm to almost the full diameter it is destined to become. Only after this dramatic increase in thickness does the stem begin to increase markedly in length.

In the great majority of plants, however, the plant body is increased in thickness by the production of new cells and tissues by a lateral meristem, the vascular cambium. Thus, the great bulk of a large oak or other tree consists of tissues (especially xylem) produced by the activity of the lateral rather than the apical meristem. The vascular cambium has a dual origin in the stem (Fig. 10–21). A portion arises within each vascular bundle, in the region between the xylem and the phloem. The remainder originates from parenchyma cells lying between the vascular bundles. In the root, some of the cambium originates from cells located on the inner side of the phloem, in the bays between the points of a core of primary xylem (Fig. 10–21). Later, additional cambium is formed by cells of the pericycle. In each organ, the two areas of cambium become joined, forming a complete cylinder of meristematic cells throughout the length of the stem and root (except the very young twigs and root tips). The cambium begins to produce new cells about the time that the primary growth (resulting from cells formed by the apical meristem) is completed, usually during the first few weeks of the growing season. On the side next to the primary xylem, the new cells differentiate into secondary xylem while those on the inner side of the primary phloem become secondary phloem.

The cells of the secondary xylem usually have heavily lignified walls, a feature that makes them hard and nearly incompressible. Those of the secondary phloem, however, have thin walls and are delicate. The secondary xylem accumulates year after year. The secondary phloem, however, is progressively crushed and destroyed as the new secondary xylem presses outward. The tree does not become devoid of secondary phloem, however, since the cambium is constantly producing new phloem during each growing season. As the secondary xylem accumulates, the cylinder of cambium increases in circumference through radial division of some of its cells. Thus, the cambium can be said to move outward as the secondary xylem increases in amount (see Fig. 10–22).

In plants growing in temperature regions, the cambium ceases producing new cells toward the end of the growing season and enters a dormant state, usually lasting until the following spring. The xylem produced by the cambium during one growth period constitutes a layer which, in transverse section, appears as a ring. Since generally only one such layer is produced annually, each is termed an **annual** or **growth ring**. One annual ring of growth can be distinguished from another because the cells produced by the cambium in the spring are larger in diameter than those formed during the summer (see Fig. 10–23). The difference in growth rate is due in part to greater rainfall in the spring and less rainfall later in the season. Since the total width of any given ring depends on the climatic condition of that particular growing season, climatologists, using borings from very old trees, can determine the climate of the earth over the past 2000 or more years.

FIG. 10–22    The anatomy of a tree. (Courtesy St. Regis Paper Company, New York.)

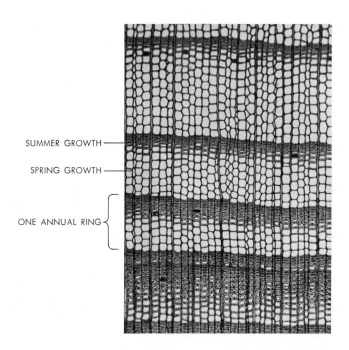

SUMMER GROWTH

SPRING GROWTH

ONE ANNUAL RING

FIG. 10–23    Cross section of stem of bald cypress (*Taxodium distichum*), a gymnosperm, showing four years' growth. Note the abrupt line of demarcation between the end of one season's growth and the beginning of the next. (Courtesy General Biological Supply House, Inc., Chicago.)

Although the secondary xylem produced each year appears as a ring in transverse sections, it is actually an open-ended cone which encloses and extends above the cone formed during the previous year. Thus, we can view the tree trunk as a series of successively longer cones of xylem stacked over each other with the big end toward the base of the tree. The cone formed last is the outermost and the longest. The secondary xylem in the roots may be visualized in the same manner, with the larger end of each xylem cone near the base of the trunk (Fig. 10–24).

**10-7
CONCLUSION**

In this chapter the structure of the plant as it has been elucidated by the use of various tools and techniques has been considered. Each individual plant, even in the embryonic stage, possesses a polarized differentiation, along an axis, into a root and a shoot with leaves joined to a stem. Each of these two basic parts of the plant body, while differing significantly in structure and function, have a common origin in the embryo. Both also appear to have had a common evolutionary origin in the leafless and rootless shoots of certain ancient plants.

During their development from the zygote, the cells of each plant differentiate into four principal tissues: meristematic, protective, fundamental, and conducting. Within each of these major kinds of tissues there is a wide diversity of cell form. Much of this diversity can be correlated with certain special functions. Although these tissues are continuous throughout the root and the shoot of the plant body, they are usually arranged in somewhat different patterns within each organ.

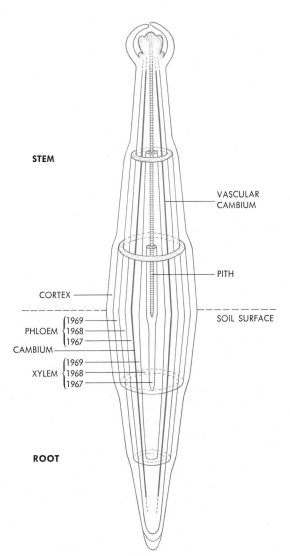

STEM

VASCULAR
CAMBIUM

FIG. 10–24   Diagram showing relative positions of secondary xylem and
phloem in a three-year-old plant.

PITH

CORTEX

SOIL SURFACE

PHLOEM { 1969
         1968
         1967

CAMBIUM

XYLEM { 1969
        1968
        1967

ROOT

Finally, several ways in which the plant increases the thickness of its body have been considered. Of particular interest is the most commonly used method—the production of secondary tissues by a lateral meristem, the vascular cambium. The reader may have noted that the treatment of plant anatomy in this chapter has been more "factual," with less emphasis on experimental work.  This is because a knowledge of the "facts" of plant anatomy must necessarily precede any meaningful experimental analysis of plant functioning or physiology.  It is to the latter, with special attention to the interrelationships between these physiological processes and the structure of the plant, that Chapter 11 will be devoted.

**EXERCISES**    1. As a one-day-old seedling (Fig. 10–25) grows into a two-day-old seedling, which of the marked regions *A* through *E* would you expect to show the greatest amount of growth relative to the others? Why?

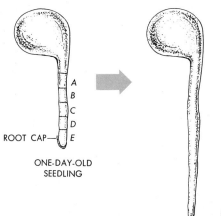

ROOT CAP—

ONE-DAY-OLD
SEEDLING

FIG. 10–25

2. How does the internal structure of the root compare with that of the stem? How do the differences show the specialized functions which each organ performs?

3. A cartoon was once published in which a man was shown going to sleep in a hammock suspended between two relatively small trees. A second frame of the cartoon showed the man awakening 20 years later and finding his hammock 15 feet off the ground. Criticize this drawing in terms of what you know about plant growth.

4. How are annual rings produced in a woody plant?

5. A special tool known as a Swedish tree borer is used to obtain cores from trees for growth ring counts and other purposes. If the tool begins boring on the outside of a tree and stops at the center of the trunk, through what tissues (in correct order) would the tool cut?

6. Is the oldest part of a tree toward the center or toward the outside? Explain your answer in terms of the way in which a plant adds new growth to its body.

7. In a cross section of a Christmas tree, a botanist counted 15 growth rings. How many rings would he see an inch or so back from the very tip of the tree?

8. In what important structural feature does a vessel element differ from a tracheid? How is this difference related to the functioning of a plant?

9. Of what significance to the tree is the vascular cambium? The cork cambium? The apical meristems of shoot and root?

10. Compare and contrast the shoot and root in regard to their external structure.

11. What is the relationship, if any, between a bud and a large stem bearing several leaves?

ESAU, KATHERINE, *Anatomy of Seed Plants* (New York: John Wiley, 1960). A comprehensive account of plant structure. Somewhat less technical than her more recently published *Plant Anatomy*, second edition.

ESAU, KATHERINE, *Plant Anatomy*, second edition (New York: John Wiley, 1965). A relatively advanced presentation of the anatomy of seed plants. Well illustrated.

LEE, ADDISON E., and CHARLES HEIMSCH, *Development and Structure of Plants: A Photographic Study* (New York: Holt, Rinehart and Winston, 1962). A paperback designed as a visual aid for students of introductory botany. Contains many excellent photographs of cells, tissues, and plant structures.

SALISBURY, FRANK B., and ROBERT V. PARKE, *Vascular Plants: Form and Function* (Belmont, Calif.: Wadsworth Publishing Company, 1964). A well written introductory account of the structure and functioning of vascular plants.

STEWARD, F. C., *Plants at Work* (Reading, Mass.: Addison-Wesley, 1964). An excellent short treatment of plant anatomy and physiology.

STEWARD, F. C., *About Plants: Topics in Plant Biology* (Reading, Mass.: Addison-Wesley, 1966). A less biochemical version of the same author's *Plants at Work.*

TORREY, JOHN G., *Development in Flowering Plants* (New York: Macmillan, 1967). Treats the development and structure of flowering plants from the fertilized egg to the formation of flowers and fruits. Some background in basic plant biology is necessary for adequate understanding.

WENT, FRITZ, *The Plants* (New York: Time, Inc., 1963). One of the *Life Magazine* special publications in natural history, this book discusses plant anatomy and physiology, as well as plant evolution. It is beautifully illustrated, well written, and nontechnical.

SUGGESTED
READINGS

The multicellular green plant is a highly specialized organism constructed of various interdependent organs. Each portion of the plant body performs special functions which benefit the plant as a whole. Each organ depends upon the others for the materials necessary for its functioning; in turn each organ supplies other organs with materials required by them. For example, water absorbed by the roots from the soil is moved through the stem to the leaves. Sugar synthesized in the leaves is transported to every living cell of the plant. Other kinds of molecules, e.g., hormones and vitamins, are manufactured in the leaves and apical meristems and are moved to various other locations in the plant. Through what tissues does this movement take place? How is it accomplished? What kinds of forces are involved? This chapter is concerned with these fundamental questions of plant physiology.

**Translocation** is the process of movement of materials from one part of the plant to another. What is the extent of translocation? How do we know the manner in which it takes place?

The fibrous root system of a single plant may be divided into two halves, and each half placed into a different beaker of water as shown in Fig. 11–1. One beaker contains only distilled water, while the other contains radioactive phosphorus ($P^{32}$) in solution. $P^{32}$ is an isotope of nonradioactive phosphorus (atomic weight 30.975). Radioactive phosphorus emits low-energy radiation in the form of beta ($\beta$) particles (in reality, electrons). By use of a Geiger counter, which is sensitive to this and other types of radiation, it is possible to track the passage of $P^{32}$ through the plant. Results of such an experiment show that after

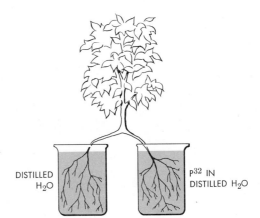

FIG. 11–1    Experiment to demonstrate the translocation of dissolved substances through a whole plant.  The radioactive phosphorus ($P^{32}$), taken in by the portion of the root system to the right, is traced through the plant by means of a Geiger counter.

DISTILLED $H_2O$

$P^{32}$ IN DISTILLED $H_2O$

a while (the time depends upon the size and type of plant, as well as certain environmental conditions) the stem and then the leaves become radioactive. We can actually track the "wave" of radioactivity as it moves through the plant.

More interesting, however, is the fact that, after a short while, radioactivity begins to appear in the roots exposed only to plain water.  This implies that $P^{32}$ from one half of the root stem has entered the main stem of the plant and has been carried down again to the roots in the other half.  The fact that some radioactivity begins to appear in the left-hand portion of the root system *before* it can be detected in the leaves implies that substances do not have to move all the way to the top of a plant in order to be transported back to the roots.

Until the 1920's, plant physiologists believed that xylem tissue was concerned primarily with the upward movement of materials, and phloem tissue with downward movement.  Yet recent investigations show that there is more to the story than this—xylem and phloem are not simple, closed conducting tubes like the plumbing system in a building.  We can get a more accurate picture of the way in which transport occurs in the living plant by considering two experiments.

One set of experiments is shown diagrammatically in Fig. 11–2.  In the first experiment (Fig. 11–2a), the outer regions of the plant stem were cut away (a process known as **girdling**); thus, both the cork and the phloem tissues were removed.  In the second experiment (Fig. 11–2b), the xylem was removed but the phloem was left intact.  The following data were recorded:

1)    Organic substances collected principally at $M$ and $P$, but some were found at $N$ and $Q$, especially when $N$ and $Q$ occurred in a region where there were leaves both above and below the girdle.

2)   Inorganic substances collected primarily at $S$ and $V$, but some accumulated at $M$, $P$, $N$, and $Q$, especially when $N$ and $Q$ were located in a region with leaves both above and below the cut.

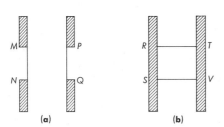

FIG. 11–2   Experiment to determine direction of flow of inorganic and organic substances through xylem and phloem.

What generalizations can we draw from these data? First, it is obvious that inorganic materials must travel principally through the xylem.  It is also clear that the principal direction of movement through the xylem is upward.  Second, we can see that phloem carries both organic and inorganic substances, and that the chief direction of transport in the phloem is downward.  However, as the data show, phloem transports materials upward as well.  Substances such as glucose move from a lower leaf to a higher leaf or flower almost exclusively through the phloem, but the transport of glucose from leaves to the roots, where it is stored, also takes place through the phloem.   Recent autoradiographic studies provide evidence that separate vascular bundles are involved in this two-directional movement (see Section 11–7).

A second set of experiments, in which radioactive carbon $(C^{14})*$ is used as a tracer, has helped to show the pathway which carbohydrates and other organic substances may take throughout the plant.  $C^{14}$ may be given to a plant in the form of carbon dioxide $(C^{14}O_2)$.  The experimental setup for "feeding" radioactive carbon dioxide to leaves is shown in Fig. 11–3.

A leaf is exposed to $C^{14}O_2$ for a short period of time.  This allows molecules of radioactive carbon dioxide to enter the plant and be incorporated into specific compounds.   In eight or ten hours, other parts of the plant are sampled to determine where radioactive sugars may be found.  For this, the Geiger counter could again be used.  However, another technique is particularly useful.  Leaves can be picked off the stem and placed between plates of photographic film for a period of several days.  The radiation emitted by the $C^{14}$ in each sample reacts with the photographic emulsion to produce a "developed" spot on the film.  If radioactive carbon atoms are spread throughout an entire leaf, the leafshape will appear as a picture on the film.  This picture is an **autoradiograph** (Fig. 11–3,

---

* Carbon normally has an atomic weight of 12.

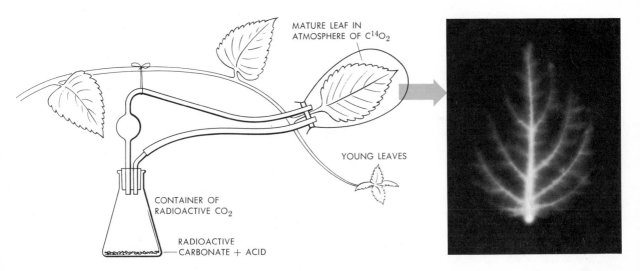

FIG. 11–3   Radioactive carbon dioxide ($C^{14}O_2$) is fed to a plant leaf by the apparatus shown above. The plant incorporates the radioactive carbon into the carbohydrates which it produces by photosynthesis. The path of these "labeled" carbohydrates can then be followed throughout the plant either by a Geiger counter or (insert) by the autoradiograph technique. (Photo courtesy Brookhaven National Laboratory.)

inset).  The lighter the picture on the autoradiograph, the greater the number of radioactive carbon atoms in the leaf.  This technique has the advantage of giving an accurate record of exactly how the radioactive materials are distributed throughout the sample.  For example, it can be shown that certain substances remain concentrated in the vascular system of the leaf (veins), whereas other substances become more concentrated in the nonvascular regions.

If we expose a young, growing leaf of a plant to radioactive carbon dioxide as described above, we find that all the radioactivity remains in that leaf. Autoradiographs of other leaves on the same stem show no image at all.  No carbohydrate is translocated by a growing leaf because all the food produced is used up by the growth of the leaf itself.  If we expose a mature leaf to $C^{14}O_2$, however, we find that some of the carbohydrate is indeed translocated.  Autoradiographs of other leaves on the stem show that most of the carbohydrate translocated by the uppermost older leaves is passed to young, developing leaves and the stem apex.  The mature leaf which was exposed to $C^{14}O_2$ still has a great deal of radioactivity, but it also passes a good deal of its newly manufactured carbohydrate along to those leaves which are still growing.  This is of definite benefit to the young leaves, since they cannot produce enough food to supply their own needs completely until they are more mature.  The lowermost leaves of a plant export carbohydrate primarily to the root.   Intermediate leaves export to the roots and the stem apex.

It is evident from the research described above that the movement of materials throughout a plant's parts is controlled quite efficiently. In the early spring, carbohydrates pass upward from the stem and root to the developing flower and leaf buds. Later, when the leaves are mature, they manufacture carbohydrate which is transported to the developing fruit. In addition, some carbohydrate is moved down to the stem and root for immediate use and for the next season's reserve supply. The ability of a plant to regulate the direction in which substances are transported implies a high degree of organization. The exact mechanisms by which the flow of organic materials such as glucose is controlled are not yet fully understood (see Section 11–6).

## 11–3 MOVEMENT OF WATER AND MINERALS INTO THE PLANT

By the end of the nineteenth century, plant physiologists had clearly demonstrated by experiments that green plants require three classes of materials from their environment: oxygen and carbon dioxide, water, and minerals (see Chapter 9). To be used by the plant, however, these materials have to be transferred from the environment into the plant body, i.e., they must be absorbed. In this section, the absorption of water and minerals will be considered; the absorption of carbon dioxide and oxygen will be discussed in Section 11–5.

It is easy to hypothesize how absorption of water could take place. Examination of young roots with a microscope reveals numerous tiny, fingerlike projections (root hairs). The presence of root hairs greatly increases the surface area of the root, making it ideally suited for the absorption of materials (Fig. 11–4). In the soil surrounding the root hairs, water is usually present in high concentration. Inside the cells, water is generally in much lower concentration. According to the simple laws of osmosis (i.e., movement of solvent (water) across a differentially permeable membrane from a region of higher to a region of lower concentration), it would be predicted that water molecules would pass into the root cells. Tracer experiments using tritiated water ($H_2^3O$) verify this prediction.

It can be hypothesized that osmosis is the only process responsible for the absorption of water by the roots. An experiment can be designed to test this hypothesis. If narrow strips of epidermis from the middle of the root hair portion of young roots are placed in different concentrations of sodium chloride dissolved in distilled water, for example, 2%, 2.5%, 3%, 3.5%, 4%, and 4.5%, microscopic examination shows that the contents of the root hair cells are contracted inward from the cell walls. In the most dilute solution, however, the root hairs are slightly swollen. In solutions of medium concentration (e.g., the 3% or 3.5% solution), the cell contents are only slightly withdrawn from the cell walls, while solutions of 2.5% concentration produce no visible effect. These observations are consistent with the hypothesis that only the physical process of osmosis is involved in the absorption of water into the root hair cells; evidently water does not pass into the cells immersed in the 2.5% solution, because there is no concentration gradient in either direction. In other words, there is no visible change of the cell contents in the 2.5% solution, because the concentration

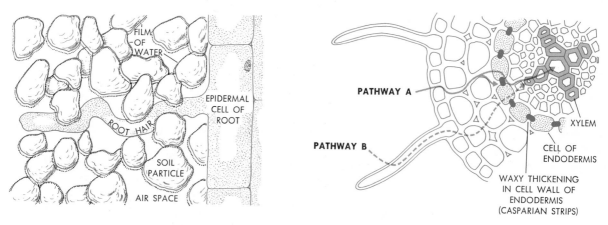

FIG. 11–4  Diagrammatic sketches of root structure and the pathways of water and mineral nutrient movement into the root. Left: In this longitudinal section, note the increased amount of surface provided by the root hair. Right: In this root cross section, water and nutrients are shown moving along pathway A through cell walls and intercellular spaces into the xylem. In pathway B, this movement takes place across cell membranes and living cells. (Drawings: left, from John W. Kimball, *Biology*, 2nd edition. Reading, Mass.: Addison-Wesley, 1968; right, adapted from Peter M. Ray, *The Living Plant*. New York: Holt, Rinehart, and Winston, 1963.)

of water inside the cell is exactly equal to the concentration of water outside in the soil. The contraction of root cell contents (inward, away from their walls) indicates that water has been removed by osmosis from these cells, since, in solutions of higher sodium chloride concentration, the concentration of water is higher inside the cells than outside. The results are thus consistent with the hypothesis and, indeed, would be predicted by it.

Attempts to establish a hypothetical generalization from these experimental results to include *all* multicellular plant species, however, run into difficulties. For example, under situations in which the "osmosis alone" hypothesis would predict water absorption, it may actually be retarded in radish root hairs. This observation makes it reasonable to suspect that some form of active transport (see Section 6–9) may be involved; it would seem that energy is expended directly or indirectly in the absorption of water, or in this case, in keeping it out.

There is also increasing evidence supporting the hypothesis that considerable quantities of water may enter the root and move across the epidermis and cortex by diffusing along the cell walls without ever actually moving by osmosis across the cell membranes. To enter the vascular cylinder, however, the water must move across the membranes of the endodermal cells (in young roots) and cambium cells (older roots); a band-like layer of waxy thickening (Casparian strips) in the radial and transverse walls of the endodermal cells functions as a barrier to the further movement of water by any other means (Fig. 11–4).

It was long assumed that absorption of water and the minerals it contains in solution takes place only in the root hair region of young roots. Recently, however, several experiments have demonstrated that considerable absorption of water occurs in the roots mature enough to possess a corky bark. Since as much as 95% of the root surface of a shrub or a tree consists of bark-covered roots, it is possible and even probable that the major portion of water and mineral absorption may not occur through the root hairs. The water probably enters through cracks and small areas of loosely organized, thin-walled cells called lenticels.

In addition to their function as water-absorbing organs, roots are involved in absorption of the mineral elements necessary for plant growth. These elements enter the plant as ions, i.e., atoms or groups of atoms bearing an electric charge. For example, phosphorus is absorbed as phosphate ions ($PO_4^{---}$), nitrogen as nitrate ions ($NO_3^-$) or ammonium ($NH_4^+$), and potassium as potassium ions ($K^+$). Some of these ions are dissolved in the soil water while others are chemically bound to soil particles.

Since the roots of the plant are in a soil environment containing various ions, it is reasonable to hypothesize that ions might move into the root by diffusion. There is, indeed, some evidence suggesting that ions in the soil solution may move into roots as far as the endodermis by diffusing along the water-saturated cell walls (see Fig. 11–4). Some ions may also enter the roots simply by being swept along with the water that is being absorbed. These processes, however, cannot account for all the ion absorption which occurs in plants. Ions continue to enter root cells even when their concentration is many times greater than in the root's soil environment. In one 24-hour water culture experiment, for example, roots of barley plants absorbed all of the potassium and 75% of the nitrate originally present in the culture solution. The absorption of these ions thus continued even in the face of an increasingly steep concentration gradient.

It seems evident, therefore, that there must be other forces at work in ion absorption. An hypothesis proposing that active transport (see Section 6–9) may be involved is a logical next step; the barley plant's root cells may be performing work in order to move ions against the concentration gradient. Support for this active-transport hypothesis comes from the observation that ions pass into the root cells against a concentration gradient only so long as the root cells remain alive. Soon after death of the root cells, the ions diffuse out until an equilibrium is established between the tissue fluids and the external medium. Further evidence that root cells are expending energy to absorb ions comes from experiments in which the rate of ion absorption is greatly reduced or even stopped when the roots are deprived of oxygen (oxygen, of course, is necessary in respiration; see Section 8–3). Still other experiments demonstrate that, when oxygen is bubbled through a culture solution in which roots are growing, the rate of ion absorption and accumulation increases. By increasing the concentration of oxygen bubbled through the solution, the rate of respiration and the rate of absorption of bromine ions are increased (Fig. 11–5).

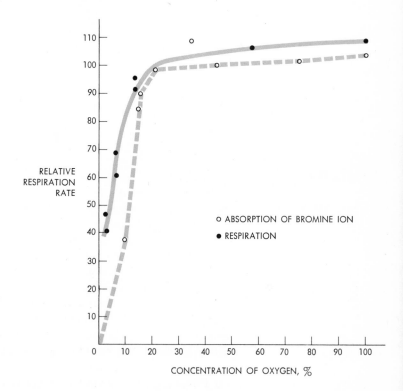

FIG. 11–5   The relationship between oxygen supply, respiration rate, and bromine ion absorption in thin disks of potato tuber (a greatly thickened stem with many root-like characteristics). (Data of F. C. Steward, from B. S. Meyer and D. B. Anderson, *Plant Physiology.* Princeton, N.J.: Van Nostrand, 1939, p. 409.)

While the roots are the principal water- and mineral-absorbing organs of the plant, some absorption of these materials is accomplished by the leaves. In fact, the only source of water and minerals for such plants as Spanish moss* (*Tillandsia usneoides*) and many species of orchids (which grow upon tree branches) is rain, water vapor, and airborne dust particles. Such plants are known as epiphytes. Epiphytes should not be confused with parasites; epiphytes make their own food and have no organic connection with the tissues of the tree on which they grow.

At times, water and minerals may also be absorbed through the stems and leaves of plants that normally grow with their roots in the soil. In one experiment, two leafy stems of a single raspberry plant were deprived of water until they wilted. After exposing one leafy stem to a continuous spray of water, both stems recovered. It seems evident that the raspberry plant must have absorbed water through the leaves and stem of the sprayed stem and then transported the water into the unsprayed stem. Another investigator was able to keep plants of several different species alive and growing for several weeks with only one or two

* Spanish moss is a common name. It is misleading in that the plant is a member of the family *Bromeliaceae* of the Anthophyta (flowering plants) and not the phylum (or division) Bryophyta which contains the true mosses.

of the leaves immersed in water (the roots and the remainder of the leaves were kept exposed to the atmosphere). There is also evidence that leaves can absorb water from dew and fog.

In recent years, it has become increasingly popular to apply minerals to shrubs and ornamental trees by spraying them on the leaves. For example, fruit trees such as apples and pears are sprayed with special preparations containing iron when the plants show symptoms of iron deficiency.

## 11–4 MECHANISM OF STOMATAL MOVEMENT

In the late seventeenth century, stomata were discovered on plant leaves (see Section 9–5). Over a century later, investigators discovered that the stomata are sometimes open and sometimes closed.

How might this stomatal opening and closing be explained? During the opening and closing of the stomata, it can be seen that the two epidermal cells surrounding each stoma have thicker walls on the side toward the opening, or stoma, than on the side away from it. Also, when the stoma is open, each of the guard cells is shaped differently than when the stoma is closed (Fig. 11–6).

On the basis of these observations, the German botanist Hugo von Mohl hypothesized that these changes in guard cell shape are due to changes in the turgidity of the guard cells. In 1856 von Mohl designed an experiment to test this hypothesis. He isolated stomata of *Amaryllis* from the adjacent cells by making razor cuts parallel with the leaf surface. The small pieces of tissue thus freed were floated in plain water and in water in which sugar was dissolved. In plain water, the stomata opened; in sugar solutions, they closed.

It seemed likely that some sort of turgor mechanism was operating here. Still to be explained, however, was how changes in turgidity of guard cells could open and close the stomata. During the 1880's, the German botanist S. Schwendener concluded from anatomical and experimental studies that the thin guard cell wall (away from the stoma) elongates as the turgor increases. Since the thickened wall bordering the stoma cannot stretch as readily as the thinner outer wall, it is therefore forced into a more semicircular shape by the expansion of the thinner wall (see Fig. 11–6).

Schwendener's hypothesis poses other problems, however. If the opening and closing of the stomata are due to changes in the turgidity of the guard cells, then what controls changes in the turgor difference between the guard cells and the other epidermal cells lying nearby? Von Mohl hypothesized that, since in the light the chloroplasts in the guard cells (see Fig. 11–6) produce sugar and starch, the concentration of water in these cells would be reduced. Water would then tend to pass by osmosis from adjacent epidermal cells (which do not contain chloroplasts) into the guard cells. This water movement would increase the turgidity of the guard cells, causing them to swell and open the stoma. At night, when photosynthesis is not occurring, the concentration of sugar in the guard cells would decrease as the food products were moved elsewhere in the plant. Thus, the concentration of water in them would increase, and water would move out of the guard cells, causing them to become less turgid and closing the stoma.

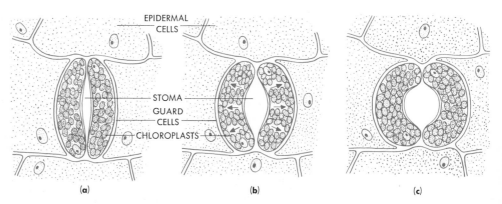

FIG. 11–6  Diagrams showing how guard cells function in regulating size of the stoma. Note that the inner walls next to the stoma are thicker than the outer walls (a). As the guard cells absorb water from the surrounding epidermal cells, they swell unevenly and the stoma is opened more widely (b). While the stoma is open (c), water vapor may diffuse out of the leaf, and the exchange of oxygen and carbon dioxide between the leaf and the atmosphere may occur.

Of course, von Mohl's hypothesis rests squarely on the assumption that photosynthesis does indeed occur in the guard cells. This assumption was not experimentally challenged until nearly a century after von Mohl first proposed his hypothesis. In the early 1950's, autoradiography experiments showed that guard cells of onion and barley plants *do* take up greater amounts of $C^{14}O_2$ in light than in darkness. However, in order to be an effective factor in the production of osmotically active material, the rate of guard cell photosynthesis must be high enough to account for the rates of osmotic pressure change actually observed during stomatal opening. In onion and barley, however, the maximum rate of photosynthesis in the guard cells is only about $\frac{1}{50}$ of the rate necessary to account for the observed osmotic pressure changes. Thus, it is obvious that von Mohl's hypothesis alone is not sufficient to account for the opening and closing of the stomata.

In 1908, the botanist F. E. Lloyd put forth a hypothesis proposing that the stomata may open in light because starch in the guard cells is enzymatically changed into sugar, thus increasing the osmotic pressure and raising the turgor. Lloyd's hypothesis was supported by his findings that, in the desert plant *Verbena ciliata*, the starch content of the guard cells was very low in the morning when the stomata opened. In the afternoon the starch content began to increase, culminating in closure of the stomata at night when the starch content of the guard cells was high.

In the 1920's, Lloyd's original hypothesis was extended by the botanist J. D. Sayre, who postulated that changes in the degree of acidity-alkalinity (pH) of the guard cell contents were involved. In experiments with *Rumex patientia*, Sayre showed that the opening of the stomata was accompanied by a decrease in guard cell starch, an increase in sugar, an increase in osmotic pressure, and a change in the pH toward alkalinity. During the night, the reverse occurred. In 1948, Sayre's hypothesis received strong support with the discovery that the guard cells of tobacco contain large amounts of phosphorylase, an enzyme that catalyzes the conversion of starch into glucose-1-phosphate. This reaction is pH-dependent: as the acidity is reduced, the activity of the enzyme is increased. The reduction in acidity would result from the photosynthetic removal of $CO_2$ which, in water, forms carbonic acid.

The Lloyd-Sayre hypothesis of stomatal movement was almost universally accepted for many years. In 1959, however, doubts began to arise when it was pointed out that the enzymatic conversion of starch to glucose-1-phosphate would produce no change in osmotic pressure of the guard cells, because for each glucose-1-phosphate molecule formed, one inorganic phosphate ion would be taken out of solution. It was suggested that, in order to raise the osmotic pressure of the guard cells, a further reaction involving glucose-1-phosphate would be necessary, and that it would require energy for the reformation of starch if the stomata were to close.

Recent evidence, however, suggests that energy is necessary for stomatal opening, but apparently not for stomatal closing. During the 1960's, the biochemistry of the guard cell mechanism has been intensively investigated, especially in the laboratory of Israel Zelitch at the Connecticut Agricultural Experiment Station in New Haven. Zelitch and his co-workers have shown evidence of a relationship between the stomatal mechanism and the metabolism of glycolic acid, an early by-product of photosynthesis. Using chemicals that inhibit the enzymatic oxidation of glycolic acid, they have found that the stomata of tobacco plants no longer open in the light as usual. These results are interpreted as indicating that the oxidation of glycolic acid in the guard cells is necessary for stomata to open rapidly in the light. Glycolic acid may be involved as a necessary intermediate in the synthesis of carbohydrate by guard cells, which would produce an increased osmotic pressure. Or glycolic acid might be involved in some kind of energy-requiring mechanism that increases the turgidity of guard cells (thus opening the stomata) through the use of ATP produced by the noncyclic reactions of photosynthesis in the guard cell chloroplasts.

The evidence in favor of the glycolic acid hypothesis of stomatal movement is considered, by Hans Meidner and his colleagues at the University of Reading in England, to be circumstantial and not entirely satisfactory. They believe that the photosynthetic production of glycolic acid or carbohydrates has only a minor effect on the turgor of guard cells. They hypothesize that it is the carbon dioxide concentration inside the guard cells which more directly changes the turgidity of these cells. To date, the various experiments designed to test this hypothesis have produced contradictory results. Further, the mechanism by which carbon dioxide might exert control over guard cell movement is not known.

Evidence that the opening of stomata may be related to the uptake of potassium was obtained in 1968 by R. A. Fischer. In his experiments, Fischer floated very small strips from the lower epidermis of the broad bean plant

(*Vicia faba*) on potassium chloride solutions of low concentrations. The stomata opened in the light when the air lacked carbon dioxide. The wider the stomata became during the opening movement, the greater the amount of potassium that entered the guard cells (Fig. 11–7). From these experiments, Fischer hypothesized that, in the light plus air free of $CO_2$, the basic mechanism of stomatal opening is stimulation of potassium absorption by the guard cells. Additional support for this hypothesis comes from observations of relatively high concentrations of potassium in the guard cells. Fischer suggested that the starch-to-sugar conversion postulated by the classical theory of stomatal movement is of only secondary importance, though perhaps closely linked to potassium absorption.

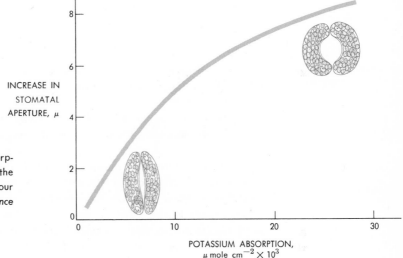

INCREASE IN STOMATAL APERTURE, $\mu$

POTASSIUM ABSORPTION, $\mu$ mole $cm^{-2} \times 10^3$

FIG. 11–7    Relationship between the absorption of potassium by guard cells and the opening of the stoma during a three-hour period. (Adapted from R. A. Fischer, *Science* **170**, 1968, p. 785, with permission.)

In summary, it is obvious that the efforts to discover the mechanism of stomatal movement have not been very successful. Much has been learned by researchers concerning the effects of light, carbon dioxide concentration, temperature, water content of the leaf, metabolic inhibitors, and other factors on the movements of the stomata. Still, the way in which the turgor of guard cells changes is not really known. Certainly both $CO_2$ concentration and starch conversion into sugar are involved. There is also good evidence that the mechanism of stomatal opening is different from that of stomatal closing, and that one is not simply a reversal of the other. Energy from ATP is probably used in the opening mechanism. This highly abbreviated account of the hypotheses put forth to account for the opening and closing of stomata does indicate the intricacy and complexity of an apparently simple biological mechanism, the turgor-operated movement of cells.

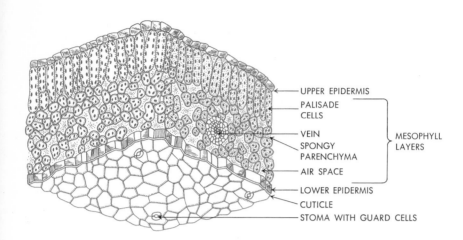

UPPER EPIDERMIS
PALISADE CELLS
VEIN
SPONGY PARENCHYMA
AIR SPACE
LOWER EPIDERMIS
CUTICLE
STOMA WITH GUARD CELLS

MESOPHYLL LAYERS

FIG. 11–8    Structure of a leaf in relation to exchange of gases with the atmosphere.

## 11–5
## THE MOVEMENT OF GASES IN PLANTS

Only a few decades after stomata were discovered in the late seventeenth century, Stephen Hales demonstrated experimentally that plants absorb and lose large quantities of water from their leaves. In one experiment, Hales measured the amount of water lost by evaporation from the aerial surfaces of a sunflower plant growing in a clay pot. When the sunflower reached the flowering stage, a sheet of lead was placed over the top of the pot and sealed tightly to the pot and the sunflower stem to prevent water loss from the soil. At intervals, a measured quantity of water was added through a corked hole in the lead covering. Each morning and night for 15 days, the pot and sunflower were weighed together. Hales discovered that during each 24-hour period the sunflower plant lost seventeen times more water per unit volume than a man. In other experiments, Hales placed leafy branches of various species of trees and shrubs into glass containers, and found that water condensed on the container walls.

Hales' contention that plants lose tremendous quantities of water by evaporation from their leaves and stems has been completely substantiated by many later investigators. In the middle 1920's, for example, one plant physiologist discovered that a single corn plant lost 54 gallons of water during its growing period from May 19 to September 2. It was calculated that the corn plants on a single acre would lose some 324,000 gallons of water during one growing season. Another investigator has estimated that a 1000-square-foot lawn loses 600 gallons of water a week. One acre of lawn loses about 27,000 gallons of water a week.

Stephen Hales also showed experimentally that the loss of water vapor from the surface of leaves is less than that from an equal area of water in an open container. Thus, it was evident that the process is not simply one of ordinary evaporation. Some hundred years later, it was pointed out that, while the loss of water from the mesophyll cells into the intercellular spaces of the leaf is evaporation, the movement of this water vapor to the exterior of the leaf is controlled by the behavior of the guard cells surrounding the stomata. Since the

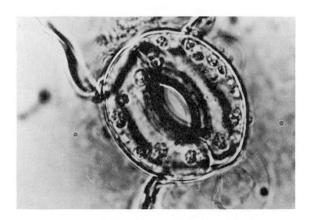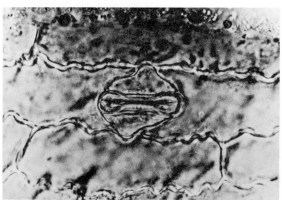

FIG. 11–9    Left, stoma and guard cells of a bean leaf. Right, stoma and guard cells of a corn leaf. Both are highly magnified. (Photos provided by the United States Department of Agriculture.)

loss of water in gaseous form from the plant differs in this respect from ordinary evaporation, the term **transpiration** came to be used for this process.

If transpiration is one of the normal functional processes of plants, what could be the cause of such a large loss of water? The simplest answer is that the plant can do very little to stop it. The leaf is an adaptation for gaseous exchange with the atmosphere; the plant requires both carbon dioxide and oxygen. A structure that is well-adapted for letting gases in and out is also an efficient device for the escape of water vapor.

A review of the structure of a leaf will aid in understanding this situation (Fig. 11–8). While the leaf structure varies greatly in different species, most leaves share a set of characteristics in relation to water loss including: a large amount of surface in proportion to mass (e.g., a sunflower plant may have 40 to 50 square feet of leaf surface); numerous stomata in the epidermis (e.g., some 428,000 per square inch in the cucumber plant); and a loosely constructed mesophyll with a sponge-like intercellular system of air spaces connecting directly or indirectly with the atmosphere via the stomata.

The system of intercellular spaces enables the leaf to have an internal surface area many times the size of the external surface area. For example, the ratio of internal to external surface in leaves of the lilac shrub has been determined to be 13:2; that of lemon, 22:2. Almost every mesophyll cell has a direct connection with the water-conveying leaf veins. Each mesophyll cell also has some of its moist surface exposed to the intercellular cavities which, again, are continuous with the external atmosphere through the stomata. Thus, leaf structure is very favorable for the loss of water by transpiration.

Since, when open, the stomata (Fig. 11–9) are the path of least resistance for the diffusion of water vapor (as well as carbon dioxide and oxygen), it is reasonable to assume that most of the water lost by the plant escapes through these openings. Support for this assumption has come from studies demonstrating that the outer surface of the epidermal cells has a waxy covering, the cuticle. Additional evidence for this hypothesis has been obtained from experiments in which a piece of transparent film was placed over a leaf. In the main, the film became clouded with water vapor only above the stomata. Experiments designed to measure nonstomatal (or cuticular) transpiration have shown that in birch trees only about 3% of the total water loss by the tree is through the cuticle. In mullein plants, transpiration through the cuticle was found to be only from one-fortieth to one-twentieth that of the total water loss.

If stomata are the principal paths of gaseous exchange between the leaf and the atmosphere, it is reasonable to ask if they possess the capacity for carrying gases from and to the leaf interior. Experiments designed to answer this question were performed in 1900 by the English botanists H. T. Brown and F. Escombe. Using the leaf of the tree *Catalpa bignonoides*, which has stomata only on the lower surface, these investigators found that, under conditions favorable for photosynthesis, one square centimeter of leaf surface absorbed 0.07 cubic centimeters of carbon dioxide per hour. During the same time period, the absorption of carbon dioxide by one square centimeter of sodium hydroxide was found to be from 0.12 to 0.15 cubic centimeters, i.e., just twice that of the plant. However, since the stomata comprise only about 1% of the area of the leaf surface (the remaining 99% being covered with cuticle), the absorption through the stomata was calculated to be at a rate fifty times higher than the rate of uptake by the sodium hydroxide solution.

To explain this seeming paradox, Brown and Escombe investigated the rate of diffusion in a model system composed of thin plates with small openings of known diameters. Using solutions of sodium hydroxide contained in test tubes covered with these perforated plates, they found that the smaller the opening, the more rapid the rate of diffusion of carbon dioxide through this opening per unit area. In addition, they discovered that the rate of diffusion through the small openings is proportional to their diameters and not to their areas.

In other experiments with this model system, Brown and Escombe discovered that diffusion was most rapid when the distances between the openings were at least eight to ten times their diameter. When the holes are closer together, the rate of diffusion is less. To explain this they hypothesized that, in still air, diffusing molecules tend to spread out like a fan as they leave small openings (Fig. 11–10a). If the holes are spaced at least 8 to 10 diameters from each other, the diffusing molecules of one hole do not interfere with those of the adjacent one (Fig. 11–10c).

Thus, by the use of a physical model, these investigators were able to calculate that stomata possess adequate capacity for carrying gases from and to the interior of the leaf. The open stomata of a sunflower leaf, for example, are able to permit the passage of three to six times as much water vapor as anyone had

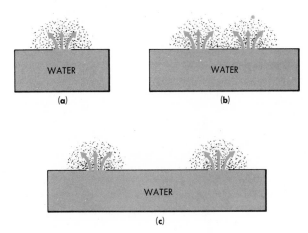

FIG. 11–10   Diffusion of water vapor from a water surface into the atmosphere.  (a) Water molecules tend to form a fan-shaped diffusion shell as they leave a small opening.  (b) If the openings are too close together, their diffusion shells overlap and the rate of diffusion is decreased.  (c) A maximum rate of diffusion occurs when the openings are well separated from one another.

ever measured.   Therefore, while stomata constitute only 1% to 3% of the epidermal surface, they possess the capacity to carry gases to a degree far greater than that required by the plant.

When the stomata are open and water vapor is diffusing through them to the atmosphere, carbon dioxide and oxygen diffuse from the air through the stomata into the intercellular spaces of the leaf.  In fact, it is very likely that the guard cell-stomata-intercellular space system evolved primarily as an adaptive device facilitating the absorption of the carbon dioxide required for photosynthesis and the oxygen necessary for respiration.  During this process, loss of water by transpiration is unavoidable.  Once inside the intercellular space system of the leaf, carbon dioxide and oxygen become dissolved in a thin film of water that encloses the mesophyll cells.  The epidermis, waxy cuticle, and guard cells of the leaf aid in protecting the gas exchange surface of the mesophyll cells from drying out.

What value, if any, is the loss of water by transpiration to the plant?  In animals, it is obvious that the evaporation of perspiration has a cooling effect upon the body.  Thus it can be hypothesized that the loss of water by transpiration from plants may also serve to cool them.  Expressed in a deductive format this becomes:

**Hypothesis:** *If . . .*   the loss of water by transpiration cools the plant,

**Prediction:** *then . . .* experimental suppression of transpiration should cause the temperature of the leaves to increase.

To test this hypothesis, leaves of tomato plants can be painted with a chemical (sodium azide) that prevents the opening of the stomata, thus suppressing the loss of water by transpiration.  Within 15 minutes, the treated leaves were found to be 4°C warmer than those of the control (in which transpiration was proceeding

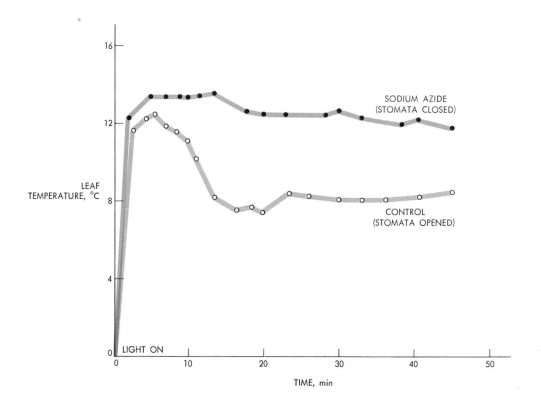

FIG. 11–11    Effect of transpiration on the cooling of leaves of tomato plants. Within 15 minutes after the stomata open, the leaf temperature drops; leaves in which the stomata remain closed due to treatment with sodium azide do not show any significant temperature drop. (After G. D. Cook *et al.*, *Science* **144**, 1964, pp. 546–547. Copyright 1964 by the American Association for the Advancement of Science.)

normally—Fig. 11–11). In other experiments, it has been discovered that, when the plant is in the sunlight, transpiration may account for almost half of the transfer of heat from its leaves. It seems clear, therefore, that transpiration serves the same function in a plant as perspiration does in an animal: to cool the organism's body.

Transpiration may also be harmful to the plant. When plants are transpiring rapidly, as in the middle of a hot, dry summer day, they may lose so much water that the cells of their leaves and young stems lose turgor, causing these structures to wilt. If the wilting is severe, the leaves and young stems may droop and the leaves become rolled or folded. Little harm is done to the plant if the tissues recover their turgidity at night. If the loss of water has been too great, however, the plant may not recover and may eventually die from dehydration.

Plant physiologists have long wondered what force moves water upwards in plants. Many explanations have been proposed; none are completely satisfactory. To be acceptable, any hypothesis of water movement through the xylem must account for the movement of water upwards to the tops of such tall trees as the giant redwood (*Sequoia sempervirens*) or the Douglas fir (*Pseudotsuga taxifolia*). At normal atmospheric pressure, a vacuum pump, attached to the top of a glass tube inserted into a bucket of water, cannot lift a column of water higher than 34 feet. Yet the California redwoods reach a height ten times this value. It seems evident that there must be several factors involved in the upward movement of water and dissolved minerals through the xylem.

Perhaps water might be "pumped" upward in the plant by the living cells surrounding the xylem. This hypothesis, first proposed in 1682 by the Englishman Nehemiah Grew, was tested by some spectacular experiments carried out in the late 1880's by the German botanist Eduard Strasburger. Strasburger used a very long vine of *Wisteria* that climbed to his rooftop. He placed a 40-foot section of the stem of this vine (between its roots and leaves) in a large kettle and killed the cells with boiling water. Strasburger then replaced the section of vine in its normal location, extending from the ground to the rooftop 40 feet above. Since the leaves did not wilt, it seemed clear that water was continuing to rise through the long stem segment, even though the cells had been killed. Evidently, other mechanisms independent of life must be operating in water movement.

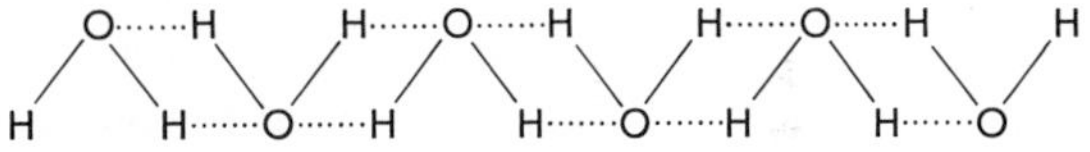

FIG. 11–12  The strong cohesion of water molecules due to the formation of a chemical bond between a hydrogen atom of one molecule and the oxygen atom of the adjacent molecule: this is known as hydrogen bonding.

It was discovered about 1850 that water molecules have pronounced cohesive and adhesive properties. It is now hypothesized that water molecules cohere or stick to each other because the hydrogen atoms of one water molecule form a hydrogen bond with the oxygen atom of the adjacent molecule (Fig. 11–12). Water molecules not only stick together, but also adhere to many other substances, such as the sides of a glass container, or the sides of a xylem tracheid.* As the diameter of the container is decreased, this effect becomes more pronounced. If the diameter in the tube is reduced to one millimeter or less, a column of water can be maintained in the tube with no outside force

---

* To observe this effect, hold a glass of water up so that your eye is on a level with the surface of the water. On either side of the glass, note how the surface turns upward. This is because molecules of water adhere to the glass.

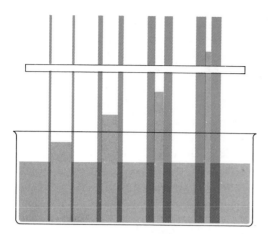

FIG. 11–13    Demonstration of capillarity.    If the diameter of a tube is small enough, a column of water may be maintained within it due to the adhesion and cohesion of water molecules.

required (Fig. 11–13).    This effect, known as **capillarity,** is produced by the combined effect of adhesion and cohesion.    It is reasonable to hypothesize, therefore, that capillarity is involved in the upward movement of water and minerals in the xylem.

According to the capillary hypothesis, the tracheids and vessels of the xylem tissue (or capillary channels within the walls of the larger bore xylem elements) would function as capillary tubes.    Experiments have demonstrated, however, that water can be maintained by a capillarity at a maximum height of only about three feet in the smaller xylem elements.    Further, neither cohesion not adhesion provides a force for moving water upward.    These intermolecular attractions simply allow a column of water to withstand many pounds of pull without breaking.    Like a fishing line, the column of water in a plant may take many pounds of pressure; however, it is the fisherman and the fish who provide the pull.    Thus, the capillary hypothesis is quite inadequate to account for the upward movement of water in plants.

In the early spring, before the leaves have yet appeared, a watery fluid can frequently be seen running out of cracks or cut stems of grape vines.    Or if the stem of a well-watered tomato plant is cut off, water will exude, or "bleed" from the stump.    If a piece of glass tubing is attached to the stump, the water may rise inside the tube to a height of several feet (Fig. 11–14).    The force producing this rise of water, called root pressure, causes water to be pushed up from the roots.*

---

* The way in which the roots of a plant exude liquid under pressure is not yet fully understood.    Involved in producing root pressure is the continuing movement of water from the soil, through the cells of the root, and into the xylem tissue.    The water already in the cells of the xylem is thereby forced upward.    The presence of living cells also seems to be necessary: if the roots are killed, root pressure stops.    In fact, even if the cells remain living but are deprived of oxygen, root pressure ceases.    Since oxygen is necessary for the respiratory production of ATP, this suggests that energy must be expended in absorbing the water placed under pressure in the xylem.

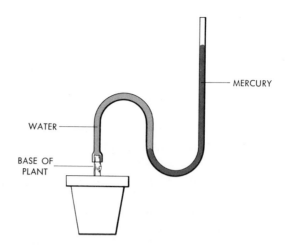

MERCURY

WATER

BASE OF
PLANT

FIG. 11–14  A diagram illustrating root pressure
due to the osmotic intake of water by the roots.  In
this apparatus, the height of the column of mercury
indicates the amount of root pressure.

Is root pressure an important factor in the upward movement of water?
In 1938, Philip White of the Jackson Memorial Laboratory in Bar Harbor,
Maine, showed that if single root tips are removed from the tomato plant (a
herb) and grown in sterile culture, each will produce root pressures sufficient to
raise water over 200 feet high.  This finding was startling to White and to the
botanists of that time.  Since tomato plants grow only a few feet in height, why
should their roots possess the capacity to generate such high pressures?  As a
result of his experiments, White recognized root pressure as an "unappreciated
force" in the ascent of water in plants.  An hypothesis that root pressure is a
major force in the upward translocation of water through the xylem became
extremely attractive.

Yet in some species, especially conifers, little if any root pressure can be
demonstrated.  Further, when the humidity of the air is low, much water is
evaporated from the leaves, and the water is moving upward rapidly in the xylem.
Under such conditions, the water inside the xylem is rarely under pressure; when
a xylem vessel is punctured with a tiny needle, the water usually does not flow
outward.  The root pressure hypothesis would predict otherwise.  Thus, this
hypothesis appears inadequate to account for the upward movement of water in
many plants, especially tall trees.

In one experiment, the tissues outside the xylem of a bean plant were removed
and a vessel element was punctured with a tiny needle.  As the investigator
watched with a microscope, the water inside the vessel snapped apart when the
needle entered the vessel.  Also, a short hissing sound was heard frequently as air
was drawn into the injured water-conducting cell.  This experiment suggests that
the water may actually be *pulled* upward through the xylem, since the column
of water would, like a stretched rubber band, be under considerable tension.

Perhaps the most dramatic support for this tension hypothesis, i.e., that the
water in the xylem is being pulled upward, comes from D. T. MacDougal of the
Carnegie Institute of Washington.  MacDougal developed an ingenious experi-

ment to test the hypothesis. He reasoned in the following way:

**Hypothesis:** *If . . .* water in tree trunks is under tension while being raised,

**Prediction:** *then . . .* the inward pull of water on the xylem vessels should decrease slightly the diameter of the tree trunk.

MacDougal knew that more water is transported upward by a tree in the daytime than at night. In the daytime, the sun increases the rate of both photosynthesis and transpiration (see Section 11–5). Thus, more water passes out of the tree during the sunlight hours.

To test his prediction, MacDougal designed a very sensitive instrument called a dendrograph. This apparatus is able to record very small changes in the diameter of a tree trunk over an extended period of time. A graph of the measurements shows that the diameter of the trunk *does* decrease in the day and increase at night (Fig. 11–15). The prediction is borne out and further validation is given to the tension hypothesis.

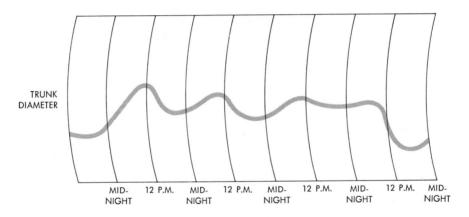

FIG. 11–15 Curves produced by a dendrograph attached to a tree trunk. Note that the tree trunk decreases in diameter in the late afternoon and early evening and increases during the morning hours to a maximum diameter just before midday.

What forces could provide the powerful upward pull of the water in the xylem, and where are those forces generated? In 1935, the German botanist Bruno Huber inserted small electric wires into tree trunks and heated the water inside the xylem elements. Then he measured the time it took for the warmed water to pass a thermocouple (a temperature-measuring device) placed a few inches higher on the tree. Huber found that, in the morning, water begins to move in the upper parts of the tree sooner than it does in the lower portion of the trunk (Fig. 11–16). This observation strongly suggested that the forces pulling the water upward are acting in the top of the tree, perhaps in the leaves.

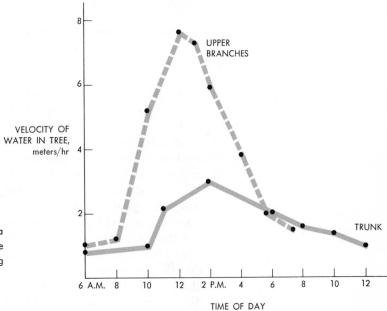

FIG. 11–16   Velocity of water movement in a tree. Note that the water starts to move in the upper parts of the tree earlier in the morning than the water in the trunk.

FIG. 11–17   The effect of transpiration on the upward movement of water in a plant is illustrated by these two experimental setups. In (a), a glass tube is filled with water, then inserted into a pan of mercury. The other end of the tube is covered with a porous clay vessel which allows water vapor, but not liquid, to pass. Evaporation through this vessel results in a column of mercury being lifted up the glass tube. In (b), a pine branch replaces the porous vessel, and evaporation of water from the pine "needles" (leaves) moves the column of mercury upward.

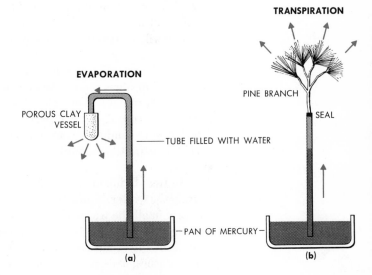

Might there be some relationship between the transpiration of water from the leaves (as well as its use in photosynthesis and other metabolic processes within the leaf cells) and the forces pulling water upward through the xylem? That such a correlation exists was demonstrated experimentally in the early 1890's by the botanists Josef Boehm of Austria, E. Askenasy of Germany, and H. H. Dixon of Ireland. Their experiments are diagrammed in Fig. 11–17. By evaporating water from the top of a closed glass tube connected to a container of mercury, a column of this heavy metal can be lifted more than 100 centimeters in the tube. A branch from a pine tree sealed into the top of a similar system is able to accomplish the same task (Fig. 11–17). This mechanical model of the xylem transport system of a tree shows that the forces pulling water upward are set in motion by transpiration of water from the leaves. In addition, the experiment demonstrates that the water is not being pushed upward by the roots (as the root pressure hypothesis maintains) since there are no roots present.

Central to the hypothesis that the water is being pulled upward in the tree is the existence of great cohesive forces between the individual molecules of water as well as adhesive forces between the water and the walls of the xylem cells. Due to the strong attraction between water molecules, the water in a closed tube, such as a xylem vessel or tracheid, behaves much like a wire and can thus be literally pulled upward. Measurements have shown that a column of water in a thin, airtight tube can tolerate a pull of 300 pounds per square inch without breaking. This force would be enough to lift a column of plant sap to the top of the tallest trees known.

In the mechanical model of the xylem water transport system shown in Fig. 11–17, the water in the tube must be previously boiled to remove all dissolved air. The formation of an air bubble in the water may break the column and the water will not be lifted. In a living tree, also, there is a possibility that air bubbles will form and break the columns of water inside the tracheids and vessels, especially during periods of strong winds and/or rapid transpiration of water from the leaves. It seems clear, however, that if a water column is broken by the formation of a gas bubble, the resulting break remains confined to that column. Thus, the presence of air in one part of the xylem does not interfere with water movement through other parts. Further, since an individual plant usually has far more conductive capacity in its xylem than is necessary for its survival, even a substantial amount of breakage of its water columns produces no serious injury.

In trees living in cold climates, however, the water in the xylem cells freezes during the winter. Since air is practically insoluble in ice, freezing causes bubbles to form in all the tracheids and vessels of the trees. How do these trees survive? One hypothesis holds that in conifers the air inside the bubbles with the xylem cells goes into solution when the ice thaws and warm weather returns. Trees such as ashes, oaks, and elms, with vessels of large diameter, replace the ruptured water-conducting system of the previous season by growing a new ring of xylem in the early spring before the leaves appear. Upward movement of the water during the summer takes place almost entirely in this new growth ring.

The concept that the water is pulled upward through the xylem does not, of course, explain a very important question concerning the ascent of sap in tall trees: how did the water get up to the tops of these trees in the first place? The water cohesion hypothesis simply attempts to explain how the water transport system is maintained within the living plant. It says nothing about the relationship between the growth of a tree and the mechanism of water movement.

One recent viewpoint holds that the water in the top of a tall tree first got up there by "growing" there! In the spring, a new layer of potential xylem cells is produced by the vascular cambium (see Section 10–6). This new xylem is located just outside the layer formed the previous year. The cells of the cambium and the immature xylem cells (being still alive) absorb water laterally from the tracheids and vessels of the older xylem. Indeed, according to this hypothesis, the new cells absorb so much water that their contents actually develop a temporary positive pressure. Supporting this contention is the observation that when these cells are punctured with a fine needle, liquid may exude from them. Once the leaves have expanded sufficiently for water to transpire from them, however, the water in the new xylem cells loses its positive pressure and a tension develops in the column of xylem liquid. According to this hypothesis, therefore, the process that initially establishes the water columns in the new xylem each year seems to be the water-absorbing activity of the living immature xylem cells. Once the water columns are formed and placed under tension generated by transpiration from the leaves and the metabolic use of water by the leaf cells, this initial role of the living cells in the water transport system ceases. Upward movement of the water columns is then maintained by the purely physical forces of evaporation and water cohesion.

**11-7
MOVEMENT
THROUGH THE
PHLOEM**

Far less is known about the movement of material in the phloem than is known about the movement of material in the xylem. One reason for this is the difficulty of studying phloem directly. The very act of trying to insert into phloem cells a micropipette which will sample their contents alters the normal functioning of the cell. The punctured cell shuts down operation, closing off the perforated sieve plates at each end.

During the 1950's, this difficulty was eliminated by using a new technique. Many organisms are known which feed on the contents of the phloem of trees and shrubs. One such organism is the aphid *Longistigma caryae* (Fig. 11–18a). This insect inserts its long feeding structure, known as a stylet, through the bark of a basswood tree and into an individual phloem cell (Fig. 11–18b). The stylet does not seem to alter the normal functioning of the cell; the aphid gets its fill from the rich contents of the phloem and then withdraws. The plant physiologist M. H. Zimmermann of Harvard University has found that if he anesthetizes a feeding aphid, he can decapitate the insect and leave the stylet still inserted in the phloem. Material continues to come out of the stylet for many hours after it is severed from the body of the insect, indicating that the phloem contents are under some pressure (Fig. 11–19).

What materials are transported by the phloem? Analysis of phloem contents collected from aphid stylets has revealed that 10 to 25% of the fluid consists of sugar (largely sucrose). In some trees, including ash, elm, and basswood, more complex sugars such as stachyose and raffinose are present. Lesser amounts of amino acids and inorganic ions, especially phosphorus, are also present in phloem sap. There is also evidence that hormones are transported in the phloem.

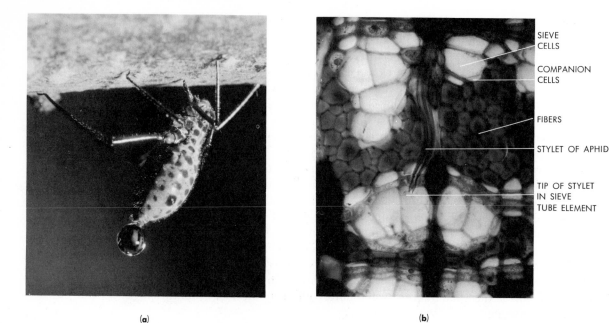

(a)                                                              (b)

FIG. 11–18    (a) An aphid feeding on phloem of the basswood tree.  The droplet of sugar solution shown here is being excreted by the insect (and serves as food for ants).  (b) Stylet of the aphid can be seen inserted into a single cell of the phloem.  (From Martin H. Zimmermann, *Science* **133**, 1961, p. 78. Copyright 1961 by the American Association for the Advancement of Science.)

How does the phloem transport materials?  This question has stimulated much of the research in plant physiology for more than one hundred years; it continues to excite the interest of both plant physiologists and plant anatomists. While much is now known about the process, no single hypothesis yet proposed has been able to account for all the various observations about the phloem transport system.

As background for a consideration of some of these hypotheses, a review of some of the observations will be helpful.  Unlike the xylem, where the cells are dead at functional maturity, living cells are necessary for the phloem transport system to operate.  In one set of experiments, the cells of bean plants were killed in a local region of the stem by heating them (with steam, boiling water, or hot wax).  While plants thus treated lived and photosynthesized for as long as 14 days, no movement of sugars took place across the damaged but still intact portion of the stem.  These results can be contrasted with the results Strasburger obtained with *Wisteria* vines (Section 11–6).

Measurements of translocation using radioactive materials or dyes show that the maximum rate of phloem transport is about 50 to 100 centimeters per hour. This is a good deal slower than xylem, which conducts at a maximum value of

FIG. 11–19   Evidence that the contents of the phloem are under pressure.  Sugar solution continues to exude from the phloem through the aphid's stylet for many hours after the aphid has been cut away. (From Martin H. Zimmermann, *Science* **133**, 1961, pp. 73–79. Copyright 1961 by the American Association for the Advancement of Science.)

60 meters (6000 centimeters or 200 feet) per hour.  Further, different materials are moved at different rates in the phloem.  In an autoradiographic experiment, the plant physiologists O. Biddulph and R. Cory, at Washington State University, sprayed a solution of $P^{32}$ in tritiated water ($H_2^3O$) on the lower surface of bean plant leaves and fed $C^{14}O_2$ to the upper surface.  They discovered that the $C^{14}$ was moved from the leaf down the stem at the rate of 107 centimeters per hour while the $P^{32}$ and $H_2^3O$ were moved only 86.5 centimeters per hour.

Through the use of $C^{14}O_2$, Biddulph and Cory further found that, when the flow of materials from a leaf reaches the phloem of the stem, it divides into an upward moving and a downward moving stream.  When one leaf is located above another, the downward flow from the upper leaf passes the upward-moving stream from the leaf below.  They also obtained evidence that this two-directional transport takes place in separate phloem bundles in the stem.  In these same autoradiographic experiments Biddulph and Cory also discovered that the upper leaves of a bean plant export materials primarily to the stem apex, the lower leaves to the root, and the intermediate leaves in both directions.  Other experimenters have observed this same pattern of transport in cotton, soybean, and tomato plants, as well as various grasses.

Though discovered in 1837, it was not until the 1960's that conclusive direct evidence of the function of sieve elements was obtained.  In one of these experiments, performed by Sam Aronoff and R. S. Gage, the leaves of cucumber were fed tritium-labeled water.  After 30 minutes, the petioles were frozen, dried, and cross-sections cut and placed in contact with a photographic film.  The radioactivity was found to be concentrated in the phloem tissue, principally in a few sieve elements.  None was present in the xylem.

In stem phloem, the movement of sugars is with a concentration gradient, i.e., from a region of higher to a region of lower concentration. In white ash, for example, Martin H. Zimmermann found a drop of some 20% phloem sugar concentration between positions 9 meters high on the trunk and 1 meter above the soil. That this gradient in sugar concentration is due to leaf activity is strongly suggested by the fact that in the autumn, after the leaves have fallen, the gradient disappears. When the investigator removed the leaves during the growing season the gradient also disappeared. In contrast, however, the movement of sugar from the mesophyll cells into the phloem of the leaf veins occurs *against* a concentration gradient.

With these observations about phloem transport serving as background, some of the hypotheses that have been proposed to explain the mechanism of the movement can be considered. One early explanation held that the translocation of sugar in the phloem was by diffusion. It was later demonstrated, however, that transport by diffusion was at least 10,000 times too slow to account for the observed rapid rates of movement of sugar. One late nineteenth century investigator suggested that perhaps diffusion might be speeded up by streaming and rotation of cytoplasm inside the phloem cells, but other botanists were unable to observe streaming in mature sieve elements, and the cytoplasmic streaming hypothesis received little support. During the 1960's, however, at least two experimenters have been able to demonstrate the movement of cytoplasm both within sieve elements and from one sieve element to the next. Thus, renewed attention is being given to the possibility that the sieve elements may play some active role in the translocation process.

In 1930, the German botanist Ernst Münch proposed that phloem translocation occurs because of a pressure or mass flow. According to this hypothesis, the force involved in moving materials through the phloem is the result of differences in osmotic pressure between leaf and root. Münch described a model system (Fig. 11–20a) composed of two sacs, each constructed of membranes permeable only to water, connected by a glass tube. One sac is filled with plain water, the other with a concentrated sugar solution. The model system is then placed in water. The water in the pan tends to flow into the sac containing the sugar solution, forcing a column of water-sugar solution through the glass tube into the other sac.

In Fig. 11–20(b), this principle is shown applied to an entire plant. The leaves, filled with carbohydrate produced by photosynthesis, are analogous to the membrane filled with concentrated sugar solution. The phloem cells can be compared with the glass tube, and the roots to the membrane filled with plain water. Because they are filled with carbohydrate, the leaves absorb water from the xylem. This, in turn, exerts a pressure, causing water to move into the phloem. Since the xylem always contains more water than the phloem, movement will always be in the direction of xylem to phloem.

The major evidence in support of the pressure flow hypothesis comes from observations that sap containing a high concentration of sugar (10 to 30%)

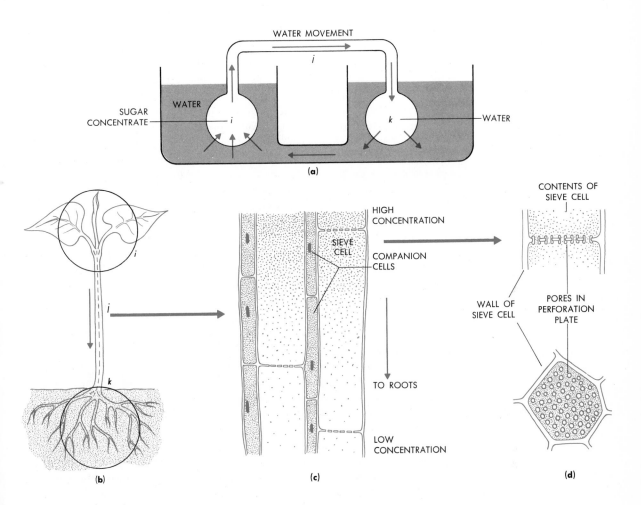

FIG. 11–20    The Münch hypothesis to explain the movement of materials through the phloem. (a) A diagram of Münch's model. An increase in the sugar content at *i* would result in an increase in the osmotic pressure in that portion of the system. The solution would then flow through *i* toward *k*. With the increased osmotic pressure at *i*, water would enter at *i* and be lost at *k*. (b) The system at work in the whole plant. Here, *i* is represented by the leaves, *k* by the roots, and *j* by the phloem tissue. (c) Details of the phloem, indicating differences in osmotic concentration in a group of cells. (d) Diagrams showing the end walls of sieve elements.

exudes from the phloem when an incision is made into the bark of various species of trees. Additional support is provided by the observation that when an aphid stylet is cut off while still inserted in the phloem, sap flows out under pressure for up to four days (Fig. 11–19). The insect relies on the pressure in the sieve elements to force the phloem sap through its stylet into its body.

However, the pressure flow hypothesis calls for a concentration gradient of sugar down the stems of trees. Such gradients are indeed present in many species of trees during the growing season when phloem translocation is active. However, if there is a pressure flow of materials in the phloem, there should be a gradient of decreasing turgor pressure from the upper to the lower portions of this tissue. Recent experiments on the phloem water relations and translocation have failed to demonstrate the existence of a gradient in turgor pressure in the phloem of tulip poplar and red maple at a time when the production and translocation of sugars would be expected to be high, during late July and early August.

Thus, the pressure flow hypothesis is not entirely satisfactory in accounting for the movement of materials in the phloem. Nor does it explain the mechanism by which sugars are moved from the mesophyll cells into the phloem (which must occur against a concentration gradient). Some experiments suggest that energy is required for this movement, and that an active transport mechanism may be operating to transfer sugars from the photosynthetic tissue to the conducting tissue.

Perhaps the most compelling objection to the pressure flow hypothesis, however, questions the capacity of the sieve tubes to pass the phloem sap along at sufficient rates. The phloem sap must pass from one sieve element to the next through extremely tiny openings in the sieve plates. From their minute size, it would appear that these openings would offer serious hindrance to the flow of material from one sieve element to the next.

In summary, the plant possesses a phloem transport system that seems entirely adequate to fulfill its functional requirements. Precisely how this system operates, however, is still not known.

**11–8
MOVEMENT OF
LIQUID OUT OF
THE PLANT**

If young corn seedlings are watered heavily and then covered with a glass jar, a watery liquid soon begins to collect as droplets at the tips of the leaves. The droplets enlarge and eventually fall off or run down the surface of the leaves. Similar droplets of water are frequently seen in the early mornings at the tips of grass leaves and along the margins of clover and other plants growing in the lawn, garden, or woods. (Some of the water droplets on the leaves at the same time are dew, which is simply water that has condensed from the moisture of the atmosphere.) This exudation of liquid water from the leaves of plants is known as **guttation** (from the Latin word *gutta*, meaning droplet). Guttation has been observed in plants of 333 genera belonging to 115 families of flowering plants (no examples of guttation are known in conifers).

The quantity of water lost by guttation from an individual plant varies greatly. A corn seedling may exude only a few drops of water. Plants of the elephant's-ear may lose 100 cubic centimeters during a single night from a young leaf tip. Chemical analysis of the exuded liquid shows that it contains in solution such inorganic substances as nitrates and calcium, and such organic substances as enzymes and amino acids.

The liquid exuded during guttation escapes from the plant through structures called **hydathodes.** Hydathodes are composed of an enlarged, stoma-like opening leading into a large chamber. Near each hydathode are tracheids and xylem vessels at the ends of the leaf veins. It has been hypothesized that liquid exudes through hydathodes due to root pressure (see Section 11–6). The liquid is assumed to be forced from the vein endings, through intercellular spaces, and out of the leaf through the hydathodes.

What role does guttation play in the life of the plant? One hypothesis holds that it may be one way in which the turgor of leaf cells can be regulated, preventing it from becoming too high when transpiration is not occurring (as at night). There is no experimental evidence to support this hypothesis, however.

Liquids of various chemical compositions are exuded from various other parts of plants, including nectar from flowers and resin from glandular epidermal hairs.

In contrast to animals, plants do not possess well-defined organs for removing potentially injurious metabolic by-products from their bodies. They have, however, evolved other ways in which toxic chemicals are made nontoxic or else transported to places within the plant where the toxicity will do little harm.

## 11-9 MOVEMENT OF METABOLIC WASTES: EXCRETION

One metabolic by-product of respiration in all living cells of the plant, carbon dioxide, probably moves in solution into the xylem and through it to the leaves. Here the carbon dioxide may either be used again in photosynthesis or may diffuse into the atmosphere via the stomata.

Some wastes are simply excreted into cell vacuoles and stored there during the active life of that cell. For example, oxalic acid is immobilized as crystals of calcium oxalate inside the vacuole. These crystals may be highly distinctive in form.

Metabolic by-products may also be excreted through the cell membrane into the nonliving cell wall. Here some of these by-products may be enzymatically converted into lignin, one of the molecular components of the cell wall. The primary function of lignin may be simply that of storing in a useful form some of the waste products of cell metabolism. Evidence for this hypothesis has come from experiments which show that some of the precursors of lignin, e.g., phenolic glycosides, may be formed as by-products of the metabolic pathways used by cells to produce the cellulose and other polysaccharide components of the cell wall. Lignin production by vascular plants, therefore, may have evolved as an adaptation enabling land plants to solve some of the problems of metabolic waste disposal. Since the presence of lignin in the cell walls gave added strength to the upright plant body, plants with the genetic ability to produce the enzymes for lignin synthesis were better adapted for land life.

Some toxic materials may be eliminated from the plant body by the leaves falling from the trees during the autumn and by the periodic shedding of the bark. One metabolic by-product, tannin, has been found in minimal amounts in the living cells of the cambium but in increased quantities in the parenchyma of the differentiating phloem and xylem. Periodically, these tannin-containing cells are shed from the plant as part of the bark. Tannin is also produced in the leaves and eliminated from the plant during the autumnal leaf fall.

Many by-products of plant metabolism are transported away from the cambium and living parenchyma of the xylem in the direction of the inner sapwood, where they are stored. Indeed, the formation of the heartwood in trees may be thought of as the result of such an excretory process. As the waste materials accumulate in the living parenchyma (both in the vertical and the horizontal rays) a toxic level is finally reached, the cells die, and the first cylinder of heartwood is produced. With time, the inward-moving waste products produce another layer of heartwood. In this manner, the sapwood-heartwood boundary moves outward as the diameter of the tree increases (see Fig. 10–22).

## 11-10
## PLANT HORMONES

**Tropisms** (from the Greek word *tropos*, "turn") have been observed in plants for many hundreds of years. Tropisms are orientation movements in response to environmental stimuli, e.g., light (**phototropism**), touch (**thigmotropism**), and gravity (**geotropism**). Intrigued by their observations, in 1880 Charles Darwin and his son Francis set out to discover why growing plants always bend toward a light source. Using seedlings of *Phalaris canariensis* (canary grass), they set up several experimental groups in the manner shown in Fig. 11–21. One group of seedlings was allowed to germinate normally; these served as controls. The tip of each coleoptile (a sheath that envelops the young leaves) in the other group was covered with a cap of very thin tinfoil. The plants were placed near a window so they would receive light from only one direction. After eight hours of daylight, the Darwins observed that the uncapped plants had curved strongly toward the light. The plants covered with tinfoil, however, grew straight up; they failed to show a response to the outside stimulus.

The Darwins then removed the caps from ten of the straight seedlings. After eight hours' exposure to the light, nine of these became greatly curved toward the light, while one curved only moderately. Coleoptiles in which the tips were cut off remained upright. From these experiments it seemed clear that the tip of the plant was somehow influential in determining the reaction to light. The Darwins hypothesized that "some influence is transmitted from the upper to the lower part, causing the latter to bend." They did not know, however, what the precise nature of the influence was, or how it acted to cause its effects.

Thirty years later, further light was shed on the problem by the Danish botanist P. Boysen-Jensen. In one type of experiment, Boysen-Jensen cut off the tips of oat coleoptiles, placed a block of gelatin on the cut surface of the stumps, replaced the tips, and illuminated the coleoptiles with a light from one side (Fig. 11–22a). The portion of the coleoptiles below the gelatin curved toward the

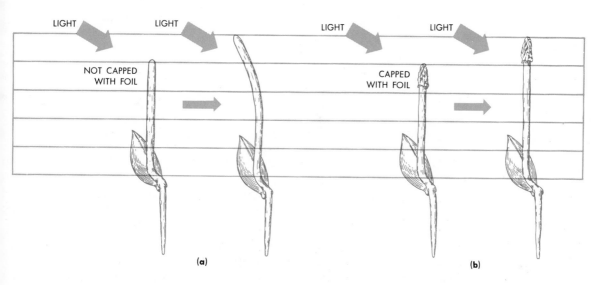

FIG. 11–21   Experiments of Charles and Francis Darwin on phototropism of canary grass seedlings. (a) The coleoptile bends toward the light.  (b) The coleoptile does not bend when its tip is covered with tinfoil.

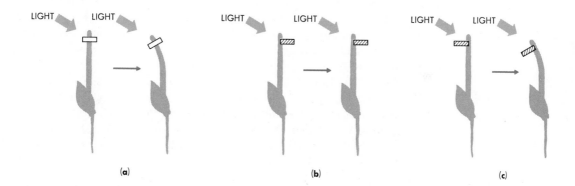

FIG. 11–22   Boysen-Jensen's experiments.  (a) When the tip of the oat coleoptile is removed and a block of gelatin is inserted between it and the stump, the coleoptile curves toward the light.  (b) If a mica plate is inserted into a transverse cut on the dark side, the coleoptile does not curve.  (c) When the mica is placed on the illuminated side, the coleoptile curves toward the light.

DARKNESS

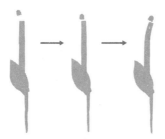

FIG. 11-23   Paál's experiment. When a coleoptile tip is cut off and replaced off center on the stump, the coleoptile curves away from the side with the tip. The curvature occurs even in darkness.

light just as did the intact coleoptiles.  It seemed clear, therefore, that the "influence" hypothesized by the Darwins had moved downward from the tip through the gelatin to the portion of the stem below.  In another experiment, Boysen-Jensen inserted a thin piece of mica (which is impermeable) into a transverse cut halfway through the coleoptile.  When the mica was on the dark side of the cut surface (away from the light), the coleoptile did not bend (Fig. 11-22b).  When placed on the lighted side, however, normal curvature occurred (Fig. 11-22c).  Boysen-Jensen concluded, therefore, that the "influence" is most likely a diffusible chemical that moves down the dark side, accelerating growth curvature toward the light.  Support for Boysen-Jensen's views was provided in 1918 by the Hungarian botanist A. Paál who showed that the "influence" could move through gelatin, but not through mica, platinum foil, or cocoa butter.

In another experiment, Paál cut off the coleoptile tips, replaced them on one side of the stumps, and discovered that the coleoptiles curved away from the side with the tips *in the absence of light* (Fig. 11-23).  It seemed clear from these experiments, therefore, that the "influence" was indeed a material substance, probably some chemical or mixture of substances.  Paál suggested that the growth-influencing material is produced in the coleoptile tip and, normally, moves downward along all sides.  If the movement of the substance is disturbed on one side, as by light or a mica barrier, the growth of the cells on that side is decreased and the coleoptile grows in a curve.

Conclusive evidence that the "influence" which moves downward from the coleoptile tip is a chemical was finally provided in 1928 by Friz Went, a young Dutch botanist who later continued his work in the United States.  From Paál's experiments, Went knew that the growth-promoting material can pass through a thin layer of gelatin between the coleoptile tip and stump.  He therefore reasoned in the following way.

**Hypothesis:** *If* . . .   the "influence" first hypothesized by the Darwins is a chemical,

**Predictions:** *then* . . .   (1) the material should collect in the gelatin when excised coleoptile tips are placed upon it, and
(2) later contact of this tip-exposed gelatin should result in growth of the coleoptile.

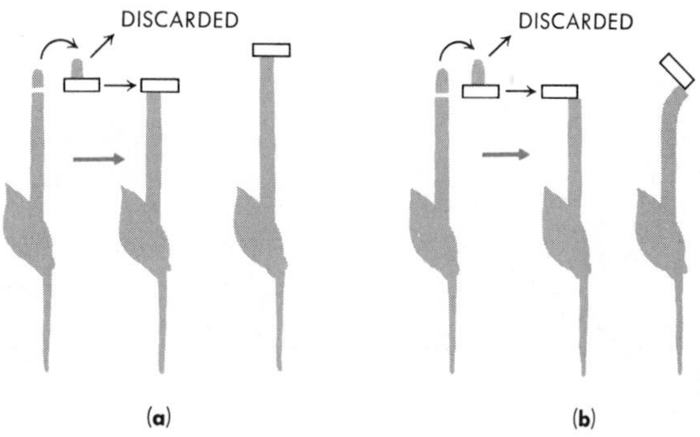

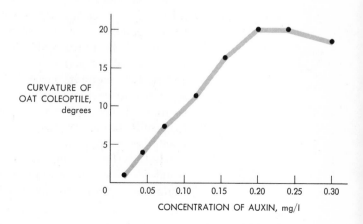

FIG. 11–24   Experiments of Fritz Went to show that a growth-promoting substance produced in the coleoptile tip is responsible for the bending activity in plants. Later, it was found that this substance is one of the auxins.

To test the correctness of these predictions, Went cut off a number of coleoptile tips of the oat plant and placed them on small blocks of gelatin (Fig. 11–24). After an hour or two, the tips were removed and the gelatin blocks were placed on the cut surfaces of coleoptile tips. The stumps resumed growth shortly thereafter. Those stumps with plain gelatin blocks (the controls) did not grow very much, however. Thus, the predictions were found to be correct and Boysen-Jensen's hypothesis that the "influence" is a diffusible chemical was verified. Since the substance acts to increase growth, it was named **auxin,** from the Greek word *auxein,* meaning to grow.

Went was also able to devise a simple test to determine the growth substance quantitatively. He placed the tips of numerous coleoptiles on a block of gelatin in order to increase the amount of growth substance collected by the block. After a period of time to permit the material to diffuse into the gelatin, the block was cut into small cubes. Each cube was placed on only one side of the cut stump of other coleoptiles. The cells beneath the block began to grow more rapidly than those on the other side and soon the decapitated coleoptile started to curve. Went was able to show that the amount of curvature was directly proportional to the concentration of the growth-promoting substance in the gelatin blocks (Fig. 11–25). This biological assay technique, which soon became known as the Avena Test (after the genus name for the oat plant), has subse-

FIG. 11–25   Evidence of auxin action in oat coleoptiles. To obtain these data, auxin was unilaterally applied in gelatin blocks to cut stumps of coleoptiles (as in Fig. 11–24). The coleoptiles responded by curving away from the treated side. The degree of curvature was directly proportional to the concentration of auxin contained within the gelatin blocks. (After Fritz Went and K. V. Thimann, *Phytohormones.* New York: Macmillan, 1937.)

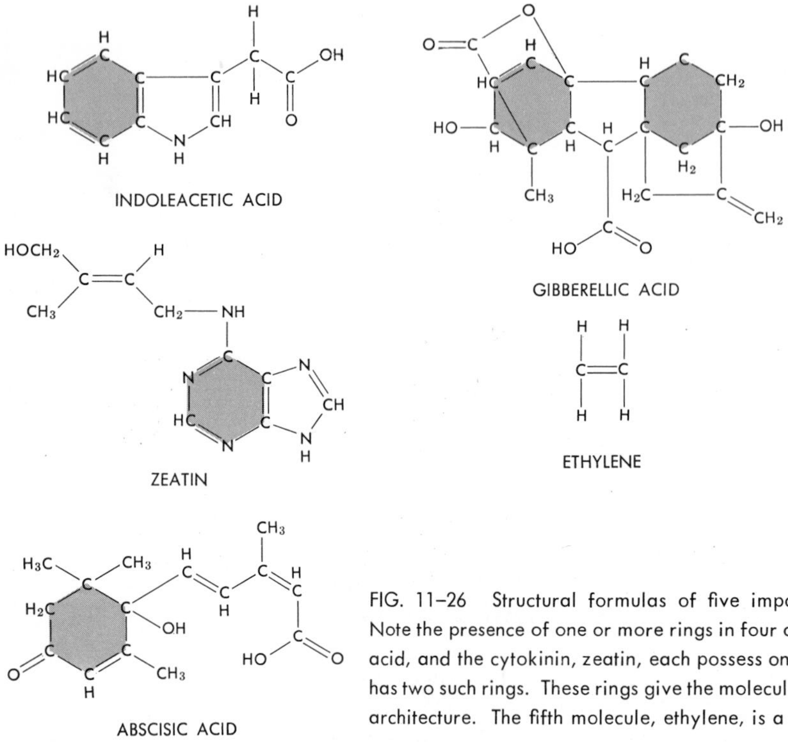

INDOLEACETIC ACID

ZEATIN

GIBBERELLIC ACID

ETHYLENE

ABSCISIC ACID

FIG. 11–26    Structural formulas of five important plant growth-regulating substances. Note the presence of one or more rings in four of the molecules. Indoleacetic acid, abscisic acid, and the cytokinin, zeatin, each possess one 6-atom ring, while gibberellic acid ($GA_3$) has two such rings. These rings give the molecule as a whole a definite shape and molecular architecture. The fifth molecule, ethylene, is a simple hydrocarbon with no rings.

quently been used extensively to measure the quantities of growth-promoting substances present in plants.

It had taken nearly 50 years of hard and painstaking work by numerous investigators to demonstrate conclusively the existence of the "influence" which the Darwins had postulated. But another problem yet remained: What is the chemical nature of this growth-promoting substance?

Went's work attracted the attention of investigators who were curious about the chemical nature of auxin. It was soon discovered that plant organs, including coleoptiles, are relatively poor sources of the material. The substance was found to be abundant, however, in malt extract (made from germinating grains), cultures of the bread mold *Rhizopus*, and, surprisingly, in human urine. In 1934, after a long series of complex experiments, two Dutch chemists, F. Kögl and A. Haagen-Smit, succeeded in isolating enough of the growth-promoting substance from human urine to permit a determination of its chemical composition. It turned out to be indoleacetic acid (IAA), a substance long-known to chemists but not recognized as possessing the property of promoting growth in plants (see Fig. 11–26).

Is IAA the substance which enhances the growth of oat coleoptiles? If IAA is indeed the growth-promoting chemical, then it should be possible to isolate it from oat and other plants. However, attempts to isolate IAA from plant tissues

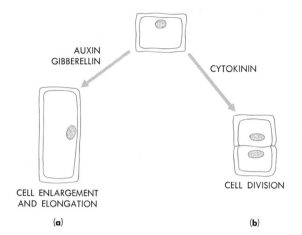

FIG. 11–27                                              FIG. 11–28

FIG. 11–27    Principal effects of growth substances on plant cells. (a) Auxins and gibberellins promote cell enlargement and elongation. (b) Cytokinins induce cells to divide.

FIG. 11–28    Promotion of root formation on cuttings of American holly by a synthetic auxin (beta-indole-butyric acid). (Courtesy Paul C. Marth and the U.S.D.A., Beltsville, Md.)

were unsuccessful until the 1940's, when minute quantities were extracted first from corn grains and later from young shoots of pineapple and from oat coleoptiles. The delay in confirmation was almost certainly due to the necessity of developing techniques and instrumentation necessary to detect very small amounts of substances in plant tissues; one investigator has calculated that the quantity of IAA present in 1000 grams of plant tissue is something like the weight of a needle in 22 tons of hay. Perhaps the main reason for such a small amount of IAA in a plant is that this chemical is constantly being destroyed by an enzyme system (indoleacetic acid oxidase).

The auxins, of which indoleacetic acid (IAA) is apparently the most important, are synthesized in the youngest, growing parts of plants, e.g., the shoot apical meristem. One of their principal properties is the ability to stimulate the elongation and enlargement of cells (Fig. 11–27a). Auxins also stimulate cell division, e.g., the initiation of roots on stem cuttings (Fig. 11–28). This property of auxin is the basis of much of the plant propagation for commercial purposes carried out by floriculturists and horticulturists. Auxins are also involved in fruit development. As the seeds develop (following pollination and fertilization), auxin is formed, first in the endosperm and later in the embryo, and it stimulates the enlargement of the cells of the ovary wall and other flower parts involved in producing the fruit. Tomato growers often deliberately initiate fruit formation through the application of auxin to the flower. Auxins also exhibit inhibitory properties, e.g., preventing preharvest drop of apples. The effects of auxins are, therefore, multiple and complex; probably they always act jointly with one or more of the other growth substances, to which attention will now be turned.

About the same time that Fritz Went was providing convincing evidence that the growth of oat seedlings is promoted by auxin, the Japanese botanist E. Kurosawa became interested in a disease of rice plants. Some of the seedlings in the fields were greatly elongated and looked almost as if they had been stretched out, for the distance between the nodes was greatly exaggerated. In 1926, it was discovered that these elongated seedlings were infected by a fungus, *Gibberella fujikuroi*. To discover the relationship between the presence of the fungus and the abnormal elongation of the rice plant stems, Kurosawa performed an interesting experiment. He isolated the fungus from the infected rice plants and grew it in a culture medium. After the addition of drops of the cell-free medium surrounding the growing fungus to healthy rice seedlings, Kurosawa observed that their stems, too, soon became greatly elongated. In 1935, the active agent was crystallized by the Japanese biochemist T. Yabuta, who decided to name it **gibberellin** (from the generic name of the fungus).

It was not until the early 1950's, however, that botanists in the Western world took notice of the Japanese research on gibberellin. Finally, in 1955, the exact chemical structure of gibberellin was determined. Subsequent research has shown that there are at least 23 gibberellins of closely similar structure. The best known of these, gibberellic acid ($GA_3$), is now commercially produced from fungus cultures by fermentation (see Fig. 11–26).

Like auxins, gibberellins are present in very small amounts within the plant. For example, 100 buds of sunflower seedlings contain only 0.001 microgram. Immature seeds and the fruits of some plants contain much larger quantities of gibberellins, however. They are synthesized in the embryo, shoot apical meristem, and the young leaves. When applied externally to plants, gibberellins can produce striking and conspicuous effects. For example, when only a few drops of a very dilute solution of gibberellic acid are applied to the apex of a genetically dwarf bush bean plant, the plant will grow as tall as a pole bean within a short time, changing from the bush to the vine habit (Fig. 11–29). The main effect of gibberellins is the stimulation of cell elongation and enlargement (Fig. 11–27).

Gibberellins are also involved in promoting the development of flowers in various plants. Even without pollination, the fruits of apples, figs, and grapes will develop following spray treatments of gibberellins (although they will contain no seeds). Gibberellins have also been found to promote seed germination. In many species of plants, the growth of the roots is inhibited by gibberellins.

A basic facet of plant growth is cell enlargement, a process regulated by both auxin and gibberellin growth substances. It seems logical, however, for the plant to possess a system of control over cell division, for without the formation of new cells, continued growth of the plant body will be severely limited. The existence of such a control system for cell division was hypothesized in 1892 by

FIG. 11–29 Effects of gibberellin on the growth of the bush bean. Left, normal growth (untreated). Right, after treatment with gibberellin, the bush habit changed to the vine form. (Courtesy S. H. Wittwer and the Michigan Agricultural Experiment Station.)

the plant physiologist J. Wiesner. About 20 years later, the German botanist G. Haberlandt found that a preparation of crushed phloem cells applied to a wound in a potato tuber provoked the parenchyma cells of the potato to undergo division. In the early 1940's, the American plant physiologist J. van Overbeek and his associates discovered that the growth in culture of embryos of Jimson weed (*Datura stramonium*) was greatly enhanced by the addition of coconut milk (the liquid endosperm of the coconut seed). They hypothesized that the milk contained a growth substance unlike any then known. Attempts to isolate the material were abandoned after a year of work, due to the lack of suitable techniques for separating the active ingredient from the other constituents of the coconut milk.

In the late 1940's, F. C. Steward and his co-workers at Cornell University greatly increased the growth of carrot root tissue by adding coconut milk to the culture medium. During the early 1950's, Folke Skoog and his colleagues at the University of Wisconsin were using coconut milk to grow pieces of tobacco tissue in culture flasks and became interested in identifying the growth-promoting substance. Since coconut milk contains large amounts of sugar and other constituents (which increase the difficulties of chemically separating the growth factor), these workers explored other possible sources. An extract of yeast was found to stimulate their tobacco tissue cultures in much the same way as coconut milk. Absorption spectra and other properties of the yeast extract suggested that the active fraction might be one of a group of chemical substances known as purines. Knowing that nucleic acids contain purines, one of Skoog's co-workers, Carlos O. Miller, looked over the laboratory supply of chemicals, found one labeled "herring sperm DNA," and discovered that this material would also stimulate tobacco cells to divide and grow. He was astonished, later, to find that freshly prepared DNA would not promote cell division. Yet when new DNA was placed in an autoclave at 15 pounds pressure for 30 minutes, it became extremely active. It was logical to conclude, therefore, that the cell division stimulant must be a breakdown product of DNA. Finally, in 1955, these workers managed to isolate a nucleic acid component, a derivative of the purine adenine, that turned out to be a long-sought promoter of cell division (Fig. 11–27b). They named the new growth substance **kinetin.** Later, several other adenine derivatives similar to kinetin were synthesized. Collectively, these substances are now known as **cytokinins.**

Due to their extremely small concentrations in the plant body, e.g., only 50 to 100 parts per billion in the phloem sap of grape, it was not until 1964 that a natural cytokinin was isolated from plant material. The structure of this substance (named **zeatin** since it was found in young seeds of corn, *Zea mays*) is shown in Fig. 11–26. Three other cytokinins have also been found in plants.

The cytokinins produce a wide variety of effects on the growth and development of plants. In addition to the promotion of cell division, cytokinins interact with auxin to induce the development of roots and shoots from tissue cultures of tobacco. If the concentration of indoleacetic acid in the culture medium is kept constant, then at low cytokinin levels, roots develop. If the concentration of cytokinin is relatively high, however, shoots develop from the tissue. Cytokinins are also involved in promoting seed germination and fruit development, enhancing flowering, and preventing the senescence of plant organs. In fact, cytokinins may well play a role in controlling nearly every aspect of plant growth. They also interact with the auxins and gibberellins in influencing growth rate and differentiation of plants. It seems clear, therefore, that plant growth and development depend on the balance between cytokinins, auxins, and gibberellins instead of the presence or absence of any one of these growth regulating substances.

While the cytokinins, gibberellins, and auxins promote plant growth and development, it seems reasonable to hypothesize that the plant must also possess some means of inhibiting its growth and developmental processes. After all, a stem or any other plant organ can enlarge to only a certain extent before it becomes disadvantageous to the plant's welfare. Then, too, it is of survival value for a plant to be able to slow down or stop its growth or reproductive functions (e.g., during the winter months in more northerly regions of the earth, or during the dry season in the tropics).

During the 1960's, several investigators offered evidence to support the hypothesis that plants contain ways of limiting their growth. In 1964, F. T. Addicott and his associates at the University of California at Davis extracted a substance from young fruits of cotton which they believed was responsible for the premature fall of the fruits from the plant; they named the substance "abscisin II." The next year, the Englishman P. F. Wareing and his co-workers isolated a substance from the leaves of birch, English sycamore, and other trees. Since it appeared to prepare the buds for winter dormancy, they named it "dormin." The chemical structure of both dormin and abscisin II was determined to be identical in 1965 by workers in both Addicott's and Wareing's laboratories (see Fig. 11–16). In 1967, both groups of researchers agreed to give the name **abscisic acid** to the substance.

In the relatively short time since the chemical nature of abscisic acid was elucidated, the number and variety of responses to this hormone have been shown to be very large and complex. As demonstrated by the early experiments of Addicott and his group, applications of abscisic acid to young cotton fruits accelerated their premature fall (**abscission**) from the plant. In addition, Wareing's laboratory showed that leaves would drop from trees prematurely after application with abscisic acid. Other investigators have discovered that abscisic acid inhibits or retards the growth of plant parts such as embryos, coleoptiles, roots, and tissue cultures. For example, J. van Overbeek and his associates have found that the growth of the small, free-floating aquatic plant duckweed (*Lemna*) is materially reduced by the addition of a concentration of only one part per billion to the culture medium. These investigators were able to keep duckweed plants in a permanent nongrowing (dormant) state with a culture solution containing one part per million of abscisic acid. Abscisic acid also inhibits seed germination of many species and may also be involved in the inhibition of flowering.

In 1910, it was discovered that the stems of pea seedlings exposed to the hydrocarbon ethylene (see Fig. 11–26), in a concentration as low as one part per million of air, underwent a decrease in length, swelled, and curved horizontally. About a quarter-century later, several investigators demonstrated that ethylene is synthesized in plant tissues; e.g., ripening apples were found to contain large amounts of ethylene, while immature fruits contained very little. This observation suggests that ethylene may be involved in the ripening process. The exact manner of this involvement is not yet known, however.

Ethylene has also been found to inhibit root growth and the formation of lateral roots. It breaks dormancy in bulbs and promotes their development. Pineapples can be induced to flower with ethylene. Flowering of the cocklebur plant, however, is inhibited by this chemical. Ethylene also acts in regulating the growth of pea seedlings subjected to physical stress. In one series of experiments, the normal elongation of pea seedlings was restricted by a mechanical barrier. Within six hours after the seedlings touched the obstruction, they were markedly curved and their production of ethylene had risen dramatically.

How do plant growth-regulating substances work? This question has proved to be one of the most formidable problems in the study of plant growth and development. A discussion of this important point must be postponed, however, until the central biological fields of genetics and development are more fully discussed in Chapters 16 through 18.

**11–11**<br>**PHOTOPERIODISM**

The developmental botanist is interested in trying to elucidate the mechanisms through which the plant grows, develops, and differentiates: processes resulting in the production of its own species-specific, three-dimensional form and structure. One of the most interesting examples of the manner in which plant form and structure can be changed and controlled is found in the transition from vegetative growth to flowering. During this process, the activity of the stem apex undergoes a remarkable change. While the plant is growing vegetatively, the shoot apical meristem produces new leaves, axillary buds, and the new tissues of the shoot. As flowering begins, however, the apical meristems undergo an extensive reorganization, a reorganization which culminates in the production of a small number of floral organs of characteristic types (sepals, petals, etc.).

What factors, both of the plant and of its environment, are involved in triggering this dramatic change in the development of a plant? It has been known for centuries that some species of plants produce their flowers early in the spring, others in the summer, and some, e.g., *Chrysanthemum*, form their flowers in the fall. Not until the early 1920's, however, was there any significant progress made in understanding the flowering phenomenon. At that time the plant physiologists W. W. Garner and H. A. Allard at the U. S. Department of Agriculture in Beltsville, Maryland, noticed that a variety of *Nicotiana tabacum* known commonly as Maryland Mammoth tobacco grew extraordinarily tall but did not flower during the summer. When they grew this tobacco in the greenhouse during the late fall and winter, instead of tall plants they obtained only short plants that flowered very quickly (Fig. 11–30). While Garner and Allard were not originally investigating flowering (they were studying a disease of this plant), the unusual flowering characteristic of the Mammoth tobacco caught their attention. Why, they asked, should this plant produce flowers during the winter in the greenhouse but not do so outdoors during the summer? They also noticed another rather significant occurrence: the plants flowered freely during the winter months. As early spring came, however, the flowering stopped and the plants resumed growth to become tall stalks.

It seemed evident that there must be some factor of the environment which forced the remarkable winter flowering. Garner and Allard hypothesized that perhaps temperature was involved in causing flowering during the winter months. It was soon clear, however, that temperature could not be an important factor, since the tobacco continued to produce flowers even when the greenhouse temperature was kept as high as that prevailing outdoors during the summer. Light was another possible factor, since the light in the greenhouse during the winter was considerably different from that of the sunlight during the summer. It was discovered, however, that the date of flowering was not materially affected by the intensity of the light.

This left the exposure to light of the plants over periods of time (which was clearly less in the winter than in the summer). Could the length of the daily exposure be responsible for the flowering?

*Hypothesis: If . . .* length of exposure to daylight during the winter is the crucial factor in regulating the flowering process,

*Prediction: then . . .* keeping a plant in the light for periods corresponding to those of winter days should stimulate the production of flowers.

In testing this hypothesis, Garner and Allard designed and constructed a dark house in which the plants could be placed for various periods of time during the summer months. By shortening the duration of the daily exposure to light, they succeeded in forcing plants of Mammoth Maryland tobacco to flower during the midsummer. The control plants did not flower until October.

FIG. 11–30  The Mammoth Maryland variety of tobacco grows tall and robust during the summer but does not flower. After transplantation to the greenhouse in the fall, the plant produces flowers during the winter. (Adapted from W. W. Garner and H. A. Allard, *Yearbook of Agriculture*. Washington, D.C.: United States Department of Agriculture, 1920, p. 399.)

Would the plants flower during the winter if artificial light was used to increase the length of the daily illumination during the short days of winter months? In another series of experiments, Garner and Allard found that by supplementing the natural length of the winter days by eight hours of artificial light, the plants did not flower, but behaved as typical, summer-grown Mam-

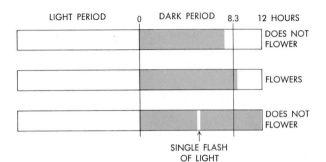

LIGHT PERIOD    0    DARK PERIOD    8.3    12 HOURS

DOES NOT FLOWER

FLOWERS

DOES NOT FLOWER

SINGLE FLASH OF LIGHT

FIG. 11–31 Summary of Hamner and Bonner's experiments showing that flowering in cocklebur (*Xanthium*) is controlled by the length of the dark period rather than the length of the day. Even a single flash of light during the long dark period keeps the plants from flowering.

moth Maryland plants. Thus, it seemed clear that the length of the day was the most important factor in inducing plants to flower. Garner and Allard suggested that the length of day favorable for the flowering of each species be called its **photoperiod**; its response to the relative length of day and night, **photoperiodism**.

Experiments with other species of plants led to the grouping of plants into three categories, *short-day*, *long-day*, and *independent*. Short-day plants are those which normally flower either in the late summer or fall, or in the very early spring. These include Maryland Mammoth tobacco, cocklebur, dahlia, chrysanthemum, aster, goldenrod and poinsettia. Long-day plants, on the other hand, are just the reverse, generally flowering in midsummer. Some well-known examples of long-day plants are clover, gladiolus, spinach, lettuce, and radish. The flowering of some species of plants, however, is independent of day length; such plants are able to flower whether the days are long or short. Some examples are dandelion, tomato, zinnia, and green beans.

In the late 1930's, Karl C. Hamner and James Bonner were studying the photoperiodism of cocklebur plants. They wondered whether the day or the night was crucial in the photoperiodic response. They added a dark period to the middle of a day, and a light period to the middle of the night. The former had no effect, the latter did. From these observations, Hamner and Bonner concluded that the initiation of flowers is controlled not by the day length, *but rather by the duration of the night* (Fig. 11–31); i.e., what matters in photoperiodism is the length of the night. Thus the names "long-day plant" and "short-day plant" are actually misleading; it would be more appropriate to speak of "short-night plants" and "long-night plants."

What part of the plant detects the photoperiodic stimulus? When all of the leaves are removed from a plant, in most instances it will not flower, even with the proper photoperiod. However, if a single leaf remains on the plant, flowers will be produced following photoperiodic treatment (Fig. 11–32). In fact, soybean plants will flower even if less than one square centimeter of a single leaf is exposed to the inducing photoperiod.

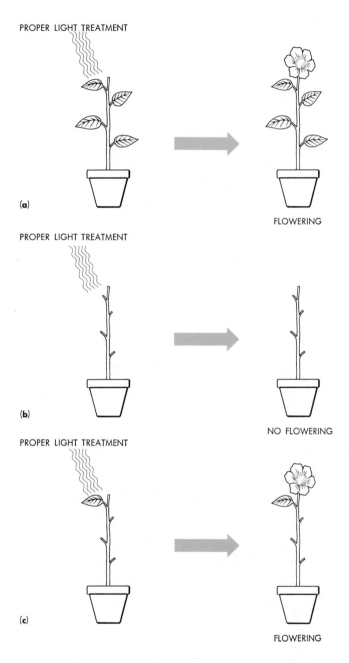

FIG. 11–32    Interpretation of experiments showing that leaves perceive the photoperiodic stimulus. (a) The intact plant flowers after exposure to correct photoperiod. (b) Defoliated plants are photoperiodically unresponsive. (c) Exposure of single leaf to photoperiodic treatment has the same effect as though the entire plant had been treated.

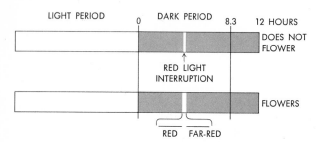

FIG. 11–33    An interpretation of experiments by Borthwick and Hendricks on the effects of red and far-red light on the flowering of cocklebur. Far-red light reverses the effect of red light.

For light to be effective in photoperiodic control, it must be absorbed by the plant. In addition, this absorbed light energy must be utilized by the plant in its measurement of the length of the dark period. A long series of experiments begun during the 1940's by F. A. Borthwick, S. B. Hendricks, and their associates at the U. S. Department of Agriculture, Beltsville, Maryland, has helped resolve these problems.    The investigators discovered that cocklebur and soybean plants would not flower if the dark period was interrupted by red light at a wavelength of about 660 millimicrons.    Later in their research, they were greatly surprised to discover that the inhibiting effect of the red light could be erased by far-red light at a wavelength of approximately 735 millimicrons. After a brief exposure to far-red light following the red light, the plants would produce flowers as if no light had been turned on them at all (Fig. 11–33).

By 1956, the work of Borthwick and Hendricks enabled them to present evidence supporting an hypothesis that the light was being detected by a pigment which existed in two states, a red light-absorbing and a far-red light-absorbing form.    Conclusive support for this hypothesis came a few years later with the isolation of a pigment called **phytochrome.**    Phytochrome proved to be maximally receptive to red light at about 660 millimicrons and to far-red light at about 735 millimicrons.    Additional biochemical studies of the isolated pigment showed it to be a protein which occurs in plant tissues at very low levels (about 1 molecule in 10 million).

As a result of this and other work, the following hypothesis was developed to explain the photoperiodic response.    Light, acting on the photoreceptive phytochrome pigment, starts a chemical reaction which goes to completion in the dark. In absorbing the red light, molecules of one form of phytochrome are converted into a second form.    This second form can be converted back to the original phytochrome by irradiation with far-red light.*

At the end of a dark period, all the phytochrome in a plant is in the 660 form.    Sunlight, which contains red light, converts most of the $P_{660}$ to $P_{735}$. At the end of the day, therefore, the plant contains mostly $P_{735}$.    During the night the $P_{735}$ is converted relatively slowly into $P_{660}$ at a rate which probably varies from one plant to another.*    The effective dark period for any one plant

---

* The two forms of phytochrome are designated by the wavelengths which each characteristically absorbs: the red-absorbing form is called $P_{660}$ while the far-red-absorbing form is known as $P_{735}$.

may well be the time required for conversion of all the $P_{735}$ to $P_{660}$. The possible phytochrome mechansim is shown here in schematic form:

$$\text{RED LIGHT} \rightarrow P_{660} \underset{\text{conversion}}{\overset{\text{slow, night-time}}{\rightleftarrows}} P_{735} \leftarrow \text{FAR-RED LIGHT}$$

A bright period in the middle of a dark period causes a plant to respond as though the dark period were short.

Florists and agriculturists use the techniques of interrupting night length in order to force plants to flower out of regular season. For example, poinsettias can be made to bloom at Christmas time, and lilies at Easter. Interestingly, although the practical application of the photoperiodic response is known, its theoretical basis is still largely a mystery. There is as yet no evidence showing how the conversion of $P_{735}$ to $P_{660}$ triggers the hormone system which is ultimately responsible for inducing flowering—in itself one of the most remarkable changes of form and structure in the life of a plant. Much research is currently being done in this area (and more is needed) in attempts to understand the exact mechanism involved.

It was seen earlier that the plant is able to detect the photoperiodic stimulus with the phytochrome system in its leaf cells. However, it is the shoot apical meristem, located some distance away, that undergoes transformation from the vegetative to the reproductive state. It seems reasonable to hypothesize that the plant may contain some substance (or substances) which transmit the photoperiodic stimulus from the leaves, down the petiole, and up the stem into the apical meristem. Evidence supporting this hypothesis has been provided by grafting experiments. A portion of the stem of a cocklebur plant which has received a photoperiod favorable for the induction of flowering (plant A) is grafted to the stem of a plant which has not been given the inductive dark period (plant B). Within a week or two, plant B begins to flower. The two plants can then be separated and a third plant (C) grafted to plant A. Soon plant C will flower (Fig. 11–34). This procedure has been continued through 8 or 10 different grafts over a long period of time, always with the same result. It seems evident that the flowering stimulus is able to pass a graft union from one plant to another.

Further support for the idea of a flowering stimulus transported from the leaves to the apical meristem has been provided by another kind of experiment. Different groups of cocklebur plants were given a favorable photoperiodic stimulus (a single, long, dark period). Immediately after this treatment, the leaves of one group were removed. Some hours later, the leaves were removed from a second group. The procedure was continued at regular intervals for several days following the long dark period. Nine days after the dark period, the plants which had had their leaves removed immediately after treatment were still

---

* An hypothesis suggesting that this phytochrome reversion system is the photoperiodic timer is no longer generally accepted. Almost certainly the phytochrome is involved, but the "clock" problem remains unresolved.

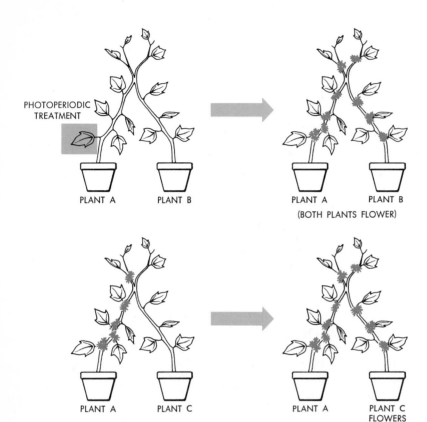

PHOTOPERIODIC
TREATMENT

PLANT A    PLANT B

PLANT A    PLANT B
(BOTH PLANTS FLOWER)

PLANT A    PLANT C

PLANT A    PLANT C
FLOWERS

FIG. 11–34 Interpretation of grafting experiments that provide evidence for the existence of a flower-stimulating substance.

vegetative. The plants which had had their leaves removed 35 hours after the dark interval, however, were producing flowers almost as well as those which retained their leaves. It therefore seems logical to hypothesize that when the leaves are removed immediately following the inductive dark period, very little (if any) of the flowering stimulus has been transported out of the leaves. However, after about 35 hours, nearly all of the flowering stimulus has been translocated from the leaves and is moving through the stem to the apical meristem.

There thus exists good evidence that some kind of chemical linkage exists between the perception of the photoperiod and the production of flowers. Yet despite the efforts of numerous investigators over a period of many years, no such substance has been isolated or extracted. One possible explanation is that such a substance may not actually exist. A flower is a highly complex structure, and it seems impossible for a single substance to induce the many changes necessary to convert a vegetative apex into a floral meristem.

There is good evidence, however, that at least two plant hormones are involved in the flowering process. Applications of gibberellic acid induce flowering in many long-day plants grown under short-day conditions. There is also the probability that a flowering *inhibiting* substance present in the apical meristem cells under noninductive conditions may keep the apex in the vegetative condition. If this is indeed the case, then the proper environmental stimulus (e.g., a favorable photoperiod) might cause the synthesis of the inhibitor to be inhibited. When the growth inhibitor abscisic acid is injected into the stem cavity of rye grass near the apical meristem, the plants do not flower, even in a favorable photoperiod. The amount of abscisic acid appears to increase in leaves of some long-day plants held under short-day conditions, thus inhibiting the production of flowers. It is possible, therefore, that both abscisic acid and gibberellic acid may be important hormonal intermediaries between the reception of the photoperiodic stimulus and the biochemical events connected with flower production by the shoot apex.

Are environmental factors other than light involved in the induction of flowering? Consider the flowering of wheat. Spring wheat produces flowers in early summer after being planted in spring. Winter wheat, however, does not normally flower until the early summer following planting the previous fall. Wheat farmers during the nineteenth century discovered that winter wheat planted in the spring would also flower, providing that the grains had been moistened and exposed to cold temperatures for several weeks prior to planting. This low temperature treatment has been called "vernalization," a word which here means "inducing spring-like behavior."

Which portion of the plant perceives the low-temperature effect? By cooling some portions of the plant while keeping the rest at normal temperature, it was found that the plant would detect the low temperature only if its shoot apical meristem was cooled. Cooling of the leaves or the roots had no effect. By placing flowers of intact plants of winter rye in vacuum bottles with crushed ice for varying lengths of time, it was discovered that the developing embryos inside the immature seeds could be successfully vernalized. In fact, the young embryos became sensitive to low temperature treatment within five days after fertilization occurred. When the plants reached maturity weeks or months later, they produced flowers. Thus the cells of the shoot apical meristem of the embryo are changed in some way by the cold, go through normal vegetative growth, and then become reproductive later in the life cycle of the plant.

The mechanism of the plant's response to cold is not yet understood. It has been found, however, that a few plants which ordinarily require low temperature for flowering can often be induced to flower without cold treatment by applications of gibberellic acid over a period of days. Thus, gibberellic acid will substitute for the cold requirement, at least in long-day plants such as carrot, cabbage, radish, and spinach. However, it has no effect on short-day plants such as soybean and cocklebur kept under long-day conditions.

**11-12**
**TROPISMS**

As we saw in Section 11–10, tropisms are movements produced by growth of the plant in response to external stimuli, e.g., light and gravity.

The reader will recall that in 1880, Charles Darwin and his son Francis studied the curvature of grass seedlings toward the light, and concluded that

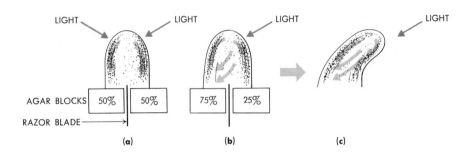

FIG. 11–35 Experiments to demonstrate the idea that light causes an uneven distribution of auxin in coleoptiles. (a) The control group, illuminated from both sides. (b) The experimental group, illuminated from only one side. (c) Growth response of an intact coleoptile, due to auxin redistribution. The agar blocks show the relative amounts of auxin which diffuse from the stem tip into them.

something moving downward from the plant apex caused the seedling to bend toward the light.

During the first quarter of the twentieth century (see Section 11–10), additional insight into the nature of the phototropic response was provided by several investigators, including Boysen-Jensen, Paál, and Went. These investigations led the Russian botanist N. Cholodny to propose a general theory of plant tropisms in the late 1920's. Cholodny hypothesized that curvatures of plant organs in response to external stimuli are due to the migration of a growth-promoting substance from one side of the stimulated plant to the other.

Almost simultaneously, Went, in the Netherlands, proposed the same idea. In addition, Went provided experimental verification. He placed coleoptile tips on razor blades so that the base of each tip was separated into two parts. The bases were then placed on top of agar blocks (a gelatinlike substance made from red algae), one block for each half of the separated coleoptile. Some of the tips were exposed to light from both sides, while others were exposed to light coming from one direction. (All the previous preparation was done in a dark room with only red light, to which coleoptiles are relatively insensitive.) After exposure, the coleoptiles were placed in the dark for about two hours. When the agar blocks were examined, Went found that the auxin content was equal in both agar blocks in the control group, which received light from both sides. In the experimental group, however, the blocks under the bases that had been facing the light contained only 25% of the auxin (Fig. 11–35).

These results indicated that light stimulates a redistribution of auxin. Soon after Went's experiments, the Dutch botanist H. E. Dolk provided similar evidence for the lateral redistribution of auxin in response to gravity. Dolk separated coleoptile tips into two parts and placed them in a horizontal position in contact with two agar blocks. After a short time in this position, the blocks on the lower side contained almost twice as much auxin as did the upper ones.

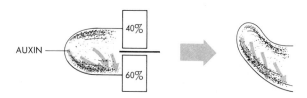

AUXIN

40%

60%

FIG. 11–36   Gravity also seems to affect auxin redistribution in stem tips. When a coleoptile is placed in a horizontal position, auxin accumulates on the lower part of the stem. It thus produces increased growth in this part, causing the stem to bend upward. It is still difficult, however, to explain the downward movement of roots on the basis of this hypothesis.

Thus, when a coleoptile is placed in a horizontal position, auxin accumulates on its lower side. This produces increased growth on that side, causing the stem to bend upward (Fig. 11–36). The results of Dolk's experiment were soon confirmed by several investigators using other organs of the plant. Recently, K. V. Thimann and his colleagues have shown that when purified carbon[14]-labeled indoleacetic acid is properly applied in small amounts to coleoptile tips, there is indeed a lateral movement of radioactive auxin during both geotropic and phototropic stimulation. It seems likely, therefore, that the Cholodny-Went theory of plant tropisms is essentially correct.

What triggers the lateral redistribution of auxin? In phototropism, it is natural to hypothesize that light is involved in some manner. As long ago as 1909, investigators of tropisms produced action spectra showing that blue light was most effective in inducing curvature of coleoptiles and that red light had little, if any, effect (hence the use of red light in dark rooms during the preparation of tropism experiments). However, if light is to be effective, it must be absorbed. This means that there must be present in the plant some kind of light receptor molecule. In 1933, it was hypothesized that this receptor might be a carotenoid pigment (carotenoids were known to exhibit action spectra similar to that which induced coleoptile curvatures). Support for this hypothesis was provided a few years later by the discovery that oat coleoptiles contain carotenoids, especially in the cells near the apex. Unfortunately, the extreme apex, which had been shown some years earlier to be the region most sensitive to light, seemed to lack carotenoids.

In 1959, it was hypothesized that another substance, riboflavin (vitamin $B_2$), might be the phototropic light receptor molecule. The plant physiologist A. W. Galston showed that the action spectrum of riboflavin resembles that for phototropism in oat coleoptiles (Fig. 11–37). He found that riboflavin is present in the coleoptile apex of a mutant strain of oats in which carotenoids are nearly

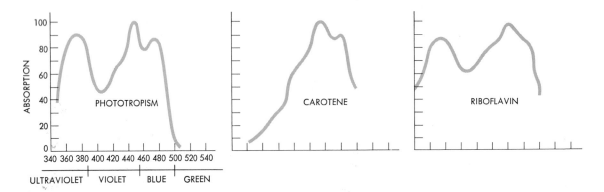

FIG. 11–37   Comparison of the action spectra for phototropism (left), carotene (middle), and riboflavin (right).

absent.   In addition, when Galston collected auxin from oat coleoptiles, he discovered that, after riboflavin was added, the auxin was oxidized in the presence of light.

More recently, the action spectra for both riboflavin and carotenoid pigments have been shown to be inexact fits for that of phototropism.   The riboflavin spectrum more closely matches the near ultraviolet peak, but not those peaks in the visible light range.   The spectrum for carotenoids fits the visible light peaks, but does not have a peak in the UV light (Fig. 11–37).   It could be, of course, that *neither* of these molecules is involved in light reception during phototropism. While plausible, this conclusion is not very helpful.   It implies that a third light receptor molecule, still undetected, exists.   This, though not impossible, is quite unlikely.   Finally, it has been suggested that perhaps both molecules may be functioning in the phototropic reaction, with carotenoid absorbing visible light and riboflavin the UV light.

Whatever the situation, it seems clear that further study must be done before the question of light absorption in phototropism can be resolved.   Then, once the nature of the light-absorbing system is determined, the mechanism whereby the light-activated chemical affects the lateral redistribution of auxin must be investigated.

As discussed earlier, the Cholodny-Went hypothesis holds that there is a lateral redistribution of auxin involved in the geotropic curvature of coleoptiles; i.e., when a coleoptile is placed horizontally, auxin accumulates on the lower side. This side then grows rapidly, causing the organ to curve upward. Can this hypothesis explain the geotropic response of roots? Since the early nineteenth century, it has been known that primary roots exhibit positive geotropism; i.e., they curve downward in response to gravity (Fig. 11–38).   In the early 1930's, it was found that when corn roots are placed horizontally for a short period of time, the lower half contains more auxin than the upper (just as in the horizontal coleoptiles).

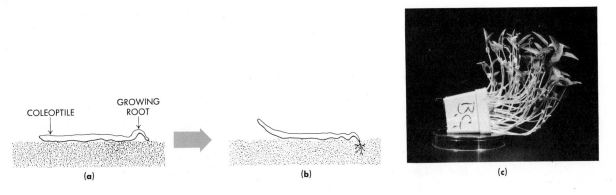

FIG. 11–38    Geotropism in plants is the response of stem and root tips to gravity.    Stems show negative geotropism; roots show positive geotropism.

Yet such a horizontal root curves downward, while the coleoptile curves upward. It seems clear, therefore, that while auxin promotes the growth of the shoot, it *inhibits* the growth of the root.

Why do auxins have an inhibitory effect on the growth of root cells and the reverse effect on stem cells? Recent experiments by Stanley P. Burg at the University of Miami may shed some light on this paradoxical situation. Burg placed excised root tips of several species of flowering plants in solutions containing various concentrations of IAA plus an energy source, sucrose. The rate of production by the roots of one metabolic product, ethylene, was determined at intervals. The roots in the control group (without IAA) produced small amounts of ethylene. In those roots treated with a low concentration of IAA, the rate of ethylene formation doubled within 15 to 30 minutes and continued to increase rapidly thereafter. Burg also discovered that the greater the concentration of IAA, the greater the production of ethylene by the root cells. In addition, as the concentration of ethylene increases, the rate of growth in length and weight of the roots is gradually inhibited. This finding suggested that perhaps the inhibition of root growth by auxin may be due to the induction by auxin of the synthesis of a growth inhibitor, ethylene. Burg also presented evidence that ethylene participates in the geotropic response of roots, but not that of stems.

This finding presents still another problem: Why does ethylene exhibit such different effects in the cells of the two organs? And there is still another problem: In what way is the auxin in a horizontally-placed root redistributed? Obviously, gravity must be involved. But how does the plant perceive gravitational forces? Around 1900, knowing that gravity affects mass, investigators postulated that perhaps the cells contain small particles which move under the influence of a gravitational field (one such type of particle could be starch grains).

A test of this hypothesis would see what response would be made to gravity by plants whose starch grains had been removed. In a recent experiment performed by K. V. Thimann, wheat coleoptiles were incubated for 34 hours at 30°C in a solution of two growth substances (gibberellin and cytokinin), both of which were known to promote growth by stimulating the enzymatic conversion of starch to sugar. After this treatment, the cells of the coleoptiles were found to be free of starch grains. When placed horizontally, these starch-free coleoptiles responded geotropically in much the same way as did the controls, which contained starch grains. The rate of curvature of the destarched coleoptiles was somewhat slower, however, than that of the coleoptiles with starch grains. It was nevertheless concluded that starch grains are not necessary for wheat coleoptiles to undergo geotropic response. It has been suggested, however, that the destarched coleoptiles responded more slowly because the postulated role of starch grains as gravity receptors was taken over by some other kind of particle inside the cell.

This last postulation of another gravity perceptive particle is a good example of an attempt to "save the hypothesis." It can be questioned whether science actually benefits from postulating the existence of such cell particles, when the only evidence for them is negative. Much time can be lost in a search for particles of this kind. On the other hand, they do occasionally turn up!

FIG. 11–39    Patterns of branching in trees. Left, excurrent branching, as in Norway spruce. Right, decurrent branching, as in sugar maple.

**11–13
APICAL
DOMINANCE AND
THE CONTROL OF
PLANT FORM**

Many plants, especially trees, possess very distinctive body forms. For example, the Norway spruce (*Picea abies*) has a pointed, spirelike form with a single main trunk, while the sugar maple (*Acer saccharum*) is much more branched and its central stem is eventually lost among the uppermost branches. The spruce tree is said to have an **excurrent** pattern of branching, whereas that of the maple is called **decurrent** or **deliquescent** (Fig. 11–39).

It has long been known that when the growing apex of a young herb, shrub, or tree is removed, many of the buds in the axils of leaves lower down on the stem begin to grow, eventually taking the place of the main stem (Fig. 11–40). This observation is the basis of the art of pruning, the practice of which enables the horticulturist and gardener to modify plant form in various ways, e.g., the square-sided boxwood hedges so often seen in formal gardens. It can be hypothesized, therefore, that the presence of the terminal bud inhibits the growth and development of the lateral buds on the stem below it.

During the early 1930's, K. V. Thimann and Folke Skoog became interested in this problem. They thought that perhaps the newly discovered auxins were involved in the domination of the apical bud over the lateral ones. They reasoned in the following way:

*Hypothesis: If* . . .    the terminal bud inhibits the growth of the lateral buds by producing a growth inhibiting auxin,

*Prediction: then* . . . decapitating the apex and replacing it with an auxin-containing agar block should result in inhibition of the lateral buds.

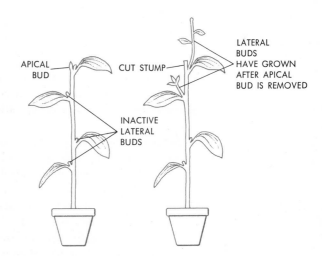

FIG. 11–40   After removal of the apical bud, some of the inactive axillary buds grow out.

In experiments to determine if auxin is produced by the terminal bud, Thimann and Skoog cut off the tips of young healthy plants of broad bean (*Vicia faba*) and placed them upon agar blocks for 4 hours. Using the Avena coleoptile curvature bioassay, they discovered that the terminal buds produced considerable quantities of growth substances. The results showed that their first prediction was a correct one.

In another series of experiments, Thimann and Skoog removed the terminal buds from broad bean plants and applied agar blocks with high concentrations of growth substance. The lateral buds on decapitated plants receiving auxin were found to be inhibited as completely as those on the intact control plants. Thus, their second prediction was verified; by means of auxin, the apical bud exerts dominance over the lateral buds (Fig. 11–41).

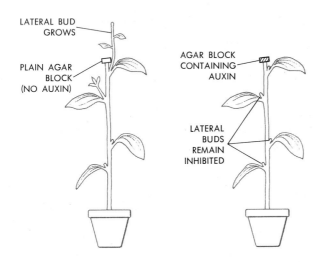

FIG. 11–41 Interpretation of experiments showing that the apical bud inhibits the lateral buds by auxin.

Thimann and Skoog's findings on apical dominance in the herbaceous broad bean plant suggested that the characteristic growth forms of trees might also be due to a mechanism involving the terminal bud and auxin inhibition. It seemed logical that if the decapitation of bean plants leads to development of the lateral buds and bushy growth, then trees such as maples with the decurrent branching pattern must not possess apical dominance, while in those trees with an excurrent pattern of branching, apical dominance must be very strong.

This rather simple interpretation of form in woody plants on the basis of weak or strong apical dominance was challenged in 1967 by the tree physiologist Claud L. Brown and his associates at the University of Georgia. After extensive observations of many species of trees, it was shown that patterns of lateral bud inhibition are actually the reverse of what one would predict from the long accepted version of apical dominance theory. In trees with the decurrent branching habit, e.g., the pecan (*Carya illinoensis*) and the oaks (*Quercus*), nearly all of the lateral buds on the current year's growth are completely inhibited, a pattern which suggests the action of strong apical dominance. Not until the second season of growth, after a period of winter dormancy, is the inhibition of the lateral buds broken and the much-branched stems characteristic of the decurrent growth form produced. In trees with the excurrent growth form such as spruce and some flowering plants, e.g. sweetgum (*Liquidambar styraciflua*) and tulip poplar (*Liriodendron tulipifera*), the lateral buds on the current year's stem grow to varying degrees. Evidently, apical dominance in these plants is rather weak.

Brown and his colleagues suggest that use of the term "apical dominance" should be restricted to the inhibition of buds on individual branches rather than extended to describe overall tree form. They propose that the term "apical control" might be more meaningful in describing the condition manifested by the excurrent or decurrent patterns of growth. Excurrent growth could be explained, therefore, by hypothesizing that the terminal leader (the central or main stem) maintains apical control throughout the life of the tree by only partially suppressing the growth of the buds beneath it. Only in this way is it possible for truly spirelike forms to originate and be maintained throughout the life of the tree.

To produce the decurrent tree forms, it was hypothesized that apical control by the terminal leader would be lost very early in life. The large, well-developed, uppermost lateral buds on the current year's growth would be strongly inhibited the first season. By the second season, however, these large buds would be able to compete successfully with the terminal bud for food, water, and growth substances. In fact, this competition may be so severe that the terminal bud is killed by the midsummer of the second growing season, producing the distinctive much-branched growth form, as in maples. After a season or two, this now-dominant lateral bud will be replaced by one of its uppermost inhibited buds. This cycle continues throughout the lifetime of the tree.

How might the bud inhibition mechanism operate? How is it possible for different lateral buds on the same plant to differ in their sensitivity to dominance? What causes some of the lateral buds to develop into branches while others remain inhibited? An early attempt to answer such questions was Thimann and Skoog's hypothesis that apical dominance operates through the inhibition of lateral buds by auxin transported from the stem apex. As we just saw, however, this hypothesis has been questioned by several investigators during the three decades since it was proposed.

In 1957, the English botanists F. G. Gregory and J. A. Veale attempted to evaluate the relative roles of auxin and nutrition using flax (*Linum*) instead of the pea plants utilized by Thimann and Skoog. In Gregory and Veale's experiments, all the buds tended to remain active as long as the supply of nitrogen was high, with apical dominance being only poorly expressed. When the level of nitrogen was low, the lateral buds were inhibited. In addition, Gregory and Veale observed that the vascular tissue extending from the stem into the dormant buds was incomplete. Perhaps, they hypothesized, auxin from the apical bud inhibited the differentiation of the vascular tissue into buds, interfered with the movements of nutrients into them, and thus prevented their growth. Auxin, therefore, was visualized as having only an indirect role in lateral bud inhibition.

In the early 1950's, Skoog and his co-workers found that the formation of buds in tobacco pith tissue cultures is controlled by both the auxin and the cytokinin in the media. This discovery led Thimann and graduate student Margaret Wickson to study the role of cytokinin in the release of buds from dominance. Using sections of pea plant stems floating on a sugar solution, these investigators discovered that cytokinin could counteract the inhibition of lateral buds by auxin. It was therefore hypothesized that apical dominance in the intact plant depends on an interaction between auxin transported polarly from the growing terminal bud and cytokinin synthesized (most likely) in the inhibited buds themselves. From observations of other species, however, it was noticed that the inhibition was sometimes only partial; some lateral buds begin to grow while others on the same stem remain completely inhibited.

In 1964, Thimann and another colleague, Helen R. Sorokin, examined the relationship between the growth of lateral buds and their anatomy, especially the development of the xylem and phloem tissue connection with the stem. In pea stem sections floated on sugar-auxin solutions, the connection between the vascular system of the stem and that of the bud was not completed. When cytokinin was added to the culture solution, the differentiation of the xylem and phloem into the bud continued to completion, and the bud began to grow. These experiments showed that Gregory and Veale were on the right track some years earlier when they postulated that a growth substance (auxin) might be functioning to inhibit the differentiation of xylem and phloem into the dormant lateral buds (at that time cytokinin had not yet been shown to occur naturally in green plants).

Recently, investigations by Thimann and his colleague Tsvi Sachs have helped greatly to clarify the mechanism by which lateral buds are released from apical dominance. In one set of experiments, a solution of cytokinin in alcohol and carbowax was applied directly to the lateral buds of pea seedlings. Within two days, the normally dormant lateral buds started growing. These buds did not elongate as much as uninhibited control buds did, however. Thimann and Sachs were able to make these buds elongate normally by applying IAA to their apices. They concluded from these experiments that the cytokinin acts to release the lateral buds from the inhibition of the growing apex, while auxin acts directly on the internodes, promoting their elongation but only *after* the initial inhibition has been removed.

With this experimental clarification of the roles of auxin and cytokinin, it is now possible to explain the importance of nutritional factors and plant vigor in the expression of apical dominance. For example, the release of normally inhibited lateral buds following high nitrogen fertilization observed by Gregory and Veale may be attributed to an increased synthesis of cytokinins in these buds (cytokinin molecules contain several atoms of nitrogen—see Fig. 11–26). Thus, nutrition influences dominance indirectly by changing the overall growth rate of the plant.

There is also evidence that auxin and gibberellin may interact in apical bud inhibition. In experiments by William P. Jacobs and his associates at Princeton University, a lanolin paste containing 1% indoleacetic acid and 1% gibberellic acid was applied to the cut surfaces of pea stems immediately following the excision of the apical bud. The resulting inhibition of lateral bud growth was found to be nearly as complete as that produced by the intact apical buds.

The growth inhibitor abscisic acid may also be involved in apical dominance. The dormancy of potato tubers as well as isolated potato buds is prolonged effectively by treatment with abscisic acid. Various species of deciduous trees have been induced to enter the dormant condition by applications of this growth inhibitor. For example, when abscisic acid was applied to the leaves of actively growing birch seedlings, the apical buds soon developed the form and structure of dormant buds.

It seems clear, therefore, that the phenomenon of apical dominance involves a highly complex interaction and balance among many factors, including auxin, gibberellin, cytokinin, abscisic acid, and nutrition.

In this chapter, the transporting systems in the plant have been examined in some detail. In the vascular plant, there are two fundamental transporting systems—two main streams of translocation which move in two different tissues. Yet the two streams are very closely interrelated; some of the water that reaches the leaves through the xylem returns to the roots in the phloem. Autoradiographic studies show that some materials, especially phosphorus, may make a circuit in the plant by being moved through both conducting tissues.

Movement of water upward through the xylem is a result of the concerted functioning of the root, stem, and leaves. Through osmotic pressure, the root provides a push. The leaves provide a pull through the effects of transpiration. The stem, through the cohesive and adhesive properties of water molecules and the narrow diameter of the xylem elements, helps maintain the column of water while it is being pulled to great heights. Food production depends on this coordinated activity, for photosynthesis can occur only if water is brought from the roots and carbon dioxide enters through the leaves. The process of respiration, which occurs in each living cell of the plant, depends upon the oxygen entering the leaves and transported through the phloem to these cells.

The metabolic activities of the living cells result in the production of various waste products which present a special disposal problem. Unlike animals which possess well-developed systems for eliminating toxic and unnecessary materials from their bodies, land-dwelling plants accumulate most of their excretory products within their tissues, e.g., in the bark and leaves (which may be shed periodically) and in the xylem (which is thus transformed into heart-wood).

Many complex plant activities such as growth, response to light or gravity, and flowering are under the control of plant hormones. The effects of hormones depend on the physiological nature of the tissues. The two main types of plant hormones are the auxins and the gibberellins. The photoperiodic response depends on a photoreceptive compound in the leaves which somehow triggers a hormone response affecting the flower bud.

1. It has been shown that when water loss from a tree exceeds water absorption, the circumference of the trunk decreases. From your knowledge of the mechanisms of water transport, suggest why this shrinkage should take place.

2. For each of the following conditions, state whether the guard cells of a leaf would be expected to be: (1) fully open, (2) partially open, (3) completely closed.

   a) Atmosphere very moist, much water in soil, sunlight plentiful.

   b) Atmosphere dry, soil quite moist, sunlight plentiful.

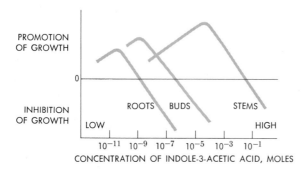

PROMOTION OF GROWTH

INHIBITION OF GROWTH

0

ROOTS  BUDS  STEMS

LOW                    HIGH

$10^{-11}$  $10^{-9}$  $10^{-7}$  $10^{-5}$  $10^{-3}$  $10^{-1}$

CONCENTRATION OF INDOLE-3-ACETIC ACID, MOLES

FIG. 11–42

c) Atmosphere dry, not much soil water, cloudy.

d) Atmosphere moist, plentiful supply of soil water, cloudy.

3. What happens to a wilted stalk of lettuce when it is placed in water to make it crisp?

4. What would happen to a crisp stalk of lettuce if it were placed in a fairly strong salt solution?

5. It is wise to recut the stems of cut flowers about an inch from the end, preferably under water. Explain why.

6. After transplanting, it is desirable to remove many of the leaves. Explain why.

7. List, in correct order, the cells and tissues through which a molecule of water travels from its point of entry into the root until it is used in photosynthesis.

8. Before the days of refrigeration, salt was used extensively to preserve meat. Explain why this process was effective (remember that spoilage and decay are the result of bacteria and other small organisms).

9. In the midwestern United States, some species of plants flower in April while others do not flower until August. Explain.

10. Tomato plants produce flowers and fruit both outdoors during the summer and in greenhouses during the winter. What does this indicate about their photoperiodic requirements?

Answer Exercises 11 to 16 on the basis of the information in Fig. 11–42,* which shows the approximate range of concentration for the promotion and inhibition of different plant organs of barley by auxins. The horizontal line marked zero indicates a point of neither inhibition nor promotion of growth. The numbers $10^{-7}$, $10^{-8}$, etc., stand for very minute fractions or amounts of the growth hormones; $10^{-7} = 1/10,000,000$; $10^{-8} = 1/100,000,000$, etc. Such small amounts have to be detected by special types of chemical analysis. Evaluate the conclusions in Exercises 16 to 21 according to the following key:

A. The data given support this conclusion.
B. The data given refute this conclusion.
C. The data given neither support nor refute this conclusion.

---

* Adapted from K. V. Thimann, "On the Nature of Inhibitions Caused by Auxin." *Amer. J. Bot.* **24:** 411, 1937.

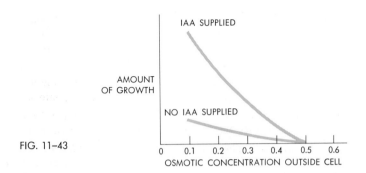

IAA SUPPLIED

AMOUNT
OF GROWTH

NO IAA SUPPLIED

FIG. 11–43

0    0.1    0.2    0.3    0.4    0.5    0.6

OSMOTIC CONCENTRATION OUTSIDE CELL

11. The best concentration of auxins for the growth of roots is between $10^{-9}$ and $10^{-8}$ molal.

12. There are concentrations of auxins that can promote the growth of stems but, at the same time, somewhat inhibit the development of buds.

13. The concentration of auxins which is best for the growth of buds (immature flowers) would prevent the growth of stems.

14. The production of auxins by the terminal bud will promote the growth of the lateral buds.

15. If the concentration of auxins in the stem is $10^{-2}$ molal, then placing the stem in a horizontal position could cause the stem tip to curve downward.

16. The best concentration of auxins for the growth of flowers is, approximately, between $10^{-4}$ and $10^{-3}$.

17. Refer to the graph of Fig. 11–43, which shows the relation between osmotic concentration outside the cell and amount of growth. Explain this graph with reference to how auxin is thought to influence the growth of plant tissues.

**ADDICOTT, F. T.,** and **J. L. LYON,** "Physiology of Abscisic Acid and Related Substances." *Annual Review of Plant Physiology* **20,** 1969. A technical review of the research on abscisic acid up to September 1968.

**BIDDULPH, S.,** and **O. BIDDULPH,** "The Circulatory System of Plants." *Scientific American,* February 1959, p. 44. A brief, well-written article surveying the general knowledge of how translocation occurs.

**BOYSEN-JENSEN, P.,** "Transmission of the Phototropic Stimulus in the Coleoptile of the Oat Seedling." Reprinted in *Great Experiments in Biology,* ed. by M. L. Gabriel and S. Fogel (Englewood Cliffs, N.J.: Prentice-Hall, 1955), pp. 146–148. Boysen-Jensen demonstrates that the phototropic response is not interfered with by a layer of gelatin separating the tip of the coleoptile from its base.

**DARWIN, CHARLES,** and **FRANCIS DARWIN,** "Sensitiveness of Plants to Light: Its Transmitted Effects." Reprinted in *Great Experiments in Biology,* ed. by M. L. Gabriel and S. Fogel (Englewood Cliffs, N.J.: Prentice-Hall, 1955), pp. 142–146. The Darwins demonstrate that the phototropic response originates in the apex of the coleoptile.

SUGGESTED
READINGS

GALSTON, ARTHUR W., and PETER J. DAVIES, "Hormonal Regulation in Higher Plants." *Science* **163**: 1288–1297, 1969. A review of the current status of research on the regulation of plant growth and development by interactions between promotive and inhibitory hormones.

GATES, DAVID M., "Heat Transfer in Plants." *Scientific American*, December 1965, pp. 77–84. An account of the ways in which a plant regulates its temperature.

GRUELACH, V. A., "The Rise of Water in Plants." *Scientific American*, October 1952, pp. 78–82. Deals with the problems of root pressure and transpiration.

HELGESON, JOHN P., "The Cytokinins." *Science* **161**: 974–981, 1968. An excellent review of current thinking concerning the nature and roles of the cytokinins in plant growth and development.

LETHAM, DAVID S., "Cytokinins and Their Relation to Other Phytohormones." *Bio-Science* **19**: 309–316, 1969. An excellent summary; well-illustrated.

STEWARD, F. C., *About Plants: Topics in Plant Biology* (Reading, Mass.: Addison-Wesley, 1966). An excellent short treatment of plant structure and function.

VAN OVERBEEK, J., "The Control of Plant Growth." *Scientific American*, July 1968, pp. 75–81. A well-written discussion of the manner in which the growth of plants is controlled in the laboratory through treatments with the proper combinations of promotive and inhibitory hormones.

ZIMMERMANN, M. H., "Movement of Organic Substances in Trees." *Science* **133**: 73, copyright 1961 by the American Association for the Advancement of Science. One of the original accounts of Zimmermann's work on removing substances from the phloem with the aid of aphids. This work is more detailed than the next article, but contains some good data on how the removal of the leaves from a tree affects the rate and type of substance moved in the phloem.

ZIMMERMANN, M. H., "How Sap Moves in Trees." *Scientific American*, March 1963, p. 133. An excellent article describing experiments using decapitated aphids for collections of phloem materials. Also presents a summary of the hypotheses involved in explaining the movement of materials throughout the plant body.

# ANIMAL ANATOMY AND PHYSIOLOGY I: CHAPTER 12
# THE INTAKE AND PROCESSING OF FOOD

Anyone who has dissected even a very simple organism cannot help being impressed by the high degree of organization he sees. In higher animals, the intricacy of structural adaptations for digestion, circulation, movement, reception of stimuli, and control of internal conditions is truly amazing. It is the purpose of the next two chapters to examine some representative (but by no means all) aspects of animal anatomy and physiology in order to give some insight into the means by which our present knowledge concerning this physiology has been gained. In earlier chapters, the complementarity of structure and function in higher plants became apparent. The present chapter will pay particular attention to this question in relation to higher animals, including man.

As with plants, no attempt will be made to describe in detail the many anatomical differences which exist between different species; rather, it is to *similarities* of structure and function that primary attention will be directed. And, as with plants, it is at the tissue level of investigation that the underlying structural similarities between different animal species must here be discussed as a necessary prologue to dealing with experimental investigations of function in this chapter and the next.

Despite the fact that higher animals seem considerably more complex than plants, the tissues that compose them can be divided into only five basic groups.

1) **Epithelial tissues.** These are the surface and lining tissues of the animal body. They form a continuous layer or sheet over the entire body surface and most of the body's inner cavities. On the external surface, epithelial tissues protect underlying cells from injury, bacteria, harmful chemicals, and drying. On the internal surface, epithelial tissues absorb water and food and give off

waste products. In the digestive tract, epithelial tissues secrete mucus to keep the passages damp and lubricated. Some places in which epithelial tissue always occurs are in the lining of the digestive tract, the air passages to the lungs, the lining of the kidney tubules, and the skin.

Epithelial tissues can be divided into three major groups, according to the shape of the cells composing them (Fig. 12–1a). **Squamous epithelium** is composed of flat cells, shaped rather like flagstones on a terrace. Squamous epithelium is found in the lining of the mouth and esophagus. In complex animals, squamous epithelium is found in stratified layers, with several of these flat cells piled one on top of the other. **Cuboidal epithelium,** as the name suggests, is made up of cube-shaped cells; it can be found lining the kidney tubules. **Columnar epithelium** also has a descriptive name. Its cells resemble pillars or columns, with the nucleus usually located near the bottom of the cell. Columnar epithelium is widespread throughout the body, forming most of the lining of the digestive and respiratory tracts.

These three types of epithelial tissue are specialized for particular functions. Columnar cells, for example, often have small hairlike projections called **cilia.** These cilia beat rhythmically, moving materials such as mucus in one direction. In the respiratory system, dust and other particles of foreign materials are removed by ciliated columnar epithelium.

Also scattered throughout the columnar epithelial cells of the respiratory passages are **glandular epithelial cells.** Here, such cells are specialized to secrete substances such as mucus. In the lining of the ear canal, glandular columnar epithelial cells secrete wax. The milk with which female mammals feed their young is produced by glandular epithelial cells. Within the skin, glandular epithelial cells secrete perspiration.

Finally, epithelial cells may be specialized into **sensory epithelium** to receive stimuli. For example, olfactory epithelium, which lines the passages of the nose, is partly responsible for the sense of smell. Other sensory epithelial cells are scattered throughout the skin, where they may be sensitive to such stimuli as heat, cold, or pressure. In the sense that all incoming stimuli must pass through an animal's epithelial tissues, such tissues can truly be called the gateway to the body.

2) **Connective tissues.** Perhaps the easiest tissues to identify, connective tissues (Fig. 12–1b) are composed of cells embedded in a nonliving matrix, one which often the cells themselves may secrete. It is the nature of this matrix, rather than that of the cells themselves, which determines the functions of the particular connective tissue. Bone, cartilage, tendons, ligaments, and fibrous tissues are all familiar examples of connective tissues which support and hold together the other cells of the animal body.

**Cartilage** and **bone** are perhaps the best-known connective tissues. The principal difference between bone and cartilage is that the matrix in which the bone cells are embedded contains calcium salts, while that of cartilage does not. These salts and organic matter together produce a structure which is hard but flexible. As the figure shows, bone is not a solid structure; the cells embedded in its matrix are alive and must be supplied with blood vessels and nerves. This function is performed by minute canals permeating the entire structure of the bone. As an animal grows, certain cells within the bone tear down the matrix while others build it up. Thus bones gradually change their shape in response to the stresses and strains of normal growth.

Cartilage, which is more elastic than bone, can be considered as bone without calcium deposits in the matrix. The skeleton of the outer regions of the nose and ears is composed of cartilage. In some animals, such as sharks, virtually the entire skeleton is cartilaginous. In higher animals, the skeleton of the developing embryo is at first entirely cartilaginous; it later becomes ossified into bone, primarily by the deposition of calcium salts.

In **fibrous** connective tissue, of which **tendons** and **ligaments** are examples, the matrix is a thick network of fibers secreted by the connective tissue cells which they surround. These stringlike tissues are found throughout the body. They hold bone to bone, muscle to bone, skin to muscle, and bind together many other structures. The toughness of leather, formerly connective tissue of an animal, testifies how well the fibrous connective tissues are constructed to serve their purpose.

**Blood** may also be considered a connective tissue, since it, too, is composed of living cells surrounded by a nonliving matrix, the **blood plasma.** Blood contains two main types of cells, red blood cells (**erythrocytes**), which carry oxygen, and white blood cells (**leucocytes**), which aid in fighting off infection. Due to its liquid nature, blood cannot perform any supportive function, but in the sense that it serves as a transport medium between the different organs of the body it is perhaps the most "connective" tissue of all.

3) **Muscular tissue.** In terms of their structural and functional characteristics, muscle tissues can be divided into three types. Most of the body musculature is composed of **skeletal muscles.** These are the muscles that move the body appendages. The cells of skeletal muscles are long and fibrous, with many nuclei located close to the surface of the cell. Under the microscope, skeletal muscle cells show stripes, or **striations,** running across the width of the cell. Indeed, skeletal muscles are often called **striated muscles.** Skeletal muscle cells are capable of quite rapid contraction and can be controlled at will by the conscious portions of the brain. They cannot remain contracted for long, however, since they are rather easily fatigued.

**Cardiac muscle** is the muscle of the heart. Like those of skeletal muscle, the cells of cardiac muscle are long and striated. There are a few differences, however. The nuclei of cardiac muscles are located in the central region of the cell. Furthermore, the long cells often branch and fuse with each other, so that an impulse can travel between cells as well as along their length. This structure helps to account for the rhythmic contractions characteristic of heart muscle. As might be expected, cardiac muscle does not fatigue easily. The short period of rest between each contraction seems to be all that it needs.

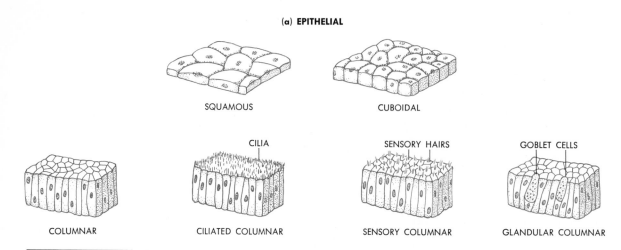

**(a) EPITHELIAL**

SQUAMOUS

CUBOIDAL

COLUMNAR

CILIATED COLUMNAR

SENSORY COLUMNAR

GLANDULAR COLUMNAR

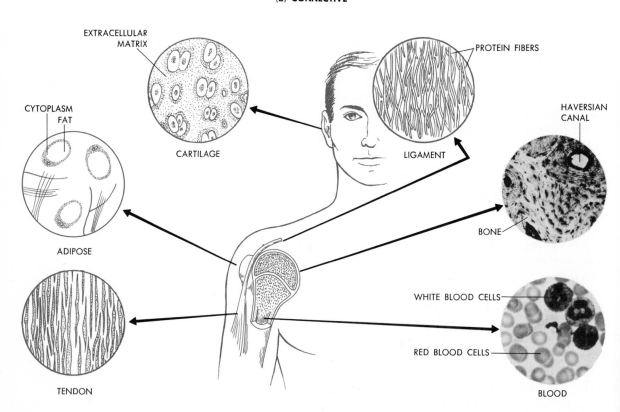

**(b) CONNECTIVE**

EXTRACELLULAR MATRIX

CARTILAGE

PROTEIN FIBERS

LIGAMENT

HAVERSIAN CANAL

BONE

CYTOPLASM
FAT

ADIPOSE

WHITE BLOOD CELLS

RED BLOOD CELLS

BLOOD

TENDON

FIG. 12–1   Animal tissues. (Photos: Bone cells courtesy Triarch, Inc., Ripon, Wisc.; the rest courtesy General Biological Supply House, Inc., Chicago.)

### (c) MUSCULAR

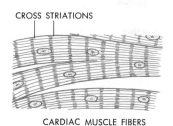

CROSS STRIATIONS

CARDIAC MUSCLE FIBERS

NUCLEI

SMOOTH MUSCLE FIBERS

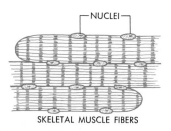

NUCLEI

SKELETAL MUSCLE FIBERS

### (d) NERVOUS

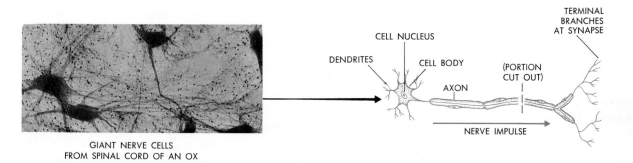

GIANT NERVE CELLS
FROM SPINAL CORD OF AN OX

DENDRITES

CELL NUCLEUS

CELL BODY

AXON

(PORTION CUT OUT)

TERMINAL BRANCHES AT SYNAPSE

NERVE IMPULSE

### (e) REPRODUCTIVE

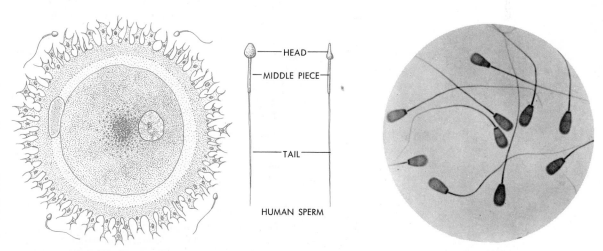

HUMAN EGG
WITH FOUR SPERM

HEAD

MIDDLE PIECE

TAIL

HUMAN SPERM

BULL SPERM

**Smooth muscle** is not striated, and thus appears smooth under the microscope. Like those of the skeletal and cardiac muscles, smooth muscle cells are elongated, but they differ in having pointed ends and only one nucleus per cell. Smooth muscle cells are found within the walls of the stomach, intestines, esophagus, etc. The smooth muscle cells of vertebrates contract rather slowly, but they can apparently remain contracted for considerable lengths of time without becoming fatigued. In some insects, smooth muscles operate the wings. Such muscles, of course, are capable of very rapid contraction.

Figure 12–1(c) shows the structural characteristics of skeletal, cardiac, and smooth muscle.

4)  **Nervous tissue.** Nervous tissue is made up of cells called **neurons,** which are cells specialized to conduct nerve impulses. Figure 12–1(d) shows a neuron and its parts. While neurons vary widely in size (and often in appearance), all of them have certain structural characteristics in common. The central cell body contains a nucleus surrounded by cytoplasm. Two types of processes, **axons** and **dendrites,** can be distinguished. Axons generally conduct nerve impulses away from the cell body, and dendrites generally conduct them toward the cell body. Impulses travel from one cell to the next by passing along the axon of one neuron and jumping a small gap (the **synapse**) to the dendrite of the next neuron. In higher animals, the nerve impulse can travel across the synapse only from an axon to a dendrite. Thus all the nerve impulses travel in only one direction. The processes extending from neurons may vary considerably in length. A nerve cell in the spinal cord may send an axon down an arm or leg for three feet or more.

Most nerve fibers are microscopic in width. The iliac nerve going down into the human leg is as thick as a pencil, but this is because it is composed of hundreds of nerve processes. Such a nerve cord is rather like a telephone cable in which many separate wires carry impulses and are insulated from each other along their length.

5)  **Reproductive tissue.** * As its name implies, reproductive tissue is composed of cells specialized to produce the next generation. In higher animals, the reproductive cells (**gametes**) are specialized into the female **egg cell,** or **ovum,** and the male **spermatozoa,** or **sperm.** Egg cells are generally spherical in shape, and contain yolk to feed the developing offspring from the moment of fertilization until it is able to obtain food in some other way. Sperm cells are far smaller than eggs, and can swim by whipping their cytoplasmic tails. The shape of the sperm cell may vary widely from one species to another. Figure 12–1(e) shows the details of these two types of reproductive tissue.

---

* It is possible to question the use of the word "tissue" in connection with the reproductive cells, since they do not function as a unit. It can be quite reasonably maintained that the reproductive cells remain a distinct group simply by virtue of not possessing features which would place them within any one of the other four tissue groups just discussed.

We stated in Chapter 1 that life without energy is a contradiction in terms. No living system can long endure without some kind of fuel—its food—to keep it running. The taking in of food we call **ingestion,** the preparation of this food for the organism's use, **digestion.**

The first process, ingestion, may vary widely from one form of organism to another. The one-celled amoeba ingests food at any point in its plasma membrane; most higher animals ingest food through a specialized opening, or mouth. Whatever the means, however, the final result is the same—the taking in of raw materials for digestion and eventual assimilation into the organism's own living material.

Digestion, too, may vary from one animal species to another. Some digestion, such as that of the amoeba or sponge, is **intracellular;** the food passes directly into the cell cytoplasm in food vacuoles and is there attacked chemically by digestive enzymes. In higher animals and many lower ones, however, **extracellular** digestion is the rule. Specialized glandular cells secrete digestive enzymes onto the food, which is usually confined by some means to a specific area of the body during the digestive process. The stomach and intestines perform this confining function in higher animals. After being digested, the food is absorbed and distributed to other body cells.

As has perhaps already been implied, digestion is primarily a chemical process. It is not entirely so, however. Mechanical digestion, the physical reduction of ingested food to smaller masses, is also important. Such a breaking apart exposes more surface area of the food material to the digestive enzymes. Teeth are probably the most familiar instruments of mechanical digestion in animals, but there are many others. Birds, who lack teeth, grind their food in the crop, a muscular sac often filled with small stones.

A change of major importance in the evolution of animals was the move from a one-opening to a two-opening digestive system. An animal such as *Hydra*, with a one-opening digestive system, must eliminate indigestable material through the same opening by which the food entered. Mixing of undigested and indigestable food material occurs, leading to considerable inefficiency in the use of the digestive enzymes. A two-opening system avoids this inefficiency. Digestion can proceed in an assembly-line fashion. Such a system is particularly advantageous in the digestion of large and complex food molecules. Proteins, for example, are first broken down into smaller units (proteoses, peptones), which are themselves then broken down into still smaller units, the peptides. The peptides, in turn, are broken down into amino acids. In a two-opening digestive system, the appropriate enzymes are secreted at different points along the route. Thus the enzymes that break large proteins into small proteoses and peptones are secreted near the beginning of the digestive tract. Those enzymes that break the proteoses and peptones down into peptides are secreted further along the digestive tract. The splitting of peptides into amino acids occurs still further along the tract. The human digestive system (Fig. 12–2) demonstrates well the efficient arrangement of digestive organs and glands.

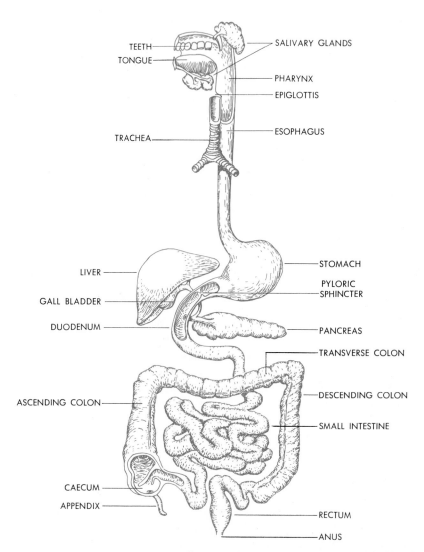

TEETH

TONGUE

TRACHEA

LIVER

GALL BLADDER

DUODENUM

ASCENDING COLON

CAECUM

APPENDIX

SALIVARY GLANDS

PHARYNX

EPIGLOTTIS

ESOPHAGUS

STOMACH

PYLORIC
SPHINCTER

PANCREAS

TRANSVERSE COLON

DESCENDING COLON

SMALL INTESTINE

RECTUM

ANUS

FIG. 12–2  The mammalian digestive system, exemplified here by that of man, is a sort of "assembly line" system. The enzymes secreted by the various organs progressively break down food substances into smaller and smaller molecular subunits.

Although ingested food contains a wide variety of minerals, vitamins, and a few miscellaneous organic compounds, its main bulk is composed of carbohydrate, fat, and protein. The first of these, being a primary source of energy for most organisms, may compose 80% of the diet.

Despite very considerable differences in the molecular structure of carbohydrates, fats, and proteins, the digestion of these three classes of nutrients proceeds by the same chemical process, hydrolysis. The reader will recall from Chapter 7 that hydrolysis involves the chemical addition of a water molecule to key chemical bond linkages. This addition results in the splitting apart of the molecule involved into small units. The process of hydrolysis can be represented diagrammatically as follows:

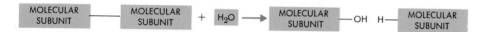

Hydrolysis will proceed spontaneously, releasing a small amount of heat energy as it does so. However, digestive enzymes (a specific one for each reaction) greatly increase the reaction rate, by lowering the energy barrier that must be cleared before the reaction will proceed. Many digestive enzymes are highly specific to the substance on which they work (their **substrate**). **Maltase,** for example, will catalyze only the reaction converting maltose to glucose; **sucrase** will catalyze only the reaction converting sucrose to glucose and fructose.

Even with enzymatic catalysis, however, the hydrolysis reactions of digestion are strongly influenced by the environmental medium of the digestive tract. Like most organic reactions, they have an optimum temperature at which they proceed best. Another important factor is pH. The enzyme **pepsin,** produced in the stomach, works best in a highly acidic environmental medium (about pH 2). The enzyme **trypsin,** secreted into the duodenum by the pancreas, works best in a slightly basic environmental medium (about pH 8).

The end products of digestion must meet two criteria. First, they must be sufficiently soluble to be absorbed and carried by the blood. Second, they must have molecular dimensions sufficiently small to pass through the walls of the digestive tract. In the case of carbohydrates, the final digestive products are generally simple sugars, such as glucose and fructose. With fats, the end products are glycerol and fatty acids. In the case of proteins, the final units are amino acids.

Several glands and other accessory organs are intimately associated with the digestive process. The salivary glands secrete saliva into the mouth. Saliva contains **amylase,** an enzyme that begins the hydrolysis of starch by converting it to the disaccharide maltose. The liver secretes **bile,** which enters the digestive tract (via the gall bladder) at the duodenum. Bile contains salts that have an emulsifying effect on fats. Emulsification separates the large fat droplets into tiny ones, making them readily acceptable to **pancreatic lipase,** the fat-hydrolyzing enzyme produced in the pancreas. Bile salts also increase the water solubility of fatty acids and substances such as vitamin K, necessary for proper clotting of the blood.

The pancreas is perhaps the most versatile digestive gland, for it produces three different enzymes. These are pancreatic lipase, the most important fat-digesting enzyme, amylase, which continues the hydrolysis of starches begun in the mouth, and **trypsinogen,** an inactive form of the enzyme trypsin. Trypsin converts protein, proteoses, and peptones to peptides. (Were the pancreas to produce trypsin, instead of trypsinogen, it would soon digest itself.) The enzyme **enterokinase,** secreted by the intestinal wall, converts trypsinogen to trypsin after it enters the digestive tract via the pancreatic ducts entering the duodenum.

Besides the salivary glands, liver, and pancreas, virtually the entire digestive tract performs glandular functions. From esophagus to anus, mucus is produced in specialized glandular epithelial cells to aid in lubrication, thus reducing friction between the food masses and the walls of the digestive tract. The stomach wall secretes hydrochloric acid (which destroys bacteria, dissolves minerals, and establishes the optimum pH for pepsin activity), **pepsinogen** (which, when converted by hydrochloric acid into the active enzyme pepsin, begins the digestion of proteins, converting them to the next-smaller molecular units, proteoses and/or peptones), and **rennin** (which curds milk proteins). To complete the digestive process, the small intestine produces many other enzymes besides enterokinase.

The small intestine is also the principal region of food absorption. With rare exceptions (alcohol is one), no foods are absorbed by the stomach. Chemical analysis of material extracted from the first few feet of the small intestine shows considerable amounts of nutrient materials still present; the same analysis run on material taken from the last few feet of the small intestine shows virtually none. The final task of the digestive tract, then, appears not to be concerned with digestion, but rather with the preparation of indigestible materials for elimination. This is primarily the role of the colon, or large intestine. Here, most of the water is reabsorbed into the blood stream. The remaining material consists mostly of bacteria and indigestible materials, such as cellulose. Bacteria are found in large numbers in the colon, where they find a suitably warm, moist, and dark environment in which to live. These bacteria may actually benefit their host by producing vitamins which can be absorbed and utilized.

The relationship of bacteria and cellulose in the stomachs of herbivorous ruminant animals, such as cattle, is an important one. The bacteria found there produce **cellulases,** enzymes capable of splitting cellulose into the monosaccharide units of which it is composed. Thus the bulk of the plant material on which these animals feed can be assimilated into their body matter, and from there, perhaps, to our own. Without these herbivorous animals—or better, without their bacteria—the vast source of energy available from plant cellulose would go virtually untapped.

**12–4
DIGESTION:
TECHNIQUES OF
STUDY**

Research on digestion spans many years. During the time of the American Revolution, the Italian scientist Spallanzani was using himself as a guinea pig to study digestion in the stomach. He swallowed small wire cages into which he had placed sponges. He retrieved the cages by means of attached strings, after the sponges had had time to soak up the gastric juice. Spallanzani found that this juice would digest the lean portions of meat (protein).

As with most systems, knowledge of the anatomy of the digestive system was acquired through dissection. Digestive physiology, however, is not so easily attacked. Information gathered from clinical reports is, of course, quite helpful. But controlled experiments can be carried out only on nonhumans, and it is often necessary to extrapolate knowledge gained from such studies to the human situation.

It was early noted by digestive physiologists that when a hungry animal is exposed to food, its stomach begins to secrete gastric juice. What factors initiate this gastric secretion? It is reasonable to hypothesize that the nervous system of the animal that sights or smells the food causes involuntary impulses to be relayed to the stomach, which then begins to secrete gastric juice. Working with dogs, the Russian physiologist Pavlov experimentally tested the nerve-impulse hypothesis as an explanation for stomach gastric-juice secretion:

*Hypothesis:* *If . . .*   gastric-juice secretion is due to impulses from the nervous system, . . .

*Prediction:* *then . . .* severing the nerves leading to the stomach should cause a cessation of gastric-juice secretion.

Yet, after the nerves were cut, gastric-juice secretion was only reduced to three-fourths of its previous amount. The hypothesis had therefore to be modified; evidently the nervous system exercises only partial control over gastric-juice secretion.

What other factors might play a role in initiating the secretion of gastric juices? Pavlov hypothesized that a hormone might be involved. He reasoned that entry of food into the stomach might cause the liberation of a hormone into the bloodstream. This hormone might act with the gastric nerves supplying the stomach to stimulate gastric-juice secretion. An ingenious experiment was designed:

*Hypothesis:* *If . . .*   a hormone is released into the bloodstream to act with the gastric nerves in stimulating gastric-juice secretions, . . .

*Prediction:* *then . . .* blood circulating from a dog which has just been fed into a dog which has not been fed should cause gastric-juice secretion in the second animal.

Two dogs, one just fed, were anesthetized and their bloodstreams joined. The prediction of the hypothesis was verified; the second dog secreted gastric juice. Since the second dog's nervous system would not be involved in its secretion of gastric juice, it would be predicted that only 75% of the normal secretion would be produced. This prediction was also verified.

How do we know that it is not some absorbed product of digestion that is causing gastric-juice secretion? If this were the case, the injection of such products into the bloodstream would initiate gastric-juice secretion. It doesn't. On the other hand, when extracts of the gastric lining on which protein digestion products have acted are injected into the bloodstream, they cause gastric-juice secretion in the stomach. This result is consistent with Pavlov's hypothesis. So, too, is an experiment in which a piece of the stomach wall is transplanted, with blood vessels intact, to the skin of the same organism. The transplant begins to secrete gastric juice soon after proteinaceous substances are placed into the stomach.

Later work showed that when food enters the stomach, a hormone (**gastrin**), is produced by glandular cells in the stomach wall. The gastrin is released into the blood, by means of which it travels all over the body. When it returns to the stomach, it stimulates the gastric glands to secrete gastric juice.

Needless to say, no such laboratory experiments have been performed on human beings. Yet, few would doubt that gastrin plays a similar role in human digestive physiology. Perhaps now is as good a time as any to insert a few words in defense of biologists against antivivisectionist claims that such experiments constitute cruelty to animals. Antivivisectionists would no doubt have protested the carrying out of this experiment by Pavlov. It is meaningless to cite the obvious benefits to human beings which accrue from the understanding of such physiological phenomena as gastric secretion, for the antivivisectionist feels that the benefits gained to man do not justify the use of other animals in experiments such as Pavlov's. It is in the charges of cruelty to animals that the antivivisectionist treads on weak ground; by making the charge, he demonstrates an ignorance of the very methods of science. Indeed, an experiment such as that performed by Pavlov is absolutely dependent on keeping the animals in a condition which is as close to their natural state as possible; any discomfort experienced is a variable which could profoundly influence the results. For purely academic reasons, then (to say nothing of humanitarian ones), the possible presence of pain in such experiments is a variable which the experimental physiologist often spends considerable time and effort to eliminate.

From the time it enters the digestive tract until it leaves, food is subjected to a considerable amount of mechanical movement. Some of this movement aids in breaking a swallowed food mass and exposing more of the surface to the digestive juices. Other movements, termed **peristaltic** movements, aid in moving the food mass along the digestive tract. Such movements can be detected either by direct observation of the organs in an animal whose abdominal cavity has been operationally exposed, or by filling the organs with an opaque substance (such as barium sulfate) and viewing them with X-rays. A third technique, which may be used to study peristalsis in either the esophagus or stomach, is to introduce into these organs a partially inflated rubber balloon attached to a hollow tube (Fig. 12–3). Any peristaltic contractions cause an increase in air pressure within the balloon, which can in turn be recorded on a mercury manometer and/or a kymograph.

Much work in the field of digestive physiology has gone into the study of the causes of movement in the organs of the digestive tract. Swallowing, for example, initiates peristalsis in the esophagus. What controls swallowing? Nerves?

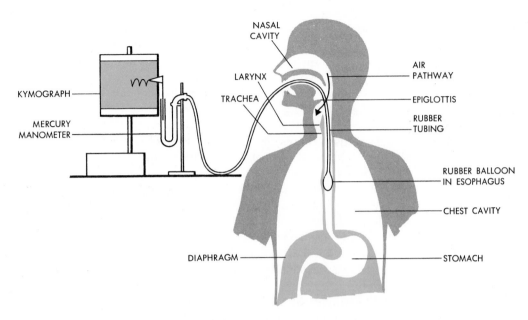

FIG. 12–3  By inserting a partially inflated balloon into the esophagus or stomach, it is possible to obtain quantitative measurements of the contractions of these organs.

Hormones? Or something else? We can begin by hypothesizing the first of these possible causes.

**Hypothesis:** *If . . .*   swallowing is controlled by nerves, . . .

**Prediction:** *then . . .* severing the nerves innervating the swallowing region should prevent swallowing.

The prediction is verified; experimental animals in which the appropriate nerves have been severed are unable to swallow. Clinical observations of human patients deprived of these nerves by accident or disease provide further evidence in support of the nerve hypothesis; such persons are also unable to swallow.

A normal person, of course, can swallow almost at will. This suggests that swallowing is under conscious control of the nervous system (as opposed to an organ like the heart, which is not). Yet, further experimentation casts doubt on this supposition. If the proper nerves are artificially stimulated, swallowing occurs automatically. This indicates that, while swallowing *is* under the control of the nervous system, it is an example of a **reflex** action, i.e., it is not necessarily under the control of the brain.

The act of swallowing is far more complex than might be thought. It involves muscles of the tongue, mouth, pharynx, larynx, and esophagus, each of which must relax and contract at the proper time and in the correct sequence.

The anatomy of the upper digestive tract seems, at first, to be designed for asphyxiation! The opening of the trachea is larger than that of the esophagus, and it would seem that swallowed food would more easily pass into it. Yet, "swallowing the wrong way" is a relatively rare occurrence. Anatomical examination of human cadavers and experimental animals reveals the presence of a flap (the **epiglottis**) which, when folded downward, effectively blocks the opening to the trachea. It is reasonable to hypothesize, then, that during swallowing, the epiglottis performs this function. Studies of the swallowing reflex in anesthetized animals support this hypothesis. But since the lowering of the epiglottis is a rather mechanical process, we might suspect that a more reliable safeguard against the possibility of food entering the respiratory tract must have evolved, especially in light of the fact that even a piece of food too small to cause choking could nevertheless initiate a serious bacterial infection in the respiratory system. Another explanation for the rarity of this occurrence must be sought.

It is known that swallowing is a reflex action involving certain nerves; therefore, it is reasonable to hypothesize that the same nerves that initiate the swallowing reflex also send to the respiratory center in the brain impulses which inhibit breathing while the food is passing the tracheal opening. Such an hypothesis can readily be tested by experiment.

**Hypothesis:** *If* . . .   the swallowing reflex involves the sending of impulses to the brain which inhibit breathing, . . .

**Prediction:** *then* . . . continued stimulation of those nerves that cause the swallowing reflex in an anesthetized animal should continue to prevent its breathing, even when the epiglottis is prevented from closing the opening into the trachea.

The experimental results support this hypothesis.

Since we know the active role played by nerves in the upper digestive tract, it is reasonable to hypothesize that similar roles are played by the nerves supplying the lower digestive tract. Anatomically, the stomach and intestines are supplied with two sets of nerves. Experimental stimulation of one set of nerves in anesthetized animals results in increased activity of the stomach and intestines; peristalsis and other characteristic churning movements increase. Stimulation of the other set of nerves tends to inhibit these movements. These preliminary observations support the hypothesis that the role of the nerves in this region is the same as that of the nerves of the pharyngeal-esophageal region. To adequately test this hypothesis, however, a crucial experiment must be performed:

**Hypothesis:** *If* . . .   the movements of the stomach and intestines are entirely controlled by nerves as are those movements of the swallowing reflex, . . .

***Prediction:*** *then* . . . severing all the nerves leading to the stomach and intestines should prevent these movements from recurring.

The experimental results contradict the hypothesis. Despite cutting of the nerves, digestive movements (slightly modified) still occur. Even isolated strips of intestine will continue to contract when placed in a proper medium. Thus the movements in this area must be controlled in a manner quite different from those of, say, the upper esophagus. In view of the rather unique structure and properties of smooth muscles (see Section 12–2), perhaps this is not too surprising.

Microscopic dissection reveals partial answers to the questions posed by these experimental results. The walls of the stomach and intestines contain vast complexes of interconnected nerve cells. Such complexes are also found in the body walls of certain primitive animals. Despite the fact that these animals have no brain whatsoever, nor any central nervous system, their body walls are capable of rhythmic contractions. It seems reasonable to hypothesize that a similar kind of control system is involved in the movement of the stomach and intestines of higher animals. Although, theoretically, experiments can be designed to test this hypothesis, it is not yet possible to separate the nerve network from the smooth muscles of the stomach and intestinal walls without damaging the latter beyond the ability to contract. Here is an example (one of many) in which the crucial test of an hypothesis must await development of new experimental techniques and technical skills.

The passage of food from the stomach into the duodenum poses another problem for the digestive physiologist. The pyloric valve consists of a ring-shaped muscle (**sphincter muscle**). When the muscle is contracted, the contents of the stomach are effectively blocked from entering the duodenum. When the stomach is full, the pyloric valve opens intermittently, allowing a spurt of semiliquid food material to enter the duodenum.* It is obviously important to the accomplishment of adequate gastric digestion that the pyloric sphincter remain closed most of the time. Also, it is obviously important that the valve open occasionally to let the digestive processes of the lower tract proceed. The question then arises: What factors control the opening and closing of the pyloric sphincter?

Preliminary experimental observations reveal the following facts:

1) The physical nature of the stomach contents influences the opening and closing of the pyloric valve. Water passes out of the stomach into the duodenum within ten minutes or less after being swallowed. Solid foods, on the other hand, may still be in the stomach five hours after being swallowed.

2) The strength of the stomach's peristaltic contractions seems to be an influencing factor. Weak stomach contractions have little effect, but a powerful

12–5
AN OPEN-AND-SHUT
CASE

---

* The reader may recall the sequence of events (established by the experiments of Bayliss and Starling and described in Chapter 4) that occur when food from the stomach contacts the duodenal wall.

wave of peristaltic contractions opens the sphincter just before the wave of contraction reaches the valve.

3) There is a considerable difference in pH between the digestive tract medium on the gastric side of the pyloric valve and that on the intestinal side. As mentioned earlier, the former is quite acid, about pH 2. The latter is slightly basic, between pH 7 and 8. These pH ranges correlate with the optimum range of efficiency for the protein-digesting enzymes. When acid is introduced into the duodenum just beyond the sphincter, the valve closes. When a basic solution is introduced in the same region, the valve opens.

These observations (particularly the last) suggest an attractive hypothesis concerning the controlling factors that open and close the pyloric valve. Strong peristaltic movements of the intestine force open the valve. This allows an acidic fluid to spurt through into the duodenum, closing the valve. Gradually, however, the acidic fluid is neutralized by the basic bile and pancreatic juice. Thus the sphincter muscle relaxes and the pyloric valve opens again. More acidic fluid spurts through, and the cycle is repeated. This is a nice, simple hypothesis, one that seems well in accord with what is known about the digestive system.

The philosopher Alfred North Whitehead once wrote, "Seek simplicity and distrust it." This statement is highly pertinent to scientific hypotheses in general, and to the one last cited in particular. It is an attractive hypothesis and, probably for this reason, has persisted. Science, however, is a suspicious discipline. More experiments show that acidic substances do, indeed, cause the pyloric valve to close, but so do strong bases; so, in fact, does almost any stimulation of the duodenal epithelial lining. Furthermore, many apparently normal persons secrete no acid at all in their stomach juices, yet their pyloric valves appear to operate normally. This of course contradicts the "nice, simple" hypothesis mentioned above.

The precise manner by which the opening and closing of the pyloric valve is controlled remains unknown. It seems likely, however, that the first two factors described above—the consistency of the stomach contents and the strength of stomach peristalsis—are more important than any pH factors that may be involved.

**12–6**
**HUNGER AND**
**THIRST**

The problems of hunger are intimately involved with the problems of digestive physiology. What is hunger? What causes hunger pangs?

Experiments on human subjects provide some answers to the last question. By the technique diagrammed in Fig. 12–3, stomach contractions of a subject can be measured and recorded on a kymograph. The subject, who cannot see the kymograph, presses a button whenever he feels hunger pangs. Almost inevitably, the pangs occur when the kymograph is recording strong stomach contractions. These results support an hypothesis attributing the cause of hunger pangs to stomach contractions.

Other observations also support this hypothesis. An empty stomach undergoes periods of quiescence in which no strong contractions occur. During such quiescent periods no hunger pangs occur.

If hunger pangs are due to stomach-wall contractions, there should be a limit to their intensity, the limit being set by the strength of the stomach-wall muscles. Hunger pangs should be no stronger after two weeks of fasting than after a two-day fast. This prediction is verified by a compilation of experimental data, plus records of the experiences of those deprived of food by being marooned or imprisoned.

It seems fairly certain, then, that the hypothesis attributing the cause of hunger pangs to stomach contractions is a correct one. However, hypotheses explaining the *causes* of the stomach contractions are on far less firm ground. The contractions do not depend on nerves, for they still occur after the gastric nerves are cut. The sugar content of the blood may be hypothesized as an influencing factor. In favor of this hypothesis are experimental data showing that when blood-sugar levels are reduced by a sizable extent, hunger pangs are initiated. Against this hypothesis can be gathered evidence to show that the fluctuations occurring in the mammalian eating cycle are very slight. Furthermore, hunger often sets in before the food ingested at the last meal is completely absorbed, an observation which does away with the "reasonableness" of the blood-sugar hypothesis.

Most puzzling is the fact that experimental methods can detect no difference between the stomach contractions that cause hunger pangs and those that occur during the end of gastric digestion, yet the latter contractions are not felt at all. To date, this puzzle remains unsolved. It is virtually certain that brain regions are involved in the hunger-eating patterns of mammals. A cat which has been fed to capacity will continue to eat if a certain region of its brain is stimulated electronically. On the other hand, a cat which has been deprived of food will not eat if a different region of its brain is stimulated.

Thirst presents another problem in digestive physiology. Physiologically speaking, water deprivation is far more serious than food deprivation. A man can live considerably longer than a month without food, but only ten days or less without water. Furthermore, unlike hunger, thirst is not intermittent, and it becomes progressively more uncomfortable. It may even be quite painful.

Certainly everyone has experienced at least a mild thirst. From this experience an hypothesis has been proposed to explain thirst on the basis of a dryness of the throat. A lowering of the water content of the body tissues in general causes a lessening in the amount of saliva secreted (saliva is mostly water). Thus the mouth and throat become dry, causing the thirst.

It is certain, however, that dryness of the throat tissue alone does not cause thirst as long as other body tissues are adequately supplied with water. Furthermore, a dog with no salivary glands drinks no more water than a normal one. A more satisfactory hypothesis to explain thirst is thus called for.

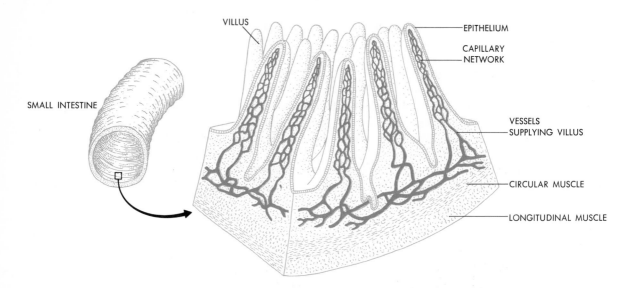

SMALL INTESTINE

VILLUS

EPITHELIUM

CAPILLARY
NETWORK

VESSELS
SUPPLYING VILLUS

CIRCULAR MUSCLE

LONGITUDINAL MUSCLE

FIG. 12–4    Villi greatly increase the surface absorption area of the small intestine.

**12-7
ABSORPTION**

Just as a finger in the hole of a doughnut cannot truly be said to be *inside* the doughnut, so food in the digestive tract of a mammal cannot truly be said to be inside the mammal; the food must first pass through the walls of the digestive tract by processes known generally as **absorption.**

It is easy to imagine how such an absorption could take place. Microscopic examination of the intestinal wall reveals it to be composed of tiny, fingerlike projections (**villi**), each supplied with vessels for the circulation of blood and lymph (see Glossary). The presence of villi greatly increases the surface area of the small intestine, making it ideally suited for food absorption (Fig. 12–4). There is also considerable evidence that the **microvilli,** which cover the surface of the villi, adsorb enzymes onto their surface, thereby greatly increasing their digestive efficiency.

In the small intestine, soluble food materials exist, of course, in high concentration. The blood supplying the intestinal lining would show a considerably lower concentration of digested food materials. According to the simple laws of diffusion and osmosis, soluble food molecules would be expected to pass into the bloodstream, and tracer experiments show that they do. It can be hypothesized that diffusion and osmosis are the only factors responsible for the absorption of foods and minerals from the lower digestive tract. An experiment must then be designed to see whether this hypothesis leads to contradictions.

Loops of the small intestine in experimental animals are tied off from the rest of the digestive tract. In some of the loops (loop A series), a 0.5% concentration of sodium chloride salt is placed (0.5 g NaCl in 100 cc distilled water). In an equal number of other intestinal loops (B), a 1.0% concentration of sodium chloride is placed. In still a third set of loops (C), a 1.5% concentration of sodium chloride is placed. Blood has a sodium chloride concentration of approximately 1.0%. Thus the concentration of sodium chloride in the loop A series is less than that of the blood supplying the intestinal loops. The concentration in the loop B series is the same as that of the blood, and the concentration of loop C series is greater than that of the blood. If an hypothesis proposes that only physical factors of diffusion and osmosis are involved in the absorption of soluble substances through the intestinal wall, it must predict that sodium chloride will not pass into the blood in the loop B series, for there is no concentration gradient in either direction. For the loop C series, the hypothesis would predict some passage of sodium chloride into the blood by diffusion, while water would be drawn from the blood by osmosis. The intestinal loops of series A would lose water to the blood by osmosis, but gain in salt content by diffusion of sodium chloride molecules from the blood.

**TABLE 12–1**   EFFECT OF CONCENTRATION OF SALT ON THE ABSORPTION OF SALT
AND WATER FROM THE INTESTINE

| SOLUTION | NaCl CONCENTRATION, % | PUT INTO INTESTINE | | ABSORBED | |
|---|---|---|---|---|---|
| | | $H_2O$, ml | NaCl, g | $H_2O$, ml | NaCl, g |
| A | 0.5 | 100 | 0.5 | 75 | 0.3 |
| B | 1.0 | 100 | 1.0 | 50 | 0.6 |
| C | 1.5 | 100 | 1.5 | 25 | 1.0 |

Table 12–1 summarizes the results of the experiment. The predictions made by the hypothesis are not verified; there is absorption of sodium chloride into the blood supplying the intestinal loops in all three series. Clearly, diffusion and osmosis alone are not sufficient to explain intestinal absorption. Yet these data do indicate that diffusion and osmosis are at least partly involved, for there is an inverse relationship between the amount of water absorbed from the solutions in the intestinal loops and their sodium chloride concentrations. There is also a direct relationship between the concentration of sodium chloride found in the various solutions and the amount of sodium chloride ultimately appearing in the blood. Both these relationships are predictable on the basis of hypothesized roles of diffusion and osmosis in the absorption process.

If blood serum from an animal is placed in an intestinal loop of the same animal, the serum is soon absorbed. Since this serum would be in perfect concentration with the blood and tissue fluids, an hypothesis proposing that only diffusion and osmosis are involved in digestive-tract absorption would predict that no absorption would occur. Clearly, this hypothesis is no longer tenable.

It is evident that there must be other forces at work in intestinal absorption of digested food. It is thus reasonable to hypothesize that active transport (see Section 6–9) may be involved; the intestinal lining cells may be performing work which results in the movement of substances against the concentration gradient. Histological examination reveals the intestinal lining cells to be of the columnar epithelial type; cytological investigation shows that such cells are liberally supplied with mitochondria. Such features are often characteristic of metabolically active cells. Further support for the active-transport hypothesis comes from the fact that substances pass through the intestinal wall against a concentration gradient only while the intestinal loop is alive. Soon after death, an equilibrium is established between the tissue fluids and the medium inside the loop.

From the observation that sodium chloride is quickly absorbed through the intestinal wall while magnesium sulfate ($MgSO_4$) is not, it is tempting to hypothesize that the intestinal wall acts as a semipermeable membrane; only molecules of the proper dimension are able to pass through it (a molecule of $MgSO_4$ is larger than a molecule of NaCl). Such an hypothesis must be quickly rejected, however; amino acids and glucose have molecules far larger than those of magnesium sulfate, yet are readily absorbed. Thus the problem of intestinal absorption becomes reminiscent of the one first posed in Chapter 6: What factors are involved in the selective passage of substances across plasma membranes? To date, no complete explanation has evolved.

**12-8**
**ELIMINATION**     In man, materials pass through the approximately 20 feet of small intestine in from four to six hours, yet take as much as 24 hours to pass through the four feet of the large intestine, or colon. This fact alone indicates that the role of the large intestine may be an important one. Yet, since chemical analyses of materials entering the large intestine from the small intestine reveal very few nutritive materials left to be absorbed, it seems equally evident that the large intestine is more concerned with unusable rather than usable materials.

Material entering the large intestine is quite watery; upon leaving, it has been formed into damp solid masses called **feces**. It is reasonable to hypothesize, therefore, that the large intestine returns much of the water used in digestion to the bloodstream. Both analytical and tracer experiments support this hypothesis. Tracer experiments also show that the fecal masses contain many of the same substances which were contained in the entering food. Such substances seem not to have been digested or absorbed. In reference to the analogy of the doughnut hole, they never really entered the body.

On the other hand, chemical analyses of fecal material leaving the large intestine reveal the presence of bacterial cell masses and of metallic ions such as calcium. Closer examination of the large intestine and its contents shows that large colonies of bacteria (mostly *Escherichia coli*) live there, metabolizing those food materials missed by the digestive process further up the tract.* This ac-

---

* Recall that in ruminants (e.g., cattle) the presence of bacteria in the stomach makes possible the metabolic utilization of sugars released as a result of the bacterial hydrolysis of cellulose. *E. coli* does not have cellulose-splitting enzymes, however, and thus, in man's diet, this material only adds bulk to the intestinal contents—a factor which may aid in the proper functioning of the large intestine.

counts for the presence of bacterial cell masses in the feces but does not account for the presence of the calcium. However, chemical analysis of blood entering the wall of the large intestine shows a higher concentration of calcium ions than is found in the blood leaving that organ. Evidently, then, the large intestine also removes excess calcium ions from the body, releasing them into the materials that pass through it.

Note, however, that there is a distinct difference between the status of material such as cellulose found in fecal material and that of the calcium ions. The former has never been "inside" the body; it was never a part of the body's metabolism. The calcium ions, however, *were* inside; they are waste-material fragments of body metabolism. In dealing with cellulose, therefore, the large intestine is acting as an organ of **elimination.** In dealing with calcium ions, however, the large intestine is one of several organs of *excretion*, a process which will be dealt with shortly.

12-9
THE TRANSPORT OF
MATERIALS:
CIRCULATION

Putting gasoline into the tank of an automobile does little good if there is no fuel line to convey it to the engine. Similarly, the digestion and absorption of foods is of little value unless the food products involved are distributed to the body cells that need them. The fuel line of a complex organism's body is the **circulatory system,** which is generally composed of the **lymphatic system** and the system that transports the blood.

The mammalian lymphatic system conveys a colorless fluid called **lymph,** composed mostly of blood plasma minus the red blood cells. Throughout most of its travels through the body, lymph simply flows freely between the body cells and tissues, helping to maintain proper osmotic balance. The lymphatic system also plays an important role in the body's defense against infection, for invading bacteria are engulfed by special **phagocytes** (see Glossary) lining the walls of the lymph node sinuses through which the lymph flows (Fig. 12–5).

Considerable amounts of blood plasma proteins pass from the blood into the lymphatic system. This loss would be a serious one were the flow to be all one way. In certain regions of the body, however, the lymph collects into ducts and, propelled mostly by ordinary body muscle movements, passes slowly through them. Special valves permit flow in only one direction. Eventually, lymph pours back into the bloodstream by way of the left subclavian vein of the shoulder region. Thus the plasma proteins are returned to the bloodstream.

The fact that the blood does, indeed, circulate throughout the body has not always been known. Many earlier scientists believed that the blood flowed from the heart through all the blood vessels and then returned through the same vessels, the action being compared to the tides of the sea. It remained for the seventeenth-century physician William Harvey to demonstrate the presence of valves in the veins of the arms, valves which allowed the blood to flow in only one direction. By cutting an artery, Harvey saw that the blood spurted out in a direction away from the heart. A cut vein gave out blood more slowly and steadily in a direction toward the heart. A cut through any large artery or vein could drain virtually all of the blood from the body.

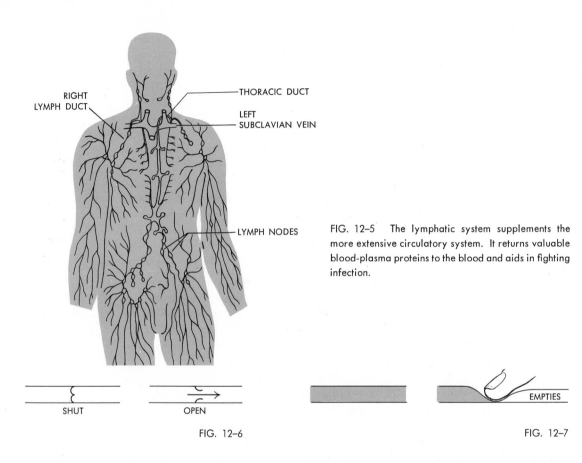

RIGHT LYMPH DUCT

THORACIC DUCT

LEFT SUBCLAVIAN VEIN

LYMPH NODES

FIG. 12–5 The lymphatic system supplements the more extensive circulatory system. It returns valuable blood-plasma proteins to the blood and aids in fighting infection.

SHUT

OPEN

FIG. 12–6

EMPTIES

FIG. 12–7

Harvey's anatomical studies of the heart led to the discovery of its valves, which allow blood to pass through its chambers in only one direction. The direction of flow can easily be established by observing the direction in which the valve opens. The valve in Fig. 12–6 opens toward the right; therefore, blood would flow through it from left to right.

Establishment of the direction of blood flow in a nonvalved blood vessel is even simpler. On blocking a nonvalved blood vessel by the pressure of a finger, one can observe that on one side of that point the blood in the vessel will flow away, leaving the blood vessel flaccid. In Fig. 12–7 this occurs to the right of the point of blockage, therefore the flow of blood must be from left to right.

Harvey's scheme for the circulation of blood through the human heart is shown in Fig. 12–8. This pattern of circulation, which is correct, was deduced by Harvey purely on the basis of his observations. One problem remained, however. If the blood left the heart through arteries and returned through veins, there must be some means for the blood to pass from the former to the latter. By dissection, Harvey could see that the thick-walled arteries became smaller and smaller as they got further from the heart and approached the organ they

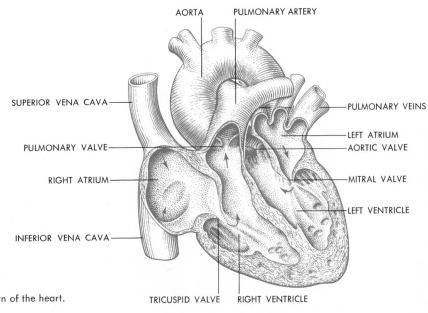

FIG. 12–8    The circulatory pattern of the heart.

FIG. 12–9

supplied. Similarly, he saw that the corresponding veins began as tiny branches of this organ, and gradually united to form the larger vessels entering the heart. But it was not until four years after Harvey's death that Marcello Malpighi discovered the blood capillaries, the link that made Harvey's chain of reasoning complete (Fig. 12–9). The general pattern of blood vessels shown in Fig. 12–9 is repeated in almost every organ or body region supplied by the bloodstream.

**12–10**
**THE HEARTBEAT**

No circulation of the blood is possible, of course, without a driving force. The origin of the forces involved in circulation are the muscular contractions of the heart. A primary problem of circulatory physiology, therefore, is to discover the cause of the heartbeat.

The fact that the heart is supplied with two main nerve trunks makes it reasonable to hypothesize that nerve impulses are the cause of the heartbeat. Preliminary experiments seem to support this hypothesis, for mild electrical stimulation of these nerve trunks in a frog heart speeds up or slows down the rate of the heartbeat, the effect depending on which trunk is stimulated. The crucial experiment is an obvious one.

*Hypothesis: If* . . .    the heartbeat is caused by impulses transmitted from the nervous system, . . .

*Prediction: then* . . . severing of nerves leading to the heart should effectively prevent the heartbeat.

The results of the experiment contradict the hypothesis; the heart continues its rhythmic beating after its nerves are severed.  The cause of the beat must therefore lie within the heart itself.  Further experiments produce another interesting bit of information.  Isolated strips of frog-heart muscle will continue to contract rhythmically.  In tissue culture, microscopically small pieces of heart tissue will continue to beat.  One is tempted to agree with Harvey that "the motion of the heart is to be comprehended only by God."

However, if quantitative measures are made of the degrees to which isolated strips of heart muscle will contract, an interesting fact appears.  Those strips showing the least activity come from the lower region, or apex, of the ventricles. Those showing the most activity come from the upper region of the atria, particularly in the right atrium near the point at which the superior vena cava enters.  Dissection in this region of the heart reveals the presence of a specialized node of tissue (the **sino-auricular node**).  From this node impulses spread into the surrounding atrial muscle.  The atrial muscle conducts impulses throughout the atria and to a second node (the **auricular-ventricular node**).  From the auricular-ventricular node, specialized fibers conduct the impulses to all parts of the ventricles.  When this pattern of branching is compared to the experimental data on the degree of contraction shown by isolated muscle strips, it becomes evident that the cells surrounded by the smallest number of fibers are capable of the smallest amount of automatic contraction.  It would seem, then, that while the nerve tracts leading to the heart are not essential for initiation of the heartbeat, the nerve tissue intrinsic in the heart itself probably is.

This hypothesis, however, defies experimental testing.  In the vertebrate heart, muscle and nerves are too intimately associated to be successfully isolated. We are forced, therefore, to extrapolate experimental results obtained from lower organisms.  The horseshoe crab, *Limulus* (Fig. 12–10), has a heart composed of muscle and nerve which can be separated easily.  We can therefore set up an hypothesis and see whether experimental results support or contradict it.

*Hypothesis: If* . . .    nerve impulses are necessary to initiate the heartbeat in *Limulus*, . . .

*Prediction: then* . . . removal of the nerves from the heart of *Limulus* should cause cessation of the heartbeat.

The hypothesis is supported.  Removal of the nerve tissue of the *Limulus* heart results in an immediate cessation of the heartbeat.

Can the experimental results obtained with *Limulus* be extrapolated to man? Ordinarily such an extrapolation is probably justifiable so long as it is remembered that a point has been stretched, and that we may possibly be wrong.  The direct relationship between the automaticity of various parts of the vertebrate heart and the amount of nerve tissue present in these parts has already been

FIG. 12–10    The heart and supplying nerves of the horseshoe crab can be separated (see text).

mentioned. This relationship tends to strengthen the bridge of reasoning that has been constructed between the heart of *Limulus* and the heart of man. Other considerations, however, rule against it. In man the sino-auricular node acts as the "pacemaker" of the heartbeat and is composed of modified muscle cells rather than nerve tissue. Furthermore, studies of developing chick embryos reveal that their heart muscle tissue begins to beat well before any nerve cells are present. It would seem, then, that automaticity of the heartbeat is an intrinsic feature of heart muscle cells, though the role of controlling the heartbeat may later reside in the heart nerve network.

It is likely that in the vertebrate heart, automaticity remains a feature of the cardiac muscle tissue. Yet, even granting this assumption, there are still several unanswered questions. A heart which has been beating for some time in a calcium-free medium will eventually stop. The addition of more calcium ions results in renewed beating activity. Does this mean that calcium ions are responsible for initiating the heartbeat? Or does it simply mean that calcium ions must be present if the heart is to respond to the true heartbeat initiator? If the latter is the correct interpretation, what *is* this "true" heartbeat initiator? Is it some yet-to-be-discovered hormone? To date, there are no definite answers to these questions, and so we can only continue to hypothesize about the nature of the primary causative agent of the heartbeat.

In Chapter 8 it was seen that respiration—the breakdown of food substances and release of the energy they contain—involves the transferal of electrons from one acceptor molecule to another.  The final electron acceptor eventually passes into the surrounding environment, such as the atmosphere or, perhaps, a liquid culture medium.  In anaerobically respiring yeast cells, for example, the final electron acceptor is pyruvic acid.  In animals, including man, the final acceptor is generally oxygen.

The primary seat of respiration, of course, is the cell.  Therefore, a major problem was the evolutionary development of respiratory exchange mechanisms capable of adequately supplying electron acceptor molecules.  For one-celled animals, this problem is solved by simple diffusion, provided that cell size does not exceed certain critical surface-to-volume ratios.  Even in organisms such as *Hydra*, composed of two cell layers, satisfactory respiratory exchange by diffusion is effected, for all of *Hydra*'s cells have their surfaces at least partially exposed to a constantly changing environmental medium.

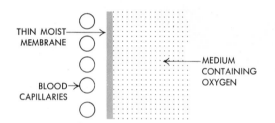

FIG. 12–11   The essential principle of operation for external respiration systems, whether respiration is by tubes, gills, or lungs.

In animals with more than two cell layers, however, more elaborate respiratory exchange mechanisms have evolved.  The earthworm absorbs oxygen and releases carbon dioxide through its skin; the movements of insects pump air directly to their body tissues through finely divided air tubes; fish exchange oxygen and carbon dioxide through gills; most other vertebrates breathe air into saclike lungs, effecting the same exchange.

Despite vast anatomical differences between such external respiratory exchange devices, all contain the same essential features (Fig. 12–11).  In mammals, external respiration involves two main phases.  In one, breathing draws oxygen-containing air into close contact with the damp epithelium of the lung, where respiratory exchange occurs.  In the other phase, oxygen and carbon dioxide are transported to and from the respiring cells.  As we have just seen, this second phase is a primary function of the circulatory system.

A major feature in the evolution of the respiratory system has been an increase in the amount of surface area available for oxygen-carbon dioxide exchange.  In fish and other marine animals, the gills may be finely branched to the point of being feathery in appearance.  The lungs of progressively complex vertebrates show a corresponding increase in the subdivisions of inner lung cavities into smaller and smaller chambers.  The simple, saclike lung of the frog

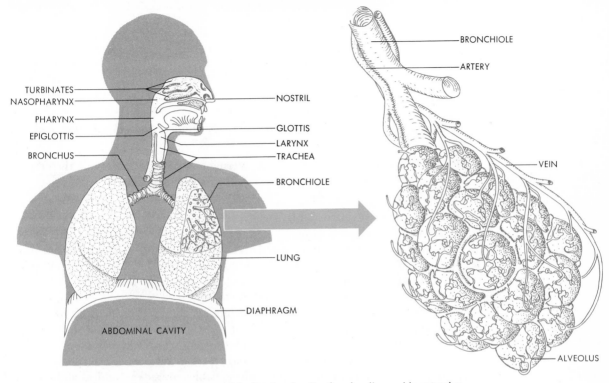

FIG. 12-12  The human respiratory system and its functional units, the alveoli, provide extensive surface area for the exchange of respiratory gases.

(which must be supplemented by cutaneous or skin respiratory exchange) is a far cry from the hundreds of thousands of air sacs (**alveoli**) found in the mammalian lung. In man, it is estimated that the alveoli provide a respiratory exchange surface fifty times greater than the area of the skin.

The basic anatomy of the human respiratory system is shown in Fig. 12-12. In all mammals, a sheetlike layer of muscle, the **diaphragm,** completely encloses the lungs in the **thoracic cavity.** The movements of the diaphragm downward, combined with upward and outward movements of the ribs, serve to enlarge the thoracic cavity. Since the thoracic cavity is closed, with only one external opening (the trachea), this increase in size results in an intake (or **inspiration**) of air from the outside. The lungs, composed of elastic tissue, are stretched by the increased air pressure within them, much like a blown-up balloon. This elasticity results in the elimination of air during **expiration.**

Obviously, not all of the air within the lungs is exhaled at any one expiration. Nor is all the oxygen removed from the air before it leaves the body. The amount of oxygen that *is* removed, however, and the amount of carbon dioxide eliminated, are well within the quantities required by the organism. Should exercise call for additional oxygen, the quantity of air entering the lungs can be increased by faster breathing rate or by deeper inhalation.

Anyone who has tried it knows that the rate of breathing can, within certain limits, be voluntarily controlled. This fact alone is justification for an hypothesis attributing full responsibility for breathing control to the nervous system.

> **Hypothesis:** *If . . .*    breathing is entirely under control of the nervous system, . . .
>
> **Prediction:** *then . . .*    experimental severing of the nerves supplying the breathing muscles should prevent breathing.

This hypothesis is supported by the experimental results: the breathing muscles of an animal in which the appropriate nerves have been severed are immediately paralyzed and unable to function. Obviously, respiratory muscle does not have the intrinsic ability to contract that is shown by cardiac muscle—a fact which might have been anticipated, given the knowledge that breathing can be controlled voluntarily, while the heartbeat cannot.

Several muscles are involved in breathing, of course. This leads us to suspect that somewhere there may be a respiratory control center, either in the brain itself or in the nerves innervating the breathing muscles. Successive experiments, involving the severing of nerve fibers and tracts in various regions, pinpoint the medulla of the brain as the locus of this control center. Anatomical and physiological experiments indicate that this center sends out periodic impulses along the respiratory nerves to initiate the sequence of events leading to inspiration.

It is reasonable to wonder what causes the cells of the respiratory center to send out these impulses. Preliminary investigation reveals that electrical stimulation of the vagus nerve fibers innervating the lungs inhibits the respiratory center; the breathing movements temporarily cease. Further investigation reveals that the same effect can be achieved by inflating the lungs. This observation leads to a promising hypothesis: Possibly the inflation of the lungs during normal inspiration causes a stretching or pressure which stimulates the vagus nerve fibers to send inhibitory impulses to the respiratory center. With the cessation of impulses from the respiratory center, inspiratory muscles would relax, leading to expiration. The resultant collapse of the lungs at expiration would cause a cessation of impulses along the vagus nerve to the respiratory center, thus freeing it to initiate another inspiration-expiration cycle.

Two experiments can be performed to test this hypothesis:

> **Hypothesis:** *If . . .*    impulses from the vagus nerve, initiated by lung inflation, are responsible for suppressing the impulses relayed from the respiratory control center, thus causing the muscle that controls inspiration to relax, . . .
>
> **Prediction:** *then . . .*    instruments designed to detect nerve impulses should register such impulses when the lungs are inflated during inspiration.

This prediction is verified; as soon as the lungs become inflated at inspiration, the instrument detects impulses traveling along the vagus nerve toward the respiratory center.

The same hypothesis leads to another interesting prediction:

*Hypothesis: If . . .*    impulses from the vagus nerve, initiated by lung inflation, are responsible for suppressing the impulses relayed from the respiratory control center, thus causing the muscle that controls inspiration to relax, . . .

*Prediction:*    *then . . .* severing the vagus nerve should result in a continuation of inspiration.

Within certain limits, this prediction is also verified. When the nerve trunk is severed, the vagus nerve impulses are unable to reach the center; thus the inspiratory muscles continue to contract and a long drawn-out breath results. The muscles do not *remain* contracted, however; eventually they relax and expiration occurs. This leads us to conclude that, while the vagus nerve normally affects the timing of impulses from the respiratory center in the medulla, the center also contains an intrinsic rhythm of impulse initiation which is independent of vagus nerve influences.

It is impossible to commit suicide by holding the breath. Ultimately, the respiratory center takes over involuntary control, and breathing resumes. The renewed breathing occurs at an increased rate and depth. It is reasonable to hypothesize that these increases may compensate for the oxygen starvation which results from holding the breath. This hypothesis is supported when we observe that the breathing slowly returns to normal, presumably because the oxygen deficiency no longer exists.

It is a simple step from such observations to an hypothesis of a chemical basis for the control of breathing, operating in conjunction with the nervous control just established. Either decreased breathing or increased muscular activity (such as in exercise) causes an oxygen deficiency in the blood, as well as an increase in the waste products of muscular activity, primarily carbon dioxide. Either a decrease in oxygen or an increase in carbon dioxide could affect the respiratory center as the blood circulated through it. But which one?

To determine this, we must experimentally increase the concentration of one, while keeping the concentration of the other constant. Oxygen is a promising first choice. Since the result of breathing is bringing oxygen and the body cells into close contact, it is reasonable to hypothesize that the rate of breathing may be related to the degree of oxygen deficiency shown by these cells. Thus as the concentration of oxygen in the blood decreases, the respiratory control center causes the rate of breathing to increase. Conversely, the higher the oxygen content of the blood, the slower the breathing rate. According to this hypothesis,

**12-13
BREATHING:
A CHEMICAL
BASIS?**

then, the relationship between the rate of breathing and the concentration of oxygen in the blood is an inverse one.

If a person breathes into a plastic bag for a few minutes, his breathing rate gradually increases. This is consistent with an hypothesis proposing oxygen as the agent whose concentration in the blood affects the breathing rate, for as breathing into the bag continues, the oxygen supply is gradually depleted. This experiment does not adequately test the oxygen hypothesis, however, for the concentration of carbon dioxide in the blood is also increasing; it may be the increase in carbon dioxide, rather than the decrease in oxygen, which is affecting the breathing rate.

A slight modification of this experiment, however, is sufficient to eliminate the carbon dioxide variable. The exhaled and inhaled air is allowed to pass over calcium hydroxide, which removes the carbon dioxide. Now the oxygen hypothesis can be adequately tested:

**Hypothesis:** *If . . .*    oxygen concentration of the blood affects the breathing rate, . . .

**Prediction:** *then . . .* breathing into a plastic bag containing calcium hydroxide (for removal of carbon dioxide) should cause an increase in breathing rate.

The prediction is not verified; no increase in breathing rate occurs.\* Evidently, then, it is the increase in the concentration of carbon dioxide in the blood rather than any decrease in oxygen concentration which influences the breathing rate, for the rate *is* increased by breathing into the bag when the carbon dioxide is allowed to accumulate. Further supporting evidence comes from experiments in which individuals are provided with above-normal amounts of oxygen, and only a slight excess of carbon dioxide. Since the excess oxygen increases the oxygen concentration of the blood, the hypothesis that there is an inverse relationship between oxygen concentration and breathing rate predicts that the breathing rate will slow down. Instead, it increases. This result is consistent with the alternative hypothesis proposing a *direct*, rather than inverse, relationship between carbon dioxide concentration (or possibly the carbonic acid it forms in the blood) and the rate of breathing.

If an anesthetized animal is given a rapid application of artificial respiration, the carbon dioxide concentration of its blood drops to a point well below normal. The result is a complete cessation of breathing activity. This result extends our original hypothesis considerably. Not only does a high concentration of carbon dioxide in the blood increase breathing; a low concentration effectively blocks it. It is intriguing that the body's physiology places such great importance on a compound which is, in essence, a waste product.

We shall return to the subject of breathing control in Chapter 14.

---

\* There may be a slight increase. However, it will not occur until the oxygen concentration is lower than it is when no carbon dioxide absorbant is used.

The forces involved in the movement of oxygen molecules from the alveoli of the lungs into the blood for transport to the body cells can now be considered. At the same time, the forces involved in the movement of carbon dioxide molecules in the reverse direction, i.e., from blood to alveoli, can be investigated.

At first glance, it seems reasonable to equate the absorption of oxygen into the blood in the lungs with the absorption of digested food substances in the small intestine. Here, recall, diffusion was only a small part of the story, with the greater portion of the absorptive process being accomplished by work performed by the intestinal epithelial cells. A histological comparison between the epithelial cells of the intestine and those lining the alveoli throws doubt on this supposition, however. The intestinal epithelial cells are columnar, the epithelial cells of the alveoli, squamous. Furthermore, the intestinal cells are richly supplied with mitochondria; the cells of the alveoli are not. From the general rule in living organisms that structure complements function, it could be concluded that little or no work is performed by the alveoli cells in regard to the movement of oxygen and carbon dioxide across them and hypothesized that only diffusion is involved. This is not an unreasonable hypothesis, since the concentration of oxygen in the blood entering the alveoli would be lower than that of the entering air and, conversely, the concentration of carbon dioxide in the same blood would be higher than that in the air. Concerning carbon dioxide removal from the blood to the alveolar air, the alternative active transport hypothesis is further weakened when it is noted that the concentration of carbon dioxide in the alveolar air is less than in the blood, instead of *vice versa*, as the hypothesis would predict. Indeed, experimentally increasing the concentration of carbon dioxide in the alveolar air actually results in a movement of carbon dioxide molecules *back into the blood*, with a resulting increase in breathing rate. Evidently, the alveoli cells can neither concentrate carbon dioxide in the alveoli nor move it against a diffusion gradient. Diffusion must, therefore, at least be primarily responsible for the movement of carbon dioxide molecules from blood to alveoli during normal respiratory activity.

Similar experiments carried out in the capillaries show that diffusion is also responsible for the movement of oxygen from the blood into the body cells and the movement of carbon dioxide in the reverse direction.

Although both oxygen and carbon dioxide will dissolve in water (which constitutes 90% of the blood plasma), they will do so only within certain limits. Yet, analysis of the oxygen or carbon dioxide content of the blood reveals amounts of these substances far in excess of those limits. Quite obviously, both oxygen and carbon dioxide must be present in the blood in another form in addition to the dissolved state.

Chemical analysis of blood provides confirmation of this. The oxygen in blood exists mostly in chemical combination with hemoglobin within the red blood cells. This chemical combination is weak enough to allow the hemoglobin to release the bound oxygen to the body cells. Carbon dioxide is found in both the plasma and the red blood cells, mostly in the form of bicarbonate ions ($HCO_3^-$).

**12-14**
**GAS EXCHANGE**
**IN THE LUNGS**

**12-15**
**RESPIRATORY**
**GASES IN**
**THE BLOOD**

The chemical reaction uniting oxygen and hemoglobin can be expressed as:

$$\underset{\text{HEMOGLOBIN}}{\text{Hb}} \quad + \quad \underset{\substack{\text{OXYGEN} \\ \text{(4 MOLECULES)}}}{4O_2} \quad \rightleftharpoons \quad \underset{\text{OXYHEMOGLOBIN}}{\text{Hb}(O_2)_4.}$$

This reversible reaction can be studied easily outside of the body, in a test tube. Hemoglobin is purplish in color; oxyhemoglobin a bright red.

Although it is obviously advantageous to the organism to have hemoglobin combine easily with oxygen in the lungs, yet release the oxygen in the capillaries, we might well ask *why* the reversible reaction behaves so conveniently. By exposing given samples of blood to various concentrations of oxygen, it can be determined that the amount of oxyhemoglobin formed is directly related to the concentration of oxygen present. Further, it can be shown that the amount of oxyhemoglobin present in a blood sample is reduced if the sample is placed in air from which most of the oxygen has been removed. Thus it can be concluded that the oxygen-hemoglobin reaction, like most biochemical reactions, undergoes equilibrium shifts to either the right or left whenever the concentration of reactants or products is changed. Thus in the lungs, where oxygen concentration is high, the reaction is strongly shifted to the right; that is,

$$Hb + 4O_2 \underset{\longleftarrow}{\rightharpoonup} Hb(O_2)_4.$$

In the body tissues, where the oxygen concentration is low, the reaction is strongly shifted to the left; that is,

$$Hb + 4O_2 \underset{\longleftarrow}{\rightharpoondown} Hb(O_2)_4,$$

and the released oxygen is free to diffuse through the capillary walls into oxygen-poor cells.

## 12-16 PARTIAL PRESSURE AND TENSION

The relationships of high oxygen concentration to oxyhemoglobin formation and low oxygen concentration to oxyhemoglobin dissociation may seem quite adequate to explain the transport of oxygen from the lungs to the body tissues. However, a bit of reflection casts doubt on this assumption. The oxygen in the alveolar air is in the form of a gas, and diffuses as such. To enter the blood, the oxygen must dissolve, and thus diffuse as a dissolved substance. In chemical combination with hemoglobin, the oxygen is essentially nondiffusible, for hemoglobin is confined within the red blood cells. Thus it is not sufficient just to consider the percentage concentration of oxygen in cases in which the oxygen diffuses from one state to another, such as from a free gas in the alveoli to a dissolved state in the blood plasma.

If the dissolved oxygen content of a body of water is compared with that of the air with which it is in contact, the difference may be as much as 100 to 1, with the air containing the greater amount. Were the physical factors the same in the liquid and gaseous state, equal amounts of oxygen would be expected in both air and water. But the physical factors are *not* the same. There are limits,

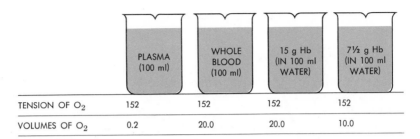

| | PLASMA (100 ml) | WHOLE BLOOD (100 ml) | 15 g Hb (IN 100 ml WATER) | 7½ g Hb (IN 100 ml WATER) |
|---|---|---|---|---|
| TENSION OF $O_2$ | 152 | 152 | 152 | 152 |
| VOLUMES OF $O_2$ | 0.2 | 20.0 | 20.0 | 10.0 |

FIG. 12–13   The concepts of partial pressure and tension must be considered in the formulation of any hypothesis dealing with the exchange of oxygen and carbon dioxide in the alveoli. Note the importance of hemoglobin to the amount of oxygen which enters the water.

for example, to the amount of oxygen which can be dissolved in water, limits dependent in turn on such physical factors as temperature and pressure.

To deal with these variable factors effectively, the physiologist calls on the concept of **partial pressures** of a gas in mixture with other gases. The concept of partial pressures can be expressed in an equation as shown below.

$$\text{PARTIAL PRESSURE GAS } a = \frac{\substack{\text{NO. OF PARTICLES} \\ \text{OF GAS } a}}{\substack{\text{TOTAL NO. OF GAS} \\ \text{PARTICLES IN MIXTURE}}} \times \substack{\text{TOTAL PRESSURE OF} \\ \text{ALL GASES IN THE MIXTURE}}$$

Thus the partial pressure of oxygen in the atmosphere at sea level (760 mm Hg) is $\frac{1}{5} \times$ 760 mm Hg (since oxygen composes about one-fifth of the atmosphere), or 152 mm Hg. Partial pressure, then, gives a numerical value for the amount of any given gas in a mixture of gases, such as the amount of oxygen or carbon dioxide in the atmosphere.

If the concept of partial pressure is to be of physiological value, it must be equated with a measure of the same gas that is in solution, such as oxygen dissolved in blood plasma, or in combination in a solution, such as the oxygen in oxyhemoglobin (Fig. 12–13). Such a measure is referred to as the **tension** of a gas. The tension of a given gas in solution is expressed numerically in terms of the partial pressure of the same gas with which it is in equilibrium. Equilibrium in this case refers to the point at which the number of gas molecules changing from the gaseous to the dissolved state is equal to the number changing from the dissolved to the gaseous state. Note that such an equilibrium by no means implies that the concentration of dissolved oxygen is equal to the concentration of oxygen in the gaseous state.

The concepts of partial pressure and tension give us parameters by which the transport of oxygen and carbon dioxide by the blood can be more readily understood. For example, experimental measurements reveal that the actual concentration of oxygen in arterial blood is *greater* than its concentration in the alveolar air. Thus any hypothesis that proposes simple diffusion to explain the

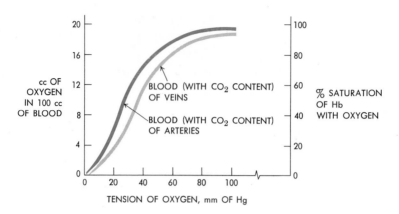

FIG. 12–14  The oxyhemoglobin dissociation curve. Note that at any given oxygen tension, arterial blood contains a greater volume percentage of oxygen than does venous blood.

entry of oxygen into the blood from the alveoli immediately encounters a contradiction. In this case, oxygen obviously does *not* move from a region of greater to lesser concentration. Indeed, it does just the reverse. The oxygen in the blood *does*, however, decrease in partial pressure, or tension, from alveoli to blood to tissues. Thus the concepts of partial pressures and tension, rather than a concept that considers only concentrations, must be incorporated into any hypothesis that explains the transport of oxygen and carbon dioxide to and from the body tissues. When this is done, the hypothesis turns out to be one that leads to experimentally verifiable predictions.

Figure 12–14 shows the **oxyhemoglobin dissociation curve.** This curve expresses the relation between the volume percentage of oxygen held in loose chemical combination with hemoglobin and the tension of oxygen to which the blood is exposed. Two curves are given, one for arterial blood and one for venous blood. Note that at the same oxygen tension, venous blood combines with less oxygen than arterial blood. Experimental investigation reveals that the addition of acid to blood lowers the amount of oxygen it can carry. This fact indicates that yet another factor aids in the dissociation of oxygen from oxyhemoglobin in the capillaries, allowing the oxygen to enter the tissues. Carbon dioxide enters the blood from the tissues in the form of carbonic acid. The increased acidity, in combination with the large difference of oxygen tension which exists between them, provides considerable impetus to the flow of oxygen molecules from blood to tissue.

The transport of carbon dioxide in the blood is different from that of oxygen. Yet, the same factors of partial pressure and tension apply. Some of the carbon dioxide in the blood is simply in a dissolved state, and this is the form in which the gas is released into the alveoli. However, this is but a small amount of the total carbon dioxide content of the blood; most is in the form of bicarbonate. Considerable quantities of dissolved carbon dioxide are converted by an enzyme (carbonic anhydrase) into carbonic acid. Finally, some of the carbon dioxide travels in combination with plasma proteins or with hemoglobin. The reactions bringing about these combinations are reversible. Concentration differences existing in the capillaries or lungs shift these reactions in the appropriate direction, causing them to release the bound carbon dioxide into solution in the blood plasma, and from there, to the alveolar air for exhalation.

An inevitable result of metabolism is the production of waste products. The process by which such waste products are removed from an organism's body is termed **excretion**. The lungs, therefore, are excretory organs which excrete carbon dioxide and water into the alveolar air, the colon is an excretory organ which excretes excess calcium and iron into the fecal material passing through it, and the liver excretes bile pigments into the duodenum via the bile duct.

In complex animals, the **kidneys** are the principal excretory organs. Within the kidneys are excreted the vast majority of the nitrogenous wastes of protein catabolism. Without kidneys, man and other complex animals would die from the accumulation of these highly poisonous wastes.

The possession of kidneys is by no means universal in the animal world, however. As with the circulatory and respiratory systems, only animals with cells that are not exposed to a surrounding watery environment have a need for any excretory system at all. A "need" for an excretory system, of course, does not result in its evolution. Natural selection favors any variation allowing a multicellular organism to eliminate its waste products more effectively. The accumulation of such variations over long periods of time would lead to the development of a complex excretory system, such as that found in mammals.

In Chapter 8 it was seen that amino acids may enter the main pathways of animal metabolism. When this occurs, the amino acids are **deaminated;** i.e., their amino groups are removed. Deamination occurs by the following two-step reaction (the R stands for the group of atoms characteristic of each kind of amino acid):

$$
1) \quad R-\underset{\underset{NH_2}{|}}{\overset{\overset{COOH}{/}}{CH}} \quad + \tfrac{1}{2}O_2 \rightleftharpoons R-\underset{\underset{NH}{\|}}{\overset{\overset{COOH}{/}}{C}} \quad + H_2O,
$$

$$
2) \quad R-\underset{\underset{NH}{\|}}{\overset{\overset{COOH}{/}}{C}} \quad + H_2O \rightleftharpoons R-\underset{\underset{O}{\|}}{\overset{\overset{COOH}{/}}{C}} \quad + NH_3.
$$

Suppose, for example, that the amino acid involved in the above reaction is alanine. In alanine, the R group is a methyl group, $CH_3$. Thus the product of the

above reaction is

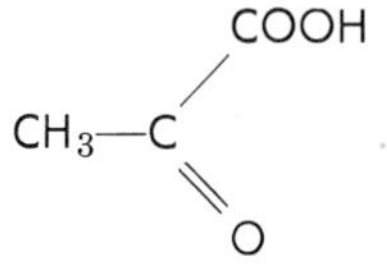

$$CH_3-C \begin{matrix} COOH \\ \\ O \end{matrix}$$

or pyruvic acid. The pyruvic acid may be used as a framework on which to build another amino acid or it may be oxidized to provide energy for ATP synthesis, just as may the pyruvic acid produced by the splitting of glucose in glycolysis (see Section 8–4).

Note, however, that in producing pyruvic acid from an amino acid rather than from glucose, a different waste product, **ammonia** ($NH_3$), is formed. Ammonia is highly soluble, a factor which aids in its transportation. But it is also highly toxic. Thus if it is to be excreted as ammonia, it must be present in the body in a very dilute solution. Large amounts of water must be available and the nitrogenous waste-containing fluid (**urine**) must pass from the body in an almost continuous flow. It is not surprising, therefore, to find that animals that excrete nitrogenous wastes in the form of ammonia are aquatic in habitat, in no danger of dehydration.

Land animals are faced with quite a different situation. Far from having a limitless supply of water surrounding them, they have a distinct problem of conserving water within their bodies. The loss of water necessary to keep the ammonia safely diluted would be fatal. These animals, therefore, convert the ammonia to either **uric acid** or **urea.**

Uric acid ($C_5H_4N_4O_3$) is found in the form of solid crystals. Being insoluble, these crystals can be stored in the body for considerable periods of time. Insects, birds, and reptiles excrete ammonia in the form of uric acid. Since these animals lay their eggs on land, the young must have a way of holding nitrogenous wastes within the egg until hatching; uric acid provides a convenient form, since its insolubility prevents reabsorption. But the insolubility of uric acid provides still another benefit; since it passes out of the body with the feces in a dry, crystalline state, water loss from the body is greatly reduced.

Urea, like ammonia, is highly soluble. However, unlike ammonia, it is not highly toxic unless present in relatively high concentrations. Urea formation is a multistep chemical process which takes place mostly in the liver. Carbon dioxide and the ammonia released by the deamination of amino acids are combined with the compound **ornithine,** as shown below.

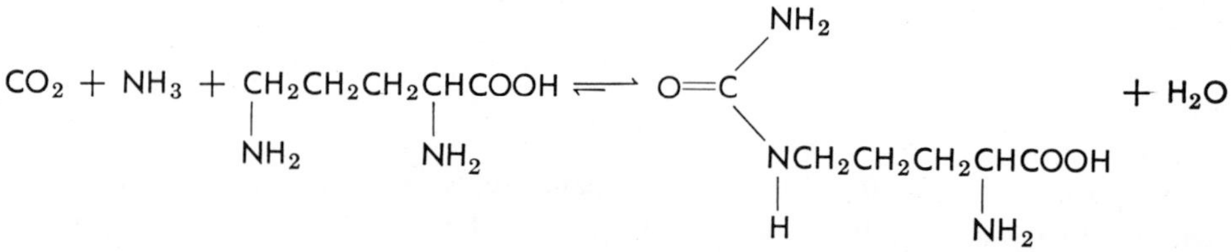

$$CO_2 + NH_3 + \underset{\underset{NH_2}{|}}{CH_2}CH_2CH_2\underset{\underset{NH_2}{|}}{CH}COOH \rightleftharpoons O=C\begin{matrix} NH_2 \\ \\ \underset{\underset{H}{|}}{N}CH_2CH_2CH_2\underset{\underset{NH_2}{|}}{CH}COOH \end{matrix} + H_2O$$

This new compound is **citrulline.** Citrulline, in turn, combines with more ammonia. This reaction also proceeds by dehydration synthesis.

$$O=C\diagdown^{NH_2}_{NCH_2CH_2CH_2CHCOOH}\quad + NH_3 \rightleftharpoons$$

(with the substituents: $O=C$, $NH_2$; $NCH_2CH_2CH_2CHCOOH$ with $H$ below N and $NH_2$ below CHCOOH)

$$HN=C\diagdown^{NH_2}_{NCH_2CH_2CH_2CH_2CHCOOH}\quad + H_2O$$

(with $H$ below N and $NH_2$ below CHCOOH)

This new compound is **arginine.** Arginine then combines with water.

$$HN=C\diagdown^{NH_2}_{NCH_2CH_2CH_2CHCOOH} + H_2O \rightleftharpoons CH_2CH_2CH_2CHCOOH + C\diagup^{NH_2}_{O}$$

(left: $H$ below N, $NH_2$ below CHCOOH; middle: $NH_2$ below CH_2 and $NH_2$ below CHCOOH; right: $C=O$ with $NH_2$)

The two compounds formed are ornithine and urea. The ornithine can be used again in the urea-forming process. Thus the formation of urea affords another good example of a biochemical reaction cycle, reminiscent of the Krebs citric acid cycle discussed in Chapter 8.

From the liver, the urea passes out dissolved in the blood, from which it is filtered and excreted. The carrying out of this filtration and the excretion of the filtrate is the job of a mammalian excretory system. The main filtering organ of this system is the kidney.

12-18
THE KIDNEYS

The anatomical relationship between the kidneys and the rest of the excretory system is shown in Fig. 12–15. In man, the paired kidneys lie in the "small" of the back, just above the hip bones. Urine filtered from the blood by each kidney passes via the ureter to the urinary bladder for temporary storage. The bladder is emptied occasionally, the urine passing to the exterior through the urethra.

Each kidney is supplied with blood by a renal artery, which branches off the aorta. Blood leaves the kidney via the renal vein and passes into the general circulation through the inferior vena cava. In relation to the size of the organ they supply, the renal blood vessels are the largest in the body. More than one-fifth of all the blood in the human body passes through the kidneys every few minutes, thereby ensuring that the concentration of urea does not reach danger-ous proportions.

Viewed in section, the kidneys themselves are seen to consist of an outer **cortex** region and an inner **medullary** region. The latter consists mostly of

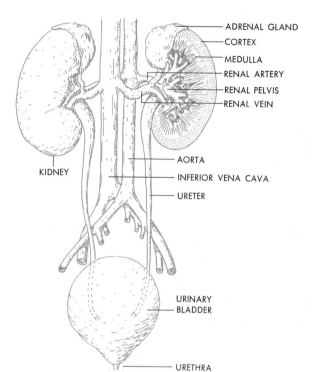

ADRENAL GLAND
CORTEX
MEDULLA
RENAL ARTERY
RENAL PELVIS
RENAL VEIN

KIDNEY

AORTA
INFERIOR VENA CAVA
URETER

URINARY
BLADDER

URETHRA

FIG. 12–15    The human excretory system and its blood vessels.

tubules running from the cortex and emptying into the renal pelvis, a cavity within each kidney leading to the ureter. It is reasonable to conclude from this arrangement that it is in the cortex that the removal of urine from the blood occurs.

Microscopic examination of the cortex supports this conclusion. The tubules of the medullary region, if traced into the cortex, are each seen to originate in a tiny, cuplike structure, **Bowman's capsule.** Each capsule, in turn, surrounds a capillary tuft, or **glomerulus.** Tracing the blood flow backward we find that the glomerular capillaries originate from the renal artery. It is between the glomerulus and Bowman's capsule, then, that the vital removal of urea and other wastes from the blood must take place. Blood leaving the glomerulus, now freed of its waste, eventually passes out of the kidney through the renal vein.

Not directly, however. The venule draining blood from the glomerulus first breaks down into capillaries. These capillaries surround the urinary tubule leading from Bowman's capsule. Shortly after leaving the capsule, this tubule follows a tortuous path, and, at one point, becomes quite thin-walled before continuing as a collecting tubule toward the medullary region. Figure 12–16 shows the relationship of a glomerulus, Bowman's capsule, collecting tubule, and the associated blood vessels. Together, these parts comprise one secreting unit, or **nephron** (of which there are approximately one million in each kidney). It is in the nephrons that the primary work of the kidneys is accomplished.

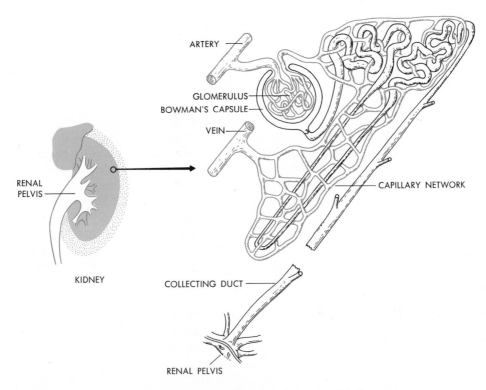

FIG. 12–16   A nephron. More than one million of these tiny filtration units are found in the cortex of each human kidney. Note that the tubule draining Bowman's capsule shows regions of specialization before emptying into a collecting duct.

Histological investigation reveals that the thin walls of Bowman's capsule closely resemble those of the alveoli. When it is recalled that the alveolar lining cells do little or no work in the movement of materials across them, it is reasonable to hypothesize that osmosis and diffusion might be sufficient to accomplish the passage of waste materials from the glomerulus capillaries to the capsule tubules. Filtration would also be involved, of course, since formed elements suspended in the plasma, such as blood cells and platelets, would not pass through the capillary or tubule wall. Nor, normally, would the proteins of which plasma is partially composed.

     The hypothesis can be formulated as follows:

*Hypothesis: If . . .*     the physical processes of osmosis, diffusion, and filtration are primarily responsible for the movements of materials from the glomerulus capillaries to the capsule, . . .

*Prediction: then . . .* the urine in Bowman's capsule should be of the same composition as the blood plasma, less its proteins.

Here is a case in which the testing of an hypothesis had to await the development of technical skills equal to the task of performing the experiment. The cavity within Bowman's capsule is less than 0.1 mm in diameter. The problem of extracting enough fluid for chemical analysis is an immense one. Nevertheless, such an extraction has been made by means of a finely drawn-out quartz tube. As predicted, the capsular fluid has essentially the same composition as the blood plasma, less its proteins.

Thus it appears that the membranes of the glomerular capillaries and Bowman's capsule serve simply as selective filters to prevent the passage into the capsular sac of the formed elements of the blood (such as the blood cells and platelets) and plasma proteins. Yet, while the physical factors of osmosis and diffusion are sufficient to account for the movements of molecules across membranes from a region of greater to a region of lesser concentration, they cannot account for the rapid passage of fluid from the blood plasma to the capsule. And as has been seen, the lining cells seem to perform no work in accomplishing this movement. Therefore, the mechanical energy for this movement can come from only one other source, the blood pressure. This one remaining hypothesis can be formulated and tested as follows:

*Hypothesis: If . . .*   blood pressure provides the mechanical energy responsible for the movement of fluid from the glomerulus blood plasma to the capsular sac, . . .

*Prediction: then . . .* urine output should show a direct correlation with blood pressure.

The experiment is performed as follows: Drainage tubes are inserted into the ureter of an anesthetized dog, and the amount of urine collected per unit time is recorded. By removal of some blood from the animal, the blood pressure can be lowered; by the administration of drugs causing constriction of the blood vessels, it can be raised. The results are as would be predicted by the blood pressure–urine output hypothesis; low blood pressure results in a sharply reduced urine output, while high blood pressure increases the flow of urine.

**12-20
REABSORPTION:
THE FINAL STEP**

Chemical analysis of urine samples extracted from any point between the medullary tubules and the urethra reveals no important differences between them. Evidently, then, the vital urine extraction and preparation processes are completed entirely within the renal cortex. Yet, a comparative chemical analysis of the fluid in Bowman's capsule and the fluid which issues from the urethra is remarkably different, indeed. First, with respect to its solutes, the voided urine is far more concentrated than the capsular fluid. To explain this, the hypothesis can be advanced that large amounts of water are reabsorbed from the capsular fluid as it passes along between the capsule and the medullary tubules:

*Hypothesis: If . . .*   water is reabsorbed from the capsular fluid as the fluid passes along the urinary tubules, . . .

***Prediction:***   *then* . . . the color of a dye which is injected into the blood and which passes into the nephron should intensify in urine samples taken at progressively greater distances from the capsule, provided the dye itself is not reabsorbed.

The reasoning here, of course, is that the reabsorption of water, if it occurs, would increase the concentration of dye molecules per unit volume of fluid, and thereby intensify the color. The prediction is verified; the hypothesis supported. More precise experimental analysis shows that in man, about 180 liters of fluid pass into the glomerular sac every day. Yet, only about 1.5 liters is excreted as urine. These results indicate a reabsorption quantity of approximately 99%.

Anatomical evidence in support of the reabsorption hypothesis is supplied by the fact, mentioned earlier, that the capillaries leaving the glomerulus do not directly leave the kidney, but rather become closely associated with the urinary tubule along part of its length leading away from the capsule. Also supportive is the thinning of the tubule at one point in its twisted path; such a thinning provides a greater surface area per unit volume for reabsorption to occur. The rather viscous nature of the blood leaving the glomerulus, in comparison to its more watery nature in the renal vein, is also consistent with the hypothesis. However, precise chemical analyses make it quite clear that water absorption alone is not sufficient to explain the difference in chemical composition between capsular fluid and urine. Certain solutes are more concentrated than others; an hypothesis that water reabsorption is the *only* factor at work would predict otherwise. For example, the sodium concentration in blood and urine is rather similar, while the urea concentration differs by a factor of approximately seventy. Bladder urine normally contains no glucose; capsular urine does. Glucose, therefore, must also be reabsorbed, *against a concentration gradient*. The cells lining the urinary tubules must therefore be performing work to move the glucose back into the blood. Cytological examination of the kidney tubule cells reveals that they are glandular in nature and possess characteristics of work-performing cells, such as being well equipped with mitochondria.

It may sometimes happen that an abnormal amount of glucose occurs in the blood. Such a situation is encountered in the case of a person with diabetes. In such cases, glucose *is* found in the urine, a fact which provides a simple test for diabetes. Evidently, if the concentration of glucose in the blood exceeds a certain value, the urinary tubule cells are unable to return all of the glucose to the blood; the excess "spills over" and appears in the urine. The same threshold phenomenon is found for other substances normally reabsorbed by the tubule cells. Yet, the concentration that represents a threshold may be quite different from one substance to another. This fact alone suggests that the reabsorption process is only part of the story, and a complete explanation must await a fuller understanding of cellular work processes in general. Recent work with isotopes, for example, indicates that the tubule cells may also perform work in moving certain substances *from the blood to the urine*, as well as the reverse. Earlier investigation of the work of the kidney by analysis of the fluids involved at various points in the process appears to have considered only the net difference between opposing flows moving across the urinary tubule walls. Such analytical work also indirectly bears on the *nature* of the reabsorptive forces involved (i.e., diffusion, active transport, etc.) as well as the factors that trigger the tubule cells to commence their work. By reabsorbing bicarbonate ions, for example, the kidney helps to keep the blood mildly basic, while at the same time secreting hydrogen ions into the urine and making it slightly acidic. Thus the kidney plays as large a role in maintaining a proper pH of the blood as any of the respiratory mechanisms, and works in a delicately balanced coordination with these mechanisms. In Chapter 14, further attention will be given to the physiological interrelations that exist between various body organs and the role these interrelations play in maintaining an internal body environment compatible with life.

**12-21
CONCLUSION**

In this chapter, the anatomy and physiology of those animal systems and organs most directly concerned with the intake and processing of food, an animal's only source of energy and raw material, have been discussed.

After ingestion, the chemical conversion of food into a form that can be absorbed (digestion) is followed both by elimination of unusable materials and by transportation and assimilation of usable materials to the body tissues. Transportation is accomplished mostly by the circulatory system, i.e., the heart, blood vessels, blood, and lymphatic system.

However, merely filling a furnace with fuel is not enough. Air must be supplied to provide the oxygen needed for the burning reaction and a means to carry waste gases away. Similarly, if an animal is to oxidize its food, an oxidizing agent must be provided and reaction by-products must be removed in order to keep the reaction equilibrium shifted in the proper direction. This oxidizing agent is oxygen; its extraction from the air, and the release of the waste carbon dioxide and water, are the job of the respiratory system. Again, the circulatory system is required to act as transportation agent between the respiratory system and the respiring cells of the animal body.

Finally, just as a man can burn some, but not all, of the material deposits in a waste basket, so oxidation fuel leaves waste products that present a special removal problem. In a living organism, these products are the nitrogenous wastes of protein catabolism. The kidney provides the special means of disposing of such wastes.

**EXERCISES**

1. Trace through the digestive system the pathway of a morsel of food containing protein, fat, and carbohydrate. Discuss the changes that take place in the types of food as this passage occurs.

2. Observe Fig. 12–17. If we calculate the amount of sugar an animal can absorb from its diet, as well as the rate at which that animal burns glucose during a twelve-hour period, the percentage of sugar in the blood should vary as curve A in the graph.

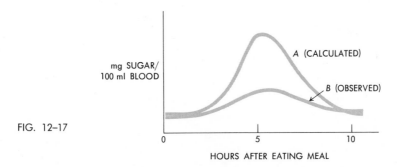

mg SUGAR/
100 ml BLOOD

A (CALCULATED)

B (OBSERVED)

0          5          10

HOURS AFTER EATING MEAL

FIG. 12–17

Actual measurements, however, show that the amount of blood sugar is considerably less. Other evidence shows that the amount of blood sugar is considerably less in the hepatic vein than in the hepatic portal vein. Offer an hypothesis to explain these results. Devise an experiment to test your hypothesis.

3. What is emulsification? Why does it precede hydrolysis during the digestive process?

4. What factors are responsible for the movement of materials across the intestinal wall (walls of the villi) during absorption?

5. How is the absorption of fats different (in terms of pathway) from that of carbohydrates and proteins?

6. After a period of starvation which depleted the glycogen from the liver, an animal was fed a meal of pure protein. Certain constituents of the blood in the hepatic vein and the portal vein were analyzed and the results were recorded as in Table 12–2. Study this table, then consider each of the statements (a) through (d). If the statement is valid according to the evidence, write A on your paper beside that statement designation; if the statement is contradicted by the evidence, write B; if the statement cannot be judged on the basis of the evidence, write C.

**TABLE 12–2**

|  | CONCENTRATION OF | | |
|---|---|---|---|
|  | AMINO ACIDS | UREA | GLUCOSE |
| HEPATIC PORTAL VEIN | 8.0 mg per 100 cc | 30.0 mg | 80.0 mg |
| HEPATIC VEIN | 6.0 mg | 30.7 mg | 81.0 mg |

a) The liver removed amino acids from the circulatory system.

b) Urea is either manufactured or stored in the liver.

c) The liver either manufactures or holds in storage a reserve supply of sugar.

d) Adrenaline was responsible for the increase in glucose content of the blood from 80 mg per 100 cc to 81 mg per 100 cc.

7. Answer the two parts of this question on the basis of the information contained in Fig. 12–18.

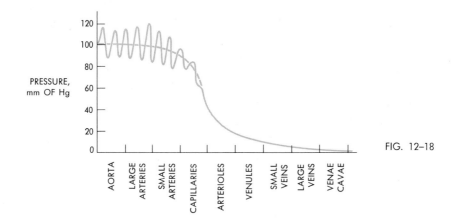

FIG. 12–18

a) Explain why the pressure curve becomes lower and lower in proceeding from the heart.

b) Since the blood pressure in the two venae cavae appears to reach the zero point, what force must be responsible for movement of blood into the left side of the heart?

8. Figure 12–19 is a schematic view of the capillary bed surrounding a group of body cells.

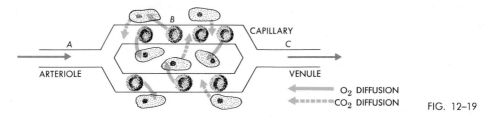

FIG. 12–19

a) Oxygen diffuses into body cells at B rather than at A primarily because:
   i) At A, the pressure from forces exerted by body cells against the outside arteriole wall is too great.
   ii) As the arteriole breaks down into numerous capillaries, the pressure becomes less at B than at A.
   iii) The blood travels too rapidly at A.
   iv) The blood travels too slowly at A.
   v) None of the above reasons.

b) Increase of blood pressure at A:
   i) Would increase the rate of oxygen diffusion at B.
   ii) Would decrease the rate of oxygen diffusion at B.
   iii) Would not affect the diffusion of oxygen at B.
   iv) Would probably rupture the artery.

c) The pressure exerted on the blood within the arteriole at A comes from:
   i) Friction alone.
   ii) Forces exerted by the surrounding body cells.

     iii) Accumulation of carbon dioxide in surrounding tissues.

     iv) The pumping action of the heart.

  d) Carbon dioxide diffuses from body cells into the capillary at $B$ because:

     i) The pressure at $B$ is less than within the body cells.

     ii) The pressure at $B$ is greater than within the body cells.

     iii) There is more concentration of $CO_2$ in the cells than at $B$ in the capillary.

     iv) All of the above.

     v) None of the above.

9. Describe the pathway that blood takes through the mammalian heart.

10. What differences in heart structure are apparent between the frog and the mammal? What is the significance of these differences?

11. Study Table 12–3, which shows the relative amounts of various gases in the alveoli and the blood (expressed as relative gas pressure), then evaluate each of the statements (a) through (d). If the statement is true according to the data, write A on your paper beside that statement's designation. If the statement is not true according to the data, write B. If the statement is in agreement with biological principles but cannot be determined from the above data, write C.

**TABLE 12–3**

| GAS | ALVEOLAR AIR | VENOUS BLOOD | ARTERIAL BLOOD |
|---|---|---|---|
| OXYGEN | 104 | 40 | 100 |
| CARBON DIOXIDE | 40 | 45 | 40 |
| NITROGEN | 569 | 567 | 569 |

  a) Oxygen tends to diffuse from the alveolar spaces (alveoli) into the capillaries of the lungs.

  b) There would be relatively greater tendency for carbon dioxide to diffuse from the venous blood into the alveolar spaces, than for oxygen to diffuse from the alveolar spaces into the venous blood.

  c) There is relatively little movement of nitrogen from alveolar spaces into the blood, or vice versa.

  d) Within normal limits, the carbon dioxide concentration of the blood is more important than that of either oxygen or nitrogen in regulating the rate of breathing.

12. A pH analysis of urine has revealed that the urine of some animals is highly acid, while that of others is highly alkaline. There is a corresponding difference in the diets of these groups of animals. Which of the following statements offers the best explanation for this difference in urine?

  a) The kidneys keep a balance in the diet by removing certain acids or alkalies from the environment.

  b) The kidneys maintain a constant pH of the blood by removing excess acids or alkalies which result from the diet.

  c) The specific pH of the urine must be a particular level regardless of the intake of acids or alkalies from the environment.

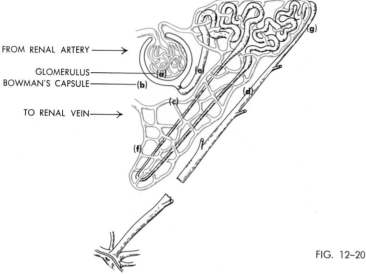

FROM RENAL ARTERY ⟶

GLOMERULUS——
BOWMAN'S CAPSULE———(b)

TO RENAL VEIN⟶

FIG. 12–20

13. Observe Fig. 12–20. Use letter designations to indicate your answer for each of the following questions.

a) In Fig. 12–20, where would you expect to find urine most similar to that which is excreted?

b) Where would you expect to find blood with the greatest concentration of urea?

c) Describe the condition of the blood at position (d) in terms of physical properties and composition of solutes.

d) Describe what happens to most of the water that passes into the glomerular filtrate.

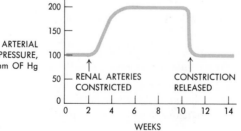

FIG. 12–21

14. When the renal arteries are restricted, the flow of blood through them is reduced to about 10% of its original amount. From the data presented in Fig. 12–21, can you explain how the kidney continues to function in an almost normal way (i.e., filtering about the same amount of liquid per unit time) under these conditions?

BEAUMONT, WILLIAM, "Experiments and Observations on the Gastric Juice and the Physiology of Digestion." An account of the fascinating observations made by physician Beaumont on Alexis St. Martin in the 1820's, after St. Martin had been wounded in the stomach by a musket wound. In Jeffrey J. W. Baker and Garland E. Allen (Eds.), *The Process of Biology: Primary Sources* (Reading, Mass.: Addison-Wesley, 1970). Also included in this book is "Gastric Juice of the Buzzard" by René Antoine Réaumur.

MAYERSON, H. S., "The Lymphatic System." *Scientific American*, June 1963, p. 80. A general discussion of the lymphatic system and its role in maintaining the "steady state" of body tissue fluids.

PONDER, ERIC, "The Red Blood Cell." *Scientific American*, January 1957, p. 95. A good summary of modern evidence on the structure and function of the red blood cell.

RUCH, THEODORE, and JOHN F. FULTON, *Medical Physiology and Biophysics* (Philadelphia: W. B. Saunders & Co., 18th ed., 1960). This is undoubtedly the best single complete text on modern human physiology. This work should serve primarily as a reference.

SCHER, ALLEN, "The Electrocardiogram." *Scientific American*, November 1961, p. 132. A good discussion of what is known today about heart function.

SCHMIDT-NIELSEN, KNUT, *Animal Physiology* (Englewood Cliffs, N.J.: Prentice-Hall, 1960). This is a brief but somewhat spotty coverage of important topics in animal physiology. Generally, the topics are well explained and require very little preliminary background.

SMITH, HOMER, *From Fish to Philosopher* (Summit, N.J.: CIBA Foundation, 1959). An excellent discussion of the evolution of renal structure and physiology.

WIGGERS, CARL. J., "The Heart." *Scientific American*, May 1957, p. 75. A review article about the structure and function of the heart. Discusses also the generation of impulses by the "pacemaker."

ZWEIFACH, BENJAMIN, "The Microcirculation of the Blood." *Scientific American*, January 1959, p. 54. This article discusses the capillary bed and how the opening and closing of capillaries is achieved.

**SUGGESTED READINGS**

# CHAPTER 13   ANIMAL ANATOMY AND PHYSIOLOGY II: MOVEMENT AND COORDINATION

**INTRODUCTION**    The release of energy in an animal is important only insofar as it can be coupled with useful activity. An animal that did nothing more than break down fuel molecules would be like an automobile whose motor is running but whose gears are not engaged. For a living organism, engaging the gears means linking vital energy-releasing processes with the energy-requiring processes associated with life. In the previous chapter, we saw how food materials were prepared for breakdown in the processes of glycolysis and fermentation by digestion, absorption, and distribution through the blood. In this chapter we shall consider the ways in which energy is used in two very important animal activities: movement and coordination.

The ability to move from place to place is a characteristic which has long been associated with the animal kingdom. To move effectively, however, requires a complex system of coordination which has reached its peak of development in the vertebrate body. Neither of these activities could occur if they were not coupled with energy-releasing processes at the molecular level. As we consider the processes of movement and coordination it will be important to see not only the way in which such coupling is thought to occur, but also the methods by which our understanding of these processes has developed.

**13-2**

**NERVES AND MUSCLES: ELECTROCHEMICAL POTENTIAL**    All cell membranes of any sort are to some degree **polarized,** i.e., there is a difference in electric potential on one side of the membrane as compared to the other. In most cases, the outside of the cell is positively charged in relation to the inside. The difference in potential is due to an unequal distribution of ions—more of certain positively charged ions are on the outside than on the inside. This results from the fact that the membrane is differentially permeable

410

to certain ions. For example, the membranes of most cells are slightly permeable to both sodium and potassium ions, but are generally more permeable to the latter. In addition, most cells actively transport ions to the outside, thus setting up a definite difference in ionic concentrations across the cell membrane. It is this difference in concentration on the two sides of a cell membrane that establishes an electric potential.

Whenever a difference in potential exists between two sides of a system, that system is capable of doing work. Doing work involves lowering the difference in potential; as water runs over the dam to turn a generator, or as one kind of ion moves from higher to lower concentration across a membrane, potential energy is lost. In both cases, an expenditure of energy is required to restore the potential. For the dam, water from lower levels must be pumped back up to the other side (or moved back up by the sun's energy through evaporation and precipitation); for the cell, certain ions must be moved out of the cell by active transport.

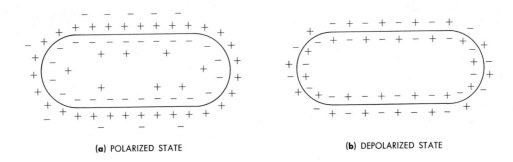

(a) POLARIZED STATE                (b) DEPOLARIZED STATE

FIG. 13-1    As shown in (a), the outside of a cell is generally positively charged in relation to the inside. This difference can usually be measured and given a value in volts (or millivolts when dealing with small potentials). In (b), the membrane potential has fallen to zero; the membrane is thus said to be depolarized. Depolarization occurs when the membrane allows the passage of ions to which it is normally impermeable. In the depolarized state, the distribution of positive and negative ions is the same on each side of the membrane.

Thus whenever a cell membrane is altered so as to allow ions to pass through which are normally kept out, the potential is lowered. This means that the concentration of certain ions is more nearly equal on both sides. When the potential drops to zero, the membrane is said to be **depolarized**. The polarized and depolarized state of a cell membrane are both shown in Fig. 13-1. Because the potential across cell membranes is associated with the distribution of ions, it is said to be **electrochemical** in nature. The electrochemical potential across the membranes of nerve and muscle cells is especially high. The high potential of nerve and muscle cells is one of their unique evolutionary adaptations.

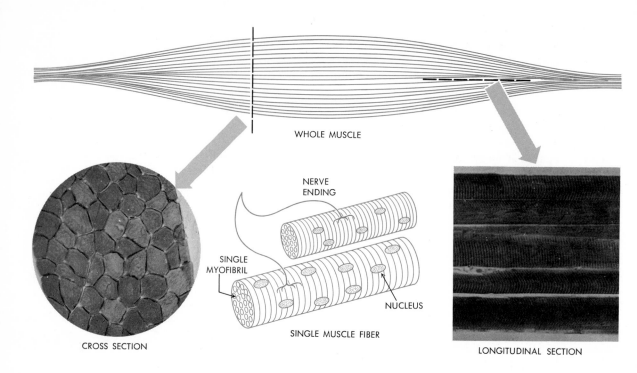

WHOLE MUSCLE

NERVE ENDING

SINGLE MYOFIBRIL

NUCLEUS

SINGLE MUSCLE FIBER

CROSS SECTION

LONGITUDINAL SECTION

FIG. 13–2  Organization of muscle tissue on the gross level.  These observations were made with the light microscope.  (Photos courtesy Professor H. E. Huxley.)

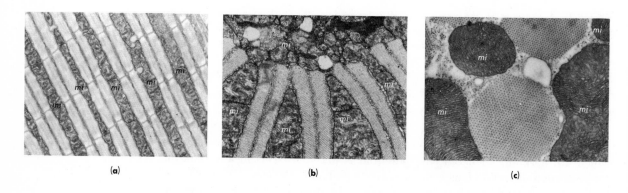

(a)                           (b)                           (c)

FIG. 13–3  The large number of mitochondria (*mi*) between these muscle fibers attests to the high degree of activity these particular fibers exhibit.  These electron microscope photographs are, left to right: longitudinal section through the flight muscle of the damselfly, ×4700; cross section through damselfly flight muscle, ×9900; and cross section through the flight muscle of an aphid, ×11,250.  (Photos courtesy D. S. Smith, University of Miami.)

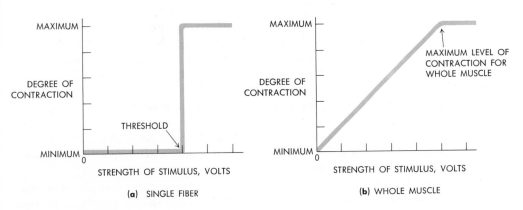

FIG. 13–4 Comparison of patterns of contraction (a) for a single muscle fiber, or motor unit, and (b) for a whole muscle. The former shows the all-or-none response, while the latter shows gradual increase in contraction compared to gradual increase in strength of stimulus.

Perhaps nowhere in the animal world is the relation between structure and function more apparent than in the study of the molecular basis of muscle contraction. A cross section through a whole muscle (such as the human biceps) shows that it is composed of many muscle **fibers** (Fig. 13–2). These fibers are arranged parallel to each other and extend from one end of the muscle to the other. Nerve fibers entering the muscle terminate in each muscle fiber. It is these nerve endings which, by activating individual fibers, bring the stimulus to the muscle as a whole. A longitudinal section through the same muscle shows the parallel fibers with alternating light and dark bands. These bands, known as striations, are characteristic of skeletal and cardiac muscle tissue (see Section 12–2).

The individual muscle fiber is the fundamental unit of structure in the intact muscle (see Fig. 13–3). It is not, however, the fundamental unit of contraction. Each nerve leading to the skeletal muscles branches out so that a number of muscle fibers receive stimuli from the same nerve (Fig. 13–2, center). This minimum unit of contraction—the group of fibers stimulated by impulses from one nerve—is known as a **motor unit.** The fewer the number of fibers stimuated by each nerve, the more precisely movement can be controlled. Thus for the muscles controlling eye movements, over which we have very precise control, a single neuron may lead to only six or ten muscle fibers. On the other hand, for muscles such as the biceps, over which we have less precise control, a single neuron may trigger several hundred muscle fibers.

Observation shows that although the whole muscle is capable of many degrees of contraction, individual muscle fibers show an **all-or-none response** (Fig. 13–4). Any fiber will respond only to those stimuli which exceed a certain

**threshold** of intensity.  Above this threshold, the fiber responds by full contraction, regardless of how far above the threshold the strength of the stimulus may have been.  The fine levels of adjustment displayed by whole muscles result from the different numbers of motor units that may be placed in operation at a given time.  The number of units in operation is determined by the number of nerve endings conveying an impulse.  Thus in a whole animal the degree of muscular response is directly proportional to the number of motor units activated by the nervous system.  It is also directly proportional to the frequency of excitation of these units.  Thus two relatively independent means for gradation of the degree of muscular contraction are available to the organism.

Each muscle fiber is surrounded by a membrane, across which an electrochemical potential exists.  The outside of this membrane is positively charged with respect to the inside.  A nerve impulse causes the membrane to become depolarized, and an **action current** sweeps the length of the entire fiber.  In some not yet clearly understood manner, reduction in membrane potential causes the muscle fiber to contract.

In the past, the question of how a muscle contracts has been approached from two quite different directions.  One approach is biochemical; it depends on the analysis of chemical changes in the muscle as a result of contraction.  The other is biophysical; it relies on the use of such techniques as X-ray diffraction and electron microscopy to study changes in the anatomy of muscle fibers during contraction.

**13-4
MUSCLE
CONTRACTION:
THE BIOCHEMICAL
APPROACH**

The first step in unraveling the problem of muscle contraction involves determining what substances disappear during the process, and what substances appear.  It can be shown that glycogen, oxygen, a phosphate compound known as creatine phosphate, and ATP are consumed by active muscle preparations, while carbon dioxide, lactic acid, and inorganic phosphate increase in quantity during muscle contraction.  On the basis of this information, a general "equation" can tentatively be established:

These are used up          These are produced

$$GLYCOGEN, O_2, CREATINE\ PHOSPHATE, ATP \rightarrow CO_2, C_3H_6O_3, P_i, CREATINE, ADP$$

where $C_3H_6O_3$ is lactic acid and $P_i$ inorganic phosphate.

In attempting to piece together a picture of the biochemistry of contraction, muscle physiologists had access to the following experimental observations:

1)  It had been observed that a muscle placed in an atmosphere rich in oxygen contracted several hundred times before becoming fatigued.  An hypothesis proposing that oxygen is essential for contraction was contradicted, however; a muscle placed in an oxygen-free atmosphere (e.g., pure nitrogen) continued to contract up to 80 times before fatigue.

2)   In the 1940's biochemist Albert Szent-Gyorgyi found that when a solution containing ATP and appropriate ions was added, extracted muscle fibers would contract and the striations would move closer together.  In another experiment Szent-Gyorgyi showed that the proteins actin and myosin were responsible for contraction in the whole muscle.

3)   Another experiment showed that even when the conversion of glycogen to lactic acid is blocked by a specific inhibitor (iodoacetate), the muscle is still able to contract.  Such a "poisoned" muscle, however, is capable of only one-third the total number of contractions of a normal muscle.

From this information it is possible to draw some conclusions.  ATP, rather than the oxidative processes associated with the breakdown of glucose, seems to be the direct source of energy for muscle contraction.  It is reasonable to infer from this that the further oxidation of glucose is responsible for regenerating the ATP consumed during muscle contraction.  The consumption of oxygen is thus required to rebuild the exhausted supply of ATP.

This is not the complete picture, however.  The compound creatine phosphate is found in plentiful supply in muscle tissue.  It seems to be used up during contraction, but what is its exact role?

The following information summarizes the observations concerning probable energy sources of muscle contraction based on studies of extracted muscle preparations where there is no permeability barrier.  (There is no way to supply ATP to an intact muscle except by the metabolism of foodstuffs.)

1)   A muscle deprived of both ATP and creatine phosphate will not contract.

2)   A muscle deprived of creatine phosphate but supplied with ATP will continue to contract until the ATP is used up.

3)   A muscle supplied with only creatine phosphate will not contract.

4)   A muscle deprived of ATP but supplied with creatine phosphate and ADP will contract.  Chemical analysis shows that ATP has been synthesized. When the supply of either ADP or creatine phosphate has been exhausted, the muscle ceases to contract.

What conclusions can be drawn from all these data?  It seems clear that although ATP provides the direct energy currency for contraction, creatine phosphate acts as a reserve of high-energy phosphate groups.  When the ATP supply runs low, high-energy phosphate groups are transferred to ADP, thus regenerating ATP.  When the muscle is resting and ATP is being reformed by fermentation and glycolysis, phosphate groups are transferred back to creatine, reforming creatine phosphate.

The relationship between these processes is summarized in Fig. 13–5.  An equilibrium must exist between the high-energy phosphate "pool" of ATP and that of creatine phosphate.  The direction of the reaction thus shifts in whichever direction the demand lies.

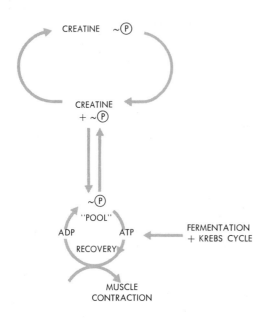

FIG. 13–5   The relation between creatine phosphate and ATP in the energy provision for muscle contraction. Creatine phosphate provides energy-rich phosphate groups to reconvert ADP, produced in muscle contraction, to ATP. High-energy phosphate bonds are ultimately generated by fermentation and the Krebs cycle.  When the ATP supply in a cell is high, the equilibrium of reaction is so shifted that the ~℗ are transferred from ATP to creatine.  When the ATP supply runs low, the equilibrium shifts back toward the transfer of ~℗ from creatine phosphate to ADP.

Since very little ATP is actually stored within the muscle itself, a sudden spurt of muscular activity might quickly exhaust the supply.  This is where creatine phosphate comes into play; it transfers its high-energy phosphate groups to ADP.  This transfer allows the muscle to work at its maximum rate for about 15 seconds.

In very strenuous exercise, however, 15 seconds is not long enough for the breathing and circulatory rates of the body to adapt to the oxygen needs of the tissues.  To meet this demand, muscle cells produce ATP by fermentation.  This fermentation yields lactic acid, with a net gain of two ATP's per glucose unit in the glycogen molecule.  As was seen in Chapter 8, however, fermentation represents a poor gain when the total amount of potential energy contained in a glycogen molecule is considered; although fermentation enables the muscle to keep going for a while, the glycogen supply eventually runs low, and lactic acid accumulates in the muscle cells and in the extracellular fluid.  The accumulation of lactic acid in the muscles produces fatigue.

Fatigue is the result of several interacting factors.  One is that the accumulation of lactic acid lowers the pH of the muscle fibers, reducing their ability to contract.  A second is that during prolonged and strenuous exercise, the muscle builds up an "oxygen debt."  The amount of the debt represents the quantity of oxygen required to oxidize the accumulated lactic acid to carbon dioxide and water.  When the muscle cell is very active, it keeps contracting on borrowed energy, i.e., on the incomplete breakdown of glycogen.  If the cell is to continue functioning it must repay this debt as soon as the body can supply the necessary amount of oxygen.  This arrangement has obvious survival value to the organism.  It allows the muscles to continue functioning at a moment of stress, even though their oxygen needs cannot be met by the body at that time. Yet, it also provides a means by which the reserves can be restored during periods of less strenuous activity.

The lactic acid which has accumulated in the muscles during exercise diffuses into the blood and is carried to the liver. Here, one-fifth of the lactic acid is completely oxidized to water and carbon dioxide, thus yielding ATP. The ATP is then used to resynthesize glycogen from the remaining lactic acid. Glycogen produced in the liver is transported back to the muscles as glucose, where it is then reformed into glycogen by dehydration synthesis.

By virtue of using one-fifth of the lactic acid to recapture the remaining four-fifths as usable fuel, muscle tissue is remarkably efficient in its energy use. This mechanism can be compared to using one-fifth of the exhaust materials on a car to reform the other four-fifths back into gasoline! The available evidence indicates that muscle contraction has a general efficiency of about 45%.

The discussion in Section 13–4 centered around one aspect of the problem of muscle contraction: the nature of the chemical reactions involved. Still left open is the problem of how the two proteins actin and myosin actually produce a contraction within the muscle fibers. The electron microscope has been of immense value in studying the molecular structure of the muscle and has thus provided a clue as to how actin and myosin might function to produce contraction.

If a single muscle fiber is viewed in cross section under the electron microscope, it is seen to consist of many **myofibrils** (see Fig. 13–6). Each myofibril, in turn, is seen to consist of alternating thick and thin filaments (see especially

## 13-5 MUSCLE CONTRACTION: THE BIOPHYSICAL APPROACH

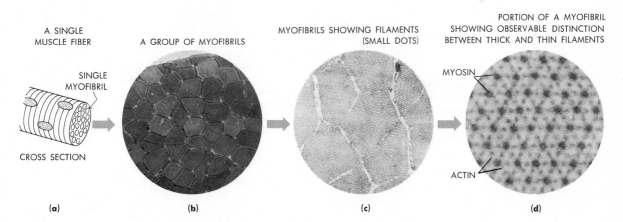

A SINGLE MUSCLE FIBER

SINGLE MYOFIBRIL

CROSS SECTION

A GROUP OF MYOFIBRILS

MYOFIBRILS SHOWING FILAMENTS (SMALL DOTS)

PORTION OF A MYOFIBRIL SHOWING OBSERVABLE DISTINCTION BETWEEN THICK AND THIN FILAMENTS

MYOSIN

ACTIN

(a)        (b)        (c)        (d)

FIG. 13–6 Successively lower levels of organization in vertebrate muscle structure, seen in cross section. (a) Diagrammatic representation of a single muscle fiber, showing myofibrils in cross section. (b) A group of myofibrils. (c) The same view but in more detail. (d) The arrangement of thick (myosin) and thin (actin) filaments can be seen in considerable detail. [Photos (b) and (c) courtesy Professor H. E. Huxley, photo (d) from *Revue Canadienne de Biologie* **21** (1962), pp. 279–301, courtesy D. S. Smith, University of Miami.]

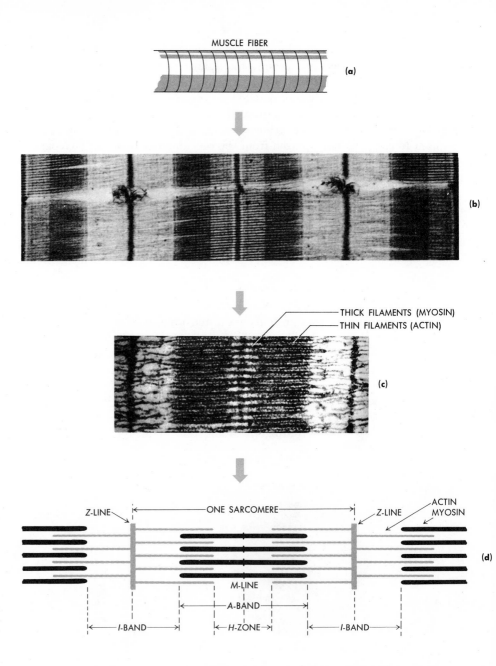

FIG. 13–7   Successively lower levels of muscle organization shown in longitudinal section. (a) A single muscle fiber with striations. (b) Photo showing the alternating bands of light and dark which create the striations. (c) Electron-microscope photo showing how the overlapping of thick and thin filaments produces the banding. (d) Schematic representation of the arrangement of actin and myosin in one sarcomere (the simplest molecular unit of contraction). Various regions of the sarcomere are labeled (Z-line, A-band, etc.) for identification. (Photos courtesy Professor H. E. Huxley.)

Fig. 13–6c, d), identified as myosin and actin, respectively. The electron micrograph in Fig. 13–6(d) shows the arrangement of actin and myosin as seen in cross section.

It was once thought that actin and myosin molecules might produce contraction by coiling or folding. Electron micrographs, however, suggest a more likely theory. Figure 13–7(c) shows a longitudinal section through a muscle fiber. Note that the dark region in the center (a striation) is caused by the overlapping of the thin filaments of actin and the thick filaments of myosin. This arrangement is shown diagrammatically in Fig. 13–7(d).

H. E. Huxley and his coworkers have observed both relaxed and contracted muscle tissue under the electron microscope. Successive stages, from relaxed to contracted, are shown in Fig. 13–8. Several important observations can be made from the photographs. It seems that during contraction:

1) The *H*-zone disappears.

2) A new dense zone appears in the center of the *A*-band where the *M*-line was normally seen.

3) The distance between consecutive *Z*-lines becomes less.

All these observations suggest the following scheme for muscle contraction. When a muscle is stimulated by a nerve or an electric current, molecules of actin and myosin interact in such a way that the thin filaments slide over the thick filaments. As the thin filaments come together the *H*-zone disappears. The thin filaments continue sliding until their ends overlap, thus producing the dense zone in the center of the *A*-band. As a result of this sliding, the distance between *Z*-bands is greatly reduced.

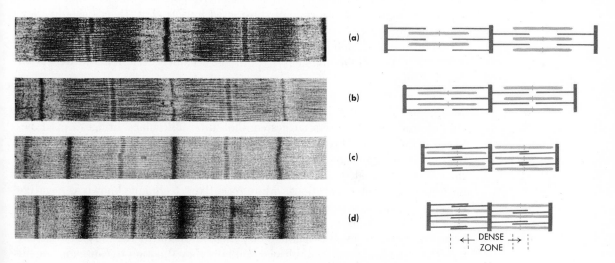

FIG. 13–8   Electron micrographs of contracting muscle, and corresponding schematic representations of filament movements. (Photos courtesy Professor H. E. Huxley.)

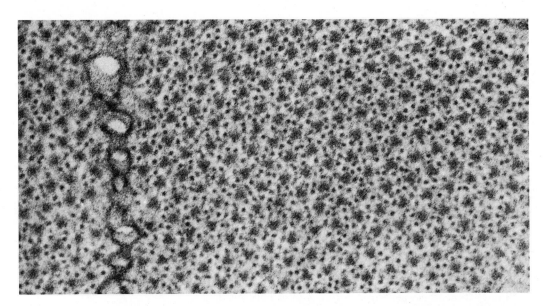

FIG. 13–9   Electron micrograph of contracted muscle cut in cross section through the dense region. Here, as predicted by the sliding-filament hypothesis, the number of thin filaments surrounding each thick filament is approximately twice as great as in relaxed muscle. (Photo courtesy Professor H. E. Huxley.)

Cross sections of relaxed muscle in the region of the $A$-band where thick and thin filaments overlap show that each myosin filament is surrounded by six actin filaments (Fig. 13–6d).   The sliding-filament hypothesis predicts that a cross section through the dense zone of contracted muscle (Fig. 13–6d) should show approximately twice as many actin filaments as were present before contraction. An electron micrograph of such a section verifies the prediction (Fig. 13–9).   It seems that the sliding-filament hypothesis accounts well for the events of contraction.

The question still remains as to the precise nature of the mechanism by which the thick and thin filaments slide along each other.   Several years ago Huxley and his coworkers suggested that intermolecular "bridges" exist between filaments of actin and myosin.   They hypothesized that these acted in a ratchetlike arrangement.   The filaments were moved across each other much as the teeth of one set of gears move another.   At the time, however, it was not possible to see such connections.   More recently, a technique known as negative staining has made it possible to get very clear pictures of ultrathin sections of muscle.   Photographs made of muscle treated in this way show that cross-bridges between actin and myosin filaments do exist in uncontracted muscle.   Exactly how the cross-bridges are established and how they function to cause movement of the filaments are not yet clearly understood.   Several hypotheses have been developed, but at the moment there is no adequate way to distinguish between them.

Let us now review the complete picture of muscle contraction as established by both biochemical and biophysical studies. It has been shown that ATP exists in muscle fibers attached to filaments of myosin. The passage of the action current down the muscle fiber somehow triggers a chemical reaction in which molecules of myosin combine with molecules of actin. The resulting compound, actomyosin, acts as an enzyme which splits the third phosphate group from the ATP molecule. This produces a complex of ADP and actomyosin, with inorganic phosphate left over. In this way the energy from ATP is specifically released to power the contraction process. The interaction of actin and myosin causes the two filaments to slide together and thus shortens each striated region of the muscle fiber. After contraction, the actomyosin-ADP complex is regenerated to form actin and myosin-bound ATP. After this short "recovery period" the muscle is ready to contract again.

Study of the nature of muscle contraction has shown how biochemistry and molecular anatomy have combined to give a detailed picture of the relation between structure and function. Many questions are still unanswered, however. As we have seen, the details of how one filament slides over the other during contraction are still unknown. Nor is it understood how actomyosin acts as an enzyme and what happens to it in the process.

The sliding-filament hypothesis as it stands today is the most comprehensive and accurate model yet developed for muscle contraction. Like all useful models or hypotheses, however, it serves mostly to organize known facts and give direction for future research.

## 13-6 VERTEBRATE MOVEMENT: THE RELATION OF MUSCLE TO BONE

Few muscle contractions, if any, produce movement directly. Most act indirectly by affecting another body part. The jellyfish, for example, contracts muscle fibers in its bell. This action squeezes water out from under the bell, thus moving the animal in the other direction by jet propulsion. An insect moves by means of the force exerted by its body muscles against the inner surfaces of its hard outer-body covering.

An unattached contracting muscle, then, moves nothing but itself. A muscle must produce a force upon an object if any useful movement of an organism is to result. In complex vertebrates such as man, muscles act by exerting force upon bones of the skeletal system (Fig. 13-10).

Muscles are attached to bones by means of tendons, composed largely of white fibrous connective tissue (see Section 12-2). One end of a tendon is closely applied to the surface of the bone, the other end to a muscle (Fig. 13-10b). The muscle, at its other end, is attached by a second tendon to another bone.

Obviously, were a muscle to be attached to two freely movable bones, its contraction would serve only to bring the two bones closer together. In order for an organism to produce motion in one direction, it must somehow exert a force against its surrounding medium (i.e., ground, water, or air) in the other

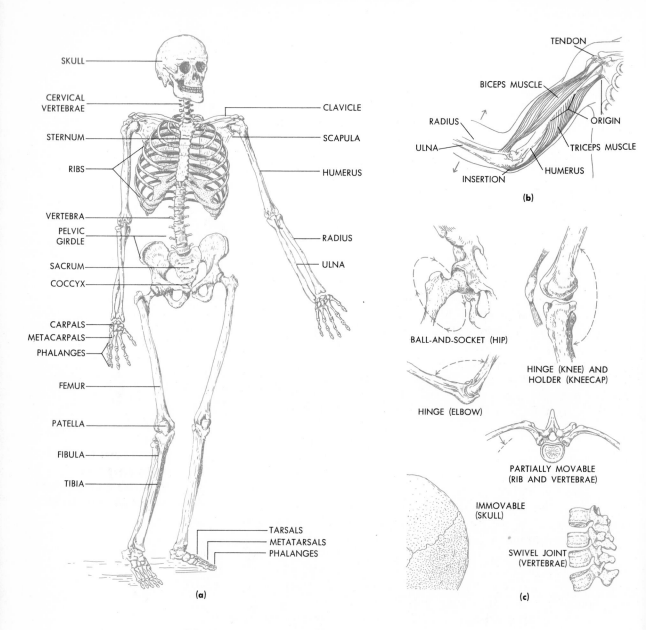

FIG. 13–10

direction. This can only be done if the muscles are anchored to a fairly immovable bone at one end and a freely movable bone at the other. Thus, for example, the tendon of the biceps muscle of the human arm is attached at one end to the relatively immovable shoulder bones. This attachment point is called the muscle's **origin.** The tendon at the other end of the biceps muscle is attached to the radius, one of the lower arm bones. This attachment point is called the muscle's **insertion.** Contraction of the biceps muscle results in movement of the bone to which it is inserted—the radius. The arm is thus bent at the elbow.

Since it is composed of cells embedded in a nonliving matrix (Fig. 12–1), bone is a type of connective tissue. Each bone is covered with a thin outer lining, the **periosteum.** Besides the strong support this system gives the body, the marrow within the bones manufactures blood cells.

The human skeleton contains approximately 200 separate bones (Fig. 13–10a), the number varying with the age of the individual. These bones are connected to each other by extremely tough white fibrous connective tissues called **ligaments.** A watery fluid secreted between the joints serves as a lubricant to reduce friction between the bones when they rub against each other. Thus the amount of force which must be exerted by the contracting muscle is considerably lessened.

There are several types of joints in the skeletal system, each specialized for a particular task. The ribs are attached to the thoracic vertebra by partially movable joints. These joints allow the limited motion necessary for breathing. Ball-and-socket joints, permitting free motion in almost any direction, are found in the hip and upper shoulder. Hinge joints, which permit free swinging movement in one main direction, exist at the elbow and knee. Finally, immovable joints are found in such places as the skull, where rigidity is necessary in order to protect the brain.

Muscles can exert a force only by contracting—that is, by pulling. They cannot push. Thus for every muscle whose action pulls a bone in one direction there must be another muscle, attached to the same bone, which works antagonistically to the first muscle by pulling the bone in the other direction. It will be seen that when one muscle is contracted, the muscle antagonistic to it must be relaxed. The strength exerted by some muscles, should they accidentally pull full force at the same time, is often sufficient to shatter the bone. This implies that there must be a system which coordinates muscle activity, causing them to contract or relax at the appropriate time. The system responsible for this coordination is the nervous system.

Like muscle cells, nerve cells have a high electric potential. The nature of this potential and the properties of the nerve impulse which result from it have been the subject of considerable investigation. In order to understand the exact nature of the nerve impulse, it will be helpful to consider some of the ways in which this problem has been approached in successive eras of biological history.

13-7
THE NATURE OF
THE NERVE
IMPULSE

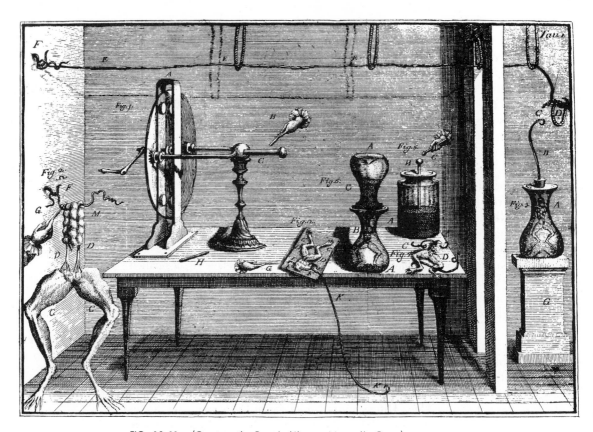

FIG. 13–11   (Courtesy the Burndy Library, Norwalk, Conn.)

The discovery that nerve cells could stimulate muscles to contract occurred completely by accident.  The Italian physiologist Luigi Galvani had been performing some routine experiments on frog muscles.  In the 1780's he wrote:

*The course of the work has progressed in the following way.  I dissected a frog . . . [then,] having in mind other things, I placed the frog on the same table as an electric machine* [Fig. 13–11] *so the animal was removed at a considerable distance from the machine's conductor* [the rod *C*, with the ball on its end] *. . .*

*When one of my assistants by chance lightly applied the point of a scalpel to the inner crural nerves* [*DD* in the figure] *of the frog, suddenly all the muscles of the limbs were seen so to contract that they appeared to have fallen in violent tonic convulsions.  Another assistant who was present when we were performing electrical experiments thought he observed that this phenomenon occurred when a spark was discharged from the conductor of the electrical machine.  Marveling at this, he immediately brought the phenomenon to my attention when I was completely engrossed in and contemplating other things.  Hereupon I became extremely enthusiastic and*

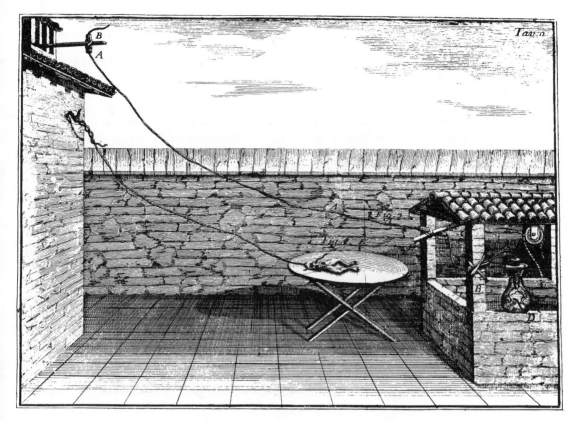

FIG. 13–12    (Courtesy the Burndy Library, Norwalk, Conn.)

*eager to repeat the experiment so as to clarify the obscure phenomenon and make it known.    I myself therefore applied the point of a scalpel first to one, then to the other crural nerve, while at the same time some one of the assistants produced a spark; the phenomenon repeated itself in precisely the same manner as before . . . I was fearful, however, that these movements arose from the contact of the point, which might act as a stimulus, rather than from the spark.    Consequently, I touched the same nerve again in other frogs with the point in a similar manner, and exerted even greater pressure, but absolutely no movements were seen unless someone produced a spark at the same time.*

To test whether the electricity of lightning had the same effect, Galvani performed another experiment.    He set up a lightning rod on a porch and waited for an electrical storm.    As soon as one arose, he attached a frog's nerve to a wire that connected to the lightning rod (Fig. 13–12):

*As we hoped, the result completely paralleled that in the experiment with artificial electricity.    Whenever lightning flashed, at the same time all the muscles fell into many violent contractions. These contractions preceded and as it were gave warning of the thunder to follow, just as the flash in illumination of lightning is wont to do.*

Using the muscle as a visible indicator, Galvani concluded that nerves could be stimulated by electricity. This discovery came at a time when many people were especially intrigued with the effects of static electricity and considered it to be the cause of a large number of biological phenomena. Galvani also noted that a nerve became excited if touched by two different types of metal, such as copper and zinc, if these metals also touched each other. From this observation he developed the idea of an innate "animal electricity." He considered that nerves could produce some type of electric current which, in turn, caused muscles to twitch.*

We see in this example some interesting reasoning. Galvani noted that two separate procedures—touching a nerve with the lead from an electric machine, and touching it with two different types of metal (not connected to or even near an electric machine)—produced the same effect (i.e., the muscle twitched). Galvani assumed that the same effect results from the same cause, and thus concluded that the nerve produced an electric current which caused the muscle to twitch. This form of reasoning is not strictly valid, however. It is not always safe to assume that the same effects *necessarily* result from the same causes. Animals do not, in fact, generate an electric current of the same sort as that produced by an electric machine. As later physiologists came to recognize, there is no such thing as "animal electricity." Nevertheless, Galvani's idea did prove valuable to later workers in nerve and muscle physiology. Thus an accidental discovery and invalid reasoning gave rise to a useful concept: *nerve conduction seems to be somehow associated with an electrical phenomenon.*

Over a generation after Galvani's experiments, the German physiologist Hermann von Helmholtz took up the same problem. Helmholtz was particularly interested in reducing biological problems to a form that would permit their study by the methods of physics and chemistry. In the case of nerve conduction, he developed the idea that the nerve impulse is propagated like an electric current running along a wire. To test this hypothesis he set out to measure the speed of the impulses along a length of nerve. He knew that the speed of a true electric current was close to that of light, i.e., 186,000 miles per second. If the nerve impulse traveled at approximately the same speed, then it would be reasonable to assume that nerves acted primarily as "wires" or conductors for a basically electrical impulse. If the speed were different in the nerve, however, then it would indicate that the nerve impulse was not the same as an electric current passing along a wire.

In a series of experiments reported in 1852, Helmholtz stimulated a nerve at various distances from its juncture with a muscle. He then recorded the time

---

* Galvani's observation about the electric current generated by two types of metals in contact through a wet medium later became the basis for the development of the battery by another Italian, Alessandro Volta.

**TABLE 13–1**

| EXPERIMENT | LENGTH OF NERVE, mm | TIME REQUIRED FOR MUSCLE CONTRACTION, sec NERVE STIMULATED AT: | | TIME DIFFERENCE, sec | SPEED OF IMPULSE, m/sec |
| | | FARTHEST POINT | NEAREST POINT | | |
|---|---|---|---|---|---|
| A | 43 | 0.04394 | 0.04219 | 0.00175 | 24.6 |
| B | 43 | 0.02585 | 0.02448 | 0.00137 | 31.4 |
| C | 40 | 0.02437 | 0.02307 | 0.00130 | 30.8 |
| D | 40 | 0.03164 | 0.03039 | 0.00125 | 32.0 |
| E | 38 | 0.03011 | 0.02880 | 0.00131 | 29.1 |

required for the muscle to contract when stimulated at the farther and nearer position. Knowing the time difference and the distance traversed (i.e., length of the nerve segment), he could calculate the speed of the impulse. He used five different nerve preparations, all between 38 and 43 mm in length. For each nerve he recorded the time required (in seconds) for the muscle to contract when the nerve was stimulated at its farther and its nearer point. The time difference was recorded and from this the speed of the impulse in meters per second was calculated from the simple formula $V = L/D$, where $V$ = velocity, $L$ = length of segment, and $D$ = time difference for nearest and farthest point stimulated.

Some of the data collected by Helmholtz are given in Table 13–1. Note that the calculations show considerable variation among the different nerve segments. Now, recall from Chapter 5 that the *variance* of a sample of data indicates how reliable the data are. Calculations from the data in Table 13–1 show that the variance is indeed quite high. (See Appendix 2 for an explanation of how to calculate variance.) This variance probably indicates that a considerable amount of experimental error was involved in making these measurements.* Since Helmholtz' time it has also been shown that rate of conduction in nerves is dependent on the type of nerve fiber and on its diameter (refer to the graph in Fig. 5–8).

However, the results of Helmholtz' experiments do show clearly that the nerve impulse is *not* transmitted like an electric current. That there is some electrical activity involved is unquestionable, since the passage of the impulse along a nerve can be recorded by the same apparatus which records an electrical impulse along a wire. But the speed of conduction in the fastest nerve fibers known (those leading to skeletal muscles in the mammal) is at best only around

---

* In view of the small fractions of seconds with which Helmholtz was working, such discrepancies in the calculated velocity are not surprising. Despite the discrepancies, the mean rate of conduction for this sample, 29.5 m/sec, is nevertheless not far from the currently accepted value of 30 m/sec for the same nerve in the frog.

FIG. 13–13   The giant nerve fiber of the squid, by virtue of its size, allows experimental testing of the "sodium pump" hypothesis. It has recently been shown with such nerves that virtually all of the cytoplasm can be removed and replaced with artificial solutions via a small glass tube. Although such a system is apparently quite lifeless, it displays all the essential behavior of a normal living nerve. This photograph shows the cytoplasm already extruded. (Photo courtesy Trevor I. Shaw, from *Discovery*, March 1966.)

120 m/sec. This is so much less than the velocity at which an electric current is transmitted that we are compelled to look to other principles in trying to understand the exact nature of the nerve impulse.

One clue is given by the fact that the rate of nerve conduction is dependent on temperature in precisely the same way as chemical reactions are. This suggests that the impulse itself may be *electrochemical* in nature. In other words, propagation of the nerve impulse may be the result of the movement of particles (molecules or ions) bearing positive or negative charges. With this hypothesis in mind, we shall turn to experimental evidence gathered in recent years, on which our current concept of nerve conduction is based.

In the last several decades physiologists have learned a great deal about the nature of the nerve impulse by experiments performed on the giant axon of the squid (see Fig. 13–13). For the nerve physiologist the squid axon is a remarkable gift of nature. Its very large diameter of 1 mm (as compared to the human nerve-cell axon, whose diameter is about 0.01 mm) makes it possible to perform detailed studies of changes inside and outside the nerve cell during conduction.

The giant axon of the squid has anatomical features characteristic of all nerve cells. The membrane of the axon is composed of layers of protein and lipid whose thickness varies from 50 to 100 Å. The membrane is quite selective as to the ions and molecules which pass through it.

Conduction in the nerve cell can be studied with an instrument known as a voltmeter. A voltmeter consists mainly of two recording electrodes, connected to a meter which records differences in electric potential between the electrodes. The instrument can be used in two different ways to study nerve impulses. In one case, both electrodes are placed on the outside of the axon. With this method any differences in potential between two parts of the outer axon surface can be measured (Fig. 13–14a). In the other case, one electrode is placed inside the axon while the other is placed on the surface (Fig. 13–14b). This arrangement makes it possible to measure changes in potential on the inside as compared to the outside at any given point on the axon. Thus the voltmeter provides a way of measuring difference in potential between any two points with which the electrodes are in contact.

The data given in Fig. 13–14(b) yield a considerable amount of information about the nature of the nerve impulse. In the top left drawing we see that the nerve impulse itself has not reached the region of the axon where the recording electrodes are located. Hence that part of the axon is in a resting condition and shows, electrically, what is called its **resting potential.** The voltmeter indicates further that in the resting condition, the outside of the nerve is positively charged with respect to the inside. The potential is measured as 70 millivolts (mv). On the graph to the right, it is shown as the horizontal part of the graph line. When the nerve impulse reaches the region of the membrane spanned by the two electrodes (middle drawing), some dramatic changes occur. The needle on the voltmeter swings first to zero, and then to the negative side of the scale. Thus the outside of the axon becomes not only as negatively charged as the inside, but *even more so.* This is represented on the graph by the sharp upswing of the graph line. The reversal of potential between inside and outside is only temporary, however. The graph line slopes down again, indicating that the original membrane potential is eventually restored (bottom drawing); the outside once again becomes positively charged with respect to the inside.

How can we account for these changes? What is happening in the nerve axon and its surrounding medium to cause the impulse to be generated and propagated down the entire axon? Once started, the nerve impulse travels the length of the axon without further stimulus from the outside. Furthermore, like a muscle cell, a nerve cell has a threshold, and fires in the all-or-nothing manner. Any theory of nerve conduction must account for all of these observations.

As has been indicated, in the resting state intact nerve (and muscle) fibers exhibit a steady difference of electrical potential across their membranes, with the exterior being positive in relation to the interior. The reasons for this polarization are revealed by investigations of the chemistry of the fibers themselves as well as the extracellular fluids which surround them. These fluids contain several positive ions, principally sodium and potassium, and negative ions, principally chloride. To differing degrees, each of these ions can diffuse across the membrane. Within the nerve cells are negatively charged ions to which the nerve cell membrane is impermeable. As a consequence of the resulting negative-inside, positive-outside electrical gradient, the negative chloride ions are excluded while the positive sodium and potassium ions tend to be drawn through the cell membrane into the cell interior. Despite this latter tendency, however,

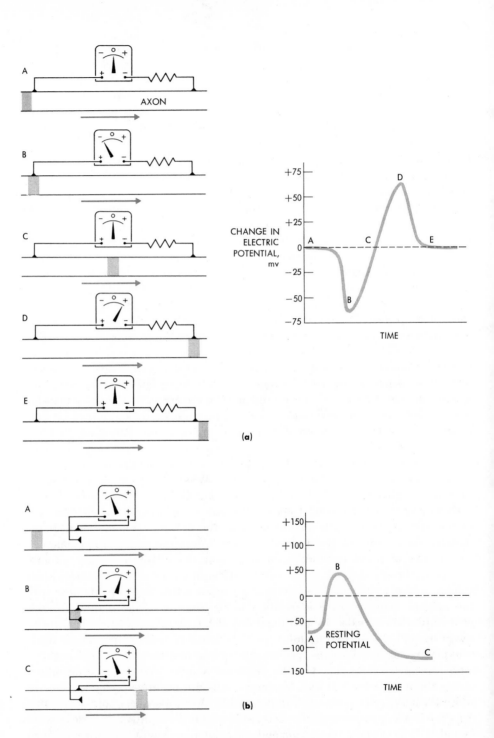

(a)

(b)

◀ FIG. 13–14     Measurement of difference in electric potential between two points on a nerve.  The gray shading on the nerve axon represents the nerve impulse.  (a) Voltmeter reading taken when both recording electrodes are placed on the outside of the axon.  (b) Reading taken when one electrode is outside and the other inside.  Neurophysiologists describe the resting potential as a negative potential, negative with respect to the internal electrode; thus the resting potential is recorded as −70 mv moving up to +47 mv.  The figures to the right represent the meter readings in graph form.

measurements of ion concentrations show that only the potassium ions are in higher concentrations inside than outside.  The sodium ions, on the other hand, are found in higher concentrations outside the cell than within it.

It is evident that since the sodium ions *can* pass through the cell membrane and since there is present within the cell a negative-charge force that would tend to make them do so, there must be present some sort of energy-expending mechanism to keep them out.  This mechanism is referred to as the "**sodium pump.**"  The result of the activity of the sodium pump is the establishment of a strong electrochemical gradient in favor of moving sodium ions into the cell.  In turn, the accumulation of positive potassium ions inside the cell because of the presence of negative ions within that cannot pass out, creates a chemical concentration gradient *favoring an outflow of potassium ions*.  The resulting deficit of positive charges accounts for the negatively charged interior of the nerve cell.  In summary, the "resting" nerve cell exhibits an equilibrium of chemical concentration and electrical gradients.  The resulting potential difference constitutes the resting potential of the nerve, e.g., as measured by the voltmeter at −70 mv in Fig. 13–14.

With the information just discussed and with the results of voltmeter studies, it is now possible to propose a hypothesis to account for the conduction of impulses along the nerve fiber.

It has already been indicated that the nerve cell membrane differs in its permeability to various kinds of ions.  Figure 13–15 shows that immediately after stimulation the nerve cell membrane suddenly becomes highly and specifically permeable to sodium ions, some of which respond by immediately moving into the nerve cell interior.  The nerve resting potential has now become an action potential.  The influx of sodium ions continues to a point which is actually *beyond* the neutral or depolarized state, and the result is the temporary reversal of polarity shown by the voltmeter in Fig. 13–14(a). However, the potential starts to be restored almost immediately, as the gradual downward slope of the graph line in Fig. 13–14(b) indicates.  These observations raise two important questions: How does the nerve impulse, once started, propagate itself down the entire length of the nerve?  And, once the membrane has undergone the reversal of polarity that occurs, how is the original potential reestablished?

The hypothesis to answer the first question is based at least partly on the observation that, when any portion of a nerve cell axon is stimulated (by a

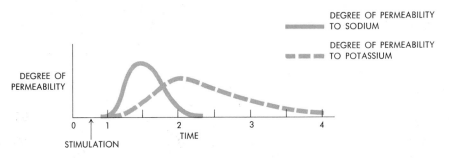

FIG. 13–15   The degree of permeability of the nerve cell membrane to sodium and potassium ions as a function of time after stimulation. These data indicate that, immediately after stimulation, sodium ion rush into the axon; this is followed slightly later by the outflow of potassium ions from the cell. (Adapted from R. D. Keynes, "The Nerve Impulse and the Squid." *Scientific American*, December 1958, p. 86.)

threshold dose of electric current, for example), the membrane seems to lose its impermeability in the region of stimulation. Depolarization followed immediately by polarity reversal of a specific region of the axon causes the area next to it to become permeable, producing reversal at that point, and so on down the axon. It is like a series of chain reactions. Once the process gets going, each stage triggers the next. Thus the nerve impulse can loosely be described as a wave of polarity reversal sweeping down the axon. If the axon is stimulated in the middle, the wave of polarity reversal spreads in both directions. If the axon is stimulated at either end, the impulse will spread in only one direction the whole length of the nerve cell. This, of course, merely describes what may happen during nerve impulse propagation along the fiber; the precise *explanation* of how this propagation may occur in terms of electrical charges, etc., still remains.

The second question—How is membrane resting potential restored after polarity reversal?—is also difficult to answer with certainty. As Fig. 13–15 indicates, the stimulus-caused change in nerve cell membrane permeability leading to sodium ion influx is followed by an outward movement of potassium ions. That it is this outward movement of potassium ions which first restores the membrane potential after polarity reversal, rather than the sodium pump, is shown by demonstrating that a nerve cell is still capable of carrying many impulses without any sodium-pump activity. It is only after a relatively long period of inactivity that the sodium pump acts to restore the original sodium-potassium ion distribution characteristic of the resting nerve cell.

The concept of the sodium pump is an excellent example of a scientific hypothetical model constructed to account for a natural phenomenon—in this case, the extrusion of sodium ions from the nerve cell against a concentration gradient. There is no requirement that the pump bear any resemblance to reality; no one actually visualizes a pump in the sense of an actual mechanical pump present in the nerve cell. It is only necessary that the model adequately account for the

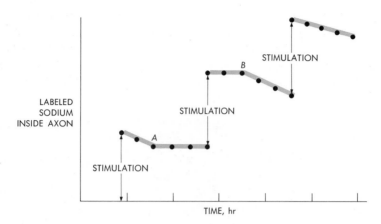

FIG. 13–16    A giant axon is placed in a medium containing radioactive sodium ions as a "tracer." When the axon is stimulated the first time, the amount of tracer sodium inside the axon increases markedly. The sodium concentration inside eventually begins to fall as a result of the action of the "sodium pump." At point A a metabolic poison known to block the production of ATP is injected into the axon. This stops the active transport of sodium ions out of the cell. At B the poison is washed out of the axon, thereby restoring its ability to remove sodium ions. (Adapted from R. D. Keynes, "The Nerve Impulse and the Squid." *Scientific American*, December 1958, p. 90.)

known data concerning sodium ion distribution as well as allow accurate predictions to be made.

Often a scientific model will also suggest additional experiments to test its accuracy. For example, all mechanical pumps require an expenditure of energy. The sodium-pump hypothetical model predicts, therefore, that, if the energy-yielding processes of the nerve cell are blocked, normal reestablishment of the resting potential will eventually be prevented. To test this hypothesis, the following experiment can be performed. If the giant axon of the squid is placed in a medium containing radioactively labeled sodium, it is possible to measure changes in the sodium ion concentration inside and outside the cell under various conditions. The results of one set of experiments are shown in Fig. 13–16. After an initial stimulation, the sodium ion concentration inside the axon is noted to rise. Immediately, however, the sodium pump begins to work and the sodium ion level drops. Presumably, energy is being expended in this process. At point A, a metabolic inhibitor known to block the production of ATP is injected into the axon. The extrusion of sodium ion soon ceases. A second stimulation causes more sodium ions to rush into the nerve cell. With the inhibitor still present, however, the sodium ions cannot be eliminated. At point B the inhibitor is washed away, thus restoring the metabolic processes which produce ATP. The sodium ion level is seen to fall. A third stimulation temporarily increases the sodium ion concentration within the nerve axon, but it is removed by the sodium pump when the stimulation has ceased. These data support the idea that the sodium pump does, indeed, exist and functions as a form of active transport.

Intriguingly, there is evidence that the idea of a molecular pump for ions such as sodium may not be as farfetched as it sounds. In 1968, Dr. A. G. Lowe of Manchester University in England put forth a hypothesis based on the idea that the ATP-splitting enzyme (ATPase) acts almost like a simple rocking-arm pump. A simplified version of Dr. Lowe's model is shown here:

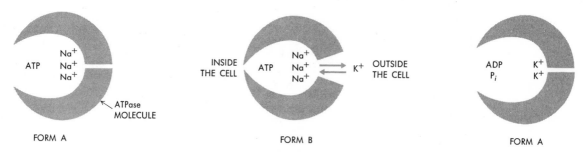

The ATPase molecule is visualized as being imbedded in the cell membrane and in contact with both the internal and external environment of the cell. In form A, the ATPase molecule allows sodium ions plus ATP to diffuse into it. As a result of binding with the ATP and sodium, the enzyme's conformation is changed to form B, making the sodium ions available for exchange with the potassium ions in the external environment but isolating the sodium ions from the cell interior. When all the sodium ions have been replaced in the ATPase molecule by potassium ions, the ATP is hydrolyzed and the ATPase returns to form A, thereby releasing the potassium ions and products of ATP hydrolysis back into the cell.

Lowe has suggested that drugs such as ouabain, known to inhibit both active transport and the ATPase enzyme, may act by "locking" the enzyme into one of its two forms (probably form B). The Lowe model is doubly interesting because, besides such phenomena as the sodium pump, it may also explain substrate phosphorylation (see Section 8–4), in which ATP is generated, by picturing the phosphorylation process as a reversal of the steps described for active transport. Such models provide valuable new ideas for future experimentation.

The current picture of the means by which a nerve impulse is conducted along the fiber can be summarized as follows:

1) Nerve stimulation results in a sharply increased permeability to sodium ions in the nerve cell membrane. Sodium ions move in, temporarily reversing the polarity of the nerve cell from negative inside and positive outside to positive inside and negative outside. *It is this "wave" of polarity reversal sweeping along the nerve fiber that comprises the nerve impulse.*

2) After polarity reversal, the membrane is first restored to its original negative-inside, positive-outside polarity by the outward migration of potassium ions.

3) The sequence of events in both (1) and (2) occurs within a few milliseconds. During a relatively long period of inactivity, the sodium pump actively trans-

ports sodium ions from inside to outside the nerve cell. This outward movement of sodium ions causes the cell interior to become highly negative again because of the negative ions within that cannot pass through the cell membrane. The positive potassium ions are thus drawn back into the cell, and the normal resting potential is restored.

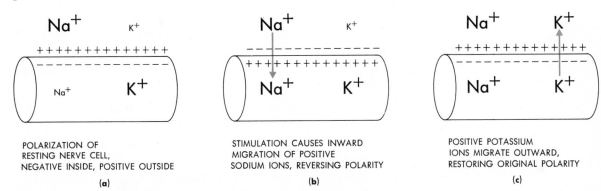

POLARIZATION OF RESTING NERVE CELL, NEGATIVE INSIDE, POSITIVE OUTSIDE

**(a)**

STIMULATION CAUSES INWARD MIGRATION OF POSITIVE SODIUM IONS, REVERSING POLARITY

**(b)**

POSITIVE POTASSIUM IONS MIGRATE OUTWARD, RESTORING ORIGINAL POLARITY

**(c)**

FIG. 13-17   Schematic illustration of the propagation of a nerve impulse down an axon. Later, the sodium pump and inward migration of potassium ions restore the original distribution of sodium and potassium ions.

The entire picture of nerve impulse conduction, summarized in Fig. 13-17, has been developed primarily within the last 25 years. Although many details have been worked out, many more problems still await answers from future researchers. For example, more knowledge is needed about the sodium pump and the nature of the nerve cell membrane. How does the membrane become more permeable to sodium ions when stimulated? How is the original degree of permeability restored? These and other questions form the basis of future hypotheses and experiments.

The nervous systems of all multicellular animals involve the complex interaction of many neurons. The nerve impulse initiated by one receptor cell (in the eye, for example) must be transmitted to secondary neurons which carry it to the brain or other parts of the central nervous system. Although each individual axon can transmit an impulse in either direction, this is not true of the intact nervous system. Here, the nerve impulses always travel on a one-way path. This one-way flow is maintained by the **synapse,** the junction between two neurons. The synapse thus plays an important role in coordination and function of the complex organism.

Neurons are situated so that the synapse represents the area where the end brush of one neuron lies next to the dendrites of another. The dendrites of any one neuron may form a synapse with the end brushes of a number of other neurons. A number of observations, both anatomical and experimental, have been made concerning the synapse. These provide the basis for formulating

**13-8
NEURON-TO-NEURON
CONNECTIONS:
THE SYNAPSE**

an hypothesis to explain how synaptic transmission of the nerve impulse may occur.

*Observation 1.* Light and electron micrographs of the synapse show that there is no direct connection (i.e., no physical contact) between the end brush of one neuron and the dendrites of the next.

*Observation 2.* The synapse slows down the transmission of the nerve impulse.

*Observation 3.* Transmission across a synapse is always one-way: from end brush to dendrite, never in the reverse direction.

*Observation 4.* Successive transmissions across a synapse bring about fatigue of the synapse area itself.

*Observation 5.* Stimulation of some nerves actually seems to inhibit the nerves which lead away from them at the synapse.

It was once thought that when a nerve impulse reached the end brush of one neuron it created an electric field across the synapse which depolarized the dendrites of the next neuron. However, this hypothesis could not explain adequately some of the observations given above. Most notably, observations 4 and 5 would not be predicted if synaptic transmission were due to creation of an electric field. There is certainly no reason why an electric field should produce fatigue at the synapse. Nor is there any satisfactory way to explain how the creation of an electric field should in some cases stimulate the postsynaptic neurons while in other cases it prevents them from firing.

A more recent hypothesis, which may be called the "chemical transmitter" hypothesis, has been proposed in an attempt to explain more adequately what happens at the synapse. It has been found that a chemical substance known as **acetylcholine** (abbreviated as ACh) is released at the synapse when an impulse reaches the end brush of the stimulated neuron. The structural formula of acetylcholine is shown below:

ACh is thought to be a transmitter substance, since it is capable of diffusing across the synaptic space. When enough molecules of ACh reach the dendrites of a second neuron, they cause that neuron to fire. Because dendrites do not release ACh, transmission of a nerve impulse at the synapse can occur in only one direction. When ACh reaches the dendrite of the postsynaptic neuron, it joins onto the dendrites at certain sensitive regions. Molecules of ACh are thought to

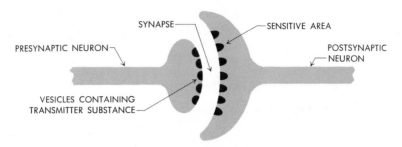

FIG. 13–18  The synapse, showing schematically the relation of presynaptic and postsynaptic neurons. The presynaptic neuron has in its end brush special vesicles in which molecules of acetylcholine are produced. When the impulse reaches the end brush, these molecules are released. They diffuse across the synaptic space and attach onto "sensitive" areas of the dendrites of the postsynaptic neuron. If enough molecules of acetylcholine are picked up by the postsynaptic neuron, it will fire. The molecules attached to the postsynaptic fiber are soon destroyed by an enzyme known as cholinesterase.

attach to the sensitive sites in much the same way as enzymes fit onto substrate molecules (Fig. 13–18). It is not known at present just how the binding of ACh to the postsynaptic neuron changes the permeability of the membrane enough to cause the neuron to fire.

If the chemical transmitter theory is correct, why do postsynaptic fibers not continue firing indefinitely once ACh molecules have attached to the sensitive sites? Neurophysiologists and biochemists have isolated and identified an enzyme known as **cholinesterase,** located in the receiving dendrite. Cholinesterase, as its name implies, acts on acetylcholine, breaking it down into an inactive form. The postsynaptic membrane can thus repair itself and be prepared to fire again if more ACh is released. All of this occurs relatively quickly in the intact organism. The distance across the synapse is about one micron, and it requires about one or two milliseconds for the ACh released by the presynaptic vesicles to reach the other side. The time required for diffusion explains why impulses which must travel across synapses take slightly longer than those traveling the same distance over single nerve cells.

Successive stimulation of a series of nerves produces fatigue at the synapse. The chemical transmitter theory accounts for this by assuming that the presynaptic vesicles contain only a limited amount of ACh. Successive stimulation uses up ACh more rapidly than the cell can synthesize it. Thus the synapse becomes fatigued, and a temporary block to further nerve conduction occurs.

Not all neurons release the same transmitter substance at the synapse. Although many release ACh or other excitatory substances, some release substances which actually make the postsynaptic fibers *less* excitable. The precise chemical nature of these inhibitory substances is not known. But a chemical known as $\gamma$-aminobutyric acid, known to be present in the central nervous systems of mammals, has such an inhibitory effect.  The structural formula for γ-aminobutyric acid is shown below.

$$
\begin{array}{c}
\quad\; H \qquad H \\
\quad\;\; \diagdown \quad \diagup \\
H \quad H \quad N \quad O \\
\;| \qquad | \qquad | \qquad \| \\
H-C-C-C-C-OH \\
\;| \qquad | \qquad | \\
H \quad H \quad H
\end{array}
$$

The acid is a definite inhibitor at certain crayfish synapses, where it diminishes the permeability of the postsynaptic dendrites to sodium ions.  This makes the cell less excitable, thus raising the threshold required for stimulation.  The value of inhibitory neurons is obvious when we consider the total coordination of the organism.  This was touched on previously in Section 13–6.  No coordinated movement would be possible if all the muscles contracted simultaneously.  Although a simple lack of stimulation can achieve this to some degree, actual inhibition of specific neurons provides more precise control over muscle activity.

**13-9
THE
NEUROMUSCULAR
JUNCTION**

The joining of a nerve end brush with a muscle fiber is called the **neuromuscular junction.**  The nerve fiber branches at its end, each branch adhering tightly to the sheath covering a single muscle fiber.  At the tips of the many nerve branches are small pockets thought to contain ACh; these are similar to ACh pockets of the presynaptic end brush.  There is also much similarity in the functioning of the neuromuscular junction and the synapse.  When a nerve impulse reaches the neuromuscular junction, a small amount of transmitter substance is released in the minute space between the end brush and the muscle fiber.  Just as at the synapse, the transmitter substance at the neuromuscular junction causes the muscle-cell membrane to become more permeable to sodium and potassium ions.  The resulting movement of ions causes depolarization at the motor end plate.  This depolarization in turn excites adjacent regions and an impulse comparable to the nerve impulse is generated.  An action current thus sweeps down the muscle fiber, stimulating the reaction between actin and myosin discussed in Section 13–5.  Soon after the transmitter substance is released at the neuromuscular junction, it is destroyed by an enzyme in the same manner as at the nerve synapse.

In mammals, two types of transmitter substances are known to be produced at different neuromuscular junctions.  One type of nerve ending produces ACh; the other produces epinephrine.*  The two types of nerves differentiated in this way form the autonomic nervous system, to be discussed in Section 13–12.

A number of drugs are known to act directly on nerves or the neuromuscular junction, e.g., nicotine and caffeine.  A person who has taken in too much caffeine

---

* This hormone is sometimes called *adrenaline,* though this term is in reality a trade name and not the scientific name.

(from coffee or various colas) often feels "jittery" because his nerves are more sensitive to stimulation and fire more readily. This is why caffeine is called a stimulant. Other drugs serve to inhibit activity at the neuromuscular junction. One powerful inhibitor is the drug curare, long known as a poison by Indians of Central and South America. The exact mechanism by which curare acts is not known, but it seems to affect muscle membranes in such a way that the transmitter substance fails to perform its task. An animal poisoned with curare dies by paralysis.

Still another class of substances acts on the neuromuscular junction—but by an entirely different mechanism. An example of such a substance is di-isopropyl-fluorophosphate (DFP for short). DFP prevents the hydrolysis of ACh by the enzyme cholinesterase, thus allowing the muscle fiber to continue firing once a single stimulus has been applied. A person exposed to DFP has prolonged muscle spasms and convulsions, leading eventually to death.

13-10
THE NERVOUS
SYSTEM

An isolated muscle, when stimulated, will contract. However, most useful muscular activity is performed by intact muscles within a living organism. Here, most of the action of muscle on bone to produce an organized movement is triggered by impulses originating within and conveyed by the nervous system. The entire system is composed of nerve cells (neurons). These can be divided into three types, according to their function:

1) **Sensory neurons.** Sensory neurons transmit information from sensory receptors such as eyes, ears, skin, etc. It is the sensory neurons which enable the detection of environmental stimuli, such as light, sound, odors, heat, cold, and contact.

No living organism is fully aware of its surrounding environment. It can only perceive that part of its world which it is equipped to perceive. Thus for the simple amoeba there is no such thing as noise, for it has no organs of hearing. For most dogs and cats there is no color, for their eyes lack the proper visual pigments to perceive it.

An environmental stimulus can be viewed as simply an expression of energy transmission. A sense organ is a sensory nerve ending specialized for the detection of one form of this energy. A noise, for example is an expression of sound energy, which is transmitted as waves of compression and decompression in a medium such as air or water; the ear is a receptor designed to detect such waves. Light is a form of radiant energy; the eye a specialized receptor for its detection. No matter what the receptor, however, its communication with the central nervous system takes place entirely via sensory nerve processes.

The specialization of sensory organs and thus of the sensory neurons which supply them is illustrated by the fact that we often must translate one form of energy into another before we are aware of its presence. Television waves, for example, are all around us. Yet, lacking the proper mechanisms for doing so, we cannot perceive them. In order to receive these waves, we must employ an instrument (a TV set) that translates them into wavelengths of visible light, which our eyes can perceive. Television sets, radios, and most scientific instruments are thus simply extensions of our biological sensory receptors. The specialization of sensory neurons to the form of energy which they detect is further illustrated by the fact that the auditory nerve, which supplies the ear, interprets pain as sound (i.e., as a ringing in the ears). On the other hand, the optic nerve, which supplies the eye, interprets pain in terms of flashes or pinpoints of light (i.e., "seeing stars").

2) **Motor neurons.** Merely sensing an environmental stimulus is only one part of the functioning of a higher organism—an active response, involving muscular contraction, may be required. Active responses are brought about by impulses conveyed to the muscles by motor neurons.

3) **Association neurons.** The roles carried out by sensory and motor neurons are quite specialized ones. Sensory neurons are quite incapable of causing motor action and motor neurons cannot detect environmental stimuli. For a sensory stimulus to be translated into action, it must be connected to motor neurons. The necessary connection is provided in the **central nervous system**—i.e., in the brain and spinal cord—by association neurons. These serve the same function as connector plugs in a telephone switchboard. Incoming stimuli from sensory neurons are hooked up to the appropriate motor neurons in much the same way that a telephone operator uses a plug on the switchboard to connect an incoming call with its appropriate destination.

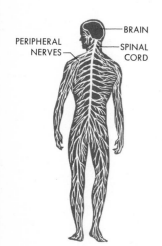

PERIPHERAL NERVES — BRAIN — SPINAL CORD

The entire nervous system of a higher animal can be divided into two regions. The first is the central nervous system, consisting of the brain and spinal cord. The second region, the **peripheral nervous system,** consists of sensory and motor neurons which extend to virtually every region of the body.

Scientific knowledge of the anatomy of the human brain has come largely through dissection. However, the functions of the parts of the brain are not so easily ascertained. A logical first step in determining the function of a body organ is to remove it and see what effect its removal has on the organism. Needless to say, such experiments cannot be carried out on human beings. Therefore, scientific knowledge concerning brain function is largely based on two sources of information. The first of these is extrapolation from studies made on experimental animals where one part or section of the brain is removed. Changes in the animal's subsequent behavior are a clue as to what part of the animal's activity is governed by that section of the brain. A second source of information is observations made by surgeons on patients suffering from brain damage (caused by an accident, by disease, or by a congenital malformation). A man deprived from birth of his cerebral cortex (the outer region of the cerebrum), is capable of performing only the most basic animal functions, such as excretion, ingestion, etc. He is in no way capable of any reasoning. It is logical to assume, therefore, that the cerebral cortex is responsible for carrying out that function. Such observations provide much valuable information concerning the function of all brain parts. They also tend to confirm the validity of extrapolating information gained from the study of other animals' brains to that of man.

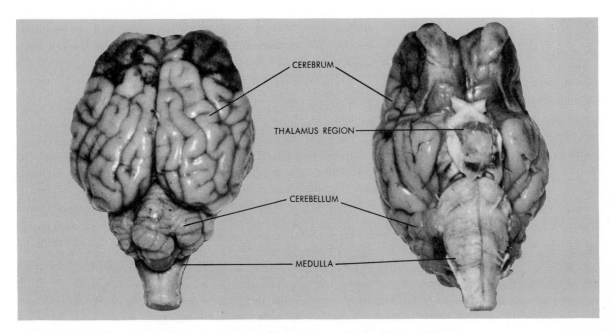

FIG. 13-19    A sheep's brain viewed from the back (left) and the front (right).  (Courtesy Schettle Biologicals.)

As Fig. 13–19 shows, most of the brain is divided into two halves, or hemispheres. The most prominent region of the brain is the **cerebrum,** composed of the cell bodies of several billion association neurons. It is to the cerebrum that signals for most (though not all) action originates. The cerebrum, then, is an "association center." It receives sensory stimuli and translates them via the motor neurons into an appropriate response.

The cerebrum also stores information gathered through the senses, and is thus the area responsible for memory. If regions of his cerebrum are touched with a needle through which a mild electric shock is applied, a human patient can be made to recall quite minor incidents in his life—incidents which he had long since forgotten. This seems to indicate that all information, no matter how trivial, is stored in the cerebrum. In view of the length of a human lifetime, and the many thousands of bits of information gathered each minute by the senses, the storage capacity of the cerebrum must, indeed, be prodigious.

There is as yet no completely satisfactory hypothesis to explain the mechanism of memory storage. Some puzzling facts emerge. For example, surgical removal of one half of the cerebrum may have little or no effect on intelligence or memory—there seems to be little need for intercommunication of the cerebral regions. Moreover, rats can be trained to a maze and then their cerebral hemispheres criss-crossed with several cuts to sever all connections between the regions, yet such rats remember their previous training as well as control rats do.

Many laboratories are now working to find a molecular basis of memory. While the results of such work have at times been contradictory, there is hope that some clues will be found in the near future. This seems to be one of the most promising areas of research in the field.

Motor impulses from the cerebrum are sent to another region of the brain, the **cerebellum.** The cerebellum "sorts out" these impulses and sends them to the appropriate muscles at the proper time in order to effect an orderly muscle response. The cerebellum improves in its performance of these duties as the organism matures and practice is gained. The helpless thrashings of a human infant show little sorting of cerebral signals on the part of the cerebellum. As the infant grows, the signals become better coordinated; the infant learns to pick things up and to crawl. Even learning to ride a bicycle, which calls for muscular coordination in response to the sense of balance, depends primarily on having the proper sequence of nerve impulses sent out from the cerebellum. Accidental damage to the cerebellum may cause a human being to lose coordinated control of his muscular activities; his motions may revert to those of an infant.

The **thalamus** is an area consisting of the thick walls of a cavity deep within the brain, below the cerebrum. This area is a relay center for incoming sensory impulses. Just under it is the **hypothalamus,** containing centers for regulating body temperature. The front part of the hypothalamus keeps the body from getting too hot; the back part keeps it from getting too cold. Also regulated by the thalamus and hypothalamus are appetite, water balance, carbohydrate and fat metabolism, blood pressure, emotional state, and sleep.

The **medulla** of the brain is the swollen area of the anterior spinal cord which connects the cord to the brain. The medulla walls are thick and composed mostly of nerve tracts leading up from the spinal cord into the higher regions of the brain. The medulla also contains nerve centers which control many involuntary physiological processes, such as breathing, heart rate, blood vessel contraction or dilation (which, in turn, raises or lowers the blood pressure), and vomiting. Certain viruses, such as those causing polio, may invade the spinal fluid surrounding the spinal cord. If the virus reaches the medulla, death may result through paralysis of important nerve tracts.

Most of the brain, as we have seen, is divided into two halves. From the top, the cerebrum is seen to be divided into right and left hemispheres. Upon entering the brain, nerve tracks from one side of the body cross with those from the other side. Thus the left side of the brain is largely responsible for the right side of the body, and vice versa. The hemispheres of the cerebellum are connected by the **pons,** a thick bundle of nerve fibers. This connection allows coordination of movement of both sides of the body.

From the mammalian brain extend twelve pairs of **cranial nerves.** While most of these nerves innervate structures in the head and neck regions, a few extend to other body regions as well. The vagus nerve, for example, innervates the stomach and heart; in the latter, it serves to slow the heartbeat.

Extending from the back of the brain is the long **spinal cord.** In vertebrates, the spinal cord runs through the hollow center of the vertebrae, and is thus protected from injury. Paired **spinal nerves** extend to each side of the body from the spinal cord, which is covered on the outside by three membranes, the **meninges.** Both the spinal cord and brain are bathed by **cerebrospinal fluid,** which contains mineral salts and traces of proteins and sugar. The cerebrospinal fluid helps to protect the nervous system from physical shock, and probably also plays a role in its nutrition.

The entire nervous system is composed, on one hand, of regions with heavy concentrations of nerve cell bodies and, on the other, of regions which are entirely composed of nerve cell processes, either axons or dendrites. In regions where nerve cell bodies predominate, the heavy concentration of cell cytoplasm gives the tissue a definite grayish color, hence the term, "gray matter." The cortex of the cerebrum is such a region. Where nerve-cell processes predominate, as in the cerebellum, the nerve tissue is called "white matter." Gray matter makes up the center of the spinal cord; here are found the cell bodies of association neurons, which make the connection between sensory and motor neurons. The outer region of the cord is composed of white matter, the axons and dendrites leading to and from the brain as well as out of the spinal cord into the peripheral nervous system.

The familiar white, threadlike nerves seen in a dissected body are only the axons and dendrites of the centrally located neurons. A cross section of such a nerve looks much like a cross section of a telephone cable carrying several wires. Each individual nerve cell process is insulated from others by fatty sheaths. The nerve cell bodies are located either within the spinal cord or just outside it in the dorsal root of the ganglion. Some of the axons of the motor neurons and the dendrites of sensory neurons—those, for example, that extend from the big toe to just outside of the spinal cord—may be as much as three or four feet long.

Suppose that a frog is decapitated, and its upper body, heart, and other organs removed so that there is little left except the backbone, spinal cord, hind legs, and a few other associated tissues. If acetic acid is applied to the hind-leg skin, the hind legs will make strenuous and well-coordinated "scratching" movements which seem aimed at removal of the irritant (Fig. 13–20). It seems evident, then, that while the brain may play a role in the initiation and coordination of muscular activity, its presence is by no means always essential for such activity to occur. By further experimentation on freshly prepared frogs, this response can be studied further, and it can be shown that only the legs, the skin to which the acid is applied, the nerves which supply both, and the region of the spinal cord to which these nerves are attached are necessary for the response to occur.

If a cat is operated upon, and the proper dorsal root of its spinal cord cut (as in Fig. 13–21), the cat will feel no pain in the appendage innervated by the cut nerve, but will still be able to move it. If, on the other hand, the ventral

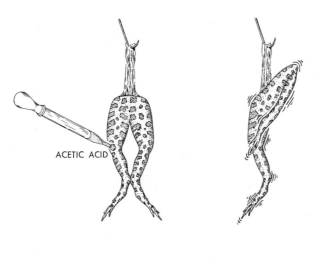

FIG. 13–20  With only the legs and spinal cord intact, a ''frog'' can still respond appropriately to a stimulus.

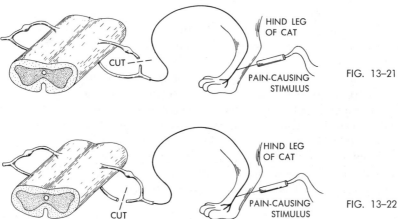

FIG. 13–21

FIG. 13–22

nerve fibers are cut (Fig. 13–22), the cat will feel pain in the affected appendage but will be unable to move it. Such studies, combined with clinical case histories of human patients, show that the dorsal root of the spinal cord is composed of incoming sensory neurons, while the ventral root is composed of outgoing motor neurons.

The dissection and microscopic examination of the gray matter of the spinal cord having revealed the presence of association and motor nerve cell bodies, we can hypothesize an explanation for the response shown by the frog and cat. Sensory neurons transmit impulses to the association neurons which in turn stimulate the appropriate motor neurons—either at the same level of the spinal cord, or via ascending and descending tracts in the white matter, to other levels. This hypothesis can be experimentally tested and supported by showing that an operational blockage of any one of the links in the hypothesized stimulus-response chain effectively prevents the typical response. Operational blockage elsewhere in the nervous system has no effect on the response.

The response shown by the frog is an example of a **reflex action,** in this case, a rather complex one. Many reflex actions are known in animals, the most familiar probably being the knee-jerk reflex in humans, which is a routine part of most physical examinations. A tap on the knee just below the kneecap results in a sudden kick by the lower leg. Like the frog's reaction to the acetic acid, the knee-jerk reflex is a stretch reflex which can be shown to be independent of the brain. The tap on the tendon below the kneecap stretches the muscle to which the tendon is attached and excites stretch receptors in the muscle. The impulse is transmitted by sensory nerve fibers to the spinal cord and from there returned to the muscle via a motor nerve, which causes contraction and movement of the lower leg. The impulses which travel to the brain do little more than inform the patient as to what has happened; the brain plays no role in bringing about the kicking response.

In some reflexes, several association neurons may be involved in conveying the sensory neuron's impulse to the motor neurons. By repetitions of the reflex action, the time which elapses between stimulus and response can be shortened. The fact that the decrease in this time interval occurs in discrete units of time, rather than gradually, supports an hypothesis proposing that shorter pathways, eliminating some of the intermediate association neurons involved, are being followed.

At times, reflex actions may be of considerable advantage to an organism. A hand placed on a hot stove will be jerked away before the brain can possibly become aware of what has happened. The time saved pays off in less damage to the hand. Care must be exercised in interpreting this fact, however. The reflex action of removing the hand from the stove is brought about by the mechanics of the system involved and *not*, in any conscious sense, for the purpose of preventing more damage. The selective advantage offered by reflex actions are obvious enough to account for their evolution without resorting to teleological explanations.

Not all reflex actions are built in, as is the knee-jerk response. Some have to be learned through repetition of a sequence of events, such as those involved in learning to play a musical instrument or to drive. The Russian physiologist Pavlov, for example, working with dogs, caused the ringing of a bell to be followed by feeding of the animals. After a time, the dogs would secrete saliva whenever they heard the bell, even though no food was given. Here was a reflex action not ordinarily present among the behavior patterns displayed by the dogs. Such experimentally established behavior patterns are known as **conditioned reflexes.**

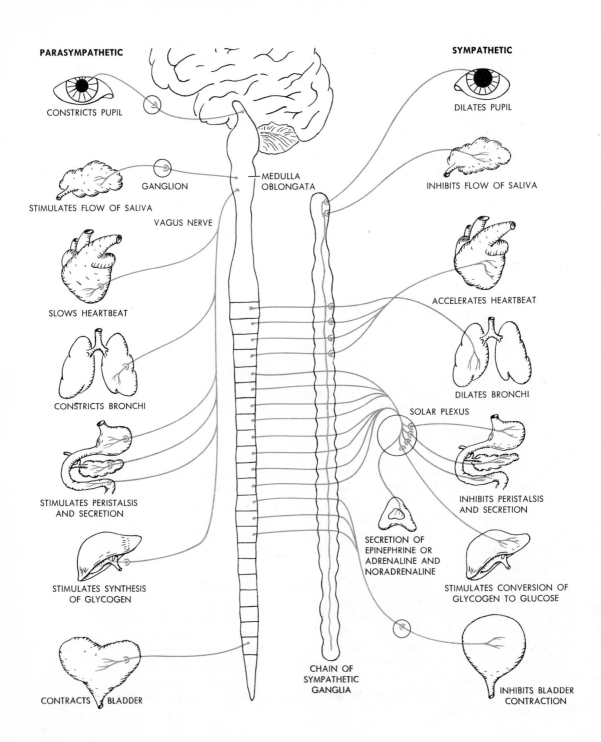

PARASYMPATHETIC

SYMPATHETIC

CONSTRICTS PUPIL

DILATES PUPIL

GANGLION

MEDULLA
OBLONGATA

INHIBITS FLOW OF SALIVA

STIMULATES FLOW OF SALIVA

VAGUS NERVE

ACCELERATES HEARTBEAT

SLOWS HEARTBEAT

DILATES BRONCHI

CONSTRICTS BRONCHI

SOLAR PLEXUS

STIMULATES PERISTALSIS
AND SECRETION

INHIBITS PERISTALSIS
AND SECRETION

SECRETION OF
EPINEPHRINE OR
ADRENALINE AND
NORADRENALINE

STIMULATES SYNTHESIS
OF GLYCOGEN

STIMULATES CONVERSION OF
GLYCOGEN TO GLUCOSE

CHAIN OF
SYMPATHETIC
GANGLIA

CONTRACTS BLADDER

INHIBITS BLADDER
CONTRACTION

◄ FIG. 13–23    The human autonomic nervous system. The parasympathetic and sympathetic nervous systems work antagonistically to each other. Note that the nerve supplying the adrenal gland does not pass through any synapses after leaving the spinal cord. (From John W. Kimball, *Biology*, 2nd edition. Reading, Mass.: Addison-Wesley, 1968.)

**13-12
THE AUTONOMIC
NERVOUS SYSTEM**

Many of man's body organs function perfectly well without any conscious effort on the part of their owner. Peristaltic contraction by the intestines, beating of the heart, and secretion activity of the pancreas all require no conscious action. Nevertheless, all the organs involved are under control of the central nervous system. That portion of the central nervous system responsible for carrying out such involuntary vital processes is called the **autonomic nervous system** (Fig. 13–23).

The autonomic nervous system consists of two complete sets of nerves. One nerve from each set runs to each body organ. Although these nerves end at the same place, they originate at different points in the central nervous system. The effects of these two nerves are generally opposite. For example, one set (the **sympathetic**) speeds up the heart and slows down digestion. The other set (the **parasympathetic**) slows down the heart and speeds up digestion. It might be hypothesized that when the heart is beating slowly, only the parasympathetic nerves are sending down impulses, and that when the heart is going fast, only the sympathetic nerve is sending down impulses. Instruments designed to measure nerve activity, however, contradict this hypothesis; both nerves are sending down impulses at the same time. When the heart is beating quickly, more impulses are passing through the sympathetic nerve than through the parasympathetic nerve. Conversely, when the heart is beating slowly, more impulses are passing through the parasympathetic nerve than the sympathetic nerve.

There are several advantages to such an arrangement. It is rather like driving a team of horses by whipping them to make them go fast while at the same time pulling on the reins in order to slow them down. Such an arrangement allows an immediate response when the actual need to slow down or speed up arises. It also provides a finer level of control, since both processes are occurring at all times. An analogous situation exists with the heartbeat. The mere slowing or stopping of impulses in the parasympathetic nerve results in an immediate increase in the heartbeat. Similarly, a slowdown of impulses through the sympathetic nerve results in immediate heartbeat decrease.

Knowing that the heart is a muscle and that its contraction therefore has a chemical basis leads us to wonder just how the parasympathetic and sympathetic nerves bring about such a fine level of regulation. In 1920 the physiologist Otto Loewi performed an experiment to test the hypothesis that the sympathetic and parasympathetic nerves leading to the heart produced different transmitter substances with opposite effects. He removed one frog's heart with its sympathetic and parasympathetic nerves attached, and another heart with no nerves attached, then placed each preparation in a saline solution. After stimulating the parasympathetic nerves of the first preparation for a considerable period of time, Loewi removed the heart and its attached nerves from the saline bath and placed the second heart into this solution. His reasoning here can be analyzed as follows:

*Hypothesis: If ...*   parasympathetic fibers release an inhibitory substance which slows down the heart rate, ...

*Prediction: then ...* traces of this substance in the saline solution bathing a heart whose parasympathetic fibers had been stimulated should slow down a fresh heart placed into the solution.

When the second heart was placed in the saline bath, the rate of beating, as Loewi had predicted, was slowed down. The opposite effect was found when the experiment was repeated but with only the sympathetic fibers stimulated. The substances released by parasympathetic and sympathetic nerves were later isolated and identified. This seems to be conclusive support of Loewi's hypothesis. From this, it was later shown that similar situations existed at many neuromuscular junctions within the autonomic nervous system.

**13-13
THE SYSTEM OF
CHEMICAL
CONTROL**

In the sympathetic nervous system there is one nerve which goes directly to the organ it affects without going through any intermediate synapses (Fig. 13–23). The organ is the **adrenal gland,** located on the anterior surface of the kidney. The adrenal gland actually consists of two entirely independent glands, the outer **adrenal cortex** and a central **adrenal medulla.** From observations of the origin of the adrenal medulla in developing embryos, the medulla is seen to develop from neural cells. The hormone secreted by the medulla, epinephrine or adrenaline ($C_9H_{13}O_3N$), is the only hormone whose secretion is brought about directly by nervous stimulation. Epinephrine is released directly into the bloodstream and circulates throughout the body. Recall that a compound released into the bloodstream by one body structure that causes an effect elsewhere in the body is called a hormone. Hormones are secreted by a group of glands which, collectively, make up the **endocrine system.**

Epinephrine produces effects which are similar to those caused by stimulation of the entire sympathetic nervous system. The heartbeat and blood pressure are increased, sugar is released by the liver into the blood stream, and blood is diverted to the heart and muscles by dilation of the arterioles supplying them and contraction of those supplying the stomach and intestines. *Thus the adrenal medulla produces a hormone with effects identical to those caused by nerve transmitter substances.* The primary difference is one of speed; the effect of nervous stimulation is almost immediate, while epinephrine cannot move any faster than the bloodstream in which it is carried. There is also a factor of specificity; sympathetic nerve stimulation can be limited to a single organ, while epinephrine must affect every body part sensitive to it.

In a sense, the adrenal medulla can be pictured as a specialized ending of the sympathetic fiber which innervates it. Just as a peripheral nerve fiber causes the release of acetylcholine to stimulate the neuron one synapse away from it, so the adrenal medulla's sympathetic nerve causes the release of epinephrine to stimulate certain other regions of the body. This suggests a close relationship between the nervous system and the endocrine system—the system of which the adrenal medulla is a part.

Other observations bear out this idea. Immediately under the hypothalamus of the brain is located the **hypophysis,** or **pituitary gland.** The anterior region of this gland develops embryologically from the roof of the mouth. The posterior region, however, develops from the brain and is composed of modified nerve cells. This portion of the pituitary produces hormones which constrict arterioles, causing a rise in blood pressure and a reduction in urine volume. Another hormone produced here causes contraction of muscles in the wall of the uterus and probably plays a role in inducing labor.

Portions of the brain which adjoin the pituitary, especially certain regions of the hypothalamus, contain large amounts of the same hormones as the pituitary. These hormones may be produced there and simply stored in the posterior portion of the pituitary gland until released into the bloodstream. Regardless of their exact role, it is again clear that there exists an intimate relationship between the nervous and endocrine systems.

Perhaps nowhere is the close interrelationship of nervous and endocrine systems so evident as in animal reproductive systems. The successful reproduction of animals depends to a considerable extent upon the proper actions and responses of mating organisms, and to no less an extent upon the proper hormonal environment within the body. Furthermore, particularly in man, certain psychological factors may enter into reproductive patterns, at times suppressing or completely blocking them.

The gamete-producing organs of both the male and female reproductive systems (the testes and ovaries, respectively) are also endocrine glands. For instance, a portion of the mammalian ovary (the corpus luteum) secretes hormones which prepare the female for pregnancy, by buildup of the uterine lining for nourishment of the developing embryo, stimulation of the mammary glands to secrete milk, etc. Special cells in the testes (the interstitial cells of Leydig) produce **testosterone,** a hormone responsible for the adult development of the reproductive organs, deep voice, growth of beard, and other such characteristic changes associated with puberty.

Research on the endocrine glands generally proceeds from the macroscopic to the microscopic level. If tissue A is suspected of having an endocrine gland function, it is surgically removed from an experimental animal to see what deficiency, if any, the animal develops. A function for gland A (assuming that it is a gland) may already be suspected. Thus the reasoning may be expressed as follows:

**Hypothesis:** *If . . .* gland A plays a role in physiological process $x$, . . .

**Prediction:** *then . . .* surgical removal of gland A should result in a cessation of process $x$.

The cessation of process $x$ is usually detected by certain deficiency symptoms, such as failure to attain sexual maturity, drop in blood pressure, etc. Should the removal of tissue A have the predicted effect, extracts of the tissue may be prepared and injected into the animal's bloodstream. If the deficiency symptoms are relieved, the extract may be analyzed chemically, and the appropriate hormone isolated and, perhaps, identified. Studies of its chemical structure may even lead to eventual laboratory synthesis.

A case study in endocrine research is found in the discovery of insulin, a hormone known to be produced in the pancreas and which regulates the blood-sugar level. In 1886 two physiologists, von Mering and Minkowski, were studying the role of the pancreas in digestion. They removed the pancreas from dogs, expecting to record upsets in the digestion of fats (since the pancreas is the only gland which secretes a fat-splitting enzyme). Instead, the dogs showed a great increase in urine output and died within ten to thirty days. Observant animal caretakers noted that ants were attracted to the urine of such experimental animals but not to the urine excreted by the control animals. Further investigation revealed the cause—the urine of the dogs whose pancreas had been removed contained sugar. The resemblance of these symptoms to those of human beings afflicted with diabetes mellitus was evident. Thus an unexpected result and a chance observation led to a rare opportunity for research on a disease fatal to man, and many investigators turned to the problem.

Histological examination of the pancreas revealed that it is actually composed of two kinds of tissue. One tissue secretes digestive enzymes. The other is found as islet tissue (called the islets of Langerhans) imbedded within the digestive tissue. But which of these tissues is the one whose absence causes the diabetes symptoms? It is not possible to remove surgically the islet tissue from the digestive tissue. If the pancreatic ducts are tied off, however, the digestive tissue degenerates, leaving only the islet cells intact. Any hypothesis proposing that it is the digestive tissue whose absence causes diabetes symptoms would predict that symptoms of the disease would occur progressively as the digestive tissue degenerates. Alternatively, an hypothesis proposing the islet tissue to be the crucial region must predict that no diabetes symptoms will appear. Experimental results have contradicted the first hypothesis and support the second. No diabetes symptoms were seen in the experimental animals.

But how does the absence of islet tissue cause symptoms of diabetes? It is reasonable to hypothesize that islet tissues secrete a hormone whose presence prevents the effects of diabetes from occurring. Accordingly, experimental animals whose pancreas had been removed were fed pancreas tissue by mouth to see whether the hypothesized hormone could be absorbed in large enough quantities to prevent diabetes symptoms. The results were negative. The hormone, if it existed, was apparently digested and thereby rendered ineffective. Pancreatic extracts dissolved in an appropriate medium were then injected into an organism, but again without effect.

About the time of this seeming impasse, a young Canadian physician named Banting became interested in the problem. It occurred to him that perhaps the digestive enzymes produced by one type of pancreatic cell might be digesting the hormone produced by the other. To get around this problem, Banting needed to find some way of isolating islet tissue without also triggering the detrimental action of the digestive enzymes of the pancreas.

One possible solution presented itself. Ligation (tying off) of the pancreatic duct leads to degeneration of the digestive tissue, but leaves the islet tissue intact. This enables the isolation of pure islet tissue. (Later, the knowledge that in embryonic development the islet tissue begins functioning well before the digestive tissue begins to produce enzymes provided still another means of separating the islets from the digestive tissue.) In collaboration with three other men, Banting extracted embryonic pancreas tissue and injected islet tissue extracts into experimental dogs whose pancreas had been removed. Diabetes symptoms subsided dramatically. Attention was then turned to isolation of the hormone produced by the islet cells. The hormone insulin was eventually isolated in pure enough form to be used on human patients. Since the insulin of one mammal is much like that of another, animal insulin can be used to treat human patients. Determination of the molecular structure of insulin by Frederick Sanger and his coworkers in the 1950's has paved the way for laboratory synthesis of this hormone on a large and commercially practical scale.

How do hormones like insulin work? Most insulin studies suggest that it is somehow involved in regulating the metabolism of sugars in the body. Diabetics not only have a high concentration of sugar in their urine but also have difficulty storing glucose as glycogen in the liver. It was once hypothesized that insulin acted on some of the enzymes involved in carbohydrate metabolism, in some way ensuring their normal function. However, no convincing experimental support for this hypothesis has ever been obtained. Recent investigations suggest that insulin acts on cell membranes, making them permeable to glucose. When the hormone is absent, glucose cannot get into the cell, and thus cannot be used as an energy source or stored as glycogen reserves. Instead, it builds up in the blood and subsequently appears in the urine.

Hormones belong to no one group of chemical compounds. Some have a relatively simple structure. Epinephrine, for example, has the formula $C_9H_{13}O_3N$, and can be produced synthetically. Other hormones, like insulin, are proteins. Still others are steroids, a class of chemical compounds with the characteristic ring configuration shown below:

The male and female sex hormones are all steroids. Just as hormones belong to a number of different chemical families, so it is hypothesized they may operate in a number of different ways. Biochemists no longer expect to find that all hormones have a similar mechanism of action as all enzymes do.

The endocrine glands form an interdependent network in relation both to each other and to the rest of the body organs. The production of the hormone thyrotropin by the pituitary gland, for example, stimulates the release of the hormone thyroxin by the thyroid gland. Thyroxin, in turn, increases the rate of metabolism in body cells in general. The increase of thyroxin in the blood has a "feedback effect" on the pituitary gland; the higher the concentration of thyroxin, the less thyrotropin produced by the pituitary gland. Thus a dynamic balance exists between all the endocrine glands. In turn, the endocrine glands affect all the other systems of the body. Thus an intricate web of chemical and physical feedback signals exists in a complex living organism. Just as a house of cards may be drastically affected by the removal of just one card, so the absence or change in the amount of just one hormone may greatly affect the physiological balance existing in the organism. The nature of this balance and its maintenance will be the topic of the next chapter.

## 13-14 CONCLUSION

Some philosophers have proposed that the existence of any environment is entirely dependent on its being perceived. Although this is a topic of lively debate, there is little denying that to an organism with little perception, the surrounding environment offers equally little stimulation. In this chapter, we have considered those systems which make animals active, perceiving, and sensitive entities.

We saw, first, that a nervous system enables animals to perceive their environment, to record this experience (memory), and to give a response. Furthermore, by effecting motion through muscles, the nervous system allows an organism to respond to its environment in an orderly way.

In our discussion of the muscular system, we have examined in some detail an hypothesis explaining how muscle contraction occurs. In studying the nature of the nerve impulse, we saw how the impulse reaches the muscle and is translated into muscle contraction. The result of muscle contraction, as we have seen, is dependent on the skeletal system's provision of muscle anchorage and leverage.

Finally, we discussed the endocrine system as a means of achieving a finer level of control over important long-term bodily processes. All of these systems show a close physiological and anatomical interrelationship, and it is this which is responsible for the great degree of coordination displayed by the higher organisms.

## EXERCISES

1. Explain the "sliding filament" hypothesis of muscle contraction. What evidence supports this hypothesis?

2. How do we know that oxygen is not necessary for the actual contraction of muscles? What, then, is the role of oxygen in muscle contraction?

3. In terms of motion of the organism, what is the relation of bones to muscles?

4. Explain the function of each of the following portions of the human brain: (a) cerebrum, (b) cerebellum, (c) thalamus, (d) medulla.

5. What would be the effects on the individual if cuts were made in the regions *A*, *B*, and *C* of the spinal cord as shown in Fig. 13–24?

6. Which of the following observations would be *correct* evidence to show that the nerve impulse is not merely electrical, but electrochemical in nature?

   a) The nerve impulse travels more rapidly along the axon than electrical current is transmitted along a suitable conductor.

   b) The nerve impulse travels more slowly along the axon.

   c) Given a certain minimal electrical excitation, a nerve fiber will always conduct a current of the same magnitude despite the strength of stimulus.

   d) The nerve fiber will conduct an impulse with a strength which varies proportionally to the intensity of the stimulus.

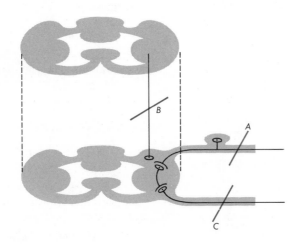

FIG. 13–24

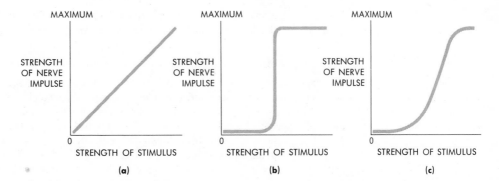

FIG. 13–25

(a)            (b)            (c)

7. Which of the graphs in Fig. 13–25 would best represent the response of a single neuron to increasing intensity of stimulus? Of an entire nerve (composed of bundles of neurons)? Explain your answer.

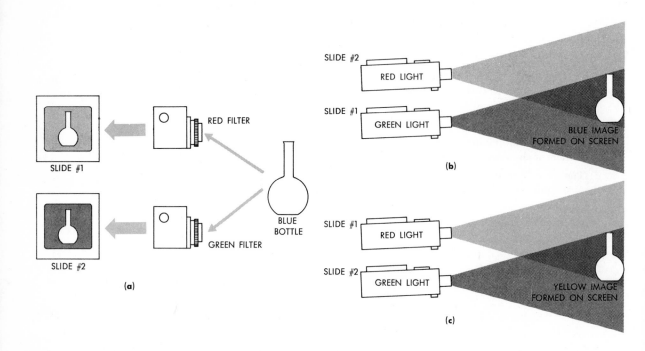

FIG. 13–26

8. Discuss what is meant by the following terms in relation to the passage of a nerve impulse along an axon: (a) threshold, (b) all-or-nothing.

9. What is the so-called "sodium pump"? How is it involved in neuron conduction? Do other types of cells show such a phenomenon?

10. How does the "chemical transmitter hypothesis" account for conduction across the synapse? At the neuromuscular junction? Design an experiment to test this hypothesis.

11. Distinguish between the parasympathetic and sympathetic nervous systems.

12. The experiments of Edwin Land (who invented the Polaroid Land Camera) on the nature of color vision are somewhat controversial. Nevertheless, they have yielded some important information on how color vision in the human eye might operate. Land photographed a colored object (such as a blue bottle) on black and white film. The photograph was taken through two different filters, one green and one red. The slides came out in different intensities of grey (Fig. 13–26a). They were then projected onto a screen so that the two images coincided. Slide #1 (taken through a red filter) was projected with a green light, and slide #2 (taken with a green filter) was projected with a red light (Fig. 13–26b). The image appearing on the screen turned out to be the original blue! Measured on an arbitrary scale, the relative amount of light coming through the green projector had a value of 3, and that through the red projector a value of 5. Land then reversed the slides, putting slide #1 in the projector with red light and slide #2 in the projector with green light (Fig. 13–26c). In this

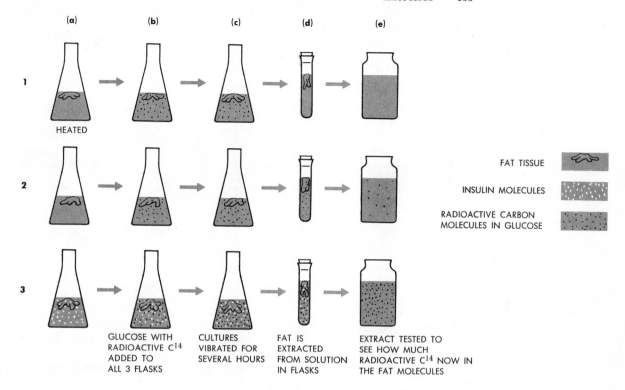

FIG. 13–27

case, the relative intensity of the red light was 3, and that of the green was 5. The projected image turned out to be yellow!

Biochemical experiments have shown that there are at least two (probably, in fact, three) photosensitive pigments in the human eye. Each pigment is thought to be located in a different type of cell in the retina, and each absorbs best at different wavelengths of light. On the basis of this information and the results of the Land experiment, offer an hypothesis to explain how the brain might interpret color from the light waves which hit the retina.

13. Explain how nerve impulses are thought to be transmitted across a synapse. What evidence supports this hypothesis?

14. Physiologists have been concerned with the question of what effect insulin has on rate of fat synthesis (i.e., conversion of glucose into fats) in mammals. In the series of experiments shown in Fig. 13–27, radioactive carbon ($C^{14}$) was used as a tracer.* Study the figure, then answer the following questions.

a) Do these experimental results support or refute the hypothesis that insulin *does* speed up synthesis of fats in mammalian tissue? Give reasons for your answer.

b) What is the function of the experiment series in row 1? What does it show in relation to the experiment as a whole?

* Adapted from Vincent Dole, "Body Fat." *Scientific American*, December 1959, p. 74.

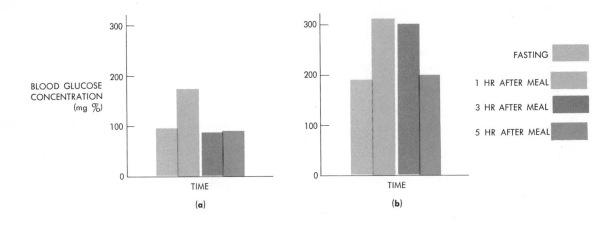

FIG. 13–28

c) It has been shown that insulin does not increase the rate of synthesis of fats from glucose under *in vitro* (test-tube) conditions—i.e., if the cells of fat tissue have been broken down, yet all the molecules from the cell are retained. Can you suggest a mechanism by which insulin could affect the rate at which glucose is converted into fats in living cells within an organism?

15. In terms of coordination, what are the relative advantages of the nervous and endocrine systems to the organism?

16. Observe the two graphs in Fig. 13–28. These graphs show the effect on blood glucose concentration of administering 50 g of glucose to two different individuals. What differences do you note in the response of the two individuals? Which of the two individuals appears to be normal? What may be wrong with the other? Give reasons for your answer.

**SUGGESTED READINGS**

BAKER, PETER F., "The Nerve Axon." *Scientific American*, March 1966, p. 74. An up-to-date account of neuron transmission on the molecular level.

BÉKÉSY, GEORG VON, "The Ear." *Scientific American*, August 1957, p. 66. This article is somewhat complex, but explains the author's work on the mechanism of hearing. A good introduction to the modern concept of ear function.

GALAMBOS, R., *Nerves and Muscles* (New York: Doubleday Anchor Books, 1962). This is one of the "Science Study Series." The book covers some of the physical and chemical principles involved in the conduction of impulses by nerves and in the contraction of muscles.

GALVANI, LUIGI, "Effects of Electricity on Muscular Motion." Translated by Margaret G. Foley. In Jeffrey J. W. Baker and Garland E. Allen (Eds.), *The Process of Biology: Primary Sources* (Reading, Mass.: Addison-Wesley, 1970). This is the most modern and readable translation of Galvani's fascinating experiments. It is well worth the time of any student who is interested in these early researches.

GRIFFIN, D. R., *Animal Structure and Function* (New York: Holt, Rinehart and Winston, 1962). This book is one of the "Modern Biology Series," currently available in paperback. It covers the basic principles of animal structure and function in a number of types of organisms. It is especially useful for comparative purposes.

HUXLEY, H. E., "The Mechanism of Muscular Contraction." *Scientific American*, December 1965, p. 18. A fine summary of current hypotheses concerning muscle contraction.

KATZ, BERNARD, "The Nerve Impulse." *Scientific American*, November 1952, p. 55. An older article than that of Keynes, this nevertheless contains a good deal of helpful information. It is well written and relatively easy to understand.

KEYNES, RICHARD D., "The Nerve Impulse and the Squid." *Scientific American*, December 1958, p. 83. A difficult article, but one which contains much information on the conduction of the nerve impulse and the biochemical mechanism by which this occurs. Well worth the time required to fully understand it.

LAND, EDWIN, "Experiments in Color Vision." *Scientific American*, May 1959, p. 84. This article discusses some recent work which shows how the eye could possibly use only two visual pigments to produce full color vision.

LEVINE, RACHMIEL, and M. S. GOLDSTEIN, "The Action of Insulin." *Scientific American*, May 1958, p. 99. This article discusses how insulin may regulate sugar metabolism by influencing the amount of sugar which passes through the walls of certain cells.

MCELROY, W. D., and H. H. SELIGER, "Biological Luminescence." *Scientific American*, December 1962, p. 76. This article shows how phosphorescent light is produced biochemically in the firefly. The article also shows the variety of organisms which produce such light by a variety of biochemical methods.

RUSHTON, W. A. H., "Visual Pigments in Man." *Scientific American*, November 1962, p. 120. Discusses three pigments seemingly responsible for color and black-and-white vision. Gives physiological and biochemical data on these pigments. This article is good for advanced students interested in the biochemistry of vision.

WILKINS, LAWSON, "The Thyroid Gland." *Scientific American*, March 1960, p. 119. This is a survey article discussing the role of the thyroid and how it chemically controls the rate of metabolism.

ZUCKERMAN, SIR SOLLY, "Hormones." *Scientific American*, March 1957, p. 76. A review article on the many vertebrate hormones, emphasizing their integrative role in physiology of the whole organism.

"The Marvel of Motion." Part I in the *Life Magazine* series, "The Human Body." October 26, 1962, pp. 76–98. Discusses the anatomy of the human body with special emphasis on its adaptations for uprightness and for motion.

"The Circuits of the Senses." Part IV of the *Life Magazine* series, "The Human Body." June 28, 1963. A discussion of the nervous system—how we receive stimuli and translate it into a response. Also includes a discussion of what can go wrong with the system from time to time.

# CHAPTER 14

**SELF-REGULATION:**
**THE PRINCIPLE OF HOMEOSTASIS**

## 14-1
### INTRODUCTION

One of the major problems facing any living organism is adjustment to a changing external environment. Changes in temperature, pH, availability of food, and the like, all have some direct effect on the life of individual cells. In a complex organism, especially in animals, cells are bathed in fluids which, to some extent, act as a buffer against such changes. These fluids form the **internal environment** of the cells.

The amazing feature of the internal environment is that it remains constant, despite rather severe changes in external conditions. Consider man, for example. The temperature outside his body may range from freezing to well over 100°F. Yet the temperature of his internal environment remains close to 98.6°F. His diet may include a great deal of sugar one day, and very little the next. Yet the amount of sugar in his blood stays the same on both days. He may exercise violently, releasing a great deal of carbon dioxide, yet the amount of carbon dioxide in the blood and tissue fluids remains fairly constant. Observations of this sort led the great French physiologist Claude Bernard (1813–1878) to say: "All the vital mechanisms, varied as they are, have only one object, that of preserving constant the conditions of life in the internal environment."

Bernard's principle of the internal environment provides a helpful way of looking at the many physiological activities within a complex organism. The cells of complex organisms can tolerate only small changes in the conditions of the fluids that reach them. As a result, many physiological controls have evolved which keep the internal environment from varying too much in any one direction. These controls come into operation in response to changes in the external environment.

One of the most interesting features of physiological control mechanisms is that they are built into the system they regulate. The controls are self-adjusting; they do not require constant monitoring by an outside agent. Such controls maintain the system in **equilibrium.** A system in equilibrium is one whose overall characteristics are not changing. It is useful to distinguish here between two general types of equilibrium: **static equilibrium** and a **steady state** (Fig. 14–1).

In the tank shown in Fig. 14–1(a), the water level remains the same over a long period of time. Because the overall characteristics of this system are not changing it is said to be in equilibrium. The equilibrium would be upset if we opened the taps at either tube $X$ or $Y$. With both tubes plugged, however, the system remains in static equilibrium; no water enters or leaves the tank.

In the tank shown in Fig. 14–1(b), the water level also remains the same for a long period of time, yet there is a continual flow of water in and out. The parts of the system are changing—they are definitely in motion—but, the over-all characteristics remain the same. This is the condition of steady state.

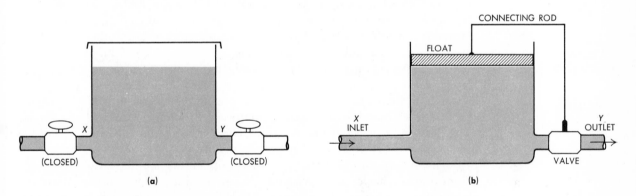

FIG. 14–1    Two mechanical systems, showing (a) static equilibrium and (b) steady state. The float, connecting rod, and valve mechanism in (b) constitute an example of a self-regulating system.

Note that the maintenance of this steady state requires a control mechanism, represented by the float, the connecting rod, and the outlet valve. Suppose the inflow of water increases. The level of the water rises, thus raising the float. The connecting rod between float and valve causes the valve to rise also, increasing the size of the valve opening and allowing more water to flow out. As the volume of outflowing water increases, the water level falls, lowering the float and, of course, the valve. This reduces the size of the valve opening and the volume of water leaving the tank. The water level increases and the cycle begins again. The reverse situation creates the same cycle with a minor difference; if the inflow of water decreases, the cycle begins at the point at which the water level falls, lowering the float.

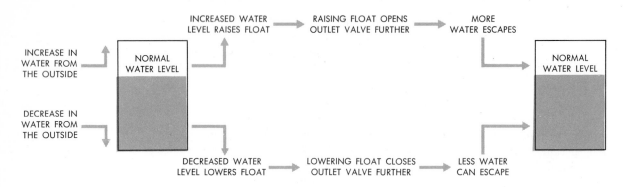

FIG. 14–2   Schematic diagram for the self-controlling system shown in Fig. 14–1(b).

It is possible to have a system in a steady state with some outside source of control. For example, if a valve were placed at the outlet pipe ($Y$), it could be adjusted in such a way as to keep the water level constant. But the important feature of the system in Fig. 14–1(b) is that the amount of water allowed to escape is controlled by a part built into the system itself. In other words, the system contains a built-in self-monitoring control (see Fig. 14–2).

The self-regulating system just examined is analogous in principle to regulatory mechanisms operating in living organisms. Maintenance of a constant water level in the tank is similar to maintenance of a constant level of some substance—carbon dioxide, salt, or glucose, for example—in the body fluids. The float and connecting rod represent body organs stimulated into action by the change in any of these substances in the blood.

The steady-state situation in living organisms is called **homeostasis.** Homeostasis is achieved by self-regulating mechanisms. It is characteristic of all homeostatic systems that they respond to an increase or decrease in the quantity of some substance in the body.

**14-3**
**A SIMPLE**
**BIOLOGICAL**
**CONTROL SYSTEM:**
**TEMPERATURE**
**REGULATION**

A good example of homeostasis is the method by which the body temperature of warm-blooded animals is kept constant.* Human beings display a relatively constant body temperature of 37°C (98.6°F). If the temperature of the external environment rises, a special region of the brain, the hypothalamus (Section 13–10), stimulates the sweat glands to perspire. The hypothalamus is composed of tissue which is particularly sensitive to changes in temperature of the blood that passes through it.

---

* The body temperature for any warm-blooded animal never varies more than two or three degrees from an average, unless some major upset occurs in the physiological processes, as in a fever. The temperatures of all warm-blooded animals are not the same, however. That of man is normally 37°C, of chickens 40 to 42°C, of dogs 39°C, of horses 38°C, and of a sloth 33 to 34°C.

Increased sweating cools the body. This is because water molecules absorb heat from the body when they evaporate from the skin surface. As the body temperature falls, the stimulation of the hypothalamus is decreased. This results in a reduced rate of sweating. As a result of this continual juggling, the body temperature is soon brought back to its normal 37°C from perhaps a slight fluctuation above this temperature (see Fig. 14–3). Sweating still occurs at normal temperatures, but much less so than at high temperatures.

If the outside temperature falls below the value of 37°, cooler blood reaches the hypothalamus. The hypothalamus responds by reducing the amount of sweating. This further reduces the amount of heat the organism loses to the outside environment. By conserving heat within the body, the hypothalamus prevents the temperature of the blood from falling to a critically low level. As the body temperature increases due to this heat conservation, the sweat glands begin to operate again, and again we see the balancing procedure involved in homeostatic systems.

Several principles emerge from this example. The first is that homeostatic mechanisms achieve their effect by modification of processes that occur continually. Sweating occurs at all times in man. The amount of perspiration released from the sweat glands depends on the amount of stimulation by the hypothalamus. This, in turn, is modified by the temperature of the blood that reaches this portion of the brain. There is a distinct advantage in using a continually occurring process as the basis for homeostatic control. It allows a more immediate response to changes in the environment. The body is continually making small adjustments in amount of sweating in response to local environmental changes. These small immediate adjustments are possible because the regulatory mechanism in the hypothalamus simply increases or decreases the rate of a process which is already in operation.

A second principle is that all homeostatic systems have a **feedback mechanism**—that is, part of the output of the system is fed back into the system as an instruction, telling it what to do. We have seen that the effect of sweating is to cool the blood as it leaves the outer regions of the body. As this cooler blood flows back to the central regions, some of it passes through the hypothalamus. This conveys a message, an instruction to the hypothalamus, that the temperature of the blood has decreased. The hypothalamus responds by decreasing its stimulatory effect on the sweat glands. Thus the process of sweating produces an overall cooling of the entire system, and a report that this cooling has occurred is fed back into the control center.

Two types of feedback can be recognized in self-regulating systems. One is called **positive feedback,** the other, **negative feedback.** Negative feedback is demonstrated when a change in the system in one direction (for example, increased sweating) is converted into a command to change that system in another direction (for example, decreased sweating). In body-temperature control, an increase in sweating lowers the body temperature. A decrease in body temperature is converted into a command (in the hypothalamus) to

decrease the amount of water excreted through the sweat glands. This contributes to a rise in body temperature and thus to increased sweating.

Negative feedback helps to keep a system in equilibrium. Positive feedback
has just the opposite effect. Suppose that the connecting rod from the float
(Fig. 14–1b) had been attached to the *inlet* (at $X$), instead of the outlet. As more
water came into the tank, and the level rose, the float would have been lifted up,
opening the inlet valve further, so that even more water could enter. This, in
turn, would have raised the level of the float, opening the inlet tube still further,
and so on. If the inlet tube were of a diameter greater than the outlet, the system
would overflow. Positive feedback produces a runaway process.

Positive feedback sometimes occurs when normal control mechanisms in the
body break down. If a man's body temperature rises much above 42°C (107.6°F)
the negative feedback mechanism breaks down and is replaced by positive feedback. High temperature brings about an increase in metabolic rate (i.e., chemical
reactions). This produces more heat, which raises the temperature, and so on.
The ultimate result of this vicious cycle is death.

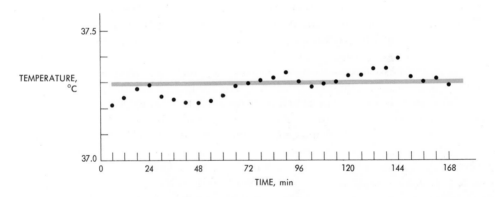

FIG. 14–3   Normal variations in mammalian body temperature with environmental temperature
held constant. It can be seen that body temperature fluctuates but is, on the average, 37.3°C.

From what has been said about homeostatic mechanisms and negative feedback, we can guess that the constancy of any system is not perfect. This, indeed,
is the case. The body temperature of any warm-blooded animal, for example,
does not remain perfectly constant. Instead, it continually fluctuates about an
average point which we speak of as "normal" (Fig. 14–3). This is true even if the
temperature of the external environment is perfectly constant. Every adjustment in one direction or the other tends to overshoot the mark. This brings the
alternative response into play. The result of this overshooting is the slight variation of the conditions in the system. Such fluctuations are characteristic of any
living system existing in a steady state.

It is a familiar fact that when a person runs up stairs, his rate of breathing increases. As soon as he is quiet again, this rate begins to return to normal. What controls this process?

A complex nerve network exists between the breathing muscles of the diaphragm and rib cage and the medulla of the brain, where the respiratory center is located (Section 12–12). This center responds to certain changes in the blood by increasing or decreasing the number of impulses sent to the breathing muscles. When we exercise, the respiratory center is stimulated, and increases the volley of impulses it transmits. When we rest, the stimulation of the center declines and the number of impulses decreases.

**TABLE 14–1** CARBON DIOXIDE COMPOSITION OF INSPIRED AIR COMPARED TO VOLUME OF AIR BREATHED PER MINUTE (AFTER HALDANE)

| $CO_2$ IN INSPIRED AIR, % | VOLUME OF AIR BREATHED, cc/min* | AVERAGE FREQUENCY, breaths/min |
|---|---|---|
| 0.79 | 111 | 14 |
| 1.47 | 137 | 13 |
| 1.52 | 128 | 15 |
| 1.97 | 128 | 13.5 |
| 2.02 | 139 | 15 |
| 2.28 | 141 | 15 |
| 2.84 | 191 | 16 |
| 3.07 | 186 | 15 |
| 3.11 | 191 | 15 |
| 3.73 | 196 | 14 |
| 4.84 | 245 | 15 |
| 5.14 | 373 | 19 |
| 6.02 | 631 | 27 |

\* Normal = 100 cc

With changes in body activity, there are changes in the amounts of oxygen used and carbon dioxide given off by individual cells. Therefore (Section 12–13), changes in either carbon dioxide or oxygen content of the blood would seem to be the major stimuli to the respiratory center. In 1905, the British physiologist J. S. Haldane carried out an experiment to test which (if either) of these gases is responsible for affecting the respiratory center. In one set of experiments, Haldane varied the amount of oxygen in the inspired air, while holding the amount of carbon dioxide constant. In another set of experiments, he did the reverse; he varied the amount of carbon dioxide while holding the oxygen constant. During these experiments he recorded the amount of air inhaled at each inspiration. These data are shown in Tables 14–1 and 14–2.

Table 14–1 shows that as the percentage of carbon dioxide in the inspired air is increased, the volume of air inhaled steadily increases. Comparing this

**TABLE 14-2**  OXYGEN COMPOSITION OF INSPIRED AIR COMPARED TO VOLUME OF AIR BREATHED PER MINUTE

| $O_2$ IN INSPIRED AIR, % | VOLUME OF AIR BREATHED, cc/min | AVERAGE FREQUENCY, breaths/min |
|---|---|---|
| 63.67 | 98 | 14 |
| 20.93 | 101 | 14 |
| 16.03 | 100.5 | 15 |
| 15.82 | 103 | 14 |
| 15.63 | 102 | 15 |
| 12.85 | 102 | 15 |
| 12.78 | 100 | 14 |
| 11.33 | 103 | 16 |
| 11.09 | 103.5 | 15 |
| 6.23 | 112 | 18 |

with Table 14-2, we can see the difference immediately. As the amount of oxygen in the inspired air is decreased, there is no noticeable change in the total amount of air breathed per minute. We can also see that there is a noticeable change in the volume of air breathed only when the oxygen content of inspired air becomes very low (somewhere between about 11% and 6%). These data show, then, that the amount of air inhaled is governed by the amount of carbon dioxide in the blood.

An interesting side issue emerges from the data in Table 14-1. Although the volume of air inhaled per minute increases as the percentage of $CO_2$ in the inspired air increases, the frequency of breathing remains fairly steady. This indicates that the medulla must respond to increased $CO_2$ in the blood first by increasing the *depth* of each inspiration. Indeed, measurements show that this is so. As shown by the table, the *frequency* of breathing does not begin to increase until the percentage of $CO_2$ in the inspired air reaches a value of 5. We can see that increasing the frequency of breathing, in addition to the depth, brings almost twice as much air into the lungs. Initially, then, the body responds to small increases in the $CO_2$ concentration of the blood by increasing only the depth of breathing. An increasing in the frequency of breathing comes into play only under more extreme conditions.

Now let us return to the problem of homeostasis as it applies to the system of respiratory control. When a person exercises, his muscle cells release some carbon dioxide into the blood. The effect is similar to that of breathing air with a carbon dioxide percentage somewhat higher than normal. Some of this carbon-dioxide-containing blood passes through the respiratory center. The center responds to this stimulus by sending to the muscles of the rib cage impulses to increase the depth of each inspiration.

More effective ventilation of the lungs increases the rate at which oxygen is taken into the alveolar sacs and carbon dioxide is given off. The system has thus responded to an increase in carbon dioxide in the blood by providing a means of eliminating it. As the amount of carbon dioxide in the blood decreases, due to

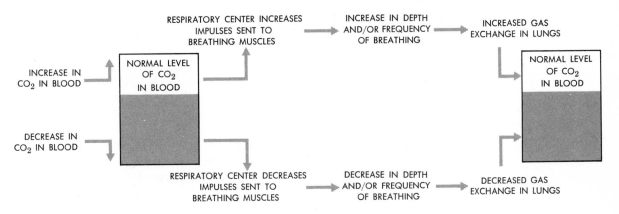

FIG. 14–4   Diagram of homeostatic control mechanisms involved in regulating gas exchange in mammals. The respiratory center is located in the medulla, part of the brain stem. It responds to the amount of carbon dioxide in the blood.

increased gas exchange, the respiratory center is less stimulated. Depth of breathing returns to normal.

The regulatory mechanism in this homeostatic system is, then, the respiratory center. Feedback occurs from the blood passing through this center. Changes in the carbon dioxide content of this blood cause the control center to increase or decrease impulses to the appropriate muscles. A diagram of the respiratory control mechanism is shown in Fig. 14–4. Carbon dioxide concentration is the major but not the sole substance in the blood which signals the respiratory center. Oxygen does play a role, as does the increase in hydrogen ion concentration. The effect of these additional mechanisms is to provide a finer set of controls for regulating the breathing process.

**14–5**
**A HOMEOSTATIC SYSTEM INVOLVING SEVERAL ORGANS: THE REGULATION OF BLOOD SUGAR**

It is important that the sugar glucose be maintained at a constant level in the blood if all cells are to function properly. This is particularly true where brain cells are concerned. A number of organs are involved in maintaining glucose at a constant level in the blood. These include the liver, the pancreas, the medullary portion of the adrenal gland, and the hypothalamus. The hypothalamus is especially sensitive to changes in the glucose level of the blood, and serves as a master regulating center.

When we eat, large amounts of glucose enter the blood through the portal vein, which runs from the small intestine to the liver. Cells of the liver metabolize glucose to glycogen, which is then stored. To keep the level of blood sugar constant, the liver releases small amounts of glucose into the hepatic vein, which runs from the liver to the heart via the vena cava. What "tells" the liver how much glucose to send out into the blood? What control mechanisms are involved?

Molecules of glucose in the blood have an effect on two parts of this control system. One organ is the pancreas, specifically the cells of the islets of Langerhans, located in the pancreas. The presence of glucose in the blood flowing through these cells stimulates them to secrete insulin. This hormone, released into the blood, is carried to all parts of the body. The major effect of insulin is to lower the amount of glucose in the blood. It is thought to accomplish this by acting on cell membranes so that more glucose molecules are allowed to pass into the body cells.*

Glucose molecules in the blood also act on the medulla of the hypothalamus itself. An increase of glucose in the blood stimulates the hypothalamus to send inhibitory messages to the liver. As a result, the liver lowers the amount of glucose it releases into the hepatic vein. On the other hand, if the blood-sugar level begins to fall below normal, the medulla signals the liver to release more glucose. Thus there are two systems in operation, each involving different control centers—the medulla and the islets of Langerhans. Yet both centers are stimulated by the same feedback mechanism—the amount of glucose in the blood.

There is yet a third mechanism, one which helps regulate the level of glucose in the blood during periods of stress or heavy exercise. Suppose we are doing some very strenuous work. Our body cells are using up large amounts of glucose. The level of glucose in the blood begins to decrease; the liver cannot release glucose as fast as it is being oxidized in the tissues. Now the hypothalamus becomes active. It stimulates the medulla or central portion of the adrenal gland to produce the hormone epinephrine (Sections 13–9, 13–13). The epinephrine enters the bloodstream, where it has a variety of physiological effects. One of those effects is to activate certain enzymes in the liver cells, the result being an increase in the rate at which glycogen is converted to glucose. Thus more glucose passes out of the liver into the bloodstream.

It is apparent that there are considerable physiological adjustments involved in keeping the blood-sugar level constant. Nearly all cells of the body can withstand low glucose levels in the blood for a short period of time; muscle can tolerate low glucose levels for several hours. But when the glucose level drops below a critical value, brain cells cannot remain alive more than a few minutes. The various control mechanisms centered in the hypothalamus and the pancreas help to prevent that level from ever being reached.

**14-6
BIOCHEMICAL
CONTROL
MECHANISMS**

The rate at which biochemical reactions occur is important to the maintenance of a constant supply of various molecules in the blood, and thus indirectly to the cells it supplies. In order for protein synthesis to proceed at a normal rate, for example, the supply of amino acids in the cell must remain at a certain level. What factors control the rate at which such reactions take place?

----

* Experimental evidence indicates that when insulin is injected into the bloodstream of an experimental animal, the amount of glucose in the blood decreases, while that in the tissues increases.

One factor is a simple chemical principle known as the **law of mass action.** Most biochemical reactions occur in a series of steps, each of which is generally reversible. The law of mass action states that at a given temperature, the rate of chemical reaction is directly proportional to the concentration of the reacting substances. In a reversible reaction, this means the substances on both sides of the chemical equation. As the end products of a series of biochemical reactions accumulate, therefore, they will tend to shift the direction of the reaction to the left, toward the reacting substances.

Consider the reactions shown below, in which original reactant A, through a series of intermediate steps involving compounds B and C, is converted into end product D:

$$A \rightleftharpoons B \rightleftharpoons C \rightleftharpoons D \quad \text{(END PRODUCT)}.$$

The accumulation of D in the cell will tend to increase the rate at which the reverse reactions occur. If there is more D than A in the cell, the reaction will run to the left. On the other hand, if there is more A than D, the reaction will proceed more to the right. By this type of built-in control mechanism an equilibrium is maintained. In this state of equilibrium, D is formed at the same rate at which it is used.

Some reactions within living systems are controlled even more specifically and delicately. The amino acid threonine, for example, is converted into isoleucine by a series of three or four reactions. One step of this series includes the production of $\alpha$-ketoglutaric acid. All these reactions are reversible, and all are catalyzed by specific enzymes. The reactions may be represented as:

$$\text{THREONINE} \xrightarrow{\substack{\text{threonine} \\ \text{deaminase}}} \underset{A}{\text{INTERMEDIATE}} \xrightarrow{\substack{\text{enzyme} \\ a}} \underset{B}{\text{INTERMEDIATE}} \xrightarrow{\substack{\text{enzyme} \\ b}}$$

$$\alpha\text{-KETOGLUTARIC ACID} \xrightarrow{\substack{\text{enzyme} \\ c}} \text{ISOLEUCINE}$$

As the reaction proceeds from left to right, isoleucine accumulates and the reaction rate begins to slow down. If only mass action were involved in this slowing down, we would expect the concentration of intermediate products to increase as an equilibrium is reached, yet this does not occur. Much work has gone into studying this and similar reactions, and at least a partial answer has been achieved.

Isoleucine, by its special molecular structure, is thought to act as a competitive inhibitor (i.e., as a "poison") for the enzyme threonine deaminase. Note that threonine deaminase is the enzyme involved in the first step of the series. Isoleucine *competes* with threonine for the active site of this enzyme. Therefore, the more molecules of isoleucine there are in the cell medium, the more molecules of threonine deaminase are temporarily knocked out of commission. Recall that competitive inhibitors do not destroy an enzyme; they only block its active site for a short period of time.

By acting as a competitive inhibitor, isoleucine regulates its own rate of production in the cell. The amount of isoleucine in the cytoplasm thus acts as a negative feedback mechanism. It is interesting that its point of action is the enzyme that catalyzes the *first step* of the reaction series. It is not known why the site of inhibition should be at this enzyme, rather than at any other. However, this seems to be a characteristic of all biochemical systems that control themselves by negative feedback.

## 14-7
## CONCLUSION

In this chapter we have discussed the principle of homeostasis and the ways by which it is maintained. We have seen that built-in control mechanisms always involve some form of feedback. All physiological control mechanisms involve negative feedback.

Homeostatic controls are found in all systems of the body. The endocrine glands, for example, all function in response to the amounts of certain substances in the blood, as well as to nervous control. The kidney operates in precise ways to control the levels in the blood of water, various salts, sugars, amino acids and the like. Indeed, homeostatic mechanisms regulate all the ways in which organisms adapt to a variety of outside conditions.

Homeostasis can even be observed in populations of organisms. As will be discussed in greater detail in Chapter 20, the size of any natural population is held constant by the availability of food and the number of predators. Increase in the size of a population will automatically increase competition among its members and at the same time encourage growth in the number of predators by providing a larger food supply. This is another example of negative feedback.

It appears that the theme of homeostasis (built-in control) is characteristic of life from the molecular to the population level. All homeostatic mechanisms are involved in maintaining a system of equilibrium. In the numbers of organisms in a population, or in the kinds of molecules within cells and body fluids, it is constancy that characterizes the living world.

## EXERCISES

1. What is meant by the term "homeostasis?" To what aspect of living organisms does it apply?

2. What are some examples of homeostatic mechanisms in organisms? Are such mechanisms found in *all* organisms, or just some?

3. What are *positive* and *negative* feedback? Describe these in terms of the following:

   a) Temperature regulation in warm-blooded animals.

   b) The regulation of breathing rate.

   c) The regulation of sugar content of the blood.

4. What are the *two* feedback mechanisms involved in the regulation of blood sugar? How do they function?

5. Using the diagram in either Fig. 14–2 or Fig. 14–4 as a model, make schematic diagrams showing homeostatic control and feedback for:

a) The biochemical control system discussed in Section 14–6.

b) The blood-sugar-level control system discussed in Section 14–5.

6. In 1858, the famous physiologist Claude Bernard put forth his idea that the major function of all physiological processes is to maintain the constancy of the internal environment. Why is it so important for the internal environment to remain constant? Offer an hypothesis explaining how homeostatic mechanisms (such as, for instance, the one involved in the regulation of breathing) could have evolved, by natural selection.

7. The pituitary gland is a small structure located at the base of the brain. It is called the "master gland" of the endocrine (hormone-secreting) system because it produces a number of specific hormones that affect other glands located throughout the body. One hormone secreted by the pituitary is known as ACTH (adreno-corticotropic hormone); this stimulates the adrenal cortex to produce its battery of hormones (corstisone, androsterone, etc.). The presence of these hormones in the blood has an inhibitory effect on the pituitary gland, however, which slows down its release of ACTH. In terms of this situation, discuss the following questions:

a) How does this system qualify as an example of homeostatic control?

b) What process in the system described above represents negative feedback?

SUGGESTED READINGS

CANNON, W. B., *The Wisdom of the Body* (New York: W. W. Norton, 1960.) This is a new edition of Cannon's 1939 work, in which he coined the term "homeostasis" and discussed the types of regulatory mechanisms found in the body. One of the important people to pick up Bernard's doctrine of constancy of the internal environment and apply it to physiological studies.

OLMSTED, J. M. D., and E. H. OLMSTED, *Claude Bernard and the Experimental Method in Medicine* (New York: Collier Books, 1952). A good discussion of Bernard with special emphasis on his experimental work.

RUCH, THEODORE, and JOHN F. FULTON, *Medical Physiology and Biophysics* (Philadelphia: W. B. Saunders & Co., 1960).

"The Life-Giving Balancing Act." Part V in *Life Magazine* series "The Human Body." Nov. 8, 1963. This article surveys a number of homeostatic control mechanisms in the body: the maintenance of $CO_2$ level in the blood, the sugar balance, the kidneys, the skin and temperature control, the fright response. There is also a discussion of how these mechanisms can break down. Well written and interestingly illustrated.

# CHAPTER 15  CELL REPRODUCTION

**INTRODUCTION**  Since in most living organisms the cell is a unit both of structure and of function, it is not surprising that so much of biological science centers upon it. In no area is this more true than in reproduction, for, in the final analysis, the reproduction of all cellular organisms must be a cellular process. For those plants or animals which reproduce asexually by fission, cell reproduction is synonymous with reproduction of the individual. For sexually reproducing organisms, the production of reproductive cells is itself the result of a specialized type of cell reproduction. Directly related to reproduction are the biological phenomena of inheritance and embryological development, neither of which can be understood without a knowledge of cellular reproduction. In this chapter, then, we shall direct our attention to cell reproduction: first to the mechanics by which it is accomplished, second to some of the questions these mechanics pose, and third to its role in the production of reproductive cells.

**15-2**
**CELL DIVISION:**
**SOME PROBLEMS**
**OF STUDY**

The first scientific paper describing the mechanics of cell division appeared in the late nineteenth century. Since then, many papers have been published on this topic. Not unexpectedly, the progress made in accurately describing what goes on inside a cell when it divides may be directly equated with improvements made in both the tools (e.g., the microscope) and techniques (e.g., micromanipulation) available to the researcher interested in the problem.

Much of the past research on cell reproduction involved the sectioning, staining, and microscopic examination of dividing cells (see Color Plate III). Unfortunately, sectioned cells do not divide. Furthermore, many of the most useful stains react chemically with certain substances in the cell, thereby changing their nature. Thus in studying cell reproduction, biologists have been plagued by an "uncertainty principle"—by virtue of the techniques needed to study the phenomenon, the conditions under which it could occur were changed to the point of being incompatible with the phenomenon itself! The problem has been only partially solved by the use of time-lapse photography which has enabled

470

biologists to telescope the often hours-long process of cell division into a few minutes of observation time.

That cell division is a dynamic rather than a static process is made evident by the techniques cited above. Although our description of the process will focus on certain distinctive phases through which cells pass during the division process, it is important to keep in mind that cell division is very much a dynamic and continuous process, and that it proceeds steadily from one phase to another.

**Mitosis** is a series of changes by which one cell nucleus becomes two. This simple definition shows mitosis to be a nuclear process, primarily concerned with the equal distribution of the chromosomes into the daughter cells. The changes which occur in the cell cytoplasm during mitosis (**cytokinesis**) are thus not directly a part of the mitotic process (although they may occur simultaneously with it).

Not all cells undergo mitosis. A mammalian red blood cell, with no nucleus, cannot divide. Nor can a highly specialized cell, such as a neuron. On the other hand, some cell types undergo mitosis quite often. In multicellular organisms, these cells are usually found in regions of growth, such as a plant root tip or a developing embryo.

Of the five main phases associated with mitosis, the longest is **interphase.** As its name implies, interphase includes the period a cell spends between one division and the next, and in this sense some biologists prefer to consider it not a part of the mitotic process. Interphase has thus often been referred to as a "resting stage." This term is a highly misleading one, however. A cell in interphase is in fact quite active, as will be seen shortly.

The cell pictured in Fig. 15–1 is in interphase.* The nucleus and nuclear membrane are clearly distinguishable. No chromosomes are seen, however, since the chromosomal material is so diffused throughout the nucleus as to be "invisible." It is only when these threads begin to condense into a tight, coil-like configuration that the chromosomes become readily visible. When this occurs, the cell enters **prophase** (Fig. 15–2).

Prophase, then, begins with the coiling of the chromosomal material (sometimes called chromatin) into compact, recognizable chromosomes. The nuclear membrane also gradually disappears, as do the nucleoli. At high magnification, the chromosomes are revealed to be doubled. There are good reasons, of course, for such a chromosome doubling or replication. Were this replication *not* to occur, the equal distribution of chromosomes to each daughter cell that occurs during mitosis would result in only half as many chromosomes in each daughter cell as in the parent cell from which it arose. The ultimate result of a series of such divisions, in each of which the chromosome number is reduced by one-half, is self-evident.

---

* For simplicity, and in view of the uncertain role it plays in the process, we have chosen to ignore the actions of the centriole during mitosis. A discussion of some current hypotheses regarding its role will be found in Section 15–4.

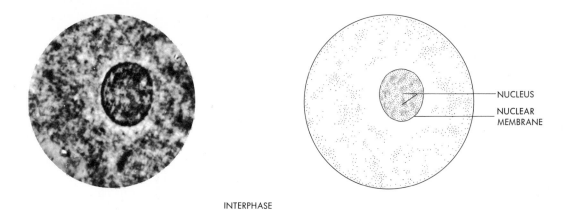

INTERPHASE

FIG. 15–1    The nucleus of an amoeba in interphase. (Courtesy Unitron Instrument Company, Newton Highlands, Mass.)

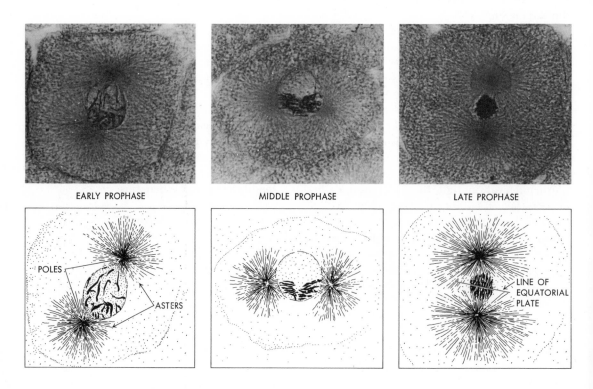

FIG. 15–2    Mitosis in cells of the whitefish. Asters are usually visible only in animal cell mitosis. (Courtesy General Biological Supply House, Inc., Chicago.)

Still closer examination of the replicated chromosomes, however, reveals that the resulting pair still remain attached to each other by a constricted region, the **kinetochore** or **centromere** (see photo at right). To these chromosome "halves," as long as they remain joined at the kinetochore, the term **chromatid** is applied. When the kinetochores separate later (at anaphase), the result is two separate, full-fledged chromosomes, each with a kinetochore of its own.

Also seen during prophase is the formation of fiberlike processes extending from the poles toward the equatorial plate of the cell. These processes are termed **spindle fibers.** Electron microscope studies have revealed that the spindle fibers are actually hollow microtubules (see Fig. 15–3 and Section 6–4). The orientation of the spindle fibers establishes the direction in which the chromosomes will later move, as well as the region where the cell will eventually divide in two. The radiating fiberlike processes surrounding each pole in animal cells and most lower plant cells are called **asters.**

**Metaphase,** the next mitotic phase, is characterized by the lining up of the chromosomes along the equatorial plate of the cell, as may be seen in Fig. 15–4.

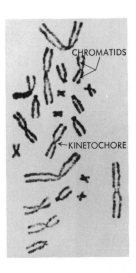

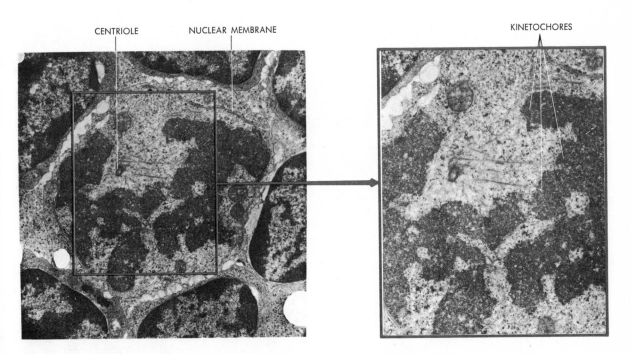

FIG. 15–3  Electron-microscope photograph of rat thymus gland cells in prophase, ×6500. Note that the nuclear membrane is still present and presents a duplicated or "stacked" appearance. A centriole can be seen cut in cross section. From the zone around the centriole, spindle fiber microtubules can be seen extending outward. The enlargement at the right (×11,000) shows more clearly that the microtubules lead to the kinetochores of the chromosomes. (Photo courtesy Raymond G. Murray, Assia S. Murray, and Anthony Pizzo, Indiana University.)

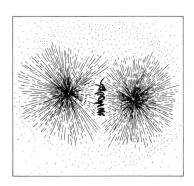 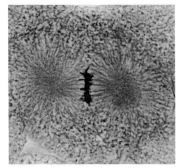 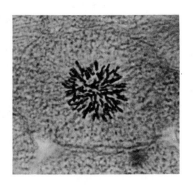

METAPHASE

FIG. 15–4    (Courtesy General Biological Supply House, Inc., Chicago.)

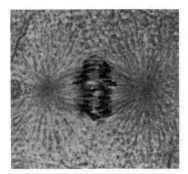 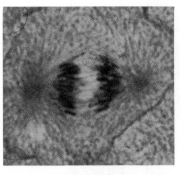 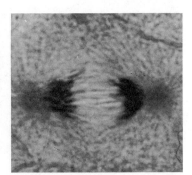

EARLY ANAPHASE                    MIDDLE ANAPHASE                    LATE ANAPHASE

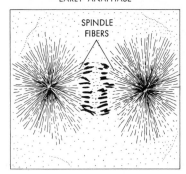 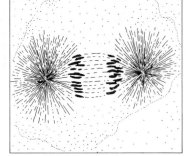

FIG. 15–5    (Courtesy General Biological Supply House, Inc., Chicago.)

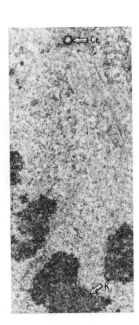

FIG. 15–6   This electron-microscope photograph shows a highly magnified (×15,000) portion of a tissue culture cell at anaphase. Clearly visible are the spindle microtubules extending from the centriole (Ce) to the centromere or kinetochore (K) of a chromosome, here seen as a dense plate separated slightly from the main mass of the chromosome. (From A. Krishan and R. C. Buck, *Journal of Cell Biology* **24**, 1965.   Photo courtesy Dr. R. C. Buck, University of Western Ontario.)

In the photograph in the center, the cell has been sectioned as in the prophase photographs, i.e., lengthwise along the polar axis.   In the photograph on the right, however, the cell was sectioned at right angles to the polar axis.   Thus the poles and asters are not seen, and the actual arrangement of the chromosomes along the equatorial plate is revealed to be circular, rather than linear as the center photo, seen alone, might indicate.

**Anaphase** follows metaphase.  Anaphase is characterized by separation of the kinetochores so that the chromosomes (formerly chromatids) are free to separate, with the two members of each pair moving to opposite poles.   The separating chromosomes move along the directions established by the spindle fibers, to which their kinetochores appear to be attached (see Figs. 15–5 and 15–6). The attachment of the chromosome's kinetochore to a spindle fiber is absolutely essential for the anaphase movement to occur.   If the kinetochore is lost, the chromatid pair cannot orient on the spindle and the characteristic separation at anaphase fails to occur.

During animal cell **telophase,** the cell undergoes the process of "furrowing," in which it pinches in on all sides until two daughter cells are formed (Fig. 15–7). During late telophase, a nuclear membrane is reformed, the chromosomes "uncoil" and disappear as distinct structures visible under the light microscope, and the cell generally returns to the interphase state.

Differences found between mitosis as it occurs in animal cells (essentially as just described) and the same process as it occurs in plant cells (see Fig. 15–8) are mostly due to the anatomical differences between the two kinds of cells.   The most notable difference, perhaps, occurs during telophase.   Since the plant cell is

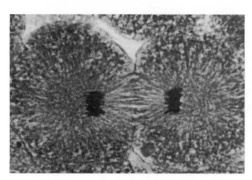 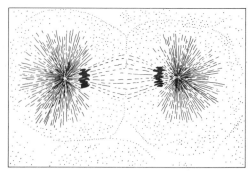

TELOPHASE

FIG. 15–7    (Courtesy General Biological Supply House, Inc., Chicago.)

generally surrounded by a nonliving cellulose cell wall, it cannot pinch inward. Instead, a **cell plate** is formed, at which a new partition of cellulose will be synthesized between the two daughter cells.

The five phases of mitosis by no means span equal lengths of time. For example, at one temperature a meristematic tissue cell in the root tip of a pea plant takes approximately 1529 minutes ($25\frac{1}{2}$ hours) to divide. Of this time, 1356 minutes are spent in interphase, 126 in prophase, 24 in metaphase, only 5 in anaphase, and 22 in telophase (Fig. 15–9). At a higher temperature, the total length of time spent by a similar cell undergoing mitosis is much shorter (952 minutes); nevertheless, the length of time spent in each phase is in the same proportion as at the lower temperature. A similar difference in phase time is shown by animal cells. A human connective-tissue cell takes 18 hours to undergo mitosis. Yet, the time span from the beginning of prophase to the end of telophase is only 45 minutes. Thus the cell spends more than 17 of the 18 hours in interphase, preparing for division. On the average, however, a cell generally spends about 10% of the cycle time in the kinetic aspects of mitosis, regardless of the temperature.

As might be predicted, cells whose main function is division spend less time in interphase than other cells. Certain cells in a grasshopper embryo, for example, complete mitosis in 208 minutes (at 38°C). Of this time, 47 minutes are spent in interphase, 102 in prophase, 13 in metaphase, 9 in anaphase, and 37 in telophase. As these figures demonstrate, the cells undergo the most kinetically active phases of mitosis in a relatively short period of time. This means that a great deal of energy is being expended per unit time by actively dividing cells. As would be predicted, the respiratory rates of such tissues as the meristem of plants or the cells of a growing animal embryo are high in comparison with

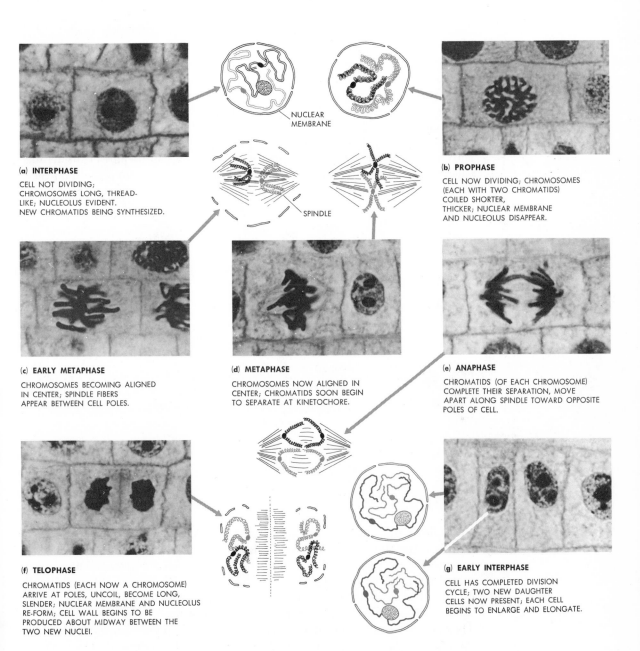

**(a) INTERPHASE**

CELL NOT DIVIDING;
CHROMOSOMES LONG, THREAD-
LIKE; NUCLEOLUS EVIDENT.
NEW CHROMATIDS BEING SYNTHESIZED.

NUCLEAR
MEMBRANE

SPINDLE

**(b) PROPHASE**

CELL NOW DIVIDING; CHROMOSOMES
(EACH WITH TWO CHROMATIDS)
COILED SHORTER,
THICKER; NUCLEAR MEMBRANE
AND NUCLEOLUS DISAPPEAR.

**(c) EARLY METAPHASE**

CHROMOSOMES BECOMING ALIGNED
IN CENTER; SPINDLE FIBERS
APPEAR BETWEEN CELL POLES.

**(d) METAPHASE**

CHROMOSOMES NOW ALIGNED IN
CENTER; CHROMATIDS SOON BEGIN
TO SEPARATE AT KINETOCHORE.

**(e) ANAPHASE**

CHROMATIDS (OF EACH CHROMOSOME)
COMPLETE THEIR SEPARATION, MOVE
APART ALONG SPINDLE TOWARD OPPOSITE
POLES OF CELL.

**(f) TELOPHASE**

CHROMATIDS (EACH NOW A CHROMOSOME)
ARRIVE AT POLES, UNCOIL, BECOME LONG,
SLENDER; NUCLEAR MEMBRANE AND NUCLEOLUS
RE-FORM; CELL WALL BEGINS TO BE
PRODUCED ABOUT MIDWAY BETWEEN THE
TWO NEW NUCLEI.

**(g) EARLY INTERPHASE**

CELL HAS COMPLETED DIVISION
CYCLE; TWO NEW DAUGHTER
CELLS NOW PRESENT; EACH CELL
BEGINS TO ENLARGE AND ELONGATE.

FIG. 15–8    Plant cell division is shown here in the apical meristem of an onion (*Allium*) root. Although
the onion actually possesses 16 pairs of chromosomes, for simplicity the accompanying drawings
show only one pair.  Note that the most evident difference between plant and animal cell division
occurs at telophase.  (Photos courtesy Carolina Biological Supply Company.)

those of less actively dividing cells.  Note, however, that this statement applies to *populations* of cells, such as found in a tissue.  In contrast, it can be shown that with *individual* cells actually undergoing the mitotic process it does *not* apply, since applications of compounds (such as azide) which inhibit respiratory activity fail to stop mitosis once it has been initiated.  The situation is somewhat analogous to the use of a playground slide by a child.  The entire activity is an energy-requiring one; the child must climb the ladder to the top of the slide.  Once started, however, no further energy input is necessary to complete the sliding activity.  Similarly, while the entire cycle of cell division requires considerable energy input, the most active phases, once initiated, are able to proceed on their own.

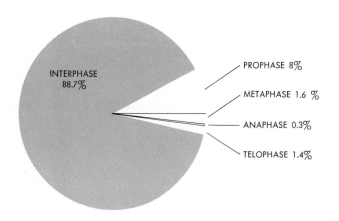

FIG. 15–9   Diagram of the percent of time spent in each phase of mitosis by a meristematic tissue cell in the root tip of a pea plant.

At least once in their life span, most cells possess the power to undergo mitosis.  Generally, however, they also have some built-in mechanism that periodically (or permanently) makes them stop dividing.  Occasionally, a cell arises which seems to have lost this regulatory mechanism.  When this cell divides, it passes on its lack of division control to its descendants. These are cancer cells.  Such cells often seem to divide in a disorderly, chaotic manner.  They may even appear to enter one phase of mitosis without completely finishing the previous one.  In carrying out this disorganized form of division, cancerous tissues require large amounts of energy.  They thus rob healthy tissues of needed nutrients.  Further, by spending so much time dividing, cancer cells fail to perform the regular body functions assigned to them.  Left unchecked, they may ultimately cause the afflicted organism's death.

Early investigations of mitosis were necessarily limited, in general, to observation. No tools and techniques had yet been developed to allow tampering with the delicate interior of a dividing cell. Of course, it is quite possible to formulate hypotheses on the basis of observation without experimentation. Furthermore, observations can also serve as a test of an hypothesis. For example, it might be hypothesized that the chromosomes are attached to the spindle fibers by their kinetochores and, during anaphase, are either pulled or pushed like puppets toward the opposite poles. This hypothesis is supported by the observation that each chromosome kinetochore does seem to follow the path established by the spindle fiber and that the ends of the chromosome trail out behind the kinetochore. Note, however, that these very observations might just as well have given rise to the hypothesis under consideration, rather than following it as a test. Thus, like the chicken and the egg, it is often difficult to tell which came first—the hypothesis or the observations which support it.

It is obvious that at some time during mitosis, the genetic material of the chromosome must replicate. Otherwise, as we pointed out earlier, each daughter cell would receive only a half-share of the genetic material. Indications of gene replication are first detected during prophase, when the doubled chromosomes are visible. It is logical to hypothesize, therefore, that gene replication is initiated either during early prophase or during late interphase. Choosing the former possibility, we might reason as follows:

*Hypothesis:* *If . . .* gene replication is initiated during early prophase, . . .

*Prediction:* *then . . .* uptake of a radioactively labeled compound unique to gene structure should occur during early prophase.

The prediction is not verified. Instead, the radioactive compound never becomes a part of the genetic material unless it is administered at a crucial period during interphase. It is evident that this crucial period is the time when gene replication must be initiated.

The role of the centriole in cell division poses another problem. In animal cells, the centrioles are involved in considerable activity during mitosis. In middle prophase the centriole (which has already replicated a division in advance) separates into its two parts, which migrate along the nuclear membrane. As they migrate toward the poles, spindle fibers appear between the centrioles, so that when the nuclear membrane breaks down the chromosomes are imprisoned within the developing spindle. The two centrioles end up at the poles of the spindle, where the fibers extending from pole to pole form the spindle, while those extending into the surrounding cytoplasm form the astral rays. The appearance of the spindle fibers between the centrioles as they migrate apart toward the poles supports a hypothesis proposing that the centrioles play a role in spindle fiber synthesis. In the light of this hypothesis, it is doubly significant that centriolelike structures have been found at the base of both cilia and flagella, themselves fiberlike structures. A serious objection to this hypothesis, however, is the fact that no centrioles have been detected in the cells of higher plants (the primary reason why they have not been mentioned until now), and yet such plant cells manage to form spindle fibers and divide quite successfully. Some investigators, however, are of the opinion that particles equivalent to the centrioles will eventually be found in such plant cells.

What supplies the energy to drive the mitotic machinery? ATP is a likely suspect; there is little reason to assume that the cell would use a less standard means of supplying energy in mitosis. An hypothesis proposing ATP as the main fuel for mitosis predicts the presence of an active enzyme in the mitotic apparatus capable of splitting ATP, and such an enzyme has, indeed, been found. Although this discovery is definitely consistent with the ATP hypothesis, it by no means provides conclusive support for it.

FIG. 15–10    An hypothesis proposing that the presence of the chromosome kinetochore is essential for chromosome movement at anaphase can be tested by the experiment diagrammed above. If exposed to ionizing radiation, normal chromosomes (1) can be broken (2). Broken chromosome ends always rejoin, but may do so in various ways. The fragments with kinetochores have joined together, as have those without kinetochores (3). The hypothesis predicts that the piece without a kinetochore will not move at anaphase, while the piece with two kinetochores will be stretched toward the opposite poles (4). The hypothesis is supported.

Another puzzle is posed by the movement of the chromosomes at anaphase. The presence of the kinetochore seems to be essential for this to take place (Fig. 15–10) and the connection of the kinetochores of each chromosome to the microtubules of the spindle has been well established by electron microscope observations, but the cause of chromosome movement along the spindle fibers has yet to be adequately explained. The fact that ordinary muscle fibers use ATP when they contract might suggest the tempting hypothesis that contraction of the spindle fibers may pull the chromosomes from the cell equator to the poles. Certain observations, however, contradict this hypothesis. For example, no thickening of the spindle fibers is seen, as might be predicted if they did, indeed, contract.

Several years ago it was discovered that application of the chemical colchicine blocks the assembly of the spindle fibers. Colchicine does not, however, interfere with the condensation of the chromosomes. As the hypothesis proposing that the spindle fibers are responsible for chromosome separation at anaphase would predict, the chromosomes do not separate. Thus when the nuclear membrane reforms, it encloses a double set of chromosomes. Such a nucleus is said to show **polyploidy.** If the cell is removed from the colchicine-containing medium, further mitotic divisions proceed normally. All the daughter cells, however, have a multiple set of chromosomes. Since the chromosomes carry the nuclear genetic material, the properties of the polyploid organism are greatly affected. Occasionally, such effects are quite favorable; many of the varieties of flowers sold by plant breeders to gardeners are polyploid. Further, the occasional occurrence of polyploidy in nature has played an important role in the evolution of various plant groups.

If there is as yet still no completely satisfactory hypothesis to explain the phenomenon of chromosome movement at anaphase, neither is there one for the causes of animal cell pinching-in at telophase. An hypothesis proposing that the mitotic apparatus (consisting mostly of the spindle fibers) may play a role seems promising, for the pinching-in at telophase always occurs perpendicular to the axis of the spindle and across its middle section. Experimentally changing the position of the spindle causes a corresponding change in the position of the plane in which the cell divides. Furthermore, if the mitotic apparatus is removed well before cell-body division is due to occur, then this division fails to occur.

However, if the same mitotic-apparatus removal operation is performed *immediately* before division, when the chromosomes are moving toward the poles at anaphase, it has no effect; cell-body division *does* occur. This observation might suggest that the control of cell-body division is transferred from the mitotic apparatus to the chromosomes at anaphase. This hypothesis is also contradicted, however; the Japanese scientists Y. Hiramoto and T. Kubota were able to remove the entire spindle and chromosomes in sea urchin eggs at a stage just prior to cell-body division—yet the division still took place. These results are important, because spindle fibers have been shown conclusively to be tiny hollow tubes or microtubules (see Section 6–4). Such microtubules are known to be associated with certain biological processes which generate movement within cells.

The Japanese results and those of other workers indicate that the causes of the pinching-in that leads to cell division in telophase may lie in the surface layers of cells, where no microtubules have been found. Acting on this suspicion, Dr. Geoffrey Selman and his coworker Margaret Perry of the University of Edinburgh, using the electron miscroscope, have studied in detail the ultrastructure of amphibian eggs just at the time when the surface of the egg dips inward to form a groove. They have detected fine filaments, only nine nanometers (approximately one-third millionth of an inch) in diameter, each oriented in the direction of the groove. Similar filaments have been found by American biologists in the eggs of jellyfish, polychaete worms, squid, and sea urchins. Dr. D. Szolloski of the University of Washington suggests that these filaments may be anchored to the microvilli which have been detected in the division groove, and that it is the gradual contraction of the filaments which causes the pinching-in of the cell. Unfortunately, to date it has proven too difficult to trace individual filaments from end to end.

It is evident that mitosis and cytokinesis, despite the detail in which they have been described, are still a very long way from being completely understood phenomena. The problems are intellectually stimulating ones, however, and will undoubtedly continue to receive attention.

## 15–5
## THE REDUCTION DIVISION: MEIOSIS

With certain exceptions, the number of chromosomes in the body cells of an organism is constant from one cell to the next. Thus, for example, each body cell of a certain gill fungus has 4 chromosomes, of an elm tree 56, and of a stalk of sugar cane, 80. In an earthworm, each body cell has 32 chromosomes, in a bull frog, 26, in a chicken, 18, and in a man, 46. Because of the chromosome duplication which occurs during mitosis, each daughter cell is assured of a full complement of chromosomes after each division is completed.

Every multicellular organism is the result of millions of mitotic divisions, starting with the first division of the fertilized egg. Take man as an example: the fertilized egg contains 46 chromosomes, of which 23 were contributed by the egg and 23 by the sperm. Thus half of the 46 chromosomes in a man's body cells are duplicate descendants of his mother's (**maternal**) chromosomes and half of them are duplicates of his father's (**paternal**) chromosomes. The 46 chromosomes are thus more accurately described as **23 pairs of homologous chromosomes.** Each pair carries many inheritance factors which influence many specific traits, such as eye or hair color. One member of the homologous pair carries the maternal factor for the trait, the other the paternal factor. The chromosome numbers given for man and the other organisms listed earlier are thus double (**diploid** or $2n$) numbers. The gametes of these organisms, however, cannot have a diploid number of chromosomes. If they did, their union at fertilization would result in a tetraploid (or $4n$) number. With each ensuing generation, the chromosome number would increase geometrically. Quite obviously, this cannot and does not occur. Rather, each gamete contains an **haploid** (or $n$) number of chromosomes. Thus in a dog, diploid number 56, a sperm and an egg each contain 28 chromosomes; in a horse, diploid number 60, a sperm and an egg each contain 30 chromosomes, and so on.

The cellular division process by which the daughter cells receive only the haploid number of chromosomes is known as **meiosis.** In animals this process takes place during the formation of the gametes (**gametogenesis**—called **spermatogenesis** in the male and **oögenesis** in the female), while in most plants meiosis occurs when spores (see Glossary) are produced (**sporogenesis**).

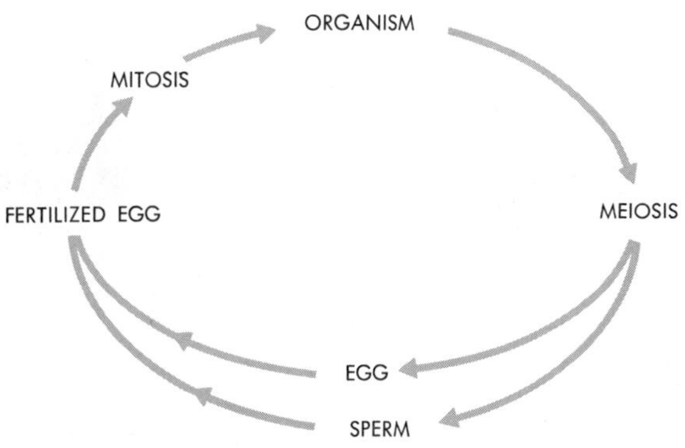

FIG. 15–11    The life cycle of a sexually reproducing animal in terms of mitosis and meiosis.  As will be seen in Chapter 25, plant groups show wide variation in the place of meiosis in their life cycles.  All of the many cell divisions undergone during embryological development and later growth are mitotic divisions.

The life cycle of a sexually reproducing animal is shown in relation to meiosis and mitosis in Fig. 15–11.

Meiosis resembles mitosis in that it, too, occurs concurrently with cell division.  Furthermore, meiosis can be divided into the same descriptive phases as mitosis, and much of the mechanics are the same—a spindle apparatus is formed, the chromosomes migrate apart at anaphase, and daughter cells result.  Yet, meiosis does differ significantly from mitosis.  Two cell divisions rather than one generally accompany the meiotic process; the actions of the chromosomes during some of the phases are quite different (see Fig. 15–12); and finally, as we have just seen, meiosis is a reductional rather than an equational process, yielding a haploid number of chromosomes as the final result.  Mitosis, on the other hand, always results in the same number of chromosomes in the daughter cells as in the parent cell.  Thus, for example, if a haploid cell divides by mitosis, the daughter cells will also be haploid; if a diploid cell divides by mitosis, the daughter cells will be diploid; if a tetraploid cell divides by mitosis, the daughter cells will be tetraploid; and so on.

The first difference between mitosis and meiosis becomes evident at the start.  Whereas both mitotic and meiotic prophase are characterized by the first visible evidence of the chromosome doubling initiated during interphase, meiotic prophase is also distinguished by a pairing of the homologous chromosomes.  During homolog pairing, the two chromosomes become closely applied to each other along their length, a factor of considerable significance in the events which follow.

The process of the pairing of homologous chromosomes during meiosis is known as **synapsis**\* (Fig. 15–13).  During the so-called S phase of interphase, DNA and histone synthesis occurred, and thus the hereditary material is already duplicated at synapsis.  The result is that each homologous chromosome has

---

\* For the sake of simplicity, only one pair of homologous chromosomes will be followed here.  The reader should keep in mind, however, that the same processes are being followed by all the other pairs as well.

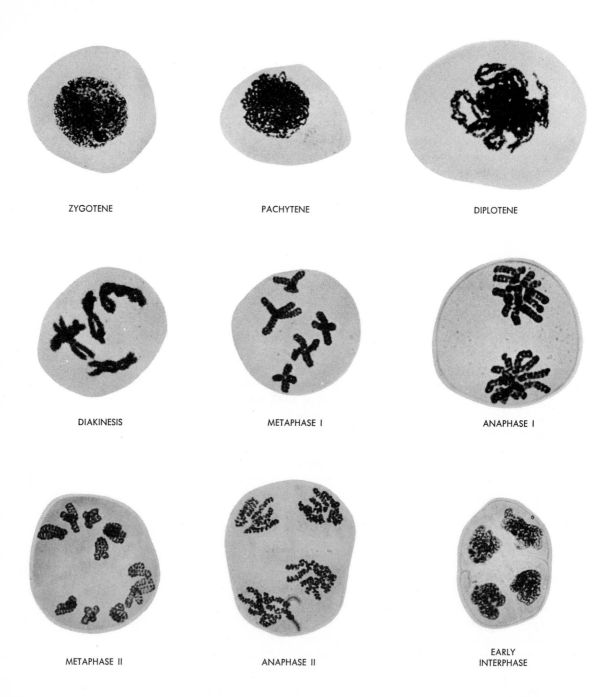

ZYGOTENE

PACHYTENE

DIPLOTENE

DIAKINESIS

METAPHASE I

ANAPHASE I

METAPHASE II

ANAPHASE II

EARLY
INTERPHASE

FIG. 15–12    Meiosis. The terms ''zygotene,'' ''pachytene,'' ''diplotene,'' and ''diakinesis'' refer to distinctive stages of prophase I.   (Photos courtesy Arnold H. Sparrow and the Brookhaven National Laboratory.)

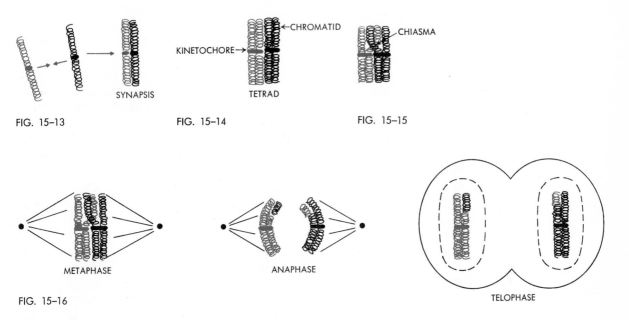

FIG. 15–13    FIG. 15–14    FIG. 15–15

FIG. 15–16

replicated, forming a four-part structure, the **tetrad** (Fig. 15–14).* Note, however, that the duplicates remain attached at the region of the kinetochore. As long as they remain so attached, each individual member of the "Siamese twin" is still a chromatid.

During tetrad formation, sections of the chromatids of different pairs often overlap or wrap around each other, forming cytologically observable patterns called **chiasmata** (sing., **chiasma**; see Fig. 15–15). As will be seen in Chapter 16, there is indirect evidence that the formation of chiasmata may be followed by chromosome breakage, *with subsequent exchange of the broken segments between maternal and paternal chromatids.* The process is known as **crossing over.** Since the evidence for it is genetic rather than cytological, a complete discussion of the significance of such crossing over will be postponed until Chapter 16. It suffices to say here that its occurrence is of primary importance to the study of both biological inheritance and offspring variation, and that it is a major selective advantage of sexual reproduction.

After tetrad formation, the homologous chromosomes line up at the cell equator in a typical metaphase, with anaphase and telophase following closely (Fig. 15–16). Note that by virtue of their being joined at the kinetochore, the chromatid pairs must travel together. Thus the maternal chromatids go to one pole while the paternal chromatids go to the other. This does not mean, however, that the resulting daughter cells will carry only maternal or paternal

* For clarity it is necessary to draw the tetrad in Figs. 15–14, 15–15, and 15–16 as if spread on a plane. In reality, it is a three-dimensional figure which in end view appears as 🕸🕸 .

inheritance factors.   If chiasmata formation followed by crossing over has occurred, as shown here, almost any combination of maternal and paternal inheritance factors is possible.

Because they are joined at the kinetochore, two chromatids form one chromosome.  Thus the division which has occurred is a true **reduction division:** the number of chromosomes in each daughter cell has been reduced by one-half, or from diploid $(2n)$ to haploid $(n)$.

A second division follows this reduction division, often without any interphase period for the daughter cells of the first division.  In this division, however, the kinetochores divide at metaphase, thus releasing the chromatids to migrate to the opposite poles at anaphase as full-fledged chromosomes.  Note that this occurrence merely retains the haploid number of chromosomes, rather than restoring the diploid number.  From each original cell at the beginning of the meiotic process, *four* haploid cells result.  In spermatogenesis, these four cells transform into sperm.  In oögenesis, the greater mass of cell cytoplasm is given to one cell, the egg (the choice being determined entirely by chance); the rest of the cytoplasm is discarded as part of the polar bodies (Fig. 15–17).

Two more important points remain to be stressed.  First, it has been expedient to describe synapsis, tetrad formation, and migration of the chromatids and chromosomes to the opposite poles during the meiotic divisions in terms of one pair of homologous chromosomes.  As has been seen, however, most organisms have many pairs, and during meiosis each of these pairs undergoes the same activity just described for a single pair.  Thus a meiotically dividing cell, particularly one containing large numbers of chromosomes, is a maze of complicated activity.

The fact that mishaps, resulting in unequal distribution of chromosomal material, occur as rarely as they do during meiosis is a testimonial to the intricate near-perfection of living systems.  Occasionally, however, offspring are born with deformities that can be traced to a failure of the chromosomes to separate at metaphase.  Thus at anaphase, both members of the pair may migrate to one pole together, and end up in one gamete.  The other gamete, of course, receives no chromosome of this pair.  This phenomenon, known as **nondisjunction,** was first identified in the fruit fly, *Drosophila melanogaster*.  More recently, nondisjunction of chromosome pair 21 has been found to be the cause of Down's syndrome, or Mongolism, in human children.  Since this discovery of the cause of Down's syndrome, several other congenital abnormalities in man have been traced to nondisjunctional occurrences of other chromosome pairs.  **Sex chromosomes** are those chromosomes which determine the sex of an organism.  In man, the sex chromosomes consist of an $X$ chromosome and a $Y$ chromosome somewhat shorter than the $X$.  The diploid cells of every woman contain two homologous $X$ chromosomes, while those of a man contain only one $X$ chromosome and a $Y$ chromosome, which pair at synapsis.  Should nondisjunction occur with the sex chromosomes rather than the other chromosomes (**autosomes**) and the resulting gametes participate in formation of the zygote, the resulting individual may have such sex chromosomal combinations as $XXY$, $XYY$, etc.

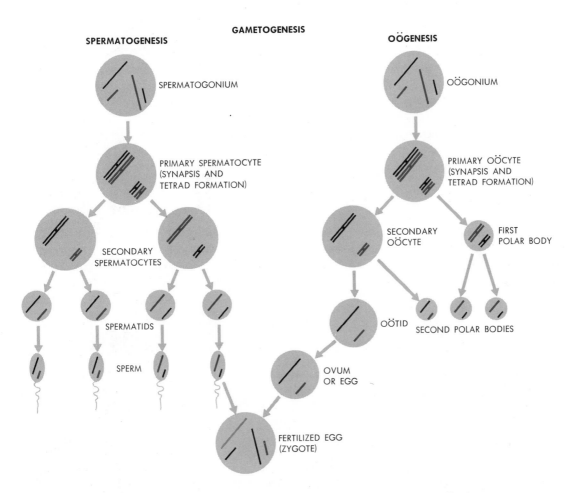

FIG. 15–17  For each cell which begins gametogenesis, four potential gametes are formed.  In oögenesis, however, only one of these matures to form the egg.  Which of the four cells becomes the egg is determined entirely by chance.  For simplicity, crossing over is not shown.

In 1961 the first $XYY$ human male was reported in the United States. Later studies of inmates of the maximum security Scottish State Hospital revealed that about 3% of the inmates were $XYY$ males, making the $XYY$ pattern approximately thirty times more common in the hospital than in the general population.  All the $XYY$ males in the Scottish State Hospital were severe psychopaths.  They had been convicted at a younger average age than the $XY$ inmates (13 as opposed to 18), were several inches taller, and tended to commit crimes of violence.  In striking contrast to the controls, the $XYY$ males came from families without any evidence of crime and from all social classes—in truth, they seemed classic examples of "the black sheep of the family."  This

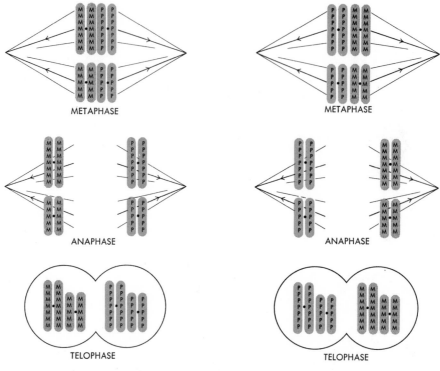

METAPHASE                                    METAPHASE

ANAPHASE                                     ANAPHASE

TELOPHASE                                    TELOPHASE

FIG. 15–18                                   FIG. 15–19

fact would lend support to an hypothesis proposing that the abnormal chromosomal makeup due to nondisjunction, rather than environmental influences, was responsible for the $XYY$ males' abnormal behavior. It must be remembered, however, that most of the $XYY$ males studied were selected for study because of behavioral abnormalities. Thus it cannot be concluded that *all* $XYY$ males will show the same behavior patterns. Indeed, some are known who appear to have formed perfectly normal social relationships. The most that can be said at present is that an extra $Y$ chromosome in the human male somewhat increases the chances of his developing psychopathic behavioral characteristics. In 1968, in Melbourne, Australia, a jury took into account an extra $Y$ chromosome in acquitting a man of a murder charge, while in France a jury decided that an $XYY$ man *was* responsible for his actions (although giving him a comparatively light sentence). The situation is obviously one of many in which biology and ethics are closely related.

Nondisjunction is also known in plants. It has been shown to occur in each of the 12 pairs of chromosomes in the Jimson weed (*Datura stramonium*). The individual plant is variously affected, depending on which pair of chromosomes is involved. If chromosome pair A is affected so that the plant has three A chromosomes (instead of two), then the plant is small, its leaves are abnormally narrow,

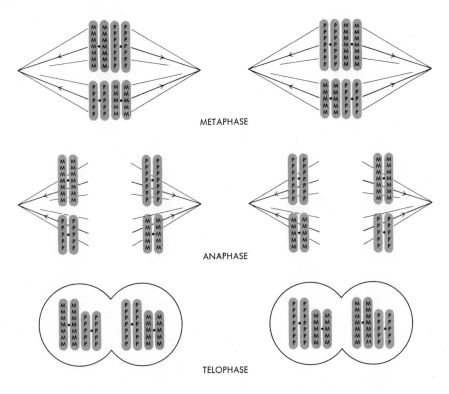

FIG. 15–20

and its fruits are tiny. Or if chromosome pair J undergoes nondisjunction, the plant has dark puckered leaves similar to those of spinach. In other plant genera, nondisjunction of chromosomes has resulted in the formation of species with fewer chromosomes than their ancestors, for example, in the false dandelion (*Crepis*), the species *C. fuliginosa* ($n = 3$) has most likely been derived from *C. neglecta* or its ancestor ($n = 4$). Through chromosome nondisjunction, numerous new species have apparently been produced in genera such as mustard (*Brassica*) and sedges (*Carex*).

The second detail that must be stressed is the relation of the chromosome pairs to each other during meiosis. At metaphase, all the chromosome pairs are lined up along the cell equator prior to separation at anaphase. For simplicity's sake, let us deal with only two chromosome pairs and assume that no crossing over has occurred. Thus each homolog carries only maternal (M) or paternal (P) genetic factors (Fig. 15–18). Note that in the figure we have arbitrarily placed the maternal chromosomes of each pair on the left and the paternal on the right. *But there is absolutely no requirement that we do so.* It would have been just as easy to reverse them, placing the paternal chromosomes on the left and the maternal on the right (Fig. 15–19). Two other combinations are also possible (Fig. 15–20). The point being emphasized here (and it is a *very* important one) is that the *direction of migration taken by one member of any chromosome pair in no way influences the direction of migration taken by a member of any other chromosome pair.* In other words, the members of individual chromosome pairs assort into their respective gametes *at random. Thus meiosis results in variability in assortments of chromosomes.* This is a factor of vast biological importance, as will become clear in Chapter 16.

**15–6**
**SELF-DUPLICATION**
**OF MITOCHONDRIA**
**AND CHLOROPLASTS**

When mitochondria were discovered in the 1890's, questions arose concerning their origin. It was hypothesized that they divide during mitosis as do cells and nuclei with one daughter mitochondrion passing into each of the two new cells. Conclusive evidence supporting this hypothesis was not obtained, however, until the late 1950's and early 1960's. Undoubtedly, the very small size of mitochondria, their great diversity in form, and lack of pigmentation contributed to the difficulty in resolving the question of their origin. In 1959, the English electron microscopist Irene Manton discovered a clear example of the origin of a mitochondrion from a preexisting one in the unicellular marine flagellate *Micromonas.* This alga contains one mitochondrion, one chloroplast, and one nucleus: the three organelles divide at the same time during cell division. Additional evidence that mitochondria arise from preexisting ones was provided in 1963 by D. J. L. Luck. This investigator grew the fungus *Neurospora* on a medium containing radioactive lecithin, a lipid component of cell membranes. The lecithin became tightly bound to the mitochondria during their early growth; later, after the mitochondria had increased in number, all were discovered to contain the radioactive lipid. These results are consistent with a hypothesis that the new mitochondria originated through the growth and division of the originally labeled organelles. Further support for the hypothesis of mitochondria self-duplication was received during the 1960's, when several investigators demonstrated that mitochondria possess their own DNA, ribosomes, and protein-synthesizing system. Recently, mitochondria have been shown to synthesize DNA.

Indeed, it has even been hypothesized that the mitochondria of eucaryotic cells form a subcellular population of semi-independent organisms living in a symbiotic relationship with the larger cell which encloses them (see Section 25–3).

During the 1880's, it was hypothesized that chloroplasts also arise by the division of a preexisting plastid. This hypothesis was based upon direct observations of division of the chloroplasts in cells of certain algae, especially in species in which each cell contains only one or a few plastids (e.g., the filamentous green alga *Zygnema*). In the unicellular green alga *Chlorella*, the single chloroplast has also been observed during cell division.

In the seed plants, however, division of mature chloroplasts appears to occur very infrequently (Fig. 15–21). In these plants, the chloroplasts usually arise from very small, undifferentiated bodies called **proplastids,** which undergo division. Proplastids may be either colorless or pale green. Internally, they have relatively little structure, with little more than a few apparently isolated

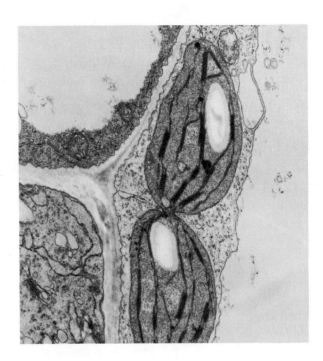

FIG. 15–21   A dividing chloroplast from leaf tissue of tobacco. (Courtesy David A. Stetler, University of Minnesota.)

flattened tubules or vesicles and, occasionally, some invaginations from the inner membrane of the plastid. In the shoot apical meristem, there may be 7 to 20 proplastids per cell. They are generally ellipsoidal or spherical in shape and may even be amoeboid. As the meristematic cells begin to differentiate into mature cells of the leaf mesophyll tissue, the proplastids begin to differentiate into chloroplasts. The internal chlorophyll-containing lamellae and grana gradually develop through invaginations of the inner part of the double membrane surrounding the plastid.

As in the case of the mitochondria, chloroplasts possess many of the attributes of independent organisms. Research during the 1960's has shown that each plastid contains its own DNA, RNA, and ribosomes as well as its own protein-synthesizing equipment. It has also been hypothesized that the chloroplasts constitute another population of semi-independent organisms living symbiotically with the green plant cell. This hypothesis is of considerable interest to biologists concerned with the evolution of plants and animals.

**15-7**
**CONCLUSION**

The processes of mitosis and meiosis are intimately connected with the phenomena of biological inheritance and embryological development.

Growth in knowledge concerning the mechanisms of mitosis has paralleled the development of tools and techniques allowing experimentation with actively dividing cells. The entire process of cell division is a dynamic one, although it has been found convenient to concentrate on certain distinctive phases in studying the process.

Equal distribution of the nuclear genetic material to the daughter cells is the primary accomplishment of mitosis. A cell undergoing mitosis usually passes through five phases: interphase, prophase, metaphase, anaphase, and telophase. During interphase, the primary genetic material is replicated. This replication later becomes evident at prophase, when the chromosomes are seen to be paired. At metaphase, the chromosomes line up at the cell equator; at anaphase, one member of each chromosome pair migrates to an opposite pole. In this case, then, separation of sister chromatids has occurred. At telophase, the cell divides into two daughter cells, which then return to an interphase state.

Research on mitosis has resulted in detailed and accurate knowledge concerning what occurs during the five phases of the process. To date, however, there are relatively few completely satisfactory hypotheses to explain how the kinetics of mitosis are brought about within the cell.

Meiosis results in reduction of the chromosome number in the daughter cells by one-half (from the diploid or $2n$ number to the haploid or $n$ number) and, most important, in chromosome assortment variability. Although meiosis passes through the same phases as mitosis, there are important differences in what occurs in some of these phases.

Two observations are of primary importance to the material on genetics which follows in Chapters 16 and 17. These are:

1) During synapsis and tetrad formation, homologous chromosome pairs may form chiasmata, break, and exchange segments with each other.

2) During separation at anaphase, the direction of migration toward a pole taken by a member of one homologous chromosome pair in no way affects the direction taken by a member of another pair. During metaphase and anaphase, then, *the chromosomes assort at random*.

**EXERCISES**    1. Identify the stages in mitosis shown in the following photographs.

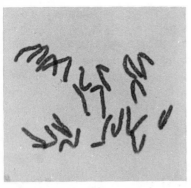
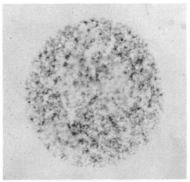

(a)    (b)    (c)

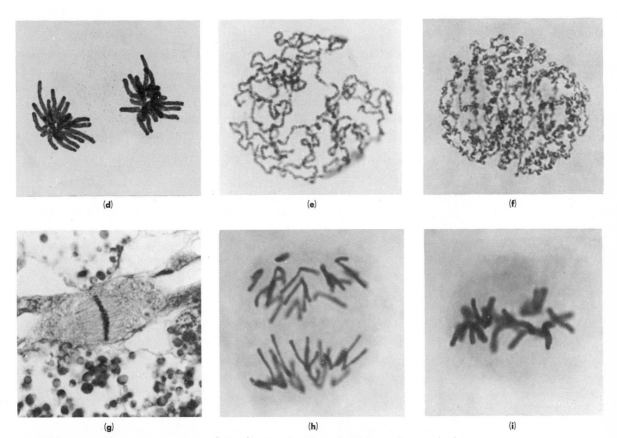

Photos (a) through (f): Preparations of lily (*Lillium*) mitosis by Marta S. Walters; photography by Spencer W. Brown, Department of Genetics, University of California, Berkeley; photos courtesy Dr. Brown. Photo (g): Mitosis in moth (*Cecropia*) tracheal cell; courtesy Dr. Spencer Berry, Wesleyan University. Photos (h) and (i): Mitosis in the onion (*Allium*); courtesy Carolina Biological Supply Company.

2. What is the basic accomplishment of mitosis as far as the genetic material is concerned?

3. Why is the duplication of the chromosomes an indispensable step in the process of mitosis?

4. How would the respiratory rate of cancer cells compare with the respiratory rate of cells in a mature, nongrowing tissue?

5. It was once hypothesized that the spindle fibers were not material structures, but merely lines of stress appearing in the cell during mitosis. Suggest an experiment to test this hypothesis.

6. It has also been hypothesized that the spindle fibers represent a magnetic field within the cell. Suggest an experiment which might test this hypothesis.

7. What is the experimental evidence for the belief that DNA replication occurs during interphase?

8. Explain why meiosis is a necessary part of the life cycle of any sexually reproducing organism.

9. In gametogenesis, how many sperm can arise from 100 spermatogonia? From 100 primary spermatocytes? From 100 secondary spermatocytes? From 100 spermatids? How many eggs can arise from 100 oögonia? From 100 primary oöcytes? From 100 secondary oöcytes? From 100 oötids? (Use Fig. 15–17 in determining your answers.)

**SUGGESTED READINGS**

KIMBALL, JOHN, *Cell Biology* (Reading, Mass.: Addison-Wesley, 1970). A highly readable account of the cell in division.

MAZIA, DANIEL, "How Cells Divide." *Scientific American* reprint #93, September 1961. Good discussion of cell division as well as of some of the investigational techniques and problems.

SWANSON, CARL P., *The Cell* (Englewood Cliffs, N.J.: Prentice-Hall, 1960), Chapter 5. This paperback book discusses in detail the several stages of mitosis, as well as the five stages recognizable in prophase of meiosis.

# GENETICS I: FROM MATH TO MENDEL   CHAPTER 16

## 16-1
## INTRODUCTION

Genetics, the study of biological inheritance, is one of biology's youngest branches—and possibly its most important. Practical applications of knowledge attained through genetic research have had considerable impact in many areas; the improvement of cultivated plant and animal stocks is but one example. On a less technological and more scientific side of the coin, genetics has provided considerable support for the theory of evolution by natural selection. Darwin was without the benefit of a satisfactory theory of inheritance, and this weakness was a point which many of his critics persistently attacked.

Since genetics deals with inherited characteristics, it must also deal with the cellular, organismal, and environmental factors influencing these characteristics. Further, genetics has found it fruitful to attack its subject matter on several fronts, ranging from the molecular to the population levels of investigation. Genetics has indeed come to occupy a central position within the life sciences (Fig. 16–1). In this and the next chapter, attention will be directed toward an understanding of the major concepts on which modern genetics is now firmly based.

## 16-2
## GENETICS:
## A MATHEMATICAL
## BASIS

It will be helpful to turn from genetics (and even biology) for a moment, and direct our attention to certain things that are determined completely by chance. The use of the word "certain" is not entirely accidental. *There are few things that are more "certain" than those based on the entirely uncertain.* Put another way, *there are few things more predictable than those based on the completely unpredictable.*

An example with which the reader may already be familiar is Charles's law. This law states that the volume of a given gas varies directly with the

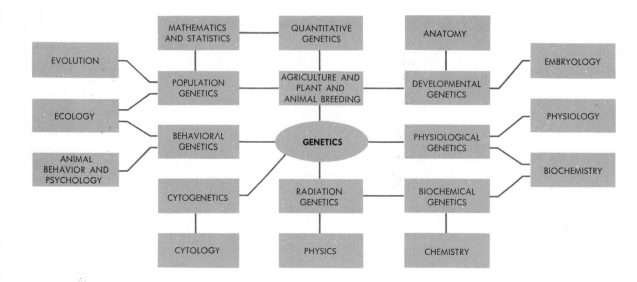

FIG. 16–1    Genetics occupies a central place in modern biological research.

absolute temperature. (See Appendix 1.) If the relationship between temperature and volume changes is graphed, a straight line is obtained, indicating perfect positive correlation (Fig. 16–2). A law giving such a correlation allows an almost certain power of prediction. Given a temperature, one has only to look at the graph in order to find the volume; given the volume, the temperature can readily be deduced.

Consider, now, the factors upon which Charles's law is based. When a gas is heated, the velocity of its individual particles (ions, atoms, or molecules) is increased. The heat energy is expressed as kinetic energy of motion. If the gas particles are in an airtight container, they hit against the sides, exerting a pressure. Thus Charles's law simply states the obvious—that the faster the particles hit the walls of their container, the greater the force upon those walls, and that the relationship is a direct one. If the container can expand, then the increase in kinetic energy results in a larger volume; if not, the pressure builds up in relation to the increase in kinetic energy of the gas particles.

However, the motion of each individual gas particle in the container is completely random. Whether a particle moves up, down, right, or left, etc., is determined entirely by chance. Since this is true for every individual particle within the container (of which there are approximately $10^{23}$) it is true for all of them as a unit. Thus we see the gas as a mass of moving particles, all traveling at very high velocities and bumping into each other, deflecting, hitting the sides of the container, returning to more collisions, and so on.

It is easy to see that Charles's law would not hold up for very long if all the gas particles in the container should suddenly start hitting only one end of the container and not the other.* Would it be possible for all the particles to do this? Yes, it would. Would it be *likely* that they would do it? Indeed *not*. As a matter of fact, the chance of their doing so is so slight as to be virtually inconceivable. The reason is that there are so many gas particles. In order for them all to hit the same side of the container at once they would all have to move toward that side at the same time. However, since their movements are entirely at random, the odds are firmly against any such unified mass movement in one direction.

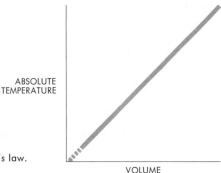

ABSOLUTE
TEMPERATURE

VOLUME

FIG. 16–2   A graphical representation of Charles's law.

Suppose, on the other hand, that there are only *two* gas particles in the container (were such a thing possible). Again, we restrict motion to only two directions and overlook the absurdity of two particles exerting "pressure." Since chance again determines the movements of each particle, it is obvious that Charles's law would not have as good a chance of being correct.† If one particle goes to one end of the container while the other goes to the opposite end, the pressure will be as uniform as can be expected under the circumstances. If both go to either one end or the other, however (as they well may), then all the pressure will be directed against the end they contact. With three, four, five, or ten particles, there are several motions that must coordinate, instead of just two, and it is easy to see that this "one-ended pressure" will be less likely to occur. In short, as the number of particles increases, so do the chances that the pressure will be uniform. With a normal state of many billions of particles, Charles's law seems perfectly safe from any failure.

Thus Charles's law is based entirely on chance. Yet this very factor makes it one of the most certain and predictable laws of science. To repeat a statement made in the opening paragraph of this section, few things are so certain as those based on entirely uncertain factors.

---

* Note that the molecular motion is restricted here to only two choices, one end of the can or the other. Such a situation does not, of course, exist. With all the possibilities of spatial movement taken into consideration, the problem becomes quite a bit more complicated.

† As a matter of fact it would be correct only 50% of the time, as will be seen shortly.

Let us turn to another example. In the tossing of coins, the laws of chance are simply and directly involved. When a coin is tossed into the air, the chances that it will fall heads (or tails) are even, or fifty-fifty (which can be expressed as $\frac{1}{2}$). Suppose that two coins are tossed simultaneously. What *now* would be the chances that both of them would fall heads (or both tails)? The answer is given by the **product principle of probability.** This principle states that *the chance that two or more independent events will occur simultaneously is given by the product of the chances that each of the events will occur individually.* In the example of the simultaneous flipping of two coins, each has a 50–50 chance of coming down heads (or tails). In other words, the probability that either coin will come down heads (or tails) is $\frac{1}{2}$. Therefore, the probability that *both* of them will come down heads (or tails) is the product of $\frac{1}{2}$ times $\frac{1}{2}$, or $\frac{1}{4}$. The probability that one coin will fall heads while the other comes down tails is $\frac{1}{4}$, and the probability that the other coin will come down heads while the first comes down tails is also $\frac{1}{4}$. Thus the total probability for a head and tail combination is $\frac{1}{4}$ plus $\frac{1}{4}$, or $\frac{1}{2}$.

Tossing of three coins then simultaneously produces the following chance distribution of results:

**THREE COINS**

| DISTRIBUTION: | HHH | HHT | HTT | TTT |
|---|---|---|---|---|
| PROBABILITY: | $\frac{1}{8}$ | $\frac{3}{8}$ | $\frac{3}{8}$ | $\frac{1}{8}$ |

**FOUR COINS**

| DISTRIBUTION: | HHHH | HHHT | HHTT | HTTT | TTTT |
|---|---|---|---|---|---|
| PROBABILITY: | $\frac{1}{16}$ | $\frac{4}{16}$ | $\frac{6}{16}$ | $\frac{4}{16}$ | $\frac{1}{16}$ |

It would be possible to go on in a similiar manner computing the chances of various head-tail distributions among the simultaneous tossings of as many coins as desired. It is obvious, however, that for a problem involving a large number of coins, the arithmetic would get a little tedious.

There is a very simple and convenient algebraic method of computing the probability of occurrence of any combination of heads and tails in any given number of coins. It consists of expanding a binomial $(a + b)$ to the $n$th power, where $a$ and $b$ are simply symbols for the two possible results (in this case, heads and tails) and $n$ represents the number of units participating in the event (in this case, the number of coins involved). In other words, any coin problem of this type is solvable by expanding $(a + b)^n$.

The reader will certainly have had enough algebra to handle simple binomial expansions. In expanding one might proceed as follows.

For $(a + b)^2$:

$$\begin{array}{r} a + b \\ \times\ a + b \\ \hline ab + b^2 \\ a^2 + ab \\ \hline a^2 + 2ab + b^2 \end{array}$$

For $(a + b)^3$:

$$\begin{array}{r} a + b \\ \times\ a + b \\ \hline ab + b^2 \\ a^2 + ab \\ \hline a^2 + 2ab + b^2 \\ \times\ a + b \\ \hline a^2b + 2ab^2 + b^3 \\ a^3 + 2a^2b + ab^2 \\ \hline a^3 + 3a^2b + 3ab^2 + b^3 \end{array}$$

This procedure is perfectly adequate and quite accurate. But it is very time-consuming. A great deal of paper would be required for a problem involving the expansion of a binomial with $n = 23$! A shortcut method, however, is available. To demonstrate this shortcut, a few binomials will be used, giving $n$ increasing values:

1) $(a + b)^2 = a^2 + 2ab + b^2$,
2) $(a + b)^3 = a^3 + 3a^2b + 3ab^2 + b^3$,
3) $(a + b)^4 = a^4 + 4a^3b + 6a^2b^2 + 4ab^3 + b^4$,
4) $(a + b)^5 = a^5 + 5a^4b + 10a^3b^2 + 10a^2b^3 + 5ab^4 + b^5$,
5) $(a + b)^6 = a^6 + 6a^5b + 15a^4b^2 + 20a^3b^3 + 15a^2b^4 + 6ab^5 + b^6$.

A careful examination of these expansions reveals several pertinent facts. First, note that the exponential values of $a$ and $b$ have a distinct ordered relationship to each other; as one decreases, the other increases. Thus, for example, in $(a + b)^4$ the $a$ goes to $a^4$, $a^3$, $a^2$, $a$ and finally disappears, while the $b$ begins at zero and proceeds $b$, $b^2$, $b^3$, and $b^4$. Note also that the exponents in each term of the expansion always add up to a number which is the value of $n$. This relationship of the exponents to the $n$ number is *not* coincidental. It is based on the fact that *the exponents represent the possible combinations that can arise in any situation given an n number.* In the flipping of four coins, for example, where $(a + b)^4$ is used, the exponents reveal the obvious; one can get four heads, three heads and one tail, two heads and two tails, one head and three tails, or four tails. With this knowledge applied to all binomial expansions, the coefficient of the expansion can be constructed by running the $a$ from $n$ down to zero and the $b$ from zero up to $n$.

For example, in $(a + b)^7$:

$$a^7 + a^6 + a^5 + a^4 + a^3 + a^2 + a^1 + a^0.$$

Next the ascending $b$'s are added as follows:

$$a^7 + a^6b + a^5b^2 + a^4b^3 + a^3b^4 + a^2b^5 + ab^6 + b^7.$$

As predicted, the exponents of each term add to $n$, or 7.

It now remains only to find the proper coefficients. There are several methods for doing this. Perhaps the simplest is the procedure outlined by the following rule: *To expand any binomial, multiply the exponent of a term by the coefficient of the term, and divide by the number of the term in the expansion.* This procedure gives the coefficient of the next term in the expansion.

In any binomial expansion, the first coefficient is always 1. Here, in the first term, $a^7$, the exponent is 7. Thus we multiply $7 \times 1 = 7$ and divide by 1 (since $a^7$ is the first term in the expansion). This gives the second coefficient:

$$a^7 + 7a^6b + \cdots$$

Working with this coefficient (7) to find the next, we multiply the exponent 6 by the coefficient 7, obtaining 42. Since $7a^6b$ is the second term in the expansion, divide 42 by 2, obtaining:

$$a^7 + 7a^6b + 21a^5b^2 + \cdots$$

Again we multiply the exponent by the coefficient, getting $5 \times 21 = 105$. Since $21a^5b^2$ is the third term in the expansion, we divide this by 3, which gives us 35, the next coefficient:

$$a^7 + 7a^6b + 21a^5b^2 + 35a^4b^3 + \cdots$$

Then, $4 \times 35 = 140$, and $140 \div 4 = 35$, the next coefficient:

$$a^7 + 7a^6b + 21a^5b^2 + 35a^4b^3 + 35a^3b^4 + \cdots$$

Continuing this process, we arrive shortly at the complete expansion:

$$a^7 + 7a^6b + 21a^5b^2 + 35a^4b^3 + 35a^3b^4 + 21a^2b^5 + 7ab^6 + b^7.$$

Note that the coefficient 1, understood in the term $b^7$, could have easily been derived by use of the rule, for $1 \times 7 = 7$. Since $b^7$ is the last and seventh term in the expansion, we would divide 7 by 7, which is, of course, 1.

This is probably the quickest method of determining the coefficients of a binomial expansion, particularly if $n$ is equal to a large number. However, there is one other means by which the coefficients of a binomial expansion can be found. Note that the coefficients go from the number 1 through a numerical sequence to a higher number, then return through the same sequence (in reverse) to the number 1. For example, in $(a + b)^6$ the coefficients run as follows:

1    6    15    20    15    6    1.

This gradation upward and downward by the coefficients was noticed by the French philosopher-mathematician Blaise Pascal (1623–1662). Pascal took a series of binomials in which the $n$ number of each succeeding binomial was one unit greater than the one before it [i.e., $(a + b)^1$, $(a + b)^2$, $(a + b)^3$] and found that if their coefficients were written one below the other, they would form a triangle with an infinitely large base (Fig. 16–3).

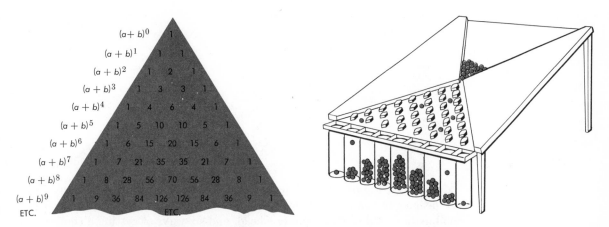

FIG. 16–3   Blaise Pascal noted that the coefficients of succeeding binomial expansions formed a triangle. Every number is the sum of the two numbers directly above it. To the geneticist, this is more than just an interesting coincidence. At right is shown a random physical system to which Pascal's triangle applies directly. The balls will be distributed in a manner proportional to the coefficients of $(a + b)^8$. The balls could just as easily represent inherited characteristics in peas, litters of mice, or many other inheritance situations.

The fact that the numbers form a triangle is merely interesting, however. The real value of Pascal's triangle lies in the fact that, given any one line in the triangle, the numbers on the line below can immediately be written, for they are the sum of the two numbers directly above. For example, in the expansion of $(a + b)^5$, the second coefficient is 5, which is the sum of the numbers 4 and 1 directly above it. The third coefficient is 10, the sum of the numbers 6 and 4 above it.

It might be wondered whether the coefficients, like the exponents, do not have some meaning also. The answer is an affirmative one; *the coefficients tell us the number of ways in which the combinations given by the sum of the exponent can occur.* Suppose, for example, that four pennies are flipped. One of the terms in the expansion of $(a + b)^4$ is $4a^3b$. Letting $a$ stand for the chance that heads will occur and $b$ for the chance of tails, the exponents show that we may get three $a$'s and one $b$ (or three heads and one tail). But the coefficient 4 tells us that there are four possible ways that this combination of three heads to one tail can be obtained. This can be seen easily if each penny is given a number label. For example, three heads and one tail might appear in any of the arrangements shown here:

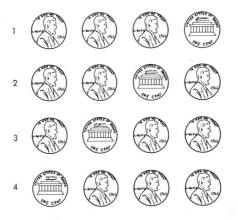

Similarly, the other coefficients indicate that there is only one way to get the pennies to come up all tails or all heads; there are four ways of getting a combination of three tails and one head, and six ways of getting a combination of two heads and two tails.

Suppose we flip five pennies and want to know the chances of getting a combination of three heads and two tails. We will let $a$ represent the chances for heads, which are 50–50, or $\frac{1}{2}$, and $b$ represent the chances for tails, which are also $\frac{1}{2}$.

Since this problem involves five pennies, $(a + b)^n$ becomes $(a + b)^5$:

$$(a + b)^5 = a^5 + 5a^4b + 10a^3b^2 + 10a^2b^3 + 5ab^4 + b^5.$$

From this expansion we select the term which gives the combination of interest to us—in this case, three heads and two tails. This particular combination is given to us by only one term, $10a^3b^2$. Substituting the known values of $\frac{1}{2}$ for $a$ and $b$ and carrying out the necessary arithmetic, we get:

$$10a^3b^2 = 10(\tfrac{1}{2})^3\,(\tfrac{1}{2})^2 = 10(\tfrac{1}{8})\,(\tfrac{1}{4}) = 10(\tfrac{1}{32}) = \tfrac{10}{32} = \tfrac{5}{16}.$$

Thus a distribution of three heads to two tails is predicted to occur $\frac{5}{16}$ of the time. Or to state it another way, out of sixteen tosses, each involving five pennies, five tosses will be expected to show a distribution of three heads to two tails. Many groups of sixteen tosses must be tossed, of course. Just as the accuracy of Charles's law is dependent on the presence of large numbers of gas particles, so the accuracy of a prediction is entirely dependent on the number of trials. Indeed, there is a positive correlation between the accuracy of the prediction and the number of trials performed.

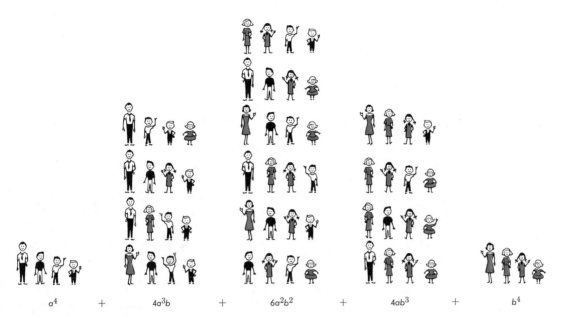

$$a^4 \qquad + \qquad 4a^3b \qquad + \qquad 6a^2b^2 \qquad + \qquad 4ab^3 \qquad + \qquad b^4$$

FIG. 16–4　When applied to the distribution of sexes in a family of four, the coefficients of the proper binomial expansion represent the arrangement(s) in which the possible sex distributions can occur.

If the binomial expansion works for coins, it should work for anything that involves two chance possibilities. Since $a$ and $b$ are merely symbols, they can be maneuvered at will. Consider, for example, the sex distribution of human infants. The chances that a child will be male (or female) are approximately 50–50 or $\frac{1}{2}$. What, then, are the chances that in a family of four children, all the children will be girls? We will let $a$ represent the chances for boys, which are 50–50, or $\frac{1}{2}$, and $b$ represents the chances for girls, which are also $\frac{1}{2}$. Using $(a + b)^n$, with $n = 4$:

$$(a + b)^4 = a^4 + 4a^3b + 6a^2b^2 + 4ab^3 + b^4.$$

Since $b$ represents the chances of girls, we want the term in the expansion that gives us 4 $b$'s. Clearly this is $b^4$. Substituting, we get

$$b^4 = \left(\tfrac{1}{2}\right)^4 = \tfrac{1}{16}.$$

In other words, the chances of getting all girls in a family of four children are the same as the chances of each child being a girl multiplied by each other child's chance of being a girl, or $\frac{1}{2} \times \frac{1}{2} \times \frac{1}{2} \times \frac{1}{2} = \frac{1}{16}$ (Fig. 16–4).

We are now ready to see how the mathematics of probability applies to the inheritance of genetic factors.

Mice are often used in genetic studies. They reproduce rapidly, are relatively inexpensive, and are easy to care for in the laboratory.

One unusual inherited characteristic in mice results in a complete lack of body hair, coupled with heavy folds or wrinkles in the skin (see Color Plate IV). For rather obvious reasons, the condition is known as rhino. Since it is inherited and easy to distinguish, the rhino condition would seem to be a good choice for use in experiments designed to shed light on how inherited characteristics are passed on from generation to generation.

Further considerations rule against this choice, however. The rhino condition couples together at least two inherited conditions, hairlessness and wrinkled skin. Further, the skin itself is a complex organ, composed of several different kinds of tissues (glandular, muscular, connective, etc.). It thus seems evident that there must be many inherited factors involved in the rhino condition. Finally, rhino mice reproduce very poorly, if at all; the very physical deformity that makes them rhino interferes with their mating capability. It is reasonable, therefore, to begin an attempt to explain the transmission of inherited characteristics by working with characteristics that are of a simpler nature.

Coat color in mice is such a characteristic. Differences in coat color are easy to distinguish and the required matings can be accomplished without difficulty. Further, differences in coat color are due to interacting factors that are far less complex than those that cause the rhino condition. In general, the coats of different-colored mice are the same; the only difference is in the pigments that are deposited in the hairs composing these coats.

A certain well-established strain of mice possesses a solid black coat of fur.* Another strain has a solid brown coat (see Color Plate IV). Since both are pure strains, crosses between black mice always yield black offspring and crosses between brown mice always yield brown offspring. It is reasonable to wonder, therefore, what would be the color of the offspring resulting from a cross between brown mice and black. Here are a few of the possibilities:

1) An intermediate color between black and brown.

2) Some black mice and some brown.

3) Spotted black and brown mice.

4) A color entirely different from black and brown.

5) All black mice.

6) All brown mice.

Several matings are made. In some, the male is black and the female brown, while in others the reverse is true. This eliminates sex as a variable in the experiment, while the large number of offspring produced by many matings allows more accurate generalizations to be made.

---

* Mice that have been mated brother-to-sister for at least twenty generations are considered to be an established inbred strain.

FIG. 16–5   A representation of the first cross of black mice with brown mice, yielding an $F_1$ of 992 mice, all black.

Figure 16–5 shows that prediction 5 is the correct one. Of 992 mice obtained (the $F_1$ generation), all are solid black and indistinguishable in appearance from their black parent.

This result raises several questions. First, what has happened to the brown color? Has it been completely destroyed by the black color? Or, is it still present but hidden? Second, does the fact that the $F_1$ black mice appear identical to their black parent mean that they are also genetically identical? Granting that crosses between two inbred-strain parents always produce black offspring, is the same true for the $F_1$ black mice? In other words, if they are crossbred, will they, too, produce only black mice?

To answer these questions, a second set of breeding experiments must be performed. The same procedure as before is followed, but this time the $F_1$ mice, all of which are black, are crossed with each other.

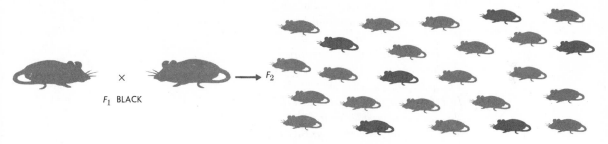

FIG. 16–6   A representation of the second cross of mice, yielding an $F_1$ of 961 black mice to 317 brown mice.

Figure 16–6 indicates the results of this cross; of the 1278 progeny, 961 are black and 317 brown.

The results answer the questions asked prior to the second crossbreeding. First, quite obviously, the brown color was not destroyed by the black. Though not in evidence, it must have been present all the time. The brown mice obtained in the $F_2$ are just as brown as the original brown parents, and when these $F_2$ browns are mated, their offspring are all brown. It can be seen, therefore, that the factor for brown coat color must be both independent of, and unaffected by, the black color.

Second, although the $F_1$ blacks are indistinguishable from their black parents in appearance, they still differ genetically. They fail to breed true, i.e., to produce only black mice.

Third, while the brown-coat factor is not affected or changed by the black-coat factor, it is still completely hidden in the $F_1$ generation. This leads us to consider the possibility that the black factor may in some way be "stronger" than the brown factor.

Often, a scientist may obtain experimental data which he himself is unable to explain. His recourse is to search the research literature. There he may find that some other scientist has obtained data similar to his and, possibly, proposed an hypothesis to explain it. A similar situation exists here. The mice-breeding experiments have yielded results that demand an explanation. The explanation applicable here was proposed a little more than a century ago.

**16–5**
**MENDELIAN**
**GENETICS**

*"You letters, you types, fruit of my research,*
*You are the rock foundation*
*On which I shall establish and upbuild*
*My temple for all time.*
*As the master willed, you shall dispel*
*The gloomy power of superstition*
*Which now oppresses the world.*
*The works of the greatest of men,*
*Which now, of use only to the few,*
*Crumble away into nothingness,*
*You will keep in the light and will preserve.*
*For in many a head still wrapped*
*In slumber, your strength will foster*
*The great, the clear, powers of the mind.*
*In brief, your coming cannot fail*
*To create a new, a better life.*
*May the might of destiny grant me*
*The supreme ecstasy of earthly joy,*
*The highest goal of earthly ecstasy,*
*That of seeing, when I arise from the tomb,*
*My art thriving peacefully*
*Among those who are to come after me."*

*Poem by Gregor Johann Mendel*
*(1822–1884), written while still a schoolboy*

The above poem seems strangely prophetic in light of the later accomplishments of its author and the subsequent fate of those accomplishments. At the age of 21, Mendel entered an Augustinian monastery in Brünn, Austria (now Brno, Czechoslovakia). That he chose this monastery was most fortunate, for there he was given a chance to go to Vienna and take courses in physics, mathematics, and zoology. Still more important, there was space in the garden surrounding the monastery for him to carry out his experiments.

It is interesting to note that Mendel twice failed to qualify for a regular high-school teacher's license. He finally gave up trying to be anything more than a substitute teacher. Particularly significant was the fact that he passed the part of the exam dealing with the more mathematical physical sciences but was unable to pass the natural history (biology) portion.

Most of Mendel's important experiments were done between 1856 and 1863. In 1865 he presented his paper reporting results obtained from thousands of tedious breeding experiments. The report was read aloud at a meeting of the Brünn Society for the Study of Natural Science and was later published in the transactions of that society. At the meeting Mendel received polite attention. However, his application of mathematics to the ratios of plant offspring seemed too much for the audience to take. Attention wandered. It is recorded in the minutes that "there were neither questions nor discussions." The fact that scientific history was made that night remained unnoticed for almost 35 years.

Gregor Johann Mendel (Photo courtesy Burndy Library, Norwalk, Conn.)

Mendel performed breeding experiments on several plants and animals. He is best known, however, for his work with the garden pea, a plant that is normally self-pollinating and hence inbred in the natural state. By close anatomical examination of these plants he was able to distinguish several distinct and inherited characteristics. Among these were the color and shape of the seeds, the positioning of the flowers on the stems (some at the end, others on the side) and the height of the plants, i.e., whether they were short or tall. In referring to Mendel's experimentation and his conclusions we will, for simplicity, deal with the characteristic of height.

Mendel crossed true-breeding tall plants with true-breeding short ones. As with the mice mentioned earlier, several possibilities were available. The plants might be all tall, all short, a mixture of talls and shorts, or they might even be of an intermediate height. Figure 16–7 represents Mendel's results; all the $F_1$ plants were tall.

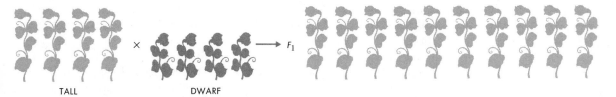

TALL          ×          DWARF        $F_1$

FIG. 16–7   A representation of Mendel's first cross of garden peas, which resulted in an $F_1$ of all tall plants.

Mendel found himself faced with the same type of questions we faced with the brown and black mice. Had the shortness characteristic been destroyed, or was it merely hidden? Were the $F_1$ tall plants genetically similar to their tall parents; i.e., would they breed true?

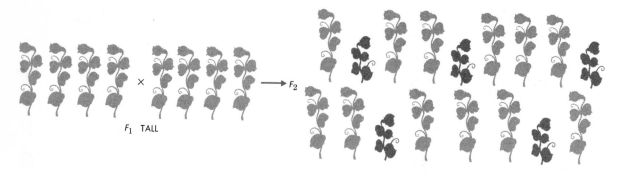

$F_1$ TALL

FIG. 16–8   A representation of Mendel's second cross of garden peas, which resulted in an $F_2$ of 787 tall plants to 277 short plants.

Mendel then crossed two tall plants from the $F_1$ generation. Figure 16–8 represents the results; out of 1064 $F_2$ plants, 787 were tall and 277 were short.

Mendel explained the results of his first cross by coining two terms which are still used in present-day genetics. Since the shortness factor was completely hidden by the tallness factor, he postulated the tallness characteristic to be **dominant** over the shortness, which he termed **recessive**. This fits well with our first cross of the mice; the black coat color must be dominant over the brown coat color, which is recessive.

It was in his interpretation of the second cross, involving the $F_1$ tall plants, that the real genius of Mendel was asserted. Long before he began his work, many people had noticed numbers like those just cited in their experimental crosses. Few, however, had bothered to look at the significance of these numbers. Fortunately, Mendel was an extremely talented mathematician, and it was this ability that enabled him to discover the prize that had so long eluded earlier naturalists.

Mendel noticed that 787 tall plants to 277 short ones constituted a ratio of 2.84:1. In similar crosses involving other characteristics of the pea plant, he obtained similar results; a dominant characteristic appeared in the $F_1$ generation, with ratios of 3.15:1, 2.96:1, 2.82:1, 3.14:1, 2.95:1, and 3.01:1 in the $F_2$ generations.

The suggestion that a ratio of three to one was predictable in the $F_2$ of such crosses was too strong to be overlooked. To Mendel, this discovery was very exciting. He recognized the ratio as being indicative of the operation of the laws of chance and probability. He therefore hypothesized as follows: Suppose that in true-breeding tall plants there is not just one factor influencing height, but *two*. Suppose further that two other factors are present in short plants. If only *one* of these factors gets into a sperm cell and only *one* into an egg cell, then the uniting of these cells will produce a plant with two factors, one from the tall plant and one from the short. Since the factor for tallness is dominant over the factor for shortness, the hybrid in the $F_1$ will be tall. If we let $T$ stand for the tallness factor and $t$ stand for the shortness factor, the first cross can be diagrammed as follows:

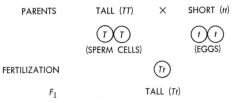

Recall that Mendel performed his experiments around 1860; such things as chromosomes were unknown to him. Yet, notice that homologous chromosomes behave suspiciously like Mendel's hypothesized factors; they occur in pairs and separate from each other during gamete formation (meiosis), one going to each gamete. Fertilization brings two homologous chromosomes together again, one from each parent.

Thus, by hypothesizing that only one factor for an inherited characteristic gets into each gamete, Mendel recognized the necessity of meiosis, though of course he knew nothing about the process. He also recognized that the factors must be paired again during fertilization when he noted the restoration of the pairing in the $F_1$ hybrid. In other words, Mendel recognized that the two factors influencing height in pea plants must separate or **segregate** from each other in the production of the germ cells and then be reunited at fertilization. This concept is known as Mendel's first law, the **law of segregation,** which states that *the factors for a pair of characteristics are segregated.*

Mendel saw that his hypothesis nicely accounted for the ratio of three tall plants to one short plant which he obtained in the $F_2$ generation. This second cross can be diagrammed as follows:

$F_1$ CROSS      TALL ($Tt$)    ×    TALL ($Tt$)

              ⓉⓉ⟋           ⓉⓉ⟋

          (SPERM CELLS)        (EGGS)

Here each parent plant can produce *two* kinds of gametes instead of only one. Half of the gametes produced will carry the tallness factor $T$. The other will carry the shortness factor $t$. Mendel saw that if two types of gametes were produced in equal numbers by both plants, his three-to-one ratio could be explained on the basis of chance and probability. Since any type of sperm cell has an equal chance of fertilizing any type of egg, there are four possible fusions that can take place.

1) A sperm cell carrying the $T$ factor may fuse with an egg carrying the $T$ factor, yielding $TT$.

2) A sperm cell carrying the $T$ factor may fuse with an egg carrying the $t$ factor, yielding $Tt$.

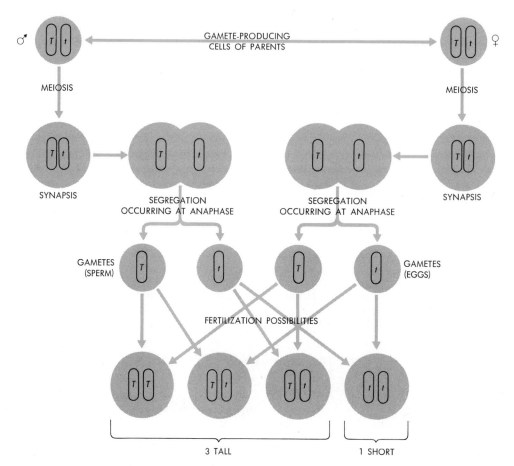

FIG. 16–9

3) A sperm cell carrying the *t* factor may fuse with an egg carrying the *T* factor, yielding *Tt*.

4) A sperm cell carrying the *t* factor may fuse with an egg carrying the *t* factor, yielding *tt*.

Since the $F_1$ generation showed that the *T* factor is dominant over the recessive *t* factor, the first three fertilization possibilities will result in tall plants. Only the fourth produces a short plant. Using present-day knowledge of meiosis, we can represent what happened in Mendel's experimental crossbreeding by means of a highly simplified diagram (Fig. 16–9).

Mendel's hypothesis provides a ready explanation for the results of a cross between two black $F_1$ mice. Note that 961 black mice to 317 brown mice closely approximates a three-to-one ratio. Therefore, it can be hypothesized that the $F_1$ male parent produced two kinds of sperm, half carrying a *B* factor for black, the other half carrying a *b* factor for brown. The female produced two kinds of

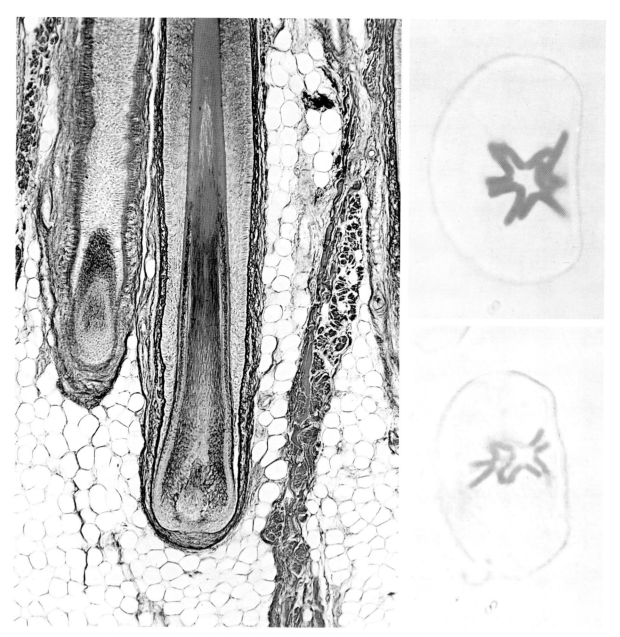

PLATE 1. Histological staining, shown in the longitudinal section of a human hair follicle at left, distinguishes one kind of tissue from another. Cytological staining, shown in the photographs at right, makes cell parts or regions stand out in contrast to each other. Top, cell exposed to a stain which turns red on contact with DNA. Bottom, the same cell exposed to a stain which turns blue on contact with histone proteins. Hair follicle photo courtesy General Biological Supply House, Inc., Chicago; others, courtesy Dr. Montrose Moses, Duke University Medical Center and the Upjohn Company.)

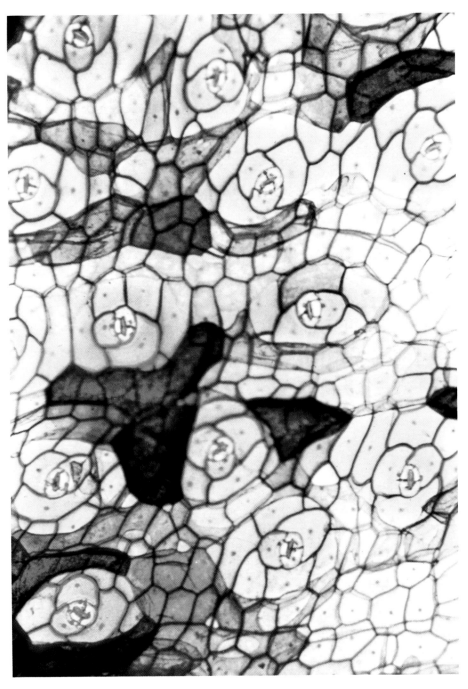

PLATE II. Leaf openings, or stomata, were discovered in the seventeenth century by Marcello Mal-pighi and Nehemiah Grew. (Courtesy Dr. Thomas Sproston, University of Vermont.)

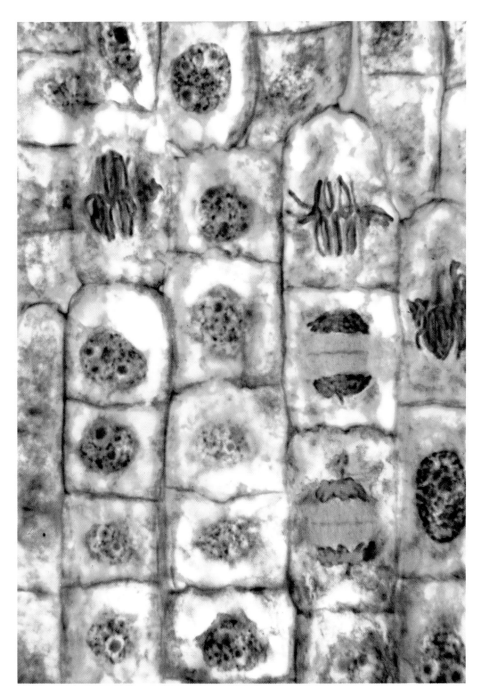

PLATE III. Mitosis in the tip of an onion root. (Courtesy General Biological Supply House, Inc., Chicago.)

BLACK

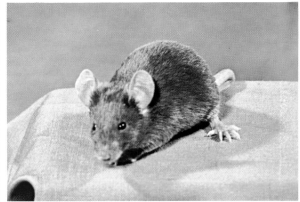

BROWN

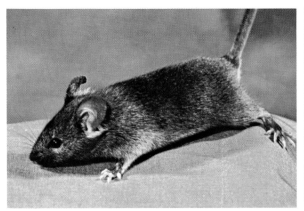

BLACK AGOUTI

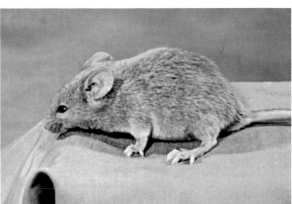

BROWN AGOUTI

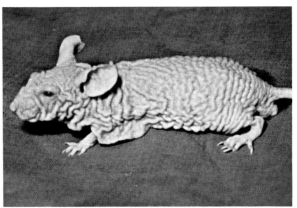

RHINO

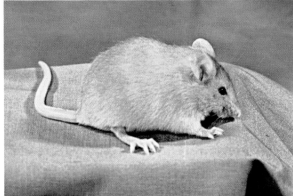

YELLOW

PLATE IV. Coat characteristics inherited in mice. (Courtesy Roscoe B. Jackson Memorial Laboratory.)

eggs, half carrying a $B$ factor, the other half carrying a $b$ factor. Given complete dominance of black over brown, and the fertilization possibilities governed by the same laws of chance and probability discussed in Section 16–2, a three-to-one ratio is readily accounted for.

As has been constantly stressed throughout this book, a good hypothesis must not only explain the observed, it must also act as a basis for accurate predictions. For example:

**Hypothesis:** *If* . . . in mice, factors for the black and brown coat colors segregate into the gametes and recombine at fertilization according to the laws of chance and probability, . . .

**Prediction:** *then* . . . assuming complete dominance of black over brown, crosses between $F_1$ black mice and brown mice should result in offspring of which one-half are black and one-half are brown.

An $F_1$ black mouse, being the result of crossing a pure black ($BB$) with a pure brown ($bb$) mouse, must carry both coat-color factors, $B$ and $b$. The dominance of black over brown makes the animal black. Half the gametes it will produce will carry the $B$ factor and half will carry the $b$ factor. The brown mouse, on the other hand, can produce only gametes that carry the $b$ factor. Since these gametes have an equal chance of fusing with either of the other gametes, a 50–50 distribution of black to brown mice is the prediction. Of the 833 offspring of such a cross, 412 were black and 421 were brown. Since the slight deviation in the predicted ratio is not statistically significant, Mendel's hypothesis is supported. Moreover, it gains stature by this experiment because his generalization concerning inheritance in a species of plant has been successfully extrapolated to a species of animal. Indeed, it will be seen that the principles of mendelian genetics play a role in the inheritance of many different species of living organisms. For, as has probably been obvious to the reader for some time, what Mendel thought of as "factors" are the hereditary units, the genes.

Not all characteristics are inherited in as simple a manner as the tallness and shortness in peas or the black and brown coat colors in mice. Indeed, simple inheritance in which only one pair of genes is involved is very much the exception, rather than the rule. Nor is it at all required for one characteristic to be completely dominant over the other. Quite often the combination of different genes tends to produce varying degrees of partial or **incomplete dominance,** with the latter usually resulting in a blending of the two genes to produce a different appearance.

An example of incomplete dominance is seen in the breeding of certain types of cattle. If a red animal is crossed with a white one, an intermediate-colored animal, a roan, is produced. No other color ever appears; however, crosses between two roans yield a ratio of one red to two roans to one white. Once again, mendelian genetics provides a ready explanation for the results (Fig. 16–10).

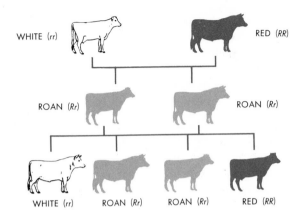

FIG. 16–10

Note that if red coat had been dominant over white (or vice versa), a 3:1 $F_2$ ratio would result. However, since the genes modify each other to produce an intermediate color, a 1:2:1 ratio is obtained. Further, in this case, the $F_1$ animals are easily distinguishable from their parents.

Note also that this 1:2:1 ratio is the same obtained in flipping two pennies simultaneously. The number of times we obtain both heads, a head and tail combination, or both tails, is 1:2:1 respectively. Further, the same mathematics discussed in Section 16–3 can be used to predict such things as the frequency of occurrence of inherited characteristics in the offspring of living organisms. Application of this principle, however, will be deferred for the time being.

Prior to Mendel it was widely believed that inherited characteristics represented a blend of characteristics shown by the parents. Undoubtedly, mulatto children produced by marriages between blacks and whites lent considerable support to this idea. It might be noted in passing that an hypothesis proposing blending of inherited traits is just as satisfactory as Mendel's particulate hypothesis in explaining the results of the cross between red and white cattle. The $F_2$ generation, however, yields results which contradict the blending hypothesis and support Mendel's particulate one.

Usually it is easier to determine the possible combinations that can occur at fertilization by arranging the gametes in a matrix, or Punnett square:

The Punnett square prevents the overlooking of a possible gamete combination, easily done in more complex crosses involving more than one pair of genes.

However, it should not be forgotten that the symbols represent gametes (sperms and eggs) and the zygotes represent the potential organisms involved.

A brief look at some genetic terminology will facilitate understanding of the material to follow. Genes that carry contrasting inheritance factors are called **alleles.** Alleles line up opposite each other during the synapsis of homologous chromosomes (Section 15–5). Genes $T$ and $t$ in Mendel's tall and dwarf pea plants were alleles. The genes $B$ and $b$ in the black and brown mice are also alleles. In the case of the pea, gene alleles $T$ and $t$ carry the contrasting inheritance factors for height; in the mice, gene alleles $B$ and $b$ carry the contrasting factors for coat color.

The term **homozygous** is used to designate an individual in which a pair of genes are identical; if the genes are different, the individual is **heterozygous.** For example, both the tall and the dwarf parent pea plants used by Mendel were homozygous, since they both contained like genes for height ($TT$ and $tt$ respectively). However, two-thirds of the $F_2$ tall plants and all of the $F_1$ plants were heterozygous (or hybrid), since they contained genes that were different ($Tt$). In the experiment with the mice, the parent black mice used in the first cross were homozygous ($BB$), as were the brown parents ($bb$). The $F_1$ blacks and two-thirds of the $F_2$ blacks were heterozygous ($Bb$). Of course, an individual may be heterozygous for some pairs of genes but homozygous for other pairs.

A distinction must be made between the *appearance* of an organism and the inheritance factors or genes that it will pass along to its descendants for, as we have already seen, one may not reveal the other. The appearance registered by means of our senses is called the **phenotype.** The phenotype of the plant $TT$ is tallness. The phenotype of the plant $Tt$ is also tallness. The plant with $tt$ has a phenotype of shortness. Similarly, mice $BB$ and $Bb$ are phenotype black, while mice $bb$ are phenotype brown.

On the other hand, the code or classification given to an organism on the basis of data from breeding experiments is its **genotype.** In other words, while phenotype is classification according to appearance, genotype is classification according to genetic makeup. For example, the symbols $TT$ represent the genotype for a homozygous tall pea plant; the symbols $Tt$ represent the genotype of a heterozygous tall pea plant. The genotype of a dwarf plant is $tt$. Likewise, in the brown and black mice, there are only three possible genotypes for coat color; $BB$, $Bb$, and $bb$.

A distinction must be made between genotype and phenotype in recording ratios given by an experimental genetic cross. In the cross between the heterozygous $F_1$ black mice, our phenotypic ratio was 3:1. But the genotypic ratio was 1 homozygous black, 2 heterozygous black, and 1 homozygous brown, or 1:2:1. In the cross between red and white cattle, yielding an intermediate phenotype of roan, the cross between the $F_1$ roans produced offspring in which the phenotypic and genotypic ratios were identical.

**16-6**
**TWO PAIRS**
**OF GENES**

Thus far, we have dealt with the principles of simple mendelian inheritance in crosses involving a single pair of genes. Relatively few inherited characteristics, however, are influenced by only one pair of genes. For example, the genes concerned with the formation and proper functioning of the pituitary gland are not directly concerned with the growth of the body. Yet, should they fail to carry out their assigned job, dwarfism results. It is often difficult to say that a certain characteristic is carried by a particular gene or genes. It is far more accurate to view it as the expression of the interaction of several groups of genes.

In addition to the black and brown coloration in mice, there is another factor that influences coat color. This factor is known as the **agouti** condition. When the agouti condition is combined with black, brown, or some other coat color, it produces a characteristic mottled appearance (see Color Plate IV). If we examine the individual hairs of the coats of agouti mice, the reason for this appearance becomes clear. The hairs of a completely black or brown mouse are solidly colored along their entire length. The hairs of an agouti animal have a distinct band across them, near the end (Fig. 16–11).

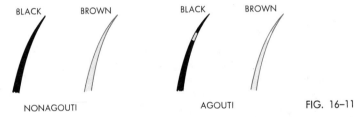

FIG. 16–11

As in the case of black or brown coat color, the inheritance of the agouti condition is dependent on one pair of genes, and is dominant. Therefore, crosses between homozygous agouti and nonagouti mice yield an $F_1$ that are all agouti. Crosses of the $F_1$ agouti animals yield a ratio of three agoutis to one nonagouti.

Such $F_2$ 3:1 ratios of black to brown or agouti to nonagouti are obtained when the characteristics are considered *separately*. Suppose, however, that they are considered *together*. In particular, consider a cross involving black agouti mice from a pure inbred strain (genotype $AABB$) with brown nonagouti mice (genotype $aabb$). Black, of course, is dominant over brown, as is agouti over nonagouti. It might be predicted, therefore, that the $F_1$ mice will show both dominant characteristics, i.e., that they will all be black agoutis. This is precisely what occurs. In a series of experiments, many matings of black agoutis with brown nonagoutis produced 1624 $F_1$ animals, all black agoutis.

Were these $F_1$ black agoutis genotypically the same as their dominant parent? If so, then crosses between $F_1$ mice should produce only black agouti mice. Previous experience, however, indicates that these $F_1$ individuals will not breed true, despite the fact that their appearance is indistinguishable from that of their black agouti parents. Past experience also leads us to expect the three-to-one ratio. *But three whats to one what?* Three black agoutis to one brown nonagouti? Or three black nonagoutis to one brown agouti? Is there any justification for assuming that the black color always appears linked to the agouti condition and the brown to the nonagouti? If not, then it must be admitted that there are *four* possible kinds of mice that we can obtain, instead of just two, namely black agoutis, black nonagoutis, brown agoutis, and brown nonagoutis.

Many such $F_1$ crosses were made, and a total of 1625 baby mice were obtained. Of these, 909 were black agouti, 304 were black nonagouti, 299 were brown agoutis, and 103 were brown nonagoutis, a ratio of 9:3:3:1.

Another examination of Mendel's work provides an hypothesis to explain this 9:3:3:1 ratio. Mendel had noticed that one inherited difference in the garden pea was seed color; some plants had yellow seeds, others green. Crosses of yellow-seed producers with green-seed producers yielded only plants that produced yellow seeds. Mendel hypothesized the dominance of yellow over green, combined with segregation of the factors for these seed colors, and saw that a three-to-one ratio of yellows to greens should result from crosses of the $F_1$ yellows. The experimental results supported this hypothesis.

However, Mendel also noticed that the pea seeds differed in still another characteristic. Some were round and smooth, while others were wrinkled or shriveled in appearance. Mendel found that crosses between plants that produced round seeds and plants that produced wrinkled seeds gave an $F_1$ of plants that produced round seeds; thus roundness is carried by the dominant gene. Crosses between plants of the $F_1$ generation produced a 3:1 ratio of round seeds to wrinkled ones.

Mendel then considered the factors of seed color and seed shape together. He noticed that crosses between two pure varieties of pea plants—one showing the dominant characteristics of round yellow seeds, the other the recessive characteristics of wrinkled green seeds—yielded an $F_1$ phenotypically identical to the dominant parent; i.e., the $F_1$ plants all produced round yellow seeds. However, crosses of these $F_1$ plants yielded a ratio of nine plants that produced round yellow seeds, to three that produced round green seeds, to three that produced wrinkled yellow seeds, to one that produced wrinkled green seeds. Notice that the ratios obtained by Mendel for the peas were the same as those obtained with the mice in the experiment mentioned above. In interpreting his results, Mendel turned his attention to gamete production. Of course, Mendel knew nothing of meiosis, but it will be helpful for us to consider his hypothesis in the light of modern-day knowledge of the process.

Recall that when Mendel was working with just one characteristic, such as tallness and dwarfness in pea plants, he hypothesized the existence of one pair

of "factors" (genes) which segregate at gamete formation. When he began
dealing with two characteristics, Mendel did not hesitate to hypothesize the
existence of *two* pairs of genes, each pair of which was concerned with the inheritance of one of the two contrasting traits (round-wrinkled and yellow-green).
The members of each of these pairs also segregate during gametogenesis, with
each seed-color gene going to a different gamete. The same is true for the genes
for seed shape; these also go into separate gametes. But, Mendel reasoned, if the
segregation of the genes for seed color is *entirely independent* of the segregation
of the genes for seed shape, and occurs *completely at random*, then once again
the mathematics of chance and probability will apply. This is known as Mendel's
second law, the **law of independent assortment.**

Mendel's first cross can be diagrammed as follows:

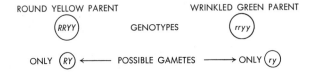

Here, $R$ = round, $r$ = wrinkled, $Y$ = yellow, and $y$ = green. Since each
parent can produce only one type of gamete, only one fertilization combination
is possible:

Note that Mendel's $F_1$ plant (producing round yellow seeds) differs genotypically from the parent that produces round yellow seeds. All the $F_1$ plants
must be doubly heterozygous, or dihybrid. Thus the $F_1$ plants produce gametes
that are unlike those of their homozygous parents. Mendel stressed completely
random distribution of the allelic genes and completely independent assortment
of the nonallelic genes. With this in mind, it becomes evident that each $F_1$
plant can produce four types of gametes:

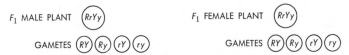

There are now several fertilization possibilities, each determined entirely by
chance. With just one pair of genes involved, only two types of gametes could
be produced by the $F_1$ hybrids. There were, therefore $2 \times 2$, or 4 fertilization
possibilities. With complete dominance, a three-to-one ratio is obtained. In
this case, however, each $F_1$ individual produces *four* different types of gametes.
The fertilization possibilities are thus $4 \times 4$, or 16. The three-to-one ratio in
the monohybrid cross yields the total number of fertilization possibilities with

one pair of genes, for $3 + 1 = 4$. The same holds true for the ratio obtained when two pairs of genes are involved, for $9 + 3 + 3 + 1 = 16$.

This $F_1$ dihybrid cross can be diagrammed by use of a Punnett square, as shown in Fig. 16–12. A count of the phenotypes reveals the experimentally obtained $9:3:3:1$ ratio.

MALE GAMETES OF $F_1$ GENERATION

|  | RY | Ry | rY | ry |
|---|---|---|---|---|
| **RY** | RRYY ROUND YELLOW | RRYy ROUND YELLOW | RrYY ROUND YELLOW | RrYy ROUND YELLOW |
| **Ry** | RRYy ROUND YELLOW | RRyy ROUND GREEN | RrYy ROUND YELLOW | Rryy ROUND GREEN |
| **rY** | RrYY ROUND YELLOW | RrYy ROUND YELLOW | rrYY WRINKLED YELLOW | rrYy WRINKLED YELLOW |
| **ry** | RrYy ROUND YELLOW | Rryy ROUND GREEN | rrYy WRINKLED YELLOW | rryy WRINKLED GREEN |

FEMALE GAMETES OF $F_1$ GENERATION

FIG. 16–12

Mendel recognized that his hypothesis had to have predictive value if it was to be accepted by his fellow scientists. Accordingly, he crossed plants of known genotypes. Before obtaining his experimental results, he determined theoretically the types of gametes that each would produce and calculated the fertilization possibilities. Mendel then recorded his predictions of the types of plants and the proportion of each that these crosses would be expected to produce. Two such crosses were as follows:

1) *Genotype RrYy with RRYY*. Mendel hypothesized that in terms of these genetic factors, the dihybrid would produce four kinds of gametes, $RY$, $Ry$, $rY$, and $ry$. The other would produce only $RY$ gametes. Thus no matter which fertilization combination occurred, the seeds of the resulting plants would all be round and yellow.

   *Results:* 192 plants, all of which produced round yellow seeds.

2) *Genotype RrYy with rryy*. Mendel hypothesized that four kinds of gametes would be produced by the dihybrid ($RY$, $Ry$, $rY$, and $ry$) and one kind ($ry$) by the other plant. By considering all the possible fertilization combinations, Mendel predicted four different kinds of plants in equal numbers.

   *Results:* 55 with round yellow seeds, 51 with round green seeds, 49 with wrinkled yellow seeds, and 53 with wrinkled green seeds.

It would take a professional doubting Thomas to question the validity of Mendel's hypothesis in the light of the extraordinary predictive abilities demonstrated by these crosses.

Lest the reader lose sight of the importance of the part played by the product principle of probability, it is worthwhile pointing out that the $9:3:3:1$ ratio could have been predicted in yet another way. A cross involving two individuals with a single pair of allelic genes ($Aa$), in which gene $A$ shows complete dominance, yields a $3:1$ ratio. The same ratio is obtained from a cross involving two individuals of genotype $Bb$ with $B$ completely dominant. By considering both gene pairs together in one cross ($AaBb \times AaBb$), we simply increase the number of fertilization possibilities from four (the sum of $3:1$) to 16 (the sum of $9:3:3:1$). If we assume, as did Mendel, that the fertilization possibilities are entirely governed by the laws of chance and probability, the product principle of probability should apply directly:

$$\begin{array}{r} 3:1 \\ \times\ 3:1 \\ \hline 9:3:3:1 \end{array}$$

And so it does.

Thus Mendel, by incorporating the mathematical laws of chance and probability into the science of genetics, provided a solid foundation upon which all later investigations in genetics could be based. Once it had been determined how genes interact with each other (i.e., whether they demonstrate dominance, incomplete dominance, etc.) reliable predictions could be made concerning the phenotypic and genotypic ratios of the progeny.

## 16-7 BINOMIAL EXPANSIONS AND MENDELIAN GENETICS

Much of the practical usefulness of genetics is based on its ability to predict the phenotypes and genotypes of plant and animal progeny. Certainly commercial breeding experiments would be of little use if it were not possible to predict the types of offspring with statistical validity.

Of particular importance to man is the application of this predictive capability to **genetic prognosis**. Genetic prognosis might be used to predict for a married or about-to-be-married couple what types of children they could expect to have. In some cases the information would be of minor interest; a blue-eyed couple probably would not be much concerned to learn that they would not be likely to have any brown-eyed children. In other cases, the questions may be more critical. It is not usually desirable to bring into the world a child with such traits as deafness, epilepsy, feeble-mindedness, or idiocy. Many couples who would be likely to have children with these or other afflictions might want to think twice before doing so. The public is largely ignorant of inherited factors, and it is probably unfortunate that more people with histories of such conditions in their families do not take advantage of the services that a geneticist trained in human prognosis can give.

Let us take a concrete example. In man, there sometimes occurs a condition known as infantile amaurotic idiocy, which results in mental deficiency, blindness, paralysis, and early death. The condition is inherited as a simple recessive trait. Thus normal parents whose family histories indicate that they are both heterozygous for the condition may expect one out of four of their children to show the condition. Suppose that such a couple goes to a genetics expert and asks for advice. They plan to get married and would like to have at least three children. However, they recognize the possibility that some or all of their children may be afflicted with this condition, and they want to find out from the geneticist what the chances are that all three of their children will be normal.

Knowing that both of these people are heterozygous for amaurotic idiocy, the geneticist can tell them immediately that three-quarters of their children can be *expected* to be normal. The Punnett square below illustrates this:

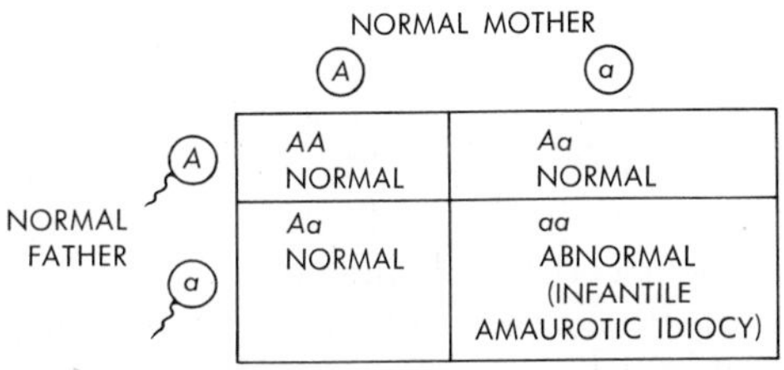

But this tells the couple very little about the matter in which they are most interested—the *chances* that all three of their children will be normal. Three-fourths of three children is a meaningless figure to most parents, as indeed it is to almost anyone.

The product principle of probability provides the answer, in this case by the binomial expansion $(a + b)^n$ with $n = 3$. Let $a$ = chances for normal children (i.e., $\frac{3}{4}$); let $b$ = chances for abnormal children ($\frac{1}{4}$). Since there are three children involved, we expand as follows:

$$(a + b)^3 = a^3 + 3a^2b + 3ab^2 + b^3.$$

We next remove that portion of the binomial expansion of interest to us, i.e., the one representing three normal children ($a^3$). Substituting the fraction $\frac{3}{4}$ as given by the Punnett square, we obtain

$$a^3 = \left(\tfrac{3}{4}\right)^3 = \tfrac{27}{64}.$$

Thus in 64 three-child marriages of this sort, 27 would be expected to have all three children normal. Thus this couple's chances of attaining their desired family size without encountering the unfavorable condition are a little less than 50–50.

As another example, suppose that a biology instructor wishes to demonstrate a 3:1 mendelian ratio to his classes by crossing two black mice, both heterozygous for brown (*Bb*). If a litter of only four mice is obtained, what are the chances that they will demonstrate this ratio?

Once again we turn to the binomial expansion and proceed as follows. Let $a$ = chances for a black mouse, or $\frac{3}{4}$; let $b$ = chances for a brown mouse, or $\frac{1}{4}$. Since there are four mice involved, we expand $(a + b)^n$, with $n = 4$:

$$(a + b)^4 = a^4 + 4a^3b + 6a^2b^2 + 4ab^3 + b^4.$$

We want to know what chance we have of getting three blacks to one brown, or, as we have symbolized it, 3 *a*'s to 1 *b*. We therefore look for the term in the expansion that gives us this ratio. Clearly this is $4a^3b$. Removing this term from the expansion, we substitute and solve as follows:

$$4a^3b = 4(\tfrac{3}{4})^3(\tfrac{1}{4}) = 4(\tfrac{27}{64})(\tfrac{1}{4}) = 4(\tfrac{27}{256}) = \tfrac{108}{256} = \tfrac{27}{64}$$

You can see from this answer that the teacher is a bit of an optimist if he expects to get a perfect demonstration with so few mice.*

In the first example discussed here dealing with infantile amaurotic idiocy, it can be seen, of course, that the chances of getting all three children normal can be derived intuitively by showing with the Punnett square that the chance that any one child will be normal is $\frac{3}{4}$, and therefore, by the product principle of probability, the chance that all three will be normal is $\frac{3}{4} \times \frac{3}{4} \times \frac{3}{4} = (\frac{3}{4})^3 = \frac{27}{64}$. For the second example, dealing with black and brown mice, it can be seen intuitively that the chance for the specific 3-black-to-1-brown combination is $(\frac{3}{4})^3(\frac{1}{4})$ and that there are four possible ways of getting this combination.

For very large numbers it is often convenient to be able to calculate the *n*th term of the binomial directly, using the formula

$$\frac{n!}{w!x!}\, p^w q^x,$$

where $n$ refers to the total number of children in the family, $w$ to the number of children with a specific genetic or phenotypic constitution having probability $p$, and $x$ to the number of children with a genotype or phenotype of probability $q$. It can thus be seen that the mathematics of genetics is essentially straightforward and, intuitively, quite reasonable.

The mathematics of chance and probability are of interest to the geneticist because they allow him to predict accurately not only the types of progeny that can be produced by individual matings, but also the frequencies of certain

---

* And even more of an optimist in expecting the mother mouse to cooperate and produce a litter of four or eight that will nicely divide into a perfect 3:1 ratio. If the teacher is blessed with the author's luck, the result will be a litter of 12 mice, all brown.

The fact that both our examples came out to be $\frac{27}{64}$ is coincidental. You should not expect all answers to come out this way.

genotypes within large groupings of mating individuals. Such information may be of vital interest to a geneticist who is breeding large numbers of animals, since it will enable him to follow the inheritance pattern of a certain gene. It is also of great importance to him if he is interested in the occurrence of certain traits within large segments of a human population. The application of genetic principles to large numbers of randomly breeding organisms is known as **population genetics,** a field that has become an increasingly useful branch of the biological sciences. Population genetics is also important to the study of evolution, for it is populations that evolve, not individuals. This point will receive further attention in Chapter 21.

**16-8
CONCLUSION**

This chapter has discussed some of the applications of genetics to human welfare and has pointed out the almost central role that genetics has assumed in biological research.

The mathematics of chance and probability were discussed in some detail, with emphasis on binomial expansions and the way in which they apply to such purely chance situations as the movement of molecules or the flipping of coins. Later, the reason for this discussion became clear. Mendel's insight into the problems posed by the results of his experiments in the breeding of garden peas was primarily a mathematical one. He recognized that the same laws of chance and probability were at work in the distribution of the "factors" controlling pea phenotypes.

By first posing the problem of breeding mice for coat color, then referring to Mendel's work in order to explain the results, we were following a pattern quite common in science. Scientists often perform experiments the results of which they are unable to explain. They may then search the biological literature to see whether some other investigator has had similar results and may possibly have put forth an hypothesis to explain them.

Mendel's "factors" were what later became known as genes. But what is a gene? Is it a definite particle on the chromosome, which we may discover simply by looking more closely? How do genes exert their influence to cause an agouti coat texture or a tall pea plant? These are topics which must be discussed in Chapter 17.

### How To Solve Genetics Problems

**EXERCISES**

The study of genetics has been the nemesis of many biology students, due mainly to difficulties they encounter in the solution of problems. On the other hand, some students who may have been doing quite poorly in a biology course suddenly blossom in the study of genetics. It is difficult to see why these differences occur; possibly it is because genetics problems, by their mathematical nature, demand very precise reasoning.

Generally, the difficulties encountered in working genetics problems are due, first and foremost, to a lack of organization on the part of the student. He reads the problem over and over, yet fails to pick out the important facts and deal with them in an orderly fashion. Yet, almost all of genetics problems encountered in introductory biology can be attacked in a simple and straightforward manner.

The following steps will help in the solution of genetics problems. They are applicable to the problems in both Chapters 16 and 17.

1)   Determine the type of inheritance dealt with in the problem; i.e., does it show complete dominance, incomplete dominance, or some other inheritance feature? Are there one, two, or more pairs of genes involved? Usually, this information is given in the problem. If not, it can be deduced from the phenotypic ratios of the offspring.

2)   Determine the genotypes of the individuals involved.

3)   Determine the types of gametes each parent can produce. Arrange them into a Punnett square and fill in the possible progeny genotypes.

4)   Count the resulting phenotypes and express them as a ratio. Often this is as far as the problem will require you to go.

5)   If chance predictions are involved, expand the binomial $(a + b)^n$ to the proper $n$th power. Substitute the fractions given by the Punnett square in step 4 and solve.

*Sample Problem:* In man, the ability to taste the bitter chemical phenylthiocarbamide (PTC) is due to a dominant gene $T$; inability to taste it is due to its recessive allele $t$. A man who can taste PTC, but whose father could not, marries a woman who can also taste PTC, but whose mother could not.

a)   What proportion of their children will probably have the ability to taste PTC?

b)   If they have five children, what are the chances that four will be tasters and one a nontaster?

*Step 1.* We determine that this is a case of simple dominance and that there is only one pair of genes involved.

*Step 2.* We determine that the man's genotype must be $Tt$ (since he is a taster, he must have at least one gene $T$, but since his father was a nontaster ($tt$), and he is the product of his father's sperm, he must also have a $t$ gene.) Likewise, the woman must also be $Tt$, since her mother was a nontaster ($tt$) and she is a product of her mother's egg.

*Step 3.* We determine that the man and woman can each produce two types of gametes, carrying either a $T$ or $t$ gene. We next put them in a Punnett square, as follows:

|   | $T$ | $t$ |
|---|-----|-----|
| $T$ | $TT$ | $Tt$ |
| $t$ | $Tt$ | $tt$ |

*Step 4.* We count up the phenotypes. In this case there are two, tasters and nontasters. The phenotypic ratio in this case is 3:1. This gives the answer to part (a); *i.e.* $\frac{3}{4}$ are tasters.

*Step 5.* We expand $(a + b)^n$ with $n = 5$ as follows:

$$a^5 + 5a^4b + 10a^3b^2 + 10a^2b^3 + 5ab^4 + b^5.$$

Letting $a$ = tasters and $b$ = nontasters, we choose the proper term in the expansion that gives us four tasters and one nontaster, i.e., four $a$'s to one $b$. Clearly this is the term $5a^4b$. Substituting the Punnett square fractions of $\frac{3}{4}$ tasters to $\frac{1}{4}$ nontasters in this term, we obtain $5a^4b = 5(\frac{3}{4})^4(\frac{1}{4}) = 5(\frac{81}{256})(\frac{1}{4}) = 5(\frac{81}{1024}) = \frac{405}{1024}$, or 405 out of 1024 chances. This is the answer to part (b).

1. Suppose you flipped five pennies simultaneously, repeating the operation many times. In one hundred tries, what are the chances of getting: (a) All five heads? (b) Four heads and a tail? (c) Three heads and two tails? (d) Two heads and three tails? (e) One head and four tails? (f) All five tails?

2. In Exercise 1, what is the total of the answers to all six parts? What is the significance of this?

3. A family planning to have three children wants two girls and a boy. What are the chances that they will get this distribution?

4. The Jones family has eight children, all of whom are girls. What is the chance that the next child will be a boy?

5. How many different ways is it possible to get a distribution of four heads and two tails in the simultaneous flipping of six coins?

6. A spotted rabbit and a solid-colored rabbit were crossed. They produced all spotted offspring. When these $F_1$ rabbits were crossed, the $F_2$ consisted of 32 spotted and 10 solid-colored rabbits. Which characteristic is determined by a dominant gene?

7. What proportion of the $F_2$ spotted rabbits in Exercise 6 would be heterozygous? Homozygous? How many of the $F_2$ solid-colored rabbits would be expected to be homozygous?

8. What method would most easily tell which of the spotted rabbits in the above problem were heterozygous and which homozygous? Is there any other method? If so, what is it?

9. If we cross a heterozygous tall pea plant with a dwarf pea plant, what proportion of the $F_1$ will be expected to be tall?

10. Suppose we cross one dwarf pea plant with another. What proportion of the $F_1$ will be expected to be dwarf?

11. A brown mouse is crossed with a heterozygous black mouse. If the mother has a litter of four, what are the chances that all of them will be brown?

12. What are the probable genotypes of the parents in a cross that gives a 3:1 ratio? A 1:2:1 ratio? A 1:1 ratio? (Use the symbols $B$ and $b$.)

13. A cross between two mice produced an $F_1$ with a ratio of one brown to one black. What are the probable genotypes of the parents? Of the progeny?

14. A mouse breeder has a pure strain of black mice that normally breed true and produce only black offspring. Occasionally, however, a brown mouse or two has appeared in the litters of some of the mice, What do you hypothesize as the cause of the appearance of brown coat color? If the brown mice are destroyed as soon as they are born, how many generations will it take to completely eliminate the brown gene from the stocks?

15. In horses, black is due to a dominant gene $B$, chestnut to its recessive allele $b$. The trotting gate is due to a dominant gene $T$, pacing to its recessive allele $t$. A homozygous black trotter is crossed with a chestnut pacer. What sort of foals will result in several crosses of this sort so far as coat color and gait are concerned?

16. If two of the $F_1$ animals from the cross in Exercise 15 are crossed, what kinds of colts can be produced? In what proportion will each phenotype be expected to appear?

17. In poultry, black color is due to a dominant gene $E$, and red color to its recessive allele $e$. Crested head is due to a dominant gene $C$, plain head to its recessive allele $c$. A male bird, red and crested, is crossed with a black, plain female. They produce many offspring, half of which are black and crested, the other half, red and crested. What would you infer about the genotypes of the parents?

18. A mating is made between two black, crested birds. The $F_1$ contains 13 offspring in the following proportions: 7 black, crested; 3 red, crested; 2 black, plain; 1 red, plain. What are the probable genotypes of the parents?

19. In man, aniridia, a type of blindness, is due to a dominant gene. Migraine, a headache condition, is the result of a different dominant gene. A man with aniridia, whose mother was not blind, marries a woman who suffers with migraine but whose father did not. In what proportion of their children would *both* of these conditions be expected to occur?

20. Suppose that a woman who was not blind, but whose parents both suffered from aniridia, goes to a genetic expert for advice. She suffers from migraine which her father also had. She wants to know what the chances are that her children will have aniridia or migraine. What would the geneticist tell her?

21. In cocker spaniels, black coat color is due to a dominant gene $B$, reddish-tan coat to the recessive allele $b$. Solid coat color is determined by a dominant gene $S$, while white spotting is determined by the recessive allele $s$. A black and white female was mated to a reddish-tan male. The litter contained five puppies: one black, one reddish-tan, one black and white, and two reddish-tan and white. What are the genotypes of the parents?

22. In summer squash, colorless fruit is due to a dominant gene $W$; colored fruit is due to its recessive allele $w$. Disk-shaped fruit is determined by a dominant gene $S$, sphere-shaped fruit by its recessive allele $s$. How many genotypes may squash plants have in regard to color and shape of fruit? How many categories of phenotypes could be expected from their genotypes? How many different homozygous genotypes are possible? What phenotypic ratio would you expect from a cross between two heterozygous plants?

**SUGGESTED READINGS**

LEVINE, R. P., *Genetics* (New York: Holt, Rinehart, Winston, 1962). This book covers modern genetics, including molecular and microbial research.

LEVINSON, HORACE, *Chance, Luck and Statistics* (New York: Dover Press, 1963). A well-written book which discusses probability in relation to many types of games. This book is highly recommended to any student who is interested in the theory of probability.

SNYDER, L. H., and DAVID, P. R., *Principles of Heredity* (Boston: D. C. Heath and Company, Fifth Edition, 1957). An exceptionally well-written genetics textbook.

A good hypothesis must explain the phenomenon to which it pertains. Mendel's hypothesis, involving the segregation and random assortment of genetic "factors," pertained to the inheritance of contrasting characteristics in peas (tall and short plants, round and wrinkled seeds, etc). His hypothesis did, indeed, account for the results very nicely; it also allowed him to predict accurately the ratios of the phenotypes of offspring resulting from crosses between parent plants of known genotypes.

However, a really good inheritance hypothesis must be applicable to more than just one kind of organism and more than just a few simple inherited characteristics. Mendel's hypothesis meets the first of these challenges, since it accounts for the inheritance of coat variations in mice. But this is still a simple inheritance situation, involving the activity of only a few gene pairs. In this chapter, attention will be directed to the applicability of Mendel's hypothesis to more complex inheritance situations. And, more important, we shall tackle the two most fundamental questions of modern genetics—What *is* a gene, and how does it work?

To account for the phenotypic ratios he observed in his pea plants, Mendel proposed a purely intellectual model, based on segregating and randomly assorting factors. Later, the behavior of chromosomes during meiosis was seen to parallel the behavior of Mendel's hypothesized factors, and thus his intellectual model seemed to attain reality.

The close parallel between the behavior of Mendel's factors (i.e., genes) and the behavior of the chromosomes during meiosis might lead to a tentative hypothesis that a gene and a chromosome are one and the same thing.

*Hypothesis:*   *If* . . .   a chromosome is the same thing as a gene, . . .

*Prediction I:*  *then* . . . chromosomes should demonstrate segregation during gametogenesis, and . . .

*Prediction II:* *then* . . . the members of separate pairs of homologous chromosomes should show random and independent assortment into the prospective gametes.

Both of these predictions are verified. Other observations, however, seem inconsistent with this hypothesis. Most obvious is the chromosome number. A red fox, for example, has only 34 chromosomes. It is difficult to imagine that all its inherited characteristics could be controlled by only 17 pairs of genes. Further, the arctic fox has 52 chromosomes. Such a wide variation in the number of "chromosome-genes" would not be predicted between these closely related forms. Finally, there seems to be no consistent principle underlying the variation in chromosome number between organisms of widely differing evolutionary status; this fact becomes extremely difficult to explain if we are to accept the hypothesis of oneness between chromosome and gene. For example, it is difficult to see why a one-celled radiolarian should have 1600 "chromosome-genes," while a crayfish has 200, and a man only 46.

There is one very simple and obvious way out of this dilemma. The hypothesis that a chromosome and a gene are one and the same thing can be modified to propose that *a chromosome represents several genes, and that these genes are located in a definite linear order along it.*

The first portion of this hypothesis, that a chromosome represents several genes, nicely overcomes the objections just raised to the one chromosome-one gene hypothesis. The second portion, dealing with the placing of genes on the chromosomes, is quite another matter. Such an hypothesis necessarily leads to certain predictions:

*Hypothesis: If* . . .   there are several genes located on a chromosome, . . .

*Prediction:* *then* . . . certain characteristics should tend to be inherited together.

The reason for this prediction becomes apparent if the chromosome is visualized as a string of beads, with each bead representing one gene. Since these genes are joined (or **linked**) together, this hypothetical model predicts that *wherever one gene on a chromosome goes, so must all the other genes on that chromosome.*

In seeking support for this hypothesis, it is reasonable to ask whether any cases have been definitely established in which one genetic characteristic always appears with another. It is easy to feel intuitively that there are such cases. In man, for example, we generally associate the occurrence of freckles with sandy or reddish hair. It might be proposed, therefore, that the genes influencing freckles and those influencing red hair are linked, i.e., that they are on the same chromosome.* However, man has many chromosomes and he cannot be bred experimentally. Thus such a linkage is difficult to establish.

It is necessary, therefore, to turn to an organism which has fewer chromosomes and which adapts more easily to controlled breeding. The tomato plant, with 12 chromosome pairs, is such an organism. In tomatoes, tall growth habit is the result of a dominant gene $D$; dwarf growth habit is the result of a recessive allele $d$. Smooth epidermis is due to a dominant gene $P$; pubescent (hairy) epidermis is due to a recessive allele $p$. As would be predicted, crosses between homozygous tall smooth plants ($DDPP$) and dwarf pubescent ones ($ddpp$) yield an $F_1$ of all tall smooth plants (genotype $DdPp$). Thus far, then, Mendel's first and second laws regarding segregation and random assortment are supported.

Assume now that a cross is made between a tall smooth $F_1$ tomato plant and a dwarf pubescent tomato plant. The $F_1$, a tall smooth plant with genotype $DdPp$, should produce four types of gametes, $DP$, $Dp$, $dP$, and $dp$. The dwarf pubescent plant could produce only one type of gamete, $dp$. The fertilization possibilities are thus:

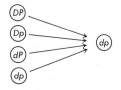

which should yield a ratio of one tall smooth, to one tall pubescent, to one dwarf smooth, to one dwarf pubescent.

Such a cross has been made, yielding 112 plants. Of these, 54 were tall smooth plants and 58 were dwarf pubescent plants, a ratio of approximately 1:1.

Clearly, Mendel's second law is contradicted by these results; random assortment of the factors for height and skin texture cannot have occurred. Instead, wherever the factor for tallness went, the smooth-skin factor must have followed. Likewise, wherever the factor for dwarfness went, the pubescent factor went also. Such a result, and the 1:1 ratio of tall smooth to dwarf pubescent plants, would be predicted by an hypothesis that the genes for tallness and smooth skin were located on the same chromosome, i.e., that they were linked. According to this hypothesis, the genes for dwarfness and pubescent skin must also be linked.

The experimental results just cited are matched by similar results obtained with certain inherited traits in other plants and animals. Such results strongly support the hypothesis of gene linkage and force us to impose a strong qualification on Mendel's second law: *Genes assort at random if and only if they are located*

---

\* It is also possible, of course, that freckles and red hair may have the same underlying genetic cause, i.e., be an example of **pleiomorphism.**

*on separate chromosomes.* Thus in many organisms, particularly those with few chromosomes, gene linkage is going to be the rule rather than the exception.

Of course, as with freckles and red hair, it may be that the genes for tallness and smooth skin are not only on the same chromosome but are actually the same gene. The same might be true for dwarfness and pubescent skin. As will be seen in the next section, however, these hypotheses yield predictions which are sharply contradicted.

If the same cross between a tall smooth $F_1$ tomato plant and a dwarf pubescent plant is carried out many times, some tall pubescent and dwarf smooth plants *do* appear. In a total of 402 progeny, a typical phenotype breakdown is as follows: 198 tall smooth, 8 tall pubescent, 6 dwarf smooth, 190 dwarf pubescent. The appearance of these recombinants contradicts the hypotheses mentioned at the end of the last section proposing that "tall smooth" and "dwarf pubescent" may each be due to one gene rather than two. Thus there seems no way to explain the appearance of these few tall pubescent and dwarf smooth recombinant plants other than to assume that occasionally, *linkage can be broken.* By itself, however, this assumption is not enough. We must go further and hypothesize not only that linkage can be broken (i.e., that chromosomes break), but that *the broken pieces must actually be exchanged between homologous chromosome pairs.* This hypothesis, posed to explain the occasional occurrence of phenotypes that an unmodified linkage hypothesis would predict to be impossible, leads us to examine the behavior of the homologous chromosome pairs themselves. Do they ever assume positions that might be conducive to an exchange of portions of their length?

The reader may recall from Chapter 15 that the answer to this question is affirmative. Prior to the first meiotic division, during tetrad formation, homologous chromosomes often form chiasmata. What might have happened with the tomato plants can be visualized as follows. Most of the time:

Therefore, only $DP$ and $dp$ gametes are produced. Occasionally, however,

   yielding, after crossing over,

Therefore, a few *Dp* and *dP* gametes are produced, as well as the *DP* and *dp* gametes.

The chiasmata formed by homologous chromosomes within living cells can be observed under the microscope. Once again, a hypothetical model constructed to explain observed genetic ratios is found to have physical reality in actual chromosome behavior.

Thus far, our tentative model for comparing the chromosome-gene relationship with a string of beads has been just that—a model. It has, nevertheless, been a useful construct. No experimental results have yet been cited to contradict it, and it readily accounts for the phenomenon of gene linkage. Perhaps intuitively, however, we have made one very basic assumption. Stemming from the concept of a linear arrangement of genes along the chromosome comes a secondary concept of *gene order*. We assume that genes are arranged along the chromosome in some sort of pattern, and that this pattern must be consistent from one homologous chromosome to another. In other words, if, in a tomato plant, gene A is located at the end of chromosome pair IX, the same gene A will not be located at the middle of chromosome pair IX in another cell of the same plant or even in another plant of the same species. This assumption of gene order stems initially, perhaps, from an inductive generalization based on many observations of living systems. All such systems show a high degree of organization and order.

To summarize, the geneticist assumes each gene to have a specific position, or **locus** (pl. **loci**) on a particular chromosome. A very useful bit of information might be gained, therefore, if the specific locus for a specific gene could be pinpointed. The process of identifying gene loci is called **mapping.**

The mapping of gene loci is not as difficult as it might seem. Indeed, the assumption of consistent gene order along the chromosome, coupled with the fact that crossing over occurs, makes it almost certain that gene loci can be determined in relation to each other. For, if genes are located in a consistent linear order along a chromosome, then the distance between any two genes and the amount of crossing over that occurs between them should be in direct proportion.

As an analogy, imagine two ropes, each of which has two knots tied in it a certain distance apart. If the ropes are tossed together into the corner of the room, they will probably fall across each other at one or more points. It is evident that they will cross each other between the knots more often if the knots are far apart than if they are close together. If the knots are tied at the ends of the ropes, many crossovers will occur between them. If the knots are side by side, crossovers between them will be rare.

Homologous chromosomes, of course, also cross over each other. And, as has already been seen, such crossovers occasionally lead to an exchange of chromosome segments between the pairs. When this occurs, the linkage between certain genes is broken and new gamete possibilities arise. The more such gametes occur, the greater will be the proportion of the offspring showing the crossover phenotype. This percentage therefore gives a direct measure of the amount of chromosomal crossing over. This, in turn, gives a direct measure of the distance between the genes involved.

Suppose, for example, that genes A, B, C, and D are linked. By carrying out many breeding experiments and recording offspring phenotypes, the following crossover frequencies are determined:

| CROSSOVER BETWEEN GENES | A and B | B and C | C and D | A and C | B and D |
|---|---|---|---|---|---|
| CROSSOVER FREQUENCY, % | 8 | 8.5 | 18.5 | 16.5 | 10 |

This information allows us to map the locus of each gene in relation to the others. Drawing a line to represent the chromosome, we can assign arbitrary positions to genes A and B, subject only to the stipulation that the distance between them be eight "map units," where one map unit equals a crossover frequency of 1%:

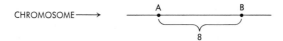

Genes B and C have an 8.5% crossover frequency. Two possibilities clearly exist:

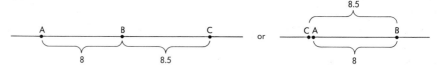

The first locus possibility predicts a 16.5% crossover frequency between A and C; the second, only 0.5%. Since the breeding experiments have already established the frequency as 16.5%, it follows that the first locus chosen for C must be the correct one.

The locus for gene D must be 18.5 map units from gene C, since the crossover frequency between them is 18.5%. Two loci satisfy this requirement, of course, but only one, which places gene D near gene A, is consistent with the 10% crossover frequency given for genes B and D. Thus the final chromosome map for these genes is:

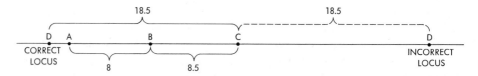

Note that we can further test the validity of our choice of locus for gene D by carrying out still more breeding experiments and recording the crossover

**TABLE 17–1**  KNOWN GENE LOCI OF SOME PLANTS AND ANIMALS
(AFTER K. F. DYER)

| ORGANISM | SPECIFIC NAME | APPROXIMATE NUMBER OF LOCI KNOWN |
|---|---|---|
| FRUIT FLY | Drosophila melanogaster | 850 |
| CORN | Zea mays | 700 |
| TOMATO | Lycopersicon esculentum | 625 |
| MAN | Homo sapiens | {575 CONFIRMED {925 TENTATIVE |
| HOUSE MOUSE | Mus musculus | 380 |
| BARLEY | Hordeum distichum | 375 |
| MOLD | Neurospora crassa | 300 |
| SILKWORM | Bombyx mori | 260 |
| A PARASITIC WASP | Mormoniella vitripennis | 200 |
| A PARASITIC WASP | Habrobracon juglandis | 200 |
| A FUNGUS | Aspergillus nidulans | 170 |
| A FUNGUS | Ascobolus immersus | 110 |
| FLOUR BEETLE | Tribolium castaneum | 90 |
| YEAST | Saccharomyces cerevisiae | 85 |
| DIPLOID WHEATS | Triticum spp. | 60 |
| RABBIT | Oryctolagus cunicula | 55 |
| PEPPER | Capsicum annum | 50 |
| RAT | Rattus norvegicus | 50 |
| FLOUR BEETLE | Tribolium confusum | 45 |
| HONEYBEE | Apis mellifera | 25 |
| DOMESTIC CAT | Felis catus | 25 |
| DEER MOUSE | Peromyscus maniculatus | 20 |
| PIG | Sus scrofa | 18 |
| COCKROACH | Blattus germanica | 16 |
| GOLDEN HAMSTER | Cricetus auratus | 10 |

percentage between genes A and D. The locus chosen predicts a 2% crossover frequency; the other locus predicts a 35% crossover frequency. The resulting breeding data, yielding a 2% crossover frequency, clearly support our choice of locus for gene D.

Using such reasoning methods, geneticists have constructed chromosome maps for several organisms, especially for those lower forms in which radiation experiments can be successfully carried out or for those organisms with a low chromosome number. Yet, despite his rather large number of chromosomes (46), and contrary to what is commonly supposed, a great deal is now known concerning gene loci in man. Indeed, if we include those genes known to be on the $X$ chromosome (though their precise location on this chromosome is not known), we know more about gene loci in man than in most other organisms. There are a large number of organisms whose genetics are relatively well known (e.g., cat, dog, cattle, horse) but whose known gene loci are very few. Table 17–1 gives a summary of the known gene loci in some plants and animals.

Note that all of the reasoning involved in mapping is indirect. The geneticist hypothesizes that a gene is on a chromosome at a particular locus in relation to other genes because, by doing so, he can explain observed breeding phenomena and make accurate predictions concerning future breedings. In mapping the gene relationships on a chromosome the geneticist is simply building a valuable hypothetical model.

**17-5**
**CHROMOSOMAL**
**ABERRATIONS**

Occasionally a broken piece of chromosome fails to become attached to another chromosome, and is simply lost. Such occurrences, called **deletions,** offer a unique chance to discover gene loci. For example, if the absence of a particular chromosome segment is always accompanied by a certain phenotype deficiency, it is reasonable to suppose that the gene normally responsible for preventing this deficiency is located on the missing piece.

A deletion may also produce evidence for the linearity of genes on the chromosomes. Assuming linearity of genes on homologous chromosomes, it follows that genes influencing the same trait will pair off opposite each other during synapsis prior to the first meiotic division.

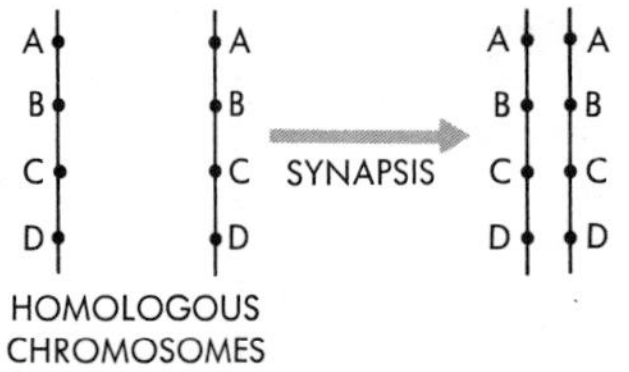

Suppose that gene B is deleted from one of the homologs. In order for similar genes to pair, an unusual synapsis figure must occur. For example:

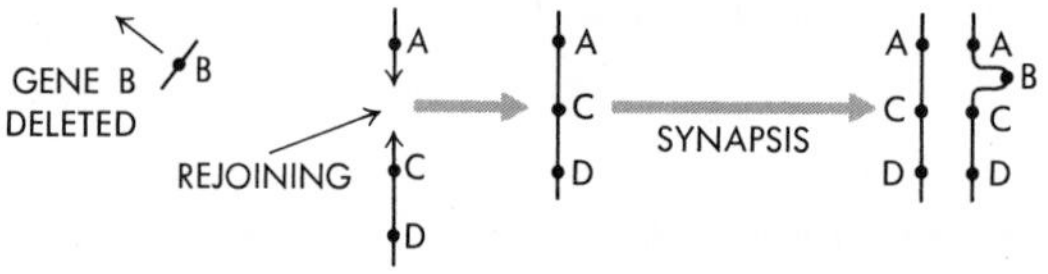

Such synaptic figures have been observed in chromosomes after a segment of one chromosome has been deleted, a fact which strongly supports the hypothesis that genes are arranged in a linear fashion on the chromosomes.

Occasionally, an entire mid-segment of a chromosome may break and rejoin in a completely reversed position:

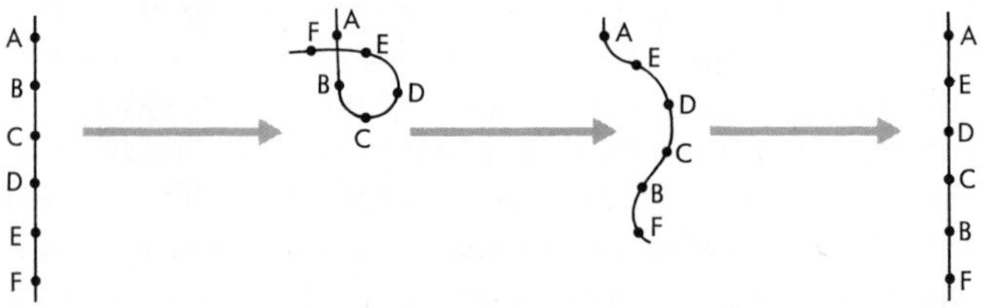

Such an occurrence is known as an **inversion.** Since it is extremely unlikely that the homolog of an inverted chromosome would undergo a similar inversion, we can predict that the chromosomes will have to be greatly contorted before proper synapsis can take place. Using line model chromosomes, one of which has the inversion shown above, at least two theoretically possible synaptic figures may be drawn as follows:

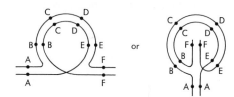

Such post-inversion synaptic figures have actually been observed in corn. Again, the hypothesis of gene linearity on the chromosome is dramatically supported.

17-6
GENETICS: THE
FRUIT FLY ERA

In the period between 1910 and 1940, geneticists turned to the fruit fly, *Drosophila melanogaster,* for an intensive study of the chromosomal basis of inheritance. This small insect, often seen around decaying fruit, has a short life cycle (approximately two weeks) and is easily raised in the laboratory. *Drosophila* also has a low chromosome number (four pairs), with each pair easily distinguishable from the others. Finally, and most important, *Drosophila* shows hundreds of inherited variant characteristics.

One such variant characteristic is vestigial wings. Flies with this characteristic have only stumps where their wings should be (Fig. 2–3). The condition is caused by the presence of a single pair of recessive genes, for crosses between vestigials yield only vestigials, while crosses of purebred winged flies with vestigials yield all winged. The $F_1$ intercross yields the familiar 3:1 ratio of dominant to recessive phenotypes.

A major center for fruit fly research was the Columbia University Laboratory of Thomas Hunt Morgan (1866–1945) and his associates. It was largely their work which, genetically speaking, made *Drosophila melanogaster* the most thoroughly understood multicellular organism in the world. A part of Morgan's work focused on the inheritance of eye color in *Drosophila*. The regular, or wild, insect has red eyes. One day a white-eyed male fly appeared in Morgan's laboratory. It was crossed with a red-eyed female and the resulting progeny were all red-eyed. The $F_1$ intercross yielded a ratio of three red-eyed flies to one white-eyed fly. It was noticed, however, that *all the white-eyed flies were male.*

Since the location of the genes on the chromosomes had already been hypothesized, it was reasonable to look for differences in the chromosomes of male and female fruit flies to explain the connection of the white-eyed condition to maleness. Morgan was already familiar with such a difference. In the male fruit fly, one pair of chromosomes is markedly different from the other three pairs. This pair consists of one normal-appearing chromosome, the $X$ chromosome, and one short, bent chromosome, the $Y$ chromosome. In the female, two matching $X$ chromosomes are found.*

Morgan saw immediately that the occurrence of white-eyed males in the $F_2$ generation could be explained by postulating the white-eye gene to be recessive and located on the $X$ chromosome. The $Y$ chromosome, being shorter, has no locus for the gene. Thus the mere occurrence of the white-eye gene would be enough to cause white eyes in the male, since no dominant gene for red eyes would be present to override it:

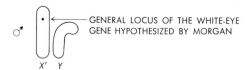

[The prime (′) symbol on the $X$ indicates the presence of the recessive white-eye gene.]

In the female, with two $X$ chromosomes, white eyes would not occur. Even should the white-eye gene be present on one chromosome, it would be masked by the dominant red-eye allele on the other, and this female would still be red-eyed:

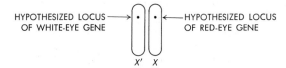

Morgan thus pictured the first cross of the white-eyed male with the red-eyed female as follows:

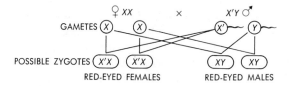

Crossing the $F_1$ flies resulted in a ratio of three red-eyed flies to one white-eyed fly, with white-eye appearing only in the male flies.

---

* At the time of Morgan's work on the white-eye condition, the $Y$ chromosome had not been detected in *Drosophila*. Morgan therefore assumed the $X$ chromosome had no homolog in the male. In terms of the hypothesis he proposed, the presence or absence of a $Y$ chromosome makes little difference, and so we shall deal with his hypothesis as if Morgan had been familiar with the $Y$ chromosome in this insect.

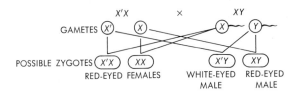

Thus Morgan's hypothesis, placing the locus of the recessive white-eye gene on the $X$ chromosome, nicely accounts for his experimental results. But it also predicts the possibility of obtaining white-eyed females.

**Hypothesis:** *If . . .*  the locus of the recessive white-eye gene is on the $X$ chromosome, . . .

**Prediction:** *then . . .* crosses between white-eyed males $(X'Y)$ and red-eyed females whose fathers were white-eyed $(X'X)$ should produce a 1:1 ratio of red-eyed to white-eyed flies. Of the white-eyed flies, half should be females.

In diagrammatic form:

|       | $X'$ | $X$ |
|-------|------|-----|
| $X'$  | $X'X'$ WHITE-EYED FEMALE | $X'X$ RED-EYED FEMALE |
| $Y$   | $X'Y$ WHITE-EYED MALE | $XY$ RED-EYED MALE |

The prediction is verified; the hypothesis is supported.

In man, both red-green color blindness and hemophilia (a condition of the blood which prevents it from clotting properly) are inherited conditions. Studies of family histories show that the conditions are recessive, are rare in females, and are transmitted to a man's grandchildren through his daughters. Morgan's hypothesis, devised solely to explain the inheritance of the white-eyed condition in *Drosophila*, also accounts for the inheritance of red-green color blindness and hemophilia in man. His work is but one of many examples of basic research that result in unforeseen benefits to man.

**17–7**

**EPISTASIS**

Certain breeds of poultry have feathers on their shanks, while other breeds do not. Crosses between homozygous feathered and unfeathered birds yield all feathered offspring. An hypothesis that one pair of genes influences feathering is untenable, however, for crosses between $F_1$ feathered birds do not yield the predicted 3:1 ratio of feathered to unfeathered birds. Instead, a 15:1 ratio is obtained. The expression of the obtained ratio in sixteenths rather than in fourths makes it evident that two pairs of genes, rather than one, must be involved. We have already dealt with cases of complete dominance involving two pairs of

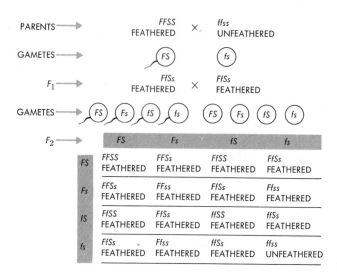

FIG. 17–1

unlinked genes, and in those cases the ratio was 9:3:3:1. An hypothesis to account for the deviant 15:1 ratio must therefore be proposed.

One such hypothesis follows directly from the assumption that Mendel's law of independent assortment holds just as well in this case as in one yielding a 9:3:3:1 ratio, but that a different sort of gene action is in effect. The crosses between the feathered and unfeathered birds can be diagrammed as shown in Fig. 17–1. It will be seen that the 15:1 ratio can be accounted for by assuming that feathering will occur even if just one dominant gene from either pair is present. In these chickens unfeathered shanks will result only from the complete absence of dominant genes. This hypothesis is supported by crosses between unfeathered birds and $F_1$ dihybrids. A 3:1 ratio of feathered to unfeathered birds would be predicted, and this is the ratio obtained.

In dogs, a cross between certain homozygous brown animals with homozygous white animals yields all white puppies. Many crosses of $F_1$ white animals yield an offspring ratio of 12 whites to 3 blacks to 1 brown.

Again a modification of the 9:3:3:1 ratio has occurred and an explanatory hypothesis is needed. The most satisfactory hypothesis is one which makes the following three assumptions.

1) Two pairs of randomly assorted genes are involved; i.e., the genes are not linked and Mendel's second law of random assortment is in effect.

2) One of these gene pairs influences coat color to the extent that it causes the coat to be black or brown, with the former being dominant.

3) The second gene pair is a gene which, when the dominant form is present in either the homozygous or heterozygous state, *inhibits* the production of any pigment at all, i.e., the animal is white.

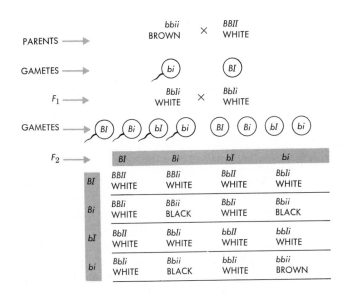

FIG. 17–2

The cross depicting this hypothesis is diagrammed in Fig. 17–2. This hypothesis, proposing a pigment-inhibiting gene, can be tested by crossing brown dogs with $F_1$ whites. The predicted 1:2:1 ratio of black to white to brown is obtained.

Feathered shanks in poultry and coat color in dogs are but two of many examples of modifications of two-pair ratios. Such examples illustrate two important points. First, what seem to be contradictions of the ratios predicted by mendelian genetics are often not contradictions at all. Indeed, close analysis reveals that these results provide still further evidence in support of mendelian genetic principles. Second, and more important, *gene pairs often work together to produce their phenotypic effects, the action of one gene pair often profoundly influencing the action of others*; e.g., the action of one gene may mask the action of another, an occurrence known as **epistasis**.

Thus far, only genes which exist in pairs have been considered. Many genes, however, have more than one allele. Besides a dominant and a recessive gene, there may be one or more intermediate genes at the same locus forming a series. Genes of this sort are called **multiple alleles**. In rabbits, for example, there is a gene $C$ which causes a colored coat; the genotype $cc$ results in albino. But two other genes at the same locus are $c^h$ and $c^{ch}$. Genotype $c^hc^h$ causes the "Himalayan" pattern, in which the body is white but the extremities, i.e., the tips of nose, ears, tail, and legs, are colored. Genotype $c^{ch}c^{ch}$ results in a "Chinchilla" pattern, a light gray color over the entire body. In this case, the genes can be arranged in a series, $C$, $c^{ch}$, $c^h$, $c$, with each gene dominant to the genes which follow it and recessive to those which precede it. In other examples of multiple alleles, the genes may be incompletely dominant, so that the heterozygote shows a phenotype intermediate between those of its parents.

One of the most prominent examples of multiple alleles in man is that of the different blood types, A, O, B, and AB, first discovered by Landsteiner in 1900. There are three alleles in the blood group series: $A$, $A^B$, and $a$. Genes $A$ and $A^B$ cause the synthesis of substances called **agglutinogens** (agglutinogens A and B, respectively). Agglutinogens, if exposed to blood of an incompatible type, cause **agglutination** or clumping of the red blood cells, and their presence makes necessary a careful matching of blood types before transfusions are attempted.

The blood types A, O, B, and AB result from different combinations of the allele genes. Neither $A$ nor $A^B$ is dominant to the other, and thus the presence of both (i.e., genotype $AA^B$) results in an individual with blood type AB. Absence of both, i.e., genotype $aa$, results in an individual with type O blood. As might be expected, the combination of a gene causing the synthesis of agglutinogens with a gene not causing their synthesis results in the synthesis of that particular agglutinogen (i.e., agglutinogen A or B). Thus individuals of genotypes $Aa$ and $A^Ba$ would have type A and B blood respectively, as, of course, would individuals of genotypes $AA$ and $A^BA^B$.

Because of their genetic basis, blood types may be helpful in settling cases of disputed parentage. However, blood tests can never prove that a certain man is the father of a child but only whether he could or, more important perhaps, could *not* be its father.

Two other blood types inherited independently are the M-N factors and the series of Rh alleles, the latter obtaining their name from the fact that they were first identified in the blood of rhesus monkeys. The **Rh factor** is another agglutinogen, and its presence or absence in the blood indicates whether the individual is Rh-positive or Rh-negative. The Rh factor may cause difficulties if an Rh-negative woman marries an Rh-positive man. Since the presence of the Rh factor (i.e., Rh-positive) is dominant, and a developing fetus develops its own blood system, the woman will carry an Rh-positive child. If, because of a defect, blood from the fetus contacts the mother's blood, her white blood cells will be stimulated to produce **antibodies** to the Rh factor. Usually more than nine months are needed for this antibody level to build up to a level sufficiently high to cause trouble. In later pregnancies, however, some of these antibodies may pass into the fetus' bloodstream and cause agglutination. The resulting condition, *erythroblastosis fetalis*, may be severe enough to cause death before birth; but more often the baby dies after birth. Familiarity with the parental blood types and knowledge of their genetic basis now generally enables afflicted infants to be saved by being given massive blood transfusions at birth.

The fact that the Rh factor was discovered in a monkey before it was known in man points up the fact that the blood groups have been helpful in establishing evolutionary relationships as well. Although many mammals and birds have substances similar to agglutinogens A and B in their blood, only in apes such as the orangutan, gorilla, and chimpanzee are such blood types as O, A, B, and AB known. The M and N substances of the chimpanzee are most like those of man, a fact that can be added to much other evidence suggesting that chimpanzees are the most human of the anthropoid apes.

Because blood types are inherited and yet play little or no role in conscious mate selection, they remain important tools in the study of gene constancy within populations, as well as in providing tests for anthropological hypotheses. It is known that the proportion of blood types in a population remains fairly constant from one generation to the next as long as there is no intermarriage with other groups; the Germans who migrated to Hungary around 1700, for example, have kept not only the language and customs, but also a blood-type frequency characteristic of the Germans in Germany.

The origin of the natives of the Aleutian Islands was long a subject of debate. Some anthropologists hypothesized that the Aleuts were derived from Eskimo-Indian crosses. Others hypothesized an Asiatic origin. Both Eskimos and Indians have a relatively low frequency of B and AB blood groups, whereas B is common in Asia. Development of a new technique allowing for determination of the blood types of mummies and skeletons paved the way for study of the blood types of 30 Aleutian mummies. They showed a high proportion of B and AB blood groups, thus supporting the hypothesis that the Aleuts were of Asiatic origin.

**17-9**
**IN SEARCH OF**
**THE GENE**

Thus far Mendel's "factors," the genes, have been dealt with in terms of an hypothesized model which pictures the chromosome-gene relationship as analogous to the one existing between a necklace and its individual beads. This model depicts the chromosome as being little more than a physical entity formed by a series of connected genes. The model is a completely satisfactory one in terms of its ability to account for random assortment, linkage, etc. And, if we make the chromosome-gene necklace the snap-in kind, in which individual beads or groups of beads can be exchanged one for another, the phenomena of crossing over, chromosomal inversions, deletions, etc., are satisfactorily pictured (though not, of course, either accounted for or explained).

Modern genetics has zeroed in on the gene itself. What is the gene composed of? What is its structure? How does it work? In answering these questions, the string-of-beads model is of little or no use. Indeed, close examination of chromosome structure casts serious doubt on whether the model is at all correct! Genes, for example, might be expected to have a rather definite chemical structure. Thus if the chromosome is simply a string of genes, it, too, should reflect gene structure. Yet chemical and physical analysis of chromosome structure does not bear out predictions based on the string-of-beads model. Instead, chromosomes are found to be composed of varying amounts of DNA and RNA, a protein of low molecular weight (histone), a more complex protein, and some lipid substances. The question then arises, *which one or more of the substances found in chromosomes represents the primary genetic material?*

In 1927, an experiment bearing indirectly on this question was performed by F. Griffith. Griffith worked with two strains of pneumonia bacteria. Strain S forms smooth colonies on a bacterial agar plate and each cell is encapsulated (i.e., surrounded by a carbohydrate wall). Strain R forms rough colonies, and R cells are unencapsulated (i.e., are not surrounded by a carbohydrate wall).

More important to Griffith's experiment, however, was the fact that strain S, when injected into mice, causes death—and this death-causing ability is inherited. The injection of strain R cells into mice, on the other hand, does not cause death. The lack of death-causing ability is also an inherited feature of these strain R bacteria.

Griffith found that when strain S bacteria were heated to 60°C they were killed. Injection of such dead strain S bacteria was no longer fatal to mice. However, if the dead strain S bacteria were injected along with some living strain R bacteria, some of the mice receiving such injections died. Further, the blood of these mice was always infected with living harmful bacteria *with capsules.*

The interpretation of these experimental results seems clear: something must have passed from the dead strain S bacteria into the living strain R to transform them from harmless, unencapsulated cells to a harmful, encapsulated kind. Further, the fact that these transformed bacterial cells passed on their new characteristics to their descendants indicated it was the genetic material of the dead strain S cells with which they were mixed before injection that must have entered the strain R cells and transformed them.

The next step was a logical one—isolate the genetic substance responsible for Griffith's bacterial transformation and chemically identify it. This task proved not to be an easy one. From the fact that the main bulk of chromosomal material is protein, it was generally thought that the genes, too, must be proteins. Yet, none of these isolated proteins caused bacterial transformation. Finally, in 1945, Avery, MacLeod, and McCarty, who were working with pneumococcus bacteria, isolated a "biologically active fraction" from encapsulated strain S bacteria. Under appropriate culture conditions, it was shown that this active fraction could genetically transform the R strain to its S strain, a strain genetically different from the former. By various chemical and physical techniques, this active fraction was found to be composed primarily of DNA. Thus Avery and his coworkers concluded their historic paper with the words:

*The evidence presented here supports the belief that a nucleic acid of the de[s]oxyribose type is the fundamental unit of the transforming principle of Pneumococcus Type III.*

It seemed, then, that DNA was the primary genetic material. By some still undetermined process, one strain of bacteria had absorbed the DNA of another strain and had thereby acquired characteristics of the donor strain. Further, and most important, this transformation of the recipient strain of cells was passed on to their descendants.

There were, however, some objections to the acceptance of DNA as the primary genetic material on the basis of these experiments. These objections were based on the fact that the transforming DNA fraction was only about 95% pure. It was reasoned that the 5% impurities (mostly protein) could be the genetically active fraction, rather than the DNA. This argument was later somewhat weakened when it was shown that highly purified DNA, containing negligible amounts of other compounds and less than 0.02% protein, was still capable of causing transformation.

The crucial experiment, however, utilized the enzyme deoxyribonuclease. This enzyme breaks down DNA, destroying its potency, but leaves other compounds, such as RNA and proteins, unaffected.

*Hypothesis I: If . . .*   DNA is the primary genetic material causing bacterial transformation, . . .

*Prediction:*      *then . . .* addition of the enzyme deoxyribonuclease to the transforming mixture before it is exposed to the recipient bacteria should destroy its ability to cause transformation.

On the other hand . . .

*Hypothesis II: If . . .*   the genetic activity of the transforming mixture is *not* due to the DNA, but rather to the protein or other impurities it contains, . . .

*Prediction:*      *then . . .* exposure of the enzyme deoxyribonuclease to the transforming mixture should have no effect on its ability to cause transformation.

The results of this experiment clearly supported hypothesis I. No bacterial transformation was caused by mixtures exposed to deoxyribonuclease.

17-10
**VIRAL AND OTHER
EVIDENCE**

The T2 bacteriophage viruses discussed in Chapter 3 provide still further insight into the possibility that DNA is the primary genetic material. These viruses become attached to the surfaces of bacteria (Fig. 3–3). After about 20 minutes, the bacteria burst, each cell releasing about 100 complete new T2 viruses. It is clear that some substance (or substances) must pass from the infecting virus into the bacterial cell and cause the formation of new viruses. This substance, therefore, must contain the genes of the virus.

Chemical analysis of the T2 virus reveals it to be composed only of DNA and protein:

DNA contains phosphorus; protein does not. Conversely, the viral protein contains sulfur; DNA does not. To the scientists Hershey and Chase, this fact suggested a crucial experiment. By tagging the DNA with radioactive phosphorus or the viral protein with radioactive sulfur, they could tell which part of the virus entered the bacterial cell and participated in the formation of new viruses. The results showed that almost all of the DNA entered the bacterial cell on infection. In contrast, only 3% of the protein did so.

The conclusion to these experiments on bacterial transformation and viruses seems inescapable: Genes, at least those of the pneumococci bacteria and T2 viruses, are made of DNA.

Note, however, that we have not yet extrapolated beyond the organisms used in these experiments. The crucial question is: Are *all* genes made of DNA? The answer is no, for there are some viruses that do not contain DNA. In such viruses, RNA has been shown to be the primary genetic material. But these viruses are certainly exceptions, comprising only a tiny fraction of the vast spectrum of life. It is in the rest of this spectrum that our greatest interest most naturally lies, for it is here that man himself is found.

What evidence is there that DNA is the primary genetic material for all other forms of life? First, as a negative form of support, there is some observational evidence that the non-DNA substances present in chromosomes are probably not the genetic material. The hypothesis proposing chromosomal RNA as the genetic material, for example, is contradicted by the observation that sperm cells contain negligible amounts of such RNA. Similarly, the histone proteins associated with DNA in sperm cells are quite different from those found in other tissues; indeed, they may not be histones at all. An hypothesis proposing histone proteins as the genetic material would certainly predict otherwise.

The alternative hypothesis is clear:

*Hypothesis: If* . . .    DNA is the primary genetic material in the majority of living organisms, . . .

*Predictions: then* . . . 1)  the quantity of DNA found in diploid cells should be approximately the same in all of them;

2)  the quantity of DNA in a diploid cell should be approximately twice that found in a haploid germ cell;

3)  the DNA from cells of widely differing species should be less alike in composition than the DNA from closely related species;

4)  the DNA from organisms within the same species should be of similar composition;

5)  among those chemical and physical agents known to alter the chemical structure of DNA without killing the organism should be those agents known to cause mutations;

6)  those wavelengths of ultraviolet light known to cause a high incidence of mutation should closely correspond to those wavelengths absorbed by DNA; and

7)  DNA should be stable; its constituent atoms should not be exchanged as rapidly as those in other cell molecules.

All of these predictions are verified. Thus, while no well-supported experiments have yet been done on higher animals with results corresponding to those obtained by bacterial transformation, it is still possible to feel reasonably confident in extrapolating from the bacterial to the higher forms of life.* It can therefore be concluded that except in the case of certain viruses previously mentioned, DNA is the substance of which the genes of living organisms are composed.

Granting that genes are composed of DNA, it is reasonable to next inquire about the molecular structure of DNA itself. The determination of this structure necessarily entails two steps:

1)  The molecular subunits of which DNA is composed must be identified.

2)  The way in which these parts are fitted together to form the entire DNA molecule must be determined hypothetically.

Step 2 is subject to two limitations. First, the hypothesized model of DNA structure must explain how genes are able to form self copies. Most certainly, if genes are composed of DNA, then DNA itself must be a self-replicating molecule. Second, the hypothesized model of DNA structure must also account for the way in which genes are able to carry out their functions leading to the expression of phenotypes they control.

Step 1 involves a chemical analysis of pure DNA. Such an analysis reveals DNA to be composed of just three different chemical substances.

1)  A five-carbon (pentose) sugar, **deoxyribose.**

2)  **Phosphates.**  Each phosphate group is composed of an atom of phosphorus surrounded by four atoms of oxygen and two of hydrogen (latter not shown).

3)  Usually four nitrogenous (nitrogen-containing) bases—**adenine, guanine, cytosine,** and **thymine.**

Adenine and guanine are **purines.**  Purine molecules are double-ring structures.

Cytosine and thymine are **pyrimidines.**  Pyrimidine molecules consist of a single ring of atoms.

Note that the pyrimidine bases are smaller than the purines. The significance of this size difference will be seen shortly.

---

* Transformation of human cells in culture has been reported, but to date the experiments have not been repeated.

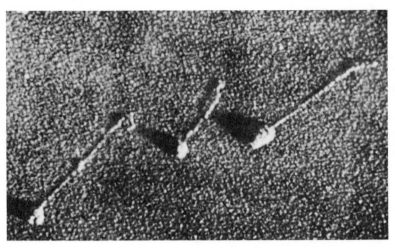

FIG. 17–3   Under the electron microscope, DNA appears long and threadlike.  At left, DNA is seen extruding from influenza viruses; at right is shown the circular DNA strand of the lambda viruses which infect *E. coli*.  Each such DNA strand is calculated to contain approximately 50,000 nucleotide pairs.  (Lambda virus photo courtesy Lorne A. McHattie and Vernon C. Bode, Harvard University Medical School.)

With these substances identified, many biologists turned their attention to the completion of Step 2—the devising of a satisfactory hypothetical model for the structure of DNA.  Among these men were J. D. Watson and F. H. C. Crick.  Using data obtained from many different experiments, Watson and Crick proposed a model of DNA structure which has proved highly successful both in its ability to account for gene replication and function and in the accuracy of the predictions that can be derived from it.

First, the physical appearance of purified DNA suggests that the molecule is long and stringlike.  When extracted and precipitated in a cold solution of ethanol sodium chloride, DNA rather resembles strands of a spider web or spun glass.  Electron-microscope photographs confirm the threadlike nature of DNA (Fig. 17–3).  Such photographs show each DNA molecule to be quite long, but only about 20 Å wide.  This latter figure is an important one, for it reveals that the DNA molecule can only be about 10 or 12 atoms across.

A second important consideration in determining DNA structure is that one must know which parts are capable of being chemically united; one does not attempt to do a jigsaw puzzle by forcing together pieces that obviously do not fit.  It can be shown that the molecular subunits of DNA are joined together into larger subunits called **nucleotides.**  Each DNA nucleotide consists of one of the nitrogenous bases, one molecule of deoxyribose, and a phosphate group.  Since there are four nitrogenous bases that are generally found in DNA, there are four different nucleotides (Fig. 17–4).

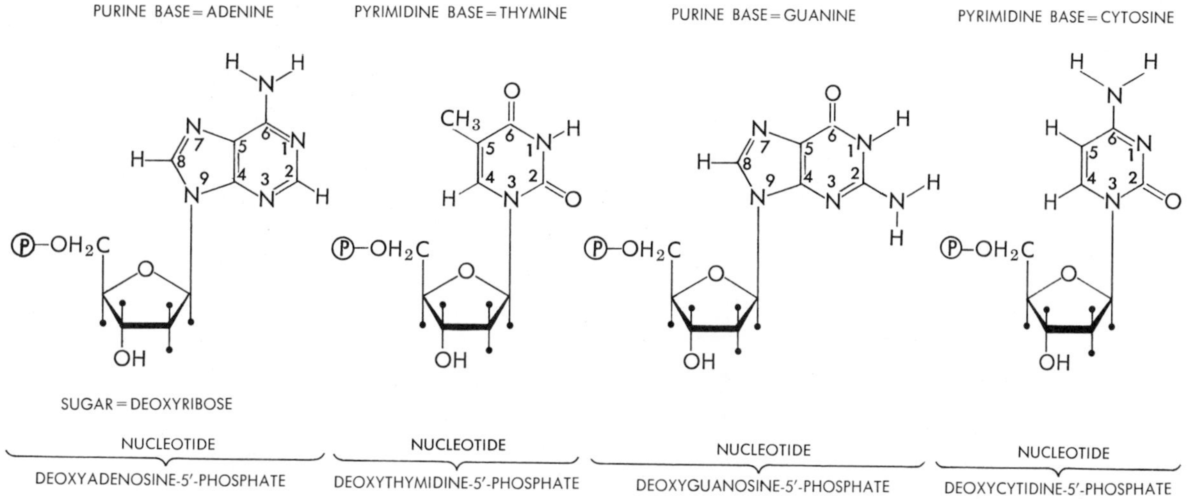

PURINE BASE = ADENINE    PYRIMIDINE BASE = THYMINE    PURINE BASE = GUANINE    PYRIMIDINE BASE = CYTOSINE

SUGAR = DEOXYRIBOSE

NUCLEOTIDE
DEOXYADENOSINE-5'-PHOSPHATE

NUCLEOTIDE
DEOXYTHYMIDINE-5'-PHOSPHATE

NUCLEOTIDE
DEOXYGUANOSINE-5'-PHOSPHATE

NUCLEOTIDE
DEOXYCYTIDINE-5'-PHOSPHATE

FIG. 17–4

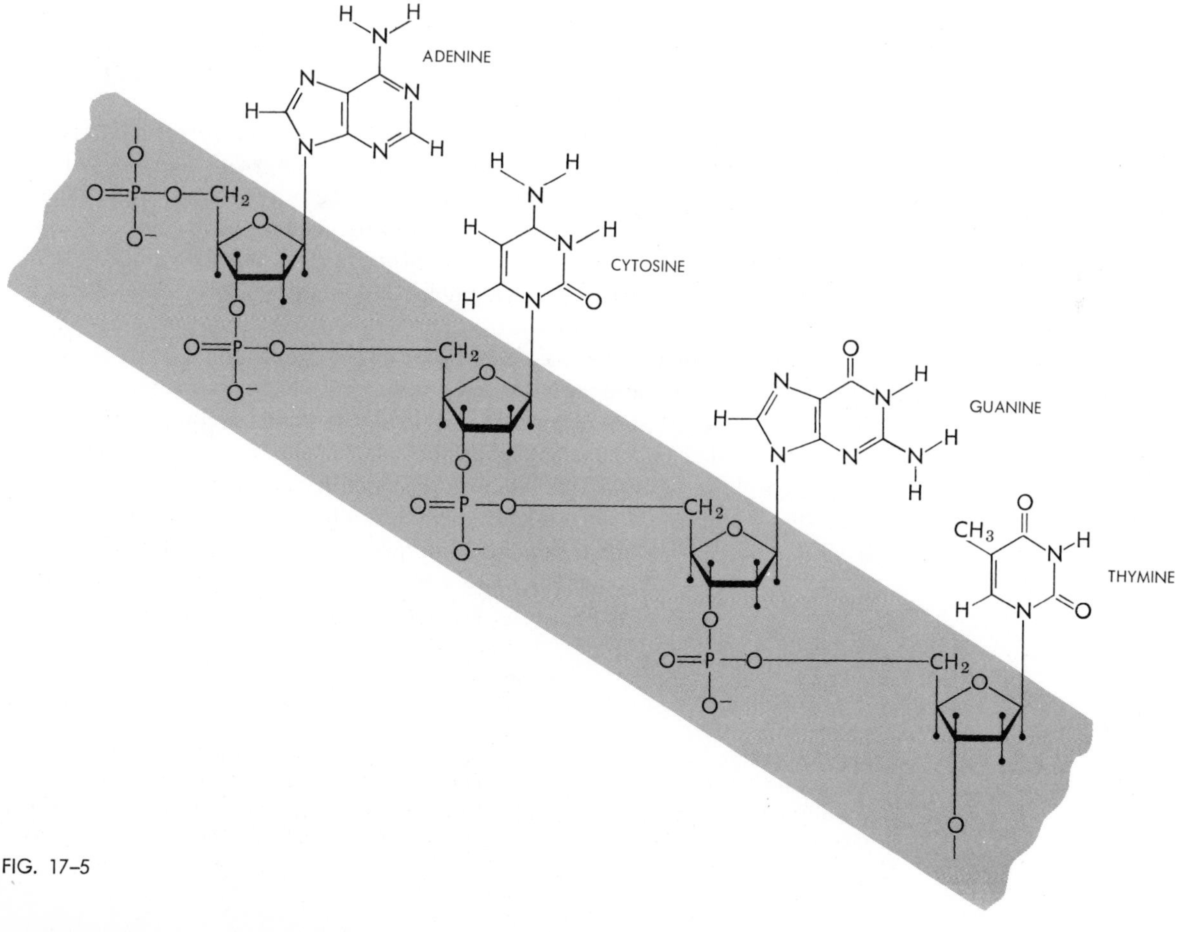

ADENINE

CYTOSINE

GUANINE

THYMINE

FIG. 17–5

It can be shown that these nucleotides will join together to form long, polynucleotide strands (Fig. 17–5). This fact suggests that the same arrangement might be found in the threadlike DNA molecule. But the distance across one polynucleotide strand is only about 10 Å, and DNA, as already mentioned, is generally about 20 Å wide. This suggests that DNA might be composed of paired polynucleotides lying side by side in chemical union.

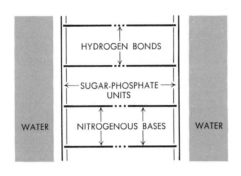

FIG. 17–6

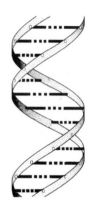

FIG. 17–7

Determination of the way in which these two strands might be oriented is based largely on information supplied by the physical chemist. First, the molecular structure and configuration of the nitrogenous bases shows them to be capable of forming weak hydrogen bonds with each other. Second, the nitrogenous bases are repelled by water (i.e., they are **hydrophobic**), while the sugar-phosphate portion of each nucleotide readily forms bonds to water molecules (i.e., it is **hydrophilic**). These facts favor an arrangement in which the nitrogenous bases face the interior of the DNA molecule (from which the water of the surrounding cellular environment would be essentially excluded) with the sugar-phosphate units on the outside. This arrangement can be tentatively represented as shown in Fig. 17–6.

The next clue to DNA structure was provided by X-ray diffraction.* Data obtained from the use of this technique on crystallized DNA showed the model to have a helical rather than a planar structure, with one complete twist of the helix occurring every 34 Å, or about every 10 base pairs. The previous representation of DNA structure in Fig. 17–6 must therefore be modified to include its helical nature (Fig. 17–7).

---

* X-ray diffraction is a technique involving the passing of X-rays through crystallized DNA and determining how they are deflected by the structure through which they pass. X-ray diffraction is *somewhat* analogous to determining the shape of an object by the shadow it casts, but the process is considerably more complex than this analogy indicates.

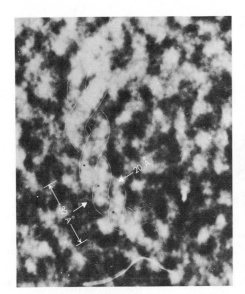
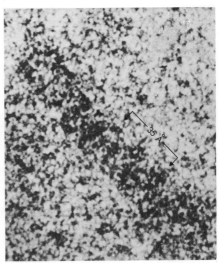

FIG. 17–8   These two photographs dramatically confirm the helical structure of DNA.   At left is
shown a short length of one DNA molecule from chromosomes of the pea.   The double-stranded helix
is plainly discernible.   For additional clarity, the artist has added white hairlines around the edge of
the helix.   At right is shown a portion of a filament of calf thymus DNA.   The double helical substructure
has the predicted diameter of 20 angstroms, with a period of approximately 35 angstroms for one
complete turn.   (Left photo courtesy Jack Griffith, California Institute of Technology; right photo
courtesy F. P. Ottensmeyer, University of Toronto.)

Obviously, a most desirable way of confirming the hypothesized helical
structure of DNA would be to take a picture of it.   This feat has just recently
been accomplished (Fig. 17–8) and the intellectual creation of Watson and
Crick given still more concrete reality.

Another problem still remains, however.   Granted that the helical strands of
DNA polynucleotides are held together by the hydrogen bonds that form between them, it must still be determined which bases pair with which.   Do they,
for example, pair purine to purine, pyrimidine to pyrimidine, or purine to
pyrimidine?

The answer is partly given by knowledge of the physical nature of hydrogen
bonds and the conditions necessary for their formation.   Besides calling for the
presence of a covalently bonded, positively charged hydrogen atom and a
covalently bonded, negatively charged acceptor atom, hydrogen bonds can only
form over certain critical interatomic distances.   Recall that the purine bases are
double-ring structures, larger than the single-ring pyrimidines.   Therefore, while
two purine bases might achieve the proper distance for a hydrogen bond to form
between them, any pyrimidine base pairs would be held too far apart for the

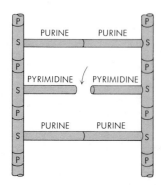

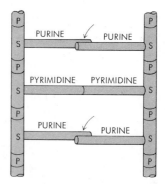

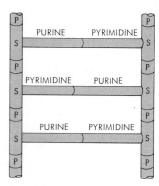

FIG. 17–9                            FIG. 17–10                           FIG. 17–11

formation of hydrogen bonds. This can be represented diagrammatically as shown in Fig. 17–9. Conversely, if the pyrimidine bases were at the proper distance for hydrogen-bond formation, the purine bases would overlap (Fig. 17–10). (For simplicity, the helical shape of DNA is ignored in these diagrams.) It might be thought that the sugar-phosphate strands could bend sufficiently to establish the proper distances for hydrogen bonding both between the pyrimidine bases and between the purine bases. However, physical and chemical considerations reduce this possibility almost to the vanishing point. One might hypothesize that infolding or puckering along the sides of a DNA molecule would allow the proper distances to be established, but electron microscope photographs fail to show any such puckering.

The alternative hypothesis, which eliminates these difficulties, is clear. Purine-to-pyrimidine bonding must occur (Fig. 17–11). However, there are two purines involved, adenine and guanine, and two pyrimidines, cytosine and thymine. A new question therefore arises: Granting a purine-to-pyrimidine base pairing, which of the two purine bases pairs with which pyrimidine? Again, the answer is provided by consideration of the factors leading to the formation of hydrogen bonds between the nitrogenous bases. The only base-pairing combinations that allow the formation of the hydrogen bonds found in DNA are those of adenine-thymine and guanine-cytosine.

It is interesting to note that the limitation of purine-pyrimidine base pairing to adenine-thymine and guanine-cytosine combinations could have been deduced from other data. Careful chemical analyses of DNA had been made earlier to determine just how much of each kind of base is present in the DNA of a particular species. The results of some of these analyses are presented in Table 17–2. Note that, in any one species, the amount of adenine equals or closely approximates that of thymine, while the amount of guanine closely approximates or equals that of cytosine, the deviations in each ratio lying well within the range to be expected from errors in experimental measurements. These results would be predicted by the Watson and Crick model, which specifies an adenine-thymine and guanine-cytosine base pairing within the DNA molecule.

**TABLE 17–2**   ADENINE-TO-THYMINE AND GUANINE-TO-CYTOSINE RATIO IN DNA

| SOURCE OF DNA TEMPLATE | ADENINE | THYMINE | GUANINE | CYTOSINE |
|---|---|---|---|---|
| BOVINE THYMUS | 28.2 | 27.8 | 21.5 | 21.2 |
| BOVINE SPLEEN | 27.9 | 27.3 | 22.7 | 20.8 |
| BOVINE SPERM | 28.7 | 27.2 | 22.2 | 20.7 |
| RAT BONE MARROW | 28.6 | 28.4 | 21.4 | 20.4 |
| HERRING TESTES | 27.9 | 28.2 | 19.5 | 21.5 |
| *Paracentrotus lividus* | 32.8 | 32.1 | 17.7 | 17.3 |
| WHEAT GERM | 27.3 | 27.1 | 22.7 | 22.8 |
| YEAST | 31.3 | 32.9 | 18.7 | 17.1 |
| *Escherichia coli* | 26.0 | 23.9 | 24.9 | 25.2 |
| *Mb. tuberculosis* | 15.1 | 14.6 | 34.9 | 35.4 |
| *Rickettsia prowazeki* | 35.7 | 31.8 | 17.1 | 15.4 |
| *Micrococcus lysodeiticus* | 15.0 | 15.0 | 35.0 | 35.0 |
| *Aerobacter acrogenes* | 22.0 | 22.0 | 28.0 | 28.0 |
| PHAGE T2 | 32.0 | 32.0 | 18.0 | 18.0 |

**17-12**

**TESTING THE MODEL**

At the start of Section 17–11, it was stated that any hypothetical model of DNA structure must account for both gene replication and gene function. Attention will now be directed to the former, with a discussion of gene function in terms of the Watson-Crick DNA model being reserved for Section 17–14.

One of the elegancies of the Watson-Crick hypothesized model of DNA structure is the way in which it immediately suggests a method of self-replication. It is quite easy to imagine that the process involves an unwinding and separation of the two DNA polynucleotide strands, with "unzipping" occurring through the breakage of the hydrogen bonds of the base pair. This mental picture is supported by the fact that the amount of energy needed to separate the DNA strands is equivalent to the amount of energy needed to break hydrogen bonds. Once separated from its partner, each unpaired base nucleotide would attract its complementary base nucleotide from the surrounding cellular medium. Thus each unpaired polynucleotide strand would build a strand complementary in structure to itself. The result would be two DNA molecules, each an exact replica of the original (Fig. 17–12).

One immediate prediction of the Watson-Crick hypothesis suggested by the diagram in Fig. 17–12 is that DNA in the process of replication should have the

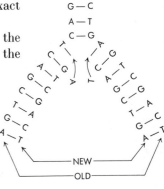

FIG. 17–12   A highly diagrammatic representation of base pairing and DNA replication as hypothesized by Watson and Crick. The four bases, adenine, thymine, guanine, and cytosine, are represented by the letters A, T, G, and C. The total length of the segment of molecule represented here would be approximately 50 Å (0.005 μ).

form of the letter Y. Dr. John Cairns of the Cold Spring Harbor Laboratory in New York has verified this prediction.

An elegant experimental test of the means of DNA replication suggested by Watson and Crick was performed by two California Institute of Technology scientists, M. Meselson and F. W. Stahl. *Escherichia coli* bacteria were grown in a medium containing glucose, mineral salts without nitrogen, and ammonium chloride ($NH_4Cl$) in which almost all of the nitrogen atoms were the heavy isotope, $N^{15}$. The bacteria were allowed to grow in this medium until fourteen generations of bacteria had arisen from those used to inoculate the culture. Hence virtually all of the nitrogen in the DNA of these bacteria was heavy nitrogen.

The key to the Meselson-Stahl experiment lay in the experimental technique. When a cesium chloride solution is spun in an ultracentrifuge at approximately 200,000 times the force of gravity, the molecules of cesium chloride can be made to begin to sediment. However, due to their relatively low molecular weight, they never sediment completely. Instead, the result is a gradation of low-to-high solution density, from the top of the centrifuge tube to the bottom. Any foreign molecule centrifuged in such a cesium chloride solution will come to rest at a level at which its density equals that of the surrounding solution. Thus DNA extracted from *E. coli* bacteria grown in a medium containing the regular light isotope of nitrogen, $N^{14}$, will form a band at a higher point in the centrifuge tube than DNA extracted from *E. coli* bacteria grown in a medium containing $N^{15}$.

After centrifuging, Meselson and Stahl removed the experimental bacteria from the heavy nitrogen medium and allowed them to undergo just one more generation, i.e., one more DNA replication. Note that as a result of this step, heavy DNA molecules containing $N^{15}$ replicated in a medium in which only light nucleotides containing $N^{14}$ were available. According to the hypothesis of Watson and Crick, the result of such replication should be "hybrid" DNA molecules, each containing one heavy polynucleotide strand and one light polynucleotide strand. After centrifugation, these hybrid DNA molecules should appear in a new band in the cesium chloride density gradient. This new band should lie in the region between the completely light DNA band formed from bacteria grown in a medium containing $N^{14}$, and the heavy DNA band formed from bacteria grown in a medium containing $N^{15}$. This prediction is verified by the experimental results.

Another test of the Watson-Crick hypothesis is to allow the $N^{15}$-labeled bacteria to undergo *two* generations in a medium containing $N^{14}$, rather than just one. Here, one would predict two DNA bands in the cesium chloride density gradient tube. Half of the DNA should be found in the area occupied by light DNA. The other half should be in the area occupied by the "hybrid" DNA. Again, the results obtained by Meselson and Stahl verified these predictions and supported the hypothesis of Watson and Crick (see Fig. 17–13).

*E. coli*, of course, is a bacterium, a fairly primitive organism. What about higher organisms, in which the DNA is located in distinct chromosomes? We

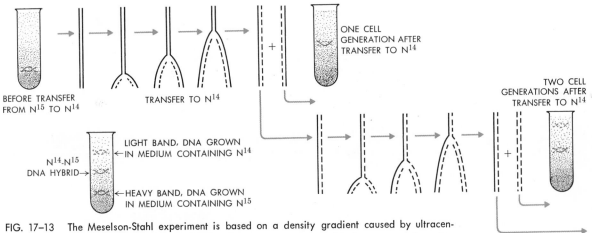

FIG. 17–13   The Meselson-Stahl experiment is based on a density gradient caused by ultracentrifugation for 48 hours in a cesium chloride solution.  When DNA molecules are spun in such a solution, they separate into regions of the centrifuge tube at which their density equals that of the CsCl solution.

have only working hypotheses to explain just how DNA is arranged within the chromosome.  However, despite this uncertainty, an experiment performed by J. A. Taylor of Columbia University sheds some light on the problem of extrapolation from the replication of DNA in *E. coli* to the replication of DNA in higher organisms.

Taylor worked with plant root tips, in which the cells constantly undergo mitosis.  He immersed these root tips in a solution containing the nucleoside thymidine, which had been labeled with radioactive hydrogen (tritium, $H^3$). The root tips were left in this solution long enough for many of their cells to double their DNA content, but not long enough for it to be doubled again.  Any DNA molecules formed during this time would incorporate the radioactive thymidine into their structure, and thus themselves become radioactive (Fig. 17–14).

As soon as the pair of daughter chromosomes became visible, they were tested by autoradiography (see Glossary).  The hypothesis of Watson and Crick predicts that the members of each pair of chromosomes should contain radioactive DNA, and that they should contain it in equal amounts.  This prediction was verified by a count of the black dots found on the photographic film where radiation had fogged it.

If one allows cells containing radioactive daughter chromosomes to undergo another cycle of duplication in a solution containing no radioactivity, the result is a completely different prediction, which provides yet another test of the Watson-Crick hypothesis.  Here, autoradiography should reveal one member of

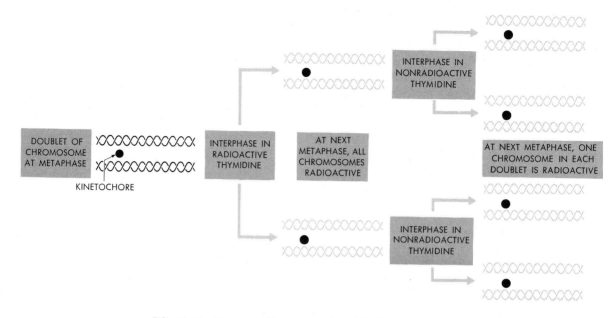

FIG. 17–14   Diagrammatic representation of Taylor's experiment with root tip cells of a pea plant. Note that the results are consistent with the Watson-Crick hypothesis concerning DNA replication. (After John W. Kimball, *Biology*, 2nd edition.  Reading, Mass.: Addison-Wesley, 1968.)

each pair of daughter chromosomes to be radioactive, and the other nonradioactive.  This prediction is verified.  Because of the many complexities involved in experimentation of this sort, which introduce the possibility of uncontrollable variables, Taylor's observations have been questioned by other investigators. However, the reported results are consistent with the Watson-Crick hypothesis, and similar experiments on human chromosomes in tissue culture yield the same results.

## 17-13
## DNA REPLICATION— SOME DOUBTS

In 1956 a team of scientists headed by Dr. Arthur Kornberg, then at Washington University in St. Louis, Missouri, succeeded in isolating an enzyme capable of synthesizing DNA in the test tube.  Kornberg named this enzyme DNA polymerase, and was awarded a Nobel prize for his accomplishments.  In the course of their work, Kornberg and his St. Louis team also confirmed another prediction of the Watson-Crick structure: that the two strands of DNA in the double helix lay "head to tail."   In chemical terms this meant that the end called 3' of one strand lay opposite the 5' end of the other (see diagram at right).  The importance of this fact will become apparent shortly.  Late in 1967, at Stanford University, Kornberg achieved another major success when he used DNA polymerase to synthesize a perfect copy of bacteriophage DNA.

However, the bacteriophage DNA synthesized by Kornberg forms a closed circle (see photo at right) and, more important, consists of a single rather than a double strand.   Most DNA is double-stranded.   Like most enzymes, DNA polymerase is quite specific in its action, not only as to substrate but also as to how it acts on this substrate.   In particular, Kornberg found that *DNA polymerase could synthesize a strand of DNA only in a manner causing the new polynucleotide chain to grow in the 5'-to-3' direction.*

Now the importance of the aforementioned "5'-to-3'" prediction of the Watson-Crick model becomes apparent.   It is easy to see how DNA polymerase could synthesize a single-stranded DNA working in one direction.   But in a double-stranded, "head-to-tail" molecule, the enzyme obviously could not replicate DNA in the usual manner (i.e., with the enzyme attaching itself to the free ends of the two strands of the helix and working up the molecule toward the fork of the Y-shaped replicating molecule); if it did so, one of the strands would be in the "wrong" direction, a direction in which DNA polymerase could not synthesize new DNA.

Faced with this dilemma, Kornberg came up with his own model for DNA replication.   The Kornberg model proposes a mechanism whereby DNA polymerase moves *up* one strand and also moves *down* the other strand in short runs (see Fig. 17–15).   As Fig. 17–15 shows, this "switch" from one strand to the other may occur either by the enzyme making a U-turn or by the double helix buckling at the fork and thus allowing the enzyme to move straight on.

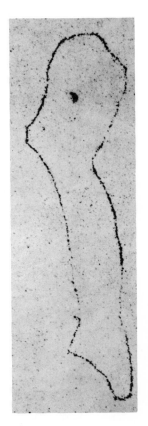

FIG. 17–15   Dr. Arthur Kornberg's hypothetical model of DNA replication.  This model suggests how the replication enzyme, though able to synthesize a new chain, only in one direction, could still replicate both strands simultaneously.  Starting at a "nick" (a), the enzyme synthesizes a new strand (indicated by the heavy colored line).  Meanwhile, the second parental strand is freed and hangs free (b).  After a certain time, the synthesizing enzyme switches strands (c).  The alternative figure in (c) shows how this switching might be accomplished without the enzyme having to make a U-turn; the double helix could hinge back on itself instead.  The newly synthesized strand is then nicked at the fork (d), and the sequence of events repeated (e).  The short lengths of the new strand are linked by a joining enzyme.

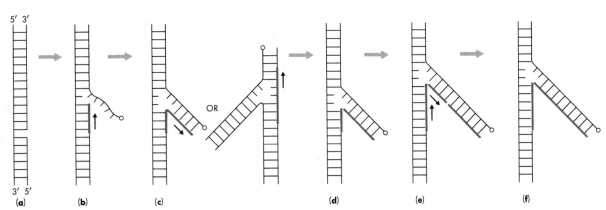

5' 3'

3' 5'
(a)          (b)          (c)          OR          (d)          (e)          (f)

The Kornberg DNA replication model leads to some interesting predictions. For one, it is obvious that DNA synthesis by this means involves the production of several disconnected lengths of single DNA strands which are only later joined into a continuous strand. But the Kornberg model also requires the presence of another enzyme, whose job it is to join the DNA strand fragments together. But at the time Kornberg proposed his model, no such joining enzyme was known.

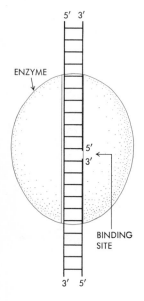

ENZYME

5′  3′

5′
3′

BINDING
SITE

3′  5′

In a few months, in several laboratories, a DNA-joining enzyme, named ligase, was found. Almost simultaneously, Dr. Reiji Okazaki and his colleagues at Japan's Nagoyo University found the predicted fragments. Further work indicated that the joining enzyme does connect the "Okazaki fragments" and, indeed, its presence is absolutely essential for DNA replication to occur. Okazaki fragments have subsequently been found in a large number of cell systems, including human ones.

In summary, then, the Kornberg model of DNA replication, though somewhat more complex than the older model, is plausible and, more important, fits the facts. Kornberg even suggested how DNA polymerase may work. He proposed that the enzyme molecule contains a groove in which the DNA double helix sits and that the enzyme attaches to the DNA either at the end of the helix or at specially created "nicks" formed in one of the strands of the double helix (see diagram at left). Kornberg has taken some electron micrographs showing enzyme molecules clearly sitting on nicks in an artificial DNA double helix.

Yet, despite the verification of predictions stemming from the Kornberg hypothetical model of DNA replication, one major objection remains: *no one has ever demonstrated that DNA polymerase can synthesize a double helix of DNA in the test tube.* The reader will recall that Kornberg achieved his DNA-synthesis feat with a bacteriophage DNA which is *single*-stranded.

Primarily because of this failure to synthesize double-helix DNA with DNA polymerase, doubts began to be expressed whether DNA polymerase was the primary DNA-replicating enzyme at all! The more the enzyme was studied, the more apparent it became that it constituted a perfect DNA *repair*, rather than replicating, enzyme. (DNA repair is a universal and vital function, involving snipping out wrongly matched sections of DNA and replacing them with sections having the correct base sequences.) The case against DNA polymerase as the DNA-replicating enzyme became greatly strengthened when, after laboriously screening almost 3500 mutants of *E. coli*, Drs. John Cairns and Paula de Lucia at Cold Spring Harbor found one that possessed less than 1% of the normal level of DNA polymerase activity yet could still carry out DNA replication perfectly well. Furthermore, the new mutant was far more sensitive to ultraviolet light than normal *E. coli*. Since ultraviolet radiation is known to change base sequences in DNA, i.e., causes "mistakes," and the mutant *E. coli* seemed less capable of repairing these mistakes, this result provides strong support for the hypothesis proposing a DNA-repair rather than DNA-replicating role for DNA polymerase.

However, the Cairns–de Lucia figure of less than 1% DNA polymerase activity is based on methods designed to test for the occurrence of that activity. But it is not always possible to assume that, because an enzyme's normal activity has not been detected, it is not there. Kornberg has suggested that mutation may have caused the loss of part of the enzyme molecule, thereby making its presence and activity undetectable by normal assaying methods. As Kornberg himself has shown, it is possible to remove up to one-third of the DNA polymerase molecule and yet show that it is not only still effective in DNA synthesis (single-stranded), but even more so. He suggests several ways in which the DNA polymerase problem might be resolved, including the genetic experiment of isolating the DNA-synthesizing activity in the Cairns–de Lucia mutant *E. coli* and determining what enzyme is responsible.

Problems similar to this are numerous in the history of science, and some drag on for many years. Often, their long lifetime is the result of the failure of anyone to come up with a better alternative. The only isolated and identified enzyme with any DNA-synthesizing abilities in cell-free test-tube systems remains DNA polymerase.

Yet there is now strong evidence that the alternative may be just around the corner—if, indeed, it has not already arrived. For some time it has been known that, in bacteria at least, DNA replication takes place on the membrane surrounding the procaryotic bacterial cells. In higher, eucaryotic cells, DNA replication may take place on the inner membranes of the cell nuclei. This suggests that the DNA-replicating enzyme sits on the membrane and perhaps forms some sort of complex with it. It also suggests a reason why no DNA-replicating enzyme other than DNA polymerase has been found. In cell-free systems, the membranes, and perhaps their associated enzymes, are discarded. Thus the possibility exists that researchers seeking the "true" DNA-replicating enzyme may have been throwing out what they were looking for.

This last-mentioned possibility has recently become a strong probability. A team of German scientists at the Friedrich Miescher Laboratory of the Max Planck Institute in Tübingen has succeeded in preparing membrane material from *E. coli* which contains no DNA polymerase. Yet, in a test-tube system, DNA is rapidly synthesized in this material. It thus seems likely that a more satisfactory DNA-synthesizing enzyme has been pinpointed and that the long-sought alternative to DNA polymerase will soon be isolated.* It is intriguing that this important work should be performed in 1970 at a laboratory named after the man, Miescher, who first discovered nucleic acids exactly 100 years before.

Note that the discovery of a replicating enzyme to replace DNA polymerase affects the Kornberg hypothetical model of DNA replication shown in Fig. 17–15

---

* It is possible, of course, that the membrane-bound enzyme may be a modified form of DNA polymerase, since DNA polymerase which is closely associated with membranes has been found.

only if the new enzyme is shown to be capable of synthesizing DNA strands in both the 5′-to-3′ and 3′-to-5′ directions—a possibility that seems remote. Even if this *were* to prove the case, there would still be left the problem of accounting for the Okazaki fragments and the necessity of the presence of the joining enzyme for DNA replication. The fact that the earlier work of Cairns, Meselson and Stahl, and Taylor supported the earlier model of DNA replication put forth by Watson and Crick is in no way detrimental to this work, although the later Kornberg model seems more in accord with now-known facts; for the results obtained by Cairns, Meselson and Stahl, and Taylor are all consistent with the prediction of the Kornberg DNA replication model *as well as* those of the Watson–Crick model. Both models, for example, predict Y-shaped conformations in replicating DNA molecules and both predict similar labeling patterns in the molecular "hybrids" produced by isotope-labeled replicating DNA molecules. Thus the work of Cairns, Meselson and Stahl, and Taylor could be said to be of value in supporting the general means of DNA replication shared by both models, but of no value in distinguishing between them.

## 17-14
## GENE FUNCTION*

The genetics discussed thus far have dealt with the end links of a three-link chain. First, we investigated the manner in which certain phenotypic characteristics are inherited (tallness and dwarfness in pea plants; red, roan, and white coloring in cattle; black, brown, and agouti coloring in mice, etc.). Most recently, we have turned our attention to the structure of the units responsible for such phenotypes, the genes. But the connecting link—the manner in which genes act to effect the expression of a phenotypic character—has thus far been neglected. It is now time to rectify this omission.

By consideration of certain facts about living organisms, it is possible to deduce a manner in which genes might work. First, it can be shown that from virus, to pea, to mouse, to man, DNA has the same essential parts arranged in the same fundamental structural pattern. It is logical to ask, therefore, "What makes these organisms different?" Again, the Watson-Crick model of DNA structure suggests an answer: *The difference between living organisms can be attributed primarily to differences in the order of nitrogenous base pairs along the DNA molecule.* The more similar the order of the base pairs, the more closely related the organisms.

It is obvious, however, that structural differences between living organisms are not expressed directly in the form of differences in the order of DNA base pairs, for DNA makes up only a tiny fraction of the cells of most living organisms. Further, many other molecules found in living organisms are not at all structurally unique to them. For example, the glucose of a yeast cell is the same as the glucose

---

* Historically speaking, the experiments described in this section predate (by about 15 years) the experiments leading to Watson and Crick's determination of gene structure. We have chosen to reverse this sequence in the interest of presenting a logical pattern in the coverage of the subject.

in a man; the fat tissue of a mouse may be quite similar to that of an elephant. Clearly, then, inherited characteristics are not initially expressed by molecules such as carbohydrates or fats. Rather, phenotypic differences between living organisms are traceable to differences in their proteins.

This fact leads to an important deduction. There must be a relationship between DNA, the genetic material, and the proteins responsible for the expression of inherited differences.

There is a condition in man known as phenylketonuria, the most prevalent symptoms of which are a severe mental deficiency and the excretion in the urine of about one gram of phenylpyruvic acid per day. Phenylpyruvic acid is derived from phenylalanine (an essential amino acid in man's diet) by replacement of the amino ($NH_2$) group by an oxygen atom.

In normal persons, phenylpyruvic acid is converted to $p$-hydroxyphenyl-pyruvic acid, which in turn is converted into another compound, and so on. Eventually the reaction series ends in the production of carbon dioxide and water. Each step in the series is catalyzed by a specific enzyme. A representation of this reaction series can be given as follows:

PHENYLALANINE $\xrightarrow{\text{enzyme 1}}$ PHENYLPYRUVIC ACID $\xrightarrow{\text{enzyme 2}}$

$p$-HYDROXYPHENYLPYRUVIC ACID $\xrightarrow{\text{enzyme 3}} \ldots \xrightarrow{\text{enzyme 4}} \ldots$

$\xrightarrow{\text{enzyme } n} \ldots CO_2 + H_2O.$

Examination of the pedigrees of human families with occurrences of phenyl-ketonuria suggests that the condition is recessive and due to a single pair of genes; i.e.,

**Hypothesis:** *If* . . .   phenylketonuria is recessive and due to a single pair of genes, . . .

**Prediction:** *then* . . . when children with phenylketonuria occur in families in which both parents are normal, they should do so in a ratio of three normals to one showing the condition.

This prediction is verified.

Early in this century the Oxford physician-biochemist Sir Archibald E. Garrod proposed that persons with conditions similar to phenylketonuria differ from normal persons only in that they lack the enzyme that catalyzes a certain vital reaction in a series. In the case of phenylketonuria, this would be the enzyme catalyzing the reaction that converts phenylpyruvic acid to $p$-hydroxyl-phenylpyruvic acid. The hypothesis selects this enzyme over the others involved in the reaction series from phenylalanine to carbon dioxide and water because only the blockage of the action of this enzyme could account for the accumulation of phenylpyruvic acid. Phenylpyruvic acid, unable to cross the energy barrier of the reaction without the aid of the missing enzyme, increases in amount and concentration within the body. This increase damages the sensitive brain tissue, thus leading to symptoms of mental deficiency. With still further accumulation, the compound spills over into the urine for excretion.

In brief, then, this hypothesis proposes that what is inherited is not phenylketonuria, but the failure of the body to produce a certain enzyme, and that this enzyme deficiency results in phenylketonuria.

It is easy to extend this hypothesis to suggest that genes carry out their action by directing the formation of enzymes (all enzymes, of course, are proteins), and that these enzymes, in turn, catalyze one step of a particular reaction series, e.g., a series leading to the production of black pigment in the hair of a mouse.

Here is an hypothesis with obvious potential for explaining a great deal about gene action. Considerable difficulty was encountered in testing it, however, a major limitation being the absence of a suitable experimental organism. The fruit fly, invaluable for examining the various ways in which phenotypic variations are inherited and in furthering the gene-on-chromosome hypothesis, is unsatisfactory here. Between the action of the genes and the formation of a vestigial wing is a broad area of very complicated chemistry, with many reaction pathways available. In the late 1930's, large numbers of investigators, attracted by the promising outlook of biochemical genetics, turned their attention to other experimental organisms. Among these were *E. coli* (about which more genetic knowledge has been accumulated than any other form of life), and the red bread mold, *Neurospora crassa*. *Neurospora*, in particular, possesses several advantages as an experimental organism. First, it has an extremely short life cycle. Second, it has a low number of chromosomes (seven pairs), on which the genes can readily be mapped. Third, its life cycle, though short, is complex, with the majority of the cycle being spent in the haploid condition. This means that any recessive gene present is immediately detectable in the phenotype, there being no dominant allele to mask it. Finally, the reproductive apparatus of *Neurospora* can be neatly dissected to isolate individual reproductive cells. This procedure, in effect, isolates a single complete set of genes.

Molds are generally thought of as being rather simple and primitive forms of life. In terms of their status on the evolutionary tree, such a concept is not without validity. Biochemically speaking, however, molds are far from simple. Indeed, they retain the ability to synthesize compounds necessary for life which man cannot synthesize and must include in his diet. Thus *Neurospora* can be grown in a laboratory on a medium containing only cane sugar, inorganic salts, and one vitamin (biotin). Such a medium is called a **minimal medium,** for it contains *only* those substances *Neurospora* needs but cannot synthesize for itself. *Neurospora* possesses, as an inherited characteristic, the ability to synthesize all the other vitamins and amino acids essential for life.

The scientists George Beadle and Edward L. Tatum devised a way to use *Neurospora* to test the hypothesis that genes act by directing the formation of specific enzymes. First, they exposed spores of *Neurospora* to X-rays or ultraviolet light. It was found that some of the molds produced by such irradiated spores could no longer grow on a minimal medium. Evidently the experimental molds had lost the ability to produce certain essential substances. By adding vitamins and amino acids to the minimal medium one by one, it could be determined which substance or substances a mutant mold had lost the ability to synthesize.

A specific example may help to make this important concept clear. Three strains of mutant molds were isolated which could no longer live on the minimal medium. The strains differed from each other in their requirements for additives to the minimal medium. Strain A would grow only if the amino acid arginine was added; strain B would grow if either arginine or citrulline were added; strain C, on the other hand, would grow with the addition of arginine, citrulline, or ornithine. The explanation for these different requirements was found by examination of the following reaction series.

It had been determined that there is a single reaction series leading to the formation of arginine. Each step is catalyzed by a specific enzyme:

$$\text{PRECURSOR } X \xrightarrow{\text{enzyme 1}} \text{ORNITHINE} \xrightarrow{\text{enzyme 2}} \text{CITRULLINE} \xrightarrow{\text{enzyme 3}} \text{ARGININE.}$$

On the basis of the gene-enzyme hypothesis, the gene responsible for the synthesis of enzyme 3 must have been mutated in mutant mold strain A to a form incapable of synthesizing the enzyme. The hypothesis proposing such a mutation predicted that the addition of any precursor compound, such as ornithine or citrulline, would have no effect on the inability of strain A to grow on the medium, since the essential reaction converting citrulline to arginine would be blocked by the absence of enzyme 3. This prediction, of course, was verified. Similar reasoning led to the hypothesis that in mutant mold strain B, the gene responsible for producing enzyme 2 had been mutated. The predictions of this hypothesis were consistent with the observation that the addition of either arginine or citrulline (but *not* ornithine) enabled strain B to grow. It was easy to see that mutant mold strain C would be able to grow with the addition of ornithine or any of the compounds coming after ornithine in the reaction series. This prediction was also verified by the experimental results: The gene responsible for producing enzyme 1 must have been mutated.

Two important steps had then to be taken to support conclusively the gene-enzyme hypothesis. First, it must be shown that the synthesis deficiency of a mutant mold strain was due to a single gene. This was done by showing that the ratios of defective to normal molds resulting from experimental crosses were those predicted by mendelian genetics for one-gene characteristics. Next, it had to be shown that the enzyme in question was, indeed, absent from molds showing the defect. Thus, for example, a biochemical analysis of mutant mold strain A, discussed previously, must reveal that no enzyme 3 is present. Similar analysis of strains B and C must show an absence of enzymes 2 and 1, respectively. In each case, the predictions of the gene-enzyme hypothesis were verified; the appropriate enzymes were, indeed, missing.

Beadle and Tatum shared a 1958 Nobel prize for their work with *Neurospora*. In a speech delivered at the award ceremony, Beadle stated:

*In this long, roundabout way, first in* Drosophila *and then in* Neurospora, *we had rediscovered what Garrod had seen so clearly so many years before. By now we knew of his work and were aware that we had added little if anything new in principle. We were working with a more favorable organism and were able to produce, almost at will, inborn errors of metabolism for almost any chemical reaction whose product we could supply through the medium. Thus, we were able to demonstrate that what Garrod had shown for a few genes and a few chemical reactions in man was true for many genes and many reactions in* Neurospora.

Garrod, however, had linked deficient or missing enzymes in man with specific *abnormal* conditions such as phenylketonuria or alcaptonuria (symptomized by a marked discoloration of the urine) only by the indirect evidence provided by mendelian ratios. The direct connection established by Beadle and Tatum in *Neurospora* still left open a wide extrapolation gap from mold to man. In 1970, however, Drs. A. Kobata and V. Ginsburg of the National Institutes of Health in Bethesda, Maryland, showed that the enzyme responsible for the synthesis of the A antigen in individuals of blood types A and AB is not present in persons with O or B blood. Thus, nearly 70 years after Garrod and 30 years after Beadle and Tatum, direct experimental evidence for the one gene-one enzyme hypothesis was obtained in normal human beings.

Despite this recent triumph, it was the Beadle and Tatum experiment that provided conclusive supporting evidence for a one gene-one enzyme hypothesis. It later became evident that certain genes control the formation of certain proteins that are not enzymes. The protein collagen, for example, is a gene-coded, nonenzyme structural protein which is the main constituent of connective tissue. Collagen accounts for aproximately one-third of the protein in the human body. Thus the one gene-one enzyme hypothesis was modified to the one gene-one protein hypothesis. As will be seen in the following section, one further modification is necessary.

## 17-15
## THE GENETIC CODE
## AND MUTATIONS

In Section 17–14 a deduction was made establishing a relationship between DNA and the protein responsible for phenotypic differences. This deduction can be made more specific: Differences in the DNA of different organisms can be traced to differences in the order of base pairs along the DNA molecule.

Similarly, differences between proteins can be traced primarily to differences in the kinds and order of amino acids along the polypeptide chains. The conclusion seems clear and inescapable: *The order of base pairs along DNA molecules must somehow control the kind and order of amino acids found in the proteins of an organism.* DNA, then, carries the **genetic code**—the blueprints establishing the kinds of proteins synthesized by the cellular machinery that make an individual organism unique.

On the basis of the results of many different kinds of experiments performed in laboratories all over the world, a model system has been hypothesized to

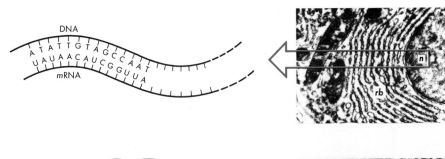

DNA

mRNA

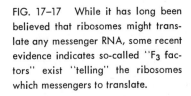

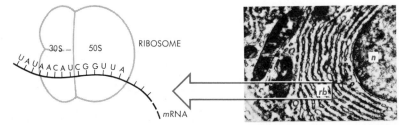

FIG. 17–17   While it has long been believed that ribosomes might translate any messenger RNA, some recent evidence indicates so-called "F₃ factors" exist "telling" the ribosomes which messengers to translate.

30 S    50 S      RIBOSOME

mRNA

explain the sequence of events comprising protein synthesis, from gene to final product.

In order to fully understand this model system, we must direct our attention toward ribonucleic acid, or RNA. Chemically, RNA molecules are very similar to those of DNA; they consist of sugar and phosphate units connected to four different kinds of nitrogenous bases. In RNA, however, thymine does not occur, its place being taken by **uracil.** Like DNA, RNA can store genetic information in its base sequence. Like the circular DNA of Kornberg's bacteriophage, RNA molecules are single-stranded. Finally, the sugar in RNA is ribose rather than deoxyribose as in DNA.

There are three types of RNA intimately involved in transcribing the genetic code into protein molecular structure. The entire process can be divided into four steps:

1) A portion of the DNA molecule "unzips," exposing a sequence of bases. Along the exposed sequence of bases of one of the two strands, a complementary strand of **messenger RNA** (*m*RNA) is synthesized (Fig. 17–16). Note that uracil, like thymine, is complementary to adenine. It is thus possible to deduce the base sequence of a DNA molecule from the sequence of bases of an *m*RNA molecule synthesized along it, just as the fender of a car tells us something about the shape of the mold in which it was fashioned. For example, if part of the *m*RNA base sequence is AUCGCUA, the corresponding portion of the DNA sequence which synthesized it must have been TAGCGAT.

2) A newly synthesized *m*RNA detaches from the DNA strand, leaves the nucleus, and becomes attached to the ribosomes (see pp. 103–104 and Fig. 17–17). There is some recent evidence indicating that hydrogen bonding may play an important role in this attachment.

FIG. 17–18

3) In the cytoplasm, free amino acids are "activated" by ATP and become attached to a second type of RNA called transfer RNA (*t*RNA), formerly called soluble RNA or *s*RNA. There are at least 20 different kinds of *t*RNA, one for each kind of amino acid. The activating enzymes are able to "recognize" both a given amino acid and its specific *t*RNA and bring about their union (Fig. 17–18).

4) Once the amino acids are attached to their respective *t*RNA molecules, they diffuse to the ribosomes. It is on the surface of the ribosomes, often connected in groups or chains called **polyribosomes** or **polysomes** (Fig. 17–19), that polypeptide synthesis actually occurs. The surface of the ribosomes, themselves composed of a third type of RNA, ribosomal RNA (*r*RNA), and protein, may serve to orient the incoming *t*RNA molecules so that they will make a proper union with the *m*RNA. There is a connection between the way in which this union is thought to occur and the structure of *t*RNA molecules. Because

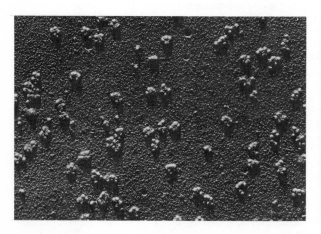
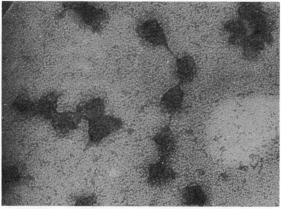

FIG. 17–19    At left is shown an electron micrograph of clusters of ribosomes, called polysomes. At right are shown polysomes engaged in the synthesis of hemoglobin polypeptides. The strand connecting the five ribosomes in the center is believed to be a molecule of messenger RNA. (Photos courtesy Dr. Alexander Rich.)

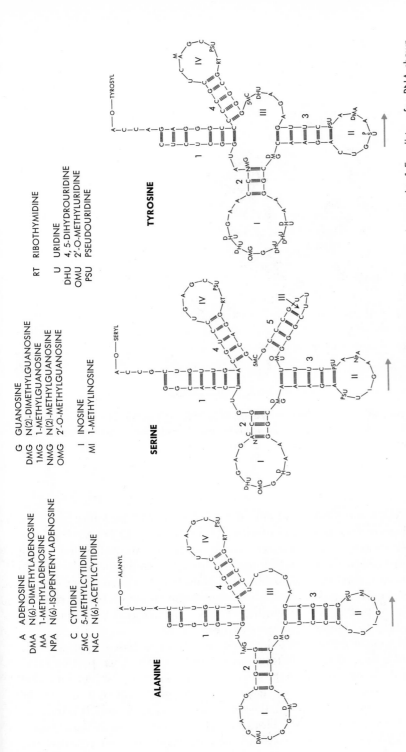

FIG. 17–20   The structure of three transfer RNA molecules. Compare these drawings with the electron micrograph of *E. coli* transfer RNA shown in Fig. 17–21.

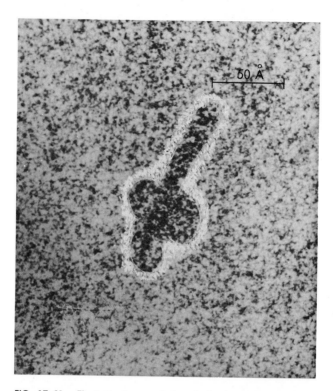

FIG. 17–21    Electron micrograph thought by some to be of *E. coli* transfer RNA, showing "clover-leaf" shape. The background has been removed in the area immediately surrounding the molecule. (Photo courtesy F. P. Ottensmeyer, University of Toronto.)

crystalized *t*RNA is difficult to obtain, determination of its structure by X-ray diffraction has not been as successful with *t*RNA as it has with DNA.  However, in 1965, after seven years of painstaking work, Dr. Robert W. Holley and a team of workers at Cornell University, by systematically breaking the molecule into fragments using highly specific enzymes, successfully determined the exact base sequences of the *t*RNA for the amino acid alanine (for this work Holley received a Nobel prize in 1968).  Since then, the structure of other *t*RNA molecules has been determined by similar techniques (see Fig. 17–20).

The *t*RNA molecule appears to be composed of a single base strand, with the strand folded into a "three-leaf clover" configuration.  The open portion of all *t*RNA molecules always contains the same base sequence: cytosine, cytosine, and adenine.  It is this end which attaches to the appropriate amino acid.  At the "cloverleaf" opposite this open end, three unpaired bases are found.  It is hypothesized that these three unpaired bases fit onto a complementary base triplet along the *m*RNA molecule.  These *m*RNA base triplets are referred to as **codons,**

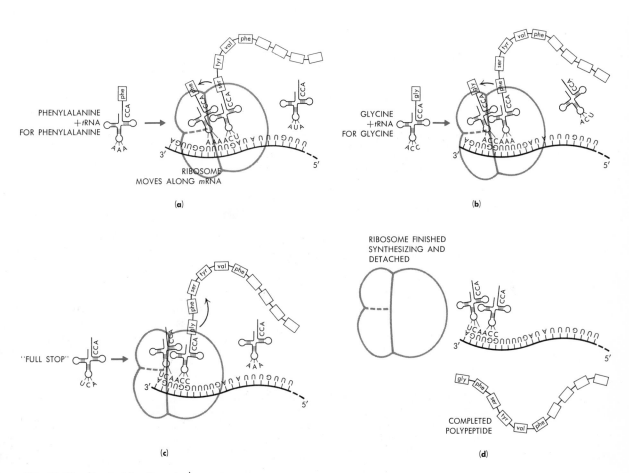

FIG. 17–22   (See text for discussion)

while the unpaired base triplets on the *t*RNA are referred to as **anticodons.**
Thus, for example, a *t*RNA molecule with the anticodon UAA would fit onto
the *m*RNA molecule where the codon AUU occurred. A *t*RNA molecule with
the anticodon ACA would fit onto the *m*RNA molecule where the codon UGU
occurred. Thus the sequence of bases along the *m*RNA molecule, originally
determined by the DNA base sequence that synthesized it, determines the kind
of *t*RNA selected. This selection, of course, indirectly selects the amino acid that
is attached to the *t*RNA molecule. Further, since the appropriate *t*RNA becomes
fitted onto the *m*RNA template, the amino acids they carry are brought into the
proper spatial alignment and spacing for peptide bonds to form between them.

5) As the ribosome moves along the *m*RNA molecule, the code is "read" by the
*t*RNA molecules and a growing polypeptide chain is formed, beginning at the
amino-terminal end. When completed, the newly synthesized polypeptide chain
is released by some as yet undetermined enzymatic mechanism (Fig. 17–22).

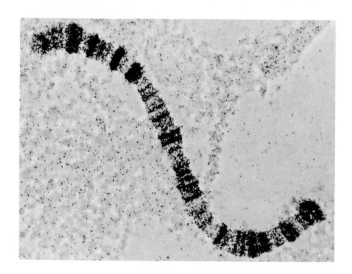

FIG. 17–23  Evidence obtained by autoradiography of the synthesis of *m*RNA at certain regions of the chromosome. (This chromosome is from the larva of a midge, *Chironomus tentans*.)  As the animal develops, the regions along the chromosome in which *m*RNA is being synthesized change, indicating that different sets of genes are called into action at different times. (Photo courtesy Dr. C. Pelling, Max Planck Institute for Biology, Tübingen.)

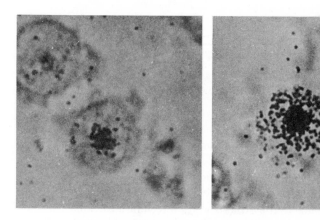

FIG. 17–24  Evidence that DNA remains within the nucleus while *m*RNA is found in both nucleus and cytoplasm is provided by autoradiography.  The moth (*Cecropia*) blood cell at left has been exposed to isotope-labeled thymidine.  Each dark spot represents the emission of electrons from the isotope, tritium ($H^3$).  Since thymidine occurs in DNA but not in RNA, the autoradiograph shows the radioactivity limited to the nucleus.  The photo at right shows the same kind of cell, but this time exposed to tritium-labeled uridine, which occurs in RNA but not in DNA.  Note the distribution of radioactivity in both nucleus (where *m*RNA is presumed to be synthesized by DNA) and cytoplasm (where the *m*RNA is presumably associated with the ribosomes during polypeptide synthesis).  See also Figs. 17–25 and 17–26. (Photos courtesy Dr. Spencer Berry, Wesleyan University.)

Thus the gene-protein hypothesis, a modification of the original gene-enzyme hypothesis, must be modified again to a "gene-polypeptide chain" hypothesis. By the series of steps just discussed, the sequence of bases along the DNA molecules specifies the kinds and sequence of amino acids along the polypeptide chain of protein molecules, thereby establishing the primary structure and uniqueness of the protein. Put more colorfully, Daddy's nose appears on baby's face because the DNA of the fertilized egg contained the particular sequences of bases which gave rise to the particular messages which were translated into the particular protein of the nasal cells that formed that particular nose.

It must be remembered that the entire protein-synthesizing process just described is still a tentative hypothetical model, subject to modification by future experimental data. Some parts of the process, such as precisely how the *t*RNA and *m*RNA are bound to the ribosome, are pure conjecture, based primarily on the fact that they appear reasonable. Other parts, however, are well supported by experimental evidence. Since it would, of course, be impossible to analyze all of the significant experiments here, only a few representative works will be cited.

In Step 1, it was proposed that DNA synthesizes an *m*RNA molecule with a complementary sequence of bases. This hypothesis can be tested by exposing chromosomes of the midge, *Chironomus tentans*, to a tritium-labeled base, uracil. Uracil, of course, would be built into any *m*RNA synthesized along the chromosome, but not into DNA (which contains thymine rather than uracil).

*Hypothesis: If* . . .     *m*RNA is synthesized by DNA along the chromosome, . . .

*Prediction: then* . . . tritium-labeled uracil should show up in the chromosome at those places at which genes are active.

Autoradiographic film will show black areas over certain regions of the chromosome (Fig. 17–23). Almost certainly, these dark areas represent points at which *m*RNA is being synthesized. Thus the hypothesis is supported.

Autoradiographic evidence has also been found that DNA remains within the nucleus while *m*RNA passes into the cytoplasm, where it transmits the genetic code to the ribosomes (see Figs. 17–24, 17–25, and 17–26).

Recently, Drs. O. L. Miller, Jr., and Barbara R. Beatty of the Oak Ridge National Laboratory in Oak Ridge, Tennessee, have obtained what they believe to be the first observations of the fine structure of individual genes in the act of synthesizing ribosomal RNA (*r*RNA) in oöcytes of the spotted newt, *Triturus viridescens* (see Fig. 17–27). Not only does the appearance of the genes at work fit with what had been expected on the basis of theoretical considerations, but measurements of the genes and their transcription products are in close agreement with those obtained by biochemical analysis. Even more recently, the

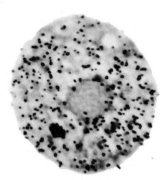

FIG. 17–25  The *Tetrahymena* cell on the left has been grown in a medium containing isotope-labeled cytidine.  Note the concentration of dark spots within the nucleus.  At right, an autoradiograph of a cell similarly exposed to tritium-labeled cytidine, but then allowed to grow further in a medium free of labeled cytidine.  Note that the pattern of dark spots supports an hypothesis proposing that nuclear-synthesized RNA passes into the cytoplasm and, it is assumed, transmits the genetic code to the ribosomes.  (Photos courtesy David M. Prescott, University of Colorado Medical School.  Reproduced by permission, from J. D. Watson, *Molecular Biology of the Gene*.  New York: W. A. Benjamin, Inc., 1965.)

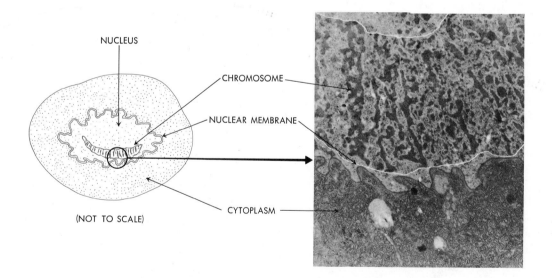

FIG. 17–26  This photograph shows a portion of an insect chromosome closely applied to the nuclear membrane.  Presumably such close application allows for easy transferal of DNA-synthesized products through the nuclear membrane into the cytoplasm.  For aid in interpretation, an artist's representation of the whole cell (not to scale) is included, and the chromosome portion visible in the photograph is outlined with a white hairline.  (Photo of chironomid cell courtesy Dr. Spencer Berry, Wesleyan University.)

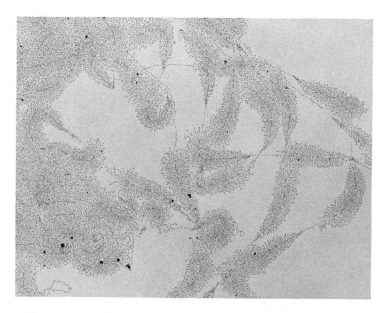

FIG. 17–27    The electron micrograph reproduced here pictures at a magnification of ×9000 the ultrastructure of extrachromosomal nucleolar genes at work. These genes, isolated from a salamander oöcyte, carry the code for ribosomal RNA (rRNA). This RNA is a major component of the ribosomes. Presumably identical genes repeat many times along the same linear DNA molecule. The genes can be visualized because approximately 100 molecules of the enzyme RNA polymerase are simultaneously transcribing the genetic code contained in each gene. The shortest lateral fibrils are attached to polymerase molecules that have just initiated reading of a gene, whereas the longest fibrils are attached to enzyme molecules which have transcribed an entire gene. As each RNA molecule is being synthesized, newly made portions are coated immediately with protein in a manner that prevents the RNA strand from extending its full length. Consequently, the ribonucleoprotein fibrils at the termination point of a gene appear considerably shorter than the length of the gene itself. Each gene is separated from its neighbors by segments of DNA that do not appear to be active in RNA synthesis. The function of this DNA is not known at present. The techniques for visualizing the ribosomal RNA genes were developed by O. L. Miller, Jr., and Barbara R. Beatty at the Biology Division of the Oak Ridge National Laboratory. These investigators believe that this work provides the first observations of the fine structure of individual genes and associated transcriptive products whose precise function is known. (Photo courtesy O. L. Miller, Jr., and Barbara R. Beatty, Biology Division, Oak Ridge National Laboratory.)

same investigators have obtained photographic evidence of the predicted type of close contact between DNA, RNA, and ribosomes (see Fig. 17–28).

What evidence is there that the genetic code is carried by a triplet of bases, rather than a single base, a doublet, or a combination larger than three? An hypothesis proposing a single base immediately runs into a contradiction; a single base would allow the selection of only four amino acids (one for each base). A doublet-code hypothesis fares little better; only $4^2$, or 16 amino acids could

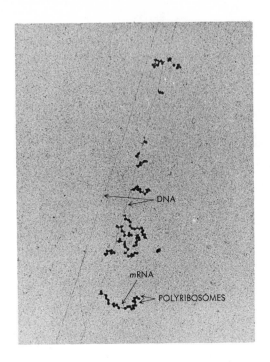

FIG. 17–28   This electron microscope photograph, magnified 36,000 times, gives dramatic support to the hypothesized roles of DNA, RNA, and the ribosomes in bacterial protein synthesis.   Shown is a portion of the single-stranded, circular chromosome of the bacterium *Escherichia coli*.   Most of the chromosome is inactive, while the active portions show *m*RNA transcribed by the chromosomal DNA attached to and interconnecting the ribosomes into polyribosomes.   This type of close contact between DNA, RNA, and ribosomes had earlier been predicted in procaryotic cells, in which there is no organized nucleus.   (Photo courtesy O. L. Miller, Jr., Oak Ridge National Laboratory; and Barbara A. Hamkalo and C. A. Thomas, Jr., Harvard University Medical School.)

be selected.  Thus the minimum number of bases that could be involved in the selection of amino acids is three (Table 17–3).  This hypothesis allows for $4^3$, or 64, selections, which are more than enough.

A more direct test of the triplet-code hypothesis is based on refined techniques, allowing bases to be inserted into or deleted from a sequence.  Invariably, to insert one, two, or four bases into a sequence, or to delete them from it, upsets the system and results in synthesis of nonfunctional proteins.  The same technique, using three bases, allows the genes to remain functional.  Each of these results is consistent with the predictions of a triplet-code hypothesis.

It is, of course, merely an hypothesis that the sequence of bases along the *m*RNA molecule plays any role at all in the determination of the amino acid selection and order in a polypeptide chain.  A solid test of this hypothesis is provided by a synthetic *m*RNA containing only uracil.

**Hypothesis:** *If* . . .   the sequence of nitrogenous bases along the *m*RNA molecule determines the choice and order of amino acids incorporated into polypeptide chains, . . .

**Prediction:** *then* . . . a synthetic *m*RNA, containing only uracil, should direct the synthesis of a polypeptide chain containing only one kind of amino acid.

The prediction is verified.  A polypeptide chain is produced which contains only tha amino acid phenylalanine.  Note that this result is consistent with an hy-

**TABLE 17–3** POSSIBLE GENETIC-CODE LETTER COMBINATIONS AS A FUNCTION OF THE LENGTH OF THE CODE WORD (A = ADENINE, G = GUANINE, U = URACIL, C = CYTOSINE) (AFTER M. NIRENBERG, 1963)

| SINGLET CODE (4 WORDS) | DOUBLET CODE (16 WORDS) | | | | TRIPLET CODE (64 WORDS) | | | |
|---|---|---|---|---|---|---|---|---|
| A | AA | AG | AC | AU | AAA | AAG | AAC | AAU |
| G | GA | GG | GC | GU | AGA | AGG | AGC | AGU |
| C | CA | CG | CC | CU | ACA | ACG | ACC | ACU |
| U | UA | UG | UC | UU | AUA | AUG | AUC | AUU |
| | | | | | GAA | GAG | GAC | GAU |
| | | | | | GGA | GGG | GGC | GGU |
| | | | | | GCA | GCG | GCC | GCU |
| | | | | | GUA | GUG | GUC | GUU |
| | | | | | CAA | CAG | CAC | CAU |
| | | | | | CGA | CGG | CGC | CGU |
| | | | | | CCA | CCG | CCC | CCU |
| | | | | | CUA | CUG | CUC | CUU |
| | | | | | UAA | UAG | UAC | UAU |
| | | | | | UGA | UGG | UGC | UGU |
| | | | | | UCA | UCG | UCC | UCU |
| | | | | | UUA | UUG | UUC | UUU |

pothesis proposing that the base triplet UUU codes for phenylalanine. Thus the sequence of bases along the coding portion of the DNA molecule must have been AAA.

All the possible codons have now been associated with specific amino acids or a role in polypeptide synthesis (see Table 17–4), although some of the codons are assigned with less certainty than others. Table 17–4 gives the triplet of base pairs for each of the 20 most common amino acids. To select the proper triplets or codons for any amino acid, simply read in order the letters appearing to the left, above, and to the right of it. Thus the codons for glycine (gly) are GGU, GGC, GGA, and GGG, while those for lysine (lys) are AAA and AAG. Some of the codons assigned here are less certain than others, and those suspected of being connected with the beginning of polypeptide chain synthesis are not included. The two codons labeled nonsense, ochre and amber (UAA and UAG), are related to no amino acid and are hypothesized to represent "punctuation" in the chain. The codon UGA is hypothesized to terminate polypeptide chain synthesis.

It is clear from Table 17–4 that the genetic code must be **degenerate;** i.e., more than one codon can select for one of the amino acids. More significant, however, is the fact that all the experimental evidence to date points toward the universality of the genetic code throughout the living world. Experiments on tissue extracts show that the triplets that select particular amino acids in mammals are identical to those that select the same amino acids in *E. coli*.

**TABLE 17–4** THE GENETIC CODE

| 1ST ↓   2ND → | U | C | A | G | ↓ 3RD |
|---|---|---|---|---|---|
| U | phe | ser | tyr | cys | U |
|   | phe | ser | tyr | cys | C |
|   | leu | ser | NONSENSE (OCHRE) | STOP | A |
|   | leu | ser | NONSENSE (AMBER) | tryp | G |
| C | leu | pro | his | arg | U |
|   | leu | pro | his | arg | C |
|   | leu | pro | gluN | arg | A |
|   | leu | pro | gluN | arg | G |
| A | ileu | thr | aspN | ser | U |
|   | ileu | thr | aspN | ser | C |
|   | ileu | thr | lys | arg | A |
|   | met | thr | lys | arg | G |
| G | val | ala | asp | gly | U |
|   | val | ala | asp | gly | C |
|   | val | ala | glu | gly | A |
|   | val | ala | glu | gly | G |

## 17–16
## THE GENE

What, then, is a gene? We have come a long way from Mendel's genetic "factors." Throughout the development of genetics, many satisfactory gene models have been proposed which, on closer analysis, later proved unsatisfactory (recall the string-of-beads model of chromosome-gene relationships). In molecular genetics, however, breakdown of the DNA molecule destroys the gene. Therefore, while much has been learned from a submolecular level of genetic analysis, it is with the intact working entity represented by the gene concept that any meaningful definition of a gene must deal.

Such a definition is now possible. The relationship of DNA to the protein whose structure it specifies can be represented as follows (the arrow encircling DNA shows that it is a template for its own replication):

$$\overset{\curvearrowright}{\text{DNA}} \xrightarrow{\text{(transcription)}} \text{RNA} \xrightarrow{\text{(translation)}} \text{PROTEIN (POLYPEPTIDE)}$$
(replication)

This representation, often simplified verbally to "DNA, RNA, protein," has been referred to as biology's "central dogma" or "Holy Trinity."

In 1965, some interesting results were reported by biochemist Dr. Howard M. Temin, now at the University of Wisconsin. As pointed out earlier, some viruses (e.g., the tobacco mosaic virus) contain RNA but no DNA. Dr. Temin noted that, when such an RNA-only virus invades a cell, strands of DNA complementary to the viral RNA can be found. The implications of this discovery were rather profound: *it suggested that these DNA fragments had been synthesized with the viral RNA as the template*, instead of *vice versa*. At the time, however, not much attention was paid to Temin's results.

In 1970, Temin and his colleague Dr. Satoshi Mizutani reported that they had found RNA-dependent DNA polymerase which would synthesize DNA upon viral RNA within cells containing cancer-causing, RNA-only viruses. Within days, similar results were reported by Dr. D. Baltimore of the Cold Spring Harbor laboratories. Still more convincing evidence followed from Dr. Sol Spiegelman's laboratory at the Columbia University Institute for Cancer Research. The four nitrogenous bases of DNA—adenine, guanine, cytosine, and thymine—were labeled with tritium and mixed with viral RNA. The labeled bases soon showed up in intact DNA. Thus the evidence seemed conclusive: viral RNA could synthesize DNA.

Not satisfied, Spiegelman went a step further, reasoning as follows:

*Hypothesis: If . . .*   the viral RNA had served as a template for DNA synthesis, . . .

*Prediction:*   *then . . .* the RNA should be complementary to one strand of the DNA and will form a double-stranded hybrid with it.

Spiegelman performed a Meselson-Stahl-type experiment (see Section 17–12). He mixed viral RNA and its hypothesized DNA product and spun the mixture in an ultracentrifuge for three days. Since RNA and DNA have different molecular weights, they will form separate layers or fractions in the centrifuge tubes. Upon inspection, these two layers were found—but so, too, was a third, intermediate layer. Undoubtedly, this third layer, lying between the other two, was the RNA-DNA hybrid.

Spiegelman has tested twelve RNA-only viruses for their ability to synthesize DNA. Eight of them can do so, four cannot. Of considerable interest is the fact that the eight that can synthesize DNA from RNA cause tumors in animals, while the four that cannot synthesize DNA from RNA do not cause tumors. With the growing evidence for the role of viruses in at least some forms of cancer, the possibility exists that identification of the enzyme responsible for RNA-directed DNA synthesis might enable the process, and thus perhaps the cancer, to be arrested. Since the transfer of genetic information from DNA to RNA can be blocked by an antibiotic which knocks out the crucial enzyme, this reverse blockage possibility does not seem too remote.

It thus seems that the representation of biology's "central dogma" must be modified to include the possibility of reverse transcription of DNA by RNA:

$$\left( DNA \xrightleftharpoons{\text{(transcription)}} RNA \xrightarrow{\text{(translation)}} PROTEIN \ (POLYPEPTIDE) \right.$$
(replication)

To date, there is no evidence that proteins might "code" for RNA. It should not take too much reflection on the part of the reader to realize that, should this ever be shown to be the case, the implications would be quite profound. However, knowing that proteins are an end product of gene action enables us to work backward to pinpoint the gene. An average-sized protein contains approximately 500 amino acids. For the selection of each of these, a triplet of three bases is required. Thus, for this protein, *the gene is a portion of the DNA molecule containing 1500 base pairs.* On the basis of average molecular weights for amino acids, it can be predicted further that this gene would have a molecular weight of approximately $10^6$. For other proteins, depending on their size, the gene is correspondingly enlarged or reduced. It is both interesting and intellectually satisfying to note that this estimate of gene size agrees well with calculations made on the basis of more macroscopic investigation, such as data obtained from genetic mapping experiments.

A more direct means of reaching the same conclusion concerning gene size is given simply by dividing the number of nucleotides in a chromosome by the number of genes located along it. (For example, there are over 70 known genes on the chromosome of the bacterial virus T4). The resulting figure, of course, represents an average number of nucleotides per gene (though there is no reason to necessarily assume that all the genes are the same size). Knowing the average size of the nucleotides allows calculations to be made concerning the size of a gene.

With this new concept of the gene, it is now possible to take a fresh and meaningful look at some phenomena associated with it. It is possible, for example, to hypothesize that crossing over involves the breakage and rejoining of intact DNA molecules, and there is solid experimental evidence to support this hypothesis. Mutations can be viewed as either a change in the order of base pairs along the DNA molecule or a change in the kinds of bases that occur there (Fig. 17–29). Either change will result in a changed sequence of amino acids in the protein synthesized, or a substitution of one amino acid for another. Sickle-cell anemia, to be discussed in Section 21–6, results from the substitution of valine for glutamic acid in but one of 200 amino acids in hemoglobin. This fact illustrates that a very slight change can have far-reaching results for the organism.

The new gene concept also enables us to picture ways in which chemical agents, such as nitrous acid, can cause gene mutations. Nitrous acid is capable of converting one nitrogenous base into another. This results in the selection of an amino acid different from the one which would normally have been selected.

Even Mendel's concept of a recessive "factor" takes on new meaning in light of the present gene concept. The recessiveness of a gene can often be viewed as its failure to produce any functional protein at all. The dominant gene, however, produces enough functional protein to hide the recessive gene's failure. There are probably enough good enzyme molecules to catalyze the metabolic reaction, even though the total number may be reduced. Or, possibly there is a control mechanism that increases the output of *m*RNA by the dominant gene to compensate for the inactivity of its recessive allele. Without this compensatory increase, an intermediate phenotype may result.

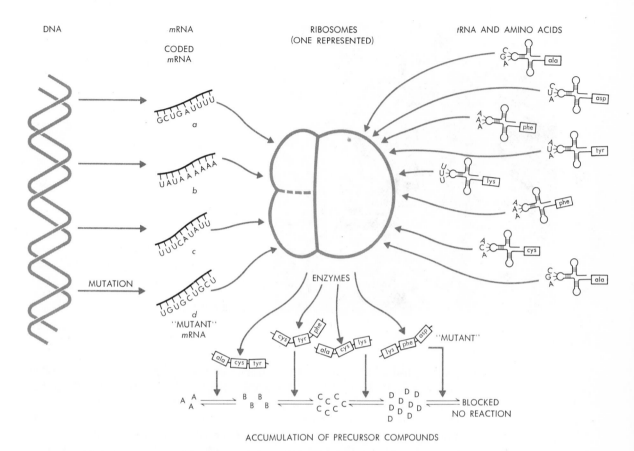

FIG. 17–29   The Watson-Crick hypothesis (that a mutation may be due to a change in the kind or order of base pairs along the DNA molecule) provides a new way to view gene mutations and their effects on the phenotype. Compound E cannot form in the above reaction series because the enzyme catalyzing its production from compound D is either absent or defective.

Biologists had long wondered if it would ever be possible to isolate an individual gene and, more important, to synthesize one in the laboratory. The answer is obviously important, for the accomplishment of these two feats might open the door to the possibility of "genetic engineering" in which man could rid himself of certain undesirable genetic traits (such as hemophilia) and even determine the kinds of children he would have.

Those who maintained that the feats of gene isolation and synthesis were impossible based their convictions on two apparently unassailable rocks. The first was that genes are so complex that their chemical synthesis and isolation is all but impossible. Genes, in other words, cannot be made to order. The second

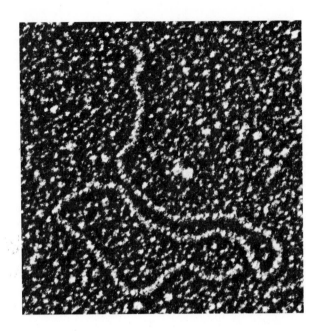

FIG. 17–30   Electron microscope photograph of an isolated gene. The gene, called the *lac* operon, is responsible for the metabolism of lactose in *E. coli.* Its calculated length is 1.4 $\mu$m. (Photo courtesy Lorne A. McHattie, Harvard University Medical School.)

argument, designed to counter suggestions that existing genes might be modified, revolved around the difficulty, if not impossibility, of identifying and altering specific nucleosides among the hundreds of millions that make up human genes. A chink in the armor of this second argument, however, developed with the demonstration by Dr. Stanfield Rogers of the Oak Ridge National Laboratory that the far simpler DNA of viruses can be chemically modified and then the genes of changed virus transduced to plants. If it can be done with plants, the possibility always exists that it might be done with animals, including man.

More important, the first "impossibility"—that of gene isolation—has now been accomplished. Successful isolation of gene material from cells of the toad *Xenopus laevis* was accomplished in 1968 by M. Birnsteil and his colleagues at the University of Edinburgh, and isolation of the DNA sequences in *E. coli* homologous to ribosomal RNA was accomplished by D. E. Kohne of the Carnegie Institute of Washington. In 1969, a team of Harvard University biologists (J. Shapiro, L. Machatti, L. Eron, G. Ihler, and K. Ippin) headed by Dr. Jonathan Beckwith announced the isolation of pure *lac* operon DNA in *E. coli.* An **operon** can be defined as a region of the DNA molecule which is simultaneously transcribed into one single messenger RNA molecule. The *lac* operon is so called because it is responsible for metabolizing lactose. The average length of the purified molecules (see Fig. 17–30) turned out to be 1.4 $\mu$m.

The gene-isolation success was followed only a few months later by announcement of the artificial synthesis of a gene by a team of University of Wisconsin scientists headed by Dr. Har Gobind Khorana, a native of India. Dr. Khorana, who had already received a 1968 Nobel prize for his work in deciphering the genetic code, developed a method of tacking together nucleosides into short lengths of DNA. The synthesized gene was built using the gene for alanine transfer RNA from yeast as a model. This transfer RNA was the first to have its structure determined (by a team of scientists headed by Dr. Robert W. Holley at Cornell University). The Wisconsin workers have shown that their artificial gene has the same parts in the same sequence and spatial arrangement as the naturally produced gene.

It still remains to be shown, however, that the artificial gene is really equivalent to the naturally produced gene in that the former can work just as well as the latter. Dr. Khorana has devised two approaches to this problem. The first is to use his "gene" to direct the synthesis in a test-tube system of a piece of alanine transfer RNA. The second is then to show that this synthesized alanine transfer RNA will function properly in making proteins. This will not be an easy task. It will mean ensuring that the protein-synthesizing system lacks a "real" or naturally produced alanine transfer RNA. Accordingly, Dr. Khorana is now working on the synthesis of another gene which codes for a modified transfer RNA from *E. coli*. This RNA, known as tyrosine suppressor transfer RNA, is absolutely necessary if tyrosine is to be incorporated into proteins in a mutant *E. coli*. Dr. Khorana can then prepare a test-tube system from the mutant—which normally cannot synthesize protein—and add the RNA whose synthesis was directed by his artificial gene. If the system can now make proteins, the artificial gene must be as good as the natural one in every respect.

Dr. Khorana claims that within the next few years it will be possible to synthesize both natural and "unnatural" genes entirely to order. Should such genetic engineering ever be perfected in man, it remains to be seen whether he will be able to adopt ethical systems to ensure that such skills are applied to beneficial uses.

One final problem remains. With the evidence firmly supporting the replication of *all* the genetic material during cell division, it is evident that each cell of a living organism contains the same complement of genes. The question then arises, "What makes these cells different?" Why, for example, do gland cells secrete certain specific protein hormones while cells of the brain do not? It seems evident that some selective mechanism must control the genes, allowing some to function and restraining others. The means by which this is hypothesized to occur will be discussed in Chapter 18.

**17-17
EXTRA-
CHROMOSOMAL
INHERITANCE**

The reader may recall from Chapter 15 that both mitochondria and chloroplasts are capable of self-replication, and possess their own DNA- and protein-synthesizing equipment. This alone shows that not all of the cell's genetic material is located within the chromosomes. As long ago as 1908, the German botanist Carl Correns, noted as one of the three biologists who in 1900 "rediscovered" Mendel's work, described the first example of a nonchromosomal gene. The explosive growth of chromosomal genetics soon eclipsed Corren's study of nonchromosomal inheritance in a number of plant species. In the 1950's, however, Dr. Ruth Sager of Columbia University and her coworkers showed that certain inherited characters in the green alga *Chlamydomonas* (see Fig. 25–7) were due to non-chromosomal genes. A nonchromosomal gene is identified by its failure to follow the mendelian pattern of inheritance, in which the genes from the male and female contribute equally to the genetic constitution of the progeny. Instead, the nonchromosomal genes from the female parent are usually transmitted during meiosis to all the progeny, while those from the male are lost. Furthermore, the data indicate that nonchromosomal genes in *Chlamydomonas* are distributed by a highly oriented mechanism, rather than at random.

The existence of such extrachromosomal inheritance has now been conclusively demonstrated for a large number of organisms, to the point that it now seems far more the rule than the exception. It is interesting to speculate on the selective value of nonchromosomal inheritance in terms of evolution. It has been shown that, unlike chromosomal replication, the replication of organelles such as mitochondria and chloroplasts is somewhat independent of cell division, and the same may be true of other cytoplasmic systems. It is not difficult to imagine situations in which the ability to increase the numbers of mitochondria or chloroplasts in a cell, independent of the division of that cell, would be of considerable adaptive value. Thus nonchromosomal genetic systems may help in providing flexibility to the manner in which an organism responds to a changing environment.

**17–18**
**CONCLUSION**   Evidence that genes are located along the chromosome in a linear order comes from investigation of linkage, crossing over, mapping, and chromosomal aberrations. The role of fruit fly genetics in establishing the inheritance of sex-linked characteristics and the advancement of modern genetics were discussed.

Examples were cited showing that genes may influence each other in their actions. The nature of the gene was traced; the ability of DNA to transform bacteria from one strain to another showed that DNA is the primary genetic material.

DNA was seen to consist of helical strands of sugar and phosphate units connected by four nitrogenous bases. The order of the base pairs was proposed as the way in which one species of living organism differs from another. The molecule was proposed to replicate by separating wherever the bases are hydrogen-bonded to each other, each single strand building its complement by attaching itself to appropriate nucleotides available in the surrounding cellular medium.

Gene function was traced from the original one gene-one enzyme hypothesis to the present concept of a one gene-one polypeptide chain. Finally, the genetic code—the means by which DNA codes the kind and sequence of amino acids in the polypeptide chain—was discussed. Also discussed were a few of the results of the research on which the hypothetical model system is based. DNA transcribes its base sequence to *m*RNA, which then carries it to the ribosomes to be put into effect.

The entire hypothetical model system, including the Watson-Crick concept of DNA structure, provides a useful construct by which the geneticist can not only explain observations and data obtained experimentally, but also predict the behavior of the genetic systems with which he works.

1. If a healthy man marries a woman who is a hemophiliac, is it possible for them to have normal children? What could you say about the sex of the normal offspring resulting from this marriage?

2. If a color-blind man married a normal, healthy woman whose father was color-blind, could they have a son with normal vision? Could they have a color-blind daughter?

3. A man and his wife both have normal vision, but their first child is color-blind. What are the chances that their next child will be a color-blind daughter? What are the genotypes of the parents of the man and his wife?

4. In man, migraine (a type of headache) is due to a dominant gene. A woman who has normal vision and does not suffer from migraine takes her daughter to a doctor for a checkup. During the examination the doctor finds his patient to be suffering from both migraine and color blindness. What can he immediately infer about her father?

5. What proportion of human progeny receive an $X$ chromosome from the father? What proportion receive one from the mother? What proportion receive an $X$ chromosome from the mother and a $Y$ chromosome from the father?

6. Ichthyosis hystrix gravior is a disease characterized by a thickened, rough, hornlike skin. It is always transmitted by a father who has the condition to all of his sons; it never occurs in girls. Form an hypothesis which will explain the inheritance of the condition.

7. The male clover butterfly is always yellow, but the female clover butterfly can be either white or yellow. White color is due to a dominant gene $W$; yellow is due to its recessive allele $w$. What is the genotype of a yellow female? Propose an hypothesis to suggest the reason why a male of the same genotype does not show the same characteristic. Plan an experiment to test your hypothesis.

8. In rats, pigmentation is determined by a dominant gene $P$, albinism by its recessive allele $p$. Black coat color is due to a dominant gene $B$, whitish color to its recessive allele $b$. For the black gene to express itself, however, the gene $P$ must be present. If a rat with the characteristics $PPBB$ is crossed with another whose characteristics are $ppbb$, what will be the phenotypes and genotypes of the first generation?

9. In the marriage of a man and woman who are both heterozygous for albinism, the distribution of their offspring will be expected to be three with normal pigmentation to one albino. However, studies of a number of families in which albinism is known turn up an interesting situation: Albinos make up considerably more than 25% of the offspring of these families. Furthermore, the fewer the children in each family, the greater the proportion of albinos among them. Geneticists, however, maintain that these results still agree perfectly with mendelian principles. Offer an explanation for this discrepancy.

10. Explain why so much is known about the means by which *Drosophila melanogaster* inherits its characteristics, while so little is known about the ways in which man inherits his.

11. Describe the major conclusions drawn from the experimental work on DNA performed by: (a) F. Griffith; (b) Avery, McCarty, and MacLeod; (c) Hershey and Chase; (d) Watson and Crick.

12. Explain the graph lines in Fig. 17–31 in terms of the experiment conducted by Meselson and Stahl to test the Watson-Crick hypothesis of DNA replication. What sort of line would be found after four generations of bacteria?

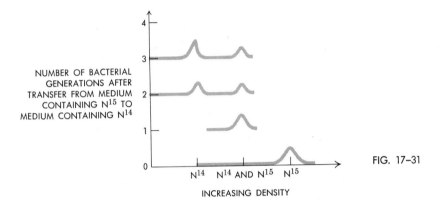

NUMBER OF BACTERIAL GENERATIONS AFTER TRANSFER FROM MEDIUM CONTAINING $N^{15}$ TO MEDIUM CONTAINING $N^{14}$

FIG. 17–31

$N^{14}$    $N^{14}$ AND $N^{15}$    $N^{15}$

INCREASING DENSITY

13. In mice, yellow coat color is known (see Color Plate IV). Crosses between black-coated and yellow-coated mice yield a 1:1 ratio of black- to yellow-coated mice. These same blacks, mated to each other, produce only black-coated young. These results are consistent with an hypothesis proposing a genotype of *BB* for the black mice and *Bb* for the yellow mice. However, this hypothesis also predicts that crosses between yellow mice should yield a ratio of one black to two yellow to one of whatever color results from genotype *bb*. This ratio, however, is not obtained. Instead, the result is a 1:2 ratio of black- to yellow-coated mice. Further investigation salvages the hypothesis, however. Dissection of the uteruses of the yellow females yielding such 1:2 ratios shows that one-fourth of the young are arrested at an early stage of their embryological development and die before birth. Evidently, then, the *bb* genotype represents a lethal combination, and the organism cannot survive. Suggest how, in terms of the modern concept of gene action, a lethal gene combination might act to produce its effects.

14. Assume that both Mrs. Baker and Mrs. Allen had babies the same day in the same hospital. After arriving home, Mrs. Baker began to suspect that her child had been accidentally switched with the Allen baby. By assigning hypothetical blood types to all four parents and the two babies, produce a combination that will show that Mrs. Baker's suspicions are correct.

15. The fruit fly, *Drosophila melanogaster*, has four pairs of chromosomes. The loci of several genes have been determined on each chromosome. Suppose you discover a new inherited trait in *Drosophila melanogaster*.

   a) How would you determine that the new trait is due to a single pair of genes?

   b) How would you determine on which of the chromosomes this new gene is located?

c) After determining which chromosome the gene is on, how would you go about determining its specific locus relative to known genes $X$, $Y$, and $Z$?

16. In cats, short hair is dominant over long hair. A long-haired male is mated to a short-haired female whose father had long hair. They produce a litter of ten kittens.

a) What proportion of their kittens would you predict to have long hair?

b) Give *two* hypotheses that might account for all ten kittens being long-haired.

c) Devise an experiment that would distinguish between the two hypotheses given in (b).

## I. On the Inheritance of Sex

MITTWOCH, URSULA, "Sex Differences in Cells." *Scientific American*, July 1963, p. 54. Discusses some of the cytological differences between male and female cells. These distinctions show how sexual differentiation is determined.

## II. On Human Genetics and Eugenics

DARWIN, MAJOR LEONARD, *What Is Eugenics?* (New York: Galton Publishing Co., 1929). A short account by a confirmed believer in eugenics.

DUNN, L. C., *Heredity and Evolution in Human Populations* (Cambridge, Harvard University Press, 1962). A well-written and interesting account of some of the recent work in human genetics and evolution. Highly recommended, nontechnical.

OSBORN, FREDERICK, *Preface to Eugenics* (New York: Harper & Bros., 1951). A more recent, but more detailed introduction to problems of eugenics than that by Darwin, listed above. It is also somewhat more technical.

REED, SHELDON, *Parenthood and Heredity* (New York: Wiley, Science Editions, 1964). A University of Minnesota professor discusses many genetic problems in human beings. The book is especially valuable and interesting because it includes many examples.

STERN, CURT, *Principles of Human Genetics* (San Francisco, W. H. Freeman & Co., 1960). A general introductory textbook on human genetics which will best serve as a reference source. It is well organized and complete.

## III. On Biochemical Genetics

BEARN, A. G., "The Chemistry of Hereditary Disease." *Scientific American*, December 1956, p. 127. This article discusses some of the most important work on the biochemistry of hereditary conditions such as alkaptonuria or Wilson's disease.

BENZER, SEYMOUR, "The Fine Structure of the Gene." *Scientific American*, January 1962, p. 70. This article discusses how the "gene" of traditional genetics has been studied in fine detail. The gene is now known to consist of smaller parts—cistrons—which it is thought represent segments of a DNA molecule.

CRICK, F. H. C., "The Genetic Code." *Scientific American*, October 1962, p. 66. Discusses how the triplet code of DNA was discovered and shows how each animo acid in a protein is coded by a specific triplet. A good survey article.

DEERING, R. A., "Ultraviolet Radiation and Nucleic Acid." *Scientific American*, December 1962, p. 135. This article shows how the effects of ultraviolet radiation on living organisms can be traced to changes in nucleic acids, especially DNA.

HURWITZ, GERARD, "Messenger RNA." *Scientific American*, February 1962, p. 41. This article discusses the basic information known both about structure and function of messenger RNA. Also discusses the general mechanism of protein synthesis.

INGRAM, VERNON, "How Do Genes Act?" *Scientific American*, January 1958, p. 68. This article discusses the problem of sickle-cell anemia and the light which it throws on how genes influence protein structure. This is still one of the best discussions of the sickle-cell problem, although the article is now somewhat dated.

NIRENBERG, MARSHALL W., "The Genetic Code: II." *Scientific American*, March 1963, p. 80. This article is a sequel to the one by Crick. This article goes into more detail on the actual mechanism of protein synthesis from the code.

RICH, ALEXANDER, "Polyribosomes." *Scientific American*, December 1963, p. 44. This article reviews the recent findings which show that ribosomes line up along a molecule of messenger RNA during protein synthesis.

SINSHEIMER, ROBERT, "Single-Stranded DNA." *Scientific American*, July 1962, p. 109. The discovery of single-stranded DNA in a bacteriophage which parasitizes *E. coli* has led to new studies on the structure of DNA and RNA. A good article for those interested in further detail about biochemistry of the DNA molecule.

STRAUSS, B. S., *An Outline of Chemical Genetics* (Philadelphia, W. B. Saunders, 1960). A very good, but difficult, survey of this new field. The text of the book is not technically written, but requires close reading. Suggested for the really interested student.

WATSON, J. D., *The Double Helix* (New York: Atheneum, 1968). A fascinating account of the discovery of the three-dimensional structure of the DNA molecule.

WATSON, J. D., *Molecular Biology of the Gene* (New York: W. A. Benjamin, Inc., 2nd edition, 1970). An excellent coverage of molecular genetics. Dr. Watson is an out-standing exception to the generalization that top-notch scientists cannot write.

# DEVELOPMENTAL BIOLOGY CHAPTER 18

18-1
INTRODUCTION

In the last chapter, we discussed the ways in which biochemical geneticists are attacking the genetic code—the means by which the genes code the construction of proteins specific to an organism. However, while biochemical genetics may dominate biology today, it cannot do so for long. By necessity, biochemical genetics is limited to a fractional portion of one cell. The biologist must go further. He must be concerned with interactions between gene and cell, cell and cell, groups of cells and other groups of cells, and, ultimately, between entire organisms and groups of organisms.

Although developmental biology deals with all kinds of living, developing systems, probably its most familiar field is **embryology.** The embryologist studies the development of plants and animals early in their lives. How is it, the embryologist wonders, that in 280 days a single fertilized human egg can become the wriggling mass of 25 million million cells we call a baby? The question is a complex one, the answers still more so. Embryology and the related fields of developmental biology tackle problems that are central to all biology. It is our purpose in the present chapter to provide a detailed discussion of some major problems in developmental biology, and the experimental means by which they are approached.

18-2
THE BACKGROUND

There are two general ways in which embryological development has been viewed historically. First, the egg could contain a tiny miniature of the adult. Under proper conditions, this miniature form would develop by simply growing larger. Since this idea involves the presence of an already-formed individual within the egg, it is called the **preformation theory.** Second, the young organism might develop from a formless mass of living material. It would develop by **differen-**

583

**tiation** of this formless material into the various body parts. This type of development is called **epigenesis**.

Which explanation is correct? The Greek philosopher Aristotle (384–322 B.C.), often referred to as the "father of embryology," watched the development of chicken eggs with fascination. From his observations, he decided in favor of epigenesis, and there the matter rested for nearly 2000 years.

In the sixteenth, seventeenth, and eighteenth centuries, attention was again turned to the problem of embryological development. Aristotle's choice of epigenesis proved unpopular, and it became a widely held belief that there was, indeed, a tiny preformed individual which simply grew in size during embryological development.

But a new problem arose. Where *was* this preformed individual? Must it necessarily be in the egg? The seminal fluid of the male had long been associated with the development of children. In fact, the word *semen* means "seed." Some men thought that the uterus simply provided the proper "soil" in which this seed from the male could grow. That this was an old belief can be seen from the fact that the Bible often refers to the seed of men, but never to the seed of women. Therefore, the preformationists became divided into two schools of thought. One group believed that the preformed individual was in the egg. The other group believed that it was in the sperm (Fig. 18–1).

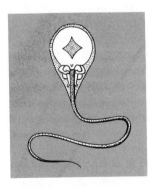

FIG. 18–1   A preformed individual in human sperm, as the seventeenth-century investigator Hartsoeker imagined he saw it.

Difficulties with these beliefs immediately arose. If there was a preformed individual within *either* the egg or the sperm, then there must be another preformed individual within the first preformed individual; within the second preformed individual there would have to be a third, and so on. Belief in preformation, then, demanded belief in a long series of progressively smaller preformed individuals, each one contained within another!

One would think that this realization would have spelled the end of the preformation theory. Not at all. Prominent men began to make guesses as to how many preformed infants Eve, "the first woman," must have carried in her ovaries (200 million was one estimate). It was thought that the world would end when this supply ran out, and predictions were made as to when this would occur.

As strange as the preformation theory seems today, these men were not ignorant. On the contrary, they made many careful observations. They were simply misled by what they saw. Chicken eggs seemed to show preformed chickens inside. Aphid eggs were observed to develop without fertilization. Preformed adult insects were seen tightly packed in insect eggs. All of this seemed to be convincing evidence for the correctness of the preformation theory.

Today, other explanations for these observations are known. The examinations of chicken eggs with "preformed individuals" were made in regions with warm climates. It is likely, therefore, that the eggs had already undergone considerable embryological development when they were examined. Aphid eggs often develop without fertilization, a phenomenon known as **parthenogenesis.** The insect eggs were probably not eggs at all, but rather the pupal stage of metamorphosis.

After 1800, more detailed observations made on the development of chicken eggs left little doubt that there were no preformed chickens inside. Aristotle's theory of epigenesis was revived.

**18–3
A NEW APPROACH**

For a long time, ideas about preformation and epigenesis were based entirely on observations of development. There was little attempt to perform experiments to support or overthrow either theory. In the late nineteenth century, however, men tired of simply observing developing eggs. They began to tamper with them. They recognized that there was an unknown mechanism within the egg that caused it to develop. This unknown mechanism could not be reached directly, so embryologists started to experiment with the environment surrounding the egg. In this way, they could observe the effects of certain environmental changes upon development. This switch to a more active means of investigation announced the birth of **experimental embryology.**

One of the first experiments performed in embryology was designed to test a modification of the preformation theory. Wilhelm Roux (1850–1924) rejected the idea of a completely preformed individual in the fertilized egg. He did, however, believe that certain *regions* in the egg were designed to become specific parts of the organism, much as individual tiles or stones contribute to a mosaic design. As a matter of fact, Roux's hypothesis is referred to as the **mosaic theory** (Fig. 18–2).

Roux tested his hypothesis experimentally. He allowed a fertilized frog's egg to divide into two cells, one of the first steps in embryological development. He then killed one of the cells with a hot needle. His reasoning was as follows:

*Hypothesis: If . . .*   there is a preformed pattern within the fertilized egg, . . .

*Prediction: then . . .* the one cell remaining alive should form only part of an embryo.

As Fig. 18–3 shows, this is precisely what occurred. Therefore, Roux felt that his mosaic theory was correct.

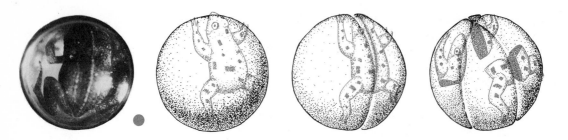

FIG. 18–2   At left is a rare photograph of the Puerto Rican frog *Eleutherodactylus portoricensis* (commonly known as the Coqui) taken just prior to hatching.  The Coqui is one of a few species of amphibians that go directly from egg to adult without an intermediate, free-swimming, tadpole stage. The circle at lower right gives the actual size of the jelly-coat sphere surrounding the animal.  At right are drawings illustrating the ''mosaic theory'' of Wilhelm Roux.  In his studies of developing frogs, Roux became convinced that certain portions of the egg were responsible for specific regions of the animal.  Thus the top half of the egg would develop into the head region, and the lower half would become the posterior region.  As cleavage continued, the duties of each cell would become more and more specific.  Thus Roux saw the early embryo as a mosaic, with each ''tile'' contributing to a part of the overall design.  (Photo at left courtesy Earl D. Hanson, Wesleyan University; specimen collected by J. J. W. Baker July 3, 1970, in Altamira, Puerto Rico.)

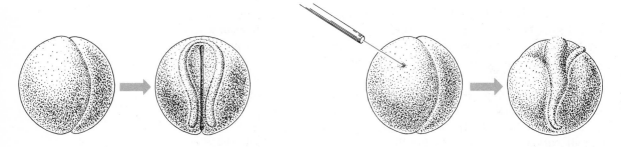

FIG. 18–3   By killing one of two cells in the early frog embryo (right), Roux at first obtained half-embryos.  Normal development is shown at left.

Roux's results were disputed by Hans Driesch (1867–1941).  Driesch performed a similar experiment, using sea urchin eggs.  However, instead of merely *killing* one of the cells at the two-cell stage, he removed one cell completely. The remaining cell grew into a complete adult sea urchin (Fig. 18–4).  This experiment seemed to completely refute the original preformation theory, as well as the mosaic theory of Roux.  If there had been a preformed individual within the egg, then only a half-embryo should have developed.

While the results obtained by Roux and Driesch were contradictory, later research showed this was not unusual.  In some species, eggs separated at the two-celled stage give rise to half-embryos; in others, complete embryos are formed.  In the sea urchin, separation of cells at even the four-celled stage gives four complete animals. On the other hand, an earthworm egg separated at the two-celled stage gives only half-embryos. Further investigation shows that in some organisms, cell materials are unequally distributed to the first cells formed, and thus complete development of separated cells does not occur.

It turned out that both Roux and Driesch were basically correct. The original idea of complete preformation was false. Yet, as the mosaic theory indicates, certain regions that are present early in the developing embryo are destined to become specific parts of the individual organism. Today, modern biochemical genetics and embryology have revived the preformation theory in a new form. It is now recognized that the embryo is "preformed" in the genetic code of DNA. In other words, the "blueprints" by which the embryo will be built are present in the genes of the fertilized egg. Since these genes are a combination of DNA that is both maternal (egg) and paternal (sperm) in origin, the offspring show features of construction resembling those of both parents. *The concern of modern embryology is the precise manner in which this construction is carried out.*

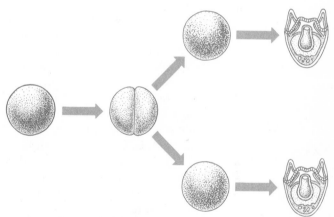

FIG. 18–4    Results obtained by Driesch on sea-urchin eggs. The two cells formed by the first cleavage after fertilization were separated, and both formed complete larvae.

While we can trace embryology back to Aristotle, most of the important work has been done in the nineteenth and twentieth centuries. Embryology developed with, and contributed to, many important generalizations of modern biology. Foremost among these are the theory of evolution, the development of modern genetics, the germ plasm theory of August Weismann (Section 2–5), and the controversy between vitalism and mechanism. In the last case, controversy arose from the experiments of Roux and Driesch. The results of Driesch's experiments seemed to him to indicate the presence of a mystical force. This force somehow kept track of the "blueprints" of the whole adult form. Driesch thus became a champion in the cause of vitalism. He was strongly opposed by Roux, and the arguments between the two men became long and bitter.

One prominent theory of the nineteenth century which contributed greatly to embryology was the **biogenetic law.** The biogenetic law was the brainchild of Fritz Muller (1821–1897) and Ernst Haeckel (1834–1919). It is often briefly stated as "ontogeny recapitulates phylogeny." As generally understood, this means that *the development of the individual (ontogeny) repeats (recapitulates) the evolutionary development of its group (phylogeny).*

The biogenetic law resulted from studies of the developing embryos of complex animals. It was noted that all embryos start out as one cell. So, it was reasoned, did the early evolution of all animals. Later, the embryo becomes a hollow, saclike form (the **gastrula**) with two main layers of cells. Animals of the phylum Cnidaria live as adults in this form. Next, the embryo develops a third layer, the **mesoderm,** which at first is relatively unspecialized. Animals of the phylum Platyhelminthes show this anatomical design. For many stages in embryological development, there seems to be an animal group with a similar adult anatomical pattern.

Considerable support was given the biogenetic law by the discovery that a human embryo, early in its development, has openings resembling gill clefts. Thus its passage through a fishlike stage was affirmed. Later, the embryo becomes covered with a fine hair. The kidney of a mammal is at first fishlike and later froglike, before its own type develops. The heart is at first two-chambered, like that of a fish, then three-chambered, like that of a frog, before it becomes four-chambered.

The development of reptilian embryos provided still more support for the biogenetic law. Snake embryos, for example, have limb buds, indicating a limbed ancestor. In some snakes, bones for these limbs are found buried within the adult as vestigial structures.

There can be little doubt that the biogenetic law did a great deal for embryology. Many talented men turned to the field for the excitement of finding more evidence to support the law. Unfortunately, in their eagerness to support it they often glossed over places where the evidence was less conclusive—or even contradictory. First of all, some stages simply are not shown by developing embryos, even though they are of such a nature that an evolving organism could hardly have bypassed them. Second, the order in which certain structures appear in embryos does not always follow the order in which they appeared in evolutionary history. In animal evolution, for example, teeth developed long before the tongue. Yet, in a mammalian embryo, the tongue appears first.

Actually, it is not at all surprising to find that the development of the embryo does not follow precisely the evolutionary path taken by its species. A developing embryo follows the most expedient path, one designed to use the available energy as efficiently as possible. It would not, therefore, repeat all the evolutionary stages of its ancestor, but only those vital to further development.

Gill clefts appear in man simply because the gene alleles influencing their development have not been eliminated by natural selection. The tissues involved in these gill clefts are used at a later stage of development to build other parts of the organism. Other stages were probably eliminated because the embryo had to adapt to the different surroundings in which it developed. For example, the reptilian embryo had to face quite different conditions within a shell on land than did its amphibian ancestor in the water. All this means that, throughout the history of animal life, embryos have had to evolve as well as adults. The embryonic development of present-day reptiles, for example, is not exactly like that of their primitive ancestors.

It is evident that the biogenetic law is not the all-encompassing concept it was originally thought to be. It contributed a great deal, however, to both evolutionary theory and embryology. When modified to fit present-day knowledge of development, the biogenetic law still serves a useful purpose.

**18–5**
**ENERGY FOR**
**DEVELOPMENT**

All living organisms require a source of energy. An embryo is certainly no exception to this rule.

The first food an organism receives in its life is often **yolk.** Yolk is a mixture of fatty compounds and proteins. The fatty compounds produce a rich source of energy and the proteins supply building materials for growth.

Almost everyone is familiar with the yolk of a chicken's egg. As in all birds' eggs, the amount of yolk is quite large. The eggs of reptiles, such as snakes, alligators, turtles, and lizards, also contain a great deal of yolk. Eggs of such animals as frogs and insects contain yolk, too, though far less than the eggs of reptiles and birds. The eggs of mammals, such as the cat, dog, rabbit, or man, contain very little yolk.

At first glance, this last statement is surprising. It seems that it would take far more energy and raw material to build a man than a baby chick, and, of course, it does. Why, then, does a human egg contain less yolk than the egg of a chicken?

The answer is quite simple. It lies in the manner in which each embryo develops. Consider first eggs with large amounts of yolk. Birds and reptiles lay their eggs with very young embryos already developing inside (fertilization, of course, has to take place *before* the shell is added to the egg). Until the egg hatches, the embryo has no source of food other than that provided by the yolk. Therefore, there must be enough yolk to supply energy and raw materials for complete development from fertilized egg to young animal.

Consider next the egg with an intermediate amount of yolk. This type of egg is produced by animals such as the frog and most insects. Like the chicken, these are complex animals, and it takes a great deal of energy to carry them from the fertilized egg to adulthood. However, the yolk of these eggs supplies just enough energy and building materials to carry development part of the way. By means of this energy, an intermediate, free-living stage is produced. This intermediate form is the **larva.** Larvae are capable of feeding, and thus storing up more food. The larva of the frog is the tadpole. Unlike the adult, the tadpole is vegetarian, and feeds on water plants. In addition, it gets energy and raw materials by gradually absorbing its tail. The moth larva, or caterpillar, is an example of an insect larva.* The caterpillar is notorious for its appetite. By feeding it stores up energy to be used for the final change into adult form. After a few weeks, the caterpillar spins a cocoon and changes into a **pupa.** Movement is at a minimum in the pupal stage; thus almost all the energy released from the food the larva ate can be used in the change to adulthood. This type of development is called **metamorphosis.** Complete or partial metamorphosis is typical of organisms that produce eggs with intermediate amounts of yolk.

Most mammalian eggs have very little yolk. Nor is there any mammalian larval stage. However, the small amount of yolk present is enough to get the fertilized egg through its early cell divisions. These divisions occur as the egg passes down the oviduct. When it enters the uterus, the egg becomes implanted in the uterine wall. Until birth, energy and raw materials come from the mother's bloodstream. In a very real sense, the developing embryo is a parasite.

Animals whose developing young are separate from the mother, and who derive their nourishment entirely from the egg yolk, are said to be **oviparous.** Fishes, amphibians, reptiles, and birds are nearly all oviparous. In some cases the young derive their nourishment from the yolk, but still develop within the mother's body. Such animals are said to be **ovoviviparous.** Two examples are the garter snake and the dogfish, or sand shark. In cases in which the embryo derives almost all of its food from the mother and develops within her body, the term **viviparous** is used. With a few exceptions, mammals are viviparous.

**18–6**
**THE BEGINNING OF**
**DEVELOPMENT**

Embryological development generally begins with fertilization. There are actually two processes involved in fertilization: first, activation of the egg, and second, uniting of egg and sperm nuclei. Since it involves the hereditary material, this last process falls within the sphere of genetics. As we learned in genetics, the meeting of gametes is a chance process. There is no evidence of attraction of one gamete by another. However, since large numbers of sperm are usually produced, since the egg is a large "target" (often thousands of times larger than the sperm), and since higher plants and animals have tubes or ducts to guide the sperm to the egg, the chances that fertilization will occur are greatly enhanced.

Once contact between the gametes is made, a chain of chemical and physical events is begun. For example, in the case of the sea urchin, the sperm become "sticky"; they clump together, or **agglutinate.** What causes sperm to agglutinate? From the fact that agglutination occurs when sperm contact the egg, it can be hypothesized that a chemical substance causing agglutination is produced by either the egg or its surrounding membranes. This hypothesis can be tested as follows.

---

* The grubs of beetles and the maggots of flies are two other examples.

***Hypothesis:*** *If . . .*    the egg or its surrounding membranes produce a chemical substance that causes sperm agglutination, . . .

***Prediction:*** *then . . .* sperm should agglutinate when placed in water which has previously held ripe eggs.

The prediction is verified; the hypothesis is supported. In 1914 a complex chemical substance composed of carbohydrate and protein and named **fertilizin** was identified as diffusing from the egg of the sea urchin. Sperm put into a fertilizin extract show agglutination. This suggests that sperm, too, may produce substances which react with the fertilizin to bring about agglutination. Extracts of sea-urchin sperm show the ability to dissolve the jelly coat surrounding the unfertilized egg. To these substances the term **antifertilizins** has been applied (Fig. 18–5). Antifertilizins and fertilizins combine in a specific way. The egg fertilizin of one species reacts best with a sperm antifertilizin of its own species. It is as if the sperm, if it is to penetrate the egg, must bring the correct "key" to open the egg's "lock."

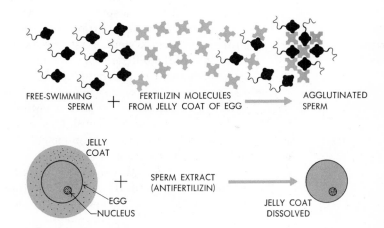

FREE-SWIMMING SPERM  +  FERTILIZIN MOLECULES FROM JELLY COAT OF EGG  →  AGGLUTINATED SPERM

JELLY COAT    +    SPERM EXTRACT (ANTIFERTILIZIN)  →  JELLY COAT DISSOLVED

EGG   NUCLEUS

FIG. 18–5   Sea-urchin sperm are agglutinated by a fertilizin extract from the egg jelly coat. In turn, sperm extract containing antifertilizins dissolves the jelly coat.

    Sperm show quite clearly a special structure, called the **acrosome,** in the tip of the head region. During sperm development, the acrosome can be shown to be derived from the Golgi apparatus. Exposed to a medium containing egg fertilizin, sperm show an "acrosome reaction"; the acrosome filament extrudes from the head end of the sperm. This filament makes the initial contact between sperm and egg, and, once contact is made, holds the sperm in place at the point of contact. It is possible that the acrosome filament may contract, pulling the sperm to the egg and bringing about the actual contact between sperm and egg cell membrane. Enzymes associated with the sperm acrosome then digest the egg cell membrane so that the sperm may enter. It is interesting that this enzyme (hyalurinodase) is the same enzyme secreted by many bacteria when they infect healthy cells.

The egg membrane responds physically to contact, also. It rises up to meet the sperm head, forming what is known as a **fertilization cone.** Formation of the fertilization cone is followed by a general lifting off of the outer egg membrane all around the cell, until a layer (the **hyaline layer**) is formed, separating the inner membrane from an outer membrane (the **fertilization membrane**). The inner membrane (the **vitelline membrane**) forms the new boundary layer of the egg cytoplasm. Thus a moat is formed after the initial contact of a sperm, and this moat serves to prevent the entry of other sperm.

The sperm cell maintains contact with the vitelline membrane so that, once the sperm cell membrane is broken, the sperm nucleus is released within the egg. The sperm centriole divides to provide the spindle for the first cleavage division. Precisely what happens to the female egg cell's centriole is unknown. There is evidence that it is present, because if the egg is caused to divide parthenogenetically, it forms a spindle of its own.

To summarize, fertilization is followed immediately by three major changes in the egg–sperm system: First, the egg membrane changes its permeability at contact so that a different sort of two-way movement in and out can take place. Second, there are drastic cytoplasmic changes; there is a considerable rearrangement of material, protein synthesis is initiated (prior to fertilization protein synthesis activity is either low or entirely absent), and the axes of the future embryo are established. Third, for many eggs, meiotic division, kept from completion until fertilization, is completed. The sperm centriole divides to form the spindle; there is a fusion of the two nuclei or, as they are termed, male and female **pronuclei.** It is at this point that the genetic material is united and the diploid or $2n$ status restored. However, the chromosomes align instantly at metaphase, since prophase and the chromosome replication which precedes prophase are already completed.

Considering the large volume of egg cytoplasm through which the sperm pronucleus must travel to get to the female pronucleus, it is a matter of some speculation as to how it manages to navigate successfully and arrive at its destination. The demonstrated presence of microtubules in the vicinity of the sperm and egg pronuclei has led to an hypothesis proposing that these microtubules may have something to do with the movement of the sperm pronucleus toward the egg pronucleus. Just how the microtubules move these sperm pronuclei is no more known than how the same types of microtubules may act to move the chromosomes at mitosis or the flagella and cilia characteristic of certain forms of animal or plant life. A "chemotaxis" hypothesis is also tempting; i.e., the egg pronucleus may give off some substance that might attract the sperm pronucleus to it. At this point the evidence is rather inconclusive, and there is still the problem of explaining the degeneration of all other male pronuclei

heading in that direction once one male pronucleus finds the egg pronucleus.*
Thus fertilization remains an area with room for almost as many hypotheses as
sperm, and to date there is a significant lack of crucial experiments to adequately
test the hypotheses now in existence.

Despite the rather obvious changes brought on by fertilization, very little
is known about what actually happens during the process. This is true even in
the much-studied sea urchin, from which most of the preceding information
concerning fertilization comes. (Figure 18–6 illustrates one hypothesis.)

FIG. 18–6    One hypothesis to account for fertilization pictures the process as a complex enzyme-
substrate reaction. The reactants are kept apart until wall B is removed. Since wall B might be removed
by a variety of chemical or physical means, this hypothesis could account for parthenogenesis as well.

That fertilization is not absolutely essential for development is shown by the
fact that some animals (aphids, drone bees) develop without it (by parthenogenesis). Parthenogenesis can also be carried out in the laboratory. Certain eggs
will begin development if pricked by a needle, exposed to chemicals or a temperature change, given electric shocks, or simply shaken. Normal frog development
has been obtained parthenogenetically in the laboratory. Two parthenogenetic
mammals (both rabbits) have been born alive. It seems certain, then, that no
one particular agent is absolutely necessary to start embryonic development.

The early development of an embryo is almost entirely epigenetic. This fact
presents a very complicated situation to the embryologist. If the embryo were
completely preformed, its development would be little more than a simple
growth in size. However, in epigenetic development, cellular differentiation
and specialization must take place at precisely the right time and place if the
individual is to be normal. Work on embryology has therefore been directed
toward the problem of just *how* complex and specialized regions of an organism
can arise from unspecialized cellular regions—for this is precisely what occurs.

In most higher organisms there are three such cellular regions, called the
**primary germ layers.** The primary germ layers are the first distinguishable

**18-7**
**EARLY**
**DEVELOPMENT**

---

* Contrary to popular belief, it is not uncommon for an egg to be entered by more than
one sperm.

TABLE 18–1  THE THREE PRIMARY GERM LAYERS AND SOME BODY PARTS THAT ARISE FROM THEM

| ECTODERM | MESODERM | ENDODERM |
|---|---|---|
| SKIN EPIDERMIS | ALL MUSCLES | LINING OF DIGESTIVE TRACT, TRACHEA, BRONCHI, AND LUNGS |
| HAIR AND NAILS | DERMIS OF SKIN | |
| SWEAT GLANDS | ALL CONNECTIVE TISSUE, BONE AND CARTILAGE | LIVER |
| ENTIRE NERVOUS SYSTEM, IN-CLUDING BRAIN, SPINAL CORD, GANGLIA, AND NERVES | DENTIN OF TEETH | PANCREAS |
| | | LINING OF GALL BLADDER |
| | BLOOD AND BLOOD VESSELS | THYROID, PARATHYROID, AND THYMUS GLANDS |
| NERVE RECEPTORS OF SENSE ORGANS | MESENTERIES | |
| | KIDNEYS | URINARY BLADDER |
| LENS AND CORNEA OF EYE | REPRODUCTIVE ORGANS | URETHRA LINING |
| LINING OF NOSE, MOUTH, AND ANUS | | |
| TEETH ENAMEL | | |

areas within the early animal embryo. They will give rise to the tissues and organs of the adult animal. The three primary germ layers are the **ectoderm** (outer skin), **mesoderm** (middle skin), and **endoderm** (inner skin). Table 18–1 shows some of the parts of the adult body that arise from each germ layer.

As we have just seen, embryological development generally begins with fertilization. The fertilized egg, or zygote, immediately becomes a beehive of biochemical activity. It soon undergoes its first mitotic division (**cleavage**). The resulting two daughter cells divide again, producing four. Each of these divides, giving eight cells. The eight soon become sixteen. As can be seen, early cleavages result in a geometric increase in cell number. Later, the increase in numbers is less precise. Eventually, however, a hollow ball of many hundreds of cells is formed.

Not all organisms show the same cleavage patterns. The amount of yolk present in an embryonic cell often determines the way in which it divides. Yolk is composed of very dense material. Thus yolk-laden cells divide more slowly than those containing less yolk. In the bird's egg, the yolk does not become divided into the individual cells at all.

The hollow ball of cells formed by cleavage is called a **blastula**. The cavity inside the blastula is called the **blastocoel**, and the blastula's cells are called **blastomeres.** It is interesting to note that the blastula, composed of many blastomeres, is often no larger than the original zygote from which it developed. There exists a critical relationship between cell size and the amount of cell membrane available for respiratory exchange. The unfertilized egg has a relatively low rate of metabolism; therefore, respiratory exchange is low. Once it is fertilized, however, things change. The zygote immediately divides several times, and these cleavages bring surface-volume proportions to a point which will sustain the greatly increased metabolic activity accompanying development (Fig. 18–7). Blastula formation also gives the embryo an adequate number of cells (essentially alike except for yolk content) for the first building blocks of the new organism.

Quite obviously the embryo cannot feed, so each cell must have its own source of energy and raw materials. Cleavage requires a great deal of energy. This energy is needed for the mechanics of mitosis and the synthesis of nucleic acid (which must occur during the chromosome replication accompanying each division). The formation of a blastula is followed by a process called **gastrulation**. The result of gastrulation is to produce another hollow ball of cells, the **gastrula**. The gastrula often resembles the blastula in appearance. Unlike the blastula, however, the early gastrula has at least *two* layers of cells, instead of only one.

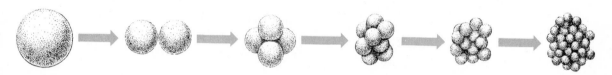

FIG. 18–7  As embryonic cleavage continues, there is little change in overall size. Instead, a greater surface-to-volume ratio is obtained—an essential factor in the respiration of active embryonic cells.

Gastrulation differs considerably from one animal to another. Once again, yolk is an important determining factor. If there is very little yolk, the side of the blastula simply pushes in, and the blastocoel is slowly obliterated. A new cavity, the **gastrocoel**, or **archenteron** (primitive gut), is formed. If there is a little more yolk, as in the frog blastula, invagination occurs more toward the top, or **animal** pole, of the blastula. The dense yolk-laden cells are concentrated at the bottom, or **vegetal** pole region. Finally, in yolk-laden eggs (birds, reptiles), invagination is greatly modified. It involves only those cells resting on top of the yolk mass.

An analogy may show how the yolk influences gastrulation. Imagine squeezing a soft rubber ball. If the ball is empty, one side can be pushed against the other. This might correspond to an *Amphioxus* blastula with little dense yolk. If the ball is half-filled with sand, only the top portion of the ball can be pushed in. This is similar to the intermediate yolk content of the frog's blastula. However, the ball almost completely filled with sand has only a small pinch of rubber at the top which can be moved. This is similar to the yolk-laden situation found in the eggs of birds. Here, invagination must be considerably modified from that which occurs in blastulas containing less yolk. However, no matter how gastrulation takes place, the net result is roughly the same; *three primary germ layers are formed.*

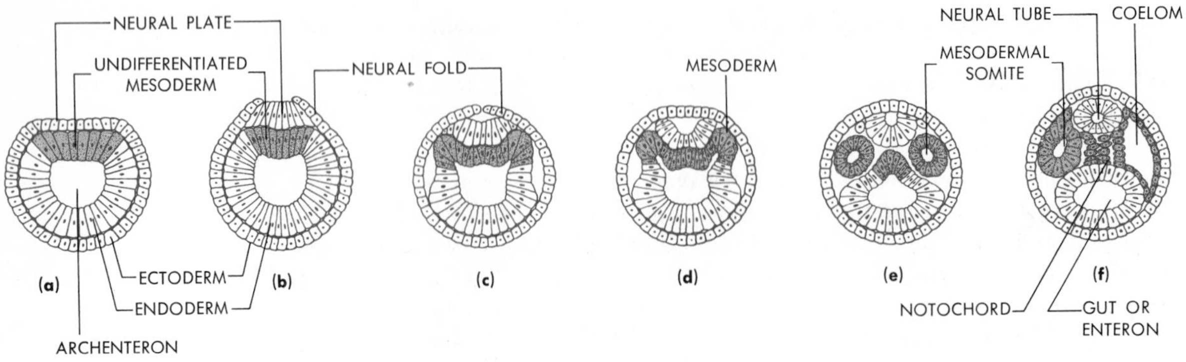

NEURAL PLATE
UNDIFFERENTIATED MESODERM
NEURAL FOLD
MESODERM
NEURAL TUBE COELOM
MESODERMAL SOMITE
ECTODERM
ENDODERM
ARCHENTERON
NOTOCHORD
GUT OR ENTERON

(a) (b) (c) (d) (e) (f)

FIG. 18–8 In *Amphioxus*, a primitive chordate, the mesoderm arises from the endoderm by pinching off, as shown. In the frog, the endoderm simply separates into two layers.

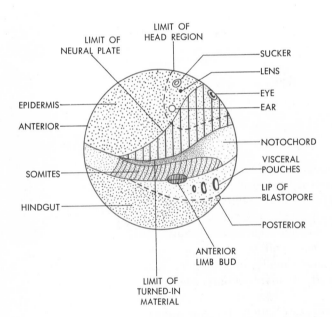

LIMIT OF HEAD REGION
LIMIT OF NEURAL PLATE
SUCKER
LENS
EPIDERMIS
ANTERIOR
EYE
EAR
NOTOCHORD
VISCERAL POUCHES
SOMITES
LIP OF BLASTOPORE
HINDGUT
POSTERIOR
ANTERIOR LIMB BUD
LIMIT OF TURNED-IN MATERIAL

FIG. 18–9 By the time the embryo is in the late blastula or early gastrula stage, it is often possible to predict what tissues and organs will be formed by many embryonic regions. (After Vogt.)

Return for a moment to the analogy of the empty rubber ball. If you squeeze it so that one wall touches the other, you eliminate the inner cavity. This corresponds to the obliteration of the blastocoel. By so doing, however, your fingers form another cavity, corresponding to the archenteron. Note that this new cavity differs from the old one in two important respects. First, it opens to the exterior. This opening corresponds to the **blastopore**. Second, the new cavity is enclosed within a *double-* rather than a single-layered wall. Similarly, in the embryo, the archenteron becomes surrounded by a double layer of cells, of which the outer layer is the ectoderm. With the formation of the mesoderm (by segregation from the endoderm in amphibians), the three primary germ layers are established. In *Amphioxus*, the mesoderm gradually spreads downward to lie between the endoderm and ectoderm (Fig. 18–8). The result is an embryo with three primary germ layers.

With the formation of the primary germ layers, a new phase of development begins. The three layers differ in their location and purpose. However, the cells of which they are composed are still very much alike in appearance.

From here on, however, *development becomes more obviously a process of cellular differentiation and specialization*, instead of simply cellular divisions and migrations. As early as the blastula stage, certain regions whose cell descendants will become part of the liver have been experimentally demonstrated. Another region in the ectoderm of the gastrula will give rise to certain cells in the brain (Fig. 18–9).

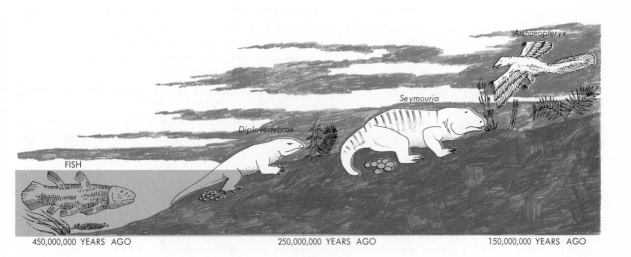

FIG. 18–10   As long as living organisms were entirely aquatic in habitat, the egg could remain relatively simple in its external design. With the evolution of land-dwelling forms, however, radical changes were necessary for the egg to survive and develop.

In the evolution of animals from water-dwelling to land-dwelling forms, many anatomical and physiological changes were necessary. The fossil record shows that it took many millions of years of natural selection to bring about a complete change from fins to feet and gills to lungs (Fig. 18–10).

Yet, if the changes were considerable for the adult body form, they were even greater for the egg. The amphibians are often considered to represent a sort of "middle-ground" form in water-to-land evolution. Yet, anatomically speaking, the toad is as terrestrial as any reptile. It is their *egg* that keeps the amphibians water bound, their *egg* that makes them as dependent on water as any fish for the continuance of their class. The amphibian egg is water-dependent from the very start.* The eggs are shed, fertilized, and develop in water. A protective jelly coat soon surrounds each, a coat formed by the absorption of water. Water supplies oxygen and carries off metabolic wastes. Water serves as a shock absorber to prevent damage to the eggs from sudden jarring. Indeed, the complexity of the amphibian egg is an *internal* complexity; on the outside, the presence of water allows the luxury of simplicity.

Not so with the land-dwellers. For them, from reptiles to the most primitive mammals, elaborate means had to be evolved to permit the development of embryos on land. An egg not directly in the water must have and hold its own fluid environment. Thus an evaporation-resistant shell is essential. An egg out of water must still get oxygen and get rid of carbon dioxide. Thus the shell must be porous, to allow exchange of gases with the atmosphere.

Nor is this all. Special **extraembryonic membranes** are necessary. In the birds and reptiles, the **allantois** is needed to hold solid, nondiffusible nitrogenous wastes until they can be discarded at hatching. In birds, the allantois also weakens the shell by reabsorbing calcium, and thus enables the young bird to peck its way out. Another extraembryonic membrane, the **amnion,** surrounds the embryo with a watery fluid to prevent damage from shock or adhesion to the shell. Finally, a **yolk sac** is necessary to gradually supply the food stored in the yolk to the developing embryo.

With the evolution of mammalian **intrauterine** (within the uterus) development, the egg, in a very real sense, returns to the sea. The bloodstream of the mother is a "sea" of great versatility. It can carry oxygen and waste materials to and from the embryo far more efficiently than any ocean. It is a sea constantly circulated by the mother's heart and kept at an even, warm temperature, ideal for the enzyme-catalyzed chemistry of development. With such a well-protected place in which to develop, the mammalian embryo makes different use of the extraembryonic membranes it inherited from its ancestors. Unlike those of the birds and the reptiles, mammalian nitrogenous wastes are excreted in a form that can be passed into the mother's bloodstream by diffusion. The allantois, therefore, no longer stores waste products, but becomes intimately associated with another membrane, the **chorion.** The chorion surrounds the embryo and sends out fingerlike projections called **chorionic villi** into the uterine wall. The fusion of a chorion with the wall of the uterus forms the **placenta,** in which the bloodstream of the embryo and mother are brought close together for respiratory and excretory exchange. Nutrients also pass from the mother to child through the placenta.

The placenta is a most remarkable organ. It is a gut, a pair of lungs, a kidney, a liver, and an endocrine gland combined into one. Many substances that reach the embryo from the mother pass through the placenta by active

---

* There are several notable exceptions, as the theory of evolution by natural selection might predict.

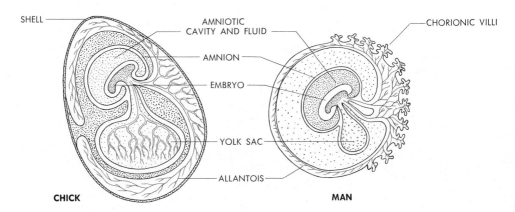

SHELL — AMNIOTIC CAVITY AND FLUID — CHORIONIC VILLI — AMNION — EMBRYO — YOLK SAC — ALLANTOIS

**CHICK**          **MAN**

FIG. 18–11   The chick and human embryo exhibit the same embryonic membranes, but make different uses of them. One major difference is the yolk sac, which in the chick supplies food and in man is a vestigial structure, serving no known function.

transport. The placental cells expend energy and do work in pulling materials out of the mother's blood and pushing them into the embryo's blood, often against a concentration gradient.

The placenta does not just function for the direct benefit of the child. It also secretes hormones which enlarge the maternal mammary glands to bring them to a condition in which they are capable of secreting milk.

The yolk sac, of course, is of no selective value to the maternally nourished mammalian embryo. As might be expected, it is only in the most primitive mammals that the yolk sac serves any purpose. In higher forms, it remains only as a small, vestigial structure. The amnion continues to serve as a shock absorber, and provides a fluid environment in which the embryo can develop (Fig. 18–11).

The experimental embryologist asks questions of nature. In asking these questions, he may subject embryos to various changes from their normal path of development. They may be exposed to chemicals, chopped into pieces, spun in a centrifuge, squeezed, stretched, twisted, crushed, shaken . . . the sky is no limit in trying to ask questions that will provide meaningful answers.

Let's just ask one deceptively simple question: What makes a tissue? It might seem that this question was answered earlier. The primary germ layers (the ectoderm, mesoderm, and endoderm) give rise to the very specialized tissues and organs of the body. Yet, we are still left with the question of *how* the primary germ layers give rise to these parts. What factors, for example, cause the descendants of certain endodermal cells to become parts of the intestinal lining, while others end up in the thyroid gland? It is perhaps understandable that in the face of such seemingly unanswerable questions, some of the early embryologists were vitalists!

**18-9
EXPERIMENTAL
EMBRYOLOGY**

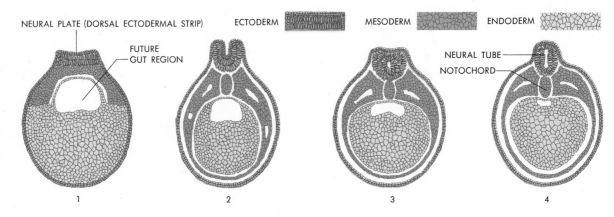

FIG. 18–12  A cross-sectional view of neural tube formation in the frog embryo. Note that the neural plate sinks inward and rolls into a tubelike shape. Later, cartilage and bone will form around the notochord and neural tube to form the spinal column.

Fortunately, however, vitalistic attitudes did not prevail for long. Soon men began to probe for better answers, answers that could be supported by experimental evidence.

In the developing amphibian embryo, the neural tube is a hollow cylindrical tissue which will eventually develop into the brain and spinal cord. The neural tube is formed from ectoderm lying on the surface of the early embryo. The ectoderm rolls into a tube and sinks into the underlying mesoderm area (Fig. 18–12). To understand the following experiment, study this figure carefully.

Since the neural tube does originate from ectoderm, it might be wondered if the neural tube would form from ectoderm which has been isolated from an embryo considerably before it begins neural-tube formation. To find out, we can remove ectodermal regions destined to form neural tubes from some frog embryos and culture them in a separate medium.

This experiment asks an important question. It seeks to determine whether the development of a neural tube is caused by intrinsic factors residing within the ectodermal region involved, or by extrinsic factors contingent upon the location of the ectodermal region within the embryo. The results of the experiment seem to provide a definite answer. In no case are neural tubes formed by the isolated pieces of ectoderm. The embryos from which the ectodermal pieces were surgically removed do not develop a neural tube either, presumably because they were deprived of cells which would ordinarily have given rise to this structure.

It seems evident, then, that extrinsic factors from the surrounding environment of the embryo's body mass are responsible for the formation of a neural tube by the ectodermal region. The next question to be posed is: From what region of the embryo do these extrinsic factors originate? A logical choice is the mesoderm, since the neural-tube-forming ectoderm rests on top of it. An experiment can be performed to test an hypothesis proposing the mesoderm as the source of these extrinsic factors:

**Hypothesis:** *If . . .*   the mesoderm contributes extrinsic factors to the overlying ectoderm to cause it to form a neural tube, . . .

**Prediction:** *then . . .* mesodermal cells, wrapped in a sheet of ectoderm isolated from an embryo at the same stage as in the previous experiment, will cause the formation of neural tissue by this ectoderm.

Such an experiment was performed by the embryologist J. Holtfreter. The results were as predicted; the sheet of ectoderm enclosing the mesoderm differentiated into neural tissues.

A truly great experimental embryologist was the German investigator Hans Spemann (1869–1941). Working with amphibian embryos (salamander and frog), Spemann set out to answer some of the questions posed by differentiation of the primary germ layer.

Spemann called the action of the mesoderm on the ectoderm one of **embryonic induction.** He hypothesized that the mesoderm *induces* the ectoderm to differentiate into the neural tube. Such inducing tissues he spoke of as "organizers," since they seemed able to organize other tissues into definite regions of the embryo. For example, Spemann knew that the eye lens in the frog, *Rana fusca*, is formed by a process of induction. Like the neural tube, the eye lens forms from ectoderm, this time ectoderm in the eye region of the embryo. However, Spemann also saw that there was not just one inductive process at work here. In eye formation, the head mesoderm induces formation of the brain, and the middle region of this brain induces the formation of the optic nerve and vesicle; the optic vesicle, in turn, induces the formation of the eye lens from the ectoderm. Working backwards, Spemann could visualize the embryo as being built by progressively less specific inducing tissues, or organizers. Thus the organizer that induces lens formation from the ectoderm is a specific organizer, with a limited range of responsibilities. The organizer that induces brain formation has a wide range of responsibilities, including in its chain of command the eye lens, as well as many other head parts. Somewhere in this chain of induction, there had to be a tissue responsible for organizing the entire organism.

In the newly fertilized frog and salamander egg, a region called the **gray crescent** appears. Spemann had experimented with the gray crescent before. He knew that if he tied a fertilized salamander egg into two halves so that a portion of the gray crescent extended into each half, two normal embryos eventually resulted. If, on the other hand, he tied the egg so that only one half had the gray crescent, only this half developed normally. The other half produced an unorganized ball of belly tissue (Fig. 18–13).

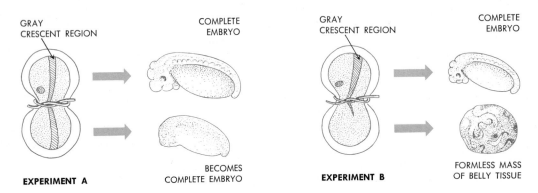

FIG. 18–13    The results of these experiments convinced Spemann that the primary organizer would be found near the region of the gray crescent. Although in experiment A only the half containing the nucleus developed at first, two complete embryos were eventually formed. (Adapted from John W. Kimball, *Biology*, 2nd edition. Reading, Mass.: Addison-Wesley, 1968.)

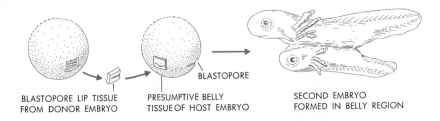

FIG. 18–14    This experiment, for which Spemann received a Nobel prize, showed the dorsal lip of the blastopore to have primary organizer capabilities.

With these experimental results in mind, Spemann turned his attention to cells associated with the gray crescent. Those cells are located on the dorsal lip of the blastopore, which is formed just below the area of the gray crescent. He considered that these cells might possibly be the primary organizers for which he was looking.

They were. Taking blastopore lip cells from one salamander embryo, he transplanted them into presumptive belly tissue of another. The host cells would ordinarily have formed the ventral areas of the salamander. However, when dorsal blastopore tissue was put among them, their future was changed. The result was not just the formation of a brain or an eye lens. Instead, a *complete new embryo* was induced, joined to the other like a Siamese twin (Fig. 18–14).

The importance of this experiment cannot be overemphasized. It, and Spemann's subsequent work, led to his receiving a Nobel Prize in 1935. Spemann published the results of his experiment in 1924, in coauthorship with his graduate student Hilde Mangold. In this one paper, he gave reality to the concept of epigenesis and supported his hypothesis of inductive organizers. *From this point on, embryologists began to picture development of the embryo as a series of inductive processes, with each member of the series being essential for the development of the members that follow it.* Thus, for example, the eye lens would not form if the optic vesicle were removed; the optic vesicle would not form if the midbrain were removed; the midbrain would not form if the head mesoderm were removed; and, finally, *nothing would form if the primary organizer, the dorsal lip of the blastopore, were removed.*

Having found the primary organizer, Spemann was at a loss to explain its nature. His experiments had not revealed the precise manner by which induction was carried out. Obviously, much more research was needed.

In the development of the neural tube, the mesoderm acts as an organizer. It provides the extrinsic factors that induce the ectoderm region to build the portion of the embryo (the neural tube) for which it is responsible. What is the nature of these extrinsic factors? *How* does the mesoderm send its instructions to the ectoderm, causing it to differentiate into neural tissue? It could not be a nervous transmission, for nerve fibers have not yet been formed. Might it be some sort of chemical transmission? Could a substance be diffusing from the mesoderm to the ectoderm, inducing it to differentiate into nerve tissue? This hypothesis deserves some testing.

If an underlying organizer tissue is separated by a thin piece of impermeable material from the tissue it is supposed to induce to differentiate, no differentiation takes place. Note, however, that although this experiment may support the hypothesis that a chemical is involved in induction, the results are far from conclusive. It may well be that physical contact between cells, rather than any chemical substance, is necessary for differentiation to occur.

If a synthetic membrane with pores so small that only individual molecules can pass through it is placed between inducing tissue and the tissue which it normally induces, differentiation *does* occur. This supports the hypothesis that an organizer substance diffuses from the inducing tissue. Yet this experiment still does not satisfactorily rule out the possibility that physical contact may also play a role.

Two embryologists, V. C. Twitty and M. C. Niu, tried a different approach. They used the hanging-drop technique of tissue culture designed by the embryologist Ross G. Harrison. The hanging-drop technique has been of great value to experimental embryology (Fig. 18–15). Into half of their hanging-drop cultures, Twitty and Niu placed organizing mesoderm. The other cultures, serving as controls, received no mesoderm. After a few hours, the mesoderm was removed from the experimental cultures, and ectoderm was placed into both experimental and control cultures. In the experimental cultures that held the mesoderm, the ectoderm differentiated into neural tissues. In the control cultures, no differentiation took place. It seemed obvious that the mesoderm released some substance into the culture medium that induced differentiation in

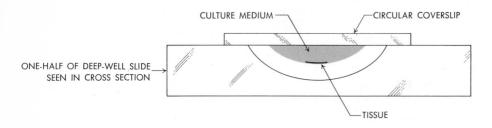

FIG. 18–15   The hanging-drop technique, developed by embryologist Ross G. Harrison.

the ectoderm. Chemical analysis of the culture medium that had held mesoderm was a logical next step. The analyses showed traces of nucleic acid.

The discovery of nucleic acid makes possible the formulation of a very tempting hypothesis. The nucleic acid might, of course, be DNA, a carrier of the genetic code for building structural proteins. Or it might be RNA, transmitter of the code from DNA to the construction sites of proteins within the cells. Due to its greater range of movement, RNA is the likelier choice of the two.

Our hypothesis, then, might go something like this: The organizing mesoderm sends out RNA molecules to the overlying ectoderm, causing it to differentiate into neural tissue. Since the RNA carries the hereditary message coded on DNA, this ensures that the ectoderm will differentiate into a neural tube typical of its own species and not that of another. This is a very workable hypothesis, since it explains both the nature of the organizer and why organisms are built according to their inherited plans.

Often, a search through the research literature in a field of science will reveal that a certain experiment provides a test of an hypothesis it was not originally designed to test. In relation to our RNA-organizer hypothesis, such an experiment was performed by the embryologist O. E. Schotté. Schotté transplanted a cell region which would ordinarily form frog flank tissue to the mouth region of an older salamander embryo (Fig. 18–16). This experiment asked an important question: Would the piece of frog tissue destined to become flank tissue still do so in the region in which a mouth is needed? In other words, do certain inherited factors within the frog tissue determine its fate, or does the environment (i.e., the surrounding salamander tissue) do so?

The experimental results showed that *the presumptive flank skin tissue of the frog formed a mouth.* This result fits well with our RNA hypothesis of the organizer. Since the RNA from the underlying salamander mesoderm would transmit the genetic code of its DNA, we would expect it to instruct the frog tissue to form a mouth. The transplanted cells seem to "listen" to what organizer substances from the salamander tissues tell them to do, rather than follow the pattern of their own normal future.

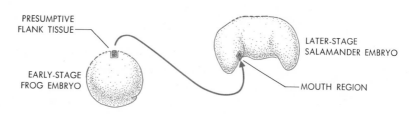

PRESUMPTIVE
FLANK TISSUE

EARLY-STAGE
FROG EMBRYO

LATER-STAGE
SALAMANDER EMBRYO

MOUTH REGION

FIG. 18–16  Oscar E. Schotté's experiment. The results indicate that while the organizer determines in general what organs are to be formed, the genes of the differentiating tissue control the details of those organs.

However, close examination of the *kind* of mouth formed showed that it was distinctly one of a frog larva, and *not* one of a salamander!  Our RNA hypothesis must therefore be considerably modified.  It is obvious that instructions from genes residing within the frog tissue were used in mouth construction, rather than those from the genes residing in the inducing salamander tissue. RNA may still be an organizer, but in a general, rather than a specific, manner.

The organizer, then, seems to give only general instructions as to what kind of structure is to be formed.  The genes of the tissue being induced determine what style of structure will be built.  The organizer might be imagined as a sort of boss who hands out general orders.  The induced tissue contains employees who are responsible for the details of carrying out the boss's orders.  The kind of job that is done depends upon the particular skills and training of these employees.

Any embryologist who might at this point have been inclined to turn to vitalistic hypotheses and attribute some mysterious or miraculous power to the primary organizer was in for a rude shock.  It was soon discovered that the ability to induce differentiation, far from being unique, was widespread.  Even chemicals foreign to living matter, such as the synthetic dye methylene blue, can induce the formation of neural tissue.  Furthermore, organizer tissues that have been subjected to a variety of physical and chemical treatments (such as crushing, freezing, heating, or killing in alcohol) can still induce some degree of differentiation.  In the light of such experiments, as well as the one performed by Schotté, it seems obvious that the action of organizing agents, whatever their nature, is trivial in comparison to the preexisting information stored within the responding cells.

## 18-10
## REGENERATION

Many embryologists never work with embryos.  They devote their full research time to studying **regeneration,** the replacement of lost parts by a living organism.

There are several reasons for this.  A developing embryo allows the study of **morphogenesis** (the development of form).  So does a regenerating organ.

A developing embryo shows cellular division, migration, differentiation, and specialization.  So does a regenerating organ.  Furthermore, a regenerating organ, such as an arm or a leg, has distinct advantages over an embryo for developmental study.  In some embryos, separation from the mother is impossible.  Many embryos are delicate, and hard to culture in the laboratory.  It is partly because they show fewer of these disadvantages that the embryos of sea urchins, starfish, frogs, salamanders, and birds are to embryology as *Drosophila melanogaster* and *Neurospora crassa* are to genetics.  Still, each of these types of embryos presents its own particular problems.

On the other hand, animals capable of regeneration are often quite hardy.  Their survival in the laboratory is good.  Furthermore, just as a regenerating limb is comparable to a developing embryo, *so the animal on which the limb is regenerating is comparable to a complex culture medium*, except that no experimenter could ever hope to provide such an ideal means of supplying the proper nutrient materials and removing wastes.  This is not to say that the processes of regeneration and embryonic development are primarily the same.  Actually, the two processes differ greatly.  Most obvious, perhaps, is the fact that a regenerating organ develops closely associated with adult tissues and, indeed, is both nourished by and develops from them.  An embryo, on the other hand, either grows apart from the adult or is separated from its tissues.  Nevertheless, there are also striking similarities which make both phenomena of tremendous interest to the developmental biologist.

We might briefly review what is known concerning regeneration.

If a sponge is chopped into a hundred parts, a hundred new sponges result.  A starfish cut in half gives two starfish.  Tear a claw from a lobster, and a new claw grows.  We might wonder, therefore, if there is any limit to the power of living organisms to repair damage.

The answer is, distinctly, yes.  In man, the limitations are quite obvious.  Anything larger than a small cut is often repaired imperfectly, leaving a visible scar.  A lost arm or leg is gone forever.  It would seem that, in general, *the lower an animal is on the scale of complexity, the greater its powers of regeneration.*  In other words, the relationship is an *inverse* one.  Thus, animals such as planaria or *Hydra* are generally capable of far more regeneration than the vertebrates.

As always, there are exceptions.  The only vertebrate that can regenerate limbs throughout its life span is the salamander.  This animal, therefore, is widely used in research on regeneration.

If the salamander can regenerate limbs, why cannot its close relatives, the Anura (toads and frogs) do so?  In the latter, limb regenerative powers are generally lost at metamorphosis (with some variations occurring from species to species).  In 1768, Lazzaro Spallanzani wrote:

*But if those species (frogs) are able to renew their legs when young, why should they not do the same when farther advanced? . . . Are the wonderful reproductions hitherto mentioned (in salamanders) only to be ascribed to the effect of water in which these animals were kept? This is contradicted in the instance of the salamander, whose parts were reproduced even on dry ground. But if the above-mentioned animals, either aquatic or amphibian, recover their legs when kept on dry ground, how comes it to pass that other land animals . . . are not embued with the same power? Is it to be hoped that they may acquire them by some useful dispositions?*

The only readily available anuran that can regenerate recognizable limbs after amputation is the South African clawed toad, *Xenopus laevis*. A number of embryologists, therefore, work with this organism.

Regeneration in *Xenopus laevis* can first be examined on the morphological level. In other words, the *form* of the regenerated limb can be compared with that of a normal limb. In this way, the overall success of the regenerative process can be estimated.

Several *Xenopus laevis* larvae are subjected to limb amputation at various times in their development. In the youngest animals, the amputated portions are simply limb buds, not yet showing external evidence of differentiation and specialization. In older larva, the amputated limbs are advanced to the stage of having the full number of toes, with webbing between them. Amputations are also performed on intermediate developmental stages at which the limbs show corresponding intermediate amounts of differentiation. The photographs in Fig. 18–17 show the results. They support the following generalization: *the capacity of the hind limb of Xenopus laevis for regeneration declines as the age of the animal increases.* In other words, the relationship is an inverse one.

Why should this be so? Why should a younger animal be better able to regenerate a lost limb than an older one? To find the answers to these questions the tissues and cells of the regenerating limbs can be studied, using the techniques shown in Fig. 18–18. By studying several slides of amputated and regenerated stumps of *Xenopus laevis* larvae, it can be seen that a sequence of events has occurred. A few hours after amputation, migrating epidermal cells form a protecting cap over the wound. Damaged and dead cells are demolished and removed. Finally, and most important, a small group of unspecialized regeneration cells appear. These cells are the beginning of a cone-shaped mass of unspecialized cells, collectively called the **blastema.** *The appearance of a blastema is typical and universal in limb regeneration. It is from the cells of the blastema that the new limb originates.*

Since this much is known, histological (tissue) and cytological (cellular) studies of limb stumps give a clue as to why younger animals are capable of more regeneration than older ones. First, as the animals get older, the number of regeneration cells that contribute to blastema formation is smaller (relative to the mass of the stump). Correspondingly, the blastema is smaller; thus there are fewer cells available to produce the new limb. Second, the regeneration cells themselves are less "embryonic" in appearance; in other words, *they are less*

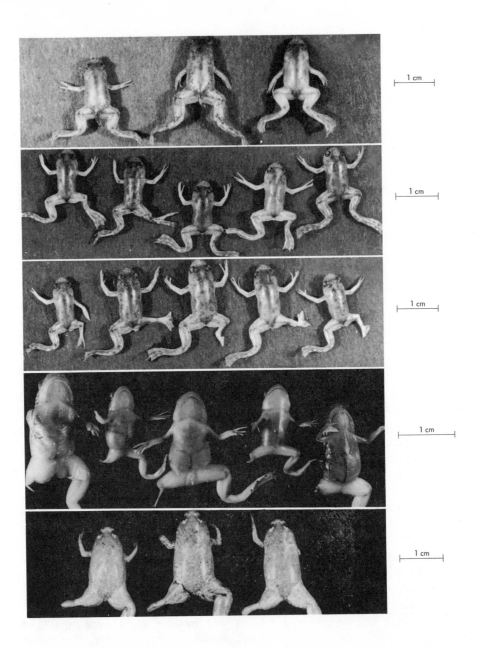

FIG. 18–17   Each of these South African clawed toads (*Xenopus laevis*) had one hind leg amputated.   From top to bottom rows, however, the amputations were done at progressively later developmental stages.   Note that as amputation was performed at later and later stages, the degree of regeneration decreased progressively.   (Photos courtesy Dr. James N. Dent, The University of Virginia.)

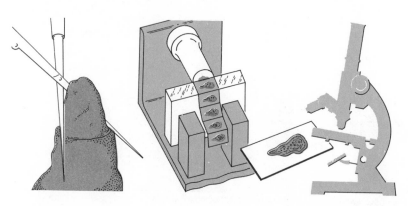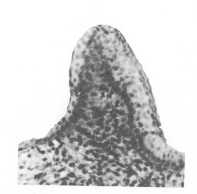

FIG. 18–18   Histological studies of regenerating limbs are prepared as shown above.   After being sectioned on a microtome, the specimen is stained and examined under a microscope.   Note the unspecialized nature of the cells in the stump.   (Photo courtesy Dr. James N. Dent, The University of Virginia.)

*undifferentiated.*   Research seems to indicate that *an animal's capacity for natural regeneration decreases as the degree of tissue differentiation increases.* From this, it might follow that a highly specialized cell, such as a neuron, would be poor at regenerating—and neurons generally are.   On the other hand, unspecialized mesenchyme cells, such as are found in sponges, have considerable regenerative ability.   For a specialized cell to regain regenerative abilities, it must first "dedifferentiate," i.e., revert to an unspecialized state.   In examining the stump cells from *Xenopus laevis* larvae whose limbs have been amputated, such a dedifferentiation is observed.   For example, muscle cells in a stump lose their striations, and seem less specialized in character.

From such studies, three tentative generalizations can be made.   First, *in general*, the lower an animal is on the evolutionary scale of complexity, the greater its powers of regeneration.   Second, there is an inverse correlation between the age of a *Xenopus laevis* larva at the time of amputation and the amount of regeneration that occurs.   Third, noting that a younger larva has more undifferentiated cells to contribute to blastema formation than an older one, we can suspect that the more differentiated a cell, the lower its potentiality for dedifferentiation and regeneration.   This third generalization is related to the first one.   The degree of cell and tissue specialization is often a distinguishing feature between lower and higher forms.   Compare, for example, the relatively simple organization of *Hydra* with the correspondingly complex organization of a mammal.

However, does the fact that certain animals (such as frogs) do not regenerate lost limbs mean that their cells have completely lost the ability to do so?   Or, might this observation simply indicate that amputation of a frog's leg, followed by no other experimental procedures, does not provide a situation in which the regenerative potentialities of its cells are aroused?   It has already been noted

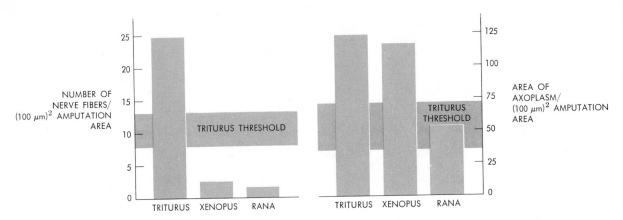

FIG. 18–19    An hypothesis proposing that it is the number of nerve fibers per unit area that accounts for the presence or absence of limb regenerative ability nicely accounts for the ability of the salamander (*Triturus*) to regenerate and the frog's (*Rana*) inability to do so.   But this hypothesis is contradicted by the South African clawed toad (*Xenopus*), which *can* regenerate (left graph).   Singer's hypothesis, proposing that it is the ratio between the cross-sectional area of the nerve and the cross-sectional area of the limb that determines regenerative ability, has greater success.   Note that the frog is on the threshold of regenerative ability, which could account for the success of Singer and others in inducing forelimb regeneration in this animal.

that a salamander will regenerate a complete new limb after amputation, while its close relative, the frog, will not.   One is naturally inclined to find out what differences might exist between these two closely related animals which could account for their dissimilarity in regenerative ability.   One such difference is purely morphological—the frog limb is quite massive; the salamander's, tiny. It had been shown as early as 1823 that even the salamander could not regenerate a limb if the nerves supplying it were first cut.   This demonstrated importance of nerve tissue to regeneration led Case Western Reserve University's Dr. Marcus Singer to hypothesize that the low ratio of nerve tissue to other tissues in the frog's limb, as compared to its relatively high ratio in the salamander's thin limb, might be responsible for the difference in the regenerative ability of the two animals (see Fig. 18–19).   His reasoning was as follows:

**Hypothesis:** *If* . . .   the differences between the regenerative ability of frogs and salamanders are attributable to differences in mass ratio between neural and other types of tissues in their limbs, . . .

**Prediction:** *then* . . . experimentally increasing the amount of neural tissue supplying a frog's limb might be sufficient to induce regeneration after amputation.

In 1954, Dr. Singer diverted the iliac nerve supplying the hind leg of a frog into its arm.   He then amputated the doubly-innervated appendage.   Regeneration occurred. Later, other investigators showed that the same regeneration would take place if adrenal glands were implanted into the stump. Thus neural tissue was not the only factor that could induce regeneration. Even before Singer, L. W. Polezhayev of the U.S.S.R. managed to achieve the regeneration of the forelimb of an adult frog by repeatedly injuring the wound, and S. Meryl Rose of the University of Illinois achieved the same result by immersing the stump many times in a strong salt solution. Thus at least some of Spallanzani's "useful dispositions" (see page 607) have been identified. In 1968 Tulane University's Dr. Merle Mizell showed that the hind legs of an immature opossum can be induced to show regenerative responses if developing brain tissues from the cerebral cortex are implanted two to four days before amputation through the implant region.

It would seem, then, that regeneration is the result of a complex interaction between organismal factors (such as the effect of the nervous and endocrine systems) rather than only of genetic conditions already determined within the cellular materials of regenerating limbs. It must be noted, however, that the regenerative frog limbs produced by the experiments of Singer and others were imperfect ones.

We might wonder *why* these limbs were imperfect. Were their imperfections due to experimental factors, or were they due to genetic factors residing within the nuclei of the cells of the regenerating stumps?

To answer this question, the problem of morphogenesis and its accompanying cell differentiation and specialization can be approached from still a different direction. An interesting situation (which is parallel to the regeneration of frog limbs under the proper experimental conditions) is found in the history of work on the organization of dissociated cells and tissue masses. In the early twentieth century, Dr. H. V. Wilson, of the University of North Carolina, squeezed living sponges through a fine cloth, obtaining a dense suspension of cells. These cells soon organized into clumps, each of which eventually developed into a complete sponge.

The sponge, however, is a very primitive animal. Since no such reorganization of separated cells into tissues had been demonstrated in higher organisms, it was assumed to be impossible in higher forms of animal life. Once again, as in the case of limb regeneration, it was assumed that higher organisms had an inherent inability to reorganize and regenerate.

Since the 1940's, this idea has been thoroughly dispelled. For example, Dr. A. A. Moscona, at the University of Chicago, has mixed suspensions of kidney-tubule-forming cells from a chick embryo with cartilage-forming cells from a mouse embryo. When such mixing is done, the chick cells clump together to form kidney tubules. The mouse cells clump together to form cartilage (Fig. 18–20).

The results of this experiment pose an interesting question. Did the chick cells clump with chick cells and the mouse cells with mouse cells because they were from the same species? Or was it because they have similar formative duties?

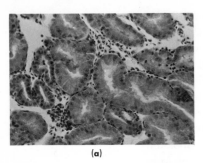
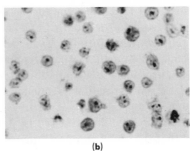
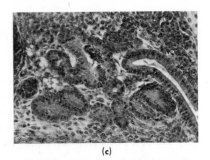

(a)                              (b)                              (c)

FIG. 18–20    Chick embryo kidney tissue consists of several cell types organized into tubules (a). Treatment with enzymes separates the tissues into individual living cells (b). Under appropriate conditions, the cells come together in masses and become organized into typical kidney structures (c). Such powers of reorganization were once thought to be limited to the simplest forms of life. (Photos courtesy Dr. A. A. Moscona, University of Chicago.)

A crucial experiment can be performed to test both suggested hypotheses:

**Hypothesis:** *If . . .*     intrinsic or inherent factors (i.e., species type) determine the reorganization fate of dissociated cells, . . .

**Prediction:** *then . . .* a mixture of embryonic chick and mouse cartilage-forming cells will segregate and clump together with those of their own species.

On the other hand:

**Hypothesis:** *If . . .*     extrinsic, or environmental, factors (i.e., some communication between cells of different species regarding their cartilage-forming role) determine the reorganization fate of dissociated cells, . . .

**Prediction:** *then . . .* a mixture of embryonic chick and mouse cartilage-forming cells will clump together to form a mosaic of chick-mouse cartilage.

Dr. Moscona has performed this experiment. Its results refute the first hypothesis and support the second; a chick-mouse mosaic of cartilage is formed. The cells involved seem to be governed more by the role they are to play in their environment (i.e., cooperating with their neighboring cells to form cartilage) than with the inherent factors (i.e., the fact that they are of different species) that might cause them to segregate.

Note, again, the close parallel between this situation and the one of the regeneration of frog limbs. From an assumption that inherent factors within the cells are of primary importance, it now becomes evident that external factors also play a definite role in the influencing of regenerating or reorganizing cells. Just as regenerating limb cells are sensitive to nervous or hormonal changes in their environments, so dissociated embryonic cells are sensitive to the formative ability of surrounding cells, and clump together on this basis. We are dealing here with a situation of heredity versus environment on a suborganismal level.

The problem of embryological development can be approached from still another direction. From an early amphibian embryo, a cell region that would ordinarily form parts of an eye can be transplanted to an embryonic region destined to become larval tail skin. This experiment attempts to answer a question similar to the one Schòtté posed in transplanting frog presumptive flank tissue to the mouth region of a salamander embryo (see Fig. 18–16). Will the transplanted tissue form what it would ordinarily form (i.e., eye parts)? Or will it readjust to its new cellular environment and form tail skin? In other words, what differentiation role will the cells of the transplant follow? The result? The cells form tail skin. Score one for environment.

The experiment is repeated. This time, however, a transplant from the eye region of an *older* amphibian embryo is placed among presumptive tail tissue of another embryo. The result? Sightless but clearly recognizable eye parts staring out of the tail of the host tadpole. Score one for heredity.

What has happened? Obviously, the transplant cells in the second experiment "lost" their ability to adjust to a new environmental situation. Or, perhaps they "acquired" the ability to override the surrounding environmental influence. In either case, they are now "committed" to forming eye parts.

The results of this last experiment force us to look once again to the differentiating cells for answers. Granting that, under certain experimental conditions, embryonic cells are not inherently determined as was once thought, there is no denying that, in normal development, they do become so. Thus, while the environment may affect their expression, there are factors residing within differentiating cells which determine their role in building the specialized tissues of an embryo or a regenerating limb.

Could the nucleus be responsible for the control of differentiation? If so, the nucleus of a fertilized egg might differ from one in the cell of an advanced embryo.

Experiments performed in the 1950's by R. Briggs and T. J. King tested this idea. Briggs and King devised the delicate experimental technique shown in Fig. 18–21. Nuclei were transplanted from the cells of older frog embryos into frog eggs from which the nuclei had been removed (enucleated eggs). Briggs and King first transplanted nuclei from blastula cells into enucleated eggs. Normal embryos resulted. Evidently, then, the transplanted nucleus was still capable of acting as a "general practitioner" of development. It could still direct (assuming it does so) the differentiation of a complete embryo, rather than merely that part of an embryo it would have acted on if it had remained in the blastula. The experiment was repeated with cell nuclei transplanted from early gastrulas into enucleated eggs. Again, normal development occurred. However, when nuclei from cells of *late* gastrula stages were transplanted, abnormal development occurred.

Do these experiments support the hypothesis that a genetic change occurs in cells as they differentiate? It may be tempting to think so, but we must not

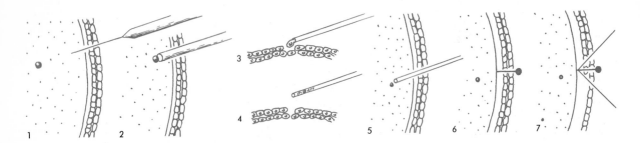

FIG. 18–21   The Briggs and King operational technique.  (1) The egg is pricked, causing the nucleus to move to the surface.  (2) The nucleus is removed with a micropipette.  (3, 4) An ectodermal cell from a blastula is drawn into the micropipette, whose diameter is so small that the cell membrane is ruptured.  (5) The cell nucleus, with most of the cytoplasm removed from it, is injected into an enucleated egg.  (6, 7) Snipping the protrusion prevents the egg cytoplasm from escaping.

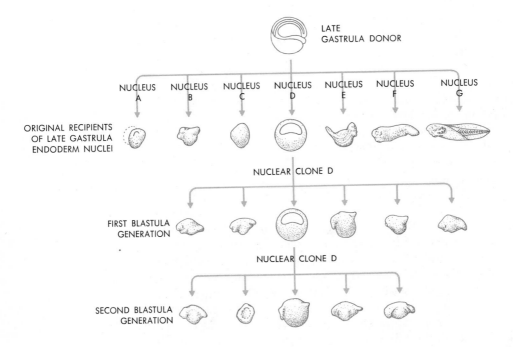

FIG. 18–22   Nuclei removed from various late gastrula endoderm cells vary widely in their ability to control embryonic development when injected into enucleated eggs.  Nucleus A, for example, seems to have lost its ability to control normal development, while nucleus G still retains the ability and causes the development of a complete embryo.  However, when descendants (clones) of any one particular nucleus are injected into enucleated eggs, they yield embryos which are uniform in the stage of development they attain.  This indicates that the genes controlling development are ''turned off'' in cell nuclei as development proceeds.

jump too quickly. Consider what a "genetic change" involves. It means a chemical change within molecules of DNA—a mutation. Yet, experimental evidence to date strongly indicates that mutations occur entirely at random (see Fig. 3–4). It is hard to base an hypothesis explaining such a highly organized process as cellular differentiation on a purely "chance" process. Besides, development is a regular and repeated *series* of events, which makes its occurrence by chance still more unlikely.

Have the nuclei from later stages in embryos lost their ability to control normal development? From these experiments, it would seem so. Yet in 1962, Dr. J. B. Gurdon and his associates transplanted to host eggs the nuclei from endodermal cells of *Xenopus laevis* donors ranging in age from late gastrula to the free-swimming tadpole stage. In some of the experimental host eggs, complete and normal development to the adult stage was obtained. In connection with the results obtained by Briggs and King it would seem, therefore, that nuclei might undergo functional but reversible differentiation (Fig. 18–22). The regeneration experiments discussed earlier showed that nuclei from the cells of adult amphibians are able to direct the differentiation necessary to grow a new appendage. If genetic change is assumed, then such cells must have undergone the proper random "unmutation." Surely this stretches the imagination too far.

It is possible that differentiation might occur because of a selective loss of DNA from cells during development. Perhaps, for example, cells of a plant destined by their position to become tracheids might lose all the DNA but that required for this particular developmental pathway. It was shown in 1950, however, that the quantity of DNA is constant in various fully differentiated cells of corn and *Tradescantia*, including those of the root, leaf, petal, and stamen hair, thus contradicting this hypothesis. Further, the amount of DNA present in the haploid cells of these plants (such as the pollen grains) was found to be precisely half that of the diploid cells. This result is to be expected, of course, since haploid cells possess an $n$ rather than $2n$ number of chromosomes.

Still more evidence against an hypothesis proposing that cells lose part of their DNA during their growth and development is provided by cell and tissue culture experiments. It has long been known that structures can be removed from the plant and grown in sterile culture in media containing combinations of inorganic salts, vitamins, growth substances, and an energy source such as sucrose. In one recent experiment (1965), A. C. Hildebrandt and Vimla Vasil at the University of Wisconsin placed small pieces of pith tissue from the stems of hybrid tobacco plants (*Nicotiana glutinosa* $\times$ *N. tabacum*) on a solid agar culture medium. After approximately a month, the tissue, now considerably increased in size, was transferred to a liquid culture medium. Following several days of growth in containers placed on a machine designed to shake them gently, the tissue dissociated into single cells and groups of cells. Using micropipettes and a dissecting microscope, the investigators picked out single cells from the medium and grew each one in a microculture, isolated from all other cells (Fig. 18–23a). Out of 150 single cells isolated, 32 underwent mitotic divisions, producing in about two weeks irregular, unorganized masses of 50 to 75 cells

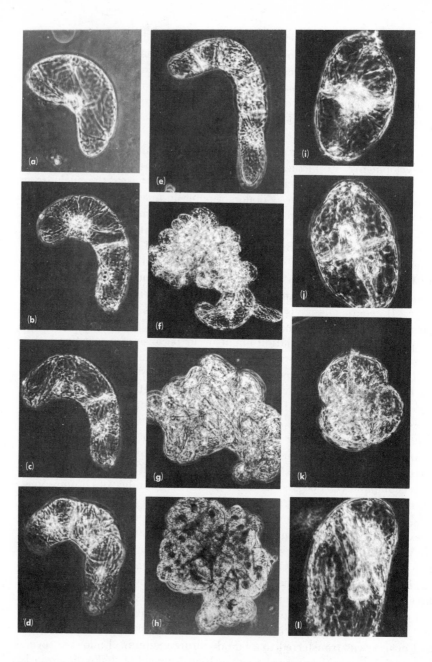

FIG. 18–23   Development of a cell cluster from a single cell of tobacco isolated from stem pith callus. (a) A single cell (×750). (b-h) Stages in the development of the cell shown in (a) into a cell cluster (b-d, ×600; e, ×470; f, ×375; g, ×300; h, ×230). (i) A single cell dividing (×750). (j) Same, now four cells (×750). (k) A cluster of cells formed from the cell shown in (i) (×300). (l) A cell soon after dividing into two cells of unequal size (×930). (Courtesy Vimla Vasil and A. C. Hildebrandt, *Science* **150**, pp. 889–892. Copyright 1965 by the American Association for the Advancement of Science.)

FIG. 18–24   Growth of tobacco plants from an undifferentiated mass of cells developed from a single isolated cell. (a) Undifferentiated mass of cells. (b) Development of several leafy shoots from a mass of cells. (c) Formation of roots by these leafy shoots. (d) Plants growing in aseptic culture ($\frac{2}{3}$ natural size). (e) Young plants transferred from culture bottles to soil in greenhouse ($\frac{1}{3}$ natural size). (f-h) Further stages in the growth and development of a tobacco plant originally transferred from culture bottles (f, $\frac{1}{2}$ natural size; g, $\frac{1}{3}$; h, $\frac{1}{6}$). (Courtesy Vimla Vasil and A. C. Hildebrandt, *Science* **150**, pp. 889–892. Copyright 1965 by the American Association for the Advancement of Science.)

(Fig. 18–23f, g, h). Each cell was then transferred to a culture bottle containing a solid agar medium. In three or four weeks, shoots with leaves arose from the mass of cells (Fig. 18–24b). The shoots were transferred to another culture medium lacking any growth substances. Under these conditions, roots formed at the base of each shoot in approximately ten days (Fig. 18–24c). Using this technique, Hildebrandt and Vasil were able to obtain hundreds of tobacco plantlets with roots and shoots (Fig. 18–24d), each having arisen originally from a single cell. To show that these plantlets were completely normal, they were transferred to sterilized soil in pots in the greenhouse (Fig. 18–24e). Several of them continued to grow and even produced flowers (Fig. 18–24h).

The results of this experiment demonstrate quite conclusively that cells do not lose any of their DNA during differentiation. The pith tissue of tobacco is fully mature and its cells are completely differentiated and specialized. Normally they would not again divide and grow. Yet Hildebrandt and Vasil's results show that by experimental manipulation the same cells can be stimulated to grow, divide, and produce a mass of cells that can be induced to grow into a whole plant. If the pith cells had lost some of their DNA during their differentiation, it seems highly unlikely that they would have been able to regenerate the entire tobacco plant.

There is another possibility, however. Abandon the hypotheses proposing either genetic change or loss of DNA during development. Assume that the nuclei of all cells retain their genetic potential to control complete and normal differentiation, but suppose that certain genes are *suppressed*, i.e., prevented from expressing themselves, and that only those genes used to perform the task at hand are allowed to remain functional.

This idea poses another question. Where and how does this gene suppression originate? Genes don't have minds of their own; they don't "know" when and when not to act. Is it not possible that elements in the cytoplasm are responsible? The fact that an enucleated egg does not develop does not mean that only the nucleus plays a role in its development, any more than the disabling of a car by removing its wheels indicates that the wheels are responsible for causing the car to move.

The logical conclusion is one we might well have been prepared for. Just as environmental factors must be considered in dealing with developing embryos and regenerating limbs, so must the nuclear environment (i.e., the cytoplasm) be considered, as well as the inherent factors residing within the nucleus.

**18–11
GENES,
REGULATION, AND
DEVELOPMENT**

In the development of the chick, the heart appears about twenty-four hours after incubation. The cells that form the heart migrate from other places into the heart-forming region.

Heart-muscle myosin (the muscle protein) can be distinguished from skeletal-muscle myosin by certain chemical tests. Thus, by chemical analysis of their proteins, presumptive heart cells can be recognized before they reach the heart region or have taken the shape of cardiac muscle cells. In other words, differentiation can be detected by looking for changes in the composition of cellular proteins.

The experiments of Beadle and Tatum, using the mold *Neurospora crassa*, demonstrated a one-to-one relationship between genes and enzymes (recall that all enzymes are proteins). A segment of DNA produces a certain polypeptide needed for the production of a certain enzyme. Each enzyme, in turn, is responsible for the catalyzing of a particular chemical reaction, perhaps one step in the production of a pigment. If the gene is absent, mutated, or suppressed, the proper enzyme is not produced. The individual produces no pigment and is thus an albino. Note the series of reactions below.

$$A \; \overset{\text{enzyme}\;a}{\rightleftharpoons} \; B \; \overset{\text{enzyme}\;b}{\rightleftharpoons} \; C \; \overset{\text{enzyme}\;c}{\rightleftharpoons} \; D \; \overset{\text{enzyme}\;d}{\rightleftharpoons} \; E$$

Suppose that compound E is needed by the organism. The rate at which the reaction of the series proceeds is proportional to the rate at which E is removed from the reaction site.

Suppose that the gene responsible for producing enzyme *c* is prevented from expressing itself, i.e., coding the construction of enzyme *c*. No compound D is formed, and thus no compound E. Compound C, unusable by the organism, accumulates. If C is poisonous in large quantities, the organism may be damaged or die. Since C is accumulating, the reaction series reverses, and the concentrations of B and A also increase. Suppose, now, that compound E is an important structural protein needed for cell differentiation. Then, suppressing one or all of the genes responsible for coding enzymes *a*, *b*, *c*, or *d* would prevent differentiation.

A brief review of current thought about gene action and protein synthesis is in order here. The gene, a part of the DNA molecule, passes on its inherited message, coded in the order of its nitrogenous bases, to messenger RNA (*m*RNA). Messenger RNA then passes from the nucleus to the ribosomes. There, the code is translated during protein synthesis, using amino acids collected and brought to the ribosomes by transfer RNA (*t*RNA). Gene activity, then, involves chemical activity. The slowing down or stopping of this chemical activity will thus effectively suppress the gene. Indeed, chemical reactions are known in which the products have a slow-down or depressant effect on the reactions that produce them. If, for example, in the reaction series

$$A \; \overset{\text{enzyme}\;a}{\rightleftharpoons} \; B \; \overset{\text{enzyme}\;b}{\rightleftharpoons} \; C \; \overset{\text{enzyme}\;c}{\rightleftharpoons} \; D$$

product D should affect the rate at which enzyme *a* can catalyze the reaction converting A to B, then D is also indirectly controlling the rate of its own synthesis. Substance D at one end of the line is having a "feedback" effect upon the first step in the series. A parallel feedback situation can be drawn which applies to development. It was established earlier that embryonic cells are sensitive to their surrounding environment as well as to their own internal one. This can be summarized diagrammatically as follows:

GENES $\rightleftharpoons$ CYTOPLASM $\rightleftharpoons$ ENVIRONMENT

The genes influence the cytoplasm. The cytoplasm, in turn, has a "feedback" influence on the genes, turning them on and off when needed. In turn, cells influence other cells and thus the composition of their environment.

In what way might this gene regulation take place? How are the genes within a cell controlled so that some of them act and others do not? Some early clues were provided during the late 1950's by experiments conducted by Jacques Monod and François Jacob at the Pasteur Institute in Paris. Jacob and Monod found that the bacterium *Escherichia coli* does not synthesize beta-galactosidase (an enzyme which catalyzes the hydrolysis of lactose sugar into galactose and glucose) in significant quantities unless lactose is present in the cell. If lactose is supplied, however, the enzyme is synthesized from amino acids already present inside the bacterium. *E. coli* can also synthesize the amino acid arginine, using raw materials from its environment. If arginine is supplied, however, the formation of an enzyme needed by *E. coli* to produce arginine is inhibited. The bacteria stop making arginine, and use that which is available from the environment. In both the lactose and arginine cases, *E. coli* is being "told" by its environment to synthesize its own enzyme for breaking down lactose or not to make an enzyme for producing arginine, etc. Might not the same principles of interaction account for the changes in potentiality shown by the differentiating cells of an embryo or the stump of a regenerating limb?

It seems clear that the environment of the bacterium containing the lactose or arginine molecules is influencing the activity of the genes, simply turning them on and off when needed. Later, Jacob and Monod found that the mechanism of gene control is far more complex than originally thought. They established that the ability of *E. coli* to break down lactose may depend on at least four genes. One of these (gene 1) may provide the information for making the enzyme beta-galactosidase, while gene 2 may code for the synthesis of another enzyme that is involved in the absorption of lactose by the bacterial cells. A third gene, in a manner not clearly known, probably controls the synthesis of yet another enzyme necessary for lactose utilization. All three of these genes are known as "structural" genes, since they determine the structure of enzymes (proteins).

Various genetic studies showed that these three structural genes are probably located close to one another on the DNA of the bacterium. In addition, Jacob and Monod uncovered evidence that the activity of all three of these structural genes may well be controlled by a fourth gene, called an operator gene, located near gene 1. The entire four-gene system is known as an **operon.** When the operator gene is "on," the three structural genes are active; when it is "off," they are inactive. Through the analysis of various *E. coli* mutations, Jacob and Monod discovered that the operator gene may itself be controlled by the combined action of two agencies: a regulator gene, located some distance away from the

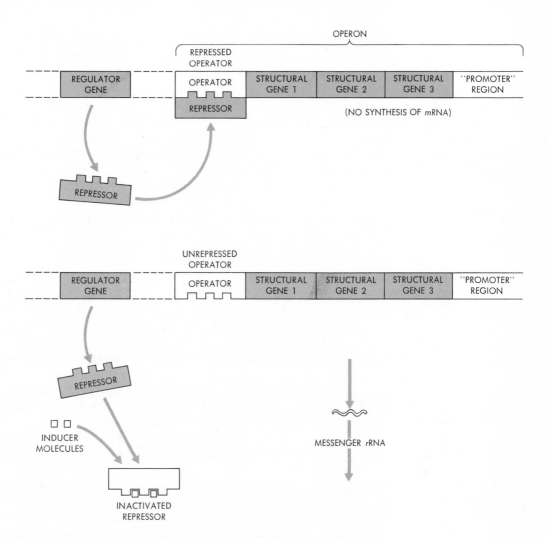

FIG. 18–25   The Jacob-Monod hypothesis of gene regulation. The three structural genes (forming an operon) are all under the control of an operator gene. When the operator is "on," the operon is active; when it is "off," the operon is inactive. Each operator gene, in turn, is controlled by a regulator gene, which produces a repressor substance capable of switching off the operator gene. Inducer molecules modify the repressor and prevent it from switching off the operon; thus, the messenger RNA can still be synthesized. This model is slightly modified from the original to include a "promoter" region.

lactose operon, and various chemical-inducing substances, such as lactose or arginine.   The regulator gene is postulated to control the manufacture of a regulator substance capable of combining with the operator gene and switching off its control over the three structural genes (see Fig. 18–25).   When this occurs, the operon is thought to be prevented from making the mRNA required for synthesis of the three enzymes involved in lactose utilization.  When an inducer substance such as lactose is supplied to the bacteria, however, it probably combines with the regulator substance and prevents it from switching off the operon.  When this happens, then enzymes for breaking down lactose are synthesized, using the $m$RNA formed by the three structural genes of the operon.  If arginine is supplied to the bacteria, however, these small molecules may react in some manner with the regulator substance, causing it to switch the operator gene off more effectively, and blocking the synthesis of the enzyme required for arginine production.

The Jacob-Monod concept of gene regulation (for which they shared the Nobel prize in medicine for 1965) is purely a hypothetical model to explain how genes may act in development.  Since first proposed in 1961, the hypothesis has undergone slight changes as more experimental evidence has become available.  The hypothesis has been very useful in explaining many observations of gene control of enzyme synthesis in bacteria.

What about gene regulation in organisms more complex than bacteria?  During the 1950's, the geneticist Barbara McClintock of the Carnegie Institution of Washington found that grains of corn (*Zea mays*) have many spots of color of various sizes and frequencies in different varieties.  Through ingenious genetic analyses, McClintock obtained evidence that these spots are due to the action of controlling elements which affect the genes for color.  One of these elements directly controls the action of the structural gene (thus is similar to the operator gene in bacteria).  Another controlling element functions in a manner comparable to the regulator gene in bacteria.  It is not at all certain, however, that the gene regulation system found in corn grains is sufficiently precise to control the orderly development of an entire multicellular plant.  The gene control systems in corn produce randomly distributed spots of color instead of predictable patterns.

Thus, conclusive evidence is still lacking for the existence in multicellular organisms of a gene control system as precise and orderly as the Jacob-Monod one.  It seems wise to be cautious in extrapolating from a unicellular organism of procaryotic cell organization to multicellular eucaryotes.  Yet it would seem reasonable to expect complex organisms to possess gene-regulating devices at least as sophisticated as those of bacteria—though, of course, they may be of a different kind.  Still, as a working hypothesis, the bacterial system is valuable for use in studies of the growth and development of multicellular organisms.

**18-12
EVIDENCE FOR
GENE REGULATION
IN GROWTH AND
DEVELOPMENT**

Is there experimental evidence that some genes are active while others are not?  Certainly this must be suspected, when the cells in the human body show such wide diversity despite their similar genetic composition.

At certain times during the development of insects, "puffs" or swellings along the chromosomes can be associated with gene activity.  The appearance of these puffs can be induced by certain insect hormones.  It might be guessed, then, that the developmental sequence of insects in metamorphosis (known to be hormonally influenced) is due to a complex interaction between genes and hormones.  If the puffs are correctly associated with gene activities, it is reasonable to hypothesize that the genes on the nonpuff regions of the chromosomes are inactive and will remain so until the proper cellular environment is established.

If a certain region of embryonic cells from a wing bud of a developing chick is removed, the adult chicken will show a particular deformity.  Chickens on which no operations have been performed have been known to have a similar deformity.  This deformity is inherited, hence it must be gene-caused.  Studies of the embryos of such chickens show that the same tissue that is removed experimentally to cause the deformity in other chickens has failed to develop in the ones that are naturally deformed.  Again, a genetic basis for morphogenesis is indicated by both experimentation and observation.

Much of the evidence for gene activation and deactivation during growth and development has come from experiments using plants in which the antibiotic actinomycin D was used to suppress the synthesis of mRNA.  Without a continuing supply of mRNA, the production of enzymes and other protein molecules ceases.  By this method, mRNA has been demonstrated to be involved in many aspects of growth and development.    It has been shown, for example, that the cotyledons of peanut seeds begin synthesizing mRNA at the onset of germination and, within a week, the content of mRNA per cotyledon doubles.  Treatment with actinomycin D, however, severely impairs the synthesis of mRNA by the cotyledons.  Actinomycin D unites with the guanine of DNA and prevents the RNA polymerase molecule from using the DNA chain in the synthesis of mRNA.  Actinomycin D has also been shown to inhibit growth of soybean hypocotyls through suppression of mRNA synthesis.  This antibiotic has been found to inhibit the synthesis of an enzyme (amylase) by germinating seeds of barley.  This sensitivity to actinomycin D suggests that the genes for RNA synthesis are being inactivated in some manner.

Further support for the hypothesis that growth and development in plants is based upon changing patterns of gene activation and deactivation has been provided by James Bonner and his colleagues at the California Institute of Technology.  Different organs and tissues from pea plants were removed and each one placed separately into a solution containing $C^{14}$-labeled leucine (an amino acid).  In a short time, the radioactive leucine was used by the organ or tissue in synthesizing protein.  Each part of the pea plants was then ground up and the proteins were extracted.  Using the radioactive leucine as a marker, the quantity of a protein known as globulin was determined for each preparation (Table 18–2).  Very little globulin was found to be present in the cells of the roots, stems, and leaves.  The protein content of the seed cotyledons, however, had as much as 9.3% globulin.  Bonner and his co-workers concluded that pea cotyledon globulin was synthesized by the cells in the developing cotyledons but not in any significant amount by cells elsewhere in the plant.

Following this experiment, Bonner and his group sought to discover the mechanism by which the genes for making globulin are able to function in cotyledon cells, but are apparently suppressed in all other cells.  To analyze the

**TABLE 18–2** SYNTHESIS OF PEA SEED GLOBULIN IN
DIFFERENT ORGANS OF PEA PLANTS*

| ORGAN | PEA SEED GLOBULIN AS PERCENT OF TOTAL PROTEIN |
|---|---|
| COTYLEDON | 4.7–9.3 |
| ROOTS | 0.18 |
| APICAL BUD | 0.15 |
| LEAVES | 0.11 |

* After J. Bonner, R. C. Huang, and R. Gilden, *Proceedings
of the United States National Academy of Science* **50**, 1963,
p. 893.

manner by which the genes of the pea plant exert control over globulin synthesis,
Bonner and his colleagues isolated chromosomes from young, growing cotyledons
and from vegetative buds of pea plants. They ground the tissues in a blender to
disrupt the cell walls and nuclear membranes. By repeated centrifugation,
chloroplasts and other nonchromosomal organelles were removed, leaving the
chromosomes virtually alone. The biochemical composition of the isolated
chromosomes was determined to be about 36% DNA, 37% histone (a type of
protein), 10% RNA, 10% nonhistone protein, and small amounts of the enzyme
RNA polymerase.

From their earlier experiments, Bonner and his colleagues knew that the
cells of pea cotyledons synthesize globulin protein, whereas the cells of vegetative
buds do not. They supplied additional RNA polymerase and the four nucleotide
building blocks of *m*RNA to chromosome preparations of buds and cotyledons,
thus producing two *m*RNA-generating systems (Fig. 18–26). Ribosomes were
then added to each preparation to establish the necessary condition for protein
synthesis by the isolated chromosomes. After 30 minutes, the chromosomes and
ribosomes were removed by centrifugation and the proportion of globulin protein
in each preparation determined. The newly synthesized proteins in the pea
cotyledon preparation consisted of about 7% globulin protein (just a bit less
than was present in the intact plant). As before, very little globulin protein was
present among the abundant proteins synthesized by the pea buds.

It is clear from these experimental results that the procedures used to isolate
chromosomes do not harm the gene or genes controlling the production of *m*RNA
for globulin synthesis. In addition, the results demonstrate that while chromosomes from both tissues support the synthesis of *m*RNA, only those of pea
cotyledons support the synthesis of the globulin protein synthesizing *m*RNA.

Thus, it can be hypothesized that the gene for globulin-making in the pea
bud chromosomes must be suppressed in some way. But what is the suppressing
agent? Since histone is present in the chromosomes in essentially the same
quantity as DNA, this protein is a logical choice for the suppressor. If the histone
is functioning in the suppression of the globulin-synthesizing gene system in the

FIG. 18–26 Summary of Bonner's experiments on synthesis of globulin protein by chromosomes isolated from pea buds and pea cotyledons. (Based on J. Bonner, R. C. Huang, and R. Gilden, *Proceedings of the United States National Academy of Science* **50**, 1963, p. 893.)

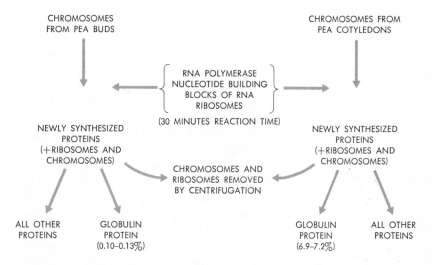

pea bud chromosomes, then chromosomes with their histone removed should be able to synthesize globulin. This reasoning can be expressed more formally as follows:

**Hypothesis:** *If* . . .  the gene for globulin synthesis in the chromosomes of pea buds is being suppressed by the histone,

**Prediction:** *then* . . . removal of the histone from the isolated chromosomes should eliminate or overcome the suppression of the globulin-synthesizing gene system.

Bonner and his co-workers designed an experiment to test this prediction. They dissociated the histone and other proteins from the chromosome preparation and separated out the heavier DNA by centrifugation. The pure DNA remaining was then used to support the synthesis of *m*RNA and ribosomal proteins in the test tube. In the absence of histone, the bud DNA now supported as much pea globulin synthesis as did the DNA from the cotyledon cells. These results strongly support the histone-gene suppression hypothesis. Histone, therefore, could be the long-sought suppressor for the synthesis of globulin protein.

 While the histone hypothesis of gene suppression is very attractive, in actuality the problem has simply been moved at least one step backward and we must now ask: what controls the histones? There is some evidence supporting an hypothesis that the histones might be under the control of some small molecule coming from outside the cells, just as the genes of the bacterium *E. coli* are influenced by the presence of lactose in their environment. Bonner and his group discovered that the buds on freshly harvested tubers of the potato plant do not grow, even if supplied with favorable conditions. Such structures are said to be dormant. When chromosomes are isolated from the cells of these dormant buds, they synthesize very little RNA, even if additional RNA polymerase is supplied. However, after treatment with gibberellic acid, a naturally occurring growth-promoting substance (see Section 11–10), isolated chromosomes supplied with the proper enzymes and building blocks synthesize RNA rapidly. It can be hypothesized that the gibberellic acid molecules may chemically bind to the histones and, in some manner, act to prevent the histones from suppressing the activity of the genes for *m*RNA synthesis. Thus, the dormancy of the freshly harvested potatoes might be broken, enabling them to commence growth.

If the histones are responsible for gene repression, it is reasonable to predict that different tissues and organs of the plant would show a wide divergence in their histone complements. Some studies made during the 1950's and early 1960's indicated that a single kind of cell contains several types of histones, and that specific organs contain their own unique histones. In the late 1960's, using more refined techniques of histone analysis, various groups of investigators were unable to demonstrate the existence of different histones in different kinds of cells. Not only are the same histones present in different organs of the same plant, but even different species of organisms possess similar histones. In addition, by use of improved methods of preparation and analysis, it has been discovered that there are very few kinds of histone molecules. There is good evidence, however, that cells in different organs do differ in the histone-DNA ratio, and there is some variation in the quantities of individual histones present in different tissues. These data suggest that, rather than specific histones regulating specific genes, the same few histones may suppress different genes in different cells. If this is so, some other type of molecule must direct the histones to the correct genes. There is growing evidence that a new type of RNA may perform this task. The relation of histones to the regulation of gene action is currently one of the most challenging and controversial topics in developmental biology.

But there are many other controversial topics in the area of the regulation of cellular differentiation. As has been indicated, the Jacob-Monod model is primarily supported by work on bacteria—primarily *E. coli.* Unfortunately, evidence of a similar sort is lacking for eucaryotic organisms, in which the nuclear material is separated from the cytoplasm by a membrane.

However, an experiment performed by Dr. Eugene Bell at the Massachusetts Institute of Technology suggests an answer. Bell incubated developing muscle cells treated with radioactive thymidine, the base found in DNA but not RNA. He found that the radioactivity—and thus the DNA—moved out into the cytoplasm, in the manner of *m*RNA. This "messenger DNA" Bell calls **informational DNA** (*I*-DNA). He found that, in the cytoplasm, *I*-DNA was firmly attached to messenger RNA and newly synthesized protein. Thus *I*-DNA shows all the characteristics to be expected of genes being actively expressed in the well-established bacterial manner. It remains to be shown, however, that Bell's experimental system was not contaminated by bacteria or viruses, and that the process of *I*-DNA formation is not just a peculiarity of embryonic cells. But Bell feels that the key events in differentiation may not be the transcription of $m$RNA by nuclear DNA, but rather the regulation of DNA replication and recombination.

The idea of multiple copies of the genes to be expressed being packaged into membrane-bound organelles (which Bell calls *I-somes*), ferried out through the nuclear membrane into the cytoplasm, and then—acting as a sort of "gene-in-residence"—synthesizing protein via the mediation of $m$RNA (as bacteria or viruses might do) is certainly an intriguing one. If this *is* the case, then it provides a means by which the genes to be used by the cell at any one time might be selected.

18-13
THE INHERITANCE
OF SEX:
A DEVELOPMENTAL
HYPOTHESIS

In Chapters 15 and 17, the chromosomal basis of the inheritance of sex was discussed. From the genetic standpoint, the inheritance of sex is adequately accounted for by the random assortment of the sex chromosomes at meiosis, and leads to quite accurate predictions.

But the conventional hypothesis regarding sex inheritance is not perfect. It fails, for example, to account for such anomalies as "intersexes"—persons who have mixed male and female anatomical and psychological characteristics *but normal chromosomal complements*.

It has long been known that during the fifth week of human embryological development a gonadal primordium—a mass of cells destined to become the sexual organs—appears. For about a week, the primordium offers no clue as to whether it will give rise to male or female sexual organs. But then the forerunners of the male testes appear. If this forerunner continues to develop, a male results. If, after making its appearance it degenerates, the female ovaries begin their development.

Acting on this knowledge, Dr. Ursula Mittwoch of London's University College suggested in 1969 that the role of the $Y$-chromosome is that of an active and "positive" factor in the survival and subsequent development of the forerunners of the male testes. She suggested that the $Y$-chromosome may cause a burst of intense cell-division activity at this critical time and place in development. Without the $Y$-chromosome (i.e., genotype $XX$), this burst of mitotic activity fails to occur, and the gonadal primordium becomes an ovary. Dr. Mittwoch pointed out that her hypothesis fits the fact that differentiation of the testes occurs before that of the ovary.

Dr. Mittwoch's hypothesis nicely accounts for sex differentiation on the basis of the presence or absence of the $Y$-chromosome. It also suggests the reason why men tend to be larger than women, and why those men with a non-disjunction-caused $XYY$-chromosome make-up (see Section 15–5) tend on the average to be larger than men with the normal $XY$-complement. Finally, the Mittwoch hypothesis suggests that one consider the inheritance of sex not just in terms of a hypothetical balance of hypothetical genes, but in terms of cell kinetics and relative growth. Thus, although it is still too early to evaluate her hypothesis fully, Dr. Mittwoch has opened the door to a fresh way of looking at an old problem of genetics and development.

Once in a while, something goes wrong. What was to have been a perfectly formed young animal turns out to be something very different.

What causes an embryo to deviate from the path of normal development? Environment? Yes, about 10% of the time. Cyclopia, a condition in which the offspring have only one centrally located eye, occurs occasionally in man, but more often in cattle. In the latter, the condition appears to be environmentally induced by the cow eating a plant called the Western false hellebore (*Veratrum californicum*) early in pregnancy. Ingestion of this plant later in the cow's pregnancy results in leg deformities in the calf. The experimental oral administration of LSD to pregnant rats has resulted in fetus death and biochemical defects in offspring, and the effect may last as long as three generations (to date, the evidence of the effect of LSD on human development is inconclusive). The Rubella virus of German measles can cause malformations if the mother has the disease early in pregnancy. The drug thalidomide is another malformation-causing environmental agent.

Heredity? Yes, again about 10% of the time. Polydactyly (extra fingers or toes) is an example of an inherited malformation. What about the other 80%? The answer should not be surprising in light of the preceding discussion of interrelationships between gene and cell, cell and cell, and cell and environment.

In mice, for example, there is a gene called Danforth's short-tail mutation, an abnormal shortening of the notochord. The notochord serves as the foundation upon which the vertebrae are built. Furthermore, the notochord is an important organizer; it induces the formation of many vital structures. From what has been discussed concerning embryonic induction, the effects of an abnormal notochord on the developing mouse embryo should be easy to imagine. The structures the notochord induces are abnormal; in turn, the structures they induce are abnormal. A "rolling snowball" effect is the result. For example, a vertebral bone produced by the abnormal notochord is misshapen; thus its articulation with the next vertebral bone is changed and the muscles that originate on this bone are twisted out of their regular position. Muscle action is therefore less effective and the mouse is crippled. At the other end of the animal, a similar sequence of abnormalities is triggered. The notochord induces the gut. If the mutant gene is present in the homozygous state, the gut shrinks. The cloaca it induces is reduced, which means that the wall between the urogenital sinus and rectum does not form, outgrowth of the ureter buds is hampered, and no permanent kidney is formed at all. Such animals, of course, cannot survive (Fig. 18–27).

In embryology, it is often necessary to deal with congenital malformations in the abstract terms of experimental biology. Yet we cannot ignore certain facts. On the molecular level, it is easy to discuss malformation in a detached manner. A change of one amino acid in a polypeptide chain of three hundred, a blockage of the synthesis of glucose-6-dehydrogenase—these may be causes. In terms of a human life, however, a congenital malformation is often a stark tragedy, extending far beyond the life or death of the afflicted individual; these are undeniable effects.

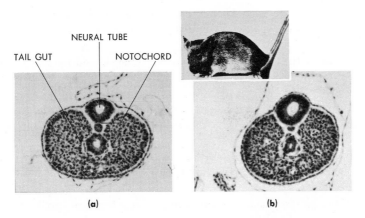
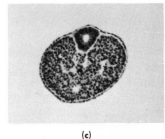

TAIL GUT        NEURAL TUBE        NOTOCHORD

(a)                    (b)                    (c)

FIG. 18–27   Danforth's short-tail mutation. (a) A cross section through the tail region of a normal mouse embryo. (b) The same section through a mouse embryo heterozygous for the condition. As the insert photo shows, such mice are crippled in the hindquarters. (c) A cross section taken from a mouse embryo homozygous for the condition. Note the progressive reduction in the differentiation of the notochord and surrounding tissue, as the strength of the gene's expression increases. Such mice cannot survive. (Photo from *Discovery*, March 1963. Courtesy Dr. H. Grüneberg.)

It would be a mistake to assign humanitarian motives to all research embryologists. Research carries its own attractions; the simply joy of discovering something new is enticement enough. Yet often such discoveries, which may at first seem trivial, open doors of immense practical value. By experimentally causing congenital malformations in laboratory animals, the embryologist constantly learns new facts which may someday be used to prevent congenital malformations in human children.

**18–15
CONCLUSION**

The questions tackled by developmental biology are central to all of modern biology. In this chapter, we have discussed a few of these questions and cited some experiments designed to provide answers to them.

To date, the answers are few. Those obtained pose still more questions. The nature of organizer tissues or inducing agents and how they work remains an open question. Regeneration research has just begun to obtain results that lend hope to the goal of a full explanation. The hypothesis of genetic "feedback" was discussed as providing many answers to questions posed by differentiation. Yet some evidence has recently been uncovered which seems to refute the feedback hypothesis. It is hypothesized instead that genes control their own timing, turning themselves on and off under some built-in time schedule.

Which hypothesis is correct? Perhaps both are. Or perhaps both are wrong and experimental evidence not yet uncovered will lead to the development of better hypotheses. Whatever lies ahead, developmental biology, despite its age of more than 2000 years, is still in a pioneering stage of development.

1. What evidence exists for the theory of preformation and the theory of epigenesis? From the type of observation that can be made with only a magnifying glass, which theory seems more reasonable?

2. Contrast the experiments of Roux and Driesch, and the interpretations that have been made of their results. What is known today that helps to explain their contradictory results?

3. As philosophical approaches to living organisms, how do mechanism and vitalism play a part in theories of embryology? Why did Driesch's experiments lead him to endorse vitalism?

4. Why is the biogenetic law not a sound principle of biology? What evidence can be marshaled against it? How can it be a useful way of looking at the development of organisms?

5. How can the amount of yolk available in a fertilized egg determine the course of embryonic development?

6. Describe the changes that occur in an egg immediately after fertilization.

7. How does the amount and distribution of yolk in the blastula affect the process of gastrulation?

8. In what several ways does the major course of embryonic development after gastrulation differ from that which precedes it?

9. What were the results of Spemann's most famous experiment? Explain the concept of embryonic induction. In terms of the direction this work gave to embryological studies, why would you say it was extremely important?

10. Explain briefly how inducing-agent substances might function. Do they seem to control directly the development in cells to which they diffuse, or do they act indirectly by affecting the genetic information of those cells? What evidence can you cite to back up your answer?

**TABLE 18-3**

| SOURCE OF DONOR NUCLEUS | TOTAL EGGS INJECTED | NORMAL CLEAVAGE | | COMPLETE EMBRYOS | |
|---|---|---|---|---|---|
| | | ACTUAL NUMBER | % | ACTUAL NUMBER | % |
| BLASTULA | 204 | 116 | 57 | 69 | 34 |
| EARLY GASTRULA | 135 | 52 | 38 | 20 | 15 |

11. Observe Table 18-3.* It refers to an experiment in which nuclei were transplanted from a donor embryo into an enucleated egg. What do these data indicate? What changes seem to occur in the nucleus as embryonic development occurs? How can you account for this?

---

*Taken from Barth, L. J., *Development, Selected Topics* (Reading, Mass.: Addison-Wesley, 1965), p. 58.

12. If a blastula nucleus from one species of frog is transplanted into an enucleated egg of another species, the development of the resulting embryo stops at an early stage. If the nuclei are taken from embryos of this kind before they die and transplanted back to enucleated eggs of the original donor species, the resulting transplant embryos develop abnormally. What do these results indicate about the relationship between the nucleus and the cytoplasm?

13. Spinal cord and notochord cells induce cartilage formation in amphibian embryos. They will also induce cells to form cartilage when cultured outside of the embryo. However, they will only induce cartilage formation in cells which would ordinarily form cartilage. Does this fact support or refute the conclusions drawn from Schotté's experiment?

Answer Exercises 15 and 16 on the basis of the following information: Fern prothallia are small, heart-shaped structures about the size of a dime. They exist as one stage in the life cycle of the fern, and are composed of all haploid cells. Prothallia live on the forest floor independent of the large fern plant. When mature, prothallia develop special gamete-producing organs, antheridia (which produce male gametes) and archegonia (which produce female gametes).

Recently much work has been done in an attempt to find out how the differentiation process (by which some cells of the prothallia give rise to antheridia and others to archegonia) is initiated. The following items of information have been obtained:

a) If a single prothallium is raised in isolation in a test tube containing appropriate growth substances, it will grow to maturity but will not produce antheridia.

b) If a number of prothallia are grown in the same test tubes, however, antheridia develop readily.

c) If a single prothallium is grown in a culture medium in which other prothallia have grown, antheridia develop readily.

d) If the growth medium in which older prothallia have developed is made very concentrated and applied to a young, isolated prothallium, the latter will develop a larger number of antheridia than normal. The number is roughly proportional (within certain limits) to the concentration of the medium. Concentration does not affect rate of growth of the antheridia, only number.

15. Offer an hypothesis to explain how differentiation of antheridia may be controlled by the plant.

16. In what ways is this similar to and different from differentiation in animal development?

17. What technical advantages are gained by studying regenerating limbs rather than embryos themselves? Explain your answer.

18. How would you account for the following generalizations?

   a) The less complex the animal, the greater its power of regeneration.

   b) The older an organism, the less power of regeneration it possesses. (Explain your answer in terms of the turning on and off of genetic information within cells.)

   Do you think that these generalizations are completely valid ones?

19. Describe how embryonic development, though it may take place within the mother's body, is still subjected to the stresses of natural selection.

20. There has been much controversy in recent years about the use of X-rays for medical examination of pregnant mothers.  Some authorities claim that this harms the developing fetus, while others claim that the effects are so slight that the medical advantages of such examinations far outweigh any disadvantages.  Table 18–4 compares stillbirths (in which the fetus is born dead), congenital defects (in which the child lives but has some malformation), and healthy children in X-rayed and non-X-rayed mothers.  Would you conclude for or against the theory that X-rays cause definite harm to the fetuses of pregnant women?

**TABLE 18–4**

|  | X-RAYED MOTHERS | NON-X-RAYED MOTHERS |
|---|---|---|
| STILLBIRTHS | 1.403% | 1.222% |
| CONGENITAL DEFECTS | 6.01 | 4.82 |
| NORMAL CHILDREN | 80.42 | 83.23 |

21. What hypothesis have the biologists Jacob and Monod suggested for the way in which certain genes come into action at one time, while others act at a later time?

22. How might studies on embryonic development (in both plants and animals) possibly give important information about cancer?

**SUGGESTED READINGS**

BAKER, JEFFREY J. W., *In The Beginning: A Survey of Modern Embryology* (Columbus, Ohio: American Education Publications, Inc., 1964).  Chapter 8 contains a discussion of the problems faced by an embryo at birth.

BARTH, L. G., *Development: Selected Topics* (Reading, Mass.: Addison-Wesley Publishing Company, Inc., 1964).  A good survey of the concepts of modern embryology.

BELL, EUGENE, ed., *Molecular and Cellular Aspects of Development* (New York: Harper & Row, 1965).  A collection of some of the most significant papers on modern developmental biology.

EBERT, JAMES D., *Interacting Systems in Development* (New York: Holt, Rinehart and Winston, 1965, Modern Biology Series).

GOSS, RICHARD J., *Principles of Regeneration* (New York: Academic Press, 1969).  A superb book on this subject; the author provides a wealth of interesting experiments.

JACOB, F., and E. L. WOLLMAN, "Viruses and Genes." *Scientific American*, June 1961, p. 92.  This article discusses some new findings on the way in which gene action is regulated in cells.

SUSSMAN, MAURICE, *Animal Growth and Development* (Englewood Cliffs, N.J.: Prentice-Hall, Inc., 1961).  A readable account of some of the more significant concepts in modern developmental biology.

# TAXONOMY: THE CLASSIFICATION OF LIVING ORGANISMS

# CHAPTER 19

*Taxonomy, or systematics, is that branch of biological knowledge which is concerned with the recognition, description, nomenclature, and classification of living organisms.*

W. T. Calman*

## 19-1 INTRODUCTION

Most sciences attempt to find an orderly pattern in certain areas of nature. The chemist, for example, tries to find relationships between the elements and compounds with which he works. He speaks of metals and nonmetals, acids and bases, and carbohydrates and proteins. The periodic table is one result of attempts to find a meaningful order among the known chemical elements. Indeed, much of man's progress through history can be seen as the results of this search for order.

Surely, one of man's greatest achievements was learning to classify things to his own benefit. Early man probably grouped animals into those which were dangerous and those which were not, those which could fly and those which could not, those which were edible and those which were not, and so on. These systems of classification, though rough, were of immediate and practical use to him. He could teach them to his children and they to theirs, adding refinements or improvements as the older criteria proved inaccurate or misleading.

Man classifies things because it makes them more orderly and easy to understand. It eliminates repetitive learning. However, the biologist is faced with a staggering task when it comes to sorting out the world of living organisms. In no other group of objects does so much variation exist from individual to individual and from group to group.

---

* W. T. Calman, *The Classification of Animals* (London: Methuen & Co. Ltd., 1949).

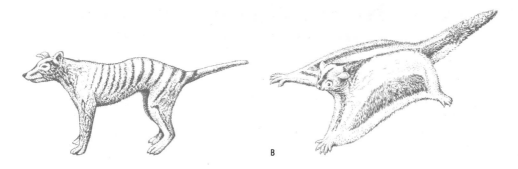

FIG. 19–1    Taxonomic problems are often caused by superficial anatomical resemblances between
two or more fundamentally distinct groups of organisms.  This is usually the result of a similarity of
ecological niches which the organisms occupy, rather than common lines of descent.  Thus organism
A appears to belong to the order carnivora, and organism B to the order rodentia, yet both organisms
are marsupials, subclass metatheria.

## 19–2 DEVELOPMENT OF TAXONOMIC SCHEMES

Attempts to classify organisms are quite old.  Theophrastus (370–285 B.C.) tried to classify all the known plants on the basis of form, life span, and habitat. Many other investigators, working with both plants and animals, followed his example.  However, the lack of communication between different naturalists made the adoption of any one system of classification impossible.  Nor was there any uniformity in the criteria by which organisms were grouped.  One investigator might classify animals by their means of movement (flying, swimming, running, etc.).  Another might choose habitat (land, sea, or air), or geographical distribution (Asian, European, African, etc.), as his criterion.

Of course, any of these criteria are perfectly adequate bases for developing a classification system.  Which system a given naturalist chooses depends on his *purpose* for making the system in the first place.  One purpose might be to classify plants for medicinal use.  Thus all plants whose extracts reduced fevers would be placed in one group, while those whose extracts eased pain would be classified in another.  The plants in a given group might have nothing in common as far as size, shape, or color are concerned.  But they would have medicinal functions closely related.  Many classification schemes were developed according to such criteria in the period before the eighteenth century.

Today, it is recognized that the many varieties of organisms on earth have evolved from common ancestors by modification, and biologists have therefore come to agree that the most useful overall classification scheme should reflect evolutionary relationships.  In general, anatomical structures seem to provide the basis for a classification system of this type.  Taxonomists have found, however, that it is never valid to use a single criterion to establish the position of any group of animals in the classification scheme.  For example, organisms which resemble each other in outward appearance are not *necessarily* closely related in evolutionary development.

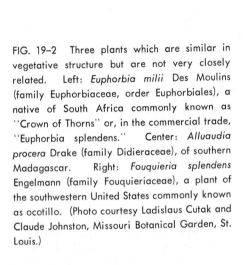

FIG. 19-2   Three plants which are similar in vegetative structure but are not very closely related.   Left: *Euphorbia milii* Des Moulins (family Euphorbiaceae, order Euphorbiales), a native of South Africa commonly known as "Crown of Thorns" or, in the commercial trade, "Euphorbia splendens."   Center: *Alluaudia procera* Drake (family Didieraceae), of southern Madagascar.   Right: *Fouquieria splendens* Engelmann (family Fouquieriaceae), a plant of the southwestern United States commonly known as ocotillo. (Photo courtesy Ladislaus Cutak and Claude Johnston, Missouri Botanical Garden, St. Louis.)

Figure 19-1 shows two organisms, of which one looks like a member of the dog family and the other a member of the order rodentia (which includes squirrels, chipmunks, and rats). On the basis of outward characteristics alone, it would seem valid to so classify them. However, the reproductive physiology of these animals reveals that they are not typical mammals (as the dog and squirrel), but marsupials. Unlike most mammals, marsupials give birth to young in a very immature form and carry them in pouches during the time needed for the offspring to complete their development. In lines of descent, then, the two organisms shown in Fig. 19-1 are more closely related to each other than to either the dog or the flying squirrel. But evolutionary adaption has brought about a chance resemblance between them and certain other, quite distinct groups of animals—Organism A, the so-called Tasmanian "wolf," occupies the same ecological niche in its native territory (Australia) as a wolf or dog in other geographic regions; Organism B occupies a niche similar to that of flying squirrels in North America.

Similar examples can be found in the plant kingdom. Figure 19-2 shows three plants that look as though they might be classified within the same family. On the basis of external characteristics of the vegetative body alone, it would seem valid to so classify them. However, study of the flowers, fruits, and other aspects of anatomy reveals differences of such magnitude as to justify separation of these plants into three separate families, each in a different order. The most likely explanation for the close similarity in vegetative features is evolutionary adaptation to similar arid environments.

The need for agreed-on criteria in any classification scheme is of obvious importance. In addition, there must be some plan of nomenclature and grouping, one that will accommodate not only all animals and plants known at present, but also those which will be discovered in the future. This need was met in 1735 by Carolus Linnaeus, when he published the first of ten editions of his work *Systema Naturae*. Linnaeus did not originate the system he presented in his book. It was the work of several men before him. However, by publishing his *Systema Naturae* he gave great encouragement to taxonomists.

The Linnaean system as it is used today consists of seven basic classifications or groupings. They are listed below in order ranging from largest to smallest:

KINGDOM
PHYLUM (plural, PHYLA)
CLASS
ORDER
FAMILY
GENUS (plural, GENERA)
SPECIES (plural, SPECIES)

Many specialists have found that these seven groupings are insufficient. Additional groupings are brought in by prefixing **super-, sub-,** and **infra-** to names given above, and occasionally even adding a side group, or **cohort.** This greatly increases the versatility of the system. Look at the following complete classification of man:

| | | | | | |
|---|---|---|---|---|---|
| KINGDOM | Animalia | (COHORT | Unfuiculata—optional) | GENUS | Homo |
| PHYLUM | Chordata | ORDER | Primata | SPECIES | *sapiens* |
| SUBPHYLUM | Vertebrata | SUBORDER | Anthropoidea | SUBSPECIES | *sapiens* |
| SUPERCLASS | Tetrapoda | SUPERFAMILY | Hominoidea | (written *Homo sapiens sapiens*) | |
| CLASS | Mammalia | FAMILY | Hominidae | | |
| SUBCLASS | Theria | SUBFAMILY | Hominidae | | |
| INFRACLASS | Eutheria | | | | |

The groups listed in this scheme form a **hierarchy.** Each group in the hierarchy includes a greater variety of characteristics than the group directly beneath it. Thus the criteria which place an organism in a given kingdom have broader applicability than those which place it in a phylum within that kingdom.

You are probably familiar with the game of "twenty questions," in which one person tries to discover the identity of an object that another has in mind by asking him twenty questions about the object. The opponent must answer these questions honestly; the fewer questions it takes to discover the identity of the object, the better the questioner's score. Now, suppose that the questioner started out by asking his opponent such questions as, "Is it a cat? . . . a dog? . . .

a doorknob? . . . a nail? . . . a chessboard? . . . a bicycle?" etc. Obviously, at this rate he would use up his twenty questions very quickly. There would be little chance of guessing the right answer, because each question would eliminate only one possibility, instead of several. On the other hand, if the first question were one such as, "Is it animal, vegetable, or mineral?" (a division, incidentally, into which Linnaeus divided all natural objects), the reply would eliminate two-thirds of the objects in the universe. Given the answer to his first question (let us say that the object is an animal), the questioner could then proceed along the same line of inquiry, trying to determine what *kind* of animal it is (bird, reptile, mammal). His questions would become progressively more definitive until the correct answer was obtained. In this way, it would usually be possible to get the answer well before the twentieth question.

The biologist who tries to identify an animal or plant that is new to him is simply playing the game of twenty questions. He begins by observing the specimen and determining the phylum (or kingdom, in some ambiguous cases) to which it belongs. In many cases, it may be very obvious where the organism belongs, from the level of phylum down to the level of order or even genus. In such cases, the biologist's past experience helps him narrow down the possibilities very quickly. He still must try to place the organism in a species, however. This involves asking specifically more and more restricted questions, until he finally reaches a category below which he cannot go. Usually—though not always—this is the species.

In taxonomy, the species is the basic unit of classification, for the species occupies a different position in the biological world than any of the higher groupings. Genera, orders, families, classes, or phyla exist only as classificatory groupings designated by the biologist. Species, however, have an important reality in nature. Members of one species are usually reproductively isolated from members of another species. Although biologists have always had difficulty formulating a species concept that will include all plants, animals and micro-organisms, it is no longer argued by competent biologists (as it once was) that species are only artificial groups set up by man.

Higher taxonomic categories such as genus or family have only what biologists think of as a historical reality. These categories are set up by man on the basis of his visual observations of structural and/or ecological similarity. Thus a genus contains a number of species which have certain characteristics in common. An order, in turn, contains a number of genera with attributes in common. For example, the order rodentia (rodents) contains a variety of different organisms, including the mouse, the squirrel, and the hamster. Each of these organisms represents a separate genus which, in turn, is composed of a number of species. However, all these groups belong to one order because they have prominent incisors (the two frontmost teeth) which are used for biting or gnawing. This is the criterion established for membership in the order rodentia. The order rodentia, in its turn, is grouped with a number of other orders in the class Mammalia. The criteria for this grouping are the form of birth and the fact that the young are nourished by their mother's milk.

In addition to advocating the hierarchial grouping system, Linnaeus supported the adoption of other rules for taxonomy. Organisms were to be identified by their genus and species names, with the latter uncapitalized. Thus man is classified as *Homo sapiens*, and the leopard as *Felis pardus*. (Compare with the listing of a name in a telephone book—for example, Smith, John.) This system of naming in taxonomy is known as **binomial nomenclature,** which means, literally, "naming with two names."

Linnaeus also insisted that all taxonomic names be latinized. He even did this to his own name (which was Karl von Linné in its unlatinized form). There were two main reasons for the choice of Latin. First of all, it was the language used by all scholars in Linnaeus' day. Secondly, since it was a "dead" language, the meanings of its words were less likely to change. The use of Latin in taxonomy does not mean that names for all organisms must come from Latin words. Many names are chosen from Greek, French, English, and other languages. But whatever their origin, the words are given Latin endings.

Certain general rules of writing taxonomic names have become generally accepted. The genus and species names are always written in italics, as in *Fasciola hepatica*, the sheep-liver fluke. A trinomial nomenclature is occasionally used. For example, Linnaeus classified the Caucasian race of man as *Homo sapiens sapiens*; one type of frog is classified as *Rana esculenta marmorata*. The third term in these cases is a subspecies designation.

Such rules as these are written and enforced by international commissions. In zoology, the first commission met in 1842, and included among its members Charles Darwin. The rules adopted by these commissions must be observed by every biologist who wishes recognition for his work. It is needless at this point to go into all the many rules of taxonomy which have been adopted. Some of them are quite legalistic and complex; in fact, many professional biologists are not entirely familiar with them. It is enough to point out that the existence of a ruling board with power to enforce is an obvious necessity to the success of plant and animal classification.

Due to the influence of the International Commission on Taxonomy, the discovery and attainment of international recognition of a new species follows a fairly standard pattern. Suppose an entomologist captures an insect which he believes to be a representative of a new species. The procedure he follows in order to have his find recognized might well be as follows:

1) *Recognition and description of the organism.* This includes studies of the anatomy, physiology, morphology, and other pertinent information that will enable the entomologist to figure out what relationship the species bears to other known groups.

2) *Placement of the animal where it belongs in the hierarchial system of Linnaeus.* This step depends on the evidence obtained in step 1, and is accomplished by "keying out" the organism—comparing its description with printed descriptions of this general type of organism down to the point at which the specimen either

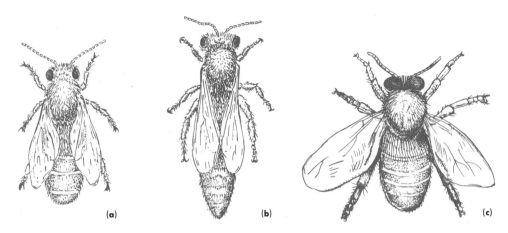

FIG. 19–3   A well-known example of polymorphism is shown by the three forms of the honeybee, *Apis mellifera.* (a) The sterile female worker bee. (b) The fertile queen. (c) The drone (male).

does or does not fit the description of a species already entered in the taxonomic key. If it does, of course, it is not a new species. An example of a key for trees and shrubs in a given region is shown in Appendix 4. The use of a key in biology is, as you can see, just a formalized game of twenty questions.

A complication in classification is encountered in species which have members that exist in many different anatomical forms. Such **polymorphism** (*poly* = many; *morph* = form) is shown by many colonial insects—for example, ants, bees, and termites (see Fig. 19–3). The worker bee, the queen, and the male (drone) are all quite different. Yet, they are obviously all the same species. The taxonomist must be careful that newly discovered types are not classified as new species when in reality they are simply different forms of a known species.

If it is revealed that the organism does not represent a new species, but an old one already described, the entomologist simply assigns the specimen its proper place within the grouping. If the organism represents a new species, however, it will not fit into the key. The entomologist must now describe it very carefully, point out how it fails to fit into the established keys, make drawings of the organism, and explain why he thinks it represents a new, undescribed species.

3) *Choice of nomenclature,* or the naming of the new species. This is the simplest step of all. The entomologist chooses a name, latinizes it, and publishes his findings in a short paper devoted to a description of the newly discovered species. Special emphasis is put on those respects in which the species differs from the most nearly similar type. Illustrations are given, with attention to *precision* rather than artistic merit (see Fig. 19–4). Often, microscopic organisms or parts are drawn with the aid of a camera lucida (see Glossary).

The biologist has long been the subject of many jokes—some good and some bad—about his choice of names for living organisms. They seem, to the

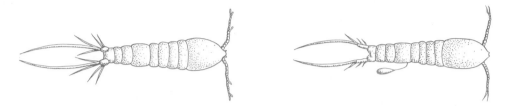

FIG. 19–4   Camera lucida drawings of two species of a small freshwater crustacean called a copepod. Such simple but accurate drawings aid the taxonomist in identifying the small anatomical differences that may distinguish one species from another.

uninitiated, needlessly complex. What the average man calls a rat, the zoologist calls *Rattus rattus rattus.* Yet, there are excellent reasons for the scientist's choice of the longer road.

First, the use of common names for organisms leads to a great deal of confusion. Often, the common name varies from locality to locality, within even a few square miles. For example, members of the insect order Odonata are commonly called dragonflies, but they are also known as horse stingers, mosquito hawks, snake feeders, snake doctors, and witch doctors. By contrast, only one name for this order of insects is used by biologists all over the world.

Second, a single common name is often used indiscriminately for a wide range of species. In fact, in common usage the name "rat" can be given to many different animals (for example, muskrat). Similarly, the term "wolf" is applied not only to the familiar wild relative of the dog, but also to the Tasmanian "wolf," which is in fact a marsupial, as we saw in Fig. 19–1. On the other hand, the biologist's term *Rattus rattus rattus* pinpoints precisely the genus, species, and subspecies he is discussing.

Biology students often become firmly convinced that taxonomic names are chosen on the basis of being difficult to learn! However, if the words seem difficult, they are not deliberately made so. On the contrary, most biological naming is done with an eye to its being both simple and descriptive. For example, the lily that is named *Tigrinum giganteum* is the giant tiger lily. The one called *Tigrinum speciosum rubrum* is a red variety. (The writers once had a student who on a test was unable to recall the species name of the common housecat, *Felis domestica.* However, he did have enough presence of mind to make his guess a descriptive one—and handed in his answer as *Felis pussicatius!*)

**19–4
THE PROBLEM OF
SPECIES
DEFINITION**

The definition of a species was far simpler in the time of Linnaeus than it is today. In the eighteenth century, it was believed that species were fixed and unchanging. Therefore, it was thought that detailed descriptions of plants and animals would apply equally well at any point in time, past, present, or future.

However, as ideas of evolution became widely accepted, and paleontological work brought to light many forms which had no counterpart among living

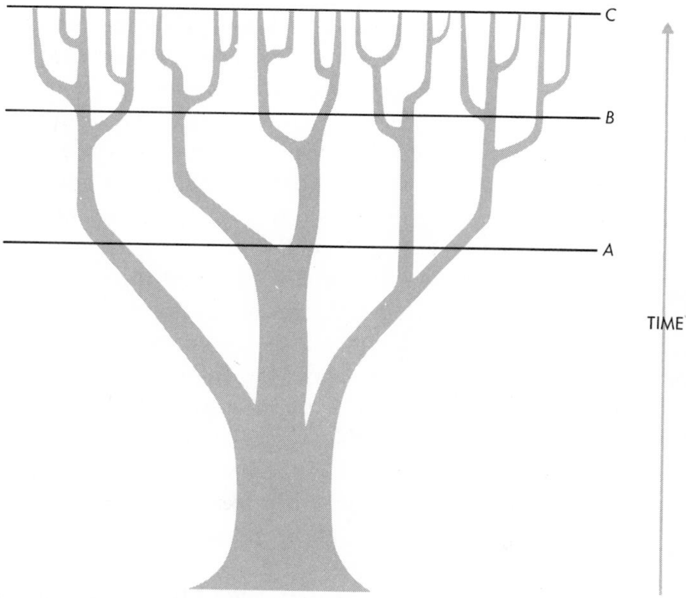

FIG. 19–5 Schematic view of the evolution of a group of species from a single common ancestor. The tops of the ''tree'' at level C represent present-day species of one particular genus. Levels B and A represent different periods of time in the geologic past. It can be seen that the number of species was smaller at time A than at time B. Species and species groups are constantly changing in time, and the techniques of modern taxonomy must allow for this.

TIME

organisms, it became obvious that the old idea of unchanging species was incorrect. Today, we think of living species as merely the top branches of a constantly growing tree (see Fig. 19–5). If we were to cut across the branches at any level, we would see the species distribution as it existed at that point in time.

The procedure followed in early taxonomy was to describe a given species in terms of a detailed anatomical study of a few "representative" specimens of that species. During the eighteenth and nineteenth centuries, examples of new and undescribed species discovered in remote areas of the world were sent back to professional taxonomists whose job it was to describe and classify the organisms. After examining a new organism, the taxonomist would decide whether it was merely a subdivision of an existing species, or was different enough to be rated as a new species. The number of specimens which the taxonomist studied, however, was usually limited to one or two of each species, and his study did not take him outside the laboratory or workroom.

Later taxonomists took to the field to study specimens, and thus were able to study species not only on a larger scale, but also on the basis of a different criterion—the presence or absence of crossbreeding. As the following example illustrates, breeding patterns reveal species distinctions that would be overlooked in a simple anatomical examination.

A number of different species of the small fruit fly *Drosophila* live in the vicinity of Austin, Texas. Many of these species are quite similar anatomically, so much so that it would take a real expert to note any distinguishing features. The differences are far less extreme, for example, than between a bulldog and a great dane, which are members of the *same* species. Yet, study of these flies in their natural habitat shows that none of these species (about 40) crossbreed with each other. Their physiological differences are great enough so that a cross-breeding, or hybridization, does not produce offspring which survive. If the older species concept had been applied to this problem, and a few flies studied anatomically under the microscope, the number of and distinction between the species would probably not have been determined. By observing the organisms in relation to their environment, a more reliable grouping of the flies into species is obtained.

The use of interbreeding as the sole criterion for species differentiation nevertheless presents certain difficulties to the modern biologist, who wishes to develop a species concept applicable to all groups in the animal and plant kingdoms. First, although interspecific breeding seldom occurs in the animal kingdom, it occurs rather frequently among plants. Two parent plants which are capable of producing hybrid offspring may frequently have to be considered separate species because they differ sharply in anatomical and other details. Taxonomists feel that if the plants do not usually interbreed in nature, a few cases of hybridization do not require those plants to be considered the same species.

An example of the reverse side of the coin is found in the animal kingdom, in the case of the grass frog. There is a continuous distribution of this amphibian from Vermont to Florida (see Fig. 19–6). Despite the fact that adjacent populations can and do interbreed, the Vermont variety cannot mate with the Florida variety if the two are brought into contact in one or the other environment. However, if specimens from Florida are first conditioned to the water temperature in which Vermont frogs live (or vice versa), then mating occurs. How, then, do we classify the Vermont and Florida varieties of the grass frog? Are they separate species? On the basis of the plant example discussed in the preceding paragraph, we might be inclined to say yes, since the two frogs generally do not mate in nature. However, taxonomists *do* consider the two varieties to be members of the same species (*Rana pipiens*). The reason is that because each geographic variety can mate with the variety adjacent to it, genetic characteristics can spread completely throughout the population, from Florida to Vermont.

Another difficulty with the criterion of interbreeding as a basis for a species concept is presented by microorganisms. Many one-celled species do not reproduce by sexual means. It is obvious that they cannot be divided into species on the basis of whether or not they interbreed. Such a criterion is, in this case, meaningless. Yet, species do exist among microorganisms as definitely (in anatomical and physiological terms) as among sexually reproducing forms.

These are just a few of the problems which are encountered in attempting to arrive at a satisfactory species definition. It is now possible to look at some of the ways in which modern taxonomists have come to view the species, and their attempts to grapple with the above problems.

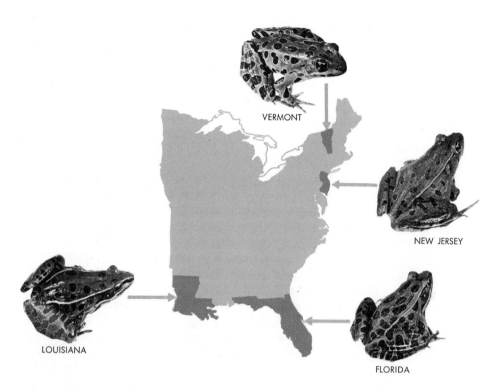

FIG. 19–6  Map of the eastern United States, showing the distribution of varieties of a single species of the grass frog, genus *Rana*. The Vermont variety and the Florida variety cannot interbreed naturally, yet they are still considered members of one species since each can interbreed with its neighboring variety. The species have spread throughout this large geographical region over the course of many thousands of years. (Photos courtesy Professor John A. Moore, Columbia University.)

Biologists think that closely related species have diverged from a common ancestor. Divergence can be seen in various stages throughout nature today. What may be only varieties of a single species, at one point in time, may become distinct species at another. For example, all housecats (Siamese, Persian, Angora) are today considered members of one species, *Felis domestica*. In the distant future, however, they may diverge enough to be considered members of separate species. The species concept developed by modern biologists tries to account for this dynamic nature of species.

The most workable species concept is that which considers the species as an active population of organisms with many anatomical, physiological, and behavioral characteristics in common. In many cases, physiological or behavioral differences can distinguish species where anatomical ones cannot. This way of looking at species may be called the **multidimensional species**

**concept.** It is based on the idea that *no single criterion* is sufficient to define a species. In accordance with the multidimensional concept, the taxonomist tries to take all an organism's aspects—morphology, behavior, physiology, and reproductive patterns—into account in asking whether two groups of organisms represent the same or different species.

**19–5
SOME MODERN
APPROACHES
IN TAXONOMY**

Modern taxonomical techniques differ considerably from those of Linnaeus' day. Part of this difference is the result of vast improvements in instrumentation and techniques. The use of computers, for example, has greatly facilitated the handling of taxonomic data. Most of the change, however, is the result of the recognition of new criteria for establishing taxonomic relationships between living organisms. Differences in behavior patterns have become one such important criterion in modern animal taxonomy. For example, differences in the mating behavior of the three- and nine-spined stickleback fish are a species-distinguishing characteristic. There is nothing else to prevent them from mating, for when their eggs are artificially inseminated, they produce healthy hybrid offspring. The three-spined male has one pattern of courtship behavior (a form of swimming "dance") which lures only three-spined females. The nine-spined stickleback has a slightly different "dance," one that attracts only nine-spined females. It is interesting to note that the dances of both males are similar at the start. Therefore, a three-spined male can hold the attention of a nine-spined female until the moment his behavior deviates from the pattern of her species. As soon as it does, she loses interest. In this manner, hybridization is prevented from occurring naturally.

Another example of the use of behavior patterns in taxonomy can be seen in Fig. 19–7. Here, analysis of sound records of cricket calls provides the basis for separation into the different species of a single genus. Cricket calls are emitted by males to attract females. A female will respond only to that call which closely resembles the pattern for her species. Thus mating does not occur between species whose patterns differ greatly from each other.

Modern biology is heavily molecular in its orientation, and taxonomy is no exception. Biochemical differences are an important means by which species may be distinguished. For example, some types of protein, such as pigments or the blood protein hemoglobin, vary in their composition from species to species. The composition of proteins can be determined by the process of **electrophoresis** (see Glossary), and the electrophoretic patterns for the same proteins in different species can then be compared. Since this technique gives quantitative results, the exact differences between two samples become apparent (see Fig. 19–8). Such biochemical studies are especially useful in work with microorganisms, notably bacteria. Two bacteria may appear completely identical anatomically. However, if the sum total of biochemical differences is great enough, they may be considered separate species.

Immunological techniques have been rather widely used in taxonomy. As a defense against infection, an organism's body reacts negatively to the introduc-

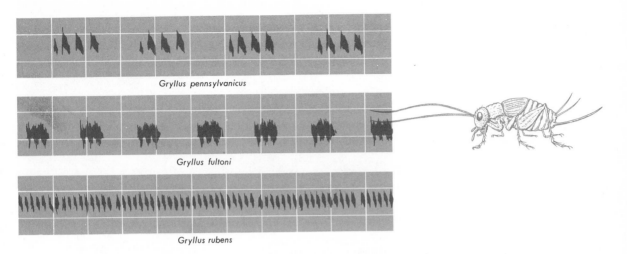

FIG. 19–7   Sound pattern recorded for three species of the common field cricket. By use of such techniques, it has been found that six different species of field cricket exist in the eastern United States alone. The use of traditional taxonomic procedures had earlier led taxonomists to believe that all the crickets in the western hemisphere were of a single species.

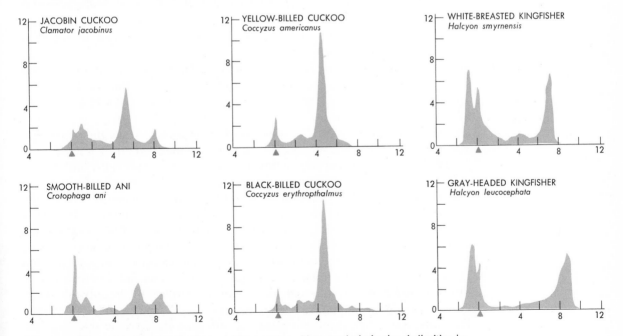

FIG. 19–8   Electrophoretic patterns of egg white proteins. Note particularly the similarities between the species of a single genus. (Based on photos in R. E. Alston et al., *Biochemical Systematics.* Englewood Cliffs, N.J.: Prentice-Hall, 1963. Courtesy Charles G. Sibley.)

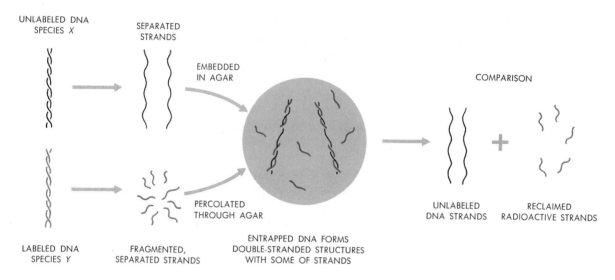

FIG. 19–9   A diagram showing how the comparison of DNA similarities can establish or confirm relationships between different groups of organisms. The DNA shown in color has been labeled with a radioactive isotope. By measuring the amount of radioactivity present in the reclaimed DNA shown on the right, the degree of relationship is established. The more DNA is reclaimed, the more distant is the relationship between the two groups of organisms.

tion of foreign protein, and produces a reaction. The more unlike its own protein the foreign protein is, the greater the organism's reaction; thus the chances of success of a transplant operation (e.g., kidney) are greater if a close relative, especially an identical twin, is used as the donor.

The immunological reaction thus has obvious taxonomical significance. For example, although the blood proteins (albumins) of man and rat show a relatively high degree of immunological reaction, far less reaction occurs between the blood proteins of man and monkey, and still less between those of man and ape. Indeed, so little reaction is shown between the blood of man and that of gorillas and chimpanzees that Dr. Morris Goodman of Wayne State University in Detroit has stated his belief that these animals should be reclassified and put into the family of man (Hominidae) rather than the family of apes (Pongidae).

The studies of blood albumin are nicely borne out by comparisons of the blood hemoglobins of the same organisms. It turns out that man and chimpanzee have identical hemoglobin; the hemoglobin of man and gorilla differ by only two amino acids, that of man and monkey by twelve. Drs. A. C. Wilson and V. M. Sarich have used this information to suggest that man and the apes diverged from the monkeys about 30 million years ago, and that man diverged from the ape around five million years ago. There is by no means total agreement on this matter, however, and since Wilson and Sarich's technique is based on the assumption that the mutation rate in any fixed interval of time is constant, there is not likely to be until other techniques either confirm or deny their results. But such work does have obvious taxonomical significance as a means of determining degrees of relationship between living organisms.

A relatively new technique for analyzing interrelationships between species involves comparison of their DNA for similarities. The technique is based upon the well-established belief that it is DNA which determines the characteristics of living organisms. The more closely related two organisms are, the more the DNA of one should resemble the DNA of the other. The DNA molecules of one species are embedded in a porous agar. Fragmented DNA molecules of the other species are labeled with a radioactive isotope and percolated through the agar. The more similar the two types of DNA, the more combinations will occur between the labeled and unlabeled DNA fragments, and the fewer radioactive DNA fragments will pass through the agar to be collected again. If the two species are not closely related, very few labeled DNA fragments will be picked up by the unlabeled DNA in the agar. In this case, most of the labeled DNA fragments will pass through the agar and be collected. The technique is represented diagrammatically in Fig. 19–9.

DNA comparison has confirmed many relationships already indicated by investigations based on anatomical or physiological similarities. DNA from the bacterium *Escherichia coli* picks up most of the labeled DNA from other bacteria, but almost none from vertebrates. About 75% of labeled DNA from mice is trapped by rat DNA, while only 60% combination occurs between the DNA of mice and hamsters. Human DNA shows 25% combination with mouse and calf DNA, but only 5% with DNA from a salmon.

**19–6
TAXONOMIC
CHARTS**

In Appendix 5 are found taxonomic charts for both the two-kingdom (plants, animals) and the five-kingdom (monera, protista, plants, fungi, animals) systems of classification. Reference must be made to them in order to do some of the exercises at the end of this chapter. Such charts are not meant to be memorized; to do so would be of little value, and would certainly not be worth the time it would require. However, the more they are used, the more familiar the taxonomic groupings will become.

Using a taxonomic chart is, therefore, like using a dictionary. No one would sit down and memorize a dictionary; most of the words learned in this way would never be put to any practical use—and besides, they would be forgotten very quickly. However, the dictionary is an extremely useful tool to be able to use when necessary. The chances are good that after a word has been looked up once or twice, and has actually been *used*, it will not have to be looked up again. A dictionary's usefulness depends only on an understanding of the principle according to which it is organized. Exactly the same applies to the use of taxonomic charts.

It must appear that much of the system of classification which biologists use is somewhat arbitrary. This is, of course, the case. Development of a system of classification represents a very characteristic aspect of scientific work: model building. Scientific models, like model airplanes or model trains, are artificial constructions that allow people to deal with various aspects of their experience in a convenient way. Most people cannot afford the space or the money to own a real airplane or a real locomotive. However, a child *can* learn something about the principles of aerodynamics from model airplanes, or he can learn about the logistics of hooking and unhooking long lines of railroad cars from a model train set.

In general, scientific models serve two purposes. One is to provide a way of organizing observations or data. The second is to provide a viewpoint from which to analyze a group of observations or phenomena, and thus give a direction for future investigation. Most scientific hypotheses are limited types of models. The more elaborate models in science are those such as the planetary model of the atom, the idea of the organism as an internal combustion engine, or the view of all species as descending by a process of modification from common ancestors.

It is characteristic of scientific models that no one claims they necessarily represent reality. They are only an artificial arrangement of parts which provide a way of looking at the world. Furthermore, there is no guarantee that the model will not break down. A child can learn a great deal about how a dispatcher in the railroad yard moves trains around from track to track, in order to hook the right cars to the right locomotives, from playing with a model train set. However, he soon learns that there are some principles about the movement of trains that the electric train set does not indicate. For instance, he may learn that the load which an electric train will pull is in no way proportionate to the load which a real train will pull. In dealing with load size, therefore, the model breaks down. In a similar way, a scientist's model may break down—he may encounter observations or phenomena that do not fit the model. When this happens, he must build a new model to account for the new information. It is not always necessary to discard the old model under these circumstances, since it may still be useful for certain purposes if not all.

The taxonomist, then, builds a scientific model when he sets up his hierarchical system of classification; he then tries to see how far it will get him in dealing with animals and plants which he collects. If the scheme allows him to place most organisms in one category or another, then the model is said to be adequate. We have noted that the only unit in the hierarchy which has any reality in nature is the species. All higher categories are parts of the classificatory model—a means of dealing with and organizing the multitude of species groups. The present classification system seems to provide a solid basis for organizing information about almost all species of organisms. It is therefore a very useful and satisfying model.

In this chapter we have been concerned with the principles of classification as they apply to the biological world. In particular, we have concentrated on the species concept and its importance in the biologist's classification scheme. We have seen that it is very difficult to develop a species concept which will apply to all forms of organisms: plants, animals, and microorganisms. Yet, at the same time, we have also seen that species are a reality in all of these types of organisms.

The modern species concept is based on a number of different criteria, such as morphology, geographic distribution, mating behavior, physiological and biochemical characteristics. It is therefore known as the multidimensional species concept. This is in contrast to the older ideas of species, which tended to establish species boundaries on the basis of a single (usually morphological) criterion.

The species is a fundamental biological unit, with each species treated as a population of interbreeding organisms. Higher categories such as genus, order, family, and so forth, represent groupings of species on the basis of similarities perceived by the taxonomist, rather than on the basis of the natural self-grouping displayed by species.

**19-8
CONCLUSION**

**EXERCISES**

1. What is the purpose of classification as a process in *any* area of human activity? Can classification schemes be arbitrary? What essential problem do biologists face which makes their efforts at classification difficult?

2. This chapter discussed at length how biologists view the concept of "species" and how they distinguish one species from another. Why do you think biologists are so interested in the question of what a species is?

3. What is meant by the term "binomial nomenclature"? Give an example of a biological species identified in this manner.

4. Describe the general practice for having the name of a new species recognized.

5. How can behavior patterns be useful criteria for distinguishing between species?

6. Give two examples of biochemical techniques which yield information of value for taxonomy.

7. In the following examples, tell whether each word represents a kingdom, phylum, class, order, family, genus, species, or subspecies. Refer to the taxonomic chart (Appendix 5) or to the reading in the chapter, if necessary. (a) Animalia, (b) Plantae, (c) Lycopodinae, (d) *Rana pipiens*, (e) *Rattus rattus rattus*, (f) Equestinidae, (g) *Bufo fowler*, (h) *Felis marmorata*, (i) Talpidae, (j) *Sorex araneus castaneus*, (k) Erinaceidae, (l) *Erinaceus europaeus* L.*

8. The genus containing the cats is *Felis*. What, then, would be the family name?

---

* The L. in this case indicates that the species was first described by Linnaeus. If it was first described by a man other than Linnaeus, and the information is deemed useful enough to be included, the man's name should be given just after the species or subspecies name, as in *Neomys fodiens bicolor* (Shaw) or *Crocidura cassiteridum* Hinton. (The presence or absence of parentheses also has meaning.)

TABLE 19–1

| ORIGIN OF SERUM | AMOUNT OF PRECIPITATE RELATIVE TO HUMAN |
|---|---|
| PRIMATES | |
| MAN | 100 |
| CHIMPANZEE | 130 (some loose pcpt) |
| GORILLA | 64 |
| ORANG | 42 |
| MANDRILL | 42 |
| GUINEA BABOON | 29 |
| SPIDER MONKEY | 29 |
| CARNIVORES | |
| DOG | 3 |
| JACKAL | 10 |
| HIMALAYAN BEAR | 8 |
| GENET | 3 |
| CAT | 3 |
| TIGER | 2 |
| UNGULATES | |
| OX | 10 |
| SHEEP | 10 |
| WATER BUCK | 7 |
| REINDEER | 7 |
| GOAT | 2 |
| HORSE | 2 |
| PIG | 0 |
| RODENTS | |
| GUINEA PIG | 0 |
| MARSUPIALS | |
| SIX SPECIES: ROCK AND NAIL-TAILED WALLABIES, KANGAROO, TASMANIAN WOLF | 0 |

9. Antihuman serum was prepared in rabbits by periodic injection with human serum. The antihuman serum was then injected into a number of organisms and the amount of precipitate recorded, as shown in Table 19–1.*

   a) From this information, construct two family trees, one for the primates and one for the carnivores.

   b) Which would be most closely related to the carnivores: the ungulates, rodents, insectivores, or marsupials?

   c) What is the chemical principle on which such serum tests are founded? What does the presence of a precipitate indicate?

---

* From G. Wald, "Biochemical Evolution," in *Trends in Physiology and Biochemistry*, E. S. G. Barron, ed. (New York: Academic Press, 1952).

Using the taxonomic chart, classify the following organisms *as completely as you can* from from the information given here and in the chart.

10. An animal with hair, which nurses its young and brings them forth alive. Its front incisor teeth are adapted for gnawing.

11. A single-celled plant, with chloroplasts, living mostly on the bark of trees, and reproducing by fission.

12. An animal with a scaly skin; cold-blooded; young hatch from eggs laid outside of the body.

13. A tree with roots, stem, leaves, and flowers. Vascular tissues in stem arranged in orderly fashion; reproductive cycle involves a true seed.

14. Land-dwelling plant. Vascular tissues in stem; reproduction by spores, and exhibits a metagenesis (alternation of generations).

15. Land-dwelling plant without vascular tissues; exhibits a metagenesis, with spore formation in asexual part of cycle.

16. Land-dwelling plant with flower and seed, and flower parts arranged in threes.

17. Aquatic plant, with cells arranged in filaments, although each cell is capable of independent existence. Reproduces asexually, by fission. Exhibits conjugation.

18. Animal with spiny skin; cold-blooded, with two-chambered heart. All aquatic or marine, and with cartilaginous skeleton.

**SUGGESTED READINGS**

MAYR, ERNST, "Difficulties and Importance of the Biological Species Concept," in Jeffrey J. W. Baker and Garland E. Allen (Eds.), *The Process of Biology: Primary Sources* (Reading, Mass.: Addison-Wesley, 1970). This is a detailed and thorough coverage of the species concept as dealt with by a specialist. The problem of "What is a species?" is discussed in relation to animals, plants, microorganisms. This work is suggested only for those who are especially interested in this topic.

SIBLEY, CHARLES G., "The Comparative Morphology of Protein Molecules as Data for Classification," in *Systematic Zoology* (part of a symposium on "the Data of Classification"). A relatively nontechnical review article of biochemical taxonomy.

# CHAPTER 20

# ECOLOGICAL RELATIONSHIPS: COMPETITION FOR ENERGY

## 20-1
## INTRODUCTION

A nineteenth-century biologist is reported to have claimed that the "glory of England" was due to its old maids! The biologist reasoned in the following manner: Healthy British men are nourished by roast beef. The cattle that supply the roast beef feed on clover. Clover is pollinated by bumblebees. Bumblebee nests are destroyed by field mice. The number of field mice in any area depends on the number of cats. Since old maids keep cats, the number of old maids ultimately determines how much roast beef is available.

As far-fetched as this argument may sound today, it nevertheless emphasizes an important principle. All organisms live in nature in a close and delicately controlled relationship with a great many other organisms. All those living things in any given area (small pond, large river, or even an entire continent or ocean) form part of a **biotic community.** In a biotic community the existence of each species, as well as of each individual, is governed to some extent by the presence of all the others. The biotic community forms a web, the structure of which depends on every single strand. If just one strand of this web is broken, the structure may assume an entirely different character. Introduction of the Japanese beetle into America and the jackrabbit into Australia has had considerable effect on the biotic communities of these countries. Introduction of nonnative organisms of this sort often invites disaster. Without natural enemies, the new organisms reproduce rapidly and can do great damage. The great numbers of jackrabbits in Australia, for example, took heavy tolls on the vegetation. This, in turn, affected a large variety of other organisms which relied on the vegetation for their food. The natural history of many parts of Australia has been altered temporarily, or even permanently, by the uncontrolled spread of rabbits after their introduction in the last century.

The study of the various relationships between organisms and their environment is known as **ecology.** The environment of any organism includes two major aspects, the **physical environment** and the **biotic environment.** Physical environment includes the presence or absence of minerals, and the amount of light or moisture as well as the temperature and pH. The biotic environment, on the other hand, includes all the various living organisms with which an animal or plant comes into contact.

Organisms in a biotic community depend on each other directly or indirectly for day-to-day existence. But although they are dependent on one another, organisms also compete for the resources available in the environment. There is competition for food, for a mineral and water supply, for sunlight and for territory. In short, and to sum up, *there is competition for energy.* For an organism to maintain itself and reproduce, a constant supply of energy is necessary. This energy ultimately comes from the environment. When plants compete for sunlight, they are in fact competing for radiant energy. When animals compete for food, they are only competing for a source of energy. One of the significant features of this competition is that the total amount of available energy is limited. For example, seed-eating birds can grow and reproduce only so long as the supply of seeds (i.e., a source of energy) lasts. The dependence of organisms on a limited food supply is one of the major principles involved in understanding how ecological relationships develop and how they are maintained.

The concepts of **ecological niche, habitat,** and **ecosystem** are very useful in describing the various relationships between organisms.

Habitat is the place in which an organism lives in the biotic community. The term may refer to an area as large as the ocean or desert, or as small as the underside of a lily pad or the intestine of a termite. Ecologists sometimes speak of habitat as the "address" of an organism within the community.

The ecological niche occupied by an organism is less easy to pinpoint than the habitat. The term "niche" refers to the role an organism plays within the biotic community. To what organisms does it serve as food, upon what organisms does it feed? What minerals does it extract from the environment? What minerals does it return to the environment? Is the organism primarily a producer, such as a green plant, or a consumer, such as an animal? Answers to such questions as these help to establish the exact niche an organism occupies. Just as an organism's habitat is spoken of as its address within the biotic community, so its ecological niche is called its "profession." Unlike its habitat, an organism's niche includes all the physical, chemical, and biotic factors the organism needs to maintain itself and to reproduce.

Organisms may live together in the same general habitat, but yet have quite different ecological niches. For example, tide pools on the coast contain a wide variety of organisms: starfish and sea anemones (animals), and "seaweed" and smaller filamentous algae (plants), all of which have roughly the same habitat. Yet within a single tide pool the algae serve as producers, since

20-2
ECOLOGICAL
NICHES, HABITATS,
AND THE
ECOSYSTEM

they can manufacture carbohydrates by using energy from the sun.  The animals serve as consumers.  They feed on smaller animals which ultimately feed on the plants.  The algae occupy a quite different ecological niche from the starfish or sea anemones.

Even more specific examples of this phenomenon can be given.  In the shallow water along the shore of a lake it is possible to observe a large variety of water insects, all of which have the same habitat.  Some of these, such as the "back-swimmer," genus *Notonecta*, serve as predators, feeding on other small animals.  Other backswimmers, of the genus *Corixa*, serve as decomposers, feeding on dead or decaying material.  Both organisms have the same habitat.  Their ecological niches within that habitat, however, are quite different.

Still another example of how specialized certain ecological niches can be is afforded by the example of African vultures, which feed on the carrion of animals that have died of natural causes, or on remains that have been left by predators.  Although large crowds of these birds can usually be seen feeding on one carcass, closer examination reveals that one species has a beak that is adapted in a manner which makes it excellent for tearing out soft flesh or intestines, another has a beak best suited to snatching flesh from others after it has been torn free, another that specializes in the hide, tendons, and ligaments, and finally a species which can reach into parts of the remaining skeleton and extract portions that none of the other species can reach.

Every environment offers a large number of niches and habitats.  In fact, the environment for any two organisms is never precisely the same, although it tends to be similar for members of a given species.  While we have seen that two species can occupy roughly the same habitat, in any given community they cannot occupy the same niche for very long.  Occupying the same niche means competing on nearly every level of existence.  Such competition generally results in the survival of one species and the elimination of the other.

The term ecosystem refers to the sum total of physical and biological factors operating in any one area.  An ecosystem is a self-sufficient unit.  Ecosystems may be very small (e.g., a freshwater pond), or very large (e.g., the Sahara Desert or the Indian Ocean).  In an ecosystem, there is a cyclic exchange of materials and energy between living things and the environment.  The minerals, the nitrogen and carbon compounds, and the water that living things require are continually recycled through the system.  If the system is a balanced one, no materials are ever exhausted.  The only requirement of an ecosystem is a constant input of energy.  The ultimate energy source is, of course, sunlight, captured by green plants in the process of photosynthesis.

A generalized ecosystem is shown in Fig. 20–1.  The living organisms in any ecosystem can be divided into three groups: **producers, consumers,** and **decomposers.**  Producer organisms are those, such as green plants, that can manufacture food substances from simple components such as water and carbon dioxide.  Plants are the ultimate producer organisms in any ecosystem.  They are the only organisms that can use the energy of sunlight to power the food-producing process.

Consumer organisms are those that feed directly on other organisms.  All animals fall into this category.  Those animals that feed on plants are called **herbivores**.  Herbivores may be considered **primary consumers**.  In other words, they feed *directly* on producer organisms.  Those animals that feed primarily on other animals are called **carnivores**.  Carnivores serve as **secondary** or **tertiary consumers,** depending on which organisms they feed on.  Alfalfa growing in a field represents a producer.  Cows, which feed on the alfalfa, are primary consumers.  Man, who feeds on the cow, is a secondary consumer.

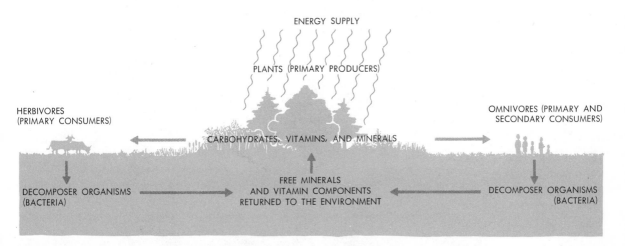

FIG. 20–1   Schematic representation of a generalized ecosystem.  All materials in such a system are constantly recycled from one organism to another, but eventually return to the environment.  To keep the system in operation, however, energy must be added continually from the outside.  The ultimate energy source for all ecosystems on the earth is sunlight.

What happens to the materials consumer organisms take into their bodies? Are the materials lost from the ecosystem? Yes, but only temporarily.  Animals are continually returning various substances to the environment by the elimination of their waste products.  Furthermore, when an animal or plant dies, the materials within its body are acted on by organisms of decay—bacteria and various other decomposers.  These organisms break down the complex proteins, fats, and nucleic acids of the dead organism and release many of the components back into the environment.  At the same time, the decomposers are gaining their own nourishment.  Decomposer organisms thus occupy an extremely important niche within an ecosystem.  Through the metabolic activity of decomposers, vital organic materials are prevented from remaining locked up in the bodies of dead organisms.

Consider an example of a typical ecosystem—a freshwater pond (Fig. 20–2). Solar radiation is the driving force that keeps any such system going.  This energy is harnessed by the producers: rooted water plants and free-floating algae.

Small organisms feed on the algae and are, in turn, fed on by larger forms. These larger forms, if they have no natural enemy, ultimately die and are acted on by organisms of decay, which break down the large organic molecules and absorb the substances they need. The rest is returned to the water. As a result, all the materials that plants withdraw from the water in the course of their normal metabolism are returned. Besides producing carbohydrates, plants often synthesize complex compounds that animals are unable to produce on their own. Thus consumers obtain from producers not only a source of energy, but also many of the substances essential for their own growth and development.

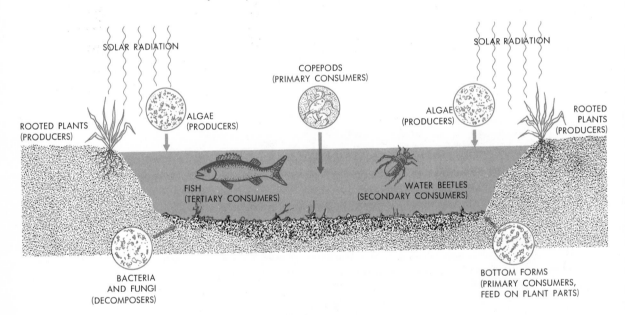

FIG. 20–2   Diagram of a freshwater pond as an ecosystem. All organisms in an eocsystem are either producers or consumers. Solar radiation energy is the driving force that keeps the system going. This energy is captured by the producers, which may be both simple algae in the water and rooted plants along the shore. Organisms such as copepod crustaceans feed directly on the algae. They therefore serve as primary consumers. Copepods, in turn, serve as food for water insects such as the predacious diving beetle or the scavenger water beetle. The beetles are thus secondary consumers. Larger fish in the pond, such as bass, feed on many of the aquatic insects. Hence fish may be considered tertiary consumers.

There is competition at all levels in any ecosystem. In a lake, algae on the surface of the water or plants around the shore compete for available sunlight and for the mineral nutrients in the water. Copepods compete for available algae, while water beetles compete for available copepods. Fish, in turn, compete for water beetles, and so on. All forms of competition are simply attempts to obtain a source of energy.

The flow of materials in an ecosystem is the result of prey-predator relationships. All animals are predators, either on other animals or on plants. A predator is an organism which feeds directly on another organism. By this definition, most plants would be preyed upon, but would not themselves be predators.* In any ecosystem, every organism serves in the capacity of either prey or predator. In most cases, an organism is both prey *and* predator, for example the scavenger beetle shown in Fig. 20–2.

Prey-predator relationships establish a long chain of events. This chain begins with the primary consumers and ends up with the tertiary or quaternary consumer. A prey-predator relationship in any ecosystem is an established, permanent relationship.

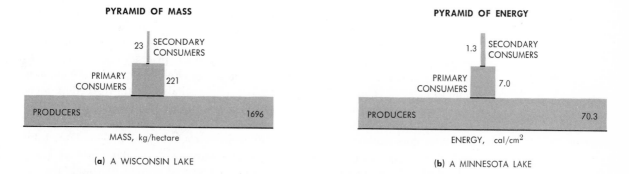

FIG. 20–3   (a) Pyramid of mass and (b) pyramid of energy. The pyramid of mass shows that the total amount of material decreases at each level along a food chain. The pyramid of energy yields similar conclusions about the amount of usable energy at each step along a food chain. A great deal of both matter and energy is required from primary producers to sustain higher-level consumers in the food chain. (Data taken from G. G. Simpson, C. S. Pittendrigh, and L. H. Tiffany, *Life: An Introduction to Biology.* New York: Harcourt, Brace & World, Inc., 1957, p. 622.)

We describe the passage of materials from producer through primary, secondary, tertiary, or quaternary consumers as a **food chain.** Like any other chain, it has a beginning and an end. The beginning is always with plants, the producers. The end is generally described as the organism that is not preyed on by any larger form. Such final links in a food chain are subject to the action of parasitic or decomposer organisms.

A food chain may be constructed in the form of a "food pyramid." This may be considered as a pyramid of mass, or a pyramid of energy. Both of these are shown in Fig. 20–3. The pyramid of mass is shown for a Wisconsin lake.

---

* The exception to this is the case of insectivorous plants, such as Venus's-flytrap. When one is dealing with animal behavior, the term predation is limited to the preying of one animal on another, and does not include the feeding by animals on plants.

This shows the amount of mass, expressed in kilograms per hectare (an area equivalent to about 2.5 acres), involved in each level of the food chain. The mass of the plant producers is given as 1696 kg. Note that the mass of the primary consumers is only 221 kg, while that of the secondary consumers is 23 kg. This means that in an area of the lake equivalent to 2.5 acres, 1696 kg of plant life will support only 221 kg of primary consumer, such as copepods, for example. In turn, the copepods will serve to sustain only 23 kg of secondary consumer, fish, for example. At each step along this chain there is a great loss of usable matter. Bypassing the intermediate steps, we can say that it takes 1696 kg of plant to support 23 kg of fish. This represents an energy transfer efficiency of about 1.3%.

A pyramid of energy (Fig. 20–3) shows much the same pattern. In this case, we are measuring the total amount of potential energy contained in the organisms making up any one level of the food chain. In the Minnesota lake of Fig. 20–3(b), the total energy of the producers (expressed as calories per square centimeter) is given as 70.3. The total energy of the primary consumers is 7.0, and that of the secondary consumers is about 1.3. Each step along the chain is able to use less than 20% of the total energy available in the preceding step. It is thus possible to see why the number of links in any food chain must be limited.

Why does each step along the food chain extract only a fraction of the total potential energy of the previous step? The decrease in available energy along a food chain is in agreement with the first and second laws of thermodynamics. The first law holds that energy cannot be created or destroyed in ordinary chemical reactions, but only changed in form. None of the energy in the universe is lost. The second law, however, states that the total amount of *usable* energy in any system tends to decrease with time. This is because no transformation of energy is 100% efficient. In a given transformation, some energy is always converted into heat.

We must thus view a food chain as one involving a series of energy conversions. With each transformation of energy from prey to predator along the food chain, there is a loss of usable energy. When a cow eats grass, for example, a great deal of the bulk consumed does not contribute to the nourishment of the cow. Much of it is indigestible and is returned to the environment in feces. In addition, the cow must move, reproduce, and carry on a great many other activities. This means that much of the carbohydrate contained in the grass must go to power such functions. Only a small amount is actually formed into structural parts of the animal that man later eats. This lack of efficiency is some indication of why the competition for energy among many groups of organisms is often so severe. This is especially true if they all occupy roughly the same consumer level on the food chain.

Three important principles emerge from this discussion of food chains. First, it can be seen that to be complete and self-containing, any food chain must always have photosynthesis at the beginning and decay at the end. In generalized form, then, a food chain may be represented as:

PHOTOSYNTHETIC ORGANISM → HERBIVORE → CARNIVORE →
ORGANISM OF DECAY.

Energy must be constantly supplied from the outside if the food chain is to keep operating. Second, we can see that the shorter a food chain, the more efficient it turns out to be. The more steps there are in such a chain, the greater the waste of energy that results. Third, we can see that the size of any population is ultimately determined by the number of steps in the food chain. With the decrease in useful energy at each step along the chain, there is very little energy available for a population of quaternary consumers. The size of a population of quaternary consumers is less than that of tertiary consumers; a population of tertiary consumers is smaller than one of secondary consumers, and so on.

In order to continue operating for any length of time, an ecosystem requires a constant input of energy. As we have seen, that energy is captured in the food-making processes of green plants. It is released again in the metabolism of both plants and animals. The *matter* (i.e., the atoms and molecules) involved in an ecosystem, however, does *not* have to be continually replenished from the outside. The chemical elements composing living organisms are constantly recirculated within an ecosystem. Several such cycles, of great importance to the maintenance of life, can be traced in nature.

**The carbon cycle.** Nearly every compound involved in the metabolic activity of living things contains the element carbon. The availability of this element in the environment is therefore a crucial factor in the maintenance of animals and plants. The continued existence of any ecosystem thus requires that the carbon "locked up" within organisms be ultimately returned to the environment. In this way, it can be used by another organism for its metabolic activity. Atoms of carbon are thus passed around in the carbon cycle.

A carbon cycle is pictured in Fig. 20–4. Let us begin with free carbon dioxide in the atmosphere. The level of atmospheric carbon dioxide is maintained by animals and plants, both of which release this gas as an end product of respiration, the process of releasing energy. Besides releasing carbon dioxide, plants have the ability to use carbon dioxide in the manufacture of carbohydrates.

The carbohydrates in plant material can follow one of several courses. If the plant is eaten by an animal, the carbohydrate is burned in the animal tissues to yield energy and release carbon dioxide back into the atmosphere. Some carbon may pass out in the waste products of animal metabolism, urine or feces. The carbon in these waste products, as well as that which is part of the animal material at death, is acted on by organisms of decay. One end product of these decay processes is carbon dioxide, which is released back into the atmosphere.

20–4
THE CYCLIC USE
OF MATERIALS

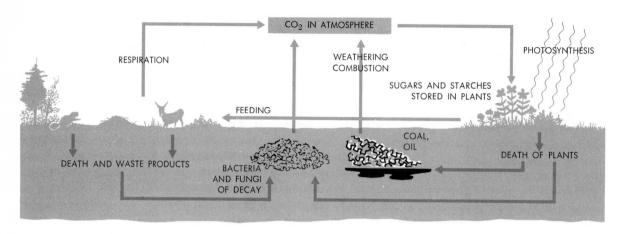

FIG. 20–4    The carbon cycle.

On the other hand, the plant may simply die, and its organic substances (carbohydrates, fats, proteins, nucleic acids, vitamins, etc.) may be acted on directly by the bacteria and fungi of decay. Sometimes, however, the plant materials may undergo a quite different process at death. By being deposited at the bottom of lakes in tightly packed layers, covered over with mud or other organic debris, and subjected to great pressure, plant parts may be turned into coal. This process requires very long periods of time, and normally occurs less frequently than decomposition by bacteria. The carbon locked in coal is taken out of the ecosystem for a long period of time. However, in due course it is returned to the atmosphere as carbon dioxide by burning or through weathering.

In all these ways, carbon taken from the atmosphere by plants in photosynthesis is ultimately returned. In the course of time, a single atom of carbon in a particular ecosystem may have existed in a variety of compounds in a variety of different organisms.

**The nitrogen cycle.** The element nitrogen is no less essential to life than carbon. In living organisms, nitrogen is found chiefly in amino acids and proteins. Since these molecules are constantly being built up and broken down in normal metabolic activity, it is essential that new sources of nitrogen be always available to an organism. Nitrogen is cycled from environment to organism back to environment by one of several paths (Fig. 20–5). Four types of bacteria are involved as key parts of the nitrogen cycle. Before considering the details of the entire cycle, it would be helpful to examine the specific nature of each of these bacteria.

1) *Nitrogen-fixing bacteria.* These bacteria live in the soil and on the roots of **leguminous plants** (i.e., plants that bear their seeds in pods, such as beans or peas), in little swellings known as **nodules** (see Fig. 20–6). Nitrogen-fixing bacteria have the ability to take free nitrogen gas from the atmosphere and

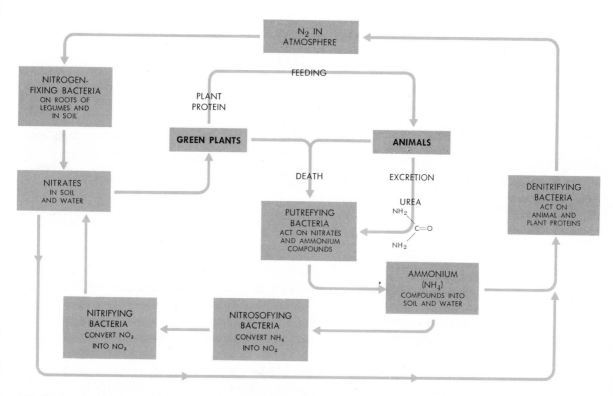

FIG. 20–5    The nitrogen cycle.

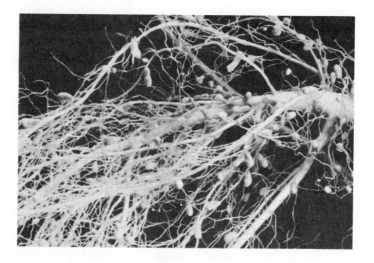

FIG. 20–6    Nodules produced on the roots of crimson clover after inoculation of the soil with nitrogen-fixing bacteria.  (Photo courtesy United States Department of Agriculture.)

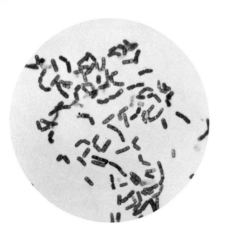

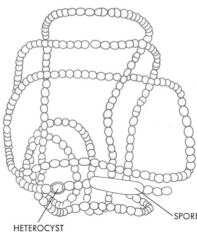

HETEROCYST    SPORE

FIG. 20–7    Two kinds of nitrogen-fixing organisms (both are procaryotes). Left: the rod-shaped bacterium *Azotobacter*. Right: *Anabaena*, a filamentous blue-green alga. (Photo courtesy General Biological Supply House, Inc., Chicago.)

convert it into soluble **nitrates** (i.e., compounds containing $NO_3$, such as potassium nitrate, $KNO_3$). Because they are soluble, nitrates can be taken into the roots of higher plants. Nitrogen-fixing bacteria and some types of algae are among the few organisms that can make use of atmospheric nitrogen (see Fig. 20–7).

2) *Putrefying bacteria.* These are bacteria found chiefly in the soil and in the mud at the bottom of lakes, rivers, or oceans. Putrefying bacteria break down animal and plant proteins, converting them into ammonium compounds (e.g., $(NH_4)_3PO_4$, ammonium phosphate). These are released into the soil or water where they can be acted on by other types of bacteria.

3) *Nitrosofying bacteria.* These bacteria (genus, *Nitrosomonas*) act on ammonium compounds such as those produced by the process of putrefaction, discussed above. By various chemical processes, these compounds are converted into **nitrites**—that is, molecules containing $NO_2$. Like nitrates, nitrites are soluble.

4) *Nitrifying bacteria.* These bacteria (genus, *Nitrobacter*) are able to convert nitrites, produced by nitrosofying bacteria, into nitrates.

5) *Denitrifying bacteria.* These bacteria convert either nitrates or ammonium compounds into molecular nitrogen ($N_2$). The denitrifying bacteria thus serve as a means of returning molecular nitrogen to the atmosphere.

Consider now how all these components fit together to form the complete nitrogen cycle. It is convenient to begin again with the atmosphere. Molecular nitrogen composes about 78% (by volume) of the earth's atmosphere. However, neither animals nor green plants use nitrogen in this form. It must first be converted into soluble nitrate compounds. This is accomplished largely by the nitrogen-fixing bacteria on the roots of leguminous plants. The nitrates produced there pass into the soil, and are absorbed by the roots of plants. Once inside the plant, nitrates can be converted into amino acids, which are, in turn, the building blocks of proteins. In this way, atmospheric nitrogen becomes incorporated into protein. It may, of course, become converted into bacterial protein without passing into green plants.

The nitrogen in plant protein may now take two different routes. If the plant is eaten by an animal, the protein is broken down and reconstituted as animal protein. In higher animals, the breakdown of proteins yields the nitrogen-containing compound urea. Lower animal forms excrete excess nitrogen in other forms, sometimes as ammonia ($NH_3$) or as a compound known as uric acid. In any case, such nitrogenous wastes are acted on by either putrefying or nitrosofying bacteria. The ultimate result is that the nitrogenous wastes are returned to the cycle either as nitrates (if acted on by nitrifying bacteria) or as molecular nitrogen (if acted on by denitrifying bacteria).

If, on the other hand, the plant dies, the proteins may be acted on by putrefying bacteria (i.e., the bacteria of decay). This changes the protein into various ammonium compounds, as well as some nonnitrogenous waste products. The ammonium compounds thus produced can be acted on by either of two types of bacteria. They may be converted into atmospheric nitrogen by the action of denitrifying bacteria, or they may be converted into nitrite compounds by the nitrosofying bacteria. Either of these processes occurs in the soil or water, as bacteria act on ammonium compounds released by the bacteria of decay. The nitrogen taken from green plants by herbivorous animals may be returned to the environment by the death of the animal. In this case, the putrefying bacteria are again the agents by which proteins are converted into ammonium.

The nitrogen cycle involves a number of organisms and a variety of pathways. There is no single nitrogen cycle; there is a group of cycles, all interacting with each other. They ultimately ensure that no atoms of nitrogen are permanently withdrawn from circulation.

The nitrogen cycle illustrates the fact that animals are unnecessary for the successful operation of an ecosystem. Only the green plants and bacteria are essential. Bacteria are needed because they can make use of the nitrogen in the atmosphere. Plants are needed because they can use sunlight to synthesize the organic compounds which, on decay, provide the bacteria with a source of energy. Animals, however, only enter the picture by feeding on plants. The nitrogen cycle, as well as the carbon cycle, would operate perfectly well without them.

**The water cycle.** Most of the water on the earth is located in the ocean. This water is constantly evaporated by the heat of the sun, and passes as vapor into the atmosphere. There, it condenses into clouds and eventually returns to the surface of the earth as rain, snow, sleet, or hail. Water falling in this way runs into streams and rivers, eventually finding its way back to the ocean. Such a pattern has become known as the water cycle. The existence of living organisms depends on relatively large and continuous supplies of water. Thus plants and

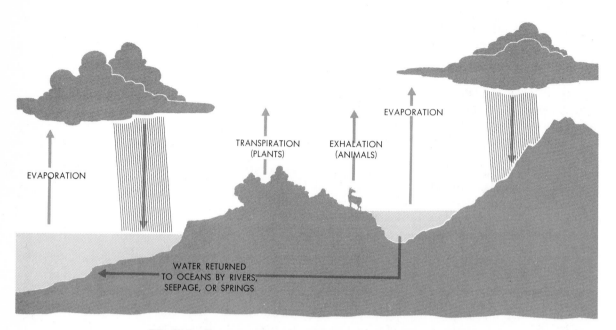

EVAPORATION

TRANSPIRATION
(PLANTS)

EXHALATION
(ANIMALS)

EVAPORATION

EVAPORATION

WATER RETURNED
TO OCEANS BY RIVERS,
SEEPAGE, OR SPRINGS

FIG. 20–8   The water cycle. From this diagram it is possible to see the number of ways in which water, once it reaches the surface of the earth, is returned to the atmosphere. The constant recycling of water is essential to the maintenance of life in an ecosystem.

animals enter into the water cycle at various points. The water cycle is diagrammed in Fig. 20–8.

Water soaking into the ground after a rain is picked up by the roots of plants. It passes into the stem and up to the leaves. Here it may be used in the process of photosynthesis. By evaporating from the leaves in the process known as transpiration, water may also pass back into the atmosphere. Animals that eat plants take some of the plant water into their bodies. This water may be returned to the environment either by excretion (mammalian urine is mostly water, with varying amounts of urea dissolved in it) or by respiration. One of the by-products of this latter process is water. This water is liberated by organisms in their excretory products, as water vapor in exhaled breath, or in a variety of other ways.

The cycles just discussed are by no means the only ones that may be traced in nature. Among other things, however, they serve to show the intricate relationships that exist between a wide variety of organisms. Each type of organism in an ecosystem requires many substances; carbon, nitrogen, and water are only three of the most important. For a source of these substances, each type of organism has come to depend on the activity of one or all of the others. Plants, and thus animals, are completely dependent on nitrogen-fixing bacteria to convert atmospheric nitrogen into soluble nitrates. In turn, the nitrogen-fixing bacteria depend on the denitrifying bacteria to return nitrogen to the atmosphere as $N_2$. This type of interdependence is part of what is meant by the term "web of life." It is characteristic of all ecosystems.

At the beginning of this chapter, it was pointed out that all organisms in an ecosystem have the same basic requirement: a source of energy. In their search for energy, organisms interact in various ways. Two of the most obvious interactions are the eating of animals by other animals and, of more interest to the botanist, the eating of plants by animals. In natural communities such as grasslands, the effects of the grazing animals on the vegetation may be minimal, since there are various mechanisms that keep the herbivores under control. When there are too many herbivorous animals living in a particular region, as often happens when men use grasslands for pasturing cattle, sheep, and goats, the plants may be greatly reduced in number or even killed. Man often fails to regulate his grazing livestock until these animals have severely harmed the vegetation. As a result, many grassland communities are now man-made deserts.

Since, by definition, a parasite is an organism which obtains its energy and matter at the expense of another, grazing animals are actually parasites upon the plants they eat. However, plants may be parasitized by other plants. Many fungi enter the tissues of living green plants and there obtain their energy. For example, the fungus *Puccinia graminis* lives one portion of its life cycle within the tissues of wheat, and another portion in barberry, producing a disease known as rust (from the rusty color of the reproductive structures of the fungus). Some species of flowering plants even live as parasites on other flowering plants, e.g., the stems of dodder (*Cuscuta*) become attached to the stems of herbs and obtain their food. During the course of evolution, such parasitic plants as dodder have even lost the genetic ability to produce chlorophyll and thus cannot manufacture their own food by photosynthesis.

Interaction between organisms in the ecosystem often takes the form of competition, an interaction wherein two individuals strive for the same resources, such as energy, matter, and space. Two kinds of competition are recognized in natural populations: intraspecific and interspecific competition. Intraspecific competition occurs between members of the same species. For example, many acorns beneath a parent tree of white oak may germinate and begin to grow. Only a very few, however, manage to survive to reproductive maturity. Those individuals with the genetic makeup enabling them to make maximum use of the available light, water, and minerals are usually those which survive; they can be said to be the more fit individuals. The less fit seedlings within the species are eliminated. Through intraspecific competition, the general character of the species may change over long periods of time.

Interspecific competition results when individuals of two different species, living in the same general area, have similar ecological requirements. The more overlap between the niches occupied by members of two species, the greater the

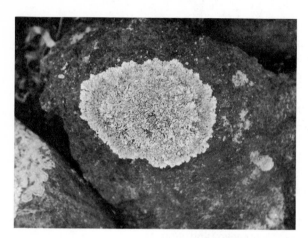
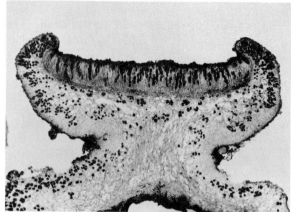

FIG. 20–9  Left: lichen growing firmly attached to rock.  Right: structural organization of a lichen.  The algae (dark round bodies) are interspersed among the fungus filaments.  The vertically aligned dark bodies in the top center are ascospores, reproductive structures of the fungus.  (Left photo from John W. Kimball, *Biology*, 2nd edition, Reading, Mass.: Addison-Wesley, 1968.  Right photo courtesy Carolina Biological Supply Company.)

degree of competition.  The frequent result of such competition is the decline and eventual elimination of one species, and the complete predominance of the other. In the wet tropical regions, for example, the seeds of various species of figs (*Ficus*) are carried to the tops of trees by birds, where they germinate and begin to grow.  Each fig seedling sends down twining roots around the trunk of the tree and leafy branches up into the tree's crown.  As the tree trunk grows in diameter, however, the pressure of the fig roots increases, and eventually the translocation of food and water within the tree trunk is shut off, resulting in death of the host tree.  Once the tree dies and falls to the ground, its space in the forest is taken over by the fig plant which now has its roots planted firmly in the soil and its leafy branches high in the canopy once occupied by the original tree.  Another equally conspicuous example of competition between individuals of different species is found in the southeastern United States.  Many years ago, plants of Japanese honeysuckle (*Lonicera japonica*) were introduced and spread over much of the region.  This plant, a vine, sprawls over low-growing shrubs and herbs and climbs high into the trees.  The shrubs and herbs are often nearly eliminated. Even tall trees may be so covered with the vine that they are eventually killed.

Interactions involving parasitism or competition might be viewed as negative interactions, i.e., one of the participants is usually affected detrimentally.  There are many cases of positive interactions within ecosystems, also.  These positive interactions involve the mutual collaboration or cooperation of two or more different species.  A good example of such mutualism is the association of nitrogen-fixing bacteria with leguminous plants (see Fig. 20–6).  The interaction of two species of plants may be so intimate as to justify the botanist's recognition of the association as a single species, e.g., lichens which consist of an alga and a fungus living in very close association (see Fig. 20–9). A lichen is actually a kind of miniature ecosystem, with a producer (the alga) and a consumer-decomposer (the fungus).

During the hundreds of millions of years since plants and animsls migrated from the seas to the land, additional, equally intricate interactions between organisms have evolved. In the largest group, the flowering plants, many of these interactions are involved with pollination and dispersal of seeds and fruits. Many species of plants are pollinated by insects; the insect obtains food in the form of pollen and nectar. This interaction has resulted in the evolutionary production of both elaborate flower structures and complex insect organs. Birds and other animals are attracted to the fleshy fruits of many plants. The seeds, resistant to the digestive juices of the transporting organisms, are thus carried from one habitat to another, where they are deposited with the feces.

There is also evidence that individuals of the same species of vascular plant may interact in a cooperative manner. It has recently been discovered that individuals of white pine (*Pinus strobus*) may be organically joined through the formation of graft unions between the roots of adjacent trees. When radioactive phosphorus ($P^{32}$) is injected into one tree, it appears later in the tissues of a nearby tree. If phosphorus can move from one tree to the next, it appears reasonable to hypothesize that other minerals, water, and perhaps even foods are shared by several trees in a forest.

Anyone who has planted a garden knows what happens if he does not cultivate it: the desired plants are soon hidden by various kinds of weeds. When a farmer allows a cultivated field to lie fallow, a crop of annual weeds grows on it during the first year and perennial herbs appear the second year. Gradually, however, the perennials are superseded as the dominant species by shrubs and trees. Such a series of changes in plant species occupying a single region is called ecological succession.

Scientific study of ecological succession began during the seventeenth century with analyses of the development of peat bogs. In the eighteenth century, attempts were made to apply to burned-over and man-disturbed areas the principles gained from bog studies. During this research, the term succession was first used to refer to changes in the vegetation. About the turn of the twentieth century, much of the modern thinking concerning succession was developed through the pioneering efforts of several ecologists, including Henry C. Cowles of the University of Chicago. Cowles described in great detail the successional changes in the vegetation of the sand dunes at the southern end of Lake Michigan. Many centuries ago, the shore of the lake extended much farther south than at present. Over the years, the lakeshore slowly retreated northward, leaving behind a series of progressively younger sand dunes and beaches. By walking from the present-day lakeshore, Cowles observed a series

**20-6
CHANGES IN
ECOSYSTEMS
THROUGH TIME:
SUCCESSION**

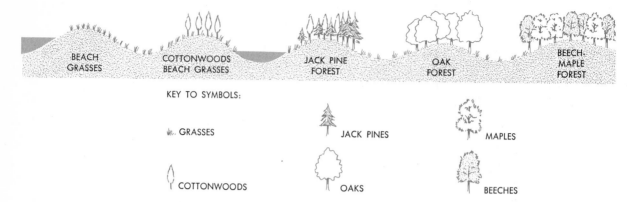

KEY TO SYMBOLS:

GRASSES          JACK PINES          MAPLES

COTTONWOODS      OAKS                BEECHES

FIG. 20–10   A highly diagrammatic portrayal of plant succession on the dunes at the southern end of Lake Michigan. (Adapted from Eugene P. Odum, *Fundamentals of Ecology*. Philadelphia: W. B. Saunders, 1959, p. 261.)

of different plant communities (Fig. 20–10). Near the edge of the water there are no plants, because of the destructive action of the waves. Higher up on the beach, where the sand is dry in summer and frequently buffeted by the waves of winter storms, a few species of succulent annual plants manage to survive. Back of the beach, the sand dunes begin. The sand dunes are rigorous environments for life, being very hot in the day and cold at night. Beach grasses survive on the dunes and actually help to secure them from the action of wind with their extensive underground stem (rhizome) systems. Various species of insects are the principal animals among the dunes.

Once the dunes are stabilized by the grasses, various species of shrubs, including cottonwoods (*Populus*), became established. The matted roots of these plants add to the stability of the dunes. On the slightly older dunes behind the cottonwood community, shrubs of other genera, including *Juniperus* and *Arctostaphylos*, and jack pine (*Pinus banksiana*) flourish. Further back from the pine woods is a forest dominated by oak trees (*Quercus*). Finally, several miles from the present lakeshore, Cowles observed forests of sugar maple (*Acer saccharum*) and American beech (*Fagus americana*) growing in deep, rich soil.

Cowles interpreted his observations of these changes in the vegetation at the southern end of Lake Michigan by hypothesizing that the series of communities represent stages in ecological succession beginning with bare beach and culminating in a well-established forest of sugar maple and beech trees. Subsequent investigators supplied support for this hypothesis by studies at other localities such as ponds, exposures of barren rocks, abandoned farmlands, and burned-over areas.

Ecological succession in ponds has been extensively studied. The first plants to colonize a newly formed pond are the planktonic algae. Vascular plants such

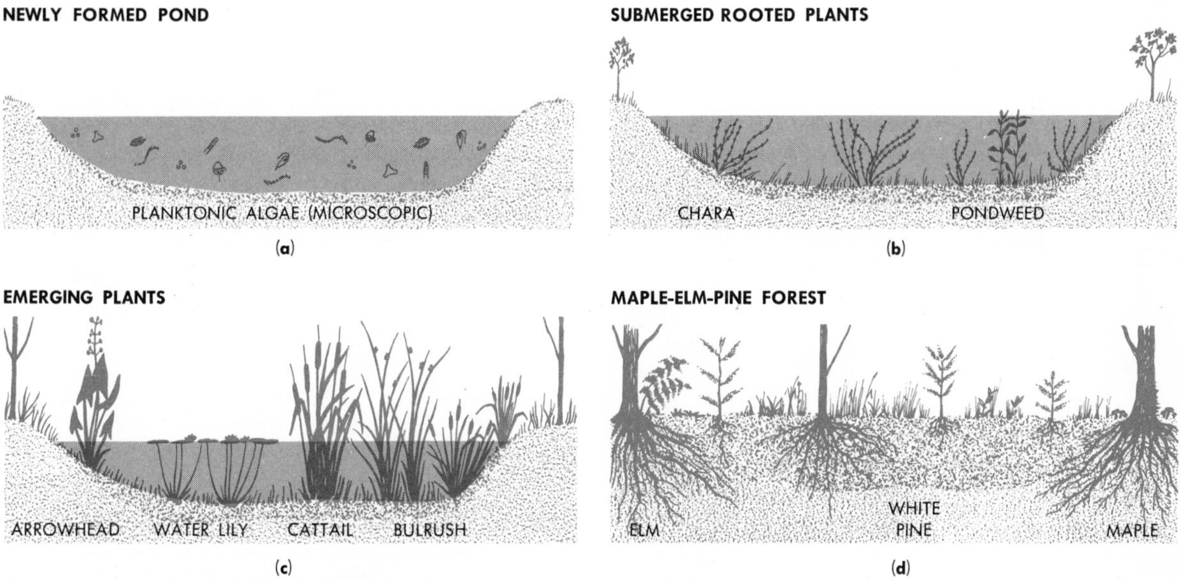

**NEWLY FORMED POND**

**SUBMERGED ROOTED PLANTS**

PLANKTONIC ALGAE (MICROSCOPIC)

CHARA        PONDWEED

(a)

(b)

**EMERGING PLANTS**

**MAPLE-ELM-PINE FOREST**

ARROWHEAD    WATER LILY    CATTAIL    BULRUSH

ELM        WHITE PINE        MAPLE

(c)

(d)

FIG. 20–11    Stages of succession in ponds.

as *Elodea*, *Myriophyllum*, and *Potamogeton* (pond weed) and the alga *Chara* soon appear in the shallow water around the margin of the pond. With the passage of time, due to the accumulation of plant remains and to soil washed by rainwater from the surrounding land, the pond begins to get shallower. The filling process is hastened by the invasion of vascular plants whose shoots extend into the air above the water, e.g., cattails (*Typha*), bulrushes (*Scirpus*), and arrowhead (*Sagittaria*). With the appearance of the plants, much of the former open water of the pond becomes a marsh. In shallower places, peat moss (*Sphagnum*) may produce a mat over the water surface which gradually adds to the filling of the pond with peat. As the pond bottom builds higher, the soil drainage improves. Terrestrial plants such as meadow grasses now enter the area. As the land becomes better drained, shrubs such as willow (*Salix*), alder (*Alnus*), and buttonbush (*Cephalanthus*) colonize the site. With the passage of years, a forest composed of various tree species, including red maple (*Acer rubrum*), elm (*Ulmus*), and white pine (*Pinus strobus*), begins to develop. This entire sequence of plant species can sometimes be observed as a nearly continuous series of zones girdling the pond. After many years, the pond disappears (see Fig. 20–11).

In this example, succession starts with open water and it takes place relatively rapidly. For example, in northern Wisconsin and Minnesota, there are numerous forested bogs that were open water lakes formed as the glaciers retreated less than 10,000 years ago. However, succession which begins on bare rock surfaces, such as those on granitic rock outcrops in the Piedmont region of southeastern

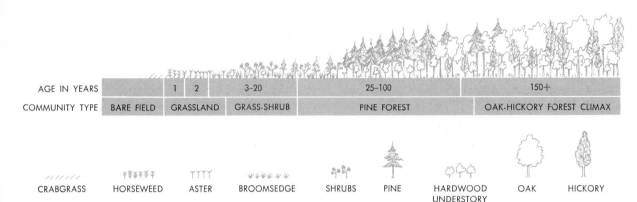

| AGE IN YEARS | | 1 | 2 | 3–20 | 25–100 | 150+ |
| COMMUNITY TYPE | BARE FIELD | GRASSLAND | | GRASS-SHRUB | PINE FOREST | OAK-HICKORY FOREST CLIMAX |

CRABGRASS    HORSEWEED    ASTER    BROOMSEDGE    SHRUBS    PINE    HARDWOOD UNDERSTORY    OAK    HICKORY

FIG. 20–12    Plant succession following abandonment of crop land in the Piedmont region of southeastern United States. (From Eugene P. Odum, *Fundamentals of Ecology*. Philadelphia: W. B. Saunders, 1959, p. 263.)

United States, is particularly slow. A rock surface is an extremely dry, harsh environment; the water escapes quickly by runoff and by evaporation. The first colonizers here are usually crust-forming lichens such as the gray-green *Parmelia conspersa*. As soil is washed by rain or blown by wind into deep cracks and depressions in the rock, plants such as black moss (*Grimmia*), hair-cap moss (*Polytrichium*), *Cladonia* lichens, and even grasses and herbaceous vascular plants become established. A gradually thickening mat of plants and soil slowly spreads over the bare rock, eventually covering the bare surface. On the more exposed sites, however, the destructive forces of water and wind remove the soil and its covering of plants, exposing bare rock again. Where the soil does accumulate to some depth, as in deep crevices, shrubs such as sumac (*Rhus*) and even trees may become established. The progress of the succession is evident as a series of girdles of vegetation. At the outer margin of the mat are the early colonizers, and each stage of succession is nearer the center, where the thickest soil is found.

The vegetation of an area may be destroyed by fire, grazing, cultivation, or roadbuilding. If the soil is not eroded away by rainwater or wind, revegetation of the area will take place relatively rapidly. The process of ecological succession on such artificially modified habitats varies considerably, depending on the climate. One well-studied example occurs in the Piedmont region of Georgia and the Carolinas on abandoned farm land (Fig. 20–12). As soon as cultivation stops, the fields are colonized during late summer and autumn by several species of herbaceous plants, including horseweed (*Erigeron canadensis*) and crabgrass (*Digitaria sanguinalis*). The horseweed lives through the winter as a dwarf rosette. The following spring, growth resumes, producing a tall, many-branched plant which flowers during the summer. While the horseweed is growing to maturity, other herbs, including white aster (*Aster pilosus*), invade the field, overwinter, and develop flowers during the second summer. By the third summer, a tall-growing bunch grass, broomsedge (*Andropogon virginicus*), appears, replacing the aster and horseweed as dominant plants of the vegetation.

By the time the broomsedge appears, seedlings of pine (*Pinus*) begin to be noticeable and, within 5 to 10 years, form a forest where once the farmer grew corn and crops. However, once the pines grow tall enough to cast a shade over the soil beneath their crowns, their own seedlings cannot grow any longer (young pine plants require almost full sunlight). Not only is there competition between the older pines and the seedlings for light, but there is also intense competition between these two growth stages for the available water in the soil. Thus, there is little or no reproduction of the pines.

The seedlings of several other tree species *can* compete successfully in the shaded environment beneath the pines, however. Broadleafed trees such as sweet gum (*Liquidambar styraciflua*), and various species of oaks (*Quercus*) and hickories (*Carya*) are able to utilize the dim light for photosynthesis as well as obtain water from deep in the soil (their roots extend several centimeters below the roots of the pines, which are confined mostly to the upper 20 or so centimeters). Thus, sweet-gum, oak, and hickory seedlings come up under the pines and, about 100 years after the field was abandoned, develop into the dominant or overstory trees of the forest. During this long interval of time, an understory of dogwood (*Cornus florida*), sourwood (*Oxydendrum*), and red maple (*Acer rubrum*) is also developing. Eventually, the old pines begin to die and are replaced by oaks and hickories so that, after about 200 years, the forest consists mostly of broadleaf deciduous trees (Fig. 20–12).

To describe ecological succession is one major problem; to explain why such successional changes occur is another. It seems clear that major changes in the vegetation of a region can only follow changes in the environment. Plants and other organisms living in a community certainly modify their environment. For example, trees shade the ground beneath them, affecting soil temperature and humidity. Leaves fall to the soil surface and undergo decay. The resulting material affects the runoff of rainwater, soil temperature, and the formation of humus in the soil. These factors, in turn, affect soil development, and alter the quantity and type of available nutrients, soil pH, and aeration. These modifications of the environment by the organisms usually make it less favorable for themselves yet, at the same time, make it more favorable for species which could have survived there earlier only with great difficulty. Thus, as organisms change the environment, they make it possible for other organisms to compete successfully with the established species. As we have just seen, the invaders may even replace the original, pioneer organisms.

The environment may be altered by forces other than living organisms. An overflowing stream, for example, may deposit fertile silt on bottomland. The soil level in a pond or lake may be raised because silt has been washed in (as often happens in bodies of water impounded by dams). The chemical content of the soil may change because of leaching. These and similar modifications of the environment are usually followed by changes in the vegetation.

Eventually, ecological succession results in the formation of vegetation existing in a steady-state equilibrium with the soil, climate, and herbivorous animals. Such a relatively stable community has less tendency than the earlier successional stages to modify its environment in a way that is injurious to itself. The plants of such a "climax community" are able to perpetuate themselves because their seedlings can survive in the competition with older plants. If environmental factors do not change appreciably, the climax vegetation will continue for centuries, not replaced by another stage. A climax community may change somewhat in the kind of plants that comprise it. For example, until about 50 years ago, the climax forests of eastern North America contained abundant chestnut trees (*Castanea dentata*). Chestnut has now been virtually eliminated by a fungus disease.

In fact, the original climax vegetation that once existed over most of North America (and the entire earth) has been destroyed by man. The normal stages in succession have been set back, modified, or stopped by such human activities as lumbering, grazing domestic animals, cultivation, urbanization, industrialization, and even radiation. In the settled regions of the earth, many of the plant communities that now exist do so not because of the natural process of ecological succession but because of man's deliberate interference. Man maintains such types of vegetation as crops, pastures, golf courses, and lawns, as well as managed forests and wildlife preserves because of his economic interests. These communities require some effort to maintain, however. Managed forests, for example, must be periodically thinned by cutting some of the trees.

## 20-7 THE GROWTH AND REGULATION OF POPULATIONS

Every type of organism has a **biotic potential.** Biotic potential is the inherent power of a population to increase in numbers, given ideal environmental conditions. Under such conditions, some types of organisms produce many more offspring than others. Jackrabbits, for example, have a very high biotic potential. They reproduce very rapidly under favorable conditions. On the other hand, populations of whooping cranes have a very low biotic potential. They produce only one or two offspring per parent every two years.

Opposing the effects of biotic potential is the **environmental resistance** any population encounters. Environmental resistance comprises all those factors in the environment that tend to prevent a population of organisms from multiplying at an unlimited rate—for example, limitation of food supply, competition with other organisms, predation, or the effects of climate.

Environmental resistance may be measured as the differences between the theoretical growth rate of a population under ideal conditions, and the observed growth rate in nature. For example, given optimum conditions, a single pair of fruit flies could yield $3368 \times 10^{52}$ offspring in a year!* The fact that the fruitfly population does not increase at this rate is a result of environmental resistance.

---

* Estimates by C. A. Villee, *Biology* (Philadelphia: W. B. Saunders, 1957, p. 577).

One of the most important problems in any ecosystem is the maintenance of a fairly constant number of each type of organism. It is apparent that an ecosystem cannot function properly if the numbers of any one organism become too great. How are populations of organisms controlled within ecosystems? What are the built-in mechanisms by which a constant number of any type of animal or plant is maintained?

The factors of environmental resistance discussed above are among the major checks to population size. If a population of organisms is introduced into a new territory where environmental conditions are favorable, the population grows rapidly. It is not that the rate of reproduction of any pair of individuals is increased, but simply that more offspring are able to survive. Figure 20–13 shows two possible population-growth curves. The solid curve shows the actual growth of the population as observed in nature. The dotted line indicates the path the curve would take if there were no environmental resistance.

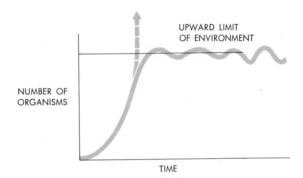

FIG. 20–13    Graph of population growth.

As the number of organisms increases, the environmental resistance begins to increase proportionately. Competition between members of the same population for food, as well as a decrease in the supply of food per organism, reduces the number of offspring that survive. The growth curve thus begins to level off. The horizontal line running across the top of the graph represents the maximum number of organisms the environment can support. In other words, it represents the maximum number of spaces in a given niche. As the actual number of organisms in the population approaches this upward limit, the environmental resistance becomes greater. When the curve levels off, and maintains itself at about the value for the maximum limit, the number of offspring that survive is very close to the number of organisms that die. The population has reached a dynamic equilibrium.

This equilibrium is not evenly maintained, however. It can be seen (Fig. 20–13) that the population size actually seesaws, first on one side of the upward limiting value, then on the other. When the population size goes over this limit, the environmental resistance has exceeded the biotic potential. The death rate increases and the population decreases. When the line dips below the limiting

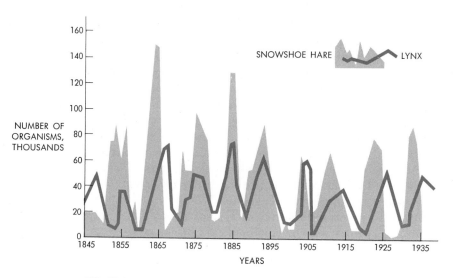

FIG. 20–14    Cyclic changes in populations of snowshoe hares and lynx in Canada from 1845 to 1935. This graph is constructed from records of the number of pelts received per year by the Hudson's Bay Company. (Redrawn by permission from C. A. Villee, *Biology*. Philadelphia: W. B. Saunders, 1957, p. 577.)

value, the biotic potential exceeds the environmental resistance. The size of the population increases.

There is also the factor of predation. Just as the size of any food population determines the size of the population that feeds on it, so the reverse is also true. In other words, the size of a food population itself is determined by the size of the population that preys on it. In a stable ecosystem, the relative ratios of prey and predator will not change much over the course of time. The graph in Fig. 20–14 illustrates dramatically how the sizes of prey-predator populations are completely interdependent. This graph shows cyclic changes in population of lynx and snowshoe hares in Canada for a period of 90 years. Three things are of importance here: First, note that on any one occasion the peak of the curve for the snowshoe hare (the prey) is always a good deal higher than that for the lynx (the predator). Second, note that the peak of the lynx population always occurs a little later in time than that of the hare population. As the number of hares increases, so does the number of lynx. This is simply due to the fact that more lynx kittens can survive when the supply of snowshoe hares is abundant. Third, note that when the number of hares decreases, so does the number of lynx.

In stable populations, predation is beneficial to the prey as a group, even though it brings about the death of certain individuals. The result of inter-

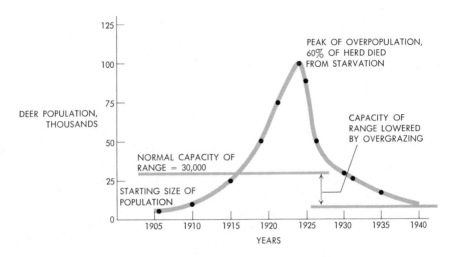

FIG. 20–15    The effect of removing predators from a stable ecosystem, illustrated by the change
in population of deer on the Kaibab Plateau of Arizona when their natural enemies (wolves, coyotes,
and pumas) were exterminated. (Redrawn by permission from G. G. Simpson, C. S. Pittendrigh, and
L. H. Tiffany, *Life: An Introduction to Biology.* New York: Harcourt, Brace & World, Inc., 1957,
p. 655.)

fering in a prey-predator relationship is illustrated by the case history of Kaibab
deer in Arizona earlier in this century. Up until 1907, the Kaibab Plateau of
Arizona sustained a healthy deer population which, by predation from wolves,
coyotes, and pumas, was kept from exceeding the supply of vegetation. As a
result of this predation there were never more deer than the vegetation could
support. A well-meaning but uninformed campaign was started, shortly after
1907, which aimed to benefit the deer by killing off all the predators. The result
was dramatic. The deer population increased from about 4000 in 1907 to 100,000
in 1924 (Fig. 20–15). The peak population for 1924 was far greater than the environment could sustain. In two winters over 60% of the herd died from starvation. The size of the deer population continued to decline, until in 1939 the
total number was back down to 10,000. This was well within the supporting
capacity of the environment as it had existed in 1907. But the large deer populations of 1924 and 1925 had been very damaging to the vegetation of the region.
During these two winters, starving deer had cropped many plants down almost
to ground level. These plants were thus unable to grow back in the spring.
The ecosystem was now caught in a vicious cycle. Even though the deer population had decreased from its peak years of 1924–1925, the vegetation was also
greatly reduced. As a result, even as late as 1939, more deer continued to die
of starvation than had been killed by predators in 1907.

A third way in which the size of natural populations may be regulated is through what are called **density-dependent factors.** Such factors are usually physiological mechanisms that go into operation within some individuals only when a population reaches a certain critical size. This generally occurs when crowding and intense competition for food exists. These built-in mechanisms function for the good of the population by killing a certain number of individuals. Let us now consider a specific example of how such density-dependent factors operate.

Referring back to Fig. 20–15, we can see that the size of the snowshoe-hare population periodically suffers a dramatic reduction. What causes this? It cannot be attributed to predation from the lynxes, since the peak of the lynx population is generally reached *after* the population of hares has begun to decrease. Many hypotheses were suggested before the cause was finally shown to be physiological. Apparently, when the population of hares reaches a critical point, the nervous strain of competition for food, coupled with the onset of a reproductive season, causes a breakdown in certain of the hormone-producing glands. In the snowshoe hare, one of the major results of this breakdown is an upset in carbohydrate metabolism. The level of blood sugar decreases, convulsions develop, and death ensues.

Other examples of density-dependent factors can be seen in the classic example of small rodents known as lemmings, living chiefly in Norway and Scandinavia. When a lemming population becomes too large, certain hormonal changes occur, and great hordes of lemmings begin to migrate from the overpopulated region. This migration is impulsive. Lemmings on the march stop neither to rest nor to eat. Frequently they bypass regions in which they could easily settle. At some point in their migration, lemmings usually encounter a lake, river or fjord. Ignoring the barrier, they usually plunge right into the water, where they drown.

This famous spectacle has given rise to a great number of romantic stories of the "lemmings' march to the sea." This is sometimes treated as though the lemmings were conscious of their purpose, to sacrifice themselves for the good of the rest of the population. In effect, this is exactly what happens, but the mass migration can best be understood as the result of physiological imbalances occurring simultaneously within a large number of individual lemmings. Such imbalances are triggered, in a way we do not yet understand, by the increase in population.

All the factors that have been discussed above are mechanisms operating on the population level. They serve to keep populations at a relatively constant level by balancing environmental resistance and biotic potential. These built-in mechanisms, which benefit the whole population by sacrificing individuals, operate on a feedback principle similar to that discussed in Chapter 14. Thus we see, again, that one of the most important and general features of living organisms is their control, on any level of organization, by feedback mechanisms.

Many of the current ecological problems of the environment are really based on rather simple ecological principles.  The balance of nature remains a balance only if there exists a proper give-and-take relationship among the following four groups:

1) the **producers,** i.e., the autotrophs, or photosynthesizing organisms that capture solar energy and use it to produce foodstuffs, directly or indirectly, for all forms of life;

2) the **consumers,** i.e., the heterotrophs, or organisms living either directly or indirectly off food products provided by the autotrophs;

3) the **decomposers,** i.e., the organisms of decay, primarily bacteria but also fungi (e.g., molds, mushrooms, etc.); and

4) the **inorganic world,** i.e., the nitrates, phosphates, carbonates, etc., all of which are needed in balanced amounts as nutritional supplements by both producers and consumers.

One thing must be made perfectly clear.  Of all the living organisms on earth, only one—man—has ever seriously threatened the delicate natural balance existing among these four groups.  He is now increasing this threat to the point that he threatens not only the existence of nonhuman organisms but also his own, for *man is the only organism that pollutes*.  He has brought about this pollution by two main means, and both are intimately connected to the fact that man is virtually the only organism that manipulates his environment to serve his own needs and desires.

First, man has vastly overstrained the food capacity of the earth by overpopulation.  His ability to conquer diseases that in the past have served to keep human population somewhat in check is a primary factor in this overpopulation.  These scientific accomplishments are admirable intellectual triumphs, of course.  However, for political, military, religious, or other reasons man has been unwilling in any significant way to use the same intellect to keep his numbers in check.

Second, human technology has enabled man to take chemical elements and compounds from the inorganic world and put them together into combinations never before introduced into nature.  He often then discards these products into the environment.  However, no decay organism has evolved that can decompose an aluminum can, a plastic toothbrush handle, dishwasher detergents, etc.  Thus these discarded items remain as pollutants and pile up in ever-increasing amounts, while the vital elements they contain remain locked within them, instead of returning to the inorganic-organic cycle.  The result is a polluted environment which contributes to a decrease in the working efficiency of the producers and decomposers at a time when a geometrically increasing human population (see Fig. 20–16) demands far *greater* efficiency.

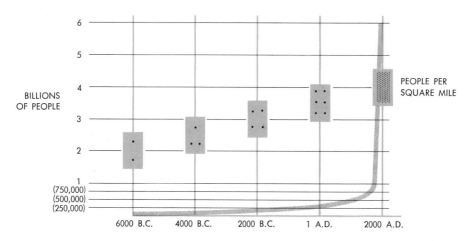

FIG. 20–16   Growth curve for the human population. The graph indicates that at present the world population is in the middle of the logarithmic growth phase. If population continues to grow at this rate, the number of people in the world will have doubled by the year 2000 A.D. (Data taken from E. S. Deevey, "The Human Population." *Scientific American*, September 1960, pp. 196, 198.)

The problem is one of man the "civilized" organism, rather than simply man the organism. There is no reason to doubt that prehistoric man lived in perfect harmony with his environment. If, at times, he preyed too heavily on the animals which served as his food, the decrease in their numbers must in turn have kept his own numbers in check. The troubles began when man began to manipulate the environment to make things a bit easier. The dawn of agriculture was undoubtedly a giant step forward in this direction; now plant food could be grown more efficiently (in terms of meeting man's needs, that is) and less human energy needed to be expended in order to forage for it. Plants, of course, need water and, if the rainfall was not sufficient, streams and rivers had to be diverted to irrigate the land. The subecosystems dependent on the diverted water supply were obliged either to perish or to become drastically changed in both the kinds and numbers of organisms composing them. Man the environmental exploiter was on his way.

This environmental exploitation on the part of man has continued unabated and at an accelerated pace ever since. The industrial revolution of barely a century ago multiplied the process a thousandfold. To protect his crops and feed his ever-growing numbers, man kills insects with powerful insecticides that pollute the rivers and seas from the Arctic Circle to Antarctica and poison his own and other animal species playing a role in maintaining the balance of nature. To manufacture his ever more powerful and polluting automobiles and airplanes and test his thermonuclear weapons of war, man has poisoned the air we breathe and surrounded the earth with a blanket of pollutants that threatens to drastically alter the earth's climatic conditions. The list of environmental abuses could go on and on, but the current increase in press coverage of the topic probably makes it unnecessary to continue. The readings suggested at the end of this chapter hypothesize various reasons for the causes of the current catastrophe facing mankind, and some possible solutions.

The human population problem has brought man face to face with the harsh realities of the laws of thermodynamics. Perhaps the most apt and colorful description of the situation is the statement, "It is the top of the ninth inning. Man, always a threat at the plate, has been hitting nature hard. It is important to remember, however, that *nature bats last.*"

At the beginning of this chapter it was stated that all organisms in an ecosystem are in competition for the same basic requirement: a source of energy. Let us now return to that point. What kinds of competition do we observe within an ecosystem? How do the various ecological relationships discussed earlier in this chapter become established in the course of time?

Two kinds of competition are recognized in natural populations: **intraspecific** and **interspecific** competition. Intraspecific competition occurs between members of the same species for a limited food supply. The result of intraspecific competition is that the less fit individuals within the species are eliminated. Through intraspecific competition the general character of the species changes over long periods of time.

Interspecific competition results when two different species, living in the same general area, have similar ecological requirements. The more overlap between the niches occupied by two species, the greater the degree of competition. The frequent result of such competition is the decline and eventual extinction of one species, and the complete predominance of the other. This has led to a formal statement known as **Gause's hypothesis,** or the **competitive exclusion principle.** This hypothesis states simply that two species with similar ecological requirements cannot successfully live together for any length of time. The results of several of Gause's experiments are shown in Fig. 20–17.

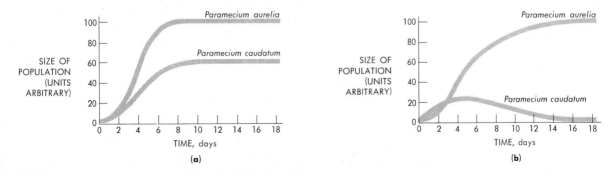

FIG. 20–17  Typical growth curves for populations of *Paramecium aurelia* and *Paramecium caudatum* (a) when each species is grown separately and (b) when the two cultures are mixed.

When one species of the protozoan *Paramecium* (in this case, *P. caudatum*) is grown alone in a nutrient culture, it shows a typical sigmoid growth curve. The same is true for another species, *P. aurelia* (both of these are shown in Fig. 20–17a). When grown together, however, *P. aurelia* has the upper hand and eliminates *P. caudatum* in the course of about 14 days (Fig. 20–17b). This results from the fact that both species compete for nearly all the same minerals and food supplies.

The evolution of interwoven ecological relationships depends on such competition. In heavily competing populations, any variations are favored which tend to reduce this competition. If *P. caudatum* is able to use some other food supply than that monopolized by *P. aurelia*, competition will be reduced. This will increase the survival rate of those individuals of *P. caudatum* that bear the variation. In nature, organisms frequently invade unoccupied ecological niches simply to avoid intense competition. Once the organism is in a new niche, any variations that allow it to exploit the available resources more efficiently will tend to be perpetuated. In this way, the population may slowly change its genetic makeup so that it becomes well adapted to a new niche.

As an illustration that such evolutionary changes actually do occur in competing populations, consider the following example. The Galapagos Islands, off the coast of South America, are populated by a number of species of finches. Two species of ground finch, *Geospiza fuliginosa* and *Geospiza fortis*, are clearly related. Both feed on seeds. The beak size (called "beak depth") of each species reflects the type of seed on which it feeds.* Figure 20–18 shows frequency graphs for the variation of beak depth (measured from top to bottom) in both species under three different environmental situations. Graphs (a) and (b) show the range and extent of variation on two islands, each inhabited by one species, but not by the other. Two features of these graphs are important. First, note that the largest number of individuals in each population (about 30–35%) have nearly identical beak depths, i.e., about 10 mm. Second, note the overall differences in distribution of beak depths between the two populations. *G. fuliginosa* has a large number of individuals (25%) with small beak depths, i.e., about 8 mm. *G. fortis* has very few individuals in this category (less than 5%). On the other hand, *G. fortis* does have a certain number of individuals with large beaks (in the 11–12 mm range), whereas none are shown for *G. fuliginosa*.

Figure 20–18(c) shows frequency distribution graphs for beak depth on two islands where both species live together. The difference between this graph and those shown in (a) and (b) is evident. Where the two species live together, there

---

* Birds with small beaks cannot crack open large seeds. Birds with large beaks find it difficult to pick up and crack small seeds without dropping them or losing the contents of the seed once opened. Birds with medium-size beaks can feed to some extent on larger seeds, and to some extent on smaller seeds. However, they are limited to a middle range, being unable to eat either very large or very small seeds.

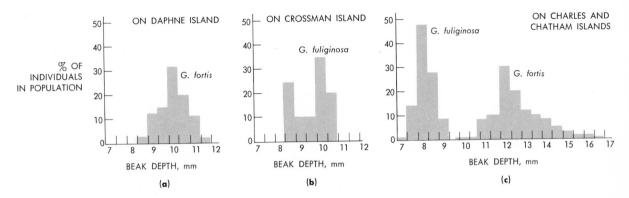

FIG. 20–18    Three frequency-distribution graphs for beak depth in two species of ground finch, *Geospiza fortis* and *Geospiza fuliginosa*. (a, b) Distribution of beak depths when the species are living without competition from each other. (c) Distribution of beak depths when the two species exist together on the same island. (Redrawn by permission from D. Lack, *Darwin's Finches.* New York: Harper Torchbooks, 1961, p. 82.)

is no overlap in beak depth. *G. fortis* has the larger beak, while *G. fuliginosa* has the smaller. How can we account for these differences?

Consider that the population of *G. fortis* from Daphne Island and *G. fuliginosa* from Crossman come together on a third island, such as Chatham or Charles. We have noted that the largest number of individuals in each of the separate populations have identical beak depths. When the two populations come together, therefore, competition between those individuals with beak depths around 10 mm will be greatly increased because of the larger numbers. The least competition would be experienced by *G. fortis* individuals with large beaks and *G. fuliginosa* with small beaks. Accordingly, these individuals would be favored, and their characteristics passed on. In time, the number of medium-sized beaks in each population would be reduced to a very low level, while the large-beaked *G. fortis* and small-beaked *G. fuliginosa* would increase. After a number of generations of such competition, the two populations would have evolved quite distinct differences in beak size.

This example illustrates how organisms can move permanently into new ecological niches. The evolution of feeding habits and physical characteristics results from such competition as that shown by *G. fortis* and *G. fuliginosa*. We can assume that when the two populations came together, their ecological requirements were so similar that they were brought into immediate competition. Variations were favored which reduced this competition and allowed individual organisms to obtain a greater amount of food. Under these conditions, the two species became more specialized. Specialization is generally nothing more than a means to avoid competition. It involves the occupation of a more restricted ecological niche.

In this chapter we have considered some of the ways in which living organisms are related to each other in biotic communities. We have seen that all animals and plants in any such community, or ecosystem, affect each other in some way. These organisms depend on each other. By their interactions they form a great and delicately balanced web. The ways in which one organism may affect another are often quite subtle and difficult to discover. In this light the example with which we began, namely that "the glory of England is due to the number of its old maids," is, in principle, not as far-fetched as it might at first seem.

One of the important features of an ecosystem is the variety of ways in which it maintains itself in a balanced state. The cycling of materials from organism to environment and back again, as well as the means for controlling population size, are only two examples of this principle. Self-maintenance and regulation is thus a characteristic not only of individual organisms, but also of whole populations and ecosystems. Regulatory mechanisms operate for the good of the ecosystem as a whole, though frequently to the detriment of certain individuals.

In conclusion, we have seen how ecological differences can develop between two species that inhabit a common territory. The historical development of such relationships (i.e., their evolution), is shown by the example of *Geospiza fortis* and *Geospiza fuliginosa*. This example also gives some indication of the role of competition in the living world; that is, it illustrates the manner in which organisms may move into different ecological niches as a means of avoiding competition.

**EXERCISES**    Figure 20–19 represents a sealed aquarium. In the figure, C represents enclosed air above the water, B the water, D the animal life in the water, A the plant life, and E the soil at the bottom. At the time it was sealed, the aquarium contained the proper balance of plant and animal life. Answer Exercises 1 through 5 on the basis of the information given above.

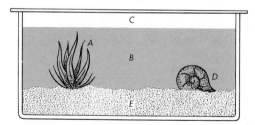

FIG. 20–19

1. How long will it be possible for life to continue in the aquarium?

   a) Until the original oxygen supply in the air above the water is used, but not longer.

   b) Until the original supply of $O_2$ dissolved in the water has been used up, but not longer.

   c) At most, not more than two months.

d) Until the original supply of nitrogen in the soil at the bottom is used up, but no longer.

e) Indefinitely, as long as the sun shines regularly on the aquarium and the temperature stays above freezing.

2. At what point within the aquarium (A, B, C, D, or E) does energy first enter the cycle?

3. At what point within the aquarium is the oxygen supply replenished?

4. At what point or points is carbon dioxide given off as a waste product: A, A and B, B and D, A and D, D and E, or D?

5. At what point is carbon dioxide utilized as a raw material?

6. What is a food chain?

7. Why is there such a great decrease in the amount of available matter or energy along each step of a food chain? How does this relate to the second law of thermodynamics?

8. On the basis of the following assumptions, calculate the overall efficiency of the energy chain leading from the sun to you.

a) Of the sun's energy, 99% goes unused.

b) Of the 1% used by plants, only about 0.6% ends up in glucose.

c) Half of this glucose is used up by the plant for its own life processes.

d) Of the glucose reaching your cells, 60% is formed into ATP.

e) Your usage of this energy is 55% efficient.

Can you detect any "energy leakages" other than those listed here?

9. Can you suggest why the poorer nations of the world must necessarily be primarily vegetarian? Give your answer in terms of the second law of thermodynamics.

10. Distinguish between the terms "habitat" and "ecological niche."

11. What is meant by the terms "biotic potential" and "environmental resistance"? How do they relate to each other?

12. Distinguish between interspecific and intraspecific competition.

13. It has generally been found that nature's most unusual organisms may be found in extreme environments (e.g., ocean bottoms, deserts, Arctic wastes). The grotesqueness and uniqueness of these organisms is generally anatomical, but may also be physiological. What reasons can you give for this phenomenon?

14. Though all of the forms living in any ecological area are seldom if ever closely related phylogenetically, they may show quite similar anatomical and even physiological characteristics. Explain why this should be the case.

An estimate has suggested that about 130 California jackrabbits eat as much forage on the open range as one cow. The cost of removing this many rabbits has been estimated at $47 (almost twice the value of a range cow). Thus a program to destroy the rabbits is not good economy. Furthermore, the rabbits, by their continual burrowing, help to aereate the soil of the range regions and also make it more porous to water. Nevertheless, despite the apparent drawbacks, a campaign against the rabbits was launched. Since the beginning of this campaign it has been observed that there is a notable decrease in the number of hawks in the region. Hawks displaced from this region have moved into others, becoming a serious problem for chicken farmers. Stopping the rabbit campaign at this point, however, presents problems. With fewer hawks in the region, the rabbit population would begin to grow rapidly as soon as extermination ceased, since rabbits reproduce very rapidly and hawks reproduce very slowly. Thus, if the campaign were stopped, the rabbit population would begin to zoom upward, with no natural checks. Answer Exercises 15–17 on the basis of the information given above.

15. The food relationships described are best indicated by which of the following food chains?

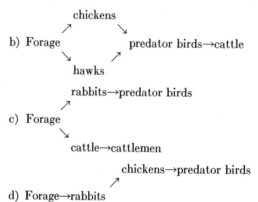

16. If the rabbit population were allowed to increase by stopping the campaign against them, what would be the first effect seen?

   a) An increase in the number of hawks.

   b) A decrease in the number of cattle.

   c) A decrease in the amount of forage available.

   d) An increase in the number of chickens in neighboring regions.

   e) A decrease in the number of cattlemen.

17. Compare this situation to the campaign against coyotes on the Kaibab Plateau earlier in this century. In what ways are the two situations similar? In what ways are they different?

18. Observe the graph in Fig. 20–20. From studying these curves, explain which organism (A or B) is the prey and which the predator. How can you tell?

19. Observe the four graphs in Fig. 20–21. Both lots of *Tribolium castaneum* (one species of flour beetle) started with 20 adults but were kept at different temperatures. The two lots of *Tribolium confusum* were kept at the same temperature but started with different numbers of adults. Evaluate the following statements using letter symbols as follows: A, The statement is true according to the data given in the graphs; B, the statement is true according to an accepted biological principle, but it cannot be shown from these graphs; C, the statement is false according to the data given

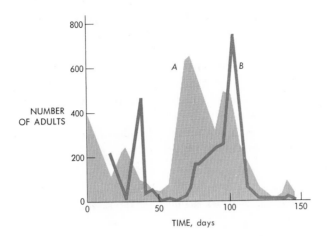

FIG. 20–20

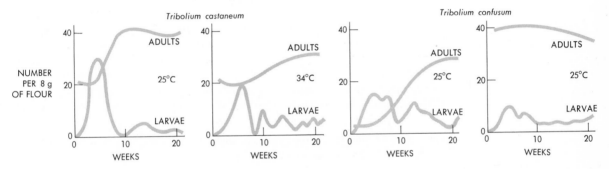

FIG. 20–21

in the graphs; D, the statement is false according to an accepted biological principle, but this cannot be shown from these graphs; E, the statement cannot be judged on the basis of the data in the graphs.

a) Adults of *T. castaneum* are more sensitive to an increase in temperature (above 25°C) than adults of *T. confusum*.

b) Adults of *T. castaneum* thrive better at 25°C than adults of *T. confusum*.

c) The larvae of *T. castaneum* are more greatly affected by a rise in temperature from 25°C to 34°C than are the adults.

d) The limiting value for the environment of these populations of adult *Tribolium* seems to be about 40 individuals.

e) There is no limit to the number of adults the environment can support, since growth rate always proceeds upward from the initial number.

f) Crowding organisms by starting a culture with an initially larger number of individuals has no effect on rate of growth of the population.

g) Starting a culture of *T. confusum* with 40 adults, as compared with four, does not significantly affect the growth of larvae and pupae.

h) In general, the growth and development of all young organisms in a population is independent of the number of adults.

i) The number of *Tribolium* larvae in the population at any one point in time never exceeds the number of adults.

j) The growth in number of larvae, as they reach their peak in any population, occurs at a more rapid rate than the growth in number of adults as they reach their peak.

k) The curve for the number of adults in each culture eventually levels off because of a limited supply of food.

**SUGGESTED READINGS**

AMOS, WILLIAM H., "The Life of a Sand Dune." *Scientific American*, July 1959, p. 91. This article discusses the many adaptations among the organisms living in a biotic community.

BAKER, JEFFREY J. W., "Science, Birth Control and the Roman Catholic Church." *BioScience*, February 1, 1970, pp. 143–151. Adapted from a speech given at the University of Puerto Rico, Rio Piedras, in March 1969, this article discusses the theological grounds cited by the Church to support its opposition to artificial means of birth control, and documents a case history of political activity by the Church in the 1960 Puerto Rican elections in opposition to birth-control-related legislation.

BRESLER, JACK B. (Ed.), *Human Ecology: Collected Readings* (Reading, Mass.: Addison-Wesley, 1966). An interesting collection of readings on ecological matters especially pertinent to man's relationship to his environment.

CLARKE, G. L., *Elements of Ecology* (New York: Wiley, 1954). A general textbook in ecology with special emphasis on marine communities.

DEEVEY, E. S., "The Human Population." *Scientific American*, September 1960, p. 194. Discusses the relations between the number of human beings and the total population of humans which the earth could support. A good review of ecological principles applied to a specific case.

EHRLICH, PAUL R., "Eco-Catastrophe!" *Ramparts*, September 1969. This provocative article (which has been reprinted by the Planned Parenthood–World Population Society, 515 Madison Avenue, New York, New York 10022) contains the author's predictions of what our world will be like in ten years if the present course of environmental destruction is allowed to continue.

EHRLICH, PAUL R., *The Population Bomb* (New York: Ballantine Books, 1968). A widely circulated book on the human population crisis. The author is an ecologist whose speeches have done much to educate the public on ecological principles.

EHRLICH, PAUL R., and ANNE H. EHRLICH, *Population, Resources, Environment: Issues in Human Ecology* (San Francisco: W. H. Freeman and Company, 1970). A textbook for general education courses designed to educate the layman about the worldwide population-ecology crisis and related social and scientific issues.

HAIRSTON, NELSON G., FREDERICK E. SMITH, and LAWRENCE B. SLOBODKIN, "Community Structure, Population Control, and Competition," in Jeffrey J. W. Baker and Garland E. Allen (Eds.), *The Process of Biology: Primary Sources* (Reading, Mass.: Addison-Wesley, 1970). An adaptation of an article by the same authors in *The*

*American Naturalist*, this work provides insight into the necessity for controlling the growth of the human population and portrays the serious consequences of over-population.

HARDIN, GARRETT (Ed.), *Population, Evolution, and Birth Control*, 2nd edition (San Francisco: W. H. Freeman and Company, 1969). This book, subtitled "A Collage of Controversial Ideas," is a collection of more than 100 articles, reviews, and criticisms presenting all shades of opinion concerning human population control.

HARDIN, GARRETT, "The Tragedy of the Commons," *Science* **162**, December 7, 1968, pp. 1243–1248. In this exceptionally stimulating article, the author argues that the current ecological crisis has no technological solution; he calls instead for a fundamental revision of human ethics and morality.

HUXLEY, JULIAN, "World Population." *Scientific American*, March 1956, p. 64. The author discusses the growing population and the problem of how to feed the world's people. Interesting, challenging, and important.

LEOPOLD, ALDO, "Deer Irruptions," in Jeffrey J. W. Baker and Garland E. Allen (Eds.), *The Process of Biology: Primary Sources* (Reading, Mass.: Addison-Wesley, 1970). A case history in ecology, dealing with population growth in deer and possible means of control.

MALTHUS, THOMAS R., "Population: The First Essay," in Jeffrey J. W. Baker and Garland E. Allen (Eds.), *The Process of Biology: Primary Sources* (Reading, Mass.: Addison-Wesley, 1970). This famous paper on population growth was cited by Darwin as being a primary contributing factor in leading him to his concept of evolution by natural selection.

ODUM, E. P., *Ecology* (New York: Holt, Rinehart, 1964). This book is one of a series, "Foundations of Modern Biology." It is a good, nontechnical survey of the field of modern ecology.

ODUM, E. P., *Fundamentals of Ecology* (Philadelphia: W. B. Saunders, 1953). A more complete textbook of ecology than the small survey published by Holt, Rinehart.

WENT, FRITZ, "The Ecology of Desert Plants." *Scientific American*, April 1955, p. 68. Shows how survival of plants in the desert is determined by the control of germination. A good study in adaptations of plants to special conditions.

WHITE, LYNN, JR., "The Historical Roots of Our Ecological Crisis," *Science* **155**, March 10, 1967, pp. 1203–1207. In this fascinating article, historian White puts forth an hypothesis proposing that western man's Judeo-Christian heritage must bear the brunt of responsibility for his exploitation of the environment for his own purposes without regard to the effects on all of nature.

ZINSSER, H., *Rats, Lice and History* (Boston: Little, Brown & Co., 1954). A well-written treatment of the effects which diseases, borne by invading animals of one sort or another, have had on the course of history. Particularly deals with the typhus infections caused by viruses borne by rats in eastern and central Europe.

# CHAPTER 21

# THE PROCESS OF EVOLUTION

The concept of natural selection is undoubtedly one of the most important generalizations in modern biology. It was introduced to the world in comprehensive form in 1859 by the English naturalist Charles Darwin (1809–1882). Darwin's book *On the Origin of Species by Means of Natural Selection* (referred to generally as *The Origin of Species*) had significant effects on the intellectual world of the mid-nineteenth century. *The Origin of Species* contained a massive amount of data supporting the concept of evolution in general, and the theory of natural selection in particular. No matter how much religious leaders and biologists might have disagreed with Darwin, they could not ignore his work.

Although Darwin's theory contained some gaps and loopholes when it was published in 1859, it has stood the test of time. Today, more than ever, evidence shows that the fundamental principles of variation and natural selection that Darwin proposed are quite valid. The present chapter will discuss the mechanism of natural selection as it is viewed by modern biologists, and the ways in which it accounts for the origin of species.

**21-2
THE EVIDENCE
FOR EVOLUTION**

There are three general kinds of explanation for the wide diversity of form in the living world. The first is the idea of **special creation,** which holds that species arose in the past as the result of a supernatural act. At the time of creation, these species possessed exactly the same characteristics they do today. The second kind of explanation is that of **spontaneous generation.** According to this idea, many species arise from previously nonliving matter, as tadpoles from mud or maggots from decaying meat. A third type of explanation is the theory of **transmutation of species,** which holds that over the course of time, one species has given rise to another. All modern theories of evolution hold to some idea of transmutation, though they may differ as to the mechanism by which one species may actually be modified to become another.

The problem in dealing with the concept of special creation is that it is inevitably linked to belief in a divine being.* Its adherents, therefore, though insistent that special creation be taught in biology courses, are not willing to submit it as a legitimate scientific hypothesis for objective testing. Such a mixing of science and religion is always unfortunate, for it makes an objective weighing of the evidence pro and con virtually impossible; the emotional attachment is simply too strong.

At times such emotional attachment can lead to tragedy. A pertinent example is that of Vice-Admiral Robert Fitzroy. Fitzroy had been captain of the *H.M.S. Beagle,* on which Darwin had sailed in 1831 on a five-year voyage which was to provide him with his evidence for evolution by natural selection. Fitzroy was an ardent believer in special creation, and Darwin had found him a valuable asset on the voyage as a source of opposing opinions against which to test the ideas that the naturalist was just then beginning to formulate in his mind.

Thirty years later, in Oxford, the famous debate between Bishop Wilberforce, representing special creation, and Thomas Huxley, representing Darwin's viewpoint, took place. A high point of the debates occurred when, in his talk, Wilberforce asked Huxley if it was through his grandmother or his grandfather that he claimed to have descended from the apes. Remarking privately to some friends that "the Lord hath delivered him into my hands," Huxley rose to reply. He stated that he would prefer to be descended from an ape than from a cultivated man who prostituted the gifts of culture and eloquence to the service of prejudice and falsehood. In brief, Darwinism triumphed. But seated in the audience was Vice-Admiral Fitzroy. He rose to his feet and, full of rage and waving his Bible in the air, shouted his regrets at having taken Darwin aboard the *Beagle* for the voyage. As long ago as 1836 Darwin had written to his sister Susan, "I often doubt what will be his [Fitzroy's] end. Under many circumstances I am sure it would be a brilliant one, under others I fear a very unhappy one." On Sunday morning, April 30, 1865, Robert Fitzroy committed suicide. It seemed that the strain between the emotional attachment to special creation and the intellectual suspicion that Darwin was right had simply been too much to bear.

The Oxford debates had a rerun in the United States in the mid-1920's with the notable Dayton, Tennessee, trial of John Scopes, a high school biology teacher. Scopes was brought to trial for teaching evolution. The prosecution engaged the services of William Jennings Bryan, three-time unsuccessful candidate for the presidency and a noted special creationist. The defense countered with the brilliant defense lawyer, Clarence Darrow. The resulting "debate"

---

* There is nothing wrong in this belief, of course; however, since the existence or non-existence of a divine being is not subject to scientific testing, an hypothesis based on its existence cannot be considered a scientific one.

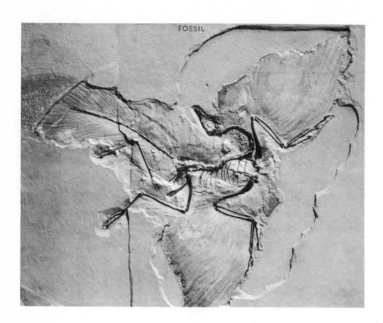

FOSSIL

FIG. 21–1   Fossil of the primitive bird *Archae-opteryx*, which clearly represents the evolutionary development of modern birds from primitive reptiles. Note the long tail, as well as the claws on the wing, which are reptilian characteristics, as contrasted with the feathers and the general structure of the appendages, which are avian features. (Courtesy American Museum of Natural History.)

was similar to the one at Oxford and in the words of the press, "Darrow made a monkey of the man." Scopes was given a minimum fine and a suspended sentence. Bryan died five days later.*

Unlike special creation, the idea of spontaneous generation *is* amenable to scientific investigation, and can be experimentally shown to give rise to false predictions (see Section 24–2).

Eventually the ideas of special creation and spontaneous generation lost ground. In the early and middle nineteenth century people became more favorably disposed to the idea of transmutation. To a large extent this was due to an increase in various types of evidence, such as the findings of paleontology (the study of fossils), taxonomy, or embryology. Evidence from various sources now strongly supports the belief that transmutation of species does occur.

One kind of evidence comes from the area of taxonomy, that division of biology dealing with the classification of organisms. It is sometimes extremely difficult to draw a distinct line between two closely related species. As naturalists accumulate more evidence about any species groups, it becomes increasingly obvious that (1) not all individuals in a single species are exactly alike, and (2) between two quite distinct species there is often a graded series of intermediate forms. Such evidence supports the idea of evolution from a common ancestor. It is difficult to account for these data on the basis of immutability and special creation.

---

* Somewhat later, Bryan College, seemingly committed to the special creation "hypothesis," was founded in Dayton—an act comparable, perhaps, to the founding of a "Napoleon Tech" at Waterloo.

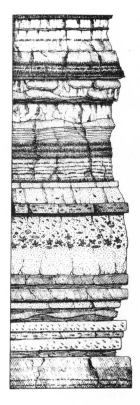

FIG. 21–2    An illustration from a study in paleontology and geology published early in the nineteenth century, showing the distinct breaks in strata, with similar changes in their fossil content, that led many naturalists to the idea of catastrophism. Distinct divisions between layers were taken to indicate great upheavals by fire or flood.

A second kind of evidence comes from the fossil record. Studying the sequence of fossils from ancient to more recent rock layers discloses several important items of information to the paleontologist. First, the sequence shows, in general, an increase in diversity as well as complexity of fossil forms. Slight modifications in fossil forms from one stratum to another seem indicative, in many cases, of the slow modification of forms over time. While this evidence does not exclude the ideas of special creation or spontaneous generation, it is certainly in direct support of the idea of transmutation. Second, some fossil forms have no living relatives; these forms are said to be **extinct.** The phenomenon of extinction shows that some species have been unable to perpetuate themselves. And, by extension, if old species die out, cannot new species originate from previous ones? Given the alternative theory of special creation, it would be necessary to suppose that the Creator whimsically allowed some species to perpetuate themselves while causing others to die off. The fact that there are many more extinct species than species presently alive on the earth would indicate that the Creator's whims must have been rather frequent. And third, the fossil records sometimes show forms intermediate between two presently living types. For example, it is now well established that birds and reptiles diverged from a common ancestor. The most convincing item of information on this score was the discovery of *Archaeopteryx*, a fossil form intermediate between these two groups (Fig. 21–1). *Archaeopteryx* had teeth and a long tail (characteristic of reptiles), and it also had feathers (characteristic of birds). Such genuine "missing links" are strong evidence for transmutation of species.

A noticeable feature of the fossil record is that it contains distinct gaps. The lines of demarcation between adjacent layers of rock are often quite sharp (Fig. 21–2). For many years (especially in the eighteenth and nineteenth centuries) these gaps posed problems for theories of evolution. Many times the fossils in one layer were totally different from those in the layer just above or beneath it. In the eighteenth and early nineteenth centuries, these gaps were thought to be the result of great cataclysms which swept the earth, destroying all or nearly all the life forms. It was supposed that after each successive cataclysm, the earth was repopulated with new forms by acts of special creation. This view of the geological record was called **catastrophism.**

More recent geological evidence has shown why such gaps occur. Changes in the level of the earth's surface cause regions to be raised or lowered from one period to another. This elevation of fossil-laden sediments exposes them to such eroding forces as wind or water. Thus whole layers, along with the fossils they contain, may be lost forever. Since such layers may represent vast periods of time, a record of considerable evolutionary history will be missing. Furthermore, a layer of sediment deposited when an area is under water will be quite different in appearance and composition from a layer deposited when the area is dry. The fossil forms will obviously be different as well.

A third kind of evidence is that of comparative anatomy. Comparative anatomy is the study of similarities and differences between the anatomical structures of two or more species. Reasoning from the hypothesis that evolution does occur, we can say:

*Hypothesis: If . . .*    organisms descend from ancestral forms by modification,

*Prediction:  then . . .* we should expect to find large groups of animals (or plants) which are anatomical variations on the same theme.

This prediction says, for example, that because the man, bat, pig, and dog are all mammals, the bone structure of their appendages should have many features in common, despite some obvious differences. The work of comparative anatomists has shown that this is indeed the case (Fig. 21–3a). Although the forelimb of each is modified for a different function (man's for grasping, the bat's for flying, the pig's and dog's for walking), the similarities in bone structure are still evident (Fig. 21–3b).

Comparative anatomy emphasizes the difference between **homologous** and **analogous** structures. Homologous structures are those which have basic anatomical features in common but which perform different functions. For example, the wing of a bat, the leg of a horse or dog, and the hand of a man show homologous bone structures. Analogous structures, on the other hand, are used for similar purposes, but are of different origin and are not necessarily built on the same anatomical plan. The wing of a bird and the wing of a butterfly are analogous, but not homologous, since they do not have any basic structural units (bones, etc.) in common.

The idea of evolution from a common ancestor is greatly supported by the study of homologous structures. In cases in which different animals have started with the same ancestor, subsequent generations show slight modifications of the basic anatomical plan. Homologous structures thus give an indication of the degree of divergence between two related forms.

The existence of homologous organs, or the existence of similarities in the structure of various body parts, does not refute the idea of special creation. There is just as much reason for believing that the Creator would choose a common plan for building His creatures as that He would choose different plans for each. However, one of the results of studies in comparative anatomy is the finding of **vestigial structures**. Vestigial structures are those which appear in the organism in a seemingly functionless role. The appendix of man, hip bones

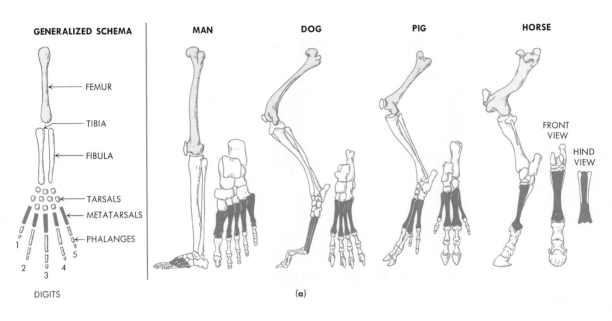

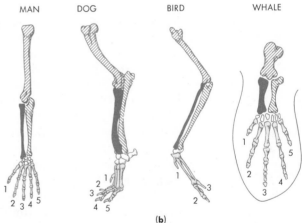

FIG. 21–3  Homologous bones in the forelimb and
hindlimb of several vertebrates. (a) Hindlimb homology. To the left is a generalized scheme for the vertebrate limb. (b) Forelimb homology. Note that
though the forelimbs of these four vertebrates are all
used for quite different functions, they nevertheless
show a similar basic pattern. (Redrawn by permission
from G. G. Simpson, C. S. Pittendrigh, and L. H.
Tiffany, *Life: An Introduction to Biology.* New York:
Harcourt, Brace & World, Inc., p. 465.)

in snakes, and rudimentary legs in whales are all vestigial structures. It is
easy to explain the existence of such structures by the idea of descent. They
represent useless or inoperative parts against whose existence natural selection
is working. By the concept of special creation, however, it is difficult to explain
why such parts exist.

Evidence from the field of genetics has made important contributions to
the idea that transmutation of species occurs. Although details of the genetic
interpretation of natural selection will be discussed in a later part of this chapter,
some mention of this important line of evidence will be made here. It has been
known since the early years of this century that genes are quite constant, and

FIG. 21–4 Charles Darwin (1809–1882), an English naturalist and author of *On the Origin of Species by Means of Natural Selection*, a work which laid the foundation for modern evolutionary thinking. (Photo courtesy the Burndy Library, Norwalk, Conn.)

are inherited on a statistically predictable basis. Generally speaking, the constancy of genes tends to keep species from changing. However, mutations do occur, introducing new heritable variations into a population. Experiments under carefully controlled laboratory conditions show that genes have different degrees of "fitness" to any given environment. If selection is practiced by the biologist, either directly (by allowing only organisms with one particular genotype to breed) or indirectly (by placing organisms in environments which will favor one genotype over another), it is possible to alter the genotype of a laboratory population in a very few generations. Experimental evidence for change of genotypes through selection gives strong support to the idea of transmutation in general and natural selection in particular.

Evidence for evolution comes from other areas as well—for example, from embryology or from the study of the geographic distribution of animals and plants. It is not necessary to go into details in these cases, since the preceding examples have provided ample evidence for the origin of species by evolution from preexisting forms. The question that arises now is: By what mechanism does evolution occur? In the history of biology there have been many attempts to answer this question. It is Charles Darwin's concept of natural selection that has provided the most satisfactory explanation.

**21-3
DARWINIAN
NATURAL
SELECTION**

The basic process of evolution by natural selection can be summarized by the following observations and conclusions.

*Observation 1:* All organisms have a high reproductive capacity. As we saw in Chapter 20, a population of organisms with an unlimited food supply and without being subject to predation, could quickly fill the entire earth with their own kind.

FIG. 21–5  On a lichen-encrusted tree trunk in nonindustrial regions of England, melanic forms of the peppered moth stand out conspicuously. The light form of the moth, however, is barely discernible (lower right). Under such conditions, the melanic form is subject to heavy predation. (Photo courtesy Dr. H. B. D. Kettlewell.)

*Observation 2:* However, the food supply for any population of organisms is *not* unlimited. The growth rate of the population tends to outrun the growth rate of the food supply.

*Conclusion 1:* The result must be a continual struggle for existence among organisms of the same kind (i.e., organisms which have the same food requirements).

*Observation 3:* All organisms show heritable variations. No two individuals in a species are exactly alike.

*Observation 4:* Some variations are more favorable to existence in a given environment than others.

*Conclusion 2:* Those organisms possessing favorable variations will be better able to survive in a given environment than those that possess unfavorable variations. Thus each successive generation will be better adapted to the environment.

To demonstrate how natural selection operates in nature, let us consider the following case. For over a century, two varieties of the peppered moth have been known to exist in various parts of England. One form, *Biston betularia*, is light-colored with small dark spots irregularly scattered over its wings and body. The other, *Biston carbonaria*, is much darker, due to the presence of the pigment melanin. This latter is often called the "melanic" form.

In the past, samples collected in the field showed that the light form was far more common than the dark. This was explained by showing that the light form was protectively colored. **Protective coloration** is the biological counterpart of military camouflage. Organisms that are protectively colored inherit certain patterns of pigmentation which allow them to blend with their backgrounds.  On tree trunks covered with lichens,* light varieties of the peppered moth are perfectly camouflaged, but the darker form stands out prominently (Fig. 21–5).  The dark form is thus more subject to predation by birds than is the light form.

Nevertheless, in the past hundred years the number of melanic moths has been observed to increase quite drastically.  In some areas the dark form has almost totally replaced the light.  A map (Fig. 21–6) comparing distribution of melanics to light-colored moths shows that the darker form predominates in the industrial centers and the regions to the southeast.  Investigation of these regions shows that the smoke and soot from factory cities has significantly darkened the natural background of these regions.  In addition, prevailing southwesterly winds have deposited a good deal of soot in the eastern regions, which themselves are not industrial.  This has been a very important factor in the evolutionary history of the peppered form.

FIG. 21–6    Distribution map of forms of the peppered moth in England.  Each circle represents a population sample taken in a given area.  The colored portion of each circle indicates the percentage of melanic forms found in the area, while the white portion indicates the percentage of light-colored forms.  (Reprinted with permission.  Copyright © 1959 by Scientific American, Inc.  All rights reserved.)

On a darker background, the light-colored moths that had previously been well camouflaged became much more visible (see Fig. 21–7).  As a result, these forms were put at a distinct disadvantage.  Being more easily detectable, the light varieties became subject to greater predation from birds.  The number of light-colored moths able to reach maturity and reproduce decreased propor-

---

* Lichens are greenish-gray growths found covering many rocks and trees.  A lichen is actually a combination of algal and fungal growths.  The moths often rest on the lichen-covered tree trunks during the day.

FIG. 21–7   On a tree trunk darkened by soot from industrial areas, the light-colored form of the peppered moth is much more visible than the melanic form.  In this situation, the melanic form has greater survival value than the lighter variety.  (Photo courtesy Dr. H. B. D. Kettlewell.)

tionately.  The genes for light color consequently reached fewer members of the next generation than before the change in background.

It might be hypothesized that the melanic form of the peppered moth arose originally by a mutation of the gene controlling coloration.  This mutation was disadvantageous on the original, light-colored background, and natural selection was unfavorable to it.  However, through the change in the environment due to industrial growth, the mutant was favored.  The result was that the melanic genes spread through the population as is shown in Fig. 21–8.  At the present time the melanic form has almost replaced the lighter form in certain areas,

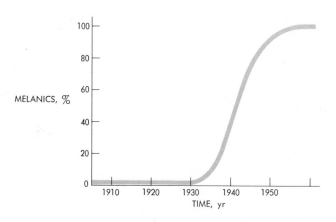

FIG. 21–8    Graph showing the theoretical increase in number of melanic moths (measured as percentage of population in a given area) over a period of years. The mutation to the gene responsible for this variety probably occurs in one out of 100,000 cases. Because this gene has a selective advantage in industrial areas, it "takes over" the population in a relatively short time. The rate of increase in percentage of melanic moths is far greater than occurs in most cases of shift in gene frequency. (Adapted from *Scientific American*, March 1959, p. 51.)

indicating the greater selective advantage of the former. Now the above hypothesis can become the basis of a prediction, as follows:

*Hypothesis: If . . .*   natural selection favors darker moths in industrial regions and lighter moths in nonindustrial regions, . . .

*Prediction:   then . . .* releasing equal numbers of light and dark forms in both regions, and recapturing the survivors after a period of time, should show definite changes. In the industrial region, far more dark forms should be recovered than light forms; in the nonindustrial areas the reverse should be true.

An experiment was designed in the early 1950's to test whether the dark form was indeed selectively favored in industrial regions as compared to nonindustrial regions. Dark and light forms of the moth were raised in the laboratory and released in roughly equal numbers into each type of environment. Before release, the moths were carefully marked with cellulose paint, a different color being used for each day of the week. In this way, it was possible to determine when a given moth had been released and how long it had survived. Other moth species were also released. (Why?)

After the experiment had proceeded for a certain period of time, large lanterns were set up in the woods at night and the surviving moths recaptured.

Table 21-1 shows the results, tabulated as percentage of moths recaptured. These data suggest that more of the darker forms survive in the industrial region and more of the light forms in the nonindustrial region. It is apparent that the differences in the pigmentation of the moths are adaptive to their respective environments. The above test therefore supports the hypothesis that natural selection does seem to favor the dark form in industrial and the light form in nonindustrial areas.

**TABLE 21-1**

|  | PERCENT OF MOTHS RECAPTURED | |
| --- | --- | --- |
| AREA | DARK FORM | LIGHT FORM |
| DORSET WOODS (NONINDUSTRIAL) | 6.34 | 12.0 |
| BIRMINGHAM (INDUSTRIAL) | 53.2 | 25.0 |

This example of industrial melanism illustrates how, by a change in the environment, a previously unfit organism (the dark form) has become *more* fit. This change likewise caused a well-adapted form (the light-colored moth) to become *less* fit. The mutant gene for melanism did not occur in response to the environmental change. As the experiments of Luria and Delbruck on bacteria (see Section 3-3) indicate, mutations are not produced in this way. The mutant gene had always existed in a small percentage of the population. Spread of the gene was possible only when changed conditions favored those organisms that carried it. In darwinian terms, it is the nature of the environment which acts as the "selecting agent."

Another example of the action of natural selection in nature was studied in a pasture in southern Maryland. The owner planted a mixture of grass and clover (*Trifolium*) seed. After the planting was completed, the owner installed a fence through the middle of the field, dividing it into two parts. One side was cut for hay a few times during the summers, while the other half was heavily grazed by livestock. Three years later, a botanist dug up plants of the various species of grass and clover and transplanted them to his experimental garden. After a period of growth under uniform conditions, a high proportion of the grasses and clover from the grazed half of the field produced a dwarf, rambling growth. However, the grass and clover plants taken from the ungrazed half were erect and vigorous (Fig. 21-9). By raising seed from these plants, the differences were found to be inherited.

What is a reasonable explanation for these observations? In the field where livestock had grazed for three years, only those plants small and low enough not to be eaten were able to produce seed. However, in the field where the plants were mowed occasionally for hay, the tall grasses and clover were able to produce seed. Thus, in this field the tall plants were favored by selection.

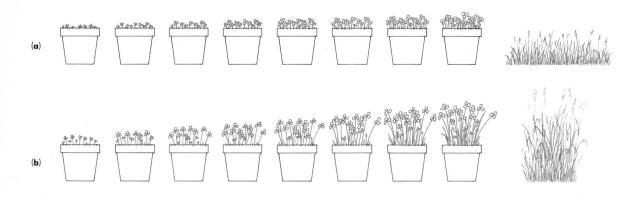

**(a)**

**(b)**

FIG. 21–9    Diagrams illustrating the action of natural selection on the growth form of different plant species. (a) Plants transplanted from grazed field and grown under uniform conditions. Note dwarf, rambling growth habit. (b) Plants transplanted from ungrazed field and grown under uniform conditions. These plants are generally much taller.

**21-4
DIRECTION OF
NATURAL
SELECTION**

The evolutionist George Gaylord Simpson has defined selection as anything producing systematic, inheritable changes in populations between one generation and the next.    This definition requires, therefore, that there be direction in the way natural selection operates.    The genetic makeup of the population may change in one direction, with respect to certain genes and genotypes.    Such **directional selection** may favor one nonaverage or extreme phenotype, pushing the population of phenotypes (and their genotypes) in the direction of this particular phenotype.    This has happened, of course, in the domestication of crop plants and animals by man.    For example, agronomists at the University of Illinois selected corn for high protein content in the grains of corn plants for 60 generations (Fig. 21–10).    Each year the ears highest in protein were chosen to plant for the next generation.    Throughout most of the 60-year period, there was steady increase in the protein content of the grains from an average of 10.9% in the original population to an average of 19.4% in the sixtieth generation after the selection began.    While this experiment was going on, the agronomists also selected for low protein content in another line originating from the same population of corn.    The protein content of this corn steadily dropped from the starting average of 10.9% to 4.9% after 60 generations of selection.    Thus, artificial selection resulted in different directions of change in the populations: the grain of one line of corn increased in protein content, while the other decreased. The agronomists were able to shift the population average for protein content of the corn from an original value of about 11% to over 19% for the upward and about 5% for the downward selection.    The populations were responding

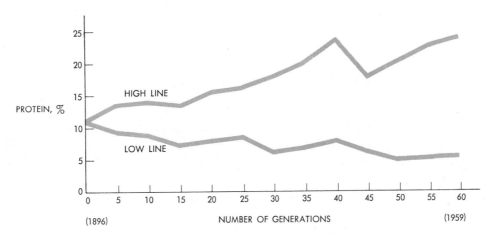

FIG. 21–10   An example of directional selection for the protein content in grains of corn during 60 generations. (Data from C. M. Woodworth, E. R. Leng, and R. W. Jugenheimer, "Sixty Generations of Selection for Protein and Oil in Corn." *Agronomy Journal* **44**, 1952, pp. 60–65.)

FIG. 21–11   Normal curves of distribution illustrating the concept of stabilizing selection. Note that the extreme variant individuals on either end of the curve are eliminated from the population each generation.

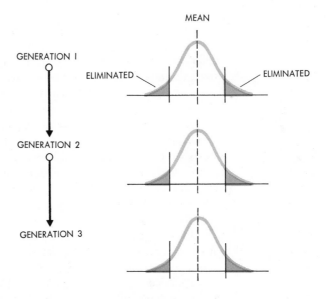

genotypically to the selection of the phenotypes. This is directional selection. In the example of the peppered moths, natural selection by birds during many generations has operated to shift the population from light-colored phenotype to dark-colored phenotype where the vegetation has been darkened by pollution.

But natural selection may also act to bring about no change in direction; in other words, natural selection may act to keep a population genetically constant.

Such **stabilizing selection** occurs whenever the population has reached a high degree of adaptation to its particular habitat and the environment remains stable for long periods of time. By favoring the average or normal individuals and eliminating the extreme variants, stabilizing selection keeps the population genetically constant (Fig. 21–11). Botanists can infer that stabilizing selection occurs in plant species. This seems to be the most likely explanation for the existence of numerous species in relatively stable habitats for millions of years without appreciable change. For example, the fossil record shows that the giant sequoia (*Sequoiadendron giganteum*), of the Sierra Nevada Mountains in California, has remained stable for millions of years.

**21-5
THE POPULATION
CONCEPT OF
EVOLUTION**

One of the most important contributions to modern evolutionary theory has come from the field of genetics. Genetics has shown how variations arise and how recombination of characteristics take place, and has provided the means of treating evolution on the *population level*. The latter contribution is of great importance to a thorough understanding of the mechanisms of natural selection.

**Population genetics** is the field of biology that studies the genetic composition of whole animal or plant populations. It is the population itself, rather than individual cells or organisms, that becomes the basic unit of biological study.

How is it possible to describe the genetic makeup of an entire population? This is not quite as difficult as it may sound. In the first place, the genetic characteristics of the population can be treated as the sum of the genotypes of all the individual members. Thus we may speak of the **gene pool** of a population. The number and kind of each allele found in the population determine the unique characteristics of the gene pool.

In the second place, population genetics uses statistical methods. Individual variations in organisms do not enter the picture unless a given variation becomes statistically significant. Only if enough organisms turn up with the same variation in a given generation will this variation become apparent as a definite and nonrandom change in the composition of the gene pool. Such methods of analysis are particularly important in studying the genetic changes involved in the evolutionary process.

By operating on individual organisms, natural selection ultimately brings about a change in the composition of a gene pool to which these individual organisms contribute. The gene pool of a population is divided up each generation and parceled out to new individual members (i.e., the offspring). Inevitably new mutations or combinations of genotypes occur which express themselves as specific individual phenotypes. As a result of natural selection, certain genotypes will leave more offspring than others. Certain genes will be passed on to the next generation in greater numbers, others in less. The composition of the gene pool will be changed accordingly.

Two opposing factors are at work on the gene pool of a population. One is natural selection, which tends to alter the composition of the gene pool from one generation to another. The other factor is expressed in the concept of **genetic equilibrium,** which holds that under very specific conditions the ratio between various alleles in a population tends to remain constant from one generation to the next. This concept applies regardless of the proportions of the genes in the initial population. The idea of genetic equilibrium was introduced into biology in 1908 by G. H. Hardy, an English mathematician, and W. Weinberg, a German physician, hence it is sometimes referred to as the Hardy-Weinberg law. Now, although it is sometimes thought (by nonbiologists) that recessive genes must eventually be wiped out of a population, according to the concept of genetic equilibrium this is not necessarily the case. For example, despite the fact that blue eyes are recessive to brown, the number of blue-eyed people in the human population remains relatively constant from one generation to another.

We mentioned earlier that genetic equilibrium would be maintained in a population *only* under very specific conditions. These are listed below.

1) *Mating in the population must be random.* That is, each phenotype must have an equal chance of reproducing. If this were not the case—if one male phenotype were more preferable to the females than another—then the favored males would leave more offspring. For example, if female birds of a given species always choose the males with red plumes, the genes producing this phenotype will spread throughout the population.

2) *All matings must yield, on the average, the same number of offspring.* Again, if this were not the case—if mating between two particular phenotypes yielded consistently fewer offspring—then the alleles of those phenotypes would decline in number with each generation.

3) *The population must be sufficiently large that chance variations in a small number of organisms do not affect the statistical average.* In small populations the effects of random mutations or immigration or emigration of a few organisms can produce statistically significant changes in gene ratios. By analogy, a failing grade in a class of three affects the class average far more than in a class of thirty (see Chapter 5).

4) *The mutation rate must have reached its own equilibrium.* This means that the frequency with which $A$ mutates to $a$ is equaled by the frequency with which $a$ mutates back to $A$. As a result, the overall ratio of $A$ to $a$ will not change from one generation to the next.

The factors just listed represent *idealized conditions* which are seldom met in natural populations. Yet, to the extent that they do occur, they tend to check or balance the opposing forces of selective mating, natural selection, small population size, or mutation. The next section will be devoted to a case study showing how the forces of natural selection and genetic equilibrium interact in a natural population.

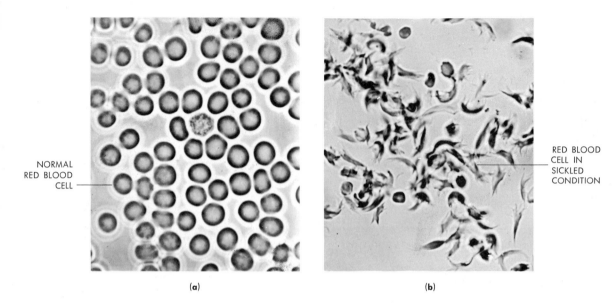

NORMAL
RED BLOOD
CELL

RED BLOOD
CELL IN
SICKLED
CONDITION

(a)                                                      (b)

FIG. 21–12    (a) Normal red blood cells and (b) cells which are sickled as a result of low oxygen tension. (Photos courtesy Dr. A. C. Allison.)

**21–6
NATURAL
SELECTION AND
CHANGES IN
GENE FREQUENCY**

Although many factors serve to upset the genetic equilibrium of a population, perhaps none is so important as the combined effect of mutation and natural selection. How this may occur in natural populations is illustrated by the human condition known as sickle-cell anemia. This condition occurs primarily among Negroes and affects the oxygen-carrying capacity of red blood cells. The biochemistry and genetics of sickle-cell anemia have been carefully studied in recent years. It is apparent that mutation of the gene for normal hemoglobin produces a slightly modified portion of the hemoglobin molecule. The mutation may be represented as:

$$Hb^A \longrightarrow Hb^s,$$

where $Hb^A$ stands for normal hemoglobin and $Hb^s$ for sickle-cell hemoglobin. When oxygen tension in the blood gets low, $Hb^s$ molecules fold up, or collapse. As a result, the red blood cells, composed of almost 100% hemoglobin, also collapse. The change in shape of the cells is a diagnostic trait of the disease (Fig. 21–12). When this folding-up occurs, it is very difficult for the affected cells to pick up oxygen in the lungs and transport it to the tissues. In many cases, reduced vigor or even death results.

Allowing *s* to represent the sickle-cell gene, and *S* the normal allele, let us see how natural selection acts on this gene in a population. With these two alleles, three combinations are possible: *ss* (individuals with sickle-cell anemia), *Ss*

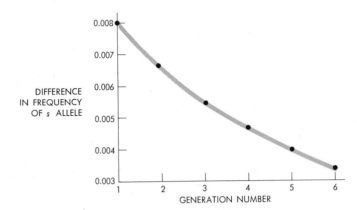

FIG. 21-13   Graph plotting the difference in frequency of s allele in successive generations.

(individuals with the sickle-cell trait, a mild form of the condition), and *SS* (individuals with normal hemoglobin). The sickle-cell alleles show incomplete dominance, hence each of the genotypes also shows a characteristic phenotype. Persons homozygous for the sickle-cell gene generally die very young and so leave few offspring, if any. Persons heterozygous for the sickle-cell trait usually live to sexual maturity, since they are affected by this condition only in cases of extreme exercise or high altitudes.

The frequency of these three genotypes among American Negroes has been studied by J. V. Neel and others. It is known that the frequency of the *s* allele is 0.05, while that of the *S* is 0.95.* According to the Hardy-Weinberg equilibrium, we should expect these frequencies to remain constant from generation to generation. However, natural selection is highly unfavorable to individuals of the *ss* genotype. It has been estimated† that a child born with sickle-cell anemia has one-fifth as much chance as other children of surviving to sexual maturity. This indicates that roughly 80% of the *ss* genotypes fail to survive beyond infancy or childhood.

Natural selection thus limits the number of mutant *s* genes passed on to the next generation. If the frequency of *s* is 0.05 in one generation, then it will be reduced by about 16% in the next generation; the frequency will thus decline from 0.05 to 0.042 in one generation. (The figure of 16% is taken from calculations based on medical records of mortality rate among *ss* individuals.) The theoretical "cutting down" effect of natural selection in this instance is represented diagrammatically in Fig. 21-13. Note that the *rate* at which the mutant *s* allele is eliminated from the population becomes slightly lower in each generation. The fewer *s* alleles in the population, the less chance they have of coming together to form the lethal *ss* homozygote. Thus selection against a

---

* In other words, the *s* gene makes up 5% of the gene pool for this allele, and *S* about 95%.
† A. C. Allison, "Sickle Cells and Evolution." *Scientific American*, August 1956, pp. 87–94.

particular gene can reduce the frequency with which it occurs in the population. However, since the rate of decrease becomes less each generation, a very long time is generally required to effectively eliminate an unfavorable gene from the population.

The case of sickle-cell anemia illustrates very well how gene frequencies vary due to differences in environmental conditions. The frequency of the *s* gene is much greater in certain parts of Africa than in other parts of the world. Investigation has shown that the areas in which the sickle-cell gene is most frequent are also the areas of high malaria incidence. It was then discovered that the heterozygous carrier (*Ss*) individuals possessed selectively greater resistance to malaria than the homozygous nonsickling individuals.* Thus in areas in which malaria exists, the sickle-cell trait has a high adaptive value to the individuals who possess it. The disadvantage of the sickle-cell trait is more than compensated for by the greater resistance to malaria.

Like melanism in moths, then, the sickle-cell trait is selectively disadvantageous under one set of conditions and advantageous under another. Therefore, natural selection tends to preserve both the *s* and *S* alleles in the population. Either homozygote is at a decided disadvantage in malaria-infested regions. Superiority of the heterozygote therefore keeps the frequency of either allele from declining to a very low level.

## 21-7
## SEXUAL SELECTION

In later editions of *The Origin of Species*, Darwin gave a great deal of emphasis to the idea of sexual selection. According to this concept, the female or male (depending on the species) selects a mate on the basis of certain distinct criteria, such as coloration or behavior. Darwin held that the male or female of a species would consistently select a mate that possessed certain specific characteristics. Sexual selection is thus a special case of natural selection. However, as a separate idea it helps to explain how characteristics such as the gaudy plumes of the peacock or the extravagant tail feathers of the bird of paradise could be of adaptive value.

In such cases, two opposing selection pressures are at work. Sexual selection tends to favor any modification that increases the attractiveness of one sex for the other. Natural selection working for survival, however, favors any modification that renders the organism less visible to its enemies. If the disadvantage of being easily spotted by predators is compensated for by the increased produc-

---

* The way in which the sickle-cell trait confers resistance to malaria seems to be something like the following. The infectious phase of the malarial protozoan enters the red blood cells as a parasite. The metabolic activity of the protozoan uses up oxygen, thus reducing the oxygen tension within the cell (i.e., the amount of oxygen). Now, molecules of sickle-cell hemoglobin collapse when the oxygen tension gets low, thereby causing the entire red blood cell to fold inward, assuming the sickle shape. Cells which have thus collapsed are, along with the parasitic protozoans within them, more readily destroyed by phagocytes. In this way the malarial parasite is prevented from spreading throughout the bloodstream.

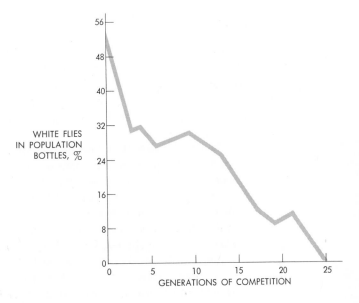

FIG. 21–14 Graph showing the result of sexual selection in a culture bottle of *Drosophila*. Since females prefer red-eyed to white-eyed males, the red-eyed males leave greater numbers of offspring, on the whole, in each generation. The culture bottle originally had about equal numbers of red-eyed and white-eyed males; the decline in percentage of the white-eyed genotype can be easily discerned.

tivity resulting from bright coloration, the latter characteristic will be favored. Genes for coloration will therefore increase in the population. However, the moment the balance swings the other way (i.e., the moment the animal becomes too easy a prey) genes reducing coloration will be favored.

A vivid example of sexual selection in a controlled laboratory situation can be seen from the data plotted in Fig. 21–14. At the beginning of this experiment, a population of *Drosophila* was set up in which the initial percentages of genes for white eyes ($w$) and normal eyes ($W$) were known. This gene is sex-linked, so by and large only males will show the white-eye trait. *Drosophila* females will not mate as readily with white-eyed males as with red-eyed ones. In other words, they show a *preference* for red-eyed males. Sexual selection operated in this case to reduce the number of $w$ genes passed on to each successive generation. The percent of individuals bearing the gene correspondingly declined over a number of generations.

Species do not generally arise from previous species at one jump. A new variation in one segment of a population does not make some of those organisms new species. A species may undergo continual change as new variations allow better adaptation to the environment. However, it is hypothesized that if one species is to give rise to two or more species, the various segments of that population must be **isolated** in some way from each other—that is, two or more segments of a population must be prevented from interbreeding, so that the "gene flow" between the two parts of the original population is stopped. This hy-

**21-8
THE ROLE OF
ISOLATION IN THE
ORIGIN OF SPECIES**

pothesis leads to the following prediction:

**Hypothesis:** *If* . . .   isolation is necessary for two or more species to arise from a single population, . . .

**Prediction:** *then* . . . we should expect to find that any two (or more) diverging populations in nature are separated from each other by some sort of barrier.

Evidence shows that all known cases of divergence (unless they occurred so long ago that the geography of the region has changed) have involved some sort of isolation. One example will show that the prediction can be verified.

Two populations of tuft-eared squirrels inhabit the north and south rims of the Grand Canyon (Fig. 21–15). These squirrels are very similar, yet there are visible differences between them. The two squirrel populations are usually considered separate species, for, although some hybridization is possible in the laboratory, little or no gene flow exists between the two populations in nature.

It seems clear that both the Abert squirrel (southern rim) and Kaibab squirrel (northern rim) arose in the past from the same population. This was apparently a freely breeding population which inhabited the entire region now

FIG. 21–15   In nature, the Abert squirrel (left) and the Kaibab squirrel (right) are not found together, as shown here. The Abert squirrel inhabits the southern rim of the Grand Canyon, and the Kaibab squirrel the northern rim. Anatomical differences indicate that these two populations diverged from a common ancestor prior to being geographically isolated by the canyon. (Redrawn by permission from G. G. Simpson, C. S. Pittendrigh, and L. H. Tiffany, *Life: An Introduction to Biology.* New York: Harcourt, Brace & World, Inc., 1957, p. 430.)

represented by the north and south rims. Widening of the bed of the Colorado River, and the subsequent formation of a deep canyon, created a geographic barrier that effectively prevented gene flow between the separate groups of organisms.

Not all geographic barriers are as spectacular as the Grand Canyon. A marshy area between two field habitats can also be an effective barrier. The question is: How does isolation produce new species? Surely the separation of the original population of tuft-eared squirrels by the Colorado River did not automatically produce two species.

Once an original population becomes divided into two isolated portions, the kind of variations that occur in each will inevitably be different. When the effect of these variations begins to become visible, we say that evolutionary **divergence** has begun. Divergence does not represent the origin of a new species. It is only the first stage. If for some reason the two populations are brought back together after only a few generations, the accumulated anatomical and physiological differences are usually not great enough to prevent interbreeding.

When divergence has continued for many generations, however, the accumulated differences may make interbreeding impossible. Once this stage is reached, we say that **speciation** has occurred. It is obvious that there can be no clear-cut dividing line between the end of divergence and the beginning of speciation. The terms are merely convenient to designate broad periods of evolutionary development.

Speciation in the tuft-eared squirrels probably started as a result of geographic isolation. In general, two or more species arise from a previous species only after some sort of physical separation of the original population into smaller groups. Then, once geographic isolation has allowed divergence and speciation to occur, a number of other isolating mechanisms come into play. These prevent the two species from interbreeding, should the populations ever come back together. Not all of these mechanisms operate in any one case, but they do serve to strengthen the boundaries between the species. Isolating mechanisms are most evident as such when two similar species are living together in the same geographic area.

Some of the various isolating mechanisms common in nature are as follows.

1) *Seasonal isolation.* Although two populations of organisms may inhabit the same geographic region, their reproductive periods may occur at different seasons of the year. As a result, members of one population cannot mate with members of the other, even though physical contact between the two is possible. This type of isolation is particularly common in plants, but is also found in certain types of insects and snails.

2) *Ecological isolation.* If two populations are capable of interbreeding, yet do not do so because they live in different ecological niches, they are said to be ecologically isolated. For example, two populations of the deer mouse *Peromyscus* are capable of interbreeding in the laboratory. One population comes

from the forest and the other from a nearby field habitat. In nature, each population remains almost completely within its own niche. The forest population rarely, if ever, enters the field and vice versa. In this situation, divergence has reached the point where the two populations are close to being completely separate species.

3) *Physiological isolation.* Probably the first differences that begin to appear in geographically isolated populations are physiological. On the basis of the ideas that genes produce enzymes, slight changes in genetic code may show up first as changes in enzyme molecules. These changes need not be great enough to produce noticeable outward (phenotypic) effects, and they will not usually prevent interbreeding should the populations come back together. However, if the changes are in some way connected with the chemistry of the gametes themselves, or of the seminal fluids, fertilization may be hindered. In sea urchins, for example, biochemical differences allow the sperm of one species to have greater success with eggs of its own species than with eggs of another. Such physiological differences prevent or greatly inhibit successful hybridization.

4) *Behavioral isolation.* In many animals, specific behavioral traits are known to be inherited. Particularly important to evolution are those behavioral patterns connected with mating. In certain birds, fish, and insects, the male and female of a given species perform highly specific and elaborate courtship rituals. Male birds may strut about in a precise pattern, displaying their plumage in hopes of attracting a particular female. Once the female becomes interested, the male begins a new behavioral ritual which ultimately leads to copulation.

That these patterns are genetic, i.e., built into each organism from the outset, has been shown by raising birds in complete isolation. In such cases, there is no opportunity for young birds to learn the ritual from older members of the species. The fact that such isolated birds still perform according to the exact behavioral pattern of other members of the species supports the hypothesis that proposes a genetic basis for such activity.

That behavioral patterns can serve as isolating mechanisms between species is shown by the courtship of several species of fish. The male three-spined stickleback (genus *Spinachia*) builds a nest attached to water plants. Then, as was noted in Section 19–5, by performing a series of zig-zag swimming motions, he induces the female of the species to lay eggs in the nest. These swimming motions are highly specific. If the male does not perform the ritual precisely, the female immediately loses interest and swims away.

In many of the rivers in which three-spined sticklebacks live, there also exists a second species, the ten-spined sticklebacks. When males of this species court females, the behavioral pattern is somewhat different from that described above. Instead of performing the zig-zag dance, male ten-spined sticklebacks bounce along vertically in the water, bobbing up and down in front of the female.

The number of bounces and the position of the male are extremely important in bringing about the egg-laying response in the female. In both species the behavior of the male sets up a reflex action in the female. In some way not yet understood, this reflex pathway in both male and female is determined by the genetic makeup of the individual. If a male three-spined stickleback courts a female ten-spined stickleback, the female fails to show the egg-laying response. The female seems to lose interest as soon as the male begins the unfamiliar zig-zag dance. Such divergence in behavioral patterns, which probably first arose from geographical isolation, serves as an effective isolating mechanism even though the geographical isolation is no longer in effect. Divergence from some ancestral stickleback allowed two courtship patterns to develop; speciation has taken place, and interbreeding has been made difficult or impossible.

**21-9**
**MIGRATION AND**
**GENETIC DRIFT**

Migration of organisms from one population to another may introduce new alleles into a population's gene pool. If these new alleles have less survival value than the ones already present, they will not spread through the population. Thus the original gene frequencies of the population will not change. However, if the new alleles are in some way more adaptive, they will tend to spread in the population. As the frequency of these genes increases, the frequency of another allele must decline. In this way, migrations *into* an established population can cause a shift in gene frequencies.

A somewhat different situation may result when a group of organisms migrate *away* from a population into new, unoccupied territory. For example, mammals are thought to have originated about 165 million years ago from a migration of small reptiles out of the lowland marshes to the highlands. This **founder population,** as the emigrants are called, was a minority group from the parent population of reptiles. As is generally the case with founder populations, they were individuals who could not compete successfully in the original environment. The gene pool and the gene frequencies of a founder population are apt to be somewhat different from the parent population. Often the effects of a new environment are to increase this difference. If isolation of the founder population from the parent population is maintained, the founder population may eventually emerge as a different species.

Gene frequencies may also shift if the size of a population becomes very small. When there are few mating organisms, the effect of a mutation or chromosomal aberration and recombination may be greatly increased. If a mutation occurs in one organism in a population of 50, its frequency from the start is obviously much greater than if the mutation took place in a population of 1000 or 10,000. Often, the result of this is to establish certain alleles in a much greater frequency than would occur in larger populations. This tendency is often called **genetic drift.**

To a certain extent, genetic drift depends on chance. A particular allele may become fixed in a population through a chance mutation occurring at one

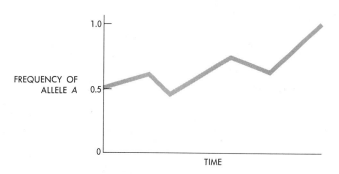

FIG. 21-16    Graph showing the changes in frequency of a given allele in the course of time. The random fluctuations at various points in time represent the great changes that occur in small populations. There is no particular "direction" to genetic drift. In small populations, however, accidental death of even a few organisms, or the occurrence of a new mutation, may produce a definite shift in frequencies.

particular time.  Or it may become established because, by chance, a certain group of organisms in the population survives while another group does not.

Figure 21–16 shows a change in frequency of a particular gene in a small population.  This graph shows that in the course of time, gene $A$ completely eliminates its allele $a$ by reaching a frequency of 1.0 (i.e., it occurs in 100% of the population).  This may be considered an example of genetic drift.  By "fixing" certain genes in the population, genetic drift tends to reduce the amount of variation that can occur.

There is debate among biologists as to whether genetic drift plays much of a role in the majority of evolutionary situations.  There has been a tendency in the past to explain many changes in gene frequency by ascribing them to genetic drift, when in reality the factor responsible was natural selection.  However, populations do exist in which the number of reproducing organisms is less than 50.  For example, at last count (1962) there were 32 whooping cranes in existence.  In a population of this size genetic drift could be an important factor in evolution.  It is certainly fair to say, however, that in the evolution of average animal and plant populations (which contain many thousands of individuals), genetic drift is usually a negligible factor.

**21-10
ADAPTIVE
RADIATION:
EVOLUTIONARY
OPPORTUNITY AND
EXPLOITATION**

All organisms are adapted to particular environments, but some are better adapted to a specific environment, or environmental niche, than others.  When a population becomes too large, it is inevitable that some organisms must either adapt to new niches or perish.  Those that can move into some area of the environment hitherto unoccupied will have a better chance of surviving.  Natural selection favors those organisms which can exploit (i.e., take advantage of) new niches in which there is less competition.  For example, if the organism has

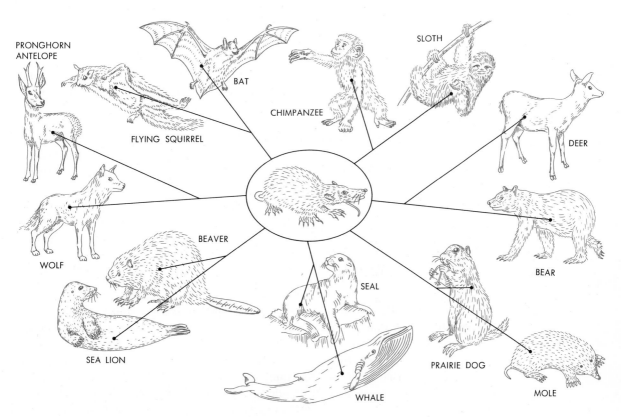

FIG. 21–17   Adaptive radiation in mammals. All the many forms of mammal living today are hypothesized to have developed from an ancestor similar to the organism pictured at the center of this diagram. By invading and exploiting varied ecological niches, mammals have become very widespread.

some chance variation that allows it to use a food source which other members of the population cannot use, it can thereby exploit this new niche. The organism has taken advantage of an evolutionary opportunity. Indeed, nature places a premium on the ability of organisms to make the most of new opportunities.

When a species is introduced into a new area, it tends to spread out and occupy as many different habitats as possible. In time, a single species will thus give rise to a variety of forms, each adapted through natural selection to a given niche. This evolution, from a single ancestral species to a variety of types, is called **adaptive radiation;** it results from the tendency of organisms to exploit unoccupied ecological niches. In a new niche, with reduced competition, an organism can produce more offspring. Variations enabling those offspring to exploit the niche further will be favored by natural selection. As a result, each population will become more and more adapted to a particular way of life. The ancestral population will give rise to a number of different populations, each with its own special adaptations. A diagram showing adaptive radiation in the placental mammals can be seen in Fig. 21–17. This represents a very extensive radiation, one which has been occurring for long periods of time. As a result, the modern forms are considerably different from the primitive mammalian ancestor.

Just how does adaptive radiation take place? In 1832 Darwin visited the Galapagos, a group of islands just off the western coast of South America (Section 20–9). There he collected some specimens of ground finch belonging to the subfamily Geospizinae. Although Darwin himself did not draw any special conclusions from study of these birds, later investigators have found in them **excellent sources of data on adaptive radiation and other evolutionary principles.**

Geological evidence shows that the Galapagos are of rather recent volcanic origin (having been formed about 1,000,000 years ago) and have never been connected to the mainland. As soon as vegetation developed on the islands, immigrant animals were free to move in and occupy the various niches. It is hypothesized that the present-day Galapagos finches (the male and the female of each species are shown in Fig. 21–18) are descended from a single type of finch which immigrated to the islands from the mainland sometime in the distant past. All attempts to find any such a mainland ancestor have, however, been unsuccessful. Perhaps this is because the ancestral finch has become extinct, or perhaps it is because the Galapagos finches have diverged so far from the ancestral traits that their relation to the mainland form is unrecognizable. **In the absence of any conclusive evidence, the former possibility seems more likely.**

An evolutionary diagram of the adaptive radiation of the finches throws light on the probable way in which divergence has occurred (Fig. 21–19). The fourteen species of finch living today can be roughly grouped into two categories: the ground finches (genus *Geospiza*) and the tree finches (genus *Camarhynchus*). In addition, there is a single "warbler" species, and one isolated species peculiar to the most distant island of the group.

Figure 21–18 indicates that the ancestral finch population very early split up into ground-dwellers and tree-dwellers. Variation and selection produced adaptations not only in foot structure, but also in the shape and size of beaks. Seeds form the major diet of ground finches, while the tree finches feed mostly on insects. Competition for food in these major niches produced further adaptive radiation within each area; all six species of ground-dwelling finches have slightly different diet preferences, even though all may be classified as seed-eaters. For example, three of the six species are specialized for specific sizes of seed (*G. magnirostris*, large seeds, *G. fortis*, medium seeds, and *G. fuliginosa*, small seeds). It is interesting that these three forms are found together on nearly all the Galapagos islands. Because these species have adapted to specific sizes of seed, competition for food between them is reduced. This subradiation occurs because

FIG. 21–18  Natural selection favors those variations which allow each organism to adapt successfully to its own niche.  All the organisms shown above occupy similar ecological niches, but each
species has evolved still further to minimize competition within its own niche.  (From David Lack,
"Darwin's Finches."  Reprinted with permission.  Copyright © 1953 by Scientific American, Inc.
All rights reserved.)

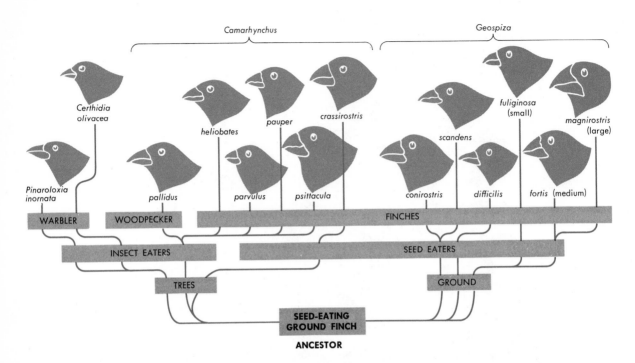

FIG. 21–19 Evolutionary history of the finches on the Galapagos. This diagram illustrates the basic radiation which has occurred at each point in time. The first radiation was between the two major habitats: ground and tree. Within each of these areas subradiations have taken place.

organisms are able to exploit numerous unoccupied niches. The other three species of ground-dwellers, on the other hand, combine seed diets with cactus pulp, or flowers.

Among the tree finches, one type feeds on seeds while the rest feed on insects. Like the ground finches, the tree finches have shown further radiation, especially in size and shape of beak. An especially interesting adaptation has occurred in one species of tree finch, *Camarhynchus pallidus*. This bird exploits essentially the same niche inhabited by woodpeckers in other geographic regions. Although it lacks the hard beak and long tongue of true woodpeckers, this finch has learned to use a cactus spine or small stick to probe insects from cracks in trees or from under the bark (Fig. 21–20). In this case, an adaptation in behavior has allowed the organism to exploit an unoccupied niche.

On the South American mainland, no species of finch has been able to undergo the great adaptive radiation seen on the Galapagos. It seems clear that on the mainland, most of the available niches are already occupied by other types of birds. The mainland forms lacked the "ecological opportunity" that makes adaptive radiation possible. The founder population that inhabited the

FIG. 21–20   The woodpecker finch, *Camarhynchus pallidus*, uses a cactus spine to pry insects from cracks in trees.  This is one of the few recorded instances of the use of tools by animals other than man or apes.  (From David Lack, ''Darwin's Finches.''  Reprinted with permission.  Copyright © 1953 by Scientific American, Inc.  All rights reserved.)

Galapagos, however, had little competition from other birds.  As a result, its members could reproduce rapidly and spread out to occupy innumerable niches.  Adaptive radiation is, then, partly dependent on the availability of a number of niches into which organisms can move.

The concept of natural selection implies that all surviving variations will in some way be more adaptive than those that do not survive.  The mechanism for evolution by natural selection is the development of adaptations.  Extinction, not evolution, is the result when organisms are unable to adapt to changing conditions of the environment.

**21-11**
**ADAPTATION AND**
**SURVIVAL**

However, some organisms adapt so well to a specific niche that when conditions change they are hopelessly unfit for a new environment. It has been hypothesized that some of the large dinosaurs of about 230 million years ago were too specialized. They lived in swampy regions, depending on water to buoy up their massive bodies. When climatic conditions changed and the region dried out, these organisms were unable to move into new territories. Nor could they survive long enough for chance variations to allow them to exploit some aspect of the changed environment. As a result, they became extinct. This hypothesis is based on the fact that one of the important features of a species is its ability to adapt to changes in the environment. If an organism cannot adapt, its evolutionary future is likely to be very dim. In evolution there is a distinct balance between specialization to one niche, and flexibility to move into a new niche if necessary. Organisms can be viewed as evolving between two opposing forces: specialization and adaptability (Fig. 21–21). Natural selection ultimately weeds out those who go too far to either side. The fact that in the history of life so many species have become extinct emphasizes how difficult it is for organisms to maintain a balance between these two pressures.

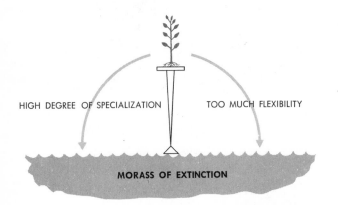

HIGH DEGREE OF SPECIALIZATION      TOO MUCH FLEXIBILITY

**MORASS OF EXTINCTION**

FIG. 21–21  Organisms evolve between two opposing tendencies. On the one hand is the advantage a species gains by specializing to a very high degree. This can lead to lack of flexibility and hence, if conditions change, to extinction. On the other hand is the advantage gained by being able to adapt to a changing environment. An organism that never specializes, however, may be unable to compete with its more specialized contemporaries under given conditions, and thus may likewise pass into extinction.

Writers who forget the importance of adaptability in the survival of new variations frequently speak of evolution as proceeding in a given direction, or for a particular purpose. The ideas of purpose and direction have long been associated with the concept of evolution. It was Darwin's work, more than that of anyone else, which showed that chance, not purpose or direction, is the basis of the origin of species. There is no evidence that evolution has any preconceived purpose, or that organisms evolve in a predetermined direction toward some absolute, ideal form. They simply undergo random variations which make them more or less adapted to given environments. Evolution along a given line, from ancestral form to the present, takes place because the environment itself does not remain absolutely constant. The types of variations that survive are those which best adapt the organism to its environment.

This chapter has provided an introduction to evolutionary theory.  We have emphasized particularly the population aspect of evolution, since genetic changes in a population over several generations provide the most accurate means of assessing the extent to which evolution is occurring.  Evolution can be studied on the population level only with living organisms.  The fossil record provides too few data to allow such treatment; it merely allows paleontologists to reconstruct the evolutionary history of animal and plant groups.  The population approach makes it possible to ask such questions as: What is the rate of evolution in a given species?  What factors influence the course or rate of evolution?  What conditions are necessary for evolution to begin or cease?

Modern evolutionary theory is strongly based on a quantitative approach.  Population genetics is especially helpful here, since it provides a way of treating evolutionary developments in a quantitative way.  The application of genetic principles and of mathematics to evolutionary theory has been of great importance in verifying and extending Darwin's original conclusions.

**21-12
CONCLUSION**

**EXERCISES**

1.  Distinguish between the ideas of evolution and natural selection.

2.  What is the value of comparative anatomy to the study of evolution?

3.  In darwinian terms, we say that the "fittest" organisms survive.  How do we determine what is meant by "fit"?

4.  Explain the process of natural selection in terms of the melanic moth.

5.  What is the role of isolation in evolution?  Can a population of organisms of the same species give rise to two separate species if no isolation occurs?  Give reasons for your answer.

6.  Occasionally, individual fruit flies are born with shortened, stubby wings, the so-called "vestigial wing."  The condition is inherited.  These organisms cannot fly, and do not survive in nature.  Design an experimental environment which would selectively favor these flies over winged ones.

7.  One criticism of darwinian natural selection centered on the evolution of such adaptive features as protective coloration.  An American biologist named MacAtee undertook a thorough study of the contents of the stomachs of birds.  He noted whether the insect forms found there were of the variety supposed to be "protected."  His data showed that, indeed, there were large numbers of "protected" insects eaten by birds.  He thus became an outspoken critic of the idea of adaptive coloration.  He claimed that there was no adaptive value in being camouflaged, and that natural selection did not produce adaptively colored individuals.

    a)  Was MacAtee's reasoning valid when applied to the mechanisms of natural selection?  Why or why not?

    b)  What further type of statistical or quantitative information is necessary before you could agree or disagree conclusively with MacAtee's findings?

8.  Another argument against the evolution of protective coloration states that because many animals survive well without it, protective coloration is not essential to survival.  Hence such coloration is not adaptive.  What is the fallacy in this argument?

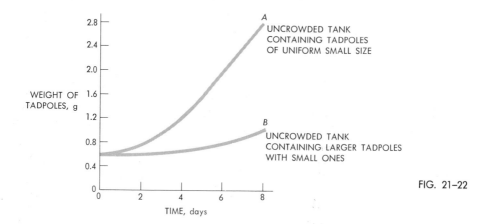

FIG. 21–22

9. Figure 21–22 shows the different rates at which tadpoles grow under different conditions. Curve A shows the growth of an uncrowded population of tadpoles all roughly the same age. Curve B shows the growth of a similar population, but in a tank in which older tadpoles were living. The available food per tadpole was the same in both cases. Scientists attempted to determine how the presence of older tadpoles could check the growth rate of smaller ones. Water from a tank in which older tadpoles had lived was placed in a tank with young tadpoles. The growth of these young tadpoles was inhibited.

a) What hypothesis can you suggest to explain how the presence of larger tadpoles can inhibit the growth of smaller ones?

b) How might this inhibition be of advantage to the survival of a population of frogs in a pond? It is obvious that this is of advantage to the larger tadpoles themselves. But since the inhibitory mechanism has obviously evolved over long periods of time, how is it of advantage to the whole population? (There are several possible ways.)

10. Two individuals heterozygous for a mutant gene become isolated. They leave two progeny. What are the chances that the mutant gene will be absent in the progeny and thus be lost (at least until a fresh mutation occurs) from this tiny subpopulation?

11. Explain why the application of population genetics to evolution by natural selection has been so useful in understanding the latter concept.

12. The situations described below are examples of specifically inherited genetic traits of populations, retained over many generations, which could hardly be adaptive to the survival of the individuals of the population. Yet the fact that these traits, involving the death or infertility of individuals, have survived in the population indicates that they must have some adaptive value. Offer an hypothesis explaining how this could be.

a) When population crowding in groups of lemmings or locusts becomes intense, definite hormonal and biochemical changes are known to occur which cause mass migrations of hundreds of thousands of individuals from the population either to new territory or, in the case of lemmings, to the sea. In either case, the phenomenon is a result of more than merely forcing out the weaker individuals; it is a definite physiological characteristic that is somehow controlled genetically.

b) Ant, bee, and wasp colonies have many sterile individuals who never reproduce during their entire lifetime.

13. Explain what is meant by the term "genetic drift." What conditions are necessary for genetic drift to have any influence on evolution?

14. Explain how the Galapagos finches seem to have developed from a single common ancestor. Discuss the stages by which this could have occurred. Include in your discussion the role played by the following: (a) adaptive radiation, (b) competition, (c) isolation (of various sorts), (d) available ecological niches.

15. To what extent has man solved the problem of specialization versus flexibility? Has his particular solution posed any additional problems?

## I. On the History of Evolutionary Theory

The history of evolutionary theory is extremely interesting, and provides many insights into just how scientific theories grow. For those interested in this topic, the following are all highly recommended.

DE BEER, GAVIN, *Charles Darwin* (New York: Thos. Nelson & Sons Ltd., 1964). Despite the great amount of attention Darwin and the idea of natural selection have been given, this is the only really modern biography of Darwin which treats his life and works as an integrated whole. The book is exceedingly well written and assumes no previous background in biology.

DARLINGTON, C. D., "The Origins of Darwinism." *Scientific American*, May 1959, p. 60. A good account of the minor evolutionists, those who suggested a concept similar to natural selection, before Darwin wrote *The Origin of Species*.

EISELEY, LOREN C., *Darwin's Century* (New York: Anchor Books, 1961). Especially pertinent are Chapters III, IV, V, VI, and VII. An excellent, readable book which covers the historical tradition before Darwin as well as concentrating on the period immediately surrounding Darwin's work. Good for interested students who wish to pursue the topic of climate of opinion in nineteenth-century biology.

NELSON, B. C., *After Its Kind* (Minneapolis: Augsbury Publishing House, 1952). This book is subtitled "The First and Last Word on Evolution." It presents the case for fundamentalism and claims to refute the theory of evolution by natural selection. While somewhat out of date in the light of isotope dating techniques which have been developed more recently, the book presents an interesting insight into the reasoning behind fundamentalism. Strongly recommended.

VORZIMMER, P., "Charles Darwin and Blending Inheritance." *Isis* 54 (1963), p. 371. An interesting article which deals with Darwin's attempts to formulate a satisfactory genetic theory to accompany his concept of natural selection.

## II. On Aspects of the Modern Theory of Evolution

ALLISON, A. C., "Sickle Cells and Evolution." *Scientific American*, August 1956, p. 87. This contains a good description of the inheritance pattern in sickle-cell anemia, and the evolutionary significance of this gene in various populations.

DOBZHANSKY, T., *Evolution, Genetics and Man* (New York: Wiley and Sons, 1955). An elementary text which covers the entire field of evolutionary theory. This is good as a reference source.

DOBZHANSKY, T., "The Present Evolution of Man." *Scientific American*, September 1960, p. 206. The author tries to show that man still evolves by selection, but that he does so in an environment which he himself has tailor-made to suit his needs.

DOWDESWELL, W. H., *The Mechanism of Evolution* (New York: Harper Torchbooks, 1960). A detailed study, but contains much specific evidence and data. Valuable primarily for data and directions for individual reports or projects.

EISELEY, LOREN C., *The Immense Journey* (New York: Random House, 1957). This is a very well-written book which deals with the evolution of life from the beginning to man. It is a very fine, highly literary treatment. Recommended for all students.

KETTLEWELL, H. B. D., "Darwin's Missing Evidence." *Scientific American*, March 1959, p. 48. This article is an analysis of the research on the melanic moth, its genetics, natural history, and evolution. Well written and illustrated, this discussion will fill in some additional details and insights to the evolution of a population.

LACK, D., "Darwin's Finches." *Scientific American*, April 1953, p. 66. This is a brief but well-written article discussing the major evolutionary adaptations of the Galapagos finches.

SIMPSON, G. G., *The Meaning of Evolution* (New Haven: Yale University Press, 1960). This book contains some very important chapters discussing topics not covered in the present text: rates of evolution, the fossil record, opportunism.

SHEPPARD, P. M., *Natural Selection and Heredity* (New York: Harper Torchbooks, 1960). This small but really excellent book covers a number of topics relating genetics, and especially population genetics, to natural selection. It is probably one of the best single treatments of evolution on a modern scale outside of the more technical writings of Fisher and Sewell Wright.

SOUTHERN, H. N., "A Study in the Evolution of Birds." *Scientific American*, May 1957, p.125. A case study in the evolution and adaptation of the guillemot, comparable with the study of Darwin's finches.

STEWARD, JULIAN, "Cultural Evolution." *Scientific American*, May 1956, p. 69. This article discusses the modern view of how culture (the use of tools, communication, art, etc.) evolved. This is a very important topic. A well-written and interesting article.

TINBERGEN, NIKO, "Defense by Color." *Scientific American*, October 1957, p. 49. An investigation of the question whether protective coloration really aids an animal in escaping from its predators.

*We often think that when we have completed our study of one we know all about two,*
*because "two" is "one and one." We forget that we still have to make a study of "and."*

Eddington

22-1
INTRODUCTION

As the reader has no doubt noticed, much of this book has been concerned with
the study of living systems on the molecular level. There are several reasons for
this, not all of which are attributable to prejudice on the part of the authors.
For one, since this book is attempting to present an accurate picture of modern
biology, it must necessarily be heavily molecular. Few biologists would deny
that the major breakthroughs of their discipline over the past three or four
decades have been primarily at the molecular level.

Yet, quite recently, the emphasis has changed dramatically. Perhaps
because of man's abuse of his environment, the focus of attack in biology has
shifted to the higher levels of biological investigation. Graduate schools are
being swamped with applicants interested in environmental biology (influenced,
perhaps, by the interest of granting agencies in funding research in this area).
Indeed, a few molecular biologists have switched to such fields as neurophysiology
and even ecology in search of new and challenging problems. In brief, the
biology of the 1970's is not the biology of the 1960's; the emphasis has shifted
to the higher levels of investigation.

What is meant by the phrase "levels of investigation"? Simply the degree of
resolution (in the microscopist sense of the word) with which the biologist studies
living matter. As has been seen, the molecular biologist attempts to study

living systems by examining the atomic and molecular interactions which go on within the systems. The cytologist operates at the cellular level of investigation; the histologist at the tissue level of investigation; the anatomist at the organ and organ-system level of investigation. It is evident, of course, that *no* biologist at *any* level of investigation can afford to remain ignorant of other levels; a cytologist, for example, who knew nothing of the very important molecular interactions occurring within the mitochondria of cells, or of the relationship of the cells he was studying to the entire organism, would be a totally obsolete one.

As was seen in Chapter 13, the movement of an appendage can be explained in terms of the contraction of certain key muscles; the contraction of these muscles, in turn, is brought about by the contraction of striated tissue of the muscle. These tissues contract because the muscle cells of which they are composed contract; the muscle cells contract because their myofibrils contract. The contraction of the myofibrils is explainable in terms of a hypothesis proposing that actin and myosin filaments slide over each other to cause contraction. What causes this sliding? Investigations are still proceeding to attempt explanations on the molecular, atomic, and subatomic levels of investigation. This tendency to move to progressively lower levels of investigation for meaningful explanations is called **reductionism.**

Yet, perhaps intuitively, even given 100% success in investigating muscle contraction at the most microscopic level, we still feel there is something more. We know, for example, that the muscle did not just contract on its own in moving the appendage; a nerve impulse triggered the action. What triggered the nerve impulse? The brain, most likely. But what triggered the brain? Probably it was an outside stimulus perceived by the organism—a noise perhaps, or the sighting of a predator. In other words, the entire system of levels of investigation has now been wrapped up into one package: **animal behavior.** *

The animal behaviorist recognizes that complete explanations are not yet available for behavioral actions at the lower levels of investigation, and perhaps will never be. But he also recognizes that there is still pertinent information that can be gathered. For example, observing a particular behavioral act such as the building of a nest by a bird, he can wonder about the selective value of building the nest always in such and such a shape, the way in which the nest-building behavior evolved, or the physiological reasons underlying the behavior. Only the last, note, is reductionist in its approach.

It is perhaps all too human a trait for many biologists to see the greatest value in that biological research which is going on at their own particular level of investigation. Thus, for example, a physiologist may place a low value on a behavioral study not reducible to physiological terms. But the same physiologist is guilty of overlooking the fact that his own research often lacks reducibility at

---

* As will be seen shortly, plants, lacking nervous systems, are not organisms which exhibit what one would generally call "behavior."

the moment to physical chemistry or quantum physics. The point—and it is a crucial one—is that *the establishing of cause-and-effect relations in biology at one level of investigation is just as scientific, interesting, and important as establishing them at another.*

The most useful scientific hypotheses are those which explain something. Indeed, some scientists refuse to apply the term hypothesis to anything which does not offer an explanation for a natural phenomenon. While this book has found it useful to apply the term hypothesis to any statement from which predictions can be drawn deductively, there is little doubt that hypotheses which attempt to explain phenomena are the most useful. Indeed, the Watson-Crick hypothesis concerning the molecular structure of DNA is *doubly* useful because if offers an explanation for both gene function and replication.

But the ability of scientific hypotheses to *predict* has also been stressed and, as must now be quite clear to the reader, it is through predictions that we test hypotheses. Here is where reductionism presents real problems. For, while moving to lower and lower levels of investigation may help to account for the muscle contraction phenomenon, *even complete explanations at one level do not provide accurate predictions at another.* As Dr. John R. Platt of the University of Michigan Mental Health Research Institute points out, there is a vast difference between explaining in detail the precise path an automobile takes in going from New York to Chicago in terms of the physics of the wheels, the bumps in the road, the guidance system, etc., and being able to *predict* the former in terms of the latter. Similarly, an exhaustive study of the physics and chemistry of a neon sign will still miss the fact that it spells "Joe's Diner" in the English language.

Platt goes on to point out that moving from one level of investigation to another involves vast changes in a scale of size. Using a hydrogen atom as a basic unit of size, investigations on the molecular level involve dimensions of roughly $10^3$ to $10^6$ hydrogen atoms; on the cellular level, $10^{15}$ atoms; on the level of the whole organism, $10^{29}$ atoms; and on the population or society level, $10^{38}$ atoms. As in the case of organized systems, moving from small sizes to big ones involves an *addition of information.* Platt maintains that hierarchical organizations develop systems properties that go far beyond the properties of the subsystems. A traffic jam cannot be predicted from the physics and chemistry of the breakdown of gasoline molecules in the cylinders of the automobiles involved; we must know such conditions as weather, traffic density, and the time of the commuter rush hour. These factors comprise the "additional information" to which Platt refers.

Animal behavior is a prime example of an "additional information" field of biological investigation. In this sense, the animal behaviorist deals with living matter at the most complex and difficult level of investigation. Some of the reasons for these difficulties will be discussed shortly. But certainly one reason is that an animal behaviorist must at least be conversant, and often thoroughly so, with the subject matter of the levels of investigation both below and above his own; he must be as knowledgeable in molecular physiology as in population biology; as familiar with the neural pathways followed by a nerve impulse as with the physical nature of the stimulus that triggered it. As Professor David Newth of the University of Glasgow puts it, "A newcomer to animal behavior might not choose to start studying hydrogen bonds, but no one could be very surprised if he found himself in their [i.e., hydrogen bonds'] company before long."

In a sense, the study of animal behavior began when primitive man first noted the behavior of the animals surrounding him. As a distinct field of study, however, it is much younger than that. While its precise beginnings are difficult (if not impossible) to pinpoint, it was almost certainly around the time of the publication of Charles Darwin's *Origin of Species* (1859). The growth of evolutionary theory and the study of behavior went hand in hand. Indeed, many if not most of the early studies of behavior were motivated by the belief that behavioral studies would provide clues to phyletic relationships. Current thought regarding the precise relationship and significance of behavior to evolution will be discussed later in more detail.

Early in this century, the field of animal behavior became divided into two prominent schools of thought. One such school of thought was given great impetus around 1924 with the publication of J. B. Watson's book, *Behaviorism*. The leading figures in this group, termed "behaviorists," were mostly American experimental psychologists. The second school of thought, mostly European, began around 1909 with the work of Jacob von Uexküll and O. Heinroth. Later, in the 1930's, important refinements and additions were made by Austria's Konrad Lorenz and Holland's Niko Tinbergen. Many scientists, mostly zoologists, became associated with this school of thought, and termed themselves "ethologists." **Ethology** may be defined simply as the scientific study of behavior.

It is important to recognize the existence of both the "behaviorist" and the "ethologist" schools of thought, for the conclusions they drew from their respective experimental work were often widely divergent and even contradictory. The behaviorists were trained in psychology and were interested primarily (if, indeed, not exclusively) in learning. Furthermore, this work was almost entirely done in the laboratory. The maze to be learned, the positive reward of food or negative one of electric shock, the "Skinner box" in which an animal learns to press a lever or peck a button for food or drink—these were the classic tools of the behaviorists. For behaviorism, ultimate success was seen in terms of accurately describing an organism's behavior patterns after training; in turn, these descriptions would enable the experimenter to increase learning efficiency and the degree of predictability. Naturally, the behaviorists preferred organisms which lent themselves well to such experimental studies, and thus the white rat became the behaviorist's *Drosophila*.

In sharp contrast, the ethologist, trained for the most part in biology rather than psychology, approached and interpreted things quite differently. Instead of working with just a few species, highly inbred for laboratory study, the ethologist studies large numbers of species under both laboratory *and* natural environmental conditions. The differences between a wild rat's behavior and that of the behaviorist's white rats are considerable but hardly surprising. The former is genetically heterogeneous and exposed constantly to highly nonuniform sequences of environmental stimuli, while the latter are genetically homogeneous and exposed to as uniformly controlled sequences of stimuli as the human experimenter can devise. With such very different approaches to such widely differing subjects, disparate conclusions were inevitable.

Not long after World War II, clashes between behaviorists and ethologists began. The behaviorists accused ethologists of ignoring the role of learning in behavioral experiments, of underestimating the role of environmental factors in influencing behavior, and of treating the word "instinctive" as both a description and an adequate *explanation* of behavior—and thus using the label too widely and too often. The ethologists returned the fire. The behaviorists were accused of unjustified extrapolation to other mammalian species from the highly untypical white rat. They were also accused of ignoring the role of instinctive or genetic factors in influencing an organism's behavior, and of thereby assuming that the environment alone provided the significant factors in this influence.

Which side was correct in its accusations? Both. The ethologists, who often tended to study mostly nonmammalian species (e.g., birds, reptiles, fishes, and insects) were thus concentrating mainly on groups whose actions *did* appear largely or entirely instinctive rather than learned. Conversely, the behaviorists *were* generally too occupied with their mazes to look at organisms in the wild (such as insects or spiders), whose behavior patterns understandably bore no resemblance to a rat which could no longer even survive outside the laboratory.

In the following years, ethologists became far more careful how they used the term "instinct." In turn, behaviorists turned open eyes and ears to other species studied under different situations. The conflict was thus a productive one. Furthermore, as will be seen in this chapter and the next, it has had some rather interesting results.

**22–3 ANTHROPOMORPHISM AND THE RAZOR'S EDGE**

Virtually everyone at one time or another has seen the cartoons of Walt Disney; the characters of Mickey Mouse, Donald Duck, and Goofy are quite familiar to most. These animal characters exhibit the full range of human emotions, experiencing anger, fear, affection, and so forth. This assigning of human characteristics to nonhuman characters (an old and deep tradition in Western literature) is called **anthropomorphism.** Since the world of Donald Duck is so plainly a fantasy, of appeal primarily to children, most educators (but by no means all) see little harm and much that is delightful in this aspect of the Disney world. After all, it is reasoned, few persons really grow up believing that ducks throw tantrums or care for mischievous nephews.

A more borderline case, perhaps, is the Walt Disney movie *Bambi*. Here, the deer family and all the forest animals are, like Donald Duck, assigned a full range of human emotions.  But in this case the situation is somewhat different; Bambi, the deer, does not live in a home with a mailbox and drive a car, but in the natural deer setting of field and forest.  Now the concept that deer, rabbits, skunks, etc., really *do* experience humanlike emotions becomes far less fantasy and far more realistic and believable.  The strong grasp that this sort of thinking can attain over the popular mind can be appreciated when one recalls the intense loyalty shown to Smoky the Bear—or to the Esso tiger when advertising men felt that the latter had served its usefulness in promoting the product and attempted to remove it from the market.  The "Save the Tiger" campaign that followed proved as successful a promotion gimmick as the original creation of the tiger itself.

In the past few years, Disney productions have started producing films utilizing real-life photography of animals in their natural environment.  It is difficult to find fault with most of the beautiful photography of films such as *Nature's Half Acre* or *The Living Desert*.  But the Donald Duck sort of anthropomorphism remains.  Thus the chase of prey by predators is depicted in a manner implying a sequence of reasoned activities on the part of both organisms, and the feeding of her young by a bird is interpreted in terms of "mother love."

No animal behaviorist today accepts such anthropomorphic explanations. Concerning the case of the bird and its "mother love," it has been shown that the same mother bird which supposedly exhibits "love" when feeding her young will kill them if they are experimentally caused to give an incorrect sequence of behavioral responses upon her arrival at the nest.  Furthermore, the concept of love is an undefined entity even in human beings, not to mention lower animals, and thus its use complicates rather than simplifies attempts to understand the feeding behavior of birds in the nest.

**"Ockham's razor"** (named after William of Ockham, who lived in the fourteenth century) is a philosophical rule which states that, given a choice of several hypotheses proposed to explain a phenomenon, one should choose the simplest one first.  Not only is the simplest hypothesis easiest to test, it is also, according to the Ockhamites, the one most likely to be correct.  While there may be some doubt about this latter assertion, Ockham's razor is so named because it cuts off the nonessential parts of hypotheses, leaving only those portions truly necessary for the explanation.  If the test of the simplest hypothesis shows it to be invalid, the next ones can be tested progressively, from simplest to most complex, until the most satisfactory one is identified.  The essential principles of Ockham's razor are widely followed in the experimental sciences, and biology is no exception.

The application of Ockham's razor to the study of animal behavior was proposed by Britisher C. Lloyd Morgan (1852–1936).  Morgan, rebelling against the anthropomorphism of his period, insisted that an animal's behavior patterns should be interpreted in terms of the simplest mechanisms which can both explain the actions and permit accurate predictions of the behavior patterns under given conditions in the future.  "Morgan's Canon" was concerned with eliminating inherently unmeasurable intervening variables (such as the concept of "consciousness") which added complexity to the behavioral phenomenon under investigation without adding precision.  The application of Ockham's razor has undoubtedly been successful in ethology, as will be seen later in this chapter. Still, anthropomorphic phrases and their frequent companions, **teleological explanations,** which ascribe purpose or goal-seeking to natural processes, are difficult for even a scientist to avoid.  Thus the authors of this book may slip and write something such as "the cell takes in glucose from its environment *in order to* increase its energy supply," thus implying thought processes and purposive action on the part of the cell.  Even ethologists coin anthropomorphic phrases such as "sham rage" to describe a characteristic behavior pattern, or use an expression such as "friendly cats turned savage after lesion of the septal area of the brain."  Certainly it is far more ego-satisfying to interpret Fido's attachment to his master in terms of intense loyalty and devotion rather than a series of unplanned reaction patterns triggered by impulses flowing along nerve pathways established early in puppyhood.  But it is the latter approach rather than the former which, scientifically speaking, is by far the more productive.

The reader is already familiar with tropisms, discussed previously in the context of plant responses to such environmental stimuli as chemicals, gravity, and light.  In the case of light, it will be recalled that plants respond to unequal stimulation on stems and leaves by turning toward the light source.  In turn, this movement is caused by auxin-controlled physico-chemical changes within the plant.

Clearly, the concept of tropistic responses nicely meets the requirements of both Ockham's razor and Morgan's Canon; the plants' movements are both explained and made predictable.  Furthermore, anthropomorphic interpretations are avoided.  This may, of course, be the result of the fact that plants do not have nervous systems; few persons worry about inflicting misery and pain when they mow a lawn.  But, on the whole, the tropism concept seems a promising one to apply to the responses of animals to their environment.

A scientist most prominent in the transferal of the tropism concept from plant to animal behavior was Jacques Loeb (1859–1924).  Loeb recognized, of course, that animal behavior was far more complex than anything seen in plants, but he felt that this greater complexity might still be interpreted on the basis of balancing interactions occurring between several tropistic responses.

Pill bugs, like green plants, orient themselves toward light.  A hypothesis proposing that the pill bug's reaction to light is a tropistic one would predict a quantitative relationship between the intensity of light and the direction in which the animal proceeds in moving toward the light; the animal should orient itself so that an equal intensity of light falls on both its sides.  For example:

*Hypothesis:*  *If . . .*  a pill bug's positive response to light is tropistic in nature, . . .

*Prediction I:*  *then . . .* a pill bug in darkness suddenly exposed to a light at one side of the animal will turn and move toward the light.

**Prediction II:** *then* . . . a pill bug exposed to light from directly above will move in random circles directly below the light source.

Both predictions are verified; the tropistic hypothesis is supported.

If a hypothesis is a good one, it must yield accurate predictions with other organisms giving other responses. The planarian *Dugesia tigrina*, by the tropistic hypothesis, would be termed negatively phototropic; i.e., it avoids light. Thus its movement pattern would be predicted to follow a path leading most efficiently toward a point where the least amount of light falls upon the light-sensitive portions of the animal's body. Again the predictions are experimentally verified.

In complex forms of life, the tropistic hypothesis can be applied to the interesting behavioral patterns exhibited by prey and predator, for example, fox and cottontail rabbit. Here it might be predicted that the rabbit will react negatively to the presence of the fox and move so as to avoid it. The fox, in turn, reacts positively upon sensing the rabbit, and moves directly to encounter it. But the predictions are not verified. In an elusive maneuver the rabbit frequently backtracks on its trail, thus temporarily moving *toward* the fox rather than away from it. Similarly the fox may stop following the rabbit's scent trail and simply lie down beside the trail to wait for it to return. Clearly any attempt to explain such behavioral interactions on the basis of even several tropistic responses will result in a hypothesis more complex than the phenomenon it purports to explain.*

With Ockham's razor and Morgan's Canon in mind, another type of explanation can be considered. In the early twentieth century, the Russian physiologist Ivan P. Pavlov (1849–1936) performed a now classic experiment which suggested another approach. Pavlov rang a bell every time he fed some dogs. The dogs soon learned to associate the sound of the bell with food. After a sufficient number of times, Pavlov showed that the dogs would secrete saliva in response to the bell alone; the sight, taste, or smell of food was no longer necessary. Such dogs were said to be "conditioned." Pavlov's work attracted much interest. Many variations of conditioning experiments were attempted and, for the most part, were successful. Furthermore, the fact that training programs based on the principles of conditioning enabled animals to learn quite complicated behavioral routines suggested that the phenomenon might also account for the complex patterns of behavior found in nature, a feat the tropistic-response hypothesis had not accomplished. Indeed, Pavlovian conditioning became virtually a third school of thought in the study of animal behavior.

But conditioning, though interesting, still provided no satisfactory explanation for many types of observed behavior. The young orb-web spinning spider

---

* The concept of tropistic movements is now generally limited to the plant kingdom, where movement is normally due to hormone-influenced differential growth patterns rather than to sensory and motor nerve impulses. The term **taxes** (sing., **taxis**) is used instead to designate the type of continuously reoriented movements the pill bug, planaria, and a few other animals employ.

FIG. 22–1   At left is shown the web of a nine-month-old female cross spider, *Araneus diadematus* Cl. (body mass 115.5 mg), raised in the laboratory and allowed to build a web every day.   Its litter-mate was prevented from building any webs by being isolated in a glass tube.   Upon release (body mass 77.8 mg), the experimental animal built the web at right.   Note that only the size, not the pattern, is the distinguishing feature.   By the time this animal had spun a fourth web, the product of its spinning was the same as that of the control's.   Further investigation revealed that the silk glands of isolated spiders slow to a low level of productivity as a result of lack of use, and that it is this factor that seems to account for the smaller web size.   When the glands regain their normal rate of silk synthesis, the web becomes the normal size.   (Photos courtesy Peter N. Witt, North Carolina Department of Mental Health, Raleigh, N.C.)

*Araneus diadematus* Cl., for example, spins a perfect web, characteristic specifically of the species, on her first try—despite the fact that she has never seen her mother perform this remarkably intricate procedure.   Even the most die-hard behaviorists, Pavlovian and otherwise, would have great difficulty explaining this phenomenon in terms of their respective lines of thought.   The fact that *A. diadematus* Cl. raised to maturity in glass tubes so small that movement is entirely restricted soon spin perfect webs when released but still kept isolated (see Fig. 22–1) appeared to make it worthless to even make the attempt.   As will be seen, however, appearances can sometimes be deceiving.

A

B

C

CAFFEINE                PHENOBARBITOL              LSD 25                 MESCALINE

FIG. 22–2   Spider web-spinning behavior is so characteristically precise that it provides a means to study the effects of drugs on behavior.   At top are shown three webs of an adult female *Araneus diadematus* Cl. (body mass 157.9 mg) built on different days.   Web A, the control, was built in approximately 20 minutes in the early morning.   At 4 P.M., the spider was given 0.1 ml of sugar water containing 1 mg of dextro-amphetamine, also known as "speed."   Web B was built approximately 12 hours later by the drugged animal; note that the web consists of only some remnants of a hub, a few irregular and frequently interrupted radii, and some erratic strands of sticky spiral.   Web C was built 24 hours later, and shows some signs of recovery.   However, several more days were required to restore the web to normal.   Since, as the other photos indicate, each drug produces a characteristic change in spider motor behavior (and thus in web design), the web pattern becomes a bioassay for drug identification.   (Photos courtesy Peter N. Witt, North Carolina Department of Mental Health, Raleigh, N.C.)

The web-spinning feat of *A. diadematus* Cl. is performed every morning by the female, who devours the old web before she spins a new one. The orb web is characteristic of several species of spiders. It is an economical one to produce; the spider covers the greatest area with as little material as possible. All other things being equal, the larger the area of the web, the greater the probability of capturing flying prey.

The web-spinning behavior of *A. diadematus* Cl. provides an excellent subject for behavioral study. For one thing, the path taken by the spider in spinning the web is faithfully recorded in its strands. The webs can later be removed and prepared for photographing by spraying with glossy white paint, spread over a dark box, and illuminated from the side. Projection of the resulting films allows precise measurements of the web's proportions. The size, number, and regularity of the web parts reveal a great deal about the motor behavior of the spider that spins the web (see Fig. 22–2).

One such revelation is the fact that web construction occurs in distinct phases. Each is executed in a different pattern of movements. The radii and frame threads are spun first, in a way that is distinctively different from the way the spirals are built. When the radii-building phase has been completed, the spider then goes into the next phase, working on the interconnections between the radii which form the spirals. This, too, is performed in a precise sequence of individual steps.

While the glass-tube isolation experiments *seem* to rule out the role of any learning or experience in web construction, the intricacies of the process certainly make it tempting to believe that there is surely some sort of reasoning involved. Teleological explanations are also tempting; the spider spins the web *in order to* trap insects most efficiently. Yet this hypothesis predicts that, if some of the web strands are destroyed, the animal will stop to repair the damage before proceeding any further with construction. This prediction is not verified. The spider does not stop to repair the damage, even if it is of such an extent as to make the web completely useless for the capture of prey.

Faced with observations of this sort, the early ethologists turned to the concept of **instinct** for an explanation. Instinctive behavior was seen as behavior coordinated in the central nervous system and not generally determined in form by external stimuli (although it might be elicited by such stimuli). *Differences* in the various kinds of central nervous systems (and thus the instinctive behavior coordinated therein) are, of course, genetically determined. To the early ethologist, therefore, instinctive behavior was "inherited" behavior, i.e., genetically programmed into the organism, and was thus the opposite of learned behavior. The instinct-versus-learning or "nature-versus-nurture" controversy was off and running.

Working first with the "instinctive behavior" hypothesis, it is possible to proceed further with an analysis of spider web-building behavior. As Figs. 22–3 and 22–4 show, the size and construction pattern of the web change as the spider

A                                    B                                    C

FIG. 22–3   Webs built by the same spider at three different ages.  Compare these with the information given in the graph in Fig. 22–4.  The age of the spider that spun web A was a few days; web B,
four weeks; web C, five months.  (Photos courtesy Peter N. Witt, North Carolina Department of Mental
Health, Raleigh, N.C.)

matures.  Now a return to a hypothesis involving some learning or conditioning
is tempting—e.g., the spider changes its web style as it "learns," with practice,
to "perfect" the web.  But this hypothesis is immediately contradicted; the first
web spun by a glass-tube-raised spider is that of a mature spider, rather than
that of a young one.

Some quantitative measurements can be made on the spider's web.  For
example, Dr. Peter N. Witt of the North Carolina Department of Mental Health
in Raleigh has measured the amount of protein material going into each web.
First, the diameter, number of radii, and spiral turns are counted.  From these
data, the thread length can be calculated.  With the aid of a spectrophotometer,
the precise amount of nitrogen each web contains can be calculated.  The quantity
of nitrogen, in turn, gives a direct measure of the amount of protein.  If it is
assumed that all the thread in one web is of uniform thickness, the quotient of
nitrogen content and thread length provides a measure of thread thickness for
any one web.  Thread thickness, in turn, gives a measure of the amount of
material per unit length.

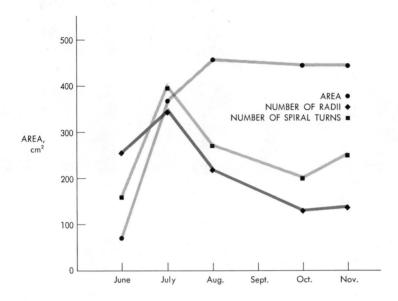

FIG. 22–4    This graph shows the changes which occur in web design as the spider grows.  Note that after an early increase the web area remains fairly constant.  In contrast, the number of radii and spiral turns declines.

   The results of these studies show that after a certain time in the spider's life, the amount of web material used (as measured by nitrogen-content analysis) remains the same.  So, too, does web area.  However, *later webs are built with shorter and thicker thread*.  The end result is webs with wider meshes.

   Why does the spider build later webs with stronger thread?  This intriguing question can be posed in two ways.  One way is *functional*, and requires demonstration of a reduced reproductive rate or increased mortality as a result of failure to build a stronger web.  But the question can also be posed as a *dynamic* one; we ask, instead, what are the immediate causes and mechanisms which promote the spinning of thicker web thread.  If this second alternative is taken, Ockham's razor can be wielded here; the simplest and most obvious fact is that the spider is growing, and thus increasing its body mass.  Therefore a stronger web, with shorter and thicker strands, is required to support the spider's greater mass.

   First, the "fact" of a relationship between body mass and web thickness must be established.  This can be accomplished as follows.

| MASS OF SPIDER | 42.4 mg | PLUS 22% | 51.6 mg |
|---|---|---|---|
| NUMBER OF RADII | 42 | | 35 |
| NUMBER OF SPIRAL TURNS | 42 | | 30 |

A                                B

FIG. 22–5    The mass of this spider has been increased approximately 22% by the addition of a lead weight (arrow). The results on web patterns are shown at right. Protein values per unit length for the experimental web B are nearly doubled. When the weight is removed, protein content returns to the level shown by the control web, A. (Photos courtesy Peter N. Witt, North Carolina Department of Mental Health, Raleigh, N.C.)

**Hypothesis: If . . .**    the mass increase of a spider causes thread thickness and mesh width changes, . . .

**Prediction:**    *then . . .* increasing an adult spider's mass with lead weights might result in even thicker thread and a web with even wider meshes.

As Fig. 22–5 illustrates, the prediction is verified, the hypothesis supported. But this hypothesis merely establishes a fact; an explanatory hypothesis based on the facts is still needed to suggest how the web-building behavior pattern may be governed.

To hypothesize that the spider "knows" it must increase thread thickness or risk breaking the web and falling is clearly both anthropomorphic and teleological; the animal is credited both with reasoning ability and with anticipation of possible future events. But such an hypothesis is unnecessary. Instead, an hypothesis proposing a sort of computerlike circuitry in the spider's glandular and nervous system can be proposed. There must be some signal which communicates to the central nervous system the amount of silk which is ready in the gland for thread production. Body mass then operates to determine thread thickness. Thus the combination of the amount of silk available and body mass indirectly determines the length of the thread the spider can spin. In turn, the length of thread used to spin the web influences web size. From all these data, the mesh width of the future web can be established in advance and programmed into the system. By doing the radii first and determining the angle between them, the spider automatically predetermines the web pattern. In the end, it will have covered the largest possible area with a web still strong enough to support its own body.

Note here the close interrelationship between biochemical processes (i.e., web material manufacture in the spider's silk glands) and motor behavior (i.e., the web-building process). The speed of protein synthesis determines the filling of the silk glands. This, in turn, regulates the motor behavior of the spider in building the web pattern. Note also the elimination of both anthropomorphic and teleological characteristics from the explanation; clearly neither are needed. Finally, note that Ockham's razor has seemingly been ignored; the hypothesis is a complicated one, with many underlying assumptions which must be tested. But if the hypothesis is complex, the behavior it attempts to explain is still more so.

It may now be quite evident to the reader that to label a behavior as "instinctive" explains no more about the phenomenon than to refer to it as "learned." For a time, there was a tendency among ethologists to label any behavior pattern in which the role of learning could not be readily demonstrated as "instinctive." Unfortunately, the term "instinctive" had in the past been applied to so many different conceptualizations of behavior (e.g., "I stepped on the brakes instinctively") that ethologists found great difficulty in freeing their own concept of the term from unwanted connotations. Partly in an attempt to give the ethological concept of instinctive behavior its own uniqueness, therefore, the term **innate behavior** was coined. Merely changing a name does not accomplish much by itself, of course. But it may often help to catalyze new thinking about a subject, or it may cause one to look at it in a new perspective.*

Consider, for example, the behavior of the female digger wasp, *Ammophila*. She must mate with a male, dig a nest hole, construct cells within it to hold the future developing pupae, hunt and paralyze with her string such prey as caterpillars and spiders, put the prey into the nest (where their state of suspended animation ensures that the young larvae will have fresh meat on which to feed before pupation), lay her eggs, and seal up the hole—all within a few weeks of summer. Since her parents died long before she was born, and there is no time to "practice," it would *appear* to be self-evident that her behavior could not be learned or be the result of conditioning. Nor is it at all helpful to say it is "instinct."

In 1935, Konrad Lorenz introduced a hypothetical model to account for such highly stereotyped behavior. Lorenz pictured an organism as possessing a

---

* In a somewhat different manner, the trend toward referring to persons as "black" rather than "Negroes" is aimed at providing a different perspective in which many members of the Negro race wish to be viewed. Words which have been around for a long time acquire distinct connotations which may influence a whole point of view. Changing a word *can* help open new ways of thinking.

very specific receiving center in the central nervous system, and applied the term **innate releasing mechanism** (IRM) to this receiving center. The innate releasing mechanism Lorenz envisioned as being triggered by some specific behavioral patterns from the environment; these he termed "releasers." With this hypothetical model, the wasp's behavior is now seen as a sequence of highly coordinated responses (mating, nest building, prey capture, etc.) put forth in response to some releaser. For example, the releaser for the example cited might be the appearance and approach of the male. Possibly this alone may be all that is needed, with the mating act, nest building, prey capture, and so on following in order in much the same way as a row of dominoes standing on end may topple in sequence if the first one is pushed over. A programmed behavioral sequence— the standing row of dominoes—has been set off by the releaser, causing the innate releasing mechanism to allow the push on the first domino.

Note that this sort of thinking allows for a regular scientific sequence of hypothesizing and testing of predictions; for example, the female wasp can be deprived of exposure to the male to see whether the rest of the sequence will follow (it doesn't). Obviously there are many different interpretations that can be placed on this experimental observation, but the point is that at least some progress has been made. Merely labeling *Ammophila*'s behavior as occurring because of "instinct" gets us nowhere at all.

It is interesting to note that the concept of releasers has led to some practical side effects in pest control. The male mosquito, for example, is attracted to the female by the sound frequency she emits in flight. Here, sound is the release mechanism which elicits the male's approach response. The male mosquito will also fly toward an electric trap and be killed if a sound source duplicating the sound frequency emitted by the female is used as "bait." No sight or odor of the female is necessary; once the releasing sound stimulus is produced, the males must topple like the dominoes. The situation is somewhat reminiscent of embryonic induction; several inducing substances (the "releasers") may act to cause the induced tissue to begin following its "innate" developmental capability.

To carry this last analogy a bit further, the reader may recall the discussion of heredity versus environment in the context of limb regeneration capability in amphibians (Section 18–10). Here the genetic ability to regenerate was shown to be greatly influenced by the environmental situation. It will come as no surprise, then, to find that the situation in behavior is quite similar. As stereotyped and "innate" as insect behavior often appears, there are many cases in which the role of learning is well documented. Tinbergen and Kruyt showed that the female digger wasp *Philanthus triangulum* learns to associate visual landmarks with the location of the hole in the ground where she makes her nest. After certain experimental landmarks around the opening (in this case, a ring of pine cones) were moved to another location a foot or so away, the wasp returned to the area encircled by the pine cones rather than to her nest. Only when the pine cones were returned to their original position was the wasp able to locate her home (see Fig. 22–6).

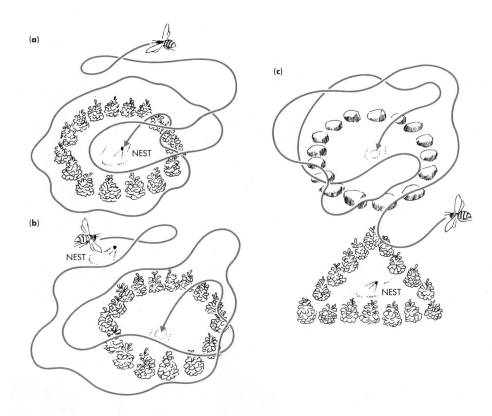

FIG. 22–6    Tinbergen's demonstration that the female digger wasp associates landmarks with nest location.  When the ring of pine cones is moved to position (b) from position (a), the wasp is unable to locate her nest.  That it is the arrangement of the cones rather than the nature of the cones themselves to which the wasp reacts is shown by the substitution of a ring of stones for the cones in (c). (Adapted from N. Tinbergen, *The Study of Instinct*.  Oxford: The Clarendon Press, 1951.)

Clearly it can already be seen that it is risky to label the actions of any species of animal as being *entirely* learned or *entirely* innate, and there is probably some truth to the statement that both psychologists and ethologists are becoming the most cautious persons to be found anywhere!

Take, for example, an experiment performed by Tinbergen and Perdeck on the feeding behavior sequence occurring between herring gulls and their chicks. The parent arrives at the nest, lowers its head, and points its beak downward in front of the chick.  The chick then pecks at the bill, occasionally grasping it and pulling it downward.  After a few occurrences of this pecking and pulling, the parent regurgitates the partially digested food.  The chick then pecks at the food, breaking it apart and eating it (see Fig. 22–7).

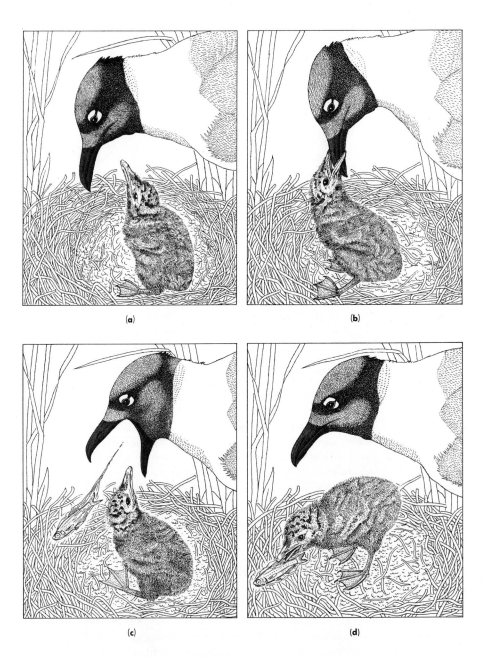

FIG. 22–7    Normal feeding behavior of the three-day-old laughing gull chick.  Components of the behavior include (a) ''begging'' peck at parent's beak when lowered, (b) grasping and stroking of beak, (c) regurgitation of partially digested food, and (d) the feeding peck.  (From Jack P. Hailman, ''How an Instinct is Learned.'' *Scientific American*, December 1969.  Copyright © 1969 by Scientific American, Inc.  All rights reserved.)

Now, it is possible to explain this parent-chick feeding sequence on the basis of releasors and innate releasing mechanisms (such as was done with wasp behavior), in which the behavior of the parent acts as a releaser to bring about the proper response on the part of the chick. This is precisely what Tinbergen and Perdeck did. By building cardboard models, which varied both in color of beak and in the position of a characteristic red patch on the lower jaw, they showed that certain features (such as the shape of the head) were unimportant, whereas the shape of the bill, its motion, and the position and color of the red patch on the lower beak yielded significant differences in the experimenter's ability to elicit the chick's feeding response. All these observations are completely consistent with an hypothesis proposing an interacting series of releasors and innate releasing mechanisms bringing about the proper responses, and it again appears quite unnecessary to suggest the involvement of any learning component in the bird's behavior.

However, as has just been seen, care must be exercised in accepting such an interpretation without reservation. In his careful studies of the laughing gull, J. P. Hailman and his associates have shown that gull chicks raised in darkness (so that no visual stimuli and thus no pecking practice was possible) differed significantly in pecking accuracy from control chicks exposed to model heads from hatching. Furthermore, a significant increase in pecking accuracy was demonstrated by chicks reared in the wild. It was found that, while a certain improvement in pecking accuracy is achieved without practice, visual experience and practice is necessary if the animal is to attain full pecking accuracy. Finally, with continuing practice and maturation in the nest, the chicks gradually responded more to accurate models of the parent gull's beak and less to innaccurate ones. The results strongly suggest that in this case, and quite possibly others, what at first appears to be instinctive or innate behavior may actually be behavior in which learning is a component of the causal factors producing the behavior. It therefore seems likely that other sequences of behavior heretofore assigned entirely to the innate behavior category can and should be reexamined.

Still more intriguing is the possibility that the Hailman hypothesis may provide answers to another perplexing problem posed by classical Pavlovian conditioning. As will be seen shortly, behavior patterns, as well as other aspects of the phenotype, evolve. But of what possible selective value is it to a dog to associate the sound of a bell with food? Certainly such unusual learning capabilities are of little use in organisms' normal activities in their natural environment. Yet the same question becomes a bit less puzzling if it is transferred from dog to gull: Of what possible selective value is it to a gull chick to associate the red patch on the mother's beak with food? Clearly, the difference between red beak pigments and food is as great as that between the sound frequencies emanating from a bell and food. Clearly, also, there is selective value in the gull chick's ability to make the red spot–food association. Thus, while it may be difficult to imagine how Pavlov's conditioning with bell and food could have any selective value in nature, it is not difficult at all to imagine how the potentiality of learning to associate seemingly unrelated stimuli might, indeed, have considerable selective value to an organism; most certainly it does to a baby gull.

The Hailman hypothesis is just that—an hypothesis, a tentative explanation. It shows promise, however, of providing a new and intellectually stimulating vantage point from which to view behavioral phenomena. Certainly the seagull example suggests that we must use extreme caution in separating behavior into learned and unlearned components, and even question whether such percentage-wise divisions between these two components are likely to be helpful. It will be necessary to return to this problem.

**22–6
BEHAVIOR:
GENETIC AND
EVOLUTIONARY
ASPECTS**

In the honeybee, *Apis mellifera* L., certain strains are referred to as being "hygienic." The name comes from the fact that, if a larva dies within its enclosing cell, the workers uncap the cell and remove the corpse. Other strains are "unhygienic"; when a larva dies, its corpse is left to decay within what has now become its tomb. The descendants of hygienic bees all exhibit the same hygienic behavior pattern; those of unhygienic strains remain, like their progenitors, unhygienic.

Certainly these are sharply contrasting phenotypes, as distinct as Mendel's tall and short peas. And, as with Mendel and his peas, a cross can be made between the contrasting phenotypes. The result is an $F_1$ which is all unhygienic; the dead larvae are left untouched, their cells capped. Clearly, the unhygienic behavior pattern, or better, perhaps, the absence of the hygienic behavior pattern, is the dominant character here. On the basis of the results thus far, tentative genotypes can be assigned:

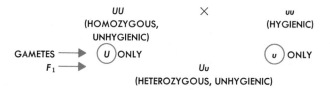

If, now, a backcross is made between the $F_1$ unhygienic hybrid, genotype $Uu$, and the recessive hygienic strain, genotype $uu$, mendelian genetics predicts a 50–50 distribution of unhygienic and hygienic bee colonies.

However, in 1964 the animal behaviorist W. C. Rothenbuhler showed that in 29 colonies of bees resulting from such a cross, the following distribution was obtained:

8 colonies: workers left cells capped and did not remove dead larvae (i.e., were unhygienic)

6 colonies: workers uncapped cells and removed dead larvae (i.e., were hygienic)

9 colonies: workers uncapped cells, but left corpses of larvae untouched

6 colonies: did not uncap cells, but would remove larvae if the caps were removed by experimenter

Clearly, it is reasonable to propose that there are two pairs of genes operating here, not one, and that the data represent a 1:1:1:1 ratio. Each pair of genes controls one of the two steps in the hygienic behavioral sequence, i.e., (1) uncapping of the cells and (2) removal of the larvae. Thus the original cross of hygienic with unhygienic must be rewritten as follows:

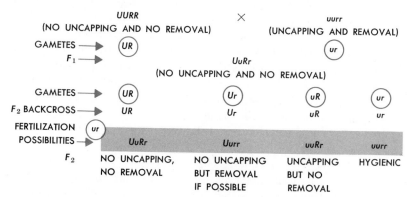

In terms of mendelian genetics, this situation works out most happily.* Not surprisingly, however, such neat results are rare in behavioral genetics. The example does show, however, that *differences* in behavior can have a genetic basis and, further, that behavioral patterns can be broken down into their component parts, e.g., the hygienic behavior pattern into (1) uncapping and (2) corpse removal.

Lovebirds are members of the parrot family. Within the genus *Agapornis* distinct evolutionary stages of nest building can be shown. In particular, two types of nest-building behavior are known. In one, strips are torn from leaves for nest-building material. The strips are then transported to the building site by being tucked underneath the rump feathers. In the other nest-building behavior pattern, however, the leaf strips are carried back to the nest one at a time in the beak or bill, not tucked into the feathers.

Dr. William C. Dilger is an ethologist who has carried out some intriguing experiments in ornithology.† Dilger wondered what would happen if he crossed "feather-carrier" lovebirds with "bill-carriers." Assuming complete dominance is involved, one would predict an $F_1$ of either all feather-carriers or all bill-carriers. With incomplete dominance, some sort of behavioral hybrid would be expected. The latter proves to be the case, and the result is a group of hopelessly confused young birds. All are completely incapable of building a nest, because they attempt a compromise between bill-carrying and feather-carrying—which

---

* It is an interesting coincidence—but only that—that besides raising garden peas Mendel was an ardent beekeeper.

† Ornithology is the study of birds. It would be difficult to find a scientific field in which "amateurs" have made any more significant contributions. The observations of members of hundreds of "bird watching societies" around the world have been invaluable in the study of behavior, especially bird migration.

means, of course, no carrying at all! A bird might begin to tuck a strip between its rump feathers, but then the bill-carrying "urge" would take over, and the strip would not be released until it was pulled back out of the feathers and dropped on the floor. Then the whole process would begin again.

Yet, again, a hypothesis proposing that nest-building behavior is entirely innate is contradicted; occasional successes were recorded when a hybrid managed to keep a strip in its beak after failing to tuck it into the feathers. After months of practice, success was achieved in more than a third of the trials. Two years later, nearly complete success was attained by the hybrid birds. Thus, once again, what seemed to be strictly innate behavior revealed, upon further examination, considerable susceptibility to learning. The "genetic factors" were not entirely suppressed, however; even hybrid birds attaining complete success in nest building still made a preliminary movement toward tucking the strip underneath their feathers before flying off with it held in their bills.

If behavior patterns have a genetic basis, they must have considerable evolutionary significance as well. At least one example has already been discussed; the different mating calls of crickets serve to isolate species which may live in otherwise overlapping habitats (see Fig. 19–7). A somewhat similar example is found in lizards of the genus *Sceloporus*. During the mating season, subtle differences in head-bobbing movements (see Fig. 22–8) serve as courtship signals as well as species-identifying signals. There are only two main groups of muscles involved in these characteristic movements, but even in this case a hypothetical model based on the concept of genes affecting nervous system thresholds can satisfactorily account for the remarkable diversity of head-bobbing behavior shown by these animals. Given more complex situations, involving many groups of muscles (more the rule than the exception), it is not difficult to picture how small accumulations of threshold changes might lead to changed behavior patterns which, in turn, might lead either to extinction or to further speciation.

Another example illustrating the evolutionary significance of behavior is pertinent here. Herring gulls remove the eggshells from the nest after their chicks have hatched. But what is the selective value of such behavior? The speckled coloring of the gull eggs before hatching gives them excellent protective coloration against the pebble-strewn background on which they are laid. The chicks, too, are protectively colored. The *inside* of the eggshell, however, is white. Thus, when the shell is broken at hatching, some fragments may lie with their inner surface exposed. This observation led N. Tinbergen to hypothesize that the white fragments might enable predators to locate the nest by sight (or even by the odor of the decaying portions of the remaining egg parts adhering to the shell fragments). This hypothesis leads to certain predictions:

*Hypothesis:*    *If* . . .    removal of eggshells from the nest after hatching aids in protecting the young from predators, . . .

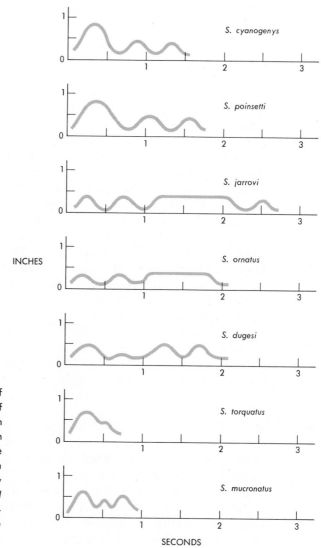

FIG. 22–8 Head-bobbing movements of some *Sceloporus* lizards. Movements of the head are represented as a line with height on the vertical axis and time in seconds on the horizontal axis. Note the variations in amplitude, speed, and length of the movements. (After Aubrey Manning, *An Introduction to Animal Behavior.* Reading, Mass.: Addison-Wesley, 1967. From Hunsaker, *Evolution* **16**, 1962, p. 62.)

***Prediction I:*** *then . . .* nests with eggshells should be preyed upon more frequently than those without eggshells.

***Prediction II:*** *then . . .* nests with eggshells left closer to them should show a higher degree of successful predation than nests with eggshells farther away.

Tinbergen tested his hypothesis with experiments conducted in the field (i.e., outside the laboratory). Both predictions were verified. Thus the seemingly energy-wasting behavior of eggshell removal on the part of parent gulls was shown to have considerable selective value.

Indeed, it seems as though *behavioral changes may be of major importance in the process of evolution by natural selection.* While stressing the primary importance of geographical isolation in the formation of new species, Professor Ernst Mayr of Harvard University states in his book, *Animal Species and Evolution:* "A shift into a new niche or adaptive zone is, almost without exception, initiated by a change in behavior. The other adaptations to the new niche, particularly the structural ones, are acquired secondarily."

If changes in behavior patterns are, as Mayr suggests, of equal or greater importance than structural ones in achieving evolutionary success, the *absence* of certain essential behavior patterns may also lead to evolutionary failure. The vestigial-winged *Drosophila melanogaster* (see Fig. 2–3) cannot generally survive very long in the wild for what seems like an obvious reason—the animals cannot fly from one food source to another. Yet, even in the laboratory, where they are well supplied with food, vestigials are unable to compete with wild-type flies. The answer is found when the sequence of *Drosophila* mating behavior is studied. At one point in this sequence, the male extends one wing out to the side and vibrates it on a horizontal plane. This movement stimulates certain sense organs at the base of the female's antennae. If this stimulation does not occur, the mating sequence cannot continue to copulation. The vestigial-winged male has far less success than a winged rival in carrying out the lateral vibration, and is therefore often unable to compete successfully. Thus it is its effect on a crucial behavior pattern rather than on flight that seems to make the vestigial character a variation doomed to evolutionary failure in the wild.

## 22–7 MOTIVATION

Most, if not all, animal behavior is goal-oriented. This statement is not necessarily teleological; it is neither necessary nor fruitful to assume conscious behavior on the part of an animal in attaining a specific goal.* Yet it is obvious that an animal may orient itself toward a specific goal—say, food—quite strongly on one occasion and quite weakly, if at all, on another. The degree of intensity of goal-oriented behavior, a degree highly influenced by an intervening variable, is termed **motivation.** Thus, if an animal is very hungry, it will be highly motivated toward the goal. If it has recently eaten, on the other hand, it will be

---

* Though the statement is not teleological, what it asserts *is*, since teleological means "goal-oriented." There is a sticky semantic problem here. Evolution is not teleological, because those organisms that survive, survive, and that's all there is to it. Certain forms of behavior, on the other hand, are teleological because of their goal-oriented nature. The key is to avoid, with Morgan, the idea of *consciousness* in such behavior. Why? Because consciousness is an undefinable entity which cannot be scientifically tested. In an effort to avoid the connotation that an animal "knows" that reaching the goal will increase the probability of its own survival and that of its descendants, the term **teleonomical** has been suggested. By definition, the concept of teleonomy filters out both conscious and evolutionary factors and simply represents the goal-directedness that remains.

far less highly motivated toward food. The time of the last feeding thus becomes the intervening variable in this case. The term **drive** is sometimes used to describe a specific motivation. Thus we often speak of hunger drive, sex drive, thirst drive, etc. Some other examples of specific motivations are fear (leading, perhaps, to an escape drive), aggression, and so on.

A major problem in dealing scientifically with motivation is that it often resists quantitative measurement and therefore must be dealt with subjectively. Thus we cannot speak of an animal as showing 90.6 or 8.03 hunger units, and therefore must resort to such expressions as "strongly motivated toward food" or "a low level of goal-oriented behavior was observed." This means that comparisons of drive intensities toward different goals are usually unprofitable; what does it mean, for example, to say that the hunger drive is stronger than the sex drive? How can the intensity of either drive be quantitatively measured? Assuming that some sort of quantitative scale *could* be established for hunger and sex drive, in what way could the scales ever be equated? Possibly the hunger drive can be placed ahead of the sex drive on the basis of the results of deprivation, one being fatal while the other is not. But most certainly this is an unsatisfactory way to compare motivation intensities.

As an example of goal-oriented behavior and motivation intensity, B. T. Gardner's work on the feeding behavior of jumping spiders can be considered. Jumping spiders do not spin webs, but rather stalk their prey. The entire sequence of jumping spider feeding behavior can be broken down as follows:

A. Orientation: The spider sees its prey (e.g., a fly) and turns toward it.

B. Pursuit:     If the spider is some distance away, it runs rapidly toward it, but slows down to a careful stalk as it approaches the fly. When it attains a certain crucial distance from the intended victim, it crouches and then jumps upon it.

—5 mm—

Gardner has shown that this sequence of steps in the overall hunting behavior of the jumping spider provides a scale by which the animal's motivation intensity can be gauged. Thus a spider which has captured enough flies to satisfy its hunger will no longer orient itself to flies. If the animal has devoured a number of flies slightly less than that necessary to completely satisfy its hunger, it may orient itself toward flies, but do no more. At a certain level of hunger, however, the spider pursues after orientation, and goes on to crouch and jump. Thus prey capture in the jumping spider provides an example of behavior in which an intensity scale can be correlated with units of time (i.e., the number of time units elapsed since the animal last fed).

Ethologists and psychologists also often quantify motivational states in terms of the degree of deprivation. For example, Dr. Martin W. Schein of West Virginia University has shown that if the dust-bathing behavior of Japanese quail is prevented for about two or three days and then allowed to occur, the behavior is measurably higher than the standard for about an hour, and then decays to the standard. A deprivation of two weeks results in a predictable, still higher increment of behavior, and so forth.

Unfortunately, not all behavioral sequences can be so neatly calibrated. Like the hunting behavior of spiders, the nest-building "drive" in birds can be separated into separate behavioral components—material gathering, transporting of the material, weaving of the nest, and so on. But it has not proven possible, in this case, to arrange the components on an intensity scale.

Model building is becoming increasingly popular in biology. Indeed it is not stretching a point too far to say that Watson and Crick achieved the Nobel Prize by essentially building a model. The requirements of a good model are the same in animal behavior as in molecular genetics—or, indeed, in any other field of science. Hypothetical models should help both to generate other hypotheses and to suggest experiments with which to test them.

It is not at all necessary for a model to bear any resemblance to reality. No biologist seriously believes that the cell membrane in any way resembles the standard artist's representation of the unit membrane concept (see Fig. 6–10) which has been put forth to account for the characteristics of cell membranes. Nor is it necessary that a model of sliding filaments devised to explain muscle contraction (see Fig. 13–7) bear any real resemblance to the actin and myosin filaments themselves. Note also that a model simply suggests *principles* by which a phenomenon occurs and says nothing at all about *how* it occurs. Thus the sliding-filament model can account for observed changes in its appearance when a muscle contracts and allows for predictions to be made, but tells us nothing about the underlying mechanisms which allow the sliding phenomenon to occur.

As examples of model building in ethology, two models will be considered here. Both were put forth to account for observations of goal-oriented behavior such as that observed by Gardner in jumping spiders.

The first model, put forth in its final form in 1950 by Konrad Lorenz, rather resembles the model given in Chapter 14. Indeed, it is often referred to as the "psycho-hydraulic" model of behavior (see Fig. 22–9).

We shall use the jumping spider's behavior to discuss this model. The increase in water level in the reservoir is caused by the constantly flowing tap. This part of the model is analogous to the increasing hunger of the spider. The outflow of water from the reservoir, analogous to motor activity behavior (i.e., fly stalking and capture), is caused by the opening of the valve, normally held shut by a spring. This opening can be brought about in two ways. In one, a sufficient water level in the reservoir (i.e., sufficient hunger) motivates hunting activity. In the other, weights on the scale pan, analogous to the varying strengths of the stimuli (the sighting of flies, their proximity, etc.), cause motor behavior to begin.

The most important and imaginative feature of the Lorenz model is the graded trough, above which is an "intensity level" scale. The stronger the hunger or stimulus (or both), the further open the valve and the faster the activity. At a 6 reading on the intensity scale, water is discharged through all the openings in the trough. At the lower 4 level of activity, shown in the figure fewer holes are used.

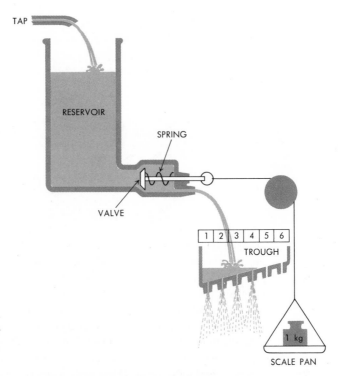

FIG. 22–9 Konrad Lorenz's "psycho-hydraulic" model of behavior (see text for explanation). (From Lorenz, *Symp. Soc. Exp. Biol.* **4**, 1950, p. 256.)

Note that this model is not only consistent with the observations of the jumping spider but, indeed, predicts them (the model preceded the publication of Gardner's work by several years). Thus an empty reservoir predicts no further hunting activity on the part of the spider, *no matter how strong the stimulus;* the behavior pattern is "exhausted." The varying intensities of hunting behavior (e.g., orientation without stalking and capture) are nicely accounted for by the different discharge intensities allowed by the holes in the graded trough. Note again, however, that this model does not possess the slightest resemblance to reality. Nor is it intended to. No one considers for one moment that any living organism contains a system of fluid-filled reservoirs, spring-controlled valves, or stimulus intensity scales. The model is helpful only insofar as it accounts for goal-oriented behavior, and, as has just been seen, it nicely does so.

But other models are also possible. J. A. Deutsch proposes a flow-chart model (see Fig. 22–10) to account for goal-oriented behavior which differs from that of Lorenz in not possessing moving parts. In the Deutsch model, a deficit in the internal medium (e.g., a food deficit) stimulates the central structure or "link," resulting in hunger. The strength of the excitation depends on the size of the deficit; in other words, the less food in the animal, the hungrier it is. The excitation of the central structure, depending on its intensity, brings about the motor behavior; i.e., if the intensity is high, the spider orients itself toward the prey, stalks, and captures; if low, it may only orient itself or show no reaction at all. As in the Lorenz "psycho-hydraulic" model, however, the

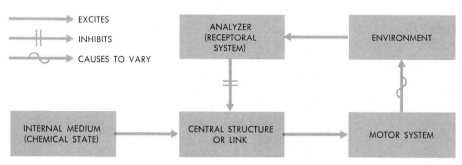

FIG. 22–10    A portion of Deutsch's model of behavior (see text for explanation).    (From J. A. Deutsch, *The Structural Basis of Behavior*.  Chicago: University of Chicago Press, 1960.)

strength of the stimulus (i.e., sighting the flies) may also cause variations in motivation intensity.  The analyzer or receptoral system represents the organism's means of detecting flies (which, in the case of jumping spider, seems to be primarily visual).  Once the animal has eaten its fill of flies, the analyzer signals the control stimulus or "link," which becomes no longer responsive to excitation from the internal medium until the proper hunger threshold is achieved again.  When this threshold is reached, the system is set in operation again and the organism begins the behavioral sequence of hunting and prey capture once again.

Which model is "correct"?  Both the Lorenz and Deutsch models are *hypothetical* models; i.e., they represent hypotheses.  Thus, as with any hypothesis, they must both be consistent with observations of the behavioral phenomena they are intended to shed light upon, and yield accurate predictions concerning this behavior.  In the case of the jumping spider, then, both the Lorenz and Deutsch models are correct.  If one model is to be discarded in favor of the other, a situation must be found in which each model leads to differing and perhaps even opposing predictions.  If this situation can be found, verification of one prediction will automatically show the other to be incorrect.  In other words, a crucial experiment is needed to test the two models.

Such an experiment is provided by the work of H. D. Janowitz and M. I. Grossman.  Dogs were operated upon so that the esophagus led out of an opening in the neck rather than into the stomach.  Thus, when an experimental animal ate, food fell outside of the body.  Because of this "sham-eating," as it was called, the behavioral act of eating could be separated from the results of doing so (i.e., the abatement of hunger).  But the stomach of these animals also led to the outside, and thus could be directly filled by the experimenter.  This meant that hunger could be satiated without the animal going through the behavioral act of eating.

Suppose, now, an animal's stomach is filled with food after several hours without eating.  Will the dog behave as if it is hungry; i.e., will it eat?  According to the Lorenz psycho-hydraulic model, the dog *will* eat, because its motivating reservoir has not been drained through the valve by either the act of eating or sight of the stimulus, food.  The Deutsch model, on the other hand, predicts that the dog will *not* eat.  The change in the environment (the change from an empty to a full stomach) activates the analyzer. The analyzer, in turn, switches off the central structure or "link." Thus no feeding activity should occur.

The results are quite clear; the experimental dogs do not eat. Thus, in this particular example of goal-oriented behavior, the Deutsch model proves to be better. The same results are obtained with "sham-drinking." Even in sexual behavior, where the relationship between behavior and physiological state is far less direct, work with fishes shows the Deutsch model of behavior to be the more satisfactory in yielding accurate predictions.

But Deutsch's model has proven to have still other qualities that work in its favor. Primary among these is that it incorporates the role of feedback from the environment, a factor we have seen to be important from genome to biome. Furthermore, it has recently been possible to identify parts of the brain whose properties closely resemble those of the components of Deutsch's model. No such success is likely in showing a counterpart to Lorenz's stored-potential-energy system as represented by the fluid-filled reservoir.

It is possible here to do some model building of our own in order to explain a "simple" behavioral phenomenon. Suppose we touch a preying mantis' leg (the stimulus). The leg is withdrawn and the animal moves away (the response). A model system can now be imagined in which the brain receives the incoming sensory nerve impulse, analyzes it as to its positive and negative aspects (i.e., food or danger?), and then sends out the proper sequence of motor nerve impulses to bring about the avoidance behavior. In this example of goal-oriented behavior, the goal is safety; the drive, an escape drive. This is a simple model, and one often invoked to explain stimulus-response behavior in organisms such as man and other animals.

Another model is also possible, however, Recall that it is not only important for muscles to contract to bring about an action, it is also essential that other muscles relax so that the muscles do not act antagonistically to each other. Thus the brain may do as much work *inhibiting* muscle contraction as it does initiating it. Impulses from the brain would then act to remove this inhibition in effecting muscle contraction. This second model is supported by K. D. Roeder's observation that a preying mantis whose brain is removed by decapitation can still perform incessant stepping movements which carry it in a circle. Still more intriguing is the fact that a decapitated male mantis is able to carry out successfully the complex sequence of behavior involved in mating. There may be some adaptive value in this phenomenon, since male mantises are occasionally decapitated by the female they are courting; speaking anthropomorphically, presumably she is more in the mood for a meal than romance. The behavioral phenomenon just cited allows for both!

Thus the second model, in the case of mantis behavior, proves the more satisfactory; indeed the first model predicts that decapitation will result in no behavior at all. But the second model also accounts for certain observations in vertebrates, e.g., that the destruction of certain areas of the brain makes some behavioral patterns easier to produce. In the case of man, it might be noted that alcohol may act to counteract inhibitions which would ordinarily be in effect.

Animals may learn in a variety of ways. A turtle will avoid an object moved toward it by withdrawing into its shell. Continued exposure to the moving stimulus results in less and less withdrawal until the response is entirely extinguished. Such learning is called **habituation.** There are clearly advantages for organisms in being able to distinguish insignificant stimuli in their environment from those which are highly significant, such as the appearance of prey or a predator.

**Trial-and-error** learning is also well known in animals. Experimentally, animals learn to move through a maze by trial-and-error; in nature, paramecia utilize the same behavior in swimming around an obstacle in their path. In each case, the technique is the same; the animal moves until progress is blocked, then backs off and tries again in a different direction until the obstacle is passed.

Far more complex is learning which seems to involve "reasoning." Perhaps for the same reasons that caused him to resist the Copernican system (which removed him from the center of the universe) and Darwinian evolution (which challenged his feeling of distinctiveness from the rest of the animal kingdom), man has been reluctant to grant reasoning powers to lower animals, despite his liking for anthropomorphism mentioned at the beginning of this chapter. It is perhaps at least partly (but only partly) in deference to this feeling that some animal behaviorists have used the term **insight learning** to refer to learning on the part of an animal where something more than simple conditioning is obviously involved. This does not always mean simply learning a difficult task. Chimpanzees can be trained to ride bicycles and play tunes on musical instruments, and the learning feats of the porpoise are well documented. But the vast majority of such learning can be accomplished by means of simple conditioning arranged in complex sequential patterns.

A situation obviously involving insight learning is one in which an indirect approach is necessary. J. Goodall effectively dispelled the myth that only man is a toolmaker with her filmed observations of chimpanzees in the wild shaping branches into slender twigs with which to probe termites out of their nest (see Fig. 22–11). In the laboratory, the chimpanzee can master quite complex tasks. Julia, a chimpanzee belonging to Jürgen Döhl of the Zoological Institute of Münster University, has convinced her owner that the ability to act intelligently and foresee the outcome of decisions is not an exclusively human characteristic, but that this feature is also present, at least in rudimentary form, in other higher animals. Julia's performance on the following task tends to support Döhl's belief.

Ten boxes were placed in Julia's cage. Each was locked but had a transparent lid. Only one contained food. The key to open this box was locked in another box. The key to this second box was locked in a third; the key to the third locked in the fourth; the key to the fourth box locked in the fifth. The key to the fifth box, however, lay in a dual selection apparatus, also under a transparent lid. The other half of this dual selection box contained a second key which was the first link in a chain leading from box six to box ten. But box ten was empty.

FIG. 22–11 It was once thought that only man could modify objects and use them as tools. Jane Goodall, who spent three years studying chimpanzees, has shown this assumption to be false. Here chimpanzees have stripped leaves from twigs and broken off bent ends, forming primitive tools, which are inserted into the nests. The insects cling to the sticks and are then withdrawn and eaten by the apes. (Photo by Jane van Lawick-Goodall. Copyright ©️ by the National Geographic Society.)

Certainly this is a terribly complex problem, for not only is it necessary to deduce the chain sequence of keys to the boxes, but the correct key that leads to the box containing food must be chosen over another one leading to the empty box ten. Despite the difficulty of the problem, and the fact that it was very different from any of her previous challenges, Julia solved it. Of some interest is the fact that she would often simply sit in front of the experimental layout and seem to "ponder" the proper procedure to take. In some cases, Julia even seemed to pursue the way back from the goal along the chain of boxes to find the beginning.

Clearly it seems difficult to eliminate the possibility of "strategy planning" and abstract reasoning in such a case as Julia's.* However, a growing number of ethologists believe that it can be done, and that an explanation for the applica-

---

* To judge from a 1964 art exhibit in Goteborg, Sweden, apes may also share man's esthetic qualities. Entries by artist Pierre Brassau received generally favorable reviews. One critic wrote: "He paints with sharp determination. Brassau's brush strokes twist with a furious fastidiousness." Another called Brassau "the Ballet Master of the canvas." A third critic, less kind, wrote: "We have seen too many painters like him in recent days." Told that Brassau's extensive use of cobalt blue showed good taste, a zoo attendant agreed, noting that Brassau usually ate more of it than he applied to the canvas. Brassau, a chimpanzee, makes both his home and his studio in the Goteborg Zoo!

tion of such responses by chimpanzees to such problems need imply no principles beyond those of operant conditioning. Further, while such feats by chimpanzees and other "higher" animals are interesting, they may also be quite misleading. It is very common to hear people speak of some species of animals as being more intelligent than others. Yet this assumption often runs into serious contradictions; rats, for example, learn complex mazes about as quickly as humans. In truth, as Dr. J. M. Warren of Pennsylvania State University has convincingly argued, the bases for comparative gauges of learning abilities and intelligence have not yet been laid. Thus at present it must be stated that the performances of animals of different species on learning sets, insight learning problems, delayed responses, and other sophisticated gauges, are not necessarily related to the species' position on a phylogenetic chart. Considering the unique nature of species-specific repertoires of motor patterns, selective responses to sensory cues, and readiness to associate particular stimuli and responses, this should not be particularly surprising. Indeed, the assumption of a connection between intelligence and phylogenetic status is more than a little bit anthropomorphic; animals are subjected to a natural selection favoring survival and reproductive success, *not* the degree to which they demonstrate progressively more human-like capacities for learning and problem solving.

A startling contrast to "insight learning" is a type of learning first described in 1890 by ethologist Douglas Spalding. Spalding noted that a baby chick which had not heard the call of its mother until eight or ten days of age would then refuse to recognize her at all, despite her coaxings. This observation was followed in 1910 by zookeeper O. Heinroth's report that young ducklings follow the first relatively large object they see moving. Heinroth labeled this rapid fixing of social preferences "prägung," the German term for "pressing" (as in the stamping of a coin). In 1935, Konrad Lorenz stressed the uniqueness of this form of learning, which he termed in translation **"imprinting."** Lorenz noted that, in geese, "imprinting" occurs rapidly, lasts a lifetime, and unlike other forms of learning does not seem to involve any "reward."

"Imprinting" is obviously of selective value, since the first moving and sound-emitting object a young bird is likely to see is its mother. Interestingly, however, young birds also become "imprinted" to objects such as toys, boxes with ticking clocks inside, and even the experimenter. Such objects, of course, bear little resemblance to the natural mother, and it is interesting to note that no matter what the object to which the animal becomes attached, the attachment is usually a lasting one. Certain male birds "imprinted" to the human hand may prefer to attempt copulation with the hand rather than with a receptive female.

Careful studies of maternal "imprinting" in goats have been carried out by P. H. and M. S. Klopfer of Duke University. It was found that contact with the young (kid) *directly after birth* is essential for the mother (the doe) to show normal maternal care patterns of behavior. If this contact is denied, the doe will reject her kid, even if it is returned to her after only an hour's separation.

However, if the doe is allowed five minutes with her kid *first*, and then separated for an hour or more, she reaccepts her kid and its littermates (if any) but will not accept a kid which is not her own.

The contrary is not the case, however. Denied her own young but allowed five minutes with an alien kid directly after birth, a doe will not only accept that alien kid as her own but will also accept her own young. However, only the alien kid to which she has been exposed is accepted; other alien kids are not. Neither the natural nor the alien kid is able to evoke the response if denied contact with the doe immediately after birth.

What is the biological basis of the differences between natural and alien kids in their ability to evoke certain maternal responses? A hypothesis proposing differences in scent of the young predicts that, if the olfactory pathways to the brain are blocked, the doe should no longer be able to discriminate between her own and alien young. This prediction is verified; application of cocaine to the olfactory membranes results in loss of the discriminatory ability. But what is the precise nature of this olfactory cue, and how is each kid individually "coded"? Also, how does this scent come to be known by the doe?

If a doe is allowed contact with her kid directly after birth and then the kid is taken from her, the doe shows obvious distress. If post-birth contact is denied, however, the doe continues as if she had never mated and given birth. It seems likely that, while the stimuli provided by the kid are obviously important, the changing internal physiological environment of the doe may be equally so. For example, although the experiment involving anesthesia of the olfactory sense of the doe shows that a scent (or scents) emanating from the kid does enhance the relative attractiveness of her own kid over aliens, the elicitation of maternal behavior itself is clearly not dependent on any special olfactory cues produced by her own kid. It is thus reasonable to look for physiological differences in the doe during the crucial five minutes after birth that might account for the fact that this period is so important to the eliciting of maternal behavior. Noting that there is a large increase in the blood level of a hormone (oxytocin) as the head of the fetus squeezes through the cervix (neck of the uterus) and passes down the vagina, and noting also that this high level of oxytocin in the blood falls to a normal level within a few minutes after birth, the Klopfers speculate that oxytocin, which apparently plays a role in bringing on the final uterine spasms which deliver the kid, may also activate maternal "centers" in the hypothalamus of the brain or elsewhere. Or, the oxytocin may change the thresholds of peripheral receptors so as to temporarily sensitize the doe to certain elements of the world about her (such as a kid). In the Klopfers' own words, "Even if oxytocin is not the keystone of mother love, its action provides us with a most useful and exciting model."

Certainly the differences between insight learning and "imprinting" are considerable. It is perhaps not surprising, therefore, that attempts to come up with a general theory of learning covering all such situations have thus far not been notably successful.

Ethologist Martin W. Schein, of West Virginia University, points out that there is a tendency to look so closely at the causes of a behavioral action and/or the behavioral action itself that the *consequences* of that behavioral action are ignored. Thus, for example, the turning red of a traffic light causes a driver to stop his car and wait for the light to turn green. Behaviorally speaking, it is relatively easy to show that this is a learned stimulus-response situation, and the cause-and-effect relationships can be detailed without much difficulty. However, to be really complete in our study of this behavioral sequence, we must look at all of the consequences of the driver's stopping for the red light: he may back up traffic for a half mile; he may cause an accident two miles back; or, if he is in a terrible hurry, he may be angry that he did not go another way to avoid the traffic-light-equipped intersection. Thus for every action there is a reaction, and this statement holds true in behavior as well as in physics and, indeed, some behavior seems geared to producing reaction. Such behavior can be termed "communicative behavior" or, simply, **communication.** Communication between animals may, of course, occur between different species (**interspecific**) or between members of the same species (**intraspecific**). Alarm signals given by African gazelles are usually detected by baboon troops foraging for food in the same area; in turn, the alarm is communicated throughout the troop and responded to accordingly. The alarm call of a crow communicates one thing to a hawk and another to other members of the flock.

Several types of intraspecific communication have already been cited; the gull chick's response to its parent's beak is an example of visual communication, while the reaction of a female cricket to the male's chirp during the mating season provides an example of auditory communication. The female cockroach communicates to the male her readiness for mating by producing a chemical attractant, and thus the olfactory system becomes the avenue of communication in this case.

At times, communication between animals of the same species appears limited to only one sense, while at others two or more senses may be involved. A mother turkey will peck at silent models of her young, yet will accept a stuffed mammalian predator if a loudspeaker within it utters the baby turkey's cries. Clearly sound, not sight, is the communication medium here. On the other hand, the complex mating behavior sequences seen in many bird species prior to copulation seem to involve both sound and visual communication. In many mammals, olfactory and visual communication is used in mating; the female first produces a chemical with a distinct odor which communicates her sexual responsiveness to the male and second performs the proper behavior patterns necessary to ensure copulation.

Occasionally, the message communicated through the channels of one sensory system is so "strong" that equally strong contradictory messages conveyed through another system are ignored. Such is the case in ants. When a member of an ant colony dies, certain chemicals produced by its decay are detected by worker ants, who remove the dead ant from the nest. Living ants coated with the same decay chemicals are likewise carried out and, despite their struggles, discarded. Upon each return to the nest by these "dead" ants, they are carried out again. Thus no matter how strongly the visual and tactile communications flash "I am alive," the olfactory message, "I am dead," is accepted.

Chemicals synthesized within a living organism's body which serve to release an immediate or belated response on the part of the organisms to which the chemicals are directed are called **pheromones.** In a sense, pheromones are "ectohormones" in that they cause their motivational effects outside instead of inside an organism's body. The parallel with hormones breaks down, however, in that some pheromones appear to "release" (rather than motivate) behavior, and thus act as do other types of taste and smell stimuli. While common in such animals as insects, pheromones are known in mammals as well, the aforementioned chemicals communicating sexual receptiveness being just one example. Some others will be discussed in the next chapter.

One of the most remarkable examples of communication postulated for any of the "lower" animals is that of the "dance language" of honeybees. This language hypothesis was a logical interpretation derived from the results of a series of ingenious experiments conducted by Karl von Frisch. Von Frisch noted that, when a food source left near the hive was discovered by one worker bee, there would shortly be hundreds at the site transporting the food back to the hive. Since the location of the food by so many bees in such a short time could obviously not be ascribed to random searching, von Frisch guessed that the forager bee that first found the food somehow communicated its discovery to the hive. By using glass-walled hives and marking the forager bees with colored paint, von Frisch was able to follow their movements upon their return to the hive. He noted that each animal ran in circles, first to the right and then to the left. This pattern was repeated many times and with much excited activity on the part of both the "dancer" and the surrounding workers. The latter would press close to the dancer and touch it with their antennae. Following this, they would leave the hive and, presumably, fly directly to the food source.

Further observations obtained by placing the food at varying distances from the hive convinced von Frisch that the dance of the bees also communicated distance. There is a variation of the dance which occurs when the food is placed some distance from the hive, and this variation is the addition of a straight-line component to the dance. When traversing this straight line, the bee wags its abdomen rapidly from side to side. Von Frisch compared the number of turns per unit time in the dance variation with the distance of the food source from the hive and found a distinct correlation (see Fig. 22–12). He also noted that the straight portion of the dance gave information concerning the position of the food in relation to the sun (e.g., opposite direction from the sun, same direction, 60° to the right or left of it). Objections to this relationship on the basis of observations that bees find the food on cloudy days just as well as on sunny days were dispelled by further experiments indicating that only a small patch of blue sky may be necessary for the bee's relatively huge compound eye to analyze the polarized light reflected from the atmosphere; this light in turn could give a bearing on the sun's position in relation to the animal. One fact which weighs

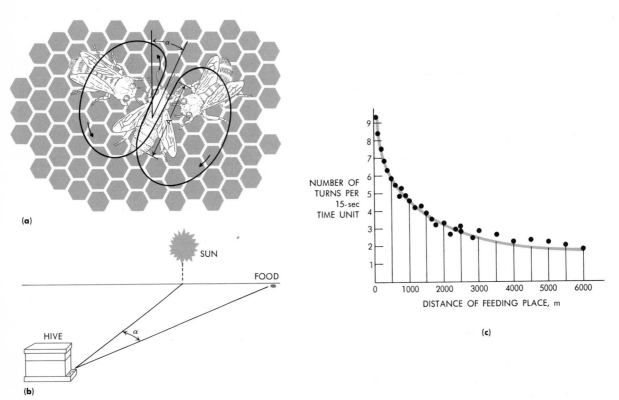

FIG. 22–12    Bee dance-language hypothesis of von Frisch.  (a) Waggle, or figure-8 dance, performed by foraging bees returning to hive.  Duration of straight-run portion of dance (A) is proportional to distance from the food, and is oriented at an angle (α) from the vertical equal to the angle
between the sun's azimuth and the food source.  (b) Beehive showing angle (α) made from point of
the bee dance to the food source and sun's azimuth.  (c) Graph showing relationship between the
number of turns per unit of time and the distance to food source located by the foraging bee.  [Parts
(a) and (b) from A. M. Wenner, "Sound Communication in Honeybees." *Scientific American*, April
1964.  Copyright © 1964 by Scientific American, Inc.  All rights reserved.]

against this line of reasoning, however, is that recruited bees succeed in finding
food sources even under complete overcasts.*

Von Frisch's analysis of the bee dance in relation to the location of the food
source has been accurate enough for biology professors to use the dance in a
laboratory exercise.  The students first observe the bees through glass-walled
hives and then must find the food (sugar water or honey) hidden somewhere

---

\* Differences between the sensory systems of experimental animals must not be overlooked
if an experiment is to be a valid one.  For example, insects can detect the fact that an
ordinary light bulb which is "on" is actually flickering on and off approximately 60 times
per second.  Man's eyes cannot detect this, and thus we see the light as continuously "on".
This factor must be kept in mind when experimenting with insects under artificial light.

on campus. Here is an example of artificially caused communication between different species, from *Apis mellifera* L. to *Homo sapiens*. The bee, of course, has no intention of communicating; the students are merely "wire-tapping."

Von Frisch's "language hypothesis" has been challenged, however, by A. M. Wenner of the University of California at Santa Barbara, P. H. Wells of Occidental College, Los Angeles, and D. O. Johnson of the Air Force Academy, Colorado Springs, Colorado. These workers maintain that there is no need to postulate the use of a language to explain the results obtained in earlier experimentation. They maintain that when they submitted the language hypothesis to a variety of tests, it consistently failed in its predictive ability. In a double-controlled experiment, for example (as against the single-controlled type of experiment used by earlier investigators), bees arrived at food sources in the field in apparent disregard of any dance information they might have acquired in the hive. Furthermore, data obtained independently by students at the California Institute of Technology indicate that recruits reach a food station only after having flown for a period several times longer than necessary for a direct flight between hive and station. For example, some marked bee recruits required up to ten minutes for a 20-second flight. Noting that an unscented sucrose solution drew few or no worker bees to it, Wenner, Wells, and Johnson set up food sources in the relation to the hive depicted in Fig. 22–13. Reasoning that the accumulation of odor in the hive should contribute to the relative success of an inexperienced worker bee locating a food source, the investigators scented

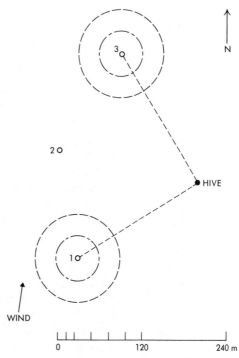

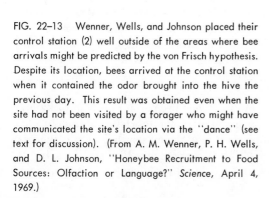

FIG. 22–13   Wenner, Wells, and Johnson placed their control station (2) well outside of the areas where bee arrivals might be predicted by the von Frisch hypothesis. Despite its location, bees arrived at the control station when it contained the odor brought into the hive the previous day. This result was obtained even when the site had not been visited by a forager who might have communicated the site's location via the "dance" (see text for discussion). (From A. M. Wenner, P. H. Wells, and D. L. Johnson, "Honeybee Recruitment to Food Sources: Olfaction or Language?" *Science*, April 4, 1969.)

the food with oil of clove for, say, three days. After this time, it was no longer necessary to add scent; the experienced bees had located the food source and "remembered" its location.

Did the recruited bees locate the food source by language or olfaction? When additional scented food is placed at a control station located well outside the areas where the language hypothesis predicts the arrival of worker bees recruited by forager bees, the result is a situation in which the language and olfactory hypotheses lead to conflicting predictions. The former predicts that recruited workers will arrive only at sites found by foragers. The latter predicts that recruits should show up at the scented control stations, even if no forager worker has been there first. The olfactory hypothesis further predicts that the number of recruited worker bees caught per unit time should not increase on days when foragers collect unscented sucrose solution, but should increase on days when odor is used in the food.

Both predictions of the olfactory hypothesis are verified. Thus the olfactory hypothesis is supported and the language hypothesis seems disproved. But Wenner, Wells, and Johnson's conclusions have been challenged in a letter to the journal *Science* by R. Dawkins of the University of California at Berkeley. Dawkins points out that von Frisch and Lindauer showed that bees exposed to a strong visual landmark (such as the edge of a forest) at times use this landmark as a guideline rather than the sun. Yet to have concluded from this investigation that bees use terrestrial landmarks rather than the sun as a compass would have been incorrect. According to Dawkins, "the artificial use of strong scent might cause olfactory cues to prevail, while the artificially engineered presence of large crowds of bees at control feeding stations might well distract foragers from other cues" (such as those provided by the "dance"). Thus, states Dawkins, the work of Wenner, Wells, and Johnson simply shows that "bees are easily distracted." However, Wenner, Wells, and Johnson do not consider Dawson's objection an important one; they maintain that, in order for the objection to be valid, it would be necessary for all the recruited bees to have been misled to the control site from their "intended" goal both upwind and downwind in equal numbers.

Which, if either, hypothesis is correct concerning food location in bees? Perhaps one and not the other, perhaps both, or perhaps neither. The problem of the bees points up the complexities and difficulties involved in dealing experimentally with animal communication in particular and animal behavior in general. It also, perhaps, points up the difficulties encountered in challenging well-entrenched scientific hypotheses.

## 22-11
## CONCLUSION

In this chapter, animal behavior or ethology has been seen as a field of biology which approaches an organism with as much attention to what it *does* as to what it *is*. The often opposing viewpoints of ethologist and psychologist in the past are explainable on the basis of their different approaches to the same subjects. Anthropomorphism might be viewed as being to ethology as vitalism is to biology—an unnecessary interpretation of living phenomena and one which is useless because it is scientifically untestable.

The concept of innate versus learned behavior was discussed, as well as some of the reasons why the concept of instinct is an unsatisfactory one in ethology. The difficulties in the design and execution of experiments that will yield clear and concise results were seen to be considerably greater in ethology than at the molecular level of investigation, especially when these experiments deal with learning or animal communication.

Finally, behavior was seen as having both genetic and environmental modifying components. The precise nature and significance of this "nature versus nurture" situation will be dealt with in the following chapter.

**EXERCISES**

1. Young Mediterranean cuttlefish (*Sepia*) raised in isolation will only attack and feed upon crustacea of the genus *Mysis* (probably their normal prey in this area of the Mediterranean). Propose hypotheses in the following three categories to answer the question: Why do young *Sepia* attack mysids?

   a) An anthropomorphic hypothesis.

   b) A teleological hypothesis.

   c) An ethological hypothesis (propose also a test for this hypothesis).

2. Lorenz and Tinbergen (1937) caused the silhouette below to "fly" on a wire extending across a pen containing geese or various game birds. When the model moved across the pen to the right (as in the illustration) no particular attention was paid to it. But when it moved to the left, the birds crouched, piled upon one another in a corner of the pen, or otherwise showed alarm. Propose a hypothesis to explain these results and outline a test for your hypothesis.

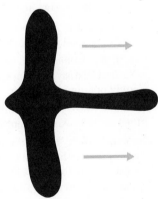

3. A mother turkey normally accepts and raises her own young with no problems. A hen turkey deafened several weeks before hatching of the eggs invariably kills all her young when they hatch. A hen turkey deafened 24 hours after hatching will raise her chicks normally. Propose a hypothesis to explain these observations and a test for this hypothesis.

4. A male and a female dove are put into adjoining cages, separated by a glass pane. At a certain period of the year, the male "displays." Following completion of the display, the female builds a nest, lays infertile eggs, and sits on them. A control female, not exposed to a male, does not exhibit this behavior.

Interpret or explain these observations. Or, in other words, what do you think this experiment demonstrates?

**SUGGESTED READINGS**

DETHIER, V., and ELIOT STELLAR, *Animal Behavior* (Englewood Cliffs, N.J.: Prentice-Hall, 1961). A good short paperback study of types of animal behavior, the genetics of some behavioral patterns, and evolution. A readable and well-illustrated text.

DILGER, WILLIAM C., "The Behavior of Lovebirds." *Scientific American*, January 1962, p. 88. An interesting case study of how behavior affects divergence in species, and thus is related to its evolutionary position.

GILLIARD, E. T., "The Evolution of Bowerbirds." *Scientific American*, August 1963, p. 38. A case study in the evolution of exceedingly complex and elaborate mating behavior. This article shows how even such activities can be adaptive for the species.

KLOPFER, PETER, and JACK P. HAILMAN, *An Introduction to Animal Behavior: Ethology's First Century* (Englewood Cliffs, N.J.: Prentice-Hall, 1967). An excellent study of animal behavior from the biological viewpoint. The book is especially good in its historical treatment of the subject.

LORENZ, KONRAD, "The Evolution of Behavior." *Scientific American*, December 1958, p. 67. An excellent article describing concisely and clearly the modern concept of the evolution of specific behavior patterns.

LORENZ, KONRAD, *King Solomon's Ring* (New York: Thomas Y. Crowell, 1952). A paperback book written by a classic investigator in the realm of animal behavior. This delightfully written and excellent book covers many topics in animal behavior.

MANNING, AUBREY, *An Introduction to Animal Behavior* (Reading, Mass.: Addison-Wesley, 1967). A good paperback introduction to ethology.

SCOTT, J. P., *Animal Behavior* (New York: Doubleday and the American Museum of Natural History). An inexpensive and highly readable description of the experimental study of animal behavior.

TINBERGEN, NIKO, "The Evolution of Behavior in Gulls." *Scientific American*, December 1960, p. 118. An excellent case study in the evolution of behavior in several species.

TINBERGEN, NIKO, *The Study of Instinct* (London: Oxford University Press, 1969). A reprinting of the original 1951 edition. This book is somewhat out of date but still good reading for the student interested in ethology.

VON FRISCH, K., "Dialects in the Language of the Bees." *Scientific American*, August 1962, p. 78. An excellent article describing a communication pattern in honeybees. Comparison of the system in closely related varieties and species shows the divergence of communication patterns due to geographic isolation.

*I have yet to see any problem, however complicated, which, when you looked at it the right way, did not become still more complicated.*

*Alderson*

No field of science, particularly at this point in human history, can long exist in complete intellectual isolation. Successful scientific hypotheses often generate highly successful technologies. A problem solved in theoretical chemistry may lead to a better glue; in biology, to better preventive medicine; in physics, to transistorized electronics and the space program. The sum total of such technological innovations is a drastically changed environment to which the organism responsible for the changes—man—must now adapt.

Along with technological plusses come serious minuses. Theoretical physics has given man nuclear weapons with which he can (and may) destroy himself. Theoretical microbiology has given us germ warfare. Theoretical biology has donated the possibility of genetic engineering, with its potential for enormous good and equally enormous bad.

Just who in a free society is responsible for the misuse of scientifically generated technologies is not clear. Is it the scientists who generate the hypotheses, the politicians who knowingly or unknowingly arrange for their misuse, or the voters who allow them to do so? The precise answer to this question, if, indeed, one is available, lies beyond the scope of this textbook. It is interesting to note, however, that while most scientists would deny their responsibility for the misuse of their ideas, the founding of a Society for Social Responsibility in Science would seem to signal a trend among scientists to assume some responsibility beyond their laboratory doors.   Thus, for example, Dr. Jonathan Beckwith, whose Harvard University research team successfully isolated and photographed a gene (Fig. 17–30), warned, in a press conference announcing the feat, of the ways in which the knowledge gained in such research might be politically misused in the future.*

In the past five years or so, certain hypotheses of animal behaviorists and workers in closely related fields (psychology, anthropology, etc.) have shown a potential for misinterpretation and resulting misuse that could have consequences as disastrous for mankind as nuclear warfare.   This "misuse potential" arises from concepts in animal behavior discussed in the preceding chapter and some to be dealt with in this one.   It is hoped that, by being exposed to this potential for misuse, the reader will better understand the concepts involved as well as attain a sufficiently broad overview of the field of behavior to see things in their proper perspective.

**23-2**
**THIS LAND IS**
**MY LAND**

As has been stressed more than once in this book, the acceptance of scientific hypotheses is often related to the times.†   Those hypotheses that do not jibe with the current trend of thinking are often ignored until their time is ripe. Thus, for example, Mendel's segregating and randomly assorting "factors" might be viewed as an idea whose time, in the mid-1860's, had not yet come.

One hypothesis which was wholly harmonious with the culture of its day was put forth to explain the fighting often observed among males of the same species during the breeding season. The reasons for this fighting seemed perfectly clear; the males were competing for a female, with the strongest claiming the prize.   The observation of such fighting was one fact among many that led Charles Darwin to his concept of "sexual selection," whereby nature allowed only the strongest to contribute to the species' future gene pool.   This concept fit in well with the chivalrous views of manhood and womanhood fashionable in the Victorian era.   And so, the concept of the female as the instigator of both aggression and sexual selection survived for many years.

In the late nineteenth century Henry Eliot Howard, an English businessman, began a detailed study of British warblers and moorhens.   An avid bird watcher, Howard spent almost thirty years carefully studying warbler behavior and making copious notes.   The result, in 1920, was a book entitled *Territory in Bird Life*.   Its message was as simple as it was refreshingly new; it is *territory*, not females, for which the male birds compete.

Slowly at first, and then with increasing rapidity, Howard's idea gained acceptance.   The aggressive behavior of other birds was observed in the fresh new light of **territoriality**, rather than femininity, as the stimulus which

---

* Hoping to play a small role in preventing such misuse, one member of Beckwith's research team has given up science in order to enter politics.
† It can be correctly pointed out, of course, that the concept of ideas having "their time" is based on whether or not they are accepted; that is, if they are accepted, the time was ripe for this acceptance, and if not, the time was not ripe. Thus the reasoning is circular.

provoked intraspecific fighting. According to the new territorial concept, the males fought for space—a tree, a meadow, a certain portion of a forest—with the winner taking a distinct and definable portion. It was the established territory, rather than any direct attribute of the male, which became the attractant that won the female.*

The basic concept of territoriality proved to have extensions beyond the class Aves (birds). On the Rio Piedras campus of the University of Puerto Rico, lizards, not squirrels, scamper through the trees and along the sidewalks. The animals are strongly territorial; the experimental introduction of one male lizard into another's territory leads to characteristic warning gestures on the part of the owner which, if unheeded, lead to combat. When more than one male lizard is kept in captivity, the cage must be large enough to allow each male to have his own territory; if the cage is too small, the loser of the fight cannot retreat out of the disputed territory to safety, and his death is the result. Invertebrates too, though less commonly, show territoriality. Male crickets, for example, fight vigorously to defend their areas against trespassers; indeed, cricket-fight matches are a popular sport in parts of the Orient. Most interesting, perhaps, is the contention of some researchers that territoriality can be demonstrated among some of man's closest primate relatives, e.g., the howler monkeys of Central America. The trespassing of one troop of howler monkeys into an area claimed by another leads to a nonviolent but deafening vocal contest which continues until the trespassers retreat. The claim that howler monkeys are territorial animals is somewhat weakened, however, by the observation that howling contests may occur even when the troops are some distance from each other. It has also been shown that the "territories" of howler monkeys are not exclusive, and that considerable overlapping occurs.

In many cases it is relatively easy to map the boundaries of the territory a particular organism considers its own simply by watching its behavior. It is far less easy, however, to understand completely the ultimate functions of territoriality. An animal expends considerable energy establishing and defending a territory, a fact which suggests that territoriality must have considerable selective value to those species exhibiting this behavior. One prevalent hypothesis proposes that territoriality serves to space out a population, and thereby helps to ensure that the available supply of food is not overexploited to the extent of jeopardizing the entire ecosystem.† But this cannot be all of the story. The spacing hypothesis nicely accounts for a hawk or eagle defending a square mile or so from being hunted over by other birds of prey, for the amount of food

---

* Speaking anthropomorphically, it is tempting to interpret this as biological verification for the linking of gold digging with femininity.

† Here is another excellent example of how attempts at brevity and conciseness in writing can lead to teleological and anthropomorphic statements. It is hoped that the reader by now understands that animals don't space out to avoid jeopardizing the ecosystem. Rather, they spread out because their ancestors did, and their ancestors were ancestors because they carved out enough of their environment to reproduce successfully.

in the area available to these animals is certainly finite. But a pair of herring gulls will defend a nesting territory of only 18 square feet or so, an area from which they certainly get no food. Here it has been suggested that the relationship among territoriality, spacing, and food supply may be an indirect one; the spacing of nests limits the size of the gull colony and thus controls the number of birds feeding in the area. This is a reasonable hypothesis when viewed from an ecologist's viewpoint, but it runs into difficulties when seen through the ethologist's looking glass. In general, seabirds do not seem to be food-limited; indeed, gulls appear to live in a superabundance of food. Most of their day is spent resting on beaches or mud flats with full bellies.

An hypothesis dealing with the functions of territoriality with which ethologists feel more comfortable comes from Tinbergen's group, which has shown that nesting territories in the black-headed gull are closely related to predation: the first occupied and most vigorously defended territories are those in areas that suffer the least predation from foxes, crows, etc. Still another advantage stemming from territoriality, but unrelated to food supply, may be the ensuring of freedom from disturbance during mating pair formation.

There is one basic fact that research on territoriality has established: territory is different things to different species. For example, as previously indicated, a hawk or eagle defends a rather wide area in which it does all its feeding. Gulls, on the other hand, show no territoriality in feeding, and it is possible that what has been interpreted as territoriality in some gulls may be little more than nest defense, especially in those species in which the nesting "territory" is only two feet or so in diameter.

## 23-3 AGONISTIC BEHAVIOR AND AGGRESSION

Ethologist Aubrey Manning of the University of Edinburgh in Scotland points out that "the first essential for a territorial animal is that it be aggressive towards others of its kind." The defense of a territory can be accomplished only if the defender shows **aggression**—i.e., initiates or gives signs of initiating an attack—against any individual entering territory claimed by the defender. Note here an almost complete reversal in the use of the term aggression in ethology in comparison to its use in international conflict. In the latter case, the nation violating the territory of another is referred to as the aggressor. On the other hand, when the invaded nation attacks the trespassing nation's forces, the action is called defensive, not aggressive. As will be seen shortly, this differing use of the same term is but one of several difficulties encountered when we move from considerations of aggression in nonhuman animals to aggression in man.

Clearly the study of aggressive behavior is one which must be approached with Professor Schein's warning (see the beginning of Section 22–10) firmly in mind. Merely to focus on the behavior patterns of an aggressive organism, without due consideration of the results of this behavior on both the aggressor and the animal which is the target of the aggression, is not sufficient.

Actually, there is a spectrum of behavior ranging in intensity from overt attack at one end of the scale to overt fleeing at the other. This spectrum of

FIG. 23–1 Agonistic behavior in mice. As a result of many encounters, the mouse at left has assumed a dominant status over the one at right, which adopts a characteristic defense posture of holding out the forefeet and moving only when attacked.

behavior is termed **agonistic behavior.** All displays of agonistic behavior (e.g., the raised and compressed body threat stance of a territorial lizard) are combinations of motivations to attack and to flee, in various absolute and relative strengths (see Fig. 23–1).

Several years of ethological research on agonistic behavior have established certain "facts" concerning it. For example, the claim has been put forth that the production and release into the bloodstream of certain hormones is associated with aggressive behavior.* Time is also often a factor; only at certain periods, such as the mating season, do some animal species show agonistic behavior. Finally, it has been established that aggression may be triggered by certain external stimuli. The male three-spined stickleback, for example, reacts violently to the visual stimulus of red on the underside of a rival male. That it is the color to which the animal reacts and not something else can be shown by experimentation. If presented with a crude model of a rival male with a red underside, the male attacks viciously. One case has even been reported in which males attempted to attack British mail trucks (which are red) driving by the window in which the aquaria containing the fish were kept. A more lifelike model, without the red underside, is not attacked. In parakeets and flickers, certain colorations or markings distinguish males from females. If the markings are changed experimentally, the males will attack their own mates (see Fig. 23–2).

Also postulated, but far less certain, is the existence of certain "aggression centers" in the brain which, when stimulated, initiate and control aggressive behavior. Supporting this "aggression center" hypothesis is the observation that electrodes implanted into certain regions of the brain release violently

---

* While there is little question that the release of certain hormones is associated with agonistic behavior, it *is* still possible to challenge the many cause-and-effect hypotheses stemming from the consequences of increased hormone output, and some ethologists have done so.

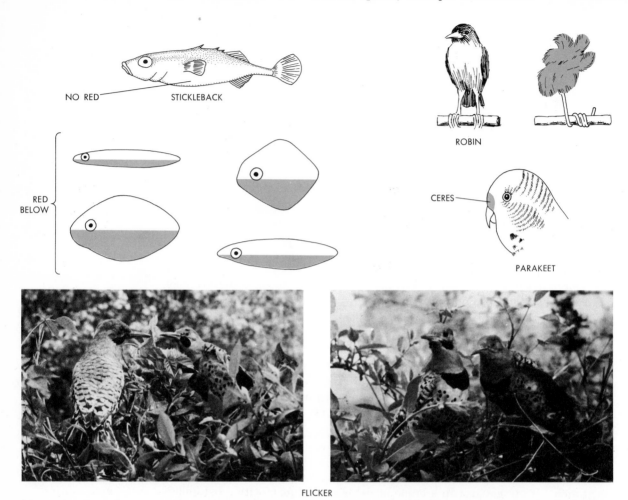

FIG. 23–2  Four examples of ''releaser'' stimuli.  Top left: The crude models of stickleback fish painted red on the underside are threatened by a male stickleback, while the true male at top with no red is ignored.  Top right: The robin will ignore an immature male without the characteristic red breast, but may attack a tuft of red feathers.  Middle right: If the characteristic color of the female parakeet's ceres is changed, her mate attacks her as if she were a rival male.  Bottom: If the black spot or ''moustache'' of the male flicker (*Coleoptus aurates*) is painted on his mate (as shown at left), he attacks her as he would a rival male.  When it is removed, he accepts her as his mate again. (Stickleback models after N. Tinbergen, *The Study of Instinct.*  London and New York: Oxford University Press, 1951.  Posed model photos courtesy Charles Tarleton, Wesleyan University.)

aggressive behavior in normally nonaggressive animals when a mild electric current is applied.  As a result of such experiments on cats, Dr. John P. Flynn of Yale University's School of Medicine believes that internal conditions, by themselves, are sufficient to produce aggressive behavior.  But psychologist R. Plotnick and neurophysiologist José M. R. Delgado, of the same institution,

FIG. 23–3   Normally placid monkey (left) shows aggressive behavior (right) when stimulated through electrodes implanted in the brain. (note thick gloves on handler's hand). (Photos courtesy Dr. José M. R. Delgado, Yale University School of Medicine.)

FIG. 23–4   José Delgado of Yale University controls a normally aggressive bull by radio transmission of a stimulus to electrodes in the animal's brain. (Photos courtesy Dr. José M. R. Delgado, Yale University School of Medicine.)

have noted in their work with rhesus monkeys (Fig. 23–3) that aggression elicited by electrode implantation and stimulation occurs *after* the stimulation, not during it. A hypothesis proposing that brain stimulation is the direct cause of aggression would predict no such delay. The contradictory results seem to suggest that the monkeys may perhaps have been hostile because they connected the stimulus with a prior disagreeable experience associated with reward-punishment training.

    It should also be pointed out that aggressive behavior can be halted as well as initiated by electrode implantation and stimulation (see Fig. 23–4). Quite recently (1970), Princeton University psychologist B. G. Hoebel has shown similar aggression initiation and suppression using chemicals applied to a specific region of the rat brain's lateral hypothalamus. Rats which normally kill mice ceased to do so when the chemical methyl atropine was applied. Conversely, rats which normally were peaceful became killers when either of the chemicals carbachol or neostigmine was applied. Carbachol is known to mimic the action of acetylcholine (see Section 13-8), normally broken down by cholinesterase. But cholinesterase is specific to its acetycholine substrate, and does not attack carbachol. Neostigmine blocks the action of cholinesterase upon acetylcholine. In both cases, the resulting high concentration of either its mimic or acetylcholine itself leads to the killing response. Atropine, on the other hand, seems to block the killing response by interfering with the action of acetylcholine. Thus, in this case, the difference between aggression and nonaggression is seen in neurophysiological terms, i.e., the relative amounts of acetycholine and cholinesterase within the brain of the rat. The social significance of such interesting findings is self-evident, and Dr. Hoebel states that "if a similar kill center can be identified in humans, it might be possible to cure pathological aggression in man." The aforementioned doubts concerning the existence of such "aggression centers" still remain, however.

Since the appearance of agonistic behavior in animals is fairly widespread, there must obviously be some selective value to such behavior. In the case of species exhibiting territoriality, it is obviously necessary for defense. Thus, in territorial species, agonistic behavior makes territoriality possible. In turn, as has been seen, territoriality may aid in spacing animals so as to prevent over-exploitation of the environment.

In some species, the relationship of agonistic behavior to territory is a remarkably close and consistent one. In the stickleback, size and strength of the fighting males is far less important than is the factor of which of the two fish invaded the other's territory. Indeed, it seems possible to show a distinct relationship between proximity to a rival's nest and the number of battles "won" or "lost" (see Fig. 23-5).

However, while agonistic behavior may at times be closely linked to territoriality, it is by no means inseparably so. Many animal species are not territorial yet exhibit agonistic behavior and *vice versa*. In certain birds, e.g., chickens, so-called "**peck orders**" are found (see Fig. 23-6). The members of a flock compete to establish a sort of class system, in which those higher in the social register get first choice of food, space, mates, etc. Once established, however, peck orders actually serve to reduce conflict, and attempts on the part of an animal to improve its standing in the order are relatively rare. Peck orders are known in primates, also, where they are usually referred to as **dominance hierarchies.** The number one or dominant male of a baboon or rhesus monkey troop is easy to spot, not only by his own behavior but by the differing degrees of "respect" shown him by animals lower down in the social order. If he so desires, the dominant male is the one who drinks first at the water hole, who

FIG. 23–5    An experiment showing a relationship between types of behavior and territory.    Male stickleback **b**, "owner" of territory **B**, is threatened by male **a** when brought into territory **A**.    When the situation is reversed, male **a** is threatened by male **b**.

FIG. 23–6    "Peck order" or dominance hierarchy in chickens.    Once the hierarchy is established, physical conflict is minimized.    Dominant hen A has just driven bottom-ranking hen E away from the food.    While A is gone, B moves in and keeps C and D away by pecks and threats.    When A returns, B will give way.

samples new food first, and who indicates when it is time for the troop to move to the safety of its sleeping quarters for the night.

If aggression at times serves a useful purpose, clearly at other times it does not. In Puerto Rico and much of Latin America, cocks have been selected for centuries for their fighting ability. The result is a fantastically aggressive animal which will fight to the death. The birds are difficult to breed, for the females are also aggressive and much time and energy is wasted in combats. In this case, agonistic behavior is almost 100% aggression, with little or no passiveness shown by animals involved in a fight.

Such is not the case in nature. Here, the balance is often swung in the other direction, with only a small proportion of the sequence of actions involved in agonistic behavior being aggressive. Equally significant is the existence of definite passive or "surrender" behavioral patterns. At times, such behavior is simply escape; the defeated animal runs away. In other cases, the adoption of a certain stance or posture turns off aggression in the rival, and the fighting ceases. More often than not, the adoption of a "threat posture" on the part of one animal is enough to cause another to back off or retreat, and thus no actual fighting takes place.

**23-4
AGGRESSION
IN MAN**

The North American frog, *Rana pipiens*, becomes dormant in winter by burying itself in the mud at the bottom of a pond or lake. Since movement is at a minimum during dormancy, the frog is able to survive by cutaneous (i.e., through its skin) respiration alone.

*Rana pipiens'* entry into dormancy seems to be dependent on temperature rather than season. If subjected in the laboratory to a gradually lowering temperature by being placed in a beaker surrounded by cracked ice and water, the frog shows a characteristic predormancy behavioral response. The animal crouches and makes movements which would cover it with mud were it in a natural setting.

In Puerto Rico, where the temperature rarely falls below 65–70°F, the native frogs never become dormant. Yet, if experimentally exposed to a lowering temperature, at least one species shows predormancy behavior. The demonstration of this behavior by the Puerto Rican frog has been attributed to the fact that, geologically speaking, Puerto Rico once had a temperate rather than a tropical climate. Thus the ancestors of the Puerto Rican frog became dormant during winter and, since there is no selective disadvantage in the retention of this unused behavior potential by its descendants, it is possible to conclude that a genetic basis for this behavior is transmitted to succeeding generations of tropical frogs.

Like hibernation in frogs, aggressive behavior seems definitely to have a genetic basis in many lower forms of animal life. But does the same situation hold true for man? There is some evidence, for example, that *Australopithecus africanus*, one of our most primitive "ape-man" ancestors, killed others of his own species. Indeed, some scientists have even suggested that it was the evolution of this behavioral trait that started man along the evolutionary path to his present dominant status over all other forms of life.

*Does* man fight and kill his own kind because of an innate tendency to do so? Or is his aggressiveness purely the result of past or present environmental influences? The state of thought existing in ethology and such related fields as psychology and anthropology can perhaps best be depicted by the following two statements:

*There can not be any doubt, in the opinion of any biologically minded scientist, that . . . aggression is in man just as much a spontaneous instinctive drive as most other higher drives.*

*Konrad Lorenz*

*. . . in the course of human evolution the power of instinctual drive is gradually withered away, till man has virtually lost all his instincts. If there remains a residue of instinct in man, they are, possibly, the automatic reaction to a loud noise, and in the remaining instances to a sudden withdrawal of support; for the rest, man has no instincts . . . . Evil is not inherent in human nature, it is learned. . . aggressiveness is taught, as are the forms of violence which human beings exhibit.*

*M. F. Ashley Montagu*

Certainly these two quotations illustrate a very wide gap in thinking concerning the origin of aggression in *Homo sapiens*. It is not surprising that it is a matter of much interest and concern which, if either, of these two schools of thought is correct. War seems always to have been part and parcel of man's heritage, and he stands now at a point in his history where his next great war will very likely be his last.

If aggressiveness in man is a highly unacceptable form of behavior in today's society, then clearly, like a disease, we should want to prevent it. But disease control is most effective when the causes for the disease are understood. One who believes man's aggressiveness toward his fellow man to be innate may well recommend a quite different treatment for the condition than one who believes aggression to be entirely the result of environmental influences. So, indeed, do the two men just quoted differ in their approach to the problem. Lorenz, believing aggression to be an innate drive which must be expressed, recommends athletic events as a specific and harmless outlet for this aggressive drive. Montagu, on the other hand, would concentrate more on finding the proper physical and cultural environment for mankind, an environment in which aggressive behavior would not be learned.

British anthropologist Geoffrey Gorer points out that the Latin proverb, *homo homini lupus*—man is a wolf to man—has been taken over by virtually every society which derives its customs, laws, or language from ancient Rome. Actually, this proverb is grossly unfair to wolves. More appropriate, ethologically, would be *homo homini rattus*—man is a rat to man. Rats do occasionally kill their own kind.*  According to Lorenz, rats are quite merciless killers of members of alien packs.  Certainly there are close similarities here to man.  Man, too, lives in "packs" or societies.  Killing of others within the pack is generally considered immoral and is subject to punishment, while killing members of other packs may not only be condoned but actually glorified.

Gorer goes on to suggest that the nation-state may be the last successful human invention for extending the size of the pack, within which killing is classified as murder.  In the past 4000 years a number of religions have been founded which would include all believers inside the pack.  However, no religion has commanded worldwide allegiance, and regularly the outcast, infidel, untouchable, or heretic has been humiliated, tortured, or burned at the stake with complete assurance of self-righteousness on the part of the believer. Buddha, Jesus Christ, and Mohammed, among others, strove to achieve a worldwide brotherhood of man, but man has thus far failed to develop the institutions these leaders envisioned, institutions which can include the enemy and the nonbeliever and provide them with the protection automatically extended to those wholly within the pack.

The establishment of nonreligious ideologies such as democracy, socialism, communism, or the United Nations has to date proven no more successful in protecting the outsider from the horrible results of righteous anger.  Indeed, this century has seen the rise of perhaps the most sinister rat pack ideology of all, in which full human status is denied to those who do not share a particular ancestry, skin color, advanced technology, etc.  Facism, Nazism, white or black supremacy —all justify hatred and contempt for those outside the pack, and recent history shows how very easily such hatred and contempt can develop into humiliation, torture, and killing.  Here we leave the rat behind; as ethologist Niko Tinbergen points out, only man is a mass murderer.

But, again, why?  Tinbergen, a coworker of Lorenz and now Professor of Animal Behavior at the University of Oxford in England, sides with his colleague. Tinbergen considers the hypothesis proposing that man still carries with him the animal heritage of group territoriality to be most likely the correct one.  He sees man as a social ape who found it selectively advantageous to turn carnivore.  In a 1968 speech, Tinbergen stated that "Ethologists tend to believe that we still carry with us a number of behavioral characteristics of our animal ancestors which cannot be eliminated by different ways of upbringing, and that group territorialism is one of these ancestral characters."  Clearly, in the "nature

---

* While falling far short of man's record, more animal species kill their conspecifics than is popularly believed.  In dogs, for example, aggressive encounters may go too far and result in death for one or both of the protagonists.  Crabs sometimes kill other crabs' young for food, and gulls often kill the young of others, though seemingly not for food. Cases of cannibalism among conspecifics of the same age have been reported in owls, and killing occurs among bees when they are invaded by members of other hives.  Finally, stressing due to overcrowding leads lemmings in the wild to kill conspecifics and causes the same effect in species which do not normally behave in this manner.  This last point will be dealt with more thoroughly later in this chapter.

versus nurture" controversy, Tinbergen seems here to have come down squarely on the side of nature.

With the last quoted statement, Tinbergen also makes plain his feeling that the majority of ethologists agree with Lorenz. A rough counting of ethologists' noses casts some doubt on this supposition, however. Indeed, despite the close parallels he sees between rat packs and man packs, Gorer states unequivocally that "Man has no 'killer instinct'—he merely lacks inhibition." Ethologist J. P. Scott of Bowling Green State University states bluntly that "the physiological evidence is against Lorenz's notion of the spontaneity of aggression and, indeed, it is hard to imagine how natural selection would lead to the development of a mechanism of continuous internal accumulation of energy which could unnecessarily put an animal into danger." Scott maintains that the weight of evidence indicates aggression is produced by an internal mechanism that is stimulated by external influences. While he admits that the hypothalamus may magnify and maintain the internal aggression mechanism, Scott denies that it initiates the mechanism's action.

Scott goes on to make another important point. He writes that "If Lorenz is right, then man can never lead a happy, peaceful existence, but must continually be sublimating the spontaneous 'drive' which accumulates within him. If the physiologists are correct, then it is theoretically possible for man to lead a happy and peaceful existence provided he is not continually stimulated to violence." Supporting Scott's pessimistic interpretation of Lorenz is Tinbergen's statement that "Lorenz, in my opinion, is right in claiming that elimination, through education, of the internal urge to fight will turn out to be very difficult, if not impossible." In other words, not only is nature powerful, but *nurture may be powerless to stop it!*

Others, however, are not so sure. Indeed, at a 1968 conference on aggressive behavior in animals held in Milan, Italy, the only universal agreement to be found among the one hundred or so biologists (representing fourteen nations) attending was that the concept of "aggressive behavior" is poorly defined and what passes for aggression differs markedly from species to species. For example, S. A. Barnett of the University of Glasgow in Scotland pointed out that the term aggressive behavior tends to lump together legal and political aspects of war, crimes against human beings, and the social behavior of animals. Thus aggressive behavior has been approached from the standpoint of human ethical evaluations rather than objective analyses. Barnett pointed out that, when two male wild Norwegian rats meet, a pattern of behavior characterized by an arched back and straight legs, with the flank turned toward the "opponent," occurs. Barnett finds it quite difficult to decide whether this behavior reflects aggression or amicability!

The Milan conference on aggression in animals also revealed a general consensus of opinion that fairly drastic measures are often necessary to induce aggression in animals. For example, Dr. Pierre Karli of the Institute for Medical Biology in Strasbourg, France, reported failure to induce a killing response in nonkiller rats, even by stimulation of those areas of the brain believed to be associated with aggressive "instincts." As was pointed out earlier, in natural "killer" rats, stimulation of the lateral hypothalamus of the brain does inhibit the killing behavior, a fact which led to the proposal of the existence of the aforementioned "aggression centers." But the ablation or destruction of the lateral hypothalamus of nonkillers did not provoke a killer reflex. Nor did destruction of the frontal lobes, long thought to act as inhibitors of the killer rat's murderous impulses. Only cutting the nerves ascending from the nose to the olfactory region of the brain induced a killing response in natural nonkiller rats. Even then, the killing behavior pattern was random biting which eventually led to the death of the victim rather than the swift, well directed kill of the natural killer. Indeed, starving, nonkiller rats would ravenously devour mice killed for them and placed in the cage. The same animals, however, would starve to death with a living mouse in the cage with them, although they might easily have killed and eaten it.

The general consensus of the biologists meeting at Milan appeared to be that if aggression was, indeed, innate it was awfully difficult to arouse. It was further agreed that aggressive behavior—or what passes for it—varies markedly betweeen different organisms, and extrapolations from one species to another may well be invalid. Ethologist P. F. Klopfer has suggested that the dilemma concerning aggression comes from our conceiving of it as a noun, and thus as a distinct entity in itself with an equally distinct causation. But such is obviously not the case; behavior which would clearly be labeled as aggressive can stem from several different emotional states, e.g., fear, rivalry, hunger, and so on.

Many ethologists believe that the concept of human aggression as innate is not only scientifically untenable but also potentially dangerous. Like the Judeo-Christian concept of original sin, which it closely resembles,* the concept of innate aggressiveness provides a simple excuse for our species' bad behavior. In turn, this belief might lead to inaction in efforts to design an environment conducive to promoting the best and suppressing the worst aspects of human behavior. On the other hand, if, as J. P. Scott and others maintain, human conflict results from defensive behavior and not from predation, lack of aggressive outlets will not, as Lorenz maintains, cause emotional damage. As Scott puts it: "This leads us to believe that we can work toward an essentially nonviolent world. We can no longer excuse human violence on the basis of our ancestry."

**23–5**
**THE DEVELOPMENT**
**OF BEHAVIOR**

It is necessary now to return one final time to the controversy over innate versus learned behavior (or "nature versus nurture"). It is essential to do so not only to put the controversy in its proper contemporary perspective as far as ethology is concerned, but also because of its obvious importance to the vital issues raised in the preceding and following sections.

The concept of the innateness of behavior, while not original with him, has perhaps been most succinctly stated by Konrad Lorenz. As his "psycho-

---

* "But I see another law in my members, warring against the law of my mind, and bringing me into captivity to the law of sin which is in my members." Romans 7:23.

hydraulic" model nicely illustrates, Lorenz visualizes the accumulation of energy for a specific innate act in a region of the brain specific for the control of that act. The act is not continuously performed, however, because it is blocked or inhibited. Only the appearance of specific stimulus patterns from the environment (e.g., the appearance of a fly in front of a hungry jumping spider, or the red belly of a rival stickleback male) causes the innate releasing mechanism to remove the inhibitor and trigger the outflow of motor impulses from the instinctive center to the muscles appropriate for that particular "innate" behavioral response.

What major criteria must be met by a behavioral action if it is to meet the requirements of the "Lorenzian innateness" hypothesis? First, the behavior must be stereotyped and constant in form. Second, it must be characteristic of the species. Third, it must appear in animals raised in isolation from others. Fourth, it must appear fully formed in animals prevented from practicing it. The reader will recall several examples of behavior (e.g., web spinning in *Araneus diadematus* Cl.) which meet all of these criteria.

But there are yet more examples. Domestic chicks, for instance, characteristically peck at objects, including food grains, soon after hatching. This behavior, like that of the jumping spider, can be broken down into highly stereotyped components—head lunging, bill opening and closing, and swallowing. This pecking behavior is stereotyped, characteristic of the species, appears in isolated chicks, is present at the time of hatching, and seems to appear without specific practice. Clearly, the Lorenzian criteria for innateness of pecking behavior are adequately met.

But *is* pecking innate? In 1932, Z. Y. Kuo showed that the three-day-old chick embryo's head is passively moved up and down by the heartbeat. The head is also rhythymically touched by the yolk sac, which is moved mechanically by amnion contractions synchronized with the heart movements. At four days, the head bends *actively* in response to this touch. The bill begins to open and close. At about eight or nine days, swallowing of fluid forced into the throat by the bill and head movements occurs. By the twelfth day, a sequence of head movement, bill opening, and swallowing has been well established. Are these embryonic movements precursors of postembryonic pecking movements? Most certainly, as a result of these observations, the "innateness" of chick pecking must be viewed in a different light. Several alternative interpretations of the embryonic development of behavior (in this case, pecking) are now possible. A whole new field, that of the developmental biology of behavior, is opened up. Despite the fact that Kuo's experiments were performed several years ago, this is an area which has yet to be adequately explored.*

---

* Kuo's papers were immediately challenged. It was claimed that the petroleum jelly he used to make the inner shell membrane transparent halted gas exchanges across the membrane, and that the reactions Kuo reported were the result of this halt. A fairly sizable bibliography on the subject of chick embryonic behavior has been prepared by Dr. Viktor Hamburger of Washington University in St. Louis.

The pecking behavior of chicks is not the only example of behavior which at first seemed obviously innate and later less obviously so. Nest building and retrieving of young to the nest after they have been removed is also an example of behavior meeting the four requirements of the Lorenzian innateness hypothesis; rats raised in isolation will still perform these functions equally well. However, if isolated rats are raised in cages where the floor is of netting (so that the feces drop down out of reach) and the food is powdered (so that no pellets are available for manipulation), normal nest building and retrieval of young does *not* occur, presumably because the adults have had no opportunity to practice manipulation of objects. The nesting material is left scattered all over the floor of the cage and the young are simply moved at random from one place to another, rather than to any one particular nesting site.

The results of such experiments have many ramifications, but in particular they force us to take a long hard look at the classical isolation experiments. As D. S. Lehrman of Rutgers University points out, "an animal raised in isolation from fellow-members of his species *is not necessarily isolated from the effect of processes and events which contribute to the development of any particular behavior pattern.* The important question is not 'Is the animal isolated?' but '*From what is the animal isolated?*' "

Thus what has been concluded from isolation experiments in the past is rather similar to what Senebier concluded from his experiments on submerged leaves (see Section 9–8). Noting that no oxygen was evolved in the absence of carbon dioxide, he erroneously concluded that the carbon dioxide was the source of the evolved oxygen. In truth, the carbon dioxide was but one of several limiting factors. So it is with isolation experiments. They may well provide negative indications that certain environmental factors are not, directly at least, involved in the origin of a particular behavior pattern. But it lies beyond the isolation experiment's nature to provide positive indication that behavior is "innate" or, indeed, any information at all about what the process of behavioral development is composed of. Even behavior which seems to be most obviously innate may well be partly learned, since learning may emerge as a factor in behavior at the earliest of embryonic stages.

Indeed, it may well be that what is innate or inherited is not simply a matter of genetics. In other words, genes may not be the only factors involved in inheritance. For example, Dr. Roger Williams, a biochemist from the University of Texas, has done some studies on "individuality." He finds a hypothesis proposing genetic bases for individual differences sadly lacking, even in "lower" animals. For example, Dr. Williams found that rats inbred for 101 generations (a degree of inbreeding which should make their genetic makeup all but identical) still varied enormously in their behavioral patterns—and even in the biochemical composition of their urine, though given identical diets.

Casting about for a better source of "identicalness," Dr. Williams selected the nine-banded armadillo, *Dasypus novemcinctus*. This animal exhibits an unusual embryological development. The fertilized egg begins cleavage and undergoes implantation quite normally, but then produces four primordial buds. These buds are formed in two stages and each will develop into a baby armadillo. Thus this animal always produces quadruplets, and since each is a descendant of the original fertilized egg, each contain identical genes. Yet, in 20 different features measured by Williams and Dr. Eleanor Shorrs (such as individual organ weight and biochemical characteristics), all varied widely within any given quadruplet set—and some varied as much as 140-fold.

If genetic differences are not the cause of this variation, what is? The environment? Williams hypothesizes that there may exist currently undetermined factors, *aside from genes and the environment*, that are involved in the intricate processes of cellular differentiation and which may affect the extent to which each of the numerous types of differentiated cells proliferates. This hypothesis would account for the fact that one armadillo could have one organ, such as a liver, much larger than that of its genetically identical littermates.

Though it is still too early to judge, the potential implications of the armadillo results are rather profound. In essence, they seem to indicate that genes are not necessarily all-important in inheritance—a fairly revolutionary notion. Many deep-seated and important characters of man, such as strength, fertility, body form, and intelligence, vary widely and continuously, even within one race. Obviously single genes fail to account for these variations, but there has been a tendency to assume that multiple-gene inheritance can do so. But in accounting for the differences between twin armadillo littermates, Williams believes that the four primordial buds that later develop into the baby armadillos receive varying amounts of these undetermined factors. If there do, indeed, exist factors outside of the genes which might control their expression, and if these factors are present in different cells in amounts wholly dependent, say, on the fairly random way that a cell's cytological contents are distributed at division, then the aforementioned human differences can be accounted for much more easily. The reader will recall that, as far as molecular biologists are concerned, factors with properties similar to those suggested by Williams, i.e., inducers and repressors, already exist (see Chapter 18).

Two interesting implications of Williams' hypothesis can be mentioned. For one, it would seem that no matter how knowledgeable about microbial genetics geneticists become—and single-celled organisms such as *E. coli* (which do not differentiate as do multicellular forms) are the main source of genetic information—we could still remain almost totally ignorant of how some of the most fundamental characteristics of mammals, for example, are inherited. Williams' hypothesis, if valid, also overthrows an assumption that for years was a mainstay of behavioral "nature-versus-nurture" experiments: that identical twins, because they have identical genes, must therefore have identical inheritance. Thus the countless numbers of identical-twin studies performed over the past decades may very well have been built upon an invalid foundation.

In summary, then, there is now a strong tendency in ethology to regard the old controversy over innate versus learned behavior as being no longer a fruitful one to pursue. Nor is it considered a worthwhile goal to establish "how much" of a particular behavioral sequence is innate and "how much" is learned. Rather, ethologists now recognize that the effects of learning and genetically determined differences in structural factors differ not only from component to component of the behavioral pattern, *but also from developmental stage to developmental stage.* Attention is therefore more apt to be directed toward analysis of the characteristics of each developmental stage and of the transition from one stage to the next. As Lehrman states it: "The interaction out of which the organism develops is *not* one, as is so often said, between heredity and environment. It is between organism and environment! And the *organism* is different at each different stage of its development."

In their systematic challenging of the concept of innateness as viewed historically in their own field, ethologists such as Klopfer are also challenging the concept of the gene as the repository of data or "blueprint" from which the organism is constructed. Rather, their work suggests that the gene is an information-generating device which exploits the predictable and ordered nature of its environment, i.e., which feeds upon negative entropy. This view fits well with the model of gene action advanced by Jacob and Monod (see Section 18-11). In their study of insect development, H. A. Schneiderman and L. I. Gilbert (1964) have shown that hormones whose synthesis can be traced ultimately to the action of particular segments of the DNA helix activate genetic transcription at other portions of the helix. As was seen in Chapter 18, the transcription products, in turn, may further exert a feedback and regulatory effect on development.

There are parallel situations at the cultural level. In discussing human development, E. Erikson (1968) writes: "The human infant is born preadapted to an average expectable environment. Man's ecology demands constant and natural historical and technological readjustment which makes it at once obvious that only a perpetual, if only ever so imperceptible, restructuring of tradition can safeguard for each new generation of infants anything approaching an average expectability of environment." Thus human behavior, as is the case with development of the embryo, is seen as the outcome of epigenetic rather than preformational processes. Epigenetic development, in turn, assures greater developmental stability, since an epigenetic system is buffered and self-correcting at several points. Thus, as with the case of aggression, behavior is, in Klopfer's terms, a *process* not a *noun*, and the hope of finding an instinct on a chromosome is illusory.

We can conclude this section by asking, then, what *is* inherited? Some investigators have gone so far as to state that only the zygote is inherited, or that heredity is only a stage of development. But it is neither necessary nor fruitful to provide a rigorous definition of heredity here. Rather, pragmatism must be ethology's guide. As Lehrman cogently points out, "to say a behavior pattern is inherited throws no light on its *development* except for the purely negative implications that *certain types* of learning are not directly involved. Dwarfism in the mouse, nest-building in the rat, pecking in the chick, and the 'zig-zig dance' of the stickleback's courtship are all 'inherited' in the sense and by the criteria used by Lorenz. But they are not by any means phenomena of a common type, nor do they arise through the same kinds of developmental processes. To lump them together under the rubric of 'inherited' or 'innate' characteristics serves to block the investigation of their origin just at the point where it should leap forward in meaningfulness."

The "peck order" shown by certain animal communities is based on the "rights" of certain individuals to be aggressive toward others. The dominance hierarchy of a baboon troop, for example, usually has a dominant male and three or so subordinates who comprise a sort of central governing body within the troop. Outside this central governing body, the dominance hierarchy continues further, with young males approaching prime usually standing higher in the order than females and aging males. The females, in turn, stand higher than the young juveniles and infants.

It would seem obvious that a social structure built upon the absolute right of aggressive dominance over subordinates could hardly be a peaceful one. Yet for animals having societies based on peck orders, peace generally rules supreme. Furthermore, it would seem obvious that the overthrow of his superior by a subordinate could occur only by violent means. Yet this, too, proves not to be the case. Rarely, for example, is a dominant male deposed by a major battle; instead, he falls from power gradually as he ages and fails to meet routine challenges and tests of his ability to carry out his responsibilities. Thus studies of baboon troops over a period of several years reveal a gradually changing structure, with dominant males being replaced slowly by younger animals and they, in turn, being replaced by those still younger. The result is a strong and continuing social order allowing high efficiency in ensuring adequate food for all and maximum protection for the weaker from predators.

However, one might observe a baboon troop for a long time without detecting the peck-order framework on which it is constructed. The reason for this is that in nature the animals forage widely for food and there is generally enough for all. Thus the competitive situations necessary to demonstrate dominance and subordination do not often occur. Rarely, perhaps, only one or two females may be in estrus (i.e., receptive for mating), in which case the males may compete for her. Or an ethologist, wishing to study the peck order, may feed the troop by scattering grain in a small area or, perhaps, by throwing it to only one animal. Under these artificially imposed conditions the troop must condense into a smaller area, and chances for contact between individual animals are greatly enhanced. Though usually mere threats are enough to prevent large-scale violence, fights under such conditions can and do occur.

Thus population density, the number of individual organisms per unit of space, definitely affects behavior. Precisely *how* it does so has recently been the object of much research, research involving many different species of organisms. With overpopulation clearly the most serious problem facing mankind, the findings of this research have obvious significance.

One of the earliest studies of this type was carried out by John B. Calhoun of Rockefeller University in New York. Calhoun first worked outdoors with the wild Norway rat. He confined a population in a quarter-acre enclosure, where the animals had no escape from the behavioral consequences of population density increase. The animals were spared, however, the normally accompanying overpopulation conditions of starvation and disease, for they were given an abundance of food and places to nest, in addition to being protected from predation. Under these "ideal" conditions, the observed reproductive rate predicted an adult population of 5000 individuals. In actuality, it numbered 150! Investigation revealed an extremely high infant mortality rate; even with only 150 adults in the enclosure, the stress of enforced social interaction led to disruption of maternal behavior. The result was death for most of the young.

Calhoun later moved his study inside and performed more sophisticated investigations dealing with the effects of population density on behavior. Again, infant mortality climbed, with levels of from 80 to 96% not uncommon. Females stopped building nests for their young (see Fig. 23–7); eating habits were changed; normally peaceful reproductive behavior patterns were disrupted and fights often resulted. Sexual deviations became common, as did cannibalism, total social disorientation, and high adult mortality rates. A startling number of these deaths occurred in females as a result of either pregnancy or giving birth.

Results such as these are troublesome, for they seem uncomfortably close to the human situation today. In heavily overpopulated Latin America, for example, despite the fact that most such deaths undoubtedly go unreported, pregnancy and childbirth deaths are high. Chile, for example, has 271.9 deaths per 100,000 births, as opposed to Sweden's 11.3. Calhoun concludes a 1962 *Scientific American* report of his work by stating: "It is obvious that the behavioral repertory with which the Norway rat has emerged from the trials of evolution and domestication must break down under the social pressures generated by population density. In time, refinement of experimental procedures and of the interpretation of these studies may advance our understanding to the making of value judgments about analogous problems confronting the human species."

Just how valid *are* extrapolations of such results to the human situation? It is difficult to judge. The results of Calhoun's studies concerning the effects of high population density on behavior are admirably supported by studies of other species both higher and lower on the evolutionary scale than the Norway rat. Most important, they seem to hold true for primate societies. When primate species normally peaceful in the wild are kept under high-population-density conditions, violence leading to maiming and death becomes quite common. Under such conditions, animals of all ranks in the peck order are thrown into

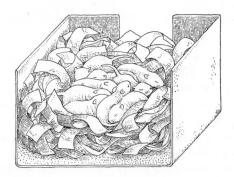

FIG. 23–7   Normal (left) and abnormal (right) rat nest-building behavior. The latter appears to be caused by disturbance of the mother's normal maternal behavior patterns by high population density pressures. The infant mortality rate may run as high as 96%. (From John B. Calhoun, ''Population Density and Social Pathology.'' *Scientific American*, February 1962. Copyright © 1962 by Scientific American, Inc.  All rights reserved.)

close proximity, and there is no escape.  Thus, instead of a situation in which, say, dominant male baboons cooperate in leading and protecting the troop, the captive animals find themselves under a tyrannical dictator.  Now the hierarchy is based on fear; subordinates direct their aggression toward animals of the next lower peck-order status, and a chain reaction of violence results.

Again, the sticky question: can we extrapolate to man? *Is* there something significant about the similarity between the abuse in captivity of his subordinates by a male baboon and the treatment of an economically poor black person by his slightly less poor white neighbor, who in turn feels put upon by others still higher on the economic ladder? *Is* there a relationship between the abuse of infant monkeys by their mothers when kept in crowded conditions and the increase in the "battered baby syndrome" (child beating and torture) reported in areas of high human population density?

It can be truthfully said that we simply do not know.  After all, Calhoun's rats, though overcrowded, were relatively "wealthy," being kept well supplied with food and water.  In man, overcrowding tends to be associated with poverty and a poor education.  If nothing else, the example points out neatly how fallible simple-appearing cause-effect relationships may often be.  Thus some scientists, such as molecular geneticist and Nobel laureate Joshua Lederberg, urge more caution in extrapolation from crowding experiments in lower animals to man.  Yet it seems certain that a large majority of scientists closest to the higher levels of biological investigation would agree with S. L. Andreski that limitation of the growth of the human population, combined with a determined attempt to bring the present majority of our population out of its present condition of misery and despair, offers the best and perhaps the only hope of abolishing war.

The opening paragraph of a book by Professor Paul R. and Ann H. Ehrlich of Stanford University states:

*The explosive growth of the human population is the most significant terrestrial event of the past million millennia.  Three and one-half billion people now inhabit the Earth, and every year this number increases by 70 million.  Armed with weapons as diverse as thermonuclear bombs and DDT this mass of humanity now threatens to destroy most of the life on the planet.  Mankind itself may stand on the brink of extinction: in its death throes it could take with it most of the other passengers on the Spaceship Earth.  No geological event in a billion years—not the emergence of mighty mountain ranges, nor the submergence of entire subcontinents, nor the occurrence of periodic glacial ages—has posed a threat to terrestrial life comparable to that of human overpopulation.*

Thus the extrapolation problem can be viewed as simply one of facing the terrifying possibilities of what may happen if, as a result of assuming that such an extrapolation is invalid, corrective action is not taken.  Initially, such problems are economic and political in nature.  Ultimately, however, all economic and political problems are biological ones.

**23–7
CONCLUSION**

In this chapter, territoriality has been discussed as a major behavioral factor in some (but by no means all) animal species.  The hypothesized role of territoriality in the spacing of organisms to prevent overexploitation of the environment was considered, along with the role of agonistic behavior in the obtaining and holding of a territory.

In dealing with agonistic behavior in general and human aggression in particular, it was necessary to turn again to the controversy over innate versus learned behavior (or "nature versus nurture").  It is hoped that, having been exposed to the controversy, the reader will be stimulated to further reading in the area (see the suggested readings on the following pages).  At this point in its development, relatively little thinking in ethology has jelled; even in the use of some of the "standard" vocabulary (e.g., "innate" behavior) there is still considerable disagreement.  While such fluidity may at times be frustrating, it merely reflects the fact that, as a field of study, ethology is still in its early and pioneering stages of development—and this is the most exciting stage of all.  Huge information gaps are evident in such areas as the development of behavior and the neurophysiological mechanisms guiding the widely divergent forms of behavior and learning already identified.

Finally, experiments and observations dealing with the effect of high population density on behavior were discussed.  These studies strongly suggest that *the most disastrous effects of human overpopulation may well be behavioral ones.*  Even if the average citizen's faith in forthcoming technological solutions to such overpopulation problems as pollution of the natural environment, scarcity of food, etc., were to prove justified (a faith seemingly not shared by a majority of the scientific community), the resulting behavioral aberrations would still be present.

In the following, read the information given, suggest an hypothesis (or hypotheses) to account for this information, design a *controlled* experiment to test each hypothesis, and state which prediction(s) is (are) being checked.

1. In the early morning, animal $A$ reacts to its detection of animal $B$ by giving behavior pattern $XYZ$. Animal $B$ reacts to its detection of $A$ by giving reaction pattern $DEF$. Animal $A$ reacts to its detection of animal $C$ by giving behavior pattern $XYZ$ and $C$ reacts to $A$ in a $DEF$ manner. Animals $B$ and $C$ do not show any discernible reaction pattern when they detect each other in the absence of $A$.

   Later in the day, animal $A$ reacts to its detection of animal $B$ by giving reaction $XYZ$, but $B$ reacts to its detection of $A$ by giving either no reaction at all or only $D$. Animal $C$, however, continues to react to $A$'s $XYZ$ reaction with $DEF$. Animals $B$ and $C$ continue to ignore each other in the absence of $A$.

   Still later, $A$ and $B$ detect each other. Animal $A$ gives the $XYZ$ behavior, $B$ gives $DE$ behavior, but not $DEF$. Animal $C$ now appears, gives no reaction to $A$, but gives reaction series $MNO$ to $B$; $B$ responds initially with $MNO$ but soon switches to $PQR$.

   Propose a hypothesis to explain these behavior interactions and the types of behavior you feel may be symbolized here. Suggest a test for your hypothesis in terms of field or laboratory experimentation.

2. Discuss briefly, but completely, the concept of "innateness" of behavior in comparison to environmental effects on behavior (i.e., "nature versus nurture") as it applies to:

   a) the formation of the neural tube in amphibian embryos from a strip of the dorsal ectoderm (see Section 18–9);

   b) early views on the nature of the ability to regenerate (or lack of it) shown by organisms at "higher" or "lower" places on the evolutionary ladder or phylogenetic tree (see Section 18–10) as contrasted with contemporary views of the same phenomenon.

3. Around 1900, there was a horse in Germany named Hans who, it was maintained, could carry out addition, multiplication, and division. He would respond to the question, "How much is $3 + 2$" by pawing the ground five times. Hans could also spell out words and sentences, pawing the ground an appropriate number of times for each letter of the alphabet. To recall that U is the twenty-first letter of the alphabet in the midst of spelling out a complicated sentence is a difficult task, yet Hans learned to do so in two years. Hans was studied by a committee of ethologists who verified Hans's ability to do the things claimed for him.

   Propose a nonanthropomorphic hypothesis to account for Hans's feats, and propose a test for your hypothesis.

4. Discuss the proposition that "Criminals are born, not made" in the light of the material discussed in this chapter.

ARDREY, ROBERT, *African Genesis* (New York: Dell, 1961). The author, a journalist with considerable writing skill, makes the case for the innateness of man's aggression toward his fellow man. Excellent reading, if accompanied by a massive grain of salt.

ARDREY, ROBERT, *The Territorial Imperative* (New York: Dell, 1966). Like *African Genesis*, a masterful job of extrapolation from lower animals to human societies and political systems. Fascinating, but not to be taken too seriously.

HARDIN, GARRETT (Ed.), *Science, Conflict, and Society* (San Francisco: W. A. Freeman, 1969). A collection of readings in the area denoted by the book's title. Included is the Calhoun study of the relation of rat population density to abnormal behavior cited in this chapter. The Calhoun paper is also available as a *Scientific American* offprint from W. H. Freeman and Co.

LEHRMAN, DANIEL S., "A Critique of Konrad Lorenz's Theory of Instinctive Behavior." *The Quarterly Review of Biology* **28,** No. 4, December 1953, pp. 337–363. An excellent presentation of the case against the concept of instinct as used by Lorenz and others.

LORENZ, KONRAD, *On Aggression* (New York: Harcourt, Brace, and World, 1966). Lorenz's most controversial book, now available in paperback. Fascinating reading by a great ethologist, but the case the author tries to make for the innateness of aggression seems not to be accepted by most ethologists.

LORENZ, KONRAD, *Evolution and Modification of Behavior* (Chicago: University of Chicago Press, 1965). Lorenz's "reply" to criticism directed against his arguments for the innateness of certain forms of behavior, but especially that of D. S. Lehrman cited in this reading list.

MONTAGU, M. F. ASHLEY (Ed.), *Man and Aggression* (London and New York: Oxford University Press, 1968). A collection of writings by fourteen ethologists, anthropologists, etc., with the stated intent to counter misleading impressions given to the general public by the wide popular distribution of Konrad Lorenz's *On Aggression* and Robert Ardrey's *African Genesis* and *The Territorial Imperative*. Reading of these last cited books should definitely be followed by the reading of this one.

The origin of life is a problem of recurring interest in the history of biological thought. From the time of Aristotle to the present it has occupied the attention of the world's most prominent biologists. How did living material come into being in the first place? When and where did it originate? Did it originate only once, or have repeated origins taken place? Such questions as these have received a variety of answers in the past. One type of answer has been a religious one: special creation (see Section 21–2). Historically, this represents an early explanation to be advanced concerning the origin of life. A second type of answer is the idea of spontaneous generation (again, see Section 21–2). This idea, advocated by Aristotle, was accepted by most people, including some eminent naturalists, up until the middle of the nineteenth century. A third type of answer makes reference to the idea of **chemosynthesis.** Chemosynthesis attempts to explain the origin of life in terms of present-day chemical and physical laws. We shall examine the second and third of these ideas in some detail.

While the idea of spontaneous generation may seem far-fetched to us today, it is not difficult to see why it gained many adherents. It is a common-sense sort of theory. If meat is left outside for a few days, maggots appear on and within it. A mud puddle is seen to have no life in it one day, and to be filled with swimming tadpoles the next day. For many years it was not known that maggots are larval flies, or that frogs lay eggs, which in turn develop into tadpoles. During those years, spontaneous generation provided the best explanation for the sudden appearance of such organisms.

Yet, the theory of spontaneous generation had weaknesses. It seemed to be applicable to only a few types of organisms. Although the late sixteenth-

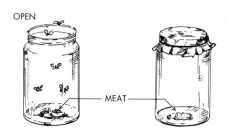

OPEN

MEAT

FIG. 24-1  Redi's experiment. The left-hand jar represents the control group, the right-hand one the experimental group. When flies are prevented from coming into contact with the meat, no maggots develop.

century alchemist Jan Baptista van Helmont (1577–1644) claimed that mice could be spontaneously generated from rags and bread in a dark corner, most of his contemporaries did not go that far. It was generally held that only lower forms of life—insects, tadpoles, certain kinds of eels—could be spontaneously generated. It was recognized that chickens developed from eggs, and calves from cows. Thus, for reasons within the nature of the theory itself, the idea of spontaneous generation became less acceptable as an effective explanation for the origin of life. Men turned to experimentation to test the hypothesis. And the experiments of Francesco Redi (1626–1697) and Louis Pasteur (1802–1895) provided conclusive evidence to refute the theory of spontaneous generation.

In 1668, Redi set up a very simple but conclusive experiment (Fig. 24–1). He placed samples of meat in two separate jars, one covered with foil, the other left open. The open flask served as the control, the covered flask as the experimental group.

Redi reasoned as follows:

**Hypothesis:** *If . . .*    maggots arise by spontaneous generation, . . .

**Prediction:**  *then . . .* they should appear on meat in both the covered and uncovered flasks.

Redi observed flies hovering about both flasks. But even after several days, contrary to the prediction, maggots appeared only in the open flask. Hence the hypothesis of spontaneous generation, at least in this case, was invalid. (Recall from Chapter 3 that if the prediction from an hypothesis is shown to be incorrect, the hypothesis must be invalid.)

Despite Redi's work, many people continued to believe in spontaneous generation. In the latter half of the nineteenth century the French bacteriologist Louis Pasteur was able to demonstrate in a convincing manner that another supposed example of spontaneous generation (in this case, microbes in decaying broth) was also invalid.

Pasteur began his experiments with the working hypothesis that all life comes from preexisting life (the concept of **biogenesis**). He placed beef broth in several flasks and boiled it. Boiling sterilized the broth. A day or two later, flasks that had been left open and allowed to cool could be seen to teem with microorganisms. Yet even months later, no microorganisms had appeared in the flasks that had been sealed immediately after boiling.

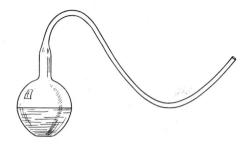

FIG. 24–2    S-shaped flask prepared by Pasteur to show that spontaneous generation does not occur.   Dust-borne microorganisms and bacterial spores are caught in the lower bend, and thus do not reach the broth.   However, air is free to pass down the neck of the flask.

However, this demonstration was not enough to convince the proponents of spontaneous generation.  They argued that boiling had altered the air in the flask, and thus spontaneous generation could not occur.

Pasteur met this argument by a new approach.   He reasoned as follows:

*Hypothesis: If* . . .    spontaneous generation requires the contact of the broths and fresh air, . . .

*Prediction:  then* . . . boiled broth brought into contact with air cleared of all its floating particles should still generate microorganisms.

To test this hypothesis, Pasteur did the following experiment.  He boiled the broth as before.  This time, however, instead of sealing the flask, he drew the neck out into a long, S-shaped tube (Fig. 24–2).  Air would still be able to pass down the entire neck of the tube and come into contact with the broth, but the lower bend in the tube would serve as a trap for all dust particles and bacterial spores.

The experimental results showed that broth in the flasks with S-shaped necks did not decay.  On examination, even months afterwards, there was no sign of microorganisms.  Several of Pasteur's flasks are still, over 100 years later, on display in the Pasteur Institute in Paris—and their contents show no signs of decay!*

To prove his point more effectively, Pasteur then took an S-shaped flask that had been sitting for several months and tipped it so that some broth ran into the lower bend of the neck.  He then allowed the broth to flow back into the main part of the flask.  Soon the broth in this flask showed signs of putrefaction.  This seemed to be dramatic evidence that for spontaneous generation to occur, something more was needed than contact between broth and air.  It appeared more likely that it was the dust particles (containing bacteria) and microorganism spores carried in the air that caused the decay of broth.

Pasteur's experiments did not disprove the idea of spontaneous generation *in general;* he did not prove that such a process *never* occurs.  Recall from Chapter 3 that such proof is impossible in science.  What Pasteur did do was to show that one supposed example of spontaneous generation was invalid.  However, this

---

* They have been resealed to prevent evaporation.  Pasteur did his original experiments in 1862.

example was so widely accepted by proponents of the theory, that Pasteur's work dealt a deathblow to the concept of spontaneous generation. Ironically, by showing that a common example of spontaneous generation was invalid, Pasteur banished the question of the origin of life from scientific investigation.

In more recent times a way out of this dilemma has been found. Chemosynthetic theories of the origin of life advocate a new variety of spontaneous generation. By claiming that organisms could arise from the nonliving environment through chemical means, they place the question of the origin of life on a rational, scientific basis. Let us examine how chemosynthesis provides an explanation for the origin and development of living organisms.

**24-3**
**THE ORIGIN OF LIFE**
**BY CHEMO-**
**SYNTHESIS**

Geological evidence has been interpreted to suggest that the early atmosphere of the earth may have contained water vapor, methane, ammonia, and perhaps some free hydrogen. These compounds provide the most essential elements found today in living organisms: carbon, hydrogen, oxygen, and nitrogen. In addition, phosphates of various sorts may have been present in the oceans. The presence of these elements set the stage for the origin of life.

**The first phase.** Before living systems could begin to develop, organic compounds such as proteins, carbohydrates, fats, and nucleic acids had to be available in the environment. The chemosynthetic hypothesis holds that these were formed from methane, ammonia, water, and hydrogen in the earth's atmosphere or on the surface of the oceans. It is hypothesized that lightning, and/or ultraviolet and cosmic radiation, provided the energy required for the formation of these complex molecules.

According to the chemosynthetic theory, probably the first molecules of any size to be produced were similar to present-day hydrocarbon chains. These consist of long strings of carbons, to which hydrogen atoms are joined:

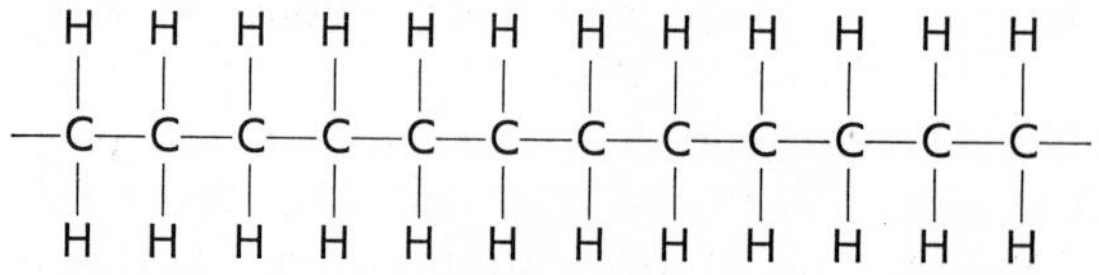

Not only do hydrogen chains form the basis of fatty acids, but by folding back on themselves they provide ring structures, such as that represented by benzene:

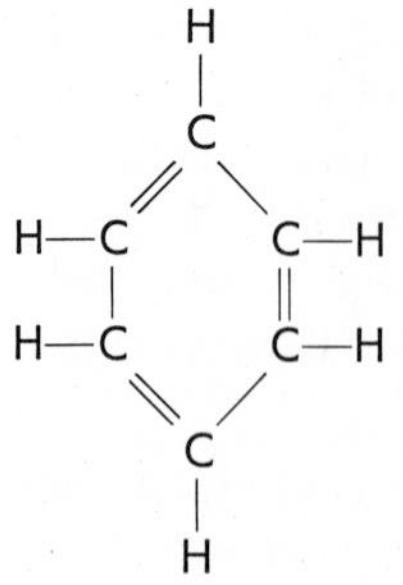

Ring structures similar to this are found in some very important biological compounds. Most notably, two types of ring molecules are the fundamental building blocks of nucleic acid.

Also formed were simple amino acids and carbohydrates. Some small peptides may have formed from the end-to-end linkage of several amino acids. There was a limiting factor on the size of molecules at this time, however. The larger the molecules became, the greater the chance that they would be broken down either by simple collision with other molecules or by the degradation effects of lightning, or of cosmic or ultraviolet radiation. While these energy sources served to build up large molecules, they were also able to break them down. Thus, during the first phase, only relatively small molecules accumulated in the oceans.

How much evidence is there that such an initial stage in the origin of life is likely ever to have occurred? The chemosynthetic theory is, in reality, no more than an hypothesis. Reasoning from this hypothesis, however, we can make a prediction:

**Hypothesis:** *If . . .*  amino acids, carbohydrates, and fatty acids could have originated from the action of lightning, etc., on methane, ammonia, water, and hydrogen, . . .

**Prediction:** *then . . .* similar energy sources acting on a mixture of these substances in the laboratory should yield the same products.

In the early 1950's a graduate student at the University of Chicago, Stanley Miller, tested this prediction in his laboratory.

Miller set up an apparatus like that shown in Fig. 24–3. Into this system he introduced the gases ammonia, methane, and hydrogen, along with water

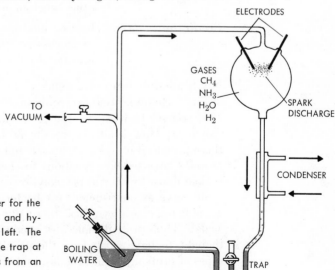

FIG. 24–3  Apparatus designed by Stanley Miller for the circulation of methane, ammonia, water vapor, and hydrogen. Water is boiled in the flask at the lower left. The products of chemical reaction are collected in the trap at lower right. Energy for chemical reaction comes from an electric discharge in the flask at upper right.

which he kept boiling in a flask. Boiling and condensation kept the substances circulating through the system. Two electrodes provided a periodic electric discharge into another flask.

After the raw material had circulated through this system for a period of time, a residue was collected from a "trap." In this residue were several amino acids, one carbohydrate (succinic acid, which occurs as an intermediate in the Krebs citric acid cycle, Fig. 8–10), and several additional organic compounds. Other workers, following Miller's procedure, have produced simple components of nucleic acid, and even ATP, by varying the type and amounts of the reactants used.

**The second phase.** As soon as amino acids, simple carbohydrates, and fatty acids or hydrocarbon chains were present, it is probable that they began to join together to produce various macromolecules. Amino acids joined end-to-end to form peptides, while glucose and other smaller carbohydrate units united to form larger sugar and starch molecules. Hydrocarbon chains, uniting with three-carbon sugars, could have yielded primitive fat molecules at this early stage. Under what conditions could these larger molecules be formed? Is there any evidence that they might have been similar to modern proteins, carbohydrates, and fats?

These questions prompted Professor Sidney W. Fox of Florida State University to conduct a series of experiments. From the hypothesized nature of the earth's environment at that very early period, he reasoned that heat might have provided the energy which drove the subunits together to form macromolecules. From this hypothesis, he could make a prediction:

*Hypothesis: If* . . .    heat energy provided the means for building proteins and other macromolecules out of their separate subunits, . . .

*Prediction:  then* . . .  heating mixtures of amino acids (or other subunits such as glucose) in the laboratory should also produce some macromolecules.

Fox heated mixtures of a number of different amino acids for varying periods of time. He found that dipeptides and even long-chain peptides were produced. This seemed to bear out the prediction. But one really important question remained: How similar were the proteins produced by thermal methods to those produced in living organisms today? Fox found that thermally produced proteins gave positive reactions to chemical tests for protein. They could be broken down by several proteolytic enzymes such as pepsin. In addition, they could serve as nourishment for bacteria. This implies that bacterial enzymes are able to break down these thermally produced proteins into individual amino acids! Thus protein molecules produced under conditions similar to what is thought to have existed on the primitive earth must closely resemble some types of protein produced today by living organisms.

Further experiments showed that the thermal production of proteins with specific and repeatable structures is not improbable. In one series of experiments, the beginning mixture of amino acids was made in the following proportions:

| | |
|---|---|
| GLUTAMIC ACID | 33% |
| ASPARTIC ACID | 33% |
| 16 OTHER AMINO ACIDS | 33% |

Every time the experiment was performed, the resulting polypeptides contained the various amino acids in the proportions:

| | |
|---|---|
| GLUTAMIC ACID | 13% |
| ASPARTIC ACID | 55% |
| 16 OTHER AMINO ACIDS | 32% |

This shows that even under prebiotic conditions, amino acids do not join together to form proteins in a purely random fashion. There is some degree of order involved. Furthermore, the polypeptides formed had a tendency to assume definite shapes (tertiary structure), thus introducing another level of order and organization.

Fox's work has been carried on by others to produce large carbohydrates and other macromolecules. It seems clear that thermal energy may well have been responsible for forming the first macromolecules in the organic soup. The second phase thus shows the production of the major organic macromolecules essential for the subsequent origin of life.

**The third phase.** Once these various organic molecules were formed, they faced two possible fates: degradation by energy sources such as ultraviolet radiation, or combination with other organic molecules to form complexes. Although degradation did occur, there were other factors working to enhance the formation of molecular complexes. Undoubtedly one of the major causes for the aggregation of macromolecules was their polarity (see Section 6–4). Several investigators have offered hypotheses to explain how these molecular aggregates could have set the stage for the origin of living organisms.

As far back as 1938 the Russian biochemist A. I. Oparin proposed what he called the **coacervate theory.** This holds that proteinlike substances in the early broth formed aggregates which tended to develop a simple membrane around them due to surface tension (something like a drop of water). Oparin showed that mixtures of gelatin and gum arabic produced small spherules of these substances. The spherules were coacervates, which simply means they were a suspension of one liquid (in this case called a colloid) in another. The coacervates were separated from the external medium by the surface layer. It is possible that fatty acids may have collected at the surface (one end of a fatty acid chain is strongly attracted to water) and thus have formed a primitive lipid membrane.

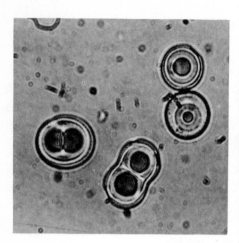
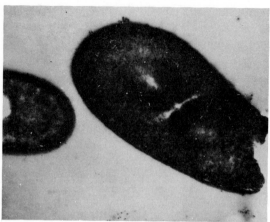

FIG. 24-4    Photograph showing both single and aggregate microspheres produced in Fox's laboratory at Florida State University. Note the regular appearance of the spheres, and their general resemblance to spherical bacteria (Fig. 25-1a). It is thought that such aggregates (mostly of protein) could represent the beginnings of organization that eventually led to life. At right are shown proteinoid microspheres produced by Dr. Fox. Note the close resemblance to the cellular structure shown by some bacteria. (Photos courtesy Professor Sidney W. Fox.)

Professor Fox has done further work based on Oparin's coacervate idea. He has shown that thermally produced proteins will form spherules with diameters about the same size as bacterial cells. Several of these spherules are shown in Fig. 24-4. These spherules, like Oparin's coacervates, are separated from the external medium by a surface layer. Addition to the medium of such salts as sodium chloride causes the spherules to shrink in size. Fox attributes this to the movement of water out of the spherule. Like living cells, the spherules show osmotic properties. In addition, two spherules can combine with each other, or one spherule can split apart upon reaching a certain critical size.

These ideas suggest strongly that something like Oparin's coacervates or Fox's spherules could have been the precursors of the first living organisms. The coacervate and spherule ideas also suggest ways in which molecular aggregates of different chemical composition could combine to produce new and better-adapted forms. Fox has shown that by starting with varying concentrations and types of amino acids, spherules with different protein characteristics can be produced. Combination of two different spherules could produce a unique form with characteristics unlike any others. This is one way in which these nonliving molecular aggregates could, step by step, begin to assume some of the characteristics which we now associate with life.

The formation of a surface layer, later followed by an actual membrane, was a great step forward. Not only did a membrane provide some protection for the macromolecules within it, it also kept the molecules it contained in close contact with each other, thus increasing the chances that chemical reactions could take place. The molecular complexes thus became more effective chemical combinations. One possible result of this would have been that combinations such as amino acids forming into proteins could use the potential energy from the breakdown of other molecules (such as phosphates or carbohydrates) as a driving force.

The third phase is thus characterized by the organization of macromolecules such as protein or carbohydrate into bodies with definite shape and unity. These bodies have certain properties that resemble those of living things.

**The fourth phase.** Up to this point, molecular aggregates lacked both a distinct, well-developed internal organization, and reproductive capacity. In general, any particular energy-harnessing reaction that a given aggregate might possess was a unique and isolated occurrence. Although an aggregate could reproduce simply by splitting in two, there was no way of determining the characteristics that the resulting parts might possess.

A real breakthrough in the origin of life occurred when nucleic acids became the major molecular "organizers" within aggregates. It is impossible to say exactly at what stage this occurred, but it was probably quite early. This contention is supported by evidence that genetic information is transmitted in the same way (by the triplet code) in all known organisms.

The appearance of nucleic acids not only provided reproductive continuity, it also directed the immediate activities of the complex. Energy-capturing systems could thus become more efficient as they also became an hereditary part of the molecular aggregates. It may be said that by the end of phase four, these molecular aggregates had become true living organisms.

**The fifth phase.** The fifth phase is characterized by the beginning of evolutionary development. Once continuity in the form of genetic control was introduced, natural selection could come into operation. No doubt one of the first results of evolution was an increased efficiency in capturing energy from carbohydrate breakdown. Those organisms that could use energy most efficiently could reproduce their kind most rapidly; hence a simple selection pressure came into operation. It was probably at this time that the processes of electron transfer and storage of energy in phosphate bonds first appeared.

The fifth phase thus saw an increase in the efficiency by which organisms could use energy sources existing in the environment. This also meant that the reproductive capacity of these organisms could increase. Thus the number of organisms in the early oceans began to rise, and competition became more intense.

**The sixth phase.** Up through the fifth phase the biotic world had been running downhill. Organisms had subsisted on carbohydrates and other energy-sources already present in the environment. These organisms were *not* self-sufficient; i.e., they were heterotrophs. Recall (Section 9–14) that a heterotroph is any organism which depends on an outside source of ready-made food. All animals today are heterotrophs.

The downhill process meant that as time went on the carbohydrate supply diminished. Competition became more and more pronounced. Under such conditions, any variation that allowed an organism to take even one step in the direction of manufacturing its own carbohydrate supply would be greatly favored. Variations must have occurred that allowed organisms to use light energy to produce carbohydrates. Thus a new form of metabolism, the process of photosynthesis, had its introduction.

The appearance of autotrophs, in the sixth phase, marked another major innovation in the early history of life. The earliest autotrophs may have resembled certain present-day bacteria. These have very simple cell structures, but a very few of them can use sunlight to produce carbohydrates. Whatever the exact structure, the appearance of a photosynthetic organism changed the biological world to a considerable extent. It provided a balance which has been characteristic of the biotic community ever since. While heterotrophs break down carbohydrates and other substances to gain energy, autotrophs capture outside sources of energy and build up carbohydrates.

It should be pointed out that any hypotheses regarding the origin of life are at best tentative, and subject to continual and frequent revision. Indeed, a fundamental aspect of the explanation outlined above has recently been called into question, for new geological evidence suggests to some workers that the chemical composition of the earth's early atmosphere contained very little ammonia or methane. Since ammonia is known to dissolve very rapidly in water, the presence of free ammonia in the atmosphere would be very unlikely. A new hypothesis proposes that a number of elements necessary for life (carbon, hydrogen, and nitrogen) were spewed forth into the atmosphere by volcanoes. Recent studies suggest that molecules such as amino acids can be produced by bombarding these elements with sunlight of a specific wavelength (2536 Å). At the present time there is no crucial test to decide which of these two hypotheses better explains how life actually did arise on the earth. New evidence will have to come from studies on the chemical composition of the earth's oldest rocks. From a detailed knowledge of their composition, it may be possible to deduce what the early atmosphere of the earth was really like.

Perhaps the most difficult problem encountered by the chemosynthetic theory is to account for the transition from molecular aggregates lacking genetic control to organized forms having this control. How likely is it that unorganized molecular groups could form some type of spontaneous organization? How likely is it that nucleic acid could become associated with these molecules in a central role?

Oparin holds that the origin of life was neither a lucky accident nor a miracle, but the result of perfectly natural and ordinary scientific laws. In other words, given the conditions that existed on earth at the time, life was bound to arise and to evolve along the lines that it has. The basis of the development of life is the result of the development of hydrocarbons, and Oparin believes that the gradual evolution in the complexity of hydrocarbons is universal. There is some geological evidence to support this claim: i.e., the older the rocks, the simpler the hydrocarbons.

In Oparin's opinion, the problem of the "primeval soup"—the sea containing dissolved organic substances, including simple polymers of amino acids and nucleic acids—has now been largely solved by the innumerable experiments of the sort performed by Stanley Miller described earlier. Such systems, however, do not exhibit any great degree of organization. To Oparin, the most difficult question is how *enzymes* first came into existence, since an enzyme's structure is adapted in a very specific way to its particular catalytic task. However, it is just this appearance of adaptiveness in the simple aqueous solution of the primeval soup, *before* the formation of such whole systems, that seems entirely improbable.

As seen earlier, to Oparin the best model to simulate the evolution of enzymes is the coacervate drop, an isolated part of the primeval soup separated from the solution by surface boundaries but able to interact with the environment. In one set of experiments, Oparin has made coacervate drops in his laboratory by polymerizing the nucleotide adenine in the presence or parallel formation of another polymer, usually histone. As soon as a certain degree of polymerization was reached, coacervate drops containing these polymers began to form. Once formed, the drops selectively absorbed and concentrated small molecules from the external medium and changed and incorporated them once they were inside the drop. Oparin refers to such coacervate drops as "protobionts." Under the influence of wave action, these protobionts can be broken up into "daughter" droplets, each with the attributes of its "parents." Once this has happened, of course, a sort of prebiological natural selection is free to operate, with the more "successful" drops (i.e., those with a greater catalytic ability to incorporate their surroundings) growing at the expense of the less successful.

Catalysts—which could only have come from the environment—thus become the telling requirement. The first of the catalysts must have been rather inefficient, like the industrial catalysts of today. However, through modification by the addition of organic molecules, their catalytic activity could have been improved a thousandfold. An enormous number of molecular alternatives must have arisen, of which only the most efficient remained. These may possibly be today's coenzymes, used now only as an aid, albeit a vitally important aid, to an enzyme's action.

Meanwhile, the random joining of amino acids could have led to primitive proteins with some form of active center. These would soon disappear, however, unless a further controlling mechanism evolved which could maintain their structure. Even at these early stages the polynucleotides, later to become DNA and RNA, might have had some organizing ability and, if they produced favorable catalysts, would have been selected. It is reasonable to assume that many millions of primitive proteins must have arisen; presumably those most successful remain today.

Oparin maintains that all these processes are subject to experimental testing despite the fact that we have no time machine to return and check them "in the field," and his laboratory is still actively engaged in research along these lines. Of course, such experiments can never *exactly* duplicate the way things actually must have happened during the time that life first appeared on earth. But even approximate experiments are extremely helpful, and studies of present-day viruses are equally so.

We saw in Chapter 1 that viruses represent a "twilight zone" between the living and nonliving worlds. They perform many of the functions characteristic of life, but they can also be crystallized and treated like a simple chemical compound.

The position of modern viruses in the history of life is uncertain. Since they parasitize living cells, it is obvious that they could not have arisen *before* cells had developed. However, recent studies on viruses have shown how macromolecules can be formed, by chemical means, into definite structures with biological functions. To understand the import of this work, let us consider some characteristics of a typical virus.

Recall that viruses are composed of two parts: a protein coat and an inner core of nucleic acid. In some ways they resemble a simple molecular aggregate. The protein coat provides a protective covering for the nucleic acid. The nucleic acid in any virus is either DNA or RNA. The rod-shaped virus shown in Fig. 24–5 contains RNA and is called tobacco mosaic virus (TMV). It normally infects only the leaves of tobacco plants. Viruses infect cells by injecting their own nucleic acid into the host cell. The viral nucleic acid "takes over" the host cell machinery, particularly ribosomes, and uses this to produce viral parts. Viral nucleic acid overrides that of the host cell. The host cell can be shown to contain messenger RNA and enzymes specific for the production of *viral* protein. This, in time, usually destroys the host cell (see Fig. 24–6).

Some interesting experiments have been performed with TMV which throw light on questions of the origin of life. By delicate chemical procedures it is possible to separate the RNA from the protein coat of TMV. It is also possible to break the protein coat down into its component units. Simple adjustments in the acidity of the medium are then enough to bring the protein units back together to form long unit aggregates. These aggregates are rods that look exactly like the intact virus. Such "empty" protein shells, however, are unable to infect plant tissues.

If the protein shells are placed in a solution of viral RNA, they form particles which behave like normal, intact TMV. The fact that a solution of this material is able to infect tobacco leaves is a good indication that the protein shells and nucleic acid organized themselves to form complete TMV particles. It is

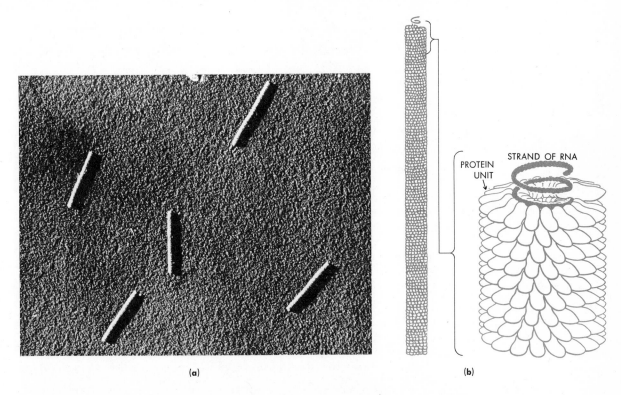

(a)                                                                (b)

FIG. 24–5    (a) Electron micrograph of rod-shaped tobacco mosaic virus. The photograph was taken after the sample had been "shadowed" with chromium to increase contrast. (Photo courtesy U. S. Public Health Service. × 67,000.)    (b) Diagrammatic representation of the structure of the same virus. Its single coiled strand of RNA is seen emerging from the stack of spirally arranged protein units in which it is embedded. All the protein units in this virus are identical. Each unit is composed of a sequence of 158 amino acids. The complete TMV has 2200 protein units. (Adapted from W. M. Stanley and E. G. Valens, *Viruses and the Nature of Life.* New York: E. P. Dutton & Co., 1961.)

known that neither nucleic acid nor protein alone is capable of producing infection. Both parts must be present for the virus to reproduce.

A second type of experiment provides even more interesting results. Heinz Fraenkel-Conrat and his associates at the University of California (Berkeley) separated the protein coats and the RNA cores from TMV viruses and from another strain of rod-shaped virus (HR). In each case, the protein coats were carefully decomposed into their individual units in such a way that the molecules of protein were not denatured. The researchers then placed the protein coats from the TMV strain with the RNA cores of the HR strain. The acidity was adjusted so as to allow the units of protein to aggregate. The result of this

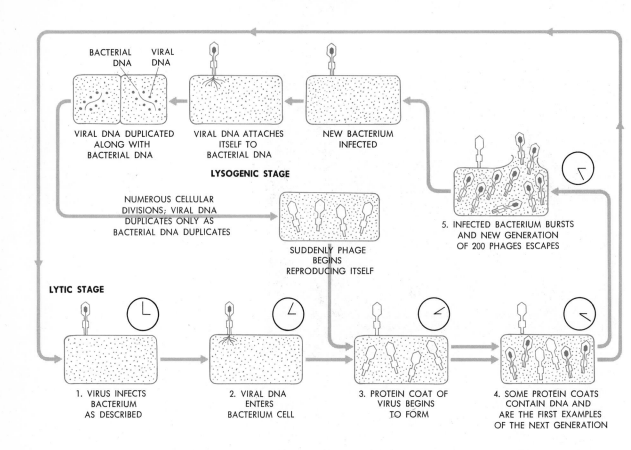

FIG. 24–6  Stages in the life history of the T2 bacteriophage, a virus which parasitizes the bacterium *Escherichia coli*. The lytic stage involves immediate infection of a single bacterium. The lysogenic stage, which occurs every so often (but not at fixed intervals), involves the "resting" of phage DNA for a period, at the end of which the phage duplicates to form new viruses, thus killing the cell.

mixture was the self-organization of a virus with a TMV coat and an HR core of nucleic acid (RNA). Here was a new type, or hybrid virus (Fig. 24–7).

In every case, the newly formed virus, when administered to plant tissues, caused an infection characteristic of the HR strain. In other words, the infection was characteristic of the type of RNA involved. This strongly supports the hypothesis that the nucleic acid of viruses is the major infective agent. The protein appears to play a passive role, perhaps as a protective cover for the nucleic acid.

As the hybrid virus was allowed to duplicate, it was noted that the new viruses developed coats of the type of protein characteristic of the HR strain. This experiment showed that in viruses, RNA contains the full genetic complement—it is coded with all the information needed for building complete viruses.

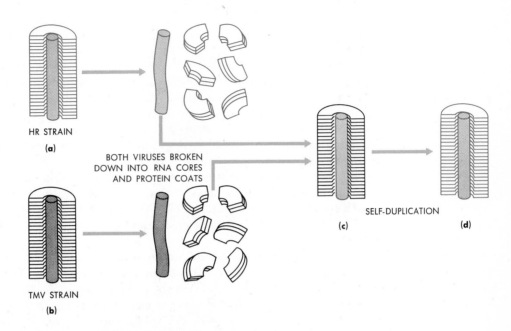

HR STRAIN

(a)

TMV STRAIN

(b)

BOTH VIRUSES BROKEN
DOWN INTO RNA CORES
AND PROTEIN COATS

SELF-DUPLICATION

(c)

(d)

FIG. 24–7    Summary diagram of Fraenkel-Conrat's experiments, showing the hybridization of viruses. The progeny at (d) have become slightly modified from their parents at (a) and (b). (Adapted from H. Fraenkel-Conrat, "Rebuilding a Virus." *Scientific American*, June 1956, p. 47.)

These experiments reveal some important principles relating to the origin of life. They show, first, that under specific conditions, a high degree of order and organization in viruses comes about spontaneously. Thus a change in the acidity or temperature of the solution can cause disordered arrays of protein to become highly ordered groupings. If such spontaneous organization comes about in the laboratory, it is reasonable to assume that it could have come about in the oceans of the primitive earth. The experiments also show that we can take a virus apart and reassemble it, which indicates that formation of objects capable of carrying on at least some complex life activities can occur by known chemical means. Provided with the right environment, such as is found inside living cells, viruses are able to reproduce new viruses with great rapidity.

Establishing a date for such events as the origin of life is quite a difficult task. The earliest types of true organisms have left little or no fossil records. The earliest traces of life are the remains of primitive plants in strata that are at least two billion years old. Life must have originated at some time considerably before that, but to find out just when, we must find some evidence in the geo-

**24-5
THE GEOLOGICAL
TIME SCALE AND
THE ORIGIN OF LIFE**

logical record.   As can be imagined, this is extremely difficult, and for this reason our estimates of when life may have originated are highly speculative.

Once fossil remains, or even traces of life, begin to appear in the strata, the history of life can be much more easily put on a definite time scale.  Geological dating procedures make it possible to establish the age of various fossils and strata with a fair degree of certainty.   One of the most prominent methods currently in use is based on the rate of **radioactive decay** of the isotopes of certain elements—for example, $U^{238}$, an isotope of uranium.  Radioactive elements undergo transmutation to more stable forms by emitting subatomic particles, such as $\beta$-particles or neutrons.  They may also emit radiant energy in the form of gamma rays.  This "decay" procedure continues until all the atoms of a given sample have been transmuted to the stable form.  For example, atoms of $U^{238}$ undergo radioactive emission and decay ultimately to the stable form $Pb^{206}$ (lead).

The critical feature of radioactive decay, so far as dating procedures are concerned, is that it occurs at a steady, measurable rate.  The rate differs for each isotope of each element.  Yet the process is so regular that, for example, we can say it takes 4.5 billion years for half of the atoms in a sample of $U^{238}$ to become $Pb^{206}$, or that it takes 15 days for half the atoms in a sample of $P^{32}$ to decay to $P^{30}$.  This period is termed the **half-life** of the isotope.

Many rock samples can be accurately dated by comparing the ratio of $U^{238}$ to $Pb^{206}$ contained in them.   $U^{238}$ is a relatively common isotope and is found in many rocks and fossils.  The basic assumption of this method is that the older the rock, the less $U^{238}$ it will contain, and the more $Pb^{206}$.  The oldest rocks known are estimated by this method to be 2.7 billion years old.  The age of the earth is estimated to be between four and five billion years.

By a variety of dating methods, but most recently by radioactive decay, geologists have established a time scale divided into eras and periods.  The various geological eras, and their major characteristics, are given in Table 24–1. This table provides a framework from which to view the evolution and development of life.  It gives some sense of the sequence of living forms on earth, and of the time scale on which they developed.

A measurement scale based on periods of time like billions or millions of years is difficult to imagine.  We can compare the whole history of life on earth to a 24-hour scale, the appearance of various forms being designated in terms of "time of day."  If we set the origin of life at one minute after midnight, the first fossils do not begin to appear until 6 P.M.  More striking, the age of mammals begins at 11 P.M. and man appears at 11:59.  The short history of our species on earth is some indication of the vastness of the time over which the origin of life and evolution to its present stage are thought to have occurred.

**24–6**
**CONCLUSION**   In the present chapter we have surveyed several theories of the origin of life. We have explored one theory, that of chemosynthesis, in some detail.  We have seen how this theory attempts to account for the origin of life by chemical and physical processes.   While the general theories of chemosynthesis are quite

**TABLE 24-1** KINDS OF LIFE IN VARIOUS GEOLOGICAL ERAS*

| ERAS† | PERIODS† | EPOCHS | AQUATIC LIFE | TERRESTRIAL LIFE |
|---|---|---|---|---|
| CENOZOIC 63 ± 2 | QUATERNARY 0.5–3 | RECENT PLEISTOCENE | Periodic glaciation | Man in the new world<br>First men |
| | TERTIARY 63 ± 2 | PLIOCENE MIOCENE OLIGOCENE EOCENE PALEOCENE | All modern groups present | Hominids and pongids<br>Monkeys and ancestors of apes<br>Adaptive radiation of birds<br>Modern mammals and herbaceous angiosperms |
| MESOZOIC 230 ± 10 | CRETACEOUS 135 ± 5 | | MOUNTAIN BUILDING (e.g., ROCKIES, ANDES) AT END OF PERIOD<br>Modern bony fishes<br>Extinction of ammonites, plesiosaurs, ichthyosaurs | Extinction of dinosaurs, pterosaurs<br>Rise of woody angiosperms, snakes |
| | JURASSIC 180 ± 5 | | INLAND SEAS<br>Plesiosaurs, ichthyosaurs abundant<br>Ammonites again abundant<br>Skates, rays, and bony fishes abundant | Dinosaurs dominant<br>First lizards: Archeopteryx<br>Insects abundant<br>First mammals, first angiosperms |
| | TRIASSIC 230 ± 10 | | WARM CLIMATE, MANY DESERTS<br>First plesiosaurs, ichthyosaurs<br>Ammonites abundant at first<br>Rise of bony fishes | Adaptive radiation of reptiles (the codonts, therapsids, turtles, crocodiles, first dinosaurs, rhynchocephalians) |
| PALEOZOIC 600 ± 50 | PERMIAN 280 ± 10 | | APPALACHIAN MOUNTAINS FORMED, PERIODIC GLACIATION AND ARID CLIMATE<br>Extinction of trilobites, placoderms | Reptiles abundant (cotylosaurs, pelycosaurs); cycads and conifers; gingkoes |
| | PENNSYLVANIAN 310 ± 10 | CARBONIFEROUS | WARM HUMID CLIMATE<br>Ammonites, bony fishes | First insects, centipedes<br>First reptiles; coal swamps |
| | MISSISSIPPIAN 345 ± 10 | CARBONIFEROUS | WARM HUMID CLIMATE<br>Adaptive radiation of sharks | Forests of lycopods, club mosses, and seed ferns<br>Amphibians abundant, land snails |
| | DEVONIAN 405 ± 10 | | PERIODIC ARIDITY<br>Placoderms, cartilaginous and bony fishes<br>Ammonites, nautiloids | Forests of lycopods and club mosses, ferns, first gymnosperms<br>Millipedes, spiders, first amphibians |
| | SILURIAN 425 ± 10 | | EXTENSIVE INLAND SEAS<br>Adaptive radiation of ostracoderms<br>Eurypterids | First land plants<br>Arachnids (scorpions) |
| | ORDOVICIAN 500 ± 10 | | MILD CLIMATE, INLAND SEAS<br>First vertebrates (ostracoderms)<br>Nautiloids, Pilina, other mollusks<br>Trilobites abundant | None |
| | CAMBRIAN 600 ± 50 | | MILD CLIMATE, INLAND SEAS<br>Trilobites dominant<br>First eurypterids, crustaceans<br>Mollusks, echinoderms<br>Sponges, cnidarians, annelids<br>Tunicates | None |
| PRECAMBRIAN 4600 | | | PERIODIC GLACIATION<br>Fossils rare but many protistan and invertebrate phyla probably present<br>First bacteria and blue-green algae | None |

* From John W. Kimball, *Biology*, 2nd ed., Addison-Wesley, 1968.
† With approximate starting dates in millions of years ago.

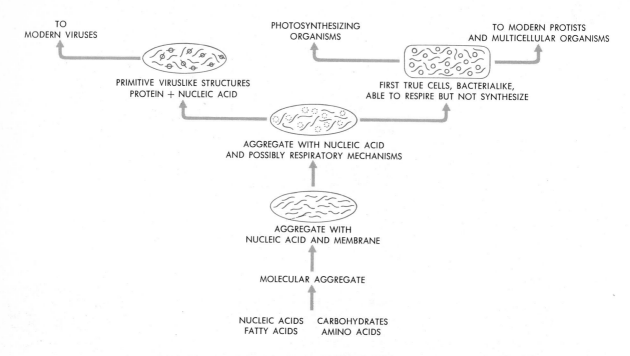

TO
MODERN VIRUSES

PHOTOSYNTHESIZING
ORGANISMS

TO MODERN PROTISTS
AND MULTICELLULAR ORGANISMS

PRIMITIVE VIRUSLIKE STRUCTURES
PROTEIN + NUCLEIC ACID

FIRST TRUE CELLS, BACTERIALIKE,
ABLE TO RESPIRE BUT NOT SYNTHESIZE

AGGREGATE WITH NUCLEIC ACID
AND POSSIBLY RESPIRATORY MECHANISMS

AGGREGATE WITH
NUCLEIC ACID AND MEMBRANE

MOLECULAR AGGREGATE

NUCLEIC ACIDS        CARBOHYDRATES
FATTY ACIDS          AMINO ACIDS

FIG. 24–8  Evolutionary tree of developments in the origin of life.  This is a very tentative arrangement.  Evidence of definite order of development, or even kinds of forms existing at any one time, can
only be hypothesized for periods where little or no fossil evidence is available.

tentative to date, they show the possibility of developing a more complete and
meaningful theory in the future.  A summary chart of the early development of
life, as outlined by the chemosynthetic theory, is given in Fig. 24–8.

We have also seen how geologists have arrived at a time scale for the various
strata.  By measuring radioactive decay, it has been possible to establish the
ages of rocks and fossils with fair certainty.  Paleontologists now have a good
idea of the age of various species, the times when certain forms appeared, and
the times when others became extinct.

**EXERCISES**    1. Explain briefly how living, cellular forms could have originated from simple organic
molecules such as amino acids, carbohydrates, lipids, and nucleic acids.

2. What is the significance of viruses, and experiments that can be done with them, to
modern hypotheses concerning the origin of life?

3. Figure 24–9 is a graph taken from the experiments of Stanley Miller, described in
Section 24–3.  Considering his work and the graph, answer the following questions.

a) Would it be reasonable to conclude that ammonia is incorporated into the formation of amino acids in Miller's experiment?  Why or why not?

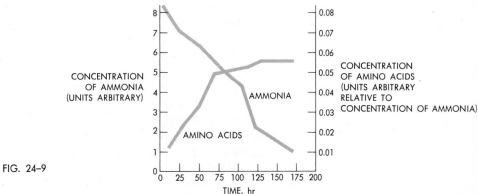

FIG. 24–9

b) The curve for concentration of amino acids is plotted on a different scale of magnitude than that for concentration of ammonia. What is the difference in magnitude? Why should this be the case? Draw the curve representing change in concentration of amino acids as plotted on the same scale as that for ammonia.

c) Methane concentration is not shown in Fig. 24–9. If it were, what shape do you hypothesize the line would have? Why?

4. Dr. Sidney Fox performed a number of experiments which were a continuation of the work of Stanley Miller. He heated a dry mixture of a number of amino acids to about 90°C. Analysis of the results showed that a number of polypeptides had been formed. He also found that if he heated the amino acids in the presence of phosphoric acid, polypeptides were formed at a temperature as low as 71°C. The polypeptides produced in this manner could be broken down by specific enzymes from animals. In addition, bacteria could use these polypeptides for food.

a) What does this experiment show about the idea that organic substances could have been formed on the primitive earth by random action? Are living organisms essential for the synthesis of organic molecules?

b) From a thermodynamic point of view, what is the significance of the fact that polypeptides form at a lower temperature in the presence of phosphoric acid?

c) What evidence from Fox's experiments suggests that the proteins formed by experimental methods are similar to native protein found in living organisms?

d) Would it be logical to conclude that proteins formed on the primitive earth (before any life appeared) were similar to the proteins that later became incorporated into the living matter of organisms? Why or why not?

5. Identify the selection pressures that may have been operating at each of the points of development listed below:

a) Formation of a membrane around nucleic acid–molecular aggregate complex.

b) Development of a definite respiratory process.

c) Development of a photosynthetic mechanism.

6. Scientists do not maintain that attempts to explain the origin of life by a concept of special creation are necessarily wrong, but only that this concept lies outside the realm of science. Why should this be the case?

7. In what ways did Redi's and Pasteur's experiments provide evidence that spontaneous generation does not occur? Were their experiments designed to support or disprove an hypothesis?

8. Why are hypotheses that explain the origin of life on earth by saying that spores were brought to the earth on meteorites unsatisfactory?

9. Describe the process of radioactive dating. On what principles is it based?

10. Although life originated on the earth two billion years ago, it required three-fourths of the time from then to the present to develop forms that would leave any significant fossils. Once this occurred, however, many diverse forms of life developed in a short period of time. Account for this slow start of life, and its subsequent rapid rate of growth.

SUGGESTED
READINGS

## I. On Theories of the Origin of Life

CLARK, F., and R. L. M. SYNG (eds.), *The Origin of Life on the Earth* (New York: Pergamon Press, 1959). This is a series of papers (and commentaries) from the first international symposium on origin of life held in Moscow, August 19–24, 1957, under the auspices of the International Union of Biochemistry. It contains many interesting articles on the origin of life, the evolution of biochemical systems, and the nature of viruses.

MILLER, STANLEY L., "The Origin of Life," in *This Is Life*, ed. by W. H. Johnson and W. C. Steere (New York: Holt, Rinehart & Winston, 1962), pp. 317–342. This article reviews the whole area of the present chapter, describing Miller's own experiments in some detail.

OPARIN, A. I., *The Origin of Life* (New York: Dover, 1953). This is a reprint of the original work of Oparin, issued in 1938. It sets forth Oparin's hypothesis in great detail, and is of interest to those wishing to pursue the topic of origin of life in some depth.

RUSH, J. H., *The Dawn of Life* (New York: Signet Library, 1963). This book, by a physicist, traces the whole story of the origin of life from the formation of the earth, through the formation of living cells, and on to the "emergence of mind." It attempts to define life, and to discuss the ways in which the brain operates like an electric circuit, or a computer. Stimulating, if on occasion too sketchy.

WALD, GEORGE, "The Origin of Life." *Scientific American*, August 1954, p. 44.

## II. On Viruses

FRAENKEL-CONRAT, H., "Rebuilding a Virus." *Scientific American*, June 1956, p. 42. This article deals with the problem of studying the way in which viruses are constructed. It describes the experiments involved in taking apart the TMV and HR strains to form the hybrid, with HR nucleic acid and TMV protein.

SMITH, K. M., *Viruses* (Cambridge: Cambridge University Press, 1962). This is an adequate, short treatment, which is especially well illustrated.

STANLEY, W. M., and E. G. VALENS, *Viruses and the Nature of Life* (New York: E. P. Dutton and Co., 1961). This is one of the best available introductions to the study of viruses. Well written, well illustrated, it is a fascinating story of the types of viruses, the methods used to study them, and the types of pathological conditions they cause in animals.

WEIDEL, W., *Virus* (Ann Arbor: University of Michigan Press, 1959). This is a very useful paperback which contains much information about viruses. Well written and interesting with good illustrations.

The great variety and number of plants which inhabit the earth today seem to have arisen from a common ancestor over two billion years ago, when a diminishing carbohydrate supply provided a selection pressure favoring autotrophic processes. Once the mechanisms for these processes had appeared, a new group of organisms—the plants—evolved. In this chapter we shall trace the evolutionary development of plants from the origin of the first procaryotic cells to the appearance of flowering plants. Although many characteristics will be discussed in relation to various representative types of plants, special attention will be paid to the evolution of reproductive processes. It is in this area, perhaps more than in any other, that critical problems of adaptation have arisen in the plant world.

Many plant biologists (botanists) consider the two procaryote groups, the bacteria (Figs. 25–1 and 25–2) and the blue-green algae (Figs. 25–3 and 25–4), to be closely related. This knowledge does not, however, indicate their order of descent. Trying to work out precise evolutionary relationships is one of the problems that evolutionary botanists face. In this case, for example, there are two alternative hypotheses:

**Hypothesis I:** *If . . .* the bacteria and the blue-green algae evolved from a common ancestor, . . .

**Prediction I:** *then . . .* they should possess many features in common.

In recent years, this prediction has been shown to be valid. The electron microscope reveals that the cell structure of these two groups of organisms is unique, differing markedly from that of all other organisms; this unique cell organization is called procaryotic (see Section 6–11). In addition, the cells of these organisms contain cytoplasm that is a rigid gel without vacuoles. This gel is resistant to

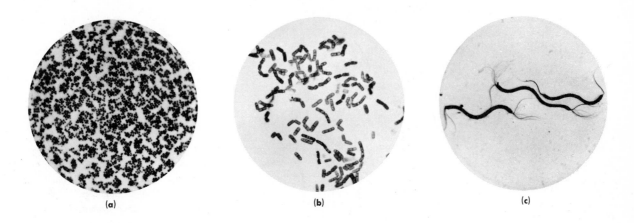

FIG. 25-1 Photographs of the three morphological types of bacteria. (a) The spherical or coccus form (*Micrococcus*). (b) The rod-shaped or bacillus form (*Azotobacter*). (c) The spiral or spirillum form (*Spirillus volutans*). (Photos courtesy General Biological Supply House, Inc., Chicago.)

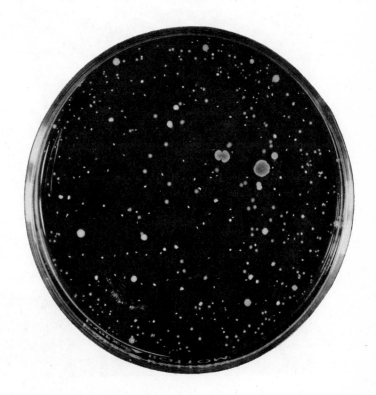

FIG. 25-2 Bacterial culture plate (petri dish) containing several colonies. Each colony descended from a single bacterium. Thus all the cells in any one colony are genetically identical.

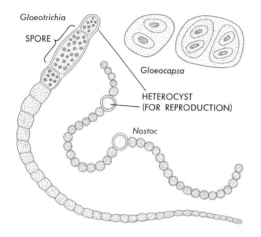

FIG. 25–3   Four genera of the phylum Cyanophyta, the blue-green algae. All these organisms possess chlorophyll *a*, plus several other pigments. One of these pigments, phycocyanin, is responsible for the blue-green color characteristic of the cyanophytes.

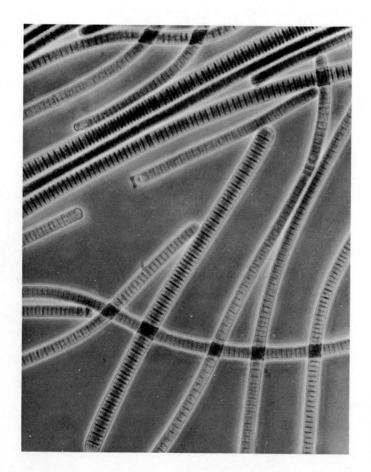

FIG. 25–4   Filaments of *Oscillatoria*, a blue-green alga (×1000). (From John W. Kimball, *Biology*, 2nd edition.  Reading, Mass.: Addison-Wesley, 1968.)

heat denaturation, drying out, and osmotic shock to a degree not present in other organisms. Finally, the cell walls of organisms in both groups are constructed of a polysaccharide-amino acid long-chain macromolecule known as mucopeptide. The possession of so many features in common certainly adds support to a hypothesis that the bacteria and the blue-green algae arose from a common ancestor, since it would be quite unlikely that so many unusual features would arise independently on more than one occasion. One possible evolutionary scheme might be:

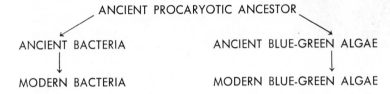

An alternative hypothesis holds that the bacteria and the blue-green algae do *not* share a common ancestry. This reasoning is as follows:

**Hypothesis II:** *If* ...   the bacteria and the blue-green algae each evolved independently, ...

**Prediction II:** *then* ... we should expect to find an array of distinctive differences between the two groups.

The blue-green algae are generally aerobic; that is, they must have oxygen to carry on their cell respiration. Many bacteria, however, are anaerobic and are capable of using substances other than oxygen as hydrogen acceptors. Nearly all of the blue-green algae use chlorophyll *a* to capture light energy in photosynthesis. In this process, they utilize hydroxide ions (derived from water) as electron donors, and produce free molecular oxygen. Only a few bacteria are photosynthetic; these lack chlorophyll *a* but do have other kinds of chlorophyll. Photosynthetic bacteria use molecules such as hydrogen and hydrogen sulfide as electron donors and do not release free oxygen (as do the blue-green algae and all other green plants). Finally, many bacteria possess flagella (Fig. 25–1c), while blue-green algae lack these structures. Proponents of this hypothesis believe that these aforementioned differences are great enough to preclude any close relationship between the bacteria and the blue-green algae. Thus, they would diagram an evolutionary scheme as follows:

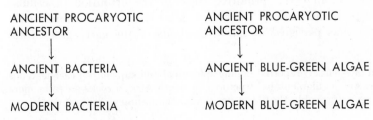

FIG. 25–5    An electron micrograph of a bacteriumlike fossil, *Eobacterium isolatum* (×66,000). (Photo courtesy Elso S. Barghoorn, Harvard University.)

It is evident that each hypothesis is supported by an impressive body of information. As yet, there is no evidence contradicting the predictions which follow the acceptance of either of the two alternative hypotheses that enables a decision between these two hypotheses to be made. To date, the fossil record is of little help in the matter; however, recent studies in paleobotany and paleobiochemistry show some promise of yielding information pertinent to the problem. In 1965, the paleobotanist Elso Barghoorn and his associates at Harvard University found organic remains interpreted as fossil bacteria in rocks from the northern shore of Lake Superior in Ontario, Canada. The remains have been dated as approximately 3 billion years in age. These investigators also discovered cellular microfossils similar in form to modern blue-green algae and green algae in one billion year old rocks of central Australia. In 1966, they found a minute, rod-shaped, bacterium-like fossil, *Eobacterium isolatum*, in rocks from South Africa; these were dated at more than 3.1 billion years in age (Fig. 25–5). Later study of these same rocks revealed spheroidal microfossils interpreted as the remnants of unicellular blue-green algae. If these remains have been correctly identified as those of blue-green algae and bacteria, then these two evolutionary lineages are the oldest known groups of organisms. Further, the presence in these rocks of organic compounds related to chlorophyll supports an hypothesis proposing that photosynthesis must have originated early in the evolution of life.*

**25–3**
**ORIGIN OF**
**EUCARYOTIC**
**ORGANISMS**

It is reasonable to hypothesize that the living bacteria and blue-green algae represent vestiges of an early, primitive stage in the evolution of cellular structure. Evidently, the procaryotic cell was a fairly successful evolutionary experiment, for it has persisted in the descendants of the early procaryotes

---

* In 1968, a team of scientists reported finding spheroidal and cup-shaped carbonaceous algalike bodies, as well as filamentous structures, in South African rocks dated at more than 3.2 billion years—probably the oldest unchanged sedimentary rocks on earth.

without significant fundamental change. At some time in the distant past history of life, however, an evolutionary advance of the greatest importance occurred— the compartmented or eucaryotic cell came into existence. This event seems to have set the stage for the processes of evolution to generate the vast diversity of life with which the modern biologist is concerned.

Did the evolution of eucaryotic organisms take place only once? Or did it occur many times? If the former alternative is correct, then all living organisms with the eucaryotic types of cell structure, including all animals and the vast majority of plants, have evolved from a common ancestor. If the latter alternative is true, then the similarities in cell organization among the various groups of eucaryotes are the result of convergent evolution, and do not indicate any close degree of relationship among the organisms.

The fossil record offers little help in resolving the problem. The oldest known fossils of unquestionably eucaryotic nature (Fig. 25–6) are from rocks of the late Precambrian period (more than 600 million years ago). They are invertebrate animals. The earliest unequivocally eucaryotic plant fossils are lime-secreting marine algae (green algae and red algae) preserved in rocks from the Ordovician period (nearly 500 million years ago).* Since the remains of these plants and animals show a very complex structural organization, it seems likely that they evolved from much older ancestors at some time during the Precambrian period.

What was the nature of the early eucaryotes? Because of the lack of an adequate fossil record, a question of this sort must be answered largely by inference from living species. One hypothesis proposes that an organism similar to the living, unicellular, green alga *Chlamydomonas* may represent a relatively unmodified descendant of the early eucaryotes. If this hypothesis is true, i.e., if *Chlamydomonas* is indeed primitive, then it is possible to infer that the early eucaryotes must have possessed many of the characteristics now present in living *Chlamydomonas*.

The single cell of an individual *Chlamydomonas* (Fig. 25–7) is usually less than 25 microns long. Two flagella protrude through the cell wall at the anterior end. Lashing movements of these flagella propel the alga through the water. Inside each cell is a single large chloroplast, usually cup-shaped, with an eyespot near its rim or apex. The chloroplast usually obscures a nucleus which lies in the colorless cytoplasm. Near the anterior (flagellar) end are two or more contractile vacuoles. Endoplasmic reticulum, Golgi complex, mitochondria, and ribosomes are present in the cytoplasm.

Using *Chlamydomonas* as a model, it can be postulated that the early eucaryotes were also unicellular, flagellated, photosynthetic organisms with at

---

* Fossils believed to be unicellular green and golden-brown algae were reported in 1969 to occur in rocks between 1.2 and 1.4 billion years old. The discoverers, a team of paleo-botanists and geologists led by Preston E. Cloud of the University of California, Santa Barbara, observed dark bodies inside the cells that suggest nuclei and other organelles. If these structures are indeed nuclei, then these fossils represent the oldest eucaryotic cells yet known.

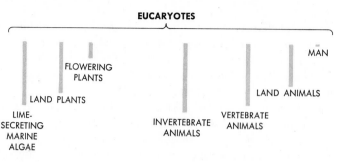

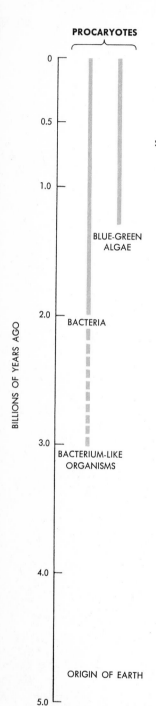

FIG. 25–6    Time of occurrence of earliest known fossils of major groups of plants and animals.

least minimum compartmentalization of their functions into organelles. The minimum structural requirements for a eucaryotic organism would appear to include at least one of the following: nucleus (with chromosomes), nuclear and cellular membranes, endoplasmic reticulum, Golgi complex, chloroplast, mitochondrion, and flagellum. It is likely that the early eucaryote may have been minute in size. Recently, an organism closely fitting this description was found as a component of ocean plankton. Being only a micron or two long, this organism, the smallest known eucaryote, was named *Micromonas* (from two Greek words meaning "small single organism"). The existence of such a minute eucaryotic organism adds further support to the above postulated primitive eucaryote. *Micromonas* (Fig. 25–8) seems even less evolutionarily modified than the larger and more complex *Chlamydomonas*. It is, therefore, conceivably far more primitive.*

Even an organism as minute as *Micromonas*, however, is a very complex organism. How might a eucaryotic cell, with its various organelles, have originated? One intriguing hypothesis suggests that chloroplasts and mitochondria may actually be minute organisms living in a mutualistic relationship with a larger organism, i.e., the cell which encloses them. According to this hypothesis, such a relationship started when a primitive one-celled blue-green alga was ingested by a nonphotosynthetic procaryote (perhaps a large bacterium) and became established. With time, the relationship between host and ingested organism developed so that both cells divided simultaneously. As more time passed, so this hypothesis maintains, the ingested cell underwent evolutionary reduction, losing certain abilities and structure but retaining its chlorophyll. Henceforth, it would function as if it were an integral part of the host cell, yet retain its own structural identity. At this stage, the eucaryotic cell would be well on the way toward being fully established.

---

* There is a possibility, of course, that both *Micromonas* and *Chlamydomonas* owe their relative simplicity and small size to an evolutionary reduction from much more complex ancestors. Even if this were the case, these organisms can still serve admirably as phylogenetic models for the postulated early eucaryotes.

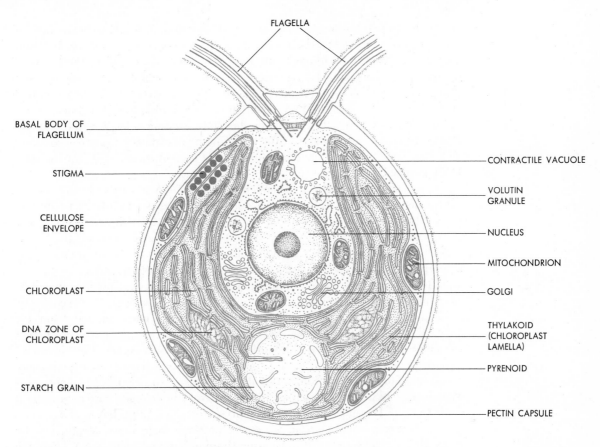

FLAGELLA

BASAL BODY OF
FLAGELLUM

STIGMA

CELLULOSE
ENVELOPE

CHLOROPLAST

DNA ZONE OF
CHLOROPLAST

STARCH GRAIN

CONTRACTILE VACUOLE

VOLUTIN
GRANULE

NUCLEUS

MITOCHONDRION

GOLGI

THYLAKOID
(CHLOROPLAST
LAMELLA)

PYRENOID

PECTIN CAPSULE

FIG. 25–7   Diagram showing structure of the unicellular green alga *Chlamydomonas* as revealed by
the electron microscope.   Only one of the two contractile
vacuoles is shown.   Volutin granules are probably
stored phosphates.   (From Keith Vickerman and Francis
E. G. Cox, *The Protozoa*.   Boston: Houghton Mifflin,
1967, p. 20; first printed in Great Britain by John
Murray, Ltd.)

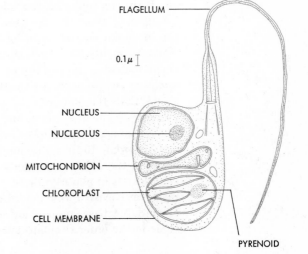

FLAGELLUM

0.1μ

NUCLEUS

NUCLEOLUS

MITOCHONDRION

CHLOROPLAST

CELL MEMBRANE

PYRENOID

FIG. 25–8   Diagram of *Micromonas*, a minute, uni-
cellular alga of the sea.   (After Peter R. Bell and
Christopher L. F. Woodcock, *The Diversity of Green
Plants*.   Reading, Mass.: Addison-Wesley, 1968, p. 5.)

Such a hypothesis may sound farfetched. If it stimulates thought and further research, however, it has scientific value. This hypothesis would predict that nucleic acids should be found inside the chloroplasts as well as in the nuclei of living plants. This prediction has been verified by several investigators in recent years. The chloroplasts of the green alga *Acetabularia* have been found to contain about $1 \times 10^{-16}$ gram of DNA—enough to code several hundred genes. Some 4% of the DNA in a cell of the green flagellate *Euglena* is located in its chloroplasts. Even the chloroplasts of the flowering plants spinach (*Spinacia oleracea*) and beets (*Beta vulgaris*) have been discovered to contain about 1% of the total DNA in a cell.

Independent support for the conclusion that DNA is synthesized inside the chloroplasts has come from electron microscope studies. Fibrils 25 to 30 angstroms thick were observed inside the chloroplasts of *Chlamydomonas*. Since these fibrils disappeared after treatment with deoxyribonuclease, they were considered to be DNA. Similar DNA fibrils have been observed in embryonic chloroplasts in the cells of the Swiss chard variety of *Beta vulgaris*.

Chloroplasts not only contain their own DNA but also possess an RNA-ribosome protein-synthesizing system. Ribosomes have been observed inside chloroplasts with the electron microscope and have been isolated from the chloroplasts. Radioautographic and radiochemical techniques have shown that the chloroplasts synthesize DNA, RNA, and protein. Again, the "invader" hypothesis of chloroplast origin is supported by the results of these experiments.

If the chloroplast is actually a small cell which once existed as an independent organism, then its nucleic acid should be different in nitrogen base composition from that of the nucleus. Recent analyses of chloroplast DNA in *Euglena*, *Chlamydomonas*, and *Chlorella* (a unicellular green alga) demonstrate it to be from 21% to 28% richer in adenosine-thymine content than DNA from the nuclei of these same organisms. Such a situation would not be expected if the chloroplasts were synthesized under control of the nuclear DNA.

If the chloroplast is an evolutionary descendant of an ancient, ingested blue-green alga, then the accessory photosynthetic pigments phycoerythrin and phycocyanin, characteristic of the blue-green algae, should be found inside it. These pigments have been discovered in the chloroplasts of red algae and the cryptomonads—but not in any other photosynthetic eucaryote. However, this apparent lack of agreement with the prediction might be explained by hypothesizing that the majority of photosynthetic eucaryotes have evolved other accessory pigment systems, and have simply lost the system inherited from their blue-green algal ancestors.

According to this "ingestion" hypothesis, there should be a close correlation between the DNA base pair composition of living blue-green algae and the chloroplasts in photosynthetic eucaryotes. This would seem to follow if chloroplasts once existed as independent blue-green algae. There is a partial matching of the DNA base composition of chloroplast DNA with the DNA of blue-green algae in the order Oscillatoriales. However, to date, too few species have been

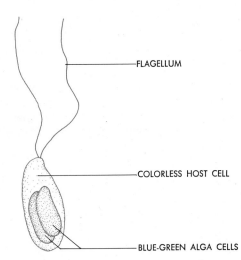

FIG. 25–9  Diagram of *Cyanophora paradoxa*, a colorless cryptomonad alga containing two unicellular blue-green algae.

investigated to make meaningful comparisons of their chloroplast DNA with that of the blue-green algae.

Actually, an hypothesis proposing that chloroplasts may once have been blue-green algae which entered the cells of nonphotosynthetic organisms and became permanently established is not as unreasonable as it may first appear. Consider an example of mutualistic relationships involving two different organisms. The cell of *Cyanophora paradoxa*, a colorless cryptomonad related to the dinoflagellates, contains a unicellular blue-green alga which has lost its cell wall and divides at the same time as its host (Fig. 25–9). Electron microscope studies show that there are no direct connections between the host cell and the blue-green alga. Apparently, the heterotrophic host obtains food manufactured by the photosynthetic blue-green alga. The alga, in turn, probably secures water, minerals, and carbon dioxide from the colorless cell. Such an example could be considered but a small step away from becoming a chloroplast. Analysis of the DNA base content of each organism has shown that the blue-green algal DNA is some 14% richer in adenosine-thymine than that of the crytomonad host cell. This finding is consistent with one of the predictions of the "invader" hypothesis. Other examples of similar mutualistic associations between blue-green algae and heterotrophic organisms include certain ciliate protozoa, corals, lichens, mosses, ferns, cycads, and flowering plants.

The "ingestion" hypothesis of chloroplast origin can be modified to explain the origin of mitochondria in eucaryotic cells. Mitochondria can be envisioned as having arisen when a one-celled bacterium was ingested by a larger organism. In time, a mutualistic relationship could be established and the ingested organism lost its ability to live an independent life. Some support for such a hypothesis comes from the discovery that, like chloroplasts, mitochondria contain their own nucleic acid-protein-synthesizing system. Additional experiments or observations designed to test this hypothesis are needed, however.

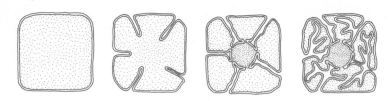

FIG. 25–10    A series of diagrams illustrating an hypothesis concerning the origin of the nuclear membrane and the endoplasmic reticulum through the infolding of the cell membrane.

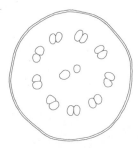

FIG. 25–11    Diagram of a cross section of a eucaryotic flagellum, showing the characteristic central pair of protein fibrils surrounded by nine fibrils.

Two other very important structures within the eucaryotic cell, the nuclear membrane and the endoplasmic reticulum, are hypothesized to have originated through evolutionary infolding of the cell membrane (Fig. 25–10). The genetic ability to produce membranes by infolding was already present in the bacteria and blue-green algae. Through natural selection, this capacity to develop internal membranes could have eventually resulted in the formation of the endoplasmic reticulum and the nuclear membrane, which have been shown to be continuous (see Chapter 6).

The eucaryotic flagellum, constructed of a core of two protein fibrils surrounded by a cylinder of nine similar strands (Fig. 25–11), may be the result of an evolutionary fusion of a cluster of bacterial flagella. Supporting evidence for this hypothesis can be derived from detailed biochemical comparisons of bacterial and eucaryotic flagella. It is difficult to comprehend the adaptive significance of the $9 + 2$ pattern of flagellar subunits—the pattern does not seem to have any inherent advantage over other possibilities.

Regardless of the correctness or incorrectness of the "ingestion" hypothesis, it is apparent that a eucaryotic cell functions as a highly complex community with two or more different kinds of separate, organized systems operating in close juxtaposition. The chloroplasts and mitochondria each constitute a semi-independent subsystem within the cell. The nucleus, endoplasmic reticulum, cell membranes, and ribosomes may comprise a third such organized subsystem. The implications of this view of the eucaryotic cell for the evolution of plants and animals are far-reaching. When did these postulated chloroplast-mito-

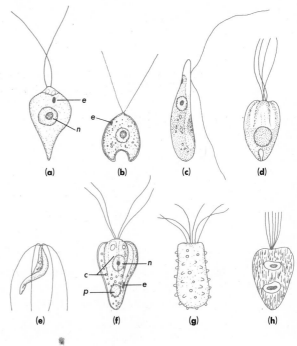

FIG. 25–12  Diagram of various members of the family Polyblepharidaceae (Volvocales, Chlorophyta). (a) *Phyllocardium complanatum.* (b) *Furcilla lobosa.* (c) *Dangeardinella saltatrix.* (d) *Pyramimonas delicatulus.* (e) *Spermatozopsis exultans.* (f) *Pyramimonas tetrarhynchus.* (g) *Pocillomonas flos-aquae.* (h) *Polyblepharides singularis.* c, chloroplast; n, nucleus; p, pyrenoid; e, eyespot. (From F. E. Fritsch, *The Structure and Reproduction of the Algae,* Vol. I. New York: Macmillan, 1935, p. 86.)

chondria "ingestions" take place? Through what stages did the ingested cell pass in evolving into a chloroplast or mitochondrion? Future studies of the cell and its subsystems may well emphasize the independence of these organelles within the cell.

If it is postulated that the original eucaryote may have been something like the unicellular, flagellated, green alga *Chlamydomonas,* then how did the evolutionary transitions to the many kinds of eucaryotes take place?

In the absence of a complete fossil record, this question can only be answered by inference from a comparative study of living species. Recently, two botanists at the New York Botanical Garden, Richard M. Klein and Arthur Cronquist, published an extensive and comprehensive review of the phylogeny of algae and fungi. In this essay, the authors hypothesized that the green algal order Volvocales may provide models for the initial stages in the diversification of the early eucaryotes. According to their hypothesis, the present-day Volvocales represent relatively unmodified descendants of a *Chlamydomonas*-like early eucaryote. The ancient Volvocales, therefore, may well be the common ancestral group which gave rise to nearly all of the major phyletic lines of eucaryotes.

Klein and Cronquist proposed that one interesting family of the Volvocales, the Polyblepharidaceae (Fig. 25–12), may provide good models for the ancestors of four phyletic lines of algae, the Euglenophyta, Pyrrophyta, Chrysophyta and Phaeophyta, the fungi, and indirectly the unicellular animals (Protozoa). Most members of the Polyblepharidaceae lack a cellulose wall. They do possess a

## 25-4
## THE ORIGIN AND DIVERSIFICATION OF EUCARYOTES: TWO ALTERNATIVE HYPOTHESES

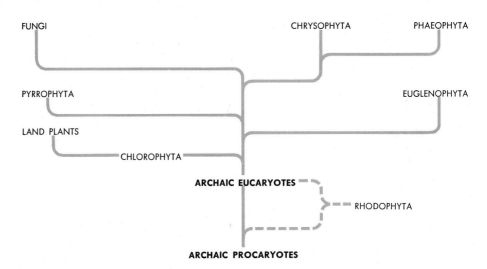

FIG. 25-13   A phylogenetic chart summarizing the hypothesis of Klein and Cronquist on the evolutionary diversification of eucaryotes. (Adapted from R. M. Klein and Arthur Cronquist, *Quarterly Review of Biology* **42,** 1967, p. 109.)

periplastic envelope, however, rigid in some species and flexible in others. Klein and Cronquist hypothesized that the organisms have lost the cellulose wall during their evolution but retain the genetic basis for cellulose synthesis (since cellulose appears in some of their presumed descendants). Contractile vacuoles and eyespots are present. Some species exhibit a tendency toward dorsiventrality (a flattening of the body) and asymmetry. Most species possess more than two flagella, while several have an inpocketing of the cell surface at the anterior (flagellar) end. Several of these features can be considered as foreshadowing attributes characteristic of one or more of these four groups of algae, fungi, and protozoa (see Fig. 25-13).

A radical alternative to the Klein and Cronquist phylogenetic model for the evolutionary diversification of the early eucaryotes was elaborated in 1968 by the biologist Lynn Margulis of Boston University (see Table 25-1). Margulis questioned the idea that the ancestor of all eucaryotic organisms was a simple, one-celled, green flagellate. She hypothesized that the ancestral eucaryote was a nonphotosynthetic amoebo-flagellate, not too dissimilar to some species of living flagellated amoebae. According to Margulis' model, this organism (Fig. 25-14) possessed mitochondria and was heterotrophic in its nutrition. Much later in evolution, some of these heterotrophic amoebo-flagellates became autotrophic cells through the ingestion of photosynthetic procaryotes resembling certain blue-green algae. Eventually, the ingested green organisms evolved into chloroplasts and the resulting photosynthetic eucaryotic organism became

**TABLE 25–1**   EVOLUTIONARY CRITERIA IN THALLOPHYTES*

| ASSUMPTIONS OF KLEIN AND CRONQUIST | ALTERNATIVE ASSUMPTIONS |
|---|---|
| 1. The basic dichotomy between organisms of the present-day world is between animals and plants. | The basic dichotomy between organisms of the present-day world is between procaryotes and eucaryotes. |
| 2. Photosynthetic eucaryotes (higher plants) evolved from photosynthetic procaryotes (blue-green algae, "uralgae"). | Photosynthetic eucaryotes (higher algae, green plants) and nonphotosynthetic eucaryotes (animals, fungi, protozoans) evolved from a common nonphotosynthetic (amoebo-flagellate) ancestor. There is not now, nor was there ever, an "uralga." |
| 3. The evolution of plants and their photosynthetic pathways occurred monophyletically on the ancient earth. | The evolution of photosynthesis occurred on the ancient earth in bacteria and blue-green algae; higher plants evolved abruptly from procaryotes when the heterotrophic ancestor (2 above) acquired plastids by symbiosis. |
| 4. Animals and fungi evolved from plants by loss of plastids. | Animals and most eucaryotic fungi evolved directly from protozoans. |
| 5. Mitochondria differentiated in the primitive plant ancestor. | Mitochondria were present in the primitive eucaryote ancestor when plastids were first acquired by symbiosis. |
| 6. The primitive plant differentiated the complex flagellum, the mitotic system, and all of the other eucaryote organelles. | Mitosis evolved in heterotrophic eucaryotic protozoans by differentiation of the complex flagellar system. |
| 7. All organisms evolved from a primitive ancestor monophyletically by single steps. | All procaryotes evolved from a primitive ancestor by single mutational steps; all eucaryotes evolved from a primitive eucaryote ancestor by single mutational steps. Eucaryotes evolved from procaryotes by a specific series of symbioses. |
| 8. Morphological, biochemical, and physiological characters are useful in classification of Thallophytes. | Only total gene-based biochemical pathways resulting in the production of some selectively advantageous markers are reliable "characters" in classification; morphology is useless in most procaryotes. |

### RESULT OF FOREGOING ASSUMPTIONS

| | |
|---|---|
| Nothing predicted; no consistent phylogeny possible, many predicted organisms not found, for example "uralgae"; no correlation with fossil record possible; no presentation of phylogeny as a function of time elapsed is possible. | Major biochemical pathways predicted; consistent phylogeny constructed; biological discontinuity at Precambrian boundary predicted. |

* This table by Dr. Lynn Margulis compares the Klein and Cronquist hypothesis concerning the evolutionary origins of organisms with the Margulis hypothesis. Note the reliance on the ability to predict as a major reason for selecting one model over the other. From Lynn Margulis, "Evolutionary Criteria in Thallophytes: A Radical Alternative," *Science*, September 6, 1968, pp. 1020–1022.

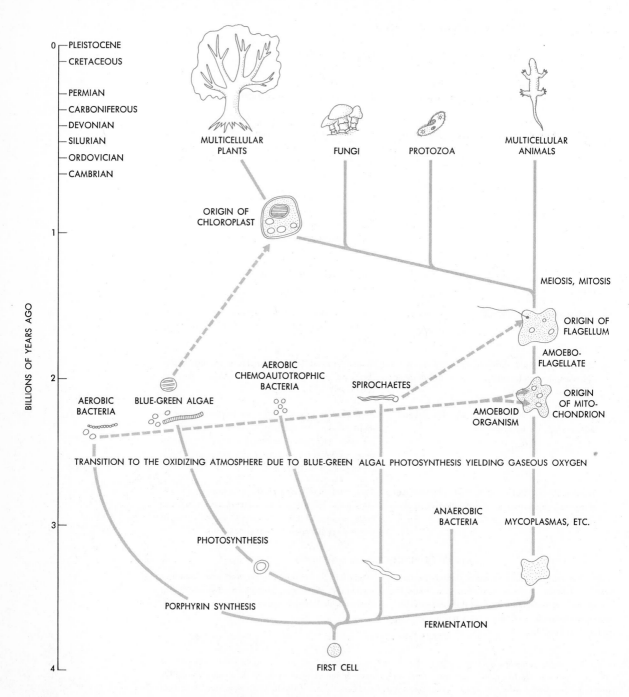

FIG. 25–14  A phylogenetic chart illustrating an hypothesis on the origin and diversification of organisms proposed by Lynn Margulis. (Courtesy of Lynn Margulis, Boston University.)

the ancestor of the eucaryotic algae and all other green eucaryotic plants (Fig. 25–14).

Margulis further hypothesized that the fungi evolved not from various algal groups as suggested by Klein and Cronquist, but from the heterotrophic amoebo-flagellate postulated to have been the ancestor of all eucaryotes. According to this hypothesis, therefore, the living fungi would be more closely related to the living protozoan animals than to the green plants (Fig. 25–14).

Phylogenetic models should help the biologist make predictions. The symbiotic theory as proposed by Margulis enables several predictions to be made. For example, all cells containing chloroplasts should also possess membrane-enclosed nuclei, and chloroplasts should contain DNA different from the DNA of the nucleus and the mitochondria. These predictions, as well as others that arise from Margulis' hypothesis, may challenge evolutionary biologists to carry out research designed specifically to test this phylogenetic model.

## 25–5 ORIGIN AND ADAPTIVE SIGNIFICANCE OF MULTI-CELLULARITY

If the diversity of plants and animals is to be explained by the hypothesis of evolution by natural selection, there must be good reasons for the retention of any distinguishing features that a species possesses. Acceptance of the hypothesis necessitates belief that at any particular point in its history, a species demonstrates the sum total of adaptive changes preserved (or at least not eliminated) by natural selection. Thus, any structural or functional characteristic incorporated into a successful organism must have some selective value—or at least be of no selective harm. If it did not meet these criteria, the feature could not have evolved.

In general, the fossil record supports the contention that those organisms which are structurally more complex originated later than the simpler forms. It is certainly reasonable to assume that complex biological systems were preceded in time by simpler ones. It is also consistent with the hypothesis of evolution by natural selection to assume that certain groups of organisms received some selective advantage in becoming more complex. Note that we are not saying here that an increase in complexity is a general trend in evolution, acting uniformly in all phylogenetic lines. Indeed, in some organisms (e.g., leaves of *Equisetum*), a *decrease* in complexity is found. We are simply stating that *for most groups* increase in complexity has been favored by natural selection.

Consider the evolution of multicellularity. Multicellular organisms must surely have been preceded by unicellular organisms. What selection pressures favored the adoption by some groups of a multicellular state? Examination of such forms reveals one possible answer. The multicellular state allows for cell specialization (i.e., some cells capture sunlight and synthesize food, some play a role in reproduction, some protect the organisms, some anchor it, and so on). The result is a corresponding increase in the ability of the organism to exploit its environment and increase its own chances for survival.

Concerning when and how multicellularity evolved, biologists can only speculate. Complex multicellular animals were already firmly established by

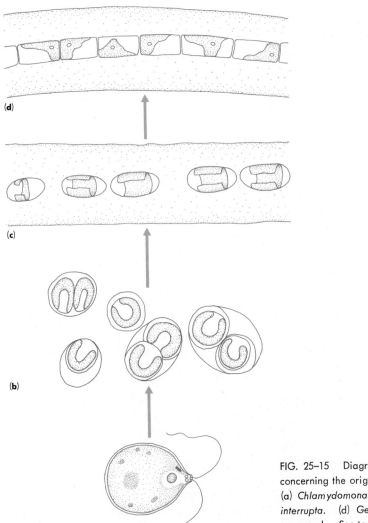

(d)

(c)

(b)

(a)

FIG. 25-15   Diagrams illustrating one hypothesis concerning the origin of the multicellular condition. (a) *Chlamydomonas*. (b) *Palmella*. (c) *Geminella interrupta*. (d) *Geminella minor*. Not drawn to same scale. See text for discussion.

the beginning of the Cambrian period, some 600 million years ago. Algae with highly differentiated multicellular bodies had evolved into at least two main groups (the green and red algae) by the Ordovician period, some 500 million years ago. Thus, the fossil record is obviously of little help. We must be satisfied to examine living organisms, such as green algae, and try to draw inferences about the nature of the first multicellular organisms that are both reasonable and fruitful.

It seems reasonable to hypothesize that the multicellular state originated through the aggregation of separate cells into a colony. Several surviving species of green algae demonstrate likely stages in this evolution. *Chlamydomonas*, for example, generally exists in a unicellular motile state (Fig. 25–15a). When conditions become unfavorable for the active condition, however, each cell loses its motility and becomes aggregated with other individuals into temporary associations. Upon the return of favorable conditions, the individual cells regain their flagella and the aggregation breaks up.

A somewhat later stage in the evolution of multicellularity may be represented by *Palmella*, which forms loose colonies of an irregular shape (Fig. 25–15b). A still closer approach to the multicellular condition is represented by *Geminella*, an alga in which numerous cells are loosely lined up within a cylindrical mucilaginous sheath, forming a simple filament. In some species, the cells lie at some distance from each other (Fig. 25–15c), while in others they are sufficiently close for their ends to touch (Fig. 25–15d). The latter arrangement would appear to be only a slight step away from that present in such filamentous genera as *Spirogyra* and *Ulothrix*, whose cells are attached to each other with a cementing material.

Another hypothesis on the origin of multicellularity maintains that the multicellular condition arose through the adherence of daughter cells after cell division. Some evidence in support of this hypothesis is provided by observations of the early growth of many filamentous algae. In these plants, the unicellular motile reproductive cells are released into the water, where they swim around for a time before coming to rest upon a rock, stick, or another alga. Upon alighting, these cells fasten themselves to the substratum by secreting a sticky material. Following cell division, the two daughter cells remain together. With further division, a row of cells is produced.

The multicellular condition may have originated by both methods hypothesized here, depending upon the particular group or evolutionary line. After all, the transition to multicellularity has taken place many times in numerous groups, among the procaryotes as well as the eucaryotes.

**25–6**
**ORIGIN AND DIVERSIFICATION OF SEXUAL SYSTEMS**

In general, sexuality as it occurs in most plants and animals does not exist among the procaryotes, presumably the most ancient group of living things still in existence. Some species of bacteria have "mating types": plus and minus strains which, by conjugation, exchange genetic material (see Fig. 25–16). This may represent the beginnings of differentiation into sexes. Conjugation lends a distinct evolutionary advantage to those species of bacteria which possess the ability to engage in it. The resulting exchange of genetic material allows for new gene combinations, hence a recombination of characteristics. Variation results, and natural selection of those proving to be the "fittest" can be effected.

There is also evidence that genetic recombination may occur in some species of blue-green algae. In one experiment, two strains of *Cylindrospermum majus*, one resistant to streptomycin, the other resistant to penicillin, were cultured

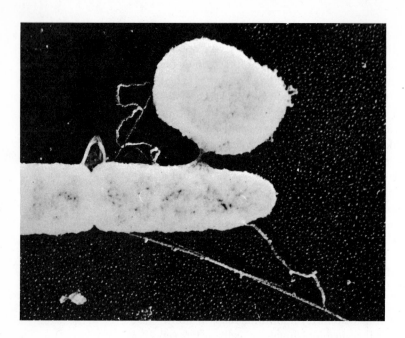

FIG. 25–16   Conjugation between two mating strains of the bacterium *Escherichia coli*. Note the conjugation bridge, a thin filament of cytoplasm connecting the two cells. Through this bridge, genetic material is exchanged between the bacteria.   (Photo courtesy Thomas F. Anderson, Institute for Cancer Research, Philadelphia.)

together in a medium containing both of these antibiotics.  In two of forty-seven culture tubes growth occurred; all the other cultures died.  The surviving algae in the two tubes were interpreted as being genetic recombinants, since they could grow in the presence of both streptomycin and penicillin.  Further evidence is needed to verify or refute this interpretation, however.

It is likely that some method of exchanging genetic material was a relatively ancient characteristic of living things.  It has been hypothesized that typical sexual systems may have evolved from an archaic sexuality at the same time that the membrane-bounded nucleus evolved.  No known living procaryotic organisms, however, survive to serve as models for the development of sexuality among the eucaryotes.  No structure even remotely resembling such complex organelles as eucaryotic chromosomes and the complex phenomena of mitosis and meiosis are known to occur in any bacterium or blue-green alga.  Perhaps when the detailed molecular and physical structure of the eucaryotic chromosome is fully understood, additional light may be cast upon the problem of the evolutionary transition from procaryote to eucaryotic sexuality.

Among living eucaryotes, the initial stage in sexual differentiation is represented by certain species of *Chlamydomonas* (see Fig. 25–17).  Two adult haploid cells (one plus and one minus, sexually) fuse, producing a diploid zygote.  The diploid zygote generally spends the winter in a dormant condition.  In the spring, the zygote undergoes meiosis and four (usually) haploid cells emerge and develop into mature individuals.  (It is characteristic of many algae that the

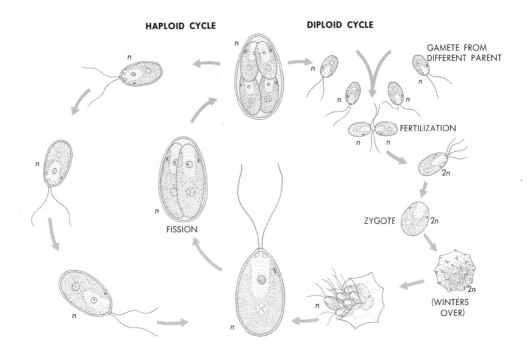

**FIG. 25–17**   Life cycle of the green alga *Chlamydomonas*, usually found in pools, lakes, and damp soil. Asexual reproduction is shown on the left and sexual reproduction on the right. At center bottom is an enlarged view of one individual. (After C. A. Villee, *Biology*, 3rd edition. Philadelphia: W. B. Saunders, 1957, p. 165.)

mature individual cells are haploid, thus carrying only one set of genes. In these species, the diploid phase is usually restricted to the dormant, inactive period.)

When two individual organisms fuse, producing a zygote, they are acting as gametes. Reproduction by two gametes that are morphologically alike, i.e., that are not differentiated in any visible way into male and female, is known as **isogamy;** the two cells involved are called isogametes. Isogamy is characteristic of many green algae.

Among the multicellular filamentous species, sexuality in its simplest form is seen in green algae like *Ulothrix*. In each filament, all the cells are haploid and structurally alike. Sexual reproduction is initiated by the formation of numerous small motile gametes by mitotic cell divisions in all cells of a given filament at the same time. After escaping from the cell, the gametes swim around in the water. Upon contact, they fuse in pairs, producing a diploid zygote. After a period of dormancy, the zygote undergoes meiosis and produces four haploid cells, each of which grows into a new filament (Fig. 25–18).

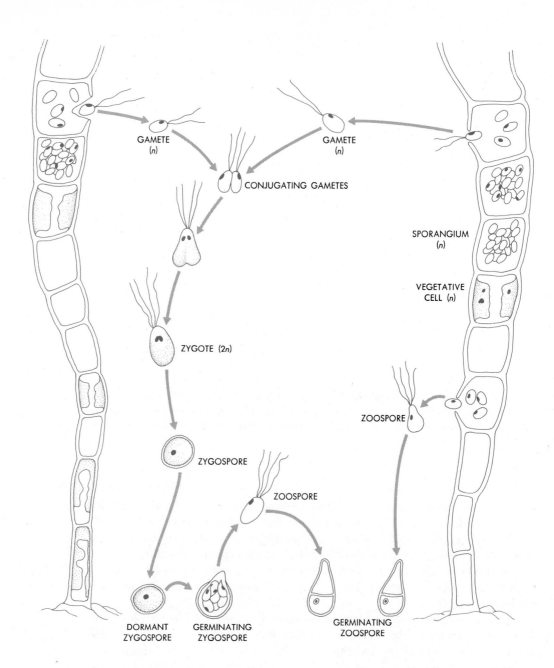

FIG. 25–18   Sexuality in *Ulothrix*.

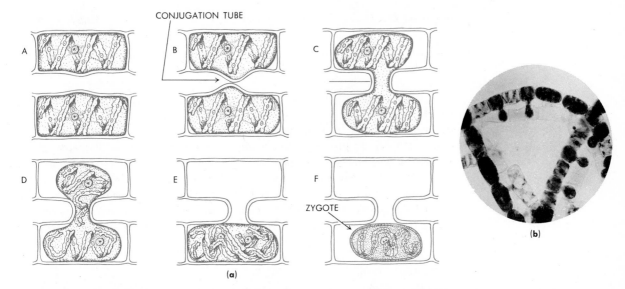

FIG. 25–19    (a) Conjugation of *Spirogyra*. Stages A–F show the progression of this process. (b) Two conjugating filaments at various stages. (Photo courtesy General Biological Supply House, Inc., Chicago. Magnification ×180.)

The green alga *Spirogyra* represents a slight advance in the differentiation of gametes.  *Spirogyra* normally reproduces asexually by cell division, the filaments growing longer until they break.  However, in the autumn, filaments of this alga undergo conjugation.  Although we have already spoken of conjugation in bacteria, the *Spirogyra* process is more complex.  At the start of *Spirogyra* conjugation, two filaments lie side by side, and a conjugation tube develops between each pair of opposite cells (Fig. 25–19).  Then the cell mass (excluding the cell wall) of each cell in both filaments rounds up into a spherical mass.  The cell mass from a given cell in one filament moves through the conjugation tube into its corresponding cell in the other filament.  Within the recipient cell, the two cell masses form a diploid zygote.  This zygote generally develops a heavy cell wall and rests on the bottom of the pond during the winter.  In the spring, it undergoes meiotic division to form four haploid nuclei.  Three of these nuclei degenerate, while the fourth grows into a mature *Spirogyra* filament.

The conjugation process in *Spirogyra* allows us to hypothesize how early differentiation into sexes might have occurred.  The following alternative hypotheses can be formulated:

**Hypothesis I:**   *If . . .*   there is no difference between two conjugating filaments of *Spirogyra*, . . .

**Prediction I:**   *then . . .* we should expect random crossover of cell masses between the two filaments.

*Hypothesis II: If . . .*    there is a difference between two conjugating filaments of *Spirogyra*, . . .

*Prediction II: then . . .* we should expect all the cells of one filament to pass over into the other filament.

As we can see from Fig. 25–19, all the cell masses of one filament do pass over and combine with the cell masses in the other filament. This observation supports the second hypothesis—that there must be some difference (not structural, therefore probably biochemical) between the two filaments of a conjugating pair. The cell masses of each filament can be considered as gametes. The active, motile cell masses may well represent a primitive type of male gamete, and the passive, nonmotile cell masses, a primitive female gamete.

Models for a more advanced type of sexuality are also present among certain species of *Chlamydomonas*. In these species, the uniting gametes are different in size (one kind is larger than the other). The two cells are called heterogametes; the process of their union, heterogamy. The smaller gamete is considered to be male, the larger, female. Both are flagellated.

Morphologically distinct male and female gametes—true sperm and egg—have evolved in some species of *Chlamydomonas* and in many filamentous algae. This condition, wherein a small motile gamete fuses with a large nonmotile gamete, is known as **oögamy.** Oögamous sexuality is well represented by the green alga *Oedogonium* (Fig. 25–20). This alga may also illustrate a stage in evolution in which the plant produces one-celled sex organs, an egg-producing oögonium and a sperm-producing antheridium which are morphologically different from the vegetative cells of the plant body. In addition, *Oedogonium* represents a stage in which the union of the gametes no longer occurs in the water. The nonmotile egg remains within the oögonium of the parent plant. The motile sperm enters the oögonium through a tiny pore in its wall and thus reaches the egg.

What is the adaptive value of having specialized gametes? For one, a passive egg can store excess food for the zygote to use in getting its start in life; only the sperm must expend energy (in order to reach the egg). In the case of isogametes, both of which are equally active, neither is able to store much food for the offspring. Providing food to get the organism off to a good start is of great survival value to a species.

**25–7**
**THE PRIMARY**
**INVASION OF LAND**

There is ample evidence that life has been in existence for at least three billion years (see Section 25–2). During five-sixths of this immense time, the land was apparently barren of life. Until about 405 million years ago, life seems to have been confined to the water. The shallow seas contained algae of various kinds including the procaryotic blue-green algae and the eucaryotic red, green, and brown algae. Invertebrate animals of many kinds flourished.

The vacant land was not to remain unoccupied much longer, however. Beginning about the close of the Silurian period, the first plants established themselves on the land. As the hypothesis of evolution by natural selection

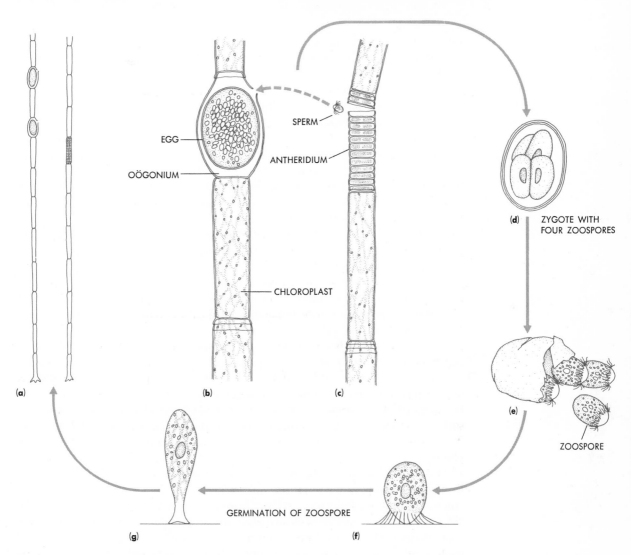

EGG

SPERM

ANTHERIDIUM

OÖGONIUM

CHLOROPLAST

(a)        (b)        (c)

(d)    ZYGOTE WITH
       FOUR ZOOSPORES

(e)

ZOOSPORE

(g)        (f)

GERMINATION OF ZOOSPORE

FIG. 25–20    Sexuality in *Oedogonium*.

would predict, the availability of so many previously unexploited ecological niches led to an adaptive radiation of immense proportions. Within about 15 million years, a wide diversity of land plants appeared, including at least four major evolutionary lines. This chapter will consider the origin and diversification of land plants with special attention to the ways in which they have solved the problems of terrestrial existence.

What algal group gave rise to the early migrants to the land? For a variety of reasons, the Phaeophyta (brown algae) and Rhodophyta (red algae) can be ruled out. For one, there exists good evidence that these algae were about as specialized in body form and reproductive methods during the Silurian period as they are today. It seems highly improbable that land plants could have evolved from such highly specialized plants.

In recent decades, a hypothesis that the ancestors of land plants were members of the Chlorophyta (green algae) has gained considerable support. For example, studies of the biochemistry and reproduction of land plants and green algae now in existence shows that both groups have the same two kinds of chlorophyll (*a* and *b*). Further, in both groups the combination and proportion of chlorophylls and carotenoid pigments is approximately the same. Both land plants and green algae store starch as a reserve food. In the land plants, sexual reproduction involves the fertilization of a nonmotile egg by a small sperm cell that is transported in some manner to the egg (oögamy); the same is also true of many green algae. The life cycle of land plants includes the alternation of a diploid, spore-producing phase (or generation) (the sporophyte) with a haploid, gamete-producing phase (the gametophyte). Several green algae also have life cycles of this type. In addition, the cell plate type of cytokinesis characteristic of land plants is present in certain green algae with parenchymatous bodies, e.g., *Fritschiella tuberosa*.

The fossil record has provided little information to either support or refute this hypothesis. While fossils of various algae have been found in pre-Devonian rocks, it is nearly impossible to determine whether the alga was indeed a member of the phylum Chlorophyta. The algal phyla are distinguished largely by biochemical characteristics. In fossils, the biochemical nature is usually not sufficiently preserved to determine whether an ancient alga was green or not. Thus, it is not possible to recognize any fossil alga as a possible ancestor of land plants.

In what environment did the ancient green algal ancestors of the land plants live? The original home of all life was undoubtedly the ocean, and the seas are still the habitat of a large proportion of both plant and animal groups. At present, 99% of the known species of brown algae live in the ocean, while 98% of the red algae do so. The present-day green algae, however, are largely inhabitants of fresh water, with only some 13% living in the seas. It is quite likely that, during Silurian times, the habitats of the red, brown, and green algae were essentially the same as those of the living species. Most, if not all, of the fossils of early land plants are found in sedimentary rocks that were probably laid down in fresh waters. Thus, it seems reasonable to hypothesize that the ancient green algae which gave rise to the early land plants also lived in fresh water.

Terrestrial existence brought with it some new and very real problems. Foremost was the danger of desiccation, or drying out. In the water, a plant is surrounded by a medium which brings all its mineral nutrients and carries away its metabolic wastes. Water and minerals enter the plant in solution at almost any point in its body. With the move to dry land, this ready supply of water and minerals was no longer available. To survive on land, therefore, a plant had to be able to reduce the water loss from its aerial parts. At the same time, it had to

be able to obtain water and minerals from the only reliable source available—
the soil in which it was growing. Once the plant secured water and minerals from
the soil, it had to be able to transport them to all parts of its body. Thus,
adaptations for obtaining these minerals from the soil, conducting them throughout the plant body, and keeping the plant from drying out must have evolved
by natural selection during the migration of plants onto the land. The land plant
also had the problem of waste disposal.

Life on land made the dispersal of spores and other reproductive units more
difficult. For organisms living surrounded by water, spore dispersal is relatively
simple, if not particularly efficient. In many species of algae, the spores are shed
directly into the water, where they are transported or swim to new areas. Water
thus serves as a transporting agent or medium for the spores. For the earliest
terrestrial plants, only air currents were available for this task. Thus, adaptations
enabling the spores to be transported by the wind were necessary.

Life on land also presented other problems. A submerged alga is buoyed up
by the water surrounding its body. On land, however, a plant is subjected to far
stronger forces of gravity and wind. However, any plant with an erect body
extending above the soil would be able to compete more successfully for available
sunlight. Height thus soon came to be of great advantage. It also increased the
need for a relatively rigid body well-anchored in the soil. To survive on land,
adaptations for resolving this dilemma were necessary.

What were the major evolutionary steps which led plants from water toward the
land and onto the land? As we saw in the previous section, there are many
structural and functional changes necessary to convert a green alga into a land
plant. It would seem, however, that any adaptations fitting the ancient green
alga for future life on dry land would have no immediate adaptive value to a
water-dweller. Of what adaptive significance, for example, would waterproof
surface layers (cuticles), or cutinized spores, or strong, rigid bodies be to a plant
submerged in water? Under normal conditions, none. It can be shown, however,
that under some special conditions such adaptations could have been of selective
value. Such a special condition may well have been seasonal drought. Geological
evidence suggests that many regions of the earth's surface may have been
subjected to prolonged seasonal droughts during the late Silurian and early
Devonian periods. During portions of the year, rainfall would be abundant (as
today in some tropical regions). At other times, the rains would cease. The
water level in the larger ponds and lakes would decrease drastically, while many
of the smaller bodies of water would undoubtedly dry up altogether.

Thus, adaptations such as cuticles, wind-blown spores, and rigid, erect
bodies may have evolved not as "preadaptations" for future life on land, but
actually as structures which would aid a water-dwelling green alga, under
seasonal drought conditions, to survive in its own proper habitat. In the early
stages of a severe drought, an alga whose body possessed some degree of rigidity
would be able to survive steadily decreasing water levels without undue difficulty.
Furthermore, with some waterproofing in the form of a cuticle, such an alga

**25–8
MIGRATION TO
THE LAND:
AN HYPOTHESIS**

would be able to keep its body from drying out as it became exposed to the air during the lowering of the water level.

What would happen if the drought worsened and the water in the ponds and lakes dried up completely? Today many species of algae manage to survive such conditions by the production of special, thick-walled, dormant spores which, upon return of favorable conditions, germinate and develop into a new individual plant. However, any plant which possesses at least the rudiments of a cuticle and some degree of rigidity of its body might be able to survive as a multicellular unit instead of a single-celled spore. Upon the return of favorable conditions, a multicellular, already established plant would obviously have the advantage over one that had first to germinate and then develop to full adult size. In addition, if in some ancient green alga cutinized windblown spores evolved, then these could be transported by the wind to regions where perhaps the drought was less severe and the ponds had not dried up completely. Thus, the species could survive in its normal watery habitat. According to this hypothesis, therefore, cutinized windblown spores, rigid bodies, cuticles, etc., were, for the time being, simply adaptations for increasing the chances that the individual alga (or species of which it was a member) would survive in its proper watery environment.

Over hundreds of generations and millions of years, the process of natural selection could easily produce plants capable of full terrestrial existence. Once the transition to the land had been accomplished, the stage was set for the relatively rapid adaptive radiation of land plants into nearly all available habitats. This radiation led not merely to the development of the familiar surviving bryophytes, club mosses, horsetails, ferns, gymnosperms, and flowering plants, but also to many groups now extinct, such as Devonian psilophytes, Carboniferous fossil club mosses and fossil horsetails, seed ferns, and fossil cycads.

## 25-9
## THE EARLY
## LAND PLANTS

If the immediate ancestors of the land plants were, indeed, ancient green algae, then one should expect the earliest known land plants to possess an algalike body composed of a slender, green, branching axis. Most likely such a plant body would not be differentiated into roots, stems, and leaves (since green algae lack those structures). Such an hypothesis was proposed in the early part of this century by the French botanist O. Lignier. Lignier visualized the earliest land plants to have had an underground anchoring and absorbing system that was merely a slightly modified portion of the main axis of the body, hardly different in its internal structure from the aerial portion (Fig. 25–21).

Support for Lignier's hypothesis came with the discovery in 1917 of some fossil plants essentially like those he had envisioned some years earlier. In northeastern Scotland near the village of Rhynie, a petrified peat bog of lower Devonian age was found to contain several species of beautifully preserved plants (Fig. 25–22). The rock containing the fossils, being extremely hard, required many months of patient and painstaking effort to prepare for study with the microscope. Successive slices of the rock were cut and ground thin

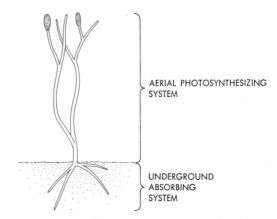

FIG. 25–21　An interpretation of the earliest land plant, postulated by Lignier. Note the lack of differentiation into leaves, stem, and roots.

AERIAL PHOTOSYNTHESIZING SYSTEM

UNDERGROUND ABSORBING SYSTEM

FIG. 25–22　A reconstruction of a landscape during the early Devonian period, showing plants of *Rhynia* and other early vascular plants in the foreground. (Landscape courtesy Brooklyn Botanic Garden.)

enough to permit light to pass through. Using this technique, the entire bodies of the plants were traced through the rock and accurate and lifelike reconstructions of these organisms were prepared (Fig. 25–23, left) by the paleobotanists Robert Kidston and William Lang.

Two species of these fossil plants were described and named as the genus *Rhynia* (after the village). One species was a small plant about 8 inches tall while the other was about 20 inches in height. The plants grew in dense aggregations in marshes or bogs which were periodically flooded with water (Fig. 25–22). Neither of the plants possessed leaves, nor were their bodies clearly differentiated into stems and roots. The erect aerial portion of these plants was apparently green and probably functioned in photosynthesis. The horizontal underground portion bore delicate rhizoids which probably served to absorb water and

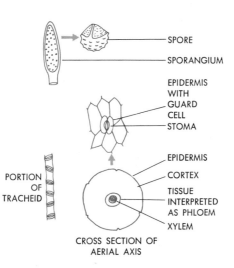

FIG. 25–23　Left: a reconstruction of *Rhynia Gwynne-Vaughani*.　Right: diagrams of various parts of the *Rhynia* body.　(Photo reproduced by permission of the Field Museum of Natural History, Chicago.)

dissolved minerals from the soil.　Structurally, however, the subterranean portion of these plants was like the aerial portion.

The *Rhynia* plants possessed several adaptations for terrestrial life.　Excessive loss of water from the aerial portion was prevented by an epidermis covered with a thick cuticle.　Entrance of oxygen for respiration and carbon dioxide for photosynthesis was facilitated by stomata scattered about in the epidermis (Fig. 25–23).　Internal to the epidermis was a broad cortex tissue with large spaces between the cells, the latter an adaptation for exposing a maximum amount of surface for the diffusion of gases into and out of the cells.　This feature suggests that the cortex functioned in photosynthesis.　In the center of the plant body was a slender cylinder of conducting (vascular) tissue composed of a core of xylem tissue surrounded by a narrow band of elongate cells that may have been phloem tissue.　The cells of the xylem tissue were tracheids, each of which possessed annular secondary wall thickening which probably functioned to keep the cell from collapsing with subsequent elongation during growth of the stem.

Species dispersal seems to have been accomplished in *Rhynia* by spores with cutinized walls, an adaptation which would permit them to be carried from one place to another by air currents without drying out.　These spores were produced inside sporangia at the tips of some of the aerial branches.　The fossils revealed nothing, however, of the gamete-producing phase.

The simplicity of the plant body of *Rhynia*, with its low degree of organ differentiation, is suggestive of many algae.　*Rhynia* possesses most of the characteristics postulated by Lignier to have been present in the early land plants or their immediate ancestors.　*Rhynia* provides an excellent example of the discovery of an actual organism which corresponds closely to one previously hypothesized to have existed.

Within a few years after Kidston and Lang completed their interpretations of *Rhynia*, many paleobotanists and plant evolutionists came to regard these plants as representing the actual ancestor of all vascular land plants. Considering the simplicity of these plants and the close agreement with the early land plant postulated by Lignier, this is perhaps understandable. The idea that, during the Devonian period, all other vascular plants evolved from *Rhynia* soon led to the classification of all vascular plants within a single division (phylum), the Tracheophyta or "plants with vascular tissues."

Actually, at the time that *Rhynia* was described, evidence was already available to show that neither it nor any other plant of the early Devonian period could possibly be the ancestor of all of today's vascular plants. In fact, Kidston and Lang found another even more complex plant in the same petrified peat bog where the two species of *Rhynia* were discovered. This plant, named *Asteroxylon* by Kidston and Lang, differed from *Rhynia* in possessing a strong central upright stem densely clothed with numerous small cuticularized leaflike structures (Fig. 25-24). Internally, the arrangement of the vascular tissues was more elaborate than that found in *Rhynia*. The xylem was conspicuously lobed when viewed in cross-section; this starlike appearance gave rise to the generic name *Asteroxylon*, meaning "star wood." In addition, the tracheid cells were more complex; on the inner surface of the cell wall were thickenings in the form of closely coiled helices (whereas those of *Rhynia* were merely rings). Originating from the arms of the xylem were very small vascular strands which traversed the cortex tissue and stopped just short of entering the leaflike structures. It seems clear that these structures, while not true leaves (since they do not have vascular tissue inside them), did greatly increase the surface of the plant exposed to the sunlight.

About fifteen years after Kidston and Lang presented their studies of *Rhynia* and *Asteroxylon*, a third, even more complex, vascular plant was discovered in Australian rocks of the early Devonian period. This plant, named *Baragwanathia* (after an Australian geologist) has the same general appearance of *Asteroxylon* but differed significantly in possessing a much thicker stem (up to about 2 cm) and slender, almost needlelike leaves which grew to a length of 4 cm (Fig. 25-25). Internally, throughout its entire length, each leaf had a slender central vascular strand. In cross section, the xylem tissue had even more lobes or arms of xylem than did *Asteroxylon* (at least 12). In longitudinal section, the xylem was composed of elongate tracheid cells, each of which had secondary wall thickenings in the form of rings.* Kidney-shaped sporangia were produced by *Baragwanathia*; whether they were attached at the base of the leaves or to the stem near the base of the leaves could not be determined because of the highly compressed state of the fossil specimens.

---

* In this feature, *Baragwanathia* was less complex than *Asteroxylon*. It is not unusual, however, for different parts of an organism to undergo evolutionary changes at different rates.

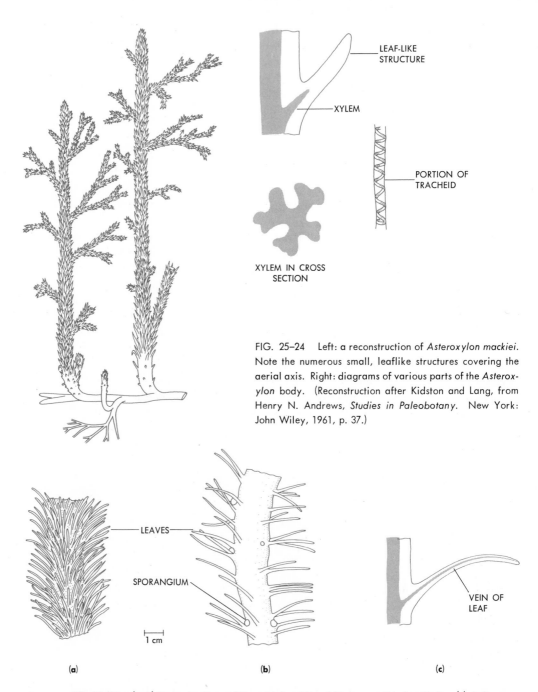

FIG. 25–24   Left: a reconstruction of *Asteroxylon mackiei*. Note the numerous small, leaflike structures covering the aerial axis. Right: diagrams of various parts of the *Asteroxylon* body. (Reconstruction after Kidston and Lang, from Henry N. Andrews, *Studies in Paleobotany*. New York: John Wiley, 1961, p. 37.)

FIG. 25–25   (a, b) Reconstructions of the aerial portion of *Baragwanathia longifolia*. (c) A diagram of a leaf of *Baragwanathia* showing the vein extending throughout the length of the leaf. (Reconstructions after Lang and Cookson, from Peter R. Bell and C. L. F. Woodcock, *The Diversity of Green Plants*. Reading, Mass.: Addison-Wesley, 1968.)

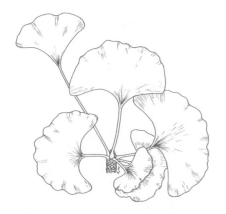
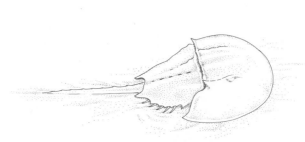

FIG. 25–26   Two contemporary examples of slowly evolving organisms.  Left: leaves of the tree *Gingko*.  Right: *Limulus*, the horseshoe "crab."  (Drawing of *Gingko* after Paul Weatherwax, *Botany*, 3rd edition.  Philadelphia: W. B. Saunders, 1956, p. 424.)

By the middle 1930's sufficient knowledge of the early Devonian land plants had been accumulated to cast serious doubt on the hypothesis that *Rhynia* was the actual ancestor of all of the land plants.  Yet, as recently as the middle 1950's some botanists still adhered to this hypothesis.  Part of the reluctance to reevaluate the concept was undoubtedly due to the fact that the precise nature of the evolutionary process, as viewed over long spans of geologic time was, until quite recently, still obscure.  Now that so much is known concerning both the diversity of the early Devonian plant life, as well as the way in which evolution operates, a reevaluation of our thinking concerning these early plants has become necessary.

If *Rhynia* and other early Devonian plants with relatively simple bodies are *not* the ancestors of all the other land plants, then how are we to view them?  A recent hypothesis proposes that *Rhynia* and its relatives (the "psilophytes") may simply be plants which persisted for millions of years as survivors of a still more ancient flora.  According to this viewpoint, these plants were able to survive with little change since they lived in rather stable, marshy environments.  Contemporary examples of other slowly-evolving organisms include *Gingko*, a tree which has remained relatively unchanged for more than 200 million years, and *Limulus*, a genus of shelled invertebrate animals hardly different today from those which lived some 400 million years ago (see Fig. 25–26).  It is thus well documented that if a species of organism is well adapted to an environment that remains constant for long periods of time, the species can remain in a stable equilibrium with this environment indefinitely, without showing any signs of evolutionary change.

While the hypothesis proposing that all vascular plants evolved from *Rhynia* is no longer tenable, these ancient, simple plants can still serve as models of an early simple stage in body development, a stage through which the ancestors of each of the several evolutionary lines of vascular plant must have passed.

25-10
EVOLUTION OF
REPRODUCTIVE
SYSTEMS IN
THE EARLY
LAND PLANTS

While changes in the entire plant body (e.g., stem, leaves, roots) were essential for adaptation to life on land, perhaps no changes equaled those in the reproductive systems. The result of these changes was greater adaptation of the reproductive methods to terrestrial existence.

There is good evidence that the earliest known vascular plants had a reproductive system which included an alternation of two distinct phases (or generations). One of these phases produced spores inside sporangia. This spore-producing plant (sporophyte) had chlorophyll and undoubtedly lived an independent existence. Nothing is known of the gamete-producing phase (gametophyte) of these ancient plants. It is possible, however, to study the reproduction of living members of these evolutionary lines. With this knowledge, the botanist can reconstruct the probable nature of the gametophyte phase of the early vascular plants.

Living ferns are good models for such an analysis. While certain tropical ferns may produce trunks as large as those of many trees, the body of most fern plants consists of an underground stem, the rhizome, from which small roots extend as adaptations for absorbing water and dissolved minerals. Growing upward from the rhizome are the leaves (fronds). The fronds not only serve for photosynthesis, but also bear spores inside sporangia. In most species, the sporangia are crowded into compact groups (sori), often on the undersides of the leaves. When mature, the sporangia burst open and expel the spores to sites often located considerable distances from the parent plant. The life cycle of a fern is shown in Fig. 25–27. If the spores fall onto moist soil, they germinate and grow into small, green structures, the gametophytes. Each gametophyte has small rhizoids on the lower surface next to the soil, and is photosynthetic. Thus, it lives on the forest floor independently of the sporophyte plant. Because the spore from which it develops is haploid, all of the gametophyte cells are haploid.

When mature, the gametophyte generally produces both **archegonia** (female gamete-producing organs) and **antheridia** (male gamete-producing organs). Sperms, produced in the antheridia, reach eggs in the archegonia by swimming through a film of water on the surface of the gametophyte, and produce diploid zygotes. By mitotic cell division, the zygote grows into the sporophyte plant. While young, the sporophyte absorbs food from the body of the gametophyte. Later, the new sporophyte becomes established as an independent plant; the gametophyte dies.

It is apparent that ferns cannot reproduce in dry habitats. They depend on an external medium for accomplishing fertilization. This fact provides supporting evidence for the hypothesis that land plants evolved from ancestral algae which lived and reproduced in the water.

In addition to most ferns, certain species of lycopods and arthrophytes possess the *homosporous* (one type of spore) type of reproductive system. The gametophytes of all of these plants produce *both* kinds of gamete-producing organs, that is, each gametophyte plant is bisexual. It seems reasonable to hypothesize, therefore, that the earliest vascular plants, known to have been

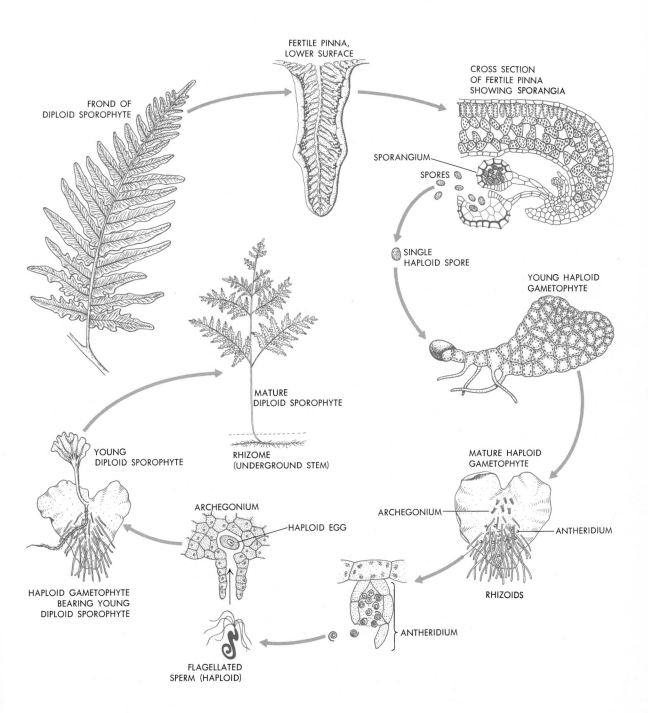

FIG. 25–27   Life cycle of a fern.

homosporous, also produced bisexual gametophytes similar in size and structure to those of the living ferns, lycopods, and arthrophytes.

While the early Devonian vascular plants produced only one type of spore (homosporous) and one kind of gametophyte (bisexual), later during the Devonian period, plants evolved which produced two kinds of spores. Certain of the sporangia on the sporophytes produced large spores (called **megaspores**) and others formed smaller spores (or **microspores**). This condition is known as **heterospory.** In many living heterosporous plants, e.g., species of the spikemoss *Selaginella*, the sporangia are borne on the upper sides of special leaves and, in many species, are aggregated into conelike structures. Some of the sporangia produce one to four large, thick-walled megaspores, while others form much smaller and numerous thin-walled microspores (Fig. 25–28). Each megaspore germinates into a many-celled, haploid, female gametophyte plant which remains within the wall of the megaspore throughout most of its development. At maturity, however, the continued growth of the female gametophyte ruptures the megaspore wall and a small portion protrudes through the break. In this exposed portion of the female gametophyte, the archegonia develop. In most species, the female gametophyte, still partially enclosed by the megaspore wall, is then liberated from the sporangium.

Each microspore also begins to germinate while still inside the sporangium, forming a male gametophyte consisting of only one antheridium filled with numerous flagellated sperm. (The remainder of the gametophyte body has apparently been lost during the course of evolution.) At maturity, the male gametophyte (still enclosed by the wall of the microspore) is liberated and transported by the wind. Upon reaching a suitable watery medium, the microspore wall breaks open and the sperms are freed. The sperms swim through the water and, if they encounter a female gametophyte, enter the archegonia and fertilize the eggs. Each zygote will develop into an independent, free-living sporophyte plant.

Heterosporous plants, such as *Selaginella*, possess several features which enable them to cope effectively with life on the land. The germination and development of the female gametophyte inside the thick megaspore wall affords the young gametophyte considerable protection. Further, a reserve of food accumulates inside the megaspore. This food is used during the early growth of the young sporophyte that develops from the zygote inside the archegonium.

The evolution from homospory to heterospory and the accompanying segregation of the sexes in the gametophytes had occurred by the upper Devonian period in several lines of vascular plants. Although there are to date still no undisputed fern fossils from the Devonian period, it is likely that this segregation of sexes had occurred in the ferns' ancestors as well as those of the gymnosperms. By the middle Carboniferous period, heterospory appeared in many species of lycopod herbs and trees. Thus it seems certain that heterospory and unisexual gametophytes have evolved independently in many different groups of vascular plants.

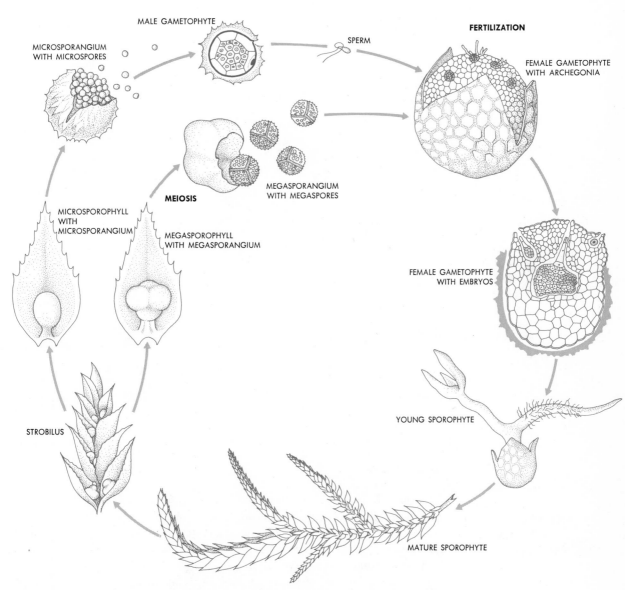

MALE GAMETOPHYTE

MICROSPORANGIUM
WITH MICROSPORES

SPERM

**FERTILIZATION**

FEMALE GAMETOPHYTE
WITH ARCHEGONIA

MEGASPORANGIUM
WITH MEGASPORES

**MEIOSIS**

MICROSPOROPHYLL
WITH
MICROSPORANGIUM

MEGASPOROPHYLL
WITH MEGASPORANGIUM

FEMALE GAMETOPHYTE
WITH EMBRYOS

STROBILUS

YOUNG SPOROPHYTE

MATURE SPOROPHYTE

FIG. 25–28   Reproduction in a contemporary heterosporous vascular plant, the spikemoss *Sela-ginella.* (After E. W. Sinnott and K. S. Wilson, *Botany: Principles and Problems.* New York: McGraw-Hill, 1963, p. 417.)

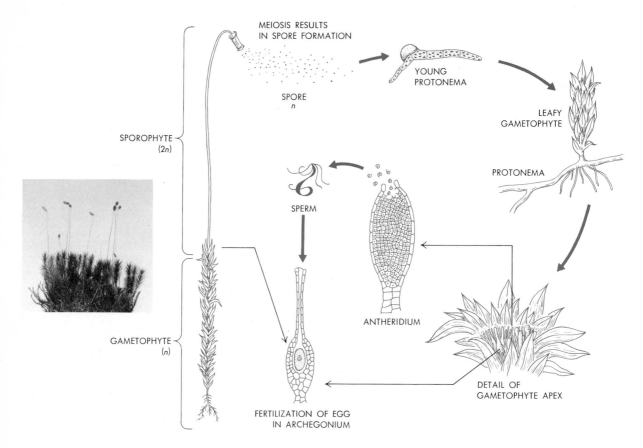

MEIOSIS RESULTS
IN SPORE FORMATION

YOUNG
PROTONEMA

SPORE
*n*

LEAFY
GAMETOPHYTE

SPOROPHYTE
(2*n*)

PROTONEMA

SPERM

ANTHERIDIUM

GAMETOPHYTE
(*n*)

DETAIL OF
GAMETOPHYTE APEX

FERTILIZATION OF EGG
IN ARCHEGONIUM

FIG. 25–29    Schematic representation of the life cycle of a moss.   At left is a photo of the moss *Polytrichum commune,* showing the sporophyte with its capsule.   (Photo courtesy American Museum of Natural History.)

## 25–11
## SECONDARY
## INVASIONS OF
## THE LAND:
## THE BRYOPHYTES

Bryophytes are much simpler terrestrial plants than the vascular plants.  They form a dominant part of the vegetation in some parts of the world, e.g., bogs in the temperate regions and at high elevations in the tropics.  Most bryophytes inhabit moist, shaded situations, possessing few adaptations for resisting desiccation.  Some species live on tree trunks and others inhabit shallow rock crevices where they are exposed to extreme temperatures and drying winds.  They grow only during periods of wet weather, but manage to survive long periods of drought.  A few species are aquatic.

Bryophytes probably evolved from ancient green algae, most likely from some of the filamentous species.  Indeed, the Bryophyta share many characteristics with the Chlorophyta, including chlorophylls *a* and *b* in the chloroplasts, cellulose in the cell walls, and starch as a food reserve.  While similar in many features, the bryophytes have evolved much more complex bodies than have the green algae.

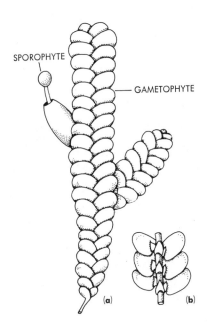

FIG. 25–30 Two liverworts. Left: gametophytes of *Ricciocarpus natans*, growing floating in pond water. Right: a leafy liverwort, *Porella bolanderi*, with dorsal view (a) of a large leafy gametophyte with small sporophyte. In the ventral view (b), the small leaves on the underside of the gametophyte are visible. (Photo courtesy William C. Steere, New York Botanical Garden; drawings from Arthur W. Haupt, *Introduction to Botany*, New York: McGraw-Hill, 1956, p. 321.)

The earliest known undisputed fossils of bryophytes are from rocks of the upper Devonian and Carboniferous periods. These fossils are very similar to present-day leaf liverworts and mosses. Undoubtedly, therefore, these plant groups had appeared at a much earlier time. While they apparently originated about the same time as the early vascular plants, bryophytes have never formed a major component of the world's vegetation. The mosses and the liverworts have been separate evolutionary lines at least as far back as the Carboniferous period. In fact, they may have originated independently from separate green algal ancestors. Neither group exhibits any obvious relationships with the vascular plants.

By contrast with the vascular plants, the gametophyte generation is the predominant phase in the mosses and liverworts. The green carpet of moss found on the forest floor is the gametophyte; it is composed of leafy, upright structures which arise from a horizontal filament, or protonema. The cells of the moss gametophyte are haploid. At the apex of the gametophyte are antheridia and archegonia. Fertilization via water occurs here, and the diploid, leafless sporophyte grows directly from the leafy gametophyte plant.

The sporophyte has a sporangium at the top in which haploid spores are produced by meiosis. When the spores are mature, the sporangium opens, the spores sift out, and are blown by the wind. When it reaches favorable conditions, each spore germinates into another gametophyte. The life cycle of a moss is shown in Fig. 25–29.

Bryophytes lack vascular tissue; thus, they have neither the means for efficient conduction of water and materials nor the supporting tissue (xylem) which would allow extensive upward growth.  For this reason, the mosses and liverworts are restricted in size.  They are literally overshadowed by most of the vascular plants in the competition for sunlight.  Like the ferns, however, mosses and liverworts (Fig. 25–30) are totally dependent on a moist habitat for the survival of the gametophyte and for effective means of fertilization.

**25–12<br>SECONDARY<br>INVASIONS OF<br>THE LAND:<br>THE FUNGI**

As green plants invaded the land, a new environment was created—one in which the fungi could compete successfully for energy and materials.  Indeed, since the decomposer organisms (fungi as well as bacteria) are fundamental components of the ecosystem, it seems only natural that the fungi would accompany or follow the green plants onto the land.  Without the decomposers, the newly evolving terrestrial ecosystems could not long continue to function.

A fungus is a unique land organism.  Unlike the vascular plants, which solve the problem of water loss by covering the aerial portions with cutin or a corky bark, the fungus escapes the problem of water loss by having the major portion of its body hidden within the soil, rotting log, or tissues of a green plant.  Like other land plants, however, fungi are dual, and have aerial as well as immersed portions.  Unlike the green land plants, however, the duality is not between the shoot and root but between the filaments (hyphae) which absorb food from the environment and the reproductive structure (e.g., the stalked mushroom) which produces and disperses the spores.

Basically, fungi may be considered as filamentous plants without chloroplasts.  Like most of the bacteria, fungi live by decaying the tissues of plants and animals (and even other fungi).  The fungal hypha is usually a very long tubular filament which branches occasionally.  A firm wall composed mainly of chitin encloses the cells of most fungi.  The partitions between the cells consist of crosswalls or "septa," each of which has a small central opening permitting cytoplasm and nuclei to move between adjacent cells.  The fungus obtains its food by secreting enzymes through the filament walls.  These enzymes break down the wood or other organic substratum in the environment, and the digested material is absorbed into the filaments.  Thus, the soft delicate hyphae of a fungus can penetrate hard wood without being damaged: they literally digest their passage into the food source.

The diversity of the fungi is tremendous.  During their adaptive radiation, they have produced some 200,000 species; each year, a thousand or more species previously unknown to mycology (study of fungi) are described.  Like any large and diverse group of organisms, the fungi present difficult problems in classification.  Complicating the task of classification is the increasing realization by mycologists that the fungi actually include several distinct evolutionary lines derived from widely differing ancestors.

The fungi include six main groups: the Chytridiomycetes (chytrids), Myxomycetes (true slime molds), Zygomycetes (bread molds), Oömycetes (water molds and downy mildews), Ascomycetes, and Basidiomycetes.  Although various species of the first four groups of fungi have evolved adaptations which enable them to survive in terrestrial environments (especially the Myxomycetes), it is the Ascomycetes and Basidiomycetes which have been most successful in making the evolutionary transition to the land. This is one main reason for considering these two groups in a chapter with the vascular plants and bryophytes. A second, equally important reason is the role of these fungi as decomposers in terrestrial ecosystems.

The Ascomycete and Basidiomycete fungi differ from most of the chytrids, bread molds, water molds, and downy mildews in that their hyphae usually are subdivided into cellular segments by septa. Since the septa are perforated, however, each segment may contain one to many nuclei. (The hyphal filaments of most other fungi are essentially long tubes with very few or no transverse walls.)

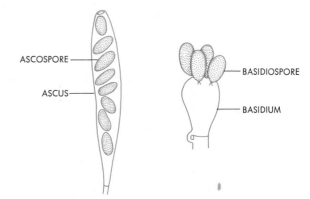

FIG. 25–31   Reproductive structures of fungi. Left: the ascus of the Ascomycetes. Right: the basidium of the Basidiomycetes.

Although similar in possessing a basically filamentous body organization and chitinous cell walls, the Ascomycetes and Basidiomycetes differ from each other in certain features of their reproductive systems (Fig. 25–31). In the former group, the meiospores (spores produced by meiosis) are formed inside special elongated, terminal hyphal cells known as **asci** (sing., **ascus**; Greek, sac). Each of the four meiospores divides once by mitosis, producing eight ascospores in each ascus. At maturity the ascospores are forcibly ejected through an opening which forms in the top of the ascus, and are blown about by the wind. The Basidiomycetes, however, produce their meiospores on minute stalks on the outside of a special terminal hyphal cell called a **basidium** (pl., **basidia**; Greek, base or pedestal). Usually only four meiospores (= basidiospores) are developed from each basidium. When mature, the basidiospores are forcibly detached from the stalks and dispersed by air currents.

Much of the evolution among the fungi of these groups has involved the fruiting body within which the spores are produced. The fruiting body evolution has resulted in the formation of reproductive structures well adapted for the rapid production of numerous spores and the efficient dispersal of the spores.

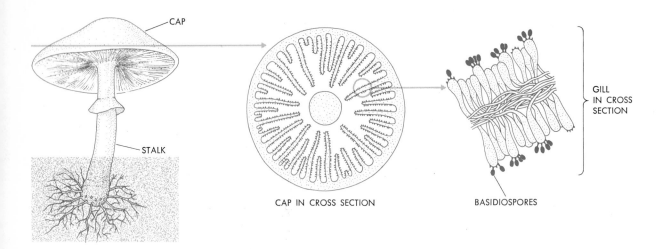

FIG. 25–32    A fungus fruiting body well adapted for the production of numerous spores and their dispersal in an efficient manner.  After being forcibly ejected from the basidia, the spores fall downward in the space between the vertical gills suspended beneath the mushroom cap.  After clearing the gills, the spores may be blown by the wind to new locations.

Consider the umbrella type of fruiting body so characteristic of many species of Basidiomycetes.  The undersurface of the umbrella is modified into flat vertical plates of tissue (gills), tubes, or spines covered with basidia; these are adaptations for increasing the spore-producing area.  Since they are located on the underside of the umbrella fruiting body, the spore-producing structures are protected from the rain.  In many species, the umbrella is elevated above the substratum by a slender to stout stalk (Fig. 25–32).  This slight elevation enables the spores to be picked up by air currents immediately after they are ejected from the basidia.  In certain species (e.g., those in the family Polyporaceae, or bracket fungi), the stalk has been lost.  Since these fungi usually grow within the trunks of standing trees or fallen logs, the fruiting bodies are already elevated enough for efficient spore dispersal.

The fruiting body, which is the only part of these fungi usually seen, is uniquely constructed of hundreds or thousands of hyphae densely aggregated into a kind of tissue (see Fig. 25–33).  Unlike the true tissue present in multicellular plants, this fungus tissue may be easily separated into the separate hyphal filaments of which it is constructed, simply by careful manipulation with a dissecting needle.

The Basidiomycetes and many of the Ascomycetes have evolved their own unique version of diploidy.  Each cell contains two haploid nuclei $(n + n)$ which

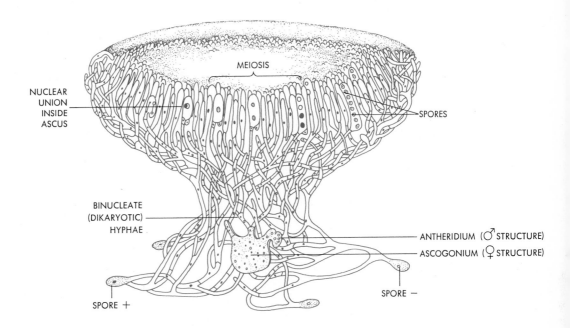

FIG. 25–33    Diagrammatic representation of the internal structure of the fruiting body of an Ascomycete fungus. Note that the fruiting body tissue consists of both uninucleate and binucleate (dikaryotic) hyphae. (Adapted from L. W. Sharp, *Fundamentals of Cytology.* New York: McGraw-Hill, 1943.)

divide at the same time but do not fuse into a diploid nucleus until the time of spore formation in the fruiting body. Binucleate or **dikaryotic** hyphae constitute the main food-absorbing stage in most Basidiomycete fungi (Fig. 25–34). In the Ascomycetes, however, the dikaryotic stage is of short duration, occurring only inside the fruiting bodies (Fig. 25–33).

One other unique characteristic of many Basidiomycetes, especially the mushrooms, bracket fungi, and puff balls, is the absence of any special sex organs. In these organisms, sexuality involves nuclei, not reproductive cells or organs as in most living things. When a haploid spore germinates, a short hypha with a single nucleus per cell is formed. If this uninucleate hypha meets another from a different spore in the soil or rotting log, they may unite at points of contact (Fig. 25–34). Nuclei from the hypha of one spore may then migrate into the hypha of the second spore. The nuclei contributed from the hypha of each spore do not fuse immediately, but remain paired side by side and divide simultaneously, making the dikaryotic hyphae that carry out the food absorption in the fungus.

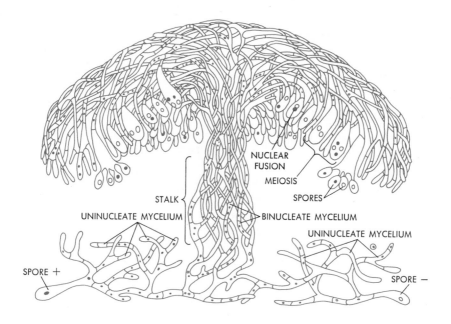

FIG. 25–34    Diagrammatic representation of the internal structure of the fruiting body of a Basid-iomycete fungus. The fruiting body consists entirely of binucleate hyphae produced from the fusion of two uninucleate hyphae, each of which developed from a haploid spore. (Adapted from L. W. Sharp, *Fundamentals of Cytology.* New York: McGraw-Hill, 1943.)

When the fruiting bodies develop, the pairs of nuclei derived from different spores finally fuse, forming a diploid nucleus inside the basidium. Through meiosis, this zygotic nucleus divides into four haploid nuclei, each of which then migrates into a tiny protrusion of the basidium wall, forming a stalked structure which develops into a basidiospore.

It seems reasonable to hypothesize that the Ascomycete and Basidiomycete fungi may not have evolved until about the time that green plants began to invade the land. Clear evidence that fungi were in existence at this time is provided by the discovery of hyphae in the fossilized remains of the vascular plant *Asteroxylon*, which grew in bogs of Scotland during the lower Devonian period. Recently, hyphae identified as being of Basidiomycete nature were found within the wood of a fern which lived during the middle Pennsylvanian period about 300 million years ago. Both of these discoveries lend support to the hypothesis that the two principal evolutionary lines of terrestrial fungi, the Ascomycetes and the Basidiomycetes, were established at an early stage in the evolution of land plants.

Any account of terrestrial plants would be incomplete without some consideration of those unique plants known as lichens. Lichens have distinctive forms and structures. For a long time, they were described as individual plants, just as any other member of the plant kingdom. During the 1860's, however, it was discovered that lichens are actually dual or composite plants composed of a fungus and an alga living in intimate association. Since then, lichens have been the center of controversy over the actual interrelationships of the two kinds of organisms which enter into their composition.

At least 26 genera of algae are known to be involved in lichen associations, including eight blue-green algae, seventeen green algae, and one yellow-green alga. The most common blue-green algae found in lichens are *Nostoc* and *Syctonema*. The unicellular alga *Trebouxia* is the most common green alga of lichens. More than 80% of all lichens involve genera of green algae.

Fungi classified in the Ascomycetes comprise most lichen associations. A few species of Basidiomycetes also produce lichens.

The lichen body is highly diverse in form and structure. Many species simply produce a powdery layer over the rock or tree bark. Others develop a thin crust which adheres closely to the substratum so tightly that the lichen appears to be painted on. Still other species of lichens grow into leafy forms which are much less tightly attached to the bark or rock surface (Fig. 20–9). Unlike the crust-formers, the leafy lichens can be carefully peeled off. The most complex lichen bodies resemble tiny shrubs, with flattened or cylindrical branches. Some species of these lichens stand stiffly erect, while others hang in long streamers from the branches of trees.

Internally, the lichen body may exhibit considerable differentiation. The algal cells may be scattered throughout or they may be restricted mainly to a specific layer. The fungal hyphae may produce tissue-like layers, including an epidermislike configuration on the surface, a cortexlike layer just beneath, and a central core or medulla (Fig. 20–9). Bundles of hyphae often form rootlike absorbing and anchoring structures on the lower surface of the lichen body.

The fungal hyphae form a close network enclosing the algal cells, often embedding the alga in a tissuelike mass. In most lichens, projections of the fungal hyphae actually penetrate the algal cells.

Investigations of lichens by numerous botanists, including intensive physiological studies by Vernon Ahmadjian at Clark University, have demonstrated that a lichen is not a simple mixture of an alga and a fungus. Not only does the lichen represent a physiological interaction between alga and fungus, but the association produces a distinctive morphological entity with features considerably different from those of the individual fungus or alga. Thus, the composite plant is different from either of its two components.

The exact nature of the interaction between the fungus and the alga comprising a lichen is only now beginning to be understood. One widely accepted hypothesis proposes that the alga, being photosynthetic, provides the fungus with organic compounds.    The fungus, in turn, provides the alga with water and minerals, as well as protection from desiccation and high light intensities.    Some support for this hypothesis has come from autoradiography.    Pieces of a lichen were provided with $C^{14}$-labeled sodium bicarbonate as its source of carbon dioxide for photosynthesis.    The $C^{14}$ rapidly appeared in various organic compounds, first in the algal layer of the lichen and, fifteen minutes later, in the hyphae of the medulla.    The movement of materials from the alga to the fungus probably occurred by diffusion from the alga and subsequent absorption by the fungus.

Much controversy has centered around the interpretation of the dual nature of the lichen.    Some investigators have maintained that both the alga and the fungus benefit from the association, i.e., the relationship is a mutualistic one. The autoradiography data demonstrating the movement of materials between the alga and the fungus offer some support for this interpretation.    Further, the algal cells within the lichen appear to be healthy and, in many areas, lichens are known to grow where neither the alga nor the fungus could survive alone.

Other investigators, however, consider the fungus to be a parasite upon the alga, the parasitism being sufficiently weak so that most of the algal cells survive.    Demonstration that the fungal hyphae actually penetrate the algal cells supports this hypothesis.    These investigators find it difficult to see any real benefit which the alga gets from the fungus, pointing out that the alga could obtain water and minerals in the free-living state just as well by itself as in association with the fungus.

As is so often the case in science, both sides of the controversy may be correct.    The diversity of lichen unions of algae and fungi is so immense, it is difficult to set up all-or-none definitions covering all cases.    In some species of lichens, the fungus is unquestionably a parasite upon the alga, while in others, the two partners exist in a relationship benefiting both.    In still other lichens, both conditions may exist: the fungus kills the algal cells at times in parts of the lichen body while it lives mutualistically with the algae in another portion of the lichen.

Indeed, it is to be expected that the nature of the lichen association would be variable, since algae and fungi vary considerably in their evolutionary origin. Thus, the evolutionary origin of lichens is doubly intriguing.    The time of origin would seem to be long after their component parts, algae and fungi, had undergone periods of differentiation.    The fossil record is of little help, since the earliest unquestionable lichen fossil is from the Mesozoic era, a time long after the algae and fungal groups had evolved and the numerous kinds of land plants had appeared and diversified.    Ahmadjian has hypothesized that the first lichen association occurred when certain fungi growing in the same habitat as algae started to parasitize the algae.    In laboratory cultures, lichen fungal hyphal tend to encircle rounded objects such as unicellular algae and actually penetrate the algal cells.    Most of the penetrated algal cells die, but the population is maintained by division of the cells not parasitized. Ahmadjian postulates that the first primitive lichen association may have started in a similar fashion. If small pieces of this early lichen happened to be moved by rain or wind onto a rock surface, where neither the alga nor the fungus could grow alone, natural selection would have eliminated all those forms in which the parasitism of the fungus was severe enough to keep the alga from surviving. Under these conditions, the initial parasitism would gradually develop into mutualism, and the alga and the fungus would become dependent on one another. Any genetic changes resulting in a more beneficial association to both organisms (e.g., the loss of the ability to synthesize certain vitamins), would have made the union more permanent. Any change resulting in a slower growth rate of the fungus would also have been selected for, since a fast-growing fungus would kill all the algal cells before a balanced relationship could be attained.

Not only are lichens highly interesting as dual or composite organisms, but they are also important members of the land flora. In the forests of Scandinavia and in subarctic Canada, lichens form extensive growth covers, providing pasture for grazing reindeer and caribou. Lichens also grow in well lighted areas such as rock surfaces and tree trunks through most of the world, and play a role in converting these substances into soil.

25–14
THE GYMNOSPERMS

The term "gymnosperm" means "naked seed"; the gymnosperms are seed-bearing plants. They began to appear in the Devonian period (about 380 million years ago). The gymnosperms or **conifers** are woody plants, containing large amounts of xylem and also some phloem. The woody tissue of conifers is composed only of tracheids, the xylem vessels found in angiosperm stems being a later evolutionary development. The increased amount of xylem has allowed the conifers to become quite large and thus to compete successfully for sunshine. The xylem increased both the amount of conduction possible and the sturdiness of the entire plant. The sporophyte generation of the conifers is dominant (the pine tree represents the sporophyte), the gametophytes being reduced to a small number of cells retained on the sporophyte itself.

The life cycle of a conifer is shown in Fig. 25–35. The spores produced on a mature pine tree are contained within cones. All conifers produce two types of spores, each in a different kind of cone. The male cones are relatively small (about $\frac{1}{2}$ to $\frac{3}{4}$ in. in length) and are located on the lower branches of the tree. The female cones are much larger (these are cones frequently used as Christmas decorations), and are located on the upper branches. Such an adaptation makes it less likely that pollen will be carried from the lower branches to the upper branches of the same tree.

The spores produced in male cones develop into winged pollen grains. They are blown by the wind to other trees, where they fall between the scales of female cones. Here, a long **pollen tube** develops from the pollen grain. The male nucleus travels down the pollen tube and is discharged into the arche-

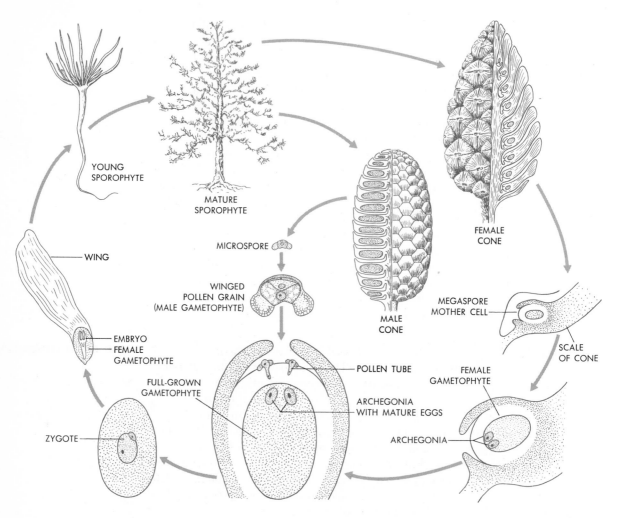

YOUNG
SPOROPHYTE

MATURE
SPOROPHYTE

MICROSPORE

WINGED
POLLEN GRAIN
(MALE GAMETOPHYTE)

MALE
CONE

FEMALE
CONE

MEGASPORE
MOTHER CELL

SCALE
OF CONE

WING

EMBRYO
FEMALE
GAMETOPHYTE

FULL-GROWN
GAMETOPHYTE

POLLEN TUBE

ARCHEGONIA
WITH MATURE EGGS

FEMALE
GAMETOPHYTE

ZYGOTE

ARCHEGONIA

FIG. 25–35    Life cycle of a pine tree (a conifer).

gonium. It unites with the egg nucleus, and the formation of the embryo begins.
Note the male nucleus itself is not motile, but merely passes down the tube to
reach the egg.

After fertilization, the zygote grows into a young embryo sporophyte.
Around the embryo a nutritive material (female gametophyte) develops, which
provides the germinating seedling with enough nutrients to carry it to the stage
where it can make its own. The embryo, the endosperm, and the seed coat make
up the seed. When the seed is fully developed, it falls away from the female
cone and is carried by the wind. If it reaches favorable ground and is exposed
to proper conditions, it germinates.

The reproductive pattern of the gymnosperms represents several distinct advances over that of the ferns. First, fertilization is independent of outside conditions of moisture. Second, the sperm nucleus is carried to the egg by the formation of a pollen tube. The pollen tube not only guides the sperm nucleus toward the egg, but also, by forming a passage through the female gametophyte tissue, provides a more protected environment for the crucial period leading up to fertilization. In the ferns, sperm must swim on the exposed surface of the gametophyte to reach the archegonia. This greatly reduces the chances of successful fertilization. Third, because the female gametophyte is retained on the parent sporophyte, the fertilized egg is given a greater amount of protection in its early stages of development. Protection of the female gametophyte, and of the developing zygote, is of great selective advantage. From the early gymnosperms, this adaptation is a universal characteristic of all higher plants. Fourth, the embryo is protected by the formation of a seed. This, indeed, represents a major evolutionary advancement. Not only does the tough seed coat provide protection for the embryo against mechanical damage, it also prevents drying out. Thus the embryo sporophyte may be able to survive until it reaches a favorable spot for germination. The seed also allows for the storage of food. Recall that young fern sporophytes have very little food reserves to call upon. They must be autotrophic almost from the very start. Providing the germinating sporophyte with a small "push"—as all seed plants do—greatly increases the survival capacity of offspring.

The term "angiosperm" means "seed borne in a vessel," that is, enclosed by definite layers of tissue. This is one way in which angiosperms differ from gymnosperms. A second way is that all angiosperms produce flowers of some kind. Although the first angiosperms appear in the fossil record in the early Cretaceous period, about 130 million years ago, they did not become dominant plant forms until the late Mesozoic and early Cenozoic eras (about 65 million years ago). During that time a great adaptive radiation took place. It appears from the fossil record that the angiosperms quickly displaced the gymnosperms as the dominant land plants.

## 25–15
## THE EVOLUTION OF THE ANGIOSPERMS

Through variation and natural selection, angiosperms have been able to show greater adaptation to land conditions than any other plant form. Their roots and stems, with well-developed xylem and phloem, provide anchorage, support, and conduction (see Chapter 10). The efficiency of conduction is further improved with the appearance of fibers and vessels as a second type of xylem cell. Flowers provide a very efficient means of pollen dispersal by attracting pollinating agents such as bees. Conifers, relying only on the wind, are much less efficient. Finally, the angiosperms produce seeds enclosed or embedded in a **fruit.** The fruit serves primarily to aid in seed dispersal. All of these factors serve to make the angiosperms eminently successful in the struggle for life.

The reproductive process of the angiosperms is somewhat more elaborate than that of the conifers. The mature plant represents the sporophyte genera-

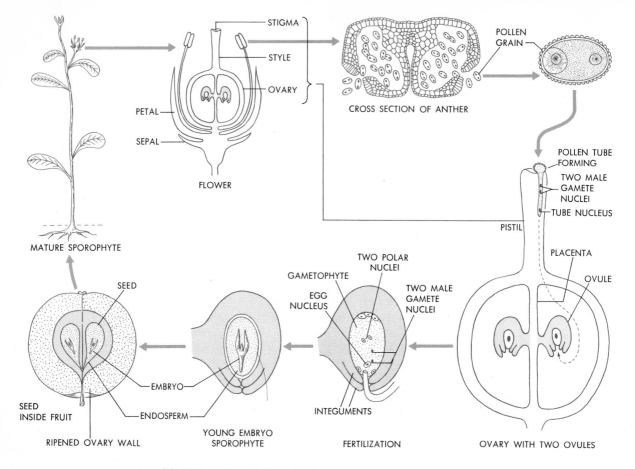

STIGMA

STYLE

OVARY

PETAL

SEPAL

FLOWER

CROSS SECTION OF ANTHER

POLLEN GRAIN

POLLEN TUBE FORMING

TWO MALE GAMETE NUCLEI

TUBE NUCLEUS

PISTIL

PLACENTA

OVULE

MATURE SPOROPHYTE

SEED

TWO POLAR NUCLEI

GAMETOPHYTE

EGG NUCLEUS

TWO MALE GAMETE NUCLEI

EMBRYO

ENDOSPERM

SEED INSIDE FRUIT

RIPENED OVARY WALL

INTEGUMENTS

YOUNG EMBRYO SPOROPHYTE

FERTILIZATION

OVARY WITH TWO OVULES

FIG. 25-36   General life cycle of an angiosperm.

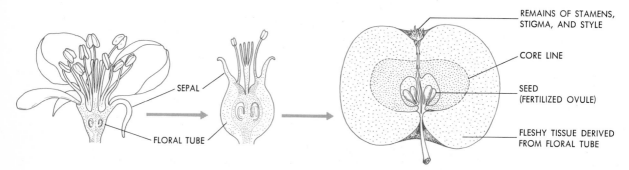

SEPAL

FLORAL TUBE

REMAINS OF STAMENS, STIGMA, AND STYLE

CORE LINE

SEED (FERTILIZED OVULE)

FLESHY TISSUE DERIVED FROM FLORAL TUBE

FIG. 25-37   A fleshy fruit, the apple, in which the edible portion develops from the floral tube, which is composed of the basal portions of the sepals, petals, and stamens. This tube is fused with the ovary wall at the core line. The core of the apple constitutes the wall of the ovary.

tion. The flower contains **pistils** and **stamens,** which produce the female and the male spores, respectively (see Fig. 25–36). The male spore is produced in the **anther,** the top part of the stamen. The male spore matures to become the pollen grain.

The pistil is composed of three parts: the **stigma** (top), **style** (thin, neck-like region), and **ovary.** Within the ovary are **ovules,** where the female spore is contained. As the flower develops, the female spore develops into the female gametophyte, composed of only eight cells. One of these is the egg cell.

Pollen is carried by the wind, insects, or other means to the stigma, where it is held by a sticky secretion. A pollen tube begins to form, growing down the style into the ovary. A tube nucleus leads the way, followed by two sperm nuclei. Upon reaching the ovule, the contents of the pollen tube are discharged into the female gametophyte. One sperm nucleus unites with the egg to produce the zygote, while the other unites with the two polar nuclei to form the beginning of the endosperm tissue. After fertilization, the female gametophyte contributes to the seed. The ovary wall now begins to grow and, as its cells increase in number, it becomes at the same time filled with sugary and starchy materials. The seed plus the ripened ovary wall form the fruit. The edible part of an apple develops from the floral tube (see Fig. 25–37).

The fleshy part of the apple does not serve as food for the young seed. But the formation of a fruit has two evolutionary advantages over the naked seed of the conifers. The first is that the fruit offers a food enticement to animals. This aids in dispersal of the seeds over a wider geographic area. Second, the fruit offers some protection to the seed until it is mature. The flesh of such fruits as the apple or pear, for example, does not ripen until the seed is mature. Animals are thus discouraged from eating such fruit until the seeds are mature enough to germinate. In both these ways, the angiosperms ensure a greater number of surviving offspring.

Thus the angiosperms seem to represent the most successful terrestrial plants. They show adaptations leading to greater efficiency in water retention, sturdiness, conduction, and exposure to sunlight, as well as remarkable adaptations in distribution of pollen and seeds.

The intricate adaptations of flowers to insects and vice versa has long excited the wonder of naturalists. One such adaptation is shown by the flower *Salvia* (a member of the mint family) to honeybees (see Fig. 25–38). When viewing such remarkable adaptations, it is perhaps easy to understand why many people refused to give up the idea of special creation as an explanation for animal and plant adaptations.

**25-16
CONCLUSION**

In this chapter we have discussed what may have been the major evolutionary pathway of early and later plant evolution, presenting some major hypothetical models put forth in an attempt to reconstruct this process. The evolution of plants constitutes a case study which illustrates some of the problems organisms

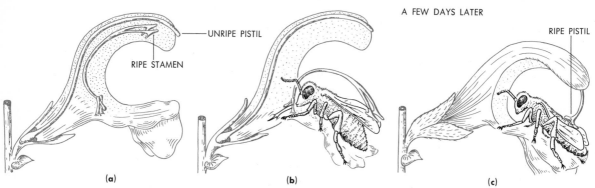

FIG. 25–38    Pollination in *Salvia*. Wide distribution of pollen and cross fertilization are ensured by: (a) maturing of the stamen before the pistil, (b) "dusting" of pollen onto the bee by a trigger mechanism, and (c) subsequent growth of the pistil so that it brushes the back of the bees who enter the flower a few days later.

encountered in the past as they invaded new ecological niches, or became more successful in exploiting old ones.

Several trends can be noted in surveying the spread of plant life over the face of the earth. One of the most obvious was the development of adaptations which enabled plants to live on land. This involved the development of protective cell walls and other covering structures which prevented water loss. A second involved the evolution of an efficient vascular system. This allowed plants to attain a much greater size. At the same time the development of supporting structures allowed plants to grow upward from the soil surface, and thus compete more favorably for sunlight. We can observe the appearance of all these trends in passing from simple algae to ferns to seed-bearing plants.

Perhaps the most significant feature in plant evolution is the trend toward a reduction in the size and duration of the haploid phase of the life cycle. Figure 25–39 compares the generalized life cycles of a primitive form (represented by an alga) and a more advanced form (represented by a seed-bearing plant). In the primitive life cycle, meiosis occurs soon after fertilization. The major part of the life of any such organism is spent in the haploid condition. In the course of plant evolution, there has been a gradual shift in the occurrence of meiosis, as shown in Fig. 25–39(b). In the life cycle of more advanced plant forms, meiosis occurs just *before* fertilization. Thus the haploid phase of the life cycle exists for only a short period of time.

It is easy to see why evolution has been in the direction of establishing the diploid phase as the major part of the life cycle. Haploid organisms lack genetic stability. Since each gene is represented only once, the genes for deleterious characteristics, which might otherwise survive as recessive alleles, have no

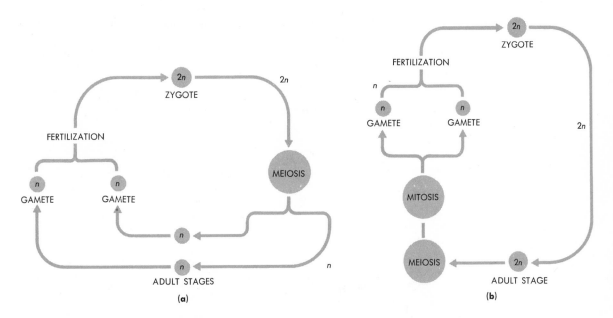

FIG. 25–39    (a) The primitive type of life cycle, where meiosis occurs soon after fertilization.
(b) The more advanced process, where meiosis takes place very close to the period of gamete production, the result being the haploid or *n* number.  The number of gametes may then be increased
by mitosis.

chance of being paired with dominant alleles capable of overriding their effects.
For this reason, haploid organisms are less able to withstand the rigors of the
environment.  The evolution of plants has thus shown a gradual reduction in
both the length of time during which this phase of the life cycle exists, and in
the degree of independence which it shows.  In all higher forms, for example,
the haploid phase is completely dependent on and protected by the diploid
organism.

    The evolution of plants shows the early development of life in the waters,
and its subsequent movement to land.  Once on land, a great adaptive radiation
occurred, and many new forms arose.

    Although we have discussed several specific evolutionary pathways, hypo-
thetical models such as those shown in Figs. 25–13 and 25–14 are still highly
tentative.  The tracing of evolutionary relationships presents many difficulties.
The fossil record for example, may be incomplete or even misleading.  The lack of
fossils for a particular form in a given stratum does not necessarily mean that
such a form did not exist at that time.  The conclusions which the paleontologist
reaches about evolutionary relationships among organisms are constantly being
revised, as more evidence becomes available to test hypotheses.

**EXERCISES**

1. What evidence supports the hypothesis that the bacteria and the blue-green algae may have evolved from a common ancestor?

2. Why are organisms such as *Chlamydomonas* and *Micromonas* of considerable interest to the evolutionist interested in the origin of eucaryotes?

3. What evidence supports the ingestion hypothesis of the origin of chloroplasts?

4. What evidence is there for the existence of sexuality in procaryotes?

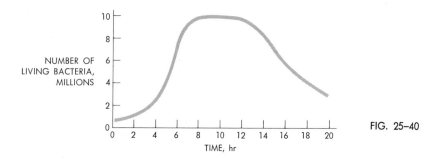

FIG. 25–40

5. On the basis of the growth curve shown in Fig. 25–40, answer the following questions.

   a) What would have happened to the shape of the growth curve if the bacterial population had been incubated at 35°C rather than 37°C?

   b) Which of the modifications suggested below would have served to make the maximum number of bacteria at the height of the growth curve several million greater? (In answering this question, consider that the high point in the curve can occur at any point in time.) Explain why you accepted or rejected each alternative.

   i) Incubating the flask at 39°C.

   ii) Inoculating the flask with more organisms at the outset.

   iii) Incubating the flask at 35°C.

   iv) Supplying more nutrient.

   c) What factors are responsible for the decline of the curve after about the twelfth hour?

6. In this chapter it was noted that plant evolution showed a trend from isogamy to heterogamy. What adaptive value might heterogamy have over isogamy?

7. What problems do terrestrial organisms face which their aquatic relatives do not?

8. Compare the life cycle of an alga such as *Chlamydomonas* with a fern's. What evolutionary developments are present? Compare both of these with the life cycle of a gymnosperm. What trends are established in the sequence from alga to conifer?

9. What is meant by "alternation of generations"? In what plants is it found?

10. What is the advantage to a plant of having the diploid generation as the dominant portion in its life cycle?

11. What evolutionary advantages to angiosperms are offered by the formation of (a) flowers, and (b) fruits?

12. Darwin was one of the first people to try to explain the intricate adaptations of some insects and flowers for the purpose of pollination. Explain how natural selection could give rise to such well-adapted and ingenious modifications on the part of both the flower and the insect (as in the case of *Salvia*).

## I. On Bacteria

RAHN, O., *Microbes of Merit* (Lancaster, Pa.: Jacques Cattell Press, 1946). A discussion of the various roles which microorganisms—especially bacteria—play in the economy of nature, and in the life of man.

SIMON, H. J., *Microbes and Men* (New York: Scholastic Book Services, Inc., 1963). An excellent little book in the series "Vistas of Science" (#5). It treats both bacteria and viruses in a well-written and informative way. There are a number of good illustrations as well.

SISTROM, W. R. S., *Microbial Life* (New York: Holt, Rinehart and Winston, 1962). This is an excellent summary book of much modern work on bacteria, with several chapters included on the bacterial viruses. It contains a good review of bacterial metabolism, and is less detailed, though also less complete, than the two references suggested above.

WOLLMAN, E. L., and F. JACOB, "Sexuality in Bacteria." *Scientific American*, July 1956, p. 109. This article shows some experiments which led to the concept of bacterial conjugation and the fate of nuclear material transferred from one bacterium to another.

ZINDER, NORMAN, " 'Transduction' in Bacteria." *Scientific American*, November 1958, p. 38. This article explains some of the experiments which showed that viruses (bacteriophages) can transport genetic material from one bacterial cell to another.

## II. On the Algae

BONNER, JOHN TYLER, "Volvox, a Colony of Cells." *Scientific American*, May 1950, p. 52. This is a well-presented article discussing the natural history of the *Volvox*, as well as some ideas as to its evolution.

DELEVORYAS, THEODORE, *Plant Diversification* (New York: Holt, Rinehart and Winston, 1965). One of the Modern Biology series, this book covers the major types of plants and their evolutionary adaptation.

ECHLIN, PATRICK, "The Blue-Green Algae." *Scientific American*, June 1966, p. 74. A well-illustrated and informative discussion of the blue-green algae. Well worth perusing.

LAMB, I. MACKENZIE, "Lichens." *Scientific American*, October 1959, p. 144. This article discusses the algae-fungi relationship which makes up the lichens. Well illustrated.

MILNER, H. W., "Algae as Food." *Scientific American*, October 1953, p. 31. This article discusses how the increasing food problem in the world can be solved by the culturing of algae.

STANIER, R. Y., M. DOUDOROFF, and E. A. ADELBERG, *The Microbial World* (Englewood Cliffs, N.J.: Prentice-Hall, 1963). This is a very complete and standard text treating all phases of bacterial life and structure. It is highly recommended for all who wish to pursue the study of these organisms in any depth. It presupposes some knowledge of physics and chemistry, but a minimum.

WEIER, T. E., and W. W. ROBBINS, *Botany* (New York: John Wiley & Sons, 1950). A good standard survey of plant anatomy and evolution. (Chapters 13–22 cover plant evolution.)

WENT, FRITZ, *The Plants* (New York: Time, Inc., 1963). This book is one of the *Life Magazine* series on natural history. Beautifully illustrated, it covers the variety of plants as well as their anatomy and physiology.

## III. On Other Plants and for General Reading

ADAMS, PRESTON, JEFFREY J. W. BAKER, and GARLAND E. ALLEN, *The Study of Botany* (Reading, Mass.: Addison-Wesley, 1970). A complete botany text. Chapters 20, 21, and 22 contain a complete discussion of plant evolution, particularly of the seeds, stem, leaves, and flowers.

ANDREWS, HENRY N., "Evolutionary Trends in Early Vascular Plants." *Cold Spring Harbor Symposia on Quantitative Biology* 24, 1959, pp. 217–234. A short but highly informative article.

ARDITTI, JOSEPH, "Orchids." *Scientific American*, January 1966, pp. 70–78. An excellent short account of orchids and some of their adaptations.

AXELROD, DANIEL I., "The Evolution of Flowering Plants," in Sol Tax (Ed.), *The Evolution of Life*, Vol. I (New York: Columbia University Press, 1960), pp. 227–305. A technical but very worthwhile discussion. Requires some background in botany.

BELL, PETER R., and CHRISTOPHER L. F. WOODCOCK, *The Diversity of Green Plants* (Reading, Mass.: Addison-Wesley, 1968). A paperback book which presents a precise account of the structure and reproduction of various groups of autotrophic plants. Well illustrated.

KLEIN, RICHARD M., and ARTHUR CRONQUIST, "A Consideration of the Evolutionary and Taxonomic Significance of Some Biochemical, Micromorphological, and Physiological Characters in the Thallophytes." *The Quarterly Review of Biology* 42, 1967, pp. 105–296. An advanced and technical consideration of one of the two hypotheses presented in this chapter.

MARGULIS, LYNN, "Evolutionary Criteria in Thallophytes: A Radical Alternative." *Science* 161, September 6, 1968, p. 1021. A brief discussion of the second hypothesis on the origin and early evolution of organisms considered in this chapter. Also considers the points of disagreement with the Klein-Cronquist hypothesis.

# THE EVOLUTION OF ANIMALS CHAPTER 26

Well over one million animal species have been described, and the list grows longer every day. These species can all be grouped into the twenty or so animal phyla generally recognized by animal taxonomists (see Appendix 5).

By itself, though, classification accomplishes little. It does, of course, establish some order out of chaos. In dealing with animals, however, the biologist wants more than order; he wants explanations—explanations that shed light on a species' past, present, and future. Such explanations Linnaeus alone was unable to provide. His classifications provided order without meaning. Since he accepted the concept of species immutability, the pigeonholes into which he placed his organisms were necessarily dead ends. The past and future of a species which is fixed and unchanging can offer little more information of interest than its present.

Following the advent of darwinism, the situation became radically changed. The static linnaean concept of the species was gradually replaced by the dynamic concept that the present form of any organism within a species is but a one-generation stop on a long evolutionary journey. By discussing certain problems posed by studies of the animal kingdom, this chapter will attempt to provide some insight into the way in which a biologist views the entire animal kingdom and the many species within it.

To the layman, matter appears in a bewildering array of different kinds and states, each with widely varying characteristics. To the chemist, the same is true. Yet, the chemist is less bewildered than the layman, for he has an underlying framework of reasoning to explain the diversity of matter and even, under varying conditions, to predict its behavior. This underlying framework is provided by the atomic and molecular theory of matter.

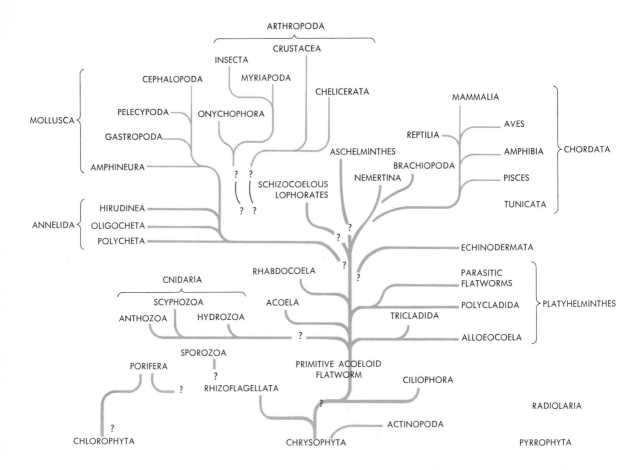

FIG. 26–1   Two phylogenetic charts. Note the similarities and differences. (Both charts from Earl Hanson, *Animal Diversity.* Englewood Cliffs, N.J.: Prentice-Hall, 1965. Right-hand chart after Marcus, 1958.)

In dealing with matter in motion, the physicist too is faced with a wide variety of behavior. Matter exists in varying masses, imparting varying amounts of energy. Masses of matter may travel at different velocities and accelerate to varying degrees when acted on by outside forces. Yet, an underlying pattern of behavior is again discernible; Newton's laws provide a means for the adequate explanation of these phenomena, and allow accurate predictions to be made concerning them.

The theory of evolution in the biological sciences corresponds to the atomic theory or to Newton's laws in the physical sciences. Indeed, evolution is the only concept in biology which is universal. The cellular nature of living organisms is an extensive generalization, but there are exceptions to it. The

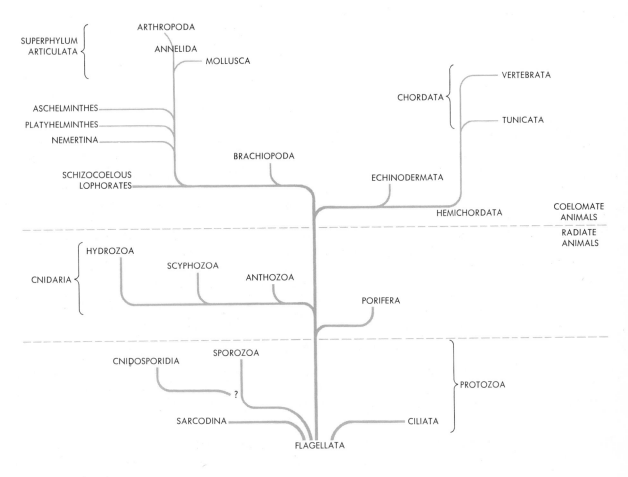

FIG. 26–1    (cont.)

concept of the role of DNA as the primary genetic material excludes certain viruses. Evolutionary processes, however, touch on all forms of life and profoundly affect them. Evolution, then, provides a logical foundation for the biologist's study of the animal kingdom.

Paradoxically, although evolution helps answer certain questions posed by animal diversity, it also raises new questions. Many phylogenetic charts have been devised by biologists in an attempt to establish evolutionary relationships between different animal phyla (Fig. 26–1); all are based on evolutionary principles, and all are far more similar than dissimilar. Nevertheless, there are differences. But the fact that no definite phylogenetic scheme is, as yet, universally accepted does not invalidate the hypothesis of evolution. On the contrary, it is the continuing changes wrought by evolution on animal species that makes the study of phyla origins so very complicated. Thus evolution encourages biologists to try to formulate hypothetical phylogenetic schemes while, at the same time, it makes it extremely difficult for them to do so.*

**26–3
EVOLUTION:
A WORKING
HYPOTHESIS**

Evolution by natural selection is an excellent working hypothesis with which to approach the problem of animal diversity. On this basis the biologist can regard any existing animal species as representing the adaptive changes thus far preserved within that species by natural selection. Note that this is a dynamic concept of an animal species, rather than a static one. Inherent within the concept is the assumption that any particular species will continue to evolve by natural selection. Thus a species may be quite different from its present form in the future, and was probably different from its present form in the past. Unlike future differences, however, those of the past can often be discovered by studying the fossil record of the group to which the species belonged. Anatomical and physiological investigations of the present form often allow inferences concerning its past. Thus, for example, the presence of vestigial limb bones in certain snakes strongly indicates that they were once limbed animals.

Once the concept of evolution by natural selection is accepted as a working hypothesis with which to approach the problem posed by animal diversity, certain predictions must follow:

*Hypothesis:   If . . .*   the evolution of any species can be considered as the sum total of the species' adaptive changes preserved by natural selection, and as the main factor leading to animal diversity, . . .

*Prediction I: then . . .* the presence of many different ecological niches (see Section 20–8) should lead to an adaptive radiation of animal forms to fill these niches.

Note that already the hypothesis is a satisfying one. It not only accounts for the phenomenon of animal diversity (since there are obviously many ecological niches) but it actually makes the diversity less an unusual phenomenon and more an occurrence that is entirely to be expected.

*Prediction II:   (then)* . . . as ecological niches change, the direction of animal evolution should change correspondingly.

This prediction is fully verified. Here, the geologist supplies the supporting observational evidence. Changes in climate from cold to tropical, or in available

---

\* In this context it is interesting to note that those who disapprove of the concept of evolution often claim that disagreements among biologists concerning animal group relationships weaken the case for evolution. Ironically, such disagreements weaken the case for special creation, for were the species fixed and immutable since their creation, it would be a simple matter to catalog them.

habitat from marine to land, or mountain to plain are often traceable in the earth's history. Such changes are usually accompanied by the predicted changes in the direction of animal evolution to fill the newly created niches.

**Prediction III:** (*then*) . . . certain animal forms will become extinct because they will be unable to adapt to new ecological niches or compete for these niches with a better adapted form.

This prediction, too, is verified. Indeed, eventual extinction seems to be the lot of all organisms. Some families have become extinct by simply evolving into new families. The majority, however, have merely dropped out of sight, without leaving descendants. In tracing these extinctions, it is often possible to connect each of them with either a corresponding loss of the ecological niche the extinct organism was adapted to fill, or the emergence of a more successful form with which it could not compete successfully.

The correlation of the extinction of animal species with changes in the earth's geologic history presents one of the more fascinating of present-day scientific mysteries. The fossil record makes it quite clear that there have been many periods in which mass extinctions of animal groups have occurred (Fig. 26–2). Nearly two-thirds of the existing families of trilobites (small, crustaceanlike animals that dominated life on earth for millions of years) disappeared at the end of the Cambrian period. During the close of the Permian period, nearly *one-half* of the known animal species became extinct! This period is one of the three periods that precede the "age of reptiles," when the dinosaurs thrived on earth. Yet, the end of the Permian was marked by a mass extinction of more than 80% of all amphibian and reptile families.

A similar mass extinction of reptiles also occurred during the end of the Triassic, the first of the three periods of the age of reptiles. Here it is tempting to hypothesize that competition with the more successful dinosaurs was an important factor in the disappearance of these early land animals. This hypothesis is weakened, however, when it is noted that many other forms, on which the dinosaurs could have had little effect, also underwent mass extinction. For example, 24 out of 25 species of ammonites, shelled marine animals, became extinct at the same time. It seems evident that some forces more extensive than species competition alone must have played a role in these events.

Best known of all mass extinctions, perhaps, is the disappearance of the dinosaurs at the close of the Cretaceous period. When one reads of dinosaurs, there is a tendency to think only in terms of the larger kinds. Certainly, reconstructions of such creatures as the carnivorous *Tyrannosaurus* or the 30-ton *Brontosaurus* do make a lasting impression. But the large dinosaurs were by no means the most numerous; there were many other species with smaller, less impressive forms. Yet, all the dinosaurs, large and small, became extinct within a relatively short period of time.

Many hypotheses have been proposed to account for such mass extinctions of animal species. One such hypothesis suggests that bursts of high-energy

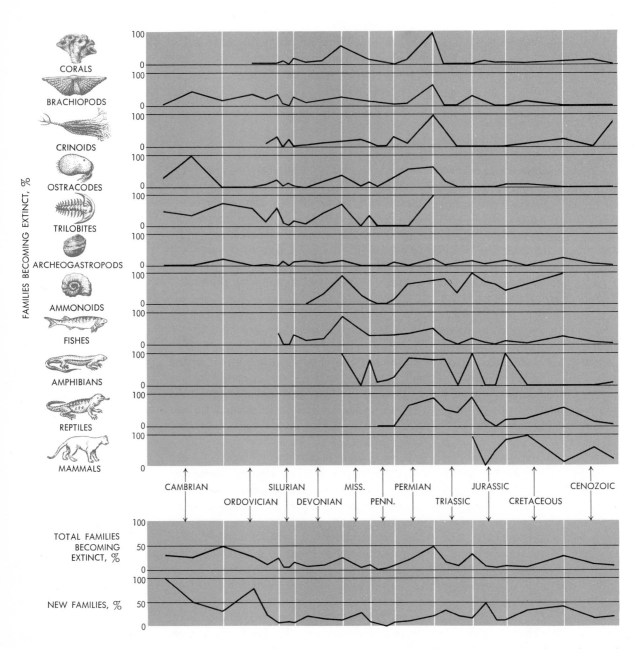

FIG. 26–2    Animal extinction, as revealed by the fossil record, makes it evident that each animal group has undergone repeated crises. Note the massive extinctions which occurred at the end of the Ordovician, Devonian, and Permian periods. A comparison of the bottom two lines indicates that periods of extinction are generally followed by periods of evolutionary activity, as would be predicted by the evolution-by-natural-selection hypothesis. (Adapted from *Scientific American*, February 1963.)

radiation from a nearby supernova might have been responsible. However, since water is a good shield against radiation, such an hypothesis must predict that terrestrial animals would be more affected than marine animals. Yet we know that in certain periods, most of the mass extinctions occurred in the sea. A much older hypothesis suggests worldwide catastrophes (i.e., floods, volcanic explosions, etc.) to account for mass extinctions. The geologic record gives no evidence of any such cataclysmic occurrences. Also old is an hypothesis proposing the exhaustion of "biological drive." This hypothesis considers an evolving group as a sort of wind-up toy, which must eventually run down. There is no evidence, however, for any such force behind evolution, nor is there any suggestion that extinction is a result of its failure.

The geologic record shows quite clearly that at various times in the history of the earth, major shifts in the earth's crust led to periods of great mountain building. Such periods were then followed by gradual erosion of the newly formed mountains. The Rocky Mountains of the western United States were formed during one such period; the Appalachians, in the east, were formed during another, much earlier one. Any attempt to establish a cause-and-effect relationship between these mountain-building periods and the times of mass extinction of animal groups, however, leads to contradictions. In general, the two do not coincide. Indeed, the most outstanding mass extinction periods have occurred during times of relative geologic quiet.

The most popular hypothesis proposed to explain mass extinction is based on climate. Briefly, this hypothesis proposes that sudden changes in the climate of the earth led to mass extinctions because the organisms involved were not able to adapt quickly enough to their changed environment. The fact that the dinosaurs were cold-blooded (and thus less able to adapt to cold climates) makes this hypothesis a tempting one. Yet, fossil plants, always good indicators of past climatic changes, do not show such changes to have occurred at the time this hypothesis would predict them. It is true that in some areas there is good geologic evidence that changes of climate in limited habitats have led to some extinctions and/or animal migrations to more favorable regions. By itself, however, the climatic hypothesis fails to account for the widespread nature of the mass extinctions to which attention has been directed here.

An interesting and relatively recent hypothesis ties the periods of crisis in the history of animal life to changes in the earth's magnetic field. The earth as a whole acts somewhat as a bar magnet and is surrounded by a magnetic field. If a hot molten mass of charged particles (ions) is allowed to slowly cool in this field, the ions align themselves according to the direction of the field. Once the molten mass has hardened, of course, the ions are "frozen" into position. Should the magnetic field change its direction, the ions can no longer adjust to it. By studying the alignment of such frozen ions in rock which was once molten lava (and by making the appropriate adjustments if the lava field itself shows evidence of having later been shifted) the direction of the earth's magnetic field can be determined at the time the lava was cooling. Since there have been many periods of volcanic eruptions over the span of the earth's existence, changes in its magnetic fields have been well recorded.

The earth's magnetic field serves to deflect radiation from outer space. During periods of field reversal, however, this shield would be effectively removed. A sudden high incidence of radiation, with a resultant high incidence of gene mutation, could conceivably result in both the elimination of certain forms and the emergence of others. This hypothesis, of course, runs into the same difficulty as the one proposing radiation from a supernova. Nevertheless, it retains a certain attractiveness, for there does seem to be a remarkable correlation between the times of magnetic field reversal and the times of mass extinctions.

Still other hypotheses remain, however. For example, the geologic evidence indicates that fluctuations of sea level have occurred often during the earth's history. A rise or fall of only a few feet is usually sufficient to drain or flood vast areas of land. Biologically speaking, one would expect such changes to have had profound ecological effects on animal communities, both land and marine. Geologically speaking, there is considerable evidence that they did. Particularly significant is the fact that evolutionary diversification was greatest during times of maximum flooding. This would be predicted by the hypothesis, since the number of available water habitats would be large. Conversely, during the major sea withdrawals, extinctions were greatly increased. This, too, would be predicted; during times when the number of available habitats was being reduced, selection pressure would be most intense.

Recall the ecological principle that no organism is stronger than the weakest link in its food chain. The welfare of any community, whatever its nature, depends on a relatively small number of key species located low on the community pyramid. The extinction of such forms cannot help adversely affecting others high on the pyramid. Thus the factors leading to the extinction of such creatures as dinosaurs and saber-tooth tigers need not act directly on them at all. The changes wrought by a shrinking coastal habitat might well have ramifications leading to the mass extinction of forms native to both land and sea.

Let us return now to our original hypothesis, in which we defined evolution as the sum total of adaptive changes preserved by natural selection and proposed it as the main factor leading to animal diversity. On the basis of this hypothesis we will make one more major prediction.

***Prediction IV:***  (*then*) . . . extinction of major groups of animals, followed by the geologic establishment of favorable environmental conditions, should result in the evolutionary emergence of other animal forms to fill those ecological niches left vacant by the extinction of earlier forms.

This prediction is also verified (Fig. 26–3). Existing at the same time as the later dinosaurs, for example, were small, rodentlike mammals. Evidently they were able to adapt to the conditions that led to the extinction of the dinosaurs.

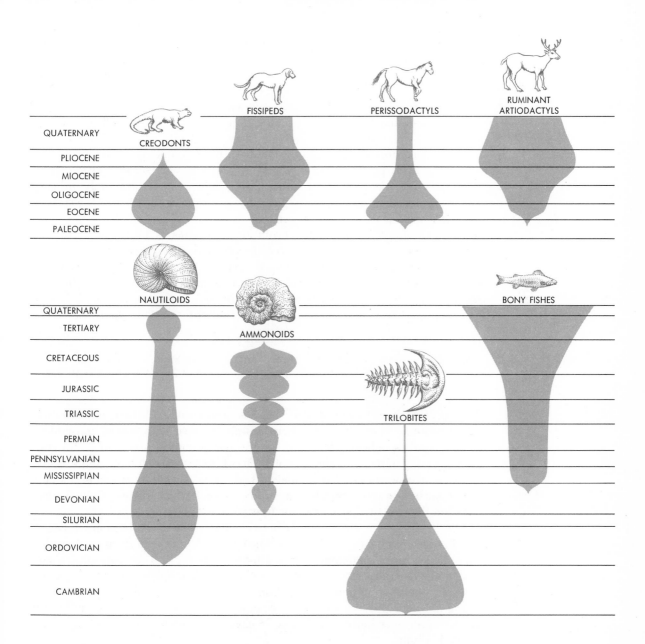

FIG. 26–3  The width of the figures on the graph above indicates the number of families in some major animal groups—the wider the figure, the larger the number of representative families.  Note that the lessening of numbers in one group (which leaves ecological niches open for occupation) is often followed by the expansion of a competing group.  Such ecological replacement is predicted by an hypothesis proposing evolution by natural selection as an explanation for animal diversity. (Adapted from *Scientific American*, February 1963.)

The fossil records show that with the removal of their major competitors for the available ecological niches, these mammals underwent an adaptive radiation of very extensive proportions, one which led ultimately to the development of man.

When evolution by natural selection is accepted as an hypothesis to explain the problem of animal diversity, the problem necessarily becomes a phylogenetic one. It is true, of course, that the biologist may well study an organism for other reasons than those of phylogeny. The frog, for example, is useful in embryological research partly because of its large and easily cultured eggs. Basic research centering on the organism itself, however, is ultimately directed toward problems of phylogeny: What is the evolutionary history of the species? To what forms is it most closely related? And so on.

As an example, consider the evolutionary origins of birds and mammals. Both of these vertebrate classes were preceded by the classes containing the fishes, amphibians, and reptiles. Since the reptiles represent the most recent and highly evolved of these three classes, it is reasonable to look first to them for the ancestors of both the birds and the mammals. We will take the birds first, and propose their evolutionary origin from the reptiles as an hypothesis:

*Hypothesis: If ...*    birds evolved from reptiles, . . .

*Prediction:*    *then* . . . the fossil record might be expected to show forms which combine anatomical features of both classes of vertebrates.

As Fig. 21–1 shows, such a fossil form has been found. Further, modern birds retain reptilian characteristics; their legs are covered with scales, and embryological studies indicate that feathers are merely modifications of scales (Fig. 26–4). Young birds, like reptiles, are often cold-blooded, becoming progressively warm-blooded as they mature. Finally, their egg-laying habits and embryological development are quite reptilian in nature, a fact which follows from modern considerations of the biogenetic law (see Section 18–4).

At first glance, it seems foolhardy to even attempt to establish any relationship between mammals and reptiles. The differences between them are considerable. Like birds, mammals are warm-blooded; reptiles, of course, are not. Mammals generally retain their young within their bodies for development, and the young obtain nourishment from their mother; reptiles lay eggs, and the young are nourished by the yolk. Mammals care for their young and suckle them; reptiles generally abandon their eggs after laying them and may never see their young.

Anatomically, the differences between mammals and reptiles are just as great. Among these differences are: the large brain case of the mammal as compared with the small one of the reptile; the single jaw bone of the mammal as opposed to the multi-part one of the reptile; the three middle-ear bones of the mammal to the one of the reptile; the differentiation of the mammal's teeth into incisors, canines, premolars, and molars, as opposed to the general uni-

FIG. 26–4   The presence of scales on their legs, as well as many features of their embryological development, strongly supports an hypothesis proposing that birds evolved from the reptiles. (Photo courtesy Dr. Daniel B. Drachman, The National Institute of Health.)

formity of reptile teeth; the differentiation of mammalian vertebrae as opposed to the lack of differentiation in reptilian vertebrae; and the uniformity of bone arrangements in mammalian fingers and toes as opposed to the variations that occur in these bones among different species of reptiles. Many more examples of anatomical differences could be cited.

All such physiological and anatomical facts would seem, at first glance, to contradict any hypothesis that mammals evolved from the reptiles. But the preceding list of differences between mammals and reptiles is based on anatomical studies of *present-day forms*. Acceptance of evolution by natural selection frees us from the present; it allows us to predict the existence of earlier forms which might combine both mammalian and reptilian characteristics. The prediction is verified; literally hundreds of fossilized remains of such mammal-like reptiles have been found (Fig. 26–5). Further, the rocks in which these fossils have been found place them precisely at the point in geologic history predicted by the hypothesis. No one reptilian type exhibits all of the mammalian characteristics, of course. As a group, however, they show a trend toward the mammalian state that is clear and unmistakable.

The hypothesis proposing the evolutionary origin of the mammals from the reptiles might predict that the mammal-like reptiles would exhibit a physiology with both mammalian and reptilian characteristics. For example, they might exhibit some tendency toward warm-bloodedness. Unfortunately, the presence of warm- or cold-bloodedness cannot be detected from fossilized remains, and so the question must be left almost totally unresolved.*

Not entirely, however. Given certain conditions which would spare an early life form from having to compete with more highly evolved forms, it is conceiv-

---

* Recently, a technique of analyzing fossil remains to determine their relative temperatures has been reported. If successful, it will be extremely useful in answering some of these questions.

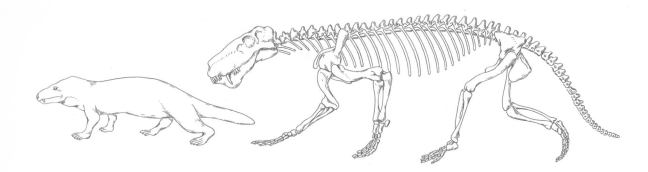

FIG. 26–5  The therapsids represent a group of mammal-like reptiles. The skeleton of one such form (*Lycaenops*) is shown here.  The smaller drawing is a reconstruction based on the remains of another form of therapsid.  Note the pair of long teeth on both forms.  (Adapted from *Scientific American,* March 1949.)

FIG. 26–6  The duckbill platypus, *Ornithorhyncus anatinus*.  This animal lays eggs like a reptile, yet nurses its young after they hatch.  In its physiological characteristics, too, the platypus combines reptilian and mammalian features.  (Photo courtesy American Museum of Natural History.)

able that some mammals might exist which would demonstrate some reptilian characteristics.  Such conditions were created by the long isolation of the continent of Australia from the mainland masses comprising the larger continents. In Australia may be found the duckbill platypus (Fig. 26–6), which is famous for the fact that it lays eggs (like a reptile) yet nurses its young (like a mammal).

Further, when the platypus is subjected to varying temperatures, its temperature also varies—not as much as that of a reptile, to be sure, but considerably more than that of a mammal such as a cat. A few other Australian forms, such as the spiny anteater, exhibit the same physiological phenomenon.

It should not be thought that the modern duckbill platypus necessarily represents a form with an evolutionary future leading to a true mammalian state. Indeed, the platypus is almost certainly a dead-end form. This is partly due to the fact that the animal itself is a highly specialized one. The fossil record is quite clear on the penalty for such specialization; it generally means eventual extinction. The unspecialized form, on the other hand, is "uncommitted," and thus is free to adapt to a changing environment. The fact that unspecialized forms enjoy certain advantages over specialized forms fits well with an hypothesis of evolution by natural selection. Indeed, such advantages are a logical consequence of the events predicted by the hypothesis.

26–5
PHYLOGENETIC
RELATIONSHIPS:
THE
INVERTEBRATES

Thus far, little attention has been directed to those animals lacking a backbone, the **invertebrates.** This is a serious omission, for of the twenty or so animal phyla, nineteen contain only invertebrates.

Invertebrate zoology has not been entirely ignored, however. The same hypothesis of evolution by natural section which was postulated to explain animal diversity among vertebrates applies equally well to the invertebrates. The principles underlying hypotheses concerning invertebrate phylogenetic relationships are the same as those concerning vertebrate phylogenetic relationships. The problems of the invertebrate zoologist are simply more complex. He deals with organisms that are far more numerous and diverse than the vertebrates. At the same time, due to the general inadequacy of the invertebrate fossil record, he lacks much of the evidence usually available to the vertebrate zoologist.

The inadequacy of the fossil record is by no means universal across the broad spectrum of invertebrate animal life. Indeed, the record of such hard-shelled forms as ammonites, clams, or brachiopods is among the most complete of any (Fig. 26–7). But the majority of invertebrates are soft-bodied and simply do not fossilize well. There are some notable exceptions; fossil jellyfish have been found that date back to the pre-Cambrian era, over 600 million years ago. On the whole, however, the fossil record of such organisms is a scanty one.

A still larger problem is posed by the fact that the most crucial periods of invertebrate evolution must have occurred long before the formation of the oldest known fossil-containing rocks. Segmented worms, for example, have been found in pre-Cambrian rocks. Since such animals had already attained a high level of complexity by the time those rocks were formed, it is evident that a long and crucial history of evolution must have preceded their development. About the conditions of this period, we can only guess. Were the vertebrate zoologist to be deprived of all fossil finds whose origin predated the appearance

FIG. 26-7   A fossil ammonite. Because of their hard shell, which is easily preserved, such invertebrate fossils are numerous. The ammonites demonstrate an exception to the general rule that evolution proceeds from a simple morphology to one more complex. (Photo courtesy Ward's Natural Science Establishment, Inc., Rochester, N.Y.)

FIG. 26-8   This fossil animal clearly exhibits external segmentation. However, such fossil remains yield little or no evidence concerning internal segmentation. (Photo courtesy *Milwaukee Journal.*)

of the first primitive mammals, he would be in a somewhat similar situation concerning the nature of mammalian evolution.

Nonetheless, for certain forms, the fossil record of invertebrate life since the pre-Cambrian is fairly complete. Like that of the vertebrates, this record clearly supports the hypothesis proposing evolution by natural selection as an explanation for animal diversity. There seems little reason to suspect, therefore,

FIG. 26–9    Segmentation, obvious in the earthworm, phylum Annelida, can also be demonstrated in the flea, phylum Arthropoda. (Photos courtesy Lynwood M. Chace, left, and Ward's Natural Science Establishment, Inc., Rochester, N.Y., right.)

that this hypothesis would be contradicted should the missing fossil records of some groups suddenly be found.

It would be clearly impossible to treat all or even most of the problems tackled by the invertebrate zoologist in establishing a satisfactory phylogeny. One example will be selected, therefore, to illustrate the reasoning behind the establishment of such a phylogeny.

As pointed out earlier, fossils of segmented animals are known from the pre-Cambrian era (Fig. 26–8). Perhaps the best-known living example of a segmented animal is the earthworm (Fig. 26–9); however, segmentation is by no means limited to the earthworm and other annelids. Indeed, although the characteristic first appears in the annelid group, traces of segmentation may be detected, by the trained eye, in every animal group ranked above the annelids, with the exception of the echinoderms.* In the vertebrates (phylum Chordata), for example, the ventral body wall muscles show a segmental arrangement, as do the branches of nerves emanating from each side of the central nervous system. The abdomen of the flea (phylum Arthropoda) is clearly segmented and, though it is more difficult to detect by sight, the segmented nature of its head and thorax can also be demonstrated.

In other groups, however, segmentation is less obvious. For example, animals of the phylum Mollusca (chitons, snails, clams and oysters, squids,

---

* The affinities of the echinoderms (starfishes, sea urchins, etc.) with other invertebrate groups is quite obscure. Segmentation in the echinoderms is clearly impossible, since they are radially rather than bilaterally symmetrical. Their embryological development, resembling that of some chordates, places them high on the list of the invertebrate phyla.

etc.) are soft-bodied forms, possessing either a shell or some modification thereof. As was emphasized in Chapter 18, similarity of early embryological development is an excellent indication of a close phylogenetic relationship. Such a similarity exists between the embryological development of the annelids and the mollusks. Yet, the annelids are clearly segmented, while the mollusks, in general, are not. To be specific, until recently segmentation was seen in the mollusks only in the eight-sectioned shell of the chitons; internally, the mollusks give very little evidence of segmentation. Nevertheless, our hypothesis predicts that segmentation must have been present at least some time during the evolution of the mollusks:

**Hypothesis:** *If . . .*   the mollusks are closely related to the annelids, . . .

**Prediction:** *then . . .* the mollusks must once have shown internal segmentation.

Note that a secondary prediction from this hypothesis would be that of similar embryological development in the annelids and mollusks. The verification of this prediction is very significant. In actuality, of course, it was the observation of developmental similarity that gave rise to the hypothesis, rather than vice versa. Still, the fact that evidence for internal segmentation is missing is disappointing; it markedly weakens an otherwise well-supported hypothesis.

The fossil record of the mollusks is of little help. Ordovician rocks contain mollusks that must be closely related to the chitons. These mollusks, however, have a single, unsegmented shell. Thus they are of even less help in establishing internal segmentation than are the present-day chitons. On the other hand, the Ordovician period was between 425 and 500 million years ago. Thus any hypothesis proposing a close phylogenetic relationship between annelids and mollusks must surely predict at least traces of internal body segmentation in Ordovician mollusks. Unfortunately, however, the soft internal body parts are not preserved in these organisms. Thus, until recently, the hypothesis remained accepted on the embryological evidence, but was essentially unsupported (though not contradicted) insofar as the prediction of internal segmentation was concerned. Were it not for the embryological evidence, the hypothesis would have been abandoned as being untestable by experimentation or observation.

Literally overnight, the picture was dramatically changed. In 1952, from an ocean depth of approximately two miles, Danish oceanographers dredged up a mollusk in the same class as the chitons. This organism was truly a "living fossil," for other members of its order are known only from Ordovician fossils! A chance to test the annelid-mollusk hypothesis was thus afforded. And—as predicted—the new-found mollusk showed clear evidence of internal segmentation.

Unfortunately, such opportune discoveries are very rare. It would hardly be reasonable to count on such finds to support many hypotheses concerning phylogenetic relationships, and zoologists do not generally do so. Nevertheless, the case does support the hypothesis of evolution by natural selection as an explanation for animal diversity. It also establishes confidence in the means to which biologists have usually had to resort in their attempts to establish phylogenetic relationships.*

If animal diversity is to be explained by the hypothesis of evolution by natural selection, there must be good reasons for the retention of any distinguishing features that a given species displays. As was seen much earlier, at any particular point in its history, a species demonstrates the sum total of adaptive changes preserved (or at least not eliminated) by natural selection. Thus any anatomical or physiological feature incorporated into a successful animal form must have some selective value, or at least be of no selective harm. If it did not meet these criteria, the feature could not have evolved.

In general, the fossil record supports the contention that those animal forms which are anatomically more complex appeared on earth later than the simpler forms. It is certainly reasonable to assume that complex biological systems must have been preceded in time by simpler ones. And, as we have seen, it is also consistent with our hypothesis to assume that to certain groups there must have been some selective advantage in becoming more complex. Note again, as with plants (see Section 25–5), that we are not saying that an increase in complexity is a general trend in animal evolution, acting uniformly on all groups. Indeed, in at least one form (the ammonites), a *decrease* in complexity is found. What we are stating is simply that *for some groups* an increase in complexity has been favored by natural selection.

Consider first the evolution of multicellularity. Multicellular organisms must surely have been preceded by unicellular organisms. What selection pressures favored the adoption by some groups of a multicellular state? Examination of such forms reveals the answer. The multicellular state allows for cell specialization (i.e., some cells capture and digest food, some play a role in reproduction, some protect the organisms, some propel it, etc.) The result is a corresponding increase in the organism's ability to explore and exploit its environment.

As to when and how multicellularity evolved, we can only speculate. Since complex multicellular animals were already firmly established in the pre-Cambrian period, the fossil record is obviously of little help. We must be satisfied to examine organisms such as *Volvox*, a simple colony of specialized cells, and suppose that this form may bear some resemblance to the first multicellular organisms.

---

* Perhaps the closest parallel example in vertebrate zoology came with the capture in 1938 off Madagascar of a living coelacanth, a fish thought to have been extinct for many millions of years. Since then, a few more specimens have been caught and studied. Of particular interest was the fact that the animal very closely resembled models which had been built of it from its fossil remains, thus attesting to the accuracy of the techniques used in such reconstructions.

Next, at some point in evolution, certain multicellular forms developed a double-layer structure. Such a structure is shown by some members of the phylum Cnidaria (Coelenterata). The **gastrovascular cavity** thus formed (Fig. 26–10) serves both a digestive and a circulatory function. Digestion can now be extracellular, with the cells lining the cavity secreting digestive enzymes directly onto a captured prey. What is the selective advantage of such an arrangement? The obvious answer is that organisms larger than those which could be engulfed by one cell can now be used for food.

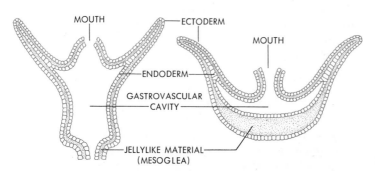

FIG. 26–10

The development of a third layer of cells (mesoderm) between the inner and outer layers is shown by all forms of life at or above the complexity of the cnidarians. Beyond a certain complexity, of course, the presence of a mesoderm establishes a need for circulatory and excretory systems; no longer are all cells exposed to a surrounding watery medium from which they can extract the oxygen and into which they can release their wastes. Again it may be asked: Of what selective advantage is the mesoderm? And again the answer seems clear—from the mesoderm develop the complex systems (such as the muscular and circulatory systems) that characterize and give such versatility to the more advanced, complex animal forms.

The preceding type of analysis may be extended to organisms throughout the animal kingdom. Given the variations found in the animal groups present on earth today, it is usually possible to discover reasons why these variations are of selective value to the organisms possessing them.

## 26–7 ANIMAL EVOLUTION: THE MOLECULAR LEVEL OF INVESTIGATION

According to Nobel laureate Jacques Monod (see Section 18–11), the greatest contribution of molecular biology to an understanding of life has been the explanation of evolution in terms of two classes of molecules, the nucleic acids (especially DNA) and the proteins, which as enzymes make certain that the gene's instructions are carried out. DNA provides a near-perfect copying mechanism by which a species preserves its uniqueness and passes this uniqueness on to subsequent generations, while natural selection is a well-honed instrument for turning to good advantage the rare but inevitable mistakes or mutations that occasionally crop up in the copying process. The resulting variant proteins test out the value of these mistakes to the organism involved in the struggle for survival.

In Chapter 22, in an introduction to animal behavior, the necessity of studying living systems at the higher levels of investigation (the level of the organism, of the population, etc.) *as well as* at the lower levels (cellular, molecular, etc.) was stressed. Certainly studies of the appearance and behavior of living organisms have contributed greatly to the observational data by which the evolutionary process has been studied. However, the data provided by such studies are still crude. After all, anatomical and behavioral characteristics are only the gross expressions of the far subtler patterns which distinguish the molecules of one species from those of another. Thus it is not surprising that many evolutionists are turning their attention to these molecular differences (or similarities).

However, unlike his colleagues working on the higher levels of investigation, the molecular evolutionist cannot take advantage of ancient life forms preserved as fossils. The biological molecules most useful from an evolutionary viewpoint do not form fossils. The molecular evolutionist can only work, therefore, with the organisms at hand today. He gets around this difficulty by using comparisons between similar molecules from different species to discover how closely the species are related (see Chapter 19). From this information he tries to extrapolate, in order to form a picture of the earlier evolutionary patterns from which present-day relationships have emerged.

The underlying unity of life is such that many genes are found to be common to most living organisms. The molecular evolutionist proceeds on the assumption that the prototypes of such "universal" genes probably arose only once, and that one common ancestor gave rise to each of the many varieties of genes distributed among today's species. He also assumes, with fairly good (but not unchallenged) evidence, that the rate at which mutations occur is constant throughout history (approximately one mutation for every hundred thousand DNA replications). Of course, most of these mutations are never selected, and are lost. For any one gene, the number of mutations which are selected, and thus become incorporated into the species, is also assumed to be constant. Thus each selected gene becomes a sort of slowly ticking evolutionary clock, with one mutation being incorporated every $x$ thousand years.

This single-gene clock keeps ticking away at its own rate even when mutations are going on in other genes—mutations which may even lead to the formation of new species. Once a new species has been formed, its own evolutionary clock, even though still ticking at the same rate, does so in its own way. In other words, the mutations affecting a gene which has become incorporated into a new species, although taking place at the same rate as those affecting the corresponding gene which has remained as part of the genetic code of the "parent" species, will almost certainly be different in kind. This means that the relationship between species can be determined by comparing the structure of a type of gene they have in common. If, for example, two species are closely related, they will have diverged relatively recently. Thus only a few mutations will have had time to take place, and the two species' "common" genes will have quite similar structures. On the other hand, if the two species converged far back in evolutionary history, large structural differences would be predicted in whatever "common" gene is chosen for comparative study.

As was seen in Chapter 18, however, it is still very difficult to determine the precise sequence of nucleotides in one gene. However, since the nature of the genetic code is such that protein structure mirrors gene structure, the gene's structure can be studied indirectly through the proteins for which it codes. Many proteins have now had their amino acid sequences worked out, and many more are added to the list every year. In a sense, then, as science writer Graham Chedd puts it, these proteins form the "hands" of the evolutionary clock.

A favorite protein for use in studies of biochemical evolution is the respiratory enzyme, cytochrome $c$ (see Section 8–3). Widely distributed in nature, cytochrome $c$ is a relatively small protein (approximately 110 amino acids) and is easily extracted from living tissue. Over 30 cytochrome $c$ molecules have had their amino acid sequences determined, in organisms as diverse as man, finback whale, Pekin duck, hippopotamus, snapping turtle, rattlesnake, baker's yeast, and bacteria.

Based on these studies, a phylogenetic tree has been constructed (Fig. 26–11) which gives both evolutionary relationships and the relative periods of time that have elapsed since the different forms diverged from each other. Unfortunately, the most important point of all—that at which the single ancestral cytochrome $c$ gave rise to the various branches—remains unlocated. However, Drs. Karl Dus, Knut Sletten, and Martin Kamen of the University of California at San Diego have determined the complete primary amino acid sequence of cytochrome $c_2$ from the primitive photosynthetic bacterium *Rhodospirillum rubrum*. Intriguingly, despite the enormous evolutionary gap between *R. rubrum* and mammals and despite the fact that cytochrome $c_2$ is involved in a photosynthetic rather than respiratory reaction, there are still definite similarities between the cytochromes $c$'s of this tiny primitive bacterium and those of man. All are obviously derived from the same gene.

Dus and his coworkers believe that the *R. rubrum* cytochrome consists of repeating units 13 to 20 amino acids in length. Furthermore, this repeating unit includes the site at which the catalytic activity of the enzyme is located. This tends to support an hypothesis proposing that the earliest biological catalysts to appear on earth were small peptides coded for by simple genes (see Section 24–3). There is much experimental evidence to show that one type of "mistake" which can occur during DNA replication is that of "gene doubling" in which two copies of a gene are made instead of just one. Different mutations occurring at different

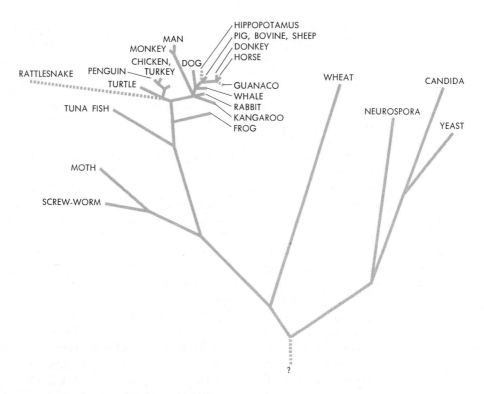

FIG. 26–11    A phylogenetic tree of organisms based on structural analyses of their respiratory enzyme, cytochrome c. The lengths of the branches give the relative times since the organisms have diverged from each other in their evolution. It is hoped that studies of the primitive bacterium *Rhodospirillum rubrum* will help to clear up most of the questions that now remain concerning the main trunk of the tree.

points in the two genes might then lead to the coding of two slightly varying proteins. These might then take on different functions, despite their structural similarities. A variation of this hypothesis suggests that a doubled gene need not separate to form identical genes, but may simply form one gene twice as long as the original, consisting of two identical halves. Such genes would then code for proteins built of peptides with repeating amino acid sequences. A continual accumulation of different point mutations provides a mechanism for the creation of complex proteins which early in their evolution show clear signs of their repeating subunit structure, but which after billions of years of mutation become so randomized that their original origin is no longer evident. This would back up the claim that *R. rubrum*'s cytochrome *c*, with its very obvious repeating sequences, is in a very primitive state. As would be expected, the cytochrome *c* from the bacterium *Pseudomonas fluorescens* differs widely in structure from that of the other organisms shown on the phylogenetic tree in Fig. 26–11. The structure of this cytochrome *c* is closer, however, to the *R. rubrum* cytochrome *c* structure. If it should prove possible, using computer programming, to work out the length and sequence of the original small peptide forms from which *R. rubrum* cytochrome *c* (and thus presumably all other cytochrome *c*'s) evolved, a great deal more will be known about the lower branches of our phylogenetic tree. It is also intriguing to think that a molecule which made the origin of life possible and which has not existed for billions of years could be created within the laboratory.

It is interesting to note that, on the whole, the results of the studies on the evolutionary relationships of organisms carried out on the molecular level tend to support rather than overthrow phylogenetic relationships determined much earlier by more traditional morphological studies. Yet such is not always the case. For example, recent studies of blood protein (albumin) structure in modern primates, carried out by Drs. Vincent Sarich and Allan Wilson of the University of California at Berkeley (see Section 19–5), establish a closer relationship between man, gorilla, and chimpanzee than had previously been suspected.

However, the most controversial aspect of the Sarich and Wilson findings is their belief that the divergence of man from ape leading to the hominid (human) line occurred only around five million years ago (see Fig. 26–12). Dr. David Pilbeam, of Cambridge University in England, states that this belief flies directly in the face of the available fossil evidence. Pilbeam maintains that the fossil called *Ramapithecus* and another discovered in 1962 called *Kenyapithecus whickevi* actually belong to the same genus and push back the evolutionary divergence of ape and man to at least 14 million years ago. Furthermore, Pilbeam suggests that *Ramapithecus* itself may have evolved from another form, *Propliopithecus*, which is distinctly hominid and which dates back some 30 to 35 million years.

Thus there exists a conflict between the biochemical evidence and the fossil evidence which is far too great to be overlooked. Some workers have suggested that Sarich and Wilson's data are correct but that their time determination is off, perhaps because of a retardation of albumin evolution in the apes and man since their divergence. Thus, although the albumins might be very similar, it would be unjustifiable to interpret this to mean that the apes and man have been evolving independently for only a short period of evolutionary time. But Sarich and Wilson have investigated the rates of albumin evolution in man and the apes, and they maintain that there is no evidence for such a slowdown in albumin evolution. They stick by their original belief that the evolutionary divergence of man and ape occurred only five million years ago. To date, this conflict between molecular and anthropological findings remains unresolved.

**26–8
CONCLUSION** An hypothesis of evolution by natural selection provides an explanation for the origin and results of animal diversity. Predictions that follow from the acceptance of this hypothesis are generally supported, while none are refuted. Accepting the hypothesis, the zoologist attempts to establish phylogenetic rela-

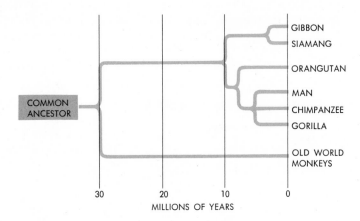

FIG. 26–12    The lineages leading to present-day man, apes, and monkeys, as deduced from the immunological data of Sarich and Wilson. The chart suggests that the lines leading to man, the modern chimpanzee, and the modern gorilla diverged from each other only about five million years ago (see text for discussion).

tionships between the various animal groups. At the same time, he recognizes that the ongoing nature of evolutionary processes make the creation of a perfectly constructed phylogenetic chart a virtually impossible task.

Acceptance of the hypothesis of natural selection to explain animal diversity leads to certain verifiable predictions concerning the relationship between the availability of ecological niches and animal evolution, extinction, emergence, etc. It also enables the zoologist to view the morphological, anatomical, and physiological features of a given animal in terms of their selective advantage in helping it to successfully occupy its particular ecological niche.

**EXERCISES**

1. What is a phylogenetic chart?
2. Why does the linnaean concept of a static, unchanging species fail to account for animal diversity?
3. Why is the hypothesis of evolution by natural selection a satisfactory way to explain animal diversity?
4. Why are there difficulties inherent in the construction of a wholly satisfactory phylogenetic chart?
5. What reasons can you suggest for the adaptive radiation undergone by the mammals at the end of the age of reptiles?
6. In terms of the exchange of materials with their environment, what advantages do protozoans have over multicellular organisms?
7. Name several disadvantages to a unicellular mode of life.

8. An obscure organism known as *Peripatus* is often spoken of as a "missing link" between the annelids and the arthropods. Read more on the structure of *Peripatus* in Buchsbaum's *Animals Without Backbones* (see reference list) or in an encyclopedia. What evidence suggests the role of "missing link" for *Peripatus?*

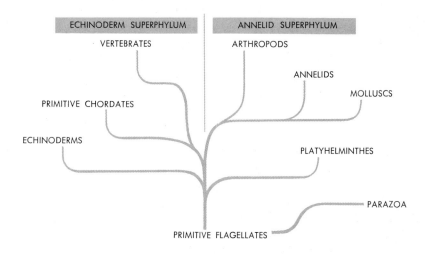

FIG. 26–13

9. Where would you place *Peripatus* on the phylogenetic chart shown in Fig. 26–13?

The invertebrates are often described as having evolved into two major groups, or "super-phyla." These two superphyla are the Annelida and the Echinodermata. Figure 26–13 illustrates this phylogenetic scheme. On the basis of the information contained in this figure, answer Exercises 10–12.

10. What evidence discussed in this chapter supports the hypothesis proposing close relationship between the annelids and the mollusks?

11. Using Buchsbaum as a reference, explain why the echinoderms are placed on the stem leading to the vertebrates, despite their radial symmetry.

12. From the construction of this chart, explain why the term "missing link" as applied to *Peripatus* is a poor one.

13. Why might we expect organisms such as *Peripatus* or the duckbill platypus to occupy a relatively minor place in the animal world today?

14. What evidence suggests that the birds evolved from the reptiles?

Table 26–1 shows a survey of many vertebrate groups for one type of visual pigment, Vitamin $A_1$ or $A_2$. The differences between these molecules are slight (only one double bond), but each has a characteristic absorption spectrum in the photometer. The presence of the pigment is indicated by a plus sign (+), and the absence by a minus sign (−). A double plus (++) indicates that where both pigments are present, one occurs in greater amounts. Study this table, then answer Exercises 15–17.

15. Construct an evolutionary tree for these organisms. Which group would you choose, on the basis of your general knowledge, as the ancestor of the others?

**TABLE 26–1**

| ANIMAL | VITAMIN A$_1$ | VITAMIN A$_2$ |
|---|---|---|
| FRESHWATER FISH | − | + |
| SALMON (LIVE IN SALT WATER, BUT RETURN TO FRESH WATER TO SPAWN) | + | ++ |
| EELS (LIVE IN FRESH WATER, BUT RETURN TO SALT WATER TO SPAWN) | ++ | + |
| FROG | | |
| TADPOLE (AQUATIC) | − | + |
| ADULT | + | − |
| NEW ENGLAND RED EFT* | | |
| TADPOLE | − | + |
| LAND-DWELLING ADULT | + | − |
| AQUATIC ADULT | − | + |
| LAND VERTEBRATES | + | − |
| MARINE VERTEBRATES | + | − |

* The red eft (a salamander) has three phases to its life cycle: the tadpole stage with gills, the adult land-dweller form with lungs, and an aquatic phase in which the adult returns to the water.

16. What do you hypothesize to have been the habitat(s) of ancestral eels and salmon?

17. Which would you hypothesize came first in evolutionary history, freshwater fish or marine fish? Explain the reasons for your choice.

**SUGGESTED READINGS**

BUCHSBAUM, R., *Animals Without Backbones* (Chicago: University of Chicago Press, 1948). A highly readable, beautifully illustrated book, which has undergone many editions since its first appearance in 1938. Deals exclusively with the invertebrates.

HANSON, E. D., *Animal Diversity* (Englewood Cliffs, N.J.: Prentice-Hall, 1965). A good, tightly written paperback which gives considerable insight into how the biologist approaches the problem of animal diversity.

ROMER, A. E., *Man and the Vertebrates* (Chicago: University of Chicago Press, 1941). Comprehensive coverage of vertebrate comparative anatomy and its significance to evolution.

SIMPSON, G. G., *Life of the Past* (New Haven: Yale University Press, 1953). A noted expert writes on the fossil record and its contributions to evolutionary theory.

# APPENDIXES

# CONVERSION OF TEMPERATURE SCALES APPENDIX 1

## Conversion of Centigrade to Absolute Temperatures

The following formula provides an easy means of converting a centigrade reading into the appropriate absolute value (K):

°K = °C + 273.

The absolute temperature is always 273° higher than the corresponding centigrade value. The absolute scale is based on the fact that when a gas is cooled, for every centigrade degree that its temperature is lowered the gas contracts to 1/273 of its volume at 0°C. Theoretically, then, a gas would possess *no* volume at −273°C. This temperature, the lowest possible in the universe, has not been obtained in the laboratory.

## Conversion of Centigrade to Fahrenheit Values

Both centigrade and Fahrenheit scales are calculated on the basis of the freezing and boiling points of water, but since intervals on the two scales are different, corresponding temperatures cannot be so readily calculated as in the conversion of centigrade and absolute temperatures. Between the freezing and boiling points of water on the Fahrenheit scale there are 180 degrees (212 − 32), or divisions. On the centigrade scale there are only 100 such divisions. One division on the centigrade scale is thus equal to 180/100 = 1.8 = 9/5 divisions on the Fahrenheit scale. Conversely, one Fahrenheit degree is equal to 5/9 of a centigrade degree. Thus, for conversion of Fahrenheit to centigrade temperatures, the following formula can be used:

°C = 5/9 °F − 32 .

The formula is reversed in converting centigrade to Fahrenheit:

°F = 9/5 °C + 32 .

### The Celsius Scale

Another temperature scale frequently encountered in scientific work is the Celsius scale. This is sometimes said to be interchangeable with centigrade, and it is true that any value given in centigrade (for example, body temperature, 37°) would read the same on the Celsius scale. Nevertheless, the two are not identical. The difference lies in the way the zero point is determined; the Celsius scale fixes the zero point by a much more accurate method. Thus the difference between the two scales is somewhat like that between a wooden yardstick and a precisely machined steel rule. Both measure the same quantities, and the divisions on the two scales are identical, but one is much more accurate. For measurements of temperature given in this book the centigrade scale is used by and large, since the difference in degree of measurement is not significant for biological problems.

# CALCULATION OF VARIANCE OF A SAMPLE OF DATA

As discussed in Section 5–4, variance can be calculated for the data on any curve of relatively normal distribution. Variance (symbolized $s^2$) is the measure of dispersion of data from the mean. It can be calculated from the following formula:

$$s^2 = \frac{\Sigma f(X - \overline{X})^2}{N - 1}.$$

In finding the variance, the difference between each observation $X$ and the mean $\overline{X}$ is obtained and squared:

$$(X - \overline{X})^2.$$

(The value is squared for mathematical reasons that we do not need to go into here. Algebraically, however, this has a practical value, since it prevents values from coming out negatively. Otherwise, positive and negative values would cancel each other, and for a normal curve the variance would equal zero.) Each squared item is then multiplied by the frequency $f$ with which it occurs; then the sum of these values,

$$\Sigma f(X - \overline{X})^2,$$

is determined and divided by the term $N - 1$, where $N$ = the total number of observations.

The following example will illustrate how to determine the variance of a distribution. From an ordinary deck of cards a hand of five cards is dealt. The number of red cards is tallied. The cards are reshuffled and the experiment is performed in the same way 29 more times, to give a total of 30 hands. The results of the tallies are given in

893

**TABLE A-1**

| NUMBER OF RED CARDS IN HAND | NUMBER OF HANDS | TOTAL |
|---|---|---|
| 0 | 1 | 0 |
| 1 | 6 | 6 |
| 2 | 10 | 20 |
| 3 | 7 | 21 |
| 4 | 5 | 20 |
| 5 | 1 | 5 |
|  | 30 | 72 |

Table A-1.* As may be easily calculated, the mean number of red cards per hand (72 ÷ 30) is 2.4.

To find the variance, we first square the difference between each recorded item and the mean. Thus in 1 out of the 30 hands, 0 red cards occurred: $(0 - 2.4)^2 = 5.76$; in 6 out of the 30 hands, 1 red card occurred: $(1 - 2.4)^2 = 1.96$. This can be continued for each number value of red cards, 0 through 5. The values obtained are given in Table A-2, second column.

**TABLE A-2**

| NUMBER OF RED CARDS (X) IN HAND | VALUE OF $(X - \overline{X})^2$ | FREQUENCY ($f$) (NUMBER OF HANDS) | PRODUCT $f(X - \overline{X})^2$ |
|---|---|---|---|
| 0 | 5.76 | 1 | 5.76 |
| 1 | 1.96 | 6 | 11.76 |
| 2 | 0.16 | 10 | 1.60 |
| 3 | 0.36 | 7 | 2.52 |
| 4 | 2.56 | 5 | 12.80 |
| 5 | 6.76 | 1 | 6.76 |

The next step, multiplying the value of $(X - \overline{X})^2$ by the frequency $f$, gives results recorded in the last column of Table A-2. All of these products are then summed, giving a value of 41.20. This is divided by $N - 1$ $(30 - 1 = 29)$,

$$s^2 = \frac{41.20}{29} = 1.42.$$

It is known from mathematical proof that the variance of a perfectly symmetrical curve of normal distribution is 1.0. The variance is judged according to its nearness to unity, or 1.0, once an adjustment has been made to the Standard Normal Distribution. A variance of 3.0 or higher represents a very great deviation from the normal curve.

---

* Data and explanation from F. Mosteller, R. E. K. Rourke, and G. B. Thomas, *Probability with Statistical Applications*, 2nd edition (Reading, Mass.: Addison-Wesley, 1970), pp. 220–221.

| NAME | ABBREVIATION | STRUCTURAL FORMULA | BALL-AND-STICK FORMULA |
|------|-------------|--------------------|------------------------|
| Glycine | gly | $H_3N^+$— $CH_2$— $COO^-$ | Key: Carbon, Oxygen, Hydrogen, Nitrogen, Sulphur |
| Alanine | ala | $H_3N^+$— CH— $COO^-$ <br> $CH_3$ | |
| Valine | val | $H_3N^+$— CH— $COO^-$ <br> CH <br> $CH_3$   $CH_3$ | |
| Leucine | leu | $H_3N^+$— CH— $COO^-$ <br> $CH_2$ <br> CH <br> $CH_3$   $CH_3$ | |

**Table of Amino Acids** (*cont.*)

| NAME | ABBREVIATION | STRUCTURAL FORMULA | BALL-AND-STICK FORMULA |
|---|---|---|---|
| Isoleucine | ileu | $H_3N^+$—CH—COO$^-$<br>HC—CH$_3$<br>CH$_2$<br>CH$_3$ | |
| Phenylalanine | phe | $H_3N^+$—CH—COO$^-$<br>CH$_2$<br>C<br>HC   CH<br>HC   CH<br>C<br>H | |
| Tyrosine | tyr | $H_3N^+$—CH—COO$^-$<br>CH$_2$<br>C<br>HC   CH<br>HC   CH<br>C<br>OH | |
| Tryptophan | try | $H_3N^+$—CH—COO$^-$<br>CH$_2$   H<br>C   C   CH<br>HC   C   CH<br>N   C<br>H   H | |
| Asparagine | asp | $H_3N^+$—CH—COO$^-$<br>CH$_2$<br>COO$^-$ | |
| Glutamic acid | glu | $H_3N^+$—CH—COO$^-$<br>CH$_2$<br>CH$_2$<br>COO$^-$ | |

**Table of Amino Acids** (*cont.*)

| NAME | ABBREVIATION | STRUCTURAL FORMULA | BALL-AND-STICK FORMULA |
|---|---|---|---|
| Serine | ser | $H_3N^+—CH—COO^-$<br>$CH_2$<br>$OH$ | |
| Threonine | thr | $H_3N^+—CH—COO^-$<br>$CH$<br>$CH_3$  $OH$ | |
| Cystine | cys | $H_3N^+—CH—COO^-$<br>$CH_2$<br>$S$<br>$S$<br>$CH_2$<br>$H_3N^+—CH—COO^-$ | |
| Cysteine | cys H | $H_3N^+—CH—COO^-$<br>$CH_2$<br>$SH$ | |
| Methionine | met | $H_3N^+—CH—COO^-$<br>$CH_2$<br>$CH_2$<br>$S$<br>$CH_3$ | |
| Arginine | arg | $H_3N^+—CH—COO^-$<br>$CH_2$<br>$CH_2$<br>$CH_2$<br>$NH$<br>$C$<br>$H_2N$    $NH_2^+$ | |

## Table of Amino Acids (*cont.*)

| NAME | ABBREVIATION | STRUCTURAL FORMULA | BALL-AND-STICK FORMULA |
|------|--------------|---------------------|------------------------|
| Histidine | his | $H_3N^+$—CH—COO$^-$<br>　　　CH$_2$<br>　　　C═CH<br>　HN　NH$^+$<br>　　　C<br>　　　H | |
| Lysine | lys | $H_3N^+$—CH—COO$^-$<br>　　　CH$_2$<br>　　　CH$_2$<br>　　　CH$_2$<br>　　　CH$_2$<br>　　　NH$_3^+$ | |

The complete key from which this sample is taken* contains 125 pairs of entries and is of the dichotomous type.  That is, the user begins by choosing between two broad alternative descriptions of the fruit specimen he has at hand, and progresses from number pair to number pair as directed, choosing always between two alternatives until he arrives at the proper identification.

1. Fruit a cone or conelike, featured by overlapping scales . . . . . . . . . . . . . . . . . . . . . . 2
1. Fruit not a cone . . . . . . . . . . . . . . . . . . . . . . . . . . . . . . . . . . . . . . . . . . . . . . . . . . . . . . 27

    2. Cone scales opposite (paired); cones small, mostly less than $\frac{1}{2}''$ long . . . . . . . . 3
    2. Cone scales alternate (in spirals); cones mostly more than $\frac{1}{2}''$ long . . . . . . . . . . 5

3. Cones oblong, at maturity yellowish brown: Arborvitae or Northern White Cedar *Thuja occidentalis* L.
3. Cones globose, at maturity bluish or purplish . . . . . . . . . . . . . . . . . . . . . . . . . . . . . 4

    4. Cone fleshy (usually not recognized as a cone); seeds wingless: Eastern Red Cedar or Red Cedar Juniper *Juniperus virginiana* L.
    4. Cones semifleshy, each scale with a small "spike" in the center, seeds winged: Southern or Atlantic White Cedar *Chamaecyparis thyoides* (L.) B. S. P.

5. Fruits or seeds have a terminal (end) wing . . . . . . . . . . . . . . . . . . . . . . . . . . . . . . . 6
5. Fruits or seeds have two lateral (side) wings or may seem unwinged . . . . . . . . . . . 22

---

* Material reproduced by permission from William M. Harlow, *Fruit Key & Twig Key to Trees and Shrubs* (New York: Dover Publications, 1959), pp. 18–25.

6. Cone falls to pieces at maturity leaving the spikelike cone axis upright on the branch . . . . . . . . . . . . . . . . . . . . . . . . . . . . . . . . . . . . . . . . . . . . . . . . . .    7

6. Cone scales persistent . . . . . . . . . . . . . . . . . . . . . . . . . . . . . . . . . . . . . . . . . . .    8

7. Cone consisting of terminally winged units, four-angled at the base: Tulip Tree or Yellow Poplar *Liriodendron tulipifera* L.

7. Cone consisting of flat scales, each bearing two winged seeds: Balsam Fir *Abies balsamea* (L.) Mill.

8. Small pointed bracts visible between scales near base of cone; cone upright on tree (Larches) . . . . . . . . . . . . . . . . . . . . . . . . . . . . . . . . . . . . . .    9

8. Bracts not visible, or lacking; cone pendent on tree . . . . . . . . . . . . . . . . . . . . . .    10

9. Cones about $\frac{5}{8}''$ long: Tamarack *Larix laricina* (DuRoi) K. Koch.

9. Cones from $1''$ to $1\frac{1}{4}''$ long: European Larch *Larix decidua* Mill.

10. Cone scales more or less thickened (Pines) . . . . . . . . . . . . . . . . . . . . . . . . . . . . .    11

10. Cone scales almost paper-thin (Spruces and Hemlocks) . . . . . . . . . . . . . . . . . .    18

11. Cones $4''$ to $8''$ long, long-stalked: White Pine *Pinus strobus* L.

11. Cones less than $4''$ long, short-stalked, or stalk lacking (sessile) . . . . . . . . . . . . . . .    12

12. Cones unsymmetrical (lopsided), usually remaining closed at maturity: Jack Pine *Pinus banksiana* Lamb.

12. Cones symmetrical, opening at maturity or during the following season . . . . .    13

13. Cone scales unarmed (no prickles), or prickles indistinct . . . . . . . . . . . . . . . . . . . . .    14

13. Cone scales with definite prickles . . . . . . . . . . . . . . . . . . . . . . . . . . . . . . . . . . . . . . . .    15

14. Scales unarmed, the outer surfaces more or less smooth and rounded: Red or Norway Pine *Pinus resinosa* Ait.

14. Scales with raised pyramid-shaped tips sometimes bearing small indistinct prickles: Scotch Pine *Pinus sylvestris* L.

15. Prickles clawlike, stout: Table-Mountain Pine *Pinus pungens* Lamb.

15. Prickles small and more slender . . . . . . . . . . . . . . . . . . . . . . . . . . . . . . . . . . . . . . . .    16

16. Prickles very slender, sometimes falling off; closed cones more or less oblong: Shortleaf Pine *Pinus echinata* Mill.

16. Prickles conspicuous; cones more egg-shaped (ovoid) . . . . . . . . . . . . . . . . . . . . . .    17

17. Open cones tend to be flat at the base; needles in threes: Pitch Pine *Pinus rigida* Mill.

17. Open cones more or less rounded at the base; needles in twos: Virginia or Scrub Pine *Pinus virginiana* Mill.

18. Cones $4''$ to $6''$ long: Norway Spruce *Picea abies* (L.) Karst.

18. Cones less than $3''$ long . . . . . . . . . . . . . . . . . . . . . . . . . . . . . . . . . . . . . . . . . . . . . . .    19

19. Cones purplish at maturity, scales with evident ragged edges: Black Spruce *Picea mariana* (Mill.) B.S.P.

19. Cones brownish at maturity, scale edges smooth or very slightly ragged . . . . . . . .    20

20. Cones about $\frac{3}{4}''$ long, or less: Eastern Hemlock *Tsuga canadensis* (L.) Carr.
20. Cones more than 1″ long. . . . . . . . . . . . . . . . . . . . . . . . . . . . . . . . . . . . . . . 21

21. Cones oblong, the scales flexible, with smooth straight edges: White
Spruce *Picea glauca* (Moench.) Voss.
21. Cones more ovoid (egg-shaped), scales brittle, with rounded, slightly
ragged edges: Red Spruce *Picea rubens* Sarg.

22. "Seeds" (nutlets) conspicuously winged (use hand lens); cone scales fall
away at maturity or during the ensuing winter. . . . . . . . . . . . . . . . . . . . . 23
22. "Seeds" not conspicuously winged; cone scales persistent (look for old
cones from previous season): Speckled Alder *Alnus rugosa* (DuRoi) Spreng.
or Smooth Alder *Alnus serrulata* (Ait.) Willd.

23. Cone matures in late spring or early summer, and then falls apart; nutlets
with hairy wings (use lens): Red or River Birch *Betula nigra* L.
23. Cone matures in autumn; nutlet wings essentially smooth (glabrous). . . . . . . . . . 24

24. Cone upright on branchlet; short-stalked; oblong; scales persistent
during part of the winter. . . . . . . . . . . . . . . . . . . . . . . . . . . . . . . . . . 25
24. Cone pendent, spreading (sideways), or somewhat upright; long-stalked;
narrowly cylindrical; scales usually falling away at maturity. . . . . . . . . . . . . . 26

25. Scales hairy (use lens): Yellow Birch *Betula alleghaniensis* Britton
(*B. lutea* Michx. F.)
25. Scales essentially glabrous: Sweet or Black Birch *Betula lenta* L.

26. Cone pendent, 1″ to $1\frac{1}{2}''$ long: Paper or White Birch *Betula
papyrifera* Marsh.
26. Cone spreading or somewhat erect, about $\frac{3}{4}''$ long: Gray Birch
*Betula populifolia* Marsh.

27. Fruit with a thin wing at the end, or encircling the seed cavity. . . . . . . . . . . . . . 28
27. Fruit not winged. . . . . . . . . . . . . . . . . . . . . . . . . . . . . . . . . . . . . . . . . . 44

28. Fruit paired (double) the two parts united at the base, but easily
broken apart (Maples). . . . . . . . . . . . . . . . . . . . . . . . . . . . . . . . . . . . 29
28. Fruit single, not in pairs. . . . . . . . . . . . . . . . . . . . . . . . . . . . . . . . . . . . 35

29. Fruit matures and is released in late spring. . . . . . . . . . . . . . . . . . . . . . . . . . 30
29. Fruit matures in autumn. . . . . . . . . . . . . . . . . . . . . . . . . . . . . . . . . . . . . 31

SOME TAXONOMIC CHARTS

As Chapters 19, 25, and 26 indicate, many different classification schemes have been proposed for living organisms. An early one was the animal-vegetable-mineral system used by Linnaeus. More recent schemes have dealt only with the biosphere or "animal-vegetable" portion of the environment, and left the nonliving portions to the other sciences.

An examination of several introductory biology textbooks or books on taxonomy will uncover several variations among modern classification schemes. There are schemes involving two kingdoms (Plantae and Animalia), three kingdoms (Protista, Plantae, and Animalia), four kingdoms (Monera, Protista, Plantae, and Animalia), and five kingdoms (Monera, Protista, Plantae, Fungi, and Animalia). The three-kingdom system, using the Protista (a category which includes organisms such as *Euglena*, which show characteristics associated with both plants and animals and are simply difficult to classify as one or the other), and the four-kingdom system are widely used in other biology textbooks, and are thus easily available to the interested reader. The authors have therefore elected to include here a modification of the two-kingdom system (which seems to be fast disappearing) and the five-kingdom system.

## THE TWO-KINGDOM SYSTEM

In the two-kingdom system, from 1883 until fairly recently, there existed for the plant kingdom a taxonomic scheme which recognized only four divisions*: Thallophyta (algae and fungi), Bryophyta (mosses), Pteridophyta (mostly ferns), and the Spermatophyta (seed plants). Modern advances in plant anatomy and physiology forced an alteration of the older two-kingdom system in which only the Bryophyta survived as a division. The Pteridophyta and Spermatophyta, formerly divisions, were brought together into one subkingdom, the Embryophyta. By contrast, the division Thallophyta was elevated to the rank of subkingdom, and ten different divisions were created out of groupings formerly considered as classes.

One advantage of the older, four-division system was that it nicely emphasized the gradual evolution of plant anatomy and reproduction (especially the latter) discussed in Chapter 25. In the representation of the two-kingdom system which follows, brackets have been used to allow the indication of elements of the older system alongside the general superstructure of the new. For example, those plants formerly classified as

---

* In botany it is conventional to use the terms "division," "subdivision," etc., in place of "phylum," "subphylum," etc.

division Pteridophyta and Spermatophyta in the older two-kingdom system have been bracketed within the new system to show the important differences that formed the basis for their previous grouping.

## KINGDOM PLANTAE

### Subkingdom Thallophyta

Completely undifferentiated plant body. No roots, stems, or leaves. No vascular (conducting) tissues; may or may not have chlorophyll. Reproduction mostly asexual by fission or spores, with gamete or spore-producing part usually unicellular.

---

SUBDIVISION ALGAE OF OLDER SYSTEM (THALLOPHYTES WITH CHLOROPHYLL)

**DIVISION CYANOPHYTA.** Blue-green algae. Without organized nucleus or plastids in cells. Immotile. Unicellular or colonial; reproduction mostly asexual. About 1500 species, found in aquatic and marine habitats, in damp soil or rocks.
EXAMPLES: *Nostoc, Oscillatoria*

**DIVISION EUGLENOPHYTA.** Euglenae. Flagellated, with bright green plastids. Reproduction asexual with longitudinal fission. Extremely motile (often classified as Animalia under phylum Protozoa). About 300 species, found in stagnant fresh water or in damp soil.
EXAMPLE: *Euglena*

**DIVISION PYRROPHYTA.** Dinoflagellates. Heavy cell wall of plates with furrows and flagella for motion. Asexual reproduction predominating. About 1000 species, mostly marine, a few aquatic.
EXAMPLE: *Peridinium*

**DIVISION CHRYSOPHYTA.** Golden algae. Many forms motile; cell wall with silicates giving varied geometrically perfect shapes. About 5000 species, marine, aquatic, and terrestrial.
EXAMPLES: The diatoms

**DIVISION PHAEOPHYTA.** Brown algae. Immotile. Sexual and asexual reproduction. About 1500 species, mostly marine.
EXAMPLES: *Fucus, Sargassum*

**DIVISION RHODOPHYTA.** Red algae. Sexual reproduction by immotile gametes. About 3000 species, marine.
EXAMPLES: All true seaweeds

**DIVISION CHLOROPHYTA.** Green algae. Contain pigments essentially the same as found in higher plants. Asexual and sexual reproduction. Unicellular, colonial, and multicellular forms known. Motile or immotile types. 5000 species, marine and aquatic.
EXAMPLES: *Protococcus (Pleurococcus), Spirogyra, Ulothrix*

REPRODUCTION ASEXUAL AND SEXUAL WITH THE LATTER OF A PRIMITIVE NATURE

**Subkingdom Thallophyta (cont.)**

**DIVISION SCHIZOMYCOPHYTA.** The bacteria. Unicellular forms reproducing asexually by fission. About 2000 species, found almost anywhere that conditions are favorable for growth.
EXAMPLE: *Diplococcus pneumoniae*
Order 1 of this phylum contains the true bacteria. A few pathogenic to man, but mostly harmless or beneficial.
Orders 2–7 contain many forms, the most commonly known of which are the viruses and Rickettsiae.

**DIVISION MYXOMYCOPHYTA.** The slime molds. Plant body a simple, undifferentiated, multinucleated plasmodium with no cell walls. Asexual reproduction by spores, sexual reproduction by flagellated gametes. Found in moist woods, on decaying organic matter.
EXAMPLES: *Physarum polycephalum, Lycogala epidendrum*

SUBDIVISION
FUNGI
OF
OLDER
SYSTEM
(THALLOPHYTES
WITHOUT
CHLOROPHYLL)

**DIVISION EUMYCOPHYTA.** The true fungi. Plant body usually composed of cobweblike threads of protoplasm called hyphae. Mostly terrestrial.

**CLASS PHYCOMYCETES.** Algal fungi. Hyphae without cross-walls. Sexual reproduction. About 1050 species.
EXAMPLES: *Rhizopus nigricans* (bread mold), downy mildews, white rust.

**CLASS ASCOMYCETES.** Sac fungi. Hyphae with cross-walls. Sexual fusion followed by ascospore formation. 12,400 species.
EXAMPLES: *Penicillium notatum, Aspergillus,* morel, cup fungi, blue and green molds, powdery mildews

**CLASS BASIDIOMYCETES.** Club fungi. Hyphae with cross-walls. Sexual fusion followed by basidiospore formation. 13,550 species.
EXAMPLES: Smuts, rusts, mushrooms, puffballs, bracket fungi.

**CLASS DEUTEROMYCETES.** Imperfect fungi. Asexual reproduction only. About 10,500 species.
EXAMPLE: Ringworm fungi

**CLASS LICHENES.** The lichens. Actually a combination of an alga (usually a green or blue-green type) and a fungus (usually an ascomycete), living in a symbiotic (mutualistic) relationship. About 16,000 species.
EXAMPLE: *Parmelia*

REPRODUCTION
ASEXUAL
AND
SEXUAL
WITH THE
LATTER
OF A
PRIMITIVE
NATURE

## Subkingdom Embryophyta

Green plants with zygote developing into a multicellular embryo while still in female sex organ (archegonium) or embryo sac.

**DIVISION BRYOPHYTA.** Mostly multicellular terrestrial plants; alternation of generations (metagenesis) with gametophyte conspicuous part of cycle. Reproduction by gametes and spores. No vascular tissue or true roots.

**CLASS HEPATICAE.** The liverworts, *Marchantia*. About 8000 species.

**CLASS ANTHOCEROTAE.** Horned liverworts. About 320 species.

**CLASS MUSCI.** The true mosses and sphagnum. About 14,000 species.

THESE FORMS WITH DISTINCT ALTERNATION OF GENERATIONS

**DIVISION TRACHEOPHYTA.** Multicellular plants with sporophyte generation as conspicuous part of cycle. Vascular tissues present, showing specialized cells for conduction (xylem and phloem). Archegonia usually present except in angiosperms.

DIVISION PTERIDOPHYTA OF OLDER SYSTEM

**Subdivision Psilopsida.** Mostly extinct simple vascular plants.
**Subdivision Lycopsida.** The club mosses.
**Subdivision Sphenopsida.** The horsetails.
**Subdivision Pteropsida.** Ferns and seed plants. Latter with an inconspicuous metagenesis.

**CLASS FILICINEAE.** The ferns. With true roots. Show obvious and typical metagenesis as the Bryophyta, but with sporophyte rather than gametophyte the conspicuous part of the cycle.

**CLASS GYMNOSPERMAE.** Large woody plants, mostly evergreen. Naked seeds, not enclosed in an ovary. No flowers present.
Order  Cycadales. The cycads.
Order  Ginkgoales. The ginkgos.
Order  Coniferales. Cone bearers, with needles or scales.
    EXAMPLES: Pine, spruce, fir, cedar, larch, cypress, redwood.
Order  Gnetales. Mostly extinct. Possible forerunners of flowering plants.

DIVISION SPERMATOPHYTA OF OLDER SYSTEM

**CLASS ANGIOSPERMAE.** The flowering plants. Seeds enclosed in an ovary which ripens into a fruit.
**Subclass Dicotyledonae.** Embryo with two cotyledons; vascular bundles in an orderly arrangement. Flower parts in fours and fives, or multiples thereof. Veins of leaves netted. Approximately 35 orders.
EXAMPLES: Buttercup, rose, elm, basswood, apple, oak, etc.
**Subclass Monocotyledonae.** Embryo with one cotyledon; vascular bundles scattered throughout stem. Flower parts in threes or multiples thereof; leaves with parallel venation. Approximately 9 orders.
EXAMPLES: Grasses, lily, iris, orchid, palm, sedge.

ALTERNATION OF GENERATIONS PRESENT BUT INDISTINCT

## KINGDOM ANIMALIA

Organisms classified as animals generally have no cellulose in their cell walls and do not contain chlorophyll.

---

**PHYLUM PROTOZOA.** Microscopic, unicellular animals, which sometimes aggregate in colonies. Some are free-living, others parasitic.

**CLASS FLAGELLATA.** Protozoa which move by whiplike protrusions known as flagella. Very primitive. May be closely related to one-celled plants.

**CLASS SARCODINA.** Protozoa which move by extending pseudopodia.

**CLASS SPOROZOA.** Parasitic protozoa reproducing by spores; no means of locomotion.

**CLASS CILIATA.** Protozoa which move by means of cilia.

**CLASS SUCTORIA.** Protozoa with cilia only in young stages, adults attached by stalk to the substrate. Some parasitic.

---

**PHYLUM PARAZOA (PORIFERA).** The sponges, both freshwater and marine. The lowest of the many-celled animals, resembling in many respects a colony of protozoans. Body perforated with many pores to admit water, from which food is extracted. There are three classes, divided primarily according to the formation of the sponge spicules.

---

**PHYLUM CNIDARIA (COELENTERATA).** Radially symmetrical animals with a central gastrovascular cavity. Body wall consists of only two cell layers. In the outer layer are stinging cells (nematocysts).

**CLASS HYDROZOA.** Hydralike animals, either single or colonial. Usually alternation of sexual (medusa) with asexual (polyp) stage in life cycle.
EXAMPLES: *Hydra, Obelia, Physalia* (Portuguese man-of-war)

**CLASS SCYPHOZOA.** Exclusively marine; polyp stage usually absent.
EXAMPLES: *Aurelia*

**CLASS ANTHOZOA.** Marine forms; solitary or colonial; without alternation of generations; tentacles.
EXAMPLES: Coral, anemones

---

**PHYLUM CTENOPHORA.** The comb-jellies or sea walnuts. Move by means of eight comblike bands of cilia.

---

**PHYLUM PLATYHELMINTHES.** The flatworms. Bodies bilaterally symmetrical, flat, and either oval or elongated, with three cell layers. All have flame cells as excretory organs. True central nervous system. No skeletal or respiratory systems.

**CLASS TURBELLARIA.** Nonparasitic flatworms with ciliated ectoderm.
EXAMPLE: *Planaria*

**CLASS TREMATODA.** The flukes. Parasitic flatworms with nonciliated ectoderm, and one or more suckers. Many are internal parasites.
EXAMPLE: *Fasciola hepatica* (sheep-liver fluke)

**CLASS CESTODA.** Parasitic forms; body a series of detachable proglottids; no intestine; head with hooks for holding on to intestinal walls.
EXAMPLE: Tapeworm

**PHYLUM NEMERTEA.** The proboscis worms. Nonparasitic, usually marine animals, with complex digestive system and proboscis armed with hook for capturing prey. Lowest group on evolutionary scale with blood-vascular system; two-opening digestive system.

**PHYLUM ASCHELMINTHES (NEMATHELMINTHES, NEMATODA).** The roundworms. An extremely large phylum, characterized by elongated, cylindrical, bilaterally symmetrical bodies; live as parasites in plants and animals, or are free-living.
EXAMPLES: Vinegar eel, *Ascaris*, hookworm, pinworm, *Trichinella*

**PHYLUM ROTIFERA.** "Wheel animals" with circular rows of cilia around the mouth which beat with a motion suggesting rotation of a wheel. Well-developed digestive system. Smallest of metazoans.
EXAMPLE: Rotifers

**PHYLUM BRYOZOA.** "Moss animals." Microscopic organisms, usually marine, form branching colonies. Have U-shaped row of ciliated tentacles by means of which they capture food.

**PHYLUM BRACHIOPODA.** Marine animals with two hard shells, superficially like a clam. Most representatives now extinct.
EXAMPLE: The lamp shells

**PHYLUM ANNELIDA.** The segmented worms, with body cavity separated from the digestive tube; brain dorsal and nerve cord ventral; body wall contains circular and longitudinal muscles.

**CLASS POLYCHAETA.** Marine worms; fleshy outgrowths, or parapodia, extending from the segments.
EXAMPLE: Sandworm

**CLASS OLIGOCHAETA.** Freshwater or terrestrial worms, with no parapodia and few bristles per segment.
EXAMPLE: Earthworm

**CLASS ARCHIANNELIDA.** Primitive annelids without bristles or external segmentation.
EXAMPLE: *Polygordius*

**CLASS HIRUDINEA.** Flattened annelids lacking bristles and parapodia, but with suckers at both ends.
EXAMPLE: Leech

**PHYLUM ONYCOPHORA.** Rare, tropical animals, structurally intermediate between the annelids and the arthropods; have an annelidlike excretory system and an insectlike respiratory system.
EXAMPLE: *Peripatus*

**PHYLUM ARTHROPODA.** Segmented animals with jointed appendages and a hard exoskeleton of chitin. Body divided into head, thorax, abdomen.

**Phylum Arthropoda (cont.)**

**CLASS TRILOBITA.** Trilobites, primitive marine arthropods that originated in the Cambrian period and became extinct in the Permian. Segmented bodies divided by two longitudinal furrows into three lobes.

**CLASS CRUSTACEA.** Mostly aquatic, breathe by means of gills; head and thorax usually fused into a cephalothorax.

EXAMPLES: Crayfish, lobster, crab, shrimp, barnacle

**CLASS CHILOPODA.** Body flattened and consisting of from 15 to 170 or more segments. Each segment has one pair of appendages.

EXAMPLE: Centipede

**CLASS DIPLOPODA.** Body more or less cylindrical, composed of 25 to 100 or more segments; most segments bear two pairs of legs.

EXAMPLE: Millipede

**CLASS ARACHNOIDEA.** Head and thorax fused into a cephalothorax. Adults have no antennae; four pairs of legs. Breathe by means of book lungs or tracheae.

EXAMPLES: Spiders, scorpions, mites, ticks

**CLASS INSECTA.** Head, thorax, and abdomen separate; three pairs of legs, one pair of antennae. External respiration by tracheae. The insects are the largest group of animals, and are mostly terrestrial. There are about 24 different orders, of which the following are most common:

Order   Orthoptera. Grasshoppers and cockroaches
Order   Isoptera. Termites
Order   Odonata. Dragonflies and damsel flies
Order   Anopleura. Lice
Order   Hemiptera. Water boatmen, bedbugs, backswimmers
Order   Homoptera. Cicadas, aphids, and scale insects
Order   Coleoptera. Beetles, weevils
Order   Lepidoptera. Butterflies and moths
Order   Diptera. Flies, mosquitos, gnats
Order   Hymenoptera. Ants, wasps, bees, and gallflies

---

**PHYLUM MOLLUSCA.** Unsegmented, soft-bodied animals, usually covered by a shell, and with a ventral, muscular foot. Respiration by means of gills, protected by fold of body wall (the mantle).

**CLASS AMPHINEURA.** Elongated body, reduced head, shell composed of eight plates.

EXAMPLE: Chitons

**CLASS PELECYPODA.** Bivalve shell; lacking head, eyes, tentacles.

EXAMPLES: Clams, oysters, mussels

**CLASS GASTROPODA.** With or without coiled shell. Head, distinct eyes, often tentacles.

EXAMPLES: Snails, slugs, whelks

**CLASS SCAPHOPODA.** Marine; body elongated, enclosed in tubular shell open at both ends. No gills.

EXAMPLE: Tooth shell

**CLASS CEPHALOPODA.** With grasping tentacles; marine.

EXAMPLES: Squid, octopus

**PHYLUM ECHINODERMATA.** Marine forms, radially symmetrical as adults, bilaterally symmetrical as larvae. Skin contains calcareous, spine-bearing plates. Possess unique water-vascular system. Respiration by skin-gills, or outpocketing of digestive tract.

**CLASS ASTEROIDEA.** Body is a central disc with broad arms (usually 5) containing double rows of tube feet.
EXAMPLE: Starfish, or seastar

**CLASS OPHIUROIDEA.** Body is a central disc with narrow arms extending.
EXAMPLE: Brittle stars

**CLASS ECHINOIDEA.** Spherical or flattened oval animals with many long spines. Tube feet with suckers.
EXAMPLE: Sea urchins

**CLASS HOLOTHUROIDEA.** Long, ovoid, soft-bodied echinoderms, usually with a ring of tentacles around the mouth.
EXAMPLE: Sea cucumbers

**CLASS CRINOIDEA.** Body is cup-shaped and attached by a stalk to the substrate. Mostly fossil; only a few living species.
EXAMPLES: Sea lilies, feather stars

---

**PHYLUM CHORDATA.** Bilaterally symmetrical animals with a notochord, gill clefts in the pharynx, and a dorsal, hollow neural tube.
**Subphylum Hemichordata.** Marine, wormlike forms resembling larval echinoderms during development. Body in three regions, with proboscis, collar, and trunk.
EXAMPLE: Acorn worm
**Subphylum Urochordata.** Marine animals with saclike adult body. Adults free-swimming or attached, often forming colonies. Larvae free-swimming, with notochord in tail region.
EXAMPLES: Tunicates, sea squirts
**Subphylum Cephalochordata.** Marine animals, with segmented, elongated, fishlike body. Burrow in the sand and ingest food by beating of cilia on anterior end. Full-fledged notochord.
EXAMPLES: *Amphioxus*, lancelet
**Subphylum Vertebrata.** Animals with definite head, vertebrate backbone, well-developed brain, and (usually) two pairs of limbs. Ventral heart and a pair of well-developed eyes.

**CLASS AGNATHA.** Vertebrates without jaws or paired fins.
EXAMPLE: Lampreys

**CLASS PLACODERMI.** Earliest fishes with jaws. Known only as fossils.
EXAMPLE: Spiny-skinned shark

**CLASS CHONDRICHTHYES.** Fishes with cartilaginous skeleton and scales of dentin and enamel in skin.
EXAMPLES: Sharks, rays, skates

**CLASS OSTEICHTHYES.** Bony fish.
EXAMPLES: Sturgeon, salmon, lungfish, perch

**CLASS AMPHIBIA.** Freshwater or terrestrial forms; gills present at some stage; skin slimy and limbs without claws; skin is scaleless.
EXAMPLES: Frogs, toads, salamanders

**Phylum Chordata (cont.)**

**CLASS REPTILIA.** Body covered with scales derived from epidermis of skin. Breathe by means of lungs and have three- to four-chambered heart. Eggs relatively large; oviparous or ovoviparous.
EXAMPLES: Snakes, lizards, crocodiles, turtles, etc.

**CLASS AVES.** Warm-blooded animals, skin covered with feathers. Present-day examples are toothless, but primitive ones possessed reptilian teeth. Forelimbs modified as wings. Four-chambered heart, and hollow bones.
EXAMPLES: All birds

**CLASS MAMMALIA.** Warm-blooded animals, skin covered with hair. Females with mammary glands which secrete milk for nourishment of young.

**Subclass Prototheria.** Primitive egg-laying forms. Mostly extinct.
EXAMPLE: Duckbill platypus

**Subclass Metatheria.** Pouched mammals. Young are born in very immature state. Complete development in pouch on mother's abdomen.
EXAMPLES: Opossum, kangaroo, koala bear, wombat

**Subclass Eutheria.** Placental mammals. Young developed within uterus of mother, obtaining nourishment via the placenta.

Order **Insectivora.** Primitive insect-eaters.
 EXAMPLES: Moles, shrews
Order **Chiroptera.** Flying mammals.
 EXAMPLE: Bats
Order **Carnivora.** Sharp teeth, cuspids for eating flesh. Claws usually present.
 EXAMPLES: Bear, raccoon, dog, cat, weasel, mink, otter, skunk
Order **Rodentia.** Mammals with incisor teeth for gnawing.
 EXAMPLES: Squirrel, woodchuck, chipmunk, mouse
Order **Cetacea.** Marine mammals with flippers replacing legs.
 EXAMPLES: Whale, porpoise, dolphin
Order **Lagomorpha.** Rodentlike animals with highly developed hindlimbs for jumping.
 EXAMPLES: Rabbit, hare
Order **Ungulata.** Hoofed mammals; vegetarians with large grinding molars. Divided into odd-toed and even-toed.
 EXAMPLES: Horse, tapir, rhinoceros (odd-toed); bison, goat, sheep, deer, pig, hippopotamus, camel, llama, antelope (even-toed)
Order **Proboscoidea.** Upper lip and nose lengthened to form long prehensile trunk; incisor teeth forming tusks.
 EXAMPLE: Elephants
Order **Sirenia.** Aquatic mammals, with finlike forelimbs and no hindlimbs. Whale-like body, with horizontal tail fin and definite neck region.
 EXAMPLE: Sea cow
Order **Primates.** Erect or partially erect mammals, with forelimbs highly modified for grasping. Highly intelligent, with greatly enlarged cerebral areas of brain.
 EXAMPLES: Monkey, gorilla, chimpanzee, orangutan, gibbon, man

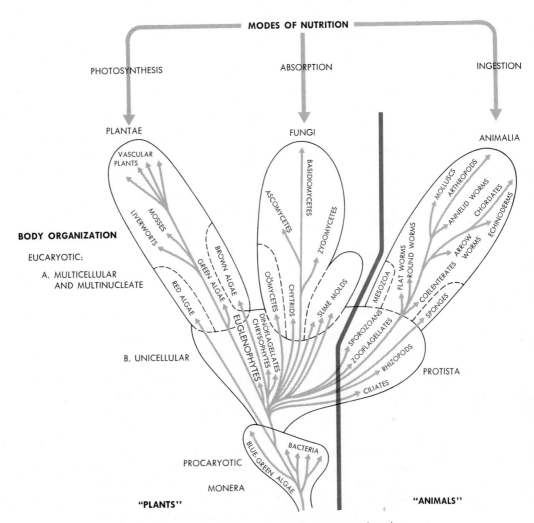

FIG. A–1    The broad interrelationships of plants and other organisms.  Five kingdoms, based on levels of body organization and modes of nutrition, are recognized in this classification system.  The organisms traditionally called "plants" in the two-kingdom system are listed on the left of the diagram, the "animals" on the right.  (Adapted from R. H. Whittaker, "New Concepts of Organisms." *Science* **163**, pp. 150–160, copyright 1969 by the American Association for the Advancement of Science.)

**THE FIVE-KINGDOM SYSTEM**

The five-kingdom system given here is adapted in part from one given by R. H. Whittaker in "New Concepts of Kingdoms of Organisms," published in *Science* (the official journal of the American Association for the Advancement of Science), Vol. 163, 1969, pp. 150–160. Besides the Protista, this system recognizes the Monera, or procaryotic organisms, as a separate kingdom.  Since the kingdom Animalia is essentially as given in the previous pages under the two-kingdom system, it is not included here.

Each taxonomic system, whether it uses two, three, four, or five kingdoms, has its own logical basis and set of criteria for the grouping or separation of organisms. Indeed, taxonomists often classify themselves—according to whether they lean toward grouping many organisms into one group or toward dividing them up into many groups—as "lumpers" and "splitters," respectively. The five-kingdom system given here tends toward the "splitter" side in terms of the number of kingdoms. Its internal logic is extremely concise, however. It is based on the criteria of levels of body organization *as well as* the different modes of nutrition (photosynthesis, absorption, or ingestion) utilized by the groups.

The five-kingdom system is summarized in Fig. A–1. Note that the colored dividing line leaves the "plants" not only the larger group but also in possession of the hypothesized ancestral forms which gave rise to both the "plants" and the "animals." (The reader may have noticed the disproportionate time spent on the evolution of plants as compared to that spent on the evolution of animals in Chapters 25 and 26. This imbalance is the result of the fact that the early ancestral forms of both the "plant" and "animal" groups fall more logically into the "plant" world.)

## KINGDOM MONERA

Organisms with procaryotic cells, lacking nuclear membranes, plastids, mitochondria, or flagella with 9 + 2 strands; body organization unicellular, colonial, or mycelial. Diverse nutritional types, including absorption, photosynthesis, and chemosynthesis. Reproduction primarily asexual by cell division; some sexual recombination known in a few species. Motile by simple flagella or gliding, or nonmotile.

---

**DIVISION 1. SCHIZOPHYTA.** The bacteria. Many species motile by simple flagella; most absorb their food, a few are photosynthetic or chemosynthetic. About 1600 species, found almost anywhere that conditions are favorable for growth.

**Order 1. Eubacteriales.** True bacteria. A few pathogenic to man, but mostly harmless or beneficial (as decomposers in the ecosystem). About 1300 species.
EXAMPLES: *Escherichia coli* and *Diplococcus pneumoniae*.

**Order 2. Actinomycetales.** The actinomycetes or funguslike bacteria. Body of elongate, tubular threads similar to (but much finer than) those of fungi. Source of many antibiotics.
EXAMPLES: the genera *Streptomyces* and *Actinomyces*.

Seven or eight other orders are usually recognized in this division. For convenience, the viruses (Virales) are usually classified near the bacteria.

---

**DIVISION 2. CYANOPHYTA.** Blue-green algae. Blue color due to pigment phycocyanin, red color to pigment phycoerythrin; nearly all are photosynthetic, producing free molecule oxygen; flagella lacking, motility (if present) by gliding. About 1500 species, found in aquatic and marine habitats, in damp soil, on tree bark, and on rocks.
EXAMPLES: the genera *Nostoc*, *Gloeocapsa*, and *Oscillatoria*.

# KINGDOM PROTISTA

Organisms with eucaryotic cells (possessing nuclear membranes, mitochondria, plastids in the plant members, 9 + 2 strand flagella, and other organelles); primarily unicellular or colonial-unicellular organisms; diverse nutritional methods, including photosynthesis, absorption, and ingestion (in a few species); true sexual processes with nuclear fusion and meiosis present in most; motile by 9 + 2 strand flagella, or by other means.

**DIVISION 1. EUGLENOPHYTA.** Euglenophytes. Flagellated unicells lacking cellulose cell walls, enclosed by a flexible or rigid pellicle; reserve food usually paramylum (a starchlike carbohydrate). About 300 species, found in stagnant fresh water or damp soil. EXAMPLES: the genera *Euglena*, *Peranema*, *Astasia*, and *Phacus*.

**DIVISION 2. PYRROPHYTA.** Dinoflagellates. Unicells with a heavy cellulose wall (in many species) sculptured into plates, others naked (unarmored); cell has two furrows, one transverse and one longitudinal, each furrow containing one long flagellum. About 1000 species, mostly marine, a few in fresh water. EXAMPLES: the genera *Ceratium*, *Peridenium*, and *Gonyaulax*.

**DIVISION 3. CHRYSOPHYTA.** Golden algae and diatoms. Golden algae have unicellular, colonial, or filamentous bodies; some have elaborate internal siliceous skeletal structure (the silicoflagellates); other have heavily calcified rings, discs, or plates embedded in the cell wall (the coccolithophores); 300 species. Diatoms have cell walls heavily impregnated with silica and highly ornamented; over 5500 species. Both groups abundant in phytoplankton. EXAMPLES: the genera *Ochromonas*, *Dinobryon*, *Synura*, *Pinnularia*, *Navicula*, and *Cyclotella*.

**DIVISION 4. XANTHOPHYTA.** Yellow-green algae. Plants yellow-green due to chlorophyll in plastids being masked by yellow carotenoid pigments; bodies mostly one-celled, a few being filamentous or tubular (coenocytic); widespread but relatively inconspicuous; grow in fresh waters and marine waters, on damp mud or moist soil; or as epiphytes on larger algae and other aquatic plants; over 400 species. EXAMPLES: the genera *Characium*, *Tribonema*, and *Vaucheria*.

Kingdom Protista also includes five phyla of protozoans and two phyla of fungus-like organisms.

# KINGDOM PLANTAE

Organisms with multicellular bodies; cells walled and frequently vacuolate; with photosynthetic pigments in plastids. Nutrition mostly photosynthetic, a very few species being absorptive. Primarily nonmotile, living anchored to the substratum. Structural differentiation leading toward organs of photosynthesis, anchorage, and support and, in most species, specialized photosynthetic, vascular, and covering tissues. Reproduction primarily sexual with cycles of alternating haploid and diploid generations, the haploid being greatly reduced in the more advanced members of the kingdom.

**DIVISION 1. RHODOPHYTA.** Red algae. Plants chiefly reddish due to the red pigment phycoerythrin; bodies vary from microscopic single cells through simple filaments to large plants over 10 feet long and with some tissue differentiation due to the aggregation of filaments; compare favorably in complexity of symmetry and branching habit with that found in flowering plants; very complex sexual reproductive systems (but no flagellated cells of any sort); grow largely attached to rocks and larger algae along ocean shores from high in the intertidal region to depths of 360 feet, especially in the tropical seas; over 3500 species.
EXAMPLES: the genera *Porphyridium, Bangia, Porphyra, Nemalion,* and *Chondrus.*

**DIVISION 2. PHAEOPHYTA.** Brown algae. Plants brownish due to the xanthophyll pigment fucoxanthin; bodies vary from simple unbranched filaments only 1 mm long to massive plants 200 feet long and with well-developed tissues (including food-conducting, sievelike elements similar to those of vascular plants); grow largely attached to rocks along ocean shores, often forming dense subtidal forests; over 1500 species.
EXAMPLES: the genera *Ectocarpus, Laminaria, Nereocystis, Fucus,* and *Sargassum.*

**DIVISION 3. CHLOROPHYTA.** Green algae. Plants bright green due to chlorophyll in plastids; body diversity is considerable, ranging from one-celled motile or nonmotile species to motile or nonmotile colonies, and from simple filaments to massive plants over 20 feet long (with tissues); wide diversity of life cycles and modes of sexual reproduction; abundant in both fresh waters and marine waters, on tree trunks, and on moist rocks, leaf surfaces, and soil; nearly 7000 species.
EXAMPLES: the genera *Chlamydomonas, Volvox, Ulothrix, Cladophora, Spirogyra, Ulva, Codium.*

**DIVISION 4. BRYOPHYTA.** Bryophytes. Multicellular terrestrial plants without vascular tissues or true roots; life cycle includes a conspicuous gametophyte with unbranched sporophyte permanently attached; sex organs (archegonia and antheridia) multicellular; reproduction by gametes and spores.

**CLASS 1. HEPATICAE.** Liverworts. Gametophyte plant body with dorsiventral symmetry; either a strap-shaped, branched thallus or leafy; sporophyte without stomata, short-lived, dying after spores mature; rhizoids unicellular; about 8000 species.

**CLASS 2. ANTHOCEROTAE.** Hornworts. Gametophyte similar to liverworts; sporophyte with stomata, continues growth for long time by addition of new cells by a basal meristem; about 100 species.

**CLASS 3. MUSCI.** Mosses. Gametophyte filamentous at first, later developing an erect stem with leaves; sporophyte often with stomata, long-lived; rhizoids multicellular; about 14,000 species.

**DIVISION 5. PSILOPHYTA.** Psilophytes. Multicellular terrestrial plants with vascular tissues; plant body consists of a sparingly branched, leafless, erect, aerial portion and a horizontal, rootless, underground portion; mostly fossil plants; only 4 living species.

**DIVISION 6. LYCOPODOPHYTA.** Lycopods or club mosses. Multicellular terrestrial plants with vascular tissues; plant body with leaves and roots; stem not jointed; spores produced in sporangia borne in the axils of fertile leaves (sporophylls); sporophylls often aggregated into clublike terminal cones (strobili); no leaf gaps; fertilized by swimming sperms; about 1300 species.

**DIVISION 7. ARTHROPHYTA.** Horsetails. Multicellular plants with vascular tissues; plant body with roots and small whorled leaves; stems conspicuously jointed; spores produced in sporangia borne on highly modified sporophylls that are aggregated into a terminal conelike structure (strobilus); no leaf gaps; fertilization by swimming sperms; about 25 living species.

**DIVISION 8. PTEROPHYTA.** Ferns. Multicellular plants with vascular tissues; plant body with large, conspicuous leaves and stem that may be much reduced, or creeping, or an erect tree (some tropical species); vascular cylinder with leaf gaps; spores produced in sporangia located usually on lower surface of the leaves; fertilization by swimming sperms; about 9000 species.

**DIVISION 9. CYCADOPHYTA.** Multicellular plants with vascular tissues; gametophyte small and physiologically dependent upon sporophyte; sporophyte large, usually woody; leaves large, fernlike, pinnately compound; ciliate sperms; seeds produced; many extinct species; about 90 living species.

**DIVISION 10. CONIFEROPHYTA.** Conifers. Multicellular plants with vascular tissues; gametophyte small and dependent upon sporophyte; sporophyte large, usually woody; leaves simple and relatively small, usually not fernlike; sperms without cilia; seeds produced; many extinct species; about 550 living species.

**DIVISION 11. ANTHOPHYTA.** Flowering plants. Multicellular plants with vascular tissues; gametophyte small and dependent upon sporophyte; sporophyte large, becoming herbaceous, shrubby, or woody; leaves usually broad; sperms without cilia, transferred to ovule by a pollen tube; seeds enclosed within an ovary which develops into a fruit.

**CLASS 1. DICOTYLEDONAE.** "Dicots." Embryo inside seed with two cotyledons; flower parts mostly in fours or fives; vascular tissue in distinct strands or bundles arranged in a cylinder or circle; leaves netveined. About 45 orders, 265 families, and over 200,000 species.

**CLASS 2. MONOCOTYLEDONAE.** "Monocots." Embryo with one cotyledon; flower parts mostly in threes or multiples thereof; vascular tissues usually in scattered bundles; leaves with parallel veins. About 16 orders, 50 families, and over 50,000 species.

## KINGDOM FUNGI

Primarily multinucleate organisms with eucaryotic nuclei dispersed in a walled and often septate mycelium; plastids and mitochondria lacking. Nutrition by absorption. Little or no vegetative body differentiation; reproductive body of more advanced species composed of tissues. Primarily nonmotile (but with protoplasmic flow in the mycelium), living embedded in a medium or food supply. Reproductive cycles usually include both sexual and asexual processes; mycelia mostly haploid in primitive species but dikaryotic in the more advanced forms.

**DIVISION 1. MYXOMYCOPHYTA.** Slime molds. *True slime molds:* body a multinucleate plasmodium without cell walls; move in amoeboid fashion; ingest solid food particles (as do amoebae) and dissolved nutrients; produce spore-bearing structures on stalks; about 450 species. *Cellular slime molds:* body one-celled during feeding stage (indistinguishable from amoebae in appearance), ingest bacteria; under certain conditions, several one-celled individuals aggregate and produce a multicellular, sluglike pseudoplasmodium which moves about as a unit and later develops into a stalked, spore-producing structure; about 24 species. Both kinds live in moist woods, on decaying organic matter, and on dung.

**DIVISION 2. EUMYCOPHYTA.** True fungi. Feeding body usually composed of cobweb-like threads (hyphae) which excrete digestive enzymes into the surrounding environment and absorb dissolved nutrients; decomposer organisms.

**CLASS 1. CHYTRIDIOMYCETES.** Chytrids. Body varies from one-celled to typical thread-like type (of hyphae); produce motile reproductive cells, each with a single, posterior, whiplike flagellum; saprophytes or parasites; mostly microscopic organisms of aquatic habitat; over 400 species.

**CLASS 2. OÖMYCETES.** Water molds, white rusts, and downy mildews. Body ranges from a single cell to a much-branched filamentous mass of hyphae (mycelium); produce motile reproductive cells, each with one tinsel flagellum directed forward and one whiplike flagellum directed backward; saprophytes or parasites (many cause serious diseases of plants).

**CLASS 3. ZYGOMYCETES.** Bread molds, fly fungi, animal trapping fungi. Body mycelial in form; produce a sexual dormant spore called a zygospore; no flagellated cells; saprophytes or parasites; some disperse spores forcefully (like a "shotgun"); some trap and digest small animals such as amoebae and nematodes in the soil.

**CLASS 4. ASCOMYCETES.** Sac fungi. Body mycelial in form (one-celled in some); produce haploid ascospores (usually 8) inside a saclike ascus (following meiosis of a zygote nucleus); spore-producing fruiting body may be large, mushroomlike, and edible (e.g., morels); over 12,000 species.

**CLASS 5. BASIDIOMYCETES.** Club fungi. Body mycelial in form (one-celled in some); produce haploid basidiospores (usually 4) on short stalks outside a club-shaped basidium (following meiosis of a zygote nucleus); fruiting body of many species is large (up to 3 feet or more in diameter) and constructed of numerous hyphae closely coherent in a pseudo-tissue; over 13,000 species.

**CLASS 6. DEUTEROMYCETES.** Imperfect fungi. An artificial group containing fungi known only by their asexual reproductive structures; known as imperfect fungi due to apparent lack of sexual phase (perfect stage); saprophytes and parasites; over 10,000 species.

The lichens (class Lichenes) are usually considered part of the fungi; body is composed of an intimate association of an alga and a fungus, the resulting structure behaving as a single plant. Over 16,000 species.

# KINGDOM ANIMALIA

See pages 906–910.

# GLOSSARY

# GLOSSARY

**absorption**  The passage of food through the walls of the digestive tract for transportation to other parts of the body.

*Acetabularia*  A single-celled marine alga composed of a stalk and an umbrellalike cap.

**acid group**  The —COOH group located on many organic molecules, especially amino and fatty acids.  The acid group ionizes at physiological pH (pH = 7.4) to yield a proton in solution as a hydronium ion:

$$\text{—COOH} + H_2O \rightarrow \text{—COO}^- + H_3O^+ \text{ (hydronium)}.$$

The acid properties of the group are a result of its ability to yield a proton in solution.

**activation energy**  The amount of energy necessary to initiate an exergonic reaction.

**active site**  The physical portion of an enzyme molecule into which a given substrate fits.  When the active site is blocked, the enzyme cannot act.

**active transport**  The movement of molecules against a concentration gradient, requiring the expenditure of energy.

**adaptation**  Any change in an organism's structure or function that allows it to better cope with conditions in the environment.

**adaptive radiation**  The development, by natural selection, of a variety of types from a single ancestral species.

**adenosine triphosphate (ATP)**  A molecule consisting of a purine (adenine), a sugar (ribose), and three phosphate groups.  A great deal of energy for biological function is stored in the high-energy bonds which link the phosphate groups, and is liberated when one or two of the phosphates are split off from the ATP molecule.  The resulting compounds are called adenosine diphosphate (ADP) or adenosine monophosphate, respectively.  (For molecular formula, see Section 8–2.)

**adhesion**  The tendency of molecules of different substances to stick together.

**adrenal gland**   A gland on the anterior surface of the kidney.   The adrenal cortex secretes the hormone epinephrine (adrenaline).

**aerobe**   An organism which requires oxygen to carry on the process of respiration.

**aerobic respiration**   A series of reactions for the breakdown of glucose in which the element oxygen is ultimately involved.

**agglutination**   The clumping of red blood cells when exposed to agglutinogens in blood of an incompatible type.

**agglutinogen**   Blood substance which causes agglutination when introduced into blood of an incompatible type.

**aggressive behavior**   Behavior in which attack is either initiated or threatened.

**agonistic behavior**   The entire sequence of behavioral events associated with aggressive behavior both on the part of the aggressor and of the organism against which the aggression is directed.

**allantois**   In bird and reptile embryos, an extraembryonic membrane for the storage of solid, nondiffusable nitrogenous wastes.

**alleles**   Genes which occupy similar loci on homologous chromosomes but carry contrasting inheritance factors.   Also, two or more genes capable of mutating one into the other.

**alternation of generations**   A characteristic of the life cycle of certain plants in which a sexual generation alternates with an asexual generation.

**alveolus**   An air sac in the lungs, thin-walled and surrounded by a blood vessel.   The hundreds of thousands of alveoli in each lung serve as the major vehicle for gas exchange in the mammalian body.

**amino acid**   The basic structural unit of proteins, having the general formula

$$\begin{array}{ccc} H & R & O \\ \diagdown & | & \diagup\!\!\diagup \\ N\!\!-\!\!C\!\!-\!\!C & & \\ \diagup & | & \diagdown \\ H & H & OH \end{array}$$

The name "amino acid" is derived from the fact that a basic amino ($-NH_2$) group and an acidic carboxylic acid ($-COOH$) are attached to the same carbon skeleton.   The R group varies from one amino acid to another, causing the differences exhibited by the different amino acids.

**amino group**   The $NH_2$ group located on all amino acids which contributes certain basic (proton-accepting) properties to the molecule.   The amino group is able to accept a proton from a hydronium ion in the following reaction:

$$-NH_2 + H_3O^+ \text{ (hydronium)} \rightarrow -NH_3^+ + H_2O.$$

At physiological pH (i.e., pH = 7.4), most amino groups are ionized in the $NH_3^+$ form.

**ammonia**   A highly toxic and soluble waste product of deamination.   In aquatic animals, ammonia passes from the body almost continuously, so that a harmlessly low concentration is maintained.   In terrestrial animals, ammonia is converted to other materials which can be safely stored in the body until excretion is possible.

**amnion**   An extraembryonic membrane surrounding the embryo and containing a watery fluid to prevent damage from shock or adhesion to the shell.

*Amoeba*   A one-celled organism of irregular shape which moves by extending part of its mass into temporary armlike extensions called pseudopods.

**anaerobe**   An organism which can carry on respiration in the absence of oxygen. Two types of anaerobes can be distinguished: facultative and obligate. Facultative anaerobes respire aerobically or anaerobically, depending upon environmental conditions (yeasts are examples of this). Obligate anaerobes can carry out anaerobic respiration only, regardless of whether there is oxygen in the environment.

**anaerobic respiration**   A series of reactions for the breakdown of fuel molecules (glucose) in the absence of oxygen.

**analogous**   Term applied to body parts that are similar in function but not in structure, e.g., the wing of a bird and the wing of a bee.

**anaphase**   The phase of mitosis characterized by the separation and movement of homologous chromosomes toward opposite poles of the dividing cell.

**angiosperm**   Flowering plant bearing ovules within a closed organ, the ovary. During the plant's development, the ovary becomes the fruit and the ovules become the seeds.

**animal pole**   The surface of an egg close to the nucleus where the yolk density gradient within the egg is smallest.

**annual ring**   The deposit of xylem (dead cells) from one growing season. The dead xylem cells remain from year to year, giving woody plant stems in cross section their patterns of concentric circles (annual rings).

**antheridium**   The male gamete-producing organ of the gametophyte generation in lower plants (some algae, the mosses, and ferns).

**anthropomorphism**   The assigning of human characteristics to nonhuman forms.

**antibody**   A substance produced within an animal which opposes the action of another substance. A globular protein which combines with and renders harmless an antigen.

**anticodon**   ("nodoc") Triplet of bases on transfer RNA complementary to the codon of messenger RNA.

**antigen**   A foreign substance, generally protein, which causes the formation of specific antibodies within an animal.

**apical meristem**   The growth region in a plant, located at the tip of each branch, where new cells are produced by rapid cell division.

**archegonium**   The female gamete-producing organ of the gametophyte in all plants. Particularly prominent in gametophytes of mosses, ferns, and their relatives.

**archenteron (gastrocoel)**   In embryology, the hollow interior of the gastrula stage, forming a primitive gut.

**asexual reproduction**   Development of new organisms without the fusion of gametes. This may occur in plants by either spore formation or vegetative reproduction. Some animals may reproduce asexually by fission or budding.

**association neurons**   Nerve cells, located within the central nervous system, which connect sensory and motor neurons.

**asters**   In the cytoplasm of dividing cells, asters are radiating, fiberlike processes, leading in different direction from the spindle fibers.

**ATP**   *See* adenosine triphosphate.

**autonomic nervous system**   That portion of the central nervous system responsible for carrying out involuntary vital processes.  The autonomic system is composed of two parts: the sympathetic system, responsible for integrating the body's many functions during an emergency, and the parasympathetic system, which counteracts the effects of the sympathetic.  Both systems operate to some extent at all times, controlling such functions as the size of the iris diaphragm, salivary secretion, heart rate, peristalsis and secretion in the stomach and duodenum.

**autoradiograph (radioautograph)**   The picture produced by the exposure of a film emulsion to radioactive particles.

**autoradiography (radioautography)**   A process whereby the location of radioactive materials is determined by use of photographic film.  When a radioactive emission (such as a $\beta$-particle) hits a photographic film, it produces an exposure.  The more particles, the "brighter" the exposure.  In biology, this process is especially useful in tracing substances throughout an organism.  The organism is fed or injected with a substance containing radioactive atoms.  Parts of the organism (a tissue section from the liver, or a leaf) are then exposed to film.  Bright spots on the film reveal the distribution of the radioactive substance in the organ or tissue under observation.

**autosome**   Any chromosome which is not a sex chromosome.

**autotroph**   An organism which can generate its own food supply from simple organic and inorganic elements (e.g., green plants).

**auxin**   The name given to a whole group of growth-regulating substances in plants.  There are a number of different molecules which serve as auxins, but all have in common the presence of one or two carbon rings.  Auxins have profound effects on the elongation of plant cells, and other growth phenomena.

**average**   The number that describes the sum total of a group of values divided by the number of values in the group (also called the *mean*).

**Avogadro's number**   The number of atoms or molecules in a gram atomic weight or a gram molecular weight: $6.023 \times 10^{23}$ particles.

**axon**   A process of a nerve cell which carries the nerve impulse away from the nerve cell body.

**bacteriophage (phage)**   A virus that attacks bacteria.  The infecting phage causes the bacterium to produce a new generation of phages; the bacterium is destroyed in the process.

**binomial nomenclature**   The system of naming in taxonomy, introduced by Linneaus, which gives both the genus and the species names for the organism; e.g., man is classified *Homo sapiens* (the genus is capitalized, the species is not).

**biogenesis**   The theory that all living things must be derived from other living things.

**biogenetic law**   A nineteenth-century theory devised by Fritz Muller and Ernst Haeckel.  This theory held that the stages of embryological development of a given organism review the stages of development that its race has undergone over a much greater period of time. This law is often stated as "Ontogeny recapitulates phylogeny." In the present view the biogenetic law is not considered to have much, if any, validity.

**biotic community**  A varied aggregate of organisms existing in a common environment. Division of labor or competition for food may be internal characteristics of a biotic community.

**biotic environment**  The sum total of living organisms with which a given plant or animal comes in contact.

**biotic potential**  The inherent power of a population to increase in numbers under ideal environmental conditions.

**blastocoel**  The cavity inside the hollow blastula stage of the embryo.

**blastomere**  The cells making up the blastula.

**blastopore**  The opening of the archenteron to the exterior in the gastrula stage.

**blastula**  The hollow, single-layered, ball-like structure forming the first identifiable phase of embryonic development. The blastula is the same size as the original zygote, but is the result of multiple cell divisions.

**blood**  A fluid connective tissue composed of living cells and a nonliving matrix. The blood carries oxygen, food, and waste products through the body.

**botany**  The study of plants.

**calorie**  The amount of heat required to raise the temperature of one gram of water from 14.5° to 15.5°C.

**cambium**  A layer of meristematic cells located between xylem and phloem which causes increase in width of stems and roots by production of secondary xylem and phloem.

**camera lucida**  An instrument, usually used in conjunction with a microscope, which by means of mirrors or a prism projects the image of an object onto a plane surface. In biology it is particularly used to make drawings of objects viewed under the microscope.

**capillarity**  An effect of the adhesive and cohesive properties of water, through which a water column may be raised in a very narrow tube.

**carbohydrates**  Compounds such as sugars, starches, cellulose, glycogen, etc., containing carbon, hydrogen, and oxygen, generally in a ratio which can be expressed as $(CH_2O)_n$. A primary energy food.

**cardiac muscle**  Heart muscle, composed of long, striated cells which often branch and fuse together. The nuclei in cardiac muscle cells are centrally located.

**carnivore**  An organism whose diet consists of meat. Such organisms usually display structural adaptations for meat-eating, such as well-developed claws and teeth.

**carotenoids**  Variously colored pigments found closely associated with the chlorophyll in green plants, and believed to be accessory to the photosynthetic process.

**catalysts**  Substances which lower the activation energy barrier of a reacting system, allowing the reaction to proceed at a lower temperature. In living systems, enzymes are the main catalysts.

**catastrophism**  A late eighteenth- and early nineteenth-century idea accounting for the changes in flora and fauna indicated by fossil records. According to this idea, from time to time great catastrophes destroyed all life on earth, and after each cataclysm, a new special creation populated the earth with new forms of life.

**cell**    A discrete mass of living material surrounded by a membrane.  The basic structural unit of life.

**cell division**    The splitting of a parent cell into two daughter cells.  This process consists of two separate phenomena: division of the cytoplasm (cytokinesis) and division of the nucleus (mitosis).  The events of the nuclear mitosis follow a regular pattern of four phases: prophase, metaphase, anaphase, and telophase.  Between succeeding nuclear divisions the nucleus is in interphase.

**cell plate**    A cytoplasmic figure formed during plant cell mitosis, at the site where a new cellulose partition will be synthesized to separate the cytoplasmic contents of the two daughter cells.

**cell wall**    A rigid structure composed of cellulose, surrounding plant cells.

**cellular metabolism**    The total process in which food materials and structural materials are broken down (catabolism) and built up (anabolism) within the cell.

**cellulase**    A bacterial enzyme capable of splitting cellulose into its monosaccharide components.

**cellulose**    A large, insoluble polysaccharide of repeating $\beta$-linked glucose molecules.  Cellulose is the major component of plant cell walls.

**central nervous system**    That part of the complete nervous system consisting of the brain and the spinal cord.

**centriole**    A small, deeply staining cytoplasmic structure with a $9 + 0$ complex of microtubules.  It is thought that the centriole performs a function in cell division; however, many higher plants, which seem to have no centrioles, still manage cell division.

**centromere**    *See* kinetochore.

**cerebellum**    A region of the brain which receives and sorts out all the impulses originating in the cerebrum, then sends them to the appropriate muscle at the proper time to effect an orderly muscular response.

**cerebrospinal fluid**    A fluid lubricating the brain and the spinal cord.  The fluid contains mineral salts and traces of protein and sugar, and may be involved in the nutrition of the nervous system.

**cerebrum**    A mass of association neurons in the anterior portion of the brain which receive sensory stimuli and translate them into the appropriate motor response.  The cerebrum also stores information gathered through the action of the senses.

**chemical bonds**    The forces of attraction between atoms which hold the atoms together in molecules.  Formation of chemical bonds is thought to be due to rearrangement of electron clouds.

**chemotropism**    The growth response of a plant to a chemical substance.

**chiasma (pl. chiasmata)**    Figure formed by chromosomes during tetrad formation which may lead to crossing over.

**chlorophyll**    A molecule based on the same ring structure (porphyrin) as hemoglobin, but with magnesium replacing the central iron atom.  Chlorophyll is found in all green plants, and gives them their color. The molecule functions in photosynthesis by absorbing specific wavelengths of sunlight, thus providing the energy for synthesis of carbohydrates. It is now known that light raises electrons of the chlorophyll molecule to higher energy levels. As the electrons return to their original level through a series of acceptor molecules, ATP is generated. It is the ATP which serves as the direct energy source for photosynthesis. Chlorophyll is one of the few molecules in the living world which can capture energy from visible light in this manner.

**chloroplast** A small plastid present in the cells of green plants. The chloroplast contains chlorophyll, which is essential for the photosynthetic activities of the plant.

**chorion** In intrauterine development, the outermost membrane surrounding the embryo.

**chorionic villi** In mammals, projections of the chorion which extend into the uterine wall. These are outgrowths of the embryonic sac (chorion), and provide the basis for surface exchange of materials between the mother and the very young embryo.

**chromatid** A term applied to each of the two parts of a chromosome after replication as long as these parts remain connected at the kinetochore.

**chromatin** A deep-staining material found in strands within the nucleus, and containing mostly nucleoprotein. At cell division, the chromatin condenses into visible structures known as chromosomes. The term is rarely used today.

**chromoplast** A pigment-containing plastid which gives color to the flowers and fruits of many plants.

**chromosome** A threadlike structure visible in the nucleus of all plant and animal cells during cell division. Chromosomes consist mostly of protein and nucleic acid, and may be thought of as bearing genes, or units of genetic information. The number of chromosomes per cell is normally constant for each species.

**chyme** Partly digested food passing from the stomach into the duodenum.

**cilium** Small, hairlike structures of living material projecting from the surface of certain types of cells. All the cilia of a given cell move together in a rhythmic fashion. The internal structure of a cilium is composed of microtubules set up in a 9 + 2 complex array.

**citrulline** A compound intermediate in the process of urea formation, created by the combination of ammonia, carbon dioxide, and ornithine.

**cleavage** The cell divisions within the mass of the developing embryo. Each cleavage approximately doubles the number of cells.

**coacervate theory** A theory of the origin of life, put forth by A. I. Oparin, based on the tendency of protein aggregates to develop a simple membrane due to the effects of surface tension.

**codon** Triplet of nitrogenous bases on messenger RNA responsible for coding specific amino acids.

**cohesion** The tendency of molecules of a single substance to stick together.

**commensalism** Relationship between two different species of organisms in which one derives benefit and the other receives no harm.

**companion cells** Nucleated cells located adjacent to sieve tubes in plant phloem tissue, and which are thought to control the cells making up the tube.

**competition**   Battle among organisms for the necessities of life.  May be intraspecific (between members of the same species) or interspecific (between two different species).

**conditioned reflex**   A behavior pattern learned through repetition of a sequence of events.

**conjugation**   A physical association and exchange of materials, leading to reproduction in certain organisms, e.g., the green alga *Spirogyra* or the protozoan *Paramecium.*

**connective tissue**   Tissue composed of isolated cells embedded within a nonliving matrix.  Connective tissues support the organism and hold its several parts together.  Bone, cartilage, and ligaments are examples of connective tissue.

**control group**   In a series of experiments, the organisms maintained under "normal" conditions, in order to serve as a basis for comparison in the evaluation of changes produced by variations in conditions with the experimental group of organisms.

**cork**   The outer protective layer of woody plants, made up of dead cells.

**cork cambium**   A special thin layer of meristematic tissue which produces the cork region on the stems and roots of woody plants.

**cortex**   In plants, the storage area of the root or stem.  In animals, the outer area of an organ, such as the cortex region of the kidney or brain.

**cristae**   Projections into the central matrix of a mitochondrion, produced by the repeated invagination of the inner mitochondrial membrane and serving to increase the membrane surface area within the mitochondrion.

**crossing over**   Exchange of chromosome segments between maternal and paternal chromatids during tetrad formation.

**crucial experiment**   An experiment which distinguishes between two hypotheses by disproving one and supporting the other.

**cutin**   The waxy secretion from leaf epidermal layers that forms the leaf cuticle.

**cytochrome**   A molecule in the respiratory assembly with the characteristic molecular structure (porphyrin) of hemoglobin.  By contrast with hemoglobin, in cytochrome the central iron atom is easily oxidized and reduced.  This allows the cytochrome to pass electrons in the electron transport chain.

**cytokinesis**   Cytological changes, usually occurring synchronously with mitosis, through which the cytoplasm of one cell is divided to form two cells.

**cytology**   The study of cells.

**cytoplasm**   All the living material in the cell that is enclosed within the plasma membrane, excluding that of the nucleus.

**deamination**   The removal of the amino group ($-NH_2$) from an amino acid by chemical oxidation.

**dedifferentiation**   The reversion of a cell from a condition of specialization to a nonspecialized, embryonic state.

**deductive logic**   A process in which a conclusion is reached by proceeding from general to specific instances.

**degradation**   The process of breaking down complex molecules to simpler ones, generally accompanied by a liberation of energy.

**dehydration synthesis**   The joining together of smaller units (such as amino acids or glucose) into a single larger molecule by the elimination of water. One of the units contributes the $H^+$, the other the $OH^-$.

**deletion**   The loss of a segment of a chromosome during crossing over, resulting in a certain phenotypic deficiency in the developing organism. Such aberrations can provide significant clues in the mapping of gene loci.

**dendrite**   A process of a nerve cell body which conducts the nerve impulse toward the nerve cell body.

**density-dependent factors**   Factors within certain individuals, operating to limit or reduce a population when it reaches some critical size, so that the population as a whole may survive.

**deoxyribose**   The five-carbon sugar in DNA (deoxyribonucleic acid). (For molecular formula, see Section 17–11.)

**depolarized**   The condition of a membrane when the distribution of charged ions is approximately the same on both sides, so that the potential across the membrane is zero.

**dialysis**   The process whereby compounds or substances in a heterogeneous solution are separated by the difference in their rates of diffusion through a semipermeable membrane. If a solution of sodium chloride and albumin is placed inside a dialysis bag immersed in water, the sodium chloride ions will diffuse outward about twenty times faster than the albumin. Thus, after a short time, the solution inside the dialysis bag will be mostly pure protein.

**diaphragm**   A sheetlike layer of muscle at the base of the thoracic cavity. Movements of this muscle control the lungs' intake and outflow of air by altering the air pressure in the cavity surrounding the lungs.

**diatom**   A form of marine alga living within a tiny, silicon-containing shell. Diatoms produce huge amounts of organic material by carrying on photosynthesis with the brown pigment fucoxanthin.

**2, 4-D (2, 4-dichlorophenoxyacetic acid)**   One of a class of growth-promoting substances known as auxins, composed of a single carbon ring and a side chain. 2, 4-D, which may be synthesized artificially, acts as a weed killer by selectively stimulating rapid growth in broad-leaved plants (most weeds are broad-leaved). Growth is so rapid that the plants are eventually killed.

**dicotyledonae (dicots)**   One of the two classes of angiosperms. Distinguishing characteristics are: two cotyledons (food leaves) in the embryo, netted venation in the leaves, flower parts in twos, fours, or fives, fibrovascular bundles in an orderly array in the stem.

**differential fertility**   A measure of the success of an inherited variation, in terms of its effects on the reproductive capacities of an organism. A variation which increases reproductive capacity is considered a successful one.

**differentiation**   The structural or functional changes which occur in cells during the embryonic development of an organism.

**digestion**   The enzymatic breakdown of food from large molecules into small ones capable of entering the bloodstream, and eventually the cells, by a process of absorption. Important organs of the digestive system include the stomach, pancreas, gall bladder, and small intestine.

**diploid**   Term applied to a cell which contains a pair of each type of chromosome. The number of chromosomes usually given for an organism is the diploid number, e.g., man has 46 chromosomes (23 pairs).

**dispersion**   In statistics, the spread of values surrounding the mean.

**dominance hierarchies**   "Peck orders" in animals, in which social hierarchies serve to maintain order, e.g., in a baboon troop.

**dominant**   In genetics, a term used to refer to an allele which always expresses itself in the heterozygous condition.

**duodenum**   That part of the small intestine closest to the pyloric valve of the stomach. Under the influence of HCl from the stomach, the cells of the duodenum secrete secretin, which stimulates enzyme release in the pancreas. A large part of the enzymatic breakdown of foods occurs in the duodenum, which in man is approximately ten inches long.

**dynamic equilibrium**   A state in which the concentration of reactants and products in a chemical reaction remains constant, though not necessarily equal.

**ecology**   The study of the relationship between plants and animals, or communities of plants or animals, and their environment.

**ecosystem**   All the interacting factors, both physical and biological, forming a biotic community.

**ectoderm**   In an embryo, the outer germ layer, giving rise to the epidermis, the neural tube, and the epithelial lining of stomodaeum and proctodaeum.

**electrophoresis**   A technique through which charged organic molecules can be separated and identified in accordance with their characteristic movement in an electric field. Particularly useful in separating one amino acid on one base in nucleic acid hydrolysis from another. An amino acid with two positive regions (i.e., two $NH_3^+$ groups) will move more rapidly toward the negative pole of the electrophoresis apparatus than one with only a single positive group. Similarly, positively and negatively charged molecules will move in opposite directions in an electric field. Thus a whole variety of molecules can be separated from each other by this technique.

**elongation region**   The region of a root, behind the embryonic area, where cells increase in length.

**embryology**   The study of the structural and functional development of an organism during its early life.

**embryonic induction**   The ability of one type of embryonic germ layer to influence the differentiation of another germ layer. According to this concept, developed by the German embryologist Hans Spemann in the early years of the twentieth century, an organizer substance (of unspecified nature) produced by one germ layer has the ability to induce the development of other tissue around it.

**embryonic region**    The growth region in roots, located just behind the root cap, where new cells are produced by rapid cell division.

**Emerson enhancement effect**    Principle stating that the rate of photosynthesis in the presence of two wavelengths is greater than the sum of the rates when the two wavelengths are applied separately.

**endergonic**    Term applied to those chemical reactions which result in an overall increase in energy among the formed products, and hence to the storage of energy (as, for example, in photosynthesis).

**endocrine system**    The sum total of hormone-secreting glands in the body.

**endoderm**    In an embryo, the innermost germ layer, which gives rise to the lining of the gut.

**endodermis**    In plants, a layer of cells separating the cortex of a root from the central cylinder (stele).

**endoplasmic reticulum**    In cells, a maze of membranes in the cytoplasm, at places continuous with the nuclear envelope. The endoplasmic reticulum may serve to increase the surface area of the cell, and thus aid in exchange of material.

**endosperm**    In plants, a triploid material developing within the embryo sac immediately after fertilization, which serves as the nutriment for the developing embryo.

**energy barrier**    The amount of energy which any nonexcited particle must gain in order to become "excited" and enter into a chemical reaction.

**environmental resistance**    Factors in the environment which oppose or limit the increase in numbers of a given population.

**enzyme**    A protein whose synthesis is controlled and directed by a specific gene. Enzymes act as catalysts, directing all major chemical reactions in the living organism.

**epidermis**    In animals, the outer covering of the body, usually several cell layers thick. In herbaceous plants, the thin (one cell thick) outer covering, which secretes a noncellular cuticle.

**epigenesis**    In embryology, the idea that an entire organism develops from an originally undifferentiated mass of living material.

**epiglottis**    In mammals and other vertebrates, a fleshy flap on the ventral wall of the pharynx capable of blocking the opening to the trachea, e.g., during swallowing.

**epinephrine (adrenaline)**    The primary hormone of the adrenal medulla. Epinephrine functions in cardiac stimulation, dilation of blood vessels leading to skeletal muscles, and constriction of vessels leading to visceral organs.

**epithelial tissue**    Surface and lining tissues of the animal body, such as the lining of the digestive tract or the lining of the air passage to the lungs.

**equilibrium phase**    The stage where growth rate in a population has leveled off, so that the appearance of new cells or organisms just equals the disappearance of old ones.

**erythrocyte**    Red blood cell. Erythrocytes contain hemoglobin (thus the red color) and serve as oxygen carriers.

**esophagus**    The structure conveying ingested material from the mouth directly to the stomach.

**ethology**   The field of animal behavior.

**excretion**   The removal of the waste products of metabolic activity. In higher organisms, the blood bathes each cell and carries away waste. This waste material is removed from the blood by the kidneys, the sweat glands, or the lungs.

**exergonic**   Term applied to those chemical reactions in which the total end products have less energy than the reactants. Thus exergonic reactions yield energy (as for example, in respiration).

**experimental group**   In an experiment, the organisms whose environment is altered so that their resulting responses may be studied.

**expiration**   The elimination of air from the lungs.

**exponent**   An integer written slightly above and to the right of a number to indicate how many times the number is to be multiplied by itself in the given expression, e.g., $X^2 = X \cdot X, 4^3 = 4 \cdot 4 \cdot 4$.

**extinct**   No longer present in the world population. Extinction is the fate of the adaptively inferior in the battle for survival.

**extrapolation**   The calculation of a value beyond a given series of values, based on generalizations made from observing the pattern of the given values.

**fats**   Lipid compounds composed of glycerol and fatty acids. Fats are energy-rich compounds, often stored in adipose tissue.

**fatty acid**   An organic molecule composed of a long hydrocarbon chain and a terminal acid (—COOH) group.

**feedback mechanism**   A self-regulating mechanism within all homeostatic systems. Part of the output of the system is cycled back into the system itself in order to regulate further function and output, as, for example, in a thermostat-furnace system.

**ferredoxin**   An iron-rich protein found in photosynthetic organisms. This compound is capable of accepting free hydrogen ions and passing them on for the reducing reactions of nutrient synthesis.

**ferredoxin-reducing substance**   Hypothesized primary electron acceptor after light absorption by chlorophyll.

**fertilization**   In sexual reproduction, the union of the male (sperm) and female (ovum) gametes to form a diploid cell (the zygote) capable of developing into a new organism.

**fertilization membrane**   A protective membrane which surrounds the egg once it has been fertilized by a single sperm, and which prevents the development of an abnormal embryo due to multiple fertilizations.

**fertilizin**   A carbohydrate and protein substance, produced by the egg, which is capable of causing the agglutination of sperm or the binding of sperm to egg.

**fibrous root**   A fairly diffuse network of roots well suited for absorption of water near the surface of the ground. Fibrous systems, characteristic of the grasses, do not penetrate deeply in the soil.

**fibrovascular bundle**   Units of vascular tissue grouped together. Fibrovascular bundles include xylem and phloem elements, cambium, and usually some supporting tissue.

**first law of thermodynamics**   No matter is either lost or gained during ordinary chemical reactions. This law may more accurately be stated as the Law of Conservation of Matter and Energy: the sum total of matter and energy in the universe remains constant.

**fission**    A rapid and efficient method of reproduction, found in many microorganisms, which involves the splitting of one cell into two, each of which receives the full genetic complement.

**flagellum (pl. flagella)**    A long, whiplike extension of cytoplasm from such a unicellular organism as *Chlamydomonas*, composed of a lipid-containing outer membrane enclosing a highly structured matrix. The matrix surrounds microtubules arranged in a circle of nine doublets with a pair of doublets inside. Three of the outer doublets contain inward projecting structures, the function of which is not yet known. The $9 + 2$ arrangement of microtubules in flagella is also found in cilia, while a $9 + 0$ arrangement is characteristic of centrioles.

**food chain**    The transfer of energy by food breakdown, starting with the independent fuel synthesis of green plants (photosynthesis).

**foramen ovale**    An opening in the fetal heart allowing blood to pass directly from the right to the left atrium, eliminating the pulmonary transit.

**frond**    The leaves of a fern growing above ground from the rhizome.

**FRS**    *See* ferredoxin-reducing substance.

**fruit**    The ripened ovary of a flower, aiding in seed dispersal.

**furrowing**    The infolding of the cell membrane by an animal cell during telophase.

**gamete**    Male or female reproductive cell containing half the total number of chromosomes (i.e., the haploid number) for any given species. These germ cells are formed by the process of meiosis (reduction division) from diploid cells. Fusion of one male and one female sex cell (fertilization) yields a diploid form, the zygote, which is capable of developing into a new individual.

**gametophyte**    The small photosynthetic haploid stage in the life cycle of lower plants such as the moss and fern. The gametophyte contains male and female gamete-producing organs.

**gastrin**    A hormone secreted by cells in the stomach wall, in response to the presence of food in the stomach. The hormone stimulates the secretion of gastric juices into the stomach for the breakdown of the food there.

**gastrula**    The embryonic structure formed in gastrulation. A hollow structure, like the blastula, but composed of at least two germ layers instead of one.

**gastrulation**    The process of embryonic development leading from the blastula to the next embryonic structure, the gastrula.

**Gause's hypothesis**    The principle of competitive exclusion, which states that two species with similar ecological requirements cannot successfully live together for any length of time, because of their competition for all the basic requirements for life.

**gene**    A part of the hereditary material located on a chromosome. The term "gene" was first used by Johannsen to mean something in a gamete which determined some characteristic of an organism. The gene concept now has been refined to the idea of a single gene as the source of information for the synthesis of a single polypeptide.

**gene pool**    The total genetic make-up of a particular population, consisting of all the alleles existing in that population at any given time, regardless of their proportions. This concept provides a way of looking at the possible genetic changes which may occur in a freely-breeding population from one generation to another. If 100 organisms (composing a hypothetical population) have 10 genes each (with 2 alleles for each gene), then the gene pool of that population consists of 2000 genes.

**genetic code**   The linear sequence of bases along a DNA molecule which in turn determines the sequence of amino acids in a polypeptide chain. The code itself consists of triplet groups, each specific three bases coding one amino acid. It has been found that more than one triplet can code for the same amino acid; thus, the term "degenerate" is used in reference to the genetic code.

**genetic drift**   A condition in which one allele becomes fixed in a population. Genetic drift is a major factor only in very small populations of organisms.

**genetic equilibrium**   The maintainence of a more or less constant ratio between the different alleles in a gene pool from generation to generation. This idea is involved in the Hardy-Weinberg Law.

**genotype**   The genetic makeup of an organism, as deduced from data yielded by breeding experiments.

**geographic isolation**   The physical division of an original population into geographically separate groups. Such isolation is usually followed by divergence and speciation.

**geotropism**   The growth response of a plant to gravity.

**germ plasm**   The term developed by August Weismann to describe the living matter of the sex cells. Weismann visualized the germ plasm as being immortal, having continuity with the germ plasms of the preceding and succeeding generations through the process of sexual reproduction. In each generation, the germ plasm gives rise to the body cells (somatoplasm), and more germ cells. Changes in somatoplasm do not affect the germ plasm.

**gibberellic acid**   The active agent, extracted from the fungus *Gibberella*, which can cause hyperelongation of the stem in certain kinds of plants. Several structural variations of gibberellic acid are known and are called, collectively, the gibberellins.

**glandular epithelial cells**   Cells of columnar epithelium specialized for secretion, as in the case of mucus- or wax-secreting cells.

**glomerulus**   A mass of capillaries enclosed within each Bowman's capsule in the kidney. This structure is responsible for the filtration of waste materials from the circulating blood.

**glycerol (glycerine)**   A compound with the formula

$$CH_2OH$$
$$|$$
$$CHOH$$
$$|$$
$$CH_2OH$$

which combines with fatty acids to form fats.

**glycolysis**   The initial stage of respiration, involving the breakdown of glucose to pyruvic acid. In aerobic respiration, glycolysis yields pyruvic acid for the Krebs cycle. In anaerobic respiration the pyruvic acid is converted to lactic acid (as in bacteria and the muscle cells of higher organisms), or into ethyl alcohol (as in yeasts).

**Golgi complex (Golgi body)** A cluster of flattened, parallel, smooth-surfaced sacs found within the cytoplasm. The Golgi complex appears to function in isolating and transporting of molecules out of the cell.

**granum** A stack of layered membranous structures containing the pigment chlorophyll, located inside a chloroplast.

**gray crescent** A surface region in the newly fertilized egg of frogs and salamanders from which the orientation of the developing embryo can be ascertained.

**growth** The enlargement in size of an organism, due to an increase in the number of cells, enlargement of cells already present, or both.

**guard cells** Cells surrounding leaf stomata, and serving to regulate the size of the opening.

**gymnosperms** The conifers and related species of plants which have naked seeds (not completely enclosed).

**habitat** The surroundings in which an organism resides—the organism's "address" in the biological community.

**half-life** The amount of time required for half the atoms of a given radioactive sample to decay to a more stable form.

**haploid** A condition in which an organism (or a single cell) bears only one copy of each gene. Most higher organisms have two copies (alleles) of the gene for any given character, and thus are called diploid. Many microorganisms, however, such as bacteria, *Paramecium*, and most algae, are haploid during most of their life span.

**heme** A complex molecular structure (a porphyrin ring) in which a central ion is capable of undergoing repeated oxidation and reduction. The heme structure is the basis of such important biological molecules as hemoglobin, myoglobin, and the cytochromes.

**herbaceous** Term applied to plants which do not contain lignin within their cell walls. These plants are less sturdy than the woody plants, which do contain lignin.

**herbivore** An organism whose diet consists exclusively of vegetation.

**heterogametes** Two gametes, structurally dissimilar, capable of fusion to form a zygote. The sperm and egg are examples of heterogametes.

**heterogamy** The condition in which gametes are differentiated into two distinct forms (generally male and female).

**heterotroph** An organism which depends on its environment for a supply of nutritive material to build up its own organic constituents and also for general energy requirements.

**heterozygous** Term for the situation in which the two members of a pair of genes located on homologous chromosomes and influencing a given characteristic are different.

**hierarchy** An arrangement of classification groups of decreasing size, with the larger groups containing the smaller.

**histogram** A graphical representation of statistical data showing frequency distribution by means of a series of rectangles. A bar graph is an example of a histogram.

**histology** The study of tissues.

**homeostasis** The maintainence of a dynamic equilibrium between the organs and systems comprising the internal environment of an organism.

**homologous**  Term applied to body parts which are similar in structure but not necessarily in function, e.g., the arm of a man and the front leg of a horse.

**homologous chromosomes**  The pair of structurally similar chromosomes within a cell which carry inheritance factors influencing the same traits.

**homozygous**  Term for the situation in which the two members of a pair of genes located on homologous chromosomes and influencing a given characteristic are identical.

**hormone**  A chemical substance produced in small quantities in one part of an organism and profoundly affecting another part of that organism.  Chemically, hormones may be proteins (insulin), steroids (estrogens), or small metabolites (thyroxin).

**hydrolysis**  The chemical breakdown of a larger molecule into smaller units by the addition of water.

**hypothalamus**  A region of the brain below the thalamus controlling certain vital bodily functions, predominantly those involving the autonomic nervous system, e.g., body temperature.

**hypothesis**  A tentative explanation suggested to account for observed phenomena.

**immunology**  The theoretical science dealing with the ability of organisms to build a chemical resistance within their bodies to various types of foreign substances (bacteria, viruses, pollen, etc.).

**imprinting**  The rapid fixing of social preferences, e.g., the tendency of a duckling to treat as its mother the first moving object it sees after hatching.

**inclusion**  Any one of a number of nonliving structures occurring within the cytoplasm of a cell, e.g., vacuoles.

**indole-3-acetic (IAA)**  A plant hormone.  The most common of the auxins, often referred to merely as auxin.  (For structural formula, see Fig. 11–26.)

**inductive logic**  A process in which a conclusion is reached by proceeding from specific cases to a generalization.

**ingestion**  The intake of food into an organism.

**innate behavior**  Ethological term which replaces the concept of instinct in that it recognizes and eliminates incorrect connotations associated with the latter term in regard to how genes influence behavior.

**innate releasing mechanism (IRM)**  Hypothesized receiving center in the central nervous system which is triggered by some external stimulus and elicits a specific sequence of behavioral events.

**insertion**  The point of attachment of a muscle to a bone whose movement is controlled by the muscle.  Usually at the distal end of the muscle.

**inspiration**  The intake of air from the outside due to an imbalance of air pressure created by an expansion of the thoracic cavity.

**instinct**  Term applied to behavior which is primarily "genetic" in nature and which seems less amenable to change through learning.

**internal environment**  The conditions generated inside an organism by the functions and interactions of cells, tissues, organs, and systems.

**interphase**  The longest individual phase of mitosis, often considered the resting phase between two active cell divisions, during which the genetic material of the cell is being duplicated.

**interpolation** The filling in of a value on a graph between two given values.

**inversion** The process of chromosome breakage and rejoining in such a way that a whole segment breaks from a chromosome and is replaced in reverse order. Thus, if the sequence of genes on a normal chromosome were represented as *abcdefghi*, and two breaks occurred, one between *c* and *d* and the other between *g* and *h*, the middle segment *defg* might turn and rejoin in reverse direction, so that the sequence of genes on the chromosome would read: *abcgfedhi*. This would constitute an inversion.

**invertebrates** Organisms composing nineteen animal phyla, characterized by the lack of a notochord.

**IRM** *See* innate releasing mechanism.

**islets of Langerhans** Groups of cells in the pancreas which secrete insulin. Lack of function of the islets causes diabetes.

**isogametes** Two gametes, which are morphologically alike, capable of fusion to form a zygote. Isogametes are not visibly differentiated into male or female forms.

**isolating mechanisms** Differences introduced by speciation and divergence during geographic isolation of two populations, which prevent interbreeding should the two populations ever come back together. Such mechanisms include seasonal isolation, ecological isolation, physiological isolation, and behavioral isolation.

**kilocalorie (Calorie)** The amount of heat required to raise the temperature of one kilogram of water from 14.5 to 15.5°C. The kilocalorie is used to measure the metabolism (energy turnover) of animals.

**kinetic energy** Energy of motion; energy in the process of doing work.

**kinetochore (centromere)** The region of the chromosome at which the chromatids remain connected following chromosome replication and to which the spindle microtubules appear to be connected during cell division.

**Krebs cycle (citric acid cycle)** A series of reactions in the oxidation of pyruvic acid, in which large amounts of energy are released. The hydrogens from pyruvic acid supply electrons for the electron transport chain.

**larva** The first free-living form of some organisms. In this stage, the organism eats extensively and stores food. It then undergoes metamorphosis into the adult form, using the stored food as an energy source.

**leaf primordia** Structure within the terminal bud of a plant from which the leaves develop.

**legumes** A certain class of vegetables which bear seeds in pods (including peas, beans, and clover). Legumes act as hosts for nitrogen-fixing bacteria.

**leucocyte** A white blood cell.

**leucoplast** A colorless plastid, thought to serve as a cytoplasmic center for the storage of certain materials, such as starch.

**lignin** A substance deposited along with the cellulose in the cell walls of woody plants, and which gives added strength to these walls.

**linkage** The location of two or more genes on the same chromosome, so that the two characteristics are passed on together from parent to offspring.

**lipids**   A group of organic chemical compounds including the fats and fatlike compounds.

**logarithm**   The power to which a given number (the base) must be raised in order to equal a certain number. Ten is the most commonly used base number. The logarithm of 100 to the base 10 is 2. This can be written: (a) $\log_{10} 100 = 2$ or (b) $10^2 = 100$. The base number is given as a subscript.

**logarithmic phase**   The phase of most rapid increase in size for a population, i.e., the area of exponential increase on a sigmoid curve.

**long-day plants**   Plants which flower when exposed to cycles of light and dark in which the dark phase is shorter than $8\frac{1}{2}$ hours.

**lymph**   A colorless fluid traveling freely throughout most of the body. It aids in the maintainence of proper osmotic balance, functions in the control of disease, and serves as the main medium of circulation for lipids.

**lysins**   A class of substances produced by sperm to dissolve the protective egg membranes and allow the sperm to enter and fertilize the egg.

**lysis**   The chemical breakdown of a cell, usually under the influence of enzymes released by the rupture of a lysosome, or by reproduction of viruses within the cell.

**lysosome**   A saclike structure containing enzymes which catalyze the breakdown of fats, proteins, and nucleic acids. The membranes of lysosomes protect the cell from being digested by its own enzymes (autolysis). Lysosomes also serve as defense mechanisms, ingesting and digesting foreign toxic agents within the cell.

**macromolecule**   A large molecule built up from small repeating units. Cellulose is a macromolecule built of repeating $\beta$ glucose units.

**mapping**   In genetics, the description of the physical order of gene loci on a given chromosome, as determined by frequency of chromosome cross-overs. The further apart two genes are on a chromosome, the greater the chance that crossing over will occur between them; thus the percentages of cross-over can be used to calculate relative distances between genes. Chromosome maps established in this way can be correlated with actual chromosome structure by a variety of cytological techniques.

**mass spectrometry**   A process which sorts streams of electrically charged particles according to their different masses by using deflecting fields. The device which accomplishes this, a mass spectrometer, consists generally of a long tube which generates a magnetic field. The particles of varying masses are passed through the tube and the degree of deflection by the magnetic field is recorded on a photographic film at the other end. Given the strength of the field and the amount of deflection, the relative masses of the particles can be calculated. Isotopes of various elements can be detected by mass spectrometry.

**matter**   That which has weight and occupies space.

**maturation region**   The area within a young root (several centimeters from the lip) where the cells reach their full size and become completely specialized.

**mechanism**   The view of living organisms which holds that life is explicable in terms of physical and chemical laws.

**medulla**   The central portion of a gland or organ.

**meiosis**  A process of cellular division which results in each of the daughter cells containing one-half as many chromosomes as the parent cell (they are said to be **haploid**). Meiosis occurs primarily in the formation of gametes (in sexually reproducing organisms) or in spore formation in organisms such as the ferns or the mosses.

**melanin**  Any of a group of dark brown or black pigments occurring in the skin as well as other parts of the body.

**meristem**  An area of rapidly dividing cells. The meristem may be a single cell, as in ferns, or it may include many cells, as in the flowering plants. Most plants have root and stem meristems.

**meristematic tissue**  In plants, any area of rapid cell division, forming a true growth region, e.g., the tips of branches and roots, or the lateral meristem (the cambium).

**mesoderm**  In an embryo, the third germ layer, lying between ectoderm and endoderm and giving rise to the connective tissue, muscle, urogenital system, vascular system, and the lining of the coelom.

**messenger RNA (*m*RNA)**  A strand of RNA synthesized in the nucleus of a cell with one DNA strand as a template. *m*RNA thus has a base sequence directly complementary to the base sequence on the DNA molecule. After its formation, *m*RNA migrates from the nucleus to the cytoplasm, where it becomes associated with the ribosomes.

**metabolism**  The sum total of chemical and physical processes within the body related to the release of energy by the breakdown of chemical fuel, and the use of that energy by the cells for their own work.

**metamorphosis**  That type of development in which the organism exists in an intermediate free-living stage (larva) prior to a change into the adult form. Metamorphosis also refers to the actual change from larva to adult.

**metaphase**  The phase of mitosis characterized by the lining up of the chromosome pairs along the equatorial plate of the cell.

**microtubules**  Tiny tubes composing such diverse structures as the spindle apparatus and the centrioles.

**minimal medium**  A medium containing only those elements absolutely essential for the growth of a particular organism, and which the organism cannot synthesize itself. Generally, minimal media contain a carbohydrate source, various inorganic salts, and sometimes a growth factor such as biotin.

**mitochondria**  Cytoplasmic organelles of a characteristic structure containing the enzymes for glycolysis and for the Krebs cycle.

**mitosis**  The series of changes within a cell nucleus by which two genetically identical daughter nuclei are produced.

**mode**  In a set of data, the item or group of items which appears most often. For example, when a set of grades for a whole class is compiled, the mode is the single grade, or group of grades, which the largest number of students obtained.

**mole**  A gram molecular weight of a substance; the molecular weight of a substance in grams. One mole contains Avogadro's number of particles ($6.023 \times 10^{23}$).

**monocotyledonae (monocots)**   One of the two classes of angiosperms.   Monocots are identified by a single seed leaf (cotyledon) in the embryo, parallel veins in the leaves, flower parts generally in threes or sixes, and scattered fibrovascular bundles in the stem.

**Morgan's canon**   Essentially, the application of Ockham's razor to ethology; i.e., an animal's behavior pattern should be interpreted in the simplest possible mechanistic terms which allow accurate predictions to be made.

**mosaic theory**   An idea most often ascribed to Wilhelm Roux, which holds that certain regions of the egg are designated to become specific parts of the organism.

**motor neurons**   Those neurons conveying impulses which bring about a bodily response to environmental stimuli.

**motor unit**   The minimum unit of contraction in a muscle, composed of all the muscle fibers activated by a single nerve.

**multiple alleles**   Sets of alleles which contain more than two members, e.g., human blood groups.

**muscular contraction**   The net effect of a change in ultrastructure of many associated muscle cells.   The agency through which movement is brought about.

**mutualism**   *See* symbiosis.

**mutation**   An inherited structural or functional variation of an offspring in relation to its parents.   Mutations are due to a change in the chemical structure of DNA, the molecule bearing hereditary information.   Once a mutation has occurred, it will be transmitted faithfully to future generations.

**negative acceleration phase**   The period of decreasing growth rate in a population, following the exponential increase that occurs in the logarithmic phase.

**negative feedback**   A mechanism of self-regulation whereby a change in a system in one direction is converted into a command for a change in the opposite direction.   A means of helping maintain a biological system in equilibrium.

**nephron**   The functional unit in the kidney, composed of a glomerulus, Bowman's capsule, and associated blood vessels.   There are approximately one million nephrons in each human kidney.

**neuromuscular junction**   The point at which a nerve end brush comes into contact with a muscle fiber.

**neuron**   One of the individual cells which make up nervous tissue.   Each neuron has a cell body, composed of nucleus and surrounding cytoplasm, and processes, varying in length and number, which carry the nerve impulse from place to place.

**niche**   The ecological position of an organism—the organism's "occupation" within the biological community.

**nitrogen-fixing bacteria**   Bacterial organisms capable of drawing free nitrogen from the atmosphere and converting it into soluble nitrates.   These nitrates can then be used by plants.

**"nodoc"**   *See* anticodon.

**nodules**   Swellings on the roots of certain leguminous plants where nitrogen-fixing bacteria reside in a symbiotic relationship with the plant.

**nondisjunction**   The failure of a pair of chromatids to separate at metaphase, creating an abnormality of chromosome number in both daughter cells.  This usually leads to deformed offspring.

**normal distribution curve**   A bell-shaped curve, more or less symmetrical, with the greatest value in the center (mean) and with values decreasing equally on both sides. Also called a normal curve.

**nuclear membrane**   The unit membrane which separates the nuclear material from the surrounding cytoplasm.  The membrane is not continuous, but rather is broken at different intervals by nuclear pores which provide a physical passage between the nucleus and surrounding cytoplasm.

**nucleoplasm**   The living material within the nucleus.

**nucleotide**   The molecule formed from the combination of a purine or pyrimidine, an appropriate sugar (ribose or deoxyribose), and a phosphate residue.  Nucleotides are the basic units of nucleic acid structure.

**nucleus (atomic)**   The dense area in the central part of an atom where all protons and neutrons are located.

**nucleus (cellular)**   A body found in nearly all cells which contains the hereditary information of the cells and is the control center of cell function.

**Ockham's razor** (often spelled **Occam's razor**)   A principle which states that the simplest hypothesis is preferable to a more complex one so long as the simplest one is not contradicted.

**oögenesis**   The process by which haploid female gametes (eggs) are produced.

**organ**   A unit composed of various types of tissues grouped together to perform a necessary function.  The liver and a plant leaf are examples of organs.

**organelle**   A small body appearing within the cell mass, with a characteristic structure and a definite, though perhaps not clearly defined, function.  Cytoplasmic organelles include mitochondria, ribosomes, Golgi complex, and the endoplasmic reticulum.

**origin**   The more fixed point of attachment of a muscle to the skeletal structure.  Usually the more proximal point of attachment.

**ornithine**   A compound necessary for one phase of the conversion of ammonia to urea. Ornithine is also an end product of the urea production process.

**osmosis**   The passage of a solvent from a region of greater concentration to a region of lesser concentration through a semipermeable membrane.

**ovary**   In plants, the basal portion of the pistil which encloses the ovules.  The ovules, in turn, contain the female spore.  After fertilization, the ovary becomes the fleshy part of the fruit, and the ovules become seeds.  In animals, the germ tissue of the female which produces the ovum, or egg.

**oviparous**   Term applied to organisms which lay eggs in which the embryo continues to develop for some period of time, while deriving nourishment entirely from the egg yolk.

**ovoviviparous**   Term applied to organisms whose young develop within the body of the mother but derive most or all their nourishment from the egg yolk.

**ovum**    The female reproductive cell containing the haploid number of chromosomes, produced from a diploid germ cell by meiosis (reduction division). The ovum is fertilized by the sperm, producing the zygote.

**oxidation**    A type of chemical reaction involving the removal of electrons. Frequently, but by no means necessarily, the element oxygen is involved.

**oxygen debt**    The amount of oxygen required to oxidize the excess lactic acid accumulated in muscle cells during strenuous exercise.

**parasite**    Organism which derives its food from another species of organism by living in or on the host organism, usually to the detriment of the host.

**parasympathetic nervous system**    That portion of the central nervous system which arises from the brain and lower tip of the spinal chord (in the region of the lumbar vertebrae), generally without passing through ganglia. It acts functionally to counteract the effects of the sympathetic nervous system; i.e., it returns the body to normal after emergency. The transmitter substance released at the nerve endings of parasympathetic fibers is acetylcholine. The vagus nerve (the tenth cranial nerve) is the most prominent parasympathetic tract.

**parthenogenesis**    The development of an egg, without fertilization, into a new individual. Parthenogenesis occurs naturally in some organisms (such as aphids, rotifers, bees, and ants) but can be induced artificially in higher forms (such as frogs) by chemical or physical stimulus to the egg.

**partial pressure**    The pressure exerted by a given component gas in a mixture of gases.

$$\text{Partial pressure of gas A} = \frac{\text{Volume gas A}}{\text{Total volume}} \times \text{Total pressure of the entire sample}$$

**pathogenic**    Capable of causing disease.

**"peck order"**    The establishment of social hierarchies, first noted in domestic chickens.

**peptide bond**    The bond, formed by dehydration synthesis (elimination of water), which links two amino acid molecules together.

**pericycle**    A root cambium. The first (outermost) layer of cells of the stele, capable of giving rise to secondary or branch roots.

**periosteum**    The thin outer layer of connective tissue covering a bone.

**peripheral nervous system**    The sum total of sensory and motor neurons.

**peristalsis**    Undulations of the digestive tract which aid in the movement of food.

**petiole**    The leaf stalk which serves to support the leaf as well as to transport water and minerals from stem to blade, and products of photosynthesis from blade to stem.

**pH**    Symbol for the logarithmic scale running from 0 to 14, representing the concentration of hydrogen ions or protons (in actuality, hydronium ions) per liter of solution. On the pH scale, 7 represents neutrality, the lower numbers acidity (acids), and the higher alkalinity (bases).

**phagocyte**    A cell in the body capable of engulfing particles from the surrounding medium into its own cytoplasm for enzymatic breakdown (phagocytosis). Phagocytes are found in large numbers lining the walls of lymph node sinuses; they destroy bacteria which have entered the body and have been picked up by the lymphatic system.  Both polymorphs and macrophages are phagocytes in man.

**phenotype**   In genetics, the outward appearance of an organism, as contrasted with its genetic make-up.

**pheromones ("ectohormones")**   Substances secreted outside the body and eliciting a particular response, e.g., the attraction of male moths to the female by the sex attractant she releases.

**phloem**   Plant vascular tissues which conduct food throughout the plant, especially from the leaves and stems to the storage areas in the roots.

**phlogiston theory**   A widely accepted seventeenth-century theory of combustion, which held that the substance phlogiston was contained in all combustible bodies and was released from these bodies upon their burning.  This theory remained strong until the later eighteenth century, when experimental work by Black, Priestley, and Lavoisier, among others, led to an oxygen theory of combustion.

**phosphorylation**   The addition of a phosphate group (e.g., $H_2PO_3$) to a compound, as in oxidative phosphorylation during respiration.

**photoperiodism**   The response of plants to day length in relation to germination and flowering.

**phototropism**   The growth response of a plant to light stimulus.

**physical environment**   All the elements surrounding an organism, excluding other living organisms.

**phytochromes**   Special plant pigments capable of light absorption at two distinct wavelengths.  Phytochromes are thought to mediate the photoperiodic response of plants.

**pinocytosis**   The process by which materials can be taken into the interior of a cell without passing through the plasma membrane.

**pituitary**   A two-lobed gland beneath the floor of the brain which secretes a number of protein hormones.  The anterior lobe produces tropic hormones (those which control the activity of other endocrine glands), as well as certain other hormones which act directly upon body function.  The anterior pituitary is the source of an antidiuretic hormone (vasopressin) and oxytocin.

**placenta**   A structure created by the fusion of the chorion with the wall of the uterus.  Respiratory, excretory, and nutritional functions of the foetus are carried on by exchanges across this structure.  The placenta also secretes hormones regulating certain aspects of foetal development.  Presence of a placenta is characteristic of all mammals except the marsupials.

**plasma membrane**   A lipoprotein of a definite structure which surrounds and contains the living matter within a cell.  The membrane has three layers: two outer protein surfaces and an inner core of lipid.  The polar part of each lipid molecule is associated with the protein on the surface, while the nonpolar portion points into the middle of the structure.  Average plasma membrane diameter is 75 Å.

**plasmagene**   A term often applied to a gene of cytoplasmic rather than nuclear origin.

**plastids**   Small bodies occurring in the cytoplasmic portion of plant cells.  Plastids are classified according to color.

**polarized**   Term applied to a cell membrane across which an electric potential exists, due to an unequal distribution of charged ions on the two sides of the membrane.

**pollen tube**   An extension of the pollen grain through the stigma and style to the ovary during reproduction in flowering plants.  The male pronucleus travels down this tube and is discharged into the ripened egg.

**polymorphism**   The existence within a single species of members showing many different anatomical forms, e.g., drone, queen, and workers in the honeybee.

**polyribosome (polysome)**   A cluster or chain of connected ribosomes.

**polysome**   *See* polyribosome.

**pons**   A thick bundle of nerve fibers which connect the hemispheres of the cerebellum.

**population genetics**   The application of genetic principles to a large number of breeding organisms.

**positive acceleration phase**   The first section of a sigmoid growth curve for a population, where the system described is just beginning to increase.

**positive feedback**   Biologically speaking, an abnormal state in which a change in a system in one direction serves as a command for continued change in that same direction. This can create a severe physiological imbalance leading to the death of an organism.

**potential energy**   Energy capable of doing work.

**preformation**   The idea that an already formed individual exists within the egg and that in embryological development that miniature individual merely increases in size.

**primary germ layers**   The first distinguishable areas within the developing embryo, namely, the ectoderm, mesoderm, and endoderm.  These areas give rise to the tissues and organs of the mature organism.

**prophase**   The first visible phase of mitosis, marked by the condensation of the chromosomal material into chromosomes and the disappearance of the nuclear membrane.

**prosecretin**   The inactive form of the hormone secretin, which can be converted into the active form by the action of dilute HCl.

**protective coloration**   Patterns of surface pigmentation which blend with the environment, allowing an organism to remain unobserved and therefore safe from predators.

**protein**   A complex organic molecule composed of amino acids joined in specific sequence by peptide bonds.  Proteins serve both structural and enzymatic functions.

**pseudopod**   An extension of the streaming cytoplasm of amoebae or other one-celled organisms which gives them their irregular shape.  In the amoeba, pseudopods function as a means of locomotion and as the tool for the intake of food from the environment.

**purine**   A class of nitrogen-containing compounds including uric acid, caffeine, adenine, and guanine.  The latter two molecules are particularly important as components of nucleic acids.  The purine structure consists of two rings with alternating carbon-nitrogen atoms.  (For structural formula, see Section 17–11.)

**pyrimidine**   A nitrogenous base combinable in two forms (cytosine and thymine) into DNA and in two forms (cytosine and uracil) into RNA.  (For structural formula, see Section 17–11.)

**pyruvic acid**    The final product of glycolysis, with the formula given below.

COOH
|
C═O
|
CH₃

**qualitative**    That which is not expressed in precise, measurable terms.

**quanta**    The tiny energy packets in which light travels.  Photons.

**quantasome**    The individual membranous structures arranged in columns within a granum.  Molecules of chlorophyll are aligned on the quantasomes.

**quantitative**    That which can be measured or given in some definite and precise (generally numerical) form.

**quantum theory**    The model which holds that light is composed of tiny energy packets (quanta, or photons) which are given off by any light emitter and which travel intact through space.

**radioactive decay**    The decrease in mass of certain unstable elements by emission of elementary particles, continuing until a stable form has been obtained.

**range**    The distribution of a group of numerical values describing specifically the lowest and highest of the included values.

**recessive**    In genetics, a term referring to the relative lack of phenotypic effect of a gene when in the presence of its dominant allele.  Thus the gene for blue eyes is said to be recessive to that for brown in the human population, because when one allele for blue eyes and one for brown eyes are present in the individual, the blue condition is masked— the individual has brown eyes.

**recombination**    In genetics, the formation of new genotypes (a combination of genes not present in either of the parents) in offspring due to independent assortment of genes and chromosomes during gamete formation.

**reduction**    A type of chemical reaction involving a gain of electrons.

**reduction division**    A division during which the number of chromosomes in each daughter cell has been reduced by one-half.  This is accomplished by nuclear division without previous chromosome duplication.

**reflex action**    A physical or chemical reaction, not necessarily under voluntary control, to a given stimulus.

**"releasers"**    Environmental stimuli which trigger the innate releasing mechanism.

**respiration**    The process whereby the energy of glucose and other fuel molecules is captured by the cells in the form of ATP.

**respiratory assembly**    A series of complex molecules (including cytochromes) capable of oxidation and reduction.  Such assemblies accept electrons from reduced coenzymes of the Krebs cycle and pass the electrons along the assembly chain, withdrawing small amounts of energy at specific points.

**response**    A change in behavior on the part of an organism (or tissue) as a result of some chemical or physical change in the environment.

**responsiveness**   A measure of the reaction of living matter to a given stimulus.

**resting potential**   The normal potential difference (electric), created by ion distribution across a cell membrane.   The term is particularly applied to nerve cells, where it refers to the potential existing across the membrane of a nonfiring cell.

**reversible reaction**   A reaction system where reactants and products are interconvertible.   If left to themselves, reversible chemical reactions reach an equilibrium point where just as much reactant is being converted into product as product into reactant.   Nearly all chemical reactions are to some degree reversible.

**rhizoid**   Small, rootlike structure extending from a rhizome and which functions in uptake of minerals and water.   Found especially in ferns and mosses.

**rhizome**   An underground stem, such as is found in ferns and iris.

**ribonucleic acid (RNA)**   A complex, single-stranded molecule consisting of repeating nucleotides.   At least three types of RNA are known, all of which are involved in transcribing the genetic code into protein molecular structure.   Messenger RNA carries the genetic code for amino acid sequence from the DNA to the ribosomes; soluble, or transfer, RNA (of which there is a given type for each amino acid) carries each amino acid to the ribosome where it is incorporated into protein in a specific place; ribosomal RNA is found only in the ribosomes and its function is not known.

**ribosomes**   Small particles found either free in the cytoplasm or attached to the outer surface of the endoplasmic reticulum.   Ribosomes contain high concentrations of ribonucleic acid (RNA), and are centers of protein synthesis.

**root cap**   The protective area at the very end of the root, composed of several layers of loosely arranged cells.

**root hair**   A structure projecting from the surface layer of cells in the maturation region. Such structures increase the absorption capacity of the root.

**root pressure**   Osmotic pressure of water diffusing into the root hairs from the soil.

**salivary glands**   Three pairs of glands (parotid, sublingual, submaxillary) surrounding the mouth, which secrete saliva into the mouth as a reflex response to the presence of food in the mouth.

**secretin**   A hormone secreted by the cells of the duodenum under the stimulus of hydrochloric acid from the stomach.   Secretin in turn causes the pancreas to secrete certain digestive enzymes into the duodenum.

**seed ferns**   Extinct organisms of the Devonian period which gave rise to both the conifers and the angiosperms.

**segregation (of alleles)**   The separation, during gametogenesis, of paired factors influencing a single condition.

**semen**   A secretion of the male reproductive organs, composed of the spermatazoa and secretions of various other glands.

**semipermeable (differentially permeable)**   Term applied to a membrane which allows some substances to pass through while prohibiting the passage of others.

**sensory epithelium**   Epithelial cells specialized for the reception of stimuli.   For example, the olfactory epithelium lining the nasal passages is in part responsible for the sense of smell. Sensory epithelial cells are connected by nerve tracts to the central nervous system.

**sensory neurons**    Those neurons capable of detecting environmental stimuli and carrying these stimuli to appropriate centers of interpretation and response.

**sex chromosome**    The chromosomes which are associated with the sex of the organism.

**shoot-tension (transpiration pull) hypothesis**    The concept that upward movement of water in plants is induced by a vacuum created when water evaporates from the leaves.

**short-day plants**    Plants which flower when exposed to cycles of light and dark where the dark phase is longer than $8\frac{1}{2}$ hours.

**sieve tube**    The most prominent type of phloem, a long tubular structure similar to xylem, but composed of living cells. The cells of the tube are connected by perforations of the cell wall.

**simple sugar**    A molecule composed of a single five- or six-carbon sugar.

**sino-auricular node**    A specialized mass of tissue on the right atrium of the heart near the entry of the superior vena cava. Impulses to the atria originate in the sino-auricular node and spread over the atria to a second node, the auriculo-ventricular node, located between the atria and ventricles. This node then stimulates the ventricles.

**skeletal muscle**    The muscles within the body which move its appendages. Because the cells of this type of muscle show striations running the width of the cell, skeletal muscles are often called striated muscles.

**smallpox**    A severe, infectious viral disease, now controlled by a cowpox vaccine.

**smooth muscle**    Muscle composed of elongated cells lacking striations and therefore having a smooth appearance under the microscope. The contraction of smooth muscle is under the control of the autonomic nervous system.

**soluble RNA**    *See* transfer RNA.

**somatoplasm**    The term used by August Weismann for all cells of an organism except reproductive cells ("germ plasm"). In each generation, the somatoplasm is derived from the "immortal" germ plasm.

**special creation**    An account of the creation of life and its diverse forms of a religious rather than scientific nature.

**specialization**    The change in cell capability from the performance of a wide range of functions to concentration on one particular activity or set of activities.

**speciation**    The process by which the accumulated effects of variation within a population make crossbreeding between two given organisms difficult or impossible.

**species**    The smallest unit of taxonomic classification, referring for the most part to a group of individuals capable of breeding among themselves. Species are defined by morphological, ecological, physiological, and biochemical criteria.

**sperm**    The male reproductive cell containing the haploid number of chromosomes, produced from a diploid germ cell by meiosis (reduction division). The sperm is divided into the head (containing the chromosomes), the neck, and the tail, which has many mitochondria. The mitochondria furnish the energy necessary for the propulsion of the sperm. The sperm fertilizes the egg, producing the diploid zygote.

**spermatogenesis**   The process by which haploid male gametes (sperm) are produced from diploid primary spermatocytes.

**sphincter muscle**   A ring-shaped muscle surrounding a tubular organ or a narrow opening, and capable of contraction.

**spinal cord**   A part of the central nervous system running down the back through the hollow center of the vertebrae, and from which pairs of peripheral nerves emerge.

**spindle fibers**   Fiberlike processes, formed during prophase, extending from the asters. Spindle fibers seem to function in determining the direction followed by the separating chromosomes in anaphase.

**spontaneous generation**   A concept according to which living organisms develop from nonliving matter.

**sporangium**   A structure in plants which produces spores. Sporangia are most commonly found in the ferns, mosses, and their relatives.

**spore**   An often thick-walled asexual reproductive cell capable of surviving adverse environmental conditions. Found particularly in bacteria, algae, mosses, and ferns. Limited in animals to one protozoan group, the Sporozoans (e.g., malarial parasite).

**sporophyte**   The diploid phase in the life cycles of ferns, mosses, and flowering plants. The sporophyte grows from the fertilized egg, and produces haploid spores which develop into gametophytes.

**standard deviation**   A statistical calculation defined as the square root of the variance (see Appendix 2). A means of showing the limits within which all items of a distribution should occur relative to the mean.

**static equilibrium**   A state of balance in which there is no activity.

**statistical analysis**   The use of mathematics to determine whether deviations from a pattern, as predicted by an hypothesis, are significant.

**stele**   The central cylinder of a root, separated from the cortex by the endodermis. The stele contains both xylem and phloem elements.

**stigma**   The top of the pistil, upon which the pollen grain lands during the events leading to fertilization.

**stimulus**   Any physical or chemical change in the environment which brings about a change in activity on the part of an organism (or portion of an organism, such as isolated tissue).

**stipule**   A small structure located on both sides of a leaf stalk, which protects the young leaf before it unfolds.

**stoma**   An opening on the leaf surface through which gas exchange and water loss take place. Guard cells control the size of the opening and thereby regulate these exchanges.

**striated muscle**   Contractile tissues in which the cells show striations running across their width. Both skeletal and cardiac muscles show such striations, but the term striated muscle is usually considered synonymous with skeletal muscle only. Striated muscle contraction is under the control of the conscious portion of the brain.

**style**   The thin, necklike region of the pistil. The style is topped by the stigma and has the ovary at its base. The pollen tube must grow down through the style to fertilize the egg within the ovary.

**substrate**  The molecule upon which an enzyme acts during an enzyme-catalyzed reaction.

**symbiosis (mutualism)**  A relationship between two species of organisms in which both derive benefits from the other, e.g., lichens.

**sympathetic nervous system**  That portion of the central nervous system which arises from the thoracic region of the spinal chord, and whose fibers pass through one synapse before reaching their sites of action.  Functionally, the sympathetic nerves prepare the body for emergencies.  They innervate the iris diaphragm of the eye (dilate pupil), the salivary glands (inhibit secretion), the heart (accelerate beat), the bronchi (dilate tubes), the stomach, pancreas, and duodenum (inhibit peristalsis and secretion), the adrenal glands (stimulate secretion of adrenaline and noradrenaline), the liver (stimulate conversion of glycogen to glucose), and the bladder (inhibit bladder contraction).  At their sites of action, sympathetic fibers generally release adrenaline or noradrenaline as a transmitter substance.

**synapse**  A small gap separating two neurons where the nervous impulse is transferred from the axon of the first neuron to the dendrite of the second neuron.  Synaptic function is thought to be carried on by chemical means.

**synapsis**  The process of the pairing of homologous chromosomes during meiosis.

**synthesis**  The process by which larger molecules can be built up from smaller molecules or atoms.  Synthesis generally requires energy.  In the synthesis of important biological molecules such as proteins from amino acids, starches from simple sugars, or fats from fatty acids and glycerol, the process involves removal of a water molecule between each two units being joined (dehydration synthesis).

**system**  An association of independent organs throughout the body for the performance of a necessary body function.  Some systems in higher animals are the circulatory, digestive, muscular, skeletal, and excretory systems.

**taproot**  A root system composed primarily of a single root which grows straight down.

**taxis (pl. taxes)**  Term applied to the simple reorientation movements of animals in response to external stimuli, e.g., the avoidance reactions of planaria to light.

**teleology**  The assigning of purpose to an action, e.g., in saying that the cell takes in calcium ions "*in order to . . . ."*

**telophase**  The final phase of mitosis, in which the cytoplasm of the dividing cell is cleaved and two daughter cells are formed.

**temporary adaptations**  Specific changes, appearing in the course of a single organism's lifetime, which are not transmitted to the next generation.

**territoriality**  The tendency of some organisms to defend a section of space surrounding them and/or their family.

**testosterone**  An androgen; a hormone produced in the interstitial cells of the testes of males, and responsible for the characteristic changes associated with puberty.

**tetrad**  The four-part structure resulting from the duplication of each pair of homologous chromosomes.

**thalamus**  Area of the brain beneath the cerebrum, serving as a relay center for incoming sensory impulses.

**thermodynamics**   That branch of physical science which deals with heat as a form of energy. It is concerned with such problems as the exchange of energy (measured always in respect to the gain or loss of heat from a system) during chemical or physical processes.

**thoracic cavity**   The chest cavity, containing the heart and lungs, enclosed by the ribs and diaphragm.

**threshold**   The lowest level of intensity of stimulation required to elicit a response. Usually applied to muscles and nerves, but also applied to such phenomena as animal behavior.

**tissue**   An aggregate of similar cells bound together in an ordered structure and working together to perform a common function. Examples: muscle, cartilage.

**tracheids**   A type of xylem tube in which each cell has a tapered end and the ends of many cells overlap to form a continuous tube. Tracheids are composed of dead cells.

**transfer RNA (soluble RNA)**   A type of RNA in the cytoplasm of which there are at least 20 varieties, one specific for each amino acid. This type of RNA unites with its specific amino acid and draws it to the ribosome during protein synthesis.

**translocation**   The movement of materials from one part of a plant to another.

**transmutation of species**   The idea of modern evolution that over a long period of time new species arise through modification of old species.

**transpiration**   The loss of water through the leaves of a plant.

**tropism**   The growth response of a plant to an outside stimulus such as light, chemicals, or gravity.

**unit membrane**   The model proposed for plasma membrane structure, consisting of phospholipid molecules sandwiched between layers of protein.

**urea**   A highly soluble conversion product of ammonia, formed mainly in the liver. This material is nontoxic if maintained in only moderate concentration. It serves as storage for waste ammonia by circulating dissolved in the blood until it is filtered out in the kidneys and is passed from the body in the urine. Urea has the following chemical structure:

$$O{=}C\diagup^{NH_2}_{\diagdown NH_2}$$

**uric acid**   A purine form, found in many organisms as the waste product of ammonia metabolism. Uric acid is highly insoluble, and its nontoxic crystals can be stored in the organism until excretion is possible. Organisms such as birds and reptiles excrete uric acid directly from the body. Mammals convert it into soluble urea.

**urine**   A watery waste containing urea in solution. Molecules of urea are produced from nitrogen-containing compounds (mostly uric acid) in the body by the liver. Urea circulating in the blood is filtered out by the kidneys and stored in the bladder until elimination.

**vacuolar membrane**   A lipoprotein structure (unit membrane) which separates the contents of a vacuole from the surrounding cytoplasm.

**vacuole**    A bubblelike structure occurring in the cytoplasm, serving as a reservoir to hold food and waste products, or as a vehicle for passage of materials across the plasma membrane of a cell.

**vagus nerve**    The tenth cranial nerve, carrying fibers to a number of important thoracic and abdominal organs. The vagus innervates the heart (slows down its beat), the bronchi (constricts the muscle in walls), the stomach, pancreas, and duodenum (stimulates peristalsis and secretion), and the liver (stimulates synthesis of glycogen).

**variance** ($s^2$)    A numerical calculation describing the extent of dispersion of data around a mean (see Appendix 2).

**vegetal pole**    The surface of an egg opposite the animal pole, on an axis running through the nucleus. The yolk density within the egg is greatest at the vegetal pole.

**vessel**    A type of xylem formed by cells with thickened walls, stacked end to end to form cylindrical tubes.

**vestigial organ**    A structure in a degenerate state which remains in an organism but has little or no purposeful function. The appendix in man is a vestigial organ.

**vestigial wing**    The effect of a mutation of a gene or group of genes controlling wing development in *Drosophila*, so as to produce short useless wings.

**villus**    A fingerlike projection from the intestinal wall, which increases the surface area of the intestine and thus facilitates absorption of food materials passing down the digestive tract. Villi are generously supplied with both blood and lymph vessels to transport absorbed materials to other parts of the body for either immediate use or storage.

**vitalism**    The view that life is an expression of something above and beyond the chemical and physical interactions of a group of molecules.

**vitamins**    Chemical substances, required in only trace amounts, which are thought to aid enzymes in catalyzing specific chemical reactions.

**viviparous**    Term applied to organisms whose embryos develop within the body of the mother and derive their nourishment from the mother.

**wavelength**    The distance between a given position on one wave and the same position on the following wave. Wavelength is often symbolized by the Greek letter lambda ($\lambda$).

**wave theory of light**    The model that depicts light as demonstrating all the properties of wave motion, analogous to waves on the surface of a body of water.

**woody**    Term applied to plants which contain the strengthening compound lignin along with cellulose in their cell walls.

**work**    An indirect measure of the energy required to move matter a given distance.

**xylem**    Plant vascular tissues which conduct water and minerals from roots to leaves.

**yolk**    Fatty compounds and proteins, stored within the egg, which serve as the first food source for the developing embryo.

**yolk sac**    An extraembryonic membrane in many kinds of eggs. It functions for the gradual supply of food material from the yolk to the developing embryo.

**zoology**    The study of animals.

**zygote**    A diploid cell, the product of fertilization formed from the union of male (sperm) and female (egg) reproductive cells (gametes).

# INDEX

# INDEX

Aberrations, chromosomal, 532
Abert squirrel, 708
Abscisic acid, 341, 349
"Abscisin II," 341
Absolute temperature, 68, 891
Absorption, 380
Acceptor, electron, 189
*Acetabularia crenulata*, 108
*Acetabularia mediterranea*, 106, 108,
    284
Acetyl coenzyme A, 201, 217
Acetylcholine, 436
Acid group, 163
Acids, amino, 162, 792
    fatty, 161
ACTH, *see* adrenocorticotropic
    hormone
Actin, 419, 724
Action current, 414
Action spectrum, 254
Activating enzymes, 562
Activation energy, 147
Active site, of enzyme, 174
Active transport, 116
Adaptation, to environment, 3, 10
Adaptive radiation, 712, 713, 866

Addicott, F. T., 341
Adenine, 543
Adenosine diphosphate (ADP), 186
Adenosine monophosphate (AMP), 186
Adenosine triphosphate (ATP), 185,
    414, 480
Adrenal cortex, 448
Adrenal gland, 448, 465
Adrenal medulla, 448
Adrenaline, 438, 448
Adrenocorticotropic hormone, 469
Aerobes, 205
Aerobic respiration, 197
Agent, oxidizing, 146
    reducing, 146
Agglutination, of blood cells, 538
    of sperm, 590
Agglutinogens, 538
Aggression, 766
Aggression center, 767
Agonistic behavior, 767
Agouti, in mice, 514
Alcaptonuria, 560
Alchemy, 229
Alcohol, 161
Alcoholic fermentation, 207

Aleutians, blood types of, 539
Algae, blue-green, 808, 825, 851
   brown, 830, 831
   golden-brown, 813
   green, 812, 813, 830, 831, 851
   red, 830, 831
   yellow-green, 851
Allantois, 598
Allard, H. A., 342
Alleles, multiple, 538
Allen, Mary B., 258
Allfrey, V. G., 227
All-or-none response, 413
Alpha-centauri, 67
$\alpha$-glycosidic bond, 160
Alpha helix, 165, 166
$\alpha$-ketoglutaric acid, 467
Alternation of generations, 840
Alveoli, 389
Amaurotic idiocy, 519
Amino acid, 162, 792
   table of, 895
Amino group, 162
Ammonia, 398
Ammonites, 867
*Ammophila*, 737, 738
Amnion, 598
Amoeba, 1
Amoeboid movement, 1, 120
*Amphioxus*, development of, 595
Amylase, 371
*Anacharis densa*, 248
Anaerobes, 205
   facultative, 205
   obligate, 205
Analogous structures, 692
Analysis, spectrum, 136
   statistical, 31
Anaphase, 475
Anatomist, 724
Anatomy, comparative, 692
Andreski, S. L., 783
Anemia, sickle-cell, 574, 704
Angiosperms, 855
Angstrom unit, 93
Animal behavior, 724
   in historical perspective, 726

Animal kingdom, taxonomic chart of, 902
Animal pole, 595
Animal tissues, 363
Annual ring, 296
Anther, 857
Antheridia, 840
Anthropomorphism, 727
Antibodies, to Rh factor, 538
Anticodons, 565
Antifertilizins, 591
Antivivisectionists, 374
Apical meristem, 272
*Apis mellifera* L., 742, 759
Apoenzyme, 179
Applied research, 46
*Araneus diadematus*, 731, 777
*Archaeopteryx*, 691
Archegonia, 840
Archenteron, 595
Arginine, 173, 559
Aristotle, 584
Arithmetic scale, 82
Arnon, D. I., 258
Aronoff, Samuel, 327
Arthropoda, 877
Ascomycetes, 846
Asexual reproduction, 7
Askenasy, E., 323
Assembly, respiratory, 195
Association neurons, 440
Asters, 473
Atomic energy, 129
Atomic radiation, effect on organisms, 78
Atomic theory, 863
Atoms, 129, 131
ATP, *see* adenosine triphosphate
Auricular-ventricular node, 386
Australia, isolation on mainland, 874
*Australopithecus africanus*, 773
Autonomic nervous system, 447
Autoradiography, 255, 304, 551, 852
Autotrophs, 262, 796
Auxin, 335
Avena test, 335
Avery, O. T., 540

Avogadro's number, 137
Axons, 368
Azide, role in respiration inhibition, 478

Bacon, Roger, 26
Bacteria, 808
    conjugation of, 825
    denitrifying, 662
    nitrate, 662
    nitrite, 662
    nitrogen-fixing, 662
    putrefying, 662
Bacteriophage, T2, 35, 541
    T4, 574
Baldwin, E., 227
Baltimore, D., 573
Banting, F., 450
Barnett, S. A., 775
Basidiomycetes, 846
Basidium, 847
Bayliss, W. M., 55, 58
Beadle, George W., 88, 558, 619
Beatty, Barbara, 567
Beckwith, J., 576, 764
Behavior, agonistic, 767
    animal, 723, 724
    goal-oriented, 746
    innate, 737
    learned, 733, 734
Behavioral isolation, 710
Behaviorism, 726
Bell, Eugene, 626
Beri-beri, 49
Bernard, Claude, 458, 469
Bertalanffy, L. von, 11
Berthollet, M., 240, 244
Beta configuration, 165
β-glycosidic bond, 160
Biddulph, O., 327
Bile, 371
Binomial expansions, 499
    and mendelian genetics, 518
Binomial nomenclature, 638
Biochemical approach to muscle
    contraction, 414
Biogenesis, 14, 788

Biogenetic law, 588
Biophysical approach to muscle
    contraction, 417
Biotic community, 652
Biotic potential, 672
Birds, evolutionary origin of, 872
Birnsteil, M., 576
Biston betularia, 695
Blackman, F. F., 248
Blade, 292
Blastema, 607
Blastocoel, 594
Blastomeres, 594
Blastopore, 596
Blastula, 594
Blending inheritance, 15, 512
Blood, 365
    types of, 538
Blood plasma, 365
Blue-green algae, 808, 825
Boas, George, 44
Boehm, Josef, 323
Bohr, Niels, 131, 132
Bond angles, 140
Bonds, α-glycosidic, 160
    β-glycosidic, 160
    chemical, 4, 136
    covalent, 139
    electrovalent, 138
    ester, 162, 187
    glycosidic, 187
    high-energy, 185
    hydrogen, 143, 165
    ionic, 138
    peptide, 164, 187
Bone, 364
Bonner, James, 344, 623
Borthwick, F. A., 346
Botanist, 268
Bowman, M., 117
Bowman's capsule, 400
Boyle, Janet, 205
Boysen-Jensen, P., 332, 350
Bracts, 291
Breathing, chemical basis of, 391
Breathing rate, control of, 390, 463
Briggs, R., 613

Bright-field microscopy, 92
*Brontosaurus*, 867
Brown algae, 830, 831
Brown, Claud L., 356
Brown, H. T., 316
Bryophytes, 844
Bud, 289
Bundle sheath, 294
Burg, Stanley P., 353

Cairns, John, 550, 554, 555
Calhoun, John B., 782
Calorie, 137
Calvin, Melvin, 255
Cambium, cork, 277
  vascular, 272
Cambrian period, 824, 867
Cannon, W. B., 469
Capillarity, 320
Carbohydrates, 159, 790
Carbon cycle, 659
Carbon monoxide, 150
Carbon-oxygen (carboxyl) group, 142,
  161, 162
Carboniferous period, 842
Cardiac muscle tissue, 56, 365
Carnivores, 655
Carotenoid pigments, 253
Cartilage, 364
Catalysts, 168
Catastrophism, 691
Cattle, incomplete dominance in, 511
Cell, 4, 12, 96
  companion, 284
  eucaryotic, 120
  fiber, 283
  procaryotic, 120
  sieve, 284
  size of, 111
Cell division, 7, 470
Cell membrane, 113
Cell theory, 90
Cell wall, 96
Cellular metabolism, 127
Cellulases, 372
Cellulose, 372
Celsius temperature scale, 892
Cenozoic era, 855

Centigrade temperature scale, 68
  conversion to Fahrenheit, 891
Central nervous system, 440
Centrioles, 101, 480
Centromere, 473
Cerebellum, 442
Cerebrospinal fluid, 443
Cerebrum, 441
Chance, in scientific experiments, 53
Charles' law, 495
Charts, phylogenetic, 20
  taxonomic, 647, 902
Chemical bonds, 4, 136
Chemical energy, 129
Chemical equilibrium, 156, 157
Chemical specificity, 164
Chemosynthesis, 787, 790
Chemosynthetic theory, 790
  objection to, 796
Chiasmata, 485
*Chironomus tentans*, 567
*Chlamydomonas*, 578, 813, 825, 826,
  830
*Chlorella*, 248, 255, 490
Chlorophyll, 100, 250
Chloroplasts, 100, 816
  self-duplication of, 490
Cholinesterase, 437
Cholodny, N., 350
Cholodny-Went hypothesis, 351, 352
Chorion, 598
Chorionic villi, 598
Chromatid, 473
Chromatin, 105, 471
Chromatography, 255
Chromoplasts, 100
Chromosomal aberrations, 532
Chromosomes, 111
  chemical composition of, 539
  homologous, 482
  maternal, 482
  paternal, 482
Chrysophyta, 819
Chyme, 56
Circulation, 383
Circulatory system, 383
Citric acid, 201
Citric acid cycle, 201

Citrulline, 399
*Cladophora*, 253
Cleavage, in embryonic development, 594
Cnidaria, 880
Coacervate theory, 793
Cocks, fighting ability, 772
Code, genetic, 560
Codons, 564
    nonsense, 571
    "punctuation," 571
*Coelacanth*, 878
Coelenterata, 880
Coenzyme, 179
Coenzyme A, 201
Collenchyma, 277
Collision theory, 147, 154
Colony, in bacteria, 825
Color blindness, red-green, 535
Coloration, protective, 695
Columnar epithelium, 364
Communication, 756
    interspecific, 756
    intraspecific, 756
Communities, 21
Community, biotic, 652
Companion cells, 284
Comparative anatomy, 692
Competition in natural populations, interspecific, 679
    intraspecific, 679
Competitive exclusion principle, 679
Competitive inhibitor, 178
Complex ion, 145
Complexity, in animals, 879
Computers, in taxonomy, 644
Conant, James Bryant, 45
Conditioned reflexes, 445
Conditioning, Pavlovian, 741
Conditions, standard, 152
Conducting tissues, 279
Configuration, beta, 165
Congenital malformations, 628
Conifers, 853
Conjugation, in bacteria, 825
    in *Spirogyra*, 829
Conjugation tube, 829
Connective tissues, 364

Conservation of energy, 130
Consumers, in ecosystem, 654
    primary, 655
    secondary, 655
    tertiary, 655
Continuity of the germ plasm, 17
Control, of breathing, 390
Control group, 50
Copper Basin, Tennessee, 21
Cork, 14
Cork cambium, 277
Cortex, 287, 289
    of kidneys, 399
Cory, R., 327
Cosmic rays, 130
Cotyledons, 291
Coupled reactions, 188
Cranial nerves, 442
Creation, special, 688, 787
Cretaceous period, 855, 867
Crick, H. F. C., 544
Cricket calls, 644
Cristae, 102
Cronquist, Arthur, 819
Crossing-over, 485
Crucial experiment, 37, 58
Cuboidal epithelium, 364
Curare, 439
Current, action, 414
Cutin, 293
Cycle, carbon, 659
    citric acid, 201
    krebs, 201
    nitrogen, 660
    tricarboxylic acid, 201
    water, 663
Cyclic photophosphorylation, 260
Cyclopia, 628
Cytidine triphosphate (CTP), 188
Cytochrome oxidase, 192
Cytochromes, 190
Cytokinins, 340
Cytokinesis, 471
Cytologist, 724
Cytology, 20, 90
Cytoplasm, 97
Cytoplasmic streaming, 120
Cytosine, 543

Dance language, of honeybees, 757
Danforth's short-tail mutation, 628
Danielli, J. F., 100
Dark-field microscopy, 92
Dark reactions, of photosynthesis, 255
Darwin, Charles, 19, 332, 349, 688, 764
Darwinism, 863
Darwin's finches, 714
*Dasypus novemcinctus*, 778
Data, variance of, 75, 893
Dating, geological, 801
*Datura stramonium* (jimson weed), 488
Davson, H., 100
Davson-Danielli, model of cell membrane, 117
Dawkins, R., 760
Deamination, 397
De Broglie, Louis, 93
Decarboxylation, 201
Decay, radioactive, 802
Decomposers, in ecosystem, 654
Dedifferentiation, 9
Deduction, 29
    in mathematics, 29
Deductive logic, 29
Deer, Kaibab, 675
Deer mice, 69
Degeneracy, in genetic code, 571
Degradation processes, 4
Dehydration synthesis, 160, 399
Dehydrogenase, succinic, 177, 219
Deletions, 532
Delgado, José M. R., 768
De Lucia, Paula, 554
Denatured protein, 166
Dendrites, 368
Denitrifying bacteria, 662
Density-dependent factors, 675
Deoxyribonucleic acid (DNA), 111, 539, 604, 798
    artificial synthesis by DNA polymerase, 553
    informational, 626
    use in taxonomy, 647
Deoxyribose, 543
Depolarization, 411

De Saussure, Nicholas Theodore, 243
Deutsch, J. A., 749
Development, genetic basis of, 618
    intrauterine, 598
Devonian period, 833
Diaphragm, 389
Dichlorodiphenyltrichloroethane (DDT), 54
"Dicots," 291
Dicotyledonous plants, 291
Dictyosome, 104, 106
*Didinium*, 88
Diet, 370
Differentially permeable membrane, 111
Differentiation, 8
    in embryonic development, 583
Diffusion, 114
Digestion, 369
Di-isopropylfluorophosphate (DFP), 439
Dikaryotic hyphae, 849
Dilger, William C., 743
Dinosaurs, 718, 867
Diphosphopyridine nucleotide (DPN), 258
Diploid, 482
Disaccharides, 159
Dissociation, 144
Distribution curve, normal, 73
Divergence, evolutionary, 709
Division, cell, 7, 470
Dixon, H. H., 323
DNA polymerase, 553
Dolk, H. E., 350
Dominance, incomplete, 511
Dominance hierarchies, 770
Dominant genes, 16, 508
"Dormin," 341
Down's syndrome (mongolism), 486
Driesch, Hans, 25, 586
Drive, 747
*Drosophila melanogaster*, 17, 486, 533, 641, 707, 726, 746
Duckbill platypus, 874
Duodenum, 56
Dynamic equilibrium, 114, 158

Earthworm, 877
Echinoderms, 877
Ecological isolation, 709
Ecological niche, 653, 866
Ecology, 21, 653
Ecosystem, 653
  typical, 655
Ectoderm, 594
Effectors, 619
Efficiency of photosynthesis, 262
Egg, 8, 368
Ehrlich, Ann H., 784
Ehrlich, P. R., 784
Eijkman, Christian, 49
Electrical energy, 129
Electrochemical nature of nerve
    impulse, 428
Electrochemical potential, 410, 411
Electron acceptor, 189
Electron microscope, 93, 94
Electron transfer, 189
Electron transition, 135
Electron transport, 188
Electrons, 129
Electrophoresis, 644
Electrovalent bond, 138
Elimination, 382
Embryology, 20, 583
  experimental, 585, 599
Embryonic induction, 601
Emerson enhancement effect, 261
Emerson, Robert, 260
Emotions, 44
Endergonic reactions, 148
Endocrine gland, 60
Endocrine system, 448
Endoderm, 594
Endoplasmic reticulum, 103
Energy, 129
  activation, 147
  atomic, 129, 130
  chemical, 129, 130
  conservation of, 130
  electrical, 129, 130
  free, 129, 149
  kinetic, 129
  mechanical, 129, 130

potential, 129
pyramid of, 658
radiant, 129, 130
solar, 130
transformation of, 130
Energy barrier, 151
Energy hill, 156
Energy levels, 132
  molecular, 136
Engelmann, T. W., 253
Enhancement effect, Emerson, 261
Enterokinase, 372
Envelope, nuclear, 104
Environment, physical, 653
Environmental resistance, 672
Enzyme inhibitors, 176
Enzyme synthesis, control of, 619
Enzymes, 147, 168, 172
  activating, 562
  active site of, 174
  constrained state of, 214
  naming of, 173
  poisoned, 172
  relaxed state of, 214
  specificity of, 173
Epidermis, 287, 289, 293
Epigenesis, 584
Epinephrine, 438, 448, 451
Epistasis, 535, 537
Epithelial tissues, 363
Epithelium, columnar, 364
  cuboidal, 364
  glandular, 364
  sensory, 364
  squamous, 363, 364
Equilibrium, 459
  chemical, 156, 157
  dynamic, 114, 158
  genetic, 703
  static, 459
  steady state, 459
Equilibrium phase, 81
*Equisetum*, 823
Erikson, E., 780
Errors, scientific, 44
Erythroblastosis fetalis, 538
Erythrocytes, 365

*Escherichia coli*, 382, 550, 555, 571, 576, 620, 779
Escombe, F., 316
Eskimos, blood types of, 539
Esophagus, 56
Ester bond, 162, 187
Ether, 45
Ethology, 726
Ethylene, 341
Eucaryotes, origin of, 812
Eucaryotic cells, 120
Euglenophyta, 819
Evolution, of development, 597
  divergence in, 709
  molecular level of, 881
  population concept of, 702
  speciation in, 709
  theory of, 19, 688, 864
  as a working hypothesis, 866
Evolutionary divergence, 709
Evolutionary origin, of birds, mammals, 872
Excretion, 3, 6, 331, 397
Exergonic reactions, 140
Experimental group, 50
Expiration, 389
Experimental embryology, 585
Experimental genetics, 504
Experimental results, interpretation of, 33
Experimental science, rational basis of, 44
Experiments, 28
  crucial, 37
Exponential scales, 83
Exponents, 83
Extinctions, mass, 870
Extracellular digestion, 369
Extracellular fluid, 6
Extrachromosomal inheritance, 577
Extraembryonic membranes, 598
Extrapolation, 77

Facultative anaerobes, 205
Fahrenheit temperature scale, 68
  conversion to centigrade, 891
Fats, 159, 160, 197
  saturated, 161

Fatty acids, 161
Feedback, enzyme, 619
  negative, 461
  positive, 461
Feedback mechanism, 461
*Felis domestica*, 643
Fermentation, 197
  alcoholic, 207
  lactic, 207
Ferns, 840
Ferredoxin, 258
Ferric ion, 192
Ferrous ion, 192
Fertilization, 8, 38, 590
  experiment concerning basis of, 39
Fertilizin, 591
Fiber cells, 283
Fibers, muscle, 413
Fibrous root, 285
Fibrous tissue, 365
Filtration, 401
Finches, Darwin's, 714
  variations in beak depth, 680
First law of thermodynamics, 130
Fischer, R. A., 312
Fission, 7
Fitzroy, Robert, 689
Flagellates, 813
Flavin adenine dinucleotide (FAD), 190, 193
Flowers, adaptation to insects, 857
Fluid, cerebrospinal, 443
Fluorescence, 257
Flynn, John P., 768
Foliage leaves, 291
Food chain, 657
Formic acid, 150
Fossils, 867
  "living," 878
Founder population, 711
Fox, Sidney W., 792, 794
Fraenkel-Conrat, Heinz, 799
Frames of reference, 66
Free energy, 129, 149
Frisch, Karl von, 757
Frog, grass, 642
Fructose-1, 6-diphosphate, 198
Fruit, 855

Fruit fly, 17, 486, 533, 606, 641, 707, 726, 746
Fumaric acid, 204, 219
Fundamental tissues, 277
Furrowing, 475

Gage, R. S., 327
Galapagos Islands, 680, 714
Galvani, Luigi, 424
Gametes, 8, 368
Gametogenesis, 482
Gametophyte, 840
Gametophyte generation, 840
Gamma rays, 130
Gardner, B. T., 747, 749
Garner, W. W., 342
Garrod, Sir Archibald E., 557
Gas, inert, 138
Gastrin, 374
Gastrocoel, 595
Gastrovascular cavity, 880
Gastrula, 588, 595
Gastrulation, 595
Gause's hypothesis, 679
Gene, artificial synthesis of, 576
    definition of, 572
    function of, 556
    structure of, 543
Gene concept, 15, 780
Gene-enzyme hypothesis, 559
Gene loci, in man, 531
Gene-polypeptide chain, 565
Gene pool, 702
Generalizations, inductive, 33
Generation, of ATP, 188
    spontaneous, 688, 787
Generations, alternation of, 840
Genes, 16, 513
    and development, 618
    dominant, 16, 508
    recessive, 16, 508
    two pairs of, 514
Genetic code, 560
    degeneracy in, 571
    universality of, 571
Genetic drift, 711
Genetic equilibrium, 703
Genetic prognosis, 518

Genetics, experimental, 504
    mathematical basis of, 495
    population, 521, 702
Genotype, 513
Geological dating, 801
Geometry, of cell, 112
Geotropism, 332
Germ layers, primary, 593
Germ plasm, continuity of, 17
German measles, 628
Gibberellic acid, 338
Gibberellins, 338
Gilbert, L. I., 780
Ginsburg, V., 560
Girdling, 303
Glandular epithelial cells, 364
Glazer, M., 117
Glomerulus, 400
Glucose, 197
    level in blood, 465
Glucose-6-phosphate, 198
Glycolysis, 197
Glycosidic bond, 187
Goethe, Johann Wolfgang von, 27
Golden-brown algae, 813
Golgi complex, 104, 105
Goodall, J., 752
Goodman, Morris, 646
Gorer, Geoffrey, 773
Grana, 250
Grass frog, 642
Gray crescent, 601
Green algae, 812, 813, 830, 831
Gregory, F. G., 357
Grew, Nehemiah, 232, 319
Griffith, F., 539
Grossman, M. I., 750
Growth, 7
Growth curve, human population, 678
Growth ring, 296
Guanine, 543
Guanosine triphosphate, 188
Guard cells, 275
Gurdon, J. B., 615
Gymnosperms, 853

Haagen-Smit, A., 336
Haberlandt, G., 339

Habitat, ecological, 653
Habituation, 752
Haeckel, Ernst, 588
Hailman, J. P., 741
Haldane, J. S., 463
Hales, Stephen, 232, 314
Half-life, 802
Hamburger, Viktor, 777
Hämmerling, experiments on
    *Acetabularia*, 106
Hamner, Karl C., 344
Haploid, 482
Hardy, G. H., 703
Hardy-Weinberg law, 703
Hare, snowshoe, 674
Harrison, Ross G., 603
Harvey, William, 383
Hasler, A. D., 32
Heartbeat, cause of, 385
Heinroth, O., 754
Helix, alpha, 165, 166
Helmholtz, Hermann von, 45, 426
Hemophilia, 535, 575
Hendricks, S. B., 346
Herbivores, 655
Herbs, 272
Herring gulls, 745
Heterospory, 842
Heterotrophs, 262, 796
Heterozygous, 513
Hevesy, George, 247
High-energy phosphate bonds, 185
Hildebrandt, A. C., 615
Hiramoto, Y., 481
Histogram, 71
Histologist, 724
Histones, in chromosome, 539
*H. M. S. Beagle*, 689
Hoebel, B. G., 770
Holley, R. W., 564, 577
Holtfreter, J., 601
Homeostasis, 460
Homologous chromosomes, 482
Homologous structures, 692
*Homo sapiens*, 773
Homozygous, 513
Honeybee, 742, 757–760
Hooke, Robert, 14

Hormones, 60
    plant, 332
Howard, H. E., 764
Huber, Bruno, 322
Hunger, causes of, 378
Huxley, H. E., 419
Huxley, Thomas, 689
*Hydra*, 369, 388, 606, 609
Hydrogen bond, 143, 165
Hydrolysis, 160, 371
Hydrophilic, 546
Hydrophobic, 546
Hyphae, dikaryotic, 849
Hypophysis, 449
Hypothalamus, 442, 461, 465
Hypotheses, 28
    false, 31
    reliability of, 34
    types of, 34

Idiocy, amaurotic, 519
"If . . . , then" reasoning, 29
Immunological techniques, 644
Immunology, 54
Impermeable membrane, 114
Imprinting, 754
Incomplete dominance, 511
Independent assortment, law of, 516
Indians, blood types of, 539
Indoleacetic acid, 336
"Induced fit" hypothesis, 175
Inductive generalizations, 33
Inductive logic, 33
Inert gas, 138
Informational DNA, 626
Infrared light, 130
Ingenhousz, Jan, 237, 250, 252
Ingestion, of food, 369
Ingestion hypothesis, 816
Inheritance, blending, 15, 512
    extrachromosomal, 577
    particulate, 15, 512
Inhibitor, competitive, 178
    noncompetitive, 178
Initial velocity, 170
Innate Releasing Mechanism (IRM),
    738
Innate response, 737

Insertion, of muscle, 423
Insight learning, 752
Inspiration, in breathing, 389
Instinct, 727, 733
Insulin, 451, 466
International Commission on
    Taxonomy, 638
Internode, 287
Interphase, 471
Interpolation, of data, 77
Interpretation of experimental results,
    33
Interspecific communication, 756
Interspecific competition, in natural
    populations, 679
Intestine, movements of, 376
Intracellular digestion, 369
Intraspecific communication, 756
Intraspecific competition, in natural
    populations, 679
Intrauterine development, 598
Inversions, chromosomal, 533
Invertebrates, evolution of, 875
Ion pairs, 144
Ionic bond, 138
Ionization, 135
Ions, 132, 143
    complex, 145
IRM (Innate Releasing Mechanism), 738
Iron, 192
Irreversible reactions, 155
Islets of Langerhans, 450, 466
Isogametes, 827
Isogamy, 827
Isolation, behavioral, 710
    ecological, 709
    experiments, 733
    in origin of species, 707
    physiological, 710
    seasonal, 709
Isoleucine, 467
I-somes, 627

Jacob, François, 620, 780
Jacobs, William P., 358
Janowitz, H. D., 750
Jellyfish, 482
Jenner, Edward, 54

Jimson weed, 488
Johnson, D. O., 759
Jumping spiders, 747

Kaibab deer, 675
Kaibab squirrel, 708
Karli, Pierre, 775
Keilin, David, 190
Kelvin temperature scale, 68
    conversion from Fahrenheit, 891
Kepler, Johannes, 44
Khorana, Har Gobind, 576
Kidneys, 397, 399
Kidston, Robert, 835
Kilocalories, 137, 186
Kinetic energy, 129
Kinetin, 340
Kinetochore, 473
King, T. J., 613
Klein, R. M., 819
Klopfer, M. S., 754
Klopfer, P. H., 754, 776, 780
Kobata, A., 560
Kögl, F., 336
Kohne, D. E., 576
Kornberg, Arthur, 552
Kornberg model, 553
Krebs citric acid cycle, 201
Kubota, T., 481
Kuo, Z.Y., 777
Kurosawa, E., 338
Kymograph, 59

Lac operon, 576
Lactic acid, 207
Lactic fermentation, 207
Lamarckism, 45
Lamellar membranes, 250
Lang, William, 835
Langerhans, islets of, 466
Larva, 589
Lateral meristem, 272
Lavoisier, Antoine Laurent, 234
Law, of independent assortment, 516
    of mass action, 212, 467
    of segregation, 509
Laws, Mendel's, 26, 509, 516
Leaf primordia, 292

Leaflets, 292
Learned behavior, 733, 734
Leaves, 270
    foliage, 291
    scale, 291
Le Châtelier's principle, 212
Lederberg, Joshua, 783
Lehninger, A. L., 227
Lehrman, D. S., 778
Lemmings, 676
Leucocytes, 365
Leucoplasts, 100
Levels of investigation, 723
Lewis, G. N., 38
Lichens, 696, 851
Life, 24-hour scale of, 802
Ligaments, 365, 423
Light, 252
    infrared, 130
    ultraviolet, 130
Light microscope, 92, 94
Light reactions, of photosynthesis, 257
Light-year, 67
Lignier, O., 834
Lignin, 331
Limitations of science, 43
Limiting factors, in photosynthesis, 249
Limulus, 386
Line graph, 73
Linkage, 525
Linnaean system, 638
Linnaeus, Carolus, 636, 863
Lipase, 162, 371
Lipids, 159, 160
    in chromosomes, 539
Liver, 465
Lloyd, F. E., 311
Lloyd-Sayre hypothesis, 312
Loci, of genes, 529
Lock-and-key theory, 174
Loeb, Jacques, 25, 729
Logarithmic phase, 80
Logarithmic scales, 83
Logarithms, 83
Logic, deductive, 29
    inductive, 33
Long-day plants, 344
Longistigma caryae, 325

Lorenz, Konrad, 737, 748, 754, 773, 776
Lotka, A. J., 46
Lovebirds, 743
Lowe, A. G., 434
LSD, 628
Luck, J. L., 490
Luria and Delbrück, experiment on mutations, 35
Lymph, 383
Lymphatic system, 383
Lysine, 173
Lysis, 104
Lysosome, 104

MacDougal, D. T., 321
MacLeod, C. M., 540
Macromolecule, 160
Malformations, congenital, 628
Malonic acid, 219
Maltase, 371
Mammalia, 635
Mammals, evolutionary origin of, 872
    and reptiles, differences between, 872
Mangold, Hilde, 603
Manning, Aubrey, 766
Manton, Irene, 490
Mapping, of chromosomes, 529
Margulis, Lynn, 820
Marsupials, 635
Mass action, law of, 212, 467
Mass extinctions, 870
Maternal chromosomes, 482
Mathematical basis, of genetics, 495
Mathematics, deduction in, 29
Matter, 129
Mayr, Ernst, 746
McCarty, M., 540
Mean, 70
Measles, German, 628
Mechanical energy, 129
Mechanism, 23
Median, 74
Medulla, adrenal, 448
    of brain, 442
Medullary region, of kidneys, 399
Megaspores, 842

Meidner, Hans, 312
Meiosis, 482, 516
Melanic moths, 695
Membrane, plasma, 113
Mendel, Gregor Johann, 15, 506, 742, 764
Mendel's laws, 26, 509, 516
Meninges, 443
Mering, J. von, 450
Meristem, apical, 272
    lateral, 272
Meristematic tissues, 272
Meselson, M., 550, 555
Mesoderm, 588, 594, 880
Mesophyll, 293
Mesozoic era, 852
"Messenger DNA," 626
Messenger RNA, 561
Metabolic activity, and cell size, 112
Metabolic pathways, 128
Metabolic rates, 81
Metabolism, 3, 4, 128
    cellular, 127
Metamorphosis, 590
Metaphase, 473
Methane, 139
Method, scientific, 27
Metric system, 67
Micromonas, 490
Microscopy, bright-field, 92
    dark-field, 92
    electron, 93, 94
    phase-contrast, 92
Microspores, 842
Microtoming, 91
Microtubules, 101, 473
Migration, of organisms in population's gene pool, 711
    of salmon, 28
Miller, Carlos O., 340
Miller, O. L., Jr., 567
Miller, Stanley, 791, 797
Minimal medium, 558
Minkowski, O., 450
Mirsky, A. E., 227
Missing link, 21, 691
Mitchell, Peter, 205
Mitchell-Boyle hypothesis, 205

Mitochondria, 101
    self-duplication of, 490
Mitosis, 471, 479
Mizutani, Satoshi, 573
Mode, 73
Models, scientific, 648
Mohl, Hugo von, 310
Molecular biologist, 723
Molecular energy levels, 136
Molecular polarity, 142
Molecule, 136
    phospholipid, 142
Mollusca, 877
Mongolism, 486
"Monocots," 291
Monocotyledonous plants, 291
Monod, Jacques, 620, 780
Monosaccharides, 159
Montagu, M. F. Ashley, 773
Morgan, C. Lloyd, 728
Morgan, Thomas Hunt, 533
"Morgan's canon," 728
Morphogenesis, 605
Morre, D. J., 106
Mosaic theory, 585
Moscona, A. A., 611
Mosses, 845
"Mother love," 728
Moths, melanic, 695
Motivation, 746
Motor neurons, 440
Movement, 6
    amoeboid, 1, 120
    through phloem, 325
    stomatal, 310
    of water and minerals into plants, 306
Muller, Fritz, 588
Muller, Johannes, 45
Muller, Paul, 54
Multicellularity, evolution of, 879
    origin of, 823
Multidimensional species concept, 643
Multiple alleles, 537
Münch, Ernst, 328
Muscle contraction, 414, 417
Muscles, 410
    cardiac, 365

skeletal, 365
smooth, 365
sphincter, 377
striated, 365
Muscular tissues, 365
Mutation rate, 78
Mutations, 17, 26, 35
    Danforth's short-tail, 628
    experiment on spontaneity of, 35
Myofibrils, 417, 724
"Myohaematin," 190
Myosin, 419, 618, 724
Myxomycetes, 846

NAD, *see* nicotinamide adenine
    dinucleotide
Natural selection, 19, 26, 694
"Nature versus nurture" controversy,
    776
Negative acceleration phase, 81
Negative feedback, 461
Nephron, of kidney, 400
Nerve impulse, 424
Nerves, 410
    cranial, 442
Nervous system, autonomic, 447
    central, 440
    peripheral, 440
Nervous tissues, 368
Netted venation, 294
Neuromuscular junction, 438
Neurons, 368
    association, 440
    motor, 440
    sensory, 439
*Neurospora crassa*, 88, 490, 558, 606,
    619
Neutrons, 129
Newth, David, 726
Newton, Sir Isaac, 27
Newton's laws, 864
Niche, ecological, 653
Nicotinamide adenine dinucleotide
    (NAD), 190, 193
Nine-banded armadillo, 779
Nitrate bacteria, 662
Nitrite bacteria, 662
Nitrogen cycle, 660

Nitrogen-fixing bacteria, 662
Niu, M. C., 603
Node, 287
Nomenclature, binomial, 638
Noncompetitive inhibitor, 178
Noncyclic photophosphorylation, 259
Nondisjunction, of chromosomes, 486
Nonsense codons, 571
Nonwoody plants, 272
*Nostoc*, 851
Nuclear envelope, 104
Nuclear membrane, 104
Nucleoli, 105
Nucleoplasm, 97, 104
Nucleoproteins, 110
Nucleotides, in DNA, 544
Nucleus, atomic, 131
    of a cell, 93, 96, 104, 110
Number, Avogadro's, 137
    turnover, 170
Numerical data, 52

Obligate anaerobes, 205
"Ockham's razor," 728
Oils, 160
Okazaki, Reiji, 554
"Okazaki fragments," 554, 556
Oögamy, 830
Oögenesis, 482
Oparin, A. I., 793
Operator gene, 620
Operons, 620
    *lac*, 576
Ordovician period, 824, 878
Organelles, of cell, 13, 97–105
Organizers, embryonic, 601
Organs, 4, 90
Origin, of muscles, 423
*Origin of Species*, 688, 726
Origin of species, role of isolation in, 707
Ornithine, in dehydration synthesis
    reaction, 398
Ornithology, 743
Osmosis, 118, 119
Osmotic pressure, 118
Otholenghi, A., 117
Ovary, 857
Overpopulation, human, 677

Oviparous, 590
Ovoviviparous, 590
Ovules, 857
Ovum, 8, 368
Oxaloacetic acid, 201
Oxidation, 127, 146
Oxidizing agent, 146
Oxyhemoglobin dissociation curve, 396

Paal, A., 334, 350
Paleontology, 20
Pancreas, 56, 450
*Paramecium*, 76, 88, 680
Parasympathetic nervous system, 447
Parenchyma, 277
Parthenogenesis, 585, 593
Partial pressures, 394, 395
Particulate inheritance, 15, 512
Pascal, Blaise, 501
Pascal's triangle, 501
Passive transport, 116
Pasteur, Louis, 54, 788
Paternal chromosomes, 482
Pauling, Linus, 175
Pavlov, Ivan P., 373, 374, 445, 730
Pavlovian conditioning, 741
$Pb^{206}$, 802
Peck orders, 770, 781
Pennsylvanian period, 850
Peppered moth, 695
Pepsin, 371
Pepsinogen, 372
Peptide, 164
Peptide bond, 164, 187
Pericycle, 287
Periderm, 277
Periodic table, 633
Periosteum, 281
Peripheral nervous system, 440
Peristalsis, 376
Peristaltic movements, 374
Permeability, differential, 114
Permian period, 867
*Peromyscus*, 69
Perry, Margaret, 481
Petiole, 292
PGA, *see* phosphoglyceric acid
PGAL, *see* phosphoglyceraldehyde

pH (hydrogen ion concentration), 154
Phaeophyta, 819
Phages, 35
Phase-contrast microscopy, 92
Phenotype, 513
Phenylketonuria, 557, 560
Pheromones, 757
*Philanthus triangulum*, 738
Philosophers, 43
Phloem, 279, 853, 855
    movement through, 325
Phlogiston theory, 45, 229
Phosphate bonds, high-energy, 185
Phosphates, in DNA, 543
Phosphoglyceraldehyde, 255
Phosphoglyceric acid (PGA), 201, 255
Phospholipid molecules, 142
Photons, 254
Photoperiodism, 342, 344
Photophosphorylation, cyclic, 260
    noncyclic, 259
Photosynthesis, 130, 228
    dark reactions of, 255
    efficiency of, 262
    light reactions of, 257
    modern view of, 249
Phototropism, 332
Phylogenetic charts, 20, 865
Phylogenetic relationships, 872
    of invertebrates, 875
Phylogeny, 872
Physical environment, 653
Physiological isolation, 710
Phytochrome, 346
Pill bugs, 729, 730
Pinocytosis, 100
Pistil, 857
Pituitary gland, 449, 469
Placenta, 598
Planaria, 606, 730
Planck, Max, 136
Plant kingdom, taxonomic chart of, 902
Plant tissues, 271
Plants, dicotyledonous, 291
    hormones of, 332
    long-day, 344
    monocotyledonous, 291

movement of water and minerals
into, 306
nonwoody, 272
short-day, 344
Plasma, blood, 365
Plasma membrane, 13, 96
Plastids, 100
Platt, John R., 725
Platypus, duckbill, 874
Pleiomorphism, 527
Plotnick, R., 768
Poisoned enzymes, 173
Polarity, 141
molecular, 142
Polarization, 410
Pollen tube, 853, 857
Pollution, 677
Polychaete worms, 482
Polydactyly, 628
Polymorphism, 639
Polypeptide, 164
Polyploidy, 481
Polyribosomes, 104, 562
Polysaccharides, 159
Polysomes, 104, 562
Pons, 442
Population, founder, 711
human, 676
Population concept of evolution, 521,
702
Population density, 781
Population genetics, 521, 702
Porphyrin ring, 192
Portal vein, 465
Positive acceleration phase, 80
Positive feedback, 461
Potential, biotic, 672
electrochemical, 410, 411
Potential energy, 129
Pre-Cambrian era, 875
Precipitate, 156
Predictions, of scientific hypotheses, 29
Preformation theory, 40, 583
Preying mantis, 751
Prey-predator relationships, 657
Priestey, Joseph, 235, 262
Primary consumers, 655
Primary germ layers, 593

Primary root, 285
Probability, in science, 33
Procaryotes, 808
Procaryotic cells, 120
Producers, in ecosystem, 654
Product principle of probability, 498
Prognosis, genetic, 518
"Proof," scientific, 29
Prophase, 471
Prosecretin, 61
Protective coloration, 695
Protective tissues, 274
Proteins, 159, 162, 369
denatured, 166
digestion of, 369
primary structure of, 165
secondary structure of, 165
tertiary structure of, 165
Protium, 131
"Proton pump," 205
Protons, 129
Pseudopods, 1
Psycho-hydraulic model, 748, 776, 777
"Punctuation" codons, 571
Punnett square, 512
Pupa, 590
Pure research, 46
Purines, 543
Purpose, in evolution, 718
Putrefying bacteria, 662
Pyloric valve, 56
Pyramid, of energy, 658
of mass, 657
Pyrimidines, 543
Pyrrophyta, 819
Pyruvic acid, 199, 201

Quanta, 136, 254
Quantasomes, 250
Quantum shift, 135
Quantum theory, 254

Rabbits, "Chinchilla," 537
"Himalayan," 537
Radiant energy, 129
Radiation, adaptive, 712, 713, 866
atomic, 78
and mice, 32

Radicals, 143
Radio waves, 130
Radioactive decay, 802
*Rana pipiens*, 642, 772
Range, of data, 75
Rates of reaction, 153
    effect of temperature on, 171
Rational basis of experimental science,
    44
Rays, of cells in xylem, 283
    cosmic, 131
    gamma, 130
    X-, 130
Reabsorption, 402
Reactions, coupled, 188
    endergonic, 148
    irreversible, 155
    rate of, 153
    redox, 146
    reversible, 155
Recessive genes, 16, 508
Recombinants, genetic, 528
Red algae, 830, 831
Red-green color blindness, 535
Redi, Francesco, 788
Redox reactions, 146
Reducing agent, 146
Reduction, 146
Reduction division, 482, 486
Reductionism, 724
Reflex action, 375, 445
Reflex arc, 443
Reflex, conditioned, 445
Regeneration, 605
    of limb, 738
Regulator genes, 621
Relationships, phylogenetic, 872, 875
Releasers, 738
Religion and science, 43
Rennin, 372
Reproduction, 3, 7,
    cellular, 470
Reproductive tissue, 368
Reptiles, evolution of, 872
    and mammals, differences between,
        872
Research, applied, 46
    basic, 46

Resistance, environmental, 672
Resolving power, of microscope, 92
Respiration, 197
    aerobic, 197
    anaerobic, 205
    efficiency of, 211
Respiratory assemblies, 102, 195
Respiratory center, 465
Respiratory exchange, 388
Respiratory gases, in the blood, 393
Response, all-or none, 413
    behavioral, 6
    innate, 737
    learned, 733, 734
Resting potential, 429
Reticulate venation, 294
Reversible reactions, 155
Rh-factor, 538
    antibodies to, 538
Rhino, in mice, 504
Rhizoids, 84
Rhizome, 840
Ribonucleic acid, 103, 539, 604, 798
    messenger, 561
    transfer, 562
Ribosomes, 103
    and protein synthesis, 562
Ring, annual, 296
    growth, 296
    porphyrin, 192
RNA, *see* ribonucleic acid
Rodentia, 637
Rodents, 637
Roeder, K. D., 751
Roentgen, 32
Rogers, Stanfield, 576
Root, 269
    fibrous, 285
    primary, 285
    system of, 285
Root cap, 272
Root hairs, 269
Roux, Wilhelm, 585
Rubella virus, 628
Rutherford, Lord, 45

Sachs, Julius, 244
Sachs, Tsui, 358

Sager, Ruth, 578
Salamander, 606
Salmon, silver, 28
Sampling error, 52, 71
Sanger, Frederick, 451
Sarich, V. M., 646
Saturated fats, 161
Sayre, J. D., 311
Scalar transformation, 81, 82
Scale, arithmetic, 82
    logarithmic, 83
Scale leaves, 291
*Sceloporus*, 745
Schein, M. W., 756, 766
Schleiden, Matthias, 15
Schneiderman, H. A., 780
Schotté, O. E., 604
Schrödinger, E., 11
Schwann, Theodor, 15
Science, limitations of, 43
Scientific method, 27
Scientific procedure, 26
Sclerenchyma, 279
Scopes, John, 689
Scott, J. P., 775, 776
Scrapie, 2
Sea urchins, 482
Seasonal isolation, 709
Second law of thermodynamics, 263
Secondary consumers, 655
Secretin, 60
Segmentation, in annelids, 877
    in arthropods, 877
    in mollusks, 877
Segregation, law of, 509
*Selaginella*, 842
Selection, natural, 19, 26, 694
    sexual, 706
Selman, Geoffrey, 481
Semen, 38
Semipermeable membrane, 114
Senebier, Jean, 241, 778
Sensitivity, 3
Sensory epithelium, 364
Sensory neurons, 439
Sex, inheritance of, 627
Sex linkage, 534
Sexual reproduction, 7

Sexual selection, 706
Shift, quantum, 135
Shoot, system of, 287
Short-day plants, 344
Sickle-cell anemia, 574, 704
Sieve cells, 284
Sieve-tube elements, 284
Sigmoid curve, 80
Silurian period, 830, 833
Simple sugars, 187
Singer, Marcus, 610
Sino-auricular node, 386
Sizes, of cells, 111
Skeletal muscles, 365
Skoog, Folke, 339, 355
Smooth muscles, 368
Snowshoe hare, 674
"Sodium pump," 431
Solar energy, 130
Soluble RNA, 562
Somatoplasm, 18
Sorokin, Helen R., 358
Spalding, Douglas, 754
Spallanzani, Lazaro, 39, 372, 606, 611
Special creation, 688
Specialization, 8, 718
Speciation, in evolution, 709
Species, 637
    concept of, 640
    multidimensional, 643
    transmutation of, 688
Specificity, chemical, 164
Spectrum, action, 254
Spectrum analysis, 136
Spemann, Hans, 601
Sperm, 8, 38, 368
    agglutination, 590
Spermatogenesis, 482
Spermatozoa, 38, 368
Sphincter muscles, 377
Spiegelman, S., 573
Spinal cord, 443
Spinal nerves, 443
Spindle fibers, 101, 473, 480, 481
*Spirogyra*, 825
    conjugation of, 829
Spontaneous generation, 688, 787
Sporangia, 840

Spores, of filamentous algae, 847
  of ferns, 840
Sporogenesis, 482
Sporophyte, 840, 853
Squamous epithelium, 363
Squid, 482
Squirrel, Abert, 708
  Kaibab, 708
Stahl, F. W., 550, 555
Staining, 91
Stamen, 857
Standard conditions, 152
Standard deviation, 75
Starches, 197
Starling, E. H., 55, 58
Static equilibrium, 459
Statistical analysis, 31
Steady state equilibrium, 459
Stele, 287
Stem, 269
Sterols, 160
Steward, F. C., 339
Stickleback, 767
  mating behavior, 644, 710
Stigma, 857
Stimulus, 6
Stipule, 292
Stomach, 372
  movements of, 372
Stomata, 232, 275, 510 (color plate II)
Stomatal movement, mechanism, 310
Strasburger, Eduard, 319
Striated muscles, 365
Striated tissue, 724
Striations, 365
Structures, analogous, 692
  homologous, 692
  vestigial, 692
Style, 857
Suberin, 277
Substrate, 371
Substrate phosphorylation, 201
Succinic acid, 219
Succinic dehydrogenase, 177, 219
Sucrase, 371
Sugars, 197
Support, of hypotheses, 29
Surface area, relation to volume, 84

Svedberg units, 104
Swallowing, 375, 376
Syctonema, 851
Sympathetic nervous system, 447
Synapse, nerve, 368, 435, 436
Synapsis, of chromosomes, 483
Syndrome, Down's, 486
Synthesis, dehydration, 160, 399
Synthetic processes, 4
Systems, 4, 90
Szent-Gyorgyi, Albert, 219, 220, 415

T2 bacteriophage virus, 35, 541
T4 bacteriophage, genes of, 574
Tasmanian wolf, 635
Tatum, Edward L., 88, 558, 619
Taxes, 730
Taxonomic charts, 647
Taxonomy, biochemical, 644
  definition of, 633
  international commission on, 638
Taylor, J. A., 551, 555
Techniques, immunological, 644
Teleological explanations, 729
Teleonomy, 746
Telophase, 475
Temin, H. M., 572
Temperature, body, 460
  regulation of, 460
Temperature optimum, 172
Temperature scales, absolute (Kelvin),
  centigrade, fahrenheit, 68–69,
  891–892
  Celsius, 892
  conversion of, 891
Tendons, 365
Tension, 394, 395
Territoriality, 764
Tertiary consumers, 655
Testosterone, 449
Tetrad, 485
Thalamus, 442
Thalidomide, 628
Theophrastus, 633
Theory, of evolution, 688, 864
  of transmutation, 228
Thermodynamics, laws of, 130, 263
Thigmotropism, 332

Thimann, K. V., 350, 354, 355
Thirst, 378
Thomson, Sir George, 27
Thoracic cavity, 389
Threonine, 467
Threonine deaminase, 467
Threshold, for muscle response, 414
Thylakoids, 250
Thymine, 543
Thyroxin, 452
Tinbergen, Niko, 738, 745, 766, 774
Tissues, animal, 363
    conducting, 279
    connective, 364
    definition, 4
    epithelial, 363
    fibrous, 365
    fundamental, 277
    meristematic, 272
    muscular, 365
    nervous, 368
    plant, 271
    protective, 274
    reproductive, 363
    striated, 724
    surface, 274
    vascular, 279, 293
TMV, *see* tobacco mosaic virus
Toad, South African clawed, 607
Tobacco mosaic virus, 572, 798
Torus, 283
Tracheids, 280
Transcription DNA, by RNA, 572
Transfer, active, 116
    electron, 189
    passive, 116
Transfer RNA, 562
Transformation of energy, 130
Transformation processes, 4
Transition, electron, 135
Translocation, 302, 319
Transmutation of species, 688
Transmutation theory, 228
Transpiration, 315
Transport, active, 116
Transport, electron, 188
*Trebouxia*, 851

Trial-and-error, 53
Trial-and-error learning, 752
Tricarboxylic acid cycle, 201
Trichomes, 275
Trilobites, 867
Triphosphopyridine nucleotide (TPN), 258
Triplet code, 564
*Triturus viridescens*, 567
Tropisms, 332, 349
"Truth," in science, 46
Truth table, 29
Trypsin, 173, 371
Trypsinogen, 371
Turnover number, 170
Twitty, V. C., 603
Typical cell, 96
*Tyrannosaurus*, 867

$U^{238}$, 802
*Ulothrix*, 825
Ultraviolet light, 130
Unit membrane, 100
Uracil, 561
Urea, 398
Uric acid, 398
Uridine triphosphate (UTP), 188
Urine, 398

Vacuolar membrane, 100
Vacuoles, 100
Vagus nerve, 58, 390
Validity, scientific, 32
Van Helmont, Jan Baptista, 230, 788
Van Niel, C. B., 246
Van Overbeek, J., 339, 341
Vapor hypothesis, 39
Variables, 29, 50
Variance, 75, 893
Vascular bundles, 289
Vascular cambium, 272
Vascular cylinder, 287, 289
Vascular plant, 269
Vascular tissues, 279, 293
Vasil, Vimla, 615
Veale, J. A., 357
Vegetal pole, 595

Velocity, initial, 170
Venation, netted, 294
    reticulate, 294
Verworn, Max, 12
Vessels, 280, 855
    xylem, 281
Vestigial structures, 692
Vestigial wing, 17
Villi, chorionic, 598
    intestinal, 380
Virchow, Rudolf, 15
Viruses, 2
    and origin of life, 798
    rubella, 628
    T2, 35, 541
    T4, 574
    TMV, 572, 798
Vitalism, 23
Vitamin K, 371
Viviparous, 590
Volta, Alessandro, 426
*Volvox*, 879
Von Bertalanffy, L., 11
Von Frisch, Karl, 757
Von Goethe, Johann Wolfgang, 27
Von Helmholtz, Hermann, 45, 426
Von Mohl, Hugo, 310

Wareing, P. F., 341
Water cycle, 663
Watson, J. B., 726
Watson, J. D., 544
Watson-Crick model of DNA structure,
    543, 549, 552, 553, 725, 748
Wave theory, of light, 252
Wavelength, of light, 252
Waves, radio, 130

Web, spider, 733
Weinberg, W., 703
Weismann, August, 17, 589
Wells, P. H., 759
Wenner, A. M., 759
Went, Fritz, 334, 350
Whatley, F. R., 258
White, Philip, 321
Whitehead, Alfred North, 378
Wiesner, J., 339
Wilberforce, Bishop, 689
Williams, Roger, 778
Wilson, A. C., 646
Wilson, H. V., 611
Witt, Peter N., 734
Wolf, Tasmanian, 635
Woodward, John, 231, 244
Woody plants, 853
Work, 127

*Xenopus laevis*, 576, 607
X-ray, 32, 130
X-ray diffraction, and DNA structure,
    546
Xylem, 279, 837, 845, 853, 855
Xylem vessel, 281

Yellow-green algae, 851
Yolk, 589
Yolk sac, 598

Zeatin, 340
Zelitch, Israel, 312
Zimmerman, M. H., 325, 328
*Zygnema*, 490
Zygote, 8

## OTHER BOOKS OF INTEREST

### THE STUDY OF BOTANY

By Preston Adams, *DePauw University,* Jeffrey J. W. Baker, *Wesleyan University,* and Garland E. Allen, *Washington University*

556 pp, 386 illus (1970)

This introduction to botany is based on the authors' conviction that although there is no one specific scientific method, there is still an underlying pattern of deductive and inductive logic in every scientific experiment or observation. The book covers a chosen number of topics in depth, emphasizing the analysis of crucial experiments and the historical development of ideas as they led to the formulation of theories, their modification, and eventual replacement.

### A COURSE IN BIOLOGY

By Jeffrey J. W. Baker and Garland E. Allen

403 pp, 187 illus (1968)

This text is a shorter version of the authors' *The Study of Biology.* It has the same approach and emphasis as the original text and also concentrates on biological principles, giving equal emphasis to plants and animals. Certain subjects have been omitted, and the authors concentrate instead on a few general topics such as the principles underlying evolution and energy change in cells. This book is particularly appropriate for one-semester or one-quarter courses for liberal arts students and prospective teachers.

### MATTER, ENERGY, AND LIFE: AN INTRODUCTION FOR BIOLOGY STUDENTS, SECOND EDITION

By Jeffrey J. W. Baker and Garland E. Allen

225 pp, 94 illus, paperbound (1970)

The second edition of this highly successful text presents the principles of physics and chemistry essential to the study of modern biology. It relates these principles to specific biological problems. Suitable for courses for prospective teachers, this book is designed specifically for introductory courses in biology. It can be used as a primary or supplementary text.